Memel Territory (1939)
Baltic Sea
Königsberg
Danzig
East Prussia
Suwałki
Danzig-West Prussia (1939)
District Zichenau
Białystok
SOVIET UNION
Annexed Nov. 1939
Bug
Vistula
Posen
Wartheland (1939)
Warsaw
Litzmannstadt (Łódź)
Lublin
Breslau
General Government (1939)
San
Zarzecze
Nisko
Vistula
Katowice
Auschwitz
Upper Silesia
Cracow
Lwów (Lemberg)
Pardubitz
Teschen
Olmütz
Teltsch
Brünn
SLOVAKIA
Subcarpathian Rus
Danube
Bratislava (Pressburg)
Vienna
Annexed by Hungary (Nov. 1938)
Budapest
HUNGARY
Tisza
CROATIA
State borders of 1937
German-Soviet demarcation line 1939–1941
Borders of the "Greater German Reich"
Annexed Territories (years of annexation in brackets)
Concentration camps
0 50 100 150 km

The Persecution and Murder of the Jews, 1933–1945

The Persecution and Murder of the European Jews by Nazi Germany, 1933–1945

Series edited on behalf of the German Federal Archives, the Leibniz Institute for Contemporary History (IfZ), the Chair for Modern History at the Albert Ludwig University of Freiburg, and the Chair for East European History at the Freie Universität Berlin

In cooperation with Yad Vashem

Volume 3

edited by
Susanne Heim, Ulrich Herbert,
Hans-Dieter Kreikamp, Horst Möller, Gertrud Pickhan,
Dieter Pohl, Hartmut Weber, and Andreas Wirsching

English edition also edited by
Michael Hollmann, Sybille Steinbacher,
and Simone Walther-von Jena

The Persecution and Murder of the European Jews by Nazi Germany, 1933–1945

Volume 3

German Reich and Protectorate of Bohemia and Moravia September 1939–September 1941

Executive Editor
Andrea Löw

Coordinator of the English-language edition
Caroline Pearce,
with the assistance of Dorothy A. Mas
and Georg Felix Harsch

DE GRUYTER OLDENBOURG

יד ושם
YAD VASHEM
THE WORLD HOLOCAUST REMEMBRANCE CENTER

THE INTERNATIONAL INSTITUTE FOR HOLOCAUST RESEARCH

ISBN 978-3-11-052374-4
e-ISBN (PDF) 978-3-11-052636-3
e-ISBN (EPUB) 978-3-11-052389-8

Library of Congress Control Number: 2019953832

Bibliographical information published by the Deutsche Nationalbibliothek
The Deutsche Nationalbibliothek lists this publication in the Deutsche Nationalbibliografie; detailed bibliographical information is available at http://dnb.dnb.de.

Typesetting: Meta Systems Publishing & Printservices GmbH, Wustermark
Cover and dust jacket: Frank Ortmann and Martin Z. Schröder
Cartography: Peter Palm
Printing and binding: Hubert & Co. GmbH & Co. KG, Göttingen

www.degruyter.com

Contents

Foreword to the English Edition

The Persecution and Murder of the European Jews by Nazi Germany, 1933–1945 presents a broad range of primary sources in a scholarly edition. A total of sixteen English-language volumes will be published in this series, organized chronologically and according to region. The series places particular focus on the countries which had the highest Jewish populations before the outbreak of the Second World War, particularly Poland and the Soviet Union. The English-language edition reproduces all the materials in the German edition and has been adapted for an English-speaking readership. Apart from those originally written in English, all documents presented here have been translated from the language of the original source. This volume, the third in the series, documents the situation of the Jews in the German Reich and in the Protectorate of Bohemia and Moravia, established in March 1939, between the start of the Second World War and September 1941.

The foreword to the first volume of the series detailed the criteria for the selection of the documents. These criteria can be summarized as follows. First, the sources used are written documents and, occasionally, transcribed audio recordings, dating from the period of Nazi rule between 1933 and 1945. The decision was taken not to include memoirs, reports, and judicial documents produced after 1945; however, the footnotes make extensive reference to such retrospective testimonies and historical accounts. Second, the documents shed light on the actions and reactions of people with differing backgrounds and convictions and in different places, and indicate their intentions as well as the frequently limited options available to them. The volumes include a variety of document types such as official correspondence, private letters, diary entries, legal texts, newspaper articles, and the reports of foreign observers. Apart from a few exceptions, the translated documents have not been abridged.

The contents of this third volume range from Heydrich's order for the arrest of Polish Jews living in the Reich to a report in the *Neue Zürcher Zeitung* on the deportation of Stettin's Jews in February 1940, to letters in which Jewish parents write to their children about the experience of living in a 'Jew house', of forced labour, and of day-to-day humiliation. A poem by a writer in exile is presented alongside the deliberations of German administrative officials concerning proposals to force Jews to wear visible identification, and a Jewish representative's written record of his summons to the Gestapo. Events and developments are thus presented from multiple perspectives. A detailed index of people, places, and institutions as well as subject-specific concepts makes it possible to locate documents by theme and emphasizes connections between them.

The editors wish to thank the German Research Foundation (DFG) for its generous funding of the German and English-language projects. The English-language volumes are produced in cooperation with the Yad Vashem International Institute for Holocaust Research. The editors are also grateful to the large number of specialists and private individuals who provided the editors with advice and comments on sources and with information for the annotations, including biographical details for the people featured in the documents. Kathleen Luft, Todd Brown, Allan Blunden, Brenda Black, Nicola Varns, Simon Garnett, Susan Pratt, David Hill, and Sage Anderson translated the German documents for this third English-language volume in the series. The Czech documents were translated by Elizabeth Spacilova and checked by Luděk Knittel. The Italian document was translated by Alex J. Kay and the Russian document by Simon Lewis. Merle Read and Alissa Jones-Nelson provided proofreading and copyediting services. Peter Palm and Giles Bennett created and advised on the map, and Frank Ortmann and Martin Z. Schröder designed the book jacket. Nora Huberty, Ashley Kirspel, Priska Komaromi, Benedict Oldfield, Charlie Perris, Barbara Uchdorf, Ana Lena Werner, and Max Zeterberg contributed to this volume as student assistants. Johannes Gamm was responsible for database management. The following people contributed to the original German volume as student assistants: Romina Becker, Giles Bennett, Florian Danecke, Bernhard Lück, Miriam Schelp, Remigius Stachowiak, and Barbara Wünnenberg. Ingo Loose, Sonja Schilcher, Gudrun Schroeter, Magda Veselská, and Maria Wilke worked on the volume in their capacity as research fellows. Follow-up research was conducted by Anat Wollenberger in Jerusalem, and by Merle Bieber, Jutta Fuchshuber, and Andreas Kern in archives in Vienna.

Despite all the care taken, occasional inaccuracies cannot be entirely avoided in a document collection on this scale. We would be grateful for any notifications to this effect. The address of the editorial board is: Leibniz Institute for Contemporary History, Edition 'Judenverfolgung', Finckensteinallee 85/87, 12205 Berlin, Germany.

Berlin/Munich/Freiburg/Klagenfurt, April 2020

Editorial Preface

This primary source collection on the persecution and murder of the European Jews should be cited using the abbreviation PMJ. This citation style is also used in the work itself where there are cross references between the individual volumes. The documents are consecutively numbered, beginning anew with each volume. Accordingly, 'PMJ 1/200' refers to document number 200 in the first volume of this edition. The individual documents are presented as follows: title (in bold type), header, document, footnotes.

The titles have been formulated by the editor(s) of the respective volume and provide information on the date of origin of the document, its core message, author, and recipient(s). The header, placed underneath the title, is part of the document itself. It specifies the type of source (letter, draft law, minutes, and so on), the name of the author, the place of origin, the file reference (where applicable), remarks indicating confidential or classified status, and other special features of the document. The location of the ministries or other central agencies in Berlin at the time, for instance the Reich Security Main Office or the Chancellery of the Führer, is not cited. The header also contains details about the addressee and, where applicable, the date of the receipt stamp, and it concludes with the date of origin and reference to the stage of processing of the source, for instance 'draft', 'carbon copy', or 'copy'.

The header is followed by the document text. Salutations and valedictions are printed, though signatures are only included once, in the header. Instances of emphasis by the author in the original document are retained. Irrespective of the type of emphasis used in the original source (for example, underlined, spaced, bold, capitalized, or italicized), they always appear in italics in the printed version. Where necessary, additional particulars on the document are to be found in the footnotes. In order to enhance readability, letters and words are added in square brackets where they are missing in the original due to obvious mistakes, or where the meaning would otherwise be unclear in the translation.

Abbreviations are explained in the List of Abbreviations. Uncommon abbreviations, primarily from private correspondence, are expanded in a footnote at the first mention in a given document.

Handwritten additions in typewritten originals have been adopted by the editors without further indication insofar as they are formal corrections and most probably inserted by the author. If the additions significantly alter the content – either by mitigating or radicalizing it – this is mentioned in the footnotes, and, if known, the author of the addition(s) is given.

As a rule, the documents are reproduced here in full. Only in exceptional cases, where individual documents are very long, for example situation reports covering extended periods of time, is the document abridged. The same applies to the written records of meetings at which Nazi policies relating to the persecution of Jews, or reactions to these policies, were only addressed within a designated part of the proceedings. Such abridgements are indicated by an ellipsis in square brackets; the contents of the omitted text are outlined in a footnote. An exception is the diary of Luise Solmitz, which has survived in both a handwritten version as well as a typewritten version compiled by Luise Solmitz herself after 1945. Since the handwritten version is very difficult to read and contains lengthy entries that are of limited historical interest, the excerpt in this volume is presented in accordance with the typescript. The author occasionally added retrospective annotations to both the manuscript and the typescript; these are marked with curly brackets: {}.

Only in a few exceptional cases is a deviation made from the chronological organization of the documents, for example with the reports written by Jewish immigrants in Palestine that provide a retrospective account of the period prior to their flight and emigration. These descriptive texts, which were written soon after the period covered but nonetheless retrospectively, are classified in some cases according to the date of the events portrayed rather than the date of origin. Where there is any uncertainty regarding the date of the documents or whether they constitute originals or copies, reference is made in the footnotes. The first footnote for each document, which is linked to the title, contains the location of the source and, insofar as it denotes an archive, the reference number, as well as the folio number(s) if available. Reference to copies of archival documents in research institutions and in the German Federal Archives in Berlin are always made if the original held at the location first mentioned was not consulted there. In the case of printed sources, for instance newspaper articles or legislative texts, this footnote contains standard bibliographical information. If the source has already been published in English in a document collection on National Socialism or on the persecution of the Jews, reference is made to its first publication, alongside the original location of the source. The next footnote places the document into context and, where appropriate, mentions related discussions, the specific role of authors and recipients, and activities accompanying or immediately following its genesis. Subsequent footnotes provide additional information related to the theme of the document and the persons relevant to the content. They refer to other – published or unpublished – sources that contribute to historical contextualization.

The footnotes also point out individual features of the documents, for instance handwritten notes in the margin, underlining, or deletions, whether by the author or the recipient(s). Annotations and instructions for submission are referred to in the footnotes where the editors consider them to contain significant information. Where possible, the locations of the treaties, laws, and decrees cited in the source text are provided in the footnotes, while other documents are given with their archival reference number. If these details could not be ascertained, this is also noted.

Where biographical information is available on the senders and recipients of the documents, this is provided in the footnotes. The same applies to persons mentioned in the text if they play an active role in the events described. As a general rule, this information is given in the footnote inserted after the first mention of the name in question in the volume. Biographical information on a particular person can thus be retrieved easily via the index.

The short biographies are based on data found in reference works, scholarly literature, or the Central Database of Shoah Victims' Names established and run by Yad Vashem. In many cases, the information was retrieved by consulting personnel files and indexes, municipal and company archives, registry offices, restitution and denazification files, or specialists in the field. Indexes and files on persons from the Nazi era held in archives were also used, primarily those of the former Berlin Document Center, and the Central Office of the Judicial Authorities of the Federal States for the Investigation of National Socialist Crimes (Zentrale Stelle der Landesjustizverwaltungen zur Aufklärung nationalsozialistischer Verbrechen) in Ludwigsburg, the latter now stored in the German Federal Archives.

Despite every effort, it has not always been possible to obtain complete biographical information. In such cases, the footnote in question contains only verified facts such as the year of birth. Where a person could not be identified, there is no footnote reference. Biographical footnotes are not added in the case of extremely well-known persons such as Adolf Hitler or Joseph Goebbels.

As a rule, in the titles, footnotes, and introduction inverted commas are not placed around terms that were commonplace in Nazi Germany, such as Führer, Jewish Council, or Aryanization, but German-language terms expressing ideological concepts of race, such as *Mischling*, are placed in italics. In line with the circumstances of the time, the terms Jew and Jewish are used for people who did not regard themselves as Jewish but were defined as such on the basis of racial legislation and thus subjected to persecution. References in the documents to the 'Gestapo', an acronym of the German GEheime STAatsPOlizei, and to the 'State Police' denote one and the same institution: the Secret State Police.

The glossary contains concise descriptions of key terms and concepts that are repeated on multiple occasions or are related to the events and developments described in the volume. All primary and secondary sources consulted are listed in the footnotes and bibliography. Where English-language versions of these sources are available, these are included. If a document has already been published in English translation but has been newly translated for this volume, this is indicated in a footnote.

This series will include two further volumes on the German Reich and the Protectorate of Bohemia and Moravia. Volume 6 covers the period from October 1941 to March 1943, and volume 11 the period from April 1943 to the end of the war.

Note on the translation

British English is used in all translations into English. Where a document was originally written in British or American English, the spelling, grammar, and punctuation of the original have been retained, with silent correction of minor typographical or grammatical errors and insertions in square brackets to clarify the meaning if necessary.

The spelling, grammar, and punctuation of the translated documents broadly conform to the guidelines in *New Hart's Rules: The Oxford Style Guide* (2014). Accordingly, the ending -ize rather than -ise is preferred throughout.

SS, Wehrmacht, and certain other ranks are given in the original German, as are titles where there is no standard equivalent in English or where there may be confusion with contemporary usage. A table of military and police ranks is included as an appendix, along with English language equivalents of these terms and an indication of their position in the National Socialist hierarchy. In addition, administrative ranks and other terms commonly used in German in scholarly literature on the period are presented in German in this volume and explained in the glossary.

All laws and institutions are translated into English in the documents; the German titles of laws can be found in the index. In the introduction and footnotes, foreign-language terms and expressions are added in brackets after the translation where this is considered important for understanding or context.

If a word or phrase appears in German in a non-German document, the German is retained in the translated text and its meaning explained in a footnote or, if necessary, the glossary. The original spelling of foreign organizations is retained in the footnotes. The titles of published works not in the English language are not translated unless the work in question is of contextual or substantial relevance.

In order to avoid confusion between British and American English, dates are spelt out in the order day, month, and year. Foreign proper names are not italicized. Thus, names of institutions, organizations, and places are written in roman type in the footnotes, but legislation and conceptual terms are in italics.

In the titles, footnotes, and translated documents, place names are generally written according to the contemporary (English) name or the variant commonly used in scholarly literature on the period. This also applies to places that have since been renamed, so, for example, 'Danzig' not 'Gdańsk'. Locations in the Czech lands had both a German and a Czech name: German speakers would, for instance, have referred to Brünn and Mährisch Ostrau, and Czech speakers to Brno and Moravská Ostrava. Usage was frequently contested depending on national affiliation. In the translated documents, these place names are given in either their Czech or their German form according to usage in the original source or the perspective of the writer. The modern English equivalent is given where this is widely used, for example Bohemia, Moravia, or Prague. The titles and subheadings use the variant of the place name(s) mentioned in the document, and the introduction and footnotes use the Czech variant. Both the Czech and German place names are given in the index. In the documents, the terms Czecho-Slovakia/Czecho-Slovak or Czechoslovakia/Czechoslovak are reproduced as in the original source; in the introduction, footnotes, and titles the terms are given as legally correct in the period under discussion. Hence, the hyphenated forms Czecho-Slovakia/Czecho-Slovak are used when referring to the period from 28 October 1918 until 29 February 1920, and from 6 October 1938 to 14 March 1939. The unhyphenated form Czechoslovakia is normally used in other cases.

Diacritical marks in languages such as Czech and Polish are retained, with the exception of the names of the extermination camps in Eastern Europe, where they have been removed in order to emphasize that these camps were established by the German National Socialist regime. Language-specific characters such as the German ß (Eszett) for ss have also been retained. Hebrew and Yiddish terms are described in the footnotes along with any other words requiring explanation.

Introduction

For the Jews in the German Reich, 1 September 1939 marked a watershed of profound significance. Long socially isolated, they were now confined within a country at war. Although they were still under pressure to emigrate, anyone attempting to do so faced ever greater obstacles. Systematically dispossessed, and at the same time confronted with strict immigration requirements in potential destination countries, most German, Austrian, and Czech Jews failed to gain entry to countries outside the sphere of German control.

Victor Klemperer, a professor of Romance languages – persecuted as a Jew under the Nuremberg Laws despite being a Protestant – predicted as early as the beginning of September 1939 that, with the onset of the war, 'a morphine injection or something similar was the best thing for us, our life was over'.[1] In the period from September 1939 to September 1941 documented in this volume, the National Socialist leadership proceeded from a policy of forced migration and repression of the Jews to mass murder. By the end of this period, the requirement for German Jews to wear a yellow star made them recognizable to everyone, and their systematic deportation to the occupied territories in the East was imminent.

With the invasion of Poland, a far greater number of Jews than before came under German control. From the very first days of the war, they were confronted with terror and violence from the German occupiers. At the same time, the authorities in the Reich used the war as an opportunity to tighten measures against perceived enemies at home – above all the Jews. Nonetheless, for a long time it was unclear what form the repeatedly invoked 'solution to the Jewish question' should actually take. This volume charts the discussions within the National Socialist leadership and administration, the implementation of anti-Jewish measures, and the consequences for the Jewish population. Diaries, letters, and reports attest to the increasing difficulties encountered by Jews in everyday life, the restrictions placed on their movement, their segregation and alienation from mainstream society, the humiliations, and the shifts between hope and despair regarding the issue of emigration. The decree of September 1941 that made it compulsory for Jews to wear a yellow star put an end to the last remaining freedoms that, up until then, one or another Jew might have taken advantage of surreptitiously.

This volume documents the early attempts by the German authorities to deport the Jews to the periphery of their sphere of control, as well as the failure of these forced displacement projects which, in turn, gave rise to increasingly radical ideas. It includes sources that illustrate the difficult situation that the Jewish organizations found themselves in. The Reich Association of Jews in Germany, the Israelite Religious Community of Vienna (IKG), and the Jewish Religious Community of Prague sought to use their limited options to help those who were persecuted, to organize Jewish life in the Reich, and, above all, to help as many Jews as possible to emigrate. But the Jewish officials were

1 Victor Klemperer, *I Shall Bear Witness: The Diaries of Victor Klemperer, 1933–1941*, trans. Martin Chalmers (London: Weidenfeld & Nicolson, 1998 [German edn, 1995]), p. 373 (entry for 3 Sept. 1939).

under constant German scrutiny and control and thus under enormous pressure, as the documents they left behind so strikingly attest.

The so-called Protectorate of Bohemia and Moravia was considered part of the Greater German Reich, even though it had a special status. Because anti-Jewish policy here followed a pattern similar to that in Germany and Austria, developments in the Protectorate are covered together with developments in the German Reich in this volume, as well as in volumes 6 and 11 of the series. In the present volume, the documentation of events in the Protectorate begins in mid March 1939, i.e. with the invasion of Prague by German troops. The account in this introduction therefore begins with the history of the Protectorate.

Bohemia and Moravia

When Hitler achieved his objective of the cession of the Sudetenland to the German Reich in the Munich Agreement of 30 September 1938, he viewed this as merely a first step towards the break-up of the Czechoslovak state. By October 1938 he had already decreed that preparations were to be made for 'dealing with rump Czechoslovakia'.[2] The main pretext was the supposed internal collapse of Czecho-Slovakia – as it was officially known after the loss of the Sudeten German territories – and the alleged repression of the German-speaking population there. On the night of 9 March 1939 the Czecho-Slovak president, Emil Hácha, dismissed the government of autonomous Slovakia, which was pursuing independence under Jozef Tiso. Tiso then travelled on 13 March to Berlin, where Hitler pressed him to proclaim the independence of his state. The next day the Slovak parliament adopted a corresponding resolution, probably also out of fear that its own national territory would otherwise be annexed by Hungary with Germany's assent. Hácha, in turn, travelled to Berlin with his foreign minister, František Chvalkovský, on 14 March. There Hitler informed him that German troops were about to invade. That same day German troops had already occupied Moravská Ostrava (German: Mährisch Ostrau). Hácha was thus forced to sign a statement in which he placed the fate of the Czech people 'trustfully in the hands of the Führer'. The Wehrmacht invaded Prague on 15 March 1939. Hitler had thereby broken his promise given in Munich that German territorial claims would be satisfied by the annexation of the Sudetenland, and National Socialist Germany had for the first time annexed a territory with a non-German-speaking majority population.[3] At the same time, around 118,000 people defined as Jews by the Nuremberg Laws were added to the German sphere of control.[4]

2 Detlef Brandes, *Die Tschechen unter deutschem Protektorat*, part 1: *Besatzungspolitik, Kollaboration und Widerstand im Protektorat Böhmen und Mähren bis Heydrichs Tod, 1939–1942* (Munich: Oldenbourg, 1969), p. 15.

3 Statement by the German and Czecho-Slovak governments, 15 March 1939, published in *Akten zur Deutschen Auswärtigen Politik 1918–1945*, series D: *1937–1945*, vol. 4 (Baden-Baden: Imprimerie Nationale, 1951), p. 235.

4 Miroslav Kárný, 'Zur Statistik der jüdischen Bevölkerung im sogenannten Protektorat', *Judaica Bohemiae*, vol. 22, no. 1 (1986), pp. 9–19; Eva Schmidt-Hartmann, 'Übersicht über die national-

Jews in Bohemia and Moravia

The Jews of Bohemia and Moravia could look back on a history spanning hundreds of years.[5] They were emancipated in the nineteenth century, during the same period as the Jews of Germany and Austria. In 1849 the Habsburg Empire rescinded the discriminatory marriage laws which, since the beginning of the eighteenth century, had meant that, at most, 8,541 Jewish families could live in Bohemia and 5,106 in Moravia, and that only one son in each family was permitted to start a family. With the creation of the Dual Monarchy of Austria-Hungary in 1867, equal rights for Jews were laid down by law throughout the state. From now on, the Bohemian and Moravian Jews enjoyed freedom of movement and could take advantage of educational opportunities and pursue careers that had previously been closed to them.[6]

In Bohemia, industrial development proceeded rapidly during the second half of the nineteenth century, and Jewish entrepreneurs had a substantial share in it, particularly in Prague. Their economic rise frequently went hand in hand with an uncoupling from Jewish traditions and with assimilation into the German-speaking middle classes – and occasionally brought them into conflict with the emerging sense of Czech nationalism. Until the mid nineteenth century, most of the population had been bilingual, but after the 1850s the use of a particular language was increasingly regarded as a form of political and national affirmation.[7]

Efforts to assimilate started to change in the 1880s. Gradually, more and more Jews began to orientate themselves towards Czech culture. In 1890, 74 per cent of the Jews in Prague listed German as their language of daily use, but by 1900 the share of German

sozialistische "Endlösung der jüdischen Frage" in den böhmischen Ländern', in Ferdinand Seibt, *Deutsche, Tschechen, Sudetendeutsche: Analysen und Stellungnahmen zu Geschichte und Gegenwart aus fünf Jahrzehnten* (Munich: Oldenbourg, 2002), p. 321.

5 On the history of the Jews in Bohemia and Moravia, see, for example, Kateřina Čapková, *Czechs, Germans, Jews? National Identity and the Jews of Bohemia*, trans. Derek and Marzia Paton (New York: Berghahn Books, 2012 [Czech edn, 2005]); Avigdor Dagan, Gertrude Hirschler, and Lewis Weiner (eds.), *The Jews of Czechoslovakia: Historical Studies and Survey*, 3 vols. (Philadelphia: Jewish Publication Society of America, 1968–1984); Ruth Kestenberg-Gladstein, *Neuere Geschichte der Juden in den böhmischen Ländern* (Tübingen: Mohr, 1969); Wilma Iggers (ed.), *The Jews of Bohemia and Moravia: A Historical Reader*, trans. Wilma Iggers, Káča Poláčková-Henley, and Kathrine Talbot (Detroit: Wayne State University Press, 1992 [German edn, 1986]); Natalia Berger (ed.), *Where Cultures Meet: The Story of the Jews of Czechoslovakia* (Tel Aviv: Beth Hatefutsoth, 1990); Tomáš Pěkný, *Historie Židů v Čechách a na Moravě* (Prague: Sefer, 2002), Ferdinand Seibt, 'Tausend Jahre jüdische Geschichte in Böhmen und Mähren', in Seibt, *Deutsche, Tschechen, Sudetendeutsche*, pp. 49–62.

6 Rudolf W. Wlaschek, *Juden in Böhmen: Beiträge zur Geschichte des europäischen Judentums im 19. und 20. Jahrhundert* (Munich: Oldenbourg, 1997), pp. 18 and 45–47, Hillel J. Kieval, *Languages of Community: The Jewish Experience in the Czech Lands* (Berkeley: University of California Press, 2000), pp. 65–67.

7 Hillel J. Kieval, 'The Lands Between: The Jews of Bohemia, Moravia, and Slovakia to 1918', in Berger, *Where Cultures Meet*, pp. 23–52, here pp. 40–46; Heiko Haumann, *A History of East European Jews*, trans. James Patterson (New York: Central European University Press, 2002 [German edn, 1998]), pp. 91–95 and 199; Michal Frankl, 'Tschechien', in Wolfgang Benz (ed.), *Handbuch des Antisemitismus: Judenfeindschaft in Geschichte und Gegenwart*, vol. 1: *Länder und Regionen* (Munich: Saur, 2008), pp. 364–370.

speakers had dropped to only slightly over 45 per cent. More than half of the Jews identified themselves as Czech, supported the Czech people's national cause, and hoped thereby in the shorter or longer term to overcome hostility. It was against this backdrop that the Czech-Jewish Political Union (Politická jednota českožidovská) came into being. The Jews of Prague, in particular, sought a greater permeability of the boundaries between the various milieus. In the academic field, the shift away from German culture and towards Czech culture did not occur until later. Most Jewish students continued to study at the German University until 1929. Thereafter, the majority opted for the Czech-speaking Charles University.[8]

In 1897 Theodor Herzl described the complicated situation of the Jews as follows:

> In Prague, they were reproached for not being Czechs, and in Žatec and Cheb for not being Germans. Poor Jews, what were they supposed to do? Some tried to become Czech, so they got into trouble with the Germans. Some tried to become Germans, so they were attacked by the Czechs as well as the Germans. It's enough to make one lose one's sanity – or to find it at last.[9]

Political parties such as the Young Czech Party took advantage of such nationalist, antisemitic sentiments, as did German *völkisch* associations and organizations. Since the 1890s, Czech and German Catholics had joined forces in Christian Social parties with antisemitic tendencies. In this political climate a so-called 'ritual murder' trial began in Polná in 1899, which resulted in a death sentence for Leopold Hilsner, a Jew.[10] The later president Tomáš G. Masaryk, then a professor at the Czech University in Prague, criticized both the accusation of ritual murder and the sentence. A second trial was held, and the following year Hilsner was convicted again. This time he was sentenced to life in prison. As a result the antisemites felt encouraged to make new accusations of ritual murder, and to attack Jews and their mostly Social Democratic advocates.[11]

In Moravia the Jews were more exposed to the influence of Vienna. As a result, they remained rooted to a greater degree in Austrian German culture. The shift towards Czech culture that took place in Bohemia was absent here. In 1900 only 16 per cent of the Jews in Moravia declared Czech to be their language of daily use. Furthermore, reli-

8 Hillel J. Kieval, *The Making of Czech Jewry: National Conflict and Jewish Society in Bohemia, 1870–1918* (New York: Oxford University Press, 1988); Wlaschek, *Juden in Böhmen*, pp. 36–37, 53–57; Haumann, *A History of East European Jews*, p. 202; Peter Demetz, *Prague in Danger: The Years of German Occupation, 1939–1945. Memories and History, Terror and Resistance, Theater and Jazz, Film and Poetry, Politics and War* (New York: Farrar, Straus and Giroux, 2008), pp. 30–31.

9 Theodor Herzl, *The Prague Jews between Two Nations* (1897), cited in Iggers, *Jews of Bohemia and Moravia*, p. 231.

10 Emerging in medieval Europe, the myth of ritual murder was used to accuse Jews of murdering Christian children as part of Jewish religious rituals and served as a pretext for the persecution of Jews. It often featured in National Socialist antisemitic propaganda.

11 Jiří Kovtun, *Tajuplná vražda: Případ Leopolda Hilsnera* (Prague: Sefer, 1994); Hillel J. Kieval, 'Death and the Nation: Ritual Murder as Political Discourse in the Czech Lands', in Maurice Godé, Jacques Le Rider, and Françoise Mayer (eds.), *Allemands, Juifs et Tchèques à Prague de 1890 à 1924: Actes du colloque de Montpellier, décembre 1994* (Montpellier: Université Paul-Valery, 1996), pp. 83–99; Michal Frankl, 'The Background of the Hilsner Case: Political Antisemitism and Allegations of Ritual Murder, 1896–1900', *Judaica Bohemiae*, vol. 36 (2000), pp. 34–118.

gious beliefs mattered more. In contrast to Bohemia, the autonomy of the Jewish communities was not abolished by the granting of legal equality in 1867. Rather, the communities remained independent until the end of the Habsburg Empire.[12]

After the First World War, Bohemia, Moravia and Moravian Silesia, Slovakia, and Subcarpathian Rus combined to form the Republic of Czechoslovakia. For all their differences, the majority of the Jews from these regions were united by their loyalty to the republic and its president, Tomáš G. Masaryk. Masaryk made them citizens with equal rights in a state in which they very soon felt firmly rooted. He was successful in defusing the anti-Jewish feeling among his compatriots to such an extent that Jewish and gentile Czechs, by and large, lived together peaceably. That was all the more important because the political elite of Czechoslovakia feared that antisemitic incidents might inflame public opinion in Western Europe and the USA against the new state.

The civil rights of the Jews were, indeed, never restricted under the First Czechoslovak Republic. The constitution made it possible officially to declare one's Jewish nationality, a step that was taken by just over 1 per cent of the population in the censuses of 1921 and 1930 (almost 181,000 and 187,000 persons, respectively). In terms of religious confession, however, approximately twice that many Jews lived in the new state, i.e. around 2.5 per cent of the population. However, there were considerable regional differences. For example, in 1930 the share of Jews in the total population of Bohemia and Moravian Silesia was slightly over 1 per cent. In Slovakia, which had formerly belonged to Hungary, it was 4.11 per cent, and in Subcarpathian Rus, 14.14 per cent.

The Jewish minority in the new Czechoslovak republic did not form a unified whole in terms of nationality, religion, or language. The Jews in the heavily industrialized regions of Bohemia, Moravia, and Moravian Silesia were, as in Austria, highly assimilated and lived predominantly in larger cities. In western Slovakia, however, Hungarian influence made its presence felt, and in the eastern part of Slovakia, as well as in Subcarpathian Rus, one was most likely to encounter those who were commonly referred to as *Ostjuden* ('Eastern Jews') and formed a group that was distinguishable from mainstream society.[13]

Tensions between assimilated and conservative Jews existed in every regional group. Franz Kafka described the associated inner conflicts and uncertainty in a letter to the writer Max Brod in June 1921:

> Most young Jews who began to write in German wanted to leave their Jewishness behind. Their fathers approved, vaguely (this vagueness was what was outrageous to them). But with their hind legs they still clung to their father's Jewishness, while

12 Kieval, 'The Lands Between: The Jews of Bohemia, Moravia, and Slovakia to 1918', p. 48; Livia Rothkirchen, *The Jews of Bohemia and Moravia: Facing the Holocaust* (Lincoln, NE: University of Nebraska Press, 2005), pp. 19–21.

13 Livia Rothkirchen, 'Czechoslovak Jewry: Growth and Decline. Part I: 1918–1939', in Berger, *Where Cultures Meet*, pp. 107–115, here pp. 108–110; Kieval, *Languages of Community*, pp. 198–216; Čapková, *Czechs, Germans, Jews?*, pp. 14–25; Martin Schulze Wessel, 'Entwürfe und Wirklichkeiten: Die Politik gegenüber den Juden in der Ersten Tschechoslowakischen Republik 1918 bis 1938', in Dittmar Dahlmann and Anke Hilbrenner (eds.), *Zwischen großen Erwartungen und bösem Erwachen: Juden, Politik und Antisemitismus in Ost- und Südosteuropa 1918–1945* (Paderborn: Schöningh, 2007), pp. 120–135.

> with their front legs they would find no new footing. The despair that ensued became their inspiration.[14]

The tendency towards assimilation was particularly strong in Prague, which was one of the most heavily secularized cities in the first decades of the twentieth century. The historian Saul Friedländer, born to German-speaking Jewish parents in Prague in 1932, recalled that although he visited a good many churches in Prague with his Czech governess, they never went to the famous Old-New Synagogue located near his parents' home, to the Jewish town hall, or to the old Jewish cemetery.[15]

Affiliation with the German or Czech nation was not the decisive issue for the Zionists. In Bohemia the Zionist group was initially so small that Max Brod spread the following joke: 'If the ceiling of a certain café falls in, then that's it for Zionism in Prague.' But gradually the movement grew. Young Prague intellectuals like the historian Hans Kohn, the journalist Robert Weltsch, and Max Brod himself felt increasingly committed to a Jewish nation and championed a modern Jewish culture. In the space of just twelve years, the Zionist Congress was held three times in Czechoslovakia: in 1921 and 1923 in Carlsbad and in 1933 in Prague.[16]

The new liberal state also gave the Jews opportunities for political expression and organization. In 1925 the Jewish Party (Židovská strana) sent two delegates, Dr Ludvík Singer and Dr Chaim Kugel, to parliament for the first time. The Zionists were united in the Central Association of Zionists, headquartered in Moravská Ostrava, with some of them supporting the Jewish Economic Party.[17]

The favourable political and social conditions allowed Jewish life in Czechoslovakia to thrive. Numerous cultural and social institutions and associations came into being. Prague, in particular, rapidly became a centre of Jewish life. Jewish writers and creative artists shaped the intellectual climate of the city, and increasing numbers of Jewish professors were appointed to both of Prague's universities. Moreover, according to estimates, 18 per cent of all university students were Jews. Many successful journalists came from Jewish families, and Jews held ministerial positions in various governments of the First Republic. According to statistics compiled in 1930, most Czech Jews were members of the middle class: 45.3 per cent worked in trade and finance, 21.6 per cent in industry and commerce, 8.9 per cent in agriculture, 7.7 per cent in public service, 2.9 per cent in traffic and transportation, and 13.6 per cent in other professions (doctors, lawyers, and so on).[18]

14 Franz Kafka, *Briefe 1902–1924* (Frankfurt am Main: Fischer, 1958), p. 337. Quotation translated from the original German. A translation can also be found in Franz Kafka, *Letters to Friends, Family and Editors*, trans. Richard Winston and Clara Winston (New York: Schocken, 1977 [German edn, 1958]), p. 289.

15 Saul Friedländer, *When Memory Comes* (New York: Farrar, Straus and Giroux, 1979), p. 6.

16 Max Brod, *Streitbares Leben 1884–1968* (Munich: F. A. Herbig, 1969), pp. 48–52, here p. 50; Hillel J. Kieval, 'Bohemia and Moravia', in Gershon David Hundert (ed.), *The YIVO Encyclopedia of Jews in Eastern Europe*, vol. 1 (New Haven: Yale University Press, 2008), pp. 202–211.

17 Wlaschek, *Juden in Böhmen*, pp. 77–87; Helena Krejčová, 'Juden in den 30er Jahren des 20. Jahrhunderts', in Marek Nekula and Walter Koschmal (eds.), *Juden zwischen Deutschen und Tschechen: Sprachliche und kulturelle Identitäten in Böhmen 1800–1945* (Munich: Oldenbourg, 2006), pp. 85–102, here pp. 86–92.

18 Wlaschek, *Juden in Böhmen*, pp. 43–44 and 90; Rothkirchen, 'Czechoslovak Jewry', p. 112; Čapková, *Czechs, Germans, Jews?*, pp. 14–25.

In 1933 democratic Czechoslovakia offered asylum to refugees from Germany – politically exposed Social Democrats and communists, writers who were unwelcome in the Reich, and Jews. The Jewish communities set up efficient structures to aid the refugees. Following the Munich Agreement, the heartland of Czecho-Slovakia was overrun by refugees from the newly created Sudetengau. Democratically inclined Sudeten Germans sought refuge, but most of those who fled were Jews – at least 15,000 by December 1938.

During the short-lived Second Czecho-Slovak Republic, however, which lasted from the Munich Agreement until March 1939, the political climate changed, as right-wing parties came to dominate events. Many Czech newspapers stirred up hatred against Jews, and there was a distinct increase in the number of antisemitic activities. Nationalist groups were in the ascendant, and the Sudeten German Party (SdP) became the dominant German party in Czecho-Slovakia.[19] On 14 October 1938, just two weeks after the founding of the republic, professional associations of lawyers and doctors issued a call for Jews to be barred from practising medicine, law, and technical professions. Because the government under Prime Minister Rudolf Beran was anxious to demonstrate through its stance on the 'Jewish question' that it was open to the policy of the German government, the Ministry of Defence suspended all officers of Jewish descent on 18 February 1939 and advised them to apply for a discharge. On 17 March 1939, one day after the establishment of the Protectorate, the Beran government met the demands of the doctors and lawyers for the exclusion of Jews from these professions.[20]

The refugees from the Sudeten German territories were only briefly out of harm's way. Max Mannheimer, who later survived the Theresienstadt ghetto and the Auschwitz and Dachau camps, recalled in his memoirs how his family initially fled to the interior of the country in the autumn of 1938. However, German troops caught up with them again in the spring of 1939.[21] Others managed to escape in the nick of time. Kafka's friend Max Brod caught the last train to the Polish border on 14 March 1939, and only just managed to get out of the country and continue his journey to Jerusalem. Later he heard that the Gestapo had gone to the editorial offices of the Zionist newspaper *Selbstwehr* on the same day that Prague was occupied to look for him and his colleagues Felix Weltsch and Hans Lichtwitz.[22]

19 Wlaschek, *Juden in Böhmen*, pp. 95–99; Helena Krejčová, 'Spezifische Voraussetzungen des Antisemitismus und antijüdische Aktivitäten im Protektorat Böhmen und Mähren', in Jörg K. Hoensch, Stanislav Biman, and L'ubomír Lipták (eds.), *Judenemanzipation – Antisemitismus – Verfolgung in Deutschland, Österreich-Ungarn, den Böhmischen Ländern und in der Slowakei* (Essen: Klartext, 1999), pp. 175–194; Frankl, 'Tschechien'; Jörg Osterloh, 'Sudetenland', in Wolf Gruner and Jörg Osterloh (eds.), *The Greater German Reich and the Jews: Nazi Persecution Policies in the Annexed Territories, 1935–1945*, trans. Bernard Heise (New York/Oxford: Berghahn, 2015 [German edn, 2010]), pp. 68–98, here p. 88.

20 Heinrich Bodensieck, 'Das Dritte Reich und die Lage der Juden in der Tschecho-Slowakei nach München', *Vierteljahrshefte für Zeitgeschichte*, vol. 9 (1961), pp. 249–261; Miroslav Kárný, 'Die "Judenfrage" in der nazistischen Okkupationspolitik', *Historica*, vol. 21 (1982), pp. 137–192, here p. 152; Frankl, 'Tschechien', p. 368.

21 Max Mannheimer, *Spätes Tagebuch: Theresienstadt – Auschwitz. Warschau – Dachau* (Munich: Pendo, 2009), p. 34.

22 Brod, *Streitbares Leben*, pp. 285–292; Demetz, *Prague in Danger*, pp. 32–33.

The Administration of the Protectorate

On the evening of 15 March 1939, after Hácha and Foreign Minister Chvalkovský had returned from Berlin, they went to Prague Castle, the president's official residence, to inform the Czech government of the German coercion. At the same time, in another part of the castle, Hitler, Foreign Minister Joachim von Ribbentrop, and State Secretary Wilhelm Stuckart were drafting – without Czech participation – the Führer decree with which Hitler, one day later, proclaimed the Protectorate of Bohemia and Moravia, which from now on was part of the German Reich. Although Article 3 stated that 'The Protectorate of Bohemia and Moravia is autonomous and shall govern itself', the next paragraph added the crucial qualification that this must occur 'in conformity with the political, military, and economic interests of the Reich'. The approximately 250,000 German inhabitants of the Protectorate were defined as 'German state subjects' (*deutsche Staatsangehörige*) and 'Reich citizens' (*Reichsbürger*), and the Czechs as 'subjects of the Protectorate' (*Staatsangehörige des Protektorats*). The position of the Jewish population was not specified in the decree. The regulation meant, in effect, that most natives of the territory now held only the status of second-class citizens. In addition, only the German residents were under German jurisdiction, whereas the others were under the jurisdiction of the Protectorate.[23]

The Protectorate was initially placed under military administration for one month. A chief of the civil administration was assigned to each of the army groups. Seasoned personnel were drawn upon for these positions. In Bohemia the Sudeten German Gauleiter Konrad Henlein performed this task; in Moravia, the Reich commissioner for Vienna, Josef Bürckel. They established a German administration and closely monitored the existing Czech administration.[24]

On 15 April, Baron Konstantin von Neurath, Germany's foreign minister until 1938, took up his position as head of the German administration in the Protectorate. He was regarded as an elder statesman with diplomatic experience and a moderate approach. Neurath had already been appointed Reich Protector by Hitler on 18 March 1939 and was directly accountable to him. Karl Hermann Frank, a former Sudeten German Party official, became von Neurath's state secretary, and from 28 March 1939 also functioned as Higher SS and Police Leader (HSSPF), holding both positions simultaneously.

Frank was born in Carlsbad in 1898. He did his utmost to become the strong man in the Protectorate and, with Heinrich Himmler's backing, succeeded in this endeavour. The office of Reich Protector was to change hands: in September 1941 Hitler replaced von Neurath – who was regarded as weak – in all but title with Reinhard Heydrich, whom he named Deputy Reich Protector. Following Heydrich's death in 1942 from the

23 *Reichsgesetzblatt*, 1939, I, p. 485; Brandes, *Die Tschechen unter deutschem Protektorat*, pp. 20–21; Wolfgang Benz, 'Typologie der Herrschaftsformen in den Gebieten unter deutschem Einfluß', in Wolfgang Benz, Johannes Houwink ten Cate, and Gerhard Otto (eds.), *Die Bürokratie der Okkupation: Strukturen der Herrschaft und Verwaltung im besetzten Europa* (Berlin: Metropol, 1998), pp. 11–25; Jan Gebhart and Jan Kuklík, *Velké dějiny zemí Koruny české*, vol. 15a (Prague: Paseka, 2006), pp. 155–192.

24 Wolf Gruner, 'Das Protektorat Böhmen und Mähren und die antijüdische Politik 1939–1941: Lokale Initiativen, regionale Maßnahmen, zentrale Entscheidungen im "Großdeutschen Reich"', *Theresienstädter Studien und Dokumente*, vol. 12 (2005), pp. 27–62, here p. 31.

consequences of an assassination attempt, Kurt Daluege was appointed his successor. Frank, however, who had made it his goal to Germanize the region, remained in office until the end of the war.

Frank built up a tight network of police surveillance. At the onset of the war, the status of the police was both legally defined and consolidated on 1 September 1939 by the Regulation on the Establishment of the Administration and the German Security Police in the Protectorate of Bohemia and Moravia. The police force was assigned to the Reich Protector, rather than subordinated to him, so that he had no managerial authority over it. Instead, the Senior Commander of the Security Police and the Senior Commander of the Order Police were responsible to Frank. The Gestapo head offices in Prague and Brünn (Brno), which were authorized to issue directives to the Oberlandräte (regional administrators), were responsible for twelve and seven Oberlandratsbezirke (administrative districts), respectively. In August 1941 the Gestapo head office in Brünn had 638 employees, while the Prague office had 812. In addition, approximately 350 SS Security Service (SD) members operated in the Protectorate.[25]

Kurt von Burgsdorff, ministerial director, later undersecretary, was appointed to serve as Frank's representative in the Office of the State Secretary. The Central Office for Bohemia and Moravia, under the direction of Wilhelm Stuckart, state secretary in the Reich Ministry of the Interior, acted as intermediary between the agencies of the Reich Protector and those of the Reich.[26]

Oberlandräte were put in charge of regional headquarters, each covering two or three Czech district administrations (Bezirkshauptmannschaften). They supervised the agencies of the Protectorate in their respective districts and submitted reports to the Reich Protector concerning developments in their area of activity.[27] Like the department heads in the Office of the Reich Protector, they were mostly Germans from the Reich. By contrast, Sudeten Germans were favoured for appointment as Bezirkshauptleute (district commissioners) and mayors, owing to their superior knowledge of the country and its people. In Prague the Czech Otokar Klapka continued to serve as mayor at first, until he was arrested in July 1940 for maintaining contacts with the resistance movement and replaced by Alois Říha. In October 1941 Klapka was executed for his links to the resistance. The Sudeten German historian and politician Josef Pfitzner functioned as his deputy and simultaneously as the government commissioner in charge of the administration of Prague. Guided by notions of Germanization much like those of Frank, he quickly

25 Copy of the regulation in BArch, R 70 Böhmen Mähren. See also Oldřich Sládek, *Zločinná role gestapa: Nacistická bezpečnostní policie v českých zemích 1938–1945* (Prague: Naše Vojsko, 1986); Oldřich Sládek, 'Standrecht und Standgericht: Die Gestapo in Böhmen und Mähren', in Gerhard Paul and Klaus-Michael Mallmann (eds.), *Die Gestapo im Zweiten Weltkrieg: "Heimatfront" und besetztes Europa* (Darmstadt: Primus, 2000), pp. 317–339, here pp. 324–325; Marc Oprach, *Nationalsozialistische Judenpolitik im Protektorat Böhmen und Mähren: Entscheidungsabläufe und Radikalisierung* (Hamburg: Kovač, 2006), pp. 47–49; René Küpper, *Karl Hermann Frank (1898–1946): Politische Biographie eines sudetendeutschen Nationalsozialisten* (Munich: Oldenbourg, 2010), pp. 146–150.

26 Brandes, *Die Tschechen unter deutschem Protektorat*, pp. 28–34; Küpper, *Karl Hermann Frank*.

27 Stanislav Šisler, 'Příspěvek k vývoji a organizaci okupační správy v českých zemích v letech 1939–1945', *Sborník archivních prací*, vol. 2 (1963), pp. 46–95.

chose Germans to fill key administrative positions in the city, whose inhabitants were mostly Czech.[28]

A Czech government operated alongside the German Reich Protectorate administration. At the meeting of state secretaries in the Reich Ministry of the Interior on 25 March 1939 (Doc. 240), Stuckart again put on record 'the will of the Führer' that 'the Reich make use of its powers [...] only to the extent that is absolutely necessary in the interests of the Reich'.[29] In practice, however, the Czech Protectorate government was forced to adjust its policies to the political, military, and economic interests of the German Reich in compliance with the wishes of the Reich Protector and his German administration. The Reich Protector was empowered to raise objections to laws and measures passed by the Czech government and to enact laws himself. Moreover, the members of the Protectorate government had to be approved by him. At the same time, it was in the interest of the German rulers to include the previous political elites, albeit with limited responsibilities, in order to ensure the continuity of administration.[30]

The 66-year-old Emil Hácha remained in office as president. Fearing that the parliament would refuse to affirm the government, he dissolved it on 21 March 1939 and established National Solidarity (Národní souručenství), a mass organization that was intended to represent all Czechs and thus to strengthen their cohesion. In doing so, he managed to prevail against both the Czech fascist organizations influenced by General Radola Gajda and the right-wing extremist Vlajka (Flag) movement, which were seeking to enter government or had attempted to seize power for themselves in the chaotic days preceding the declaration of the Protectorate. Hácha established a fifty-member Committee of National Solidarity, into which he incorporated political figures from the period before the Munich Agreement. At its first meeting on 21 March, this body accepted the president's proposal for the founding of a unity party. Numerous members of the resistance movement also aligned themselves with National Solidarity; however, it increasingly came under German surveillance, and many of its officials were arrested by the Gestapo.

General Alois Eliáš, formerly a delegate to the League of Nations and minister of transport in the Beran government, served as prime minister from 27 April 1939. His great ambition was to regain state sovereignty. To that end he worked in secret, until his arrest in autumn 1941, with the Czechoslovak government in exile in London and with the resistance movement in the country itself. In June 1942 he was executed for 'high treason'. Minister of Agriculture Ladislav Feierabend and the head of the Supreme Board

28 Vojtěch Šustek, 'Die nationalsozialistische Karriere eines sudetendeutschen Historikers', in Alena Míšková, Josef Pfitzner, and Vojtěch Šustek (eds.), *Josef Pfitzner a protektorátní Praha v letech 1939–45*, vol. 1 (Prague: Scriptorium, 2000), pp. 71–109.

29 NAP, 109-1/88, fols. 1–8a. Published in Miroslav Kárný and Jaroslava Milotová (eds.), *Anatomie okupační politiky hitlerovského Německa v 'Protektorátu Čechy a Morava': Dokumenty z období říšského protektora Konstantina von Neuratha* (Prague: Ústav Českosloven. a Světových Dějin ČSAV, 1987), doc. 2, pp. 4–17, here p. 6. On this meeting, see also Wolf Gruner, *The Holocaust in Bohemia and Moravia: Czech Initiatives, German Policies, Jewish Responses* (New York/Oxford: Berghahn, 2019).

30 Brandes, *Die Tschechen unter deutschem Protektorat*, p. 32; Brandes, 'Politische Kollaboration im "Protektorat Böhmen und Mähren"', in Joachim Tauber (ed.), *'Kollaboration' in Nordosteuropa: Erscheinungsformen und Deutungen im 20. Jahrhundert* (Wiesbaden: Harrassowitz, 2006), pp. 453–462, here pp. 458–459.

of Prices,[31] Jaromír Nečas, had fled in January 1940; they later became part of the government in exile.[32]

The president, the government, and the prime minister cooperated with the German rulers in the hope of thereby being able to stave off more serious consequences for the Czech population. Indeed, life under German rule was tolerable for most Czechs at first. However, plans were emerging for the Germanization of what the National Socialists regarded as Lebensraum: the long-term goal was to establish a German region here. Czechs considered incapable of assimilation were to be expelled and those deemed 'hostile to the Reich' were to be murdered; the others were to be made into Germans. The latter course of action seemed feasible, as Czechs ranked higher in the National Socialist racial hierarchy than, for example, their Polish neighbours. Moreover, it was necessary for pragmatic reasons. Czech industry would, after all, have collapsed without its workers, and Czech industrial facilities were of considerable significance for the German wartime economy. According to estimates, 9 to 12 per cent of the industrial production of the German Reich came from the Protectorate.[33]

The Czech government hoped that the German occupation would be of limited duration. It endeavoured to play for time and, through its contacts with the government in exile, to begin making arrangements for a time when sovereignty would be regained. Often the same individuals were active in the government and in the resistance movement. However, the Protectorate government also sought to adjust to the German administration, and took pains to secure Czech participation in Aryanization measures. Ultimately, it even sought to control the course of 'Jewish policy' in the Protectorate.[34]

The Persecution of the Jews in the Protectorate of Bohemia and Moravia

After the Wehrmacht invasion the initial targets of persecution were predominantly politically suspect Czechs and refugees from Germany. Using a list previously compiled for Operation Grid (*Aktion Gitter*), two Einsatzgruppen (mobile task forces) of the Security Police arrested alleged and genuine opponents, including at least 4,376 people in

31 An institution responsible for setting retail prices.

32 Helmut Heiber, 'Zur Justiz im Dritten Reich: Der Fall Eliáš', *Vierteljahrshefte für Zeitgeschichte*, vol. 3 (1955), pp. 275–296; Brandes, *Die Tschechen unter deutschem Protektorat*, pp. 24–52 and 97–106; Vojtěch Mastný, *The Czechs under Nazi Rule: The Failure of National Resistance, 1939–1942* (New York: Columbia University Press, 1971), pp. 155–165; Pavel Maršálek, *Protektorát Čechy a Morava: Státoprávní a politické aspekty nacistického okupačního režimu v českých zemích 1939–1945* (Prague: Karolinum, 2002), pp. 57–64.

33 Václav Král, *Otázky hospodářského a sociálního vývoje v českých zemích v letech 1938–1945*, 3 vols. (Prague: Nakladatelství Československé akademie věd, 1957–1959); Peter Němec, 'Das tschechische Volk und die nationalsozialistische Germanisierung des Raumes', Bohemia, vol. 32 (1991), pp. 424–455; Isabel Heinemann, *'Rasse, Siedlung, deutsches Blut': Das Rasse- und Siedlungshauptamt der SS und die rassenpolitische Neuordnung Europas* (Göttingen: Wallstein, 2003), pp. 127–186; Chad Bryant, *Prague in Black: Nazi Rule and Czech Nationalism* (Cambridge, MA: Harvard University Press, 2007), pp. 84–89 and 104–138; Küpper, *Karl Hermann Frank*, pp. 158–178.

34 Brandes, 'Politische Kollaboration', pp. 458–462; Bryant, *Prague in Black*, pp. 41–45.

Bohemia alone, 747 of whom were German émigrés, as well as numerous Jews. At least 1,000 German émigrés were arrested in Moravia.[35]

Yet the first attacks deliberately targeting the Jews took place as early as March 1939. Not only Germans but also Czechs set fire to synagogues in several cities, looted shops, and stole objects of value (Doc. 239).[36] The initial period of German occupation was marked above all by looting. 'Even before the Germans had ensconced themselves here, it was clear that their version of occupation was actually an enormous plundering raid,' wrote Václav Černý, a Czech literary scholar and vice chancellor of Prague's Charles University; 'this was the first thing to really emerge'.[37] The writer Jiři Weil, who later feigned suicide to avoid being deported and survived in hiding, similarly wrote that the German occupiers 'thought only of how they could enrich themselves, [...] and were willing, for the sake of worldly goods, to murder, loot, and steal'.[38]

However, to prevent the sort of unauthorized Aryanizations by freebooting profiteers that had occurred in Vienna after the Anschluss,[39] on 16 March 1939 Hermann Göring, in his capacity as Plenipotentiary for the Four-Year Plan, ordered in an express letter that the 'restructuring of ownership' in the Protectorate was to be controlled by the Reich Ministry of Economics (Doc. 237). In addition, with the appointment of Hans Kehrl, he put in place an agent of the Reich Ministry of Economics who was to pursue, from Prague, the economic integration of the Protectorate into the Reich. A turf war over these matters quickly flared up among various German and Czech authorities. The heads of the civil administration, Henlein and Bürckel, announced that no one was empowered to Aryanize Jewish businesses without their authorization.[40]

The government of the Czech Protectorate now also took action against Jews. As early as 17 March 1939 it stripped Jewish physicians and lawyers of their licences to practise, as noted, mandated the exclusion of Jews from top positions in industry, and ordered that Jewish shops be identified as such.[41] In doing so, it complied with the wish of the German rulers, who were anxious to make the Czechs accomplices in their anti-Jewish policy. A directive from Hitler was announced at a meeting of state secretaries in the Reich Ministry of the Interior on 25 March 1939. This made it clear that although the Jews were to be 'excluded' from public life in the Protectorate, this was to be the task of the Protectorate government 'and not the direct responsibility of the Reich', as the 'Jewish question' in the Protectorate would presumably 'develop of its own accord' (Doc. 240). In May, von Burgsdorff affirmed: 'The Führer has ordered that the Czechs should deal with the Jewish question themselves and that we should not interfere' (Doc. 245).[42]

35 Sládek, *Zločinná role gestapa*, p. 66; Küpper, *Karl Hermann Frank*, pp. 146–147.

36 Jens Hampel, 'Das Schicksal der jüdischen Bevölkerung der Stadt Iglau 1938–1942', *Theresienstädter Studien und Dokumente*, vol. 5 (1998), pp. 70–99, here pp. 74–78.

37 Václav Černý, *Kultur im Widerstand: Prag 1938–1945*, vol. 1: 1938–1942 (Bremen: Kafka-Presse, 1979), p. 193.

38 Weil, Jiří, 'Klagegesang für 77 297 Opfer', in Jiří Weil, *Leben mit dem Stern*, trans. Bettina Kaibach (New York: Farrar, Straus and Giroux, 1989 [Czech edn, 1949]), pp. 337–386, here p. 340.

39 See PMJ 2, p. 39.

40 Brandes, *Die Tschechen unter deutschem Protektorat*, p. 33; Kárný, 'Die "Judenfrage" in der nazistischen Okkupationspolitik', pp. 145–151; Gebhart and Kuklík, *Velké dějiny zemí Koruny české*, pp. 192–193.

41 Gruner, 'Das Protektorat', p. 33.

42 Kárný, 'Die "Judenfrage" in der nazistischen Okkupationspolitik', pp. 160–161.

Beyond the disputes over economic decision-making, a number of different offices sought to secure their influence over other contested policy areas. On 11 May 1939 Prime Minister Eliáš submitted to the Reich Protector the draft of a government regulation on the status of the Jewish population in which the definition of the term 'Jew' was based on religious criteria (Doc. 246). Although the draft envisaged extensive restrictions for Jews, the German side viewed it as too moderate. The Senior Commander of the Security Police, Walter Stahlecker, thus told Frank on 1 June: 'As experience has shown that it is precisely the rich and influential Jews who have abandoned the Mosaic faith, these persons would thus not be treated as Jews according to the draft.'[43] The Reich Protector resolved both disputes on 21 June 1939 by announcing a regulation on Jewish assets. In it he determined that the Nuremberg Laws should also apply in the Protectorate (Doc. 247). To ensure that the looting of the Jewish population would benefit the German Reich, the Reich Protector appropriated for himself all authority for Aryanization. As a result, the instructions to leave the 'Jewish question' to the Czechs were rendered completely obsolete. At a single stroke the Reich Protector had resolved outstanding disputes over areas of responsibility in favour of the German powers.[44]

This pattern was repeated in similar instances. In the summer of 1939 the Czech Protectorate government drafted a government regulation on the legal status of Jews in public life. Because German permission was delayed, however, it was not made public until 24 April 1940, and with several major amendments. For example, paragraph 3 of the regulation had originally granted the Czech president the right to declare Jews who, in his opinion, played an important role in the country to be 'honorary Aryans'. The revised version of this paragraph stated that this required the consent of the Reich Protector. Von Neurath rejected every single application (Doc. 296).[45]

Strengthened by von Neurath's regulation of 21 June 1939, Germans became the major beneficiaries of Aryanization in the Protectorate. The Group for Trade and Industry in the Office of the Reich Protector set up a 'de-Jewification' (*Entjudung*) section, which was headed first by Siegfried Ludwig and then, from the autumn of 1939, by his deputy Rudolf Stier, who had previously worked in the corresponding department under the Reich commissioner for the Sudetenland. In April 1941 the section took stock of its achievements:

> The goal of de-Jewification was to place all applicable businesses, trading firms, etc. in German hands. In selecting the applicants for Jewish businesses, importance was

43 Letter from the Senior Commander of the Security Police to K. H. Frank, dated 1 June 1939, NAP, ÚŘP, 3b 5801, box 388.

44 Miroslav Kárný, *'Konečné řešení': Genocida českých židů v německé protektorátní politice* (Prague: Academia, 1991), pp. 18–75; Jaroslava Milotová, 'Die Zentralstelle für jüdische Auswanderung in Prag: Genesis und Tätigkeit bis zum Anfang des Jahres 1940', *Theresienstädter Studien und Dokumente*, vol. 4 (1997), pp. 7–30, here p. 8; Jaroslava Milotová, 'Zur Geschichte der Verordnung Konstantin von Neuraths über das jüdische Vermögen', *Theresienstädter Studien und Dokumente*, vol. 9 (2002), pp. 75–115; Helena Petrův, *Právní postavení židů v Protektorátu Čechy a Morava (1939–1941)* (Prague: Institut Terezínské iniciativy, 2000); Jörg Osterloh and Harald Wixforth, 'Die "Arisierung" im Protektorat Böhmen und Mähren', in Harald Wixforth, *Die Expansion der Dresdner Bank in Europa* (Munich: Oldenbourg, 2006), pp. 306–350, here pp. 307–308.

45 Miroslav Kárný, 'Die Ausschaltung der Juden aus dem öffentlichen Leben des Protektorats und die Geschichte des "Ehrenariertums"', *Theresienstädter Studien und Dokumente* (1998), pp. 7–40.

> attached to enabling Germans from Protectorate territory to obtain a secure livelihood and allowing as many German Volksgenossen as possible from the so-called Altreich or abroad to transfer their place of residence to the territory of the Protectorate, so that they could establish a new sphere of activity here. As a result, there has been considerable ethnopolitical activity and the German Volkskörper in the territory of the Protectorate of Bohemia and Moravia has been enlarged.[46]

The transfer of assets to Germans was furthered not least by the appointment of German trustees. At the end of June 1940, of the 1,205 trustees in the operational sphere of the Oberlandrat in Prague, 1,109 were Germans and 96 were Czechs.[47] In early October 1940 the Böhmische Escompte Bank reported that, in the Protectorate, 'there is no longer any significant de-Jewification property available to new applicants'.[48] Although there had been complaints at first about the lack of success of Aryanization (Doc. 268), the newspapers in the Protectorate were soon full of notices announcing changes of ownership (Doc. 294).

German ethnopolitical measures in the Protectorate also included efforts to increase the pressure on Jews to emigrate. At the same time, however, it was to be guaranteed that the Protectorate Jews would not compete with the Jewish emigrants from the Old Reich for the few possible havens of refuge. Only under this condition did Reinhard Heydrich, the Chief of the Security Police and the SD, who initially wanted to prohibit emigration from the Protectorate, consent to the establishment of a Central Office for Jewish Emigration here as well. In late June 1939 his 'resettlement expert', Adolf Eichmann, came to Prague and set up the office together with Stahlecker. The Protectorate government also sent staff. In July a delegation of members of the Czech government travelled to Vienna, where it gathered detailed information about the work of the Central Office in Vienna (Docs. 252, 255). Through the Reich Protector's regulation of 5 March 1940 on the supervision of Jews and Jewish organizations, the Central Office was granted oversight of all Jewish communities in the Protectorate.[49] It exercised control through the Prague Religious Community, which was charged with ensuring that the directives were also implemented throughout the territory. The Jewish representatives in Prague often only received their orders orally from the Central Office (Doc. 263). Hence, it is difficult to find evidence of many of the anti-Jewish regulations in the Protectorate. The Central Office's exploitation of the Prague Religious Community for its own ends resulted in a dilemma: many Jews viewed the Community as the originator of restrictive regulations.

46 'Bericht: Die Kapitalverflechtung zwischen dem Protektorat und dem Reich nach dem Stand vom Frühjahr 1941', published in Kárný and Milotová, *Anatomie*, pp. 187–199, here p. 197; Frank Bajohr, 'Die wirtschaftliche Existenzvernichtung und Enteignung der Juden: Forschungsbilanz und offene Fragen', *Theresienstädter Studien und Dokumente*, vol. 13 (2006), pp. 348–365.

47 Report by the trustee supervision for the Oberlandrat in Prague, 26 June 1940, NAP, ÚŘP, I–1a 1803, box 279, fol. 303.

48 Helma Kaden (ed.), *Europa unterm Hakenkreuz: Die faschistische Okkupationspolitik in Österreich und der Tschechoslowakei (1938–1945)* (Berlin: Deutscher Verlag der Wissenschaften, 1988), doc. 82, pp. 156–157.

49 Milotová, 'Die Zentralstelle für jüdische Auswanderung in Prag', p. 23.

Eichmann left the Protectorate towards the end of 1939 and transferred to the Reich Security Main Office (RSHA). Stahlecker moved to Norway as Senior Commander of the Security Police in April 1940. His successor was Horst Böhme, who had a background in commerce. However, it was Hans Günther, a former colleague of Eichmann's in the Vienna Central Office, who actually ran the Central Office in Prague. While Böhme went on to command SS Einsatzgruppe B in Belarus in 1943, Günther remained in office until the end of the war and became one of the main persons responsible for anti-Jewish policy in the Protectorate.[50]

The German Reich and Heightening Persecution of the Jews

Since the November pogroms of 1938, the German government had greatly intensified its efforts to exclude the Jews from the economy and had thus deprived most of them of their livelihood. The authorities pursued two main objectives: first, to dispossess the Jews, and second, to force them to emigrate. However, these two purposes contradicted one another, and the Jews were caught in the middle, for they needed money to be able to emigrate. Jews without means had scarcely any chance of gaining entry to another country.

There was little enthusiasm for the war among the German population in September 1939. The horrors of the First World War had by no means been forgotten. In the course of these new preparations for war, therefore, the National Socialist leadership endeavoured to avoid any dramatic fall in the standard of living, lest the loyalty of the population be jeopardized. Yet this approach was compatible only to a limited extent with the increased build-up of arms and the allocation of economic resources for the war. The German Reich had neither adequate foreign-exchange reserves nor a balanced budget at its command, and raw materials and manpower were in short supply. The break-up of Czechoslovakia, which gave the Reich access to the Czech industrial regions, was thus of great economic significance for overcoming bottlenecks. The expropriation of the Jewish population was justified on grounds of (wartime) economic necessity, as were the compulsory deployment of the Jews as forced labour and their eviction from their homes, which were then allocated to non-Jews. Moreover, propaganda blamed 'the Jews' for the war and thus provided the rationale for depriving them of their rights.[51]

With the invasion of Poland, the German state leadership tightened its policies on various levels. The German occupation of Poland was marked by terror and unprecedented violence. Even in the first weeks of the war, police and Wehrmacht units murdered a great

50 Ibid.; Gabriele Anderl, 'Die "Zentralstellen für jüdische Auswanderung" in Wien, Berlin und Prag: Ein Vergleich', *Tel Aviver Jahrbuch für deutsche Geschichte*, vol. 23 (1994), pp. 275–299.

51 Jutta Sywottek, *Mobilmachung für den totalen Krieg: Die propagandistische Vorbereitung der deutschen Bevölkerung auf den Zweiten Weltkrieg* (Opladen: Westdeutscher Verlag, 1976); Ludolf Herbst, *Das nationalsozialistische Deutschland 1933–1945: Die Entfesselung der Gewalt. Rassismus und Krieg* (Frankfurt am Main: Suhrkamp, 1996), pp. 251–255; Adam Tooze, *The Wages of Destruction: The Making and Breaking of the Nazi Economy* (London: Allen Lane, 2006), pp. 326–357; Kim Christian Priemel, *Flick: Eine Konzerngeschichte vom Kaiserreich bis zur Bundesrepublik* (Göttingen: Wallstein, 2007), pp. 390–431.

many Jews and Poles. Military expansion provided the planning staff of the newly established Reich Security Main Office, the SS Race and Settlement Main Office, and other German institutions with completely new alternatives for action. The bilateral agreements with the Soviet Union, for example, created the opportunity for large-scale population transfers and Germanization projects. The implementation of the agreements, however, soon caused new problems, which resulted in partial revisions, so-called interim solutions, and repeated population displacements, thereby further increasing the pressure to act. The brutal eviction of Poles and Jews in favour of German settlers was made easier by the fact that worldwide public attention was focusing on the war. The German warlords now had to make far less allowance for international reactions to their crimes than had been the case in peacetime.[52]

In the period from September 1939 to spring 1942, various institutions and authorities in the Reich devised a host of plans – correspondingly adjusted as the war progressed – for a 'solution' to the Jewish question. The plans were often tested only in rudimentary fashion and were withdrawn in some cases. Although the individual operations and concepts sometimes overlapped chronologically, this period of approximately two and a half years can be divided into five phases.

In the first phase, up to the early summer of 1940, large-scale resettlement projects were attempted in the occupied territories under the direction of the SS. At the same time, the Reich Security Main Office organized the first deportations of Jews from the so-called Old Reich, the Protectorate, and Austria to the occupied Polish territories.

Second, between early summer and approximately November 1940, the military victories in Western Europe led the German state leadership to contemplate for the first time an overall European 'solution to the Jewish question' which would consist of deporting all Jews to the French colonial island of Madagascar.

With the failure of this project and the start of preparations for the invasion of the Soviet Union from late 1940, the vague notion of a 'territorial final solution' gained acceptance. The plan was no longer to deport the European Jews to Madagascar, but instead to the Soviet territories that Germany was expecting to conquer. In this third phase the term 'final solution to the Jewish question' cropped up with increasing frequency in the plans, without systematic mass murder necessarily being meant at this point. Nevertheless, both 'territorial solutions' assumed the death of a large number of Jews.

The decisive shift towards radicalization came about with the invasion of the Soviet Union in June 1941. In the very first days of the war of annihilation (*Vernichtungskrieg*), Einsatzgruppen and police units began to shoot thousands of Jewish men in the occupied Soviet territories. In August they also began to murder women and children. During this fourth phase Hitler agreed to make it compulsory for Jews in the Reich to wear a yellow star as identification. In contrast to his initial plan, he also agreed for them to

52 Peter Longerich, *Holocaust: The Nazi Persecution and Murder of the Jews*, new edn, trans. Shaun Whiteside (Oxford: Oxford University Press, 2010 [German edn, 1998]), pp. 229–230; Götz Aly, *'Final Solution': Nazi Population Policy and the Murder of the European Jews*, trans. Belinda Cooper and Allison Brown (London: Arnold, 1999 [German edn, 1995]); Klaus-Michael Mallmann and Bogdan Musial (eds.), *Genesis des Genozids: Polen 1939–1941* (Darmstadt: Wissenschaftliche Buchgesellschaft, 2004); Jochen Böhler, *Auftakt zum Vernichtungskrieg: Die Wehrmacht in Polen 1939* (Frankfurt am Main: Fischer, 2006). On developments in Poland, see the Introduction to PMJ 4.

be deported to the East while the war was still ongoing. The present volume documents these developments up to September 1941.

Finally, between autumn 1941 and spring 1942 the decision to systematically deport and murder millions of European Jews assumed concrete form within the National Socialist leadership. This development is described in detail in volume 6 of the series.[53]

Between the Onset of War and the Summer of 1940

After the Munich Agreement, Hitler confronted Poland, which he had planned to make a junior partner and a staging area for war against the Soviet Union, with ultimatums. His demands included extraterritorial access through the 'Polish Corridor' to East Prussia, the incorporation of the Free City of Danzig into the Reich, and the accession of Poland to the Anti-Comintern Pact. When the Polish government refused, Hitler gave orders in early April to commence preparations to invade Poland ('Case White') and abrogated the non-aggression pact of 1934 between the two countries. To general amazement both at home and abroad the Soviet Union, previously stylized as the great ideological enemy, now became the ally of Germany, which saw this as a way of keeping its options open. On 23 August 1939 the respective foreign ministers, Joachim von Ribbentrop and Vyacheslav M. Molotov, signed a non-aggression pact containing a secret protocol in which the two countries staked out their spheres of influence in East Central Europe and, in particular, divided up Poland between themselves.

When the Wehrmacht invaded Poland one week later, France and Britain quickly responded by declaring war on the Reich, but did not attack Germany. In the following weeks, German troops occupied around half of the national territory of Poland.[54]

Terror in the Reich

The opportunities afforded by the war in Poland developed a dynamic of their own within the German Reich as well. While preparing for war, the regime had already created the domestic political prerequisites to crush all resistance if Germany went to war. Construction of new concentration camps to detain 'enemies of the Reich' had started as early as 1937. The relevant ministries created new and more punitive legislation for

53 On developments between autumn 1939 and spring 1942, see, for example, Raul Hilberg, *The Destruction of the European Jews*, 3rd edn (New Haven, CT/London: Yale University Press, 2003 [1961]); Leni Yahil, *The Holocaust: The Fate of European Jewry, 1932–1945*, trans. Ina Friedman and Haya Galai (New York: Oxford University Press, 1990 [Hebrew edn, 1987]); Longerich, *Holocaust*, pp. 131–310; Christopher R. Browning, with contributions by Jürgen Matthäus, *The Origins of the Final Solution: The Evolution of Nazi Jewish Policy, September 1939 – March 1942* (Lincoln, NE: University of Nebraska Press, 2004), p. 19; Saul Friedländer, *Nazi Germany and the Jews*, vol. 2: *The Years of Extermination, 1939–1945* (New York: HarperCollins, 2007).

54 Gerhard L. Weinberg, *A World at Arms: A Global History of World War II*, 2nd edn (Cambridge: Cambridge University Press, 2005); Browning, *The Origins of the Final Solution*, pp. 15–16; Richard Overy, *1939: Countdown to War* (London: Allen Lane, 2009). See also the Introduction to PMJ 4.

the start of the war. The Wartime Special Penal Regulation (*Kriegssonderstrafrechtsverordnung*), issued in August 1938, took effect on 1 September 1939.[55] A few days later, on 4 September, it was followed by the Wartime Economy Regulation (*Kriegswirtschaftsverordnung*),[56] and the next day by the Regulation against *Volksschädlinge* ('vermin'; people considered harmful to the German *Volk*).[57] This ensured that the death penalty could be imposed even for loosely defined crimes and thus more frequently than before. A substantial percentage of all offences were now tried before special courts (*Sondergerichte*). After German military courts in Poland had attempted, during the first weeks of war, to pass sentence on SS men for the crimes committed there, Hitler issued a secret amnesty decree on 17 October 1939 that placed all members of the SS and the police under special jurisdiction, and thus granted them extensive immunity from prosecution.[58]

On 27 September 1939 the Reich Security Main Office was created by merging the SD and the Security Police (Gestapo and Criminal Police). It now also assumed responsibility for the occupied territories, where it quickly expanded its powers. Its Einsatzgruppen took action against the political and social elites of Poland and terrorized the populace. In establishing the Reich Security Main Office, Himmler and Heydrich also created an authority that directed German operations against the Jews in the Reich and in Europe during the war.[59]

Right from the start of the war, the regime toughened its anti-Jewish policy in the Reich, often with the argument that the 'provocative behaviour' of the Jews aroused public indignation and could not be tolerated now that Germany was at war. On 6 September 1939 the Gestapo announced key measures against Jews to be taken by the relevant ministries (Doc. 5). One day later the Gestapo targeted those Polish Jews who had not been expelled in October 1938.[60] Heydrich ordered all male Polish Jews in the territory of the Reich to be arrested and sent to concentration camps (Doc. 6). One of the approximately 2,000 to 3,000 men arrested was Leon Szalet. He later recalled how, along with other Polish Jews, he was taken from Stettin railway station in Berlin to Sachsenhausen concentration camp. No sooner were the prisoners aboard the train than SS men began to beat them. 'When the train started to move, our composure and powers of

55 *Reichsgesetzblatt*, 1939, I, pp. 1455–1457.

56 Ibid., pp. 1609–1613.

57 Ibid., p. 1679.

58 Uwe Dietrich Adam, *Judenpolitik im Dritten Reich* (Düsseldorf: Droste, 1972), pp. 274–275; Gerhard Werle, *Justiz-Strafrecht und polizeiliche Verbrechensbekämpfung im Dritten Reich* (Berlin/New York: Walter de Gruyter, 1989). See also the Introduction to PMJ 4.

59 Hilberg, *Destruction of the European Jews*, pp. 292–297; Ulrich Herbert, *Best: Biographische Studien über Radikalismus, Weltanschauung und Vernunft 1903–1989* (Bonn: J. H. W. Dietz, 1996), pp. 230–249; Michael Wildt, *An Uncompromising Generation: The Nazi Leadership of the Reich Security Main Office*, trans. Tom Lampert (Madison, WI: University of Wisconsin Press, 2010 [German edn, 2002]).

60 Yfaat Weiss, *Deutsche und polnische Juden vor dem Holocaust: Jüdische Identität zwischen Staatsbürgerschaft und Ethnizität 1933–1940* (Munich: Oldenbourg, 2000), pp. 195–217; Gertrud Pickhan, '"Niemandsland": Die Briefe der Greta Schiffmann und das Schicksal einer jüdischen Familie, ausgewiesen aus Dortmund im Oktober 1938', *Beiträge zur Geschichte der Stadt Dortmund und der Grafschaft Mark*, vol. 91 (2001), pp. 170–201; Jerzy Tomaszewski, *Auftakt zur Vernichtung: Die Vertreibung polnischer Juden aus Deutschland im Jahre 1938* (Osnabrück: Fibre, 2002). See also PMJ 2, p. 53.

resistance were at an end. Men began to sob like children; those who were injured whimpered in pain. Hopelessness, fear, and despair gripped everyone on the train.'[61]

On 10 and 11 September, the Gestapo arrested a total of 1,048 Polish Jews in Vienna and held them in the Prater Stadium. Scientists from the Natural History Museum in Vienna subjected 440 of the prisoners to racial-anthropological examinations. For six days, they measured and photographed the prisoners and made plaster masks to add to an exhibition that had opened in May 1939, *The Psychological and Racial Appearance of the Jews*. At the end of September, the Gestapo deported these Jews to Buchenwald (Doc. 33). By the summer of 1940, more than two thirds of them were no longer alive.[62]

In October 1939 Himmler ordered that Jews who failed to obey state instructions or exhibited 'behaviour hostile to the state' were to be imprisoned in concentration camps (Doc. 20). On 10 April 1940 he decreed that Jewish concentration camp prisoners were not to be released from the camps for the duration of the war (Doc. 67). The concentration camp system was further expanded, and the number of inmates soared. During the preparations for the war, two large concentration camps – Mauthausen near Linz and Flossenbürg in eastern Bavaria – had already been built on the periphery of the German Reich. In the substantially enlarged sphere of control, Stutthof near Danzig, Auschwitz on the western edge of the Polish town of Oświęcim, Neuengamme in Hamburg, Natzweiler in occupied Alsace, and Groß-Rosen in Lower Silesia were added by the summer of 1941.[63]

Before the war, it was almost exclusively Germans and Austrians who had been interned in the concentration camps. However, following the arrest of thousands of Poles and Czechs on the basis of pre-prepared lists, foreigners were to make up the majority of the prisoner population soon after the onset of the war.[64] In late 1940, German

61 Leon Szalet and Winfried Meyer, *Baracke 38: 237 Tage in den 'Judenblocks' des KZ Sachsenhausen* (Berlin: Metropol, 2006), p. 28.

62 Doron Rabinovici, *Eichmann's Jews: The Jewish Administration of Holocaust Vienna, 1938–1945*, trans. Nick Somers (New York: John Wiley, 2014 [German edn., 2000]), p. 88; Claudia Spring, 'Vermessen, deklassiert und deportiert: Dokumentation zur anthropologischen Untersuchung an 440 Juden im Wiener Stadion im September 1939 unter der Leitung von Josef Wastl vom Naturhistorischen Museums Wien', *zeitgeschichte*, vol. 32, no. 2 (2005), pp. 91–110; Margit Berner, '"Judentypologisierungen"' in der Anthropologie am Beispiel der Bestände des Naturhistorischen Museums, Wien', ibid., pp. 111–116.

63 Jane Caplan and Nikolaus Wachsmann (eds.), *Concentration Camps in Nazi Germany: The New Histories* (London: Routledge, 2010); Falk Pingel, *Häftlinge unter SS-Herrschaft: Widerstand, Selbstbehauptung und Vernichtung im Konzentrationslager* (Hamburg: Hoffmann und Campe, 1978); Ulrich Herbert, Karin Orth, and Christoph Dieckmann (eds.), *Die nationalsozialistischen Konzentrationslager: Entwicklung und Struktur*, 2 vols. (Göttingen: Wallstein, 1998); Helmut Krausnick, Martin Broszat, and Hans-Adolf Jacobsen, *Anatomy of the SS-State*, trans. Richard Barry, Marion Jackson, and Dorothy Long (London: Collins, 1968 [German edn, 1965]); Karin Orth, *Das System der nationalsozialistischen Konzentrationslager: Eine politische Organisationsgeschichte* (Hamburg: Hamburger Edition, 1999), pp. 67–68 and 95–97; Wolfgang Sofsky, *The Order of Terror: The Concentration Camp*, trans. from German by William Templer (Princeton: Princeton University Press, 1999 [German edn, 1993]); Nikolaus Wachsmann, *KL: A History of the Nazi Concentration Camps* (London: Little, Brown, 2015).

64 Karel Kašák, 'Češi v koncentračním tábore Dachau', in *Almanach Dachau: Kytice událostí a vzpomínek* (Prague: Calve, 1946), pp. 14–22; Detlef Brandes, 'Nationalsozialistische Tschechenpolitik im Protektorat Böhmen und Mähren', in Detlef Brandes and Václav Kural (eds.), *Der Weg in die Katastrophe: Deutsch-tschechoslowakische Beziehungen 1938–1947* (Essen: Klartext, 1994), pp. 39–56, here pp. 39–42.

concentration camps held around 53,000 prisoners. Jews ranked at the bottom of the prisoner hierarchy and were usually assigned to the most physically demanding and dangerous labour squads. An individual's chances of survival depended on his or her position within this hierarchy.[65]

'Euthanasia'

The first systematic mass murder in the Reich was set in motion shortly after the war began. The killing of persons regarded in the National Socialist state as 'unworthy of life' (*lebensunwert*) had been planned for some time. As early as the spring of 1939, the Chancellery of the Führer had established the Reich Committee for the Scientific Registration of Severe Hereditary and Congenital Illnesses, a front organization that arranged for the murder of newborns and infants with serious physical deformities, the so-called child euthanasia programme. On 18 August 1939 the Reich Minister of the Interior introduced the compulsory reporting of such 'malformed' newborns. Very quickly the murder programme was extended to include disabled adults as well. In addition to the Chancellery of the Führer, the Ministry of the Interior and specially selected heads of institutions and medical experts played a part in formulating the programme.[66]

In late September, information was gathered on all institutions housing patients with physical or mental disabilities or psychiatric illnesses (*Heil- und Pflegeanstalten*), and patient reporting forms were sent out in October. Presumably during the same month, Hitler signed the authorization for mass murder:

> Reichsleiter Bouhler and Dr Brandt are given the responsibility for extending the authority of individual physicians, to be specified by name, so that patients who, according to human judgement, are incurable can, after a most careful diagnosis of their medical condition, be granted a mercy death.[67]

The official letter of authorization was backdated to 1 September 1939 to link the murder of patients to the war. During the First World War eugenicists had already been warning against the 'national biological' consequences of war. Because it was precisely the healthiest and most capable men who were most likely to be killed in combat, they argued, the genetic substance of the nation was at risk of impairment. Such considerations bur-

65 Orth, *Das System der nationalsozialistischen Konzentrationslager*, p. 105; Jürgen Matthäus, 'Verfolgung, Ausbeutung, Vernichtung: Jüdische Häftlinge im System der Konzentrationslager', in Günter Morsch and Susanne zur Nieden (eds.), *Jüdische Häftlinge im Konzentrationslager Sachsenhausen, 1936 bis 1945* (Berlin: Hentrich, 2004), pp. 64–90; Dieter Pohl, 'The Holocaust and the Concentration Camps', in Caplan and Wachsmann (eds.), *Concentration Camps in Nazi Germany*, pp. 149–166, here p. 151.

66 Henry Friedlander, *The Origins of Nazi Genocide: From Euthanasia to the Final Solution* (Chapel Hill: University of North Carolina Press, 1995); Longerich, *Holocaust*, pp. 135–136; Ernst Klee, *'Euthanasie' im Dritten Reich: Die 'Vernichtung lebensunwerten Lebens'*, 2nd edn (Frankfurt am Main: Fischer, 2010 [1983]).

67 BArch, R 3001/4209. A facsimile of the original letter is printed at the beginning of Friedlander, *Origins of Nazi Genocide*.

geoned after the onset of the Second World War and provided the advocates of an 'eradication of the inferior' with a rationale.

In the newly created Gaue of Danzig-West Prussia and Wartheland, psychiatric patients were murdered immediately after the entry of German troops and independently of the centralized 'euthanasia' campaign. Even during this early phase, however, the murders were not limited to former Polish territories. The Gauleiter in Pomerania, Franz Schwede-Coburg, saw an opportunity to get rid of the patients in his Gau. He promised Himmler that he would place several hospitals at the disposal of the newly created Waffen SS in exchange for permission to have the patients removed. The patients were shot. Two hospitals were converted into barracks for the Waffen SS, and the other three continued to operate as psychiatric hospitals. It had quickly become clear to a number of powerful local and regional leaders just how much the war had broadened their opportunities.[68]

In the Reich the programme of murder was coordinated by the Chancellery of the Führer. For this purpose, it set up an organization later known as 'T4', a reference to its headquarters in a villa at 4 Tiergartenstraße in Berlin. Over time, six killing centres were established, where the victims were asphyxiated with poison gas: in Brandenburg an der Havel; Grafeneck; Hartheim, near Linz (Austria); Pirna-Sonnenstein; Bernburg on the Saale river; and Hadamar, near Limburg. On 18 January 1940 the first transport with twenty-five men from the Eglfing-Haar psychiatric institution arrived in Grafeneck. The first patient on the list for this transport, and thus the first 'euthanasia' victim in the Reich, was a Jew: Ludwig Alexander, born on 1 September 1895.[69]

At first the procedure for the Jewish patients was officially the same as for the non-Jewish ones, though the dates of the transfer and killing of the Jews allow the conjecture that, even during this early phase, racial classification had greater significance than the medical condition.[70] Very soon the doctors in charge of the selections also distinguished between Jews and non-Jews. They assessed non-Jewish patients in terms of their chances of being cured and their fitness for work, and they spared those who did not require permanent care. However, if the patient was a Jew, this alone was regarded as a sufficient criterion to mandate his or her killing. In retrospect this practice can be

68 Volker Rieß, *Die Anfänge der Vernichtung 'lebensunwerten Lebens' in den Reichsgauen Danzig-Westpreußen und Wartheland 1939/40* (Frankfurt am Main/New York: Peter Lang, 1995); Friedlander, *Origins of Nazi Genocide.*

69 IfZ-Archives, NO-3356; Hans-Walter Schmuhl, *Rassenhygiene, Nationalsozialismus, Euthanasie: Von der Verhütung zur Vernichtung 'lebensunwerten Lebens' 1890–1945* (Göttingen: Vandenhoeck & Ruprecht, 1987); Friedlander, *Origins of Nazi Genocide*, p. 271; Brigitte Kepplinger, Gerhart Marckhgott, and Hartmut Reese (eds.), *Tötungsanstalt Hartheim* (Linz: Oöla, 2008). On the National Socialist 'euthanasia' programme, see also Robert Lifton, *The Nazi Doctors: Medical Killing and the Psychology of Genocide* (New York: Basic, 1988); Robert Proctor, *Racial Hygiene: Medicine under the Nazis* (Cambridge, MA: Harvard University Press, 1989); Götz Aly and Peter Chroust, *Cleansing the Fatherland: Nazi Medicine and Racial Hygiene* (Baltimore, MD: Johns Hopkins University Press, 1994); Susan Bachrach and Dieter Kuntz (eds.), *Deadly Medicine: Creating the Master Race* (Washington, DC: United States Holocaust Memorial Museum, 2004).

70 Annette Hinz-Wessels, 'Jüdische Opfer der "Aktion T4" im Spiegel der überlieferten "Euthanasie"-Krankenakten im Bundesarchiv', in Maike Rotzoll et al. (eds.), *Die nationalsozialistische 'Euthanasie'-Aktion 'T4' und ihre Opfer: Geschichte und ethische Konsequenzen für die Gegenwart* (Paderborn: Schöningh, 2010), pp. 143–146.

identified as a significant step towards the indiscriminate murder of Jews, irrespective of age, state of health, or gender. Only the Jews who were brought to the psychiatric hospital in Bendorf-Sayn from December 1940 (Doc. 127) were not yet included in this murder programme. They were deported and murdered in 1942 along with the Jews from Koblenz.[71]

On 15 April 1940 Herbert Linden, the section head responsible for the 'euthanasia' programme in the Department for Health in the Ministry of the Interior, instructed local health centres to register all Jewish patients. From June 1940 these patients were taken to the 'euthanasia' facilities, where they were murdered. To conceal the facts, relatives who made enquiries were informed that the patients had been taken to the hospital in Chełm, in the Lublin district of the General Government. The death certificates were also posted from there. However, the hospital in Chełm no longer existed and the Polish patients had already been killed in January 1940. The deception also served the purpose of enrichment. The Reich Association of Jews in Germany had to pay fake invoices for months of supposed care for 1,050 patients who had actually long since been murdered.

The representatives of the Reich Association stumbled into a truly tragic situation. Although some of them were evidently aware of the murder of the Jewish patients, they were nonetheless obliged to pay the bills. Conrad Cohn, the head of the Welfare Department, informed the district offices of the Reich Association of this duty in August 1941 (Doc. 201). Less than two months later, he wrote a memo to Paul Eppstein, the official in charge of social welfare at the Reich Association: 'The invoices received here so far relate to around 1,100 patients, 1,050 of whom were deceased at the time of invoicing.'[72]

In the Protectorate of Bohemia and Moravia, most Jewish patients were unaffected by the 'euthanasia' programme. There too, however, they were segregated from the other patients. From the autumn of 1939 they were only supposed to be treated in new so-called Jew wards. The hospital management in Jihlava even went so far as to provide separate toilets and washbasins for Jewish patients and had their dishes washed separately (Doc. 262). After the closure of this psychiatric clinic, its Jewish patients, like most of the others, were placed primarily in two institutions: the Bohemian patients in the regional hospital in Prague-Bohnice in 1940 and the Moravian ones in the regional hospital in Kroměříž in 1941. Jewish patients were also placed in hospitals run by the churches as well as in the hospitals operated by the Jewish Religious Community of Prague. The majority were subsequently deported and murdered.[73]

71 Friedlander, *Origins of Nazi Genocide*, pp. 281–282.

72 Dr Conrad Israel Cohn's note to Dr Eppstein, dated 2 Oct. 1941, BArch, R 8150/7, fol. 221; Beate Meyer, 'Der Traum von einer autonomen jüdischen Verwaltung: Die Reichsvereinigung der Juden in Deutschland. Auswanderer und Zurückbleibende in den Jahren 1938/39–1941', in Susanne Heim, Beate Meyer, and Francis R. Nicosia (eds.), *'Wer bleibt, opfert seine Jahre, vielleicht sein Leben': Deutsche Juden 1938–1941* (Göttingen: Wallstein, 2010), pp. 21–38, here p. 27.

73 Tomáš Fedorovič, 'Jüdische geisteskranke Patienten aus dem Protektorat Böhmen und Mähren zwischen nationalsozialistischer "Euthanasie" und Holocaust (1939–1945)', in Michal Šimůnek and Dietmar Schulze (eds.), *Die nationalsozialistische 'Euthanasie' im Reichsgau Sudetenland und Protektorat Böhmen und Mähren 1939–1945* (Prague: Mervart, 2008), pp. 199–236.

Jewish Self-Administration

After the outbreak of war, it became virtually impossible for Jewish organizations to carry out their main task, which was to arrange for the emigration of as many Jews as possible. It also became increasingly difficult to provide supplies to the impoverished population. The Reich Association of Jews in Germany, which had its headquarters in Berlin; the Israelite Religious Community in Vienna; and the Jewish Religious Community of Prague also had to struggle with these fundamental problems. In addition, they had to cooperate in the implementation of anti-Jewish measures. In doing so Jewish organizations were under the strict control of the Gestapo and the SD or of the Reich Security Main Office.

Eichmann repeatedly summoned the heads of the Jewish institutions in Berlin, Vienna, and Prague to the Reich capital for joint meetings and also made sure that they passed on instructions to each other. Ever since the spring of 1938, when he reorganized the Israelite Religious Community of Vienna, headed by Dr Josef Löwenherz, in such a way that it basically implemented his instructions, he had viewed this type of subordinated self-administration as a model for dealing with other Jewish organizations too. The Reich Association had been formed in February 1939 from what was previously the Reich Representation of Jews in Germany, a step that was established by law in July 1939 with the Tenth Regulation on the Reich Citizenship Law. Every Jew now had to belong to this umbrella organization, in whose decisions the communities and district offices of the Reich Association had no say. The restructuring entailed only minimal changes in personnel.[74]

The Jewish organs of self-administration had no significant influence over the decisions of the Reich authorities. Nonetheless, whenever they conscientiously carried out Gestapo directives in order to prevent the Gestapo itself from intervening, they had to justify themselves to the Jewish population. Their situation is comparable to that of the Jewish Councils in occupied Eastern Europe. They felt obliged to cooperate in order to prevent things from getting worse.

Moritz Fleischmann, who worked for the Israelite Religious Community of Vienna, reported that for its senior official, Josef Löwenherz, 'every approach to Eichmann was the road to degradation'.[75] A colleague wrote in retrospect about Paul Eppstein, one of the leading representatives of the Reich Association: 'Eppstein, who was the liaison to

74 Anderl, 'Zentralstellen für jüdische Auswanderung', p. 297; Avraham Barkai, Paul Mendes-Flohr, and Steven M. Lowenstein, *Deutsch-jüdische Geschichte in der Neuzeit*, vol. 4: *Aufbruch und Zerstörung 1918–1945* (Munich: Beck, 1997), pp. 338–342; Meyer, 'Der Traum von einer autonomen jüdischen Verwaltung', pp. 26–32. See also PMJ 2, pp. 62–64.

75 Moritz Fleischmann, testimony at the Eichmann trial, 26 April 1961, cited in David Cesarani, *Eichmann: His Life and Crimes* (London: William Heinemann, 2004), p. 72; Rabinovici, *Eichmann's Jews*, pp. 40–42. On the situation in Prague, see Margalit Shlain, 'Jakob Edelsteins Bemühungen um die Rettung der Juden aus dem Protektorat Böhmen und Mähren vom Mai 1939 bis Dezember 1939', *Theresienstädter Studien und Dokumente*, vol. 10 (2003), pp. 71–94, here pp. 78–79; Ruth Bondy, *'Elder of the Jews': Jakob Edelstein of Theresienstadt* (New York: Grove, 1989).

the Gestapo, came back from every meeting drenched in sweat.'[76] Similarly, Berthold Simonsohn, who worked for the Jewish welfare programme in Stettin and Hamburg, recalled:

> Whenever Eppstein was summoned to the Gestapo, he never knew whether he would come back, and he always carried a capsule of potassium cyanide with him to put an end to his ordeal should there be an attempt to force him into things he could not reconcile with his conscience and with his sense of responsibility towards the Jews as a whole.

A steady stream of new, arbitrary directives or sudden arrests meant that even the less prominent employees of the Reich Association were under enormous strain. 'Everyone knew back then that one day the bell would toll for them too.'[77]

In another respect, too, the example of Paul Eppstein may illustrate the dilemma in which the Jewish officials found themselves. Eppstein and his wife, Hedwig, had moved from Mannheim to Berlin in 1933. He sought to establish a smoothly running Jewish administration and, like many of his colleagues, felt such a sense of responsibility that he allowed the opportunity for emigration to pass him by. His brother Lothar and sister-in-law Paula managed to reach the USA via France and Lisbon. In reply to Lothar's reproach that it had been irresponsible to postpone emigration, Hedwig Eppstein said:

> Precisely the opposite is the case with P[aul]. You know him well enough, in this respect too, to appreciate that P. cannot work just for the sake of eating and sleeping. That is unthinkable for him. For him, work has to be placed in a greater context, and clearly this context is present here in our situation. The burdensome nature of a job does not diminish the experience of its value.

Hedwig Eppstein herself organized the emigration of young Jews to Palestine as part of the Youth Aliyah. Perhaps she would have liked to leave, as she wrote to her brother-

76 Kurt Goldmann, 'Hechaluz und Jugendaliyah in Deutschland von 1936 bis Ende 1939', YVA, O.1/204, fol. 6, cited in Meyer, 'Der Traum von einer autonomen jüdischen Verwaltung', p. 29. On the history of the Reich Association, see Herbert Strauss, 'Jewish Autonomy within the Limits of National Socialist Policy: The Communities and the Reichsvertretung', in Arnold Paucker, *Die Juden im nationalsozialistischen Deutschland, 1933–1943 / The Jews in Nazi Germany, 1933–1943* (Tübingen: J. C. B. Mohr, 1986), pp. 125–152; Otto Dov Kulka, 'The Reichsvereinigung and the Fate of the German Jews, 1938/1939–1942', ibid., pp. 353–363; Beate Meyer, 'The Fine Line between Responsible Action and Collaboration: The Reichsvereinigung der Juden in Deutschland and the Jewish Community in Berlin, 1938-1945', in Beate Meyer, Hermann Simon and Chana Schütz (eds.), *Jews in Nazi Berlin: From Kristallnacht to Liberation*, trans. Caroline Gay and Miranda Robbins (Chicago: University of Chicago Press, 2009 [German edn, 2000]), pp. 310–363; Beate Meyer, *A Fatal Balancing Act: The Dilemma of the Reich Association of Jews in Germany, 1939–1945*, trans. William Templer (Oxford: Berghahn, 2013 [German edn, 2011]).

77 Berthold Simonsohn, 'Sein Andenken wird weiterleben', *Jüdische Sozialarbeit*, vol. 4, no. 3/4 (18 Sept. 1959), pp. 23–26, here p. 24. The obituary was composed in 1945.

in-law: 'I would have no objections to a somewhat happier life.'[78] However, the couple stayed in Germany and faced tasks that were ultimately impossible. Paul Eppstein had to coordinate every undertaking and all expenditure with the Reich Security Main Office, which steadily pressed for cost-cutting. When he refused to support a precarious ship transport for the purposes of illegal – because of the British Mandate prohibition – emigration to Palestine, he was himself placed in 'protective custody'. He had to produce a written record of his own summons to the Gestapo Central Office regarding his detention (Doc. 128). After his release, Eppstein was no longer permitted to handle emigration matters. In this way the Reich Security Main Office made it clear to the Jewish officials how subordinate they were. At the same time, it constantly utilized them to publicize new regulations, to organize the first deportations and the enforced relocations to 'Jew houses' (*Judenhäuser*), and to collect statistical data concerning the Jewish population.

The Reich Association, as well as the Jewish Religious Communities of Vienna and Prague, had to maintain homes for children and the elderly, operate soup kitchens for those in need, and ensure the care of invalids without financial means. More and more financial aid was needed on account of the growing impoverishment and the increase in the percentage of the elderly caused by the emigration of mostly younger Jews. In late 1939, 52,000 persons, more than a quarter of the Jewish population of the Reich, were receiving aid from the Reich Association.[79] In November 1939 the head of the General Public Welfare Department, Hannah Karminski, described the conflict of Jews willing to emigrate

> who, before their emigration, confided to us their last and greatest cause of worry: the mother or – more rarely – the elderly father left behind. They always had the intention of sending for their elderly relatives as soon as possible, but for the time being they had to remain behind on their own.[80]

When she wrote these lines, Karminski could not know that most of the older Jews would never succeed in leaving Germany, nor would she herself. In December 1942 she was deported to Auschwitz, where she was murdered the next year at the age of 45.[81]

The Jewish institutions also tried to maintain educational and cultural organizations. At the start of the war, all events of the Jewish Culture League were initially prohibited, but they had resumed by the end of September 1939, albeit on a limited scale (Doc. 14). The Culture League had branches in several major cities, and the one in Frankfurt was

78 Letter from Hedwig Eppstein to Lothar and Paula Eppstein, dated 21 Sept. 1938, StA Ma, Eppstein Collection, Zug. 27/2002, no. 11.

79 Wolf Gruner, *Öffentliche Wohlfahrt und Judenverfolgung: Wechselwirkung lokaler und zentraler Politik im NS-Staat 1933 bis 1942* (Munich: Oldenbourg, 2002), p. 245; Gudrun Maierhof, *Selbstbehauptung im Chaos: Frauen in der jüdischen Selbsthilfe 1933–1943* (Frankfurt am Main/New York: Campus, 2002), pp. 174–175.

80 Hanna Sara Karminski, 'Die Jüdische Winterhilfe beginnt', *Jüdisches Nachrichtenblatt* (Berlin edn), no. 88 (3 Nov. 1939), p. 1.

81 Beate Meyer, 'The Fine Line between Responsible Action and Collaboration', p. 352.

particularly active. Outside Berlin, however, generally only smaller events and cinema screenings, as well as guest appearances by performers from Berlin, continued to take place. The Gestapo shut down the organization on 11 September 1941.[82]

The First Deportations

On 6 October 1939 Hitler announced in the Reichstag that 'a new order of the ethnographic situation' was to take place in Eastern Europe. A large-scale 'resettlement of nationalities' was intended to ensure 'peace and order' in Germany's relations with its new ally, the Soviet Union.[83] To secure long-term German domination in the recently conquered territories, Hitler planned a mass resettlement in these territories of members of minority populations of German descent living in other countries. The following day he placed the Reichsführer SS Heinrich Himmler in charge of the practical implementation of this programme for the 'strengthening of Germandom' (Doc. 18).

By the end of October, Hitler had divided up the conquered territories. The Gaue of Danzig-West Prussia and Wartheland were incorporated into the German Reich; the eastern part of Upper Silesia was integrated into the Gau of Silesia; and the administrative district of Ciechanów (renamed Zichenau) became part of East Prussia. The police border between former Poland and the Reich, however, remained in effect, with an altered course. One of the reasons for this was to prevent an uncontrolled migration of Polish citizens from the newly incorporated territories into the Old Reich. On 26 October 1939 the remainder of the German-conquered Polish territory, known as the General Government and headed by Governor Hans Frank, became a vaguely defined colonial borderland. The 'undesirable elements' from the Reich, including the newly incorporated territories, were now to be deported to this zone in order to make room for settlement of the ethnic Germans (*Volksdeutsche*). By the end of September, the German Reich and the Soviet Union had agreed upon a large-scale population transfer. Hundreds of thousands of Germans who had come under Soviet control during the occupation of eastern Poland and the Baltic states were now to be brought 'home to the Reich'. Additional pressure to act was created by Himmler's plan to resettle approximately 200,000 South Tyroleans in the German Reich. On 21 October 1939 Hitler and Mussolini concluded an agreement whereby the German-speaking minority in South Tyrol would have to choose between emigrating to the German Reich or staying in South Tyrol but giving up the German culture and language. More than 85 per cent of those questioned opted for resettlement in the Reich. However, it was by no means clear just where they were to go.[84]

82 Herbert Freeden, *Jüdisches Theater in Nazideutschland* (Tübingen: Mohr, 1964), pp. 150–169; Volker Dahm, 'Kulturelles und geistiges Leben', in Wolfgang Benz (ed.), *Die Juden in Deutschland 1933–1945: Leben unter nationalsozialistischer Herrschaft* (Munich: Beck, 1988), pp. 75–267, here pp. 244–257; Sylvia Rogge-Gau, *Die doppelte Wurzel des Daseins: Julius Bab und der Jüdische Kulturbund Berlin* (Berlin: Metropol, 1999); Michael Brenner, 'Jewish Culture in a Modern Ghetto: Theater and Scholarship among the Jews of Nazi Germany', in Francis R. Nicosia and David Scrase (eds.), *Jewish Life in Nazi Germany: Dilemmas and Responses* (New York: Berghahn, 2012), pp. 170–184; Rebecca Rovit, *The Jewish Kulturbund Theatre Company in Nazi Berlin* (Iowa City: University of Iowa Press, 2012).

83 See PMJ 4/17.

84 See the Introduction to PMJ 4 and Aly, *'Final Solution'*, pp. 14–81.

Even before detailed plans for the scheme had been formulated, it was determined that large parts of the Jewish population were also to be deported from Reich territory in the course of the resettlements. At a meeting of department heads and Einsatzgruppen commanders on 21 September 1939, Reinhard Heydrich announced that Hitler agreed to the deportation.[85]

Adolf Eichmann, who headed the Central Offices for Jewish Emigration in Vienna and Prague, was put in charge of organizing the deportations. On 6 October 1939 Gestapo chief Heinrich Müller gave Eichmann the task of initiating the resettlement of Jews from Katowice and Moravská Ostrava to the General Government. Eichmann also decided to include the Viennese Jews, and the local Gauleiter, Josef Bürckel, readily authorized him to do so. While the Gestapo offices were in charge of the deportations in the Old Reich, in Vienna this task was taken on by the Central Office for Jewish Emigration (Doc. 24).[86]

The Israelite Religious Community of Vienna was required to assist and sometimes even to compile the deportation lists itself, as well as to inform those concerned. Its representatives repeatedly emphasized

> that the involvement of the Religious Community in these actions did not stem from its own initiative and was guided solely by the intention to nominate the transportees and to implement the execution of the transports in a manner that avoided hardships as far as possible.

Nonetheless, the Religious Community drew criticism from many Viennese Jews as a result of its role.[87]

Beginning on 18 October 1939, around 5,000 Jews from Vienna, Moravská Ostrava, and Katowice were deported in five transports to the region around Nisko on the San river, near Lublin, in the east of the German-occupied part of Poland. In Zarzecze, near Nisko, the first Jews deported from Moravská Ostrava were ordered to build a barracks camp. Those unfit for work, together with most of the Viennese Jews, were driven further eastwards and left to their fate. Some stayed in the area; others crossed the demarcation line into the Soviet-occupied part of Poland, where the Soviet authorities apprehended many of them and put them in labour camps.[88]

85 Minutes of the conference, dated 27 Sept. 1939, in Tatiana Berenstein and Adam Rutkowski, 'Dokument o konferencji w Urzędzie Policji Bezpieczeństwa z 21 IX 1939 r.', *Biuletyn Żydowskiego Instytutu Historycznego*, vol. 49, no. 1 (1964), pp. 68–73. See also PMJ 4/12.

86 Hans Safrian, *Eichmann's Men*, new edn, trans. Ute Stargardt (New York/Cambridge: Cambridge University Press, 2010 [German edn, 1993]), pp. 72–86; Browning, *Origins of the Final Solution*, pp. 65–69; Gabriele Anderl, Dirk Rupnow, and Alexandra-Eileen Wenck, *Die Zentralstelle für jüdische Auswanderung als Beraubungsinstitution* (Vienna: Oldenbourg, 2004), p. 264.

87 Letter from the Israelite Religious Community of Vienna to Siegmund Flieger, dated 7 Jan. 1940, CAHJP, AW 2747, copy in Archiv der IKG Wien, MF W 1, fr. 126; Andrea Löw, 'Die frühen Deportationen aus dem Reichsgebiet von Herbst 1939 bis Frühjahr 1941', in Heim, Meyer, and Nicosia (eds.), *'Wer bleibt, opfert seine Jahre, vielleicht sein Leben'*, pp. 59–76.

88 Seev Goshen, 'Eichmann und die Nisko-Aktion im Oktober 1939', *Vierteljahrshefte für Zeitgeschichte*, vol. 29 (1981), pp. 74–96; Jonny Moser, *Nisko: Die ersten Judendeportationen* (Vienna: Steinbauer, 2012). Of the Jewish men detained in Zarzecze, 198 returned to Vienna in April 1940 after the camp was closed; of the 1,291 men from Moravská Ostrava, 460 returned. See Alfred Gottwaldt and Diana Schulle, *Die 'Judendeportationen' aus dem Deutschen Reich 1941–1945* (Wiesbaden: Marixverlag, 2005), pp. 31–33.

One of the Jewish officials required to accompany the transports in the autumn of 1939 was Jakob Edelstein. Born in Horodenka, Galicia, in 1903, during the First World War he had moved with his family to Brno in Moravia, where, from 1926, he was active in Zionist organizations. From 1933 he headed the Palestine Office in Prague, which sought to arrange for emigration to the British Mandate. After seeing the conditions in Nisko, he did his utmost to save the Jews in the Protectorate from deportation to the East, convinced that most of them would not survive. He wrote an account of his experiences which, along with statements by Jews who had fled, formed the basis for an article written by Sir Lewis B. Namier for the British newspaper *The Times* in December 1939. The article stated that the project to construct a 'Jewish reserve' in the area around Lublin was about creating a 'place for gradual extermination, and not what the Germans would describe as a *Lebensraum*' (Doc. 38).[89]

The authorities in Vienna had assumed that 65,000 Jews would be deported, yet already the third Viennese transport, planned for 31 October 1939, failed to depart for technical reasons. Müller, the Gestapo chief, had ordered that all transports had to be authorized by his office in the future, and on 21 December he announced that Himmler had forbidden the deportations from continuing 'until further notice' (Doc. 40).[90] For the Reichsführer SS, who, since October 1939, had simultaneously functioned as Reich Commissioner for the Strengthening of Germandom, moving the inhabitants out of the annexed Polish territories and settling ethnic Germans there took priority. Shortly thereafter, Eichmann transferred to Berlin, where he headed Section IV D 4 (Evacuation Matters and the Reich Central Agency for Jewish Emigration) in the Reich Security Main Office which, from now on, was to coordinate the deportations.[91]

On 30 January 1940 Heydrich announced at a meeting in the Reich Security Main Office that, in mid February, 1,000 Jews from Stettin, whose apartments were urgently required for reasons relating to the war economy, would be evicted and deported to the General Government.[92] The first deportation of Jews from the Old Reich, on 12 February 1940, involved almost the entire Jewish community of Stettin (Pomerania). Precise guidelines governed every detail of the expulsion (Doc. 52). According to a deportation list commissioned by the Jewish Council in Lublin and subsequently drawn up by the deportees themselves, 1,120 people were deported to Lublin from the Regierungsbezirk Stettin. They had to make their way on foot or in sledges from there to Głusk, Bełżyce, and Piaski. Some froze to death en route. Over the course of the next month, further deportees fell victim to the cold weather and malnutrition. At the end of February, approximately 160 Jews were deported from Schneidemühl, though apparently not to the

89 Bondy, *'Elder of the Jews'*, pp. 149–165; Livia Rothkirchen, 'Zur ersten authentischen Nachricht über den Beginn der Vernichtung der europäischen Juden', *Theresienstädter Studien und Dokumente*, vol. 9 (2002), pp. 338–340; Shlain, 'Jakob Edelsteins Bemühungen', pp. 71–94, here pp. 81–84.

90 Himmler's letter to Bürckel, dated 9 Nov. 1939, ÖStA/AdR, Reichskommissar Bürckel/Materie, 2315/6, fol. 25; circular decree from the RSHA (S-IV II Rz), dated 21 Dec. 1939, cited in Wolf Gruner, 'Von der Kollektivausweisung zur Deportation der Juden aus Deutschland: Neue Perspektiven und Dokumente', in Birthe Kundrus and Beate Meyer (eds.), *Die Deportation der Juden aus Deutschland: Pläne – Praxis – Reaktionen 1938–1945* (Göttingen: Wallstein, 2004), pp. 21–62, here pp. 34, 36.

91 Aly, *'Final Solution'*, pp. 59–66; Browning, *Origins of the Final Solution*, pp. 59–63.

92 PMJ 4/82.

Lublin district but rather to places including the retraining camps (*Umschulungslager*) in Rietz-Neuendorf, near Fürstenwalde, and Radinkendorf in Brandenburg.[93]

When it came to the second deportation from Pomerania, the Reich Association of Jews in Germany managed to negotiate a reduction of 150 deportees. A short time later the association learned of plans to deport the approximately 1,000 Jews of East Frisia to the Lublin district. With the help of local Jewish community leaders Max Plaut, who headed the district office of the Reich Association in north-western Germany, succeeded in persuading the Gestapo not to deport the Jews. Instead, they were to be rehoused within three weeks, so that their apartments would become vacant. Most of them moved to Berlin, Hanover, and Hamburg.[94]

Swiss press reports on the transports from Pomerania (Doc. 53) aroused concern in the Reich Foreign Office. State Secretary Ernst von Weizsäcker asked whether it was true that the deportations from Stettin were the prelude to extensive expulsions. He was informed by the Reich Security Main Office that they were an isolated action for the purpose of creating space to house resettled Baltic Germans.[95]

On 23 March 1940 Göring banned further transports of Jews from the Reich. Because the General Government under Hans Frank was resisting the deportation into its territory with increasing vehemence, the plan for a 'Jewish reservation' in the Lublin district had to be shelved. The Soviet Union was also unwilling to accept Jews. Eichmann and Stahlecker had evidently proposed this to the Soviet Resettlement Commission in the course of the German–Soviet population transfer of 1939/1940. After the deportations to the Lublin district ceased, Eichmann had the idea of making the German, Austrian, and Czech Jews emigrate to the Soviet Union or of expelling them there (Doc. 48). These deliberations, however, came to nothing.[96]

This first attempt to deport Jews en masse from the Reich to the East was a failure – primarily because it had not been made absolutely clear how the General Government was to be dealt with in the future. The regional German authorities throughout the annexed and occupied territories were now pressing to 'get rid of' 'their' Jews as soon as possible. For the time being, however, it remained an open question how this was to be done and where the Jews were to go.

Bans, Forced Labour, and 'Jew Houses'

The initial experiments in deportation had failed. The Jews remained in the Reich and in the Protectorate. A vast number of rules regulated even the tiniest details of the Jews' daily life. Food rations for Jews were reduced, and when Goebbels decided in mid November 1939 that they should no longer be allocated ration coupons for the purchase of

93 *Die Namensliste der 1940 aus dem Regierungsbezirk Stettin deportierten Juden* (Rostock: Geschichtswerkstatt Rostock, 2009); Gottwaldt and Schulle, '*Judendeportationen*', p. 35.

94 Meyer, 'Der Traum von einer autonomen jüdischen Verwaltung', p. 33.

95 Christopher R. Browning, *The Final Solution and the German Foreign Office: A Study of Referat D III of Abteilung Deutschland, 1940–1943* (New York: Holmes & Meier, 1978), pp. 20–21.

96 Pavel Polian, 'Hätte der Holocaust beinahe nicht stattgefunden? Überlegungen zu einem Schriftwechsel im Wert von zwei Millionen Menschenleben', in Johannes Hürter and Jürgen Zarusky (eds.), *Besatzung, Kollaboration, Holocaust: Neue Studien zur Verfolgung und Ermordung der europäischen Juden* (Munich: Oldenbourg, 2008), pp. 1–19.

chocolate products, the Reich Ministry of Food issued a corresponding order two weeks later, on 2 December 1939. Furthermore, soon Jews were permitted to shop only at fixed times and in specific shops. When, as in Breslau, shopping was allowed only during the middle of the day, working women encountered problems. If the shopping hours were limited to the late afternoon, they had to rush from one shop to the next after work, and frequently could not get everything done in the hour permitted, or found themselves faced with empty shelves. In Munich the shops assigned to Jews were situated in distant neighbourhoods. After mid 1941, when Jews were no longer allowed to travel by tram, they thus had to cover distances of many kilometres on foot. Some shops displayed signs reading 'Goods in short supply are not sold to Jews'. In addition, Jews could obtain ration coupons for shoes and clothing only in limited quantities, if at all.[97]

In the Protectorate, both German and Czech authorities introduced, in quick succession, measures similar to those in the Old Reich and Austria, and the accumulation of prohibitions brought some to the point of despair. Max Mannheimer, who undertook forced labour in road construction near the spa town of Luhačovice, noted in his diary:

> My lodging during the week is a wooden shack behind the tool shed. From there, despite the 8 p.m. curfew and the ban on entering the grounds, I go to the spa gardens. I count the 'Off limits to Jews' prohibition signs. There are six of them. Later, towards 11 p.m., I pull all the prohibition signs out of the ground and throw some of them into the bushes, some into a stream. All my bravery was in vain. The next evening, all the signs were back up again. I could not muster the courage to pull them out a second time. I am simply not a hero.[98]

Sometimes people had no idea what was permitted and what was not. If the directives and prohibitions were published at all, then it was in the *Jüdisches Nachrichtenblatt*, which was issued in different editions in Berlin, Vienna, and Prague. Both the Propaganda Ministry and the Reich Security Main Office censored the newspaper.[99]

The exploitation of the Jews followed a two-pronged strategy that involved dispossessing them and utilizing them as a workforce. For the most part the Jews had already been forced out of their occupations and made to give up their businesses.[100] Now, the tax authorities attempted to take possession of almost all their assets. On 15 November 1939 the Reich Minister of Finance increased the so-called Levy on Jewish Assets (*Juden-*

97 Peter Hanke, *Zur Geschichte der Juden in München zwischen 1933 und 1945* (Munich: Stadtarchiv, 1967), p. 274; Marion A. Kaplan, *Between Dignity and Despair: Jewish Life in Nazi Germany* (New York: Oxford University Press, 1998), pp. 150–153; Abraham Ascher, *A Community under Siege: The Jews of Breslau under Nazism* (Stanford: Stanford University Press, 2007).

98 Mannheimer, *Spätes Tagebuch*, pp. 37–38.

99 Ruth Bondy, 'Chronik der sich schließenden Tore: Jüdisches Nachrichtenblatt – Židovské listy (1939–1945)', *Theresienstädter Studien und Dokumente*, vol. 7 (2000), pp. 86–106; Clemens Maier, '*Das Jüdische Nachrichtenblatt* 1938–1943: Instrument der Verfolgung und Mittel der Selbstbehauptung', in Eleonore Lappin and Michael Nagel (eds.), *Deutsch-jüdische Presse und jüdische Geschichte: Dokumente, Darstellungen, Wechselbeziehungen*, vol. 2 (Bremen: Lumiere, 2008), pp. 163–179.

100 Christoph Kreutzmüller, Ingo Loose, and Benno Nietzel, 'Nazi Persecution and Strategies for Survival: Jewish Businesses in Berlin, Frankfurt am Main, and Breslau, 1933–1942', *Yad Vashem Studies*, vol. 39, no. 1 (2011), pp. 31–70. See also PMJ 1, pp. 49–52, and PMJ 2, pp. 14–15.

vermögensabgabe) (Doc. 25), which had been imposed on the Jews as an 'atonement fine' after the November pogroms of 1938.[101] In addition, from December 1940, Jews were obliged to pay a 15 per cent 'social compensation tax' (*Sozialausgleichsabgabe*). The remainder of their assets were held in blocked accounts, and they were only permitted to access a fixed amount each month.[102]

In September and October 1939 representatives of various ministries, of the Plenipotentiary for the Four-Year Plan, and of the Reich Security Main Office continued the discussion they had begun before the war regarding the formal introduction of forced labour for Jews, which was already established practice by then.[103] As a result of rearmament efforts and conscriptions, the notorious labour shortage in the Reich had become considerably more acute. The National Socialist leadership endeavoured to solve this problem both by deploying foreign labourers and by making Jews carry out forced labour.[104] In the spring of 1940 the set of persons used for such labour was expanded. All Jewish men between 18 and 55 and Jewish women between 18 and 50 were now required to register, regardless of whether they drew welfare benefits or not. With the deportations having failed for the time being, forced labour was planned as a longer-term measure. While they were previously more likely to be used as casual workers, from May 1940 Jewish labourers also had to work in industry. Jewish institutions had to reduce their staff in order to detail employees for forced labour. Young Jews preparing for emigration in retraining camps were forced to replace absent agricultural workers and harvesters or to work in nearby factories. In any case, the age limit offered no guarantee that younger or older people would not also be conscripted for compulsory labour.

The working conditions and pay varied, depending on the employer. Some employers gave the Jews primarily the hardest and dirtiest of jobs, spurred on by the propaganda that always emphasized that now, in wartime, the Jews too would learn to work 'at last'. Frequently the employers were at pains to ensure that the Jews came to the firms in segregated groups and did not use the staff canteens. Sometimes the Jews even had to use separate toilets.[105]

Some cities did indeed pay standard wages, but the Jewish forced labourers often received only a fraction of the pay due to them, and sometimes nothing at all. They were,

101 PMJ 2/142.

102 Hilberg, *Destruction of the European Jews*, vol. 1, pp. 140–152; Avraham Barkai, *From Boycott to Annihilation: The Economic Struggle of German Jews, 1933–1943*, trans. William Templer (Hanover, NH: University Press of New England, 1989 [German edn, 1988]), pp. 188–191; Benno Nietzel, 'Die Vernichtung der wirtschaftlichen Existenz der deutschen Juden 1933–1945: Ein Literatur und Forschungsbericht', *Archiv für Sozialgeschichte*, vol. 49 (2009), pp. 561–613.

103 On the pre-war situation, see PMJ 2/119.

104 Ulrich Herbert, *Hitler's Foreign Workers: Enforced Foreign Labor in Germany under the Third Reich*, trans. William Templer (Cambridge: Cambridge University Press, 2006 [German edn, 1999]); Wolf Gruner, *Jewish Forced Labor under the Nazis: Economic Needs and Racial Aims, 1938–1944*, trans. Kathleen M. Dell'Orto (New York: Cambridge University, 2006 [German edn, 1997]).

105 Konrad Kwiet, 'Nach dem Pogrom: Stufen der Ausgrenzung', in Wolfgang Benz (ed.), *Die Juden in Deutschland 1933–1945: Leben unter nationalsozialistischer Herrschaft* (Munich: Beck, 1988), pp. 545–659, here pp. 574–589; Gruner, *Jewish Forced Labor*, pp. 118–142; Trude Maurer, 'Vom Alltag zum Ausnahmezustand: Juden in der Weimarer Republik und im Nationalsozialismus', in Marion Kaplan (ed.), *Geschichte des jüdischen Alltags in Deutschland: Vom 17. Jahrhundert bis 1945* (Munich: Beck, 2003), pp. 347–470, here pp. 455–458; Moshe Zimmermann, *Deutsche gegen Deutsche: Das Schicksal der Juden 1938–1945* (Berlin: Aufbau, 2008), p. 72.

as a matter of principle, relegated to the most disadvantageous tax bracket, and were required to pay the 'social compensation tax'. The wages of some were merely credited to a blocked account, which they required authorization to access.[106] That was the experience of some of the women who undertook forced labour with Elisabeth Freund at a commercial laundry in Berlin. Freund wrote about the general system of wages there: 'When we started here, we were not told what we would get for this work. We have to do forced labour and have to be glad to get anything at all. Then, on the first payday, we found out: around 12.50 Reichsmarks weekly for a married female worker' – about half as much as non-Jewish colleagues. Unmarried women, who did not have pay deducted for being in a double-income household, earned at most 14 Reichsmarks. That was not enough to live on. Underpaying the Jews, Freund also conjectured, was a way of forcing them to use up any remaining savings they might have had. 'And the ones who have no reserves can surely turn to the welfare office of the Jewish community, which is always supposed to provide support for everything.'[107]

German Jews were never deployed on a large scale as forced labourers. In the territory of the Old Reich, around 60,000 Jews had been classified as fit for work in February 1941. Of that number, approximately 54,000 had to carry out forced labour.[108]

In the Protectorate, individual municipalities drew on the Jewish population for labour as early as 1940, long before this policy became standard. On 10 January 1941 the Reich Protector forbade the Jews in the Protectorate to engage in any independent economic activity. On 23 January the Czech government mandated the deployment of all Jews between the ages of 18 and 50 for forced labour, and in August it expanded the measure to include all those between 16 and 60. By 1 April 1941, 70 per cent of the Jewish men in the latter age group were forced labourers. The same month, the Reich Protector aligned the practices with those in the Reich. Now, only the employment offices were supposed to select the places of work. In addition, there was a requirement to ensure strict segregation between Jews and non-Jews (Doc. 305). Nonetheless, in the Protectorate too, the economic significance of forced labour remained relatively small. According to statistics from the Jewish Religious Community of Prague, the number of Jewish workers peaked at 13,623 on 1 December 1941.[109]

Traditionally, the Jewish population in the territory of the Reich lived predominantly in cities, and persecution had only reinforced this tendency. An ever-increasing number of Jews moved into the large cities in the hope that anonymity would afford them protection. In Austria almost all Jews were by now living in Vienna. From April 1939 the Law on Tenancy Agreements with Jews made it possible to place Jews in special houses (*Judenhäuser*) and thereby segregate them from the rest of the population.[110] In the Sude-

106 Barkai, *From Boycott to Annihilation*, pp. 173–181.

107 Carola Sachse (ed.), *Als Zwangsarbeiterin in Berlin: Die Aufzeichnungen der Volkswirtin Elisabeth Freund* (Berlin: Akademie, 1996), pp. 56–58.

108 Gruner, *Jewish Forced Labor*, p. 4.

109 'Jüdische Kultusgemeinde Prag: Arbeit', published in Helena Krejčová, Jana Svobodová, and Anna Hyndráková (eds.), *Židé v Protektorátu: Hlášení Židovské náboženské obce v roce 1942. Dokumenty* (Prague: Maxdorf, 1997), pp. 105–116, here p. 106; Gruner, *Jewish Forced Labor*, pp. 141–159; Gruner, 'Das Protektorat', pp. 4–45.

110 PMJ 2/277; Gerhard Botz, *Wohnungspolitik und Judendeportation in Wien 1938 bis 1945: Zur Funktion des Antisemitismus als Ersatz nationalsozialistischer Sozialpolitik* (Vienna/Salzburg: Geyer,

tengau and in Vienna, this practice began in the summer of 1939. After the onset of the war, the number of so-called Jew houses increased rapidly. In Vienna the heads of the local NSDAP branches, the mayor, and Reich Commissioner Bürckel vied with each other in proposing ways to remedy the housing shortage by crowding the Jewish population even more closely together (Doc. 16).[111]

The forced changes of residence involved an uprooting that was difficult to bear, especially for older people. They had to leave behind their usual surroundings and often familiar objects, and reduce their private sphere to a minimum. In this situation some viewed taking their own lives as the only remaining avenue of escape.[112] In her reminiscences about Vienna, Ruth Klüger describes how she and her mother moved into ever worse apartments, increasingly dark and cramped, which they had to share with one or two other families – and with unwelcome 'pets': 'You turn off the light and imagine the bugs crawling out of the mattresses. Then you get bitten, turn on the light and wail loudly, because the disgusting vermin are actually walking around in the bed.'[113] In Dresden, Victor Klemperer described his new lodgings on 6 June 1940: 'Superior concentration camp.'[114]

Klemperer lived in a so-called non-privileged mixed marriage. His wife was not Jewish and the Klemperers had no children. Such couples were subject to the anti-Jewish measures. Their assets were blocked and they were forced to live in 'Jew houses'. Later the Jewish spouses and the children also had to wear the yellow star. Those in a so-called privileged mixed marriage (between a man of 'German blood' and a Jewish woman or in a mixed marriage with children who were baptized) were not forced to do this, and these families were also allowed to stay in their homes. The non-Jewish spouses reacted in various ways: some went along with the relocation to the 'Jew house' and shared in all the harassment, while others initiated a separation.[115]

When they were called up at the beginning of the war, many men who had been classified as *Mischlinge* under the Nuremberg Laws clung to the hope that they could gain membership of the *Volksgemeinschaft* by serving in the Wehrmacht. On 8 April 1940, however, Hitler excluded *Mischlinge* of the first degree from the Wehrmacht, along with men who were married to Jewish women (Doc. 66). Only in exceptional cases, in

1975); Marlis Buchholz, *Die hannoverschen Judenhäuser: Zur Situation der Juden in der Zeit der Ghettoisierung und Verfolgung, 1941 bis 1945* (Hildesheim: A. Lax, 1987); Hubert Schneider, *Die 'Entjudung' des Wohnraums –'Judenhäuser' in Bochum: Die Geschichte der Gebäude und ihrer Bewohner* (Berlin/Münster: Lit, 2010).

111 Herbert Rosenkranz, *Verfolgung und Selbstbehauptung: Die Juden in Österreich 1938–1945* (Vienna/Munich: Herold, 1978), pp. 210–215, 229–231; Wolf Gruner, *Zwangsarbeit und Verfolgung: Österreichische Juden im NS-Staat 1938–45* (Innsbruck: Studien, 2000), pp. 127–134; Osterloh, 'Sudetenland', pp. 84–85.

112 Konrad Kwiet, 'The Ultimate Refuge: Suicide in the Jewish Community under the Nazis', *Leo Baeck Institute Yearbook*, vol. 29 (1984), pp. 135–167; Kaplan, *Between Dignity and Despair*, pp. 180–184; Christian Goeschel, *Suicide in Nazi Germany* (Oxford/New York: Oxford University Press, 2009), pp. 96–118.

113 Ruth Klüger, *Landscapes of Memory: A Holocaust Girlhood Remembered* (London: Bloomsbury, 2004 [German edn, 1994]), p. 61.

114 Klemperer, *I Shall Bear Witness*, p. 417 (entry for 6 June 1940).

115 Beate Meyer, *'Jüdische Mischlinge': Rassenpolitik und Verfolgungserfahrung 1933–1945* (Hamburg: Dölling und Galitz, 1999).

which he attested that *jüdisch Versippte* (persons related to Jews by marriage) exhibited particular valour, were these persons allowed to remain in the armed forces. They were told that they would be assessed after the war to establish whether they could be put on an equal footing with 'persons of German blood'.[116]

Early Summer to the End of 1940: The Madagascar Plan

In April 1940 the Wehrmacht occupied Denmark and Norway. On 10 May the offensive in Western Europe began, and Luxembourg surrendered that same day. On 15 May the Netherlands capitulated, and on 28 May Belgium followed suit. On 22 June, Germany and France signed an armistice. Approval of Hitler's policies reached its peak among the German population. Germany saw itself on the way to being a world power.[117]

As had been the case with the conquest of Poland, the victory over France led the National Socialist leadership to devise scenarios for a 'territorial solution' to the so-called Jewish question. After the victory over the colonial power in the summer of 1940, the idea of deporting the Jews to the French colony of Madagascar seemed to be within the regime's grasp. In mid May 1940, Himmler had already noted briefly in his position paper 'Some Thoughts on the Treatment of the Ethnically Alien Population in the East': 'I hope to see the term Jew completely eradicated through the opportunity presented by a large-scale emigration of all Jews to Africa or some other colony.'[118]

The proposal was not new. Antisemites had already promoted it in the late nineteenth century, and in the 1930s there had also been deliberations in Poland, France, and Britain about using Madagascar as a place to settle certain groups of Jews. Even the American Jewish Joint Distribution Committee had briefly contemplated such a project.[119] In the summer of 1940 the initiative was seized by the Reich Foreign Office, or, to be more precise, its Department for Germany, whose Section D III was in charge of all matters pertaining to Jews. On 3 July 1940 Franz Rademacher, the head of this section, suggested to his superior, Martin Luther, that Madagascar was a possible destination for the re-settlement of the 'Western Jews' from Europe. Only a short time later, Hitler too expressed an intention to resettle the European Jews in Madagascar.[120]

Heydrich intervened and pointed out to the Reich Foreign Office that he himself had been tasked by Göring with coordinating Jewish emigration. Subsequently, both the

116 Rudolf Absolon, *Die Wehrmacht im Dritten Reich*, vol. 5: *1. September 1939 bis 18. Dezember 1941* (Boppard am Rhein: Boldt, 1988), pp. 148–151; Meyer, *'Jüdische Mischlinge'*, pp. 230–237; Bryan Mark Rigg, *Hitler's Jewish Soldiers: The Untold Story of Nazi Racial Laws and Men of Jewish Descent in the German Military* (Lawrence, KS: University Press of Kansas, 2002).

117 Andreas Hillgruber, *Die gescheiterte Großmacht: Eine Skizze des Deutschen Reiches 1871–1945* (Düsseldorf: Droste, 1980), pp. 95–99.

118 Cited in Helmut Krausnick (ed.), 'Denkschrift Himmlers über die Behandlung der Fremdvölkischen im Osten (Mai 1940)', *Vierteljahrshefte für Zeitgeschichte*, vol. 5 (1957), pp. 194–198, here p. 197.

119 Magnus Brechtken *'Madagaskar für die Juden': Antisemitische Idee und politische Praxis 1885–1945* (Munich: Oldenbourg, 1997), pp. 116–119.

120 Leni Yahil, 'Madagascar: Phantom of a Solution for the Jewish Question', in George Mosse and Bela Vago (eds.), *Jews and Non-Jews in Eastern Europe* (New York: Wiley, 1974), pp. 315–334; Browning, *Origins of the Final Solution*, pp. 81–89.

Reich Foreign Office and the Reich Security Main Office drew up plans and obtained expert opinions. In his expert's report, the geologist Friedrich Schumacher concluded that Madagascar was sufficiently worthless for Jews to be settled there, as it had no significant natural resources. The demographer Friedrich Burgdörfer also viewed the project positively. Plans were made to relocate 4 million Jews to this Indian Ocean island within the next four years. They would eke out an existence there under the supervision of the SS – it was assumed that many of them would not survive under the envisaged conditions (Docs. 92, 94, 99).[121]

However, the project did not prove viable. Without an armistice or even a victory over Britain, it was impossible to gain the requisite control over the sea routes. Nonetheless, from then on the Germans responsible for resettlement plans never abandoned the basic idea of deporting all the Jews within the German sphere of control to a remote region.[122] At first there were thoughts of resettling Jews within Europe. When the victory over France allowed Alsace and Lorraine to be annexed by the Reich and incorporated into the Gaue of Baden and Saar-Palatinate, the respective Gauleiter, Josef Bürckel and Robert Wagner, suggested that all the Jews from their Gaue be deported to France, a proposal that Hitler endorsed. On 22 October 1940 more than 6,000 Jews from the Baden and Saar-Palatinate regions were transported to southern France (Docs. 112, 113).

The Vichy government protested against the unannounced deportations into its territory and demanded that the Jews be returned to the Reich. As a result, the planned deportation of Jews from Hessen was postponed. Like Hans Frank in the General Government, the Vichy government was disinclined to make its territory available for a solution to Germany's 'Jewish question'.[123] It interned the German Jews in the camp at Gurs and later in Rivesaltes, at the foot of the Pyrenees.[124]

121 Browning, *Final Solution and the German Foreign Office*, pp. 39–40; Brechtken, '*Madagaskar für die Juden*'; Hans Jansen, *Der Madagaskar-Plan: Die beabsichtigte Deportation der europäischen Juden nach Madagaskar* (Munich: Herbig, 1997).

122 Ian Kershaw, *Fateful Choices: Ten Decisions that Changed the World, 1940–1941* (London: Penguin, 2007), pp. 447–449.

123 Jacob Toury, 'Die Entstehungsgeschichte des Austreibungsbefehls gegen die Juden der Saarpfalz und Badens (22./23. Oktober 1940 – Camp de Gurs)', *Jahrbuch des Instituts für deutsche Geschichte Tel Aviv*, vol. 15 (1986), pp. 431–464; Erhard R. Wiehn (ed.), *Oktoberdeportation 1940: Die sogenannte 'Abschiebung' der badischen und saarpfälzischen Juden in das französische Internierungslager Gurs und andere Vorstationen von Auschwitz* (Konstanz: Hartung-Gore, 1990); Gerhard J. Teschner, *Die Deportation der badischen und saarpfälzischen Juden am 22. Oktober 1940: Vorgeschichte und Durchführung der Deportation und das weitere Schicksal der Deportierten bis zum Kriegsende im Kontext der deutschen und französischen Judenpolitik* (Frankfurt am Main/New York: Peter Lang, 2002). On the policy towards the Jews in the Vichy government, see also Michael Robert Marrus and Robert O. Paxton, *Vichy France and the Jews* (New York: Basic, 1981); Susan Zuccotti, *The Holocaust, the French, and the Jews* (Lincoln, NE: University of Nebraska Press, 1999), pp. 65–80; Browning, *Origins of the Final Solution*, p. 91.

124 Over the course of 1941, some of the German Jews were sent to other camps in south-western France. Approximately 1,500 prisoners managed to escape or emigrate to other countries, and a total of around 1,000 died in the camps. On the camps, see Claude Laharie, *Le camp de Gurs, 1939–1945: Un aspect méconnu de l'histoire du Bearn* (Pau: Infocompo, 1985); Anne Grynberg, *Les camps de la honte: Les internés juifs des camps français 1939–1944* (Paris: La Découverte, 1991); Denis Peschanski, *La France des camps: L'internement, 1938–1946* (Paris: Gallimard, 2002); Jean-Marc Dreyfus, 'Alsace Lorraine', in Gruner and Osterloh, *The Greater German Reich and the Jews*, pp. 316–339, here p. 327.

Protests against the deportation of German Jews also occurred in Germany. Otto Hirsch of the Reich Association of Jews in Germany complained to the SD, saying that after the 'resettlement' of the Stettin Jews in the spring of 1940, the board of the Association had been assured that no more Jews would be deported (Doc. 111). The Reich Association also alerted the Jews who had not been at home at the time of the 'operation', advising them not to return. All the Jewish communities proclaimed a day of fasting as an expression of mourning, rabbis offered prayers for the deportees during worship, and cultural events were cancelled for an entire week. The lawyer Julius Seligsohn, also an official of the Reich Association, was one of the driving forces behind the board's efforts to mark the deportations with acts of mourning and with warnings for the future. As a result, the Gestapo imprisoned him in Sachsenhausen concentration camp. At the same time, Paul Eppstein was still being held in 'protective custody' (Doc. 128). Whenever he was summoned to the Gestapo, Otto Hirsch tried repeatedly to bring about the release of his colleagues. Not long thereafter, he himself was arrested by the Gestapo because he had allegedly tried to leak news into foreign countries about the situation of those deported to France.[125]

Academics and policymakers worked hand in glove, and not only to prepare the Madagascar Plan. Military expansion broadened the planning horizons of the regime and simultaneously increased its need for policy advice from the academic world. Economists, sociologists, and historians, with their project for a New Order inspired by population economics and racist theory, paved the way intellectually for radical solutions to the 'Jewish question'. Prominent examples included the numerous ideas for resettlement and Germanization of the occupied territories, which later culminated in the 'General Plan East'.[126]

At the Frankfurt-based Institute for the Study of the Jewish Question, work on a 'general European solution to the Jewish question' had been under way since the summer of 1939 under the patronage of Reichsleiter Alfred Rosenberg. The deliberations were published in the institute's journal, *Weltkampf* (Doc. 171). At the inaugural conference, which did not take place until March 1941, all the speakers addressed the topic of a future 'final solution', though without defining it in concrete terms.[127]

Scholars from various disciplines knew how to utilize the military situation for the purposes of their own research, as well as the climate generated by initial military suc-

125 Esriel Hildesheimer, *Jüdische Selbstverwaltung unter dem NS-Regime* (Tübingen: Mohr, 1994), pp. 192–202; Meyer, 'Der Traum von einer autonomen jüdischen Verwaltung', pp. 34–35.

126 Max Weinreich, *Hitler's Professors: The Part of Scholarship in Germany's Crimes against the Jewish People* (New York: Yiddish Scientific Institute, 1946); Alan Steinweis, *Studying the Jew: Scholarly Antisemitism in Nazi Germany* (Cambridge, MA: Harvard University Press, 2006); Isabel Heinemann, 'Wissenschaft und Homogenisierungsplanungen für Osteuropa: Konrad Meyer, der "Generalplan Ost" und die Deutsche Forschungsgemeinschaft', in Isabel Heinemann and Patrick Wagner (eds.), *Wissenschaft – Planung – Vertreibung: Neuordnungskonzepte und Umsiedlungspolitik im 20. Jahrhundert* (Stuttgart: F. Steiner, 2006), pp. 45–72; Jan Eike Dunkhase, *Werner Conze: Ein deutscher Historiker im 20. Jahrhundert* (Göttingen: Vandenhoeck & Ruprecht, 2010), pp. 35–67. See also the Introduction to PMJ 4.

127 Hans-Christian Petersen, *Bevölkerungsökonomie – Ostforschung – Politik: Eine biographische Studie zu Peter-Heinz Seraphim (1902–1979)* (Osnabrück: Fibre, 2007); Dirk Rupnow, *Judenforschung im Dritten Reich: Wissenschaft zwischen Politik, Propaganda und Ideologie* (Baden-Baden: Nomos, 2011).

cesses, which was pervaded by fantasies about what could be achieved. Economists developed concepts for a European economic area under German leadership harnessed to the needs of the war (*Großraumwehrwirtschaft*), and physicists worked on new weapons systems and more powerful aircraft. Agronomists sought to make Germany 'blockade-proof' by exploring possibilities for increasing agricultural production and by attempting to replace imports, for which large amounts of foreign exchange were needed, with domestic substitutes. Eugenicists and human geneticists provided the expertise for the policy on hereditary health. Meanwhile, the mostly foreign prisoners in the greatly enlarged concentration camps served as test subjects for human experiments conducted by medical professionals. The consequences for the prisoners' health were grave, sometimes fatal. By such means, research on chemical weapons and on tuberculosis gained fresh momentum. Neuroscientists and anatomists utilized the victims of executions and 'euthanasia' murders to obtain findings that, had the research been carried out in peacetime and with the proper legal safeguards, would only have been possible through the protracted and uncertain process of animal experimentation.[128]

The Jews in the Reich: Desperate Attempts to Emigrate

Between 1933 and 1939 approximately 247,000 Jews had managed to emigrate from Germany. Around 80,000 left the territory of the Old Reich alone in the eight months between January 1939 and the onset of war. After that, only 30,000 to 35,000 Jews succeeded in leaving the Old Reich, Austria, and the Protectorate before October 1941, when emigration was prohibited. Moreover, following the renewed territorial expansion through conquest in the spring of 1940, almost all the neighbouring countries were occupied by German troops. As a result of the war, established escape routes were often blocked off, available ship capacity reduced, and maritime routes became increasingly unsafe.

After the outbreak of war, the situation in Britain became markedly more difficult for the Jews who had fled from the Reich. When imposing restrictions, the British government did try hard to distinguish between Jewish Germans and Germans loyal to the

128 Christian Pross and Götz Aly, *Der Wert des Menschen: Medizin in Deutschland 1918–1945* (Berlin: Hentrich, 1989); Götz Aly and Susanne Heim, *Architects of Annihilation: Auschwitz and the Logic of Destruction*, trans. A. G. Blunden (London: Weidenfeld & Nicolson, 2002 [German edn, 1991]), pp. 215–233; Doris Kaufmann (ed.), *Geschichte der Kaiser-Wilhelm-Gesellschaft im Nationalsozialismus: Bestandsaufnahmen und Perspektiven der Forschung* (Göttingen: Wallstein, 2000); Susanne Heim (ed.), *Plant Breeding and Agrarian Research in Kaiser-Wilhelm-Institutes 1933–1945: Calories, Caoutchouc, Careers* (Dordrecht: Springer, 2008); Gerhard Baader, 'Auf dem Weg zum Menschenversuch im Nationalsozialismus', in Carola Sachse (ed.), *Die Verbindung nach Auschwitz: Biowissenschaften und Menschenversuche an Kaiser-Wilhelm-Instituten* (Göttingen: Wallstein, 2003), pp. 105–157; Francis R. Nicosia and Jonathan Huener (eds.), *Medicine and Medical Ethics in Nazi Germany: Origins, Practices, Legacies* (New York/Oxford: Berghahn, 2004); Wolfgang U. Eckart, *Man, Medicine and the State: The Human Body as an Object of Government Sponsored Medical Research in the 20th Century* (Stuttgart: Steiner, 2006); Mark Walker, Karin Orth, Ulrich Herbert, et al. (eds.), *The German Research Foundation, 1920–1970: Funding Poised between Science and Politics* (Stuttgart: Steiner, 2013); Paul Weindling, *Victims and Survivors of Nazi Human Experiments: Science and Suffering in the Holocaust* (London: Bloomsbury, 2015).

regime. However, when it ordered the internment of so-called enemy aliens in the early summer of 1940, many German Jews were affected. Moreover, once the war had begun, the British government stopped issuing Jews from the territory of the Reich with certificates for emigration to Palestine. As a result, it was only possible to emigrate there via neutral countries or by illegal means (Docs. 120, 121). Elisabeth Freund, who was later able to escape to Havana, described in retrospect her efforts to leave Germany. On 1 September the onset of war had thwarted her emigration to Britain, which had already been approved. She continued her endeavours:

> In the spring of 1940 we got an entry permit for Portugal. We got everything ready at once, applied for our passports – then the German troops invaded Holland, Belgium, and France, a flood of refugees poured into Portugal, and the Portuguese government sent out telegrams cancelling all the permits that had been issued. We were still lucky that we had not yet given up our apartment and sold our furniture.[129]

Many non-Jews took advantage of the Jews' predicament and gained possession, at a price well below the original value, of furnishings and valuables that the Jews either could not take or were not permitted to take with them (Doc. 179).[130]

The more countries the German Wehrmacht attacked, the more cautiously the neutral states, particularly the USA, approached their immigration policy. Politicians and journalists were worried, fearing a 'fifth column' of German spies. Julius Seligsohn of the Reich Association of Jews thus had to state in a pamphlet in 1940:

> In early July 1940, the government in Washington instructed the consular representations to apply a strict standard to the verification of immigration requirements. If there is any cause for doubt, the visa is not to be issued, even if the tightened verification procedures should result in immigration quotas not being met.[131]

Julius Seligsohn never left Germany. He died in Sachsenhausen concentration camp on 28 February 1942.

129 Sachse, *Als Zwangsarbeiterin in Berlin*, p. 74.

130 Herbert A. Strauss, 'Jewish Emigration from Germany: Nazi Politics and Jewish Responses', parts I and II, *Leo Baeck Institute Yearbook*, vol. 25 (1980), pp. 313–361, and vol. 26 (1981), pp. 343–409; Werner Röder and Sybille Claus (eds.), *Biographisches Handbuch der deutschsprachigen Emigration nach 1933* (München: Saur, 1980–1983); Susanne Heim, 'Vertreibung, Raub und Umverteilung: Die jüdischen Flüchtlinge aus Deutschland und die Vermehrung des "Volksvermögens"', in 'Flüchtlingspolitik und Fluchthilfe', special issue, *Beiträge zur nationalsozialistischen Gesundheits- und Sozialpolitik*, vol. 15 (1999), pp. 107–138; A. Beker (ed.), *The Plunder of Jewish Property during the Holocaust* (Basingstoke: Palgrave, 2001); Gregg J. Rickman, *Conquest and Redemption: A History of Jewish Assets from the Holocaust* (Piscataway, NJ: Transaction, 2014).

131 Julius Ludwig Israel Seligsohn, *Die Einwanderung nach U.S.A.* (Berlin: Jüdischer Kulturbund in Deutschland, 1940), pp. 9–10. Also see David S. Wyman, *Paper Walls: America and the Refugee Crisis, 1938–1941* (Amherst: University of Massachusetts Press, 1968), pp. 172–176; Deborah E. Lipstadt, *Beyond Belief: The American Press and the Coming of the Holocaust, 1933–1945* (New York: Free, 1986), pp. 128–131; Richard Breitman and Alan M. Kraut, *American Refugee Policy and European Jewry, 1933–1945* (Bloomington: Indiana University Press, 1987); Hans-Ullrich Dillmann and Susanne Heim, *Fluchtpunkt Karibik: Jüdische Emigranten in der Dominikanischen Republik* (Berlin: Links, 2009), pp. 70–71, 127–128; Saul Friedman, *No Haven for the Oppressed: United States Policy toward Jewish Refugees, 1938–1945* (Detroit, MI: Wayne State University Press, 2017).

The principles governing the issuing of visas were not usually revealed to the applicants (Doc. 29). In letters from Jewish parents to their children who had emigrated before the war, efforts to emigrate and the failure thereof are the dominant theme, as in the correspondence of Amalie and Paul Malsch, a couple living in Düsseldorf (Docs. 186, 207). The children, still trying hard to find their place in a new environment, felt responsible for enabling their parents to emigrate, but in most cases their endeavours were unsuccessful.

Despite the dwindling opportunities for emigration, anti-Jewish policy continued to focus on expulsion. It was a contradiction that the Jewish officials were supposed to resolve, yet they were completely unable to do so. Because emigration from the Old Reich and Austria had precedence over that from the Protectorate, Eichmann's Central Office in Prague had little success in bringing it about. The monthly emigration figures failed to rise after the establishment of the office.[132]

Even after the war began, Jewish representatives travelled abroad at the behest of Eichmann to ask the representatives of international Jewish organizations for help with their emigration efforts. Leading members of the Reich Association would have had a chance to emigrate. On the one hand, the Reich Security Main Office prevented them from doing so by confiscating their passports and not allowing their spouses to accompany them on trips abroad. On the other hand, like board member Otto Hirsch they felt a sense of obligation: 'Not everybody can leave; after all somebody has to take care of the old people!' He himself lost his life in Mauthausen on 19 June 1941.[133] Jakob Edelstein, who, as head of the Palestine Office in Prague, travelled abroad on a number of occasions (Doc. 250), came back every time and made tireless efforts to enable Jews from Bohemia and Moravia to emigrate and thus to save their lives. He was deported in December 1941 to Theresienstadt, where, as the first Jewish elder, he had to organize life in the ghetto. On 20 June 1944 he was shot dead in Auschwitz, along with his wife and son. Paul Eppstein, who replaced Edelstein in January 1943 as Jewish elder in Theresienstadt, was shot and killed there at the age of 42. His wife, Hedwig, perished in Auschwitz.[134]

In March 1940 Eichmann had appointed Berthold Storfer of the Israelite Religious Community of Vienna to serve as coordinator for the refugee ships that sailed illegally, mainly to Palestine.[135] Storfer then organized crossings on the *Pacific*, the *Milos*, and the *Atlantic*, which took on board Jews from Germany, Austria, and the Protectorate. When the three ships reached the port of Haifa in late 1940, the British authorities ordered all the passengers to be combined aboard the *Patria*, which was supposed to set sail immediately for Mauritius. The British Mandate wanted to prevent the refugees from entering Palestine and so the intention was to intern them on Mauritius. The Jewish underground organization Haganah tried to prevent the ship from leaving Haifa through an act of sabotage. But the effects of the charge that exploded aboard the *Patria* on 25 November 1940

132 Bondy, *'Elder of the Jews'*; Shlain, 'Jakob Edelsteins Bemühungen', pp. 81–87; Anderl, 'Zentralstellen für jüdische Auswanderung', p. 283.

133 'Zur Gedenkfeier für Dr. Otto Hirsch', in *Schawe Zion*, July 1941 (no author named), YVA, O.1/267, fol. 3, cited in Meyer, 'Der Traum von einer autonomen jüdischen Verwaltung', p. 26.

134 Meyer, 'Der Traum von einer autonomen jüdischen Verwaltung', pp. 31–35.

135 On Storfer and illegal immigration to Palestine, see PMJ 2, p. 47. See also Gabriele Anderl, *9096 Leben: Der unbekannte Judenretter Berthold Storfer* (Berlin: Rotbuch, 2012).

had been miscalculated – it sank the ship within a matter of minutes. More than 250 of the 1,800 passengers lost their lives, many of them in view of family members waiting on shore. The authorities took the survivors to the Atlit refugee camp (Docs. 120, 121). Zionist leaders such as Chaim Weizmann and David Ben-Gurion, who felt compelled to compromise with the British mandatory power, criticized illegal immigration into Palestine and as a result triggered impassioned debate within Jewish communities.[136]

Another illegal refugee transport, carrying 822 Jews mostly from Vienna, but also from Berlin and Danzig, had left the Danube metropolis in November 1939 and made an intermediate stop in Bratislava to take on board an additional 100 passengers from Prague and from Bratislava itself. However, they got no farther than the Yugoslav port of Kladovo on the Danube, where they were allowed to go ashore after spending several weeks on the ship. Most now lived in a camp composed of tents and barracks. In September 1940 the refugees were taken to the Serbian town of Šabac, their hopes of a quick resumption of their journey repeatedly dashed. Other Jews gradually joined the group, which thus grew to include around 1,400 people. Approximately 200 to 280 of them, members of the Youth Aliyah in particular, managed to escape, with the help of Palestine certificates, shortly before the German invasion of Yugoslavia. The others fell into the hands of the German troops in April 1941 and were among the first Jews from the Reich to be victims of systematic mass shootings in October 1941.[137]

While Jews were dependent on financial assistance from Jewish organizations to support their emigration efforts, non-Aryan Protestant Christians found support for various matters, including emigration, from the Pastor Grüber Office in Berlin, a relief organization of the Confessing Church (Doc. 47). On 19 December 1940 the Gestapo arrested Heinrich Grüber and in early 1941 ordered the work of the office to be officially discontinued. Grüber was sent to a concentration camp and not released until June 1943.

Catholics who were persecuted as Jews received assistance with their emigration efforts from the St Raphael Society[138] until it was banned in June 1941, along with the Relief Agency of the Episcopal Ordinariate in Berlin. In addition, relief agencies were established in destination countries. On instructions from the Vatican, they worked together with the St Raphael Society and endeavoured to help the refugees after arrival.[139]

136 Jürgen Rohwer, 'Jüdische Flüchtlingsschiffe im Schwarzen Meer – 1934 bis 1944', in Ursula Büttner (ed.), *Das Unrechtsregime: Internationale Forschung über den Nationalsozialismus*, vol. 2: *Verfolgung, Exil, belasteter Neubeginn* (Hamburg: Christians, 1986), pp. 197–248; Dalia Ofer, *Escaping the Holocaust: Illegal Immigration to the Land of Israel, 1939–1944* (New York: Oxford University Press, 1990).

137 Gabriele Anderl and Walter Manoschek, *Gescheiterte Flucht: Der jüdische 'Kladovo-Transport' auf dem Weg nach Palästina 1939–1942* (Vienna: Gesellschaftskritik, 1993); Dalia Ofer and Hannah Weiner, *Dead-End Journey: The Tragic Story of the Kladovo-Šabac Group* (Lanham, MD: University Press of America, 1996).

138 The St Raphael Society for the Protection of Catholic German Emigrants was founded in 1871 in Mainz. Its president was the bishop of Osnabrück. The German authorities banned the society on 25 June 1941.

139 Eberhard Röhm and Jörg Thierfelder, *Juden – Christen – Deutsche*, vol. 3: *1938–1941* (Stuttgart: Calwer, 1995); Jana Leichsenring, *Die Katholische Kirche und 'ihre Juden': Das 'Hilfswerk beim Bischöflichen Ordinariat Berlin', 1938–1945* (Berlin: Metropol, 2007); Hartmut Ludwig, *An der Seite der Entrechteten und Schwachen: Zur Geschichte des 'Büro Pfarrer Grüber' (1938 bis 1940) und der Ev. Hilfsstelle für ehemals Rasseverfolgte nach 1945* (Berlin: Logos, 2009).

Reactions to 'Euthanasia' and Persecution of the Jews

Beginning in the summer of 1940, rumours of the 'euthanasia' crimes were circulated, first in the vicinity of the killing centres, but soon thereafter throughout the entire Reich. In Laubach (Hesse), the lawyer Friedrich Kellner noted in his diary on 28 July 1941 how the crimes were already attracting attention through mix-ups at the centres:

> The 'institutions for patients with physical or mental disabilities' have turned into killing centres. As I am informed, one family had brought their mentally ill son back home from such a facility. After some time, this family received [from the facility] a notification to the effect that their son [was] deceased and the ashes were being delivered to them! The office had forgotten to cross his name off the list of the dead. The plans for premeditated murder thus came to light.[140]

'Euthanasia' had become an open secret, and the rumours were also fuelled by fears that the killing programme would be expanded. Bishop Clemens August, Count von Galen, made it perfectly clear in a sermon in St Lambert's Church in Münster on 3 August 1941: 'If one establishes and applies the principle that "unproductive" human beings may be killed, then woe betide us all when we become old and frail! [...] and woe betide our brave soldiers who return home gravely injured, crippled, as invalids.'[141]

Public unrest was presumably one reason why Hitler ordered a halt to the centrally organized gassings in the 'euthanasia' facilities in the Reich around 24 August 1941. More than 70,000 people had already been killed by this time. Those responsible were now given the task of setting up killing centres in Eastern Europe.[142]

There were influential protests against the killing of patients with physical and mental disabilities. Probably no other National Socialist crime aroused so much indignation among the German population as the 'euthanasia' programme. Even though, until mid 1941, the Jews were 'only' being persecuted and not yet systematically murdered, there was no stirring of comparable indignation. Although the degree of approval or repudiation within German society is difficult to ascertain, many had obviously accepted the notion that Jews could not be part of the *Volksgemeinschaft*. In addition, the progressive

140 Friedrich Kellner et al. (eds.), *My Opposition: The Diary of Friedrich Kellner – a German against the Third Reich* (Cambridge: Cambridge University Press, 2018), p. 176.

141 Sermon at St Lambert's, 3 August 1941, published in Peter Löffler (ed.), *Bischof Clemens August Graf von Galen: Akten, Briefe und Predigten 1933–1946*, vol. 2: *1939–1946* (Mainz: Matthias-Grünewald, 1988), pp. 874–883, here p. 878.

142 Kurt Nowak, 'Widerstand, Zustimmung, Hinnahme: Das Verhalten der Bevölkerung zur "Euthanasie"', in Norbert Frei (ed.), *Medizin und Gesundheitspolitik in der NS-Zeit* (Munich: Oldenbourg, 1991), pp. 235–249; Friedlander, *Origins of Nazi Genocide*, pp. 111–114; Hugh Gregory Gallagher, *By Trust Betrayed: Patients, Physicians, and the License to Kill in the Third Reich* (Arlington, VA: Vandamere, 1995); Michael Burleigh, *Death and Deliverance: 'Euthanasia' in Germany, 1900 to 1945* (London: Pan, 2002); Winfried Süß, *Der 'Volkskörper' im Krieg: Gesundheitspolitik, Gesundheitsverhältnisse und Krankenmord im nationalsozialistischen Deutschland 1939–1945* (Mun ich: Oldenbourg, 2003), pp. 127–151; Götz Aly, *Die Belasteten: 'Euthanasie' 1939–1945. Eine Gesellschaftsgeschichte* (Frankfurt am Main: Fischer, 2013); Nathan Stoltzfus, *Hitler's Compromises: Coercion and Consensus in Nazi Germany* (New Haven, CT/London: Yale University Press, 2016), pp. 174–206.

isolation of this already very small group made it easy to block out their fate. Jews lived in houses designated solely for them, they were not seen either at the cinema or the theatre, they did their shopping at other times and to some extent in other shops, and even at work they were usually segregated from colleagues.[143]

The situation in the Protectorate was similar, as the writer and historian H. G. Adler, who survived Theresienstadt and later published a major work on the ghetto, wrote in a letter in 1947:

> Restrictions and torments, slowly increasing, increasingly unbearable, increasingly inhumane. Kindness, but also cowardice and the venal mentality of lackeys on the part of a great many Czechs. Moral degeneracy and inhumanity on the part of the Germans. Only a very few friends on either side kept faith with each other.[144]

From the End of 1940 to June 1941: Preparations for the War of Annihilation

On 18 December 1940 Hitler signed Directive No. 21, 'Case Barbarossa'.[145] The decision to attack the Soviet Union had thus been taken. For the European Jews, it was a decision of dire significance. Given a successful outcome of the war, millions of them would fall under the German sphere of influence. Even without concrete plans, the National Socialist leadership expected that the anticipated rapid victory over the Soviet Union would make resettlement projects possible on a scale far greater than before.[146]

At the end of 1940 and beginning of 1941, new versions of a 'final solution [*Endlösung*] to the Jewish question' were also under discussion. The term was used with increasing frequency in internal discussions, although its meaning only gradually became clear. When Eichmann noted in December 1940 that the Jews should be deported 'to a territory yet to be determined' (Doc. 125), his choice of words suggested that it was no longer Madagascar that was in question. Himmler himself, who had requested Eichmann's

143 Otto Dov Kulka, '"Public Opinion" in Nazi Germany and the "Jewish Question"', *Jerusalem Quarterly*, vol. 25 (1982), pp. 121–144; David Bankier, *The Germans and the Final Solution: Public Opinion under Nazism* (Oxford: Blackwell, 1992), pp. 159–170; Susan Bachrach and Dieter Kuntz, *Deadly Medicine*; Eric Arthur Johnson and Karl-Heinz Reuband, *What We Knew: Terror, Mass Murder, and Everyday Life in Nazi Germany. An Oral History* (Cambridge, MA: Basic Books, 2005); Frank Bajohr, 'Vom antijüdischen Konsens zum schlechten Gewissen: Die deutsche Gesellschaft und die Judenverfolgung 1933–1945', in Frank Bajohr and Dieter Pohl, *Der Holocaust als offenes Geheimnis: Die Deutschen, die NS-Führung und die Alliierten* (Munich: Beck, 2006), pp. 15–79, here pp. 26–27; Bernward Dörner, *Die Deutschen und der Holocaust: Was niemand wissen wollte, aber jeder wissen konnte* (Berlin: Propyläen, 2007), pp. 71–75; Ian Kershaw, *Hitler, the Germans, and the Final Solution* (New Haven: Yale University Press, 2008), pp. 119–234.

144 Cited in Franz Hocheneder, *H.G. Adler (1910–1988): Privatgelehrter und freier Schriftsteller* (Vienna: Böhlau, 2009), p. 69.

145 The directive is published in H. R. Trevor-Roper (ed.), *Hitler's War Directives, 1939–1945* (London: Pan, 1966), pp. 93–98.

146 Andreas Hillgruber, *Hitlers Strategie: Politik und Kriegsführung 1940–1941* (Frankfurt am Main: Bernard & Graefe, 1965), pp. 352–397; Aly, *'Final Solution'*, pp. 124–128; Browning, *Origins of the Final Solution*, pp. 213–224.

comments in preparing for a speech to the Reichsleiter and Gauleiter, summed up the current state of thinking: 'Jewish emigration and thus additional space for Poles' (Doc. 126). He addressed the connection between the resettlements in German-occupied Europe and the 'final solution to the Jewish question', but did not name a specific target region. When Theodor Dannecker, in his function as official in charge of Jewish affairs (*Judenreferent*) for the representative of the Chief of the Security Police and the SD in Paris, discussed future plans on 21 January 1941, mention was made only of the 'yet to be determined territory' (Doc. 138).

During this phase, on 30 January 1941 Hitler again recalled his 'prophecy' of 30 January 1939 that a world war would result in the annihilation of European Jewry (Doc. 142). On 18 March 1941 Goebbels reported on a meeting with Hitler and Governor General Frank: 'Vienna will soon be entirely free of Jews. And now it is to be Berlin's turn. I am already discussing this with the Führer and Dr Franck [*sic*]. He is putting the Jews to work, and they are compliant, too. Later they must be out of Europe altogether.'[147]

There were still approximately 60,000 Jews living in Vienna. After Gauleiter Baldur von Schirach, in office since August 1940, had complained to Hitler in October about this state of affairs, in early December Hitler gave his consent to deportation even while the war was still ongoing (Doc. 123). Consequently, in February and March 1941, the deportation of the Viennese Jews was incorporated into the third 'short-term plan' (*Nahplan*), a gigantic resettlement programme to take place on Polish territory. Approximately 5,000 people in Vienna were affected. Families were selected for deportation to the General Government by the Central Office for Jewish Emigration, headed by Alois Brunner. Prior to their deportation, they were held in improvised and crowded assembly camps (*Sammellager*) (Doc. 151). The Israelite Religious Community of Vienna had to play a part in making the arrangements. Because preparations for the invasion of the Soviet Union took precedence over further deportations in the period that followed, there were no further deportations from Vienna for the time being.[148]

Hans Frank, who had earlier placed great hope in the Madagascar Plan, viewed the military planning against the Soviet Union as a new opportunity to deport the Jews living in the territory under his control towards the East. His protests against resettlements of Jews in the General Government intensified the pressure on Berlin to find other solutions. At a government meeting in Cracow on 25 March 1941, he reported on a preceding visit to Berlin, where 'the Führer had promised him that the GG [General Government] would be the first territory to be made free of Jews'. With the loss of the General Government as a deportation destination, however, a territorial 'solution to the Jewish question' had become virtually impossible.[149]

On 20 March 1941 Eichmann declared to representatives of the Propaganda Ministry that Heydrich 'was tasked by the Führer with planning the final evacuation of the Jews',

147 Cited in *Die Tagebücher von Joseph Goebbels*, Elke Fröhlich ed., part 1: *Aufzeichnungen 1923–1941*, vol. 9: *Dezember 1940 – Juli 1941* (Munich: Saur, 1998), pp. 191–194, here p. 193; see also Susanne Heim and Götz Aly, *Bevölkerungsstruktur und Massenmord: Neue Dokumente zur deutschen Politik der Jahre 1938–1945* (Berlin: Rotbuch, 1991), pp. 22–25; Aly, *'Final Solution'*, pp. 124–128.

148 Rabinovici, *Eichmann's Jews*, pp. 99–102; Löw, 'Die frühen Deportationen', pp. 71–75.

149 Quotation in Werner Präg and Wolfgang Jacobmeyer (eds.), *Das Diensttagebuch des deutschen Generalgouverneurs in Polen, 1939–1945* (Stuttgart: Deutsche, 1975), p. 337; see also Hilberg, *Destruction of the European Jews*, pp. 220–221; Aly, *'Final Solution'*, pp. 161–162.

but his proposal that the Jews now be deported had not been accepted, because the General Government could not currently take in any Jews or Poles. In a memorandum dated 26 March 1941 concerning a conversation with Göring, Heydrich himself wrote that his draft must be reworked in view of the responsibilities assigned to Alfred Rosenberg, who had already been designated to serve as the future head of the Reich Ministry for the Occupied Eastern Territories. Now, therefore, the 'territory yet to be determined', in which the 'final solution' was to be carried out, was defined, at least in broad terms: it was the yet to be conquered East, with the Pripet Marshes in southern Belarus the specific focus of discussion.[150] The plans concerned all the Jews of Europe. On 20 May 1941 the Reich Security Main Office gave instructions for further emigration from Belgium and France to be halted 'in view of the undoubtedly imminent final solution to the Jewish question' (Doc. 182). In France, Heydrich's former deputy Werner Best, who headed the Military Commander's administrative staff, had noted as early as 4 April 1941: 'The German interest consists in a progressive removal of Jewry from every country of Europe, with the aim of completely de-Jewifying Europe.'[151]

In parallel with these plans, Heinrich Himmler tackled an additional project in early 1941. As the numbers of prisoners in the concentration camps were increasing, he sent an enquiry at the beginning of the year to Philipp Bouhler in the Chancellery of the Führer, asking how the 'euthanasia' headquarters could be used to unburden the concentration camps.[152] The programme of murder that was developed by the organizers of 'euthanasia' at Himmler's behest under file reference 14f13 targeted prisoners of various nationalities who were deemed politically or racially undesirable, infirm, or no longer fit for forced labour. In most cases the Jews fell victim to indiscriminate preselection by the camp administrators. From the spring of 1941 the 'euthanasia' assessors visited the concentration camps and selected prisoners. In September 1941 the physician Friedrich Mennecke wrote from Dachau to his wife: 'There are only 2,000 men and the job will be finished really quickly, as they are simply glanced at as they pass by, like on a conveyor belt' (Doc. 214). When, after one year, 'Operation 14f13' was discontinued in the spring of 1942, the doctors had been responsible for the death of at least 10,000 people.[153] In addition, in the spring of 1941 – independently of this operation – first 425 and then, in the summer, more than 200 Dutch Jews were deported to Mauthausen concentration camp, where most of them were murdered within a few weeks. Approximately 1,600 Jews perished there in the course of 1941.[154]

150 See PMJ 7/1; Aly, *'Final Solution'*, pp. 171–177; Peter Longerich, *The Unwritten Order: Hitler's Role in the Final Solution* (Stroud: Tempus, 2001), pp. 57–62.

151 Best's meeting schedule for the Military Commander in France for discussion with Xavier Vallat, dated 4 April 1941, cited in Michael Mayer, *Staaten als Täter: Ministerialbürokratie und 'Judenpolitik' in NS-Deutschland und Vichy-Frankreich: Ein Vergleich* (Munich: Oldenbourg, 2010), p. 206.

152 Friedlander, *Origins of Nazi Genocide*, p. 142.

153 Walter Grode, *Die 'Sonderbehandlung 14f13' in den Konzentrationslagern des Dritten Reiches: Ein Beitrag zur Dynamik faschistischer Vernichtungspolitik* (Frankfurt am Main/New York: Peter Lang, 1987); Friedlander, *Origins of Nazi Genocide*, pp. 142–150; Pohl, 'Holocaust and the Concentration Camps', p. 151.

154 Pingel, *Häftlinge unter SS-Herrschaft*, p. 96; Hans Maršálek, *Die Geschichte des Konzentrationslagers Mauthausen: Eine Dokumentation* (Vienna: Österreichische Lagergemeinschaft Mauthausen, 1980); Eberhard Jäckel, *Hitler's World View: A Blueprint for Power*, trans. Herbert Arnold (Cambridge, MA: Harvard University Press, 1981 [German edn, 1969]), pp. 89–122.

In the meantime, the war had also reached south-east Europe. Admittedly, Hitler's plan to clear the way for the invasion of the Soviet Union by quickly defeating Britain had failed. But on 27 September 1940 he had successfully concluded the Tripartite Pact with Italy and Japan, an agreement discussed as early as 1939. By 25 March 1941 Hungary, Romania, Slovakia, Bulgaria, and Yugoslavia had joined the alliance. A coup in Belgrade on 27 March against the participation in the Tripartite Pact was used by Hitler as an opportunity to have German troops invade Yugoslavia on 6 April. The Yugoslav government capitulated on 17 April. In Greece the Wehrmacht came to Mussolini's aid and, on 27 April, German soldiers occupied Athens. On 10 April, Croatia declared itself an independent state, allied with the Axis Powers.[155]

As a result, almost 3 million Jews were now living under direct German rule: 675,000 in the Greater German Reich, including the annexed territories, as well as 2,250,000 in the occupied territories. German influence on Slovakia, Romania, and Italy posed a direct threat to hundreds of thousands more Jews.[156]

Preparations for the invasion of the Soviet Union made it clear from the outset that this would be a war of annihilation, in which the conventional rules of warfare would no longer apply. While the Wehrmacht and SS units had differed in their approach in Poland, the boundaries now began to blur. In April 1941 the Wehrmacht destroyed an entire Serbian village, Donji Dobrić, as 'retribution' for the shooting of a German officer. In May 1941 the commander of the Second Army, Field Marshal Maximilian von Weichs, announced the shooting of 100 Serbs for an attack on German soldiers and made it known that, in the future, 100 Serbs would be shot for every German soldier killed.[157]

At this time, and in close cooperation with Hitler, the Wehrmacht developed corresponding guidelines for the war against the Soviet Union. On 3 March 1941 Hitler sent back a draft directive from the Wehrmacht High Command (OKW) with addenda for the revised version: 'This coming campaign is more than just a struggle of weapons; it also heralds a confrontation of two world views. [...] The Jewish Bolshevist intelligentsia, hitherto the "oppressor" of the people, must be eliminated.'[158]

At the instruction of Hitler, Himmler and Heydrich set up Einsatzgruppen of the Security Police and the SD which, having been field-tested in the Poland campaign, were now supposed to secure the rear area in the wake of the invading army. On 26 March 1941 Göring instructed Heydrich to prepare a short handout 'for the troops about the

155 Detlef Vogel, 'German Intervention in the Balkans', in Militärgeschichtliches Forschungsamt (ed.), *Germany and the Second World War*, vol. 3: *The Mediterranean, South-East Europe, and North Africa, 1939–1941*, trans. Dean S. McMurry, Ewald Osers, and Louise Willmot (Oxford/New York: Oxford University Press, 2001 [German edn, 1984]), pp. 449–556, here pp. 451–526; Weinberg, *A World at Arms*, pp. 142–161, 215–224; Alexander Korb, *Intertwined Genocides: Mass Violence in Western Yugoslavia during the Second World War* (Oxford: Oxford University Press, 2019).

156 Yahil, *The Holocaust*, p. 143.

157 Walter Manoschek, *'Serbien ist judenfrei!' Militärische Besatzungspolitik und Judenvernichtung in Serbien 1941/42* (Munich: Oldenbourg, 1993), pp. 31–32.

158 War Diary of the Wehrmacht High Command, vol. 1, p. 341 (3 March 1941), cited in Percy E. Schramm (ed.), *Kriegstagebuch des Oberkommandos der Wehrmacht (Wehrmachtführungsstab)*, vol. 1: *1. August 1940–31. Dezember 1941*, compiled and annotated by Hans-Adolf Jacobsen (Frankfurt am Main: Bernard & Graefe, 1965), pp. 340–343, quotation p. 341; Christian Streit, *Keine Kameraden: Die Wehrmacht und die sowjetischen Kriegsgefangenen 1941–1945*, 4th edn (Bonn: Dietz, 1997 [1978]).

dangerous nature of the NKVD [Soviet secret police], the political commissars, Jews etc., so that they know whom, in practice, they have to put up against the wall'.[159] Dated the same day is the draft of an order by Quartermaster General Eduard Wagner, in which he stated, following talks with Heydrich, that the Sonderkommandos of the Security Police (SD) should carry out their assignments 'on their own responsibility' and, in so doing, be authorized to 'take executive measures' with regard to the civilian population. This order was issued one month later.[160] Shortly thereafter, on 13 May, Wilhelm Keitel, the chief of the Wehrmacht High Command, issued the so-called 'Decree on Exercising Military Jurisdiction in the Area of Barbarossa and Special Measures by the Troops' (Barbarossa Decree). He thereby delivered the practically defenceless populace into the hands of the invading troops, for members of the Wehrmacht no longer had to answer before a military court after an attack upon civilians.[161] On 19 May he ordered his officers and men to 'crack down ruthlessly and vigorously on *Bolshevist agitators, irregulars, saboteurs, Jews*'.[162] And finally the 'Commissar Order' (*Kommissarbefehl*) of 6 June 1941 stated that 'political commissars' were to be shot.[163] In addition, one thing was certain: the anticipated prisoners of war, as well as the population, would go hungry. At a meeting on 2 May 1941, the state secretaries of the key ministries confirmed that, in view of the plans to feed the German army 'off the land' and also to send foodstuffs to the Reich, it was clear that 'countless millions of people [would] starve to death'.[164]

Even before the German invasion, therefore, it was established that an extralegal area would be created in the occupied territory. Hitler's phrase 'Jewish Bolshevist intelligentsia' was accepted by the Wehrmacht and the Einsatzgruppen alike. Moreover, it was sufficiently imprecise to make it possible to keep expanding the set of persons classed as enemies.[165]

159 PMJ 7/1.

160 Army High Command/Army General Staff/Quartermaster-General of the Army/Department for Wartime Administration, Nr. II o.Nr./41 geh. vom 26.3.1941, BArch, RW 4/v.575, cited in Jürgen Förster, 'Operation Barbarossa as a War of Conquest and Annihilation', in Militärgeschichtliches Forschungsamt, *Germany and the Second World War*, vol. 4: *The Attack on the Soviet Union*, trans. Dean S. McMurry, Ewald Osers, and Louise Willmot (Oxford: Oxford University Press, 1996 [German edn, 1983]), p. 491.

161 The decree is published in Reinhard Rürup (ed.), *Der Krieg gegen die Sowjetunion 1941–1945: Eine Dokumentation* (Berlin: Argon, 1991), p. 45, and in Ian Kershaw, *Hitler 1936-1945: Nemesis* (London: Penguin, 2009), p. 601.

162 PMJ 7/3; Hans-Adolf Jacobsen, 'Kommissarbefehl und Massenexekutionen sowjetischer Kriegsgefangener', in Martin Broszat, Hans-Adolf Jacobsen, and Helmut Krausnick, *Anatomie des SS-Staates*, vol. 2 (Olten/Freiburg im Breisgau: Walter, 1965), pp. 161–279, here pp. 213–214.

163 The order is published in Rürup, *Der Krieg gegen die Sowjetunion*, p. 46.

164 File note regarding a meeting of state secretaries on 2 May 1941 about the economic objectives of the war aims against the Soviet Union, published in *Trial of the Major War Criminals before the International Military Tribunal Nuremberg, 14.11.1945–1.10.1946*, vol. 31 (Nuremberg: Internationaler Militärgerichtshof, 1948), p. 84.

165 Hillgruber, *Hitlers Strategie*, pp. 516–532; Mechthild Rössler and Sabine Schleiermacher (eds.), *Der 'Generalplan Ost': Hauptlinien der nationalsozialistischen Planungs- und Vernichtungspolitik* (Berlin: Akademie, 1993); Browning, *Origins of the Final Solution*, pp. 213–234; Johannes Hürter, *Hitlers Heerführer: Die deutschen Oberbefehlshaber im Krieg gegen die Sowjetunion 1941/42* (Munich: Oldenbourg, 2006), pp. 205–265; Friedländer, *Nazi Germany and the Jews*, vol. 2, pp. 129–138.

For Himmler, as Reich Commissioner for the Strengthening of Germandom, the impending war in the East also afforded an opportunity for large-scale demographic projects intended to dwarf all the previous ones. From as early as the autumn of 1939, the agronomist Konrad Meyer, head of the Main Department for Planning and Soil in the office of the Reich Commissioner for the Strengthening of Germandom, had been making calculations relating to extensive population displacements. In June 1941 Himmler assigned him the task of developing a 'General Plan East' adapted to the new circumstances. Meyer submitted an initial version on 15 July 1941. This early draft also envisaged the resettlement of 5 to 6 million Jews. In a later version, the Jews were no longer mentioned. The authors obviously assumed that there were no longer any Jews left in these regions.

June to September 1941: The War of Annihilation Begins

On 22 June 1941, the day that Germany invaded the Soviet Union, Hitler declared in his 'Proclamation to the German Nation' that 'the hour has now come in which it has become necessary to oppose this conspiracy of the Jewish-Anglo-Saxon warmongers and likewise the Jewish ruling powers in the Bolshevist control centre in Moscow'.[166]

Anti-Jewish propaganda, which had noticeably diminished in the first two years of war, now received a new thrust. To prevent the USA from entering the war, in the summer of 1940 Goebbels had ordered that verbal assaults on America and the Jews there must cease. In addition, the stereotype of 'Jewish Bolshevism' could not be employed in German propaganda as long as the non-aggression pact with the Soviet Union was in effect. Nonetheless, the Propaganda Ministry had not wholly renounced anti-Jewish agitation and had also used films for this purpose. *Jud Süß* (Jew Süss) became mandatory viewing for SS men (Doc. 119) and was a great popular success, far outstripping the ratings for *Der ewige Jude* (The Eternal Jew), which was advertised as a documentary (Docs. 124, 135).[167]

At the end of May and beginning of June 1941, the ministry had meanwhile already instructed the press to emphasize that Britain and the USA – in National Socialist terminology, the 'plutocracies' – were governed by Jewry. On 22 June 1941 linguistic restraint was abandoned altogether. At a press conference that day, Goebbels announced: 'Finally, an absolute clarification of the nature of plutocracy and Bolshevism is necessary. Both have a Jewish origin.'[168] The media were instructed to report at length on the massacres

166 Cited in Max Domarus and Patrick Romane (eds.), *The Essential Hitler: Speeches and Commentary* (Wauconda, IL: Bolchazy-Carducci, 2007), p. 765.

167 Karl-Heinz Reuband, '"Jud Süß" und "Der ewige Jude" als Prototypen antisemitischer Filmpropaganda im Dritten Reich: Entstehungsbedingungen, Zuschauerstrukturen und Wirkungspotential', in Michal Anděl et al. (eds.), *Propaganda, (Selbst-)Zensur, Sensation: Grenzen von Presse- und Wissenschaftsfreiheit in Deutschland und Tschechien seit 1871* (Essen: Klartext, 2005), pp. 89–148; Jeffrey Herf, *The Jewish Enemy: Nazi Propaganda during World War II and the Holocaust* (Cambridge, MA: Harvard University Press, 2006), pp. 14, 92; Bill Niven, 'Preparing Genocide: The Nazi Films *Jew Süss* and *The Eternal Jew*', in *Hitler and Film: The Führer's Hidden Passion* (New Haven/London: Yale University Press, 2018), pp. 163–184.

168 BArch, ZSg. 102/32, 22.6.41, cited in Peter Longerich, *'Davon haben wir nichts gewusst!': Die Deutschen und die Judenverfolgung 1933–1945'* (Munich: Siedler, 2006), p. 159.

carried out by the NKVD before its retreat from eastern Galicia. On 9 July 1941 Goebbels issued the slogan 'The Jews are to blame', which would from then on exert a crucial influence over media reporting. Goebbels said that he had been given explicit instructions by Hitler. The *Völkischer Beobachter* newspaper reacted promptly, featuring headlines about 'Jewish Bolshevism' and the 'Jewish world conspiracy'.[169]

A welcome opportunity for a further tirade was afforded by a pamphlet, *Germany Must Perish*, that Theodore N. Kaufman, the owner of an advertising agency in Newark, New Jersey, had issued through a publishing firm founded especially for this purpose. In this pamphlet, which attracted no further attention in the USA, Kaufman called for the sterilization of all German men. German propaganda made out that Kaufman was a close friend of Roosevelt's speechwriter, and on 24 July 1941 the *Völkischer Beobachter* ran the headline 'Roosevelt demands the sterilization of the German people' and claimed that the 'The Jewish-American war aim, under this plan, is "Utter extinction of the German nation!"'[170]

Newsreels showed photos '*of the victims of Bolshevik terror in Lemberg*', which allegedly expressed the '*true nature of Bolshevism and Jewry*'. The SD called for them to be '*shown again and again*, so that each and every Volksgenosse may be convinced, through this cool and objective factual material, of the danger which Jewish Bolshevism harbors'.[171]

The equation of Bolshevism and Jewry was enormously significant for subsequent developments. Like the Red Army's political commissars, the Soviet Jews were soon to be murdered as, after all, they supposedly embodied the 'Jewish Bolshevist' threat. On 2 July 1941 Heydrich informed the Einsatzgruppen: 'All the following are to be executed [...] Jews in Party and state posts, and other radical elements (saboteurs, propagandists, snipers, assassins, rabble-rousers, etc.).'[172] The group of persons to be shot was only vaguely outlined, and, more importantly, by means of the 'etc.' at the end Heydrich gave the commando leaders the opportunity to expand this group continually. Many commandos and police units took advantage of the ensuing leeway as early as July 1941, by indiscriminately shooting the male Jewish population of the places into which they advanced. They also initiated and supported pogroms conducted by local militias. Independent initiative from below and constant pressure from above were mutually reinforcing factors in this process. In the meantime, Himmler was manifestly emboldening the German units in Białystok, in eastern Poland, to take a more radical line of action. Be-

169 *Die Tagebücher von Joseph Goebbels*, part 2: *Diktate 1941–1945*, vol. 2: *Juli–September 1941* (Munich: Saur, 1996), p. 35 (entry for 9 July 1941). For newspaper headlines, see, for example, *Völkischer Beobachter* (North German edition), 10 July 1941, p. 1: 'Der Bolschewismus enthüllt sein jüdisches Gesicht' ('Bolshevism reveals its Jewish face'); Longerich, *'Davon haben wir nichts gewusst!'*, pp. 159–160; Richard J. Evans, *The Third Reich at War, 1939–1945* (London: Allen Lane, 2008), pp. 244–246.

170 *Völkischer Beobachter* (North German edition), no. 205, 24 July 1941, p. 1; Friedländer, *Nazi Germany and the Jews*, vol. 2, pp. 205–206.

171 RSHA, Amt II (SD): Meldungen aus dem Reich, cited in Otto Dov Kulka and Eberhard Jäckel (eds.), *The Jews in the Secret Nazi Reports on Popular Opinion in Germany, 1933–1945*, trans. William Templer (New Haven, CT/London: Yale University Press, 2010 [German edn, 2004]), doc. 554, pp. 527–528.

172 PMJ 7/15.

tween 8 and 11 July, members of Police Battalions 316 and 322 shot at least 1,000 Jews in the Białystok area.[173] It is against this backdrop that, on 17 July, an order was issued that Heydrich had drafted as early as 28 June 1941: all Jewish prisoners of war in the Soviet Union were to be shot.[174]

Hitler also expressed himself with undisguised candour during this phase. On 10 July he likened himself to Robert Koch and praised himself, saying that he had recognized the Jew as a 'bacillus'.[175] Then, on 16 July, at a meeting in the Führer Headquarters, he commented on Stalin's appeal for partisan warfare on 3 July, saying that it 'enables us to exterminate everyone who opposes us'. The necessary pacification 'is best effected by shooting everyone who even looks sideways at us'.[176]

The mass shootings of Jewish men during the first weeks of the war led to a new problem for German occupation officials in the Soviet Union. The families whose men had been murdered now lacked breadwinners. Consequently, the Germans began to consider whether one should also shoot those Jewish women and children who could not provide for themselves. In any case, large portions of the indigenous population, as well as the Soviet prisoners of war, were not being provided with adequate food supplies by the German authorities. In the feeding hierarchy, the Soviet prisoners of war and the Jews ranked at the bottom. The latter were regarded as 'useless eaters' (*unnütze Esser*), given the supply shortfalls. Alternatively, if they sought to help themselves, they were viewed as looters and black marketeers.[177]

On 1 August 1941 Himmler ordered that Jewish women, too, were no longer to be spared: 'Explicit order from the Reichsführer SS. All Jews must be shot. Herd Jew-women into the swamps.'[178] From mid July 1941 onwards Jewish women and children also fell victim to the SS and police units in increasing numbers of communities. The Kamianets-Podilskyi massacre in western Ukraine marked a tragic culmination of these operations. After Hungarian authorities had deported approximately 10,000 Jews from Subcarpathian Rus to the town, its Jewish population had grown to 23,600. The local German field commandant's office, fearing supply shortfalls and epidemics, pressed for a 'solution'. The task was assigned to Friedrich Jeckeln, the HSSPF for southern Russia, who had all Jewish men, women, and children in the area murdered between 26 and 28 August 1941. This massacre marked the beginning of the systematic eradication of Jewish

173 Jürgen Matthäus, 'Operation Barbarossa and the Onset of the Holocaust, June–December 1941', in Browning, *Origins of the Final Solution*, pp. 244–308, here p. 257.

174 PMJ 7/9.

175 'Tagebuch von Walther Hewel', in Peter Longerich (ed.), *Die Ermordung der europäischen Juden: Eine umfassende Dokumentation des Holocaust 1941–1945* (Munich/Zurich: Piper, 1989), p. 76.

176 PMJ 7/28.

177 Hillgruber, *Hitlers Strategie*, pp. 518–532; Jürgen Förster, 'Ideological Warfare in Germany, 1919 to 1945', in Militärgeschichtliches Forschungsamt, *Germany and the Second World War*, vol. 9/1: *German Wartime Society, 1939–1945: Politicization, Disintegration, and the Struggle for Survival*, trans. Derry Cook-Radmore, Ewald Osers, Barry Smerin, and Barbara Wilson (Oxford: Oxford University Press, 2009 [German edn, 2004]), pp. 485–670, here pp. 537–558; Hürter, *Hitlers Heerführer*, pp. 262–263; Longerich, *Holocaust*, pp. 192–255. On the mass murders in the individual regions, see the Introduction to PMJ 7.

178 Radiogram to the Cavalry Division, 2nd SS-Cavalry Regiment, 1 August 1941, 10 a.m., BArch, RS 3-8/36. See PMJ 7/51.

communities in Ukraine,[179] which claimed the lives of more than 100,000 people – men, women, and children – by the end of September. Over the course of two days in late September 1941, the remaining Jews in Kiev – over 33,000 in total – were murdered at the Babi Yar ravine by members of Sonderkommando 4a of Einsatzgruppe C and the headquarters company of the HSSPF for South Russia.[180]

The escalating violence in the Soviet Union was instrumental in the decision to murder the European Jews. The events there led to a radicalization throughout Europe and accelerated the decision-making process in Berlin. A climate arose in which proposals for mass murder were discussed with increasing openness, and in which both the regime's leadership and various officials in the areas concerned could assume that everything was now possible.

On 16 July 1941 the chief of the SD headquarters in Poznań and of the local Central Resettlement Office, Rolf-Heinz Höppner, informed Eichmann how, in his opinion, the crowded ghettos and tens of thousands of starving and ill Jews in the Gau Wartheland should be dealt with:

> This coming winter there is a danger that it will no longer be possible to feed all of the Jews. One should seriously consider whether the most humane solution would be to use some kind of fast-acting means to finish off the Jews who are no longer fit for work. At any rate that would be more pleasant than letting them starve to death.[181]

One day later, on 17 July 1941, Governor General Frank explicitly declared in Cracow that he wanted 'no ghettos to be formed, because, according to an explicit statement by the Führer on 19 June of this year, Jews will be removed from the General Government in the foreseeable future, and the General Government is only to be a sort of transit camp'.[182]

On 20 July 1941 Goebbels threatened European Jewry in an article: 'Just as the fist of an awakening Germany once slammed down upon this racial filth, the fist of an awakening Europe will one day slam down upon it as well' (Doc. 193). Although Hitler told Croatian marshal Slavko Kvaternik on 21 July 1941 that the Jews of Europe would be sent to Madagascar or Siberia once the Eastern Campaign was over, by now he was probably using 'Madagascar' merely as a metaphor for his objective that there must no longer be any Jews, at least in Europe.[183]

179 PMJ 7/67 and 70; Klaus-Michael Mallmann, 'Der qualitative Sprung im Vernichtungsprozeß: Das Massaker von Kamenez-Podolsk Ende August 1941', *Jahrbuch für Antisemitismusforschung*, vol. 10 (2001), pp. 239–264.

180 See the Introduction to PMJ 7, and PMJ 7/84, 94, and 141; Dieter Pohl, 'The Murder of Ukraine's Jews under German Military Administration and in the Reich Commissariat Ukraine', in Ray Brandon and Wendy Lower (eds.), *The Shoah in Ukraine: History, Testimony, Memorialization* (Bloomington: Indiana Univ. Press, 2008), pp. 23–76.

181 PMJ 4/314.

182 Präg and Jacobmeyer, *Diensttagebuch des deutschen Generalgouverneurs*, p. 386.

183 *Akten zur Deutschen Auswärtigen Politik 1918–1945*, series D: *1937–1941*, vol. 8/2, appendix III, p. 835–838.

In Serbia the German occupiers now proceeded to shoot Jews in retaliation for attacks by partisans. Hence, on 25 July 1941, 100 Jews were shot in Belgrade, and on 19 July '122 communists and Jews [were] executed'.[184]

On 31 July 1941 Heydrich submitted to Reich Marshal Göring a letter for him to sign, drafted in advance, in which Göring empowered Heydrich afresh 'to make all necessary preparations from an organizational, material, and financial perspective for a comprehensive solution to the Jewish question within the German sphere of influence in Europe' (Doc. 196). Heydrich later enclosed this letter with the invitation to the Wannsee Conference on 20 January 1942. It was intended to establish him as the organizer in charge of the 'final solution to the Jewish question'.[185]

In every part of Europe occupied by the Wehrmacht, the Germans in authority now required that their spheres of influence be 'cleansed' of Jews. On 21 August 1941 the official responsible 'for Jewish and Freemason questions' at the German embassy in Paris, Carltheo Zeitschel, noted to his superior:

> As far as the occupied territories such as Holland, Belgium, Luxembourg, Norway, Yugoslavia, and Greece are concerned, the Jews could simply be removed to the new territory in mass transports by means of military orders, and the other countries could be urged to follow the example and deposit the Jews in this territory.

He added: 'We could then have Europe free of Jews in a short period of time.'[186]

At this point, mass murder had already begun in the territories to which the Jews were to be deported. Still unresolved was the question of what was to be done with the German Jews.

The Situation in the Territory of the Reich

Meanwhile, a debate was developing in the Reich over whether to make it compulsory for Jews to wear visible identification. On 16 July 1941 Karl Hermann Frank had proposed to the Head of the Reich Chancellery, Hans-Heinrich Lammers, that such a step be taken in the Protectorate.[187] Two weeks later, he urgently sought permission to implement this. Lammers forwarded the request to the Ministry of the Interior. In his reply, State Secretary Stuckart asked whether it could be made compulsory for Jews throughout the

184 'Tagesmeldungen des Armeeoberkommandos 12 an Wehrmachtführungsstab/Abt. Landesverteidigung: Erschießungen in Serbien, 1941', in Longerich, *Die Ermordung der europäischen Juden*, pp. 285–286.

185 Eberhard Jäckel, 'Der Mord an den Juden als historisches Problem', in Eberhard Jäckel and Jürgen Rohwer (eds.), *Der Mord an den Juden im Zweiten Weltkrieg* (Frankfurt am Main: Fischer, 1987), pp. 15–16; Browning, *Origins of the Final Solution*, pp. 315–316; Longerich, *Holocaust*, pp. 260–261.

186 Cited in Kurt Pätzold (ed.), *Verfolgung, Vertreibung, Vernichtung: Dokumente des faschistischen Antisemitismus 1933 bis 1942* (Leipzig: Reclam, 1991), pp. 305–306, quotation p. 305.

187 Letter from State Secretary Karl Hermann Frank, SS Gruppenführer, to Reich Minister Hans Lammers, dated 16 July 1941, published in Pätzold, *Verfolgung, Vertreibung, Vernichtung*, p. 294.

Reich and the Protectorate to wear visible identification.[188] On 15 August, Goebbels convened a meeting on the subject in the Propaganda Ministry (Doc. 203). The matter was to be presented to Hitler, whom Goebbels met in the Führer Headquarters on 18 August 1941. Goebbels documented the meeting in his diary:

> We also talk about the Jewish problem. The Führer is convinced that his earlier prophecy in the Reichstag – that if Jewry should succeed in once again provoking a world war, it will end in the extinction of the Jews – is coming true. It is coming true during these weeks and months with an almost uncanny certainty. In the East, the Jews must foot the bill; in Germany they have already paid it in part and will have to pay even more of it in future.

At the meeting, Hitler agreed to make it compulsory for Jews to wear identifying stars (Doc. 206). On 1 September 1941 the requirement was introduced in the Reich and the Protectorate. All Jews over the age of six had to wear a yellow star (Doc. 212). Many Germans who had previously largely ignored the marginalization of the Jewish population could no longer do so. Some looked away when a 'star-wearer' came their way, while others reacted with outrage and sympathy. Some tried to help, for example, by slipping food to a Jew in the street, offering their seat on the tram to a Jew, or simply stopping and assuring a Jew how greatly they disapproved of the measures. Writing in the spring of 1942, Erich Frey, a Berlin Jew, recalled: 'In contrast, the population kept calm and, with very few exceptions, took no notice of the star, in some cases even responded favourably to it.' In Prague many Czechs greeted the Jews wearing stars in a warm and friendly manner (Docs. 318, 319).[189]

However, there were also malicious and hateful reactions. For the Jews, the mandatory wearing of the star was a heavy blow. Those who had previously still been bold enough to violate the prohibitions, by shopping at non-approved times or possibly by going to a theatre or cinema, were now identifiable immediately and ran the risk of being denounced. Else Behrend-Rosenfeld wrote in Munich in September 1941: 'Again one sees the Jews walk through the streets with stony faces, with eyes that seem to see through everything and everyone, many with their head sunken, but some also, and I am among them, with their heads proudly held high.'[190]

The US ambassador in Berlin reported to Washington that the 'Jewish question' had now 'come back into public focus very prominently', and at the end of the month both the ambassador and the US press predicted that 'even more radical measures' were obviously in the offing. Since the onset of the war, the fate of the Jewish population had only

188 Hilberg, *Destruction of the European Jews*, vol. 1, pp. 177–178.

189 Erich Frey, letter to his daughter (April/May 1942), in Michael Kreutzer, *'Die Gespräche drehten sich auch vielfach um die Reise, die wir alle antreten müssen.' Leben und Verfolgtsein der Juden in Berlin-Tempelhof: Biographien, Dokumentation* (Berlin: Evangelischer Kirchenkreis Tempelhof, 1988), pp. 91–104, here p. 100; Detlef Brandes, 'Deutsche Propaganda und Stimmung der tschechischen Bevölkerung im Protektorat Böhmen und Mähren 1939–1945', in Anděl et al., *Propaganda, (Selbst-)Zensur, Sensation*, pp. 149–178, here p. 172.

190 Quotation from Else R. Behrend-Rosenfeld, *Ich stand nicht allein: Erlebnisse einer Jüdin in Deutschland 1933–1944* (Cologne: Europäische, 1979), p. 114; Kaplan, *Between Dignity and Despair*, pp. 157–158.

rarely been consciously made a subject of discussion abroad. The press was more likely to report on the general concern about an expansion of the war and about the oppressed peoples, including the Jews, in their entirety. And even now, news about the fate of the Jews rarely made it into the headlines. The *New York Times* placed the article about the introduction of the yellow star on page 14.[191]

For the Czech government in exile, which the Allies had recognized in December 1939 as a national committee, in June 1940 as the provisional Czech government, and in July 1941 as the legitimate Czech government, dealing with the Jews in the Protectorate was likewise not a central focus until the autumn of 1941. Rather, priority was assigned to the question of how an end could be put to German rule and to plans for the post-war period. In London there were disputes with regard to whether and how many Jewish delegates should be represented in the local parliament in exile. The introduction of the requirement to wear the yellow star, however, motivated Hubert Ripka, the foreign minister of the government in exile, to take a clear position in favour of the Jewish population in the Protectorate (Doc. 317).[192]

Until the autumn of 1941, forced resettlement within the cities, which had begun with the 'Jew houses', became increasingly radical in practice. In September 1941 more than 1,000 Jews in Hanover had to leave their homes within 24 to 48 hours and move into 16 buildings that had been allocated within the city (Doc. 215). In some cities the local government began forcing Jews to move into barracks camps (Doc. 213). The largest such camp was in an old fort in Cologne-Müngersdorf, where 2,000 Jews were housed in 100 rooms. The barracks reminded Klara Caro of the Roman catacombs: 'Due to the dripping water, the damp odor of mold spread. Everything needed to serve the most primitive needs was missing.' From the autumn of 1941, many of these barracks camps were repurposed to serve as assembly points for deportation.[193]

In September 1941 Hitler changed his mind about the deportation of the Jews from the Reich. Although he had emphasized one month earlier that this would not be a possibility until the war was over, he now ordered it to be set in motion after all (Doc. 223). The deportation of hundreds of thousands of Volga Germans to Siberia ordered by Stalin in late August may have been a deciding factor. Above all, however, various Gauleiter had long been urging that their cities be made 'free of Jews', including Goebbels in Berlin, Baldur von Schirach in Vienna, Karl Hanke in Breslau, and Karl Kaufmann in Hamburg. Kaufmann later boasted to Göring:

> In September 1941, after a heavy air raid, I approached the Führer to request that the Jews be evacuated to enable at least some of the bombing victims to be assigned a

191 Lipstadt, *Beyond Belief*, pp. 140–154.

192 Avigdor Dagan, 'The Czechoslovak Government-in-Exile and the Jews', in Avigdor Dagan, Gertrude Hirschler, Lewis Weiner et al. (eds.), *The Jews of Czechoslovakia: Historical Studies and Surveys*, vol. 3 (Philadelphia: Jewish Publication Society of America, 1984), pp. 449–495; Jan Němeček, 'Das tschechoslowakische politische Exil in London und die "jüdische Frage"', *Theresienstädter Studien und Dokumente*, vol. 9 (2002), pp. 347–366; Rothkirchen, *Jews of Bohemia and Moravia*, pp. 160–186; Bryant, *Prague in Black*, pp. 89–95.

193 Quotation from Kaplan, *Between Dignity and Despair*, p. 155. See also Hanke, *Zur Geschichte der Juden in München*, pp. 282–283, and Buchholz, *Die hannoverschen Judenhäuser*.

> new apartment. Without hesitating, the Führer acted on my suggestion and issued the corresponding orders for the removal of the Jews.[194]

The chief reason for Hitler's reversal of opinion, however, was probably the international situation, which was increasingly threatening for Germany. There were increasing signs that the USA would enter the war. On 11 March 1941 President Roosevelt had signed the Lend-Lease Act, on the basis of which the USA supplied arms and equipment to Britain. In the early summer of 1941, supplies for the Soviet Union followed. In mid August, Roosevelt and Churchill met off the coast of Newfoundland and, in the joint declaration known as the Atlantic Charter, threatened Germany with certain defeat. Hitler, who viewed Roosevelt as a tool of the Jews, believed that he could exert pressure on the American president by taking drastic steps against the German Jews, and in this way deter him from entering the war.

The deportation of the German, Austrian, and Czech Jews seemed to represent a suitable signal for that purpose. In addition, the end of the war, to which the 'solution to the Jewish question' was supposed to have been deferred, was still not in sight.[195] On 18 September 1941 Himmler informed the Gauleiter of the Warthegau, Arthur Greiser, that the deportation of 60,000 Jews to Litzmannstadt (Łódź) was imminent (Doc. 223).

The German Jews had no knowledge of all these discussions and decisions. While tens of thousands of Jews fell victim to the mass shootings in the occupied Soviet territories in August 1941, the letters written by German Jews to their relatives abroad still mostly centred on their greatest concern: would they succeed in emigrating (Docs. 186, 192, 207, 211)? Nonetheless, news from the front did make its way to the Reich. The historian Willy Cohn noted in Breslau at the end of July 1941: 'Professor Hoffmann also told me the horrific news, barely comprehensible, that 12,000 Jews have been shot in Lemberg. The SS is said to have done this' (Doc. 195).

Most of the German, Austrian, and Czech Jews whose letters and diary entries are documented in this volume were deported and murdered. The question of whether and when Hitler gave an order for the murder of all the European Jews, and whether he had to do so at all in order to set the systematic mass murder in motion, has been the subject of historiographical debate. Without his consent, such a step is unthinkable. At this stage, the events in the Soviet Union and the experiences in the Reich were interdependent. In August and September 1941, the mass murders in the occupied Soviet Union had assumed gigantic proportions, and simultaneously a great many persons in authority in the Reich and in the rest of occupied Europe were pressing for a more radical course of action against the Jews. All the plans they had previously pursued – emigration, deportation to Madagascar or to a 'Jewish reservation' in the General Government – had come

194 Kaufmann to Göring on 4 Sept. 1942, cited in Frank Bajohr, 'Hamburgs "Führer": Zur Person und Tätigkeit des Hamburger NSDAP-Gauleiters Karl Kaufmann (1900–1969)', in Frank Bajohr and Joachim Szodrzynski (eds.), *Hamburg in der NS-Zeit: Ergebnisse neuerer Forschungen* (Hamburg: Ergebnisse, 1995), pp. 59–91, quotation p. 81; Ascher, *A Community under Siege*, p. 214; Kershaw, *Fateful Choices*, p. 462.

195 Christian Gerlach, 'The Wannsee Conference, the Fate of German Jews, and Hitler's Decision in Principle to Exterminate All European Jews', *Journal of Modern History*, vol. 70, no. 4 (December 1998), pp. 759–812; Longerich, *Holocaust*, pp. 265–271; Browning, *Origins of the Final Solution*, pp. 375–377.

to naught. Mass murder, which had long since been under way in the Soviet Union, thus became a feasible 'solution' in other parts of Europe as well.

Clearly, a turning point was reached in the autumn of 1941. At the same time as Operation Typhoon, the advance on Moscow in early October 1941, German units carried out massacres of Jewish men, women, and children in eastern Poland and in parts of the Wartheland. In Serbia, Jewish men were murdered during 'anti-partisan combat'. Plans for the deportations from the Reich and the Protectorate were moving ahead at full speed. In October, preparations were made to build the extermination camps at Chelmno in the Warthegau and Belzec in the General Government. Killing facilities were installed at the Auschwitz concentration camp.

Willy Cohn could not have known this when he wrote the following diary entry on 27 September 1941: 'In my opinion, it is certain that, unless there are radical changes, the Germans will continue to vent their rage on the Jews! We must be prepared for that.'[196] Two months later, on 25 November 1941, he was deported from Breslau to Kaunas with 1,000 other men, women, and children. On 29 November he was shot dead there in the so-called Ninth Fort.

196 Willy Cohn, *No Justice in Germany: The Breslau Diaries, 1933–1941*, trans. Kenneth Kronenberg (Stanford, CA: Stanford University Press, 2012 [German edn, 2006]), p. 381.

List of Documents

Part 1: German Reich

18 With his Decree for the Strengthening of Germandom, issued on 7 October 1939, Adolf Hitler places Heinrich Himmler in charge of the racial policy plans for settlement on German-ruled territory

19 On 9 October 1939 Adolf Eichmann's deputy secures the assistance of the Wehrmacht and the civil administration for the planned deportation of Jews from Kattowitz

20 On 12 October 1939 the Cologne Gestapo announces that Jews are to be immediately arrested if they disobey ordinances

21 In October 1939 Rica Neuburger takes her own life as a result of the harassment of Jews

22 On 13 October 1939 Friedrich Kellner fulminates against wars started in breach of international law and the disenfranchisement of the Jews

23 On 16 October 1939 Adolf Eichmann informs Criminal Police Chief Arthur Nebe that carriages containing 'Gypsies' can be coupled to the deportation trains travelling to Poland

24 On 16 October 1939 details of the deportation of Viennese Jews to Poland are discussed at the Central Office for Jewish Emigration in Vienna

25 On 19 October 1939 the Reich Minister of Finance increases the Levy on Jewish Assets

26 On 21 October 1939 the Jewish Community of Cologne announces restrictions on the purchase of food

27 On 21 October 1939 Martha Svoboda writes in her diary about the deportation of her brother from Vienna to Nisko

28 *Mansfelder Zeitung*, 26 October 1939: article on the conviction of David Naruhn, who lived illegally with an Aryan woman

29 On 2 November 1939 the Emigration Advice Service of the Jewish Economic Aid Association in Dresden asks the American Joint Distribution Committee to speed up the issuing of visas by the US consulate general in Berlin

30 On 10 November 1939 a Jewish woman from Vienna writes to Josef Löwenherz, asking him to prevent girls under the age of 18 from being deported to Poland

31 On 17 November 1939 the Innsbruck Gestapo informs the Landeshauptmann of Tyrol about the membership and assets of the Jewish Community in Innsbruck

32 On 18 November 1939 the SD District Leipzig writes to the Reich Security Main Office, proposing a travel ban on Jews

33 On 20 November 1939 Josef Löwenherz informs the Vienna Gestapo of fatalities in Buchenwald and requests the release of Jews who are able to emigrate

34 On 24 November 1939 an SD informant complains about the behaviour of the Berlin Jews

35 On 25 November 1939 Jolan Thorn from Vienna tells her sister in New York about her difficulties in making arrangements for emigration

92 On 3 July 1940 Franz Rademacher makes proposals at the Reich Foreign Office for settling all the European Jews on the island of Madagascar

93 Report by a German Jewish woman to a London immigrant organization regarding the situation of Frankfurt am Main's Jewish population up to 11 July 1940

94 On 17 July 1940 the statistician Friedrich Burgdörfer calculates how many Jews could be deported to Madagascar

95 On 18 July 1940 the mayor of Leipzig informs Saxony's Minister of Economics about the provisioning and labour deployment of the Jewish population in Leipzig

96 On 29 July 1940 the Reich Postmaster General orders that Jews' telephone lines be cancelled

97 *New York Times*, 2 August 1940: article on export bans, shopping restrictions, and prohibited areas for Jews in Germany

98 On 15 August 1940 Hitler's plans to deport all the Jews from Europe after the war become known in the Reich Foreign Office

99 In mid August 1940 the Reich Security Main Office plans the deportation of the European Jews to Madagascar

100 On 21 August 1940 a refugee committee in Shanghai explains immigration requirements to the Jewish Religious Community of Vienna

101 In late August 1940 Legation Counsellor Franz Rademacher of the Reich Foreign Office makes suggestions for the implementation of the 'Madagascar Plan'

102 In August 1940 Herbert Gerigk writes about the role of Judaism in music

103 During a meeting at the Reich Ministry of Propaganda on 6 September 1940, Reich Cultural Administrator Hans Hinkel reports on the planned deportation of Berlin's Jews

104 On 9 September 1940 Emilie Cassel asks the Stettin Chief of Police for permission to purchase a 'people's receiver', despite her husband being non-Aryan

105 On 12 September 1940 Hermann Samter, editor at the *Jüdisches Nachrichtenblatt*, writes to Hanna Kobylinski about the activities of the Jewish Culture League in Berlin

106 On 30 September 1940 the mayor of Misdroy asks the German Council of Municipalities whether a Jewish woman who lives in the town may be committed to an institution

107 On 2 October 1940 the head of the Swiss Police for Foreign Nationals urges the Swiss ambassador in Vichy to ensure that Jewish refugees from Germany receive transit visas

108 On 4 October 1940 the Reich Trustee of Labour for the economic area of Styria and Carinthia justifies low pay for Jewish workers

109 On 7 October 1940 the Reich Minister of Aviation informs Luftgaukommando VII that Jews are to be allowed entry to public air-raid shelters

110 On 22 October 1940 Heinrich Himmler, addressing the NSDAP Country Group in Madrid, announces the deportation of all Jews from the Greater German Reich to the General Government

Part 2: Protectorate of Bohemia and Moravia

DOCUMENTS

Part 1
German Reich

DOC. 1

The writer Walter Tausk records his experiences in Breslau on 1 September 1939, the day the war broke out[1]

Diary of Walter Tausk,[2] entry for 1 September 1939

Friday, 1 September 1939
There is absolutely no doubt that it has started. Yesterday, for example, the entire Jewish hospital was evacuated without notice, apart from the gynaecology unit, hospices, and homes for the elderly, in order to free up 380 beds. While there has been rigorous cost-cutting at other hospitals in the city in recent weeks, here the Gestapo and the military were making a 'negative exception', i.e. they outdid themselves in their inhumanity; anyone who didn't have a fever was sent home, put out onto the street, or otherwise 're-located' (some to private accommodation, some to the empty rooms of the Community hall on Wallstraße; serious and critical cases were moved to the gynaecology unit). Patients recovering from recent operations (e.g. appendixes) who were barely capable of being transported were evacuated; old people, over 80, who were supposed to live out their days in the converted attics of the hospital, were thrown out with all their possessions and moved in with the terminally ill: everything mixed up haphazardly, in addition the mad and the half-mad. And in the afternoon a long downpour, while the evacuation was under way. A preview of how things will be in the coming days, and of what 'Schittelhuber's war'[3] will bring for the unsuspecting mass of humanity.

The prospects for my emigration are now zero. On 17 August *the most important thing, the fare,* was not paid out to me (see the papers attached)[4] and so I really am the victim of my 'dear co-religionists' (may Heaven continue to protect me from them) and my own impecuniousness.[5] *Postal correspondence with England is no longer possible.*[6]

This morning, between around ¼ to 5 and 7, planes flew non-stop over the city; bombers, fighters, and other aircraft, all heading east. At 8:30 a.m. the caretaker appeared with a circular decree from the police: 'Get everything ready for sudden blackouts and air raids. Prepare water supplies, above all keep bomb shelters in good condition', etc.[7]

1 Biblioteka Uniwersytecka we Wrocławiu, Ako. 1949 KN 1351–1354. Published in Walter Tausk, *Breslauer Tagebuch 1933–1940*, ed. Ryszard Kincel ([East] Berlin: Rütten & Loening, 1975), pp. 229–230. This document has been translated from German.

2 Walter Tausk (1890–1941), trade representative and writer; converted from Judaism to Buddhism in 1917; wrote articles for Buddhist magazines; casual worker from 1933; deported from Breslau on 25 Nov. 1941 to Kaunas, where he was murdered; author of *Olaf Höris Tod: Skizze zu einer Vollmondphantasie* (1924).

3 Tausk means 'Schicklgruber'. Hitler's opponents commonly referred to him by his father's surname, as a way of pointing out his father's lower-class rural origins and extramarital birth, the latter being cause for suspicions about Jewish ancestry.

4 The enclosure is not in the file.

5 Walter Tausk had been attempting to emigrate since 1936. On 17 July 1939 he received an entry permit for Britain; the travel costs were to be paid by the Relief Association of German Jews.

6 The postal service to Britain was suspended on 1 Sept. 1939 for the entire duration of the war. In the middle and the end of that month, telegraph and telephone services were also suspended.

7 Tenth Implementing Regulation to the Air-Raid Protection Law, 1 Sept. 1939, *Reichsgesetzblatt*, 1939, I, pp. 1570–1572.

Eleven o'clock in the morning: from ten up to now a speech by '*him*' broadcast from the Reichstag can be heard over the loudspeaker nearby. For years the same old story: no other nation and no other statesman is more innocent, more misunderstood, betrayed, and maligned than '*him*' and 'his people'; no nation and no statesman so exclusively peace-loving, etc. The voice: gurgling, rasping, choking, droning, whining, beseeching, arousing sympathy, and then back to ranting, only to choke again soon after. And of course, everything is the Poles' fault.[8]

Then, of course, the Horst Wessel song was also sung: 'Comrades shot by the Red Front … march in spirit within our ranks.'[9] This, despite the pact with the Russians.[10] Schittelhuber also laid down the dynastic sequence for the 'cast-iron 1,000-year Reich', 'in case something happens to me' (he wants to 'take to the field as an ordinary private'). After him, the private, comes Field Marshal Göring, and after him (in case of 'something happening') the former medical auxiliary Hess. The house droned with applause, as ever. – At the same time, the troops everywhere were already invading Poland.

DOC. 2

On 1 September 1939 Emilie Braach from Frankfurt writes to her émigré daughter in Britain, describing how everyday life is changing with the start of war[1]

Letter from Emilie Braach,[2] Frankfurt am Main, to her daughter Bergit[3] in Britain, dated 1 January 1939

My dear Bergit,

Today I want to begin a series of letters, though I have no idea when, if ever, you will read them.[4] I can only hope that one day they reach you, so that you hear about the

8 In his speech to the Reichstag on 1 Sept. 1939, Hitler blamed Poland's alleged violation of the border for the outbreak of war: *Völkischer Beobachter* (Berlin edition), 2 Sept. 1939, pp. 1–2.

9 The full line is: 'Comrades shot by the Red Front and reactionaries / March in spirit within our ranks.' Horst Wessel had published the text of 'Die Fahne Hoch' ('Raise the Flag!') in 1929 in the NSDAP newspaper *Der Angriff*. After Wessel's violent death in Feb. 1930, the poem was set to music and became a kind of party anthem for the NSDAP.

10 Tausk means the German–Soviet Non-Aggression Pact of 23 August 1939.

1 ISG Frankfurt, S1/379, Nr. 1. Published in Emilie Braach, *Wenn meine Briefe Dich erreichen könnten: Aufzeichnungen aus den Jahren 1939–1945*, ed. Bergit Forchhammer (Frankfurt am Main: Fischer, 1987), pp. 15–17. This document has been translated from German.

2 Emilie (Mile) Braach, née Hirschfeld (1898–1998), author; wrote for various magazines from 1927; banned from publishing in 1935 because she was classified as a so-called *Mischling* of the first degree; branch manager at the Kalasiris corset shop, 1935–1945; co-owner and manager of a leather wholesaler's, 1946–1988; gave talks in schools and elsewhere about her experiences under National Socialism; awarded the Federal Cross of Merit (*Bundesverdienstkreuz*) in 1990 and the Johanna-Kirchner Medal in 1994.

3 Bergit Forchhammer, née Braach (1921–2011), teacher and journalist; emigrated to Britain, 1939; returned to Germany with the US Civil Censorship Division in 1945, and was in American employment until 1948; teacher in Denmark, 1961–1967; lived in the US until 1969, and in Tanzania, 1969–1974; subsequently worked as a teacher at the Danish International School in Copenhagen and as a correspondent.

4 See Doc. 1, fn. 6.

events, both big and small, that move us, that on the one hand concern and worry us, and on the other hand make us happy in small ways. Today, however, it seems like a miracle or, rather, a dream that only the evening before last Imme[5] and I were sitting together playing music. And it is no less unbelievable that only yesterday we were sitting comfortably on Mother and Father's[6] veranda enjoying the cool evening air.

Today? The war has started. There is a blackout in Frankfurt and all the towns and villages in the country. I'm sitting in the dining room, which I've fitted out with all the most necessary precautions, and have resolved to have a faultlessly blacked-out room ready by Sunday, in which there is a shimmer of light *more* than half a metre in diameter. Today I'm satisfied with that. What wouldn't one be satisfied with today? I've even reconciled myself to my cup of reheated tea, after heavily depleting my coffee quota due to all the anxiety of late. However, I also have to be careful with the tea ration of 20 grams a month.[7] But that's all trivial compared to world affairs and the bloodshed. And anyway, I'm lucky this evening because I can sit at home. I almost had 'air-raid duty' already at our shop on Kaiserstraße today. How that's supposed to work is still unclear to me. Four people are supposed to keep watch all night every night. Well, we will see what chores await. Above all, I'm curious to see how the mostly very young and inexperienced girls master their task, and if they are able to do watch duty at all. I myself am such a night owl that I won't feel it that much. Last night I was up listening to the radio until three o'clock and was still up very punctually this morning, in order to see as caretaker that everything was shipshape. But now I absolutely must get myself relieved of this function. After all, I'm not here in the daytime. And if I do ever visit Erna[8] or Mother and Father in the evening, I'll sleep there, because a completely blacked-out city has something really spooky about it. Particularly now, with such a storm raging outside that the paper I've put up as an imperfect blackout on the windows is almost coming away.

At work there's constantly something to do. All the questions about [ration] coupons have been especially stressful. Hopefully that's now over, because I heard earlier that bras and corsets are now freely available again. [Other] underwear, on the other hand, can only be obtained in exchange for coupons. And then there are all the questions and above all the gossip. Everyone has their own opinion, everyone knows something different, has heard something or other, clings, or rather clung, to another hope. Now there's no longer even the smallest of branches to cling to. You've no idea how many people lately I've had to console, how many people try on their new corset in tears. As you know, I'm quite unsympathetic in such situations. If you really are that upset and tearful, then the last thing on your mind is shopping and the like. That's how I'd feel at least, and in the last few days it certainly wouldn't have occurred to me to buy a hat or

5 Imogen (Imme) Werkhäuser (1926–1981) was the daughter of Emilie Braach's sister Erna Werkhäuser, née Hirschfeld (1902–1995).

6 Otto Hirschfeld (1866–1952), leather goods manufacturer, and Marianne Hirschfeld, née Könitzer (1872–1952), were evicted from their apartment in Sept. 1941 and subsequently moved in with their daughter Emilie Braach. Otto Hirschfeld was registered at her address without the affix 'Israel' to his name, which was compulsory for Jews. Following his summons by the Gestapo in March 1945, Emilie Braach found a hiding place for her parents with an acquaintance in Bad Homberg; she also went into hiding until the liberation.

7 Rationing on staple foods was imposed on 27 August 1939: *Reichsgesetzblatt*, 1939, I, pp. 1498–1505.

8 Erna Werkhäuser.

pair of gloves. With or without coupons. I'm more impressed by people who try on corsets stark naked in peaked caps and knee-high boots. How we used to laugh. One day not long ago I had to listen to three stories about people dying! All in minute detail, with all the stages repeated. Not even the [deathbed] confessions were left out. I was completely exhausted. I'd almost rather have someone who spends three hours trying on corsets and then says it's a relief she doesn't have to buy one every day. –

Today the whole of Frankfurt was occupied with the blackout. Every other person was carrying a roll of black paper under their arm, and in the shops people were starting to queue up for it. I'd sent Anneliese[9] shopping three days ago, hoping that the expense would turn out to be unnecessary. Anneliese is coming along well, by the way, and is a good companion and decent sort. In the last three weeks during Mrs M.'s absence she's developed very nicely in lots of ways and has come to be a real support. Let's hope she doesn't fall back into her old sloppiness. I've had to provisionally let our good housekeeper Mrs Jäger go, because I just can't predict how the business is going to develop.

Twenty past ten: I've just heard the news, although it wasn't very exhaustive. There will probably be bulletins later, like last night. The only interesting thing was the ban on listening to foreign radio stations.[10] But that's no doubt the same in every country. By the way, I'm so tired that if I had to speak I'd only be able to babble. So tonight I definitely would've been no good for keeping watch, and I'm soon going to turn in for the night. I'll let Füchschen and Klettchen[11] come too, as an exception. Last night they were allowed to as well. In tense and extraordinary times like these one can allow oneself such things.

DOC. 3

On 2 and 3 September 1939 the historian Arnold Berney, an émigré in Jerusalem, records his gloomy prognoses on the outbreak of war[1]

Diary of Arnold Berney,[2] Jerusalem, entries for 2 and 3 September 1939

2 September 1939

The Reich German National Socialist short-wave station reported on numerous border skirmishes, adding that these demonstrated the inner disintegration and demoralization of the Polish army.

If you are so brave, so soldierly, so chivalrous: why then this weak, pathetic, and furthermore stupid and fatal belittling of the enemy? But that's how you are: you also didn't defeat your internal enemies in a manly fashion, nor did you chivalrously allow

9 Anneliese was an apprentice at the corset shop.

10 Regulation on Extraordinary Radio Measures, 1 Sept. 1939: *Reichsgesetzblatt*, 1939, I, p. 1683.

11 Emilie Braach's two cats.

1 CAHJP, P/179, box 1, folder 3. This document has been translated from German.

2 Dr Arnold Berney (1897–1943), lawyer and historian; adjunct professor in Freiburg im Breisgau from 1927; had his teaching permit revoked in 1935; professor at the Higher Institute for Jewish Studies in Berlin, 1936–1938; in 1938 emigrated via Switzerland to Palestine, where he worked as a private tutor.

them some kind of right to exist afterwards; instead, you plagued them, defiled them, tortured, slandered, and robbed them, and then banished them. Even now the (shockingly hysterical) voices of your radio announcers shriek into the microphone, 'the Jews are to blame'. In this, too, you are blind and cowardly. You would do better pointing out that it is nothing other than the hulk of the old Entente that is revolting against a violently ascendant Germany – but also a Germany very much in need of growth. Why do you mislead your people (possibly towards new pogroms)? Where is your much-touted political intelligence, your soldierly sense, your Germanic cleanliness? One fights the enemy; however, when one refrains from abusing him and insulting him, one respects in him one's own manliness that has been forced to fight.

From Chamberlain's speech yesterday afternoon it's clear that England and France will fight.[3] I no longer dare to think that this battle might be replaced by a blockade of Germany, for example, and instead [think] that England and France are getting ready to enter the war, and that means at best systematic air raids and the tying down of major forces at the West [...][4] means at worst a French-English offensive in the West, Italy's entry into the war, and fighting in the Mediterranean. Turkey will then no longer be able to remain neutral. One can be relaxed about the Turkish decision only if it means neutrality.[5]

3 September 1939
England has declared war on the German Reich.

When a loved one passes away after lengthy suffering and after lengthy and searing uncertainty for their family, the first thing felt by those closest to them is liberation. Pain, sorrow, worry, loneliness, desperate homesickness – all that only begins *later*. War is the death of peace – and, seen from here, the boundless sorrow now being invoked across the Occident has begun its wild, unstoppable campaign of conquest in utterly terrifying silence. Like a giant barely awakened, calamity is stretching itself, roaring from its oft-interrupted slumber. Inconceivable to hear the noise from the streets, the chatter of children playing, to hear a Bach fugue being practised on the sixth floor, to eat one's dinner (still plentiful, but for how long?) from a white-clothed table, and to know that thousands are already lying in their own blood, wounded, maimed, or dead – that houses are already collapsing again, their smouldering walls pointing up into the sky – that tormented women and frightened children are screaming, that farmers are fleeing along country lanes on overloaded carts.

Despite knowing all too well that National Socialism has incurred blood guilt, lies, and deception, I have no side in this war. In 1914 and again in 1916, when I was a soldier, I had a fatherland, which, like the other 70,000 German Jews that fought, and like the

3 The British prime minister, Neville Chamberlain, announced to the House of Commons on 1 Sept. 1939 that France and Britain would lend military support to Poland if German troops failed to withdraw. Since Germany had, he said, refused to enter into negotiations on the peaceful resolution of the German-Polish conflict, it bore sole responsibility for the imminent war. See 'Prime Minister's Indictment of Germany', *The Times*, 2 Sept. 1939, p. 5.

4 One or two words are illegible.

5 Turkey maintained its neutrality until 23 Feb. 1945; only then did it declare war on Germany and Japan.

10,000 that fell, I unthinkingly and enthusiastically served.[6] Now I have been hounded to the far end of the Western world, and live within a Jewish society that has barely begun. I look back: I do not weep for past 'happiness', I do not blame anyone for anything, I am free from resentment, I feel no hatred towards others. 'Blessed is he who walks apart, though no hate he bears.'[7] Walking apart is allowed, of course – and blessedness impossible for anyone. But the state of 'not bearing hatred' (and resisting all forms of fanatical partisanship) is like a spiritual home which, despite feeling as though I am covered up and buried, despite 'having' nothing, despite seeing neither a way forward nor a use for myself, I wish to build for myself.

DOC. 4
On 5 September 1939 the State Commissioner for Private Industry to the Reichsstatthalter of Vienna proposes that the Viennese Jews be confined to forced labour camps[1]

Letter (confidential) from the State Commissioner for Private Industry (Rf/K.)[2] to the staff office of the Field Marshal,[3] for the attention of Ministerialdirigent Dr Gritzbach,[4] forwarded to Deputy Regierungspräsident Barth[5] for his information, dated 5 September 1939 (carbon copy)

Dear Party Comrade Dr Gritzbach,

Recent events have created a need to take prompt new measures to remove the Jews from Vienna. I have been informed that the appropriate Reich agencies will be notified

6 Of a total of more than 100,000 Jews who served in the First World War, around 12,000 are likely to have fallen on the front line; the figures vary from source to source. The Reich League of Jewish Front-Line Soldiers recorded around 10,200 dead: Reichsbund jüdischer Frontsoldaten, *Die jüdischen Gefallenen des deutschen Heeres, der deutschen Marine und der deutschen Schutztruppen 1914–1918: Ein Gedenkbuch* (Berlin: Der Schild, 1932).

7 Johann Wolfgang von Goethe, 'To the Moon' (1789): 'Blessed is he who walks apart, / though no hate he bears, / Holds a friend within his heart; / And with him shares ...'.

1 ÖStA/AdR, Reichskommissar Bürckel/Materie, 2160/7. This document has been translated from German.

2 Walter Rafelsberger (1899–1986), engineer and chemist; joined the NSDAP in 1933 and the SS in 1934; appointed Gau economic advisor in Vienna, 1938; head of the Vienna Asset Transfer Office; state commissioner for private industry to the Reichsstatthalter; president of the Vienna Chamber of Commerce; briefly arrested in 1947, then went into hiding; chief agent for the Jenbacher engine works in South Tyrol, 1966.

3 Hermann Göring.

4 Dr Erich Gritzbach (b. 1896), civil servant; joined the SS and the NSDAP in 1933; chief commissioner for the Olympic Games, 1933–1936; ministerial director, 1936; SS-Gruppenführer, 1938; head of the staff office of Minister President Göring, 1938–1945; editor of the journal *Der Vierjahresplan: Zeitschrift für nationalsozialistische Wirtschaftspolitik*; interned by the US authorities in 1945, then worked as a senior executive with the European Coal and Steel Community.

5 Dr Karl Barth (1896–1962), lawyer; joined the NSDAP in 1935; from 1938, head of department for the Reich commissioner for the reunification of Austria with the German Reich, as well as deputy Regierungspräsident; general representative of the Reichsstatthalter in Vienna, 1939; Regierungspräsident of the Palatinate, 1939, and of the Westmark, 1940; interned, 1945–1948; regional councillor in Saarbrücken, 1956.

of the situation in the coming days, and asked to take immediate remedial action, by the Gauleitung of the NSDAP, by the mayor of Vienna,[6] and certainly by the Reichsstatthalter.[7] I consider it necessary, in consultation with these agencies, to inform you and thus the Field Marshal about this new situation and the measures needed to address it.

As we all know, the removal of Jews from private-sector enterprises is effectively complete.[8] However, as a result of the approach hitherto adopted, more than two thirds of non-agricultural Jewish property holdings in Vienna are still in Jewish hands. For this sector the measures already proposed by us on numerous occasions must be put in place, come what may, i.e. the appointment of non-Jewish property managers and the taking over of such property holdings by a finance syndicate (the insurance companies would make most sense).

Even more urgent is the immediate removal of the 150,000–180,000 Jews remaining from the original 300,000 or so, who are still living in the country as pensioners or proletarians. At the present time this large number of Jews represents a significant political threat. We have already ensured that they are kept totally separate from the non-Jewish population when doing their daily shopping and collecting their ration coupons.[9] We are also taking steps to exclude them from cafés and restaurants.[10] However, we cannot prevent this large number of Jews, who effectively have nothing else to do, from continually establishing local centres of resistance in the working-class districts and heavily populated areas. It has also been observed that in recent days the Jews have been behaving in an increasingly insolent manner. As a result of this, there is a risk that the populace might once again take matters into its own hands,[11] which would be particularly unwelcome at the present time.

In our view, the only effective way of countering such threats right now would be to send the majority of Jews to forced labour camps, which would have to be set up

6 Dr Hermann Neubacher (1893–1960), forestry engineer and economist; joined the NSDAP in Austria in 1933; director of the GESIBA housing association in Vienna, 1921–1934; mayor of Vienna, March 1938 to Dec. 1940; special commissioner for the South-East, 1940; from 1943 representative of the Reich Foreign Office seconded to the military commander in Serbia; sentenced to twenty years' imprisonment in Yugoslavia in 1951 and released in 1952; then worked as a building contractor in Salzburg; consultant for the development of public administration in Ethiopia, 1954–1956.

7 Josef Bürckel (1895–1944), teacher; joined the NSDAP in 1921; Gauleiter of Rhineland-Palatinate, 1926–1936; member of the Reichstag, 1930–1944; Reich commissioner for the reintegration of the Saarland, 1935–1936; Gauleiter of Saarpfalz and Reich commissioner for the Saarland, 1936–1940; SA-Obergruppenführer, 1936, joined the SS, 1937; Reich commissioner for the reunification of Austria with the German Reich, 1938–1940; Gauleiter of Vienna, 1939–1940; Reich commissioner for Saarpfalz, 1940–1941; head of the civil administration in Lorraine and Gauleiter of the Westmark, 1940–1944; he is thought to have taken his own life.

8 See PMJ 2/20 and 2/62.

9 On instructions issued by Mayor Neubacher, special opening times for shops (2–4 p.m.) and skilled craft enterprises (5–6 p.m.) were introduced for Jews in nearly every municipal district of Vienna on 6 Sept. 1939. As of 8 Sept. 1939 separate counters for the issue of ration coupons were also set up. *Jüdisches Nachrichtenblatt* (Vienna edition), 8 Sept. 1939, p. 3.

10 According to the Police Regulation on the Conduct of the Jews in Public, issued on 28 Nov. 1938, the mayor of Vienna was authorized to impose such restrictions on Jews: *Reichsgesetzblatt*, 1938, I, p. 1676.

11 This is a reference to the pogroms that followed the annexation of Austria in March 1938: see PMJ 2/27, 2/31 and 2/33.

throughout the Reich. They could be put to work on road-building projects or in brickworks and all sorts of other large-scale undertakings that could employ Jews in segregated work squads. My own personal view is that it would be absolutely essential to house these Jews in camps and keep them under guard. An uncontrolled dispersal of the Jews throughout the country would diminish the political threat in Vienna, but at the cost of spreading it to the whole of the Reich. Proposals along these lines are currently being drawn up in consultation with the employment office and the organizations concerned with the economy, and these will shortly be submitted to the relevant agencies. I would be grateful if you could lend support to these efforts of ours yourself, and also procure the support of the Field Marshal.[12]

Heil Hitler!

Your very devoted

DOC. 5

On 6 September 1939 the Gestapo Central Office instructs its regional branches to prevent acts of violence against Jews, and announces pending anti-Jewish measures[1]

Telex (no. 191 087 6.9.39 1600) from the Gestapo Central Office, Berlin (II B 4 Nr. 982/39 J.), unsigned,[2] to all State Police (head) offices, for the information of the inspectors of the Security Police, dated 6 September 1939 (copy)

Re: anti-Jewish measures.
Case file: none.
As the reports from various State Police offices indicate, the Jews have adopted a higher public profile in recent days, and in several instances their behaviour has been provocative.

I must point out that no acts of violence against the Jews should be perpetrated under any circumstances, for obvious reasons, and to that end I would ask you to liaise immediately with the appropriate Party agencies. Discussions are currently taking place between the various ministries concerned regarding general measures to be taken against the Jews. In particular, general arrangements for the labour assignment of all able-bodied Jews are likely to be announced in the near future.[3] Further discussions will also take

12 Proposals for interning the Jewish population of Vienna in labour camps had already been submitted by Rafelsberger in Oct. 1938: see PMJ 2/111. The matter was also discussed by other agencies as a response to housing problems: see Doc. 16, especially fn. 4. The plan became redundant, however, when Eichmann announced the deportation of the Viennese Jews in the autumn of 1939.

1 BArch, R 58/276, fol. 231. Published in H. G. Adler, *Der verwaltete Mensch: Studien zur Deportation der Juden aus Deutschland* (Tübingen: Mohr, 1974), p. 42. This document has been translated from German.

2 In 1939 Wilhelm Hülf (1907–1954) headed Section II B 4 of the Gestapo Central Office (Gestapa), which was responsible for Jewish affairs.

3 In the spring of 1940, all Jewish men between the ages of 18 and 55 and all Jewish women between 18 and 50 were ordered to report for labour deployment. However, there were local differences in the way the order was enforced.

place on arrangements for supplying the Jews with food, on the presence of the Jews in public life in general, and on other such matters.[4] I will issue further instructions as soon as these questions have been settled in principle.

DOC. 6

On 7 September 1939 Reinhard Heydrich orders the arrest of all male Polish Jews over the age of 16 in the Reich[1]

Telegram marked 'secret' from the Chief of the Security Police and the SD (NUE 191 332, 7.9.29.2115 = KR.), signed Heydrich,[2] to all Gestapo (head) offices, for the information of the inspectors of the Security Police, received by the Weimar Gestapo, 7 September 1939, 23:01 hours (receipt no. 9342), dated 7 September 1939 (copy)[3]

I hereby issue the following order:
(1) All male Jews of Polish nationality are to be arrested. Their dependants (wife, children up to the age of 16) are to be registered by name only. Where necessary, conditions are to be imposed on adult family members (residency ban, compulsory registration, etc.).[4] –
Any available assets are to be provisionally confiscated, and only such portion thereof may be released as is deemed necessary for the maintenance of dependants. –
(2) The names of all Jews who previously held Polish nationality or who come from Poland are to be registered as discreetly (underlined) as possible. –
The intention is, as far as possible, to deport these Jews and the Jews of Polish nationality already arrested under section (1) at some future date to those parts of Poland that we are not planning to occupy.[5] For this reason the State Police (head) offices are required to provide me with the following information by 12 September 1939 at the latest:
(A) The number of Jews arrested under section (1) (with the number of dependants in each case). –
(B) The number of Jews recorded as having previously held Polish nationality or as having come from Poland. –

4 See Doc. 36, fnn. 4 and 7.

1 ThHStA, MdI, P 94, fol. 33. This document has been translated from German.
2 Reinhard Heydrich (1904–1942), career officer; served in the German navy, 1922–1931; joined the NSDAP and the SS in 1931; appointed head of the SD in 1932 and in 1933–1934 tasked with the centralization of the Political Police forces of the different German states; in 1934 he became head of the Gestapo Central Office (Gestapa) in Berlin, which was initially responsible only for Prussia; chief of the Security Police and the SD, 1936–1942; chief of the Reich Security Main Office (RSHA), 1939–1942, and from Sept. 1941 also Deputy Reich Protector of Bohemia and Moravia; following an assassination attempt in Prague, he died of his injuries on 4 June 1942.
3 The original contains handwritten annotations.
4 When circulating Heydrich's order, the Potsdam Gestapo, for example, also stipulated on 8 Sept. 1939 that family members were not allowed to leave the local police district, and furthermore were 'required to report to the police three times a day': BLHA, Pr. Br. Rep. 6 B Kreisverwaltung Beeskow-Storkow 634.
5 Heydrich is presumably referring to those parts of Poland not intended for incorporation into the Reich, i.e. the General Government, which was established in Oct. 1939.

(3) The arrest records of persons taken into protective custody under paragraph (1) are to be forwarded in the normal way to the Gestapo Central Office, section Roman 2 D.[6] Section Roman 2 D will issue instructions on a case-by-case basis as to whether an individual is to be sent to a concentration camp.[7] –
Those Jews of Polish nationality, or formerly of Polish nationality, who are needed – for example – to assist with the general emigration of Jews from the Reich, are *not* to be arrested.–
Note for the Vienna State Police head office: please liaise with SS Hauptsturmführer Eichmann, SD Main District Danube.[8]

DOC. 7
On 8 September 1939 Walter Grundmann reports to Reich Minister of Church Affairs Hanns Kerrl on the work of the Institute for the Study and Elimination of Jewish Influence on German Church Life[1]

Letter, signed Dr Grundmann,[2] Jena, to Reich Minister Kerrl,[3] Berlin, dated 8 September 1939 (copy)

Esteemed Reich Minister,

At a moment when world Jewry, consumed by its hatred of the German nation, is about to deliver a decisive blow, and the German nation is engaged in a struggle to defend its rights and its very existence, I turn to you in my capacity as academic director of the De-Jewification Institute,[4] which has been established with your consent by a group of regional churches.

6 Section II 1 D is meant here: protective custody, concentration camps.
7 Between 2,000 and 3,000 Polish Jews were subsequently interned in concentration camps.
8 In Vienna the Gestapo arrested a total of 1,048 Polish Jews on 10/11 Sept. 1939, holding them initially in the Prater Stadium, and transported them to Buchenwald concentration camp at the end of the month: see Introduction, p. 31, and Doc. 33.

1 EZA, 7/4166. This document has been translated from German.
2 Dr Walter Grundmann (1906–1976), Protestant theologian; joined the NSDAP in 1930; in 1932, head of the National Socialist Pastors' League in Saxony, where in 1933 he co-founded the Saxon branch of the German Christians movement; professor in Jena, 1936–1945; academic director of the Institute for the Study and Elimination of Jewish Influence on German Church Life in Eisenach (hereafter Eisenach Institute), 1939–1943; served in the war, 1943–1945; in Soviet captivity, 1945; under the name 'Berg' he was an unofficial informer (IM) for the East German Ministry of State Security (Stasi), 1956–1969; rector of the theological seminary in Eisenach, 1957–1975; church councillor, 1974.
3 Hanns Kerrl (1887–1941), judicial officer; joined the NSDAP in 1923; member of the Landtag in Prussia, 1928–1933; head of the NSDAP district branch in Peine, 1929–1941; member of the Reichstag, 1933–1941; appointed Reich commissioner for the Prussian Ministry of Justice, March 1933, then Prussian minister of justice until June 1934; Reich minister of church affairs, and head of the Reich Office for Spatial Planning, 1935–1941; SA-Obergruppenführer, 1936.
4 The Eisenach Institute was inaugurated on 6 May 1939 at a ceremony conducted at Wartburg Castle. More than 50 professors of theology, dozens of young academics, and some 100 pastors and bishops, as well as many lay persons, affiliated themselves with the new institution. In 1940 the institute published a revised version of the New Testament for the first time, under the title *Die Botschaft Gottes* (God's Message): see PMJ 2/307.

We have set about the work of the institute in the firm belief that the Jewish influence on all areas of German life – including religion and church affairs – must be unmasked and crushed. An age that overlooked the Jewish question was not capable of carrying out this task. Both theology and ecclesiastical practice are therefore now faced with critical tasks that have only emerged as a consequence of the radical transition in Germany. We are determined to tackle these tasks. We are guided by the belief that Christianity, as its history in the first centuries shows, developed in opposition to Judaism, and imparted a crucial truth to the Germanic tribes as they evolved towards nationhood and historical power and influence. Our forefathers did not fall victim to a concealed Judaism, but faithfully and devoutly received a truth that nourished them. Nevertheless, in the cause of developments, and indeed from the very beginning, certain thoughts and ideas took root and led to the emergence of forms that do not derive from the fundamental truth of Christianity, but from an alien, and in part Jewish, spirit and character. These are the source of the ongoing tensions between church and state throughout the course of German history. Furthermore, in the nineteenth century in particular, the evil spirit of Judaism brought its influence to bear on German life, firstly through religion and later through philosophy, giving birth to the devastating philosophy of materialism and its religious nihilism. To identify the innate principles that drive German religious life and German Christian experience, and to unmask the degenerate and dangerous alien influences: such is the mighty and all-encompassing task that lies before us, the accomplishment of which, given the times we face, is to our mind absolutely imperative.

Today, after just six months of intensive work, I venture to say that the establishment of this institute has created a platform that did not previously exist within ecclesiastical and religious life. This platform is not a specifically German-Christian affair in the narrow sense of one particular group. The impetus to found this institute did indeed come from the German Christians,[5] and it was they who set about planning it and bringing it into being. It could not be any other way, since the German Christians, as National Socialists, were the first to recognize and detect the enemy of German life in his cloak of religion, and to realize that the continuation of the Reformation in the present times must start here. But, from the outset, the platform they created broadened to such an extent that able and knowledgeable persons from every quarter have joined it to collaborate and contribute. Letters have been received from all sections of the German population, confirming support for our initiative in tackling these tasks.

I would like to cite a number of examples to illustrate the above. A study group that I initiated and lead is investigating the history of the beginnings of Christianity with reference to the influence of Judaism and the conflict with Judaism. The study group is planning a major work in several volumes, which will examine these issues with German

5 The pastor Joachim Hossenfelder (1899–1976) founded the German Christians in 1932 as a faith movement within the German Protestant Church. The pro-NSDAP movement set itself the objective of dissolving the separate state churches and establishing a national Reich Church that would exclude 'non-Aryan Christians'. The movement won the church elections in the summer of 1933 and soon had a membership of 1 million. But its radical demands were too much for many members, who left the movement. Over the next few years, the German Christians fragmented into various splinter groups.

academic rigour.[6] Collaborators on this project include university professors Dr Bertram (Giessen),[7] the only German expert on Hellenistic Judaism, which has had a profound influence on the cultural life of the Western world, a subject that has only really been studied by Anglo-Saxon scholars; Dr Preisker (Breslau);[8] Dr Schneider (Königsberg),[9] one of the leading experts on the religious world of Hellenism; the young rabbinical scholar Lic. habil.[10] Rudolf Meyer[11] in Leipzig; and a number of other young scholars. Another study group is working on the problem encapsulated by the name 'Spinoza', examining the influence of this man on the nineteenth century, and in particular on the emergence of materialism. This study group is headed by Professor Redeker at Kiel University.[12] The problem that has beset the history of religion, that of Semitic versus Aryan forms and principles of religion, has been addressed jointly by a group that includes Professor Hempel,[13] Berlin, the Giessen lecturer Lic.[14] Dr Euler,[15] and a number of other colleagues.

6 The study group led by Grundmann and Herbert Preisker sought to eliminate 'Jewish influences' from the New Testament. By 1942 Grundmann had published three volumes of conference proceedings on the relationship between 'Christianity and Judaism' (1940) and 'Germanic Civilization, Christianity and Judaism' (1942, 2 vols).

7 Dr Georg Bertram (1896–1979), Protestant theologian; professor in Giessen, 1925–1946; worked with the Eisenach Institute from 1939, and became its academic director in 1943; professor in Frankfurt am Main, 1955–1965; author of works including *Volkstum und Menschheit im Lichte der Heiligen Schrift* (1937).

8 Dr Herbert Preisker (1888–1952), Protestant theologian; active in pastoral ministry; professor in Frankfurt an der Oder, 1934, in Göttingen, 1935, and in Breslau, 1936–1945; from 1939, military chaplain and an associate of the Eisenach Institute; professor in Jena, 1947–1952, and in Halle, 1952; author of works including *Deutsches Christentum* (1934).

9 Dr Carl Schneider (1900–1977), Protestant theologian; joined the NSDAP in 1933; professor in Königsberg, 1935–1945; associate of the Eisenach Institute from 1939; after 1945, cultural advisor to the city of Speyer and head of the Protestant Academy in Enkenbach; author of works including *Das Frühchristentum als antisemitische Bewegung* (1940).

10 Licentiate degree allowing one to teach at a German university.

11 Dr Rudolf Meyer (1909–1991), Protestant theologian; research assistant at the University of Leipzig, 1934–1939; associate of the Eisenach Institute from 1939; served in the war and was later captured, 1939–1945; professor in Jena, 1947–1975.

12 Dr Martin Redeker (1900–1970), Protestant theologian; joined the NSDAP in 1933; professor in Münster, 1934–1936, and in Kiel, from 1936; worked for the Eisenach Institute from 1939; from 1942 served as a military chaplain; lecturer and professor in Kiel, 1945–1969; member of the Landtag for the Christian Democratic Union (CDU) in Schleswig-Holstein, 1954–1967; awarded the Great Cross of the Order of Merit of the Federal Republic of Germany in 1967. In July 1939 Redeker had given a paper on Spinoza at a conference organized by the Eisenach Institute: see PMJ 2/307.

13 Dr Johannes Hempel (1891–1964), Protestant theologian; professor in Halle, 1924, Greifswald, 1925, Göttingen, 1928, and Berlin, 1937–1945; from 1939, headed the Old Testament study group at the Eisenach Institute; served as a military chaplain, 1939–1945; pastoral administrator in Salzgitter, 1947–1958; honorary professor in Göttingen, 1955–1958; editor of the *Zeitschrift für die alttestamentliche Wissenschaft* (1927–1959).

14 Licentiate.

15 Dr Karl Friedrich Euler (1909–1986), Protestant theologian; lecturer at the University of Giessen, 1936–1946; joined the NSDAP in 1937; worked for the Eisenach Institute from 1939; assigned to the Inspection Office for Foreign Mail in Berlin in 1940; pastor at the University Hospital in Giessen, 1949–1967.

In Heidelberg a study group made up of philologists and religious scholars is working on material documenting the influence of Judaism on the ancient world, and is in the process of preparing the first annotated edition of this source material.[16] The group is headed by Prof. Kiefer, who has been studying this material for the past decade.[17] This example illustrates how the quiet endeavours of individual German scholars flow together in this institute and have an impact. The problem of Judaism and Christianity in German literature and art will be addressed with the particular input of Dr Wilhelm Stapel (Hamburg).[18] The new church historian in Vienna, Lic. Opitz,[19] editor of the *Theologische Literaturzeitung*, is leading a study group that focuses primarily on the question of the Catholic Church. And a team of legal experts is addressing the whole issue of ecclesiastical law.

The results of all these scholarly endeavours will be put to practical use. We are planning to publish a book of devotions for the household and family.[20] In words and pictures the German people will be able to learn about its religious faith – and the dangers that now threaten it. Everything is aimed at creating a unified German Christian Church, which seeks to come into being in the German people. And it will come into being by capturing the vitality of Christian faith as mediated through the German character, and by sweeping away all that is alien.

Having presented the facts here, I believe that the claim made at the beginning is warranted: that a platform has been established here which is broad enough to encompass the various forces that may gather and have already gathered around it; clear enough for real inner forces and clarity to flow from it into German religious life; determined enough for the key issues to be addressed impartially and brought to a resolution. I would be delighted to come and present our work and plans to you in more detail, esteemed Reich Minister. On behalf of the colleagues who have come together here, and who are ready to devote their efforts to this cause, I commend this institute to your attention and humbly request your support for the important work that we are doing. I may also add that within the ranks of the German clergy, who are awaiting a leadership that looks to the future and tackles the questions of our age with earnest intent, there is

16 The planned work for which source material was being gathered here – 'Das Urteil über die *Juden* und das *Judentum* in der griechisch-römischen Spätantike und dem Mittelalter bis zum 16. Jahrhundert' – was never published.

17 Erwin Oskar Kiefer (1895–1973), Protestant theologian; city pastor in Karlsruhe, 1919–1920, and in Bruchsal, 1920–1923; rector of the Melanchthon Seminary in Wertheim, 1924–1934, and city pastor of the town from 1928; held lectureship in Hebrew at the theological faculty of the University of Heidelberg, 1934–1945; worked for the Eisenach Institute from 1939; joined the NSDAP in 1940.

18 Dr Wilhelm Stapel (1882–1954), journalist, editor of the arts journal *Kunstwart*, 1911–1916; editor of the journal *Deutsches Volkstum*, 1919–1938; worked for the Eisenach Institute from 1939; worked as a freelance writer and translator after 1945.

19 Dr Hans-Georg Opitz (1905–1941), Protestant theologian; research assistant at the University of Berlin from 1931; worked for the Eisenach Institute from 1939; taught in Vienna, where he became professor in 1940; joined the NSDAP in 1940; called up for military service in 1940; killed in action.

20 The 'book of devotions', under the title 'Der Ruf des Lebens' (The Call of Life), was to have contained a selection of texts from religious thinkers such as Martin Luther, Matthias Claudius, and Johann Peter Hebel. Although the project was at an advanced stage, the book was never published. A regulation issued by the Reich Press Chamber on 1 June 1941 effectively meant the end of publishing on Church matters in Nazi Germany.

a lively interest in and response to this institute – and not only in the German-Christian section of the German clergy, as recent conferences have demonstrated.

Hoping for your attention and support, as requested above, I remain,

Respectfully yours,

Heil Hitler![21]

DOC. 8
On 10 September 1939 Willy Cohn writes in his diary about the increasingly antisemitic atmosphere in Breslau[1]

Handwritten diary of Willy Cohn,[2] entry for 10 September 1939

Breslau, Sunday.

Yesterday afternoon first at the barber's, then a walk with Trudi.[3] But it was not very pleasurable; the atmosphere has become very antisemitic; a woman called out behind us: Jewish low life. I very much expect that the atmosphere will become more antisemitic in line with the extent to which the people are affected by the wartime shortages and the losses increase.

People blame the Jews for this war, because they believe that they supported England and Poland. In addition, the Jewish men have not been called up.

One must be ready for anything. Yesterday six Jewish women who were sitting on a bench in Hohenzollernstr. were arrested. Someone had claimed that they had laughed in front of the hospital where the wounded soldiers are.

The women have to report to the Gestapo today. I heard this story from a Mrs Freund, who spoke to me as I came from Mother's in the evening. It's true that our people don't really need to sit in a group of six on a bench on Hohenzollernstr., but this small and insignificant incident is proof of the sentiment against us – it can be compared with the atmosphere during the Coalition Wars, when the emigrants in France were held responsible for the wars against that nation.[4]

By the way, it is difficult to convince Jews that the boycott of Germany was a tactical error.[5]

21 The request for support was successful to the extent that in Jan. 1940 Kerrl abandoned his opposition to the use of church taxes to help fund the work of the institute. He is thought to have initially opposed this form of funding because he wanted to limit the influence of the Protestant Church on the institute.

1 CAHJP, P 88/90, fols. 67–72. Abridged English translation in Willy Cohn, *No Justice in Germany: The Breslau Diaries, 1933–1941*, ed. Norbert Conrads, trans. Kenneth Kronenberg (Stanford, CA: Stanford University Press, 2012 [German edn, 2006]), p. 274. This document has been newly translated from the original German.

2 Dr Wilhelm (Willy) Cohn (1888–1941), teacher and historian; Zionist; member of the Social Democratic Party of Germany (SPD); from 1919 until his forced retirement in 1933, secondary school teacher in Breslau; subsequently earned his living as a visiting lecturer on Jewish history; his plans to emigrate to Palestine failed; on 25 Nov. 1941 he was deported to Kaunas, where he was murdered.

3 Gertrud Karoline Cohn, née Rothmann (1901–1941), secretary; second wife of Willy Cohn; in Nov. 1941 she was deported along with her husband and two youngest daughters to Kaunas, where she was murdered.

Besides, in spite of all the successes in Poland, I now no longer have any hope that the war can be localized. It seems to be gaining force in the West now as well. Two French planes have been shot down over German territory. England will surely wage war most tenaciously. It's good that it is not possible to see the future. Still no news from my boys.[6] I wrote to Rufs[7] again.

Breslau, Sunday afternoon.
Today I did not receive any post from my sons, either; the only thing was a returned card that I had sent to Wölfl a week ago. One must resign oneself.

In the morning busy with Thomas Aquinas; later a walk with Susannchen.[8] We sat first for a while at the depot in Gräbschen.[9] Susannchen brought the trolley along; I read the newspaper.

In the West three French planes have been shot down over the German lines. In the East it is said that they occupied Łódź today. Since early morning the air has constantly been full of air traffic. One hears the buzzing of the heavy motors constantly.

Sat later with Susannchen on Leedeborntrift.[10] Had a conversation with an Aryan woman sitting there with a small child. She was full of praise for the Jewish paediatricians: Weigert,[11] Pogerschelsky,[12] Leichtentritt.[13] She said that her child had been seriously hurt as a result of a mistake by an Aryan physician, the adjunct professor Dr Klinke;[14] he waited too long to pierce the ear drum to relieve a middle ear infection and the child got meningitis.

4 During the Coalition Wars (1792–1815), also known as the French Revolutionary Wars (1792–1802) and the Napoleonic Wars (1803–1815), France condemned French emigrants for betraying their homeland. Because they had joined the counter-revolution abroad, Napoleon's French commander Maximilien Foy even accused them of having brought the war to France.

5 After the boycott of Jewish businesses in the German Reich in April 1933, Jewish organizations abroad called for the governments of their respective countries to boycott German goods in response. The German government used this in its antisemitic propaganda.

6 The reference is to Willy Cohn's sons from his first marriage. Wolfgang (Wölfl) (b. 1915) studied at university in Paris from 1933; Ernst Abraham (1919–2008) obtained a youth certificate which allowed him to emigrate to Palestine in 1935.

7 Rosette Ruf, née Lewy, was a childhood friend of Willy Cohn in Frankfurt; she lived with her husband Leon Ruf in St Gallen, Switzerland. She was thus able to receive messages from Willy Cohn's son Wolfgang; the German Reich blocked all post from France after the start of the war.

8 Susannchen is the diminutive form of Susanna. Susanna Cohn (1932–1941), daughter of Willy and Gertrud Cohn; on 25 Nov. 1941 she was deported with her parents and her sister Tamara (1938–1941) to Kaunas, where she was murdered.

9 City district with a park and manor house. It had been incorporated into the city of Breslau in 1911 and was located near Willy Cohn's apartment.

10 Correctly: Ledeborn-Trift, a street in a Breslau park.

11 Dr Richard Weigert (1875–1948), physician; paediatrician in Breslau; emigrated to Uruguay.

12 Correctly: Dr Herbert Pogorschelsky (b. 1897), physician; paediatrician in Breslau; probably emigrated in 1938. In Oct. 1940 his doctorate was revoked, and his subsequent fate is unknown.

13 Dr Bruno Leichtentritt (1888–1966), physician; paediatrician at the University Children's Hospital in Breslau, 1919–1928, associate professor in 1926; emigrated to the USA in 1938.

14 Probably Dr Karl Klinke (1897–1972), physician; was removed from his position at the University Children's Hospital in Breslau in 1934 due to 'political unreliability'; military physician, 1939; lecturer at the University of Breslau, 1941–1943; professor in Rostock, 1944–1947; director of the paediatric clinic of the Charité hospital in Berlin, 1947–1951; director of the University Children's Hospital in Düsseldorf, 1951–1965.

Her husband has not yet been called up; he is a Polish-language interpreter. Then she tried to extract from me some judgement of the situation, but I did not say anything. The Aryans are beset with a great fear about what could happen if the West intervenes.

The newspaper today said that it is possible that ration cards for bread will be introduced.[15] Cocoa, the purchase of which does not require stamps, is impossible to get: the hoarders have squirrelled it away.

DOC. 9
On 11 September 1939 the NSDAP Kreisleitung for Kitzingen-Gerolzhofen reports on attacks on Jews and calls for the incarceration of all Jews in a concentration camp[1]

Report on morale compiled by the NSDAP Kreisleitung for Kitzingen-Gerolzhofen, Gau of Mainfranken, unsigned,[2] to the Gauleitung of Mainfranken, Würzburg,[3] dated 11 September 1939[4]

Last night an air-raid siren went off in Kitzingen. No enemy aircraft were sighted. The alarm passed off without incident. It turned out that the number of air-raid shelters, particularly the public ones, is far too small. The absence of an air-raid shelter in the vicinity of the railway station was particularly noted. There are a lot of complaints that no gas masks of any kind have been issued in Kitzingen, and none are available to buy either.

In Kitzingen and Marktbreit there were outbreaks of violence against the Jews at the weekend. In Kitzingen the notorious Jew Moses Meier was beaten up. The perpetrator was taken into protective custody, but released immediately at the instigation of the Party. No charge was brought.

In Marktbreit a crowd of over 100 angry people gathered outside the house of a Jew and dragged the Jew's housekeeper – a German woman from Veitshöchheim – outside.[5]

A few windows were broken and the house sustained some other minor damage. The Jew himself was unhurt. The miscreant housekeeper was collected by her son within one hour and driven off in a motor vehicle.

Nevertheless, it is noted that the Jews are still heavily involved in spying activities. There are still a lot of Jews hanging around the railway station, and on the main roads where troop units are passing through. There are also a lot of Jews moving from village to village, and some of them are going to inns and restaurants out in the country again.

For example, I have had a report from Großlangheim that the Jew Ackermann has been seen in the 'Zum Adler' inn. This inn is very popular with the aircrew based nearby. I am certain that Ackermann only goes to Großlangheim in order to spy. Ackermann

15 On 8 Sept. 1939 a front-page report in the *Jüdisches Nachrichtenblatt* (Berlin edition) announced that mandatory ration cards had been introduced for a number of products, including bread and flour.

1 StA Wü, NSDAP Gau Mainfranken Nr. 8. Extracts are published in Martin Broszat (ed.), *Bayern in der NS-Zeit*, vol. 1: *Soziale Lage und politisches Verhalten der Bevölkerung im Spiegel vertraulicher Berichte* (Munich: Oldenbourg, 1977), p. 480. This document has been translated from German.

2 The NSDAP Kreisleiter of Kitzingen from 1932 to 1945 was Wilhelm Heer (1894–1961).

3 The NSDAP Gauleiter of Mainfranken from 1935 to 1945 was Otto Hellmuth (1896–1968).

4 Parts of the original are underlined and annotated by hand.

5 Since 1 Jan. 1936 it had been forbidden for Jews to employ Aryan female domestic staff under the age of 45: Law for the Protection of German Blood and German Honour, 15 Sept. 1935, *Reichsgesetzblatt*, 1935, I, pp. 1146–1147; see also PMJ 1/199.

himself comes from Kleinlangheim. As was reported some time ago, this Jew was chased out of his village by the local Party branch leader in Wiesenbronn, Fröhlich,[6] just as he was setting out for Rödelsee. We have noticed that this Jew is always going to the villages by the airfield in Kitzingen.

In my opinion the time has come to round up all the Jews at last and put them in a concentration camp, so that they really cannot have any more contact with German Volksgenossen. It has also been reported that the Jews are buying up goods in the grocery shops, especially at Kupsch, Backdie, etc., and they are especially stockpiling items that can be bought without ration coupons.

Morale among returnees remains low, not least because the majority of them do not have any cash. They also lack the most essential items of clothing, as we have already reported. There is an acute shortage of work clothing. Since it has been known for many months that these returnees would be arriving, and indeed that this had already been organized, arrangements should have been made to provide sufficient clothing and shoes for the returnees, come what may.[7]

Most returnees have no winter clothing at all, and action is urgently needed now to make sure that the poor devils don't freeze this winter, on top of everything else. It seems to me that if we can spend up to 90 billion [Reichsmarks] on armament and many, many billions more to fight this war, then it should be possible to find one or two billion to provide the returning migrants with food and clothing.

As they have been promised, the returnees want to be found work again, the whole lot of them, and it is highly regrettable that the employment offices have still not been given the necessary instructions. As far as looking after the returning migrants is concerned, the cooperation between Party, state, and Wehrmacht has left a great deal to be desired. This is one area where we would be ideally placed to do some serious damage to our main enemy, the politicizing Church.

From time to time we still get the odd person claiming that things will turn out the same way they did in the 1914–18 war, when those who had money – and an elastic conscience – were able to line their pockets at the expense of the general population, and duck out of military service. On this subject I would like to refer you to the report that was sent off today to the Reich Propaganda Office for Mainfranken, about the behaviour of the sons of Ökonomierat Lang, who lives on Untere Neue Gasse in Etwashausen.[8] It is appalling to think people might be saying that agencies of the military, the Party, or the economy could be corrupted again in this war too.

6 Georg Fröhlich (1899–1966), businessman and wine retailer; joined the NSDAP in 1932; local Party branch leader in Wiesenbronn from 1933 to 1945; interned after 1945.

7 When war broke out, the civilian population had to vacate the 'Red Zone', the area between the reinforced German line of defence (the 'Westwall' or Siegfried line) and Germany's western border. Hundreds of thousands were evacuated en masse to the interior of the country, and they were not allowed to return until the end of the campaign against France, in the summer of 1940. The source uses the term 'Rückwanderer' to describe the returnees.

8 Georg Lang (1872–1944) was awarded the title of Ökonomierat for services to the agricultural industry. His sons, Georg Friedrich (1903–1973) and Georg Heinrich (1900–1970), had initially been exempted from military service. This is said to have provoked 'great outrage and bad feeling' in Kitzingen's garden suburb of Etwashausen, where Lang had a large market garden business: letter from the Kreisleitung of Kitzingen-Gerolzhofen to the Reich Propaganda Office of Mainfranken, dated 11 Sept. 1939, StA Wü, NSDAP Gau Mainfranken Nr. 8

DOC. 10
On the basis of a denunciation, on 13 September 1939 the Munich Gestapo accuses Felizi Weill of inciting hatred against the German state leadership[1]

Gestapo interrogation report from the Gestapo Head Office in Munich (B. Nr. II. B), signed Detective Constable Schipferling,[2] dated 13 September 1939[3]

Subject: 1. Last name (and maiden name, in the case of women): *Weill*, née Hamburger; first and middle names (underline name normally used): *Felizi* Sara.[4] 2. Date of birth: 22 March 1903; birthplace (parish, administrative district, country, if abroad): Bad-Kissingen. 3. First name and surname (a) of father: Nathan *Hamburger*; (b) of mother: Pauline, née Wimmelsbacher; occupation and place of residence of parents: family butcher's business in Bad Kissingen. 4. Marital status: single, *married*, widowed, divorced. 5. (a) Occupation; (b) capacity (self-employed, salaried employee, manual worker and service or post; in the case of wives the name, occupation, capacity, date of birth, and birthplace of the husband must also be stated): wife (husband: Eugen Israel *Weill*). 6. Place of residence and address (or address of last overnight stay): 12/3 Albanistr., Munich. 7. Nationality (foreigners must also state their home parish): Reich subject. 8. Identification papers (type, issuing authority, date and number): identity card no. Munich 05 352, issued 27 March 1939. 9. Driving licence: –; *regarding:* violation of the law of 20 December 1934.[5]

According to confidential information received here, the Jewess *Felizi* Sara *Weill*, resident at 12/3 Albanistr., Munich, made inflammatory and derogatory remarks about the [German] state at around 2 p.m. on 29 August 1938,[6] while she was putting her washing through the mangle in the *Kegel* laundry at 9/o Entenbachstr. Among other things, she is alleged to have said, quite unprompted: 'Now there's another war coming. If they bomb us, there'll be nothing left of Munich after four weeks. Let's hope we're still around to see all the high-ups snuff it. People care more about dogs than they do about us Jews.' The housemaid Luis *Rehl*,[7] of the Kegel laundry at 9/o Entenbachstr., Munich, was cited as a witness.

1 StA Mü, Staatsanwaltschaften Nr. 5463, fol. 6r–v. This document has been translated from German.

2 Georg Schipferling (1900–1945), police officer; joined the NSDAP in 1933; SS-Untersturmführer; declared dead in 1945.

3 At the end of the report, which was written on a standard form, is a typewritten note accompanied by the stamp of the Munich Gestapo (B.Nr. 35 766 II B), Schi., 13 Sept. 1939: 'Forwarded, with ID card no. Munich 05 352 and interrogation transcripts, to *Munich* Local Court – for the attention of the investigating judge – while the accused is transferred pending a decision on her arrest.'

4 Felizi Weill, née Hamburger (1903–1980), housewife; emigrated to the USA in March 1940 together with her husband, Eugen Weill (b. 1896).

5 The Law against Treacherous Attacks on State and Party and for the Protection of the Party Uniform (*Heimtückegesetz*), enacted on 20 Dec. 1934, prescribed a jail sentence of up to two years for 'malicious, inflammatory, or vulgar' comments about the Reich government and the NSDAP: *Reichsgesetzblatt*, 1934, I, pp. 1269–1271.

6 Date as in the original. The alleged offence was presumably committed in the summer of 1939.

7 Correctly: Luise Rebl, married name Eder (1918–1980), had worked in the laundry since March 1938.

When questioned, *Rehl* confirmed the alleged remarks by the Jewess cited in the confidential communication, and added that the Jewess *Weill* had also said:

> When a dog dies in the road these days, they care more about the dog than about us Jews. But hopefully the high-ups will soon drop dead too – I hope that we will get to see that happen before long. Now they want to throw me out of my apartment too – I might as well jump straight in the Isar [river]. They've taken all my silver, and now my gold too;[8] they'll be wanting my clothes next – I wouldn't put anything past them.

The main door to the laundry was open, apparently, so that anyone walking past in the street could have overheard the conversation, especially as the Jewess was talking very loudly.

The owner of the laundry, *Kegel*,[9] described the Jewess *Weill* as very loud-mouthed and aggressive. She had already made it clear to the Jewess that she would prefer it if she didn't come to her shop again, but the Jewess kept on coming regardless, in typical Jewish fashion.

When questioned, the Jewess *Weill*, who was very loud and outspoken with the officials, denied that she had made the alleged remarks, and said, quite unprompted, that she was not in the habit of conversing with such a common girl. By this she meant the female witness of German blood, Luise *Rehl*, who at the time in question had to help her put her washing through the mangle. From the results of our enquiries and the behaviour of the Jewess herself, it is apparent that at every available opportunity, and in typical Jewish fashion, she seeks to incite the German-minded populace against the state leadership, and to do serious damage to the welfare of the Reich and the standing of the Reich government by causing the people to lose confidence in the Reich leadership. *Further details can be found in the attached documents.*[10]

8 According to the Third Directive based on the Regulation on the Registration of Jewish Assets, issued by Göring on 21 Feb. 1939, Jews of German nationality were required to surrender all gold, platinum, or silver items, as well as precious stones and pearls, within two weeks, in return for financial compensation which was to be specified: *Reichsgesetzblatt*, 1939, I, p. 282: see also PMJ 2/258

9 Rosa Kegel, née Dobmeier (1898–1975), had owned the laundry since 1929.

10 StA Mü, Staatsanwaltschaften Nr. 5163, fol. 6r–v; in addition to the interrogation transcripts, the file contains documents relating to subsequent proceedings, which were suspended on 15 Jan. 1940 – after three months in 'protective custody' – in accordance with the so-called Führer amnesty issued on 9 Sept. 1939 (*Reichsgesetzblatt*, 1939, I, p. 1753). Felizi Weill had booked a crossing to New York with her husband, and on 22 Jan. 1940 she was to finalize her travel arrangements at the US consulate general in Stuttgart.

DOC. 11
Aufbau, 15 September 1939: article on the significance of this war for the future of the Jews[1]

'Chosen' again – in this conflict too!
The fate of all Jewry hangs in the balance

m.g.[2] Now the world has its war. The war that it wanted to prevent – and which it did nothing to prevent. Selfish social interests and an almost inconceivable stupidity in grasping the situation on the one hand, megalomania, bloodlust, and a manic imperialism on the other, have contrived to turn Europe into a battlefield. A bloody sky hangs over the entire continent. And it weeps bloody tears over its lost child, the earth.

We Jews stand between the warring nations. We are so remote from these events that not even Hitler has exposed us to the horrors that are now unfolding, other than through a few bellowed platitudes. We are so remote from them, and yet so near, that the body of our people will be no less torn apart and shattered, tortured, and mutilated, by fire and by lead, than that of other nations.

If anyone had cause to tremble at the prospect of this war, because he was afraid for his brothers, it was the Jew. There may be some among us who, out of unbridled hatred and a natural thirst for revenge, watched with joy and excitement as the world's arsonists in Berlin stumbled into their most fearful trial to date, but anyone who could see beyond himself and his own impure and confused feelings knew from the very start that even if the Jews have nothing to do with this war, their fate depends on its outcome. No one can or will escape this war. Most people have barely begun to understand. This is the second part of the World War, and its consequences will continue to destroy the ways of life to which we are accustomed. To an irreparable extent and degree. The horrors that have already occurred are just child's play compared with what is to come. The present theatres of war are narrow little enclaves compared with the vast extent of the battlefields where the final outcome will be decided. To put it in biblical terms: it is fair to say that a last and extreme trial of hellish proportions is upon us, and that over large areas of the earth not one stone will be left standing upon another.[3]

None of us knows what the world will look like at the end of what has now begun. Some statesmen are talking about fighting 'to the bitter end'.[4] They are still able to pic-

1 '"Auserwählt" – auch in diesem Kampf!', *Aufbau*, no. 17, 15 Sept. 1939, pp. 1–2. This document has been translated from German. *Aufbau* appeared from Dec. 1934 and was published by the German-Jewish Club in New York– fortnightly until 1939, and thereafter weekly. Circulation rose from 500 to 8,000 in 1938.

2 Probably Dr Manfred George, born Manfred Georg Cohn (1893–1965), lawyer, journalist, and writer; worked for the Ullstein publishing house, 1917–1923, and for the Mosse publishing house, 1923–1928; co-founder of the Republican Party of Germany (RPD), 1924; features editor for the *Tempo* newspaper, 1928–1933; emigrated to Czechoslovakia in 1933, and to the USA in 1938; editor-in-chief of the journal *Aufbau*, 1939–1965; author of *Theodor Herzl: Sein Leben und sein Vermächtnis* (1932).

3 The allusion is to Jesus's prophecy of the destruction of Jerusalem: 'For the days will come upon you when your enemies will […] surround you and close in on you from every side; they will demolish you – you and your children within your walls – and they will not leave you one stone upon another, because you did not recognize the time of your visitation from God' (Luke 19:43–44).

ture what that might mean. Everything that is happening now is imaginable – for now. But soon it will all be unimaginable! What is happening in Poland now, this trampling of an entire country, where even the unborn child is no longer safe, and hospitals for girls suffering from tuberculosis are already being targeted by dehumanized airmen; what is going on in this country, whose fields and inhabitants are being cooked up together in a red pulp of shattered human flesh and churned-up earth – this is only the beginning. The deadly gases have yet to be released, the flamethrowers are not yet pumping out fire, the rivers have not yet been poisoned, and germ warfare has not been unleashed.

This war will be the bloodiest and most comprehensive slaughter that the world has ever seen. It is bound to be, because it was started by the bloodiest and most relentless murderers who have ever put themselves at the head of a nation. Not for nothing has Hitler pronounced the barbaric Genghis Khan to be a 'Nordic Aryan'. He needed a suitably racist moniker for his role model.

We Jews must brace ourselves for such a war. We are powerless, and weaker than ever. In Poland alone, 3 million of us are facing the guns of our deadly enemies at this moment. Millions are scarred with the leprosy of their wretched refugee status, scattered to the four winds, and not knowing which frontiers they will be hounded across tomorrow. Only a small fraction are living under more propitious skies. And even Palestine, the land of the future for young Jews, is bristling with arms, and these arms are carried by Jews.

That is why this war, which is not of our making either in its causes or in its aims, is also our war. Because our lives are now at stake. The fate of Jewry will be decided in this war, far more definitively than the fate of other peoples. The future of each and every one of us depends on the outcome of this war. We cannot grasp this vital truth early enough, nor deeply and earnestly enough. For those forces that win this war – and nobody knows which forces it will be – will largely determine the entire future of the Jews.

This war is, of course, not just a war involving human bodies, but a war of fundamental moral attitudes, even if it has burst upon this warm, sunny autumn like an explosion of gases from a cesspool filled with immorality. And so, to the sympathy and the action that we bring to the battle against evil, we must add one more thing: the belief in the value that we, as a people bound together by a godly morality, represent for this world of ours, in which all that was once held true has now been cast into doubt. If the concept of being 'chosen', hopelessly misunderstood as it so often is, has any temporal meaning at a time like this, when chaos threatens to engulf us, then it is this: that as well as being willing to fight with every ounce of strength, and with everything that we are and everything that we possess, we are also faced with a challenge a thousand times more difficult, namely to salvage from the tumult our faith in humanity, justice, and morality. Not just for us, but for the whole world.

Such is the significance of the great hour of destiny that has now struck for us with a fearsome, thunderous toll.

4 The British secretary of state for the dominions, Anthony Eden (1897–1977), had declared in a radio address on 11 Sept. 1939 that the Commonwealth would, if necessary, fight to the bitter end to free the world from Hitler: 'Nazi Leaders' Illusions: Mr. Eden on British Determination', *The Times*, 12 Sept. 1939, p. 8, and 'Text of Anthony Eden's Address', *New York Times*, 12 Sept. 1939, p. 18.

DOC. 12

On 16 September 1939 the Plenipotentiary for the Four-Year Plan hosts a meeting in Berlin to discuss the emigration of the Jews and their deployment as forced labourers[1]

Notes compiled by the Reich Ministry of Finance (Section V/3), Berlin, signature illegible, dated 16 September 1939 (copy)[2]

Re: emigration of the Jews.
Notes: The above matter was the subject of a meeting attended by representatives of the departments involved, which was hosted by Staatsrat Wohlthat[3] in his capacity as representative of Field Marshal Göring.

1. The first item discussed was the organization of labour deployment for able-bodied Jews. The representative of the Chief of the Security Police reported on this subject. He summarized the situation as follows:
According to provisional investigations, it seems likely that approximately 60 per cent of the Jews cannot be deployed as labour, as they are either under the age of 16 or over the age of 55. Relatively few Jews are currently in employment at all. Estimates indicate that there are still around 50,000 men and 60,000–70,000 women who could be conscripted for work. The total number of Jews still living in the Reich is not yet known. Aside from that, the Führer reserves the right to take a decision on the employment of the Jews. That decision has not yet been made.

2. The political departments argued that further Jewish emigration is desirable, regardless of whether the destination is neutral or hostile countries. At present, Jewish emigrants receive in foreign exchange only 4 per cent of the money provided by them in Reichsmarks, instead of the 6 per cent previously allocated. The Reich Ministry of Economics will obtain a decision on the issue of whether it is still possible to grant the 4 per cent without prejudice to our foreign-exchange holdings.
It is assumed that under the present circumstances, foreign countries will be more willing to assist and support Jewish emigration from Germany. If it is decided that Jewish emigrants should not be allocated any foreign exchange at all, the question arises as to what should happen to their residual assets (after deduction of all charges). Leaving these residual assets untouched, e.g. in blocked accounts, would be problematic, because the Jews might try to gain access to their money from abroad. This being the case, it

1 BArch, R 2/14195, fols. 17–18. This document has been translated from German.

2 The original contains handwritten annotations and underlining. According to the distribution list at the end of the document, copies were sent to 'Sections Uhlich, Prause, Schmidt-Schwarzenberg, Richter'.

3 Helmuth Wohlthat (1893–1982), economist; worked as a businessman, 1920–1933; headed the Reich Office for Foreign Exchange Control in the Reich Economics Ministry from 1934 to 1938; worked in the Prussian Ministry of State and in the office of the Plenipotentiary for the Four-Year Plan, 1938–1945; joined the NSDAP in 1940; commissioner at the Dutch Central Bank, 1940–1941; head of delegation for economic negotiations in Eastern Asia, 1941–1945; cleared by a denazification tribunal, 1948; served thereafter on the supervisory board of various companies.

would be preferable to insist that the Jews hand over their residual assets to the Reich Association of Jews in Germany. The Reich Association is required to fulfil various tasks associated with the Jews, and adequate financing of its work from Jewish resources is in the interest of the Reich, since the responsibility for providing support would ultimately rest with the Reich.

Those present at the meeting also agreed that it would not be appropriate at present for the German government to provide additional support for emigration through the formation of a special trust fund by way of levies on Jewish assets.[4] This cannot be entertained for reasons of financial and foreign-exchange policy.

For submission by the State Secretary[5] to the Minister,[6] for his information and attention.

DOC. 13

On 19 September 1939 year 8 school pupils practise writing 'barefoot Polish wenches and greasy caftan Jews'[1]

Excerpt from a school exercise book belonging to Ruth Senger (copy)[2]

7.[3] *A war correspondent reports*

Heavy convoys rumble over the bumpy cobbles of a Polish city, bearing munitions, food, and supplies of all kinds. Motorcycle troops speed by, men from the signal corps lay cables, orderlies hurry to receive orders. In the schoolhouse the army commander's staff are busy with the large map sketches. At this moment, a truck drives past the house, taking captured Polish soldiers to be interrogated. Filthy uniforms sagging on gaunt bodies, hollow cheeks, staring eyes.

Staff officers come and go. In the next street a medical squad moves into a house that is at least halfway clean. Steaming field kitchens are parked in the orchard. The hum of motors in the air. From the nearby airfield a line of reconnaissance planes ascends, pushes on towards the front. Barefoot Polish wenches and greasy caftan Jews shuffle along against the walls of the houses. A mass of ragged women and children in a courtyard. The NSV distributes food. The Field Police ensure order is maintained.

4 In the negotiations with the Intergovernmental Committee on Refugees, which had been established in 1938 at the Evian Conference, Wohlthat had agreed to the establishment of such a trust fund: see PMJ 2, p. 48, as well as PMJ 2/207 and 2/230.

5 The incumbent at the time was Fritz Reinhardt (1895–1969).

6 Count Johann Ludwig Schwerin von Krosigk: see Doc. 25, fn. 3.

1 'Diktatheft Nr. 1 (8. Jahrgang)', dictation dated 19 Sept. 1939, AdK, Berlin, Kempowski-Biographienarchiv, 4128. The dictations were typed up by the author's husband. This document has been translated from German.

2 Ruth Stephan, née Senger (1925–1992); attended school in Eichstätten (Kaiserstuhl); compulsory service year, 1940, then apprenticeship in an office of the Wuppertal city administration; employed at the registry office in Freiburg, 1943; later a secretary at the Birklehof private school, Hinterzarten; moved to Halle (Westphalia) and gave birth to a son in 1950.

3 The numbering was presumably added afterwards, during transcription.

DOC. 14

Jüdisches Nachrichtenblatt, 22 September 1939: the Jewish Culture League announces that the Film Theatre is to resume film screenings[1]

The Jewish Culture League in Germany[2]

The Film Theatre in Berlin will start screening films again on Sunday, 24 September 1939.[3] Because of the blackout, the screenings will begin at 3 p.m. and 5 p.m. (weekdays and Sundays). Arrangements have been made to ensure that the second screening will finish before 7 p.m. Because of the holidays, the screenings of the film *Das Ekel* will take place only on Sunday, 24 September, Monday, 25 September, and Tuesday, 26 September, at 3 p.m. and 5 p.m. On Sunday, 1 October, Monday, 2 October, and Tuesday, 3 October, the film *Renate im Quartett* will be shown.[4] The reopening of the Jewish Film Theatre means that the general public will once again have the opportunity to see outstanding films that offer both instruction and entertainment. Especially at a time like this, everyone will welcome the fact that the Jewish Culture League in Germany is giving the public a chance to escape for a while from the burdens of everyday life through the medium of art. Nothing is better suited to distract people from their cares and worries than artistic performances of the highest calibre. The Jewish Culture League in Germany has demonstrated a reliable and good taste in giving its public what it needs.

We have no doubt that when the Film Theatre of the Jewish Culture League in Germany reopens, it will draw audiences just as large as before. Tickets for both films go on sale from 10:30 a.m. on Friday, 22 September, at the film box office, 58/59 Kommandantenstr. (tel. 17 69 43). On weekdays tickets can also be purchased in advance from the following outlets: members' office, 57 Kommandantenstraße (tel. 17 31 16), Monday to Thursday, 9 a.m. to 6 p.m., and Friday, 9 a.m. to 4 p.m.; cashier's office at 18 Aschaffenburger Straße, Monday to Friday, 10 a.m. to 5 p.m.

1 'Jüdischer Kulturbund in Deutschland e.V.', *Jüdisches Nachrichtenblatt* (Berlin edition), 22 Sept. 1939, p. 1. This document has been translated from German. The newspaper was published twice weekly from Nov. 1939 to 1941 – duly censored by the Reich Ministry of Public Enlightenment and Propaganda – as the newsletter of the Reich Association of Jews in Germany.

2 The Jewish Culture League (Jüdischer Kulturbund) was founded in Berlin in June 1933 as the Culture League of German Jews (Kulturbund deutscher Juden). Under the direction of Dr Kurt Singer it created work opportunities for Jewish artists. It was the model for similar culture leagues in other towns and cities, which organized theatre and opera performances, concerts, film screenings, lectures, and exhibitions: see PMJ 1/71 and 1/84. The Gestapo dissolved the Culture League in Sept. 1941.

3 With the outbreak of war all events organized by the Culture League had initially been banned.

4 *The Scoundrel*, directed by Hans Deppe, and *Renate in the Quartet*, directed by Paul Verhoeven, were German feature films released in 1939.

DOC. 15

On 28 September 1939 Martin Striem from Berlin writes to his émigré son Rolf about being required to move into a 'Jew house'[1]

Handwritten letter from Martin Striem, formerly Max Ehrlich,[2] 190a Köpenicker Straße, Berlin SO 16, to Rolf Striem,[3] dated 28 September 1939

My dear boy,

Once again a week has passed without news from you. Hopefully you are in good health and have a satisfactory position, one that is also materially more lucrative and secures your livelihood. We, my dear boy, are in good enough health, but at the moment everything is in a terrible commotion. Yesterday and today the removal man was here and has now packed everything in boxes and crates, and on 3 October the move will take place; we wish that it were behind us already. We were only able to sell a few odds and ends, and we have far too many things for the cramped apartment, which in addition is disproportionately expensive, and on top of that there are the other tenants, to whom we must still become accustomed.[4] I hope that you enjoyed all the holidays, if you were at all in a position to celebrate them. Bernhard Baer preached on Yom Kippur, and the chairman [of the Jewish congregation] voiced his appreciation. I have something to tell you, my boy, that will surely sadden you: the radio is no longer in our possession and there is no prospect of getting it back again.[5] It had always offered us some diversion and variety in spite of everything; however, one must be resigned to all that happens. Naturally we have not had any news from San José, either, and we must remain patient until we are able to hold a letter from you in our hands again.[6] Apart from this there is nothing of importance to report, only that James Rothschild[7] has found work. Uncle

1 Jüdisches Museum Berlin, Sammlung Familie Korant Schwalbe Striem, 2006/57/873. This letter has been translated from German.

2 Martin Striem, born Amandus H. Striem (1871–1942), retailer; married to Gertrud Striem, née Dombrowsky (1883–1942); both were deported on 14 August 1942 to Theresienstadt and from there on 26 Sept. 1942 to Treblinka, where they were murdered. It is unclear why 'formerly Max Ehrlich' was added to the letterhead.

3 Rolf Striem (1907–1985), lawyer; employed at Berlin courts; dismissed on account of being a Jew, 1933; subsequently a sales representative; emigrated in 1939 via Paris to Bolivia, where he taught German and English; professor, 1951; spoke out against National Socialist movements in Bolivia; after death threats emigrated to the USA in 1961; taught German in Colorado and at the Michigan Technological University.

4 The Law on Tenancy Agreements with Jews (30 April 1939) reduced the protection of Jews from eviction and stipulated that 'a Jew must, when so required by the municipal authority, take in Jews as tenants or subtenants': *Reichsgesetzblatt*, 1939, I, pp. 864–865; see also PMJ 2/277. Many Jews were required to move into so-called Jew houses (*Judenhäuser*).

5 On 16 Sept. 1939 the Chief of the Security Police and the SD, Heydrich, reported in an express letter that Himmler, with the approval of Hitler, had ordered the Gestapo to confiscate radios, though without making a public announcement to this effect: IfZ-Archives, PS-2161.

6 Martin Striem's nephew Dr Herbert Schwalbe (1899–1963), dentist, had settled in San José, California, in 1939 with his family.

7 James Rothschild (b. 1909); deported to Auschwitz on 28 June 1943.

Bernhard is coming here on Saturday. I have spoken to him already on the telephone; he sends his greetings to you, as do all our acquaintances and relatives. May you remain in good health, with the warmest greetings and kisses from your loving father.[8]

DOC. 16

On 2 October 1939 the head of the local NSDAP branch, Emil Rothleitner, argues the case for deporting all Jews from Vienna[1]

Report by the head of the local NSDAP branch for Vienna-Alserbach (R/R), signed Rothleitner,[2] to Kreisleitung I in Vienna, Kreisleiter Berner[3] (received on 4 October 1939), dated 2 October 1939[4]

Subject: the problem of Jews and housing
I hereby present my report on the current status of the Jewish problem in the area controlled by the local NSDAP branch in Alserbach in particular, and in the Gau of Vienna in general, and submit the suggestions below for your consideration.

The local branch area comprises 5 cells with 2,313 households and 6,178 residents, who are distributed across the individual cells as follows:

	Households Aryan	Households Jewish	Households Total	% Jewish	Persons/[household] Aryan	Persons/[household] Jewish	Residents Aryan	Residents Jewish	Residents Total	% Jewish
01	306	89	395	23	2.6	2.7	785	240	1,025	23
02	447	84	531	16	2.7	3.5	1,227	290	1,517	19
03	378	72	450	17	2.7	2.7	1,040	194	1,134[5]	17
04	344	88	432	20	2.7	2.9	917	259	1,176	22
05	462	43	505	9	2.4	2.8	1,104	122	1,226	10
Branch	1,937	376	2,313	16	2.6	2.9	5,073	1,105	6,178	18
Branch	fall in the number of Jewish households since the revolution:[6] approx. 150.						Fall in the number of Jewish residents since the revolution: minimal.			

An analysis of the tables reveals the following:

1. The number of Jewish households has fallen considerably (by 30 per cent), but the number of Jewish residents has not significantly declined.

8 On the back of the letter is a handwritten letter from Rolf Striem's mother dated the same day, as well as greetings from Leo Dombrowsky, a relative.

1 YVA, O.30/88. Extracts published in Gerhard Botz, *Wohnungspolitik und Judendeportationen in Wien 1938 bis 1945: Zur Funktion des Nationalsozialismus als Ersatz nationalsozialistischer Sozialpolitik* (Vienna: Geyer, 1975), pp. 80–86. This document has been translated from German.

2 Emil Rothleitner (1909–1987), teacher; joined the NSDAP in 1933; head of the Vienna-Alserbach branch of the NSDAP from 1938; worked for the Asset Transfer Office in Vienna, 1939, and for the Price Setting Office in Linz, 1940; called up for military service, 1942; held in US military captivity, 1945–1947.

2. The average number of persons living in Jewish homes is not significantly higher than the number living in Aryan homes (2.9 as opposed to 2.6).
At first sight these two points appear contradictory, but in actual fact they are not. In March 1938 a Jewish household numbered approx. 2.0 persons, so that when 150 households were broken up, 300 persons had to be rehoused in the remaining 376 households, thereby causing the number of persons per household to increase from 2.0 to 2.9, giving a total again of around 300 persons. Jews moving in from other local branch areas in Vienna made up for the number of Jews who moved out of the area.

It is good news that 150 homes have become available for Aryans, but very bad news that the overall *number* of Jews has not fallen. Because this is the crux of the matter. Party comrades and the vast majority of our Volksgenossen desire nothing more fervently than to see the day when the last Jew has vanished from sight. They know very well what dangers lie in living in apartment buildings alongside Jews.

The Jews are the authors and disseminators of rumour and counter-propaganda. The foreign Jews continue to listen to enemy radio broadcasts, and in next to no time they are telling others what they have heard – greatly assisted in this by the telephone. The fact is that Jews are seldom prepared to give up their telephone, because it greatly facilitates contact with other Jews and with Aryans. The Jews make every possible effort to maintain their contacts with Aryans, which they manage to do by dint of various tricks – mainly by evoking sympathy (they are all 'sick' and 'suffering') and by disguising their attire (easily done) and their speech (dialect). The aim is to influence Aryans by means of disinformation and rumour, in order to undermine the morale of the German people. The danger should on no account be underestimated; the number of Volksgenossen who do not go out of their way to avoid consorting with Jews is still fairly large. This is how rumours suddenly appear and spread to large sections of the population.

A further danger is race defilement, which occurs continually as long as Jews are living in proximity to Aryans. It should also be pointed out that the number of Jewish prostitutes is constantly growing. For the rest, the pernicious effects of the Jewish presence within the German Volkskörper are so well known that I do not need to say any more.

It turns out that the number of Jews in Vienna has not fallen as far or as fast as we would wish. There were close to 250,000 Jews living in Vienna. Since the revolution, probably a third of these at most have moved away, which means that the majority are

3 Hans Berner (1901–1986), pharmacist, Protestant curate, and writer; joined the NSDAP in 1930; carried out extensive illegal propaganda activities during the period when the NSDAP was banned in Austria; NSDAP Gau superintendent for Vienna, 1938–1939; NSDAP Kreisleiter of the Vienna I district, 1939–1942; worked in the Party Chancellery from 1942; Reich office head, 1944; briefly interned by the Americans after the war; later worked as a writer in Germany.

4 The report was written on the official notepaper of the Vienna Gauleitung. This was one of several reports dating from Oct. 1939 in which heads of local NSDAP branches reported, at the request of their Kreisleitung, on the housing problems within their local branch area, and proposed solutions detrimental to local Jewish residents; extracts are published in Botz, *Wohnungspolitik*, pp. 79–88.

5 The numbers of residents in this line (1,040 Aryan and 194 Jewish) do not add up to the total given, which means the percentage is also incorrect.

6 The author means the National Socialist Anschluss of Austria in March 1938.

still here.[7] Emigration is now completely out of the question. Nevertheless, there is a widespread view among the population that the time is ripe for another decisive push to get the Jews out of Vienna, as it is thought that certain allowances that have hitherto had to be made will shortly be swept aside.

Suggestion I:
Consequently, many Party comrades and Volksgenossen have suggested that we should seize this favourable opportunity to take radical action and deport all the Viennese Jews to what is now the German part of former Poland. This would be both a radical solution and an ideal one for *Vienna.* In principle it is not impossible. At a rough estimate, there are now 2 million Jews living in the German part of Poland, so another 170,000 will make no difference; but it does make a difference if there are 170,000 Jews living in Vienna – all of them agents of Mr Churchill – or none at all. The claim that this would not be feasible for technical reasons would make no sense to the National Socialist-minded population of Vienna, given that many more than 170,000 *Germans* have recently been forced to flee from Czechoslovakia and Poland.[8] It must surely be possible – so the argument goes – to carry out an organized resettlement of such a large number of people. People are even thinking about how such an operation could work in practice. Some think the Jews should be dispersed across the former Polish towns and cities, while others think it would be better to concentrate them in certain areas, such as the territory between the Bug and the Vistula; but in both cases, those who are fit for work would have to be confined in camps. In any event, the view of many National Socialists is that *when* the right moment comes, the opportunity should not be passed up.[9]

Suggestion II:
If this radical solution proves impracticable, I suggest that we exhaust all available options for reducing the number of Jewish residents *and* households. Those options are:
(1) Facilitating emigration.
(2) Concentrating the younger, able-bodied elements in camps.
(3) Sending Jews who moved to Vienna from formerly Polish areas back to their municipalities of origin.
(4) Expelling Jews of foreign nationality wherever possible (Slovakia, Hungary, Romania, etc.).
(5) Housing Jews who are over 70 and frail in Jewish care homes – as many of them as the Israelite Religious Community can accommodate.
(6) Reorganizing the concentration of the remaining Jews in large Jewish apartments.

7 By the end of July 1939, 104,000 Jews had emigrated from Vienna. In Dec. 1939 the head of the Israelite Religious Community of Vienna, Josef Löwenherz, put the number of Jews still living in the city at 58,000: Josef Israel Löwenherz, *Vollständiger Bericht von Dr. Löwenherz über die Tätigkeit Eichmanns und Brunners in Wien–Prag–Berlin, 1938–1945*, compiled by Tuviah Friedman (Haifa: Institute of Documentation in Israel, 1995), p. 20. By this time some 1,600 Viennese Jews had already been deported to the region around Nisko on the River San: see fn. 9.

8 In 1938–1939 there were attacks on local German-speaking minorities in Czechoslovakia and Poland, in the wake of which many ethnic Germans (*Volksdeutsche*) fled these territories. Nazi propaganda exaggerated the attacks and used them to justify Germany's war policy.

9 In the autumn of 1939 over 5,000 Jews were deported from Vienna, Moravská Ostrava, and Katowice to the area around Nisko on the River San: see Introduction, p. 39; Docs. 19, 24, 38, and 264.

I would like to expand on this last point:

Two persons can easily be housed in an average living room, so that 8 or 9 persons living in a 4- or 4½-room apartment is not excessive. Within my own local branch area this would mean the following: if we assume that 30 per cent of my 1,100 Jews can be got rid of by the measures itemized under points 1–5 of Suggestion II, we will be left with 770 Jews in the local branch area. To house them, I would need 385 rooms, or in other words 128 3-room apartments or 96 4-room apartments, which is to say around 100 large apartments. I am quite sure I can find these 100 among the 376 Jewish-occupied apartments currently listed for the local branch area. Thus, at a single stroke I would not only free up 276 apartments, or 70 per cent of the total (most of them small apartments) for Aryans, which would be a considerable propaganda coup, but I would also be ensuring that many hundreds of Volksgenossen were no longer exposed to the pernicious influence of Jews.

This idea is not at all new, and the Vienna municipal housing office has already tried something similar.[10] Unfortunately, however, this has met with little success – otherwise the occupancy rate per apartment would not be as low as 2.9 Jews. The reason for this lack of success is, firstly, that the housing office is not able – and on occasion, perhaps, not willing – to cope with the volume of work that this project entails. And secondly, the necessary legal mechanisms are not in place, or only imperfectly so. What good is it, after all, if the housing office instructs the landlord to give his Jewish tenants notice to quit, and he does so (which counts as a success in itself), but the Jew is then free to take his eviction notice to court, appeal against it, and get an extension of six months or more from the judge? At the end of the six months he is often granted a further extension. And in many instances the landlord's action for eviction, brought on official instructions, is simply thrown out. Here is a case in point: the property manager of the apartment building at 2 Pasteurgasse, Vienna 9, a certain Dr Heinrich Höfflinger,[11] who resides at 19 Praterstrasse, Vienna 2, was instructed by the housing office to evict the Jew Taussig,[12] who occupies apartment no. 13 (3 rooms) on his own together with an Aryan housekeeper. The first time, the action for eviction was dismissed by the judge of the Josefstadt District Court, Dr Walter Unger,[13] on the grounds that the Jew had been served with the papers on the 4th of the month instead of the 3rd. In the case of the second eviction notice, served 'in a timely manner', the property manager had to apply during the hearing for a stay of proceedings in order to save costs, since the same judge declared at the hearing that he would not evict the Jew, as he was married to an Aryan woman, and the marriage had

10 In the spring of 1939 the Vienna housing office had collaborated with the Gestapo to start the compulsory resettlement of Jews, who had to move into 'collective' apartments and housing blocks within the city area. The Law on Tenancy Agreements with Jews of April 1939 provided the legal basis for this measure: *Reichsgesetzblatt*, 1939, I, pp. 864–865: see also PMJ *2/277*.

11 Dr Heinrich Höfflinger (1882–1963), officer, bank director, and landowner; served as commercial governor of the Equestrian Order of the Holy Sepulchre of Jerusalem, 1943–1949, and as regent, 1949–1951.

12 Correctly: Paul Thausig (1868–1942), stockbroker. In July 1941 he was forced to move to Schwarzspanierstraße, and he died in Jan. 1942 of natural causes. He was married to the Gentile Henriette Thausig, née L'Herbier (1864–1904), with whom he had a daughter.

13 Dr Walter Unger (1910–1968), lawyer; appointed to the Vienna Inner City District Court in 1937; assistant judge in the regional civil court, 1937–1938, and in Josefstadt District Court from 1938; served as district court judge in Mistelbach (Lower Austria) from 1940, then in Vienna; called up for military service in Dec. 1942.

produced a child who was not classed as a Jew. The judge cited paragraph 7 of the relevant law, which can only mean that Mischlinge, who are not classed as Jews, are to be protected *if they are living at the address to which the eviction notice applies*, which of course is not the case here. Paragraph 7 cannot be taken to mean that protection should be extended to a Jew who in our eyes is a race defiler.[14] Whether this was intentional or whether the judge simply failed to understand the law, I cannot say. But if he did act in accordance with the law, then the law needs to be amended or explained.

Similar complaints can be heard from any landlord who has taken his action for eviction to court on instructions from the authorities. As a consequence of this we should insist either that the law should be changed to deny Jews the right to appeal against an action for eviction initiated on instructions from the authorities, or that responsibility for enforcing the notice of eviction should be taken away from the courts and handed over to the police. I understand that suggestions along these lines are already under consideration.

To ensure that evictions of Jews and their rehousing are not carried out in an aimless and haphazard manner, however, we should seek the collaboration of those agencies that are most familiar with the problem, namely the local branches of the NSDAP. The idea is *not* that they would be *actively* involved in serving notice themselves, but *rather* that they would take charge of the *planning*, deciding which homes are to be vacated, and where the evicted Jews are to be rehoused. It would then be the responsibility of the police or the housing office to evict these Jewish tenants. At the same time, every local Party branch must have the right to make *binding* recommendations to the housing office for replacement tenants, nominating Volksgenossen in its area who are clearly living in substandard accommodation. It would not be necessary to carry out a survey for this purpose, since every cell leader already knows who has serious damp problems, and where there are children with rickets living in dank basements. Any abuse of this right, for which the head of the local Party branch would be personally responsible, would have to be severely punished (also a chance to get rid of bad apples). For the rest, the housing office would be free to allocate the majority of the vacated Jewish dwellings as it saw fit.

The fact that some of the apartments in Vienna formerly occupied by Jews have now been vacated – 30 per cent within my own local branch area, for example – is, of course, entirely due to the efforts of the NSDAP, even if the methods used were not the right ones and left a great deal to be desired.[15] But there is no good reason why the problem cannot be solved in a proper manner, without infringing current legal regulations, which will have to be put in place accordingly. I should also like to point out that one often hears people saying, 'when the Party had the homes, you could always get one'. I am aware that these suggestions will not end the housing shortage by themselves, and that they are far from perfect. I do, however, believe that they are calculated to significantly

14 The Law on Tenancy Agreements with Jews (30 April 1939) stripped the Jews of their legal rights as tenants. Paragraph 7 stated that the regulations did not apply if a Jewish tenant had children from a so-called mixed marriage and these children were not classed as Jews: *Reichsgesetzblatt*, 1939, I, pp. 864–865; see also PMJ 2/277.

15 Local NSDAP agencies, the Gestapo, and the housing office worked together to register 'Jew apartments' (*Judenwohnungen*) and evict the tenants. In practice this meant that tens of thousands of dwellings were 'unofficially Aryanized': landlords, Party members, SA men, or private individuals simply evicted Jewish tenants by force and without any legal grounds, and in many cases installed themselves as the new occupants.

alleviate the housing shortage within a short space of time. But for *now* the most important thing is speed: he who gives quickly gives twice.[16]

I have reported at some length here on the twin problems of the Jews and housing, which are directly linked, because the issue is of very great concern to me, as it is to all National Socialists.

Heil Hitler!

DOC. 17

On 4 October 1939 Gerdrut Günsburg from Apolda writes to the Foreign Exchange Office in Thuringia, asking it to lift the security order against her husband[1]

Letter (reference number I.I. 338 Bo/Ho) from Gerdrut Günsburg, née Halbauer,[2] Apolda, to the Regional Tax Director of Thuringia in Rudolfstadt (received on 5 October 1939),[3] dated 4 October 1939

You have issued my husband[4] with a security order.[5]

I would like to inform you of the following: my husband cannot set up a 'security account with restricted access' because he possesses no cash and also no material assets, save the clothes he wears. The existing savings bank accounts have nothing to do with my husband, nor do they run under his name, because the savings do not come from him. However, the savings bank accounts will be kept, and I and my children will, if necessary, pay for essentials from these savings.

I have already informed you about the sums held in the savings books belonging to my son Heinz,[6] my daughter Liesbeth,[7] and me. The 311.23 Reichsmarks belonging to

16 Latin proverb: 'Bis das, si cito das'.

1 ThHStA, Der Oberfinanzpräsident Thüringen Nr. 703, fols. 98–99. This document has been translated from German.

2 Gerdrut Günsburg, née Halbauer, officially registered as Beatrice Alice Gertrud Ginsburg (1890–1969), pattern cutter.

3 Dr Theodor Hillmer (1881–1961), lawyer; Regierungsassessor, 1906; district head in Rüstringen from 1914 and in Jever from 1919; president of Oldenburg regional tax office, 1922–1933, and president of Schleswig-Holstein regional tax office from 1933; joined the NSDAP in 1933; regional tax director of Thuringia and Central Germany, 1936–1945.

4 Salomon Günsburg, also Ginsburg (b. 1891), master tailor; after the November pogroms of 1938 imprisoned in Buchenwald; released one year later at the request of the Günther company in Apolda in order to work in the tailor's workshop there; deported to Auschwitz in May 1944; declared dead in 1950.

5 The regulations governing security orders (*Sicherungsanordnungen*), which were introduced in 1936 to access the capital of Jewish emigrants, were tightened with the Law on Foreign Exchange Control (12 Dec. 1938). Jewish taxpayers subsequently had to transfer their capital to security accounts at banks licensed to deal in foreign exchange, and required authorization to access it: *Reichsgesetzblatt*, 1938, I, pp. 1734–1890, esp. p. 1742. On 28 Sept. 1939 Salomon Ginsburg was instructed via security order to set up a security account within five days, from which he could withdraw RM 250 a month without requiring permission: ThHStA, Der Oberfinanzpräsident Thüringen Nr. 703, fols. 95–96v.

6 Heinz Friedrich Günsburg, also Ginsburg (1920–2000), police officer; undertook forced labour from 1941 for the Buna Works in Schkopau and in the Dreiwegelager, a camp in Weißenfels, from 1944; escaped during an air raid; member of the German People's Police (Deutsche Volkspolizei), 1945–1950; security officer at the Apolda knitwear and hosiery company from 1951, and after that clerk for the city council: tax collector at the district church office in Jena, 1964–1981.

7 Liesbeth Günsburg, also Ginsburg (1923–2002).

my daughter Liesbeth come from confirmation presents and, in addition, savings from wages. The 423 Reichsmarks belonging to my son Heinz have been saved from wages. He had already saved 120 Reichsmarks of this prior to his confirmation. My savings of around 900 Reichsmarks have been saved out of my own wages by going without. For as long as I have been married I have gone to work in the factory. My husband has no right to these savings; I have earned them entirely alone.

We have no debts at the moment.

In 1938, my husband earned as a self-employed tailor	RM	298.50
then as an outworker for the Günther company	RM	778.54
total for 1938	RM	1,077.04
In 1938 I myself earned	RM	1,011.34

I ask you to inform me whether, under these circumstances, the security order is unfounded. I am a German Aryan woman of old German stock. I have incurred no guilt on account of my marriage; when I married, there were no race laws and no race war.

Heil Hitler![8]

DOC. 18

With his Decree for the Strengthening of Germandom, issued on 7 October 1939, Adolf Hitler places Heinrich Himmler in charge of the racial policy plans for settlement on German-ruled territory[1]

Decree for the Strengthening of Germandom, issued by the Führer and Reichskanzler.
7 October 1939

The consequences of Versailles in Europe have been eliminated. The Greater German Reich is now able to take in and to settle on its territory German people who until now have had to live in foreign lands, and to organize the settlement of racial groups within its sphere of interests so as to achieve better dividing lines between them. I commission the Reichsführer SS[2] to carry out this task according to the following stipulations:

8 In response to this letter, the Foreign Exchange Office in Thuringia lifted the security order against Salomon Günsburg on 13 Oct. 1939: ThHStA, Der Oberfinanzpräsident Thüringen Nr. 703, fol. 100r–v.

1 BArch R 186/2, fols. 447–448. Published in Herbert Michaelis and Ernst Schraepler (eds.), *Ursachen und Folgen: Vom deutschen Zusammenbruch 1918 und 1945 bis zur staatlichen Neuordnung Deutschlands in der Gegenwart*, vol. 14: *Das Dritte Reich: Der Angriff auf Polen. Die Ereignisse im Winter 1939–1940* (Berlin: Wendler, 1969), pp. 85–86. An English translation is available in Robert Lewis Koehl, *RKFDV: German Resettlement and Population Policy, 1935–1945. A History of the Reich Commission for the Strengthening of Germandom* (Cambridge: Harvard University Press, 1957), pp. 247–249. This document has been newly translated from the original German.

2 Heinrich Himmler.

I

According to my instructions, the Reichsführer SS will be asked:

(1) to repatriate Reich and ethnic Germans living abroad who are eligible for returning home to the Reich permanently,
(2) to eliminate the damaging influence of such racially alien parts of the population that pose a danger to the Reich and to the Volksgemeinschaft,
(3) to create new German settlement regions through relocation, in particular through the settlement of Reich and ethnic Germans returning home from abroad.[3]

The Reichsführer SS is authorized to issue all general directives and executive measures necessary to carry out these duties. In order to fulfil the tasks appointed to him in paragraph 1 no. 2, the Reichsführer SS may assign eligible parts of the population to particular residential areas.

II

In the occupied former Polish territories, the chief of the Upper East administration[4] will carry out the tasks appointed to the Reichsführer SS in accordance with the latter's general directives. Their implementation will be the responsibility of the Upper East chief of administration and the subordinate administrative chiefs of the military districts. Measures are to be adapted to the needs of the military leadership. Persons issued with special instructions for carrying out these tasks will not be subject to Wehrmacht jurisdiction in this respect.

III

Insofar as the creation of a new German farming class is concerned, the tasks delegated to the Reichsführer SS are to be carried out by the Reich Minister of Food and Agriculture,[5] in accordance with the Reichsführer SS's general directives. In all other respects the Reichsführer SS will make use of the existing Reich, state, and local authorities and institutions, as well as other public bodies and housing associations, to fulfil his task within the territory of the German Reich. In cases where an agreement between the Reichsführer SS and the highest Reich authority in charge (in theatres of operations, the Commander-in-Chief of the Army)[6] is required by law and administrative practice but

3 German-speaking minorities from abroad were resettled in German-occupied western Poland in order to permanently 'Germanize' the region.

4 The term 'Upper East' (*Ober-Ost*), which had been introduced during the First World War, denoted the territory under military administration supervised by the Commander-in-Chief of the German Armed Forces in the East. The head of the administration at the time was Hans Frank (1900–1946), who acted as governor general of occupied Poland from 26 Oct. 1939. The commander-in-chief East was Johannes Albrecht Blaskowitz (1883–1948).

5 Richard Walther Darré (1895–1953), agronomist; joined the NSDAP in 1930 and the SS in 1931; member of the Reichstag, 1932–1945; chief of the SS Race and Settlement Main Office, 1932–1938; Reich minister of food and agriculture and Reich farmers' leader from 1933; SS-Obergruppenführer, 1934; suspended from all posts in 1942; interned by the US in 1945; sentenced to seven years' imprisonment at the Nuremberg Military Tribunals in 1949; released in 1950.

6 Walther von Brauchitsch (1881–1948), professional soldier; general staff officer, 1914–1918; transferred to the Reichswehr, 1921; brigadier, 1932; commander-in-chief of the army, Feb 1938–Dec 1941; military commander in France, 30 June–25 Oct 1940; promoted to field marshal on 19 July 1940; died in British captivity.

no such agreement can be reached, a decision must be obtained from me through the Reich Minister and Head of the Reich Chancellery.[7]

IV

Negotiations with foreign government agencies and authorities as well as with ethnic Germans, so long as they are still abroad, are to be conducted in agreement with the Reich Minister of Foreign Affairs.[8]

V

Insofar as land is needed within the territory of the Reich for the settlement of returning Reich or ethnic Germans, the acquisition of the required land will be regulated by the Law on Land Procurement for the Purposes of the Wehrmacht, 29 March 1935 (*Reichsgesetzblatt*, I, p. 467) and the provisions for implementation issued in connection with it.[9] The responsibilities of the Reich Office for Land Procurement will be taken over by the agency designated by the Reichsführer SS.

VI

The funds necessary for the implementation of these measures will be made available to the Reichsführer SS by the Reich Minister of Finance.[10]

Berlin, 7 October 1939

The Führer and Reich Chancellor
signed Adolf Hitler
The Chairman of the Ministerial Council for the Defence of the Reich
signed Göring
Field Marshal
The Reich Minister and Head of the Reich Chancellery
signed Dr Lammers
The Chief of the Wehrmacht High Command
signed Keitel[11]

7 Dr Hans Heinrich Lammers (1879–1962), judge, legal scholar, and politician; judge at a regional court from 1912, at the Reich Ministry of the Interior from 1920; member of the Stahlhelm, 1923–1933; joined the NSDAP in 1932 and the SS in 1933; head of the Reich Chancellery, 1933–1944, with the rank of Reich Minister from 1937; sentenced to twenty years in prison at the Nuremberg Military Tribunals in 1949; sentence reduced to ten years in 1951; released in Dec. 1951.

8 Joachim von Ribbentrop.

9 This law allowed the Reich Ministry of War and the Wehrmacht High Command (OKW) to expropriate land in exchange for 'fair compensation' in consultation with the Reich Ministry of Food and Agriculture; see also the first and second provisions for the implementation of and addition to the Law on Land Procurement for the Purposes of the Wehrmacht, 21 August 1935, *Reichsgesetzblatt*, 1935, I, pp. 1097–1102, and 13 Feb. 1937, *Reichsgesetzblatt*, I, pp. 253–255.

10 Count Johann Ludwig Schwerin von Krosigk.

11 Wilhelm Keitel (1882–1946), military officer; served in the military from 1901; head of the Army Organization Department at the Troop Office (Truppenamt), 1925–1927 and 1929–1933: head of the Wehrmcht Office in the Reich Ministry of War, 1935–1938; promoted to the rank of full general in 1937; chief of the Wehrmacht High Command (OKW) and Hitler's closest military advisor, 1938–1945; joined the NSDAP in 1939; promoted to the rank of field marshal in 1940; sentenced to death by the International Military Tribunal at Nuremberg and executed in 1946.

DOC. 19

On 9 October 1939 Adolf Eichmann's deputy secures the assistance of the Wehrmacht and the civil administration for the planned deportation of Jews from Kattowitz[1]

Notes by Rolf Günther,[2] Mährisch-Ostrau, dated 28 October 1939

Re: meeting with Major General von *Knobelsdorf*[3] and the head of the civil administration, President *Fitzner*,[4] in Kattowitz on Monday, 9 October 1939.

I. *Notes:*

On Monday, 9 October 1939, SS-Hauptsturmführer *Eichmann*[5] and SS-Hauptsturmführer *Günther* had an audience in Kattowitz with Brigadier von *Knobelsdorf*, Border Section Command III, in order to conduct negotiations about the removal of Jews from Kattowitz and the surrounding region. SS-Hauptsturmführer Eichmann briefed Major General von Knobelsdorf in detail about his assignment and requested assistance from the military authorities, which the brigadier pledged unequivocally in every respect for

1 NAP, 101-653-1. Published as facsimile in Gedenk- und Bildungsstätte Haus der Wannsee-Konferenz, *Die Wannsee-Konferenz und der Völkermord an den europäischen Juden: Katalog der ständigen Ausstellung* (Berlin: Gedenk- und Bildungsstätte Haus der Wannsee-Konferenz, 2006), p. 75. An abridged translation is published in House of the Wannsee Conference, *The Wannsee Conference and the Genocide of European Jews: Catalogue of the Permanent Exhibition*, trans. Caroline Pearce (Berlin: House of the Wannsee Conference, 2009), p. 141.This document has been translated from German.

2 Rolf Günther (1913–1945?), commercial employee; member of the SA, 1929–1937; joined the NSDAP in 1931, and the SS in 1937; employed by the Erfurt Gestapo from 1935; worked at the Central Office for Jewish Emigration in Vienna after 1938; Eichmann's deputy at the Reich Security Main Office; worked at the Central Office for the Settlement of the Jewish Question in Bohemia and Moravia, 1943–1944; at the RSHA, Section IV B 4 (Jewish affairs and evacuation affairs), 1944; presumed to have committed suicide.

3 Correctly: Otto von Knobelsdorff (1886–1966), professional soldier; joined the military in 1906; became a major in 1929, brigadier in 1939, and major general in 1940; commander of the 19th Infantry/Panzer Division in France and the Soviet Union, 1940–1942; general of Panzer forces, 1942; commander-in-chief of the First Army, 1944; prisoner of war in US captivity, 1945–1947.

4 Otto Fitzner (1888–1945?), mine director; member of a Freikorps (paramilitary group), 1919–1920; technical director of the Georg v. Giesches Erben zinc company, Breslau, after 1925; joined the NSDAP and the SA in 1931; head of the Silesia Chamber of Commerce and president of the Chamber of Industry and Commerce in Breslau in 1935; chief of the civil administration in Border Section Command 3 in Katowice from Sept. 1939; war economy leader (*Wehrwirtschaftsführer*); Gau economic advisor in Lower Silesia from 1941.

5 Adolf Eichmann (1906–1962); began his career as a sales representative; joined the NSDAP and the SS in 1932; worked at the SD Main Office, 1934–1938; after summer 1938 managed the activities of the Central Office for Jewish Emigration, first in Vienna and from March 1939 also in Prague; after Dec. 1939, special expert at the RSHA on the evacuation of the annexed Eastern territories; then head of Section IV D 4 (evacuation affairs and Reich Central Agency for Jewish Emigration); by March 1941, head of IV B 4 (Jewish affairs and evacuation affairs); attended the Wannsee Conference in 1942; imprisoned in 1945; escaped in 1946; in hiding in Argentina, 1950–1960; in 1960 abducted to Israel, where he was condemned to death in 1961 and executed.

the area under his command. Brigadier von Knobelsdorf appointed Captain Count *Bückler-Burksdorf*,[6] who was also present at the meeting, as his deputy.

During the meeting the head of the civil administration, President *Fitzner*, arrived in the brigadier's office; it was thus possible to brief him regarding the planned transport of the Jews as well. President Fitzner also declared his readiness to assist with the preparations and the implementation of the transport in every way.

SS-Hauptsturmführer Eichmann reported that for the time being two transports from Mährisch-Ostrau and from Kattowitz are planned. After their completion a report must be submitted via the Chief of the Security Police for the Reichsführer SS and Chief of the German Police. This will probably be passed on to the Führer. We must then wait until the order is given for a general evacuation of the Jews.

For the time being the Führer has ordered the transfer of 300,000 Jews without means from the Old Reich and the Ostmark.[7]

At the end of the meeting both Major General von Knobelsdorf and the head of the civil administration asked to be kept informed about developments.[8]

DOC. 20

On 12 October 1939 the Cologne Gestapo announces that Jews are to be immediately arrested if they disobey ordinances[1]

Letter from the Gestapo, State Police office in Cologne (II B 3585/39), signed by Isselhorst,[2] to the Landräte of the district, dated 12 October 1939 (copy)[3]

Re: sanctions against Jews.
Case file: none.

From numerous reports it is evident that the Jews are not exercising the restraint that is required when they appear in public and on multiple occasions also disregard or attempt

6 Probably: Count Carl Friedrich von Pückler-Burghauss (1886–1945), officer and farmer; member of the German National People's Party (DNVP), 1919–1931; joined the NSDAP and the SA in 1931; member of the Reichstag, 1933; farmer, 1934–1937; office head in the Supreme SA Command, 1937–1939; transferred to the Wehrmacht, 1939; joined the SS in 1940; deputy of the Higher SS and Police Leader (HSSPF) for Central Russia, 1941–1942; commander of the Waffen SS in Bohemia and Moravia, 1942–1943; major general in the Waffen SS, 1944; military commander in Bohemia-Moravia, 1945; committed suicide.

7 This could not be verified.

8 At the end of the document: 'II. *Z.d.A.: II/1-7[1], II/1-8*'; countersigned twice.

1 LAV NRW R, 18/3, fol. 332. This document has been translated from German.

2 Dr Erich Isselhorst (1906–1948), lawyer; joined the NSDAP in 1932 and the SS in 1934; head of the State Police office in Erfurt, 1935–1936, in Cologne, 1936–1939, and in Munich, 1939–1942; after Feb. 1942 on the staff of Einsatzgruppe B (EG B), where he led Einsatzkommando 8 (EK 8) from Sept. to Nov. 1942, and EK 1 of EG A until June 1943; commander of the Security Police in White Ruthenia from June to Oct. 1943; senior commander of the Security Police in Straßburg, 1944; sentenced to death by a French military tribunal and executed.

3 The Landrat of the Oberbergisch district forwarded the copy for the attention of the district mayor on 16 Oct. 1939 (d. Nr. L.I. 610/39, signed p.p. Frank, received by the office of Lieberhaus on 17 Oct. 1939).

to contravene existing ordinances. It goes without saying that such behaviour on the part of the Jews can by no means be tolerated. The RFSS[4] has issued the mandate that Jews and Jewesses who violate any ordinance or otherwise engage in behaviour harmful to the state are to be arrested without exception.

I will have the apprehended Jews taken into protective custody. The proceedings of the arrest along with the transcripts of the interrogation are to be submitted to me in duplicate without delay.

DOC. 21
In October 1939 Rica Neuburger takes her own life as a result of the harassment of Jews[1]

Report (unsigned) on the suicide of Rica Neuburger,[2] dated 13 October 1939[3]

Mrs Rica *Neuburger*, 72 years old, had for some time been suffering from a heart condition.

She lived with her sister[4] at 161 Zeppelinstr. The housing issue[5] caused her great concern and anxiety.

She was afraid of being unable to find suitable accommodation and reportedly often said, 'I won't let myself be pushed around like this.'

The confiscation of her radio set on the highest Jewish holiday[6] upset her deeply.

She had to take to her bed for the last four weeks. Because as an invalid she could barely care for herself, her sister almost never left her alone at home.

On the first day when her condition began to improve and when, with the support of a stick, she could walk a few steps alone, she urged her sister to go and make some purchases in town.

When her sister came home at around 6 p.m. and found the invalid neither on the sofa nor in bed, she opened the kitchen door. The invalid was sitting there on a chair, her head bent over the gas stove. The gas valve was open. A doctor was called immediately but could only pronounce her dead.

A note was found pinned to her dress. It read as follows:

> The housing issue and all that they are doing to us and forcing on us is too cruel and difficult and I can't survive it. Dear Rosa, thank you for caring for me, farewell with all my love. It's better there than it is here. I can no longer bear the way they are oppressing us. Please forgive me for taking this step!
> Rica

4 Reichsführer SS, Heinrich Himmler.

1 Archives of the Leo Baeck Institute, New York, at the Jüdisches Museum Berlin, Karl Adler Collection, MF 572, reel 2, box 3, folder 1. This document has been translated from German.
2 Probably Rica Neuburger, née Metzger (1867–1939).
3 The author of the report is not evident from the original.
4 Probably Rosa Adler, née Metzger (b. 1874); deported to Theresienstadt on 22 August 1942 and from there on 29 Sept. 1942 to Treblinka, where she was declared dead.
5 Following the Law on Tenancy Agreements with Jews (30 April 1939), many Jews were forced to leave their apartments: see Doc. 15, fn. 4.
6 Radio sets had to be handed in on Yom Kippur, which in 1939 fell on 23 Sept.: see also Doc. 15, fn. 5.

DOC. 22
On 13 October 1939 Friedrich Kellner fulminates against wars started in breach of international law and the disenfranchisement of the Jews[1]

Handwritten diary of Friedrich Kellner,[2] Laubach, entry for 13 October 1939

Human beings are very peculiar creatures indeed. Now that the war is under way and people are talking among themselves about war and peace, not a single supporter of the war is to be found. But when it's peacetime, warmongers are ten a penny. The statesmen say: the nations long for peace and the nations don't want war. Who the devil is waging the war, in that case? It must be possible to ascertain. Has it been started by a single ruler? That's certainly not the case. If I'm planning to do something unusual, for example go on a long trip, then I will always talk first to people who have the necessary experience in the field. It's the same with 'war'. The specialists are the officers. In a stricter sense, the general staff. That's where the people with influence are. That's where the plans are hatched. And it's from there that an irresponsible, war-hungry tyrant can be steered and guided, for better or for worse.

It is by no means necessary that every lover of peace attack the general staff and kick it out, on the assumption that doing away with it will bring peace for all time. For the purposes of defence against a mad assailant there has to be an institution that occupies itself with things to do with the military, should the need arise.

The way out of the confusion points urgently to two issues: *attack* and *defence*. Can a single country or nation decide what is attack and what is defence? No! Because the arts of inversion turn attack into defence and vice versa. In a legal conflict, each party considers itself to be in the right.

It's not the party that decides, but the judge. What determines individual life must also go for a nation. So-called 'honour' and 'national sentiment' must get used to submitting to the world order. That's the crux of the matter.

If the world as a whole doesn't want to go off the rails, then the troublemaker or troublemakers must be put before an international court, come what may. This court must examine the reasons that cause the country in question to attempt, through violence, to bring about a change in existing relations. If the examination concludes that everything arose solely from an attempt to conquer, or from a morbid desire for notoriety, then all nations will turn against this new troublemaker. All nations are duty-bound, according to their size, to provide assistance. Militarily, economically, and financially.

It cannot be permitted that one nation (for example the Japanese) claims the right to deal with its boundless population growth simply by attacking another nation (the Chi-

1 The original is privately owned; copy in Archiv der Arbeitsstelle Holocaustliteratur an der Justus-Liebig-Universität Gießen. Published in Friedrich Kellner, *'Vernebelt, verdunkelt sind alle Hirne': Tagebücher 1939–1945*, ed. Sascha Feuchert, Robert Martin Scott Kellner, Erwin Leibfried et al. (Göttingen: Wallstein, 2011), pp. 36–38. This document has been translated from German.

2 Friedrich Kellner (1885–1970), judicial inspector; member of the Social Democratic Party of Germany (SPD) since the 1920s; acting judicial inspector at Laubach local court, 1933–1948; temporarily SPD chairman in Laubach after 1945; council official of the town of Laubach, 1945–1946; employed at Gießen District Court, 1948–1950; deputy mayor of Laubach, 1956–1960.

nese), and then to rule over this nation or get rid of it for its own benefit.[3] Such selfishness is impossible.

These Japanese first of all have to impose limitations upon themselves. Reason and good sense cannot be allowed to assist rampant expansion. It is up to Japan to find the ways and means as far as this is concerned. At any rate, nature has given them an island to live on. A change to this situation can be achieved only through *peaceful* routes in association with *assenting* nations. There is absolutely no place for violence. After all, I can't violently 'conquer' an apartment in some other house I don't know. The contractual consent of the owner or proprietor is the first condition for the use of the apartment. Especially if it is important to me to stay in the rooms for longer than one day. This goes without saying for every cultured person. But why are the simplest of legal concepts contravened by the sum of such people, who then refer to themselves as a 'nation'? Because they feel stronger as a mass, at any rate. Hence the theory: violence precedes law.

However, civilization and the progress of mankind depend upon respect for the law. This is so important that it should be hammered into people's heads like a daily prayer. Each Volksgemeinschaft, the state, must lead by example. *It must inviolably guarantee the basic rights of its citizens.* This ought to be sacred and eternal law!!!

How do things stand in Germany today (1939) on these points? Miserably! A people without a constitution! A nation of slaves! Serfs without rights!! When will Germany rise up?? Out of the darkness and into the light of a better future?

I don't yet dare to imagine how things will turn out. Too many problems have been tackled in the past six years. However, not one of them has been solved. Attempts to deal with the Jewish question were brutally rigorous and one-sided. But as to where the Jews are supposed to live, the Nazis haven't given that any thought. They generously leave that to other countries. The Jew is plundered without the least respect for the law, and then allowed to leave. Not even the Gypsies have received such treatment. At least they were assigned fixed places to live.[4] No objections can be raised to this when it comes to maintaining order in the state. But when the Jews, who in economic life have proved for centuries to have contributed to the development of society as a whole, are denied their rights, then that is a deed unworthy of a cultured nation. The curse of this evil deed will forever rest upon the whole German nation. The perpetrators (the National Socialists) will one day have disappeared, but their deeds will live on.

3 In 1931 Japanese troops began to occupy Chinese territory, eventually triggering the Second Sino-Japanese War in July 1937. The following winter they carried out a massacre in what was then the Chinese capital, Nanjing, killing tens of thousands of people. In Germany the events became known via the German retailer John Rabe, who returned from Nanjing in the spring of 1938.

4 From 1936 onwards, internment camps were set up in several German cities for members of the Sinti and Roma ethnic groups, who were classified as an 'alien race' (*fremdrassig*). The camps enabled them to be registered and isolated. From 17 Oct. 1939 Sinti and Roma were no longer permitted to leave their place of abode: see Doc. 23.

DOC. 23
On 16 October 1939 Adolf Eichmann informs Criminal Police Chief Arthur Nebe that carriages containing 'Gypsies' can be coupled to the deportation trains travelling to Poland[1]

Telex from the SD District Danube (no. 7743), signed SS-Hauptsturmführer Eichmann, to the Gestapo branch office in Mährisch-Ostrau, for the attention of SS-Hauptsturmführer Günter,[2] Mährisch-Ostrau, dated 16 October 1939[3]

With reference to the telex message[4] sent to you from the [office of the] Head of the Security Police, [by] SS-Oberführer Nebe,[5] it is requested that the following answer be sent by telex to SS-Oberführer Nebe.

Concerning the deportation of gypsies, it is announced that the first transport of Jews will leave from Vienna on Friday, 20 October 1939. Three or four carriages of Gypsies can be coupled to this transport.

Transports will now be departing at regular intervals, provisionally from Vienna for the Ostmark, from Mährisch-Ostrau for the Protectorate, and from Kattowitz for the former Polish territories.[6] Concerning the onward transportation of Gypsies, I suggest that officials at the Criminal Police head offices in Vienna contact, for Vienna, SS-Obersturmführer Günther,[7] 22 Prinz-Eugenstraße, Wien 4, and for Mährisch-Ostrau and Kattowitz, SS-Hauptsturmführer Günther[8] at the Gestapo branch office, so that detailed measures can be taken by the authorities that have been tasked by me.

As already stated, the simplest method is to couple several carriages of Gypsies to each transport. Since these transports depart more or less according to schedule, no

1 NAP, 101-653-1, fol. 96r–v. This document has been translated from German.
2 This refers to Rolf Günther.
3 The telex was printed on paper with the letterhead of the Gestapo, State Police Office Brünn. The original contains handwritten annotations, an official stamp, and, at the end, the following note: 'To the Chief of the Security Police, Reich Criminal Police Office, for the attention of SS-Oberführer Nebe. Re: transportation of the Gypsies.'
4 On 13 Oct. 1939 the SD Main Office had forwarded to Eichmann via telex a telephone enquiry from Nebe from the previous day about 'when he can send the Berlin Gypsies'. Nebe was worried that the city would have to build camps for them if the deportation was delayed: telex from the SD Main Office, signed SS-Hauptsturmführer Braune, to the State Police branch office in Moravská Ostrava, NAP, 101-653-1, fol. 87.
5 Arthur Nebe (1894–1945), police officer; worked for the police from 1920; joined the NSDAP and the SA in 1931; chief of the Prussian Regional Police Office and deputy chief of the Office of the Criminal Police Office in the Security Police Main Office in 1935, and chief of the latter from 1936; joined the SS in 1936; chief of the Reich Criminal Police Office, 1937–1944; in Office V of the Reich Security Main Office from 1939; chief of Einsatzgruppe B in 1941; executed in March 1945 because of connections to the conspirators behind the plot to assassinate Hitler on 20 July 1944.
6 See Docs. 19, 24, and Introduction, p. 39.
7 Hans Günther (1910–1945?), accountant; member of the SA, 1928–1937; joined the NSDAP in 1929; worked for the Erfurt Gestapo, 1935–1937; joined the SS in 1937; worked at the Central Office for Jewish Emigration in Vienna, 1938–1939; head of the Central Office for Jewish Emigration in Prague from 1939 (renamed Central Office for the Settlement of the Jewish Question in Bohemia and Moravia in 1942); thought to have had the idea for the propaganda film about Theresienstadt (1944–1945).
8 Rolf Günther.

complications are expected in carrying this out. As regards the matter of the Old Reich, be informed that this will not be addressed for another three or four weeks.[9]

The duplicate of this telex is to be presented when I travel through Mährisch-Ostrau on 17 October 1939.

DOC. 24

On 16 October 1939 details of the deportation of Viennese Jews to Poland are discussed at the Central Office for Jewish Emigration in Vienna[1]

Memorandum from the Head of the Central Office for Jewish Emigration,[2] signed Brunner,[3] Vienna, to SS-Hauptsturmführer Eichmann, Mährisch Ostrau, SS-Obersturmbannführer Vollheim,[4] IV, 16 Theresianumgasse, SS-Sturmbannführer Polte,[5] IV, 16 Theresianumgasse, dated 17 October 1939

Re: discussion between SS-Hauptsturmführer Eichmann, Dr Ebner[6] from the Gestapo office, Vienna, and Dr Becker[7] of the staff of the Reich Commissioner.

On 16 October 1939 a discussion took place at the Central Office between the aforementioned individuals, during which Dr Becker from the Gauleitung explained to

9 Apart from the deportations from Pomerania in Feb. 1940 (see Docs. 52 and 53) there were no transports from the Old Reich to occupied Poland until autumn 1941: see Introduction, p. 41.

1 NAP, 101-653-1a. Published in Dokumentationsarchiv des österreichischen Widerstandes, *Widerstand und Verfolgung in Wien 1934–1945: Eine Dokumentation*, vol. 3: *1938–1945* (Vienna: Österreichischer Bundesverlag, 1984), pp. 284–285. This document has been translated from German.

2 The Central Office for Jewish Emigration (Zentralstelle für jüdische Auswanderung) was founded in Vienna on 20 August 1938.

3 Alois Brunner (1912–c.2010); retailer; joined the NSDAP and the SA in 1931; joined the SS in 1938; worked as a salesman and decorator until 1938; worked at the SS Security Service (SD) and the Central Office for Jewish Emigration in Vienna from 1938; head of the latter from 1941; organized the deportation of Jews from Austria in 1939 and 1941–1942, from Berlin in 1942–1943, from Greece in 1943, from France in 1943–1944, and from Slovakia in 1944; lived under a false name near Essen from 1947 to 1954; sentenced to death in absentia in Paris in 1954; fled to Syria.

4 Friedrich Vollheim (b. 1907), navy officer; worked for the Reich navy, 1925–1933; joined the SA in 1933 and the SS in 1935; worked at the SD Main District Rhine in 1935, then at the SD Main Office from 1936; joined the NSDAP in 1937; worked at the SD Main District Danube, Vienna, from 1938; appointed SS-Obersturmbannführer in 1939; worked at the Reich Security Main Office (RSHA), Office VI, from 1941.

5 Friedrich Polte (1911–1946), historian; joined the SA in 1932 and the SS in 1933; worked at the SD from 1934; joined the NSDAP in 1936; head of Section II 211 (scholarly affairs) at the SD Main Office in 1936; worked from 1938 at the SD Main District in Vienna, which he led from 1939 to 1941; head of the SD Main District in Berlin from 1941 to 1945; appointed SS-Obersturmbannführer in 1942; sentenced to death and executed in Yugoslavia in 1946.

6 Dr Karl Ebner (1901–1983), lawyer; from 1929 worked for the Austrian Federal Police; joined the NSDAP in 1936 and the SS in 1937; from 1938 worked for the Gestapo in Vienna; from 1939, head of the 'section for Jewish affairs'; played a major role in the deportation of Viennese Jews; in 1942, Oberregierungsrat and deputy head of the Gestapo; in British internment after 1945; sentenced to twenty years' imprisonment by the Vienna People's Court; released in 1953; from 1955 to 1968 housing administrator in Vienna.

7 Dr Eugen Becker (1897–1969), lawyer and economist, joined the NSDAP in 1933; head of the Economic Office of the City of Vienna, 1939–1940; deputy leader of the Reconstruction Office in the Gau Westmark, 1940–1945; city commissioner of Metz, 1941–1942; senior civil servant, 1943; in French internment, 1945–1948; after that, economics editor of various newspapers and managing director of the Regional Association of Saar Retailers.

SS-Hauptsturmführer Eichmann that the latter has personally received from Gauleiter Bürckel complete authorization for the resettlement operation to Poland and that Eichmann has even requested that the resettlement from Vienna be accelerated. Dr Becker explained that for the benefit of resettlement he will remove all bureaucratic and other hurdles (putting together trains, appointment of a team of urban police to accompany the transport, procurement of foodstuffs, registration of Jews, and assignment of housing office assistants) directly via Gauleiter Bürckel.

Dr Becker also said that he had already reported to Gauleiter Bürckel about the meeting on 7 October 1939[8] and that the Gauleiter is more than happy that the planned relocation of the Jews into barracks need not take place, since the costs for the construction of the barracks alone would have amounted to 500 Reichsmarks per head. Dr Becker will also, if possible, arrange to report to Gauleiter Bürckel on the morning of 17 October 1939. If not, SS-Obersturmführer Günther liaises between the Gauleitung and the Central Office for Jewish Emigration, and in the event of any difficulties can always contact Dr Becker.

Dr Becker requested the dispatch of a register for each transportation of Jews relocating to Poland, in order to be able to manage the housing appropriately and to prevent the possibility of disorderly Aryanizations. Dr Becker also said that the entire real estate of the Viennese Jews was to be handed over to a trust company that transfers the corresponding payments to the Central Office for Jewish Emigration, also in order to avoid the rushed Aryanization of Jewish homes. Dr Becker also agreed to immediately exclude the state commissioner[9] for the General Foundation for Jewish Welfare in Vienna,[10] so that there will on no account be any delays in the resettlement.[11]

Dr Ebner of the Gestapo was also present during the negotiations and emphasized in particular that unless an immediate stop is put to the disorderly Aryanization of homes and the Aryanization of real estate, then the events of November[12] might be repeated. Dr Ebner also promised to put his entire apparatus to work on the resettlement and to take the necessary measures for the registration of the Jews. He also requested that in the second transport preference be given to stateless Jews[13] in custody and that

8 On 7 Oct. 1939 Eichmann had spoken with leading members of Bürckel's staff about the planned deportation of Jews from Vienna.

9 Karl Beranek (1900–1945), company secretary; bank clerk, 1917–1925; owner of a taxi business, 1925–1938; joined the SA in 1932 and the NSDAP in 1933; auditor from 1938 to 1942 and head of the Audit Office of the National Socialist People's Welfare Organization in Vienna from 1939; briefly state commissioner of the General Foundation for Jewish Welfare in Vienna in 1939; auditor at the Gau Treasury Office in Vienna in 1942, and at the Gauleitung of the Sudetenland from 1943 to 1945; died in internment.

10 From March 1938 onwards nearly all Jewish foundations and funds were gradually closed down. Their assets were transferred to the General Foundation for Jewish Welfare in Vienna and were used mainly to finance care for children, the elderly, and the infirm, but also for deportations. The foundation was shut down at the end of 1941.

11 Beranek had unsuccessfully demanded an itemization of the individual assets of the dissolved foundations, to which end he had Josef Löwenherz arrested. Eichmann took over Beranek's responsibilities on 7 Dec. 1939 and delegated these to Anton Brunner in Feb. 1940.

12 This refers to the November pogrom of 1938, during which looting and rioting against Jews and Jewish establishments took place on a vast scale throughout the Reich: see PMJ 2, pp. 54–56, and esp. PMJ 2/123–138.

13 See Docs. 33 and 41.

those in concentration camps also be added immediately. Dr Ebner will also ensure that all Jews currently being held in custody by the regional courts and the various local authorities are quickly released via the resettlement. Dr Ebner requests that for all Jews resettled in Poland a per capita list for each transportation be sent to the Gestapo.

It can therefore now be assumed that there are no insurmountable difficulties standing in the way of two transportations per week, each with 1,000 Jews. The first transportation leaves at 22:00 on Friday, 20 October 1939, from Aspang Station.[14]

DOC. 25
On 19 October 1939 the Reich Minister of Finance increases the Levy on Jewish Assets[1]

Second Implementing Regulation to the Atonement Fine for Jews, 19 October 1939

Pursuant to § 2 of the Regulation on an Atonement Fine for Jews of 12 November 1938 (*Reichsgesetzblatt*, I, p. 1579),[2] the following is hereby decreed:
(1) In order to reach the sum of 1 billion Reichsmarks, the Levy on Jewish Assets is to be increased from 20 per cent to 25 per cent of the property.
(2) The difference of 5 per cent of the property is to be payable by 15 November 1939.
(3) The payment is to be made without special prompting.
Berlin, 19 October 1939
The Reich Minister of Finance
Count Schwerin von Krosigk[3]

14 After the second transportation from Vienna the deportations were stopped again. On the deportations to Nisko in the Lublin district, see Doc. 16, fn. 9.

1 'Zweite Durchführungsverordnung über die Sühneleistung der Juden', *Reichsgesetzblatt*, 1939, I, p. 2059. This document has been translated from German.
2 The Regulation on an Atonement Fine for Jews of German Nationality (12 Nov. 1938) imposed a compulsory levy of 1 billion Reichsmarks on Jews in the Reich. § 2 of the regulation stipulated that the Reich Minister of Finance was authorized to enact legislation for the implementation of the regulation: *Reichsgesetzblatt*, 1938, I, p. 1579; see also PMJ 2/142.
3 Count Johann Ludwig (Lutz) Schwerin von Krosigk (1887–1977), lawyer; Prussian public servant from 1909; worked at the Reich Finance Ministry from 1920, as head of its finance department from 1929; Reich finance minister, 1932–1945; interned by the Americans in 1945 and sentenced to ten years' imprisonment at the Nuremberg Military Tribunals in 1949; released in 1951; subsequently worked as a writer; author of works including *Es geschah in Deutschland* (It Happened in Germany) (1951).

DOC. 26

On 21 October 1939 the Jewish Community of Cologne announces restrictions on the purchase of food[1]

Circular issued by the board of the Jewish Community of Cologne,[2] dated 21 October 1939

To all Jews of the city of Cologne.
From Monday 23 October there will be a comprehensive change to the purchasing regulations concerning the supply of food for Jews in Cologne.

The authorities will take care of the allocation of food to us. It is therefore expected that all persons strictly adhere to every aspect of the following official regulations, especially since infringements incur serious consequences for the transgressor.

1. *All* foodstuffs may be bought *only* in the designated sales outlets, and *only* between *13:00 and 15:00.*
2. Aside from grocery stores, bakers, butchers, and fruit and vegetable shops have now also been designated as sales outlets. Purchases may not be made at markets, at fruit and vegetable stalls, or from itinerant traders. Insofar as designated groceries also stock fruit and vegetables, these may be bought there, but after that not at another fruit and vegetable shop.
3. No shops are assigned for fish and poultry. The purchase of fish and poultry is not permitted at the outlets designated for other articles. This does not pertain to tinned fish available at the designated outlets.
4. The purchase must be made at the nearest designated shop. The previous choice of designated outlets therefore no longer applies.
5. The purchase of all other non-food items may be made at other hours of the day.

For *mixed marriages*, the following regulation applies:

It is assumed that the purchase of food is the task of the housewife. If the housewife is Jewish according to the relevant laws,[3] then the purchase can be made only in the designated shops during the time stipulated. If the housewife is an Aryan, then the purchase can take place in groceries of choice, so long as the purchase is made by Aryans alone. Household employees are considered to be acting under orders and therefore have no right to shop freely for the family. Insofar as Mischlinge do not yet possess rights as citizens of the Reich, their right to purchase is based on that of the member of the family whose status determines the family's position.

1 NS-Dokumentationszentrum Köln, Nachlass Corbach, E 798. This document has been translated from German.

2 In 1939 the chairman of the Jewish Community of Cologne was Georg Fröhlich (b. 1899?). From 1939 his deputy was Dr Albert Kramer (1887–1942), lawyer; from 1920–1933, municipal director in Cologne, foreign-exchange advisor for Jewish emigrants, and chairman of the Rhineland-Westphalia Regional Organization of the Zionist Federation for Germany; on 30 Oct. 1941 he was deported to the Lodz ghetto, where he perished.

3 § 5 of the First Regulation on the Reich Citizenship Law stipulated who was to be deemed a Jew: *Reichsgesetzblatt*, 1935, I, pp. 1333–1334; see also PMJ 1/210.

For the purpose of informing the authorities, the attached slip is to be filled out in full and returned to the secretary of the Jewish Welfare Office, 33 Rubensstr., by Thursday, 26 October, at the latest.[4]

For the suburbs not covered, we are attempting to gain authorization for retailers for the next allocation of supplies.

Also note that the registration for the purchase of food, particularly at butchers, must take place by Monday, or Wednesday at the latest, so that supplies are not interrupted.

DOC. 27

On 21 October 1939 Martha Svoboda writes in her diary about the deportation of her brother from Vienna to Nisko[1]

Handwritten diary of Martha Svoboda,[2] Vienna, entry for 21 October 1939

Uncle Paul[3] left yesterday. On an 'officially authorized emigrant transport' to Poland.[4]

Ten days ago he was summoned to the Religious Community, together with many other fellow sufferers, where they were told to register voluntarily for emigration to Poland; the first transportation was going in a few weeks. If not enough people registered, then the Gestapo would 'take matters into their own hands'.

On Sunday the call came to get ready for impending departure and the day before yesterday the order to be at the station the next day!

Our collective dismay was indescribable. All the necessities had to be bought from one day to the next, which was very difficult, given the terrible shortages of food and other goods.

But we were lucky, given the circumstances, to have the friends we do! Thanks to their help we were able to equip Uncle Paul for his sad journey.

The farewell was brief, but our hearts were heavy. Who knows when we will see each other again.

One day, perhaps when you grow up, my child, such things will, so I hope and believe, be unthinkable: to tear completely innocent people away from their families and to transport them like criminals to an unknown destination in a foreign country and have them do forced labour there.

If there were no signs that all this pain may soon come to an end, it would be almost unbearable.

4 The file does not contain this slip.

1 The original is privately owned; copy in IfZ-Archives, F 601. This document has been translated from German.

2 Martha Svoboda (1900–1984), housewife, lived in Vienna in a so-called privileged mixed marriage. She wrote her diary for her child.

3 Paul Müller (b. 1905), upholsterer, was Martha Svoboda's brother. He was deported to Nisko on 20 Oct. 1939 and fled in the direction of Lwów; he is thought to have died in 1941.

4 On the deportations, see Doc. 16, fn. 9.

DOC. 28
Mansfelder Zeitung, 26 October 1939: article on the conviction of David Naruhn, who lived illegally with an Aryan woman[1]

Local news

Halle. David the Jew believed he was an Aryan. The 44-year-old stateless Jew David Naruhn[2] of Plötz was born in Lithuania, fought in the World War for the Russians, and came to Germany as a prisoner in 1915. Released after the end of the war, in 1919 he returned to Germany, where he made a good living. For formality's sake he also got himself baptized, and perhaps he would never have fallen foul of the law were it not that, at the bottom of his heart, he remained a true Jew.

In April 1937 he lost his wife and in May found a housekeeper via an advertisement. Naruhn didn't care that the woman wasn't yet 45 years old and that he therefore wasn't allowed to employ her in his household.[3] This breach of the law was soon followed by the more serious one of race defilement, because soon they were living together out of wedlock, until Naruhn was arrested. Now he had to answer to the great First Grand Criminal Chamber in Halle.

David feigned ignorance, claiming to believe that he had become an Aryan through baptism, all the more so since he'd always 'fought against the Jews'! Though unable to deny that he himself was descended from pure-blooded Jews, he pretended not to know anything about the Nuremberg Laws, although he has been resident in Germany for twenty years. But when the Jew realized that his evasions weren't being believed, he let the mask slip and showed his true race. He accused the woman of soliciting him and of cheating him over household expenses. The whole show of calm and nonchalance was over; he was once more the dyed-in-the-wool Jew ready to use any means to save his skin.

The accused was sentenced to one year and four months of penal servitude and three years' loss of civil rights, taking into account time already spent in custody.

1 'Aus dem Kreise', *Mansfelder Zeitung*, 26 Oct. 1939, p. 3. This document has been translated from German. The *Mansfelder Zeitung* was one of the local editions of the *Mitteldeutsche Zeitung*, which was founded in the nineteenth century.

2 David Naruhn (1895–1942) was deported on 19 Oct. 1942 to Auschwitz, where he perished.

3 According to § 3 of the Law for the Protection of German Blood and German Honour (15 Sept. 1935), Jews were forbidden from employing female German household workers under the age of 45: see Doc. 9, fn. 5.

DOC. 29

On 2 November 1939 the Emigration Advice Service of the Jewish Economic Aid Association in Dresden asks the American Joint Distribution Committee to speed up the issuing of visas by the US consulate general in Berlin[1]

Letter (via airmail) from the Emigration Advice Service of the Jewish Economic Aid Association in Dresden,[2] unsigned, to the American Jewish Joint Distribution Committee, New York, dated 2 November 1939 (copy)[3]

Re: issuing of visas at the American consulate general in Berlin.
The process of checking affidavits by the consulate general in Berlin gives us cause to write to you today.

The difficulties that the consulate has been creating for visa applicants for quite some time now are increasing daily. There is barely a single case in which the petitioner is issued with a visa in Berlin without there being some complaint or other. Either [the sum stated in] the affidavit is not high enough, or the relation of the issuer of the affidavit to the recipient is not close enough (cousins do not suffice), or the issuer of the affidavit is too old. In all these cases, the petitioner is first denied the visa and either they must provide a *supplementary affidavit* or a security deposit is demanded of *$1,000* upwards per person. In one case it was even required that the American relative provide a will favouring the visa applicant, and when this was presented to the consulate, having been obtained with great difficulty, it was rejected, because the will was not certified as irrevocable. In one case an American friend of a gentleman from here, whose affidavit from a relative was not high enough, provided a passbook for the sum of $1,250, with the stipulation that when he reached America he could withdraw his monthly expenses from the credit. This fact was confirmed to the consulate general in Berlin by the bank at which the passbook was deposited. The Consul General[4] rejected this measure with the stipulation that $1,250 should be deposited under the name of the emigrant and the authorization be issued to him allowing him to withdraw a monthly sum.

This handling of matters by the American consulate general in Berlin creates such difficulties that emigration from here will become illusory if these measures continue. It requires so much work and such psychological pressure for those seeking help that we cannot simply remain silent, if we are to avoid being jointly responsible for these methods.

1 JDC Archives, AR 33/44, 658. This document has been translated from German.
2 The Jewish Economic Aid Association (Jüdische Wirtschaftshilfe) was founded in 1933 in response to the economic marginalization of the Jewish population in Germany. It concentrated primarily on supporting German Jews by means of advice, retraining, and recruitment. Alongside the Central Office of Jewish Economic Aid in Berlin, branches were set up in all the larger municipalities.
3 The original contains handwritten annotations.
4 Dr Raymond Herman Geist (1885–1955), diplomat; US consul from 1924 to 1929 in Alexandria and from 1929 to 1939 in Berlin, where he was acting consul general from 1937 to 1939 and first ambassadorial secretary from 1938 to 1939; worked at the US State Department in Washington from 1940 to 1945; ambassadorial secretary in Mexico City from 1945 to 1948; awarded the Federal Cross of Merit (*Bundesverdienstkreuz*) in 1954.

For this reason we have described to you the above, and politely request that you do everything in your power to put an end to this absurd business.[5]

With the highest esteem[6]

DOC. 30

On 10 November 1939 a Jewish woman from Vienna writes to Josef Löwenherz, asking him to prevent girls under the age of 18 from being deported to Poland[1]

Handwritten letter from a Jewish woman from Vienna, unsigned, to Dr Josef Löwenherz[2] in Vienna, dated 10 November 1939

Noble sir
Dr Josef Löwenherz
Vienna

A desperate mother implores you in the name of many other mothers to do your utmost to at least stop girls under 18 years of age from being sent to Poland.[3] They could, after all, be put to work here in other ways.

This small concession could surely be achieved if you were to seek it, and therefore with all my heart I again implore you to act.

An unhappy mother

5 Immigration visas for the USA were issued only by the consulates in Berlin, Hamburg, Stuttgart, and, from 1938, also Vienna. Applicants had to present a valid passport and a police certificate as well as proof of financial security (affidavit) once in the USA. The decision on whether an affidavit was acceptable was at the discretion of the consuls. After 1933 they tended towards a restrictive interpretation of the regulations and often accepted affidavits only from first-degree relatives. Even if all the required documents had been presented, it took time for visas to be issued. When the war started, the entry conditions were made stricter still, on the grounds of security considerations, such as fear of German spies.

6 It is not known if the letter received a reply.

1 CAHJP, A/W 2747; copy in Archiv der IKG Vienna, MF W 1, fr. 71. This document has been translated from German.

2 Dr Josef Löwenherz (1884–1960), lawyer; delegate at the Tenth to the Fifteenth Zionist Congress, 1911–1915; lawyer in Vienna from 1918; vice president of the Israelite Religious Community of Vienna (IKG), 1925–1937, and director of the same, 1937–1942; commissioned by Eichmann to reorganize the Jewish Community of Vienna in May 1938; after its dissolution he was officially nominated as Jewish elder (*Judenältester*) in Vienna on 1 Jan. 1943; imprisoned by Soviet soldiers for collaboration in 1945 and released after three months; lived in New York after 1945.

3 On the deportations to Nisko, see Doc. 16, fn. 9. The third transport from Vienna, planned for 31 Oct. 1939, did not depart, because the deportations had in the meantime been suspended for technical reasons.

DOC. 31
On 17 November 1939 the Innsbruck Gestapo informs the Landeshauptmann of Tyrol about the membership and assets of the Jewish Community in Innsbruck[1]

Letter from the Gestapo, State Police office in Innsbruck (II B 35/39), p.p. signature illegible, to the Landeshauptmann of Tyrol,[2] Innsbruck, Landhaus, dated 17 November 1939[3]

Re: Jewish religious communities in the Ostmark.
Reference: Your letter of 8 November 1939, B. Nr. III – 4535/11[4]
Enclosure: 1
I am sending you enclosed a list of the thirty Jews who are currently still living in Innsbruck.[5]

I am unable to give any precise information about the whereabouts of the assets of the former Israelite Religious Community in Innsbruck. All we know is that at the time of the protest in November 1938,[6] the district leadership of the Hitler Youth took possession of an iron stove and an upright piano. A number of metal objects (wrought-iron candelabra, a metal goblet, a metal plate with chain, and similar items, all of very little scrap value) were seized by the Gestapo at this time. These objects are currently still in the Gestapo's possession. The other fixtures and fittings from the synagogue which were temporarily seized at the time were handed over on 8 December 1938 to the then secretary of the Israelite Religious Community, Burin,[7] who has since emigrated.

The cash assets of the Israelite Religious Community in Innsbruck were seized by the Gestapo and used in part to further Jewish emigration, in part (on instructions from the Gestapo Central Office) to pay for the maintenance of individual Jews who were elderly and without means, and in part (on instructions from the inspector of the Security Police

1 YVA, O.30/43. Published in Dokumentationsarchiv des österreichischen Widerstands, *Widerstand und Verfolgung in Tirol 1934–1945: Eine Dokumentation*, vol. 1 (Vienna/Munich: ÖBV/Jugend und Volk, 1984), p. 464. This document has been translated from German.
2 Franz Hofer (1902–1975); businessman; joined the NSDAP in 1931; NSDAP Gauleiter of Tyrol, 1932–1934; arrested in 1933; member of the Reichstag from 1938; Gauleiter, Landeshauptmann, and from 1940 Reichsstatthalter of Tyrol-Vorarlberg; interned, 1945–1948; escaped, sentenced in absentia in Munich and Innsbruck to ten years' hard labour and to death, respectively, 1949; sentenced by the Munich appellate tribunal to three and a half years' hard labour in 1953; acquired a metal fittings factory in Mülheim an der Ruhr in 1957.
3 The original contains handwritten notes.
4 This letter is not in the file.
5 YVA, O.30/43; according to this list, the majority of the persons named had been baptized as Christians.
6 On the November pogroms, see PMJ 2, especially Docs. 123–138.
7 Karl Burin (b. 1905), retailer; born in Germany; in 1936 moved to Innsbruck, where he worked as a salesman; in Nov. 1938 he was taken into protective custody, and on 31 Dec. 1938 he was forcibly relocated to Vienna; in April 1939 he emigrated to Britain with his wife.

in Vienna[8]) transferred to the Israelite Religious Community in Vienna. A balance still held by the Gestapo will be administered, on instructions from Gestapo Central Office, for the purpose of maintaining the necessary welfare services for Jews.

We have no knowledge here of any legal representative of the former [Israelite] Religious Community in Innsbruck, and such a person probably does not exist. The Gestapo has instructed the Jew and licensed legal consultant Dr Paul Israel Kühne, born 2 June 1892 in Klagenfurt, resident at 10 Egger-Lienzstraße in Innsbruck,[9] to pass on any instructions that it may issue to the remaining Jews living in Tyrol and Vorarlberg.

DOC. 32

On 18 November 1939 the SD District Leipzig writes to the Reich Security Main Office, proposing a travel ban on Jews[1]

Letter from the Security Service of the Reichsführer SS (II 112 C 422–1 Hi./Bö.), Head of the SD District Leipzig, SS-Sturmbannführer Hayn,[2] to the Reich Security Main Office in Berlin, Office II, Section II 112,[3] dated 18 November 1939

Re: travel ban on Jews.
Case file: none.
During the recent concerted series of arrests, it became clear that quite a number of Jews could not be arrested because they had been travelling for varying lengths of time without any known destination.

It therefore seems advisable to impose a travel ban on Jews, similar to the existing 8 p.m. curfew, or at least to require Jews to report to the appropriate authority before they embark on any journey, however short, stating their exact destination, and to report in again immediately upon their return.

Our experience shows that the Jews think they can avoid arrest by embarking on a journey at times when they feel particularly under threat.[4]

8 Probably Dr Franz Walter Stahlecker (1900–1942), lawyer; joined the NSDAP for the first time in 1921 and rejoined in 1933; head of the Political Police in Württemberg, 1934–1937, and of the Breslau Gestapo office, 1937; head of the SD for the SS Main District Danube and inspector of the Security Police in Vienna, May 1938–June 1939; senior commander of the Security Police and the SD (BdS) for Bohemia and Moravia, 1939; Ministerialrat in the Reich Foreign Office from 1940; appointed BdS for Norway in 1940; head of Einsatzgruppe A in June 1941 and BdS for Ostland in autumn 1941; shot and killed by Soviet partisans.

9 Dr Paul Kühne (1892–1945), lawyer; had lived in Innsbruck since around 1910; worked as a lawyer after the First World War; forcibly relocated to Vienna on 1 Jan. 1941, and emigrated in March 1941 to Shanghai, where he died.

1 RGVA, 500k-1-659; copy in USHMM, RG-11.001M01, reel 9. This document has been translated from German.

2 Gustav Hayn (b. 1902), commercial employee; worked for various firms in Breslau, 1919–1934; joined the NSDAP and the SA in 1931 and the SS in 1935; head of the SD Sub-District Liegnitz from 1935 and of the SD Sub-District Leipzig from 1938; SS-Sturmbannführer, 1939; served in the Wehrmacht and Waffen SS, 1940–1941.

3 Section II 112 at the Reich Security Main Office (RSHA) was responsible for 'Jewish affairs'.

4 A general travel ban for Jews was only imposed in Sept. 1941, with the issue of the Police Regulation on the Visible Identification of Jews: see Docs. 212 and 222.

DOC. 33

On 20 November 1939 Josef Löwenherz informs the Vienna Gestapo of fatalities in Buchenwald and requests the release of Jews who are able to emigrate[1]

Letter from the Head of the Israelite Religious Community of Vienna, Dr Josef Israel Löwenherz, to the Gestapo in Vienna, dated 20 November 1939

During the month of September 1939 a series of stateless persons who had previously held Polish citizenship were taken into protective custody, and after a temporary period of incarceration in various Viennese prisons they were sent to the concentration camp in Buchenwald, near Weimar.[2]

The Israelite Religious Community of Vienna has since been bombarded with requests from the relatives of these persons to petition the relevant authority for their release. In the meantime, a number of families have been informed by the administration of Buchenwald concentration camp that their relatives held there in protective custody have died, and their ashes have been sent to Vienna for burial. It is apparent from the records kept by the Cemeteries Department of the Israelite Religious Community of Vienna – which are of course confidential – that a total of 199 urns from Buchenwald have been interred in Vienna. This high mortality rate is due to the fact that among those taken into protective custody there are a large number of persons whose health is seriously impaired by incarceration, either because of old age or for other reasons.

It is clear from the report dated 16 November of this year,[3] prepared by the Israelite Religious Community of Vienna, that many of these prisoners are in possession of entry visas that would allow them and their families to leave the territory of the Reich within a relatively short space of time. There is no doubt that others would also be in a position, in the event of their release, to secure entry visas, enabling them to emigrate with their families. This would significantly increase emigration numbers and make the work of the Israelite Religious Community of Vienna much easier.

It is therefore requested that individual cases of persons held in protective custody be reviewed, and the release of prisoners authorized.[4]

1 The original is privately owned: copy in DÖW, 8496. Published in Dokumentationsarchiv des österreichischen Widerstandes, *Widerstand und Verfolgung in Wien*, vol. 3, p. 266. This document has been translated from German.

2 On 7 Sept. 1939 Heydrich had ordered the arrest of all male Jews of Polish nationality and the confiscation of their assets: see Doc. 6. In Vienna a total of 1,038 men were arrested and sent to Buchenwald concentration camp. By the summer of 1940, two thirds of them had died.

3 This report could not be found.

4 There is no known response to this letter.

DOC. 34
On 24 November 1939 an SD informant complains about the behaviour of the Berlin Jews[1]

Report from an informant, signature illegible, dated 24 November 1939[2]

In substantial sections of the population there are growing complaints about the insolent behaviour of the Jews in Berlin, which is becoming increasingly intolerable. At the marketplace, at the baker's, and in other shops, wherever you care to look, the Jews are pretty full of themselves again, and often start making inappropriate comments in a rather arrogant way about the food-stamp system, living conditions, etc. In some places, e.g. the area around Kurfürstendamm, the talk one hears is deliberately defeatist. In the following instances I have been able to ascertain specific names:

Widow of Leonhard Brasch, Berlin-Charlottenburg, 4 Clausewitzstraße (owner of a house at 39 Lehrterstraße), is the sole occupant of a nine-room apartment, with two sons who have emigrated to England.[3] According to reports, this woman seems able to get hold of all the foodstuffs she wants, delivered direct to her door. They say she also keeps large stocks of supplies at home, tips generously, etc.

The Schlüter apartment block in Berlin-Charlottenburg, 43 Schlüterstraße, still has many Jewish residents, who occupy the most expensive apartments. The *caretaker Schröder* is described as a typical Jews' lackey, who is constantly getting tips from the Jews and always defending the Jews against the Aryan tenants. During the last air-raid warning he even put Aryans and Jews in the same air-raid shelter, whereupon the Jews, who were in the majority, behaved in an insolent and provocative manner, making jokes about the Führer to their general merriment. The Volksgenossin who told me this is the wife of an SA-Sturmführer, who is currently serving on the Western front. She didn't dare say anything, knowing that the caretaker always sides with the Jews, and she registered her protest by leaving the air-raid shelter. If necessary, she can be called as a witness.

Something absolutely must be done about the Jews, as they are now deliberately starting to spread their defeatist talk again, channelling and disseminating rumours, and influencing public morale.

1 RGVA, 500k-1-396; copy in USHMM, RG-11.001M01, reel 5. This document has been translated from German.

2 The report was forwarded to Section II 112 of the Reich Security Main Office on 5 Dec. 1939: RGVA, 500k-1-396.

3 Bianca Brasch, née Lazarus (1877–1943), wife of the businessman Leonhard Brasch, who owned a liqueur factory and wholesale wine business in Berlin and had died in 1929; on 29 Jan. 1943 she was deported to Auschwitz, where she was murdered in March of that year. Her sons Arno (b. 1904) and Martin (b. 1907) emigrated to the USA and Britain, respectively. The wine cellars of the family business were located at 39 Lehrter Str.

DOC. 35
On 25 November 1939 Jolan Thorn from Vienna tells her sister in New York about her difficulties in making arrangements for emigration[1]

Letter from Jolan Thorn,[2] Vienna, to Sofie Neufeld,[3] New York, dated 25 November 1939

My dear Sofie,

Your letter of the 11th, sent by clipper, arrived yesterday, having been checked by the censorship office. It finds us still here, unfortunately. I have written to you less frequently of late, because all our correspondence, which is now quite extensive, has had to be done by hand since we sold our typewriter, and that takes up a lot of time. You probably think I've got nothing else to do, but that's not quite true.

Now for the most important news: the Bolivian project has just been resurrected[4] from its state of suspended animation or complete demise. The passage has to be paid for in foreign exchange, which we cannot get hold of here. Our religious community is not so flush with dollars that they could afford to give our party the necessary sum.[5] In the telegram he sent to you Fr.[6] asked you to put pressure on a certain person who is close to the JDC [to send] the prepaid answer to a telegram. Unfortunately without success, following your change of address. Now at long last, when the whole thing has almost ground to a halt because of sabotage by certain people, a representative of the JDC is due to come, and the decision about the passage rests in his hands. Maybe he will have to make enquiries in NY first, which will mean more delays.

Our whole project looks completely different from one day to the next. So it's hardly surprising that it is not possible to describe each phase exactly and give an account of it. But time is pressing, and we don't have much time any more to sit around and wait. So we've decided that if necessary we can go to Pal[estine] instead, and Fr. has already arranged for us to join one of those transports.[7] This plan should become a reality within the next three weeks or so, i.e. before the close of this year's Danube navigation season. I can't tell you how tough it is on the nerves, waiting to actually achieve something in all this. All the endless 'ifs' and 'buts', all the headaches and worrying. But we really

1 YVA, O.75/529.4. This letter has been translated from German.

2 Jolan Thorn, née Spielmann (1892–1940), industrial employee; employed by the paper manufacturer Vereinigte Papier- und Ultramarinfabriken; dismissed as a non-Aryan on 30 June 1938; died of pneumonia and meningitis. Her husband Siegfried Thorn (1885–1942) was deported on 11 Jan. 1942 to Riga, where he perished.

3 Probably Josefa Neufeld, née Spielmann, later Josie Newfeld, also Neweld (b. 1903), the sister of Jolan Thorn; emigrated to the USA in Sept. or Oct. 1938.

4 At least 12,000 Jews escaped to Bolivia, which was beyond the sphere of control of the German Reich.

5 Jolan and Siegfried Thorn were planning to emigrate together with Jolan's mother, Luise Spielmann, née Fürst (b. 1871).

6 Probably Friedrich (Fritz) Spielmann (b. 1900), the brother of Jolan Thorn. On 15 Feb. 1941, he was deported to Opole Lubelskie together with his wife, Hilda Spielmann (b. 1901), and his mother, Luise Spielmann. Luise Spielmann's last letter from there was dated 30 August 1941.

7 The reference is to an illegal transport to Palestine – in this case, possibly the paddle steamer *Grein*, which arrived in Budapest on 17 Dec. 1939 with refugees from Vienna. In the Romanian port city of Sulina they were transferred to the *Sakarya*. The vessel sailed in Feb. 1940 and reached Haifa the same month.

shouldn't complain at all; we just need to keep going and not lose heart. One day the sun will shine for us again – and hopefully a warmer sun at that. Anyway, we'll keep you updated, if only from here and then when we reach our destination, because while we are travelling it will not really be possible to write – for reasons which I'm sure will be unclear to you – if we decide to go with project no. 2. But please do carry on writing until you hear something definite from us.

I must also thank you for all you have done for Eslo.[8] We have recently had some more news of him, the last just eight days ago. He writes that he is very well, but so far we have not received any reports from the doctors about his actual state of health, which I asked them to send. I just hope and pray that the dear little soul didn't suffer any lasting damage!! That's my greatest worry now, and obviously I shall be terribly anxious until I hear some good or positive news.

I'm so grateful to you and Coca! Please write to the boy as often as you can, and don't wait for him to reply first. In the hospital E. used to write long letters, but they were not sent, as his illness was infectious, of course. Later he sent us birthday poems, which either arrived too late or too early! It was really sweet.

If you are going to see Coca some time soon, please tell her that I visited Mama again yesterday.[9] She's upset that she hasn't heard from Coca since 8 August. She is well, but feels very lonely.

We have more or less packed our bags, and are waiting to see how things turn out. We've pared things down pretty much to the bare minimum.

The weather here is wretched at the moment, just rain and snow or snow and rain. But it's all the same to us, of course.

By 4 p.m. it's already evening. We don't venture out later than that anyway, but it means the lights are on for a very long time.

Evi must be an all-American little girl by now! She is so cute!! Can she even speak German any more, I wonder?

My brain is frazzled now, so I'll finish for today and send you fondest kisses – Your Jolan.

Warmest greetings from your little brother-in-law Willy.

Give […][10] a prod – she writes a couple of words every four months!

8 Erich Paul Thorn (1929–2005), literary scholar, the son of Jolan and Siegfried Thorn; he travelled on a Kindertransport to Montmorency in France, where he arrived on 14 March 1939; from the autumn of 1939 to July 1941 he was housed in the Château de Chaumont home, run by the Jewish aid organization OSE; in Sept. 1941 he was sent by sea to the USA on board the *SS Serpa Pinto*; after the war he served in the US Army in Germany until 1953; lecturer at Marshall University, WV, 1956–1996.

9 Luise Spielmann; see fn. 5.

10 Name illegible.

DOC. 36

In his diary entry for 8 December 1939 Jochen Klepper describes how his family in Berlin is being progressively deprived of the necessities of life[1]

Diary of Jochen Klepper,[2] Berlin, entry for 8 December 1939

8 December 1939, Friday
Therefore be ye also ready: for in such an hour as ye think not the Son of man cometh. Matthew 24, verse 44

The Lord is nigh unto them that are of a broken heart; and saveth such as be of a contrite spirit. Many are the afflictions of the righteous: but the Lord delivereth him out of them all. Psalm 34, verses 19 and 20.[3]

The antisemitic measures continue to progress despite the annihilation of Jewry: not only no clothes and no linen, but no sewing materials either. And no soles for shoes.[4]

And today Dr Edzards[5] (NSV) was here, genuinely agitated and worried, having come to bring me the new food ration cards. Now there are special rules for Hanni and Reni on this, too, where it really hits us hardest.[6] Apparently they're supposed to have a red J stamped on their cards now, they can only go shopping at certain times, the ration of chocolate and gingerbread is to be withdrawn, etc.[7]

The Jews will be told the details next Tuesday, when they go to collect their ration cards. Let's just hope the food rations are not cut even more drastically – !

1 Deutsches Literaturarchiv Marbach, record group A: Klepper, ZN: 77 3346. Published in Jochen Klepper, *Unter dem Schatten deiner Flügel: Aus den Tagebüchern der Jahre 1932–1942* (Giessen: Brunnen, 1997), pp. 481–482. This document has been translated from German.

2 Jochen Klepper (1903–1942), journalist and writer; member of the Social Democratic Party of Germany (SPD), 1933–1935; worked in radio broadcasting in Berlin, 1933–1935; was employed by the Ullstein Publishing House from 1933 to 1935, and thereafter worked as a freelance writer. In 1937 he was about to be expelled from the Reich Chamber of Literature on the grounds that he was 'intermarried with a Jew' (*jüdisch versippt*), but was then granted a special exemption; served in the military, 1940–1941; took his own life. Author of works including *Kyrie: Geistliche Lieder* (1938).

3 Correctly: verses 18 and 19. From 1933 Jochen Klepper began every diary entry with Bible quotations taken from the compilation published by the Moravian Church.

4 On 7 Dec. 1939 the Reich Ministry of Economics ordered the withdrawal of clothing coupons that had previously been issued to Jews; on 23 Jan. 1940 it prohibited the issue of ration coupons for clothing and shoes to Jews and decreed that the Reich Association of Jews in Germany had to assume responsibility for supplying the needs of Jews.

5 Wife of Dr Hermann Edzards (b. 1879), veterinarian.

6 Jochen Klepper's wife Johanna, née Gerstel (1890–1942), widowed during her first marriage, in which her married name was Stein, and her daughters Brigitte (b. 1920) and Renate Stein (1922–1942), were regarded as Jews. Brigitte Stein emigrated to Britain in May 1939, but her sister's emigration plans were thwarted (see fn. 15). When the SD ultimately refused her an exit visa in Dec. 1942, Renate Stein and Jochen and Johanna Klepper committed suicide.

7 On 11 March 1940 the Reich Ministry of Food and Agriculture excluded all Jews from extra allocations of food rations and introduced a nationwide requirement for Jews to have their ration cards marked with a 'J'. The setting of separate shopping times for Jews was left to the local food offices: Decree on Food Supplies for Jews, 11 March 1940, IfZ-Archives, MA 1555–118, NID-14581. In Berlin the chief of police did not take action on shopping hours until 4 July 1940, when Jews were restricted to the hour between 4 and 5 p.m.: Police Regulation No. 543 on Shopping Hours for Jews, *Amtsblatt für den Landespolizeibezirk Berlin 1940*, pp. 202–203.

When will it all end?

But what a blessing that everybody around here is of one mind in these matters. In other parts of the city, things might be very different.

I hope the shops don't make any difficulties for us; but Hanni has a favourable impression of the people. Zimmermanns,[8] Moltkes,[9] Anni,[10] Mrs Edzards, Karbe;[11] they're all really appalled. The thing is, it is no longer possible to remain anonymous. – As far as Mrs Edzards knows, there are now only three Jewish families living in the whole of Nikolassee.[12]

Since the antisemitic measures *have become* so unpopular, they are no longer publicized. They give out little red leaflets instead.[13] Today my complimentary copies of *Vater* arrived, 30,000 copies have now been printed.[14]

My life runs along strangely contradictory lines. It's very difficult to write under these circumstances.

There's still no movement on Renate's case in Switzerland. But the Tappolets did send us a little tin of coffee today.[15]

Now it is cold, overcast, and gloomy; but when the sun rose it was a glorious bronze colour, and for a few moments everything was bathed in a bright glow.

8 Dr Carl Zimmermann (d. 1960), civil servant and Oberregierungsrat; appointed vice president of the German Research Foundation (DFG) in 1939; administrative head of the Reich Institute of Physics and Technology. He and his wife lived on the top floor of the building where the Kleppers resided.

9 Gertrud von Moltke (b. 1891) and Wilhelm von Moltke (b. 1881), a retired army major who joined the NSDAP in 1933; neighbours of the Kleppers.

10 Anni Tiecke was the Kleppers' housekeeper.

11 Dr Hans Karbe (1905–1999), farmer, businessman, and art historian; joined the NSDAP in 1937; editor of the *Essener Nationalzeitung*, 1939–1942, and the weekly *Stern* in 1939; worked for the Reich general director of film; lived in Switzerland from 1945 onwards, and became a freelance artist in 1976. Before Jochen Klepper committed suicide, he gave the diary to his neighbour Hans Karbe and asked him to hide it in his home.

12 An exclusive residential district in the south-west of Berlin.

13 New laws affecting the Jews were not generally published in daily newspapers. Many measures were either not publicized at all or only announced in the *Jüdisches Nachrichtenblatt* bulletin; in many cases, however, people only heard about them through word of mouth or circulars.

14 Jochen Klepper's *Der Vater: Roman eines Königs* was first published in 1937. Despite Klepper's exclusion from the Reich Chamber of Literature, the novel was selected as 'recommended reading' for the Wehrmacht.

15 At the end of Nov. 1939 the Kleppers tried to find accommodation for Renate Stein in Sweden or Switzerland, as this was a requirement for the issue of an immigration permit. At the end of Dec. 1939 the family of Walter Tappolet (1897–1991), church organist, theologian, and writer, agreed to take her in. However, Renate Stein's application for immigration was refused by the Swiss immigration authorities on 10 May 1940.

DOC. 37

In a letter dated 11 December 1939 Max Wiener tells Ernst Grumach in Berlin that there is little prospect of his securing a post at an American university[1]

Letter from Max Wiener,[2] 29 W. Daniels Street, Corryville, Cincinnati, Ohio, USA, to Ernst Grumach[3] in Berlin, dated 11 December 1939

Dear Mr Grumach, I was looking forward with great excitement to receiving your letter of 11 November (which only reached me about twelve days ago), and I fell upon it eagerly, hungry to hear your news. Firstly, on the point that specially concerns you, and therefore interests me greatly: looking at things entirely dispassionately, and with the benefit of two months' experience, I have to say that I think it very unlikely that the College[4] *here* will issue further invitations before the fate of the previous ones is resolved. Apart from me, who am lucky enough to have eight hours' teaching, even if not in my own subject, Landsberger is here,[5] as you know, who was an associate professor of art in Breslau until '33 and then a museum director with the Jewish community in Berlin, and a Dr Werner[6] from Breslau, a musicologist and – so he likes to think – an authority on religious and especially Jewish music. None of us have come over as a result of successful lobbying by the College. In my case, as you know, I had a regular employment contract, which fully satisfied the requirements of immigration law. In London, L.[7] was the guest of Murray,[8] who used his personal influence at the consulate and persuaded them to issue the visa. Werner was here as a visitor[9] in the autumn of last year, which of course made things very much easier, and because he had been teaching music at the Breslau seminary for the last few years, he was given an employment contract here, on the strength of which he was able to immigrate from Cuba, perfectly legally, as a non-quota person.[10] A few

1 CAHJP, P 205/14. This document has been translated from German.
2 Dr Max Wiener (1882–1950), rabbi and philosopher of religion; rabbi and teacher of religion in Düsseldorf, 1909–1912; rabbi to the Jewish Community of Stettin, 1912–1926; lecturer at the Higher Institute for Jewish Studies in Berlin, 1925–1939; rabbi to the Jewish Community in Berlin, 1926–1939; member of the presidium of the Jewish Culture League, 1933; emigrated to New York in 1939; taught at the Hebrew Union College in Cincinnati from 1939 to 1941; assistant rabbi in New York, 1943–1950.
3 Dr Ernst Grumach (1902–1967), classical philologist; taught at the University of Königsberg, 1930–1933; taught at the Higher Institute for Jewish Studies, 1937–1942; was forced to work for the central library of the Reich Security Main Office (RSHA), 1941–1945; professor at the Humboldt University in Berlin, 1949–1957; research fellow at the Berlin Academy of Sciences, 1949–1959; edited the Akademie edition of Goethe's works from 1952 onwards.
4 English in the original here and in the following.
5 Dr Franz Landsberger (1883–1964), art historian; professor in Breslau, 1918–1933; director of the Jewish Museum in Berlin, 1935–1938; incarcerated in Sachsenhausen in Nov. 1938; emigrated to Britain in 1939, and then to the USA; professor at the Hebrew Union College in Cincinnati, 1939–1958.
6 Dr Eric Werner (1901–1988), musicologist; professor in Saarbrücken, 1926–1933, and in Breslau, 1934–1938; emigrated to the USA in 1938; professor at the Hebrew Union College in Cincinnati; dean of faculty at the University of Tel Aviv, 1966–1971.
7 Franz Landsberger.
8 Dr George Gilbert Aimé Murray (1866–1957), classical philologist.
9 English in the original.
10 His immigration was authorized extra to the immigration quota.

days ago I heard that Dr Sonne,[11] who was teaching at the seminary in Rhodes, and then went to Palestine when it was closed down, has received his visa on the basis of a job offer he received some time ago. Gottschalk[12] and Franz Rosenthal[13] seem to have had firm rejections; as far as Spanier[14] and Lewkowitz[15] are concerned, both of whom are in Holland, the principal[16] told me at the beginning of October that favourable reports have been sent to the consuls from Washington, where he went in person to support their applications. But I still haven't heard any positive news. With regard to Alexander G.,[17] the principal told me yesterday that everything was going very well, apart from one small thing – yet again, the consulate has not received the necessary documents from here, although they were definitely sent. So they had to be sent again. What will happen then, and whether they will satisfy the consul, is very much open to question. I have the impression that the consuls are completely independent agents in such matters, and are not easily persuaded from here to go against their own inclinations. So this is not very encouraging, and the matter has probably not been handled from here with the requisite forethought – perhaps that is asking the impossible anyway. But under these circumstances, clearly, there won't be a new round of job offers any time soon. Our colleague Eugen[18] has left people here in a state of uncertainty, just as he has shrouded himself in mystery over there. – In your case, my dear Grumach, two conditions would need to be met: a non-specialist college would need to hire you as a philologist, perhaps, assuming that your track record at Königsberg University, supported by your teaching experience

11 Dr Isaiah Sonne (1887–1960), historian; from 1925, professor at the Rabbinical College in Florence; director of the Jewish Theological Seminary on Rhodes, 1936–1938; lecturer and librarian at the Hebrew Union College in Cincinnati, 1939–1940.

12 Dr Walter Gottschalk (1891–1974), orientalist and librarian; worked at the Berlin State Library, 1919–1935; emigrated to Belgium in 1939, then to Turkey in 1941; professor in Istanbul from 1949; helped to develop the Turkish library system; returned to Germany in 1954.

13 Dr Franz Rosenthal (1914–2003), orientalist; taught at the Higher Institute for Jewish Studies in Berlin, 1937–1938; emigrated to Sweden in Dec. 1938, from there to Britain in 1939, and finally to the USA in 1940; lecturer at the Hebrew Union College in Cincinnati, 1940–1948; worked for the Office of Strategic Services (OSS), 1943–1945; professor in Philadelphia, 1948–1956, and at Yale University, 1956–1985.

14 Dr Arthur Spanier (1889–1945), philologist and librarian; worked at the Berlin State Library, 1921–1935; lecturer at the Higher Institute for Jewish Studies, 1935–1938; incarcerated in Sachsenhausen concentration camp in Nov. 1938; emigrated to the Netherlands in 1939; deported to Westerbork in June 1943, and from there to Bergen-Belsen, where he perished.

15 Dr Albert Lewkowitz (1883–1954), theologian and rabbi; military rabbi, 1914–1916; taught in Breslau from 1914 to 1939; emigrated to the Netherlands in 1939; deported to Westerbork in Sept. 1943, and from there to Bergen-Belsen in Jan. 1944; in the summer of 1944 he went to Palestine on an exchange arrangement; became a rabbi and lecturer in Haifa.

16 English in the original here and in the following.

17 Dr Alexander Guttmann (1904–1994), theologian and rabbi; lecturer in Berlin, 1927–1932, where he was appointed a professor at the Higher Institute for Jewish Studies in 1935; emigrated to the USA in 1940, and taught as a professor at the Hebrew Union College until 1978; visiting professor at the Higher Institute for Jewish Studies in Heidelberg, 1981.

18 Dr Eugen Täubler (1879–1953), historian; founder and director of the Central Archives of German Jewry, 1906–1918; lecturer at the Higher Institute for Jewish Studies in Berlin, 1910–1916 and 1919–1922; associate professor in Zurich from 1922, in Heidelberg, 1925–1933, and at the Higher Institute for Jewish Studies, 1933–1941; emigrated in 1941 to the USA via Sweden, and was a professor at the Hebrew Union College until 1953.

at the Higher Institute [for Jewish Studies], would be an adequate European basis. Is there such a place? If your salary could be guaranteed for two years, possibly by a third party, which is permissible, then it should be just about manageable. But where would you find someone willing to put up a sum of at least $3,500–4,000 à fonds perdu?[19] When I think of your wife[20] and her extraordinary ability and her handicraft skills, there is every chance that such a sum would not be perdu[21] at all. But although *I myself* believe this, will a prospective donor believe it too? Or do you happen to have a wealthy uncle living here, whom you could let me loose on? – I know of a case in Berlin where that turned out to be just the answer. But of course all this is just speculation. And for the moment you still have work over there at our institute. One solution that I wouldn't dismiss out of hand would be for you and your wife to go to one of the South American countries. From what I hear about conditions over there, you would certainly not be at a loss there. Who knows how things are going to turn out in Europe? Without wishing to get your hopes up, I suggest you send me everything that you've done. (I'd also be very grateful if you could let me have some of my own writings that you have there with you – or you could ask the Higher Institute for Jewish Studies to send them to me as printed matter. I don't have any of my own writings here. I'd also be grateful if you would look through my selected Luzzato letters[22] and tell me the numbers of the ones I translated from Hebrew or Italian, etc. I might do an English edition here.) Today I received the proofs of my essay for the *Monatsschrift*. Are they now going to send the entire volume? I won't be returning the corrected proofs; it would just take too long. I'm very sorry that Gross[23] and Joseph[24] have given up their certificate 'for personal reasons', especially in the case of Gross. What does Dr Fabian[25] say about it, after he invested so much time and effort in trying to help Gross make his Aliyah? Please send my warmest regards to both of them, and of course to our other colleagues and students! If only one knew what to do with these young fellows! I've often talked with the principal about this. He takes the view – which cannot be argued with – that if dozens of mature colleagues have come over and continue to do so, and there is absolutely nothing else that can be done with them apart from giving them very lowly positions in their line of work, which is extremely difficult in itself, then there is no chance of bringing over young

19 French in the original: 'with no prospect of repayment'.

20 Margarete Grumach, née Breuer, lived with Ernst Grumach in a so-called non-privileged mixed marriage.

21 French in the original: 'lost'.

22 Samuel David Luzzato (1800–1865), philosopher and Bible commentator; regarded as one of the fathers of Jewish studies. Many of his letters were published in various journals. In one of the last editions of the *Almanach des Schocken Verlags* an edition of his correspondence, translated and annotated by Wiener, was announced, but it was never published: Robert S. Schine, *Jewish Thought Adrift: Max Wiener (1881–1950)* (Atlanta: Scholars, 1992), pp. 131–132.

23 Manfred Gross (b. 1918), rabbi; deported from Berlin to Auschwitz in March 1943.

24 Probably Peter Joseph (b. 1920), rabbi; qualified as a rabbi at the Higher Institute for Jewish Studies, 1941; worked thereafter as a rabbi in Berlin; deported to Auschwitz on 29 Nov. 1942.

25 Probably Dr Hans-Erich Fabian (1902–1974), lawyer; dismissed from the judiciary in 1933; appointed general secretary of the Higher Institute for Jewish Studies in Berlin in 1938; head of the organizational department of the Reich Association of Jews in Germany; deported to Theresienstadt in June 1943, but quickly brought back to Berlin, as the Gestapo needed him to wind up the assets of the Reich Association; chairman of the Jewish Community of Berlin from 1946; emigrated to the USA in 1949.

persons who could still be retrained for other work, quite apart from the almost insuperable difficulties associated with their immigration. – Please tell Baeck[26] from me that I have gathered from a letter sent here by his son-in-law that his family are evidently doing well. He's not able to hear from them directly, of course. – The institute still looks pretty impressive, I think. This place is just a teaching set-up, of course – so basically aimed at persons of average ability, and operating on the principle that young people (so it is claimed) have to be forced to learn. – Tell Schaefer – and please give him my regards – that he should write to me from the school and tell me about himself! – You write that you have been teaching Latin, standing in for Strauss. So where is Strauss, then?[27] – I haven't seen his obituary in the [*Jüdisches*] *Nachrichtenblatt*, which I get regularly. What you read in there is not even the bare bones of what's happening in the community. One hears the odd thing or two from letters etc., but otherwise it's a blanket of silence. So I should be delighted if you would write me another letter soon which is not just a reply to the various queries and suggestions in these lines. – My wife and I send warmest greetings to you and your wife and child.

Yours

DOC. 38

The Times, 16 December 1939: article on the situation of the Jews deported to the Lublin district[1]

Lublin for the Jews.
The Nazi Plan. A Stony Road to Extermination[2]

From a Correspondent[3]
Poland under German occupation has an area of about 70,000 square miles and a population of 22,500,000. The Provinces which had been Prussia before 1918 – Posnania, Pomorze, and Upper Silesia – have been incorporated in the Reich, and so has the northern fringe and a wide belt in the west of what had been Russian Poland before the last

26 Leo Baeck (1873–1956), rabbi; Reform rabbi in Oppeln and Düsseldorf, 1897–1912, and in Berlin, 1912–1942; lecturer at the Higher Institute for Jewish Studies, 1913–1942; served as chairman of the General Association of Rabbis in Germany from 1922; grand president of the German District of the B'nai B'rith Lodge; president of the Reich Representation of German Jews and subsequently the Reich Representation (later, Association) of Jews in Germany, 1933–1943; deported to Theresienstadt in 1943; emigrated to London after 1945; author of various works, including *The Essence of Judaism* (1936 [German edn, 1905]).

27 Herbert A. Strauss (1918–2005), historian; assistant rabbi and deployed as a forced labourer in Berlin, 1939–1942; fled to Switzerland in 1943; emigrated to the USA in 1946; professor in New York 1960–1972, where he founded the Research Foundation for Jewish Immigration in 1972; director of the Center for Research on Antisemitism in Berlin, 1982–1990; co-editor of the *Biographisches Handbuch der deutschsprachigen Emigration nach 1933*.

1 *The Times*, 16 Dec. 1939, p. 9. *The Times*, founded in 1785 as *The Daily Universal Register*, has appeared since 1788 as a daily newspaper in London under its current name. In the 1930s it had a circulation of 190,000 copies.

War: together an area of about 27,000 square miles, with a population of nearly 8,000,000. The remainder is appositely described by the Nazis as the Polish *Reststaat*.[4]

In this 'Remainder State' an area in the barren district round Lublin is to be set aside as a Jewish reserve (*Judenreservat*). Forecasts on the intended size of this concentration area differ widely; some put it at a few hundred square miles, others at 3,000 and more; not that this matters much, as it is clear that the scheme envisages a place for gradual extermination, and not what the Germans would describe as a *Lebensraum*. The maximum deportation programme comprises all the Jews now under German control: 180,000 from the original Reich, 65,000 from Austria, 75,000 from the Czech Protectorate, some 450,000 from the annexed Provinces of Poland, and nearly 1,500,000 from the Polish *Reststaat*. These figures are merely approximate even as a statistical survey. Will non-Aryan Christians be included? And how many Jews have by now perished in Poland under German occupation or have succeeded in escaping across the Russian frontier?

The number of the dead rises into tens of thousands, and of refugees into hundreds of thousands. But again the size of the programme is very nearly irrelevant: it amounts to a mass massacre such as Nazi imagination can conceive but even Nazi practice can hardly carry through in full. Meanwhile it serves as a means of torture for many thousands and of terror for all the rest.

Some Who Escaped

It is impossible to ascertain how many Jews have by now been deported to the Lublin *Reservat*.[5] Exact figures could be supplied only by the German authorities or by the Jewish communities which are forced to cooperate in this gruesome work; but the Nazis will not say, and the Jews do not dare to speak. Reliable information about these transactions is mainly derived from people who have succeeded in escaping across the Russian frontier. They know the size and fate of their own transports, and as much about others as they were able to collect from people with whom they happen to come in touch; but none of them can survey the entire enterprise. A few weeks ago the figure of 45,000 gained currency in the world Press, which seems to have been an exaggeration; at that time the number of Jews deported to the Lublin area can hardly have exceeded 10,000. So far transports are known to have reached the *Reservat* from Vienna, Mährisch-Ostrau in Moravia, Teschen and Katowice in Silesia; none apparently from the old Reich or the Polish *Reststaat*.[6]

The first purpose is to make room and obtain loot for Germans in the parts which have been singled out for systematic Germanization. Therefore, while the sadism of local Nazis, for instance in Vienna, may result in a transport being sent, the danger of system-

2 The article is illustrated with a map.

3 The author was Sir Lewis B. Namier, born Ludwig Bernstein Namierowski (1888–1960), historian; grew up in Galicia; emigrated to Britain in 1907; worked for the British Foreign Office, 1915–1920; worked as political secretary for the Jewish Agency for Palestine, 1929–1931; professor in Manchester, 1931–1953; active in refugee aid for the Jewish Agency in London, 1938–1945.

4 German: a remainder or rump state.

5 German: reservation.

6 Until the plan was discontinued, around 5,000 Jews from Vienna, Moravská Ostrava (Mährisch-Ostrau), and Katowice were deported to Nisko in the Lublin district in Oct. 1939.

atic evacuation seems greatest in the Czech Protectorate and in the western provinces of Poland.

The following account is compiled from information supplied by 'evacuees' who succeeded in reaching a neutral northern country by way of Russia. Early in October the Jewish community of Mährisch-Ostrau was ordered to compile a register of all male Jews between the ages of 17 and 55, and to call for volunteers for a 'retraining camp' in connexion with the proposed Jewish reservation round Lublin. Very few having responded, the Nazis ordered all Jews between 17 and 70 to register and to parade on October 17, at 8 a.m., at the Ostrau riding school.

A Closed Train

Each man was ordered to take a knapsack, a suit case, food for three days, a maximum of 300m.[7] They were told to take leave of their families at home, as no one would be allowed to accompany them and strict silence would be enforced at the school. There was to have been a medical examination, and men adjudged invalids were to be dismissed; but the so-called examination was a farce, and even serious diseases were not considered sufficient ground for exemption. About 1,000 men were taken in buses to the railway station. As that ghoulish cortège proceeded through the streets of Mährisch-Ostrau non-Jewish Czechs, and even some German women, were seen crying bitterly.

The train remained in the station till the next morning. The journey to Nisko, southwest of Lublin, took three days. After Cracow it was forbidden to open the windows or obtain water at railway stations. At Nisko the transport was divided into two groups. About 650 younger men for work were sent to Zarzecze, and some 450 old men and invalids to Pysznica. At Zarzecze the younger men were mustered in a field adjoining a peasant farm. The S.S. guards were lodged in a barn; the doctors in another outhouse; the men were ordered to start building barracks under the direction of Jewish engineers included in the transport. Tired out by the journey, in pouring rain, inexperienced at the work, they had to begin. Three days and nights were spent in the open, and it took two or three weeks before the barracks were tolerably habitable. No wages were paid and no food was supplied. The Jews had to live on the means they had brought with them. The party, composed of elderly men and invalids, which was sent to Pysznica, was the first night attacked by local bands of peasants. One Jew was killed, another gravely wounded, and all were robbed of their belongings. They scattered in the dark, some losing their way in the surrounding marshes and forests.

A few days later further transports arrived from Vienna and Katowice, including some small children. Distributed to various townships and villages, the Jews were attacked by the local peasants, and about 15 were killed. Then the Jews made contact with the Polish mayors and clergy, and secured some help and protection in return for medical service rendered where epidemics are rife and doctors scarce. But the peasant guards did not prove invariably reliable. In one case they led a party of Jews into a marsh, robbed them, and left them to their fate; six men perished.

7 300 Reichsmarks.

Next the Jews organized their own self-defence, and this, combined with the rendering of medical help, enabled them safely to proceed further afield towards the Russian frontier. Considerable numbers, especially of the younger and more enterprising, have since succeeded in crossing that frontier into a land which, by comparison, is to them one of freedom and safety. But whether such mass escapes will be possible when the numbers of deportees increase seems doubtful. There is another camp at Tomashov,[8] near Lublin, where some 700 Jews are kept under strict discipline by the S.S.; and although they do not seem to be subjected to physical ill-treatment, they are slowly being starved to death.

In No Man's Land

Here is another account from a man included in the Teschen transport. The Jewish community of Teschen was ordered within 48 hours to muster all men between 14 and 60, and send them to the railway station; 145 were gathered from Teschen, and about 350 from the surrounding district. Every man was allowed to take 600 Polish zlotys and 60lb. luggage, but a short distance farther, at Bielitz, they were robbed of all their money and belongings. Next, in spite of severe weather, they were put into open cattle trucks, 90 to 100 men in each: they had to stand all the way. This transport was sent to Ulanov, near the River San. They camped for a few days in the open. Afterwards the younger and stronger were picked out and put to work, while the older and weaker were marched off, and when after three hours they reached the river, which forms the frontier with Russia, they were shown two directions in which they were to proceed to clear out of the German occupied territory. They were told that if they returned they would be shot. Some have reached Lvov, but of a good many nothing has been heard since; they may have been drowned or shot, or may be wandering about somewhere in No Man's Land.

In some camps in the Lublin area the Jews are allowed occasionally to write home; in others, all intercourse with the outer world is forbidden. None the less, news about conditions in the Lublin concentration area has spread throughout the Jewish communities under Nazi rule, and men who are threatened, or think themselves threatened, with transportation very often disappear or commit suicide. The fear of Lublin is sometimes deliberately exploited by the Nazis. In Vienna the Jews were told by one of the Nazi chiefs that by February the town must be judenrein (cleansed of Jews); they have to emigrate, or will be sent to Lublin, or combed out in other ways. But where are they to go?

8 The author means Tomaszów Lubelski.

DOC. 39
On 19 December 1939 the Reich Security Main Office plans a meeting of departmental heads to discuss a 'Jewish reservation'[1]

Letter from the RSHA, II/II 112 (Dö.),[2] Berlin, to the Head of Office II of the RSHA,[3] dated 19 December 1939

Re: key points for consideration at the meeting of departmental heads regarding the issue of Jewry.
Case file: your circular of 18 December 1939[4]
Final solution to Germany's Jewish problem.

I. *Jewish reservation in Poland.*
The question arises as to whether a Jewish reservation should be established in Poland, or whether the Jews should be relocated to the future [General] Government of Poland. If it is planned to establish a reservation, then we need to consider whether it should be administered by Jews or by Germans from the Reich. A Jewish administration would be more advantageous, as fewer German administrators would then be required. Only managerial posts would need to be filled by Germans. A further decision would then have to be taken about overall control: to whom would the administration be accountable?

It would make sense to leave the administration under the control of the Security Police until such time as the relocation of the Jews from the Reich, the Ostmark, and Bohemia/Moravia has been completed.

II.
In this regard, a definitive decision would have to be taken about Jewish emigration: should it be continued, if this reservation is going to be established?

1 BArch, R 58/544, fol. 218r–v. Published in Kurt Pätzold (ed.), *Verfolgung, Vertreibung, Vernichtung: Dokumente des faschistischen Antisemitismus 1933 bis 1942* (Leipzig: Reclam, 1991), p. 253. This document has been translated from German.

2 Karl Döscher (b. 1913), businessman; joined the NSDAP and the SA in 1932, and the SS in 1934; worked initially in the SD Main District East; transferred to the SD Main Office, Section II 112 (Jewish questions) in May 1938, and was appointed head of this section in the Reich Security Main Office (RSHA) in Sept. 1939; SS-Obersturmführer, 1940; police officer in Göttingen, working in a managerial capacity after 1945.

3 Dr Franz Alfred Six (1909–1975), lawyer; joined the NSDAP in 1930, the SA in 1932, and the SS in 1935; from 1935 worked in the SD; professor in Königsberg, 1938, and in Berlin, 1939; head of Office II (research on adversaries) in the RSHA, 1939; head of the Advance Commando Moscow within Einsatzgruppe B, 1941; head of the Cultural Policy Department in the Reich Foreign Office, 1942; sentenced to twenty years' imprisonment at the Nuremberg Military Tribunals in 1948; released in 1952; advertising consultant at Porsche-Diesel-Motorenbau, 1956–1963; management consultant in Essen from 1963.

4 On 18 Dec. 1939 Six had written to all departments of Office II in the RSHA, announcing a meeting of departmental heads to be held on 20 Dec. 1939, and requesting them to draft a discussion document: BArch, R 58/544, fol. 217.

In foreign policy terms, a reservation would also be a good way of bringing pressure to bear on the Western powers. And perhaps, following on from this, the question of a global solution could be broached when the war ends.[5]

DOC. 40

On 21 December 1939 the Reich Security Main Office informs all Gestapo offices that Himmler has suspended the deportation of Jews to the General Government[1]

Letter from the RSHA Berlin (S-IV [II Rz.] 565/39), signed Müller,[2] to all State Police offices and head offices, for the information of the inspectors of the Security Police and SD (received at the State Police head office in Stettin on 23 December 1939), dated 21 December 1939[3]

Re: deportation of Jews from the Reich to the occupied Polish territories.
Case file: none.
The Reichsführer SS and Chief of the German Police has ordered that all deportation of Jews from the Old Reich, the Ostmark, and the Protectorate to the occupied Polish territories must cease until further notice. I am writing to inform you of this, and request that the order be strictly adhered to.

p.p.
signed *Müller*

5 The meeting ultimately took place a day early, on 19 Dec. 1939; immediately afterwards, Eichmann was appointed by Heydrich as 'special expert' for dealing with the centralized Security Police arrangements as the clearance of the eastern territories was carried out. Cited in Peter Longerich, *Holocaust: The Nazi Persecution and Murder of the Jews*, new edn, trans. Shaun Whiteside (Oxford, Oxford University Press, 2010 [German edn, 1998]), p. 156.

1 RGVA, 500k-1-324; copy in USHMM, RG-11.001M04, reel 72. This document has been translated from German.

2 Heinrich Müller (1900–1945), originally an aircraft fitter; worked at the police headquarters in Munich from 1919, and from 1929 was responsible for monitoring communist organizations for the Political Police; joined the SS in 1934; transferred to the Gestapo Central Office (Gestapa) in Berlin; deputy head of the department of the Political Police division in the Main Office of the Security Police, 1936; joined the NSDAP in 1938; managing director of the Reich Central Agency for Jewish Emigration and chief of Office IV (Gestapo) in the RSHA, 1939; attended the Wannsee Conference in 1942. Missing, presumed dead, since 1945.

3 The original contains handwritten annotations and underlining, and carries the official stamp 'RFSS u.Ch.d.DtPol. im RMdI' (Reichsführer SS and Chief of the German Police in the Reich Ministry of the Interior), as well as the note: 'Witnessed: Dietrich, Chancellery clerk'.

DOC. 41
At the end of 1939 the dramatic situation of the Jews in Vienna is depicted in a report for the American Jewish Joint Distribution Committee[1]

Anonymous report for the American Jewish Joint Distribution Committee, undated[2]

The Jews in Austria at the End of 1939
There are still about 60,000 Jews in Vienna living under the saddest imaginable conditions. Most of them have been evicted from their apartments and are compelled to find lodgings as sub-tenants. In the 2nd and 20th districts two or three families comprising 8 to 12 people must sometimes live herded together in a single room.

Officially, three months' notice should be served on Jews,[3] which is the regular period, but in practice Jews are asked to come to the Vienna Municipal Lodging Office and are compelled to promise to leave their homes 'voluntarily' in one or two weeks. This is brought about by use of all the well-known Nazi methods of pressure.

The men have to face the wall for hours and hear threats that they are to be shot that very day. They are beaten up by the S.S. and S.A. men on guard, made to wash the stairs, run about and curse and spit at one another. New lodgings are given arbitrarily and are often already occupied, with the result that those living in them must clear out. It therefore happens that poor people must change the rooms they live in as sub-tenants several times in a few months, a process which costs them their last savings.

On the outbreak of war, men of Polish nationality and stateless of Polish origin were arrested and placed in primitive provisional centres. About 2,000 persons, aged 16 to 87, were arrested and about half of these were sent to the Buchenwald concentration camp early in October; as to conditions there, it suffices to say that within 6 or 7 weeks, about 300 persons died. The relatives in Vienna receive telegrams daily from the Camp Commandant, informing them that a father, brother or son has passed on. With the excuse, possibly true, that there is an epidemic of dysentery at Buchenwald, all communication with the prisoners is forbidden and they are not even allowed to receive small amounts of money or packages. With the epidemic, the bad weather and the treatment meted out (they are compelled to sleep in unheated tents), there is a great danger that those still alive are condemned to death.[4]

There are also about 200 persons at Dachau and Buchenwald who were there before the war. They are lodged somewhat better, but there is hardly any hope that they will be released in the near future.

Late in September the Viennese Jewish Community was ordered to list the men between 18 and 60 and to send them to Poland under the supervision of the Central Office for Jewish Emigration. Instructions were to the effect that two transports of 1,000 persons each were to leave weekly. The first two transports, composed only of men, were

1 JDC Archives, AR 1933/45, 440. The original document is in English.
2 The text is described as a 'translation'. The original, presumably German, has not been found.
3 On Jews being forced to move out of their apartments, see PMJ 2/277. In accordance with § 2 of the Law on Tenancy Agreements with Jews, the legal period of notice could be ignored if the shelter of the tenant was assured: *Reichsgesetzblatt*, 1939, I, pp. 864–865.
4 See Introduction, p. 31, and Doc. 33.

to be followed by others with women and children. It may be said that similar transports were ordered in Bohemia and Moravia and actually sent. Through the efforts of the Viennese Jewish Community, only 1,500 men in two transports were sent to Poland in 4 weeks, instead of the 8,000 who were supposed to go. During this time 3,500 were sent out of Bohemia and Moravia. A third transport, comprising men, women and children, was cancelled at that last moment and the people were interned in the Refuge of the Jewish Community. According to the authorities, they will only be freed if they can show a permit to enter another country. The transports to Poland have been postponed and are to be resumed in March.[5] There are various rumours concerning the reasons for the postponement. It is said that the military authorities are opposed to these transports and the settlement of the Jews in the territory between the San and the Vistula (Nisko, Lublin). This territory is not at all suited to the settlement of large masses. Most of the villages and towns are in ruins and living quarters are not to be found, while means of earning a living are non-existant. Food supplies are short and difficult to obtain. Bands of Polish peasants roam the roads and woods and rob the Jewish traveller, taking from them most of the 50 kg. baggage the German authorities allowed them to take along.

Only 400 to 500 artisans can be placed in the single labour camp at Nisko and all the other Jews have had to go North and East of Nisko without knowing whither they were drifting. Most of those brought to Poland left their baggage and walked 60 to 80 km. to the Russian border, which they crossed clandestinely. Little is known regarding their fate.[6]

The organization of these poorly prepared transports is naturally considered a great misfortune by the Jews in Vienna and they regard the possibility of their resumption in March 1940 with dread. The German authorities do not know themselves how the transfer is to take place and it seems that this is a planless action carried on without care for the results. A number of Jews committed suicide to avoid being deported to Poland.

Immediately after the war started, the Jews in Vienna were prohibited to appear on the streets after 8 o'clock in the evening. After the attempted assassination on the 9th of November in the Bürgerbräu Keller in Munich, the curfew of the Jews was fixed at 4 o'clock in the afternoon.[7] These measures are extremely trying because they leave the Jews only a few hours to make their purchases and take care of personal affairs.

The food cards issued to the Jews were stamped with a 'J' in November.[8] In spite of these cards, however, Jews find great difficulty in purchasing provisions. Many shops have signs to the effect that nothing will be sold to Jews, and Jewish women, desiring to make purchases, during the hours permitted, often hear that there is nothing left because

5 See Doc. 40.

6 See Doc. 38. Many of the Jews deported fled to the German–Soviet demarcation line or fended for themselves in other places in the area. When the camp in Zarzecze near Nisko was closed in April 1940, around 500 inmates returned to Vienna or Moravská Ostrava.

7 On 8 Nov. 1939 the carpenter Johann Georg Elser had attempted to assassinate Hitler by planting a bomb in the Bürgerbräu beer hall in Munich. Following the outbreak of war, a night time curfew was imposed on Jews: see the Karlsruhe Gestapo decree concerning a directive of the Reichsführer SS and Chief of the German Police issued on 10 Sept. 1939, instructing that the Jewish community be informed of a curfew for Jews after 8 p.m., published in Sauer (ed.), *Dokumente über die Verfolgung der jüdischen Bürger in Baden-Württemberg*, no. 397, p. 176. The existence of a curfew starting at 4 p.m. could not be verified.

8 See Doc. 36, fn. 7.

the Aryans have already bought up everything. It goes without saying that Jews are not allowed to go to restaurants, cafés or other public places.[9] They have been excluded from cinemas and theatres for a long time.[10] All Jews have been compelled to turn over their radios to the Gestapo.[11]

Mortality among the Jews is increasing in spite of the fact that two-thirds of the population have already emigrated. Undernourishment is commencing to make its effect felt, especially among the children.

Summarising, it must be said that the Jews in Vienna are living under dreadful conditions and that the spiritual torture to which they are subjected is unbearable. Robbed of their property, homeless and without any possibility of earning a living, they are scarcely able to stand up against the constantly increasing pressure and await their emigration with longing. This pressure on the part of the authorities started with the Anschluss in March 1938 and has continued ever since. Authorities state frankly that Austria must get rid of its Jews and that they will not be permitted to remain in the country after 1940.

Emigration therefore remains the only possibility of salvation for the Jews; a large number have already left and, if we consider those who will have to remain and die in Austria, only about 30,000 people are involved. Of this number, 10,000 hope to go to the United States in 1940, 5,000 to Palestine and 4,000 to 5,000 to Shanghai and Central and South America. Establishment of a transit camp in one of the neutral countries for approximately 10,000 people is an absolute necessity and possible without expending very much money. This would permit the complete solution of the question of Jewish emigration from Austria in the year 1940 and would prevent the execution of the plan to deport the Jews to Poland.

DOC. 42

Washington Post, 14 January 1940: article on the increasing exclusion of Jews in Germany[1]

Reich Denies Meat, Clothes Cards to Jews. Persecution Pressed In Many Ways to Drive Out Race

By Louis P. Lochner,[2] Associated Press Staff Writer

Berlin, Jan. 13. – Germany's Jews, already subjected to extensive restrictions, have received another shock in calling for ration cards for the period of January 15 to February 11.

9 See Doc. 4, fnn. 9 and 10.

10 On 15 Nov. 1938 Goebbels had decreed that Jews be forbidden from entering theatres, concerts, lectures, film screenings, dance performances, and exhibitions: *Amtliche Mitteilungen der Reichsmusikkammer*, no. 22, 15 Nov. 1938, p. 77.

11 The Reich Security Main Office (RSHA) issued a decree on 19 Oct. 1939 ordering the confiscation of wireless radio sets from Jews and *Mischlinge*: see Doc. 15, fn. 5.

1 *Washington Post*, 14 Jan. 1940, pp. 1 and 4. The *Washington Post* was founded in 1877 and is the largest daily newspaper in Washington, DC. In 1931 the morning edition had a circulation of 75,000 copies.

They found that coupons for a total of 125 grams (almost 4½ ounces) of meat and all coupons for podded vegetables – such as peas, beans and lentils – were invalidated as far as they were concerned.
They further were denied general ration cards recently issued to all other Germans to enable them to obtain certain extras when the Nazi regime finds itself able to grant something beyond the ordinary daily allotment.
Jews must have the letter J stamped on their ration cards,[3] enabling a tradesman to declare he has not in stock what the Jews ask for or in other ways to discriminate against them.
For certain foods not yet rationed one must enter his name on his grocer's or butcher's list.
Poultry and fish, for instance, are obtained after registration. Tradesmen, with but few exceptions, will not register Jews.
Jews are barred from appearing in stores or at markets before noon and after 2 p.m.[4] Most of the supplies on the market have been sold by noon or only second-rate goods may be left.
Every German must have a clothes card to obtain wearing apparel but Jews have been denied such cards.[5]
Those still possessing adequate clothing say they will not be able to buy thread or yarn and they do not know how their shoes can be repaired once the soles are worn out.
Jews are required to remain indoors after 8 o'clock each night but the hardship of this is less than it might be since they are barred anyway from the theater, concerts and the opera.[6]
However, many are now required to stay in apartments which often are crowded since the Jews are becoming herded together in smaller living space than they formerly had.
Just how many landlords have availed themselves of the possibility given under Nazi law of breaking leases with Jews cannot be determined.[7]
The Nazi idea is that any apartment house constitutes a miniature community in which the Jew will be a disturbing factor.
Originally it was intended to establish virtual ghettos in all cities where Jews were left. But this idea apparently has been abandoned. Major effort is aimed at ridding Germany of Jews.
Of Berlin's 59,000 Jews, some 20,000 have been assigned to street cleaning, snow shoveling, road building and other manual work, including forestry and gardening tasks.

2 Louis P. Lochner, born Ludwig Paul Lochner (1887–1975), American journalist and author; worked for the Associated Press in Berlin from 1924 and was head of the Berlin bureau of the Associated Press from 1928 to 1942; president of the US Chamber of Commerce in Germany, 1936–1941; Pulitzer Prize for his reporting from Nazi Germany, 1936; interned in Germany, Dec. 1941 until May 1942; correspondent for the National Broadcasting Company (NBC) and Associated Press (AP) from 1943; war correspondent in Europe, 1944–1945; editor of *The Goebbels Diaries, 1942–1943* (1948).
3 See Doc. 36, fn. 7.
4 On restrictions to shopping hours, see Doc. 36.
5 On the withdrawal of clothing ration cards, see Doc. 36, fn. 4.
6 See Doc. 41, fnn. 8 and 11.
7 Law on Tenancy Agreements with Jews of 30 April 1939, *Reichsgesetzblatt*, 1939, I, pp. 864–865; see also PMJ 2/277.

Jewesses, ousted from work earlier in the Nazi regime, have been pressed into work, serving chiefly as maids, farmerettes and textile workers.[8]

Apparently early morning raids upon the Jews and their imprisonment in concentration camps no longer occur wholesale.

It has been pointed out that the regime knows the status of every Jew, has seized virtually all Jewish wealth and has but one more interest therefore, namely to get the Jew out of the country.

Jews who are delivered to concentration camps meet with stern treatment which is even more severe if the warden is particularly anti-Semitic.

But no Jew likes to talk about his experience in such a camp and generally speaking, the non-Jewish Germans know little about the status of the Jews since restrictive measures no longer take the form of decrees but rather orders for [wh]ich the Gestapo holds officers of the Jewish community responsible.

Each Jew, therefore, learns of new measures by letter from the leaders in his community.

Adolph[9] Hitler, in his Reichstag speech of last January 30, threatened:

'Today I will once more be a prophet: If international financiers[10] in and outside of Europe should succeed in plunging nations once more into a world war, then the result will not be the bolshevization of the earth and thus a victory of Jewry, but the annihilation of the Jewish race in Europe.'

Apparently his followers are taking those words rather literally so far as conquered Poland is concerned, for such details as do leak out indicate short shrift is given any Jew who runs afoul [of] Nazi orders.

Disease is a potent ally in the elimination process, and wholesale smuggling of Polish Jews from the German-occupied portion of Poland to Russia further rids the German conquerors of responsibility for many Jews.

Polish Jews are being ousted rapidly from areas annexed permanently by the Reich. Lublin evidently is being converted into a Jewish reservation.

Since the movement of several thousand Jews from Vienna, Prague and Maehrisch-Ostrau, however, apparently no efforts are being made to send others from greater Germany to the reservation.[11]

In the Bohemia-Moravia protectorate, the Jewish community has been informed that all Jews under 60 must leave before the end of May. Those left when the deadline is reached face the threat of being imprisoned in concentration camps.[12]

8 On labour service, see Introduction, pp. 42–43.
9 Spelling as in the original.
10 The wording in Hitler's speech of 30 Jan. 1939 is 'international Jewish financiers': see PMJ 2/248.
11 On the deportations to Nisko in the Lublin district, see Doc. 16, fn. 9.
12 This measure was not carried out.

DOC. 43

On 19 January 1940 Margarete Korant from Berlin tells her daughter how she was humiliated while shopping[1]

Handwritten letter from Margarete Korant,[2] Berlin, to her daughter Ilse Schwalbe,[3] 251 South 15th Street, San José, California, USA, dated 19 January 1940

My dear child,

I had only just put a letter to you in the postbox when I received your airmail letter of 21 December. I won't reply to it for a few more days now, as this present letter is going off with the normal post. Since I can't send you the right heel-pads, because they won't take samples of no commercial value, I'll send a couple of different ones, which are not so practical, but may do the job anyway. Unfortunately you have to stick them into the shoe, which means you can't change them later. The letter J is meant for your coat; I wear one myself. There are so many things available here, even flowers that light up, which have spawned an entire industry.[4] It is bitterly cold again ([minus] 15–20°), and I am very glad of my electric fire. The heating is wretched – today, for example, it's not working again – but we've had some coal via h.s.d.,[5] so I expect things will be better again tomorrow. This time we were given one less food ration card, a so-called supplementary card for non-rationed food items (i.e. no card required), which include pulses, rice, chocolate, game, poultry, herrings, etc. As I was on a customer list for the last item, I went to go and get some, but the woman took a very snide tone with me and said I surely must know that non-Aryans are not getting supplementary food items any more. It goes right through me, every time I hear something like that; you never get used to this kind of thing. In our neighbourhood we are not allowed to go to the markets and many of the shops before noon,[6] and you can probably imagine how much is still left on the market by that time. I'm really sorry I haven't received the pictures of you and little Steffi;[7] it's appalling, the amount of post that goes astray. Auntie Dussel has been ill for several days now; I shall go and visit her later. We had another long letter from C's, addressed to O. again; they have already received at least four letters, and can't bring

1 Jüdisches Museum Berlin, Sammlung Familie Korant Schwalbe Striem, 2006/57/209. This document has been translated from German.

2 Margarete Korant, née Apt (1882–1942); lived initially in Dresden, but at the age of 12, following the death of her parents, she and her two sisters went to live with an uncle in Breslau. In 1903 she married Georg Korant and in 1910 moved to Berlin, where Georg Korant died in 1937; on 25 Jan. 1942 deported to Riga, where she was murdered.

3 Ilse Schwalbe, née Korant (1904–1992), secretary; worked in her uncle's leather goods shop in Oppeln, 1923–1924; in 1926 married Herbert Schwalbe, who then emigrated to Palestine in 1933 and in 1938 to the USA; secretary at the Child and Youth Aliyah in Berlin, 1934–1939; emigrated to the USA in March 1939, where she held posts including that of secretary to the Jewish Community in San José.

4 No further details are available. The requirement for Jews to wear identifying markers was not introduced in the Reich until 1 Sept. 1941; see Doc. 212.

5 No further details are available.

6 See Doc. 42.

7 Stephanie Wells, born Steffi Brigitte Schwalbe (b. 1931), teacher; granddaughter of Margarete Korant; emigrated to the USA in March 1939 with her mother and her brother Reiner Max; after graduating from university she worked as a teacher of German and Spanish.

themselves to reply. If they would only write to me instead, they'd get a quicker response, but they've obviously completely forgotten that I even exist. Auntie Ellen[8] has visited the boy and writes that he looks great, and he seems to be doing very well. I do hope you receive this letter and its various enclosures. Hugs and kisses to you all, I miss you all so very much – with fondest love,

Your Grandma-Mummy

As the letter is double the standard weight, I'll send you two rather than just the one. Hopefully they'll both get to you.

DOC. 44
On 27 January 1940 Alfred Rosenberg describes in his diary how he joked with Hitler about antisemitism in Russia[1]

Diary of Alfred Rosenberg,[2] Berlin, entry for 27 January 1940

27 Jan.
At lunch today the Führer was very jovial again. The imprudent admissions of Lord Lloyd[3] that Poland had only been a pretext for the British to pursue their war policy have pleased him greatly. Also, the other, very confused voices showed, as he said, that things are not going well for the English. They are reported to have lost 60 per cent of their feed imports and want to reduce this loss to 40 per cent.[4]

During the meal the Führer talked about Poland: the small, previously ruling class had regarded the land as a plantation, while it mostly lived in Paris rather than in the [Polish] countryside. I commented that the Counter-Reformation [in the sixteenth and seventeenth centuries] had only achieved a deliberate process of eradication here;

8 Ellen Cohn, née Apt (b. 1887), sister of Margarete Korant; emigrated to Britain in July 1939.

1 USHMM, RG-71 Acc. 2001.62.14, published in *Das Politische Tagebuch Alfred Rosenbergs aus den Jahren 1934/35 und 1939/40. Nach der photographischen Wiedergabe der Handschrift aus den Nürnberger Akten*, ed. Hans-Günther Seraphim (Göttingen: Musterschmidt, 1956). Published in English in *The Political Diary of Alfred Rosenberg and the Onset of the Holocaust*, ed. Jürgen Matthäus and Frank Bajohr (Lanham, MA: Rowman & Littlefield, 2015), pp. 184–186. This document has been newly translated from the original German.

2 Alfred Rosenberg (1893–1946), architect and publicist; was born in Reval (Tallinn), grew up in Riga, and studied at university in Moscow until 1918; joined the SA in 1921; participated in the Beer Hall Putsch in 1923; joined the NSDAP in 1925; editor-in-chief, 1923–1924 and 1926–1937, and editor, 1938–1945, of the *Völkischer Beobachter*; member of the Reichstag from 1930; head of the Foreign Policy Office of the NSDAP, 1933–1945; plenipotentiary of the Führer for the supervision of the entire intellectual and ideological training and schooling of the NSDAP (Amt Rosenberg), 1934–1945; Reich minister for the occupied eastern territories from July 1941 to 1945; sentenced to death by the International Military Tribunal at Nuremberg in 1946 and executed.

3 George Ambrose Lloyd (1879–1941), politician; governor of Bombay, 1918–1923; high commissioner in Egypt, 1925–1929; secretary of state for the colonies and leader of the House of Lords, 1940–1941.

4 The former Liberal prime minister David Lloyd George (1863–1945) had given a speech in the House of Commons criticizing Britain's lack of preparations for ensuring food and feed supplies in the event of war. Britain's guarantee in March 1939 to provide military assistance to Poland was a sign that the government had known for months that war was inevitable: *The Times* (parliamentary reports), 26 Jan. 1940, p. 3.

the dominant group remaining was a stratum with a thin veneer of social culture, one capable of some courageous outbursts but incapable of constructive development. – In Poland a real show of resistance was not to be expected, the Führer said, and slapped me on the arm and said laughingly: The only resistance left is that of the Balts. Yes, if you give them *one* business, they want the next one, etc. I said: That is perhaps not entirely true. For example, the owner of a leather factory is to be given a shoe repair shop, a hotel owner is offered a job as a waiter, etc. And then those affected complain that this was surely not the point of the [resettlement] exercise.[5]

Only an hour previously I had sent Himmler a factual letter along with some enclosures.[6] The Balts are surely not to be dealt with so easily as the Volhynian Germans,[7] who gave up little and were always smallholders. The Balts know, of course, that they once stood for culture, and strong personalities do not want to simply allow themselves to be pushed back and forth by bureaucrats like a herd of refugees. – Himmler simply has an aversion to the Balts, so it may be assumed that he has made a few plain remarks to the Führer in specific form about the cold, the winter baggage that cannot be found, etc.

In closing I asked the Führer to receive Dr Lammers and me so that we could present the draft of the assignment. Because Hess[8] happened to be standing nearby, the Führer asked if he was in agreement. H[ess] said he had not yet read the most recent version. I said: It is still the same one used by *you*. The Führer: Then it is fine; if Hess agrees then you can finalize the matter. After all the attempts to delay it, however, I will not rest easy until the signature is really on the document.[9]

By the by, Hess gave the Führer the report of a German captain who had been in Odessa again after many years. The man said that in contrast to earlier times he had not encountered a single Jew in the government agencies. This gave rise to one of the now frequent observations about *whether* in this respect there is *really* a transformation under way in Russia. I remarked that if this trend was really starting it would end with a terrible pogrom against the Jews. The Führer said that perhaps in that case a frightened Europe

5 Beginning in Oct. 1939, in accordance with a secret protocol added to the German–Soviet Non-Aggression Pact, the German minority living in Estonia and Latvia were resettled to the annexed eastern territories, where they were allocated the apartments, farms, and jobs of the expelled Jewish and non-Jewish Poles.

6 These could not be found.

7 Ethnic Germans from the region of Volhynia, which was divided between Poland and Russia following the First World War.

8 Rudolf Hess (1894–1987), businessman; member of the Thule Society; joined the NSDAP in 1920, participated in 1923 in the Beer Hall Putsch, for which he was imprisoned in Landsberg am Lech; Hitler's private secretary; Deputy of the Führer, 1933–1941. On 10 May 1941 Hess secretly flew to Scotland to visit the Duke of Hamilton, apparently in order to attempt to initiate peace negotiations; remained a prisoner in Britain until the end of the war; in 1946 was sentenced to life imprisonment by the International Military Tribunal at Nuremberg; committed suicide while serving his sentence.

9 Presumably Rosenberg was hoping that Hitler would consent to his plans for an Advanced School (Hohe Schule). On 29 Jan. 1940 Hitler – bypassing the Reich Minister of Education – officially tasked Rosenberg with preparations for the creation of an NSDAP Advanced School, which was to be 'the central facility for National Socialist research, teaching, and education'; order, signed by Hitler, V 6/40, re: creation of an NSDAP Advanced School, 29. Jan. 1940, BArch, R 43 II/604, fol. 14.

would come begging *him* to ensure humanitarianism in the East … Everyone laughed. F[ührer]: And Rosenberg would have to be the secretary at the congress presided over by me on the humane treatment of the Jews. And incidentally, a new Russian film has been released that deals with earlier Polish–Russian conflicts.[10] I said: Yes, I had heard about it; it also looks at the policy of the Vatican during that period. F[ührer]: Would it be possible to show this film sometime? I replied, sorrowfully: Anything that discusses the Vatican can of course not be shown here [in Germany]. This naturally gave rise to more laughter. Bormann[11] nudged me, laughing: It is only possible to see such a thing in Russia – alas!

DOC. 45
In January 1940 the Gleiwitz District Office of the Reich Association of Jews in Germany provides information about the emigration levy[1]

Bulletin of the Gleiwitz District Office of the Reich Association of Jews in Germany, signed by Judicial Counsellor Adolph Israel Kochmann,[2] dated January 1940

Bulletin concerning the Jewish emigration levy
In order to obtain a certificate of receipt for passports, each emigrating person must pay to the Reich Association of Jews in Germany an emigration levy of an amount stipulated by the government.[3]

For the calculation of this levy the following documents are *absolutely* necessary:
1. Income tax assessment from the relevant tax office for the years 1937, 1938, 1939.
2. Assets tax assessment valid as of 1 January 1940.
3. Confirmation from the relevant Jewish religious association that the membership fees and other dues, such as Jewish Winter Relief, burial services, etc., have been paid for the years 1938, 1939, and 1940 (through to 31 December 1940). The confirmation must indi-

10 This presumably refers to the period film *Minin i Pozharskii* (1939), which portrays the popular uprising against the invasion of Russia by Polish troops in 1611.
11 Martin Bormann (1900–1945), labourer; sentenced to one year's imprisonment in 1924 for incitement to murder; joined the NSDAP and the SA in 1927; main department head in the Reichsleitung of the NSDAP from 1933; chief of staff for the Deputy of the Führer, 1933–1941; member of the Reichstag, 1933–1945; joined the SS in 1937; member of the personal staff of the Führer, 1938–1945; SS-Obergruppenführer, 1940; head of the Party Chancellery, 1941–1945; Hitler's secretary and personal adjutant, 1943–1945; committed suicide.

1 AŻIH, 112/3, fol. 158. This document has been translated from German.
2 Dr Arthur Adolph Kochmann (1864–1943), judicial counsellor; member of the Landtag for the German Democratic Party (DDP) in Prussia, 1919; city councillor for many years; honorary citizen of Gleiwitz; chairman of the synagogue congregation; representative for Upper Silesia in the Reich Representation of German Jews after 1933; lawyer and notary in Gleiwitz until 1938; deported on 24 Dec. 1943 to Auschwitz, where he perished.
3 In addition to the Reich Flight Tax (*Reichsfluchtsteuer*), Jews were required to pay an emigration levy (*Auswanderungsabgabe*); this was calculated according to income and assets and was intended to enable poorer Jews to emigrate. The levy, which increased each year, was payable to the Deutsche Golddiskontbank. The Deutsche Golddiskontbank, a subsidiary of the Reichsbank created in 1924 for financing raw material imports, was dissolved in 1945.

cate the records that were used and the amount of the fees that were calculated for each year, because a verification of the information will be undertaken.

4. If it is not possible to provide a property tax assessment valid as of 1 January 1940, the valuation must be made on the basis of the most recent property tax assessment. In such cases a reduction of assets may be taken into account, provided there is *documentary evidence* to demonstrate this.

5. *Upon application*, the following will be considered in relation to the emigration levy:

(a) a transfer via the Golddiskontbank to be undertaken, envisaged, or already carried out in connection with the emigration,

(b) the costs of transporting goods to the emigration destination and the cost of the journey, if these are paid for in Reichsmarks,

(c) any duties paid to the Golddiskontbank (gold duty),[4]

(d) any outstanding tax payments (state taxes),

(e) cost of living from the day of the application until the moment of emigration, in accordance with the social and financial circumstances of the applicant.

Evidence must be provided for all claims listed under 5.

6. As a general rule, the payment of the emigration levy is to be made in cash. Only if cash payment is not possible will securities be accepted.

7. Applications for the issuing of an emigration levy certificate must be submitted in a timely manner and *all required documents must be included*. In such cases the certificate will be issued within approximately three days. Missing documents will delay the processing of applications.

Certificates of receipt for passports will be issued *only after payment of the emigration levy* during working hours in the morning. The office is not open to the public in the afternoon.

DOC. 46

In late January 1940 employees at a retraining camp in Vienna send Gauleiter Josef Bürckel suggestions for the further deployment of Jewish workers[1]

Letter from the staff of the Retraining Camps for Non-Aryans, 11 Universitätsstraße, Vienna I, to Gauleiter Josef Bürckel (received on 31 January 1940), undated[2]

The staff of the Emigrant Retraining Camps for Non-Aryans who have been employed there since it was established would like to present the following remarks and request a decision.

4 Jews were permitted to take personal possessions and valuables out of the country only after they had paid their levy to the Golddiskontbank. Any cash transfers to their destination country also had to be made – with substantial deductions – via this bank.

1 ÖStA/AdR, Reichskommissar Bürckel/Materie, 2160/12. This document has been translated from German.

2 The original contains handwritten annotations.

This office was established on 29 Oct. 1938 under the leadership of retired Mayor Ernst Dürrfeld[3] for the following purpose: to group unemployed Viennese Jews in a provisional camp located in the wider surroundings of Vienna and, using this labour force, into which as many corresponding Jewish skilled craftsmen as possible were to be incorporated, to set up within a short time an initial camp[4] for about 400 people, and then to attach this initial camp to a large-scale camp in order to accommodate entire Jewish families in it.

The objectives were as follows:
(1) to free up apartments in Vienna
(2) to train Jews in suitable health for labour or to retrain them for agriculture and skilled trades, and
(3) to facilitate the emigration of these people.
This planned camp construction was, however, only completed to the point of establishing the initial camp, which was occupied initially in February 1939 with some 130 Jews. Due to the ordered downsizing of the office, all but 50 of these Jews were dismissed. In March and April 1939 new appointments then took place until the number of camp occupants totalled 160. Because the intended expansion of the camp did not take place, however, on orders of the employment office some 120 of these trained workers were released to the employment office of Vienna for productive labour deployment near Wels, in Stubachtal, in the Harz Mountains, and on the Dutch border. The remainder, approx. 40 men, were used for work in the fields and in road construction near Gänserndorf, for already in the harvest weeks even before the outbreak of war a shortage of Aryan labour was evident. During the period from the beginning of July to 13 October 1939, these people earned RM *3,688* by means of their labour deployment, although the wages, accommodating the rural population, only amounted to about RM 2 per person per day.

Since the outbreak of war the labour shortage has naturally grown even more and is evident in the increasing requests for labour submitted to the camp command by the farmers, for bringing in the root crops and the necessary tilling of the fields. For this purpose 40 new Jews were taken on via the employment office, and they lent such assistance to the remaining work in the fields that the district farmers' association expressed its gratitude to the camp command at the end of the work. As a consequence of the bad weather and the labour shortage setting in, another 50 Jews were removed as of 11 December 1939, so that the current number of Jews was 30, of whom today 20 are still working in the Angern distillery and the rest are utilized for tasks within the camp and snow [clearance] work. The wages received for the mandatory labour between October and *c.*20 December 1939 amount to around RM *4,850*. This year [it was] around RM *300* per week.

Since the funds that were provided for the office and the camp personnel have now been exhausted, and the negotiations for acquiring the camp for the purposes of the

3 Ernst Dürrfeld (1898–1945), unskilled worker; joined the NSDAP in 1922; local branch head, 1926–1935; later Kreisleiter of the NSDAP in Kaiserslautern; mayor of Saarbrücken, 1935–1937; member of the Reichstag from 1935; head of the Retraining Camps for Non-Aryans in Austria from 1938; economic advisor and department head in the Warsaw city administration, 1940–1944; at the Reich Ministry of Armaments and War Production, 1944–1945.

4 *Aufbaulager*: a camp set up to accommodate inmates who had the task of building a new camp.

DAF[5] or the municipality of Vienna must be considered to have failed – insofar as both solutions being pursued would not have conformed to the fundamental purposes of the camp – we request that the following suggestion meet with a favourable response. With the arrival of spring there will surely be an increased shortage of farm labour. Therefore, starting on 20 February of the current year, the size of the camp is to be increased to about 250 and these people are to be given preliminary training as labourers straight away in preparation for the coming spring field work, so that it is certain that no cultivated fields will be left unused due to a lack of labourers. With the completion of this work and the gradual increase [in numbers] and work training, by the end of April of the current year a workforce of about 400 serviceable Jews could be available. These Jews would either, as happened in 1939, be placed in different positions by the employment offices, thus taking them off unemployment benefits, or it might be possible to permanently relocate these Jews, fully capable of being put to work, to Poland along with their families, where they would have the entire period until the winter of 1940/41 at their disposal to establish a new residence under the appropriate supervision.

It goes without saying that each occasional departure from the camp would have to be replaced immediately, so that there would constantly be trained transports ready to move.

It would thereby be feasible, although – due to the size of the camp – only to a limited extent, to achieve the following:

(1) to gradually bring under control those Viennese Jews capable of work and to train them to carry out manual labour, so that, if need be, they may be available to the employment office or the resettlement authorities;

(2) to exert renewed pressure on the Jews as a whole to actively prepare and ready themselves for their own emigration;

(3) to disrupt their continued leisurely existence in Vienna.

The provision of usable material[6] could be secured by the employment office and the police. This should, however, in contrast to previous practice, also be extended to those Jews who are not in the records of the employment office, since these surely constitute the more dangerous subversive elements.

The expenses for their upkeep in the camp would, as now, if not completely, then at least in large part be covered by the payment of those requesting their labour.

In any case, through this continuity in the use of the camp at Gänserndorf, on the one hand, the purpose of the camp would remain ensured, and, on the other hand, it would demonstrate to the Jews that nothing has changed in the judgement and the attitude towards them. This would be lost in the case of a closure of the camp or an alteration of its purpose, since the large numbers of Jews still present in Vienna would then have outlasted the existence of the camp in Gänserndorf after all.

Heil Hitler![7]

5 Deutsche Arbeitsfront: German Labour Front.

6 This means the recruitment of Jewish labourers.

7 The letter was unsuccessful. Subsequently the greatly underfunded camp was no longer utilized, either as a station of departure for forced labour transports or as a transit camp for deportations to Poland. On Bürckel's orders the work camp was closed on 1 April 1940: Wolf Gruner, *Zwangsarbeit und Verfolgung: Österreichische Juden im NS-Staat 1938–45* (Innsbruck: StudienVerlag, 2000), pp. 97–102 and 146–147.

DOC. 47

On 2 February 1940 Pastor Heinrich Grüber criticizes the Protestant Higher Church Council for its discrimination against pastors regarded as *Mischlinge* or who live in mixed marriages[1]

Letter from Pastor Heinrich Grüber,[2] 12a Dorfstraße, Berlin-Kaulsdorf, to the Protestant Higher Church Council, for the attention of Vice President Dr Hymmen,[3] 3 Jebensstraße, Berlin-Charlottenburg 2, dated 2 February 1940[4]

Dear Vice President,

The pastors who have not produced an Aryan certificate for themselves and their wives have received a new request in combination with a statement, signed by you, from the Protestant Higher Church Council.[5] Due to the nature of the work that I am carrying out at present,[6] a number of my colleagues have sought my advice. I would thus like to voice an opinion on your statement and the stance of the Protestant Church of the Old Prussian Union, which I will also send to these colleagues.

You surely do not have the impression, Vice President, that the statement of the EOK[7] has in any way weakened the objections of the BK.[8]

Your recent comments, to the effect

> that the Church, when choosing the persons to whom it entrusts the task of proclaiming the Word, that is, entrusts them with the mission and the duty of relaying the ministry of the Word in public worship to a *particular* circle of people that is

1 EZA, 7/1960. This document has been translated from German.

2 Heinrich Grüber (1891–1975), Protestant pastor; pastor in Berlin-Kaulsdorf from 1934; head of the Church Aid Office for Protestant Non-Aryans from 1938 to 1940 (disbanded in 1940), which supported emigration, also by making efforts to obtain false passports; imprisoned in Sachsenhausen and Dachau concentration camps, 1940–1943; provost for Berlin after 1945; representative of the Protestant Church in Germany (EKD) to the East German government, 1949–1958.

3 Dr Johannes Hymmen (1878–1951), Protestant theologian and pastor; military chaplain, 1916–1918; pastor in Blankenstein and managing director of the Inner Mission in Westphalia, 1923–1925; consistory councillor and lecturer at the University of Münster from 1926; higher consistory councillor, 1932; appointed in 1934 to the Protestant Higher Church Council in Berlin, where he was vice president for matters of spiritual welfare from 1936; retired in 1945.

4 The original contains handwritten underlining, notes, and a stamp: 'Passed through the president's office.'

5 Although the Protestant Church had included the information from the national census of 17 May 1939 about 'racial belonging' in the personnel files of its pastors, the Church Chancery required in May 1939 that a separate Aryan certificate be provided for all pastors, and distributed questionnaires. In connection with this, Hymmen had commented on 22 Dec. 1939 that non-Aryan clergymen were received with hostility and mistrust, and consequently one should no longer confer the office upon them. The Aryan certificate, he had said, was 'on the same level as the certificate of Reich citizenship and a university degree in theology': EZA, 7/1960.

6 The reference is to Grüber's leadership position in the Church Aid Office for Protestant Non-Aryans.

7 Evangelischer Oberkirchenrat: Protestant Higher Church Council.

8 Bekennende Kirche: Confessing Church. Protestant movement led by Martin Niemöller and others, founded in 1934 to oppose attempts to bring the Church under the control of the Nazi regime and in line with Nazi ideology. The conflict between the Confessing Church and the Nazi-oriented 'German Christian' movement, both of which remained part of German Protestantism, was termed the 'Church struggle' (*Kirchenkampf*).

> more or less *delimited in terms of location or individuals*, has, from time immemorial, seen to it that this person should be skilled in the office, that is to say: the person should, in human terms, have the aptitude and the task of bringing the Word to the largest possible audience and as convincingly as possible within the sphere of activity assigned to them

misunderstand the meaning of ordination and conferral of office. The supervisory authorities of the Church can neither restrict nor withdraw the powers of the office so long as the holder of the office has not given cause due to their teaching or way of life. They cannot demand that a pastor be required to undergo a new qualifying exam after performing his duties for some period of time. The most recent statements would only be meaningful if there were still pastors in the office of preaching who did not belong to the Volksgemeinschaft. It is surely well known to you that all pastors who are to be considered Jews according to the Nuremberg Laws no longer hold office in Germany, but that they have, in part, been received by other Protestant churches of the world and been engaged to carry out the office.

The planned census therefore only concerns those people who, according to the clear will of the lawmaker, should remain untouched, namely the Mischlinge and those ethnic Germans living in marriages of mixed race. The Nuremberg Laws clearly and precisely indicate that the greater division is not that between ethnic Germans and Mischlinge, but rather between Mischlinge and Jews. In the civil service and positions within the Reich, Mischlinge and ethnic Germans living in mixed marriages are to remain undisturbed in their offices, just as these persons are also called up for military and labour service and can belong to the German Labour Front and the Hitler Youth.

The most recent decrees of both the Ministry of Food and the Ministry of Economics demonstrate that both groups of people are considered as belonging fully to the nation as a whole.[9] I do not need to draw your attention specifically to the decree of the Deputy of the Führer of 2 September 1938 or the edicts of the Reich Ministry of Economics of 28 October 1936 and 3 August 1938, since I expect you are aware of them.[10]

I believe that the Protestant Church has more important things to do during such times than providing occasion for people to be exposed to defamation who, according to the clear will of the state leadership, should continue to remain unhindered from doing their work.

I can discern nothing in the entire proceedings but a pandering to the favour of those entities who ultimately reject the Church, and who would like to see it eliminated sooner

9 The decree issued by the Reich Economics Ministry (RWM) on 23 Jan. 1940 regarding the revocation of clothing stamps excluded Jews living in so-called privileged mixed marriages: on the decree see Doc. 36, fn. 4. The same was true for the measures mandated by the Reich Ministry of Food and Agriculture on 11 March 1940, after this letter was composed: ibid., fn. 7. It is possible that instructions to this effect had been issued and implemented locally at an earlier date.

10 On 28 Oct. 1936 the RWM dictated that in the commercial sector '*Mischlinge* with provisional Reich citizenship' and people 'of German blood' were of equal status: BArch R7/1219. On 3 August 1938 it was ordered by decree that *Mischlinge* of the first degree were not to be discriminated against in the economic sphere: Bernhard Lösener and Friedrich A. Knost (eds.), *Die Nürnberger Gesetze mit den Durchführungsverordnungen und den sonstigen einschlägigen Vorschriften* (Berlin: Decker, 1942), p. 277.

rather than later, and an attempt to introduce the Aryan Paragraph into the Church through administrative channels.

Allow me to draw your attention to one more thing. The treatment by the official Church of the pastors who are considered Jews according to the Nuremberg Laws has damaged the Protestant Church, especially in the eyes of the neutral church leaders who are well disposed towards Germany, to a greater extent than is realized in Germany. This new lack of charity, which has been revealed through the survey and the introduction of which it is not possible to explain by invoking any clear will on the part of the state leadership, will become an even greater hindrance to cooperation between the Protestant churches of the world, which is of course urgently necessary not only in times of war and in the case of possible peace negotiations, but also in the times of peace to come. The Christian churches must at all times remain the conscience of the world, and they will refuse to stand together with a church leadership that allows its actions to be dictated not by a conscience bound to God, but by some opportunistic reason or another.

Out of love for my affected brothers and out of responsibility towards the Protestant Church of Germany, I cannot fill out the questionnaire, and I ask all my brothers, who appeal to me in this matter, to likewise refrain from doing so.

Heil Hitler![11]

DOC. 48

On 9 February 1940 the Soviet Population Transfer Directorate informs Chairman of the Council of People's Commissars Vyacheslav M. Molotov about German proposals for the deportation of Jews to the Soviet Union[1]

Letter from the Population Transfer Directorate of the Council of People's Commissars of the USSR (no. 01 471s), signed by its head, Chekmenev,[2] to the Chairman of the Council of People's Commissars (entry no. 3440), V. M. Molotov,[3] dated 9 February 1940, with six attachments[4]

The Population Transfer Directorate of the SNK[5] of the USSR has received two letters from the Berlin and Vienna offices[6] for population transfer regarding the question of organizing a transfer of members of the Jewish population from Germany to the USSR – specifically, to Birobidzhan and Western Ukraine.

11 The file contains a draft of a response from March 1940. In it the Supreme Church Council assumed that due to the transmission of various documents, the 'expressed misgivings' submitted by Grüber 'have become obsolete'. However, on account of misgivings on the part of Church Council President Friedrich Werner (1897–1955), the letter does not appear to have been sent: EZA, 7/1960.

1 RGASPI, 82/2/489, fol. 1. This document has been translated from Russian closely following Pavel Polian, 'Hätte der Holocaust beinahe nicht stattgefunden?', p. 1.

2 Evgenii M. Chekmenev (1905–1963), agricultural economist; joined the All-Union Communist Party (Bolsheviks, VKP(b)) in 1927; head of the population transfer directorate attached to the Council of People's Commissars, June 1939 – April 1941; then deputy people's commissar of the USSR for agriculture and later deputy president of the Gosplan planning agency; deputy chairman of the procurement committee from 1961.

3 Vyacheslav M. Molotov, born Skryabin (1890–1986), politician; member of the Central Committee from 1921 and of the Politburo of the VKP(b) from 1926; chairman of the USSR Council of People's Commissars, 1930–1941; Soviet foreign minister, 1939–1949 and 1953–1956.

According to the agreement in place between the governments of the USSR and Germany on the evacuation of populations,[7] only Ukrainians, Belarusians, Rusyns,[8] and Russians can be evacuated to the USSR.

We believe that the proposals of the above-named population transfer offices cannot be accepted.

Please provide instructions.[9]

DOC. 49
On 10 February 1940 the local NSDAP branch on Hainburgerstraße in Vienna complains to the District Propaganda Office about the Jew Steffi Walther[1]

Letter from the Hainburgerstraße local NSDAP branch, signed by Propaganda Chief Kuchinka,[2] to the District Propaganda Office in Vienna, for the attention of Party Comrade Starrach (received on 10 February 1940),[3] dated 10 February 1940[4]

The communication below, which I hereby relay, was forwarded to me by the propaganda manager of the NSV.

Re: conduct of the Jewess Walther, Steffi.[5]
The neighbours of the Jewess in the building at 27 Wassergasse are agitated by the provocative behaviour of the Jewess. She comes home every day loaded with provisions while the other residents have to make do with a tiny fraction of this amount. It would be good if the matter were to be thoroughly investigated. One constantly hears the complaint that provisions are being sold surreptitiously. If one were to take a particular case, such as the one described, a house search would surely be appropriate.

4 These letters were not in the file.
5 Sovet narodnykh komissarov (Council of People's Commissars).
6 The author means the Reich Central Agency for Jewish Emigration (Reichszentrale für jüdische Auswanderung) in Berlin and the Central Office for Jewish Emigration (Zentralstelle für jüdische Auswanderung) in Vienna under Eichmann and Brunner; the letters were not found. They relate to the German–Soviet population exchange of 1939–1940.
7 The Boundary and Friendship Treaty of 28 Sept. 1939 contained provisions on the demarcation line in Poland and a substantial population exchange: the German-speaking minorities that had fallen under Soviet rule were to be resettled to the west.
8 An eastern Slav ethnic minority inhabiting Subcarpathian Rus.
9 A response was not found. The German proposal was evidently not accepted.

1 ÖStA/AdR, SD Leitabschnitt Wien ZB 7050 A.12, fol. 445. This document has been translated from German.
2 Franz Kuchinka (1889–1968), hairdresser; joined the NSDAP in 1933; propaganda chief of the Hainburgerstraße local NSDAP branch, Vienna, 1939–1943.
3 Walter Starrach (1904–1980), graphic designer; joined the NSDAP in 1930; after 1932, involved with propaganda work; after 1934, district propaganda chief and later district office head; was imprisoned between 1935 and 1938 for a total of seventeen months; joined the SS in 1941 and the SA in 1943; imprisoned, 1946–1947; sentenced to fourteen months in prison in 1949 by a People's Court.
4 The original contains handwritten annotations and underlining, as well as the official stamp of the Hainburgerstraße local NSDAP branch in Vienna.
5 Stefanie Walther, née Sebenka (1898–1972), housewife; lived with her Protestant husband, Friedrich Walther (b. 1890), a customs inspector, at 27 Wassergasse in the years 1919–1961.

Re: Caretaker Fischer, Johann,[6] in the same building.
Fischer is described as a great complainer. And yet he was unemployed for a long time during the Systemzeit[7] and he has only done well since the revolution.[8] He is even said to earn RM 100 per week. But although he is doing so well as a result of National Socialism, he thinks it is right that he does not make any donations, not to mention sacrifices. He even refuses to donate on the Sunday of Sacrifice.[9] All of this inexplicable behaviour becomes clear once one knows that Mrs Fischer spends her time with the Jewess Walther. They're Jew helpers, who have no business living with us.

One should certainly take radical action to ensure that things are put in order.

Heil Hitler

DOC. 50
In an internal police memo dated 12 February 1940 the Reich Security Main Office stipulates that the Jewish population is to be concentrated in certain areas for the purposes of better surveillance[1]

Express letter from the RSHA (IV–D3c–553/39), Berlin, signed p.p. Müller, to all Gestapo offices except Posen and Danzig, for the information of the inspectors of the Security Police and of the SD and all Gestapo offices except those in the former Polish territories, dated 12 February 1940[2]

Re: restriction of the freedom of movement of Jews on Reich territory and consolidation in larger municipalities.
Case file: none.
Enclosures: 1 overview.
In a number of Reich districts, directives have been issued by various local offices, as a result of which the freedom of movement of Jews has been restricted. Recently, as a result of such directives, there have been difficulties in providing accommodation for Jews because these directives have taken into account only purely local interests and were not aligned with the concerns of the rest of the Reich.

Because, on the other hand, the Jews evade the necessary surveillance due to their free and uncontrollable movements from place to place, I intend to regulate this matter uniformly throughout the Reich and over time work towards the Jews being concentrated at suitable locations within a given province. In these locations the Jews can be more

6 Johann Fischer (1901–1957), locksmith; his wife Marie Fischer, née Zwiefelhofer (1891–1941), was caretaker of the building, 1939–1941.

7 German for 'system era'; a term used by the National Socialists to refer disparagingly to the period of the Weimar Republic.

8 The author means the National Socialist assumption of power in Jan. 1933.

9 Germans were encouraged to eat a cheap stew or 'one-pot' (*Eintopf*) meal one Sunday a month, and to donate the money thereby saved for welfare purposes. In 1940 the 'One-pot Sunday' was renamed the 'Sunday of Sacrifice' (*Opfersonntag*).

1 RGVA, 503k-1-385; copy: USHMM, RG-11.001M04, reel 74. This document has been translated from German.

2 The original contains handwritten annotations and underlining, as well as the official stamp of the Gestapo.

easily monitored in preparation for their emigration and also for general domestic policy reasons than is possible if they live scattered throughout the Reich. Under consideration as destinations are the cities listed in the enclosed overview.

For the time being, however, I ask for a report by 27 February 1940 as to whether and, if so, for what particular reasons there are concerns about relocation to the cities listed.[3] Where applicable, other suitable locations are to be named, whereby it is to be taken into account that Jewish school facilities must be available. Furthermore the report should indicate whether it will be possible to accommodate the Jews present from the individual provinces or states in the locations designated in the enclosed list. If necessary additional suggestions should also be made in this regard.

This matter is to be kept strictly confidential for now. It may not be passed on to other offices.

Addendum for the State Police head office in Düsseldorf:
For the report dated 11 January 1940 – II B4 /71.02/4258/39.[4]
Enclosure to Decree IV D 30 Nr. 553/39 dated 12 February 1940
Overview
of the locations under consideration for receiving relocated individuals.

Province	East Prussia	Königsberg
»	Brandenburg	Berlin to a limited extent
	and the city of Berlin	Frankfurt an der Oder
Province	Pomerania	Schneidemühl
»	Silesia	Breslau
		Liegnitz
		Oppeln
»	Saxony	Magdeburg
		Halle
		Erfurt
»	Schleswig-Holstein	Lübeck
»	Hanover	Hildesheim
		Osnabrück
		Stade
»	Westphalia	Arnsberg
		Münster
		Dortmund
		Bielefeld
		Gelsenkirchen
		Witten
		Hagen

3 The circular decree issued by the Reich Security Main Office (RSHA) was evidently interpreted in many locations as stipulating that Jews were to be concentrated in the listed locations at once. Therefore the RSHA issued a correction in a letter dated 15 March 1940 stating that this decree was only designed to create a basis for a later assessment of the resettlement question; no measures were to be taken, therefore, until the issuing of specific instructions: RGVA, 503k-1-385.

4 This report could not be found.

"	Hesse-Nassau	Fulda
		Marburg
		Frankfurt am Main
Rhine Province		Duisburg
		Krefeld
		Mönchen-Gladbach
		Rheydt
		Wuppertal-Barmen
		Wuppertal-Elberfeld
		Siegburg
		Düren
State of Bavaria		Munich
		Regensburg
		Bamberg
		Fürth
		Aschaffenburg
		Augsburg
State of Saxony		Chemnitz
		Dresden
		Leipzig
State of Württemberg		Stuttgart
		Ulm
State of Baden		Heidelberg
		Mannheim
		Pforzheim
State of Thuringia		Meiningen
State of Hesse		Bingen
		Darmstadt
State of Mecklenburg		Rostock
Sudetenland		Aussig
Ostmark		Vienna
Bremen		Bremen
Hamburg		Hamburg

DOC. 51

On 12 February 1940 the lawyer Alfred Panz petitions the Reich Minister of Finance to give preference to Sudeten German applicants in the Aryanization of a brickworks[1]

Letter from the lawyer Dr Alfred Panz,[2] Mies, p.p. Hans Demal, Wenzel Lappat, Josef Süss, estate of Franz Stell, to the Minister of Finance[3] in Berlin (received on 16 February 1940), dated 12 February 1940[4]

Re: de-Jewification of the company Wilhelm Salz and Sons Ring Kiln Brickworks in Staab.[5]
Franz Stell, retailer in Staab, sought authorization for a purchase agreement on 27 January 1939 from the Reichsstatthalter in Carlsbad,[6] with which he had purchased the ring kiln brickworks of the company Salz and Sons. Since he had been advised that he should not take on the brickworks by himself because his own capital was not sufficient for such an acquisition, Messrs Hans Demal, Wenzel Lappat, and Josef Süss, all from Staab, joined the venture. From all those who applied, the Regierungspräsident in Carlsbad in a reply dated 27 June 1939 granted the four applicants named above authorization to negotiate with the Jewish company.

The negotiations proved to be very difficult because the Jews did not wish to sign a new purchase agreement, although an agreement had been reached regarding the purchase price. When the signing was finally due to take place in Prague, one of the signatory partners left on a plane to London the same day.

With the consent of the Regierungspräsident office in Carlsbad a second contract was then presented in addition to the first, by means of which Franz Stell transferred three quarters of the property to the three additional partners. Thereupon a valuation was carried out in order to determine any surcharges that might be owed. As of December 1939 the final authorization had not yet been issued.

In this month the assets of the company Salz and Sons were then confiscated by the Gestapo on behalf of the German state. The four applicants expected that the acquisition would thereby now finally be expedited. However, it turned out that new difficulties arose in the form of new applicants. As was determined by Department 161 under the regional tax director in Carlsbad, a purchaser from the Old Reich is tendering for this brickworks and is offering a significantly higher price than its estimated value.

The four applicants, whose Aryanization applications were already submitted to the Regierungspräsident in Carlsbad and are pending settlement, are Sudeten Germans, all four of whom were active in the ethnic struggle in the linguistic border area before the

1 BArch, R 2/25023, fols. 39–41. This document has been translated from German.
2 Dr Alfred Panz (b. 1905), lawyer; joined the NSDAP in 1938.
3 Count Johann Ludwig Schwerin von Krosigk.
4 The original contains handwritten annotations and underlining.
5 The company was one of the largest brickworks in Bohemia during the interwar period.
6 Wilhelm Sebekovsky (1906–1981), lawyer; head of the press office of the Sudeten German Home Front from 1933, later the Sudeten German Party (SdP), of which he was a founding member; member of the Prague parliament after 1935; joined the NSDAP in 1938; Regierungspräsident in Carlsbad, 1938–1940; joined the Wehrmacht in 1940; after the end of the war worked as a lawyer in Essen; founding member of the right-wing Sudeten German Witikobund organization in 1947.

liberation of the Sudeten Gau. Thus, Hans Demal was Gau chairman of the West Bohemian gymnastics association for many years until the annexation of the Sudeten district and last German mayor of the city of Staab as leading candidate of the Sudeten German Party. He fought at the front and is a lieutenant in the German army. Wenzel Lappat is now local head of the NSDAP in Staab and currently lieutenant in the German army. Josef Süss is a veteran member of the DNSAP,[7] then member of the SdP, and now member of the NSDAP. He is temporary manager of the brickworks and has run the brickworks, which was idle in October 1939, so magnificently that the plant will be nominated by the DAF[8] for the Gau prize for the Gau Sudetenland. Franz Stell was the last district manager of the SdP in Staab. He died last year; consequently, his estate is taking on his interests.

The four applicants have already incurred quite substantial costs connected with the preparations of the contract, and they are convinced that the Minister of Finance will come to the same decision as that which the Regierungspräsident has already made provision for, and that no applicant now turning up and insisting on his greater financial capacity will be given preference. It is obvious that the state cannot give anything away and that the four applicants are increasing the originally agreed-upon purchase amount to the already officially determined purchase price, which amounts to some 700,000 Reichsmarks, since the applicants would have to pay a surcharge according to the proper Aryanization process. The state, however, surely also has measures in place to prevent the officially determined prices from being exceeded, particularly when it happens that a new applicant only intends to transform his surplus cash into tangible assets.

The Sudeten Germans did not have the good fortune to be able to reap the benefits of the economic growth of the last seven years in the Old Reich. During this time they were still engaged in the very challenging ethnic struggle, which demanded that personal interests simply could not be realized in such a way that they would be able to compete with Reich German applicants in terms of purchasing power above the normal price.

Therefore, it is requested that the four Sudeten German applicants be given consideration as purchasers of the brickworks.

1 enclosure in triplicate[9]

7 Deutsche Nationalsozialistische Arbeiterpartei: German National Socialist Workers' Party.

8 Deutsche Arbeitsfront: German Labour Front.

9 Enclosed was a copy of a letter in which the Carlsbad Gestapo informed the company Salz and Sons on 1 Feb. 1940 that the company's assets had been seized for the benefit of the Reich. Henceforth the regional tax director in Carlsbad would be responsible for these assets. The Reich Ministry of Finance also forwarded Panz's letter to the regional tax director on 10 April 1940 'for further action': BArch, R 2/25023, fol. 47.

DOC. 52

Selected NSDAP members receive instructions on how to proceed during the night before the deportation of the Stettin Jews on 12 and 13 February 1940[1]

Instruction sheet, unsigned, undated

Instructions
You have been selected by your Kreisleiter to take part in an important operation.[2] The aim is to make the Regierungsbezirk Stettin free of Jews if possible. Together with one or two Party comrades or SA men, you will be assigned a particular Jewish family by your Kreisleiter. You are to go to their home on 12 February 1940 at 8.00 p.m., act according to these instructions, and remain with the Jews in their apartment until you are collected. This will be between 3.00 and 6.00 a.m. on the 13th. I expect you to carry out this order with the required severity, diligence, and discretion. The Jews will attempt to make you waver with pleas or threats or by other means, or they will be obstreperous. You must not allow yourself to be influenced by this in any way or to be hindered from carrying out your duties.

These instructions tell you what you have to do. The rules laid out here can, of course, only be very *general*. In your individual case, you will have to decide for yourself what needs to be done to ensure the task is duly carried out. Arrangements have been made for patrols to come to the Jew apartment while you are there. You will inform these patrols, who will identify themselves by showing their detective or SD badge, about any difficulties or queries that have arisen. The patrols have been briefed in detail about precisely which departments are on alert and will summon these for your assistance (e.g. doctors, ambulances, NSV, people to transport pets, etc.). If there is a telephone in the Jew apartment, you can also contact the State Police head office in Stettin (tel. 3 52 31, ext. 770) with queries. A slip of paper with the most important extensions for you to contact in case of any queries will be delivered to you together with these instructions.[3] The most expedient way for you to proceed is as follows:

(1) At 8.00 p.m. make your way to the Jew apartment assigned to you. Before entering the Jew apartment make contact with the caretaker and see to it that the front door of the building will not be locked during the night. One of you will subsequently have to check occasionally whether the front door is still open. This is necessary to ensure that the patrols can get to you. If the Jews refuse to let you in and do not open up, one of you is to remain at the residence, while the other immediately informs the nearest police station. In the Jew apartment, summon all family members and *read out* the 'State Police order' that was delivered to you along with these instructions.[4] The Jews are henceforth

1 RGVA, 503k-1-337; copy: USHMM, RG-11.001M04, reel 72. This document has been translated from German.
2 The Gestapo organized the Stettin deportations in collaboration with the NSDAP Kreisleitung.
3 The slip of paper is not in the file.
4 According to the State Police order, the Jews concerned had seven hours to pack essential articles including clothing, blankets, and tableware, but not bonds, foreign currency, jewellery, etc. They were also instructed to wear a tag with their name and date of birth around their neck: RGVA, 503k-1-337.

to remain in *one* room, which you will assign to them. The SA member(s) or Party comrade(s) assigned to you will remain with the family members of the Jew for the entire time until their removal. You are to approach the head of the household of the Jewish family yourself.

(2) Go through the apartment with the head of the household. If there are heated stoves in the apartment, no more fuel is to be added. If these are slow-burning stoves (tiled stoves or similar), the oven door is to be unscrewed so that the fire will go out during the time in which you are in the Jew apartment. When you leave the apartment, the fire must be extinguished.

(3) Then, apply yourself to packing with the head of the household. Make sure the Jews only take the items listed in the State Police order. You must ensure that valuables etc. which, according to the order, must not be taken along are not put into the luggage. Should it be necessary to ask other family members any questions, you will return to the room where all the Jews are present with the head of the household and have them tell you what else is to be packed. If necessary leave the head of the household in that room and go with the Jewess to pack. If you are assigned two Party comrades or SA men to assist you, one of these can also pack together with a family member. However, it is vital to ensure that the remaining family members also remain under supervision and are not left alone for even a moment.

(4) Blankets that may be taken must be rolled up or folded in such a way that they can be transported without difficulty.

(5) Go through the apartment with the head of the household (including the basement and loft space!) and establish what foodstuffs, livestock, or pets are in the apartment. You and the head of the household are to take these items into one room, if it is possible to do so. Inform the patrols and have the items removed.

(6)
(*a*) Fill out the attached declaration of assets[5] with the Jew. This declaration must be completed by every family member separately. Here you must be particularly vigilant that the Jew does in fact actually declare everything that he has. Receivables and debts must also be declared precisely. This is absolutely imperative. Furthermore, remember that many Jews have opened dummy accounts. Point out that they are obliged to declare these dummy accounts as well. In many cases, the Jews have taken out mortgages etc. on their property, which are either not genuine or do not correspond to the amount listed in the land register. Here, too, you must point this out to the Jews and insist that everything is declared to you. Also ask the Jews whether they perhaps have any secret compartments in the apartment, whether in the walls, in cupboards, tables, or elsewhere. These, too, must be declared. It is also necessary to declare if the Jew has any valuable artworks or particularly valuable furniture. Should valuables be found in the apartment

5 The declaration of assets is not in the file.

that are not covered by the questions contained in the attached declaration of assets, you are to add these to the questionnaire accordingly. The questionnaire is to be filled out for each family member in quadruplicate. Pay attention that the sheet is filled out clearly and legibly. If the Jew cannot write properly, you take over this task. The questionnaire is to be signed by you and by the Jew.
(*b*) *All* valuables (e.g. rings, jewellery, bowls, earrings, goblets, etc. made of precious metals) are to be gathered together by the Jew. This also includes bank savings books, mortgage certificates and other securities, and cash. These objects are to be placed in a bag. If no such bag is to be found in the Jew apartment, a suitcase, pillowcase, or some other item of sufficient size is to be used. If these items include larger objects, care must be taken to ensure the container does not rip. An exact list must be compiled in triplicate of all the items that will be taken along. In it, everything must be listed precisely, e.g. the (exact!) number of silver teaspoons and silver tablespoons or silver and gold rings, the number and type of savings books etc. The list is to be signed by the block leader who negotiated with the head of the household and by the Jew in question. These lists are to be marked with the exact address and placed with the valuables.

(7) Have the Jew show you his identification papers. For any Jew over 14 years of age who is not in possession of an identity card, two photographs are to be brought along (if possible passport photos; if no passport photos are available, any pictures in which the Jew alone is shown. If such are also not on hand, then a group photo surely will be. A picture of the Jew is to be cut out of this).

(8) All items (suitcases, blankets, livestock and pets, the receptacle mentioned in 6 (b), as well as the house keys, which you are to remove and hand over to the police – see no. 9! –) are to be labelled with durable tags, upon which the name and the exact apartment address of the Jewish owner is to [be][6] indicated. These tags must be securely affixed so that they will not come off under any circumstances. The inscriptions must be clearly legible. You must prepare the tags while still in the apartment and [attach][7] them to the aforementioned articles. Furthermore *every* Jew must wear a tag around his neck, upon which his name and date of birth are indicated.

(9) When you have finished drawing up the inventory, and the inspection of the apartment and attic and basement spaces, which – I reiterate – must be undertaken only together with the Jewish head of the household, continue to wait in the apartment. At 3 a.m. at the earliest, you will then be picked up by an automobile. Please note *that by this time everything in the apartment must have been taken care of!* So you must have made certain that the fires have been extinguished, the electric light has been switched off, that gas and water have been turned off, and the windows are closed in all rooms except for the one where you are with the Jews. In the room in which you are waiting with the Jews the fire must also have gone out by three o'clock. When you are then picked up, take the collected valuables and exit the apartment together with the Jews. Lock the apartment door. Take charge of the apartment key, likewise the key to the door

6 This word is partially illegible in the original.
7 A word is illegible in the original.

of the building, after you have attached a corresponding tag (cardboard or similar) [with][8] the apartment information to this key as well. Then seal the apartment according to the instructions you will receive from the Kreisleiter. In addition, you must note the time you exited the apartment on the seal and draw two crosses in ink which extend as far as the wooden doorposts on either end. Only then may you make your way on to the street.

It may of course also be the case that the Jew lives as a lodger. In this case, of course, only the door of the apartment in which the Jew lives must be sealed. However, you must not only take the key belonging to this door, but also the keys to the corridor and the building which the Jew was issued by the landlord. If, on the other hand, Aryans are living in the apartment of the Jew as lodgers, all of the doors of the apartment are to be sealed. The keys to the individual rooms are to be labelled with a tag in the manner described above. If it is the case that an Aryan family is sharing a kitchen with the Jews, the objects belonging to the Jew are to be retrieved from the kitchen and brought into the living space. In such cases you are also to ascertain where the gas and electricity meters are located and write this on a slip of paper along with the name and apartment information of the Jew. If there are any doubts as to such arrangements, contact the patrol or the State Police head office directly.

(10) The journey from the Jew apartment to the port will only be accompanied by the block leader who negotiated with the head of the household. Anybody else will be discharged at this point. Upon arrival at the port, the block leader will register his Jews and hand over the package with the valuables and the keys. These instructions, the State Police order – which is to be read to the Jews – and any unused seals or adhesive strips are also to be returned! He will learn about everything else once he is there.

The execution and progression of the operation must remain strictly confidential, even afterwards. You are expressly reminded of your obligation to secrecy.

DOC. 53
Neue Zürcher Zeitung, 16 February 1940: article on the deportation of the Jews from Stettin[1]

The deportation of the German Jews

Berlin, 15 February. *(Tel. from our local correspondent.)* After a number of transports of Jews from Austria and the Protectorate of Bohemia and Moravia to the *region of Lublin* in Poland were already sent off before the new year,[2] the deportations from the Old Reich territory have now also begun. This new operation indicates that the project of a

8 A word is illegible in the original.

1 'Die Deportation der deutschen Juden', *Neue Zürcher Zeitung*, 16 Feb. 1940 (morning edition), p. 1. This document has been translated from German. The daily *Zürcher Zeitung* was founded in 1780 and renamed *Neue Zürcher Zeitung* in 1821.

2 On the deportations to Nisko, see Doc. 16, fn. 9.

Jewish reservation in the eastern part of the General Government between the Bug and San rivers continues to be pursued and is being implemented contingent on the availability of means of transport. During the night of 12 and 13 February, as reported before,[3] all the Jews in *Stettin* were apprehended by members of the SS and the SA, as well as officials of the NSDAP. Each apartment was occupied by two men, who informed the families in question that they must leave their apartments that same night and would be transported to an unknown destination. They were to put on warm underclothes, insofar as such were available. In terms of baggage, each person was allowed to take only one suitcase. Any remaining furniture had to be left behind. Likewise, the Jews had to hand over any available cash and their valuables, with the exception of a wedding ring and a watch. If they owned *bank accounts* or *real estate*, the Jews in Stettin were made to sign a *waiver relinquishing* these assets.[4]

The Jews were not permitted to take food or travel provisions with them. Any food still in the apartments was confiscated. Between three and four o'clock in the morning two guards each from the SS and SA fetched the Jews with their wives and children from their apartments and took them to the Stettin freight yard, where the *transport* to eastern Poland began in the early morning hours on Tuesday. The residents of the two Jewish homes for the elderly in Stettin, some eighty individuals, were also deported. If they were no longer capable of walking, they were taken to the freight yard on stretchers. In Stettin and the surrounding area, more than 1,800 people were deported. Among them were former veterans from the World War. Every Jew had a cardboard tag hung around his neck, which listed his name and deportation number. In response to the question as to whether there was accommodation waiting in Poland, the accompanying contingents of guards gave evasive answers. In response to the subsequent question as to how long the transport would last, they responded: 'Three to four days.' The deportees attempted to send a request for help to President Roosevelt via an intermediary, in which they asked for expedited permission to enter the United States in order to save the Jews from their fate.[5] In *Danzig*, *Königsberg*, and other cities in northern Germany the deportations are to begin in the coming weeks. All the preparations there have already been made by the Gauleitungen of the Party and by the police departments.[6] In these places, too, the deportation will involve the confiscation of all valuables.[7]

3 'Abtransport der Juden aus Stettin?', *Neue Zürcher Zeitung*, 14 Feb. 1940 (noon edition), p. 3.
4 See Doc. 52.
5 Else Meyring was evidently the only one of the deportees who managed to emigrate. She later wrote an account of the deportation from Stettin: Else Meyring, 'Deportation aus Stettin', in Andreas Lixl-Purcell (ed.), *Erinnerungen deutsch-jüdischer Frauen 1900–1990* (Leipzig: Reclam, 1992), pp. 307–332. Other attempts to leave the Lublin district failed: see Doc. 134.
6 At this point only the deportation of East Frisian Jews was planned. Following the intervention of the Reich Association of Jews in Germany, however, the deportation was never carried out: see Introduction, p. 48.
7 In response to this article the Reich Foreign Office asked the Reich Security Main Office (RSHA) whether additional deportations were in fact planned; however, it received the response that the operation in Stettin had been a one-off measure because space had been needed there for the Baltic Germans: see also Introduction, p. 41.

DOC. 54

On 20 February 1940 Johanna Simon asks the Israelite Religious Community of Darmstadt to continue to pay her for her work in the soup kitchen[1]

Handwritten letter from Johanna Simon,[2] 27 Kasinostraße, Darmstadt, to the board of the Israelite Religious Community of Darmstadt,[3] 15 Bleischstraße, dated 20 February 1940

As you are aware, I have assisted in the local soup kitchen since 15 June 1936. The compensation for my work in the amount of 20 [Reichs]marks, in words twenty marks, was paid for by the local religious organization until 31 December 1939. For both of the last months, January and February of this year, I still have not received any remuneration. Since you are surely well aware of my economic situation, I most courteously request that you continue to grant me the above sum each month for my work in the soup kitchen.

Respectfully[4]

DOC. 55

On 22 February 1940 Hofrat Julius Munk from Vienna petitions the Reich Office for Kinship Research to grant him *Mischling* status[1]

Letter from Hofrat and retired district chief police physician, signed Dr Julius Munk,[2] 47 Alserstraße, Vienna VIII, to the Reich Office for Kinship Research, 2 Bräunerstraße, Vienna I, dated 22 Feb. 1940

Since I have not yet succeeded in providing all the documents verifying my Aryan descent, I was obliged to take the name Israel when the decree regarding the forenames of Jews was published,[3] and heretofore I have had to submit to all regulations applying to Jews. As indicated by the enclosed birth and baptismal certificate from the Roman Catholic parish office in Wischau, I was born on 2 June 1857 and am thus 83 years of age, and on 6 June 1857, four days after my birth, I was baptized according to the Roman

1 CAHJP, D/Da1/21. This document has been translated from German.

2 Probably Johanna Simon (1881–1943), who was deported to Theresienstadt on 27 Sept. 1942 and perished there on 30 August 1943.

3 In Feb. 1940 the liberal religious community and the Orthodox religious organization merged into a single community. The board comprised three representatives from each of the previous individual communities. Its head was Karl Benjamin (1876–1944), retired bank director; deported on 27 Sept. 1942 to Theresienstadt, and from there on 28 Oct. 1944 to Auschwitz, where he was murdered.

4 In its reply dated 26 Feb. 1940, the religious community declined Johanna Simon's request. She was, however, granted permission to eat lunch there free of charge as before if she continued to work there: CAHJP, D/Da1/21.

1 DÖW, 4666. Excerpts published in Dokumentationsarchiv des österreichischen Widerstandes, *Widerstand und Verfolgung in Wien*, p. 320. This letter has been translated from German.

2 Dr Julius Munk (1857–1940), physician.

3 According to a regulation issued on 24 Jan. 1939, Jews in Austria and the Sudeten German territories were required to use the compulsory forenames 'Israel' and 'Sara' starting on 1 April 1939: *Reichsgesetzblatt*, 1939, I, pp. 81–82.

Catholic rite. My father, Dr Johann Wilhelm *Munk*, municipal physician in Wischau, was likewise Roman Catholic, as was my mother Amalia, née Granitzer. I have not been able to acquire the additional required documents of my grandparents or the marriage certificates. This can be ascribed to the fact that it is a very long time ago, well over a hundred years, and the applicable offices are small municipalities and small parishes in Moravia. It must also be borne in mind that the Napoleonic Wars were taking place in this region during this period. Around the time of my birth my father was serving as a military physician in the army of Field Marshal Count Radetzky as the head of a military hospital in Verona.

Since I am not able to procure and present the certificates in the manner required by regulations, I find myself obliged to seek the path of clemency, and plea that in my case the Reich kinship authority be lenient with me regarding the presentation of the certificates and documents and concede me, if not the rights of an Aryan, then at least those of a Mischling.

I justify my plea as follows:

My father before me had already proved his worth as a physician. After his return from Italy he was posted as a cholera doctor to Galicia and subsequently, as municipal physician, headed the Prussian cholera military hospital in Wischau. With respect to his political disposition, he was always a good German in bilingual Wischau, and played an active role as a co-founder of the German Party.

I myself completed grammar school at the Vienna Piaristen-Collegium, sat the school-leaving exam here, attended the Vienna medical school, was then a trainee for one and a half years at the general hospital, an assistant physician for two years at the Lower Austrian Maternity and Foundlings' Home, assistant physician, first grade, at the St Anna Children's Hospital for five years, and filled in for the imperial-royal paupers' physician in Gumpendorf for about half a year, after which I became a medical assistant for the Lower Austrian governor's office. After the reorganization of the police district physicians I was named police district physician in Vienna and served until 1923, in which year I was pensioned off after being awarded the title of Hofrat.

During my period of service as police district physician I had assignments as an institutional physician in a school association for daughters of civil servants for more than thirty years, as a school physician at the Robert Hamerling Grammar School for twenty-three years, as theatre physician in the Theater in der Josefstadt, and as physician for the apprentices' medical insurance company of the Tailors' Cooperative, for the creation of which I provided the impetus.

Of my brothers, two were physicians. The youngest, who received his doctorate *sub auspiciis imperatoris*,[4] was a lawyer and died nine years ago as president of the Administration for Austrian State Debt with the title of head of department in the Ministry of Finance and having been elevated to the lowest level of the peerage.

4 Latin for 'under the authority of the emperor', indicating a doctoral title that was considered a particular honour. Until 1918 Austrian universities were allowed to award it at most once a year – in Vienna a maximum of three times a year. The successful candidate, who had to have obtained the highest mark in all the examinations, received a diamond ring with the imperial initials during the degree congregations.

I was married to a Mischling of the second degree.[5] My son was likewise a police physician. I have been living in my present home since 1891, that is, for almost forty-nine years, and I will have to leave it because I could not provide a certificate of Aryan descent. Noting my advanced age and my services to the state and to humanity, and noting further my current state of ill health and my honourable ancestors, I venture to most humbly repeat the attached plea.

One enclosure.[6]

Registered.[7]

DOC. 56

On 6 March 1940 a senior diplomat at the US embassy in Berlin briefs Secretary of State Cordell Hull about the situation of Jews in Germany[1]

Letter no. 2024 (confidential) from Alexander Kirk,[2] chargé d'affaires ad interim (840.1 JDB/mhg), Berlin, to the US Secretary of State,[3] Washington, DC, dated 6 March 1940[4]

Subject: Situation of Jews in War-Time Germany.

Sir:

With reference to the Embassy's telegram No. 529 of March 1, 2 p.m.,[5] and previous recent telegrams dealing with developments affecting the Jews in Germany, I have the honor to submit herewith, for the possible convenience of the Department, a recapitulation of the situation of the Jews in Germany in war-time. This survey is based on information obtained in Berlin and while it touches upon conditions in Austria, in the Protectorate of Bohemia and Moravia and in Poland, it relates particularly to the status of the Jews in the territory formerly comprising the 'Old Reich'.

As a result of the anti-Jewish legislation enacted late in 1938,[6] the German Jews, i.e., those persons legally defined as Jews on the basis of having three or more Jewish grandparents or of belonging to the Jewish faith, have been virtually eliminated from com-

5 Hermine Munk, née Kugel (1866–1939/1940?); the Munks had married in 1891.

6 The enclosure is not in the file.

7 The Reich Office for Kinship Research rejected Julius Munk's request on 4 March 1940 on the grounds that petitions for leniency were not within its remit. The baptismal certificate was returned to him with the message that according to the records he was considered a Jew: DÖW, 4666. The response is published in Dokumentationsarchiv des österreichischen Widerstandes, *Widerstand und Verfolgung in Wien*, pp. 320–321.

1 NACP, RG 59, decimal file 862 4016/2161. Published in Confidential U.S. State Department Central Files, Germany: Internal Affairs, 1930–1941, Frederick, MD, reel 58, fr. 00 080–00088.

2 Alexander Kirk (1888–1979), lawyer and diplomat; worked at the US Department of State from 1915; chargé d'affaires at the US embassy in Berlin, 1939–1940; later worked in Egypt; from 1944, ambassador in Rome; returned to the USA after retirement.

3 Cordell Hull (1871–1955), lawyer and politician; representative in the US Congress, 1907–1931; senator, 1931–1933; secretary of state, 1933–1944; awarded the Nobel Peace Prize, 1945.

4 The original contains handwritten remarks, the stamp 'strictly confidential', and various other official stamps.

5 In his telegram of 1 March 1940, Kirk had reported on the deportation of Jews from Stettin and Schneidemühl: NACP, RG 59, decimal file 862 4016/2161.

merce, trade and the professions, except medicine, which they may practice among themselves. Many Jews consequently live upon savings or upon the charity of the central Reich Association of Jews in Germany, which is the body authorized by the German Government to administer the public affairs of the Jews and to levy contributions upon them for Jewish relief. During the late summer months of last year, and particularly since the outbreak of the war, some twenty thousand Jews have been re-employed as day laborers in industry and have been put to work on land improvement and outdoor construction projects. Jews are not accepted for army service.

Shortly after the outbreak of the war the German Government authorities instructed the various Jewish agencies that they should continue to promote emigration by every means possible. This has proved, however, to be more difficult than formerly, owing to the closing of enemy countries as direct areas of reception, as well as owing to new obstacles arising from complications regarding transportation and the acquisition of foreign exchange. With respect to the emigration of German national Jews from the territory of the Old Reich, the Government has as yet imposed no restrictions based upon age or profession or other considerations.

There is presented below a table indicating the number of Jews (i.e., Jews in the sense of the definition mentioned above), still left in various German territories, following reductions brought about by emigration or flight. These statistics, which have been obtained from the central Jewish Association in Berlin, are more or less exact as regards the Old Reich, while with respect to the other districts they represent approximate estimates.

Jewish Population in the German Reich (Old Reich)		
Number beginning of 1933		522,700
in the census of June 16, 1933	499,682	
plus in the Saarland	*5,000*	504,700
Number End of 1939		202,400
Emigration from the beginning of 1933 to the end of 1939		281,900
Emigration since the beginning of the war:		
a) to the end of 1939		6,000
b) January and February 1940 together		2,000
Excess of deaths over births from the beginning of 1933 to the end of 1939		38,400
Jewish Population in the Ostmark		
Number in 1933		191,481
Before incorporation in the German Reich		170,000
Present number		56,000
In particular in the City of Vienna:		
Number in 1933		176,034
Before incorporation in the German Reich		160,000
Present number		55,000

6 Following the November pogroms, Göring chaired a conference at the Reich Aviation Ministry in Berlin on 12 November 1938. See PMJ 2/146.

Jewish Population in the Protectorate	
Before affiliation with the German Reich	250–270,000
Present number	160,000
Jewish Population in Danzig	
Former number	8–10,000
Present number	1,400

In general the treatment of the Jews in the Old Reich has not changed to any great extent since the beginning of the war. As a rule they receive the same food rations as the rest of the population, although they are subjected to petty discriminations in being compelled to call at the Government Food Offices for their ration cards and in being forced to make their purchases at specified hours. The Jews, moreover, do not receive supplementary rations for comestibles such as chocolate, honey and cakes, and extra meat rations, and furthermore they have for the time being been refused clothing ration cards.[7] In certain sections of Berlin coal deliveries have not been made to Jewish families nor apartment houses predominantly occupied by Jews. During the recent severe weather several thousand Jews in Berlin were enlisted for forced work for the cleaning of snow and for the loading and unloading of coal trucks.

The situation of the so-called 'crossbreeds' and half-Jews, of whom there are perhaps a million in the Old Reich alone, would appear to vary locally. On the whole they are treated somewhat better than the full-blooded Jews, but in certain districts they are understood to suffer unofficially imposed disabilities.

With respect to Austria, the legal status of the Jews there is now practically assimilated to that prevailing in the Old Reich, and the same process is apparently under way in the Protectorate of Bohemia and Moravia. The Reich Association of Jews in Germany is not permitted to concern itself with the welfare of the Jews in either Austria or in the Protectorate, and it is understood that, owing to the still comparatively unsettled state of National Socialist Party discipline in these areas, and particularly in Austria, the Jews are subjected to considerably severer extra-legal persecution and restrictions than in the Old Reich.

Shortly after the conquest of Poland reports circulated that plans had been made for a general deportation of the Jews in Germany to the new Jewish 'reservation' established in Eastern Poland in the district around Lublin. A detailed statistical survey carried out by the police of Jewish families in the Old Reich was thought to portend such a development. With the exception of Stettin, however, the Jewish population of the various Reich German cities have so far been permitted to remain in Germany.

In Stettin the entire Jewish population of some 1,200, including casual Jewish visitors to the city and Jews who had completed preparations to emigrate abroad, were assembled on seven hours' notice during the night of February 12 and were shipped off by special train to Poland. They were permitted to take with them only small quantities of baggage and, following their departure, their houses were sealed and it was officially stated that their belongings in Stettin would be liquidated and the funds thereby realized would be placed in a blocked account. It is learned that the Stettin Jews have arrived in Eastern Poland, with at least one death occurring en route, and that they are now settled

7 See Doc. 36.

in the towns of Piaski, Biala and Terespol in the Lublin district. They are being cared for by already existing Jewish communities in these cities and it is said that they are experiencing considerable hardship and distress.[8]

The central Jewish Association in Berlin was officially informed that this action had been initiated by the *Gauleiter* of the Stettin district, Herr Schwede-Coburg,[9] and that although the Reich authorities were not 'responsible' therefor, they could not rescind the action already taken. It was furthermore stated that the Stettin Jews would have to remain in Poland and that for the time being permission to leave could not be given to those who had completed their preparations for emigration abroad. On or about February 15 an order was issued in Schneidemühl, which is also within Herr Schwede-Coburg's district, that the Jews in that city should prepare for deportation within a week's time, presumably also for Eastern Poland. The Jewish authorities learned after inquiring in Berlin that Herr Schwede-Coburg planned that all Jews should be evacuated from the *Grenzmark*,[10] the region lying on the former Polish frontier and including Schneidemühl, and that their place here, as well as in Stettin, should be taken by returning Baltic Germans.[11] The central Jewish authorities have apparently succeeded in obtaining a modification of the original plan to send the Jews from Schneidemühl to Poland and arrangements are now being considered whereby these Jews should be sent farther back into the Reich, where they will be settled in small towns on Jewish-owned farms.[12]

Information is not available as to how many Jews in all have been sent to the Lublin reservation. It is known that approximately 4,500 have been despatched from Vienna and 1,000 from Mährisch-Ostrau in the Protectorate.[13] There have also been heavy deportations of Jews from the former Polish territories, in particular the Corridor[14] and the Posen areas, including Lodz, now formally annexed to the Reich; the Jews, together with a large number of Poles, are being removed from these districts to make room for Baltic Germans.[15] Official intimations have also been given that some 1,400 Jews from Danzig, as well as the Jews in East Prussia, will be moved to Poland in the early spring.

According to German official estimates there are some two million Jews within the former Polish territory now comprising the General Government.[16] As far as can be

8 Stettin's Jews had been brought to Piaski, Bełżyce, and Głusk in the Lublin district of the General Government: see Docs. 52 and 53.

9 Franz Schwede-Coburg (1888–1960), machine fitter; in the navy, 1907–1921; joined the NSDAP in 1922; worked at an electricity plant, 1922–1929; city councillor, 1924–1930; mayor of Coburg, 1933–1934; member of the Bavarian Landtag, 1930–1933; member of the Reichstag from 1933; NSDAP Gauleiter and Oberpräsident of Pomerania from 1934; SA-Obergruppenführer, 1938; interned by the British, 1945–1947; sentenced to ten years' imprisonment in 1951 by Coburg Regional Court.

10 German: frontier area.

11 See Introduction, p. 40.

12 The Jews of Schneidemühl were brought to Neuendorf and to the Radinkendorf estate in Brandenburg.

13 On the deportations to Nisko, see Doc. 16, fn. 9.

14 The Polish Corridor was a strip of territory that gave the newly reconstituted state of Poland access to the Baltic Sea after the First World War. It divided the bulk of Germany from the province of East Prussia.

15 See the Introduction to PMJ 4.

16 Approximately 1.5 million Jews lived in the territory which became the General Government in autumn 1939.

ascertained there has as yet been no large scale transfer of Jews within the General Government to the Lublin reservation which, in addition to the Jews sent from Stettin, Austria and the Protectorate, comprises many Jewish communities which have been settled there for a long period of time. The Jews in the General Government are compelled to wear arm bands and are subject to a forced labor obligation, as well as many restrictions.[17] Although they have been forced out of leading positions in commerce and industry, they apparently still continue to be active in trade. Those Polish Jews who were caught in Germany at the outbreak of the Polish war were immediately imprisoned, some of them being confined in work camps from which they have been subsequently released to be sent back to Poland, and some of them being detained in concentration camps, where a number estimated between one and two thousand still remain.[18]

Although government officials in Berlin have assured the central Jewish Association that no plan is being entertained at present to deport Jews from the Old Reich to Eastern Poland, the Jewish authorities are apprehensive that steps along these lines may be taken in the course of this year. Among the factors which encourage such an apprehension are the following: 1) the recent completion of the already-mentioned statistical survey of Jewish families in the Reich, the exact purpose of which, although undefined, would appear to be adapted to just such an aim as mass deportation; 2) the possibility that other *Gauleiter* may be tempted to rival each other in following the precedent set in the district of Stettin; 3) reports concerning the construction of barracks in small towns in Poland which are reputedly for the reception of Jews, who would be put to work on land improvement projects in the surrounding countryside; 4) the fact that an example for the removal and transfer of populations has been set in the case of the Baltic Germans and the Germans from Russian Poland,[19] and the fact furthermore that the organization and equipment which would be necessary for the deportation of Jews has thus, so to speak, been tested and tried and would be ready for use. Although it is learned that pressure from radical Party circles is increasing in favor of a mass removal of the German Jews to Poland particularly in view of the slackened rate of emigration resulting from the war, no definite decision in the matter is known so far to have been taken, and it is thought likely that further consideration of possible action along this line may be postponed at least until the spring when a change in the weather would be conducive to further transfers of populations.

Respectfully yours,

17 Governor General Hans Frank had decreed work for Jews compulsory on 26 Oct. 1939, while the wearing of a distinguishing mark had been mandatory since Dec. 1939. The situation in the General Government is covered in detail in PMJ 4 and PMJ 9.

18 See Introduction, p. 30, and Doc. 6.

19 Also known as Congress Poland, this was the part of central Poland, including the capital Warsaw, that had been attached to tsarist Russia as a formally independent kingdom at the Congress of Vienna in 1815. After the Polish uprisings of 1830 and 1863, the name and the territory's self-governing bodies were abolished.

DOC. 57

On 8 March 1940 Max Seelig contacts the Gestapo seeking the return of his children, after they were deported from Stettin to Piaski[1]

Handwritten letter from Max Seelig,[2] 7 Marienstraße, Kolberg, to the Gestapo, Stettin, dated 8 March 1940

I have learned that my children Edith Sara Seelig, born 25 Oct. 1926 in Kolberg, [and] Ursula Sara Seelig, born 12 Sept. 1928 in Kolberg,[3] were taken on the transport to Piaski, near Lublin, by mistake.[4] They were in Stettin to attend school and at the boarding house of A. Barnitz, 18 Breitestr., Stettin. All the other children from Kolberg and Berlin who were there to attend school were sent back to their parents. Only my two children were, I assume, inadvertently taken along.

Approximately three weeks ago now I wrote to the police administration in Stettin regarding this matter and requested the return of the two children, but I have not yet received a response.[5] I therefore ask most humbly for the children to be brought back and returned to their parents.

At the same time I emphasize that I will pay the costs of this. I am also prepared to come and fetch them and [I request] that an attestation be issued to me, showing that I have the authorization to fetch the children, if it should be necessary to fetch the children.

Moreover I ask to be sent an affirmative response as soon as possible.[6]

1 RGVA, 503k-1-385; copy: USHMM, RG-11.001M04, reel 74. This letter has been translated from German.

2 Max Seelig (b. 1886), estate agent; was released from Sachsenhausen concentration camp on 14 Dec. 1938 after temporary imprisonment; deported on 3 Feb. 1943 with his wife, Doris Seelig, née Markus (b. 1890), and oldest daughter, Margot (b. 1924), to Auschwitz, where he perished.

3 Edith and Ursula Seelig were deported to Piaski on 12 Feb. 1940; their subsequent fate is unknown.

4 On the deportations to Stettin, see Docs. 52 and 53.

5 Seelig's letter to the police administration is in the file: RGVA, 503k-1-385.

6 Handwritten comment: 'Out of the question. Parents should move to join their children'; initials illegible, 9 March [1940]. The State Police in Stettin noted on 13 March 1940: 'A return of the children is out of the question,' and instructed the State Police office in Köslin on the same day to inform the parents of this 'and suggest that they move to join the children': RGVA, 503k-1-385.

DOC. 58

On 12 March 1940 Charlotte Wollermann from Düsseldorf denounces the Protestant pastor Gottfried Hötzel for having given a pro-Jewish sermon[1]

Note by Detective Constable Eisel,[2] Düsseldorf, dated 12 March 1940

Re: Pastor *Hötzel*, Düsseldorf-Oberkassel.[3]

The wife of Hans *Wollermann*, Charlotte, née Marten, born 5 April 1902 in Braunsberg, residing in Düsseldorf-Oberkassel, 7 Achillesstr., communicated the following:

Around April 1939, together with her husband, Senior Consistory Councillor Dr Hans Wollermann,[4] she attended a service at the Protestant church in Düsseldorf-Oberkassel. There Pastor Hötzel gave the sermon.

Throughout his sermon Pastor Hötzel discussed the Jewish question. He began with a Bible passage according to which Christ once said that the Jews are the children of the Devil.

Pastor Hötzel explained in his comments that this remark has been abused by many. Pastor *Hötzel* essentially said the following: 'It is not the Jews who are the children of Satan, but those who are persecuting the Jews.'

Pastor Hötzel championed the Jews in his sermon to such a degree that she was extremely incensed about his sermon.

The statements of Mrs Wollermann seem entirely credible.

She is a Party member and in the National Socialist Women's League.[5]

1 LAV NRW R, RW 58/3911. This document has been translated from German.

2 Werner Eisel (1910–1947), police officer; joined the SS in 1933; was employed at the Düsseldorf Gestapo from 1933; joined the NSDAP in 1937; with the commander of the Security Police (KdS) in Cracow in 1941, then in the Einsatzkommando for Special Assignment Lemberg; head of the counter-intelligence section of the KdS in Galicia; SS-Obersturmführer in 1942; head of the Security Police in Czortków after Oct. 1943; with the Senior Commander of the Security Police (BdS) in Hungary; returned to the Düsseldorf Gestapo in Sept. 1944.

3 Hugo Karl Gottfried Hötzel (1880–1940), Protestant theologian and pastor; missionary and teacher in China, 1906–1914; pastor in Düsseldorf-Heerdt-Oberkassel after 1917; member of the Confessing Church from 1933; took part in public protests after the November pogroms in 1938; provided support for Protestant non-Aryans in the Grüber Office in 1939; imprisoned from Feb. 1940 to 9 April 1940, and released upon the condition that he was to be banned from Rhineland and Westphalia and from public speaking; died following a stroke.

4 Dr Hans (Johannes) Wollermann (b. 1895), lawyer; at the Protestant Consistory in Königsberg, 1927–1933; consistory councillor in the Higher Church Council in Berlin, 1933–1937; at the consistory in Düsseldorf, 1937–1946; served in the war, 1940–1945; prisoner of war, 1945; later worked in schools in Düsseldorf.

5 The complaint was made to the police only after Hötzel had been arrested following a lecture he gave to the German Protestant Women's League.

DOC. 59

On 15 March 1940 Ferdinand Itzkewitsch writes to his son from Buchenwald, asking him to seek assistance from the Relief Association of Jews in Germany for his emigration[1]

Handwritten letter from Feibusch Israel Itzkewitsch,[2] no. 1925, block 9, Buchenwald, to his son Horst,[3] dated 15 March 1940[4]

My dear Horst,

I have received your letters and money, and I was pleased that you and your dear mother are well. The reason for today's letter is to request that you write again urgently on my behalf to the Relief Association in Hanover, so that [they] provide me with these as quickly as possible,[5] since I am not able to obtain the foreign currency for this, as is known to the Relief Association, for I have written to them but not received any answer. It seems that double standards are in effect there. Get in touch with Dr Villsen, lawyer, as well. Perhaps he can help with this. I would also be agreeable to being relocated to my home town[6] and I leave it to you, or rather to the Relief Association, to immediately undertake the necessary steps for this, since I have been expelled.

Arrange for the Relief Association to answer me at once and inform me of the ship's departure. Likewise I await from you prompt handling [of this matter] and a response. Regards to your mother, best wishes and kisses to you

Your faithful, never-to-be-forgotten

Papa

1 BwA, 52 11 914. Published in Harry Stein, *Juden in Buchenwald 1937–1942* (Weimar: Gedenkstätte Buchenwald, 1992), pp. 106–107. This letter has been translated from German.

2 Ferdinand, also Feibusch, Itzkewitsch (1891–1941), shoemaker; Russian citizen and prisoner of war in Germany in the First World War, settled in Germany after his release; imprisoned from summer 1937 to Oct. 1938 for committing so-called race defilement with his non-Jewish partner, Gertrud K.; imprisoned in Buchenwald from 10 Nov. 1938; deported on 15 July 1941 to the 'euthanasia' killing centre Pirna Sonnenstein, where he was murdered.

3 Horst Itzkewitsch (b. 1923).

4 The letter was written on the stationery of Buchenwald concentration camp, which includes the printed text an 'excerpt from the camp regulations'.

5 As in the original.

6 In the 1920s Lipsko-born Ferdinand Itzkewitsch had submitted an application for citizenship which was, however, rejected. This is probably the reason for his suspicion that 'double standards' were being applied.

DOC. 60

Jüdisches Nachrichtenblatt, 19 March 1940: notification from the Reich Association of Jews in Germany that the compulsory first names must henceforth be included in telephone book listings[1]

Announcements from the Reich Association
Correction of telephone book listings
The Reich Association of Jews in Germany announces:
It is essential that all Jewish telephone subscribers have their name listing corrected in the telephone books for the next edition of the telephone book by entering the additional first names 'Israel' or 'Sara'.[2] We strongly recommend that the application required is submitted in a timely manner.

It is known that a new edition of the telephone book is currently being produced for the district of the Reich Post Office Headquarters *Berlin*, and the deadline for applying for changes has, strictly speaking, already passed as of 9 March 1940. However, we have been informed by the office responsible that applications for correction of first names will still be accepted if they are received without delay. If no application has yet been made to correct the listing of Jewish telephone subscribers in the Berlin district, the *application* must now be submitted *by 22 March 1940 at the latest* to the telephone directory office in Berlin C 2, at 13/14 Spandauer Straße.[3]

DOC. 61

On 29 March 1940 Salomon Samuel from Berlin thanks Mr and Mrs Schubert in Essen for their sympathy and support[1]

Handwritten letter from Dr Salomon Samuel,[2] Berlin-Grunewald, to Else Schubert,[3] dated 29 March 1940

Esteemed Mr[4] and dear Mrs Schubert,

I am returning you most warmly the greetings you sent me from your Easter walk in the Botanical Gardens. I can report that we are currently experiencing a return of winter, with snow and ice for the umpteenth time this year. Nevertheless, the sun's strength has not faded. It shines radiantly into our rooms, which since 21 March have been elevated to the status of a summer residence, and which will look so cheery and bright for the next six months with all the greenery at the windows when things start coming out, and

1 'Mitteilungen der Reichsvereinigung: Berichtigung der Eintragungen im Fernsprechbuch', *Jüdisches Nachrichtenblatt* (Berlin edition), 19 March 1940, p. 1. This article has been translated from German.

2 According to the Second Implementing Regulation to the Law on Changes to Surnames and Forenames (17 August 1938), Jews were forced to assume the additional names 'Sara' and 'Israel': *Reichsgesetzblatt*, 1938, I, p. 1044.

3 On 29 July 1940, Jews' telephone lines were cancelled altogether: see Doc. 96.

1 Alte Synagoge Essen, AR.4733. Excerpts published in Angela Genger (ed.), *Durch unsere Herzen ziehen die Jahrtausende: Briefe von Anna und Salomon Samuel 1933–1942* (Düsseldorf: Patmos, 1988), pp. 114–115. This letter has been translated from German.

which give us some relief from the hostility of our wider surroundings. We are by no means certain whether and for how long we will be able to enjoy the peace of our dwelling. Any day, a new operation could flush us out. Even the day ahead is precarious and uncertain. Let us not harbour any illusions. If you, dear Mrs Schubert, want to grant us the pleasure of a visit in May – and we will ask around regarding where you could stay – then that means you expect to find *us* here. And indeed we also believe that we will be able to persevere. But it is not down to us. That's simply the way it is: we are slated for emigration or misery. Is it not enough that a benevolent fate has led some two thirds of the Jewish people out of Old Germany and rescued them? The remainder are facing a sorrowful fate, if Heaven does not have mercy on them too. Do not feel too sorry for us, dear friends. If *we* have the courage to bear such a fate, then others should likewise not be faint-hearted and not make us faint-hearted.

But they can and may do something else: they can make this fate easier for us. And you have been doing that, dear friends, throughout all these difficult years of persecution. It has been a great comfort and support to me, and it has given me hope. It will also not have been in vain even when the ultimate fate can no longer be averted for us. I often think about the days in Essen, few, but filled with so much. And, all things considered, we made as much use of them as we possibly could. And the two of you were as friendly towards me as all of the others together. And that is saying a lot, for I was quite satisfied with the reception from my old congregation. Dear Mrs Kirschstein[5] surpassed all the others.

Today I received a letter from Dr Norden,[6] who is so diligently exercising his duties in H[am]b[ur]g and sent me the text for the address he is giving today entitled 'And Aaron was silent'. It is all too appropriate for the congregation in its beleaguered situation. I fear that it will elicit many sighs. He himself is valiantly stifling his yearning for his loved ones far away. His Hanna[7] is happily married in Tianjin. I hope that your three children continue to have favourable things to report.[8] I hope in particular that fate will be kind to Konrad. Dr Walter has hopefully got over his illness. We would be delighted to read a longer account of his personal experiences. And how are things in Jugenheim?

2 Dr Salomon Samuel (1867–1942), rabbi; rabbi of the Jewish congregation in Essen, 1894–1932; co-founder of the Union for Liberal Judaism in 1908; worked for the newspapers *Israelitisches Familienblatt* and *Jüdisch-Liberale Zeitung*; lived in Berlin after 1933; deported to Theresienstadt in 1942, along with the residents of the Jewish home for the elderly in Köpenick; died in Theresienstadt; author of *Geschichte der Juden im Stadt- und Synagogenbezirk Essen* (1913).

3 Else Schubert-Christaller (1891–1982), writer; addressed questions of Jewish faith in her works; author of *In deinen Toren Jerusalem: Jüdische Legenden* (1929).

4 Martin Schubert, mechanical engineer.

5 Johanna Kirschstein (b. 1890); lived in Essen; deported from Düsseldorf to Minsk on 10 Nov. 1941; declared dead.

6 Dr Joseph Norden (1870–1943), rabbi; served in Neustettin from 1897 to 1899, in Myslowitz, Upper Silesia until 1907, and then in Elberfeld; co-founder of the World Union for Liberal Judaism; returned after retirement in 1935 to his home town of Hamburg, where he worked for the Hamburg Temple, 1939–1942; deported in July 1942 to Theresienstadt, where he perished.

7 Joseph Norden's youngest daughter, Hanna Hochfeld (1919–2011), emigrated to Tianjin, China, on 13 June 1939 with her husband, Josef Hochfeld (1912–2004), a pharmacist; after 1948 they lived in the USA.

8 Else and Martin Schubert's children Konrad, Armgard, and Hedwig.

Here, my wife Anna is overseeing the brisk circulation of the much-loved series of books by Helene Christaller.[9] Keep on adding to your collection, dear Mrs Schubert! Fortunately you are down-to-earth people. At some point in the future you will surely have a place of your own on more content German soil rather than having to keep renting rooms from strangers. And the 'Samuel family' and all that is connected with them will occupy a little corner there. That will ensure that we are remembered positively and that nobody can influence how we are remembered. Even the most powerful lie is *in*effective when confronted with realities. Mr Buchthal[10] shows himself to be so very attentive: do you want to learn what is befitting etc.[11] – We have just been reading *Measure for Measure* by Shakespeare, not a masterpiece, but rich in ideas.

With best wishes for a peaceful Sabbath

Much refreshed by the lovely spring letter, I am sending you with warm greetings the requested poem. Will write more soon, yours truly[12]

DOC. 62
On 30 March 1940 the Ministry of Domestic and Cultural Affairs in Vienna dissolves the Jewish communities in the Ostmark[1]

Letter from the Ministry of Domestic and Cultural Affairs (IV-K/c-10224/1940), Vienna, signed p.p. Krüger,[2] to the State Administration of the Reich Gau of Vienna, Section I/6, 2 Ballhausplatz, Vienna I, dated 30 March 1940 (copy)

Dissolution of the representative bodies of the Israelite religious communities in the Ostmark and appointment of a representative of the same.

Since, as a result of the emigration of the Jews from the Ostmark, those Jewish religious communities in the Ostmark that have not yet been dissolved are no longer capable of governing themselves in accordance with the laws or statutes and also cannot lawfully represent themselves to the outside world, I hereby, in accordance with § 30 of the law issued on 21 March 1890, *Reichsgesetzblatt*, no. 57,[3] dissolve the hitherto existing *repre-*

9 Else Schubert-Christaller's mother, Helene Christaller, née Heyer (1872–1953), who lived in Jugenheim an der Bergstraße; considered one of the most important Lutheran writers of her time.
10 Albert Buchthal (1876–1942), businessman; owned a fuel wholesaler in Essen; deported to Theresienstadt on 20 July 1942, and from there two months later to Treblinka, where he was murdered.
11 The reference is to Carl Schütte, *Willst Du erfahren, was sich ziemt? Ein lustiges und lehrreiches Handbuch für die Jugend im Dritten Reich* (Do You Want to Learn what is Befitting? An Entertaining and Educational Handbook for Youth in the Third Reich) (Caputh: Klaus Hans/Erlitz, 1934).
12 The initials are illegible.

1 DÖW, 9887. This letter has been translated from German.
2 Kurt Krüger (1906–1987), lawyer; joined the NSDAP in 1925; co-founder of the NSDAP and SA in Danzig; Regierungsrat in Danzig, 1934; joined the Reich Economics Ministry in 1935; in charge of education and religion at the Ministry of Domestic and Cultural Affairs in Vienna after 1938; Ministerialrat and main office head for church and school affairs in the Munich NSDAP central office from 1940; lawyer in Nuremberg after 1945.
3 According to § 30 of the Law concerning the Regulation on the Legal Status of the Israelite Religious Community (21 March 1890) the state was allowed to disband congregations: *Reichsgesetzblatt*, 1890, pp. 109–113, here p. 113.

sentative bodies of the not yet dissolved Israelite religious communities in the Ostmark, with the exception of the Israelite Religious Community in Vienna. Concurrently with this, I appoint the head of the Israelite Religious Community in Vienna, Dr Josef Israel Löwenherz, as the representative of all the existing and not yet dissolved Israelite religious communities in the Ostmark. This representation will take effect on 15 April 1940.

All the Israelite religious communities in your administrative area that have not yet been dissolved are to be informed of this *immediately*, if necessary by applying § 29 of the *AVG Bundesgesetzblatt*, no. 274/1925.[4]

I request that you have a formal appointment decree issued and presented to Dr Josef Israel Löwenherz *immediately*.[5]

DOC. 63

On 5 April 1940 the board of the Reich Association of Jews in Germany discusses ways of increasing the number of Jewish emigrants[1]

Minutes of the board meeting of the Reich Association of Jews in Germany, Friday, 5 April 1940, (I/Dr. Hi/Kl.), 158 Kantstraße, Berlin-Charlottenburg, signed Dr Hirsch,[2] dated 9 April 1940[3]

(1) Dr Hirsch and Dr Eppstein[4] reported on discussions with the staff of the migration organizations regarding the number of allocations to the Central Office for Jewish Emigration which can still be met. After detailed discussion, in which nearly all attendees participated, unanimity was reached regarding the following:

(a) To speed up the process, the work of the emigration department in establishing the progress of the emigration preparations of the Jews in Berlin should proceed in a decentralized manner in the individual districts. The most important factors are the

4 According to § 29 of the General Administrative Procedure Law (*AVG*), official notifications for people or groups of people whose place of residence was unknown could be anounced by posting a public notice: *AVG*, 21 July 1925, *Bundesgesetzblatt für die Republik Österreich*, no. 274/1925, pp. 945–958, here p. 949.

5 The letter was forwarded on the same day by Krüger to the Landeshauptmänner 'with the request, […] to *immediately* inform all the Israelite religious communities in your administrative area that have not yet been dissolved', and to the 'General Plenipotentiary for the Assets of the Israelite Religious Communities in the Ostmark, SS-Hauptsturmführer *Eichmann*': DÖW, 9887.

1 BArch, R 8150/1, fol. 184r–v. This document has been translated from German.

2 Dr Otto Hirsch (1885–1941), lawyer; active in Jewish organizations from 1919; Ministerialrat in the Württemberg Ministry of the Interior from 1920; executive chairman of the Reich Representation of German Jews from 1933; arrested in 1941 and murdered in Mauthausen concentration camp.

3 The meeting was attended by Dr Baeck as chairman, Dr Eppstein, Henschel, Dr Hirsch, Philipp Kozower (1894–1944), Dr Arthur Lilienthal (b. 1899), Dr Seligsohn, Dr Berliner, Brasch, Dr Cohn, Paula Fürst (b. 1894), Fuchs, Hannah Karminski (1897–1942), Löwenstein, Lyon, Paul Meyerheim (1896–1944).

4 Dr Paul Eppstein (1902–1944), sociologist; member of the board of the Federation of Jewish Youth Associations; Zionist; adjunct professor at the Mannheim Commercial College, 1926–1933; dismissed in 1933; taught sociology in the 1930s at the Higher Institute for Jewish Studies in Berlin; social welfare officer in the Reich Representation of Jews in Germany and their liaison to the Gestapo from 1935; deported on 26 Jan. 1943 to Theresienstadt, where he was the Jewish elder from Jan. 1943 to 27 Sept. 1944; murdered on 28 Sept. 1944.

potential destinations and whether individuals have contacts in form of friends and relatives in neutral countries. To this end, voluntary staff should be recruited immediately and the required rooms be made available in consultation with the municipality.

(b) In light of the importance of providing consolidated training for the emigrants before their emigration, in particular in connection with language skills, geographical knowledge, questions of hygiene and economics, the residents of the Hachsharah and other training institutes who are prepared for emigration, and furthermore, as much as possible, also the individual emigrants from the Reich who are in emergency accommodation in Berlin, are to be brought together for training courses lasting around four weeks and instructed to submit their application for a passport to the Central Office during their residency in Berlin. Concerning the emigration of families, it must be determined whether it is necessary for the entire family to take up residence in Berlin or only the head of the family.

We expect to be able to allocate around 400 people per month to the Central Office as a result of this measure. The Palestine Office and the Relief Association department are authorized to confirm special transports to Palestine[5] and to approve foreign currency for the passage, dependent in appropriate cases on participation in the training courses.

(c) It was affirmed that the emigrants need to already have obtained their tax clearance certificate and other documents, and have their permission to pack up their belongings some time before the passport is issued. Therefore, it should be arranged, on the basis of the observations made in connection with (a), for those persons who are emigrating in the course of this year to file their application for emigration documents with the Central Office with the exception of the passport application. The number of allocations made possible through this measure is also estimated at 400–500 per month. Provided that the implementation of the measures in (b) and (c) is authorized, a daily allocation of 40–50 persons in the second half of April and an average allocation of 60 persons in May can be undertaken.

(2) The board noted that Mr Paul Israel Hirschfeld[6] has resigned from his office as chairman of the Jewish Religious Community of Stettin in a written declaration submitted today. However, he has declared his willingness to carry out special tasks, while refraining from exercising all other duties, until his resignation has been processed and until arrangements have been made for his successor. These arrangements will be made in consultation with the head of the district office of Hamburg, Dr Plaut.[7]

5 See Doc. 120.

6 Paul Hirschfeld (b. 1893), clothing manufacturer; from Nov. 1938, on the board of the Jewish Community of Stettin and head of its welfare department; deported from Berlin to Auschwitz on 29 Jan. 1943.

7 Dr Max Plaut (1901–1974), bank clerk, lawyer, and economist; secretary of the Jewish Community of Hamburg, 1933; chairman of the Jewish Religious Association of Greater Hamburg, 1938–1943; head of the north-west German district office of the Reich Association of Jews in Germany, 1939–1943; was imprisoned multiple times; went to Palestine on an exchange transport in 1944; between 1950 and 1965 lived in Bremen, where he worked as a company manager and in other posts; involved in promoting Christian–Jewish understanding in Hamburg, 1965–1974.

(3) Brasch[8] reported that the Gestapo head office in Berlin has granted permission for the curfew to begin at 10 p.m. rather than at 8 p.m. on the two evenings of Seder (22 and 23 April 1940). Requests from other religious communities that have been received and continue to be received by the Reich Association are to be answered accordingly.

(4) Dr Cohn[9] reported on the links between labour deployment and vocational training. The discussion will be continued at the next board meeting.

DOC. 64

On 7 April 1940 the SPD in exile reports on the desperate situation of the Jews in the German Reich[1]

Sopade report on Germany, 7 April 1940

[...][2]

III. The persecution of the Jews

We most recently reported on the situation of the Jews living under National Socialist rule in issue 7/1939 (pages A 80–119), that is, in our last publication before the war.[3] While the situation of the Jews was already desperate enough at that time, since then even worse things have occurred. Since the invasion of Poland the persecution of the Jews has entered its final, most horrifying stage.

Because the majority of the German people are less sympathetic than ever to the antisemitic excesses, the National Socialists are endeavouring to incite hatred of the Jews by blaming them for the war. Julius Streicher[4] in particular has resumed his

8 Dr Martin Brasch (1906–1941), lawyer; consultant for economic aid with the Jewish Community of Berlin from 1933; executive chairman of the Jewish Culture League and board member of the Jewish Community of Berlin from Sept. 1939; arrested on 7 May 1941 and hospitalized shortly afterwards on account of blood poisoning.

9 Dr Conrad Cohn (1901–1942), lawyer; worked at the Higher Regional Court in Breslau from 1928; banned from practising law in 1933; subsequently worked for the Religious Community of Breslau; member of the directorate of the Reich Representation of Jews from 1937; head of the welfare department of the Reich Association of German Jews/Jews in Germany from 1939; deported to Sachsenhausen concentration camp on 20 June 1942 and from there to Mauthausen concentration camp on 8 August 1942; probably took his own life.

1 Deutschland-Berichte der Sozialdemokratischen Partei Deutschlands (Sopade), vol. 7, 1940, no. 4, IfZ-Archives, Z 1527, fols. A 43–A 47. Published in Klaus Behnken (ed.), *Deutschlandberichte der Sozialdemokratischen Partei Deutschlands (Sopade) 1934–1940*, vol. 7 (Frankfurt am Main: Zweitausendeins, 1980), pp. 256–260. This report has been translated from German.

2 Part I outlines the general situation in Germany; part II describes the economic situation.

3 See PMJ 2/287 and 316.

4 Julius Streicher (1885–1946), teacher; member of the German Socialist Party (DSP), 1919–1921; joined the NSDAP and the SA in 1922; took part in the Beer Hall Putsch, 1923; was suspended from teaching; editor of the magazine *Der Stürmer*, 1923–1944; Gauleiter for Northern Bavaria, 1925–1928; dismissed from the teaching profession, 1928; Gauleiter for Nuremberg-Fürth, 1928–1929, and for Franconia, 1929–1940; imprisoned for antisemitic agitation in 1930; relieved of his position as Gauleiter due to personal enrichment in 1940; sentenced to death by the International Military Tribunal at Nuremberg in 1946 and executed.

bloodthirsty rabble-rousing once more after a short period of silence. Since the start of the war, the widely disseminated *Stürmer* has been tirelessly publishing variations on the theme that the Jews are to blame for the war, in red banner headlines repeated on every page, as well as in page after page of accompanying articles, all with loathsome illustrations. Letters, supposedly from soldiers in Poland, which the *Stürmer* claims to have received in September and October, contained accounts of Jewish atrocities against the invading German troops, of poisoned wells and of all sorts of cowardly murders committed by Jews.[5] The radio supported the work of Julius Streicher with extensive Jew-baiting, and in his speech to the Reichstag on 6 October 1939 Hitler himself spoke of the 'Jewish capitalists and journalists' who were to blame for the war and who could profit more in war than in peace.[6] At present the German press is striving above all to provide evidence for a Jewish admixture in the bloodlines of the democratic statesmen, or at least a Jewish intermarriage. As far as we are able to survey the effects of the propaganda, this war-blame exercise is not making much of an impression on the German people, and there is still opposition to the persecution of the Jews. It is admittedly different in the case of the young people who have grown up under National Socialist leadership, who have for the most part fallen under the spell of the antisemitic propaganda and also, whenever there is an opportunity, participate in great numbers in the excesses against the Jews.

1. The Jews in the Reich

The main act of this horrifying drama is playing out on Polish territory. In the Reich itself, from which the flow of direct news about the fate of the Jews is scarce, the primary weapons against the Jews who have not yet been shipped off are evidently hunger and cold. The Jews are categorically discriminated against in the allocation of food, coal, and all other rationed articles. Two reports on this follow:

Berlin: 1st report. The fate of the Jewish families – in the main these now consist only of the elderly and children – is very harsh. The Jews are barely considered when foodstuffs are allocated. They receive meat rarely, and in very small quantities, and no fish, poultry, milk, or butter. But even the procurement of the most simple provisions such as legumes and potatoes is difficult for them, because they are restricted to designated shopping hours. They are only allowed into the shops shortly before closing, after everything nourishing and good has already been bought up and only scraps are left. The Jews' ration cards are marked with a 'J'. They do not get any special rations, which are occasionally distributed.

Anyone who had even any bits of coal left in the house at all during the coldest period could not be sure that they would be able to keep them. Many Jews have had their fuel reserves simply 'confiscated'. You are probably already aware that the Jews do not receive any clothing rations. They receive a roll of sewing thread every quarter to mend their

5 In the column 'Das ist der Jude: Frontsoldaten schildern ihre Erlebnisse' ('That's what the Jew is like: soldiers at the front describe their experiences'), *Der Stürmer* published alleged letters from front-line soldiers from the beginning of the war. The letters were given titles such as: 'Assassins!', 'Apartment Looters and Thieves!', or 'Devil's Spawn': *Der Stürmer*, Oct. 1939, p. 10.

6 See PMJ 4/17.

worn-out things. 'Jewish' shoes may not be resoled; laundry items may not be replaced.[7] The elderly have suffered particularly from the bitter cold. Fortunately there are frequently courageous – one might almost say utterly fearless – Aryan friends who do not forsake the unfortunate souls and secretly slip them one thing or another.

2nd report. Mrs X. reports terrible things from the hell of Berlin. The Jews really do not know any more what they are or are not allowed to do. Groceries are available for Jews only after 12 o'clock; everywhere there are signs that Jews are prohibited from entering shops before 12. Jews who are on the streets after 8 p.m. are arrested. Mr ... had his coal supplies simply taken away.[8] It is absolutely ghastly there. Did you know that the Nazis made arrests again on 9 November, especially in Breslau, in 'remembrance' of last year's pogrom?[9]

The Jews who are, so to speak, at liberty are treated scarcely better than prisoners. On this point, too, two reports provide additional details:

Southern Germany. The snow-shovelling 'Jewish work squads' have done nothing to lighten the mood here. These emaciated figures are enough to make a dog howl. Jewish forced labourers between 16 and 60 years of age are now being deployed to carry out the most strenuous tasks: road construction, unloading railway freight, etc.[10] There are many intellectuals among them, doctors, lawyers, writers, etc. They say that some of them collapse while working. I have not seen this myself, but how could this not be the case? These people are even more undernourished than the average German; their clothes are torn and fall off and they do not receive any new ones, not even any work clothes. Their remuneration is handled in a variety of ways. Here the Jewish squads may receive an entirely inadequate meal in the canteen, but no wage in cash. Elsewhere they are said to be paid a pittance, but no food at all is provided. The German authorities are endeavouring to encourage and occasionally force Jewish emigration in spite of the war. But where are the Jews to emigrate to? First their money is taken away, and when no other country is willing to receive the destitute and worn-down people, it is claimed that the Jews are not pursuing their departure energetically enough, that they like being in Germany far too much. This – at least in substance – was actually printed in our newspaper not long ago.

Most of all, the Jews are afraid of being sent to the 'Jewish reservation' in Lublin.[11] Some have even committed suicide for fear of this fate.

South-western Germany. In ... the following incident played out. Here a senior Aryan civil servant was married to a Jewish woman for thirty years. She lacked the external characteristics of her race to such an extent that even after the death of her husband her parentage remained completely concealed. The two children of this marriage dared to

7 See Doc. 36, fnn. 4 and 7.

8 Ellipses here and subsequently as in the original.

9 On 8 Nov. 1939 the attempt by Georg Elser (1903–1945) to assassinate Hitler in the Munich Bürgerbräukeller failed. Subsequent to this some 150 Jews were also arrested in Breslau.

10 On the expansion of forced labour in 1940, see Introduction, p. 64.

11 It was originally intended to establish a 'Jewish reservation' in the area around Lublin, but this plan was later abandoned: see Introduction, p. 41, and PMJ 4/65.

conceal their half-Jewish ancestry under Hitler. The daughter was a municipal librarian until the end, while the son held a well-paid post as an engineer. Mother, daughter, and son literally no longer had a moment's peace and were terrified of being found out, because they were constantly making themselves liable to prosecution under the National Socialist legislation. At the beginning of the war the son was conscripted and killed in action in Poland. When the pension entitlements for his wife were being calculated everything was revealed: the mother and sister poisoned themselves with gas at the end of January.

The *economic dispossession* of the Jews continues; in other words, it is approaching its end, as already at this stage there are only tiny remnants of Jewish property left. The work of the Jewish welfare organizations is made extremely difficult. If the buildings belonging to the Jewish communities have not yet been requisitioned, they are gradually passing into the possession of the state and the municipalities. Thus, for example, the Israelite Hospital in Leipzig has been taken over by the city and transformed into a municipal hospital, as reported by the *Leipziger Neueste Nachrichten* in mid January. The Jewish patients had to be removed.[12] The Jewish school buildings in Berlin were already requisitioned in October and used to house evacuees from the Rhineland.[13]

The Jews have been removed from their private residences too, without their seeing any possibility of finding alternative accommodation.

Hamburg. A long-established Jewish family – the husband, 66 years old; the wife, 64 – once wealthy, has been in living in a large apartment for 14 years. On 1 March 1940 the landlord gave them notice to leave their apartment by 31 March 1940. Contrary to the terms of the rental contract, no reason was provided.[14] They are unable to obtain a new apartment. A 77-year-old relative has been living with the family for many years. He is thus also sharing the same fate.

Saxony. A Jewish family had their lease terminated as of 1 April 1940 by the landlord without any reason being given. They cannot get a new apartment. The husband is not a Jew; only the wife is Jewish. He, a foreigner, received German citizenship during the Weimar period. The Third Reich expatriated him several months ago. The wife is 40 and the husband 45 years old.

If up to now some few Jews have managed to escape the worst, it is thanks to the fact that German antisemitism is not genuine, but rather artificially fostered by the Party. A small example of this is provided in the following report:

Central Germany. A number of Jewish engineers have worked for a long time in a large machine factory in X. They were able to keep their positions because, with the consent of the German Labour Front, they were recognized as employees on account of their

12 *Leipziger Neueste Nachrichten*, 28 Dec. 1939, p. 3: 'Das Israelitische Krankenhaus von der Reichsmessestadt übernommen' ('The Israelite Hospital taken over by the Reich Trade Fair City'). The hospital had already been evacuated on 15 Dec. 1939.

13 This could not be verified. On 1 Oct. 1939 responsibility for Jewish schools was passed to the Reich Association of Jews in Germany; they were not banned until 1942.

14 See Doc. 16, fn. 15.

specialist expertise. During the pogroms in November 1938 their apartments were also spared from the 'outburst of public anger'. But eventually the Party intervened and demanded that a 'solution' must be found. The plant manager found one as follows: he declared that the Aryan engineers could not be expected to continue working together with the Jewish colleagues – and rented special office spaces for them, where they continue in their work for the facility uninterrupted.

[…][15]

DOC. 65

On 8 April 1940 Max Inow from Wuppertal updates his daughter Grete in Palestine on the scattered family members and his own endeavours to emigrate[1]

Handwritten letter from Max Inow,[2] Wuppertal, to his daughter Grete,[3] Palestine, dated 8 April 1940

Dear Grete,

We were delighted to receive your last letter. Since I play cello nearly every evening, which gives me some variety and stimulation, I was really interested in your account of the concert you listened to. We often speak about you, dear Grete, and how well you could recite the music you heard. Through practising diligently I have also regained my familiarity with the instrument. I have so many grateful listeners in the house. I don't charge entrée.[4] All free of charge. If I should happen to skip an evening, there are protests the next day.

We had dealt with your enquiry about the letter to the address. We had let ourselves be photographed especially for this purpose. Mother's photo was particularly good.[5]

In April there was a succesion of birthdays; we wrote to all. I assume, at any rate, that our birthday greetings reached you on time.

15 The remainder of the document describes the situation of the Jews in the Protectorate of Bohemia and Moravia, in Vienna, and in Poland, followed by a discussion of German war production. See also Doc. 263 for the period up to the beginning of Oct. 1939.

1 The original is privately owned; copy in IfZ-Archives, F 601. Published in Ulrike Schrader (ed.), '*… so froh, dass Ihr draußen seid': Die Briefe der Familie Inow, Wuppertal* (Plauen: privately published, 2005), pp. 125–126. This document has been translated from German.

2 Maximilian Inow (1877–1942), businessman; co-owner of the company Gebrüder Inow, founded in 1919, which sold knitted goods and hosiery; owner of an antiques and handicraft store after 1931. In 1937 the Wuppertal municipal utility services terminated Max Inow's lease on the shop; he was deported from Düsseldorf to the Lodz ghetto on 27 Oct. 1941, and from there in May 1942 to Chelmno, where he was murdered.

3 Margalit Harlev, née Grete Inow (1921–2015), teacher; emigrated to Sweden in 1937; attended a Hachsharah boarding school in Västraby; emigrated in Jan. 1940 to Palestine, where she held various posts, for example in a kitchen and in an office of the British navy; employed as a teacher, 1958–1980; lived in Haifa.

4 French in the original: entrance fee.

5 Beatrice Inow, née Michels (1887–1942), housewife; deported with her husband to Lodz and from there to Chelmno, where she was murdered.

Alfred[6] had not yet written about his change of job. He writes, amongst other things, that Renate,[7] whom he visits every fortnight, has grown tremendously.

To return to your request: I went to the P. Office[8] in person and filled out the relevant forms and included the photos. However, there are thousands of requests before ours, so that some time will probably pass before an answer comes.

I find your endeavours to find and foster contacts very appropriate. That sort of thing has never done any harm. It is always a way to get rid of a certain one-sidedness, and that is very good right now.

Someone has just turned up to watch; I am to play Bach's prelude.

We are well, keep healthy, enjoy nature, continue to take pleasure in music. Lots of kisses, Father.

Good night

DOC. 66
On 8 April 1940 Hitler issues a ruling on Jewish *Mischlinge* serving in the Wehrmacht[1]

Order from the Chief of the Wehrmacht High Command (file ref. 121 10–20 J [Ic], No. 524/40 secret), signed Keitel, Berlin, dated 8 April 1940[2]

Secret!
Re: treatment of Jewish Mischlinge in the Wehrmacht
The Führer and Supreme Commander of the Wehrmacht has reached the following decision:

1. The 50 per cent Jewish Mischlinge or men who are married to 50 per cent Jewish Mischlinge or to Jewish women are, depending on their age (§§ 10 and 11 of the Military Service Law),[3] to be assigned to Replacement Reserve Force II or Reserve Force II, but with the respective notation 'n.z.v.',[4] in order to set them strictly apart from the other conscripts in these categories. Exempted from this are officers who, on the basis of the Führer's ruling (OKW–WZ (II)/ J–no. 651/39, dated 13 March 1939),[5] have remained in

6 Alfred Inow (1922–1998), gardener; son of the Inows; attended a technical school in Turin in 1933; in 1935 returned to Germany and worked as a gardener in Haan; was arrested at the time of the November pogroms in 1938 and imprisoned in Dachau for four weeks; emigrated to Britain in 1939; after the beginning of the war detained as an 'enemy alien'; subsequently joined the British army; worked for a horticultural firm after the war.
7 Renate (Renie) Inow (b. 1929), daughter of the Inows; came to Britain on 17 May 1939 with a Kindertransport; lived in Israel, 1952–1955, and afterwards in London; worked for the Jewish Agency, 1960–1970, and for London city government, 1971–1993.
8 Palestine Office.

1 BArch, R 187/240b. Published in Adler, *Der verwaltete Mensch*, p. 295. This document has been translated from German.
2 The original contains two receipt stamps dated 8 Sept. 1941 and 10 Sept. 1941, as well as handwritten annotations.
3 §§ 10 and 11 of the Military Service Law of 1935 governed the use of conscripts in the Replacement Reserves and the Reserve Force (Landwehr): Military Service Law, 21 May 1935, *Reichsgesetzblatt*, 1935, I, pp. 609–614, here p. 610.
4 *Nicht zu verwenden* = not to be used.
5 This ruling could not be found.

the peacetime Wehrmacht. In special cases, the Führer reserves the right to make exceptions, which must be applied for through the OKW.[6]

2. The 25 per cent Mischlinge and members of the Wehrmacht who are married to 25 per cent Mischlinge remain in the Wehrmacht and *can, in wartime*, by way of exception, be promoted and utilized as superiors if proven to have acquitted themselves particularly well. In addition, former non-commissioned officers, civil servants, and officers who are 25 per cent Mischlinge, or who are married to 25 per cent Mischlinge, can be utilized in the Wehrmacht in wartime *with sufficient justification*. Every application for promotion or reappointment must be submitted to the Führer, through the OKW, for his ruling.

To ensure that the prescribed measures are expedited, prompt announcement of the order above is requested.

The orders OKW no. 190/40 J (Ic) dated 16 January 1940 and OKW no. 280/40 J (Ic) dated 20 January 1940, the latter with the exception of the provisions applicable to Freemasons, are herewith superseded.[7]

DOC. 67

On 10 April 1940 Heinrich Himmler orders, for the duration of the war, a ban on the release of Jews imprisoned in concentration camps[1]

Wireless message from the Reich Security Main Office, IV C 2[2] (Allg. Nr. 28/731/40 KL. G), unsigned, to all Gestapo head offices and Gestapo offices, dated 10 April 1940[3]

Urgent – Present immediately – *Secret* –
The Reichsführer SS and Chief of the German Police has ordered, for the duration of the war, a general ban on the release of all Jewish (underline) prisoners who are in concentration camps. At the same time, however, he has had it made known that he consents to the release of Jews whose emigration has already been arranged and who can emigrate in the near future – in Apr[il] – provided there are no political or other objections – All applications now on hand here for release of Jewish prisoners have thereby been dealt with –

6 Oberkommando der Wehrmacht: Wehrmacht High Command.

7 The two OKW orders governed the deployment in wartime of members of the Wehrmacht who were married to Jewish women or *Mischlinge* or who fell under the provisions applicable to Freemasons. While the deployment of Wehrmacht civil servants and officers who were married to '25 per cent Mischlinge' was not subject to any restriction, former non-commissioned officers and ordinary servicemen returning to service who were married to Jewish women or *Mischlinge*, or who fell under the provisions applying to Freemasons, could be promoted to a rank no higher than sergeant: *Allgemeine Heeresmitteilungen*, 7 March 1940, p. 119.

1 BArch, R 58/276, fol. 252. This document has been translated from German.

2 Section IV C 2 was in charge of so-called protective custody affairs and was headed by Dr Emil Berndorff (b. 1892).

3 The wireless message was sent out in Berlin on 10 April 1940 at 9:35 a.m. and received by the Gestapo in Düsseldorf. It contains handwritten notes.

DOC. 68

On 12 April 1940 Marianne Wachstein describes to Hofrat Wilhelm how she and other women were mistreated in Ravensbrück concentration camp[1]

Handwritten letter (regarding 104c Vr. 2782/39, Hr. 11/40)[2] from Marianne Wachstein,[3] room 24, second floor, hospital, Vienna, to Hofrat Dr Wilhelm, at this hospital, ward 104 c, Vienna, dated 12 April 1940[4]

Hofrat Dr Wilhelm, Noble Sir,

Regarding the above matter, the undersigned ventures most respectfully to present the following:

By way of introduction I must say the following, to ensure a clearer understanding. The Ravensbrück concentration camp near Fürstenberg in Mecklenburg is a forced labour camp.[5] The tasks that I saw women perform there – I myself suffer from a nervous illness and am unable to work – are, for example: there are two stone road-rollers, a so-called small one and a big one, and around these road-rollers are ropes; each rope has a cross-handle, and the women had to grasp this cross-handle and pull the road-rollers. They also had to shovel sand, and others carried it away in wooden boxes that rest on two wooden base supports, etc. In summer the working day was nine hours long; on Saturday the work lasted until noon.

Three times a day and twice only on Saturday and Sunday there is a so-called roll call, that is, the whole camp, every block (a block holds around 140–150 persons, who are quartered in a wooden barracks) has to line up in front of its barracks, one behind the other in rows of four, stand to attention next to each other like soldiers, hands at their sides, and stand silently until the whole camp is counted by the matron[6] and an overseer, i.e. each block warden (the person in charge of the whole block) announces to the aforementioned the number of persons present. Every roll call always lasts 20 minutes.

The camp contains 17 barracks, each with space for around 150 persons, and of which one is a barracks for Jews. In addition there is a dungeon, completed in the summer

1 YVA, O.33/3262. Published in Irith Dublon-Knebel, 'Der Bericht der Marianne Wachstein', in *Schnittpunkt des Holocaust: Jüdische Frauen und Kinder im Konzentrationslager Ravensbrück. Wissenschaftlicher Begleitband zur Ausstellung* (Berlin: Metropol, 2009), pp. 87–106, here pp. 92–102. This document has been translated from German.

2 File number of an Austrian court in the first phase of a proceeding.

3 Marianne Wachstein, née Kobler (1895–1942), arrived at Ravensbrück on 27 July 1939; was taken to Vienna in Feb. 1940 for questioning and brought back to Ravensbrück a few months later; murdered in the 'euthanasia' facility in Bernburg on the River Saale in the course of Operation 14f13.

4 The receipt stamp on the original cannot be deciphered.

5 Ravensbrück concentration camp was the largest concentration camp for women on the territory of the Old Reich. It was set up in 1939 near the town of Fürstenberg in the area bordering the states of Brandenburg and Mecklenburg.

6 This refers to the senior guard Johanna Langefeld, née May (1900–1974), matron; joined the NSDAP in 1937; guard, 1938, and senior guard, 1939, at Lichtenburg concentration camp; from May 1939 at Ravensbrück and from March to Oct. 1942 at Auschwitz-Birkenau, at which point she returned to Ravensbrück; arrested in the spring of 1943; released after a trial before an SS and police court in Breslau and worked for BMW in Munich; arrested in 1945; having been extradited to Poland in 1946, fled, went into hiding, and returned to Munich in 1957.

of 1940, which is still very dank. Among other things, I was, for example, in solitary confinement in cell 15 of the building, which was so damp that the wall where the window was was covered with patches of black mould. In solitary confinement, with the exception of one prisoner or another, one is not allowed to pursue any activity, even reading, nor writing either, nothing at all, just sitting all day on a stool; taking a walk is not allowed either.

Shortly before I (on 23 February 1940) boarded my transport from Ravensbrück to here, to the LG[7] in Vienna, orders were given for me to be put in detention again, specifically for twenty-eight days, again completely unjustified. Detention in Ravensbrück consists of the following:
1) A hard bed daily.
2) Food only every fourth day (and then only the same ration as those who get food every day, which approximately equals the daily food here in quantity and quality), the three days in between just the bread ration alone (approximately as much as we get here in addition to food), and twice a day, black coffee (it is prohibited to drink the water there because it causes diarrhoea).
3) A damp, pitch-dark jail cell, one floor below ground level, in the aforementioned jail built in the summer of 1940. As the day wears on, one can make out the toilet and washbasin.
4) [It is] unheated (with the climate there still quite harsh and this year's winter especially severe). Of the twenty-eight days I served only four, [and] on the fifth day God led me out, bringing me here; during the first two days there was no heat at all, [and] on the third and fourth days, in my estimation, including the time in which the heat was dissipating, there was heating for approximately one hour in total, that is, it was completely inadequate.
5) No opportunity for activity, even the slightest.
6) No taking a walk. All this together is labelled with the simple little word 'detention'.
I came to have this detention as follows. At the time when I was admitted to the camp, there was a doctor who examined me, like every new arrival, and on the basis of the examination he gave me an exemption from standing in formation for roll call. I was allowed to participate while seated and was not made to work. This doctor was even so kind as to prescribe cold sponge baths for me three times a day, because at that time, as a result of all the agitation, I was almost unable to walk and stand. One day I was brought before a new doctor,[8] who among other things took away the dispensation cards. In those days, people with dispensation stayed in the block and did not participate at all in the roll call, which took place outdoors. It was the deep of winter. As soon as I entered the surgery, this doctor, without examining me in the slightest, snarled: 'You have to take part in your roll call.' This was Saturday, 10 February 1940. Because I suffer from a nervous

7 Possibly 'camp prison' (*Lagergefängnis*), 'regional court prison' (*Landgerichtsgefängnis*), or 'military hospital prison' (*Lazarettgefängnis*).

8 In the initial phase there were two camp doctors: Dr Erika Jantzen, née Köhler (b. 1911), camp doctor first at Lichtenburg concentration camp and then at Ravensbrück from Jan. 1938 to Nov. 1940; terminated her service in the concentration camps after her marriage in Nov. 1940; also Dr Walter Pfitzner (1910–1946), who joined the NSDAP and the SS in 1933; camp doctor at Lichtenburg concentration camp and then at Ravensbrück from May 1938 to Feb. 1939; when the war started, joined the Waffen SS as the medical officer of a division; committed suicide.

illness, I cannot possibly stand for such a long time, because three times, this is almost an hour a day, I can't even stand for twenty minutes. So I asked the doctor to examine me, saying I could not possibly do this. In reply, he snarled at me again: 'You will take part in your roll call.' I replied that it was a matter of inability to perform and asked him once again to examine me. Despite my request for an examination, he insisted, without examining me in any way, that I had to stand, and rudely said something derogatory about 'Jews', and the nurse at the desk in the surgery seconded it by sneering. At this, I retorted, in my adversity: 'I will tell people abroad, too, how one is treated here in the concentration camp.' Then the military doctor in black grabbed hold of my back and roughly threw me out of the surgery, without having performed even the slightest examination. My ribs hurt, but I said calmly: 'I will report that too.' Outside in the anteroom, however, in my distress at the treatment and because of the pain in my ribs, I shouted loudly that I would relate this everywhere. My ejection took place before a vast number of prisoners, as it is customary in Ravensbrück that, every Saturday, those who want to see the doctor have to form a queue and wait their turn. I took part, for example, on one such Saturday (admittedly, I sat) – a crowd of prisoners were queued up from around 8 a.m. to noon, after which a great many still had not been dealt with, when the nurse quite simply came out and said: 'Go home and come back next Saturday.'

A female prisoner, who was in room B of the block for Jews and is called 'Rike', told me that she heard what had taken place. Who the many prisoners in the queue were, I do not know.

Then I was led back to the block and gave an account of the incident to a number of prisoners in room B of the Jews' block and also to the room elder, Miss Hertl (or something like that), as well as the block elder, Miss Paula Kemmelmayer, both Aryans, adding the following: 'The doctor has sworn a spondeum[9] and must examine me, the Jewess, just the same as an Aryan, to assess whether inability to perform is present or not.' I was understandably in a dither about it, because I had once had the experience that, when I collapsed in solitary confinement, the guard Mrs Zimmer[10] ordered water to be poured on me through the opening where the food is shoved in, and when this was of no avail, she instructed the prisoner Mrs Kaiser (everyone knows her, she counts all the prisoners every day when work commences), who is now no longer in the camp, to hit me with a stick like a broomstick through the aforementioned opening. Then, when the blows of the stick brought me to consciousness – how many I received, I do not know – I was quite wet and had to spend several days in the deep of winter in my wet dress and wet slippers (shoes are no longer permitted in solitary cells), because the stove was broken, and thus [the cell was] completely unheated and nothing would dry. By the way, Mrs Zimmer also forgot for several days to turn on the heat for me; I did not even know that [it] worked and not until the changeover of the guards, when Miss Mandl came[11] – she

9 'Spondeum' (derived from Latin *spondeo*: solemnly swear) probably stands for the Hippocratic oath and the associated ethical obligations of every physician.

10 Emma Zimmer (1888–1948); ran the punishment block at Ravensbrück, 1939–1942; deputy senior guard from mid 1940; joined the NSDAP in 1941; made senior guard at Ravensbrück in March/April 1942, and deputy senior guard at Auschwitz from Oct. 1942 to the end of 1943; sentenced to death by a British military tribunal in July 1948 and executed.

11 Maria Mandl (1912–1948); initially worked as a cleaner and post office clerk; guard at Lichtenburg concentration camp from Oct. 1938; guard at Ravensbrück from May 1939; joined the NSDAP in

asked me whether it was warm enough for me, and turned on the heating. Also, I often saw how a young girl from the neighbouring block (a Gypsy) was forced to stand again and again, despite continuing seizures, which in my opinion were epileptic in nature, and in our Jews' block too, Mrs Schenk[12] frequently had serious attacks of convulsions, followed by rigidity of her limbs, and nonetheless was repeatedly forced to stand. Because, all my life, I have fainted after standing for a prolonged time, I naturally was quite afraid of the roll call, all the more so as I now have even more trouble standing, as a result of all I have been through since the overthrow,[13] because my knees will not hold me.

I cite as witnesses to the fact that, at that time, after I was seen by the doctor on 10 February 1940, my utterances had to do only with the fact that I, as previously mentioned, gave an account of the incident and referred to the spondeum: Miss Paula Kemmelmayer, Miss Hertl, both Aryans, further the prisoners Ida Steinhardt, Else Boschwitz, Edith Weiss, Blumenthal, Modesta Finkelstein, Kaufmann, Leontine Kastenbaum,[14] Rike, and other prisoners who were in room B of the Jews' block. It is possible that one or another of the prisoners listed was not in the room at that moment, but these are the ones who sat nearest me. The aforementioned utterances or account of the incident were interpreted as verbal abuse of the state and, I think, also of the leadership. One 'camp mate' went to the guard, who interrogated me, then the senior guard interrogated me, and I was put in solitary confinement the same day. To prove that I was not possibly trying to protect myself from the freezing temperature, I declared to the block elder, Miss Kemmelmayer, that I was willing to take part in the roll calls outdoors, while seated.

Around one week later I was taken out of solitary confinement and brought to the director.[15] Because I was suffering from a nervous illness and in an even worse state after the commotion, and could not walk quickly in slippers, the guard (name unknown, the woman who assumed responsibility for me in solitary confinement on 10 February 1940 and subsequently was the guard in solitary confinement and detention)[16] grabbed me from behind and kept pushing me forward, forcing me to walk quickly; I stumbled, lost a slipper, barely managed to stop myself from falling, and begged: 'I can't walk that quickly, please slow down.' The director immediately yelled at me: 'Why did you shout like that?' although I had merely made my request in a very calm tone of voice, because I was always afraid there. Our path led just across the corridor. I replied calmly that I

1941; made senior guard at Ravensbrück in April 1942; then at Auschwitz-Birkenau from Oct. 1942; headed the women's section in the Mühldorf camp complex, one of the Dachau satellite camps, from Nov. 1944; US prisoner of war; extradited to Poland in 1946; sentenced to death in Cracow in 1947 and executed.

12 Cäcilie Schenk, née Lewin (1896–1942); lived in Berlin; was murdered on 14 Feb. 1942 in the 'euthanasia' facility in Bernburg on the River Saale.

13 The author is referring to the National Socialist entry to power in Jan. 1933.

14 Correctly: Kestenbaum.

15 Max Koegel (1895–1946); originally worked as an Alpine shepherd and deliveryman; joined the NSDAP and the SS in 1932; worked at Dachau concentration camp from 1933, commandant of the protective custody camp at Lichtenburg concentration camp from 1938; then at Ravensbrück in May 1939, and officially appointed as commandant in Jan. 1940; commandant of Lublin-Majdanek concentration camp from the summer of 1942 and of Flossenbürg concentration camp after May 1943; was captured by US forces in June 1946 and committed suicide.

16 At the time the reports on the numbers of persons in detention were usually signed by Johanna Langefeld.

had not shouted. The director now read aloud to me a piece of paper stating that, on 10 February 1940 in the block, I had verbally abused the state and, I think, the leadership as well. I responded politely that I had only talked about the incident, as previously mentioned, and about the spondeum. The director picked up the file in front of him and hit my hands with it several times. I saw that I was not permitted to defend myself. Two days later, the senior guard had me brought before her, and read aloud to me as the director had done and said that I was getting twenty-eight days in detention as a result. I said: 'It is not true that I verbally abused the state or the leadership, but I can't defend myself, of course.' At that, the senior guard replied: 'This has come to you from the director,' and I was immediately led off to detention, *regardless of the fact that my feet were bleeding and blue with cold, that I had already lost so much weight that every one of my ribs could be counted, my skin was hanging like an empty sack in some places, my legs were slender in the morning when I got up and quite swollen a short time later – (I don't know whether my flesh has already turned fluid or whether it is tissue fluid), my flesh is coming away from my bones, and one can also tell immediately from my face and neck area what a bad state I am in.*

I served four days of these twenty-eight days of detention; on the fifth, thanks to Almighty God, I had to be transported to Vienna. The first two days there was no heat at all; the third and fourth days, in my estimation, including the reduction of the heat, it was heated for around one hour, which naturally was completely inadequate. Although I am a very hardy person, I was miserably cold, with my teeth chattering, I sat there starving in the pitch-dark with bleeding feet all day long. From outside, the electric light can be switched on at any time.

While I was in the Polish prison at Alexanderplatz in Berlin[17] for three and a half days during transport and had to wait for fourteen days in Plauen in the Vogtland region, because there was no prison vehicle and no room, respectively, I had the good fortune to encounter generous doctors and guards. Through the doctor in Berlin I obtained from the guard chilblain ointment dressings for both feet; in Plauen, also through the doctor, [I obtained] ointment dressings from the guard and in addition even daily alternating footbaths throughout the entire fortnight. My toes and feet healed again as a result, and today the skin merely remains sensitive and there are small scabs in a few spots.

In Berlin and especially in Plauen (there I was apparently in the court prison) I had plenty of good food, for breakfast every day even genuine rye bread with either butter or fine, sweetened jam, so much that I still had enough for a break-time snack with coffee. Nevertheless, I could not recover.

I already had – I think, on 28 August 1939 (I noted the date because two days previously, while still in the block, I read about the non-aggression pact with Russia in the newspaper) – to serve forty-two days in solitary confinement with a break of two and a half days, after I had four days of detention in the block immediately before that; the latter was a punishment that the whole block got, as a camp mate told me, because two were unwilling to work any more. In Ravensbrück it is also common practice to punish the entire block for the actions of individuals. I got the forty-two days of detention (which at that time was still without the hard bed and in a wooden barracks that was

17 The writer means the police headquarters at Alexanderplatz, which also contained the city jail. From 1935 the building was used by the Gestapo.

divided into cells by wooden walls on both sides, with a central corridor) as follows. I was led into the office, where a number of printed pages were placed before me and I was required to sign in acknowledgement of their receipt. I asked to be allowed to read them before signing, but I was told that it was just identification papers. Nonetheless I did not want to sign without reading them, and when I was pressed to sign, I said point-blank that I would not sign without reading, that I [...][18] did not want any help through them. God would help me, I said, and added that the communists would indeed exact vengeance for whatever happened to us. After that I was led away to detention in darkness, which at that time was still semi-darkness (shortly after that it was made entirely dark by boarding up the window from outside), and in the wooden barracks as previously mentioned.

It was the first time that I was put in detention, and I did not yet know what that meant. A short while after I was there, the guard Mrs Zimmer opened the door again; a man in uniform was next to her and shouted in to me: 'Now you'll rot there, starve, you'll not get out of there alive.' (As I later heard, this must have been the driver of the men – soldiers – present in the camp.[19]) Because I am devoutly religious, I answered calmly: 'If it is God's will that I die, then I will die here.' Then the man left and the guard locked the door. About an hour later the guard Mrs Zimmer opened the door again, and told me to come out. In the corridor she told me to undress completely down to my chemise; I did so, whereupon I was forced to put on a straitjacket (at that time still unfamiliar to me; the straitjacket is a popular means to exacerbate punishment in Ravensbrück). My hands were bound so tight that my right hand was swollen for around fourteen days and my body was also strapped tight, even at the neck, then I was led back into the cell and lay on the floor, tightly wrapped into a parcel. I had not raged about in the least, but had sat meekly and quietly in my cell for the hour, which witnesses brought in as a result will confirm. Because of the tight restraints, I felt very queasy, I lost consciousness, now I am said to have had a screaming fit. I was shaken until I came round; in front of me stood Mr Sill in uniform (said to be an SS-Hauptsturmführer; I am not familiar with uniforms).[20] I [was] lying on the floor in a short chemise and over it only a straitjacket, then I heard the woman in detention in the next cell (later I learned that her name is Annemarie Vancotic or Vankotic) call over to us: 'She lives only for religion and communism'; in reply Mr Sill: 'Indeed, we know that,' and his fist smashed down hard on my nose, which I continued to feel for many weeks afterwards, his foot landed hard two or three times on my bare calf, and at the same time the guard Mrs Zimmer roughly grabbed my hair from behind; my body, my hands hurt from the tight restraints – all that was done to me, a helpless, tied-up parcel. I lost consciousness again, woke late in the evening, tormented by pain, soiled with my own faeces. Then they came

18 One word is illegible here.

19 The SS driver was Ludwig Sauerbrey (b. 1912), a journeyman butcher; joined the NSDAP and the SA in 1933 and the SS in 1935; worked full-time in the service of the SS from 1935; driver at Lichtenburg concentration camp in 1938; then at Ravensbrück from 1939; became SS-Hauptscharführer in 1943.

20 Correctly: Egon Zill (1906–1974), baker; joined the NSDAP and the SA in 1923 and the SS in 1926; worked at various camps from 1934, including as camp commandant at Flossenbürg from Sept. 1942 to May 1943; then in the Waffen SS; arrested in 1953 and sentenced in Munich to life imprisonment in 1955; the sentence was reduced to fifteen years, and he was released in 1963.

to untie me. In total, I must have lain there in the straitjacket for around six hours. I had to spend the following night dressed only in a nightshirt (I had been made to remove my clothes, shoes and stockings and leave them outside), without blankets, without a straw mattress, without pillows, just lying on the bare floor, my teeth chattering with cold. The summer nights there are also very cold; the camp is situated partly in a pine forest, a lake on one side, and supposedly the camp is on very low ground. By the next night I was given blankets; starting the third night, pillows, with covers. During the first two days there were instructions that I was to be given nothing at all to eat, only black coffee twice daily, no bread either. (The water there cannot be drunk because it causes diarrhoea.) But no one had said a word to me about this being only for three days. Now one can imagine what effect this has on an inexperienced person when he is put into such a dark cell the first time, and is yelled at: 'Now you'll rot there, starve, you'll not get out of there alive,' and then is brought nothing to eat for three days, no bread either, without being told that beginning on the fourth day he will get bread every day and water every four days.

Several days later it was read out to me that because of my statements in the office I was getting three weeks in detention and another three weeks in detention for my shouting and soiling myself with my faeces. The fact that both took place while I was unconscious was not taken into account.

Two and a half days interrupted the two lots of three weeks, that is, forty-two days in solitary confinement, and after serving the forty-two days I was locked in a cell with a madwoman named Apfel. Before transfer from the solitary detention cell to the cell with the madwoman, the guard Mrs Zimmer read aloud to me that I was getting solitary confinement for life. I immediately had the feeling that God would not allow this, and replied: 'Go right ahead,' whereupon she corrected herself: 'That is, as long as you are alive and healthy and here!' Also a fine prospect, if one were not devoutly religious, if one knows that people may be kept there for years, as one stays there for an unspecified period without a trial, without a sentence, without knowing when one will get out. Not long before I came to Vienna, for example, a woman named Silberberg (or something similar) was released; she is said to have been there for five years. She was a Jewess.

I was, as previously mentioned, locked into the cell with the madwoman Apfel after serving the forty-two days in detention. My complaints and requests to be removed from the cell because she was insane were of no avail. After the first night (this was during the two and a half day break from detention) the guard Mrs Zimmer asked, when she unlocked the door to hand in the coffee (there were no hatches there for pushing food through; this detention centre was only a temporary space until construction of the jail was completed): 'Well, have you given one another a good beating?' The madwoman welcomed me primarily by pouring a big washbasin of water on me from behind, she spat in various directions every few minutes, at the window, on to my straw mattress, the door, the floor, wherever she happened to strike, she – pardon the expression – soiled herself with diarrhoea, which she did not wash away but simply allowed to run down her legs, she did not wash herself but spat into her hands and rubbed the spittle on her face and hands: that was her way of washing herself. At night she sat down on my bed, fidgeted constantly, which I put up with for an hour, and then when I asked her to get up because I could not sleep, she tore the blankets from me and pulled the pillows and bed sheet out from under me. She tore her bread into bits and threw it out of the window, she poured her coffee on the floor and waited for me to slip and fall, she made speeches for hours at night, wild speeches, she cursed God day and night. Her hands, her arms and legs were already as thin as a spider's. Because of the noise she made for hours on end every night, everyone in detention or solitary confinement – both categories were housed in the same barracks – was unable to sleep. It was all dreadful. The guard did not have the courage to come into the cell. On the third day of the break in my detention, the madwoman roared and bellowed so that the guard came into the barracks as a result – not into the cell. – The madwoman was sitting on her upper bunk (as in a sleeping car, she had the upper bed, I the lower one), had poured her coffee on my head, and was in the process of aiming missiles which she had taken up to her bunk (food bowl, tin plate, coffee mug) at me; I had held up a washbasin in front of me as a shield and had fled to the farthest corner of the cell – the madwoman uttered threats, demanding that I put down the washbasin shield. The guard Mrs Zimmer, who had unlocked the door, remained outside the door herself and ordered me to put down the washbasin. Mrs Kaiser joined her. I had to put down my shield, then Mrs Zimmer locked the door again, and I was left in the cell. A few minutes later she came back and led me out of the cell – at Mrs Kaiser's urging, I assume. Despite all that, and although Apfel at that time, as camp mates informed me, had already spent a year in solitary confinement and was known by everyone to be insane, after I had served the three weeks in detention Mrs Zimmer locked me in with Apfel again and I was, I believe, in [the same] cell with her for another ten to fourteen days. Even before I left Ravensbrück, Apfel was in solitary confinement. I was, as previously mentioned, in detention again before coming here, before that in solitary confinement again in the new jail building, and heard Apfel screaming at night, this time no longer like a human being but like an animal. I suspect, however, that there is a second madwoman there, because another voice was heard that had lost all its human qualities – I do not think that this also was Apfel's voice.

As witnesses *for everything* that took place in the previous detention or solitary confinement and everything I wrote about the new detention or solitary confinement, I cite: the Jehovah's Witnesses and Aryans Toni Hahn, Anny Schmauser, Luise Olschewsky, Käthe Riskal, further the communist and Aryan Suse Benesch, the Aryans Annemarie Vancotic, Pepi Koppelhuber, Anny Kraushaar (the latter three will only know about some parts; they will all know many interesting things in addition).

To find the truth, however, it would be necessary to bring the witnesses away from Ravensbrück in order to interrogate them because no one would have the courage there to tell the truth, because there are medieval punishments there, for example, as described, the straitjacket, further the flogging, twenty-five blows, enforced standing for long periods. The latter consists of standing outdoors for four hours a day (after working hours and roll call) in the evening, without supper. I don't believe that a single day goes by without women being forced to stand as punishment. I saw prisoners standing in the pouring rain. During the coldest part of the year, the standing punishment took place indoors, rather than out in the open, for a time. A Jewess named Rosenberg, who at that time was housed in B wing of the Jewish block, said that, despite her ulcerous breast, she was subjected to the standing punishment in this draughty room, in which the windows and doors were open in the freezing cold.

One gets this [punishment] for two or three weeks in a row and, for example, for the following. The beds have to be made exactly as ordered, with no creases, all the same, the bed sheets tucked into the iron at the bottom, in an extremely meticulous manner, the pillows squared, the blanket on top, a nice line, all the same. Anyone who fails three times to accomplish that in the time available can certainly get standing punishment. But for other things too. It also had a very severe effect on my nerves that, in the previous detention and solitary confinement in the wooden barracks, one often heard the screams of prisoners in detention who were attacked and beaten in the dark by the prisoners who brought the food or emptied the pails, over something they said or for some other reason. (The guard Mrs Zimmer knew this, because she was the only one who could open the cell doors.) For example, Alma Schulze, an Aryan, was beaten so badly on one occasion that she screamed constantly, even during the night: 'My eyes, my eyes,' and she feared she would lose her sight.[21]

Hedwig Peter, who is back in the camp again after trying to escape during a stay in the public hospital, served at the old detention and solitary confinement centre for a time. It would probably be quite interesting to hear what she has to say.[22]

The new detention and solitary confinement building is serviced by the prisoner Neumann, and the aforementioned prisoner Mrs Kaiser, who is no longer in the camp, also worked for a time in the new building.

When I was seen by the female doctor before I was transported here to Vienna, a nurse, I believe it was nurse Erika in the anteroom, who brought me out of detention, asked the guard Mrs Mandl (who, by the way, has always behaved fairly and correctly, through and through, towards me): 'How are things with you?' As an illustration, I mention this in addition: the guard Mrs Kolb[23] was doing the duties of the guard Mrs Zimmer on her Sunday afternoon off. She opened the door of my cell and said, 'It stinks in there,' and quickly shut the door. To that, I said: 'Excuse me, Mrs Guard, it can't stink, I wash my body three times a day.' Her reply: 'All Jews stink,' and I had the feeling that one more word from me and she would hit me. I fell silent again. The next time, when she opened the door again to bring food, she repeated, 'It stinks in there', and closed the door quickly.

A man in uniform came to my solitary cell to notify me that there was a cash remittance for me. Through the food hatch, he tossed the receipt stub to me, saying 'Jewish pig.' Another time, again a man in uniform, [I] don't know whether it was the same one, asked me to sign for a cash remittance with these words: 'Write straight, or else you'll get slapped.' Fellow inmates said this probably was Mr Schneider.[24]

It is also of interest that I made my journey from Vienna to Ravensbrück dressed only in a nightgown and over it a petticoat (combination) and sandals – nothing else, no dress, no trousers, no stockings, no coat, nothing. My last memory before my journey from Vienna to Ravensbrück is of events in the police station in Vienna's 9th District. There I remember the female guards Langer, Hahn, Borowitz, Petersam, Gaisa, Lock, and the senior guard Mrs Mayer. Then all I recall is suddenly waking up in the police van, dressed as described above, alone in a two-person cell. I clutched and pinched my

21 Alma Schulze, née Waldmann (1907–1942), murdered on 19 Feb. 1942 at the 'euthanasia' facility in Bernburg on the River Saale.

22 Hedwig Peter (1911–1942) perished at Ravensbrück in June 1942.

23 Katharina Kolb: no biographical information located.

24 Karl Alfred Schneider (b. 1910), SS-Hauptscharführer; in charge of managing the prisoners' money.

arm, I thought I was dreaming, but it was reality, not a dream. I travelled dressed in that way, passed through the railway stations, and was delivered to Ravensbrück dressed in that way, as is also made clear by the book there, where a record is made of what the prisoners hand in before they put on institutional clothing.

At the time my nerves were in a very bad state. In the police van I asked what was happening to me and was told that I was going to a psychiatric hospital, which I was glad to hear. But when we had gone past Salzburg and the journey continued, I realized that I was being deported to the Old Reich. This upset me so much, so that I could no longer stand unassisted at all, or walk either. In the police van on the Salzburg–Munich route – I learned from camp mates that it was in this area – one of the two transport officials (the one with the round face and blue eyes) approached us and barked at me: 'Get up!' I said that, because I had a nervous illness, I could not stand unassisted. After making this demand twice, he said he would hold me up and he did actually put his hand under mine; I stood up, he immediately pulled his hands away, I fell to the ground and could not get up again. He barked: 'Stand up!' I: 'But I can't.' He: 'Stand up!' and all the while he was hitting me hard on the back of my head, trying to make me stand up. But I could not. Then I began to vomit and I vomited and vomited, got all soaked, and it would not stop. Then he grabbed me, pulled me to my feet, threw me onto the bench and slammed the door (witness to the fact that I was beaten: the Jehovah's Witnesses and Aryans Stadtegger, or Stadtecker, and Mollenhofer, who were taken to Ravensbrück on the same transport). Later, I felt quite nauseous when I was asked everywhere what my name was, etc., I could not remember anything, not even my name, and when I was told my name, it sounded so strange to me and I denied that that was who I was. And that's how I ended up being sent to Ravensbrück. I was not able to write to any of my relatives, because I could not recall a single name, a single address, not even who my husband was. Then Leontine Kestenbaum came to the camp from Vienna. She knew me from the LG and also from the Vienna police, where she was a trusty:[25] she knew a great deal about me; she told me all sorts of things and slowly, slowly my memory returned. She also told me that I was taken from my bed, on which I had lain unconscious for two days, and, still unconscious, put into the transport, that she wanted to put stockings on me at least, which she was not allowed to do, however, and that I had even been beaten. But I cannot remember that. The guards were always very good to me, all of them.

By way of illustration, I will add the following to show, for example, how things are done in Ravensbrück. The window of my detention cell in the old detention centre was a normal one, opaque at the bottom, darkened at the top with a sheet of asbestos or some similar material with holes in it, through which the tiny amount of light came in and through which one, by standing on the stool, could look into the work area. That was prohibited. But one day a Jehovah's Witness called to me, saying I should quickly look out of the window. As a result of the cold ablutions prescribed by the first doctor and carried out for two months before my detention, my feet were much improved. I looked out and saw the following: a frail young woman – as I later heard, she is said to be named Langer, to have lupus, and to have already had a piece of her nose replaced with sewn-on flesh – was refusing to shovel sand. She was given a thorough beating but

25 *Fazi:* Austrian term for a prisoner who helped to distribute food, emptied the toilet pails, and performed other duties.

still did not pick up the shovel. Someone grabbed her – the prisoner Lohmann, a work-squad leader, is said to have done this – dragged her to a fountain, held her tight, and let the powerful stream of water pour down all over her. Completely drenched, she was buried in a pile of sand, only her head poking out, and then, over and over, someone covered her head and face with sand. She freed herself each time, and after this game had continued for quite some time, she was dug out and made to stand with her face to the wall. (The whole thing lasted so long that in the meantime I had got up from my stool and sat down again dozens of times.) The guard observed all of this, and sometimes I also saw a man from the military. Witnesses: Anny Schmauser, Annemarie Vainatic, possibly also Toni Hahn, Benesch. Also of interest is the fate of Resi; the previously listed witnesses can provide information.

Once, after a woman – Else Marta (or something similar) – had escaped, the entire camp had to stand for thirteen hours in succession, with no food, without a break (with the exception of those who were excused from standing in formation for roll call at the time), and the block from which the escapee came had to stand for another three hours. Then, the next day, only the block from which she came [had to stand] just a short time again, then the captured escapee was brought back, and the people who had been forced to stand so long on her account savaged her.

Gertrud Etzel, a diabetic missing five toes on one foot, one on the other, had to take part in roll calls. J'accuse.[26]

Regarding Case 104 c Vr 2782/39, I feel guilty, also in the machine matter.[27]

DOC. 69

On 16 April 1940 Martha Svoboda from Vienna writes in her diary about the effect the propaganda is having[1]

Handwritten diary of Martha Svoboda, Vienna, entry for 16 April 1940

How much longer will the war last? Last week, when I received the news of the audacious onslaught on Norway and Denmark,[2] I thought it must be over soon, the world must at last resist and finally do away with these villainous methods. But thus far nothing of the sort has happened. Denmark is calmly putting up with the 'protection'; only Norway is fighting for its freedom. How is it possible, I ask myself again and again, that millions of people silently impose the most terrible sufferings upon themselves, quietly allow themselves to be violated?

26 French: 'I accuse.' This was the heading of the writer Émile Zola's open letter in 1898 taking the side of Alfred Dreyfus, a Jewish French army captain who was wrongly convicted of espionage. Since that time, the phrase has stood for courageous opposition to government abuse of power.

27 File number of the court proceeding. It is unclear what is meant by 'machine matter'.

1 The original is privately owned; copy: IfZ-Archives, F 601. This document has been translated from German.

2 On 9 April 1940 German troops invaded Denmark and Norway. Denmark capitulated the same day and armed resistance in Norway ended on 10 June.

It can only be the lies that exert this enormous influence, the lies that are hammered into people's heads every hour of every day by the newspapers and radio, saying that everything that is happening is the best and finest, indeed, absolutely the only possible thing. And unfortunately there are more than enough stupid people who believe it all; they don't even notice what is really going on around them. The few Jews who are still here are tormented in the most outrageous way, the rest of the population are being squeezed to the utmost by taxes and collections. How much longer?

DOC. 70

Leitmeritzer Tagblatt, 19 April 1940: article about Marie Pick, who was convicted of an offence against the Law on Treachery[1]

The Abusive Jewess[2]

The special court in Leitmeritz has sentenced Marie Sara Pick,[3] *a Jewish citizen of the Protectorate, to seven months in prison for violating the Law against Treacherous Attacks.*[4]

She owns a residential building in Komotau, which she purchased for 143,000 korunas after the divorce from her husband in 1930 and which now, while under temporary administration, is to be put up for sale. The tax inspector Karl Zebisch was interested in purchasing the building, which was valued at 13,580 RM, and had already obtained the consent of the regional council. On 24 September, Zebisch negotiated with the owner of the building, who nonetheless demanded a larger sum because another party allegedly had already offered her around 20,000 RM. When Zebisch pointed out to her that her demand was outrageous and illegal, she was incensed and declared that the Jews, including her, were being cheated, and she indulged in abusive language, rebuking the Führer. She said she had relatives in England and America and would make sure that the whole world would know about her being double-crossed. At the same time, she predicted that both Zebisch and all those who cheated the Jews would be subject to punishment by God. At the main trial, the Jewess did attempt to deny having made the especially venomous utterances against the Führer and about the official regulations. However, the panel of judges issued a guilty verdict, as requested by the public prosecutor, on the grounds of the wholly credible witness statements and the fact that two married daughters of the accused have left Prague for an unknown destination and are probably overseas.

F. R.

1 'Die schimpfende Jüdin', SOAL pobočka Most, OLG, inv. č 517, Kt. 382, fol. 43. This article has been translated from German. The *Leitmeritzer Tagblatt* was founded in 1871; in 1935 it reached a circulation of 6,500 copies. The newspaper was the predecessor of the *Elbetalzeitung*, the official daily of the NSDAP in the Gau Sudetenland.

2 The article belongs to a series, each part of which was published under the title 'The Abusive Jew' (*Der schimpfende Jude*) or 'The Abusive Jewess'.

3 Possibly Marie Picková (1892–1942), deported on 9 Jan. 1942 from Theresienstadt to Riga, where she perished.

4 'OStA beim SG Leitmeritz, Anklageschrift gegen Marie Pick', 2 April 1940, SOAL pobočka Most, OLG, inv. č 517, Kt. 370, fols. 26–27.

DOC. 71

On 24 April 1940 Gestapo chief Heinrich Müller specifies which categories of Jews are permitted to emigrate in wartime and to which destinations[1]

Letter from the Reich Security Main Office (IV D 4–2 [Rz] 1275/40), p.p. signed Müller, to all State Police head offices in the territory of the Reich, for information to the SD (main) districts in the territory of the Reich, Berlin, dated 24 April 1940[2]

Re: guidelines for the emigration of Jews.
Case file: none.
To guarantee a uniform approach, below are my comments on the overall problem of Jewish emigration from the territory of the Reich.

1) *Jewish emigration from the territory of the Reich must continue to be pursued to an increased extent, also during the war.* The Chief of the Security Police and the SD has informed Minister President Field Marshal Göring, with whose explicit consent Jewish emigration continues to take place, *that Jews who are fit for military and labour deployment must not, if at all possible, be allowed to emigrate to other countries in Europe and under no circumstances to the hostile European countries.* On this point, I note that every case of emigration, unless it involves overseas destinations, must be examined according to the principles stated above and must be decided on one's own responsibility. Jews living in mixed marriages may on no account be pressed to emigrate.

2) A pronounced increase of *emigration to Palestine* is undesirable for foreign policy reasons.[3] I have established extremely strict conditions to deal with all the ensuing difficulties, and I have reserved for myself the right to take a decision on the authorization of transports after these conditions have been met. I ask that the respective branches on no account permit Jews to join such special group transports to Palestine[4] until my explicit consent for the implementation of such a transport has been given. In the process, care must be taken that, if at all possible, middle-aged male Jews are excluded.

The Reich Transport Group 'Providers of Ancillary Travel Services' will for the time being accept, with my consent, applications from travel agencies for the implementation of special group transports and will forward them, once all the required documents are in place, to Section IV D 4 of the Reich Security Main Office[5] for a decision. The actions of licensed travel agencies that deal with emigration on the part of individual Jews must not be obstructed.

1 RGVA, 500k-1-324; copy: USHMM, RG-11.001M04, reel 72. Reproduction of a version that was reworked to produce a decree of the State Police head office in Düsseldorf, published in Hans Mommsen and Susanne Willems (eds.), *Herrschaftsalltag im Dritten Reich: Studien und Texte* (Düsseldorf: Schwann, 1988), pp. 460–462. This letter has been translated from German.

2 The original contains handwritten notes and underlining, the official stamp of the Gestapo and next to it 'Certified: Signature illegible', and, at the bottom, typewritten: 'State Police II B 4-2788/40. 1. Acknowledged; 2. II B 4: For removal of the second copy to the reference files for II B 4; 3. To be filed, p.p.', signature illegible.

3 The Reich Security Main Office (RSHA) did not wish to provoke the Arab population of the British Mandate for Palestine against Germany.

4 See Doc. 120.

5 Section IV D 4 (emigration and evacuation) under Adolf Eichmann was responsible for all issues related to the emigration and deportation of the Jewish population.

3) For *Jews who are or once were Polish nationals* and are now confined in concentration camps, emigration is out of the question at present. Jewish women and children, male Jews over the age of 60, cripples, etc. who formerly held Polish nationality can be permitted to emigrate.

4) I have noted that rumours are repeatedly surfacing about a state-sanctioned *deportation of Jews from the territory of the Reich into the General Government. On this point I note that, for the time being, deportations of Jews, regardless of nationality,* from the territory of the Reich into the General Government are not to occur. In addition, all voluntary emigration of Jews to the General Government is prohibited. I am to be informed immediately, by express telex, about every attempt that becomes known to deport Jews on one's own authority to the General Government, irrespective of their nationality or statelessness.

5) In order to gain an overview of the status of the efforts being made by the Jews in the individual districts to emigrate and of the extent to which they are able to emigrate, I ask that each appropriate district or local office of the 'Reich Association'[6] be instructed to perform a thorough review of the status of the emigration efforts undertaken by every single Jew present in the districts. Particular emphasis must be placed on extending the possibilities that arise as a result of requests for families or relatives [to join emigrants overseas], and through the procurement of monies to fund passage by ship or provide evidence of funds. Please inform me of the result by 15 May 1940.

6) I ask that I be informed by the same date of what has been undertaken thus far on individuals' own initiative within the local area of responsibility in order to facilitate and increase Jewish emigration.

Addendum for the State Police head office in Munich: to telex no. 10 113, dated 9 April 1940.

Addendum for the State Police head office in Frankfurt am Main: to local letter II B 2 1936/40, dated 22 April 1940

Addendum for the State Police head office in Hamburg: to local letter II B 2 641/40, dated 18 March 1940, and telex no. 6616, dated 28 March 1940

Addendum for the State Police head office in Aachen: to local telex no. 1665, dated 27 March 1940[7]

6 Reich Association of Jews in Germany.
7 These are not included in the file.

DOC. 72

On 26 April 1940 Aron Menczer forwards a report to Josef Löwenherz concerning the proposed reopening of retraining sites in Vienna[1]

Letter from the Youth Aliyah advisory centre, 5 Marc-Aurel-Straße, Vienna I, signed Aron Menczer (AM/Qu.),[2] to the office director Dr Josef Löwenherz, 42 Nussdorferstraße, Vienna, dated 26 April 1940

We venture to present to you the enclosed report concerning the reopening of the Hachsharot.[3]

With Zion's greetings[4]

Vienna, 25 April 1940
Report on the reopening of the Hachsharah (agricultural redeployment programme) by the Youth Aliyah advisory centre in Vienna

The plan for reopening the Hachsharah for young people that is run by the JUAL (Youth Aliyah advisory centre in Vienna)[5] is outlined briefly below. –

The report is divided into the following sections:

1) Reasons for the necessity of the Hachsharah
2) Experiences of the Hachsharah
3) Technical execution
4) Financial structure

Re 1) The necessity of the Hachsharah, particularly for the young people concerned, who range from 14 to 17 years of age, is probably so well known to all the offices interested in youth emigration that the reasons will only be listed according to key points.

a) For the young people who emigrate through the JUAL, completion of a Hachsharah programme for the purpose of agricultural training is absolutely essential, according to the regulations of the Jewish Agency. It must be noted, especially in view of the recent news regarding the issuance of a schedule, that the number of young people in Hachsharah training within Irgun towns[6] will play a decisive role in calculating the various ratios used to allocate the available JUAL certificates.

b) It is our task to train young Jews to become productive, free, independent, and healthy fellow workers, and the Hachsharah is greatly suited for this purpose. At the same time, it should be noted that we generally take these young people – for a few weeks at least –

1 CAHJP, A/W 2508; copy in Archiv der IKG Wien, MF U 52, fr. 466–470. This letter has been translated from German.

2 Aron Menczer (1917–1943), educator; head of the Zionist socialist youth movement 'Gordonia' in Vienna; head of Youth Aliyah in Vienna from Sept. 1939; deported on 25 Sept. 1942 to Theresienstadt, where he carried out youth welfare work and was a Hehalutz board member; deported on 5 Oct. 1943 to Auschwitz, where he was murdered.

3 Plural of Hachsharah. These agricultural retraining camps had been shut down shortly after the war began, when the British Mandate Authority prohibited direct emigration into Palestine from the German Reich: see Introduction, p. 50. The term Hachsharah is both a noun describing the training establishments and a verb referring to the retraining process.

4 Handwritten addition: 'Best wishes for your recovery and regards to your wife! Aron.'

5 The acronym JUAL stands for the German term Jugendalijah (Youth Aliyah)

out of a parental setting that, under present circumstances, can be viewed as of little benefit to a young person's development. Apart from this, the easing of the social burden on the family in question is also significant.

c) Also in cases where young people are at risk as a result of statelessness, labour conscription, etc. the Hachsharah offers the only chance to keep this risk at bay. Moreover, proof of full labour deployment is provided through our young people assisting with farm work and harvesting.

d) The running of agricultural redeployment camps has a very favourable effect on foreign countries, particularly on Zionists outside Germany.

e) As a result of the Hachsharah, the JUAL advisory centre, that is, the central sponsor of Vienna's Jewish youth, can also organically continue with its educational activities, which add practical and pedagogical aspects to the theoretical work of our school.

Re 2) In connection with the Hachsharah of Hehalutz, the past year has probably not brought about the great success that one justifiably anticipated. Concerning this point, the following fundamental points should be raised:

a) We do not identify with the style and management of all the other organizations that ran Hachsharah programmes previously.

b) We support the Israelite Religious Community controlling our Hachsharah sites financially and economically, as has been the case in our office and in the school and workshop for several months now, to our mutual satisfaction.[7]

c) The centralized grouping of our youngsters in two, at most three, camps also ensures efficient management in every respect.

d) Despite the fact that experiences with the Hachsharah programmes held last year were not always satisfactory, it can be unequivocally stated that in many hundreds of cases the agricultural retraining has had a productive effect on our youth.

Re 3) We suggest at present that we begin on a trial basis with one site, which should accommodate around 100 young people. We suggest a practical implementation as follows:

a) The young people should complete a temporary preparatory camp over a period of four weeks. They will work for half of each day in agriculture, horticulture, and housekeeping and will be deployed everywhere, in accordance with their strengths. – The working time is to be approximately four to five hours per day (this depends on the circumstances of the site and the season).

b) The second half of the day is to be filled with the study of the Hebrew language, Jewish history, and other subjects needed for future life in Eretz, and additionally with theoretical education in agricultural and technical subjects.

c) Camp life should foster a sense of community and Jewish nationhood.

d) On days off, as well as to some extent during the morning hours of working days, the greatest emphasis should be placed on physical education, all the more so because for

6 The military underground organization the Irgun Tzva'i Le'umi in Palestine had split off from the Haganah in 1931. This organization, a precursor of the Herut party, committed several acts of terrorism against the British and the Arabs, and from 1934 was involved in organizing illegal emigration to Palestine. 'Irgun towns' refers to towns where the Irgun had strong support.

7 The Israelite Religious Community (IKG) had officially taken over Youth Aliyah and its school operations on 1 Jan. 1940.

quite some time now the Viennese youngsters have had little opportunity to keep physically fit.
e) The camp (below, it is always the first camp that is under discussion) should be run, in both an administrative and an economic respect, by a professional who has many years of experience managing an agricultural property, and who will be named in this capacity to the authorities. In addition, the camp management will consist of the teachers and youth educators who stay in the camp at all times and look after the youngsters.
f) A trained female cook will be brought in to run the kitchen. It will also be her task to familiarize the young girls with household management, to train them to do kitchen work, and, in particular, to teach them the essentials of running a communal kitchen.
g) Further, a trained nurse from the IKG hospital of the Israelite Religious Community will be available to our youngsters. In cases of illness and injury, she will step in until medical help arrives.
h) The camp is authorized by the appropriate local group of the NSDAP, as the superior authority.
i) The property belongs to a man who is no longer in Vienna, and it is managed by an Aryan commissioner whose powers are laid out in an official contract.
j) Dealings with the rest of the population are scrupulously avoided. The camp provides a self-contained territory for its occupants, and one may only leave the premises with a pass from the camp administration.
k) The aforementioned retraining camp is situated in Moosbrunn, at no. 9 (the former Schumann factory), and it belongs to the district of Gramat-Neusiedel. Hehalutz had a campsite there last year. The fact that the number of camp occupants is being reduced from 260 in 1939 to around 100 this year will minimize some of the difficulties that arose the previous year.
l) The Central Office for Jewish Emigration has granted general approval for the setting up of Hachsharah sites. In the case of Moosbrunn, final confirmation must still be obtained, but statements made by Commissioner Brunner[8] indicate that this will happen.
m) No investments are needed. According to the IKG's warehouse manager, furnishings are still available from the holdings of the Hachsharot that have closed down (beds, tables, benches, and cupboards are also on hand). The question of procuring work clothing, footwear, etc. is a different one, which would have become pertinent even without the opening of the Hachsharah programme. This matter must be dealt with separately.
Re 4) The financial management of the first Hachsharah site will probably entail a number of difficulties, but these can be kept to a minimum by extreme thriftiness and efficient leadership.
a) We calculate for the first month, for food supplies and other expenses (such as minor expenditure, repairs, trips, and the like), around RM 45 per youngster; clearly, an exact amount can be given only after the first month has elapsed.

For 100 camp occupants	*c.* RM 4,500
b) The rent for the buildings, incl. light, water, etc. amounts to and must be paid monthly.	RM 300

8 Alois Brunner.

c) Personnel:

1 operations manager 1 instructor 1 cook 1 nurse 3 teachers	*c.* RM 600
In total	RM 5,400
But with an anticipated number of 100 [camp] residents, we will probably have enough with the sum of	*c. RM 5,000*

For Moosbrunn, however, it must also be noted that a one-off sum of RM 380 would have to be paid as annual rent for the use of the gardens and meadows.

We envisage raising of the RM 5,000 as follows:

1.) By payment from the individual haverim,[9] whereby we expect on average RM 3 per child per month, that is	RM	300
2.) Through a monthly Keren Kayemet[10] grant in the amount of	"	500
3.) Through a monthly Keren HaYesod[11] grant in the amount of	"	500
4.) By cutting back on the JUAL classes, closing the workshops, and the resulting absence of tram expenses, wages, etc. *c.*	"	1,500
In total *c.*	RM	2,800

If these sums are raised, the amount still required would decrease to around RM 2,200, although it must also be noted that the Community would have to cover costs to a certain extent if the children remain in Vienna, such as youth welfare, free meals, and the like. With an increased outlay of just RM 2,000 to 3,000, the Religious Community would thus help to create something that is of decisive, even vital, importance for the continued training and preparations of our youth.[12]

9 Plural of haver, Hebrew for 'friend'; in Zionist discourse also member, comrade.

10 Keren Kayemet LeIsrael (Hebrew: Jewish National Fund); the organization, founded in 1901 at the Fifth Zionist Congress in Basel, was responsible for buying land in Palestine.

11 Hebrew: Foundation Fund; the institution was founded in London in July 1920 to finance the projected immigration and settlement schemes in Palestine after the Balfour Declaration of 1917.

12 Such a camp was never set up. Instead, the Youth Aliyah children were integrated into retraining courses run by the Religious Community.

DOC. 73

On 29 April 1940 Moritz Weinberg from Cologne writes to Bruno Kisch in New York about his efforts to emigrate[1]

Letter from Moritz Weinberg (Dr W/Da.),[2] legal consultant,[3] 8 Hardefuststraße, Cologne, to Prof. Bruno Kisch,[4] 514 West 114 Str., Ap. 21, New York City, dated 29 April 1940

Dear Prof. Kisch,

The visit today from your mother-in-law,[5] from whom I have got your new address, gives me occasion to write a few lines to you once again. The reason for the aforementioned visit was the customary security order from the local foreign exchange office regarding your mother-in-law's assets, which unfortunately are no longer very substantial. I helped her deal with the applicable regulations, as she was not familiar with them. I am glad to hear that you and your wife are doing well. The circle of persons around us has become relatively small. Doubtless we too would have long since received authorization for an intermediate stay, pending further emigration to our ultimate destination, the USA, if the war had not almost completely eliminated this possibility. Consequently we are forced to wait for our waiting-list number, which is now just over 26,000, at the American consulate in Stuttgart. We have now been separated from our children for more than 15 months. While we hear good news regularly from our daughter in Holland,[6] very little information is sent by our son, who will soon be 14.

Emigration is made difficult, as you know, by the impossibility of paying in Reichsmarks for travel by ship and the embargo on transport. Nonetheless, we very much hope that our friends will make these expenditures possible for us in due course. A far more difficult problem, if we obtain the entry visa for the USA, is the choice of a vocation, as one naturally would not wish, with a family of four, to be utterly dependent on grants and welfare. Perhaps you are in a position to give me some pointers in this respect, for which I would be very grateful to you.

With best regards, also to your wife, and also on behalf of my wife, I remain,

Yours truly,

1 CAHJP, P 80/71. This letter has been translated from German.

2 Dr Moritz Weinberg (1888–1944), lawyer; practised law in Cologne from 1924; responsible for managing the confiscated assets of deported Jews, which delayed his own deportation; deported with his wife Hilde (1902–1944) and daughter Marie Luise to Theresienstadt on 18 June 1943, and from there in Oct. 1944 to Auschwitz, where he perished.

3 Under the Fifth Regulation on the Reich Citizenship Law (27 Sept. 1938), Jews were barred from the legal profession. A very limited number were allowed to represent Jewish clients exclusively as so-called legal consultants (*Rechtskonsulenten*): *Reichsgesetzblatt*, 1938, I, pp. 1403–1406.

4 Dr Bruno Zacharias Kisch (1890–1966), physician; professor of physiology at the Cologne Academy from 1924; dismissed in 1936; emigrated to the USA in 1938; professor of cardiology at Yeshiva University in New York, 1938–1961; co-founder and president of the American College of Cardiology; regularly visited the Federal Republic of Germany as a guest scientist from 1952.

5 Probably Karoline Cohn, née Neumann (1858–1942); deported from Cologne to Theresienstadt on 15 June 1942, and three months later to Treblinka, where she was murdered.

6 Marie Luise Weinberg (b. 1929); deported with her parents on 18 June 1943 to Theresienstadt and on 19 Oct. 1944 to Auschwitz, where she perished. On the repatriation of children from the occupied territories, see Doc. 111.

DOC. 74

On 30 April 1940 the Commissioner for the Supervision of Jewish Welfare Institutions in Frankfurt gives a report to the city's Mayor[1]

Report by the Commissioner for the Supervision of Jewish Welfare Institutions in Frankfurt am Main, signed Holland,[2] 29 Röderbergweg, Frankfurt am Main, dated 3 May 1940[3]

Re: verbal report to the Mayor[4] on 30 April 1940.

1. *Migration*

In the period from 1 April 1939 to 31 March 1940, around 8,500 Jews have departed from Frankfurt am Main.

Of that number, around 500 Jews [emigrated] in the first quarter of 1940. Around 11,500 Jews are still living in Frankfurt am Main at present.

In comparison with other large cities in the Old Reich, the number of Jews in Frankfurt am Main remains quite high in proportion to the German population, although the Jewish Community in Frankfurt has been very successful in its efforts to promote emigration.

At present there are limited opportunities for emigration, because, with the exception of the USA, almost all countries are reluctant to take in additional Jews. Immigration into the USA is made quite difficult by the demand of the US government that the sponsors deposit fairly substantial sums of money on behalf of the immigrants.

2. *Labour deployment*

(a) *Men*. As migration was only possible for persons who were healthy and fit for work, the number of Jews who are fit for labour has greatly decreased. Those remaining are predominantly elderly or frail (for example, men injured in the World War). As of 29 April 1940, the following numbers have been recorded by the Jewish Public Welfare Office, Dept of Labour Deployment, 29 Röderbergweg, Frankfurt am Main:

Men between 17 and 50	1,121	
Of these, working:	724	
At present unfit for work		397

1 ISG Frankfurt, Magistratsakten 8718. Published in Kommission zur Erforschung der Geschichte der Frankfurter Juden, *Dokumente zur Geschichte der Frankfurter Juden 1933–1945* (Frankfurt am Main: Kramer, 1963), pp. 456–459. This report has been translated from German.

2 Ernst Holland (b. 1898), retailer; joined the NSDAP in 1930 and the SS in 1931; ancillary employee of the Frankfurt municipal administration from 1933; SS-Untersturmführer, 1936; administrative inspector, 1939; Gestapo commissioner for the supervision of Jewish public welfare from 1940; drafted into an SS medical unit, Oct. 1943; missing in action; classified in absentia as a 'major offender' by a denazification tribunal.

3 The original contains handwritten notes.

4 Dr Friedrich Krebs (1894–1961), lawyer; worked as a judge in Frankfurt am Main and other cities from 1923; regional court judge in Frankfurt, 1928–1933; joined the NSDAP in 1929; member of the Prussian Landtag, 1932; NSDAP Kreisleiter from 1933; mayor of Frankfurt, 1933–1945; joined the SA in 1937; interned by the US, 1945–1948; classified as a 'lesser offender' by a denazification tribunal in 1947; elected to Frankfurt City Council for the national-conservative German Party (DP) in 1952; stepped down after protests; worked as a lawyer after 1953.

Men between 51 and 60	840	
Of these, working:	222	
At present unfit for work		618
[In total] now unfit for work		1,015

The return to fit-for-work status of the aforementioned persons who are currently unfit for work is being steadily monitored, as is the opportunity to find jobs for persons with limited fitness for work.

Those mentioned above who are working are employed as follows:

(a) at the Jewish Community and its welfare facilities	around 400
(b) placed in productive jobs in March/April 1940 (brickyard, excavation, etc.)	331
(c) other jobs (carrying coal etc.)	215
In total:	946

At present, the Jewish Welfare Office is no longer supporting any persons fit for labour deployment.

Negotiations are currently pending with the employment office in Frankfurt am Main with a view to placing persons not in receipt of support who are fit for work.[5]

(b) *Women.* Placing women in productive labour proved quite difficult, as a great many of them are demonstrably busy looking after older family members who are in need of care. Of 142 registered women, only 39 could be made available to the forestry department of the municipal building office to do planting work in the municipal forest.

3. *Savings due to labour deployment*

Ongoing support by Jewish Welfare Office for March 1940	RM 65,242.45
Ongoing support by Jewish Welfare Office for April 1940	" 50,322.40
	RM 14,920.05

4. *Soup kitchen*

The soup kitchen provides 500 meals daily for distribution to benefit recipients. Until now, in addition to a monthly contribution to the soup kitchen in the amount of RM 0.30 for each family, the amount of RM 0.10 per meal was collected. For January 1940, a subsidy for the soup kitchen from the Jewish Public Welfare Office was necessary, amounting to RM 2,600. As a result, Jewish welfare recipients were better off, by RM 5.20 a month, than German welfare recipients. Beginning on 11 March 1940, the price was set at RM 0.30 per meal, so that for March 1940 a subsidy of only RM 1,053.69 was required. Since 1 April 1940 a subsidy from the resources of the Jewish Public Welfare Office has no longer been necessary.

5. *Hospital of the Israelite Community, Frankfurt am Main, 36 Gagernstr.*

During an inspection of the stocks of rice and pulses for Jewish winter relief that are stored on the premises of the Hospital of the Israelite Community, the Food Office con-

5 Further negotiations turned out to be unnecessary as Jews throughout the Reich who were not in receipt of public funds were also called up for forced labour from spring 1940.

fiscated the following for the benefit of the Main Association of the German Grains and Animal Feed Industry:

Rice:	34 sacks	3,124.25 kg,
Lentils:	8 sacks	566.00 kg,
Beans:	9 sacks	249.05 kg.

The decision of the Main Association of the German Grains and Animal Feed Industry is still pending.[6]

The inspection of the food stores of the Hospital of the Israelite Community and the food management led to complaints from the Food Office. Objections were made to:
(a) the fact that in some cases employees and workers at the Hospital of the Israelite Community received food individually by using food ration cards, while others were included in the allocation of foodstuffs purchased using coupons;
(b) the fact that around twenty so-called pensioners lived in the hospital, although they were not in need of hospital care;
(c) the fact that two kitchens were operated that did not properly monitor food requirements.
The deficiencies were remedied, so that now, with respect to food supply, there should no longer be a risk of concealing the facts in order to improve the situation of hospital staff and patients.

Re (a) The provisioning of the personnel and the patients now takes place in a uniform way, according to ration coupons that have been applied for.

Re (b) The so-called pensioners moved out on 1 April 1940.

Re (c) The ritual kitchen at the Hospital of the Israelite Community ceased operation on 7 April 1940. Patients who want kosher food are being admitted to the Rothschild Hospital on Röderbergweg. Only ritually prepared food is provided in this hospital.

The closing of this kitchen is financially advantageous as well, as it employed thirteen persons to feed an average of around ten patients.

Because the overall size of the workforce at the Hospital of the Israelite Community was too large relative to the number of patients, forty-two persons in total were placed in other jobs.

6. *My position on the State Police*
In a discussion with Regierungsrat Weiß-Bolland[7] before I took up the position of commissioner for the supervision of the Jewish welfare institutions in Frankfurt am Main, I was given oral instructions, in consultation with the welfare administration, to the effect

6 The decision by the Main Association of the German Grains and Animal Feed Industry could not be found.

7 Correctly: Anton Weiß-Bollandt (1909–1973?), lawyer; joined the NSDAP and the SS in 1930; worked at the Gestapo Central Office (Gestapa) from 1936; with the Vienna Gestapo from March to August 1938; deputy head of the Gestapo from Sept. 1938; on secondment to Schneidemühl as head of the Gestapo in Frankfurt from August to Dec. 1939; SS-Sturmbannführer, 1939; head of the Frankfurt Gestapo from April 1940 and of the Osnabrück Gestapo from 1941; worked for the commander of the Security Police in Simferopol, 1942; interned, 1945–1948; classified as a 'follower' during denazification proceedings.

that I, as a civil servant in the Welfare Office of Frankfurt am Main, must oversee the efficient use of the funds made available to the Jewish welfare institutions by the Reich Association of Jews in Germany, Berlin, and must ensure in particular that the budget of the Jewish welfare institutions in Frankfurt am Main is not exceeded. In October 1939 the accounting office of the Jewish welfare institutions prepared a budget proposal for the first six months of 1940, a copy of which I am enclosing, and submitted it for approval to the Reich Association of Jews in Germany, Berlin.[8] Approval is still pending at this time, so it was not possible for me to examine it in accordance with the instructions issued to me. I worked and adopted my measures from the perspective of whether they were directly or indirectly in the interest of the City of Frankfurt am Main, and I will continue to work along these same lines.

A set of instructions, which the administration of the Welfare Office and the Gestapo intended to prepare jointly, has not reached me thus far, as the Gestapo has not completed a corresponding draft.[9]

DOC. 75

On 3 May 1940 the Gau economic advisor in Aussig urges the Reich Minister of Finance to accelerate the Aryanization of real estate in the Sudetenland[1]

Letter from the NSDAP Gau economic advisor, Gauleitung Sudetenland, signed Engineer Wolfgang Richter,[2] 59 Große Wallstraße, Aussig, to the Reich Minister of Finance (received on 7 May 1940),[3] dated 3 May 1940[4]

Subject: utilization of the confiscated Jewish property in the Sudetenland.

According to existing regulations, the de-Jewification of enterprises and plots of land is the responsibility of the Reichsstatthalter and the three Regierungspräsidenten in the Sudetengau. Exempt from this arrangement are the properties that were seized by the Gestapo and entrusted to the regional tax directors in Carlsbad and Troppau.

Although Jewish property was thereby signed over to the regional tax directors on a large scale, the process of utilizing the property and transferring it into German hands is proceeding very slowly. This appears to be attributable on the one hand to the absence of certain standard operating procedures. On the other hand, it can be stated that the regional tax directors are extraordinarily reluctant when it comes to the utilization and de-Jewification of the property entrusted to them. The de-Jewification of real estate in

8 ISG Frankfurt, Magistratsakten 8718.

9 The set of instructions mentioned, which amounted to subordinating Holland to the Gestapo rather than the Welfare Office, was issued on 31 May 1940.

1 BArch, R 2/25023, fol. 62r–v. This letter has been translated from German.

2 Wolfgang Richter (1901–1958), engineering graduate; Sudeten German Party (SdP) delegate in Prague, 1935–1938; joined the SA and the NSDAP in 1938; member of the Reichstag, 1938–1943; war economy leader, 1942–1945; Reich plenipotentiary for total war in the Sudetenland, 1944–1945; in hiding until 1947, then manager of the hosiery firm Opal Strumpfwerke GmbH in Hamburg.

3 Count Johann Ludwig Schwerin von Krosigk.

4 The original contains handwritten notes and underlining, as well as the official stamp of the NSDAP Gauleitung in Sudetenland.

particular is proceeding extremely slowly, which seems to be due to the desire to create apartments for Reich civil servants in the confiscated Jewish buildings. However understandable this endeavour is in view of the extraordinary housing shortage, for economic and political reasons one cannot approve of commercial buildings in particular losing their intended economic purpose as a result. The seizure of Jewish property is surely not intended as a means of transferring ownership of land and buildings to the Reich. Rather the purpose is doubtless to channel the proceeds of utilizing the confiscated assets to the tax office.

Because complaints are coming to me from Carlsbad in particular, referring to the aforementioned state of affairs, I request that you ask the regional tax directors in Carlsbad and Troppau to carry out the sale of the confiscated Jewish real estate as quickly as possible in line with economic necessities in the Gau Sudetenland. The justified wish to acquire or retain apartments for Reich civil servants can surely be taken into account in the process through issuing appropriate instructions.

Heil Hitler!

DOC. 76

On 3 May 1940 SS-Sturmbannführer Heinrich Heckmüller refuses to revoke orders issued by him with respect to Jewish labourers in Eisenerz[1]

Letter (marked 'registered!') from SS-Sturmbannführer Heckmüller (He/G),[2] Eisenerz, to the Gestapo, for the attention of Oberregierungsrat Dr Noske,[3] 4 Parkring, Graz, dated 3 May 1940[4]

Re: employment of Jewish labourers

The arrival of the Jewish labourers in Eisenerz was communicated to all possible offices several days in advance. It was variously requested that directives necessary for the security of Eisenerz be issued as quickly as possible. It was also requested that the arrangements be made so as to prevent any insult to German Volksgenossen by the Jewish labourers. For every decent German must regard it as an insult whenever Jews are in the same waiting room at the doctor's surgery, in the same ward in hospital, or in the same

1 Steiermärkisches LA Graz, L., Reg.IA.Pol. 386 Ju 1/1940, fols. 4–6. This letter has been translated from German.

2 Heinrich Heckmüller (1906–1959?), metalworker; joined the SA and NSDAP in 1929 and the SS in 1930; from 1932, full-time SS officer, SS-Sturmbannführer, 1939; intelligence officer and head of plant security for Alpine Ore Mines in Eisenerz from 1939; with the Waffen SS, 1941–1944.

3 Correctly: Gustav Adolf Noßke (b. 1902), lawyer; joined the SA and the NSDAP in 1933; with the Gestapo in Aachen from 1935; joined the SS in 1936; head of the Gestapo in Frankfurt an der Oder from Sept. 1936; after 1939 in Graz, and later in Aachen and Düsseldorf, in 1941–1942 head of Einsatzkommando 12 of Einsatzgruppe D; SS-Obersturmbannführer, 1942; head of Section IV D 5 (Occupied Eastern Territories), 1942, and head of Group IV D (Occupied Territories) at the Reich Security Main Office (RSHA), 1943; sentenced to life imprisonment at the Nuremberg Military Tribunals in 1948; sentence later reduced to ten years; released in 1951.

4 Carbon copies went to the Reichsführer SS, SS-Gruppenführer Rodenbücher, the Landrat in Leoben, and the SD – Security Main Office in Berlin, the SD in Graz, and Captain Kissling.

restaurant as he. Similarly, one cannot expect German Volksgenossen to listen to the same bandstand concert and use the same esplanade here in Eisenerz as the Jews, especially as the latter do not appear singly but rather en masse. We have only one street in Eisenerz, and it is unavoidable that German Volksgenossen will encounter Jews here and brawls will result.

Because we currently employ 340 Jews and get new transports daily (in total, 750 Jews), and no directives have been issued thus far, despite our repeated requests to various offices, I felt compelled to contact your office directly. On the basis of this, I received authorization by telephone to issue provisional regulations for the Jews. I also arranged for this to be done immediately – see the carbon copy – and forwarded a carbon copy of the provisions to the individual offices concerned.[5]

On 3 May 1940 I was informed by telephone that these regulations must be revoked. I therefore feel compelled to inform you that I categorically reject any responsibility for operational security and workplace order in Eisenerz. I must assign this responsibility to those who always know how to cause trouble. If the Landrat[6] had contacted me on the basis of the carbon copy, which he received immediately after the decree, it would certainly have been possible to achieve a better outcome. In any event, I must declare the approach now described to be completely wrong, as it will only result in causing great confusion, which can have catastrophic effects for us. For if the Jews realize from the outset that we are at odds over their treatment and are not taking strict measures immediately, they will surely be acting up with us before long. It will most certainly be difficult to take them strictly in hand again after the event.

When the directive I had issued was withdrawn, I was also informed that I should have the camps guarded by the plant's security guards. I must tell you, however, that this is impossible, as this unit is not meant to guard other firms, because (1) it is not large enough for such a task; (2) it does not have financial responsibility; and (3) guarding the camp in the absence of any kind of directives would also be impossible, unless a machine gun is placed in every corner. From a purely military standpoint, one can never guard a camp without issuing the requisite camp rules. My directives were not intended for Eisenerz, but solely as camp directives. With this camp directive, I can easily conduct a loose supervision of the camps with the Prebichl patrol as a plant guard force and with the Prebichl patrol as a police force.[7] Guarding a camp without camp rules, however, is impossible. It is equally impossible to guard a camp in which Germans are also present unless the persons to be guarded are outwardly marked.

5 On 29 April 1940 Heckmüller had ordered that the Jewish workers be housed and fed separately, identified with a 'five-pointed star on the back' or a 'yellow armband with a black star', and forbidden to leave their camp area. In an almost identical police order issued one day later, the mayor of Eisenerz, Rudolf Walcher, also forbade Jews to enter any pub or shop or to engage in 'any dealings whatsoever with non-Jews': Reg.IA.Pol. 386 Ju 1/1940, fols. 7 and 11.

6 Dr Wilhelm (Willi) Kadletz (1895–1966), painter and lawyer; worked first for the Leoben agricultural district authority and district commission; joined the NSDAP in 1938; Landrat, 1938–1945, and police chief of Leoben from 1941; joined the SS in 1942; worked as a local history researcher after the war.

7 Also Präbichl: a mountain pass near Eisenerz, where the Jewish workers were deployed and housed.

To this day I have always ensured, in the individual operations too, that peace and order prevail in Eisenerz, no matter whether Alpine's own firms or firms that worked for Alpine were concerned.[8] But as cooperation between the separate official agencies seems impossible because everything that is proposed by Alpine is categorically rejected, I am forced in future to concern myself solely with the mining operation. But for the future as well, I must assign the responsibility to the Landrat in Leoben. The main responsibility for operational security, however, also hereby devolves down to him, as the vast majority of our camps and workers are in Eisenerz and are in close contact with Poles and Jews.

It would be advisable to implement a definitive arrangement for Eisenerz at long last and not to keep dodging this issue. Because either one is in charge of overall operational security and responsible for it, and then, of course, one also requires corresponding authority, or else a civil servant is deployed here who then assumes responsibility. But I have been working here in Eisenerz for one year (and can indeed claim with a clear conscience that something has been accomplished during this year) without having been granted even the slightest authority. Thus far all my work has met with approval, and this is the first time I have had to withdraw a regulation. For the future, I am forced to decline responsibility for such work without the necessary authority, because I have no desire to open myself up to ridicule. The responsibility then falls, as previously stated, upon those who are responsible for it.

Heil Hitler![9]

8 From 1923 the Austrian Alpine Mining Company (Österreichisch-Alpine Montangesellschaft) controlled practically the entire crude-iron production of Austria. The German steelworks Vereinigte Stahlwerke AG acquired a majority of the shares in 1926, and in 1938 the Alpine Mining Company was absorbed by the Hermann Göring Works. The concern, which was nationalized in 1946, became a component of VOEST-Alpine AG in 1973.

9 In his reply on 4 May 1940 Noßke referred to the remit of the Reichsstatthalter and criticized Heckmüller for acting without due authorization. The office of the Reichsstatthalter took the view that the Jewish labourers did indeed have to be segregated, but otherwise were not be treated any worse than the regular workforce. After intervention by the RSHA, however, the restrictions were regarded as lawful from June 1940: Reg.IA.Pol. 386 Ju 1/1940, fols. 2–3 and 41–51.

DOC. 77
On 3 May 1940 Göring's representative for the Aryanization of the Petschek group submits his final report[1]

Report (confidential) from the Ministerial Director for Special Assignment (W. XII/1128), signed Wohlthat, to Minister President Field Marshal Göring, Berlin, dated 3 May 1940[2]

Submitted to Minister President Field Marshal Göring for his attention.

Final report on the de-Jewification of the Ignaz Petschek group[3]

I. *Assignment*

In the spring of 1938 Field Marshal Göring assigned me the task of de-Jewifying the property of the Jewish families of Julius and Ignaz Petschek that is situated in Ger-

1 PA AA, R 99 365. This report has been translated from German.

2 The original contains handwritten notes.

3 The Petschek group was the largest single enterprise to be targeted by Aryanization: see also PMJ 2/91.

4 Established in July 1937 as the Hermann Göring Reich Works AG for Ore Mining and Iron- and Steelworks, the state-owned group added dozens of subsidiaries in the course of Germany's expansion; in July 1939 a reorganization created the Hermann Göring Reich Works Holding AG and, with the relocation to Salzgitter in 1941, the Reich Works were restructured and split into three sections: mining, arms production, and shipping. In August 1944 the concern, which was the largest and financially strongest in the Reich, comprised 260 enterprises. It was dismantled by the Allies after the war and its holdings were transferred to Salzgitter AG in 1953.

5 PA AA, R 99 365.

many.[6] If transfer problems make it impossible to acquire the properties in Germany by means of purchase, then the controlling stake over the two groups, which is indispensable in Germany's interest, should be gained in another way.

II. *Separate actions against the Julius and Ignaz Petschek groups*
The families of Julius and Ignaz Petschek had been quarrelling for a generation. Nonetheless, it seemed advisable to first de-Jewify the smaller properties of *Julius Petschek* to avoid creating a common front of Jewish interests abroad. This problem was solved by July 1938, in closest cooperation with Mr Flick.[7] In the process, paying off an American creditors' group with a certain sum in foreign currency was unavoidable. By contrast, the valuable lignite holdings of the Julius Petschek group were transferred into German ownership. The task of de-Jewifying the Ignaz Petschek group was addressed as soon as there was evidence that de-Jewification had been successful in the case of Julius Petschek.

III. *Situation in the Ignaz Petschek group*
The companies designated as the *Ignaz Petschek group* were represented as follows in the lignite briquette manufacturing sector:

in the Ostelbisches Braunkohlensyndikat[8]	with	57	per cent
in the Mitteldeutsches Braunkohlensyndikat[9]	"	20	per cent
in the Rheinisches Braunkohlensyndikat[10]	"	1.39	per cent

6 Ignaz Petschek (1857–1934), banker and industrialist; founder of the Petschek group; principal shareholder of Phönix AG, along with his brother Julius Petschek, from 1926; of the mine Ilse Bergbau AG, and the Eintracht lignite plant and briquette factory, from 1927; of the Vereinsglück AG lignite company, Leonhard AG, the mining company Ernst Herzog AG, and the Kraft mine, from 1931; and of the mining companies Anhaltische Kohlenwerke AG and Niederlausitzer Kohlenwerke AG, from 1932.

7 Friedrich Flick (1883–1972), entrepreneur; from 1913, business director of the ironworks company Eisenindustrie zu Menden und Schwerte AG; board member and majority stockholder of the Charlottenhütte AG steel company, 1915; founder of the steelworks Mitteldeutsche Stahlwerke AG, 1926; later, owner of one of the most important mining concerns in the German Reich; joined the NSDAP in 1937; in 1947 sentenced at the Nuremberg Military Tribunals to seven years in prison and to expropriation; released from prison, 1950; subsequently rebuilt the Flick corporation and amassed a second fortune.

8 The Ostelbisches Braunkohlensyndikat (East Elbe Lignite Syndicate) was founded in 1928 and included, at least for a time, all the Lower Lusatian coal companies. The syndicate, which had as many as seventeen shareholders and was headquartered in Berlin, focused on the commercial exploitation of the coal of Lower Lusatia. It was liquidated in 1946 by order of the Soviet military administration.

9 The Mitteldeutsches Braunkohlensyndikat (Central German Lignite Syndicate) originated in 1909 from the sales association of the Thüringische Braunkohlenwerke (Thuringian Lignite Works) and the sales association of the Sächsische Braunkohlenwerke (Saxony Lignite Works). It included nine coalfields and one of its tasks was to regulate the transport of rough coal, briquettes, and coke. It was liquidated in 1946 by order of the Soviet military administration.

10 The Rheinisches Braunkohlensyndikat (Rhineland Lignite Syndicate) existed from 1915 to 1945 and had twenty-nine members in three groups (Rhineland, Westerwald, Hesse). In 1950 it was re-established as Rheinische Braunkohlenbrikett-Verkauf GmbH.

In addition, there were the *Oehringen* and *Preußengrube*[11] hard-coal mines in Upper Silesia, and a major coal trading company, *Deutsche Kohlengesellschaft mbH*,[12] with numerous participating interests. The pre-eminent position of the concern in the East German lignite region was tantamount to a formal monopoly on distribution. The corporation had vast intermediary-trade profits. The mid-tier coal business in the East Elbe lignite mining district was to a great extent dependent on the Petschek firms.

The members of the *family of Ignaz Petschek* (consisting of the four sons of Ignaz Petschek, who died in 1934: Karl, Franz, Wilhelm, and Dr Ernst Petschek)[13] held *Czechoslovakian citizenship*. Although assets in the German Reich were estimated in business circles at more than *200 million* Reichsmarks, within the borders of the German Reich only a small fraction could be conclusively identified as Jewish Petschek assets. In the main, in the case of the coal companies under Petschek influence, foreign banks and other foreign companies with unknown shareholders emerged as beneficiaries. The international business relationships were spread among *Germany, Czechoslovakia, Holland, Switzerland, Luxembourg, England*, and *Poland*. The demonstrable Petschek shareholdings in German companies, too, had been largely taken abroad.

Given this state of affairs, the process of de-Jewification encountered almost insurmountable problems. All attempts after 1937 to wage the struggle against the Petscheks by appointing commissioners were directed against individual shortcomings within the group, and these attempts failed because of the highly diversified structure of the trading and industrial interests in Germany and because central positions of power in holding companies were anchored abroad.

IV. *Execution of the assignment in cooperation with the Reich Ministry of Finance, the Reich Ministry of Economics, and other ministries*

Tax auditors worked for years on ascertaining the tax situation of the Petschek family. The audits repeatedly turned up causes for suspicion, which focused on the question of whether the seat of a unified management of the diverse business interests was in Berlin, or whether there was truth to the Petscheks' claim that individual enterprises were mainly managed from abroad. Only in the 1937–1938 audit, which was in progress when the de-Jewification assignment was issued, was there success in obtaining adequate documentary evidence of tax offences committed by the Petscheks. The *demands for back taxes* now amounted to around *80 million Reichsmarks*. In order to clarify all the factual and legal circumstances that were important for de-Jewification,

11 Oehringen Bergbau AG (Oehringen Mining AG) was founded in Nov. 1921. The following month it purchased from Hohenlohe-Werke AG the Sosnitza shaft mine and brick factory, the Oehringen shaft mine, and the Järischau clay pits. Until 1938 the company belonged to the Petschek group, and it was dissolved at the end of 1939. Preußengrube AG emerged in 1922 from the assets of mining and iron- and steel-making enterprise Kattowitzer AG für Bergbau und Hüttenbetrieb.

12 The Deutsche Kohlenhandelsgesellschaft mbH managed the assets of the Petschek group in Upper Silesia.

13 Karl, also Charles, Petschek (b. 1890) and Wilhelm, also William, Petschek (1896–1980) emigrated to the USA in 1938/1939. Dr Ernst Friedrich Petschek (1887–1956), chemist; board member of Deutsche Industrie AG; chairman of the supervisory board of Leonhard AG; emigrated to the USA in 1938 after the Aryanization of the Petschek group of companies.

I worked in closest cooperation with the *Reich Ministry of Finance* and the tax authorities from the outset.

A succession of valuable supporting documents fell into the hands of the tax authorities as a result of the *occupation of the Sudetenland in October 1938, Czechoslovakia in March 1939, and Poland in September 1939*. The Petscheks had always speciously claimed that the hub of their activities was situated in *Aussig*. Evidence to the contrary was produced there and then after the occupation of Aussig. In the Protectorate, *many crates of books and pieces of evidence*, which had been taken from the Sudetenland to Czecho-Slovakia by the Petscheks, were *confiscated shortly before dispatch to Switzerland*. In Poland, evidence was found that the Petscheks had carried out prohibited foreign exchange transactions involving the misuse of Polish company names. The additional foreign currency misconduct by the Petscheks, already established during the initial phase of the investigations (obtaining, under false pretences, foreign currency permits to move shares abroad), made it necessary to involve the Reich Ministry of Economics and the Foreign Exchange Office in Berlin. In addition, I was continuously involved in the most important negotiations: with the *Reich Ministry of Economics* (regarding questions of de-Jewification and the coal industry), the *Reich Ministry of Justice* (regarding the intricate legal questions), the *Reich Foreign Office* (regarding political questions that spread into the area of foreign relations), the *Reich Ministry of Public Enlightenment and Propaganda* (regarding the question whether the business affairs of the Petscheks should be dealt with in the German press during the de-Jewification process), and *the Gestapo* (regarding the large number of questions concerning individuals that arose due to numerous prominent Aryans being used to serve the business interests of the Petscheks).

V. *Impossibility of reaching a settlement via negotiations with the Petschek brothers*

By concealing their holdings, using convoluted foreign holding-company structures, and allegedly divesting key interests abroad, the Petscheks took precautions against having to appear in person as negotiating parties in a de-Jewification procedure. They *left Germany* in *September 1938*, shortly before the Czech crisis. Alleged owners and purchasers of the Petscheks' properties appeared in their place, including *Englishmen* (Sir Oliver Duncan, Sir Jonah Walker Smith[14]), *Swiss persons* (D. Baur-Steffen – as head of the Swiss company Helimont – and Dr Hänggi[15]), *various foreign banks*, and *other foreign firms*. The attempt made by the Reich Ministry of Finance to bring the Petscheks to the negotiating table in person in place of their lawyers fell through, although the prospect of safe conduct had been presented to them. Until the spring of 1939, before the collapse of the Czech lands, the Petscheks still felt so secure that they believed they could exercise control of their properties with the help of the German representatives of their foreign holding companies, through their middlemen's well-networked connections with the highest levels of the German administration, and they envisaged a failure of the new de-Jewification operation as well. Under these circumstances, there was no alternative but to push through a settlement without the Petscheks.

14 Sir Jonah Walker Smith (1874–1964), Conservative politician in the British Parliament.

15 Dr Paul Hänggi, Basel, held shares with a face value of 2.4 million Reichsmarks in the Hubertus lignite holdings in the Rhineland, which belonged to the Petschek group.

VI. *Verification of Jewish property in the firms of the Petschek group*
The tax audit revealed that the Petscheks controlled German firms in the lignite and hard-coal mining industry and in the coal trade with a share capital of 136 million Reichsmarks. Of that amount, shares worth 36.7 million Reichsmarks were held domestically in a complex structure of lignite mines and trading companies, while shares worth 47.3 million Reichsmarks were held abroad, and the remainder, shares worth 52 million Reichsmarks, belonged to domestic, probably mostly Aryan, shareholders. Significant portions of the shares abroad were in two holding companies, Helimont AG in Glarus (Switzerland) and Park Trust in Monte Carlo. Also with Helimont AG were the shares of Deutsche Industrie AG, Berlin,[16] where the domestic trade interests were consolidated, in particular through complete control of the Deutsche Kohlengesellschaft mbH. The intrinsic value of the businesses that were controlled by the Petscheks can be estimated at around 300 million Reichsmarks. The mines were impeccably run, from a technical standpoint. The trading companies operated with large inter-company earnings and were safeguarded with respect to their revenue by control of the Ostelbisches Braunkohlensyndikat and by substantial influence in other syndicates. The coal trade formed the basis of the position of power built up by Ignaz Petschek. The mining companies and thus the interests in syndicates had been acquired in order to ensure profitable dealings. The four sons of Ignaz Petschek essentially administered the inherited legacy and did not make their mark with new industrial acquisitions.

VII. *Plan for proceeding against the Petschek group*
In the summer of 1938 the *decision* was taken to have the Reich Ministry of Economics declare the *top level of the trade organization* of the Petscheks, the *Deutsche Kohlengesellschaft mbH, to be a Jewish business*. At that time the conscious decision was taken to refrain from declaring all the Petschek firms to be Jewish businesses, in order to allow the industrial enterprises to continue operating undisturbed and to avoid unsettling the economy. The Deutsche Kohlengesellschaft mbH was selected as a point open to attack, as the Petscheks had *run their entire group from here as if from a trust bank*. Systematically and according to plan, all the firms in the Petschek group were checked using their resources available under tax and foreign-exchange laws, and the essential business transactions within the group, the methods used by the Petscheks to run the enterprises, and the connections to foreign countries were ascertained during these procedures.

VIII. *Evidence of the Jewish character of the firms in the Petschek group*
In the course of methodical investigations over a period of eighteen months, the tax auditors, using the confiscated documents and the numbered lists that were located in banks, were able to identify *the shareholdings of the Petscheks almost completely* and proved, with the help of these findings, the Jewish character of the businesses under the Petscheks' influence. Moreover, actual evidence emerged, indicating that the Petschek brothers had retained central management in their hands until the time of their emigration, although after 1936 they no longer represented the firm to the outside as promi-

16 Deutsche Industrie AG was a part of the Petschek group in Bohemia; see also PMJ 2/91.

nently as before. The *facts of Article I § 3 of the Third Regulation on the Reich Citizenship Law of 14 June 1938* ('A business is deemed to be Jewish if it is effectively under the controlling influence of Jews')[17] were therefore present.

IX. *Declaration of the Jewishness of the Deutsche Kohlengesellschaft mbH and the other trading companies of the Ignaz Petschek group*

The declaration that the first Petschek companies were Jewish immediately ran into great difficulties. The Deutsche Kohlengesellschaft mbH had already been declared a Jewish business in the spring of 1938. At that time, however, the influence of the Petscheks had succeeded in having the declaration retracted through their German and Swiss Aryan middlemen. *As a result of the declaration of 'Deutsche Kohlengesellschaft' to be Jewish, more than thirty of the trading concerns it controlled were likewise declared to be Jewish.* Because the shares of 'Deutsche Kohlengesellschaft' were completely owned by *Deutsche Industrie AG* (DIAG), this company too, which had the character of a holding company, was declared to be Jewish. Now *Helimont AG in Glarus*, as the owner of almost all the shares of DIAG and thus as the company at the head of the concern, argued that, *since May 1938, 75 per cent of its own shares* (that is, 450,000 Swiss francs out of 600,000 Swiss francs) had been in English hands (*Sir Oliver Duncan*), and that as a result the corporation controlled by DIAG and 'Deutsche Kohlengesellschaft' had passed into the possession of English Aryans before the enactment of the de-Jewification regulation on 14 June 1938.[18] In response to this argument, I demanded proof of the particulars of the transfer of ownership, including submission of the original documents. At first an *incredibly low purchase price* of 350,000 Swiss francs was alleged to have been paid for the shares in Helimont, that is, not even half a million Swiss francs. In response to the information that, given this low purchase price for the company at the top of the Petschek group, the seriousness of the entire purchase transaction must be called into question, the representatives of Helimont attempted to convince the German authorities of progressively higher purchase prices. The demand by the German authorities to have the written documents and entries in the books verified there and then in London by an accounting expert acceptable to the German authorities was rejected by the representatives of Helimont. The lawyer engaged to represent Helimont and the alleged English purchaser attempted to prove to me the bona fide nature of the purchase transaction by *submitting photocopies of correspondence* concerning the transaction. These documents could not be recognized as authentic because the decisive company names had been cut out of the photocopies and were not indicated. In other respects, too, the documents were not conclusive. The lawyer stated during the negotiations that he must decline to give further information because it could be interpreted by the tax authorities to the disadvantage of his clients. In addition, *personal negotiations with Sir Oliver Duncan* concerning his relinquishing his rights to an agency to be designated by the German authorities were unsuccessful. Under these circumstances, the Reich Minister of Economics rejected Helimont's arguments against the decision to declare it to be a Jewish business.

17 *Reichsgesetzblatt*, 1938, I, 15 June 1938, pp. 627–628.
18 See ibid. and PMJ 2/42.

X. *Declaration of Jewishness and trusteeship for all companies in the Petschek group*
In December 1938 and January 1939 all the companies in the Petschek group were declared to be Jewish, and each was put under the control of a *trustee, one for the trading companies and one for the industrial enterprises*. The previous Petschek majority owners, led by alleged legal successors, sought to appear at the general meetings of shareholders in the Petschek companies over the course of 1939. The issuing of foreign exchange directives served to prevent such influence from being exerted and to stop any payment of dividends on Petschek shares held abroad. The persons concerned acquiesced to their exclusion from the general meetings without instigating legal proceedings, although there were *a few written protests*, for example, by the *Swiss legation*, which were made without instigating legal proceedings. In no case thus far could a bona fide purchase of Petschek stocks be proved.

The Reich Minister of Economics took the view that the legal validity of the purchase of either a majority or a sizeable parcel of shares in a German company must be repudiated, given that the foreign-exchange permits were obtained under false pretences. Despite all the efforts of the Petscheks to the contrary, the companies controlled by them could therefore be treated as Jewish. A few weeks later, the *administrative trustees* received *the order and the authority to sell the businesses*, because the companies declared to be Jewish did not comply of their own volition with the directive ordering the sale of their businesses to Aryans.

XI. *Sale and liquidation of the Petschek companies with special consideration of the interests of the Hermann Göring Reich Works*
The de-Jewification of the Petschek companies gave the *German coal industry* great opportunities to *restructure* the ownership of lignite resources, the organization of the coal trade, and the policy of the syndicates. The *Mining Department of the Reich Ministry of Economics* collected all the proposals from interested parties and guided the individual operations towards a *regeneration of the coal industry in accordance with overriding economic principles*. In this context, plans were also made to utilize the Petschek lignite resources – which had to come under the control of the tax authorities in order to pay the tax obligations and the anticipated penalties for violating currency regulations – so as to procure for the *Hermann Göring Reich Works* the *hard-coal supply* it had lacked thus far, *by exchanging it for lignite*. By order of Field Marshal Göring the majority of the lignite resources were therefore sold to the Hermann Göring Reich Works, in order to provide it with resources which can be swapped for hard coal.

The *trustees* of the companies in the Petschek group *sold, in September 1939, the businesses* with all their assets and debts (material assets) to the German mining concern *Deutsche Kohlenbergbau GmbH*, the *receiving company* which had been founded by the Reich. Excluded from this transaction were *Ilse Bergbau AG*[19] and *Preußengrube AG*, which could be de-Jewified by selling the shares that were tied to the group, and *the*

19 Ilse Bergbau AG, founded in 1871 to the north of Senftenberg, expanded from 1888 to become the most important lignite mining company in Lower Lusatia. In 1927 Ignaz Petschek acquired the majority of the share capital. As a result of the forced sale of the corporate shares held by Petschek, the company avoided divestiture. While the Ilse works were expropriated in the Soviet zone of occupation in 1947 and converted into state-owned enterprises, the company was reactivated and partly resumed operations in the West.

Hubertus Lignite Holdings in the Rhineland, which reverted to the Aryan founding families. *The receiving company sold the businesses in December 1939 to the Hermann Göring Reich Works AG* for the same price the receiving company itself had been charged. The sales prices must be paid to the receiving company by 31 December 1940.

When the Reich Ministry of Economics *set the prices*, it was taken into account, on the one hand, that the *Aryan shareholders* who had to be paid off should receive a fair price, and, on the other hand, that in a process of *de-Jewification* a modest current value must be taken as a basis. The prices that were set are consistently higher than the latest stock-market rates, so that the Aryan shareholders are not disadvantaged.

In all property transfers, the *social needs of the workforces* were safeguarded through imposing conditions.

The *Petschek (parent) companies*, with the exception of Ilse Bergbau AG and Preußengrube AG, are being *wound up* (liquidated). Starting at the end of 1940, they will distribute their assets, from the sales prices for their material assets, amounting to *around 160 million Reichsmarks.*

Vereinigte Industrie-Unternehmungen AG [VIAG] (a Reich corporation)[20] has acquired the *majority of the shares in Ilse Bergbau AG* during the de-Jewification process. The *years of struggle between the Petschek group and 'Viag' have been decided in favour of the Reich.*

The *majority of the shares of Preußengrube AG* have passed into the possession of the *Hermann Göring Reich Works.* Likewise, the Hermann Göring Reich Works acquired the existing business (material assets) of *Oehringen Bergbau AG* (hard-coal mine, Upper Silesia).

The *Hermann Göring Reich Works AG* has used the greatest part of the purchased lignite mines for the conversion of *Westphalian hard-coal mines* held by *Flick and Salzdetfurth.*[21]

The total assets of the former Petschek companies in liquidation, now in the possession of the receiving company German Coal Mining GmbH, consisting of the price paid for businesses that were sold, must firstly be used to pay off the *domestic Aryan shareholders.* Their claims are estimated at *60 million Reichsmarks at most.*

The *liquidation proceeds of around 100 million Reichsmarks* that are due to the *Petscheks* and their front men are not to be paid out because of the substantial *outstanding taxes and financial penalties due to the Reich.* Seizure through actual confiscation of the shares is not possible because the share certificates are located abroad. The seizure of the liquidation proceeds due to the Petscheks will take place during criminal prosecution for breach of foreign-exchange regulations, around 50 per cent of which will be obtained by confiscating either actual cash values or the replacement values that substitute actual cash values

20 Vereinigte Industrie-Unternehmungen AG (VIAG) was founded in Berlin in 1923 as a holding company for investments in companies from the arms industry of the First World War. In the 1930s it expanded to the energy and aluminium sector and was one of Europe's leading electricity producers. After 1945, VIAG lost more than half of its assets due to war damage and losses in East Germany, but by the beginning of the 1990s it was once again among Germany's twenty largest industrial enterprises.

21 The Petschek family held shares in the mining and drilling company Salzdetfurth AG, which was founded in Goslar in 1889. In 1899 it was renamed Kaliwerke Salzdetfurth (Salzdetfurth Potash Works).

(claims to the liquidation proceeds). The remainder of the liquidation proceeds will not be sufficient to cover the anticipated penalties associated with foreign-exchange and tax violations. Moreover, the Reich Ministry of Finance has already *seized other property assets of the Petscheks* in the amount of approximately *15 million Reichsmarks.*

XII. *Summarizing implementation report*

Through purposeful collaboration by all the offices concerned, the plan drawn up for the de-Jewification of the Ignaz Petschek group in the summer of 1938 was successfully carried out in its entirety, against the opposition of the Petscheks, who drew in part on the services of foreign and German representatives. The result of this work, which took more than eighteen months, is as follows:

The Petscheks no longer hold sway over the lignite industry. Not one of the successors has received such a decisive share that it would be possible for him to continue the efforts to achieve a monopoly in the lignite industry. The Petscheks' *eastern German production of lignite and briquettes*, along with the associated trading interests, is now divided up between '*Viag' and Flick. The Reich* (Viag) is thereby ensured a sufficient *lignite supply for its power stations and aluminium plants*. The Flick holdings are made more complete with the aid of the new business and can be made more efficient. In central Germany, unified *resources* have been obtained *by Salzdetfurth*, whereby an economically beneficial rationalization process was made possible by combining these resources with the previously existing brown-coal resources of Salzdetfurth.

The *Hermann Göring Reich Works* have gained the *hard-coal resources desired by the state* by exchanging the Petscheks' lignite mines for the Westphalian hard-coal mines, which are well located for the Salzgitter company, along with the Petscheks' hard-coal mines in Upper Silesia (Oehringen and Preußengrube), which were directly transferred to the Reich Works.[22] The transfer of *Hohenlohe (Kattowitz)* out of the Petscheks' ownership is still pending. The Hermann Göring Reich Works still control a few Petschek businesses in central Germany, which they should either transfer back to the receiving company if they do not need them for their own purposes, or resell to other buyers with the consent of the Reich Minister of Economics.

This result in the de-Jewification of the Petschek group was achieved with existing legal instruments, without any cash movements required thus far and avoiding all transfers, without any disruption to the production and distribution of coal, without impairing the social interests of the employees, with the protection of the Aryan German shareholders, and without the Petscheks' cooperation and, furthermore, in the face of their resistance. Looking back, it must be stated that *the power of authority granted by the Field Marshal* has been *a determining factor in this achievement*. This authority enabled me, in the crucial months of the autumn and winter of 1938/39, to take a stance that a civil servant in a single ministry could not have maintained, given the complicated nature of the matter, which was only ever partly under his remit. This authority made it possible to attack the central position of the Petscheks' Deutsche Kohlengesellschaft–DIAG–Helimont concern and to maintain the declaration of the group's Jewishness in the face of the protests from the English. During the course of the procedure, proof of the sus-

22 In arms production, high temperatures for steel-making could be reached more quickly by using hard (bituminous) coal as a fuel.

pected strategies and management practices of the Petscheks' business fell into our hands, with the result that we can compile a virtually complete set of evidence.

This report addresses the largest *single case of tax or currency violations* that has been handled thus far in Germany, and these proceedings will result in more than 100 million Reichsmarks entering the Reich treasury. The *economic assets* that pass into Reich ownership as a result of the de-Jewification of the Ignaz Petschek group must be valued at a *substantially higher figure.*

In this report, I cannot list all the ministerial staff who have contributed to these proceedings; however, I wish to mention by name the gentlemen from the Reich Tax Authorities who, under the guidance of Ministerialrat Gebhardt,[23] have made an outstanding contribution through their expertise: Senior Tax Inspector Krause,[24] who has been conducting the tax audit in the Petschek case since 1936, Senior Tax Inspector Lübke, who had varied tasks to perform in eliminating Jewish and foreign influences, and Senior Customs Inspector Gaede, to whom the difficult task of tracing the foreign-exchange offences was assigned.

DOC. 78

On 5 May 1940 the physician Max Schönenberg from Cologne writes to his brother-in-law Julius Kaufmann in Shanghai about the curtailing of his medical practice[1]

Handwritten letter from Max Schönenberg,[2] Cologne, to Julius Kaufmann,[3] Shanghai, dated 5 May 1940

Dear Julius,

A few days ago I asked you on behalf of Dr Cobliner whether the land route to there is feasible, and above all, whether Manchukuo[4] grants transit visas to Jews. If that

23 Joseph Gebhardt (1887–1976), lawyer; from 1918, with the Bavarian financial supervisory authority; at the Reich Ministry of Finance, 1930–1942/43, where he was responsible for audit investigation and financial and company audits, and ultimately held the post of ministerial director; joined the NSDAP in 1933; chief judge at the Reich Fiscal Court, 1942/43 to 1945; judge at the Supreme Fiscal Court in Munich, 1949; from 1951 president of the Bayerische Landesanstalt für Aufbaufinanzierung, a Bavarian state-owned bank funding economic development.

24 Friedrich Krause, tax inspector at the Regional Tax Office in Berlin.

1 NS-Dokumentationszentrum Köln, Briefe Max Schönenberg, record group: 46. Excerpt published in Martin Rüther, *Köln im Zweiten Weltkrieg: Alltag und Erfahrungen zwischen 1939 und 1945* (Cologne: Emons, 2005), p. 533. This letter has been translated from German.

2 Dr Max Schönenberg (1885–1943), physician; served in the First World War as a senior physician, then had his own practice in Cologne; visited his son in Palestine together with his wife Erna in June 1939 but they returned to Cologne; deported to Theresienstadt on 15 June 1942, where he perished on 8 Jan. 1943.

3 Dr Julius Kaufmann (d. 1965), lawyer; Zionist; practised law; editor of the *Israelitisches Gemeindeblatt* in Cologne; worked in a welfare office for emigrants from 1933; was briefly imprisoned in Dachau concentration camp in Nov. 1938; emigrated to Shanghai shortly before the outbreak of war in 1939, and later to Palestine.

4 The Empire of Manchukuo in north-eastern China was a puppet state of Japan between 1932 and 1945. It was recognized by the German Reich in 1938.

enquiry has not yet reached you, please give him a reply in response to this letter. He can have the money for the proof of means wire-transferred to an account there.

In future, please do not stick on to the envelopes any stamps that you would like to have back. I read yesterday that exchange of stamps with addressees in other countries is undesirable and that letters with stamp enclosures will no longer be conveyed (or returned?) in the near future. I hope this does not affect my last or next-to-last letter, which contained three envelopes from you and on to which I had stuck special-issue stamps (and which contained several group photos of us). My practice will soon be a lot quieter. As a result of a new directive, all my patients, since 1 May, have been excluded from the private health insurance schemes.[5] Now, many a person will think twice before consulting a practitioner for the sick,[6] and if he does make up his mind to do so, he may well lack the money to pay. I expect a further loss as a result of the fact that the male Jews who are fit for work (whether it will apply to women, I don't yet know, but it would not affect Erna,[7] as she works as a housewife, or Grete either, as she is employed in the office of the shelter) and are between the ages of 16 and 55 are being conscripted for labour and thus must be covered by health insurance, and hence are eliminated from my pool of patients.

In general we are not dissatisfied with this measure. Even though it is not easy for many people from business or academic professions to adjust to physical labour, most of the people with whom I've talked are pleased that the enforced idleness has ceased. And once they've got through the initial stages, most of them also feel quite good about the new activity, and for many it is really a piece of good fortune that they can earn something again.

Previously, we had a different vision of what constituted good fortune. Now it is only three more weeks until we hope to have a reply from Mortimer.

Stay well and happy.

Warm regards

[…][8]

5 On 13 April 1940 the Reich Supervisory Office for Private Insurance had ordered that Jews be excluded from private health insurance as of 1 May 1940: *Jüdisches Nachrichtenblatt* (Berlin edition), no. 42, 24 May 1940, p. 1.

6 With the Fourth Regulation on the Reich Citizenship Law, Jewish physicians lost their licence to practise medicine with effect from 30 September 1938. A few were allowed to continue working as 'practitioners for the sick' (*Krankenbehandler*) but could only treat Jewish patients.

7 Erna Schönenberg, née Kaufmann (1882–1944), housewife; wife of Max Schönenberg and sister of Julius Kaufmann; deported on 15 June 1942 to Theresienstadt and on 9 Oct. 1944 to Auschwitz, where she was murdered.

8 The blank margins of the two-page letter and the foot of the second page were used by Erna and Max Schönenberg, as well as Erna Schönenberg's mother, for short notes with purely private contents. Max Schönenberg dated his note 6 May 1940.

DOC. 79

On 15 May 1940 the SD Main District Stuttgart permits the Jewish Liaison Office to place Jews with local farmers in preparation for their emigration[1]

Letter from the Head of the SD Main District Stuttgart (II/112 – Ri./Sta.)[2] to the Jewish Liaison Office in Stuttgart,[3] dated 15 May 1940 (copy)

Re: emigration of Jews – placement of Jews in agricultural occupations
Case file: various discussions.
Encl.: none.
Following consultation with our office, the regional employment office, the regional farmers' association, and the NSDAP have consented to the deployment and training of Jews in farming and horticultural enterprises. The regional farming association will issue corresponding instructions to the district and local farmers' leaders, stating that Jews may be set to work as unskilled agricultural labourers for wages based on the standard rates for unskilled agricultural workers. The Jews under consideration are mainly to be deployed in agriculture in their place of residence. The remaining Jews must under no circumstances be permitted to live in the farmers' homes. Instead, they must be quartered in the home of a Jew in the locality or nearby. The farmer is responsible for feeding the Jew. However, the Jew will naturally not eat his meal at the same table as his employer. Instead, he must completely avoid the family unit. After the Jew has completed his agricultural training, the appropriate farmers' leader will issue him with the certificate required for his emigration. If possible, Jews are to be assigned only in farms where no Poles are deployed.

It is requested that the placement of Jews in agriculture be undertaken without delay and that a report be submitted on what has been set in motion. Should difficulties arise in implementing these instructions, notification must be given at once.

1 Archives of the Leo Baeck Institute, New York, at the Jüdisches Museum Berlin, MM92. This letter has been translated from German.

2 Eugen Steimle (1909–1987), grammar school (*Gymnasium*) teacher; joined the NSDAP and the SA in 1932, and the SS in 1936; head of the SD sub-district in Württemberg, 1936–1939; head of the SD Main District Stuttgart, 1939–1943; headed the Sonderkommando 7a of Einsatzgruppe B in 1941 and the Sonderkommando 4a of Einsatzgruppe C from 1942–1943; head of Group VI B of the Reich Security Main Office (RSHA), 1943–1945; SS-Standartenführer, 1944; sentenced to death at the Nuremberg Military Tribunals in 1948 but the sentence was later commuted to a prison term of twenty years; granted early release in 1954; teacher in Wilhelmsdorf/Württemberg, 1955–1975.

3 The Jewish Liaison Office (Jüdische Mittelstelle), headed by Karl Adler (1890–1973), a branch of the Reich Association of Jews in Germany, had the task of organizing the emigration of Stuttgart's Jews. It was under the strict supervision of the Gestapo and the SD.

DOC. 80

On 17 May 1940 the Reichsführer SS urges the Reich Minister of Finance to initiate the rapid seizure of the assets of Jewish emigrants remaining in the country[1]

Letter from the Reichsführer SS/Chief of the German Police (S.I A 11 Allgem. 1427), p.p. signed Dr Bilfinger,[2] to the Reich Minister of Finance[3] (received on 18 May 1940), dated 17 May 1940[4]

Re: confiscation of assets of Jewish emigrants.
Case file: none.
The cases of revocation of German nationality under § 2 of the law of 14 July 1933 (*Reichsgesetzblatt*, I, pp. 480 ff.)[5] that are to be viewed as crucial to the war effort and thus to be attended to with the utmost energy and speed include those in which an emigrant is still in possession of substantial assets in this country which the Reich would lose if the emigrant, by becoming naturalized in a foreign country, evades the revocation procedure and the related declaration of forfeiture of assets. In the latter cases, it is imperative to accelerate the confiscation process, in particular because the longer an emigrant has resided abroad and possibly fulfilled the foreign residence requirements of the host country, the greater the risk of such naturalization. In all cases in which Jews residing abroad have submitted lists of assets in accordance with the regulation of 26 April 1938 (*Reichsgesetzblatt*, I, p. 414),[6] I have therefore directed all State Police head offices to ascertain quickly whether the prerequisites for the revocation of German nationality and for the associated confiscation and declaration of forfeiture of assets have been met.

At the urging of the tax office in Moabit West, I request in this connection that all tax offices be instructed until further notice to reject, in the interests of state policy, all applications for a refund of overpaid levies on Jewish assets, as well as applications for the issuance of tax clearance certificates for Jews residing abroad, to the extent that this concerns enabling access to capital assets in order to prevent assets being transferred to the disadvantage of the Reich. Tax clearance certificates would thus be issued by the tax

1 BArch, R 2/5979, fols. 289–290. This letter has been translated from German.
2 Dr Rudolf Bilfinger (1903–1998), lawyer; joined the NSDAP in 1923, the SA in 1933, and the SS in 1939; worked for the Gestapo in Stuttgart, 1934–1937; at the Main Office of the Security Police from 1937, then at the Reich Security Main Office (RSHA) as head of Section I B 1 (Organization of the Security Police); head of administration in the office of the senior commander of the Security Police in Cracow, 1940; SS-Obersturmbannführer, 1941; at the RSHA, 1941–1943; commander of the Security Police in Toulouse, 1943, and in Cracow, 1944; interned in France in 1945 and sentenced to eight years in prison in 1953 (classed as time served); later, senior administrative judge in Mannheim.
3 Count Johann Ludwig Schwerin von Krosigk.
4 The original contains handwritten annotations, underlining, and official stamps of the Reichsführer SS and Chief of the German Police.
5 Under § 2 of the Law on the Revocation of Naturalization and the Deprivation of German Nationality (14 July 1933), the citizenship of Reich subjects residing abroad could be revoked and their assets confiscated for the benefit of the Reich: *Reichsgesetzblatt*, 1933, I, p. 480.
6 The Regulation on the Registration of Jewish Assets required Jews to disclose their financial circumstances; failure to comply was punishable by a fine or prison term: *Reichsgesetzblatt*, 1938, I, pp. 414–415; see also PMJ 2/29.

offices solely for payments that are essential for the preservation and management of the assets. I request that you send me, in due course, a copy of your instructions to the subordinate authorities.

DOC. 81

On 24 May 1940 Günther Troplowitz from Berlin asks the Reich Foreign Office about the possibility of settling the Jews in future German colonies[1]

Letter from Günther (Israel) Troplowitz,[2] 119 Manfred v. Richthofenstraße, Berlin-Tempelhof, to the Reich Foreign Office, dated 24 May 1940[3]

I hereby venture to advance a proposal with the following remarks, in the belief that I can assume the Reich Foreign Office to be the relevant authority in this matter.

To resolve the question of the non-Aryans, to the extent that they are Jews or are deemed such under the law, I most respectfully ask whether settlement in future German colonies would be possible, specifically for those who:
(1) are members of a Christian denomination,
(2) preferably have one or two Aryan grandparents,
(3) are married to Aryan women,
(4) can prove that their ancestors held, before 1812, German nationality or that of one of the former constituent states,
(5) have no criminal record and are not politically incriminated in any respect,
(6) can demonstrate that they have a certain number of Aryan guarantors,
(7) have lost close relatives (fathers or brothers) in the war of 1914–1918 or in the present campaign,
(8) did not belong to a leftist party during the Systemzeit[4] or earlier, or to a [Masonic] lodge. These reflections do not emanate from new insights on my part, based on the undoubted outcome of the present European conflict, but rather from a conviction that I have held for as long as I can remember. Allow me to cite excerpts from a letter that I sent on 11 May 1939 to Pastor Grüber[5] in Kaulsdorf, whose Berlin office deals with the care of non-Aryan (Protestant) Christians:

> thus I must say, at least as far as I am concerned, that a solution within the German Reich Association [of Jews in Germany] would be the most desirable thing, from a purely emotional standpoint … Perhaps I am a poor optimist, but I simply cannot

1 PA AA, R 99 353. This document has been translated from German.
2 Günther Troplowitz (b. 1900), sales representative; regarded as a *Mischling* of the first degree; lived with his non-Jewish wife, Emmy, née Wenzel (b. 1904), and his father, Wilhelm (1862–1940), in Berlin-Tempelhof; later did excavation work, and was conscripted in Oct. 1941 for labour service; survived the war in Berlin, where he later resumed his work as a sales representative.
3 The original contains handwritten notes.
4 German for 'system era', a term used by the National Socialists to refer disparagingly to the period of the Weimar Republic.
5 The reference is to the Grüber Office, which assisted Protestant Christians persecuted on grounds of race to emigrate from Germany. See Glossary.

> believe that the state should not have a certain interest in our circle after all. The fact that I continue to cherish this hope also has to do with my belief that all of us who, compelled by circumstances, seek to build a new, modest life for ourselves somewhere else, as best we can, are more or less an object of political agitation and will continue to be so. And in all probability we are approaching an inner conflict with respect to whether we ought to oppose our homeland … I am convinced that Germany, in the foreseeable future, will also regain its African territories, one way or another! We should be placed there. The vexatious question of capital would be resolved at a single stroke. The circles that believe they absolutely must be rid of us would be relieved of us more quickly than otherwise, and we, on the other hand, would have an opportunity that does not utterly detach us from our homeland, which will perhaps be restored to our descendants some day … Perhaps you will say that I lack a sense of dignity. In reply, I can only tell you that for me it is not a matter of my dignity, my pride, my self-respect, but rather it is about Germany! … I can only state what I believe I can answer for to God and my conscience. In so doing, success or failure can never ever be the decisive factor. Instead, it must always be only one's moral foundation that is decisive.[6]

Unfortunately, I did not receive a reply to the letter. On 25 August 1939, as a war veteran, I volunteered. However, on 25 October 1939 I received a letter of rejection. On 19 April 1940 I repeated my request. During a personal consultation at Recruiting District Headquarters VII, Colonel Hoffmann told me that there had been no change in the existing requirements. I mention this solely to show that I was adamant in holding fast to my attitude and was also willing to take up arms to defend it. And I believe I may say that I am not alone in my stance and that for persons in the aforementioned circle – and it is only for them that I can speak, I believe – it is a largely undeserved punishment and hardship to be inescapably embedded in a society from which, however, everything separates them and must separate them.

I can be only a suppliant, strengthened solely by the awareness of never having done anything that goes against the interests of my country. I know that more important problems exist aplenty. And I nonetheless ask that my proposal be examined, and if the possibility of carrying it out arises, then I ask that the deployment of men fit for military service to the front be made possible during the campaign and that, after the war, courses be held at colonial schools.

In conclusion, I venture to ask also, if the Reich Foreign Office is not the appropriate authority for this matter, that this letter be kindly forwarded to the proper office.

Most respectfully,[7]

6 Ellipses as in the original.

7 The file does not contain any response to this letter.

DOC. 82

On 29 May 1940 the Reichsstatthalter announces that the Reich-wide laws pertaining to Jews will not be adopted in Danzig, as there will soon be no Jews left there anyway[1]

Letter from the Reichsstatthalter of Danzig-West Prussia (I A 1–4800), p.p. signed Huth,[2] to all departments of the Reichsstatthalter with printed documents for the subordinate departments, dated 29 May 1940[3]

Re: application in Danzig of the Reich German legislation pertaining to Jews

Under § 4 of the Law on the Reunification of the Free City of Danzig with the German Reich, 1 September 1939 (*Reichsgesetzblatt*, I, p. 1547), the entire body of Reich law and Prussian regional law entered into force in the former Free City of Danzig on 1 January 1940, unless it was stipulated by the relevant Reich ministers that specified Reich laws or Prussian regional laws are not to take effect. Because the Reich German provisions and the Danzig provisions largely coincide in the matter of laws pertaining to the Jews insofar as the exclusion of Jews from economic life and their use for special services are concerned, and because the introduction of the Reich German provisions would require changeover provisions and transitional rules in many cases, I have encouraged the Reich Minister of Economics to issue a regulation stating that the Reich German provisions should not take effect and that the Danzig regulations should continue to remain effective. The Reich Minister of Economics,[4] by means of the decree of 16 March 1940 (III L 5/7791/40),[5] has fundamentally endorsed this view and stated that, given that the process of excluding Jews from Danzig's economic life is almost complete, it would needlessly burden the authorities involved if, for the relatively short time still required to completely cleanse Danzig of Jews, they had to apply the regulations valid in the rest of the Reich

1 Archiwum Państwowe w Gdańsku, 263/2, fols. 145–146. Published in Erwin Lichtenstein, *Die Juden der Freien Stadt Danzig unter der Herrschaft des Nationalsozialismus* (Tübingen: Mohr, 1973), pp. 231–232. This letter has been translated from German.

2 Wilhelm Huth (1896–1982), engineering graduate; with the Mechanical Engineering Office in Danzig-Cracow, 1927–1932; joined the NSDAP in 1930 and the SS in 1932; Danzig Senate delegate, 1933–1939, and its vice president from 1934; Regierungspräsident and deputy Reichsstatthalter of Danzig-West Prussia, 1939–1945; after 1945 worked in the insurance industry in Hamburg.

3 The letter was also sent to the Higher SS and Police Leader of Danzig-West Prussia, SS-Gruppenführer Richard Hildebrandt (1897–1952), with printed documents for the subordinate bodies, to the regional tax director, Julius Hoppenrath (1880–1961), to President of the Higher Regional Court Walter Wohler (1893–1968), to the chief public prosecutor, Curt Graßmann (1882–1941), to the Reichsstatthalter (Reich Propaganda Office), to the Reich Labour Service, to the head of Labour Gau II Danzig-West Prussia Dr Hermann Wagner (1896–1970?), Zoppot, 7 Ernststraße, and to the mayors and Landräte in the territory of the former Free City of Danzig.

4 Walther Funk (1890–1960), journalist; editor-in-chief of the *Berliner Börsenzeitung*, 1922–1930; joined the NSDAP in 1931; Hitler's personal economic advisor from 1931; press chief of the Reich government from 1933; state secretary in the Reich Ministry of Public Enlightenment and Propaganda; Reich minister of economics, 1938–1945; president of the Reichsbank from 1939; was sentenced at the International Military Tribunal at Nuremberg to life imprisonment in 1946, and released in 1957.

5 Letter from the Reich Minister of Economics, dated 16 March 1940, re the introduction in Danzig of the laws on Jews; Archiwum Państwowe w Gdańsku, 263/2, fols. 139–140v.

territory, in addition to the numerous implementing regulations and decrees. The Reich Minister of Economics, however, in consultation with the Plenipotentiary for the Four-Year Plan,[6] has deemed it unnecessary to decree, by issuing formal legislation with retroactive effect, that the provisions concerned should not take effect in Danzig as of 1 January 1940. It is instead to remain the case that the regulations in question, together with the other Reich laws, have entered into force in Danzig, and the special circumstances with respect to de-Jewification in Danzig are taken into account solely through regulating the implementation accordingly.

This regulation is then set out in detail in the decree of 16 March 1940. As appropriate, the application of the Danzig regulations will essentially continue. Considering that the decree is in the main only of significance for the representative in charge of furthering and ensuring Jewish emigration, no copy is being provided.[7] However, it is left to your discretion – particularly in case of doubt – to consult Department I of the Office of the Reichsstatthalter.

DOC. 83

On 30 May 1940 Paul Eppstein records details of a summons to the Gestapo, during which there was mention of forced labour by Jews[1]

File note on a summons on 30 May 1940, 10:30 a.m., to the Gestapo Central Office, to see Regierungsassessor Jagusch,[2] signed Dr Eppstein, dated 31 May 1940

1. *Labour deployment*

It was stated that at twelve o'clock today a consultation was scheduled in the Reich Ministry of Labour (Oberregierungsrat *Letzsch*)[3], during which difficulties that have arisen thus far with regard to the labour deployment of Jews outside Berlin were to be discussed. Regierungsassessor Jagusch declared that there are no objections to this discussion, that in the discussion it should be pointed out that case files regarding labour deployment are available from the supervisory authority, and that general arrangements for labour deployment and job training are being instituted, regarding which a direct

6 Hermann Göring.

7 This post was held by Oberregierungsrat Walther Hildebrandt, who worked in the Danzig Senate's department for economics.

1 BArch, R 8150/45, fols. 198–201. This document has been translated from German.

2 Dr Walter Jagusch (1912–1981), lawyer; SA member, 1932–1933; joined the NSDAP in 1933 and the SS, possibly in the same year; at the Gestapo Central Office from 1939, then at the Reich Security Main Office (RSHA); headed Section IV A 5 (emigrants); also responsible for 'Jewish affairs' from 1940; served temporarily as head of the Gestapo in Strasbourg from the end of 1940 to 1942; led an Einsatzgruppe against partisans in Riga, 1942–1943; at the SS and Police Court in Metz from May 1943; in hiding after the war ended; lawyer in Bielefeld after 1952.

3 Correctly: Dr Walter Letsch (b. 1895), political scientist; headed the employment office in Waldenburg, 1928–1934; joined the NSDAP and the SA in 1933; specialist at the regional employment office in Silesia, 1934–1936; worked at the Reich Institute for Labour Placement and Unemployment Insurance, 1936–1938; at the Reich Labour Ministry from 1939; Ministerialrat, 1941; worked for the Reich Plenipotentiary for Labour from 1942.

agreement between the Reich Security Main Office and the Reich Ministry of Labour will follow. A discussion about these general arrangements was postponed. It was stated that Jews who are fit for work are to be used for work, whether in labour service or in the facilities for vocational training. Regierungsassessor Jagusch requested a written report on the outcome of the consultation in the Reich Ministry of Labour.[4]

2. *Visible identification of Jews deployed as labour*
The facts of the matter were presented. Regierungsassessor Jagusch remarked that a similar case from Cologne has come to his attention.[5] He requested submission of a report that also provides the commentary from the central department for Jews at the employment office in Berlin,[6] so that a review by the [supervisory] authority can be arranged. It was explained that such visible identification is not consistent with the statement that had been issued on the occasion of the temporary introduction of measures to visibly identify Jews in the eastern territories in Peiskretscham, according to which such a measure was not to apply to Jews in the Old Reich.[7] It was stated that because the Jews deployed for labour service are accustomed to working in separate groups anyway and at a distance from the other workers, it seems unnecessary to make them wear identifying markers, especially in the form of a yellow Star of David that must be worn on the chest and the back. Remedial action is therefore being requested. Regierungsassessor Jagusch will firstly get in touch with the employment office.

3. *Supervision of the Jews in Eupen and Malmedy*
The letter of enquiry from the district office in Cologne was presented.[8] Now that the region of Eupen and Malmedy has been legally annexed, Regierungsassessor Jagusch expressed no opposition to allowing the Jews living there to be looked after by the Reich Association [of Jews in Germany] or by the district office in Cologne.[9]

4. *Requirements of Gestapo authorities for reports on the emigration tax*
It was stated that a number of Jewish religious congregations have been notified of requirements imposed by Gestapo offices with respect to the tax levied on emigrants. In Cologne, for example, every exemption from the emigration tax that the Religious Community files for with the Reich Association must be authorized in advance by the Gestapo. Although the Reich Association in Bremen does not levy the emigration tax, at the behest of the Gestapo it must provide the religious congregation with a fund of RM 10,000, from which the Gestapo reserves the right to grant sums of money. In Magdeburg and Chemnitz a special fund in addition to the emigration tax is to be set up at the behest of the Gestapo. Additional reports have been received thus far from Leipzig,

4 This report could not be found.
5 The Cologne firm Glanzstoff-Courtaulds GmbH used badges to identify more than 200 Jewish workers.
6 This report could not be found.
7 This statement could not be verified.
8 This enquiry could not be found.
9 The Eupen-Malmedy region was annexed to the German Reich after the invasion of Belgium in May 1940.

Hanover, and Stolp. Regierungsassessor Jagusch asked for a written summary, which should be sent at the same time to Section IV D 4.[10]

5. *Hiring of an infant nurse from Kattowitz*

It was stated that the Jewish Community of Berlin intends to hire, for its Berlin-Niederschönhausen nursery for infants and small children, a certified infant nurse who presently resides in Kattowitz, as suitably qualified personnel are not available in the Old Reich. Regierungsassessor Jagusch raised no objections to the appointment in this exceptional case.

6. *Accommodation of a war invalid, currently in Neuendorf, in the home of relatives in Berlin*

It was stated that among the Jews who were grouped together in Schneidemühl and then taken to Neuendorf is the Jewish war invalid Ernst Israel *Levin*, along with his wife and daughter.[11] He is very easily aggravated as a result of his war injury and therefore it will be extremely difficult for him to fit into the community in Neuendorf. Permission to house him separately in Berlin was requested. In view of the special circumstances, Regierungsassessor Jagusch expressed no objection to this plan, but stated that it must remain an exception.

7. *Stettin*

In response to the questions from Regierungsassessor Jagusch, a report was given concerning the current status of the acquisition of fabrics and footwear from the apartments of the Jews deported from the Regierungsbezirk Stettin, in particular concerning the result of the negotiations of the Reich Association representative with the trustee Dr Lenz. In the process, it was stated that a purchase of the items from the apartments by the Reich Association, to the extent that a collective shipment of items to Lublin had been promised in principle, is contradictory in the sense that the Reich Association would then be indirectly paying the recipients for the items that are to be sent to Lublin. For this reason, it was asked that the following proposal be considered: that the valuation and handover of the items be completed as scheduled. After the handover, the items are sorted for the collective shipment. The estimated value of these items is offset against the total estimated value. Then only the difference is transferred by the Reich Association into the blocked account of the individuals who have been deported to Lublin. It is allocated proportionally to the payments that should have been made in accordance with the total estimated value.

Regierungsassessor Jagusch regarded the implementation of this arrangement as possible: accordingly, the items in the collective shipment are thus to be taken over at no charge by the Reich Association and sent to Lublin as soon as the requisite permission

10 This report could not be found. Section IV D 4 of the RSHA operated until March 1941 under the name 'Emigration, Evacuation' and was headed by Adolf Eichmann.

11 Probably Ernst Lewin (b. 1895) from Falkenburg in Pomerania; was deported from Berlin to Theresienstadt on 3 Oct. 1942 and from there to Auschwitz on 6 Oct. 1944. Neuendorf was a Hachsharah camp near Fürstenwalde. On the deportations from Schneidemühl, see Introduction, p. 40.

of the regional tax director (Foreign Exchange Office) in Stettin has been obtained. A written report is to be submitted about this.[12]

8. *Trustee for Breslau*
(a) Trustee for the community in Breslau
Regierungsassessor Jagusch said that he had already forwarded the case file in the manner stated to the Reich Ministry of Economics and the Gestapo head office in Breslau. It was stated that in the meantime there had been no change in the functions of the trustee. Regierungsassessor Jagusch agreed to another letter of enquiry directed to the Reich Ministry of Economics.[13]
(b) Trustee for individuals
Regierungsassessor Jagusch said that he had instructed the Gestapo head office in Breslau that the appointment of individual trustees is being discontinued. It was stated that, according to a report submitted yesterday by the board of the Jewish Religious Association in Breslau, the appointment of trustees for individuals has thus far not been revoked. It was therefore requested that the matter be checked again.

9. *Synagogue buildings*
Regierungsassessor Jagusch enquired about the utilization of the synagogue buildings that burned down in November 1938 or the utilization of the corresponding plots of land. It was reported that in the Reich the synagogues have already been demolished in most cases, and in Berlin negotiations regarding the sale of the land are pending.

Regierungsassessor Jagusch requested a written report on the disposition of the plots of land, specifically in Berlin. Now that a sufficient number of synagogues have been approved again for religious services, care must henceforth be taken to ensure that the other properties are put to use as soon as possible.[14]

10. *Release of Dr Lamm from prison*
The facts were presented and the written report was submitted.[15]

11. *Jewish convalescent clinic in Warmbrunn*
The correspondence with the mayor of the town of Warmbrunn was submitted and discussed in detail. Regierungsassessor Jagusch was of the opinion that the calculation of the capitalized value must be disregarded in determining the purchase price, and that the sale should be based on the assessed value. A request was made for a decision or direct instructions to the mayor of Warmbrunn.

The other pending matters (expansion of Neuendorf, contract for Berkaerstraße, identification papers for employees, automobile use, curfew in Münster, emigration tax for persons who have emigrated) were postponed until the next discussion.

12 This report could not be found.
13 This enquiry could not be found.
14 Reports are available in BArch, R 8150/4, fols. 199–208, for various places in the Reich, and fols. 209–212, for Berlin.
15 Probably Dr Fritz Lamm (1876–1942), head of the Welfare and Youth Services Office of the Reich Association of Jews in Germany; taken hostage in exchange for Reich Association employees who were designated for deportation and had gone underground; shot dead on 1 Dec. 1942.

DOC. 84

Jüdisches Nachrichtenblatt, 31 May 1940: announcements from the Israelite Religious Community of Vienna concerning travel restrictions and the emigration requirement for Jews[1]

Announcements

It is announced that, by virtue of the existing restriction order, travel may be undertaken only to perform an official assignment or in connection with emigration.

Israelite Religious Community of Vienna.

It is pointed out that persons who are conscripted for *labour deployment* by the relevant employment offices must *still make preparations for emigration*. If this is impossible as a result of absence from Vienna, *relatives* remaining in Vienna are asked to seek advice in the individual departments of the Israelite Religious Community of Vienna concerning the steps to be taken.

Israelite Religious Community of Vienna.

DOC. 85

On 5 June 1940 the Grafeneck Regional Hospital for the Disabled informs Moritz Fleicher of the death of his son[1]

Letter from the Grafeneck Regional Hospital for the Disabled, Münsingen, signed Dr Keller,[2] to Moritz Israel Fleicher,[3] Stuttgart, 9 Reuchlinstraße, dated 5 June 1940

Dear Mr Fleicher,

We regret to inform you that your son Ferdinand Israel Fleicher,[4] who had to be transferred to this institution by ministerial order on 20 May 1940, in accordance with instructions from the commissioner for the defence of the Reich, passed away unexpectedly on 4 June 1940 as a result of acute cerebral swelling.[5] Given his serious, incurable illness, his death constitutes a release for him.

At the instruction of the police authority, the deceased had to be cremated immediately in order to protect public health. We ask that you tell us to which cemetery we should have the police authority transport the urn with the mortal remains of the depart-

1 'Verlautbarungen', *Jüdisches Nachrichtenblatt* (Vienna edition), 31 May 1940, p. 1. This document has been translated from German.

1 Archives of the Leo Baeck Institute, New York, at the Jüdisches Museum Berlin, Karl Adler Collection, MF 572, reel 2, box 3, folder 1. This letter has been translated from German.

2 The physicians in Grafeneck signed letters to relatives of the murdered patients with the pseudonyms 'Dr Keller' or 'Dr Jäger'.

3 Probably: Moritz Fleischer (1872–1944), resident of Stuttgart; was deported in August 1942 to Theresienstadt and in May 1944 to Auschwitz, where he perished.

4 Correctly: Ferdinand Fleischer (1907–1940), who was deported from the Weissenau Psychiatric Hospital (Ravensburg) on 20 May 1940 and murdered in Grafeneck the same day.

5 The standard letters to relatives gave fictional causes of death. The patients had in fact been murdered during the 'euthanasia' operation.

ed. If we have received no information from you within fourteen days, we will have the urn interred elsewhere at no charge. The clothing of the deceased, which had no particular value and was damaged during the disinfection process, will be transferred to the NSV.

We enclose two death certificates, which you should carefully retain for submission to public authorities, should this be required.[6]

DOC. 86
On 7 June 1940 Valerie Scheftel from Berlin writes a yearning letter to her sweetheart Karl Wildmann in the USA[1]

Letter from Valy Scheftel,[2] Berlin, to her boyfriend Karl Wildman in the USA,[3] dated 7 June 1940

My darling, only boy!

You'll be with me in this world! This one sentence from your last letter is with me all the time, wherever I am. I hear it, see it, feel it. Whenever I do what I did on all the previous days too, when I bandage children, when I'm called to them at night, when I can't sleep afterwards and sit at the window, sick with longing. I'm always consoled by your words: You'll be with me … They comfort me and torment me at the same time, for *when will* I be with you, tell me, I beg you, darling, when? *I* have no answer to that question, and the consulate just says something about 1 to 2 years, so that is infinite, unimaginable, inconceivable, the same as 100 years for me. I must be with you in the shortest time possible, immediately, now.

The third summer without you is beginning now. And instead of going swimming with you now, boating, going to the woods and experiencing with you all the lovely things there are here, as it goes without saying, I am sitting here and tapping away at the typewriter, feeling incredibly sad and angry. And yet the summer is so marvellous, especially this year. Oh, I have quite a lot more to tell you: my mum[4] has been assigned the management of a home for the elderly in Babelsberg, near Potsdam (an hour from Berlin).[5] And

6 These death certificates are not included in the file.

1 The original is privately owned; copy in IfZ Archives, F 601. This letter has been translated from German. For further letters from Valerie Scheftel to Karl Wildmann between 1939 and 1942, see Sarah Wildman, *Paper Love. Searching for the Girl My Grandfather Left Behind* (New York: Penguin, 2014).

2 Valerie (Valy) Scheftel (b. 1911), physician; lived in Troppau in 1938; moved to Berlin in 1938 or 1939; worked as a nurse in the Jewish Hospital, as an unskilled worker, and as a teacher in the Jewish nursery school workshop; made unsuccessful efforts to emigrate to the USA; in Jan. 1943 married Hans Fabisch (1921–1943), who was deported on 29 Jan. 1943 with her from Berlin to Auschwitz, where she presumably perished, although her date of death is unknown.

3 Karl Wildmann, also Wildman (1912–1990), physician; emigrated to the USA in Sept. 1938, where he worked as a general practitioner. Valerie Scheftel and Karl Wildmann had been students together in Vienna; she wrote to him regularly from Dec. 1939.

4 Hanna T. Scheftel, née Flamm (b. 1885), known as Toni, was deported to Auschwitz on 12 March 1943 and presumably perished there.

5 The home for the elderly at 1 Bergstraße, now Spitzweggasse, in Potsdam-Babelsberg was established in 1940; it later served as an assembly camp prior to deportations and was then used by the Gestapo until 1945; the building was torn down after the war.

this home is accommodated in the villa of a former Russian diplomat. The building is in a fabulous location. At the highest point in the town, directly next to the university observatory, surrounded by an enormous, completely overgrown, jungle-like, magical garden. The building itself is built like a fortress (I am widely known here as 'the damsel'). At the very top there is a big dome, a blue room with many, many little windows, formerly a music room. And this is where I like to be best. Here I sing Solvey's Song[6] and all the songs you loved so much. I sit here for hours on end and dream of you. And then I go up to the roof or climb to the very top of the dome. From here one has an incredibly beautiful view over villas, forests, and lakes. It is quite unfathomably beautiful. And it hurts so much that I have to see all that alone and can't show it to you. I will have to bring people out here. Perhaps, if I'm not alone, I will be able to forget now and then that you're not the one who is here with me …

In purely objective terms, the transfer of the position of manager of the home to my mother has provided a wonderful solution. Although she receives only a small wage, it means that we are at least rid of the really bad, nagging, and sometimes quite drastic worries about our livelihood. And my mum has a job that is appropriate for her once again, and the value of that must not be underestimated. She has a management position again. She can organize, direct, solve a task set for her in the best way possible, and she is up to her neck in work and has absolutely no free time once again. And that is wonderful! There is a great deal of work here, but I hope she can accomplish it without excessive strain. And for her free time – brief though it is – she has the garden and balconies. I am happy beyond belief and grateful that it all came about, that is, that my mother got this position.

Unfortunately, I can't live in Babelsberg. I've had to rent a small furnished room for myself near the hospital – the first furnished room for me alone without you – but I come out here every weekend, sometimes during the week too.

Professionally, I am doing well. I have just finished running the children's ward on my own for two weeks. One doctor was on holiday, the other was ill. During this time I also lived at the hospital. Unfortunately, that is over now. At the exact time that I was covering for the other doctors, there was an exorbitant amount to be done in the ward. We had – multiplicity of cases – three empyemas,[7] two serous pleuritides,[8] two serious cases of pneumonia with premature births – besides the usual things: otitis,[9] bronchitis, glandular abscesses, eczema, etc. It was a real trial of strength! I would never have thought that I would survive it. And yet I did survive it, quite well in fact! Naturally the head of the ward came for an hour-long medical round every day. But he did not come more often or stay any longer than if the ward physician had been present. The nurses were one of my most difficult problems: nurses like these, at least in the children's ward, are a separate breed of human beings. In private they are all really nice, but on the ward it is the matron who calls the shots, first and foremost, and then, a long way down, the

6 This is a reference to 'Solveig's Song' from the stage music composed by Edvard Grieg for Henrik Ibsen's drama *Peer Gynt*.

7 Cases of accumulated pus in a body cavity.

8 Plural of pleuritis: inflammation of the pleura, the lining of the lung.

9 Ear inflammation.

other nurses, and then we, right at the bottom of the pile, might have a say too. They will perish of importance one day, these nurses!

Darling, I have already asked so often when my number[10] will come up. But I am always told in such a dilatory way that it might happen in one or two years. But you probably won't have to extend the affidavit. That is apparently not necessary now. But all that, of course, is unfortunately by no means up to date. However, I will go back to the consulate and enquire again.

Please write to me soon, and write a lot. You have no idea how indescribably happy your letters make me! Please write very soon. I would so like to know what is going on with your medical practice and what other plans you have. How is your dear mama? Please give her my very warmest regards. And Zilli and Karl[11] too. Do you get together with colleagues of ours? Is Lonka Schlüssel already in the USA? Please give her my kind regards as well!

And now goodbye – for today, and endless kisses,

Yours, Valy

Darling, I just learned from Mr Jurmann, Paula's brother-in-law, that our affidavits have to be separated, that is, one for me alone and one for my mother alone, and that this can only be applied for in the USA. These transactions often take a very, very long time, and it is better and saves more time if all these administrative matters can be undertaken right away and are already done when my turn is called. And then he thought that several good affidavits from relatives naturally improve one's chances. Could you please let me know the precise degree of kinship of the people providing my affidavits, because I don't know these relatives all that well, of course, and one is required to give precise information about the degree of kinship. And please be a dear and arrange – if necessary – for a separation of our affidavits.

Once again, lots of love!

Yours, Valy

Please forgive me, dearest, if this sheet of paper is crumpled. I was writing on the roof terrace during a strong wind – which did not do this piece of paper any good. I can't make the decision to stop writing to you. I want to at least stretch out, for as long as possible, this intense thinking about you and this being with you in my thoughts! My darling, only boy, I yearn so much to join you! – Every day brings me closer to coming there. And now another day will soon be at an end.

Perhaps it will happen some day after all?!

Kisses and good night![12]

10 The consulates issued waiting numbers for departure to the USA.

11 Celia (Zilly) Feldschuh, née Wildmann (1910–2000), the sister of Karl Wildmann, and her husband Karl.

12 The last paragraph was added in handwriting in the left margin of both sheets of writing paper.

DOC. 87

On 13 June 1940 Reinhard Heydrich makes it clear that he alone is in charge of the emigration of Jews from the territory of the Reich[1]

Letter from the Reich Security Main Office, IV D 4–2 (Rz) 1746/40, signed Heydrich, to the Reich Office for Emigration Affairs, for the attention of Ministerialrat Dr Müller,[2] Berlin NW 40, at 6 Königsplatz, dated 13 June 1940, forwarded (marked 'confidential!'), p.p. signed Müller,[3] to all Gestapo (head) offices in the territory of the Reich (marked 'excluding new Gaue in the East!'), for information to all SD (main) districts in the territory of the Reich (marked 'excluding new Gaue in the East!'), on 23 June 1940[4]

Re: work of the Reich Office for Emigration Affairs
Case file: none.
Below I call to your attention a copy of a letter of crucial importance addressed to the Reich Office for Emigration Affairs.

Re: Jewish emigration from the territory of the Reich
Case file: none
A questionnaire from the Cologne Public Advisory Centre for Emigrants, of which you are in charge, has been presented to me.[5] I gather from this document, which is primarily concerned with Jewish emigration to the USA, that a direct influence on the Jewish communities is being exerted from there.

In the interest of achieving a uniform focus with respect to the overall problem of Jewish migration in the territory of the Reich, I would like to point out that the work of the advisory centres for emigrants must take place exclusively in accordance with the guidelines laid down by the Field Marshal[6] in his directive concerning the founding of the Reich Central Agency for Jewish Emigration, dated 24 January 1939.[7] Accordingly, the Reich Office for Emigration Affairs, along with the offices within its remit, operates in the field of Jewish emigration only to the extent that it, together with the Reich Central Agency, identifies appropriate destination countries.

Pursuant to the mandate of the Field Marshal, I alone am responsible for the implementation and control of all Jewish emigration from the territory of the Reich. I there-

1 RGVA, 503k-1-385; copy in USHMM, RG-11.001M4, reel 74. This document has been translated from German.

2 Dr Adolf Müller (1886–1974), lawyer and administrative official; worked at the Bavarian Regional Statistical Office from 1914; at the Reich Statistical Office, 1919–1921, and the Reich Ministry of Food and Agriculture, 1921–1922; specialist for economic affairs for the occupied Rhineland territories in the Reich Ministry of the Interior, 1922–1933; deputy director of the Reich Office for Emigration Affairs, 1933–1944; founder of the Social People's League of Hesse-Palatinate (Sozialer Volksbund Hessen-Pfalz) after 1945.

3 Heinrich Müller.

4 The original contains annotations, the official stamp of the Gestapo, and a receipt stamp dated 24 June 1940.

5 This questionnaire could not be found.

6 Hermann Göring.

7 See PMJ 2/243.

fore request that in future you act only in the closest consultation with the State Police (head) offices, which in turn I will continue to provide with special guidelines.

The matter of Jewish emigration from the territory of the Reich is one that can by no means be managed along the lines of the former practice applied in the case of emigration by German individuals, for example to overseas destinations. Therefore, to my mind, the Emigration Law of 1898 cannot apply here either, as all the prerequisites ordained by the lawmakers at that point cannot pertain in the field of 'Jewish emigration'.[8] Instead, in each particular case my offices must reserve the right to examine undertakings on an ad hoc basis and, if necessary, assign the technical implementation of emigration to Jewish official agencies and non-Jewish private agencies, and to monitor their actions. I can view an involvement of the Reich Office for Emigration Affairs as being justified solely with respect to the business methods of such operators.

I request that your offices be instructed accordingly.

signed Heydrich.

I ask that, in future, the handling of Jewish emigration be approached in accordance with the clarification of the areas of work that has thus been provided.

DOC. 88

On 16 June 1940 an anonymous writer describes the living conditions of Jews in Munich and Berlin[1]

Letter from F., dated 18 June 1940 (copy)[2]

My dears,

... On 7 May I left Munich, spent one more day with G. and went with her to visit her friends and Aryan relatives, whom she frequently sees. Of all of us, she still has the best place to live, always had enough to eat, and even used to send quite a bit to us in Berlin. We also got by there, of course, but shopping even for the most basic vegetables was a daily struggle, which became even more difficult for the Jews because, during recent months, they were not permitted to enter grocers' shops and even a large percentage of the other shops until after midday.[3] A large number of retailers and market vendors did set goods aside for their old Jewish clientele, and there were indeed lots of

8 Correctly: Reich Law on Emigration (*Reichsgesetz über das Auswanderungswesen*), 9 June 1897. This law, the first uniform one throughout Imperial Germany, focused on the centralized control of emigration from German territory. However, the law was also supposed to achieve the 'preservation of Germandom among the emigrants and [the] utilization of emigration for the interests of the motherland': *Reichsgesetzblatt*, 1897, pp. 463–472. See also Paul Goetsch, *Das Reichsgesetz über das Auswanderungswesen vom 9. Juni 1897* (Hamburg: Lütcke/Wulff, 1898), p. 207.

1 Wiener Library, Doc 1656/3/1/620. This letter has been translated from German. Dr Alfred Wiener founded the Jewish Central Information Office in Amsterdam in 1933. After his emigration to Britain in the spring of 1939, it was reopened in London on 1 Sept. 1939 and soon thereafter renamed the Wiener Library. Wiener and his associates gathered accounts written by refugees from Germany to inform British government offices about the persecution of the Jews.

2 Ellipses as in the original.

3 On restricted shopping hours, see Doc. 36, fn. 7.

touching scenes in general, as the traders were in the main quite embittered, but nonetheless still suffered these circumstances.

In Munich there was far more for sale and without having to queue up for hours, but here the Jews were forced to buy their groceries in a limited number of shops, which were specially selected for this purpose, and they were expelled from their homes or restricted to separate rooms, along with other types of harassment.[4] In addition, in all the smaller and medium-sized towns, all assets were confiscated and only a little money to live on was released. In Berlin this was not as comprehensive, though it did affect most of the well-to-do.

I fear that the food supplies of city dwellers were even more depleted during the last offensive, as everything available went to the front, where all the soldiers were well fed. Well, it will still be bearable, especially as the invasion of France will likely have created new reserves for the military and the civilian population, and now that France has succumbed, there is no need to establish additional food reserves. In fact, there was virtually nothing left to buy anywhere. No shop could keep going unless it had reserve supplies. Industry has been completely transformed to meet wartime or combat needs, and it will take months for private industry to get going again, particularly if England does not yield. Just as I was leaving, the Jews were asked to report to the employment office: men up to the age of 55, women up to 50.[5] Many welcomed this, as they no longer had anything to live on, but many had been working even before, in factories and road construction, shovelling snow in winter, etc. Now, unfortunately, the fear is that all Jews will be thrown out of all the enterprises again, to make room for the droves that are returning. It would be even more dreadful if, at the same time, a general evacuation into Polish areas were to begin. The levels of misery which the Jews from Stettin were plunged into at that time is ghastly.[6] In the meantime, in mid May, the Jews from eastern Upper Silesia were also taken to the vicinity of Cracow or some other place.[7] These resettlements continually loomed over us and were probably always cancelled only because there was still a desire to keep using the Jews for labour. Perhaps better arrangements have been made for this resettlement by now, so that constructive development is possible in the new territories. But even old and sick people have been sent away thus far, irrespective of their circumstances. E. particularly feared this, because in Breslau they were harassed even more severely and were summoned to the Gestapo to be pressed into emigration …

G., in Munich, who is almost on an equal footing with the Aryans as a result of her earlier mixed marriage, and even received a clothing ration card, while the other Jews were suffering an acute shortage, and did not even get thread and darning needles (only a small amount and only just recently),[8] will probably not be taken either if there is an evacuation …

4 See also Docs. 15 and 26.

5 The order was published in the *Jüdisches Nachrichtenblatt* (Berlin edition), no. 41, 21 May 1940, p. 2.

6 On the deportations from Stettin to the Lublin district in Feb. 1940, see Doc. 52 and Introduction, p. 40.

7 At the end of April 1940 the Gestapo in Kattowitz had given instructions for the Jewish population to be expelled from eastern Upper Silesia: see PMJ 4/112.

8 See also Doc. 36, fn. 4.

Before I start reporting on what is going on here, I will add the following: in better German circles, people have been saying: for better or worse, we just have to win the war that has been brought upon us, but afterwards the Hitler system will have to go. …

With warm regards to everyone,

Yours, F.

DOC. 89

On 24 June 1940 Reinhard Heydrich urges the Reich Minister of Foreign Affairs, Joachim von Ribbentrop, to consider a 'territorial final solution'[1]

Letter from the Chief of the Reich Police and the SD (IV D 4–1574/40), signed Heydrich, to the Reich Minister of Foreign Affairs, SS-Gruppenführer Joachim von Ribbentrop,[2] dated 24 June 1940 (copy Pol. XII 136)

Dear Party Comrade von Ribbentrop,

The Field Marshal,[3] in his capacity as Plenipotentiary for the Four-Year Plan, tasked me in January 1939 with implementing Jewish emigration from the entire territory of the Reich.[4] Despite major difficulties in the period that followed, it was possible to proceed successfully with Jewish emigration, even during the war. Since my office assumed responsibility for this task on 1 January 1939, more than 200,000 Jews in total have thus far emigrated from the territory of the Reich. *However, the problem as a whole* – this already involves around 3¼ million Jews in the territories *presently* under German jurisdiction – can no longer be solved *by emigration*. A territorial final solution has thus become necessary.

I request that I be involved in any discussions on the final solution to the Jewish question that you may be planning to hold in the near future.

Heil Hitler!

DOC. 90

New York Times, 25 June 1940: interview with Nahum Goldmann from the World Jewish Congress in which he warns of the extermination of 6 million European Jews[1]

Nazi Publicity Here Held Smoke Screen. Propaganda Called Cover to Destroy Democracy

The Nazi regime's attempts to conquer America by propaganda and anti-Semitism are only the smoke screen for its ultimate aims to destroy democratic institutions, it was

1 PA AA, R 100 857, fol. 192. This letter has been translated from German.
2 Joachim von Ribbentrop (1893–1946), businessman; joined the NSDAP in 1932 and the SS in 1933; Hitler's foreign policy advisor (Bureau Ribbentrop) from 1934; ambassador to London, 1936–1938; Reich minister of foreign affairs from 1938; was arrested in 1945, sentenced to death at the International Military Tribunal at Nuremberg, and executed.
3 Hermann Göring.
4 See PMJ 2/243.

1 *New York Times*, 25 June 1940, p. 4. The daily newspaper the *New York Times* has appeared since 1851.

said yesterday by Dr. Nahum Goldmann,[2] chairman of the administrative committee of the World Jewish Congress, who arrived here last Friday from Switzerland.

'Six million Jews in Europe are doomed to destruction,' Dr. Goldmann said in an interview at the Hotel Astor, 'if the victory of the Nazis should be final. The only hope for them lies in a British victory.'

He called upon American Jews to follow the example of the American people and urged them to create a united defense. He announced the formation of a Pan-American Jewish Congress for the protection of Jewish rights and said that this body, with the participation of Latin-American delegations, would soon hold its first session in this country.[3]

'The chances for mass emigration and resettlement of European Jewry seem to be remote, and European Jews face the danger of physical annihilation,' he said. 'Even the 4,000,000 Jews under Soviet rule, although free today from racial discrimination, are not safe in the event of a final Nazi victory.'

Dr. Goldmann said that the principal offices of the World Jewish Congress will be established in the United States, supplementing already existing offices in London and Geneva, in addition to a newly organized bureau in Buenos Aires. The Paris offices of the organization were closed the day the Nazis occupied Paris, he said.

DOC. 91

On 3 July 1940 Adolf Eichmann asks Jewish officials from Berlin, Prague, and Vienna to prepare a position paper on the emigration of all Jews from Europe[1]

File note no. 44 regarding a consultation in the Reich Security Main Office involving Jakob Edelstein,[2] Prague, Dr Franz Weidmann,[3] Prague, Dr Josef Löwenherz, Vienna, and Dr Paul Eppstein, Berlin, on 3 July 1940, 3:30 p.m.

I. With Hauptsturmführer Eichmann

1. *Activity reports*

At Hauptsturmführer Eichmann's request, activities in the fields of emigration, organization, and finances were reported on.

Within the next four weeks Dr *Löwenherz* is to present statistics on the Jews living in the Ostmark to the Central Office for Jewish Emigration in Vienna, organized according to the occupations they last pursued before the radical transition in 1938,[4] in addition to

2 Dr Nahum Goldmann (1895–1982), lawyer; editor of the *Encyclopaedia Judaica*; board member of the Zionist Federation for Germany, 1926–1933; emigrated to Switzerland, 1933; representative of the Jewish Agency for Palestine at the League of Nations, 1934–1940; founding member and then chairman of the executive committee of the World Jewish Congress, 1936; president of the World Jewish Congress, 1951–1977, and of the World Zionist Organization, 1956–1968.

3 The first pan-American conference of the World Jewish Congress took place in Nov. 1941 in Baltimore. The demands issued at the conference included aid and compensation payments for victims of National Socialism, the recovery of equal rights for Jews, and that Jews participate in a possible peace conference: *New York Times*, 25 Nov. 1941, p. 6, and 26 Nov. 1941, p. 9.

1 Copy in IfZ-Archives, Eichmann-Prozess, T-1143. This document has been translated from German.

a list of names of Jews with foreign nationality who are still in the Ostmark, not including those who are stateless. Dr Löwenherz was further ordered to dismiss an additional 100 employees of the Israelite Religious Community of Vienna within the next four weeks.

Following a report by Dr Löwenherz on the sale of the property on Müllnergasse, Vienna IX, which is due to be sold to a private individual for RM 40,000, although a different buyer is now offering RM 60,000, Hauptsturmführer Eichmann ordered that a report on this matter be presented to the Central Office for Jewish Emigration in Vienna, along with a request that the case be resubmitted to him for review.[5] Hauptsturmführer Eichmann also stated that no further sales of the properties owned by the Israelite Religious Community of Vienna and the General Endowment will take place on his instructions. The management of these properties and of the securities will be in the hands of the Israelite Religious Community of Vienna as trustee under the control of the Central Office for Jewish Emigration [...].[6] The sums already paid into a special account from the security of the purchase price for the sold-off properties in the countryside and in Vienna, as well as the purchase-price sums that are still being paid in, will be paid out by special intervention to the Religious Community for emigration and welfare purposes, following calculation and payment of the development fee. These sums can be made available to the Religious Community only after the authorization of Hauptsturmführer Eichmann has been obtained. With respect to the finances of the Religious Community, Dr Löwenherz has been summoned to meet with Hauptsturmführer Eichmann on 4 July at 11 a.m.

2. *Special transports to Palestine.*
A report on the feasibility of special transports to Palestine is to be made tomorrow after consultation with Mr Berthold Israel *Storfer*,[7] who is scheduled to arrive in Berlin this evening.

2 Dr Jakob Edelstein (1903–1944), lawyer and Zionist official; worked in the headquarters of Hehalutz from 1929; head of the Palestine Office in Prague from 1933; leading representative of the Czech Jews to the German administration and responsible for emigration issues; on 4 Dec. 1941 deported to Theresienstadt, where he was Jewish elder from 1941 to Jan. 1943; deported in Dec. 1943 to Auschwitz, where he was shot dead on 20 June 1944, along with his wife and son.

3 Franz, also František, Weidmann (1910–1944); head of the Kapper student association; headed the Jewish Religious Community of Prague after the emigration of his predecessor Emil Kafka in 1939; deported to Theresienstadt on 28 Jan. 1943; member of the Council of Elders there; deported on 28 Oct. 1944 to Auschwitz, where he was murdered.

4 The reference is to the Anschluss of Austria by Nazi Germany.

5 The property at 21 Müllnergasse was owned until 1939 by the Israelite Prayer House Association Chevra Beth Hatfila. After the association was disbanded, the property was transferred to the Israelite Religious Community of Vienna. On 23 Sept. 1940 it was sold to the baker Alois Stefan. In Dec. 1947 it was returned to the Israelite Religious Community of Vienna by decision of the Restitution Commission.

6 A word is illegible.

7 Berthold Storfer (1880–1944), businessman; awarded the title of Kommerzialrat ('commercial counsellor', honorary title bestowed upon businessmen and philanthropists) in 1928; co-owner of several enterprises until 1938; delegate of the Viennese Jews at the Evian Conference in 1938; as head of the committee he set up for Jewish overseas transports, he organized the illegal immigration of Jews into Palestine; in the summer of 1943 he was deported to Auschwitz, where he was shot dead in Nov. 1944.

3. *Persons in protective custody*
It was urgently requested that petitions for release of persons being held in protective custody in a concentration camp be allowed. Hauptsturmführer Eichmann stated that this is not possible at the moment. For the time being, the same applies to the additional request that young persons in protective custody be released.[8]

4. *Emigration question*
Hauptsturmführer Eichmann, after receiving the reports on the current state of emigration, stated that efforts to arrange emigration via the Far East and also via Lisbon are to be continued.

After the end of the war, however, an overall solution to the European Jewish question will probably have to be sought. This would affect around 4 million Jews in the European countries concerned. Individual emigration will not be sufficient for the settlement of these Jews, even though individual emigration will still be allowed in special cases. Hauptsturmführer Eichmann asked whether considerations or plans in this regard have already been discussed. This question was answered in the negative. Hauptsturmführer Eichmann ordered a short memorandum to be prepared, summarizing the general viewpoints that would have to be taken into account with such a scheme.[9]

It was pointed out that such a plan is feasible only with regard to a specific area for settlement; with guaranteed funding, especially through public funds, for both emigration and settlement; and with an organized settlement procedure. Hauptsturmführer Eichmann stated that at the moment it should only be a case of setting up guidelines that would make it possible to execute such an emigration scheme without any friction for either party and without any hardships within a period of approximately three to four years.

The significance of Palestine was addressed in this context. It was pointed out that Palestine, with not[10] approximately 500,000 Jews, is probably the most important starting point for the admission and settlement of sizeable numbers of Jews, and that the cooperation of Jewish aid organizations would probably be most readily obtainable for a large settlement scheme in Palestine. Hauptsturmführer Eichmann stated that there are as yet no definite plans regarding the settlement area and the form of settlement. The point of the position paper is solely to express a few pivotal ideas for such a plan. The position paper is to be submitted by the afternoon of 4 July.

II. *With Obersturmführer Dannecker*

5. *Emigration question*
Obersturmführer Dannecker[11] offered a number of comments on the requested memorandum. The difficulties of presenting such a plan within the short period of time were expanded upon. Obersturmführer Dannecker observed that the memorandum should merely be seen as an initial statement regarding the overall problem. This document, he

8 See Doc. 67.

9 Josef Löwenherz evidently submitted the requested report one day later: *Vollständiger Bericht von Dr. Löwenherz*, p. 27.

10 Use of the negative as in the original.

said, may very well take the example of one country as a starting point, even if a concrete region is not yet certain.

In this context, the discussion about Palestine as an area of settlement was resumed. (Obersturmführer Dannecker commented on the question to the effect that Palestine does not have sufficient capacity and that the Arabs may also prove difficult. The response to this was that Palestine at its present size should have capacity for around 3 million Jews, and with the addition of Transjordan could even solve the existing overall problem.)

6. *Passports for subjects of the Protectorate*
It is requested that passports without a J and without the additional given name be issued to Protectorate subjects in Prague. Obersturmführer Dannecker confirmed that a corresponding instruction will be issued to the Central Office for Jewish Emigration in Prague, as pursuant to the legal provisions there are no objections to the issuance of such passports.

7. *Assistance for Jews in the Protectorate who are not of the Mosaic faith*
In reply to an enquiry, Obersturmführer Dannecker stated that support by the Pastor Grüber Office for the work of the Jewish Religious Community of Prague's department for Jews not of the Mosaic faith can be effected only through the Central Offices for Jewish Emigration in Berlin and Prague.

8. *Passage to the Far East*
(a) Obersturmführer Dannecker noted that, with respect to the distribution of passages obtained by the Reich Association of Jews in Germany into the Old Reich, Ostmark, and Protectorate at a proportion of 47:37:16, there is complete agreement among the persons involved.[12]
(b) Obersturmführer Dannecker agreed to allow an employee of the Jewish Community of Prague to come to Berlin approximately once every two weeks for discussion of all relevant questions with the Reich Association. A report on this must be submitted on each occasion to the Central Office for Jewish Emigration in Prague.
(c) Applications for issuance of letters of recommendation by the Reich Foreign Office for Jews from the Ostmark should be submitted directly to the Central Office for Jewish Emigration in Berlin by the employee of the Israelite Religious Community of Vienna who is based in Berlin. The Israelite Community of Vienna shall inform the Central Office for Jewish Emigration in Vienna about these submitted applications.
(d) The Emigration Department of the Reich Association submits applications filed by Jews in the Protectorate for letters of recommendation from the Reich Foreign Office.

11 Theodor Dannecker (1913–1945), businessman; joined the NSDAP and the SS in 1932; worked at the SD from 1936; responsible for the 'Jewish question' in SD Section II 112 and Section IV B 4 of the Reich Security Main Office (RSHA) from 1937; 'advisor for Jewish affairs' with the Senior Commander of the Security Police and SD (BdS) in occupied France from Sept. 1940; organized the deportation of the French Jews in 1942, the deportations from Bulgaria in 1943, and the deportations from Italy and Hungary in 1944; taken prisoner by US troops in 1945, and committed suicide.
12 See Doc. 178.

9. Brochure about American immigration laws
It was reported that Dr Julius L. Israel *Seligsohn*[13] has prepared a brochure on American immigration laws, that the Ministry of Propaganda has agreed in principle to the publication of this brochure by the publishing division of the Jewish Culture League, and that the copy-editing of the brochure is being assigned to the Central Office for Jewish Emigration in Berlin. The Ministry of Propaganda will therefore forward the brochure during the next few days to the Central Office for examination.[14]

DOC. 92
On 3 July 1940 Franz Rademacher makes proposals at the Reich Foreign Office for settling all the European Jews on the island of Madagascar[1]

Notes by Legation Counsellor Franz Rademacher,[2] Reich Foreign Office (D III 200), dated 3 July 1940

The Jewish question in the peace treaty
The imminent victory gives Germany the opportunity and in my view also the duty to find a solution to the Jewish question in Europe. The desirable solution is for all Jews to be out of Europe. In this regard, it is the task of the Reich Foreign Office:
(a) to anchor this demand in the peace treaty and to assert the same demand through separate negotiations with the countries in Europe that are not affected by the peace treaty;
(b) to guarantee, in the peace treaty, the necessary territory for settlement of the Jews and to define the principles for cooperation by the enemy nations in resolving this problem;
(c) to specify the constitutional position of the new Jewish overseas settlement area;
(d) as groundwork:
  (1) clarification of the wishes and plans of the concerned domestic German [Nazi] Party, state, and academic bodies and tailoring of these plans to the wishes of the Reich Minister of Foreign Affairs, further including:
  (2) creation of an overview of the documentation available from the individual bodies (number of Jews in the individual countries), liquidation of their assets through an international bank;

13 Dr Julius Ludwig Seligsohn (1890–1942), lawyer; board member of the Jewish Community of Berlin from 1924; lawyer in Berlin until 1933; member of the executive committee of the Reich Representation of German Jews and member of the executive committee of the Relief Association of German Jews from 1933; board member of the Reich Association of Jews in Germany after its establishment in 1939; arrested in Nov. 1940 after calling for a memorial day for Jews deported from Baden and the Palatinate; deported on 18 March 1941 to Sachsenhausen, where he perished on 28 Feb. 1942.
14 Dr Julius L. Israel Seligsohn, *Die Einwanderung nach U.S.A.* (Berlin: Jüdischer Kulturbund in Deutschland e.V., 1940).

1 PA AA, R 100 857, fols. 230–231. Published in *Akten zur Deutschen Auswärtigen Politik 1918–1945*, series D: *1937–1945*, vol. 10 (Göttingen: Vandenhoeck & Ruprecht, 1963), pp. 92–94. This document has been translated from German.
2 Franz Rademacher (1906–1973), lawyer; member of the SA, 1932–1934; joined the NSDAP in 1933; in the diplomatic service from 1937; between 1938 and 1940 in Uruguay; legation counsellor, 1940;

(3) initiation of negotiations with our friend Italy regarding these questions.

Concerning the initiation of the groundwork, Section D III, through the Department for Germany, has already approached the Reich Minister of Foreign Affairs[3] to offer proposals and has been tasked by him with setting this groundwork in motion without delay. Discussions with the Office of the Reichsführer SS, the Ministry of the Interior, and several Party offices have already taken place. These offices endorse the following plan put forward by Section D III:

Section D III suggests, as a solution to the Jewish question: in the peace treaty, France must make the island of Madagascar available for the solution of the Jewish question and must relocate and compensate the approximately 25,000 French residents there. The island will be assigned to Germany as mandated territory. Diégo Suarez Bay, which is important in terms of naval strategy, and the port of Antsiranana will become German naval bases (it may be possible to expand these naval bases, depending on the German navy's wishes, also to the ports – open roadsteads – of Tamatave, Andevorante, Mananjara, etc.). Besides these naval bases, suitable parts of the country will be taken away from the Jewish territory for installation of air bases. The part of the island not needed for military purposes will be placed under the administration of a German police governor who is accountable to the administration of the Reichsführer SS. In other respects the Jews obtain self-governance within this territory: their own mayors, their own police, their own postal and railway administration, etc. The Jews, as joint debtors, will be held responsible for the value of the island. To this end, all their previous European assets will be transferred to a European bank, which is to be established, for liquidation. If these assets are not sufficient to pay for the land values that the Jews get hold of and for the purchase of goods in Europe that are needed for development of the island, the same bank will make loans available to the Jews.

As Madagascar will be only a mandate territory, the Jews residing there will not acquire German nationality. All Jews deported to Madagascar will, however, from the time of their deportation, be stripped by the individual European countries of their nationality in these countries. Instead, they will be subjects of the Madagascar Mandate.

This arrangement prevents the Jews from founding something like a Vatican State of their own in Palestine and thus being able to harness for their own purposes the symbolic value that Jerusalem possesses for the Christian and Mohammedan parts of the world. In addition, the Jews remain in German hands as collateral for future good conduct by members of their race in America.

One can utilize as propaganda the magnanimity that Germany displays towards the Jews by granting them cultural, economic, administrative, and judicial self-governance, and in so doing can emphasize that our German sense of responsibility to the world prohibits us from immediately bestowing an independent state upon a race that has not possessed statehood for thousands of years. A period of historical probation is required before that can happen.

headed the section for Jewish affairs (D III) in the Reich Foreign Office, 1940–1943; became a naval officer in April 1943; sentenced to three and a half years in prison by Nuremberg Regional Court in March 1952; temporarily released in July and fled to Syria; returned in 1966.

3 Joachim von Ribbentrop.

DOC. 93

Report by a German Jewish woman to a London immigrant organization regarding the situation of Frankfurt am Main's Jewish population up to 11 July 1940[1]

Report by an anonymous author, undated

Report on Frankfurt-on-Main in July 1940

The following report originates from a young lady about 20 years old, recently arrived in this country. She left Frankfurt on July 11, 1940, and travelled via Siberia and Japan to the United States. It is to be noted that the young lady left Frankfurt before the intensive British air raids began.

1. Food situation: The food supply was sufficient for non-Jews as well as Jews. Prices were well regulated and not above the pre-war standard except for such things which were not rationed. For instance the price for a simple silk dress was between $30.00 and $50.00 (pre-war price $4.00–$10.00); the average income of a German middle-class citizen is $80.00–$100.00 per month. The shortage of certain kinds of food and materials such as fat, coffee, clothes etc. is well known and need not to be repeated here.

2. Spirit of the population: No remarkable opposition was noticeable within the population. Not even the German victories in Poland, Belgium, the Netherlands and especially in France could stir the German hearts. This is particularly interesting if one recalls how such victories were celebrated between 1914–1918. It seemed as if everybody would be happy if this war would soon end. This feeling may have increased in the meantime, since the amazing resistance of Great Britain could not be foreseen in July 1940.

3. Air-Raids: in Frankfurt. Air raid alarms could be heard every night. Everybody – except for the old and sick – was forced by law to go to the shelters.[2] The visible damage was very slight. At one time a tremendous fire broke out in the administration building of the I.G. Farben Werke (Chemical Dye Trust) but was quickly extinguished. Fire started in the Osthafen region where large oil storages were situated. At that time daylight air raids did not occur. Some damage was done to the E. Merck Chemical Factory at the outskirts of Darmstadt.

Air raids: in Hamburg. The situation in Hamburg was different from that in Frankfurt. Air raid alarms sounded day and night. Many people spoke about the damage inflicted upon ship yards, oil storages, etc. The shelters in Hamburg were particularly large and comfortable. Air conditioning, gas proof doors, ventilation systems, comfort stations and many emergency exits were built in. Jews, in Frankfurt too, were permitted to go to the public shelters which bore no signs prohibiting them from entering. In apartment houses, however, there were generally cellars for Jews. If a building did not possess two shelters, Jews had to go to a Jewish shelter in the neighbourhood.

1 Wiener Library, Doc 1656/3/1/617; copy in YVA, O.2/423. The original document is in English. On the reports from the Wiener Library, see Doc. 88, fn. 1.

2 Instructions on conduct during an air-raid warning were given in § 2 of the Tenth Implementing Regulation to the Air-Raid Protection Law: *Reichsgesetzblatt*, 1939, I, pp. 1570–1572.

4. *Situation of the Jews in Frankfurt*: The Jews lived in their houses absolutely separated from the other population, without telephone, without radio, without public baths, without any possibility of visiting cafeterias, restaurants, theatres, movie houses, public parks etc. This situation could almost be compared with a typical ghetto. The Jews left their apartments only when absolutely necessary. They had to stay at home from 7 p.m. in the winter and 8 p.m. in the summer until dawn. Not more than eight Jews were allowed to gather without special permission, which was only granted for religious purposes or community work.[3] Furthermore no Jew was allowed to stay in the apartment of another Jew during the night. Punishment was severe for breaking of regulations.

For example, a Jew entered the front garden of his home three minutes past 8 o'clock, and in front of his housedoor he met a Gestapo (Secret Police) man who, because of the blackout, was not visible to him. He was imprisoned for four weeks for this offence. This was the usual penalty for such a 'crime'.

A certain measure was carried out concerning libraries in Jewish households. Beginning June 1940, the Jews were forced to make lists of all their books. It was announced that nobody who listed so-called forbidden books was to receive punishment, but was threatened with punishment if such books were found later on. The Gestapo (Secret Police), however, confiscated numerous books found in many homes.[4]

In the spring of 1940, all male Jews between the ages of 18 and 40 were compelled to do forced labour. Most of them were without a job at the time. They had to work very hard, although they were not used to such labour. In most cases they were treated decently and received additional food cards.[5]

Some Jews were still members of the hospitalization insurances (Krankenkassen). They were allowed to consult only Aryan physicians. Because of the shortage of physicians this regulation was changed and they could then consult the few Jewish doctors who were still practising. The Jews could buy bread and meat at certain hours only and in certain stores where they were registered. Of course, they could only buy such things that were left over by the Aryans. Chain grocery stores often set aside one store for Jewish customers. Other stores, such as candy stores, 5 and 10 stores,[6] stationery and others used to ask whether the customer was Aryan or Jewish; they did not sell to Jews. Clothes could not be bought since Jews did not receive ration cards. If they needed clothes they had to go to the Jewish community who examined the application and sold or gave them the required article. The Jewish community obtained such clothes from those Jews who had left Germany and to whom the Gestapo (Secret Police) permitted only a few belongings to take away. These people could themselves not decide to whom the clothes to give but were forced to give them to the Jewish community without pay. Those who left via Siberia were permitted 50 kilos as freight and 20 kilos as hand luggage.

3 This meant that the holding of every Jewish religious service required special permission, as otherwise the minyan – a quorum of ten male adults required by Jewish law to conduct a communal religious service – could not be achieved.

4 These measures were linked to the creation of a central Jewish library and a Jewish archive by the Security Service under the direction of Dr Franz Alfred Six (1909–1975), the head of Office II, Research on Adversaries, in the Reich Security Main Office. By early 1939 the library already contained almost 200,000 volumes, and during the war whole libraries arrived from the occupied countries.

5 On the expansion of forced labour in spring 1940, see Doc. 5, fn. 3.

6 Stores offering a wide assortment of inexpensive items for personal and household use.

DOC. 94
On 17 July 1940 the statistician Friedrich Burgdörfer calculates how many Jews could be deported to Madagascar[1]

Expert opinion of the Director of the Bavarian Regional Statistical Office, Munich, signed Dr Burgdörfer,[2] dated 17 July 1940 (copy)[3]

On the question of resettling the Jews
Any attempt to assemble information about the total number of Jews currently living in the various parts of the world will understandably encounter substantial difficulties.[4] Statistical surveys concerning the number of Jews in terms of blood have thus far been conducted only in Germany (1939).[5] Otherwise one must rely on information about religious affiliation, i.e. on identification of the Jews by faith, which generally detects only a part of the Jews by race – even though this is by far the greatest part, as the German census of 1939 has shown. In a number of countries, however, such as France, England, the United States of America, etc., religious affiliation is not among the types of information sought in the population censuses. In those cases one has to rely on surveys, estimates, or calculations provided by Jews or non-Jews, some of which refer to the Jews by race, while others limit themselves to counting the Jews by faith, and, besides, are more or less unreliable.

In 1939 the Reich Statistical Office attempted to obtain an overall picture of Jewry by gathering and critically inspecting the available materials. The numbers were published in issue 12 of *Wirtschaft und Statistik* (1938)[6] and then evaluated by me in the aforementioned paper. These numbers are reproduced in column 1 of the following table and, wherever possible, have been converted to take into account the present territorial status. Column 2 contains the numbers that P.H. Seraphim has presented in a recently published paper based on a calculation published by a Jewish party.[7] In column 3 I have attempted – by taking into account the political events and migration movement during the past years and by evaluating the latest results of statistical surveys or partial surveys –

1 PA AA, R 99 335. This document has been translated from German.
2 Dr Friedrich Burgdörfer (1890–1967), statistician; department head in the Reich Statistical Office, 1925–1939, responsible for the specific recording of Jews in the censuses of 1933 and 1939; director of the Bavarian Regional Statistical Office, 1939–1945; made an honorary member of the German Statistical Society in 1960; author of works including *Volks- und Wehrkraft, Krieg und Rasse* (1936).
3 The original contains handwritten notes and marking.
4 The original contains the note: 'Cf. F. Burgdörfer, Die Juden in Deutschland und in der Welt, *Forschungen zur Judenfrage* (The Jews in Germany and in the World, *Research on the Jewish Question*), vol. 3, published by the Reich Institute for History of the New Germany.' The volume was published in Hamburg in 1938. Burgdörfer's article, subtitled 'Ein statistischer Beitrag zur biologischen, beruflichen und sozialen Struktur des Judentums in Deutschland' ('A Statistical Contribution to the Biological, Occupational, and Social Structure of Jewry in Germany'), can be found on pp. 152–198.
5 This refers to the population census of 1939: see PMJ 2/36.
6 The article 'Die Zahl der Juden auf der Erde um das Jahr 1937' ('The Number of Jews on Earth c.1937') appeared on 5 July 1938 in *Wirtschaft und Statistik*, the journal published by the Reich Statistical Office, pp. 500–502.
7 Note in the original: 'P. H. Seraphim, Die Wanderungsbewegung des jüdischen Volkes, *Schriften zur Geopolitik* (The Migration Movement of the Jewish People, *Writings on Geopolitics*), no. 18, Heidelberg 1940.'

to estimate the *current number of Jews* in the individual countries, based on the present territorial status.

The Jews in the world

Countries *of Europe*	Publication of Reich Stat. Office, *W. u. St.*[8] 1938, no. 12 1	Seraphim, Migration of the Jewish People 2	New estimate based on current territorial status (1940) 3	Remarks on column 3
German Reich:				
Old Reich	420,000	500,000	233,973	Census of 17 May 1939 (*W. u. St.* 1940, no. 5/6, p. 84)
Austria	200,000	191,000	94,270	
Sudeten territory	*[9]		2,649	
Protectorate rein-	*	118,000[10]	87,000	
corporated eastern territories	*	632,000[11]	600,000	
Memel and Danzig	13,000			
Gen. Gov. Poland		1,269,000	1,200,000	
Total, current Reich territory	*	2,710,000	2,217,892	
Belgium	80,000	50,000	70,000	
Brit. Empire (Europ. parts)		345,000	397,000	400,000
Bulgaria	50,000	50,000	50,000	
France	280,000	200,000	250,000	
Greece	90,000	75,000	90,000	
Italy	52,000	48,000	50,000	
Yugoslavia	75,000	68,400	75,000	
Lithuania	175,000	250,000	250,000	1940 incl. Vilnius area
Latvia	96,000	100,000	100,000	
Netherlands	135,000	112,000	120,000	
Poland	3,300,000	*	*	See Germany, Russia, and Lithuania
Romania	1,050,000	829,000	700,000	1940 not incl. Bessarabia and Bukovina

8 *Wirtschaft und Statistik.*
9 This may mean that no numbers are given in the publication concerned.
10 The information includes 'Sudeten territory' and 'Protectorate'.
11 This information and the information in the line that follows include, respectively, the annexed territory of western Poland, described as 'reincorporated eastern territories', and 'Memel and Danzig'.

Switzerland	*	18,000	20,000	
Slovakia	*	137,000	170,000	
Soviet Russia (Europ.)	2,950,000	2,860,000	2,900,000	
plus Russ. area of interest in Poland	*	1,214,000	1,300,000	
Bessarabia and Bukovina	*	*	350,000	
Spain	*	12,000	12,000	
Czechoslovakia	385,000	*	*	1940 see German Reich, Slovakia, and Hungary
Turkey (Europ. part)	60,000	80,000	70,000	
Hungary	450,000	547,000	550,000	
Other countries	64,000	37,600	50,000	

Continents	Publication of Reich Stat. Office, *W u. St.* 1938, no. 12 1	Seraphim, Migration Movement of the Jewish People 2	New estimate based on current territorial status (1940) 3	Remarks on column 3
Europe[12]	10,270,000	10,000,000	9,800,000	
Asia	939,000	900,000	1,000,000	
Africa	666,000	475,000	700,000	
America	5,110,000	4,600,000	5,250,000	
Australia	30,000	30,000	30,000	
	17,015,000	15,975,000	16,880,000[13]	

The most significant changes in comparison with earlier compilations emerge for the German Reich, and indeed these changes can be demonstrated with great certainty owing to the survey of descent that was carried out as part the population census of 17 May 1939. According to this census, which recorded not only the Jews by faith but also all the Jews by race, in the Old Reich the number of around 500,000 Jews (by faith) in 1933 has decreased to 234,000 Jews (by race), and in the Ostmark it has decreased from around 200,000 Jews (by faith) to 94,000 Jews (by race). It has presumably dropped still further since then as a result of additional emigration (at least up to the outbreak of war). Yet it seemed advisable to me to use these effective findings of 17 May 1939 as a basis for the calculation. If one also adds in the Sudeten territory with 2,600 Jews, the Protectorate of Bohemia and Moravia with an estimated total of 87,000 Jews and the reincorporated eastern territories, including Memel and Danzig, with an estimated total of 600,000 Jews, the total number of Jews within the Greater German Reich would amount to around 1 million. In this case, the numbers given for the Protectorate of Bohemia and Moravia

12 The numerical values given in this line are not based on the exact sum of the figures above, but rather have obviously been roughly rounded up or down on the basis of those figures.

13 Correctly: 16,780,000.

and the Eastern territories roughly equate to the numbers residing in the areas concerned before the present war. I am unable to judge the extent to which these numbers have decreased in the meantime as a result of the military and political events in the regions concerned. The same is true for the Jews in the General Government in Poland, whose number is estimated at 1.2 million. If one includes them, 2.2 million Jews would be incorporated within the Greater German Reich up to the eastern boundary of Germany's sphere of interests. In Europe as a whole, the number of Jews is estimated at around 10 million. These are divided between:

Soviet Russia	2,900,000
The Russian sphere of interest in former Poland	1,300,000
Bessarabia and Bukovina	350,000
In total:	4,550,000

All told, that would amount to around 4½ million Jews within Russian territory, whose number increases to 4.9 million, that is, close to 5 million, if one adds in the Baltic states (Lithuania with 250,000, Latvia with 100,000 Jews). If the Jews in this territory were not to be considered for resettlement, there would still remain around 5 (more precisely, 4.9) million Jews from the rest of Europe who would be under consideration for resettlement. As for the Jews outside Europe, their number can be estimated at 7 million in total, of whom around 5¼ million are in America (4.6 million of them in the United States), and they can probably not be considered for resettlement to Madagascar either. Accordingly, there would still remain around 1¾ million non-European Jews, who are distributed approximately as follows:

Asia:	1,000,000	Jews
of which Palestine	430,000	»
Iraq	120,000	»
Iran	60,000	»
Soviet Russia, Asian part	130,000	»
Turkey	30,000	»
Africa:	700,000	»
of which Egypt	70,000	»
French possessions	350,000	»
Italian possessions	125,000	»
Union of South Africa	150,000	»
Australia:	30,000	»

I am unable to judge the extent to which these 1¾ million non-European Jews can be considered for resettlement. If they all come into question (again with the likely exception of the Soviet Union), the following overall picture emerges:

(1) Jews from Europe (excluding the territory of Soviet Russia)	4.9 million
(2) Jews from the remaining continents, excluding America and the Soviet Russian part of Asia	1.6 million
Total:	6.5 million

Accordingly, around 6½ million Jews can be considered for resettlement.

Madagascar, according to the last census (1 July 1936) had 3.8 million inhabitants, that is – given a total area of 616,000 square kilometres – 6.2 per square kilometre. According to the figures, the number of Jews in line for resettlement would be only 2.7 million more than the current population of the island. If one were to reserve the island exclusively for Jews, with 6.5 million Jews on the island there would still only be a population density of 10 per square kilometre. If one wanted to put the 6.5 million Jews there while also keeping the long-established population, the average population density would increase to around 16 persons per square kilometre, that is, to the level of population density that has been ascertained as the overall average for the surface of the earth and somewhat more than one tenth of the population density of the German Reich. This number, too, should fit within the natural capacity of the island.

DOC. 95

On 18 July 1940 the mayor of Leipzig informs Saxony's Minister of Economics about the provisioning and labour deployment of the Jewish population in Leipzig[1]

Letter from the mayor of Leipzig, signed Freyberg,[2] to the Saxon Minister of Economics Lenk,[3] 2 Carolaplatz, Dresden N 6, dated 18 July 1940 (copy)[4]

Dear State Minister,

With reference to your telephone conversation yesterday regarding the deployment of Jews and the food rations for Jews, I hereby report the following:

The Law on Tenancy Agreements with Jews dated 30 April 1939 gave the lower administrative authorities a suitable weapon for tackling the problem of the Jews in a more resolute way than was previously possible under the existing legal regulations.[5] Since that date, in consultation with the Kreisleiter, I have entrusted the handling of this task to an official with the Leipzig municipal administration, who is simultaneously the head of the local NSDAP branch.

Processing the tenancy affairs of the Jews inevitably entailed the handling of other tasks, such as the supervision of those businesses that are undergoing liquidation or are scheduled for liquidation, the labour deployment of the Jews who have become available as a result of giving up their businesses, prohibition of the presence of Jews in ornamen-

1 StA Leipzig, Kap. 1, Nr. 122, fols. 263–264. This letter has been translated from German.
2 Alfred Freyberg (1892–1945), lawyer; joined the NSDAP in 1925; practised law in Quedlinburg, 1926–1929; city councillor and notary at the Higher Regional Court, 1929–1932; minister president in 1932 and state minister in Anhalt from 1933; joined the SS in 1933; member of the Reichstag, 1936–1945; mayor of Leipzig, 1939–1945; SS-Gruppenführer, 1942; committed suicide.
3 Georg Robert Lenk (1888–1945), businessman; in 1911 founded an underwear factory; joined the NSDAP in 1930; city councillor in Plauen, 1930–1932; member of the Reichstag, 1930–1944; Gau economic advisor for Saxony, 1931–1933 and 1936–1941; Saxon minister of economics, May 1933 to March 1943; joined the SS in 1934; went to the Waffen SS in 1944; died in Soviet captivity.
4 A copy was sent for information to the main administrative office. The original contains a handwritten annotation.
5 See Doc. 15, fn. 4, and PMJ 2/277.

tal public squares, parks, and woodlands, and then, since the onset of war, supplying the Jews with specially marked food ration cards, distributing coal, creating sales outlets engaged in various lines of business and designated specifically for Jews, etc. As a result of the very extensive and rigorous tackling of these tasks, more than half of the approximately 6,000 Jews still in Leipzig on 1 June 1939 have emigrated or moved away thus far, so that there are around 2,300 Jews still here at present.

During the last two visits of the Gauleiter[6] to Leipzig in the winter of 1939/40 and the spring of this year, the official in charge had occasion to report to him concerning, among other things, the decline in the numbers of Jews, at which the Gauleiter expressed his satisfaction.

When food rationing measures were introduced, I had ordered that Jews must not receive any special allocations. Those who were ill or frail, pregnant women and nursing mothers, as well as women who had recently given birth, were treated no better than the average consumer, even upon presentation of a certificate. Those performing heavy manual labour or working long shifts or at night (there were and are some) received no additional ration cards and no ration cards for extra allowances. In addition, the Jews were allotted absolutely no shoes or textile materials in exchange for ration coupons.

I was forced to change the directive regarding food distribution because of the decree of the Reich Minister of Food and Agriculture dated 11 March 1940 (II C 1–940) which was mandatory for me.[7] Since then the Jews have received the same standard rations as other persons entitled to sustenance, and the provisions for the ill, frail, etc. apply to them also, in accordance with the directive.

Considering this decree, I have forwarded to the relevant trade inspectorate all the petitions for the granting of additional allowances for long-shift workers filed by Jews who work in the city administration or elsewhere and are away from home for at least eleven hours per day (that is the prerequisite laid down throughout the Reich), and have asked this authority 'for a resolution'. Considering the aforementioned decree of the Reich Minister of Food and Agriculture, the State Trade Supervisory Office has approved extra ration cards for Jews who work long shifts.

I gathered from your statements during yesterday's telephone conversation, dear State Minister, that you do not wish the State Trade Supervisory Office to handle the matter in this way, despite the decree of the Reich Minister of Food and Agriculture. I venture to propose that the State Trade Supervisory Office be instructed in accordance with your wishes.

As mentioned above, it was necessary to ensure that Jews were brought into the work process. Particularly after the beginning of the war, given the shortage of manual labourers, one could not justify allowing Jews to be idle or to pursue their previous business

6 Martin Mutschmann (1879–1947), textile worker; from 1907 owner of a lace factory in Plauen; joined the NSDAP in 1922; Gauleiter of Saxony, 1926–1945; member of the Reichstag, 1930–1945; Reichsstatthalter in Saxony, May 1933 to 1945; tasked with heading the Saxon state government, 1935–1945; arrested in 1945; sentenced to death in Moscow in 1947 and executed.

7 According to a decree issued by the Reich Ministry of Food and Agriculture concerning the food supply of the Jews, they were supposed to receive – with the exception of special food allocations – the same food rations as average consumers. Additional allowances could be granted to those who were ill, pregnant women, nursing mothers, and those who performed physically taxing manual labour: see Doc. 36, fn. 7.

openly or covertly and thereby keep state and municipal supervisory bodies constantly busy. There was only one way to address the situation in a radical way, and that was to occupy the Jews in a physically taxing manner and for as long as possible each day. The requisite steps were taken, in consultation with the employment office, and Jews were set to work in groups and kept separate from the staff. The director of the Saxon Regional Employment Office[8] had envisaged, for the labour deployment of Jews, jobs including excavation, road construction, and work in market gardens. I also considered this sort of labour deployment to be useful in the local area. I therefore allocated a number of Jews, including Jewesses, to the municipal forestry commission office to do reforesting work. A larger number were allocated to the municipal labour centre (splitting wood), while others dug trenches and made communication trenches for use in air raids next to the large covered market, and others still were at work on the new, large rubbish tip, tasked with picking textile waste and scrap metal out of the ashes delivered there. An additional group was used for levelling, digging, and gardening work in the individual Leipzig cemeteries, including the South Cemetery. Finally, to relieve a pressing need, Jews were allocated to private refuse collection services.

Previously I paid wages of 10, 20, or 24 pfennigs per hour to the Jews who did compulsory labour for the city. This directive had to be changed, because the Leipzig Employment Office lodged a complaint against it and referred me to provisions that stipulate payment according to standard rates.

Currently seventy-four Jews in total are working for the cemetery office, fifty-one of them at the South Cemetery, fifteen at the construction site for the West Cemetery, and eight in the parks in Richard-Wagner-Hain.[9] The work that the Jews must perform there is decidedly dirty work, for which city employees would have to be given protective clothing, in addition to the bonus for dirty work. Neither is granted to Jews. At the South Cemetery they are mainly working on the sewer system. They have to clear the sluices of the sewage pipes leading to the main road, clean silted-up pathways, tidy up overgrown communal grave sites, and remove thistles and other weeds from embankment slopes covered with wild roses.

At the new construction sites in the West Cemetery, the Jews must do levelling work and, because the water supply system is not yet functioning, must bring water from far away in pails in order to water the ornamental gardens. There too, as in Richard-Wagner-Hain, they perform weed control. In addition, the rough work of building paths must be done there, and stones must be broken for this purpose. Jews, therefore, contrary to the assumption you imparted to me yesterday, have not been used either in the South Cemetery or in other cemeteries for the tasks of digging or filling in graves.

Heil Hitler!

Your very devoted

8 Johannes Hardraht (1880–1940); Regierungsrat in the Grimma district administrative office; district administrator in Grimma, 1919–1932; Ministerialrat in the Saxon representative office from 1932; director of the regional employment office in Saxony from 1936.

9 Park in Leipzig.

DOC. 96

On 29 July 1940 the Reich Postmaster General orders that Jews' telephone lines be cancelled[1]

Letter from the Reich Postmaster General,[2] Min-Z (Lb) 1035–0, p.p. signed Risch,[3] to the directors of the Reich Post Office Headquarters, dated 29 July 1940

Exclusion of Jews from telephone communication

In future the Jews are to be barred from being telephone subscribers. Exceptions are authorized only for:

(1) Jewish legal consultants,[4]
(2) Jewish practitioners for the sick[5] and hospitals,
(3) the Reich Association of Jews in Germany, including its subsidiary organizations,
(4) privileged mixed marriages; these are mixed marriages:
  (a) from which children have resulted who are not considered Jews within the meaning of § 5 of the First Regulation on the Reich Citizenship Law of 14 November 1935,[6] regardless of whether it is the father or the mother who is Jewish;
  (b) which are childless and in which the *husband* is of German blood;
(5) Jews with foreign nationality.

Specifically, the following action is to be taken.

For telephone subscribers who are known to be Jews or are deemed Jews under § 5 of the First Regulation on the Reich Citizenship Law of 14 November 1935 (*Reichsgesetzblatt*, I, p. 1333), unless they come under the exception in (5), *all* main telephone lines must be cancelled by the end of next month, even if the minimum subscription period has not yet elapsed.[7] Because, under Regulatory Statute 1 for § 18 of the Telephone Code, in the case of a branch exchange the cancellation of all main lines also includes the cancellation of all telephone extensions and other facilities, there is no need for a

1 BArch, R 4701/11160, fols. 43 and 45. Published in Wolfgang Lotz (ed.), *Die Deutsche Reichspost 1933–1945: Eine politische Verwaltungsgeschichte. Ausgewählte Dokumente* (Koblenz: Bundesarchiv, 2002), pp. 481–482. This document has been translated from German.

2 The Reich postmaster general from 1937 to 1945 was Wilhelm Ohnesorge (1872–1962).

3 Dr Friedrich Risch (1895–1965), lawyer; with the Freikorps Epp, 1919; employed by the Reich Postal Service from 1924; joined the NSDAP in 1933; from 1936 at the Reich Postal Ministry; head of the Berlin Post Office Directorate, 1938; ministerial director and head of the Central Department of the Reich Postal Ministry, 1939; head of the Foreign Department, 1941; joined the SS in 1942.

4 Under the Fifth Regulation on the Reich Citizenship Law (27 Sept. 1938), Jews were barred from the legal profession. A very limited number were allowed to represent Jewish clients exclusively as so-called legal consultants (*Rechtskonsulenten*): *Reichsgesetzblatt*, 1938, I, pp. 1403–1406.

5 Under the Fourth Regulation on the Reich Citizenship Law (25 July 1938), the medical licences of Jewish physicians were revoked as of 30 Sept. 1938. Only a few Jewish doctors, as so-called practitioners for the sick (*Krankenbehandler*), were allowed to provide medical care to Jewish patients: *Reichsgesetzblatt*, 1938, I, pp. 969–970. See also PMJ 2/76.

6 § 5 of the First Regulation specified who was to be regarded as a Jew within the meaning of the Reich Citizenship Law: *Reichsgesetzblatt*, 1935, I, pp. 1333–1334. See also PMJ 1/210.

7 Owing to the short deadline for submitting the application for exemption, the Reich Postal Ministry decreed on 15 August 1940 that the cancellations should take place not at the end of August 1940 but one month later instead: Order of the Reich Postal Ministry to the Directors of the Reich Post Office Directorates, BArch, R 4701/11160, fol. 46.

separate cancellation of any branch exchange that is linked with the cancelled main lines. In the case of private branch exchanges, it is incumbent upon the subscribers to deal with the private contractors. Also to be cancelled are branch exchanges that a subscriber has ceded to Jews for permanent use – Telephone Code § 15(2).[8]

It is prohibited to list Jews who do not come under (1) to (5) as co-users (Regulatory Statute 2 for § 40 of the Telephone Code)[9] in official or private telephone directories (*ÖFB, HGBV*).[10]

If there are doubts whether a telephone subscriber is a Jew or is considered a Jew, the State Police (head) office must be consulted in the first instance. If applicable, the telephone lines of these subscribers must be cancelled as well. Jews who are foreign nationals, if this fact is known, are not to lose their telephone service, but service must be cancelled for stateless Jews.

The exemptions must be pointed out in all official cancellation letters. If Jews apply for an exemption within the meaning of (1) to (4), they must verify this application by means of a certificate issued by the Reich Association of Jews in Germany and furnished with the notation 'Agreed' by the appropriate local State Police (head) office. Jews who are foreign nationals must attach a certificate from their consulate. Upon submission of such certificates, the cancellations are to be revoked.

New connections for Jews may be established only in the exceptional cases defined in (1) to (5) and upon submission of a joint certificate from the Reich Association of Jews in Germany and the appropriate local State Police (head) office, or upon submission of a certificate from the consulate.

All telephones that are the property of the post office are to be removed promptly after expiration of the notice period. Payment is waived with respect to the remaining fees for any minimum subscription period that has not yet elapsed.

In the case of companies that are undergoing de-Jewification, the transfer of the telephone service is to be initiated by the trustee or, if the business is already being run by the prospective non-Jewish buyer, transfer is to be initiated by him.

Any difficulties should be reported.[11]

8 Telephone Code with Regulatory Statutes (*Fernsprechordnung mit Ausführungsbestimmungen*), 1940, pp. 19, 21.

9 Ibid., p. 38.

10 *ÖFB*: *Örtliches Fernsprechbuch* = local telephone directory; *HGBV*: *Handels-, Gewerbe- und Berufsverzeichnis der Fernsprechteilnehmer* = commercial and professional telephone directory.

11 On 12 Sept. 1940 the Reich Postal Ministry supplemented its order as follows: 'Exceptions are permitted only for: 1. Jewish legal consultants and foreign exchange advisors, 2. Jewish practitioners for the sick and midwives, hospitals, and private Jewish old people's homes, 3. The Reich Association etc., 4. etc., 5. etc. The telephone connections temporarily left in place for seriously disabled Jewish ex-servicemen are henceforth to be cancelled as well': BArch, R 4701/11160, fol. 44.

DOC. 97

New York Times, 2 August 1940: article on export bans, shopping restrictions, and prohibited areas for Jews in Germany[1]

New Curbs Placed on Jews in Reich.

Emigrants Forbidden to Take More Than Most Essential Articles of Clothing. Shopping Limited to Hour. Jewish Community's Hospitals Forbidden to Paint Red Crosses on Roofs

Berlin, Aug. 2 (AP) – A general tightening of restrictions affecting Jews in Germany was marked today by regulations issued to emigrants forbidding them to carry out of the country more than two suits of clothes, one pair of overalls, one sweater and one overcoat.[2]

Hitherto the emigrating Jew could invest his remaining marks in personal equipment calculated to relieve him of worries in the country of his adoption. Now he may take only the most essential objects of wear.

Under the new regulations an adult Jewish woman, for instance, may take along two dresses, two professional robes, two aprons, one pullover, one raincoat or costume, one Winter coat or cape, one pair of Winter gloves, three pairs of drawers, two nightgowns or pajamas, two underskirts, six pairs of stockings, two bedsheets, two bed covers, two pillowcases, one pillow, two quilts, one set of mattresses or a straw bag, two pairs of street shoes, one pair of house shoes or gymnasium slippers, three personal towels, three dish towels, two scrubbing rags, two dust rags.

For Jews unable to emigrate – and very few can make the grade now – further restrictions came in city police orders, of which those in Berlin are typical.

Jewish telephone subscribers received notices today cancelling their service save for calls to doctors, nurses and hospitals. Where Jews have extensions to apparatus subscribed to by 'Aryans,' the latter were requested to sever the connections.[3]

Jewish hospitals have been forbidden to paint the red cross on their roofs.[4]

Jews here may purchase their necessities only between 4 and 5 p. m. This applies not only to all shops but even to private and public markets, and Jews complain it often is impossible to complete shopping within an hour when long queues are standing. Gentiles are forbidden to shop for Jews except between 4 and 5 o'clock.[5]

Before the present hostilities began Chancellor Hitler stated publicly that another war would mean the elimination of the Jews.[6] Now city after city is systematically being cleared of Jews.

1 *New York Times*, 3 August 1940, p. 18. The original document is in English.
2 The circular decree 'concerning withdrawal of citizenship for Jewish emigrants, in particular the auction of property' dates from 1 August 1940; this decree could not be located. It was preceded by an earlier decree issued by the Reich Economics Ministry on 16 July 1940 regarding the relocation of household goods by emigrants: BArch, R 2/56066.
3 See Doc. 96.
4 The existence of such a ban could not be verified.
5 See Doc. 36, fn. 7.
6 See PMJ 2/248.

The latest is the case of Breslau, where all Jews have been ordered to leave by Autumn.[7]

Repression of the Jews also extends to the German-occupied portion of Poland, as is shown by an official notice in the *Warschauer Zeitung*, daily paper in Warsaw printed in German. According to this notice, Jews are forbidden to enter Warsaw parks or sit on benches placed for the convenience of the public in various parts of the city.[8]

A number of streets and public places in Warsaw also have been designated as forbidden to Jews. Here Jews may not even tread. The only exception to the general rule are benches located in a restricted area of Warsaw designated as a Jewish reservation, in other words, a ghetto.[9]

Like Berlin, there formerly were a few benches in the parks and public squares for Jews, but these mostly have disappeared since the war.

The curfew for Jews in most German cities is at 9 p.m.[10]

DOC. 98

On 15 August 1940 Hitler's plans to deport all the Jews from Europe after the war become known in the Reich Foreign Office[1]

Message (marked 'strictly confidential') from Martin Luther,[2] Reich Foreign Office, Department for Germany, to Legation Secretary Franz Rademacher, Reich Foreign Office, dated 15 August 1940[3]

(1) On the occasion of a meeting with Ambassador Abetz[4] in Paris, the latter told me that when he gave his presentation on France around two weeks ago, the Führer informed him that he intends to evacuate all the Jews from Europe after the war.

7 From 1939, and especially from 1940, Jews in Breslau had to move out of their houses and apartments, and were concentrated in several streets and 'Jew houses' (*Judenhäuser*). The complete evacuation of Jews from the city as mentioned in this article, however, had not been decreed.

8 This notice could not be found.

9 On 18 July 1940 Ludwig Leist, the governor of the city of Warsaw, announced a 'ban on Jews entering public spaces', which applied to all parks outside the designated 'epidemic quarter' (*Seuchenviertel*) for Jews: *Mitteilungsblatt der Stadt Warschau*, no. 27, 1 August 1940, p. 1.

10 The curfew usually applied after 8 p.m.

1 PA AA, R 100 857, fol. 194. This document has been translated from German.

2 Martin Luther (1895–1945); originally worked as a furniture haulier; joined the NSDAP and the SA in 1932; chief specialist in the NSDAP's foreign policy office, the Bureau Ribbentrop, from 1936; transferred in 1938 to the Reich Foreign Office, where he was head of the Department for Germany; SA-Oberführer, 1940; undersecretary, 1941; representative of the Reich Foreign Office at the Wannsee Conference, 1942; arrested after a plot against Ribbentrop, 1943–1945; died shortly after the end of the war.

3 The original contains handwritten annotations and underlining, as well as receipt stamps of the Reich Foreign Office; date illegible.

4 Otto Abetz (1903–1958), art teacher; grammar school (*Gymnasium*) teacher in Karlsruhe between 1927 and 1934; specialist for France in the Reich Youth Leadership in 1934, and in the Bureau Ribbentrop from 1935; joined the SS in 1935 and the NSDAP in 1937; ambassador in France from 1940; SS-Brigadeführer, 1942; arrested in 1945 and sentenced in Paris in 1949 to twenty years of forced labour; released in 1954.

(2) Ambassador Abetz also told me that they have confiscated the entire registry of the Freemasons in France and have placed it for safekeeping in a building next to the embassy.

DOC. 99
In mid August 1940 the Reich Security Main Office plans the deportation of the European Jews to Madagascar[1]

Draft by the Reich Security Main Office, forwarded by SS-Obersturmführer Theodor Dannecker to Legation Counsellor Franz Rademacher, Reich Foreign Office (received on 21 August 1940), dated 15 August 1940

Dear Comrade Rademacher,

By messenger I am sending you your personal copy of the draft of the 'Madagascar Project'. I ask that it be treated as especially confidential.

Heil Hitler!

Yours, Dannecker

Originally submitted to Envoy Luther for information, with return requested. The plan itself was forwarded directly by Gruppenführer Heydrich to the Reich Minister of Foreign Affairs,[2] from there through Kult E to D III, and then directed by me to Pol XII.[3] In the meantime, I had directly received the enclosed item. I had been informed of Heydrich's intention, which I immediately communicated to you in Fuschel by telephone.[4]

Reich Security Main Office:
Madagascar Project
Contents

1 PA AA, R 100 857, fols. 197–214, annexes fols. 215–219. Published in excerpt in Adler, *Der verwaltete Mensch*, pp. 75–79. This document has been translated from German.
2 Joachim von Ribbentrop.
3 Section Kult E was in charge of emigration affairs; D III, of areas including 'Jewish affairs'; and Pol XII, of peace questions.
4 Correctly: Fuschl am See, situated in Austria's Salzkammergut region. The original contains handwritten annotations.

I. *Situation and basics*

(a) With the establishment of the General Government in Poland and the incorporation of the new German Gaue in the East, large numbers of Jews came under direct German sovereign authority. In addition, there are the Jews who reside in the territories under German military sovereignty.

Practical experience to date has shown that even in the territory of the Reich, including the Protectorate of Bohemia and Moravia, it will be difficult to *bring the Jewish problem to a definitive resolution in the foreseeable future by means of emigration*, due to the difficulties that arise everywhere (tightening of immigration laws in overseas countries, the difficulty of obtaining passage and foreign currency, etc.). After the addition of the masses in the East, resolving the Jewish problem by means of emigration has become impossible.

(b) In total, the number of Jews amounts to around 4,000,000 at the moment, consisting of the following:

(1) Germany	approx.	743,000 (incl. the new Gaue in the East – 500,000)
(2) General Government	approx.	2,300,000

5 *Absetzung* in the original German; probably refers to settlement.

(3) Protectorate	approx.	77,000
(4) Belgium	approx.	80,000
(5) Holland	approx.	160,000
(6) Luxembourg	approx.	2,500
(7) Denmark	approx.	7,000
(8) Norway	approx.	1,500
(9) Slovakia	approx.	95,000
(10) France	approx.	270,000
		3,736,000[6]

(c) The following report reflects the preliminary work done thus far by the Security Police on the project to place these approximately 4,000,000 Jews in *Madagascar.* To avoid other people constantly coming into contact with Jews, an overseas solution *involving an island* must be favoured over any other.

II. *Physical features* (For map see Annex I.[7])

(a) *Climate*

The coasts of the island are unhealthy for Europeans because of the high temperature and the constant humidity. A large part of the interior forms an elevated plateau with an average height of 800–1,500 metres. This zone is suitable for Europeans.

The high levels of precipitation account for the presence of numerous streams and swamps. As a result, naturally, there is a danger of fever in the low areas. Through drainage, the spread of epidemic diseases could be controlled to the greatest possible extent. Here alone there are major tasks to be dealt with for a labour programme.

(b) *Population and land*

The territory of the island, totalling almost 600,000 square kilometres, is comparable to the size of France, Belgium, and Holland together. In total, there are 3.8 million inhabitants, including 3,660,000 Malagasy, 11,000 Indians and Chinese, and 24,000 Europeans, mostly French.

(c) *Economy*

Industries are present only to a small extent.

Besides rice, which is grown in every part of the country, the crops include manioc (or cassava, a tuberous root that replaces the potato there) and potatoes, as well as cotton, peanuts, maize, sugar cane, coffee, tea, cloves, and vanilla. Plants used in perfumes and for medicinal purposes are exported. At altitudes up to 1,000 metres, bananas, oranges, lemons, coconut palms, mangos, lychees, avocados, and pineapples thrive. The large numbers of livestock, totalling around 7 million head of cattle, make it possible to export meat at present. The food supply is thus ensured, even with the addition of 4 million Jews.

There are some ore deposits, but inadequately developed.

6 This number was added by hand.

7 The annex contains a map of Africa with statistical information on the development of the former German colonies in Africa: PA AA, R 100 857, fols. 197–214, annexes fols. 215–219.

(d) *Transport routes*

The railway network of the island is only 600 kilometres long. An extensive network of durable road infrastructure, paths, and bridges must still be built in large quantities. Flood control of waterways is needed, as far as possible. A large-scale programme of work to develop the transport routes would create jobs for years to come.

The local leadership of the territory would have to strive to make the economy of this country self-sufficient, so that the possibility of international trade links between the Jews and the rest of the world will be ruled out. Wherever this cannot be achieved in the initial phases, German trust agencies must be used to solve these problems.

III. *Constitutional structure and territorial division*

(a) Madagascar, because it is an island, is suitable for the creation of a Jewish reservation. Every attempt at Jewish statehood must be prevented, by determining the constitutional structure in advance. At the same time, it is necessary to prevent all potential objections, especially on the part of the USA. For these reasons, the creation of a Jewish home under German sovereignty seems appropriate as the constitutional structure. However, this mandate would in fact have to be organized internally as a *police state.*

The requisite bases and airfields will be kept open for the German navy and Luftwaffe.

(b) The overall territory of the island must be subdivided expediently into four districts, for organizational reasons and considering the large distances in particular. While a *Jewish Council of Elders*, yet to be formed, is at the disposal of the *main placement staff* as an organization for the performance of central tasks, *Jewish district communities*, which in turn are subdivided into regional and local communities, are to be formed at the headquarters of the *district staffs*.

The local French administrative apparatus would have to continue functioning temporarily, under the direction of the German authorities. As a result, an easing of the official burden on the placement staff, as on any other German authorities present, will be accomplished.

IV. *Organization* (For organizational plan see Annex II.[8])

(A) *Overall leadership*

Overall control is in the hands of the Chief of the Security Police and the SD, who has already been appointed by order of the Reich Marshal on 24 January 1939 as special commissioner for Jewish emigration.[9] He is responsible for the centralized management of the entire evacuation and placement process, for coordinating the transports, for all financing matters both of the transports and of the placement– and for overseeing the surveillance by the Security Police.

(B) *Evacuation*

(1) *Technical execution*

For the technical execution of the evacuation, the following evacuation staff units will be formed:

West: for France, Belgium, Holland, Luxembourg.

8 PA AA, R 100 857, fols. 197–214, annexes fols. 215–219.

9 See PMJ 2/243.

Central Area: for the Old Reich plus the Sudetenland, including the new German Gaue in the East, the Ostmark, the Protectorate of Bohemia and Moravia, Slovakia, Denmark, Norway.

East: for the General Government in Poland

(2) *Individual details*:

(a) *Old Reich, Sudetengau, new German Gaue in the East*

Central coordination is in the hands of the Reich Central Agency for Jewish Emigration in Berlin. The Security Police and the SD are in charge of implementation in this case. They will become executive organs through their subordinate offices. With respect to execution, they draw in particular on the district organizations or local federations of the Reich Association of Jews in Germany or, in the Gaue in the East, on the Jewish Council of Elders.

(b) *Ostmark*

Central coordination is in the hands of the Central Office for Jewish Emigration in Vienna. The Israelite Religious Community of Vienna with all its personnel and resources is at its disposal for implementation in individual cases. (This only concerns around 50,000 Jews there.)

(c) *Protectorate of Bohemia and Moravia*

Central control is in the hands of the Central Office for Jewish Emigration in Prague, which is directly subordinate to the Senior Commander of the Security Police and the SD. The State Police head offices in Prague and Brünn are responsible for the individual aspects of implementation. As the central body organizing all Jewish life in the Protectorate, the Jewish Religious Community of Prague is in charge of the work on the ground.

(d) *Slovakia*

Based on the model of the Central Office for Jewish Emigration, a special emigration staff will be set up in Pressburg[10] with the assistance of the local authorities. The office will be accountable to the Chief of the Security Police and the SD.

(e) *Denmark*

While the implementation of the evacuation in the territories listed under (a), (b), (c), and (d) is larger in scope, the evacuation in Denmark, where there are only around 7,500 Jews, can take place by having a representative of the Central Area staff, together with the local Danish police authority, carry out the tasks, which can be completed in a short period of time.

Jewish communities or organizations, if there are any, must be involved here in the specifics of implementation.

(f) *Norway*

Here there are only around 1,500 Jews, who can be evacuated in a *single* transport.

(g) *France, Belgium, Holland, Luxembourg*

In each case, the evacuation staff for the West will assign a representative for each of the relevant police authorities of these countries. Implementation in detail will be the responsibility of the lower administrative or police authorities of the four countries.

In the process, the Jewish organizations or communities are to be used as auxiliary offices, following their reorganization along the lines of the structure of the Israelite

10 Bratislava.

Religious Communities in Vienna and Prague or the Reich Association of Jews in Germany.

(h) *General Government in Poland*

Overall responsibility for evacuation in the General Government is in the hands of the evacuation staff for the East, which operates within the staff of the Senior Commander of the Security Police and the SD in Cracow. District representatives are based in the individual districts to implement the evacuations with the support of the local offices of the Security Police and the SD. In the process, the Jewish Council of Elders must carry out the preliminary work for specific implementation, as far as possible.

(3) *Preliminary work*

(a) All offices tasked with implementation must first undertake a precise classification of the entire Jewry in their territory. They are responsible for requesting and executing all necessary preliminary work related to the evacuation of the Jews, such as acquiring documents for individual Jews, registering and liquidating assets, and including them in transports. The first transports should contain mainly farmers, construction specialists, craftsmen, and manual labourers' families up to the age of 45, in addition to physicians. These will then be sent ahead and put in place as a sort of vanguard for the purpose of preparing accommodation for the masses that will follow.

(b) The Jews are permitted to take along up to 200 kg of non-bulky luggage per person. Jewish farmers, craftsmen, physicians, etc. *must*, where applicable, take along all equipment in their possession and necessary for the pursuit of their occupation. With regard to taking along cash and objects made of precious metal, the respective provisions apply.

(c) The remaining assets of the evacuated persons are to be reported to the 'Trust Agency for Jewish Assets', which is to be set up for this purpose in each country. The total proceeds from the sale of the immovable assets will then be transferred into a central evacuation fund, which will be created along the lines of the emigration fund in Vienna or in Bohemia and Moravia. It will draw on these funds and, where applicable, on other regional funds under its authority.

(C) *Transports*

(1) *Shipping space*

To give a rough overview of the shipping space required, the following estimate is presented, based on an average capacity of 1,500 persons per ship: if one assumes around 60 days for the round trip, including the necessary stopovers, then the result is that with 120 ships of similar capacity, two transports per day could be carried out, with a total of 3,000 Jews, according to these calculations. On an annual basis, this would amount to around 1 million Jews per year. The time required for implementation of the entire project could thus be set at around 4 years.

After peace has been concluded, the German merchant fleet will undoubtedly be very heavily utilized elsewhere. It will therefore be necessary to stipulate in the peace treaty that both France and England will make available the requisite shipping space for the solution of the Jewish problem.

(2) *Financing of transports*

The peace agreement should stipulate that the cost of the transports is essentially to be borne by the Jews residing in the territories of the Western powers, as compensation for the harm inflicted on the German Reich economically and otherwise by the Jews in the aftermath of the Treaty of Versailles.

(D) *Placement*

(1) *Main Placement Staff*

The office directly responsible to Berlin for overall management of the placement process will be the Main Placement Staff of the Chief of the Security Police and the SD. It is yet to be established where this staff will be based. It will be responsible for the entire security system, the admission and distribution of transports (immigration contingents), the registration and information system, food supply system and agriculture, health services, financial system and currency questions, communication, and the establishment of control over the Jewish community.

(2) *Placement staff units*

Placement Staff Units I–IV, which will operate in the districts and whose locations have yet to be decided, bear responsibility for the proper execution of the orders of the Main Staff and for unconditional compliance with the general guidelines issued by them in their districts. The Jewish district communities will be directly accountable in each case to the placement staff, who in turn will make the necessary individual decisions on the ground, in accordance with the guidelines it is given. The main task of the placement staff in the districts is, further, to oversee the suitable placement of Jewish work squads with the aim of ensuring that accommodation is provided for the subsequent transport in order to secure immediate integration into the production process, to the extent necessary to cover the Jews' own requirements.

(3) *Procedure*

As a basis, the presumed capacity will be roughly determined by an advance squad after the district borders have been established. At this point, the numbers for the individual districts will be allocated. Once the allocation numbers have been announced, the placement staff units in the districts can begin large-scale planning, keeping the main placement staff constantly involved.

(E) *Jewish community*

As previously stated, an operational Jewish organizational body will be set up, whose main work will consist in enforcing the directives of the placement staff units as quickly as possible. This method has proved highly successful in the work of the Central Offices for Jewish Emigration, and it shifts a large share of the work on to the Jews themselves.

The Jewish district communities must organize the regional and local communities down to the last detail, so that a smooth execution is guaranteed during the placement process. Furthermore, Jewish construction specialists and trained farmers, who enter the country with the vanguard, must immediately set about expanding and developing agricultural settlements within the individual Jewish communities and creating a transport network in the country. In addition, the Jews must ensure a well-ordered food supply by setting up a distribution system on a *cooperative* basis. To ensure medical care to some extent, the Jewish offices must be vigilant with respect to the correct distribution of all available physicians within the territories.

(F) *Funding*

Implementation of the proposed final solution requires significant funds. One must distinguish between funds that are raised for the evacuation of the Jews from the territory of the Reich, including the Protectorate of Bohemia and Moravia, the new German eastern territories, and the General Government, and funds under consideration for the evacuation of the Jews from those countries that are to be factored in for the final solution. The latter funds could be raised by stipulating corresponding provisions during the peace treaty negotiations, for example, a levy on Jewish assets in these countries.

These funds raised through contributions can doubtless be much more generous than those to be raised within the territory of the Reich, including the Protectorate of Bohemia and Moravia, even taking into account the inclusion of all Jewish assets in the territory of the Reich, the Protectorate of Bohemia and Moravia, the new German eastern territories, and the General Government. The requisite balance between these two funding streams must be brought about by an appropriate method of apportionment. Also still to be clarified would be the question of whether, with regard to the raising of funds in the territory of the Reich, in the Protectorate of Bohemia and Moravia, in the new German Eastern Gaue, and in the General Government, expropriation measures seem appropriate, or alternatively whether these funds should be raised in the form of voluntary legal transactions by involving the Jewish religious communities of Prague and Vienna, the Reich Association of Jews in Germany, and the Jewish Councils of Elders in the eastern territories.

(G) *Advance measures*

In the event of the definitive designation of Madagascar as a home for the Jews, it is suggested that a Security Police commando comprising the appropriate expertise be put in place there.

The mission of this advance commando is to establish the following information:

(1) Overall capacity.

(2) Potential for enlarging capacity by setting up camps and the like.

(3) Usefulness of the lower French administrative authorities with respect to distributing and placing transports when they arrive.

(4) General food-supply situation.

(5) Agriculture and economy in general; labour deployment.

(6) Landing sites; transport routes.

Once the report of the advance team is submitted, preparatory work will be started involving the local French administrative authorities.

It is suggested that a representative of the Reichsführer SS and Chief of the German Police also be included in the peace negotiations for the area pertaining to this matter.

DOC. 100

On 21 August 1940 a refugee committee in Shanghai explains immigration requirements to the Jewish Religious Community of Vienna[1]

Letter from the Committee for the Assistance of European Jewish Refugees in Shanghai, Immigration Department,[2] Room 177, Entrance A, Embankment Building, signature illegible, to the Jewish Religious Community of Vienna (foreign correspondence no. 6320, received: 14 September 1940), dated 21 August 1940

The numerous letters and telegrams inquiring about permits, some of which come directly to us and others to individuals currently here, are frequently written in such a way that it is entirely impossible to fulfil the wishes expressed therein. We therefore feel compelled to explain once again what the situation is like.

A. The International Settlement mainly[3] issues permits if a landing charge of at least US$400 is on hand here for the expected immigrant. Possession of the landing money alone absolutely does not guarantee admission to Shanghai. The money must be transferred here without fail, and a permit must be applied for here on the basis of the deposited landing money. If the presumptive immigrants have relatives or acquaintances here who can take the necessary steps for them, the money can be transferred to these individuals, who can then make the payment to the committee. If the persons concerned have no contacts here, however, the sum must be transferred to Chase Bank Shanghai, Account Speelman for (name of the immigrant), naturally with corresponding notification sent to us. In these cases it is also the committee that makes the submission to the authorities. In all cases it is advisable to transfer an additional four to five US dollars per person to cover the fees and costs associated with the permit department.

An additional option is for persons here to request a permit for close relatives, if they are able to prove that they have the means to support the potential new immigrants. Applications based on contracts of employment have almost no prospect of a positive outcome. On average, one must expect the handling of the matter to take one to two months.

B. To obtain a permit from the Imperial Japanese Consulate General the absolute prerequisite is that the applicant must live in the Japanese-occupied region of Shanghai and be registered with the Japanese authorities. Registration took place during approximately a one-year period. A retroactive registration is performed only for persons who enter the country on the basis of a permit issued by the Japanese Consulate General. The possibility to apply to the Japanese authorities for a permit based on landing money does not exist at present.

1 CAHJP, A/W 2546, 2; copy Archiv der IKG Wien, MF U 8, fr. 595–596. This document has been translated from German.

2 The Committee for the Assistance of European Jewish Refugees in Shanghai (CAEJR) was founded on 19 Oct. 1938 to help the mainly impoverished German and Austrian immigrants, for example by setting up collective accommodation and soup kitchens.

3 Within Shanghai the International Settlement and the French Concession constituted independent administrative districts. The Chinese part of the city was under Japanese control from 1937.

In practice, therefore, only those cases come into consideration in which an application is made for relatives, with proof of means of [financial] support. Unfortunately, it is not possible to provide reliable information about how long it takes to process applications to the Japanese authorities. Likewise, we are not able to say reliably from here whether the necessary transit visas for the journey via Siberia are obtainable on the basis of a settlement permit. The local Japanese Consulate General, however, has repeatedly assured us that it has requested the Japanese consular authorities in Germany to put all types of permits on an equal footing with the Japanese permits.

The large number of previously issued immigration permits is proof of the extraordinary goodwill of the local authorities. But it is not possible to submit applications with any prospect of success beyond the scope of the rules or without complying with the conditions imposed. We ask you to pass on this information to all interested parties that come into consideration, in order to prevent completely unfulfillable wishes from being presented in letters or telegrams.

Only the undersigned Immigration Department is in charge of immigration questions. It is therefore advisable to address correspondence concerning these matters only to this office, PO Box 1024.

Respectfully

DOC. 101

In late August 1940 Legation Counsellor Franz Rademacher of the Reich Foreign Office makes suggestions for the implementation of the 'Madagascar Plan'[1]

Reich Foreign Office paper, signed Rademacher, Berlin, presented to Martin Luther on 30 August 1940[2]

Previous development of the Madagascar Plan of Section D III

The idea of moving the Jews to Madagascar was first published in the twenties by the old Dutch antisemite Beamish.[3]

After the Reich Minister,[4] acting on the suggestion of the Department for Germany, decided that the solution to the Jewish question in the peace treaty should be worked on by Section D III in the Department for Germany, in consultation with the offices of the Reichsführer SS, I drafted the following plan for the solution to the Jewish question in the peace treaty.

1 PA AA, R 100 857, fols. 195–196. This document has been translated from German.

2 Parts of the original have been underlined by hand.

3 Henry Hamilton Beamish (1873–1948), British founder of the antisemitic organization 'The Britons' in 1919, was regarded as one of the first in the 1920s to advocate 'getting rid' of the Jews by sending them to Madagascar, an idea that went back to Paul de Lagarde (1827–1891). Beamish issued an article in the publishing arm of The Britons to this effect in 1923. Three years later an article appeared on the front page of the *Völkischer Beobachter*, probably written by Beamish, entitled '"Madagaskar" (Von einem Engländer)' ('Madagascar' (by an Englishman)): Magnus Brechtken, *'Madagaskar für die Juden': Antisemitische Idee und politische Praxis 1885–1945* (Munich: Oldenbourg, 1997), pp. 32–38.

4 Reich Foreign Minister Joachim von Ribbentrop.

This plan divides up practical responsibilities as follows:
(1) Leadership of negotiations with the enemy powers on the basis of the peace treaty and with the other European states on the basis of special treaties – Reich Foreign Office.
(2) Registration of the Jews in Europe, their transportation to Madagascar, their resettlement there, and the future administration of the island ghetto – Reich Security Main Office.
(3) Registration of Jewish assets in Europe, foundation of an inter-European bank, which, acting as a trust, is to administer and utilize these assets, as well as to manage the financing of the resettlement enterprise – Office of the Four-Year Plan, Staatsrat Wohltat.
(4) Preparing propaganda and safeguarding the plan against a possible smear campaign from the USA:
 (a) for the interior, the Ministry of Propaganda, Oberregierungsrat Dr Taubert, with his 'Antisemitic Action';[5]
 (b) for abroad, the Information Department of the Reich Foreign Office.

I approached the individual offices in accordance with this plan. The Madagascar Plan of the Reich Security Main Office was then formulated in response to my initiative and in close consultation with me.[6] The plan of the inter-European Bank, in the form it appears here, was drawn up by me. I have sent it to Staatsrat Wohltat, who will check it for practicability and assume the task of implementing it.[7] Antisemitic Action is preparing of its own accord a propaganda plan for the domestic sphere. During the preliminary talks with inner-German offices, Senior Division Head Brake[8] of the Chancellery of the Führer (Bouhler staff)[9] suggested that the organization of transport, which he has developed as a special assignment from the Führer for wartime, subsequently be deployed for the transport of the Jews to Madagascar.[10] I advised Senior Division Head Brake to contact SS Gruppenführer Heydrich in this regard. In my view, his plan is certainly

5 Dr Eberhard Taubert (1907–1976), lawyer; joined the NSDAP and the SA in 1931; from 1933 section head at the Reich Ministry of Public Enlightenment and Propaganda, where his responsibilities included anti-Jewish propaganda; in 1934–1935 founded the Institute for the Study of the Jewish Question, which was renamed Antisemitic Action (Antisemitische Aktion) in 1939; honorary judge at the People's Court from 1938; wrote the screenplay for the film *Der ewige Jude* (The Eternal Jew); Ministerialrat, 1942; immediately after the war went into hiding; founded the People's League for Peace and Freedom in 1950; later psychological warfare consultant to the Federal German armed forces.

6 See Doc. 99.

7 Rademacher's plan was that the bank would centrally administer the assets of the European Jews and thereby meet the costs of deportation and resettlement: 'Gedanken über die Gründung einer intereuropäischen Bank für die Verwertung des Judenvermögens in Europa', 12 August 1940, PA AA, R 100 857, fol. 228r–v.

8 Correctly: Viktor Brack (1904–1948), economist; joined the SA in 1923 and the NSDAP and the SS in 1929; employed at NSDAP headquarters in Munich from 1932; chief of staff from 1934 and deputy head from 1936 of the Chancellery of the Führer, where he was liaison officer to the SS, member of the People's Court; appointed SS Oberführer in 1940; closely involved in the 'euthanasia' murders; orderly officer in the Waffen SS, 1942–1944; sentenced to death at the Nuremberg Military Tribunals in 1947 and executed.

9 Brack was on the staff of the head of the Reich Chancellery, Philipp Bouhler (1899–1945).

10 The reference is to Gekrat (Gemeinnützige Kranken-Transport GmbH), an organization that transported victims to the 'euthanasia' killing sites. On 'euthanasia', see Introduction, p. 32 and Glossary.

noteworthy. A well-attuned organization with a wealth of experience can be deployed more rapidly than a new entity, which will naturally encounter teething problems. In order to move the plan forward efficiently, it is now necessary:

(a) to summon the aforementioned inner-German offices for a meeting at the Reich Foreign Office and to assemble a preparatory commission;
(b) to approach the French, so that they allow this commission to enter Madagascar;
(c) to send the commission to Madagascar for one or two months, in order to identify at first hand individual issues associated with resettlement and to prepare for it.

It can already be affirmed that all the European Jews, the total number of whom is estimated at 6.5 million at the most, can be accommodated in Madagascar alongside the native population. Reports by Professor Burgdörfer of the Bavarian Regional Statistical Office and Dr Schumacher of the Freiberg Academy of Mining, commissioned by me, confirm this.[11] The fact that, because of their swampy climate, large parts of the island are currently to be regarded as harmful to health does not contradict this. This failing can be easily rectified by drainage work, as demonstrated in the Portuguese colonial territory of Mozambique, which is directly opposite the island, and in South America in the Port of Santos. The average population density would be around 16 per km^2, in other words equal to the current average population density for the earth's surface.

Herewith

presented to the envoy Mr *Luther*, with the request that he secure approval from the Reich Foreign Minister for the proposed procedure.

DOC. 102

In August 1940 Herbert Gerigk writes about the role of Judaism in music[1]

Preface to *Lexicon of the Jews in Music* by Herbert Gerigk,[2] dated August 1940

The cleansing of our culture and thus also of our musical life of all Jewish elements is now complete. Clear legal regulations in Greater Germany guarantee that, in the artistic fields, the Jew cannot be publicly active either as a performer or as a creator of works,

11 On Burgdörfer's report, see Doc. 94. The report by the geologist Friedrich Schumacher (1884–1974) dealt with the question of Madagascar's mineral resources: 'Zusammenstellung der mineralischen Bodenschätze von Madagaskar', 29 July 1940, PA AA, R 100 857, fols. 223–225.

1 *Lexikon der Juden in der Musik: Mit einem Titelverzeichnis jüdischer Werke*, Veröffentlichungen des Instituts zur Erforschung der Judenfrage Frankfurt a. M., vol. 2 (Berlin: Hahnefeld, 1940), pp. 5–9. Published as facsimile in Eva Weissweiler, *Ausgemerzt! Das Lexikon der Juden in der Musik und seine mörderischen Folgen* (Cologne: Dittrich, 1999), pp. 185–189. This document has been translated from German.

2 Dr Herbert Gerigk (1905–1996), musicologist; joined the NSDAP in 1932, the SA in 1933, and the SS in 1935; director of the Cultural Policy Archives head office at the office for ideological education and training of the NSDAP (Amt Rosenberg), 1935–1939, and the Main Office for Music in the Rosenberg Office, 1935–1945; from 1940 also in charge of the Special Staff for Music within the Rosenberg Task Force, where he was tasked with the confiscation of Jewish property; appointed SS-Hauptsturmführer, 1942; co-editor of *Lexikon der Juden in der Musik*; music critic for the newspaper *Ruhr Nachrichten* after 1945.

either as a writer, a publisher or an entrepreneur. The names of the 'greats' from the period between the end of the World War and the new order of the Reich have disappeared. Indeed, they have been forgotten to such an extent that, should such a name accidently resurface, some will barely be able to recall that it concerns a notorious, once oft-cited Jew. This will be particularly the case for members of the younger generation, who did not consciously experience that degenerate era, in other words people whose work began during the period of reconstruction. Moreover, because of the large number of names, it is entirely natural that, here and there, doubts continue to arise about the descent of a composer or person otherwise active in the musical field.

This situation made it necessary to set about creating a reference work that, despite the complexity of the material, flawlessly reflects the state of our knowledge. It was necessary to locate the most reliable sources in order to give the musician, the music educator, the politician, and also the music lover the absolute certainty that must be required with regard to the Jewish question.

Such a lexicon will continue to be significant in the future, when the Jewish question in German art one day comes to constitute a distant historical episode. Creating a lexicon of Jews prominent in the field of music is above all important for academia, so that facts and contexts can be passed down and explained that may prove impossible to recognize and investigate so thoroughly in the future. With this discovery, the academic world thereby receives a valuable tool to aid its reorientation along the lines of race.

Nowhere can there ever be a genuine connection between the German and the Jewish spirit. Recognition of this prompts us to draw as clear a distinction as possible, all the more so since the preceding years have shown us how things develop as soon as Jewish elements are tolerated or even placed in positions of authority. The world outside Germany has only understood this to a minimal extent, and on the whole there is an unwillingness to understand it at all. People do not want to see that, for us, it is never about judging *individual* Jews, be it in music or anywhere else, but rather that the Jewish question forms, in our view, an indivisible whole. For that reason, the question that occasionally arises as to the worth or worthlessness of individual achievements is wrong from the outset, since it misses the point. We measure by the standards of *our* race, and it is then that we do indeed reach the conclusion that the Jew is uncreative, and that in the field of music he is only capable of advancing to a certain degree of technical ability through imitation. His capacity for empathy enables him as a virtuoso to achieve astonishing things; however, on closer inspection these turn out to be without substance, especially since it is inevitable that his oriental perception will perpetually distort the content of occidental musical creation.

In our era the connections between music and race are being scientifically and systematically investigated for the first time. It took a long time for Richard Wagner's polemic essay 'Judaism in Music',[3] which in the mid nineteenth century emphatically directed attention to the racial question in music, to be followed up in a positive sense. The pioneering work done by Richard Eichenauer in his 1932 book *Music and Race*

3 Richard Wagner's antisemitic essay 'Das Judenthum in der Musik' first appeared in 1850 under the pseudonym K. Freigedank in the *Neue Zeitschrift für Musik*. *Das Judenthum in der Musik* was published under Wagner's name in 1869 as a pamphlet.

remains useful, regardless of some of his controversial and debatable observations.[4] Karl Blessinger dealt with Judaism in particular in his work *Mendelssohn, Meyerbeer, Mahler.* In it, he attempted a debate in a scientific sense, so far as is possible on the basis of existing preliminary research.[5] Various lexicographical attempts have also already been made: however, these have shortcomings consisting either in an unconsidered inclusivity regarding the names to be registered or in grave omissions. This lexicon aspires to the highest standards of reliability. This entailed initially omitting all names that could not be proved with sufficient certainty to be Jewish. The descent of by far the largest part of the Jews and half-Jews entered can be proved by official documents (quarter-Jews and persons intermarried with Jews were not taken into account, although given the sensibility of the artist, extensive influence on the Aryan spouse must be assumed). Even in the case of persons widely known to be Jews, a cross has been added to their name if there is no incontestable documentary evidence about their lineage and therefore reservations exist. It is therefore in the common interest that as many users as possible forward any additions and corrections to the existing names to the address provided, as well as details about Jewish musicians not yet taken into account. A supplement will include this material at a later date.

The difficulties are considerable when researching earlier centuries in particular. Jewish sources are unreliable, since some authors deliberately want to claim Aryans for the purposes of Judaism. Alfred Einstein, for example, includes Hugo Kaun in his *Jewish Lexicon*.[6] The notorious Adolf Kohut[7] claims the most famous female singers for the Jewish race. Here a great deal still needs to be checked. Changes of name and the fact that many Jews, even when working for a long time in one place, tend not to register with the police, as is required, make collecting data a lengthy process, even for periods close to the present day.

Now that the compilation of material has been concluded for the time being, it will be possible to begin with constructing an overarching account of the role played by Jewry in music.

For the purposes of this lexicon, it seemed sufficient in the case of Jews who have emigrated that generally their last domicile in the territory of the German Reich be recorded. In order to prevent the book becoming unnecessarily voluminous, indexes of works and exhaustive bibliographic entries have been left out. Clarity would otherwise have suffered, and after all our aim is not to immortalize Jewish creations but rather to

4 Richard Eichenauer, *Musik und Rasse* (Munich: Lehmann, 1932). Eichenauer (1893–1956) attempted to apply the racial theory of H. F. K. Günther (1891–1968) to music. The book was soon criticized for its amateurish and unscholarly approach.

5 Dr Karl Blessinger (1889–1962), musicologist and composer; teacher at the Academy of Musical Arts in Munich, 1920–1945; joined the NSDAP in 1932; appointed professor in 1942; published works including *Mendelssohn, Meyerbeer, Mahler: Drei Kapitel Judentum in der Musik als Schlüssel zur Musikgeschichte des 19. Jahrhunderts* (1939).

6 Dr Alfred Einstein (1880–1952), musicologist; editor of the *Zeitschrift für Musikwissenschaften*, 1918–1933; editor of the *Riemann Musiklexikon*, 1919–1929 (referred to incorrectly as the *Jewish Lexicon* in this document); critic at the *Berliner Tageblatt*, 1927–1933; emigrated to Britain in 1933, to Italy in 1935, and to the USA in 1938; lecturer in Northampton, MA, 1939–1950. Hugo Kaun (1863–1932), composer, conductor, and educator.

7 Dr Adolph, also Adolf, Kohut (1847/1848–1917), writer, journalist, and literary and cultural historian.

provide a guide to enable the swiftest possible elimination from our cultural and intellectual life of all remnants that have been mistakenly maintained up to now. As masters of camouflage, individual Jews still manage to slip through the net here and there, even now.

The lexicon is intended to be a reliable guide for politicians working in the field of culture, stage directors, and conductors, for the radio, for leading figures in the offices of the Party organs and affiliated organizations, and not least for the directors of light music orchestras. Moreover, for the first time it provides both the music educator and the scholar with a reliable guide. The index of Jewish stage works can in some cases make the work significantly easier.

The main work on the lexicon was accomplished by Dr Theo Stengel.[8] However, the work in its present form would not have been possible without the extensive assistance of the Reich Office for Kinship Research. We are also grateful to those registry offices and administrations that very willingly provided information and documents. Valuable work was carried out by the members of the office of Reichsleiter Rosenberg – Dr Lily Vietig-Michaelis,[9] Dr Wolfgang Boetticher,[10] and Dr Hermann Killer.[11]

The lexicon will, for its part, offer illuminating and educational material for an important branch of our artistic life.

8 Dr Karl Theophil Stengel (1905–1995), musicologist; joined the NSDAP in 1931; from 1935 employed at the legal department of the Reich Chamber of Music, and later section head for ancestral documentation; served in the Wehrmacht, 1941–1944; briefly in US internment in 1946; later a music teacher near Heidelberg; co-editor of the *Lexikon der Juden in der Musik*.

9 Dr Lily Vietig-Michaelis (b. 1912), musicologist; head of political education in the National Socialist Association of Students; joined the NSDAP in 1937; employee at the Main Office for Music and in the Rosenberg Task Force from 1939; lived in Bad Schwartau after 1945.

10 Dr Wolfgang Boetticher (1914–2002), musicologist; joined the NSDAP in 1937; employee at the Main Office for Music from 1939/1940; as member of the Special Staff for Music within the Rosenberg Task Force, involved in the confiscation of Jewish property in the occupied territories; lecturer from 1948 and appointed professor in Göttingen in 1956; banned from teaching by the university administration in 1998 because of his National Socialist past.

11 Dr Hermann Killer (1902–1990), musicologist; joined the SA in 1933 and the NSDAP in 1937; wrote for the *Völkischer Beobachter*; director of the Cultural Policy Archives head office in the Amt Rosenberg, 1939–1945.

DOC. 103
During a meeting at the Reich Ministry of Propaganda on 6 September 1940, Reich Cultural Administrator Hans Hinkel reports on the planned deportation of Berlin's Jews[1]

Report on a meeting at the Reich Ministry of Public Enlightenment and Propaganda, unsigned, dated 6 September 1940

10:45 – meeting on 6 September 1940

1. Now that, following the abdication of the Romanian king, there is no longer any obligation to show consideration, at least some of the more radical papers in Germany should, if possible, probe into the character of this corrupt monarch and stress that he was the one who had the Romanian patriots shot. Moreover, his relationship with Mrs Wolf-Lupescu[2] needs to be brought to light, along with the fact that he arranged for his mistress to marry his minister of court, in order to live with the former under the same roof, and that he then wanted to use this very minister as head of the anti-Jewish movement.[3]

2. Mr Fischer (press)[4] should see to it that only a few factual reports reach the press about the trip of the Czech journalists, and that they don't focus too much on individual Czechs. In Berlin, on the other hand, the Czechs should be received in a way intended to create an impact, if possible at Aviators' House.[5]

3. Major Martin[6] reports that, as required by the Hague Convention, the English and French prisoners in Germany are receiving the same rations as reserve troops catered for by the home military, in other words the same as the German civilian population. He adds that in workplaces involving heavy labour, in order to extract sufficient work

1 BArch, R 55/21220. Published in Willi A. Boelcke, *Kriegspropaganda 1939–1941: Geheime Ministerkonferenzen im Reichspropagandaministerium* (Stuttgart: Deutsche Verlags-Anstalt, 1996), pp. 491–492. This document has been translated from German.

2 Correctly: Magda-Elena Lupescu (1896–1977), third morganatic wife of King Carol II (1893–1953). The supplement 'Wolf' (Romanian: *lupu*) was intended as an allusion to the family's Jewish descent.

3 The cession of territory to the Soviet Union in June 1940 and the Second Vienna Award of 30 August 1940, in the course of which Romania lost a third of its territory, led to political unrest. On 6 Sept. 1940 Carol II, who after 1938 had opposed efforts to form a government by the fascist Iron Guard, abdicated in favour of his son Mihai I (b. 1921). General Ion Antonescu (1882–1946) de facto assumed power. Carol II and his staff, including his former minister of court Ernest Urdăreanu (1897–1985), fled to Portugal.

4 Erich Fischer (1908–1996?); worked as a surveyor until 1931; joined the NSDAP and SA in 1927; head of the NSDAP Press and Propaganda Department in 1935; section head of the Reich Press Office, 1937–1939; in the Reich Ministry of Public Enlightenment and Propaganda from 1939; joined the SS in 1940; Ministerialrat and head of the German Press Department, 1942; publishing manager of *Der Spiegel* magazine in Düsseldorf from 1952.

5 In Sept. 1940, on Goebbels's invitation, a group of thirty-four Czechs who, alongside prominent journalists, included the poet Josef Hora (1891–1945) and the literary critic Jaroslav Durych (1886–1962), travelled through the German Reich. The aim was to encourage them to collaborate with the German occupation regime.

6 Hans-Leo Martin (b. 1899), military officer; group head of propaganda in the Wehrmacht High Command; military liaison officer to the Reich Ministry of Public Enlightenment and Propaganda, Feb. 1940 to mid 1944.

from the prisoners, it will even be necessary to give the prisoners the same supplements for heavy labour. The Minister[7] wants the OKW to write a memo about this matter, which can be passed on to the Gauleiter in order to communicate the information orally within the Party.

4. In response to a letter from the Commander-in-Chief of the Luftwaffe,[8] the Minister makes it clear that war reporters assigned to propaganda companies of the Luftwaffe should under no circumstances be pointlessly deployed to carry out some task or other unless there are compelling military reasons for doing so.

5. In the light of particular circumstances, the Minister points out the confidentiality of the 10:45 meeting, stressing that statements he makes about persons not present at the meeting, which moreover are also not to be taken as personal judgements, may under no circumstances be communicated to those persons.

6. The Minister approves of reporting within Germany the news of the torpedoing of a 12,000-tonne troop transporter,[9] since otherwise rumours would only be encouraged. In this context, he suggests above all to the Luftwaffe that, should the daily tally of downed aircraft ever be to our disadvantage, it publicize this fact plainly, since doing so would especially highlight the credibility of the German OKW reports.

7. Mr Hinkel[10] reports on the deportation of Jews from Vienna and Berlin. Of the 180,000 that formerly lived in Vienna, there are now 47,400, of whom two thirds are women and only around 300 are men aged between 20 and 35. It has been possible, even during wartime, to deport a total of 17,000 Jews via the south-east.[11] In Berlin, there are still 71,800 Jews left. In the future, 500 Jews per month are also to be sent from here to the south-east. Mr Hinkel reports further that all preparations have been made so that – as soon as transportation becomes available after the war – 60,000 Jews can be removed from Berlin within four weeks, [and sent] primarily towards the east. Within another four weeks, the remaining 12,000 will also have disappeared.

7 The Reich Minister of Public Enlightenment and Propaganda, Joseph Goebbels.
8 Hermann Göring.
9 In early Sept. 1940 a German transporter belonging to a convoy heading to Norway was sunk by the British navy at Skagerrak.
10 Hans Hinkel (1900–1960), journalist; joined the NSDAP in 1921; took part in the Beer Hall Putsch in 1923; member of the Reichstag from 1930; joined the SS in 1931; state commissioner in the Prussian Ministry of Culture, 1933–1935; at the Reich Ministry of Public Enlightenment and Propaganda from 1935, responsible for the supervision of the cultural activities of non-Aryans; general secretary of the Reich Chamber of Culture, 1941–1944: Reich Film Director, 1944; extradited to Poland in 1947; classified in absentia as a 'major offender' by the Munich main denazification tribunal in 1949; released to the Federal Republic in 1952.
11 After war broke out, thousands of Jews were able to flee the German Reich on refugee ships that sailed down the Danube to Yugoslavia. From there they hoped to reach Palestine via the Black Sea: see Docs. 120 and 121.

DOC. 104

On 9 September 1940 Emilie Cassel asks the Stettin Chief of Police for permission to purchase a 'people's receiver', despite her husband being non-Aryan[1]

Letter from Emilie Cassel, née Bannert,[2] 10. I. Harkutschstrasse, Stettin, to the Chief of Police in Stettin,[3] dated 9 September 1940

Application for permission to be allowed to buy a radio/people's receiver:[4]
The signatory is the daughter of the Aryan master turner Johannes Bannert, who died in 1905. My husband, to whom I have been married for nearly forty years, is non-Aryan by birth and belongs to a family that has lived here for centuries. He left the Jewish association after the Führer's seizure of power in February 1933.[5] Since his two brothers are also married to Aryans, we barely had any relations with Jews even before that. The national reliability of my husband is indisputable; I vouch for that. He fought in the World War for over four years, is a long-standing member of the Stettin Gymnastics Club (corps),[6] and was a member of the German Navy League to the end. Our only son is a recognized Volksgenosse, has been married to an Aryan for eleven years, is a member of the German Labour Front, and, after signing up voluntarily, was conscripted in the defence of the Fatherland in February this year. He took part in the advance on Holland and is currently a soldier in France (field post no. 06 942).

After asking for my radio to be returned to me on 25 September and 24 October [1939], I was promised that this would happen, but unfortunately I have not received it.[7] I now assume that for technical reasons a return is no longer possible, so I ask for permission to be able to purchase another set without foreign reception, so that I can follow national events, which understandably interest me all the more given that my son is in the field.

Moreover, like my husband, I will soon be 68 years old, through an accident have lost my left leg, and, as a result of this physical handicap, am almost permanently housebound. Hence, I also have a 48-year-old Aryan home help, who is also only 50 per cent fit to work. Also living in my home is an Aryan lodger of nearly 84 years of age, and for

1 RGVA, 503k-1-385; copy in USHMM, RG-11.001M04, reel 74. This document has been translated from German.
2 Emilie Cassel, née Bannert (1872–1943); deported at the end of August 1942 to Theresienstadt, where she perished in March 1943.
3 Wilhelm Jahn (1891–1952), bank clerk; joined the NSDAP and the SA in 1922; electrical goods and car salesman in Osnabrück, 1922–1930; full-time SA officer from 1931; chief of police in Halle, 1936–1939, in Stettin, 1939–1942, and in Königsberg, 1942–1943; leader of the SA Group Elbe from Dec. 1943.
4 *Volksempfänger*: an inexpensive radio which had a limited range, making it difficult to pick up foreign broadcasts. The Ministry of Propaganda promoted the manufacture and sale of these radios with the aim of increasing the number of radio listeners, transmitting national propaganda, and encouraging collective listening.
5 Alexander Cassel (1873–1943); at the end of August 1942 deported to Theresienstadt, where he perished.
6 Meaning is possibly that the club was organized on military lines.
7 This correspondence is not in the file.

all four persons a radio would be the sole joy and diversion during the long winter evenings to come. I therefore again ask for permission to be able to buy a radio set as soon as possible.[8]

DOC. 105

On 12 September 1940 Hermann Samter, editor at the *Jüdisches Nachrichtenblatt*, writes to Hanna Kobylinski about the activities of the Jewish Culture League in Berlin[1]

Letter from Hermann Samter,[2] 18 Schillstrasse, Berlin W. 62, to Hanna Kobylinski,[3] Copenhagen, dated 12 September 1940

Dear Hanna,

It is years now since I last heard from you. And then a few days ago I received a letter from my aunt, Cläre Samter from San Domingo,[4] in which she mentioned in passing that Eva had written to Liesel Feist saying that she should make an effort to get you entry to the USA. Attached to my aunt's letter was a note to the Friedländers. When passing it on I took the opportunity to ask the Friedländers for your address. Not long ago I made another effort to find out your address, by the way: on your birthday I travelled to Heidelberg. On the way it occurred to me that I hadn't heard from you for so long. But how was I to get your address? I recalled that eleven years ago I was often with Richard[5] at your relatives, the Jablonskis.[6] And so I decided to go to them. Although they couldn't remember who I was, they were very nice to me. However, they couldn't tell me your address because they knew very little about you all. Thus, it was only from me that they heard that your parents are not with you in Copenhagen, as they had supposed. Their own son is also where your parents are,[7] by the way, while his young wife lives with them.

8 At the end of the document there is a note from the State Police II B 4 dated 17 Sept. 1940: 'According to the decree of the Reich Security Main Office Berlin dated 1 July 1940 (IV A 5 b – 982/39–2) permission to receive radio signals is to be refused if the head of the household is a Jew. This applies here. The applicant has been duly informed.'

1 Holocaust Memorial Center, Farmington Hills, MI; copy in YVA, O.2/30, fol. 1. Published in Hermann Samter, *'Worte können das ja kaum verständlich machen': Briefe 1939–1943*, ed. Daniel Fraenkel (Göttingen: Wallstein, 2009), pp. 60–62. This document has been translated from German.

2 Dr Hermann Samter (1909–1943), journalist and economist; worked for the *Jüdisches Nachrichtenblatt*, 1939–1942, then for the Reich Association of Jews in Germany; he and his wife Lili Samter, née Landsberger (1919–1943), were deported on 12 March 1943 to Auschwitz, where they were murdered.

3 Dr Hanna Kobylinski (1907–1999), historian and sinologist; emigrated to Denmark in 1933; fled to Sweden in 1943; returned to Copenhagen after the war and worked as a historian.

4 Cläre Samter (1881/1882–1972?); emigrated to the Dominican Republic in spring 1940; later joined her son Dr Max Samter (b. 1908), doctor and allergist, who had emigrated to the USA in 1937.

5 Richard Kobylinski (b. 1911), brother of Hanna Kobylinski; emigrated in the 1930s to Britain, where he completed his medical training.

6 Probably Lora Jablonski, née Reis (1877–1944), and Leo Jablonski (1873–1942); both were deported to the Gurs camp on 22 Oct. 1940. Leo Jablonski perished in the Récébédou internment camp; Lora Jablonski perished in Gurs.

7 This is probably a reference to Britain.

Yes, much has changed since we last saw each other. How long ago is that, in fact? You must have heard from your parents that at the time of their emigration I was also making great efforts to get to South America. For a time last year it looked quite promising; however, then everything went wrong. I'm lucky, at least, to have had almost continuous employment. In November 1938 the Berlin newspaper *Jüdisches Gemeindeblatt*, along with all the other Jewish newspapers, ceased to exist.[8] But by the beginning of January 1939 I already had another position, at the newly established *Jüdisches Nachrichtenblatt*. This job is pretty much like the previous one. We occupy the rooms which belonged to the *Jüdische Rundschau*. The paper is printed at the – now Aryan – printworks of the *Israelitisches Familienblatt*. The staff comes from the various newspapers and the Culture League. That enterprise – the Jewish Culture League – is a very interesting outfit. It is divided into an 'artistic division' (film and other events such as theatre, concerts) and the 'publishing house'. The publishing house, here on Meinekestrasse, is divided into a newspaper and a book publisher. Since all Jewish publishing houses and bookshops have closed, all books and their distribution have been transferred to the Culture League. In our building there are around forty employees. – In August I had a fortnight's holiday and, as I mentioned, travelled to Heidelberg. I only knew it from the eight days when I was there at Richard's in 1929. Back then, I was in and out of lectures non-stop and only got to know Heidelberg a tiny bit. So when I arrived this time, everything was more or less new to me. It was the university holidays, although even so I don't think you see nearly as much activity at the university as before. Back in 1929, I also had no idea of what the situation would be when I would return one day. I made the most of the fourteen days and was out and about practically all the time. I liked Heidelberg so much that I stayed literally until the last minute: I arrived at Anhalter train station [in Berlin] an hour before work. Life is good there. I often thought it was like a fairy tale that something like that is still possible today. It now seems to me as if it was years ago. Instead of the Neckar valley, I now have to content myself with the Havel and the Spree. The beautiful surroundings of Berlin are indeed all that one has left. Today, I can appreciate it better than before. Therefore I go out into the countryside every Sunday. There aren't many other diversions. Once a week I go to the cinema at the Culture League, which often shows the films at the same time as the theatre premieres. Every two months there is a new play, much more primitively staged than two years ago, of course. And, finally, strangely enough I still have a range of acquaintances whom I often meet up with; it is strange in that most of the sensible ones emigrated a long time ago.

My aunt writes that she hasn't heard from her sister Mrs Feist for a long time and has no idea whether she is still in Copenhagen. You are no doubt often at the Feists. How are the Wechselmanns? And above all, I am interested to hear about what has become of your work. Hopefully it hasn't stopped. So please, tell me very soon and in detail! I

8 In early November 1938 the Gestapo Central Office (Gestapa), in consultation with the Reich Ministry of Public Enlightenment and Propaganda, banned all Jewish newspapers and magazines. The final issue of *Jüdisches Gemeindeblatt* appeared on 6 Nov. 1938 (no. 45) and the first issue of the *Jüdisches Nachrichtenblatt* appeared on 23 Nov. 1938.

haven't heard from Lotte for a long time. She probably wasn't with your parents much, since the travel costs are too expensive for her.[9]

Warm regards

DOC. 106

On 30 September 1940 the mayor of Misdroy asks the German Council of Municipalities whether a Jewish woman who lives in the town may be committed to an institution[1]

Letter (no. 121–3) from the mayor of Misdroy,[2] p.p. signed Schubbe, alderman,[3] to the German Council of Municipalities, 7 Alsenstraße, Berlin NW 40 (received on 3 October 1940), dated 30 September 1940[4]

Re: institutional care for Jews
Case file: publication no. 823 in the *Nachrichtendienst des DGT* of 20 September 1940.[5]
The above publication gives me occasion to make the following enquiry:

Here in Misdroy lives a Jewess who was born on 12 October 1880.[6] Up to the time of the ruling that the Reich Association of Jews is to provide welfare for Jews in need[7] she was a state pauper,[8] and had been for the last thirty years.

The Jewess is a prime example of Jewish filth. When she shuffles through the streets, she desecrates the entire appearance of the street. In summer, during the main tourist season in Misdroy, the police have placed restrictions on how long she may stay out on the streets. With typical Jewish brazenness, however, she exploits the restrictions to the full. She also knows that everyone avoids her; but that doesn't shame her in the least. She also does her shopping with the same shamelessness.

9 Charlotte (Lotte) Blumenfeld, née Samter (1907–1989), Hermann Samter's sister; emigrated in June 1939 with her husband Paul Blumenfeld (1901–2001), a cellist, to Britain; she worked there as an administrative assistant at a lawyer's office.

1 LAB, B Rep. 142/ 7, Nr. 1-2-6–1. This document has been translated from German.
2 Dr Helmut Szpitter (1898–1944?).
3 Fritz Schubbe (b. 1881), publican; joined the NSDAP in 1933; in Szpitter's absence he was evidently formally in charge of the administration.
4 Parts of the original have been annotated and underlined by hand.
5 The *Nachrichtendienst des Deutschen Gemeindetags* ('News Service of the German Council of Municipalities') states the following on 'institutional care for Jews': 'If negotiations with the Reich Association of Jews in Germany over covering the costs of Jewish institutional care fail to reach a satisfactory conclusion, it is recommended […] that an enquiry be placed with the German Council of Municipalities'; *Nachrichtendienst des Deutschen Gemeindetags*, 1940, p. 198.
6 Probably Johanna Zobel (b. 1880), deported to the Warsaw ghetto on 14 April 1942. Her subsequent fate is unknown.
7 According to the Tenth Regulation on the Reich Citizenship Law, 4 July 1939, the Reich Association of Jews in Germany was required 'to support Jews requiring welfare sufficiently so that public welfare need not intervene'; *Reichsgesetzblatt*, 1939, I, pp. 1097–1099, here p. 1098.
8 *Landarme*: pauper eligible for poor relief from the public relief fund in the province in which they resided.

When reading your publication, I wondered whether it would be possible to place this Jewess in a Jewish institution. I would be grateful if you could give me a response to this as soon possible.[9]

DOC. 107

On 2 October 1940 the head of the Swiss Police for Foreign Nationals urges the Swiss ambassador in Vichy to ensure that Jewish refugees from Germany receive transit visas[1]

Letter from the head of the Police Division of the Swiss Department of Justice and Police, signed Rothmund,[2] Bern, to the ambassador of Switzerland in Vichy, Stucki,[3] dated 2 October (carbon copy)[4]

Today, the first transport of German refugees is travelling from Geneva in transit through France to an overseas destination. A total of fifty-two persons are undertaking the journey in two buses. In order to obtain a precise insight into how the transport proceeds as well as experience for the future, we have tasked the secretary general of the Department of Justice and Police of the Geneva canton, Mr Guillermet,[5] and one of his section heads, Mr Déléaval,[6] with accompanying the transport. Mr Guillermet is travelling with a diplomatic pass. He will go as far as Barcelona. Mr Déléaval has a public service pass. We have told the gentlemen that they should contact your embassy if anything goes wrong.

9 Because, in his judgement, this woman was not in need of welfare, the specialist for Jewish affairs at the German Council of Municipalities, Döbereiner, saw no possibility of committing her to an institution. However, he did suggest checking whether there were 'policing grounds' for doing so: letter of the German Council of Municipalities, p.p. signed Döbereiner, to the mayor of Misdroy, dated 10 Oct. 1940, LAB, B Rep. 142/ 7, Nr. 1-2-6-1.

1 Archives d'Etat de Genève, E2001D 1000/1553, Bd. 271, Az. B.41.21.02, 'Wiederauswanderung politischer Flüchtlinge (jüdische Emigranten) nach überseeischen Staaten', 1938–1947. Published in Nationale Kommission für die Veröffentlichung diplomatischer Dokumente der Schweiz, *Diplomatische Dokumente der Schweiz 1848–1945*, vol. 13: *1939–1940* (Bern: Benteli, 1991), doc. 391, pp. 957–962. This document has been translated from German.

2 Dr Heinrich Rothmund (1888–1961), lawyer; joined the Swiss federal administration in 1916; head of the Swiss Federal Headquarters of the Police for Foreign Nationals, 1919–1929; head of the Police Division of the Swiss Federal Department of Justice and Police, 1929–1954; in this position in charge of the Swiss Police for Foreign Nationals from late 1933.

3 Dr h.c. Walter Stucki (1888–1963), lawyer and diplomat; secretary general of the Swiss Federal Department of National Economics, 1917–1920; director of the Swiss Federal Department of Trade, 1925–1935; representative and delegate of the Swiss Federal Council for Foreign Trade from 1935; Swiss ambassador to Paris in 1937; Swiss Federal Council delegate for special questions after 1945.

4 The carbon copy was sent to the Swiss Federal Political Department, the Section for Foreign Affairs in Bern, the Swiss Federal Prosecutor in Bern, and Regierungsrat Briner, president of the Swiss Central Office for Refugees in Zurich.

5 Arthur Guillermet (1891–1981), lawyer and civil servant; secretary general of the Department of Justice and Police, 1919?–1933 and 1936–1955; secretary general of the Department of Trade and Industry in the canton of Geneva, 1933–1936; member of the Liberal Party.

6 Eugène Déléaval (1897–1970), civil servant; as a member of the canton administration of Geneva, 1915–1962, held various posts dealing with the policing of foreign nationals and residence issues.

Thanks to your efforts, for which we are most grateful, the Reich Foreign Office authorized the embassy in Bern to issue up to 150 transit visas to the refugees expelled by the Germans, who are now waiting in Switzerland to continue their journey. However, this is just the beginning. It is crucial that we succeed in persuading the French government to give the embassy in Bern the general instruction to issue transit visas to these foreigners, regardless of their number and their destination. Even if the transports were not being accompanied at our expense, and we were not issuing return visas just in case, we should be able to expect this. After assuming responsibility from France for ensuring the completion of these transits and simultaneously guaranteeing that we will take back these foreigners should, contrary to all expectations, the onward journey be impossible despite the Spanish visa, or should one of the refugees escape the closed transport while in France, further difficulties from the French side would appear not only incomprehensible but also as an explicit act of hostility towards Switzerland. This would especially be the case in view of the assistance provided by our country to our neighbours in need through the acceptance of around 8,000 civilians and over 40,000 military refugees in June of this year,[7] the donations of the Swiss Red Cross, the Swiss relief to refugees in France, the willingness to hospitalize 800 French children in Switzerland etc.,[8] and not least the great friendship of the Swiss people towards the French.

The skewed perception of this issue is probably a result of the fact that your first steps towards authorizing the transit of refugees from Germany go back to the beginning of the war. At that time it was a question of allowing German citizens to travel through France, despite the two countries being at war. That was also the reason why we offered France such extensive guarantees for the supervision of the transit, and initially only discussed a limited number of persons making the transit. However, the situation has changed significantly since the conclusion of the armistice. Today, the issue might arise for France as to how the Germans regard the transit. Indeed, at a breakfast yesterday at the French embassy, Ambassador Gazel[9] explained to the signatory that it would probably be important for Vichy to have a communiqué from the German government to the effect that it has no objections to the transit. In September 1938, during negotiations in Berlin on the control of the entry of German refugees into Switzerland, it was explained to the signatory by representatives of the Reich Foreign Office and the Ministry of the Interior (Gestapo) that Germany had not the slightest interest in having these people in neighbouring countries. On the contrary, they preferred them to be accommodated in countries as far away as possible. The same thing was repeated to the signatory very recently by the German ambassador in Bern. Indeed, at our request, the German envoy[10]

7 From 19 June 1940, following the defeat of the French army, 42,500 soldiers and around 7,500 civilians fled from France into Switzerland within the space of a few days.

8 See fn. 20.

9 Armand Gazel (b. 1896), diplomat; consular attaché in Budapest, 1922–1924; subsequently member of the French foreign missions in Brussels and Madrid; represented the Vichy government in Bern, 1940–1942; changed to the side of the French Committee of National Liberation, the government in exile in June 1943; continued in diplomatic service after 1945, appointed commander of the Legion of Honour in 1956.

10 Dr Otto Köcher (1884–1945), lawyer and diplomat; joined the NSDAP in 1934; consul general in Barcelona from April 1933 to Nov. 1936; German envoy in Bern from April 1937; committed suicide in US internment.

recently asked the Foreign Office in Berlin to communicate to the Spanish government via the German embassy in Madrid that Germany has no interest in applications for travelling through Spain made by refugees resident in Switzerland being checked individually by the central authorities in Spain, as is currently the case where applicants do not possess a German passport. Therefore, you can tell the French government that we know for sure that Germany does not intend to cause any difficulties in the slightest in allowing the passage of refugees from Switzerland, but on the contrary also sees this as being in its own interests.

Allow us once again to briefly sum up our understanding of the problem of refugees as regards transit through France. From the very outset, in April 1933, when the first measures against the Jews were taken in Germany, a statement published in the press[11] announced that Switzerland could only offer these foreigners temporary refuge, without work permits; residence in our country may be used solely to prepare for onward emigration. The short-term tolerance permits were extended only if proof could be provided that the applicant had done everything in his power to prepare for onward emigration. We reviewed the issue of continued emigration permanently, in close contact with the private organizations that had taken on these refugees, but especially with the head of the Swiss Federation of Jewish Communities.[12] We were also in contact with the organization in London that grew out of the Evian Conference,[13] where I took part in a conference in July 1939, using the opportunity to draw attention to the particularly difficult situation in which the small transit countries had found themselves in as a result of taking in refugees, and where, accompanied by the Swiss Federation of Jewish Communities, visits were also made to English and international private organizations.[14] In April 1940 we went to Basel to meet the former Belgian president van Zeeland, who had been tasked by the London committee with looking into new possibilities for resettlement.[15] Incidentally, the leaders of the London committee had an audience with President Roosevelt in Washington in October 1939. These consultations prompted the representatives of England and France to issue the declaration, which was disseminated by the press, to the effect that both countries would leave it to the small transit countries of Switzerland, Belgium, and Holland to organise the onward journey.[16] England had authorized the entry of a large number of refugees from Germany in 1939. France had also already taken in a great many. Both countries reckoned with long stays, if not the permanent presence

11 This statement could not be found.

12 The Swiss Federation of Jewish Communities (SIG) was founded in 1904 as an umbrella organization for the Jewish communities in Switzerland. The president of the SIG in the years 1936–1942 was the textile trader Saly Mayer (1882–1950); as honorary representative of the American Jewish Joint Distribution Committee (JDC) in Switzerland from 1940 and its European coordinator from 1943, Mayer played an important role in supporting Jews in the German-occupied territories of Europe.

13 The Evian Conference in July 1938 established the Intergovernmental Committee on Refugees (IGCR). Its task was to negotiate with the German government over the transfer of the assets of emigrating Jews, and with other governments over possibilities for resettling Jewish refugees: see PMJ 2, p. 48.

14 The third IGCR conference was held in London on 19–20 July 1939.

15 Paul van Zeeland (1893–1973), lawyer, economist, and politician; professor in Löwen; Belgian prime minister from March 1935 to Nov. 1937; foreign minister, 1935–1936; president from 20 July 1939 of the Coordinating Foundation, which was set up to explore resettlement possibilities for Jewish refugees; member of the Belgian government in exile from 1941; foreign minister again, 1949–1954.

16 This declaration was not found.

of these foreigners. France, whose strength never lay in organization, thus undertook no preparations for the onward journey of the refugees resident in that country.

When the war broke out, obliging us to fear that we would have to keep these foreigners for a relatively long period of time, without being able to allow them to work, we explored together with the army the question of setting up labour camps. This was based on the consideration that physically strong emigrants used to heavy work would be more readily admitted as immigrants by overseas destination countries. It was estimated that employing 800 men for one year in labour camps would cost 1.5 million francs.[17]

The efforts of individual emigrants to prepare for onward emigration, which were often targeted towards a very wide range of countries and exploited all former relationships, whether family, friends, or professional contacts, took a great deal of time. Given the increasing closure of destination countries to immigrants, particularly Jews, these efforts were not particularly successful and at any rate unpredictable. This also goes for the United States of North America. We are thus not in a position to predict how many refugees will succeed in obtaining entry permits to an overseas country. The total number of persons still resident with us lies between 7,000 and 8,000. We soon hope to be in a position to provide a precise figure; a full collection of data is under way. From this account you may surmise that the notion of the French Ministry of the Interior that 'our' emigrants could take away the overseas places of refugees resident in France is mistaken. This is certainly not the case for the United States. The quota reserved for Germany is divided among the various European countries. When one of the latter registers less emigration from Germany, then the remainder of the quota allocated to that country cannot be transferred to another.

The situation in San Domingo might be different. A company has been founded in New York for setting up a Jewish colony in San Domingo, provisionally limited to 100,000 persons. A representative of that country came to Europe to seek out the first qualified colonists in the various European countries. He initially wanted to select ten persons from Switzerland. After visiting our labour camps and seeing that their inmates were receiving the best possible preparations as future colonists, he immediately decided to pick a hundred people. We reckon with certainty on bringing a relatively large number to San Domingo, and for that reason have adapted our labour camp wholly to this project. Here, France might rightfully be worried about Swiss competition. We have continued to keep Dr Trone, the representative of the 'Dominican Republic, Settlement Association, New York', from travelling to Vichy to negotiate with the French government about the transit, because with his interesting project he may very well have reinforced the view of the Ministry of the Interior about Swiss competition.[18] That is one

17 On 12 March 1940 the Swiss Federal Council resolved to set up labour camps for male émigrés aged between 16 and 45 years. There were subsequently up to 50 labour camps, usually accommodating 100–200 refugees. In return for a small wage, they were put to work mainly in agriculture or infrastructure schemes. In some camps, women did sewing and washing for refugees in other camps.

18 In 1938 the Dominican Republic had offered to admit 100,000 Jewish refugees. The JDC founded and financed a resettlement society and in 1940 sent Trone and his wife Florence to Europe to select suitable settlers from the refugee camps. In total, however, no more than 500 Jews ever lived in the settlement. Dr Solomon Trone (1872–1969), engineer; born in Latvia; member of the Communist Party; emigrated to the USA in 1916; until 1931 employee of General Electric, for which he ran major projects for the electrification of the Soviet Union; member of the Allied Reparations Commission from 1945; lost US citizenship in 1953 during the McCarthy era and went to live in London.

reason why we urged you so strongly to obtain French approval for the transit, and why today we must entreat you to even greater haste. As long as we have Mr Trone, who is by the way a very assiduous man with considerable influence in San Domingo, in our vicinity, we can develop a more extensive plan for Switzerland–San Domingo with him. However, Mr Trone intends to travel to Portugal soon and to stop in Vichy on his way. Before he arrives, which he is expected to do the week after next, we must at all costs obtain the general assurance from the French government for the transit of our refugees.

The emigrant problem has significant financial implications for Switzerland. Between 1937 and 1939, the charities spent roughly 7 million francs, 5½ million of which [was paid] by the Jewish refugee relief. Part of these funds comes from America. However, Swiss Jews have so far donated more than 4 million francs. Since we too have only a small number of well-off Swiss citizens among the Jews, and probably none that are very wealthy, this has to be seen as an extremely heavy burden. However, the state cannot contribute to support in Switzerland, if only because doing so would cause private initiatives to cease entirely. As explained above, we do, however, finance the labour camps. On top of this are federal contributions to onward emigration, which are also steadily increasing. Today they amount to 400 francs per person, in other words 2,000 francs for a family of five. We must reckon with a very high sum, which can amount to millions, but we are resolved to propose spending so much because the removal of emigrants, 90 per cent of whom are Jews, is absolutely essential for demographic and general domestic and foreign policy reasons. That political reasons are currently at the forefront is something we need not emphasize. We merely point to the fact that we still wish to solve the problem on our own initiative so that we can reject any kind of foreign interference.

From a discussion with Mr Coulondre[19] at yesterday's breakfast at the French embassy, it emerged that the ambassador strongly supported our request to his government in Vichy. He, too, is unable to understand the attitude of his government.

Yesterday we also had the visit from the delegate of the French Red Cross to the military refugees in Switzerland; he is from Alsace and a Swiss citizen, domiciled in Basel. Mr Bernheim took on the task of speeding up preparations in Vichy for the dispatch of French children to be hospitalized in Switzerland by the Swiss Committee for War-Damaged Children.[20] We briefed Mr Bernheim about the difficulties France is causing us concerning the transit, and that we are resolved to force the transit by refusing the children permission to enter the country or by closing the border, should the French government fail to grant our self-evident request at last. However, we also told him that we have good reason to hope that you will be successful in getting our wish granted, without our having to use coercive means.

19 Dr Robert Coulondre (1885–1959), lawyer and diplomat; worked in the French diplomatic service from 1909; deputy head of the Trade Department of the Ministry of Foreign Affairs from 1927; second director of the Political Department from 1933; ambassador in Moscow, 1936, in Berlin, 1937–1939, and in Bern from May to Oct. 1940.

20 Correctly: the Swiss Working Group for War-Damaged Children (SAK). Founded in 1940, the SAK had the role of enabling children from countries involved in the war to spend time convalescing in Switzerland. At the request of the Swiss Police for Foreign Nationals, Jewish children were exempted from these convalescence trips. In 1942 the SAK merged with the Child Relief of the Swiss Red Cross: Antonia Schmidlin, *Eine andere Schweiz: Helferinnen, Kriegskinder und humanitäre Politik 1933–1942* (Zurich: Chronos, 1999), pp. 131–150.

As explained above, we are unable to inform you, for the attention of the French government, about how many refugees will pass through France and when they will receive permission to enter the country of destination, nor when all the other formalities will have been completed. Currently, around 180 persons are ready to travel. As far as we understand from today's press, the French Council of Ministers is considering a race law that will divide the Jews into various categories.[21] It is possible that an attempt will be made to thwart your efforts on these grounds. It will not be difficult for you to counter this objection.

We hope that, with these explanations, we have provided you with all the possible arguments that can be deployed in order to finally achieve a fundamental concession from the French government. Our account of our efforts concerning emigration to San Domingo is of course intended for you alone, in order to make it clear to you why we need to press for a speedy guarantee from the French government.

We ask you to ensure that the French government takes action to authorize the embassy in Bern to provide all refugees issued with Swiss return visas travelling through France on group transport accompanied at our cost – whether by coach or perhaps later by train – with transit visas in the form of a list. There should be no restriction with regard to numbers. Nor should the French government concern itself with the final destination of the refugees. It must suffice that the onward journey to Spain is guaranteed by the Spanish entry or transit visa. The French Ministry of the Interior can ensure that it has control over every transit that takes place by having one of those stamped lists drawn up by the French border authority at the point of entry showing entries, and another at the point of exit drawn up by the border authority showing entries and departures, and stamped by both authorities. It is thus unnecessary for the embassy to send the lists to Vichy by a certain time prior to the departure of the transport, as was the case before today's transport. The embassy had expressly explained to us that Vichy only needs the lists in order to be able to send them to the French border authorities, not, however, to double-check the question of the transit of the persons on the list.

We would like to reiterate the extreme importance and urgency of this matter. We would therefore be extremely grateful if you could do all in your power to obtain the definitive agreement of the French government to our proposal by the end of next week at the latest. If you should need to use coercion, then you have at your disposal the refusal to allow the entry of the children requiring hospitalization and, second, a complete visa embargo on France. We leave it to you to judge whether these means ought to be used.[22]

21 On 2 Oct. 1940 various newspapers reported that, the day before, the Vichy government had approved the draft of the Statute on Jews, which divided Jews into various categories. Jews born in France who had served in the army were classified most favourably; Jews who had arrived as immigrants received the least favourable classification: 'Vichy Drafts Plan to Deal with Jews', *New York Times*, 2 Oct. 1940, p. 8. On the Statute on Jews, see also Doc. 138, fn. 8.

22 Those Jewish refugees from Switzerland whom Trone had recruited for the resettlement project in the Dominican Republic were eventually granted the French transit visa.

DOC. 108

On 4 October 1940 the Reich Trustee of Labour for the economic area of Styria and Carinthia justifies low pay for Jewish workers[1]

Letter from the Reich Trustee of Labour for the economic area of Styria–Carinthia (no. 25 B l T/B),[2] p.p. signed Tremesberger,[3] Graz, to the Reichsstatthalter in Styria, Dept. Ia[4] (received on 7 October 1940), dated 4 October 1940[5]

Re: your letter of 23 August 1940, Ia Pol-386 Ju 1/16–1940.[6]

On the basis of your above mentioned letter the director of the regional employment office[7] has asked me, as the person responsible, to respond to this matter.

The report of the Landrat of Kreis Leoben on 15 August 1940 to the effect that construction companies are not meeting their financial responsibilities towards Jews is factually incorrect. Jews were hired for the standard wage: however, it turned out that the performance of the Jews is exceptionally poor. The construction companies hoped that, after the induction period of six to eight weeks, the output of the hired Jews would reach normal standards. However, they were disappointed in this respect. The Jews' output remained the same. The companies have now developed performance-based rates and submitted these to me for approval. The rates were calculated so that employees would, with average output, be able to earn at least 20 per cent more than the standard wage. For that reason, I approved the use of these rates. By introducing these performance-based rates, employers could prove that Jews often only achieved between one third and one fifth of the output of a normal worker, if not less. The employers could therefore no longer be expected to pay Jews the standard wage after the relatively long induction period, despite their minimal output. For example, as a result of paying the standard wage, the STUAG firm made losses of approx. RM 20,000.[8] I have therefore exempted Jews from the standard wage regulation and authorized managers to only pay them for their actual output on the basis of the perfor-

1 Steiermärkisches LA Graz, L., Reg.IA.Pol. 386 Ju 1/1940, fols. 64–65. This document has been translated from German.

2 The Reich Trustee of Labour and director of the Styrian Regional Employment Office from 1940 was Dr Walter Opitz (b. 1891).

3 Dr Georg Tremesberger (1905–1971), salaried employee; joined the NSDAP in 1930.

4 The department responsible for general and internal administrative affairs was headed by Oberregierungsrat Dr Albert Wöhrer (b. 1896). The Reichsstatthalter in Styria from March 1940 was Dr Siegfried Uiberreither (1908–1984).

5 The original contains handwritten annotations.

6 The Reichsstatthalter had forwarded a letter to the Regional Employment Office from the Loeben Landrat Wilhelm Kadletz, requesting a response. According to Kadletz, 36 of the 622 Jewish workers employed in Eisenerz and Prebichl had fled within a short space of time. He suspected the cause to be their low pay and asked for it to be checked whether the workers could be accommodated on the same basis as prisoners of war: Reg.IA.Pol. 386 Ju 1/1940, fols. 56–58.

7 Dr Walter Opitz: see fn. 2.

8 The road-building and underground construction company STUAG-Bau AG was set up in Vienna in 1928. Österreichische Länderbank took over the company in 1976; STUAG became part of the construction company STRABAG in 1999.

mance-based rates. I myself have on many occasions watched Jews at work and have observed that they are ridiculously lazy. I am sure that this is a case of malicious refusal to work.

DOC. 109

On 7 October 1940 the Reich Minister of Aviation informs Luftgaukommando VII that Jews are to be allowed entry to public air-raid shelters[1]

Letter from the Reich Minister of Aviation and Commander-in-Chief of the Luftwaffe and Inspectorate of Civilian Air-Raid Protection[2] (41 d. 18.12 Nr. 4949/40 [2 I B]), p.p. signed Großkreutz,[3] to Luftgaukommando VII,[4] dated 7 October 1940 (copy)[5]

Re: use of air-raid shelters by Jews
In consultation with the Deputy of the Führer,[6] you are hereby advised that during air-raid warnings Jews cannot be denied entry to public air-raid shelters and other shelters, since otherwise a detrimental state of affairs is to be feared that could also have an adverse effect on the German-blooded population. Where several air-raid shelters exist, Jews should be accommodated separately. If only one air-raid shelter is available, it will be advisable to partition off a part of the shelter, so as to allow Jews to use the air-raid shelter while remaining segregated from the German-blooded inhabitants of the shelter.

1 BArch, R 58/276, fol. 257. This document has been translated from German.
2 Hermann Göring.
3 Hans Großkreutz (1881–1948), military officer and civil servant; major, 1920; archivist at the Reich Archives, 1919/1920–1933; employed at the Reich Ministry of Aviation, 1933–1944; departmental head from 1936 and Ministerialdirigent from 1941.
4 A Luftgaukommando (aerial Gau command) was a Luftwaffe division responsible for the ground organization of aerial operations within a certain geographical area. Luftgaukommando VII encompassed southern Bavaria, Baden, Württemberg, Tyrol, and Salzburg.
5 The original contains annotations. The copy was forwarded by the Regierungspräsident in Augsburg (Nr. Lu 1260/40) to the Landräte – except in Nördlingen – and the mayor of Kempten on 21 Oct. 1940, with the comment: 'for your attention, to be implemented'.
6 Rudolf Hess.

DOC. 110

On 22 October 1940 Heinrich Himmler, addressing the NSDAP Country Group in Madrid, announces the deportation of all Jews from the Greater German Reich to the General Government[1]

Report (marked 'confidential') on Heinrich Himmler's speech in Madrid on 22 October 1940 (copy)[2]

Himmler on settlement questions
EP.[3] Madrid, 22 October.
At a reception of the Country Group of the NSDAP[4] held at the German House, Reichsführer SS Himmler gave a speech about modern problems of settlement and issues regarding the territory in the European East. He began his speech by observing that the purification of Germandom by the Nuremberg Jewish Laws and the rebuilding of the economy and the military, as well as the unification of the entire Germandom through the solution of the Austrian, Bohemian-Moravian, and Polish questions, were the hallmarks of the new political course. 'A victorious war', continued Himmler, 'consists not in gaining people of other ethnic groups, but in gaining land.[5] Although Germany has had to take over 8 million people from foreign ethnic groups as a result of its military victories in the East, the preparations have already been made to clearly segregate the different ethnicities. All foreign ethnic groups and particularly the Jews will, in the future, be placed in the General Government, meaning that between 500,000 and 600,000 people are to be resettled, with the Jews – that is to say, all the Jews from the Greater German Reich – in a separate ghetto. To date, around 250,000 ethnic Germans from Bessarabia, South Bukovina, and Dobruja have been installed in the new eastern provinces on plots of land corresponding to their former property, partly under significantly better conditions.[6] The resettlement is taking place on the basis of the most recent research and will bring revolutionary results, not only because it transplants ethnic contingents, but also because the landscape is being completely reshaped. Windy steppes are being made usable through various forms of forestry. Through the confiscation of brick factories, it has so far been possible to manufacture and store 750 million bricks. Next year this will increase to 1.3 million, and immediately after the war the bricks will be used to build model settlements, farming villages, and towns. The general plan for the reshaping of a territory of around 200,000 square kilometres is complete and will be put into effect in the first half of

1 BArch, R 49/20, folder 'Reden führender Personen über die Umsiedlungsaktion 1939–1942'. Published in Rolf-Dieter Müller, *Hitlers Ostkrieg und die deutsche Siedlungspolitik: Die Zusammenarbeit von Wehrmacht, Wirtschaft und SS* (Frankfurt Main: Fischer, 1991), doc. 8, p. 139. This document has been translated from German.
2 The speech was published in slightly abridged and altered form in the *Neue Zürcher Zeitung* (morning edition), 24 Oct. 1940, pp. 1–2, although another surviving version of the source indicates that the excerpt was not intended for publication: BArch, Filmsammlung, Nr. 16 789.
3 Probably the initials of the author.
4 The country groups (*Landesgruppen*) were subdivisions of the Foreign Organization of the NSDAP.
5 The original does not indicate where the quote ends.
6 On these resettlements, see the Introduction to PMJ 4.

next year. This will make Germany the strongest country in the world and the German people the healthiest and most productive. Alongside this large-scale internal colonization is the colonial problem, which will be solved through other means. The colonies, which Germany will reacquire, are primarily to be used for the production of additional economic products and raw materials, without Germandom putting down roots there and thus becoming lost to the home nation. Here, too, methods are being used for the first time. Himmler concluded: 'There will no longer be a homeland abroad, because home can only ever be the eternal Greater Germany. There will no longer be colonies that open up the possibility for all manner of illusions, but only economic territories supervised according to a clear plan. That is the true meaning of the war forced upon Germany.'

DOC. 111
Otto Hirsch describes how he protested to the Gestapo on 26 October 1940 against the deportations from Baden, the Palatinate, and the Saarland[1]

File note by Otto Hirsch regarding his summons to the Gestapo Central Office to see Regierungsassessor Jagusch, on 26 October 1940

1. *Deportation of Jews from Baden, the Palatinate, and the Saar region*
I requested permission to express our sorrow at the events in Baden, the Palatinate, and the Saar region. This distress has resulted in my asking the Culture League[2] to suspend performances for a week. I said that it was terrible that in the course of a single day and without any preparations, over 7,000 people were expelled and sent to an unknown destination.[3] Following the incidents in Stettin, the Reich Association[4] was, I said, informed that something like this would not occur again, and in the case of Schneidemühl and Breisach,[5] the central authorities took immediate action to remedy the situation. I said that the events that have now occurred strike at the heart of the Reich Association. I urgently requested to be told where the people have gone to, what we can do for them, and whether these things will continue.

Regierungsassessor Jagusch replied that this was a case of orderly emigration and that the Reich Association was to be involved towards the end of the coming week. The emigrants had been issued with power-of-attorney forms based on those drawn up by us for Stettin, naming the Reich Association. This means that, in many cases at least, the Reich Association will act as authorized representative. The result of this will be that, in

1 BArch, R 8150/45, fols. 132–134. This document has been translated from German.
2 Culture League of German Jews.
3 On the deportations to France, see Docs. 112 and 113.
4 Reich Association of Jews in Germany.
5 On the deportation of the Jewish population from Stettin to the Lublin district, see Doc. 52; on the deportations from Schneidemühl, see Introduction, p. 40. Following the occupation of Alsace by German troops in the summer of 1940, the Breisach municipal administration authorized the deportation of Jews remaining in the town to the psychiatric clinic in Rufach in Alsace; approximately one month later they were allowed to return to Breisach. Among the Jews deported to Gurs in Oct. 1940 were 34 Breisach Jews.

many cases at least, the Reich Association will have power of attorney. How one will proceed where this is not the case is not yet clear. Assessor Jagusch was unable to answer my question as to whether such things would continue. I then explained that immediately after receiving the initial news on Tuesday I had attempted to call in person and that I had wanted to submit a report, but this request was refused. Regierungsassessor Jagusch requested that I give it to him, which I did, while pointing out the size of the population. Upon reading Dr Lilienthal's file note, Regierungsassessor Jagusch underlined the words 'southern France'.[6]

The question then arose as to whether Mr Joachim[7] would be able to deal with all the powers of attorney issued, as had been the case with the people from Stettin or the present emigrants, or whether, as a result of the considerably larger numbers and the associated work, somebody else or an office would be necessary. I replied that I felt Dr Eppstein should be appointed to do this, as it was without doubt a difficult and responsible task, which was in any case separate from emigration-related questions. Regierungsassessor Jagusch completely agreed with this plan, so I also requested Regierungsassessor Jagusch to support Dr Eppstein's prompt release, particularly as his wife's mother and sister were among the evacuees from Baden. Regierungsassessor Jagusch expressed his willingness to do so.[8]

2. *Journey to Lisbon*

When, in conjunction with the need for the prompt release of Dr Eppstein, I mentioned that in the near future I would have to travel to Lisbon to meet the deputy of the JDC, Regierungsassessor Jagusch declared that it would be impossible to do so. He said that I was indispensable at this time. He had to have a responsible representative of the Reich Association here, particularly as the journey to Lisbon was not likely to be of short duration. He said that the interests of the Reich Association would then have to be attended to by Dr Löwenherz, Vienna. I objected strongly, pointing out that Dr Löwenherz was not familiar with our circumstances and that it was his right and duty to protect the interests of the Jewish Religious Community of Vienna. The current opportunity to meet with Mr Troper[9] would be the only chance for a long time, and I requested most humbly to be allowed to point out that, as a result of years of cooperation, I enjoy a measure of trust with Mr Troper that would be beneficial to our work. Were I not to attend the meeting myself, I would have to fear that the interests of the Reich Association would inevitably suffer. Regierungsassessor Jagusch insisted, however, that I was indispensable

6 Artur Lilienthal had informed the Reich Association of Jews in Germany the previous day about the deportations: minutes of the Reich Association board meeting, 25 Oct. 1940, BArch, R 8150/45, fol. 82.

7 Dr Richard Joachim (1891–1942), lawyer; member of the Social Democratic Party of Germany (SPD); lecturer at the Trade Union University in Bernau; Regierungsrat, Oberregierungsrat, and then Ministerialrat in the Reich Foreign Office until 1932; president of the senate at the Reich Social Insurance Office until 1933; worked for the Reich Association of Jews in Germany after 1933; shot as a hostage in place of Jews who did not turn up for deportation in Oct. 1942.

8 Paul Eppstein had been in protective custody since 15 August 1940; see Doc. 128, fn. 6.

9 Morris Troper (1892–1962), lawyer; legal practitioner and auditor in New York; worked for the American Jewish Joint Distribution Committee (JDC) from 1920; chairman of the European Executive Council of the JDC, 1938–1942; officer in the US Army, 1942 to 1948.

here. He was insistent that a colleague be sent to Lisbon, and recommended that I discuss the matter with Hauptscharführer Hartmann.

3. *Warm clothes for persons held in protective custody*
The petition dated 24 October was handed over.[10]

4. *Membership of the Jewish subjects of the Protectorate in the Reich Association and their obligation to pay the emigration levy on relocation to the Protectorate*
The petition dated 25 October was handed over.[11]

5. *Return of children from the occupied territories*
In response to my enquiry, Regierungsassessor Jagusch disclosed that a letter had now been sent to all German offices abroad (Belgium, occupied France, Holland), stating that there were no concerns regarding the return to their families in Germany of children aged up to 16 currently attending school or vocational training courses in the occupied territories. They are to contact the local office abroad in order to obtain a permit. Permission from the authorities in Germany was not required nor was it necessary to make a formal enquiry to them. It is simply a matter of normal registration with the police. However, as he, Regierungsassessor Jagusch, has not yet had any feedback from the offices abroad regarding the circular, one should wait until next week before communicating with our district offices and branches with regards to this announcement. He advised us to enquire again.

6. *Stettin*
Regarding the Stettin Jews in the Lublin district, it was stated that a group report was still pending. Regierungsassessor Jagusch informed me that he has instructed the Regierungspräsident, so that once the report has been received a summary can be sent to the Reich Association. In response to my enquiry, it was also stated that no directive has yet been received concerning the repatriation to Germany of the minors from the Lublin district.[12]

7. *Missing persons enquiries by the Red Cross*
The enquiries submitted by the Polish Red Cross that were handed over to us during the consultation on 26 September 1940 were returned,[13] and in the case of these and other incoming enquiries of the Red Cross it was stipulated that the Red Cross be instructed to contact the police authorities either in the last place of residence, or at the presumed current abode.

8. *Auditing*
On the basis of the letter dated 24 October from the German Auditing and Trustee Company,[14] the meeting held with its representatives was reported on. Regierungsassessor Jagusch requested that the employee from the German Audit and Trustee Company designated to run the audit at the Reich Association attend a meeting with him on Wednesday, 30 October, at 4 p.m., to discuss the scope and nature of the audit.

10 No further information could be found on this.
11 No further information could be found on this.
12 On the rejection of such applications, see Doc. 57.
13 These enquiries are not in the file.
14 This letter could not be found.

9. *Question regarding the incorporation of the Ludwig Philippson Lodge of the IOBB, Bonn am Rhein*[15]
The report dated 23 October was submitted.[16]
10. *Request by Sally Danziger, Berlin, concerning a welfare issue*
Regierungsassessor Jagusch will hand over the letter from the afore-mentioned individual dated 28 August 1940 to the 'Reich Commissioner at the Reich Ministry of the Interior for Jewish Affairs', requesting immediate action.[17]
11. *Lodge home of the IOBB, Berlin*
Regierungsassessor Jagusch requested a report about the legal status of the named organization, in particular about whether the Jewish Community of Berlin has been appointed as trustee. This relates to an enquiry made by Charlottenburg Local Court under the file reference number 49 C 616/40.[18]

DOC. 112

On 29 October 1940 Reinhard Heydrich informs the Reich Foreign Office that the deportation of the Jewish population from Baden and the Palatinate took place on Hitler's orders[1]

Letter from the Chief of the Security Police and the SD (IV D 4 2602/40), signed Heydrich, to the Reich Foreign Office, SA Standartenführer Envoy Luther, dated 29 October 1940[2]

The Führer ordered the deportation of the Jews from Baden via Alsace and the Jews from the Palatinate via Lorraine. Following implementation of the operation, I can inform you that on 22 and 23 October 1940, seven deportation trains left Baden, and on 22 October 1940, two trains left the Palatinate, transporting a total of *6,504 Jews* into the unoccupied part of France via Chalon-sur-Saône. The operation took place in consultation with the local duty stations of the Wehrmacht and without the French authorities being informed in advance.

The deportation of the Jews was executed smoothly in all parts of Baden and the Palatinate and passed without incident. The course of the operation itself was barely noticed by the population. The registration of the Jewish financial assets as well as the

15 The Independent Order of B'nai B'rith (IOBB) was a Jewish humanitarian Freemason lodge founded by German Jews in New York in 1843 and in Germany in 1882. In 1934 a private Jewish school was housed in the building of the Ludwig Philippson Lodge in Bonn and lessons were held there even after the nationwide dissolution of the IOBB in 1937. The school was incorporated into the Reich Association of Jews in Germany on 1 Oct. 1939: Stadtarchiv Bonn, Pr 40/2460.
16 This report could not be found.
17 This letter could not be found.
18 This report could not be found.

1 PA AA, R 100 869, fol. 14r–v. Published in Gerhard J. Teschner, *Die Deportation der badischen und saarpfälzischen Juden am 22 Oktober 1940: Vorgeschichte und Durchführung der Deportation und das weitere Schicksal der Deportierten bis zum Kriegsende im Kontext der deutschen und französischen Judenpolitik* (Frankfurt am Main: Peter Lang, 2002), pp. 346–347. This document has been translated from German.
2 The original contains handwritten annotations.

manner by which they will be held in trust and utilized will be carried out by the relevant Regierungspräsidenten.

Jews living in mixed marriages were excluded from the transports.

DOC. 113
Report, dated 30 October 1940, on the deportation of German Jews to southern France[1]

Report, unsigned, Karlsruhe, dated 30 October 1940[2]

Report on the evacuation of Jews of German nationality to southern France.[3]
On the order of Gauleiter and Reichsstatthalter *Josef Bürckel*, currently based in Metz, and Gauleiter *Wagner*,[4] currently in Strasbourg, all the Jews from Baden and the Saar-Palatinate were, during the night of Monday 21/Tuesday 22 October 1940 and on the following day, arrested in their apartments by the Gestapo and by members of the auxiliary police, and immediately thereafter evacuated in the trains provided. In the Saar-Palatinate a *deportation* order from the Gauleiter and Reichsstatthalter responsible, dated in *Metz* on 20 October 1940, was delivered by the police to the individuals concerned.[5]

On the basis of an agreement between the Wiesbaden Armistice Commission[6] under General von Stülpnagel[7] and the French delegation under General Huntziger[8] and the Vichy government, all Jews of *French* nationality from Alsace and Lorraine are to be sent

1 BArch, R 3001/20052, fols. 107–108. Published in Teschner, *Die Deportation*, pp. 348–349. This document has been translated from German.
2 The report was forwarded 'Most respectfully to Ministerialrat Schoetensack: regarding local events', BArch, R 3001/20052, fol. 106. This document contains handwritten annotations. Hermann Schoetensack (b. 1893), lawyer; regional court judge in Aurich and senior regional court judge in Emden, 1926–1933; joined the NSDAP, 1933; higher regional court judge in Celle, 1933–1937; Ministerialrat in the Reich Justice Ministry from 1938; Reich Supreme Court judge, 1944.
3 See Docs. 111 and 112.
4 Robert Wagner, born Robert Backfisch (1895–1946), soldier; in the Reichswehr, 1914–1924; took part in the Beer Hall Putsch, 1923; joined the German Workers' Party in 1924 and the NSDAP in 1925; NSDAP Gauleiter of Baden, 1925–1945 (from 1941, Baden-Alsace); member of the Baden Landtag, 1929–1933; member of the Reichstag and Reichsstatthalter in Baden, 1933–1945; chief of the civil administration in Alsace, 1940–1944; sentenced to death by a French military court and executed.
5 This could not be verified.
6 The German–French Armistice Agreement of 22 June 1940 provided for an Armistice Commission based in Wiesbaden. It monitored compliance with the agreement.
7 Carl Heinrich von Stülpnagel (1886–1944), professional soldier; in military service from 1904; infantry general, 1939; chairman of the German–French Armistice Commission, 1940; commander-in-chief of the Seventeenth Army in the Soviet Union, 1941; military commander in occupied France, 1942–1944; executed as a co-conspirator in the assassination attempt on Hitler on 20 July 1944.
8 Charles Léon Clément Huntziger (1880–1941), professional soldier; divisional general of the French colonial troops, 1933; commander of the Second and then the Fourth Army Group in northern France, 1940; signed the armistice agreement; minister of war in the Vichy government from Sept. 1940; killed in a plane crash.

to the unoccupied area of France, and the French authorities are obliged to take in the evacuees. This provision was analogously applied by the two Gauleiter, who are Gauleiter of Baden and the Saar-Palatinate respectively, to *all Jews of German nationality* resident in the area of Saar-Palatinate and Baden. At that point approximately 6,300 German Jews in Baden and 1,150 in the Saar-Palatinate were then deported to southern France.[9] As it is also the intention to deport the remaining Jews from the Old Reich, the Ostmark, and the Protectorate of Bohemia and Moravia to France – a total of 270,000 people, most of whom are of advanced age – the Vichy government has expressed its concern at this measure. As a result the planned deportation of Jews from Hesse has been postponed for the time being.

The deportation of Jews from Baden and the Saar-Palatinate took place in the form that, according to the orders of the two Gauleiter, 'all persons of Jewish race, *as far as they are able to be transported*,' had to be deported, without any consideration of age or gender. Only existing mixed marriages were excluded. Even men who had fought on the German side in the 1914–1918 war and, in some cases, officers of the old armed forces had to be deported. The homes for the elderly in Mannheim, Karlsruhe, Ludwigshafen, etc. were evacuated. Women and men who could not walk were transported to the trains on stretchers, as per the orders.

The oldest deportee was a 97-year-old man from Karlsruhe.[10] The time the deportees were given to prepare varied, depending on location, from a quarter of an hour to two hours. A number of women and men chose to commit suicide during this time in order to escape deportation. In Mannheim alone, by Tuesday morning, *eight people* had committed suicide, and in Karlsruhe, three had done the same. Wehrmacht vehicles were made available for the transportation from remote areas to the assembly points. The deportees had to leave all their belongings, capital assets, and property behind, as per the orders. These will be held in trust until a final decision is taken by the two Gauleiter. Since the deportations in many cases did not occur in an orderly manner, i.e. legal requirements such as payment of the Reich Flight Tax were not fulfilled, all assets have been secured in the meantime. The deportees were permitted to take a sum of money of between 10 and 100 Reichsmarks, which was, depending on availability, converted into French francs. Luggage weighing up to a maximum of 50 pounds could also be transported. The apartments were sealed by the police.

According to the available reports, the transports, consisting of twelve sealed trains, arrived at concentration camps at the foot of the Pyrenees in southern France after a journey of several days. Since there is a shortage of food and appropriate accommodation for the mainly elderly male and female deportees, the French government, as far as we know, is planning to send the deportees to Madagascar as soon as the sea routes are opened up.[11]

9 The numbers are too high; a total of 6,500 Jews were deported.

10 According to a report, dated 1946, by the Mannheim paediatrician Dr Eugen Neter, the oldest deported man was 98 and the oldest woman 97 years old: Stadtarchiv Mannheim, *Die Judenverfolgung in Mannheim 1933–1945*, compiled by Hans-Joachim Fliedner, vol. 2: *Dokumente* (Stuttgart: W. Kohlhammer, 1971), doc. 38, pp. 78–95, here p. 80.

11 The Vichy government interned the German Jews in the Gurs camp and later in Rivesaltes. In the course of 1941 some were moved to other camps in south-western France. While approximately 1,500 prisoners managed to escape or emigrate, a total of approximately 1,000 people perished in the camps.

DOC. 114

On 2 November 1940 the Bielefeld Gestapo announces that all Jews between 18 and 55 years of age are to be enlisted for segregated labour deployment[1]

Order no. 101/10 (marked 'confidential! extremely urgent!') circulated by the Gestapo office in Bielefeld (II B 4–4042/40), signature illegible, to the Landräte and mayors of the district[2] and to the branch offices in Paderborn, Detmold, and Bückeburg, dated 2 November 1940[3]

Re: labour deployment of Jews
Case file: none
It is planned to enlist Jewish men and women aged between 18 and 55, who are currently not in employment but are *fully fit for work*, for segregated labour deployment.

In order to first obtain an overview of the Jewish men and women still not in full employment but able to work, I request to be informed by 12 November 1940 at the latest on:

(a) the number of Jews – separated according to gender – who have already been assigned to work by the employment office;
(b) how many Jewish men and women, aged between 18 and 55 and without occupation but fully fit for work – separated according to gender – are available for segregated labour deployment.

Wives who have to run a household and are thus classified as fully employed, as well as Jewish men and women living in a mixed marriage, are not to be included.

The assessment is to be made in consultation with the relevant employment office.

I would ask that special care is taken to comply with the deadline given above.

1 BArch, R 58/276, fol. 258. Extracts published in Pätzold, *Verfolgung, Vertreibung, Vernichtung*, pp. 276–277. This document has been translated from German.
2 Added to the original: '(with carbon copy for the local police authorities)'.
3 The order was also sent for information purposes to the Regierungspräsidenten in Minden, the state governments in Detmold and Bueckeburg, and the SD district office in Bielefeld.

DOC. 115

On 3 November 1940 Esther Cohn, living in Munich, writes in her diary about her desperation at the deportation of her mother and sisters to France[1]

Handwritten diary of Esther Cohn,[2] Munich, entry for 3 November 1940

3 Nov. 1940
Oh, something terrible has happened since I last wrote in here! All the Jews from Baden have been taken away, it happened on 22 October.[3] It is really dreadful, absolutely unbelievable! It's been almost a fortnight, and I still don't have an address. I cannot take much more of this life! Many people have written to me but what help is that? When will I see my sweet Musch and siblings again?[4] Will I ever see them again? Oh, dear God, please let us be together again soon, or if it is not to be, bring my poor life to an end. What have I got if I no longer have anybody? Oh, I wish I had never been born rather than endure such misery! My poor sweet father is not here either[5] – hopefully I will soon hear something from him and my loved ones, who probably now have to stay in the south of France.

Dear God, please protect and take care of the only people I love; give them enough to eat and a bed to sleep in. With every mouthful I take, I wonder if my mother also has something to eat. Oh, what a terrible fate! Dear God, please let us be together again soon. I cannot and will not live alone like this. Oh, Mum, why didn't we get on better during the holidays? Now, when I need you so much!!!

On 18 October I became unwell, my Mum would want to know about that. 13 November will be Miss Bendix's birthday and we are supposed to perform something again. If only it were already over![6]

1 YVA, O.33/1666. Published in Esther Cohn and Martin Ruch, *'Inzwischen sind wir nun besternt worden': Das Tagebuch der Esther Cohn (1926–1944) und die Kinder vom Münchener Antonienheim* (Norderstedt: Books on Demand, 2006), pp. 72–74. This document has been translated from German.

2 Esther Lore Cohn (1926–1944), born in Offenburg; lived in the Jewish children's home on Antonienstraße, Munich, from 1939 to 1942 and obtained her school-leaving certificate from the Israelite Primary School in Munich. She was deported to Theresienstadt on 29 July 1942, then on 16 Oct. 1944 to Auschwitz, where she was murdered.

3 See also Doc. 111, Doc. 113, and Introduction, p. 47.

4 Musch: Esther Cohn's mother Sylvia, née Oberbrunner (1904–1942), housewife; began writing poetry when she was a schoolgirl; was deported from Baden to Gurs in southern France in Oct. 1940, together with her daughters Myriam (1929–1974) and Eva (b. 1931). Sylvia Cohn was initially taken to Rivesaltes, then deported on 13 Sept. 1942 via Drancy to Auschwitz, where she was murdered a short time later. With the help of the French children's aid organization OSE, Myriam and Eva succeeded in reaching Switzerland, where they were taken in by the Lilly Volkart children's home in Ascona. They emigrated to Britain in October 1945.

5 Eduard Cohn (1898–1976), sales representative and retailer; member of the Offenburg Zionist Association; following the November pogroms he was arrested and imprisoned in Dachau concentration camp until 20 Dec. 1938; emigrated to Britain in May 1939; foreman in a factory manufacturing springs, 1945.

6 Alice Bendix (1984–1943), educator; from 1933, deputy director, and from 1935, director, of the Jewish children's home in Antonienstraße; in 1942 sent with the remaining children and staff to the Milbertshofen Home, and from there to the Berg am Laim assembly camp; on 3 March 1943 deported with the children to Auschwitz, where she was murdered.

Now I'm already a teenager. – Miss Rubens, our English teacher, is giving me a lot of English to read, with the result that I have given up reading novels completely. Günter has tried offering me one many times, but I always stick to my guns and say no.[7] I am now very pleased that I have given it up.

At the moment, Günter is the only one for me. I care for him more than anyone else. The others can make fun of me for it as much as they like, I really don't care.

I have recently read two wonderful books: *Abraham* and *Dienst auf den Höhen*. They are both sublime.[8] Tomorrow school does not start until 8:50. It will be like that all winter. Also tomorrow, two new girls are coming to the home. We call them the 'Ruthenburgs'. I like them very much. They were in Mirz's class.

Well, goodnight for today, dear diary.

I cannot stand Günter any more.[9]

DOC. 116

On 8 November 1940 Adolf Hitler gives a speech in Munich on the rise of the National Socialist movement and the 'struggle against Jewry'[1]

Hitler's speech at the commemoration of the march on the Feldherrnhalle[2] in 1923, delivered in the Löwenbräukeller in Munich on 8 November 1940[3]

My fellow Party members and comrades!

We have gathered together to commemorate the 9th of November once again, just as we gathered together back then, on the day before the rally. For us, the year 1923 marked a climax in the struggle for power in Germany. That struggle, and hence the significance of the day that we now commemorate, can only be understood by those who recall the time in which we were then placed, and in particular by those who think back to the prehistory of this whole mighty conflict.

When we entered the political life of the nation, our names were unknown. The majority of us, I myself first and foremost, were not even members of a party. Most of us had been soldiers, and we came back from the Great War with our hearts filled with

7 Günter Pollak (1926–1941); lived in the Jewish children's home in Antonienstraße, 1935–1941. He was deported on 20 Nov. 1941 to Kaunas, where he was murdered.

8 Ernst Furstenthal, *Abraham* (Berlin: Jüdische Buch-Vereinigung, 1936), Martha Wertheimer, *Dienst auf den Höhen* (Berlin: Jüdische Buch-Vereinigung, 1937).

9 Sentence presumably inserted at a later date.

1 DRA, 2 743 247. An edited version was published in *Völkischer Beobachter* (northern German edition), 10 Nov. 1940, pp. 3–4. This document has been translated from German.

2 In what is known as the Beer Hall Putsch, on 8 November 1923 Hitler proclaimed the start of a 'national revolution' at a gathering in the Bürgerbrau Beer Hall in Munich and called for support to topple the government in Berlin. The next day several thousand supporters, many heavily armed, took part in a march to Munich's Feldherrnhalle (Field Marshals' Hall). The coup was crushed by the Bavarian police and fifteen of the supporters were killed. After 1933 the National Socialists honoured these 'martyrs' on 9 November every year.

3 The printed text follows the audio recording of the speech; total length: 105 minutes and 30 seconds.

rage or despair. The situation of our people, of the German Reich, appeared desperate, and for many it seemed hopeless.

The Germany of the years prior to 1914 is no longer our Germany. Nonetheless, we still feel a sense of connection with that Germany, too, for it already embodied the unity of a large section of the German people. It was a land of work, and also a land of welfare. In the German Reich of that time, whatever else might be said against it, the beginnings of social legislation can be identified. In that Germany, for the very first time, people took a stance on problems to which today, nearly thirty years later, the so-called democracies remain deaf and blind. Of course, these problems were solved from the perspective of the times – how could it be any other way? – and by its very nature the profoundly capitalistic state could only take a half-hearted and hesitant approach to solving social problems, which, in order to be successful, would have required the state, the Volksgemeinschaft, to have had a very different character. This was not the case.[4] Hence, it is all the more remarkable that people back then took any kind of interest in such problems, and sought to solve them with the resources available at the time.

Incidentally: back then Germany was still a land of democrats. In this country, perhaps more than in any other, democracy ran riot. This was the land of freedom. Everyone could do whatever he wanted, however he wanted. This freedom extended so far that in those days even the borders of the Reich were left open for anyone to enter. But not like America, the so-called land of boundless freedom. There, every immigrant had to pass an extremely difficult examination before he was granted permission to set foot on the hallowed ground of democracy, even though there were scarcely 10 residents per square kilometre.[5] Here in Germany – with a population density even back then of more than 130 persons per square kilometre – no such measures were put in place. We were so free that every Jew, every Polack,[6] could enter the country at will and immediately be granted a fully equal status. Germany had to pay dearly for this at a later stage. This period saw the gathering of that international horde – international in its character and origins – that raised the flag of revolution in 1918.

But above all, the Germany of that time was undoubtedly a land of peace. People were content to live their lives and earn a living. It was understood that war in general is bad for earnings. So they hoped for peace, to the point where, at a time when the rest of the world was undoubtedly arming itself against Germany, they let every favourable moment for initiating conflict slip by. When the war did finally come, it found Germany utterly ill-equipped.

I am no critic of those times, although I could be; for more than anyone else in history, perhaps, I have learned lessons from the past, and taken them to heart. And I have been at pains not to let the German people face danger in the same sort of state as it was in back then.

And back then, England was already our enemy.

4 The text following 'problems' ('which, in order ... not the case.') was omitted from the transcript printed in the *Völkischer Beobachter*.

5 From 1917 potential immigrants to the USA were tested on their reading and writing ability, and a quota system limiting the number of immigrants was also introduced.

6 Pejorative term for Pole.

When I say 'England', I know very well that in that country, too, the people and their leaders are not the same thing. A small clique of international democrats, Jews, and plutocrats rules that country, and this clique was behind the rush to war in those days too. In fact, they are the same people now as they were back then. Today's Mr Churchill was already one of the biggest warmongers at the time,[7] and some who are now old were at it back then in their youth. Back then, too, the British warmongers succeeded in mobilizing the whole world against Germany.

And thus came the war that Germany had not wanted. For it would have had better opportunities to wage this war on its own initiative. And even though the German Reich of those days was poorly armed and equipped – we can say that openly now – that same Germany held out for more than four years.

And as a former soldier of the World War, and the supreme commander of the German Wehrmacht today, I can say quite openly that they would not have beaten Germany back then if their ally within had not broken us. They tried for four years, and even then they had to conjure up an American priest-magician who then came up with the formula that the German people fell for, trusting in the word of honour of a foreign president.[8] When they claimed later that they would have beaten us anyway, then one is bound to ask: so why, then, did they call forth that spirit to beguile and deceive us, if they could have managed it anyway?

Germany was laid low by a gang of conspirators who were able to plot and scheme among our people and in our land. And then we paid the price for our gullibility.

The 8th and 9th November 1918 and the days that followed are a warning to our German people for all time.[9] Not a single promise made by the victors at that time has been kept. The biggest breach of faith in history originated there. Then began the period of suffering and misery, and consequently of despair in our people. There were, no doubt, many people at that time who lost the will to live. The figures for suicides rose to over 20,000 a year. To most of them, a life that offered no prospect of ever regaining equal rights, and therefore freedom, for the German people no longer seemed worth living.

It was then that our struggle began.

It was a noble struggle, for it was a struggle waged against all probability. When I first started speaking publicly in this city, and many of you here today began to follow me, even some of my closest friends had given up on me. They could not understand how an otherwise sensible man could suddenly take it into his head to battle alone against an entire world of realities. They said: 'What is this pathetic creature after? He has no money, and nobody has heard of him. Not a single newspaper is backing him, he has no party,

7 Winston Churchill (1874–1965) was first lord of the Admiralty from 1911 to 1915, in charge of the Royal Navy; he subsequently left the cabinet and sat as a backbench MP, before serving as minister for munitions from 1917 to 1919.

8 Hitler is presumably referring here to Woodrow Wilson (1856–1924), US President, 1913–1921, and to the fourteen-point programme devised by him, which formed the basis of the peace negotiations between the victorious Allies and the defeated nations after the First World War.

9 In Oct. 1918 sailors in Wilhelmshaven and Kiel mutinied. Their protests triggered uprisings of soldiers and workers throughout the country, demanding an end to the war and political change. The German republic was proclaimed in Berlin on 9 Nov. 1918. In Jan. 1919 the German National Assembly was elected and subsequently constituted in Weimar.

and everyone out there is against him. He wants to fight everybody. He wants to fight the business owners, and he wants to fight the proletarians as well. He wants to fight against the democratic Reich of the day, but also against the states. He wants to fight against all religious denominations, he wants to fight against organized capitalist society as we know it today, but he also wants to fight against organized trade unions. There is nothing that this man is not intent on fighting. He wants to construct a new state, a new society, and he has absolutely nobody to back him – a madman who dares to go forth alone and declare war on a tightly grouped majority in every area of society.'

This fight was not so easy, and yet gradually we started to see successes. The young movement began to make headway against the tactic of ignoring us, then making fun of us and ridiculing us, and later on against the flood of lies and slander, and finally against the terror tactics. All of you have lived through this, as you found your way to me, one by one, in those days. Some of you came in 1919, others in 1920 and 1921. And all of you felt in your heart of hearts at the time: we will win this struggle for power in Germany, despite everything. It may well be hard. But we have reason on our side, the validity of our principles, and the knowledge that the state as it is now cannot be upheld for long, that it is only a matter of time before it breaks apart in one way or another. It is also the sense of the need to rethink many received ideas.[10] Finally, it was also what I am tempted to call a 'mystical belief' in the immortality of our ethnic community, an ethnicity that would, nonetheless, have been destroyed had we maintained the status quo.

And so we gradually grew, viewed by some with indifference, persecuted with fury by others, hated by many, simply because it was the easy option. So many citizens back then, watching us on the street from their windows, nursed a quiet rage within them, because they thought: 'This constant unrest – if only they would leave us in peace. And there's all this fighting and brawling going on, simply because they can't leave it alone! They should just knuckle down – that's what we do, after all. People can think what they like, but they don't need to keep on saying it out loud – they should keep it to themselves. You can still be a decent citizen. We protest too, but we protest privately, quietly, and only in our thoughts. But they always wade in straightaway with violence. They know that the others will respond with violence – so the wiser course is to back down.' But we did not take the wiser course. Even as a boy, I never did. I have always rejected the view that it is wiser to back down; on the contrary, I have always preferred not to back down, even at the risk of others saying 'He was foolish'.[11] So we didn't back down then, either! (Laughter and applause.)

And we kept on disturbing the peace of these citizens, we never yielded, and we continued to rebel; and as a result we have gradually succeeded in conquering the streets and conquering the squares, taking possession of the towns and villages one by one.

And then the struggle began to push outwards beyond the confines of our homeland.

More especially, this was a struggle against the people that seemed to be virtually all-powerful in our country: the struggle against Jewry. And what that meant is something that people who are born today will simply not be able to understand in the future. A satanic power, which had taken possession of our entire nation, which had gained control of all the key positions in intellectual, political, and economic life. And which kept

10 This sentence is omitted from the text printed in the *Völkischer Beobachter*.
11 The *Völkischer Beobachter* notes at this point: 'General mirth.'

the entire nation under surveillance from these key positions. A power that also possessed the influence to pursue with the full force of the law, where necessary, anyone who dared to join the struggle against this power, and who was prepared to oppose the continuing expansion of this power.

This all-powerful Jewry declared war on us back then – and as you know, I have always taken the view that there is no more stupid people than the Jews, but also none more corrupt and unscrupulous. (Isolated applause.[12]) And I have always taken the view that the time will come when we shall remove these people from our ranks. This is a view which I still hold today, now that we have gained victory here in Germany.

We have declared war on everybody who sustained this state at that time, and who led this state. And we have devoted ourselves to one thing, and one thing only – namely, the German people. We have known only one goal: to be of use to the German people, and to serve them – and for that we were prepared to shoulder every burden. [...][13]

DOC. 117
On 9 November 1940 the Reich Security Main Office invites its staff to apply for apartments formerly occupied by Jews[1]

Letter from the RSHA (Office IV, IV.Gut. – B. Nr. 1310/40), signed p.p. Pieper,[7] to all sections of Office IV,[3] dated 9 November 1940[4]

Re: Jew apartments

To alleviate the present housing shortage affecting members of the Security Police and the SD, a number of apartments formerly occupied by Jews have been made available, following an agreement reached between the Inspector General of Building[5] and the Chief of the Security Police and the SD.[6] In order to identify the most deserving applicants for

12 The *Völkischer Beobachter* notes at this point: 'Thunderous applause.'

13 Hitler then goes on to recapitulate the rise of his party leading up to the so-called seizure of power (*Machtergreifung*) and lists the achievements of his time in government. He describes his failed attempts to persuade Britain to enter into an alliance with Germany, and claims that Britain is responsible for the war. He then reminds his audience of Germany's successful conduct of the war, and predicts the destruction of Britain: DRA, 2 743 247.

1 BArch, R 58/276, fol. 260. This document has been translated from German.

2 Hans Pieper (1902–1980), bank official and policeman; worked for the Political Police in Berlin from 1931; joined the SS in 1935 and the NSDAP in 1937; police superintendent at the Gestapo Central Office (Gestapa) from 1938; SS-Sturmbannführer, 1941, headed the administrative office of Section IV in the Reich Security Main Office (RSHA) from May 1942; after the war, executive director of the People's League for Peace and Liberty.

3 Office IV (Combating Adversaries – Gestapo) was headed by Heinrich Müller.

4 Parts of the original are annotated and underlined by hand.

5 Albert Speer (1905–1981), architect; joined the NSDAP and the SA in 1931; planner and architect of major construction projects from 1934, including the new Reich Chancellery; inspector general of building for the Reich capital from 1937; appointed Reich minister of armaments and war production in 1942; sentenced to 20 years' imprisonment at the International Military Tribunal at Nuremberg in 1946; released in 1966.

6 Reinhard Heydrich.

these homes, which are in limited supply, I would ask that staff members seeking accommodation submit their applications to the administrative office of Section IV. Applications should be presented in accordance with the following list of categories:

(A) Married persons who do *not* have an apartment of their own in Berlin.

(B) Married persons who have an apartment of their own in Berlin, but have to move house for pressing reasons.

(C) Unmarried persons who are about to marry, and do not yet have an apartment of their own.

For persons in category *C*, this will be a provisional registration, as generally it will probably not be possible to allocate apartments to this group of persons. This will depend mainly on how many applications are received from persons in categories *A* and *B*.

The application form should be completed with care, since Section IV D 4 will be using the information supplied to ensure that the *most suitable* dwelling is made available via the Reich Association of Jews, and to prepare the tenancy agreement for signature.

Given the urgency of the matter, enquiries are to be made as soon as possible and the applications submitted to the administrative office of Section IV no later than 15 November 1940.

DOC. 118

On 13 November 1940 the Main Trustee Office East writes to the Chief of Police in Berlin about the sale by auction of the plot of land owned by Chaim Goldfarb[1]

Letter from the Plenipotentiary for the Four-Year Plan, Main Trustee Office East (9 930 312), signed p.p. Dr Krahmer-Möllenberg,[2] Berlin, to the Chief of Police in Berlin,[3] dated 13 November 1940

In accordance with the Regulation on the Handling of the Assets of Former Polish Nationals issued on 17 September 1940 (*Reichsgesetzblatt*, I, p. 1270), the Main Trust Agency (East), Berlin, is responsible for the confiscation and sale of property owned by Poles.[4]

I intend to issue an instruction for assets covered by the aforementioned regulation to be registered in writing. However, in order to prevent any transfer of assets in the meantime, Polish assets are to be confiscated in advance.

According to a private communication sent to me, the property listed under *Land Registry No. 70-2083, N. 58, 23/23a Griebenowstr.*[5] appears to be owned by the Polish national *Leib Goldfarb Warczawa, 40a Nowalipie.*

1 BADV, HTO 10 028 Goldfarb, Chaim Lejb. This document has been translated from German.

2 Dr Erich Krahmer-Möllenberg (1882–1942), lawyer; worked in the Prussian interior administration, 1918–1920; board member of the Deutsche Stiftung, a covert government organization for the support of German minorities abroad, 1920–1940; deputy director of the Main Trustee Office East (Haupttreuhandstelle Ost) from 1940.

3 Count Wolf Heinrich von Helldorf (1896–1944), farmer; took part in the Kapp putsch in 1920; joined the NSDAP in 1930 and the SA in 1931; chief of police in Potsdam, 1933–1935, then in Berlin, 1935–1944; executed for his involvement in the failed plot to assassinate Hitler on 20 July 1944.

4 The so-called Polish Assets Regulation covered not only the confiscation and sale of real estate, but also the entire assets of Polish nationals. In the case of non-Jewish Poles the confiscation could be carried out 'for the public good' or 'in the interests of strengthening Germandom'; in the case of Jews, it was mandatory: *Reichsgesetzblatt*, I, 1940, p. 1270, § 2. In practice the regulation legitimized a process that had been underway since the autumn of 1939.

With reference to section 7 of the Reich Marshal's directive on the Main Trust Agency (East), issued on 12 June 1940, *Dt. Reichsanzeiger* No. 139/40,[6] I request immediate clarification as to whether the aforementioned property does or does not belong to the Polish national.[7]

DOC. 119

On 15 November 1940 Heinrich Himmler instructs all members of the German police to go and see the propaganda film *Jew Süss*[1]

Screening of the film Jew Süss[2]
Circular decree from the Reichsführer SS and Chief of the German Police, dated 15 November 1940 – OKdo WE (2) No. 275/40

I want all members of the German police to see the film *Jew Süss* over the winter, and am therefore issuing the following instructions:
1. The state police authorities will make arrangements with local cinema operators to hold special screenings for those members of the Order Police and Security Police who have not yet seen the film.
2. Members of the gendarmerie who are not familiar with the film are to be shown it during a district staff meeting. The commander of the gendarmerie will make the necessary arrangements with local cinema operators. Members of the Security Police will also attend these screenings.
3. The municipalities can make the same arrangements as listed under sections 1 or 2 above for the urban police in the municipalities, the fire protection police, and members of the voluntary fire services. If the number of officers is not sufficient for a special screening, joint screenings are to be organized in conjunction with the gendarmerie.
4. SS agencies should be consulted regarding the participation of SS members in the screenings organized for police officers.
5. Members of the Order Police and Security Police who attend the special screenings are required to pay the cost of admission themselves. Cinema operators will make tickets available at reduced prices for these special screenings.
6. Family members may also attend these screenings.
For distribution to all police authorities.

5 Handwritten note in the original: 'identical to 241/42 Schwedterstr.'.
6 Under § 7 of the directive, all Reich, regional, and local authorities and their subordinate agencies were required to provide administrative support. The police authorities were 'placed at the disposal' of the Main Trustee Office East in consultation with the Reichsführer SS and Chief of the German Police: *Deutscher Reichsanzeiger und Preußischer Staatsanzeiger*, no. 139, 17 June 1940, p. 3.
7 On 12 Dec. 1940 the Main Trustee Office East approved the forced sale of the plot of land in question 'for the benefit of the German Reich': BAIDV, HTO 10 028 Goldfarb, Chaim Lejb.

1 *Ministerialblatt des Reichs- und Preußischen Ministeriums des Innern*, vol. 47 (1940), p. 2116b. This document has been translated from German.
2 The German feature film *Jud Süß*, directed by Veit Harlan, premiered on 5 Sept. 1940. On the critical reception of the film, see Introduction, p. 59.

DOC. 120
Michael Meyer describes how he emigrated to Palestine on a series of refugee ships in the autumn of 1940[1]

Talk given by Dr Michael Meyer[2] on 21 August 1941, following his release from Atlit,[3] to the Working Group of B'nai B'rith from Central Europe[4]

A migration to Eretz Israel in 1940
Before we embarked on our journey, I had given my wife a small travel *tefillah*[5] at her request. Inside I had written the dedication: 'lo Yanum velo Yishan schomer Jisrael.'[6] This passage from the prayer liturgy of our people, which I had deliberately chosen as a kind of mantra for our journey into the unknown, turned out to be true from beginning to end. Miracle upon miracle occurred, which I can only put down to an invisible being, which held a protective hand over us and averted the dangers that constantly beset us.

However, it is not my intention here to lose myself in transcendental observations. I just wish to relate the facts, and I leave it to you to square these facts with your philosophy or beliefs, or simply to take note of them.

The backdrop to emigration in 1940, emigration from Germany to a distant land, was the situation of the Jews at that time under the Nazi regime. I think it is important to say a few words as a reminder of that situation, so that you can imagine the stress under which we were living prior to our emigration.

Following the promulgation of the Nuremberg Jewish Laws in September 1935 and the associated implementing regulations, things went fairly quiet again in the period between the summer of 1937 and the summer of 1938.[7] The Jews were pretty much left to their own devices within the boundaries that had been set for them. In the Jewish Culture League, the Jewish house of learning, and the synagogues, they were free to live as they wished. The only thing that was taboo, and dangerous, was any encroachment on the Aryan sphere of life. But Jews were quite free to take Aryans to court, for example. In non-political matters, Jews could successfully assert their rights in court like anyone else. Several such judgements are filed in my packing case in Hamburg. (If by some miracle we ever get the packing case back, I would be happy to hand the documents over to the national library, if it wants them.)

I'd like to give you one example that shows what life was like in the period up until the middle of June 1938. It's something that relates to us personally, but it had happened just one month previously, and as I say, it really shows what life was like at the time. In

1 Wiener Library, Doc 1656/2/6/214; copy in YVA, O.2/283. This document has been translated from German. On the accounts from the Wiener Library, see Doc. 88, fn. 1.
2 Dr Michael Meyer, lawyer; practised law in Berlin.
3 The British Mandate power used a section of the fortress of Atlit, built in 1218 by the Knights Templar some 20 kilometres to the south of Haifa, to intern refugees who had entered Palestine illegally. Today the fortress is a restricted military area.
4 Jewish fraternal organization founded in New York for 'benevolence, brotherly love, and harmony' by German migrants in 1843. The first branch in Germany was established in 1882 in Berlin.
5 Hebrew: prayer (book).
6 Hebrew: 'the Lord will neither slumber nor sleep' (Psalm 121:4).
7 On the Nuremberg Laws, see Glossary and also PMJ 1/198, 199, and 210.

mid May 1938 we were still able to celebrate the bar mitzvah[8] of our son in our apartment on Niebuhrstraße, Charlottenburg, without any difficulties at all. Nonetheless I had been careful to ask the [NSDAP] cell leader who lived in our building whether it was permitted to invite a hundred or so relatives and friends into our apartment for a religious celebration marking our son's coming of age. The Nazi man told me: 'We have no objection to Jewish religious celebrations.' I also asked the other occupants of the building, all of them Aryans, whether they minded. None of them had any objections. Some of them even wished our son well for the future, including a Ministerialrat from the Ministry of Finance. In the event we had not just a hundred people from the synagogue on Pestalozzistraße at the reception, but over three hundred. However, as I said, it all went off without a hitch.

The circumstances as I have described them changed suddenly in mid June 1938. The situation of the Jews became significantly more difficult and dangerous.[9] The Nazis had undoubtedly been emboldened by the fact that after the annexation of Austria, which took place a few months earlier, in March, they had tackled the Jewish question there with a shockingly naked display of brutality, without encountering any protest from the civilized peoples of Europe. So they judged that they could get away with tearing down the great synagogue in Munich,[10] and dragging all the patrons out of Jewish cafés and restaurants on the evening of 17 June, hauling them off to police headquarters in trucks, and sending anyone with any kind of criminal record on to concentration camps. In order to give this inhuman behaviour a semblance of legality, they invoked a regulation that gave the police authorities the right to put asocial elements into labour camps. In the weeks that followed, thousands of Jews who had been convicted of any offence, however minor, were arrested on the strength of this regulation, and sent to Sachsenhausen, Buchenwald, or Dachau.[11]

Further restrictions now followed in quick succession: the exclusion of Jews from many business enterprises, the withdrawal of licences to practise medicine as of 30 September 1938, followed by the withdrawal of licences to practise law as of 30 November 1938, and other measures besides.[12] The line the Nazis were taking very soon became clear. They wanted to bring about a mass emigration of Jews by terrorizing them and taking away their livelihood. And some of them did decide to emigrate, but only a minority, largely confined to the criminals who had been put into concentration camps. But the number of emigrants was clearly not enough to satisfy the Gestapo. So they stepped up the pressure. On 28 October 1938, out of the blue, Polish Jews were expelled from Germany and promptly deported over the border to Poland. But only a few trains managed to get across the border. The Polish authorities resisted further deportations.[13]

8 The bar mitzvah is a ceremony to celebrate a boy's religious coming of age at the age of 13. On the occasion he reads from the Torah in the synagogue for the first time.

9 The introduction of harsher anti-Jewish measures in 1938 is documented in detail in PMJ 2.

10 See PMJ 2/40.

11 The June Operation was part of Operation Work-shy Reich (*Arbeitsscheu Reich*), in the course of which some 10,000 people were incarcerated in the camps at Buchenwald, Dachau, and Sachsenhausen. In June 1938 approximately 1,500 Jews were affected: see PMJ 2, pp. 22–23, and PMJ 2/88.

12 See for example Doc. 96, fnn. 4 and 5.

13 On the deportation of Polish Jews, see PMJ 2/113, 118, 122, and 203.

Then came the terrible night of 9/10 November and all that followed: the destruction of synagogues, the bestial murder of many Jews, especially in the provinces, the demolition of homes and businesses, the incarceration of tens of thousands in concentration camps, the systematic robbery of Jews through the 'atonement fine',[14] through the removal of all tax concessions, through pressurizing them to sell businesses, factories, and land well below their market price, through forcing them to surrender gold and silver, and much else besides. You know about what went on, even if you didn't experience these things in person. A few key words are enough to bring it all back. And you also know that all these atrocities were attributed to the mood of the people, which had allegedly reached fever pitch once again because of the shooting of the embassy official Rath by Grünspan.[15] In reality, all these measures had been prepared long before the attack, and it was just a matter of waiting for the right moment to unleash the *furor teutonicus*.[16]

All the horrors I have touched upon eventually led to the mass emigration that the Gestapo had wanted. But my wife and I had already decided to emigrate before 10 November 1938. Our boy had already entered the country in March 1939 through the Youth Aliyah. He had been attending the Zionist School in Berlin since 1931. For my wife and me, too, Eretz Israel was the only possible destination. I had been a member of the Zionist organization since 1917, and had been active in the Zionist cause since 1911. We had deliberately raised our son from the outset to make his Aliyah at some future date.

I took the decision to make Aliyah back in July 1938, just after the passing of the laws excluding Jews from economic life. I realized this step marked a radical shift, and I also expected an early ban on the practice of law by Jews. Since genuine capitalist certificates[17] were hard to get through the normal channels, even back then, I applied to an agency that I had come across in the course of my legal practice, which I knew could obtain, or broker, Basel capitalist certificates against payment of certain sums. Hitherto this procedure had always worked like a charm. I was told by the agency that I would have to wait until a certain Mr Stein or his fiancée came to Berlin from Darmstadt. I was asked, however, to have the requisite 2,000 Reichsmarks (in cash) available at all times, so that our business could be concluded as soon as Mr Stein arrived. A few months later, Mr Stein's fiancée duly came to Berlin. We arranged to meet and I handed over the 2,000 Reichsmarks – without a receipt, of course. She made a few notes and simply told me that the money would be transferred secretly to Palestine. In due course, probably some time in December, I would be notified by the Palestine Office in Basel that a certificate of application from a relative was ready for us. The certificate would have to be

14 On the 'atonement fine' (*Sühneleistung*), see Doc. 25, in particular fn. 2. On the November pogroms, see Glossary, also PMJ 2, pp. 53–56, and especially PMJ 2/123–126, 128–131, and 133–138.

15 On 7 Nov. 1938 Herschel Grynszpan, also known as Grünspan (b. 1921), shot the junior diplomat Ernst vom Rath in the German embassy in Paris, presumably after learning that his family had been deported from Hanover. Rath was critically wounded in the attack and died the next day. The same day the German press was instructed to make much of the incident in its reporting, and to blame it on the Jews. Grünspan was initially imprisoned by the French, and then handed over to the Germans. He is thought to have perished in Sachsenhausen, probably in 1945: see also PMJ 2, pp. 53–54.

16 Latin expression referring to the ferocity of the German tribes during the Roman Empire.

17 On payment of 1,000 pounds sterling, Jews could immigrate into Palestine with so-called capitalist certificates.

designated as such for the benefit of the German tax authorities, but in reality it would be a capitalist certificate.

I thought I had now done everything I could to make our Aliyah happen. My optimism was entirely justified, based on previous experiences of these Basel certificates. However, 10th November thwarted our plans. Among the masses who were then searching desperately for ways of emigrating, several hundred were trying to get hold of Basel certificates. This possibility, which up until then only a select few had known about, had now become general knowledge. And the managers were unscrupulous enough to promise a certificate to everybody who applied for one. While they may have voiced certain reservations, they took people's payments all the same, and after the catastrophe of 10 November these generally amounted to considerably more than 2,000 marks. These people didn't think twice about exploiting people's desperation. It gradually emerged that the senior manager behind all this was a certain Brender, who apparently was officially resident in Palestine. So this type of certificate became known as a 'Brender certificate'.[18]

In January 1939 Brender himself came to Berlin, and here he was besieged by those who had been promised certificates by his agents. It was perfectly clear that promises on such a scale could not possibly be fulfilled. In Basel the number of such certificates available had always been relatively small. These were the certificates that were not used in Switzerland, because there was no significant demand there from emigrants. The same was true of countries like Belgium and Holland. So Brender tried to get hold of unused certificates in these countries too, with the help of the local Palestine Offices there, in order to satisfy at least some of his customers.

I won't take up your time by relating the full story of how we and several hundred others failed to receive a 'Brender certificate'. It is a particularly sad story, which is also the subject of various lawsuits that are still pending here. Brender, who I estimate has transferred at least 400,000 Reichsmarks, at an exchange rate of 20 Reichsmarks to the pound, as I know very well, which means he has collected at least £20,000 without doing anything much in return, is refusing to give any refunds. And so far, I'm sorry to say, the courts have dismissed the actions brought against him. They take the view that no claims relating to transactions that are prohibited under German foreign exchange laws can be pursued in this country either.

So there was no Brender certificate to be had. In the meantime, the new war had broken out, and now many of those for whom certificates had already been properly issued – or at least approved – through the proper channels were left empty-handed, now that the English consulates in Germany were closed. Apart from very special exceptions, there was now only one way to get to Eretz Israel: a so-called 'S.H. passage'. S.H. stands for *Sonder-Hachsharah*.[19] The name was chosen to disguise the fact that this is

18 Naftali Hirsch Brender (b. 1908), businessman; as a young man he worked in his father's textile company in Karlsruhe; sentenced to two months' imprisonment in 1928 for falsifying documents, and fled abroad; after 1933 he was frequently in Germany, where he encouraged Jews to emigrate to Palestine. He returned to Karlsruhe in 1949 and set up two companies; when investigation proceedings were initiated in 1950, following allegations including embezzlement of funds, he fled the country again.

19 German: 'Special Hachsharah'.

about illegal Aliyah. For the same reason, the Palestine Office in Berlin, which in fact organized this illegal Aliyah, also known as 'Aliyah B', together with its subsidiary organizations, the *Hehalutz* and the *Youth Aliyah*, did not officially associate itself with this project. Officially, the transports were organized and carried out by a so-called 'Committee for Jewish Overseas Transports'.

The transports were of course illegal only in the eyes of the English.[20] In Germany they were legal and could not be anything else, since all Jewish agencies operated under the supervision of the Gestapo, and, apart from a few isolated exceptions, emigration was only possible with the knowledge and assent of the authorities. Prior to the outbreak of war, two such transports had already been organized by the Berlin Hehalutz, and these had been a success. Those who sailed with this S.H. 1 and S.H. 2 had come ashore after experiencing all kinds of hardships and dangers, without falling into the hands of the English.[21] S.H. 3 set sail after the outbreak of war, in October 1939, and likewise arrived safely three months later, but this time the party was captured by the British, who interned it in *Atlit*; the women were released soon afterwards, the men after six months. This party had likewise endured many dangers and hardships, including an outbreak of fire on the ship, which was promptly put out, but it cost a young girl her life.[22]

S.H. 4 set out in November 1939. Winter came early, and in the severe weather the ship became ice-bound on the Danube off the Yugoslavian coast. The passengers, mostly young people, were taken to a camp in *Cladowe*[23] in *Yugoslavia*, where they endured many hardships due to hunger, cold, and the wretched living conditions. Several attempts were made to help them continue their journey, but these came to nothing. It was only in the spring of this year, when the Nazis were getting dangerously close to Yugoslavia too, that the young people from this transport entered the country on the strength of Youth Aliyah certificates,[24] for which we have to thank the tireless efforts of Miss *Szold*.[25]

S.H. 5 was not organized from Berlin, but from *Vienna*, by the Committee for Jewish Overseas Transports, located on Rote Turmgasse. This transport departed from Vienna on the *Pencho*, sailing down the Danube. I will say more later about the sad fate that

20 In May 1939 the British Mandate government published its White Paper, which strictly limited Jewish immigration into Palestine. Jewish organizations sought to circumvent this policy by the use of these *Sonder-Hachsharah* transports.

21 S.H. 1 was en route from 4 to 15 March 1939. The participants travelled by rail to Yugoslavia, and from there by ship to Palestine. Those who travelled with the second transport crossed illegally into Belgium and sailed from Antwerp on board the *Dora* on 16 July 1939; they reached Palestine on 12 August 1939.

22 The emigrants on the S.H. 3 transport left the German Reich on 13 Oct. 1939 and travelled via the Romanian port of Sulina; their onward passage on the Greek steamer *Hilda* was delayed, in part because the Danube was frozen over. In the second half of Jan. 1940 the ship was captured by British coastguards off the coast of Palestine.

23 Correctly: Kladovo.

24 At the beginning of March 1941 another 200 to 280 young people were able to emigrate and travel to Palestine. The refugees who remained in Kladovo were later murdered: see Introduction, p. 52.

25 Henrietta Szold (1860–1945), social worker and writer; secretary of the Jewish Publication Society of America, for which she translated many books; founder of the Zionist women's organization Hadassah; emigrated from the USA to Palestine in 1920; director of the Children's and Youth Aliyah from 1934.

befell those on board. S.H. 6 was likewise organized from Vienna. I know nothing of its fate, or nothing that I can now recall.

I come now to *S.H. 7*. This is the S.H. that my wife and I joined. As I have already mentioned, there was no alternative once the war had broken out. We applied for an S.H. transport in the full knowledge of the dangers and hardships that this would entail. I was fairly well informed about these things, as I had been doing volunteer work in the Berlin Palestine Office since the spring of 1939, and the reports on earlier transports had come to my attention.

It was not easy to join S.H. 7. There was a huge rush of people applying for places. Hitherto, the knowledge that such transports existed had been largely confined to Zionist circles – and more particularly, to Hehalutz circles, which by and large organized them only for the *halutzim*[26] youth. But since February 1940 their existence had become widely known throughout Germany. At that time Hapag approached the Palestine Office in Berlin and offered to make ships available for the illegal transports to Palestine. At first the Palestine Office was wary of this offer, fearing that the Gestapo was behind it, and that it was all a ploy to deport a whole load of undesirable people. But after some negotiation, it was agreed that applications to join a transport should be submitted to the Palestine Office, which would be solely responsible for deciding which persons to take. The Palestine Office was now inundated with applications from all over Germany. In the course of two or three months, around 30,000 applied for the 'Apala'. Apala was the name suggested by Hapag for the transports; it did not want its own name to be publicly associated with the venture. Many of those who applied probably had no real intention of emigrating to Palestine: they simply wanted to be able to show the Gestapo evidence of their attempts to emigrate. The vast majority of applicants, however, were genuine.

The Palestine Office now appointed commissions to examine the applications and approve or reject them, setting out guidelines for this purpose. These stipulated that the only persons who should be accepted were essentially those with a track record of working for the Zionist cause, or who had accommodation already arranged in the country. In order to be accepted one also had to be fit enough to cope with the journey and with the country itself, and able to raise the cost of the passage in dollars. The dollars were necessary because the emigrants themselves had to raise a total of 80,000 dollars. As a rule, older persons were asked to pay 200 dollars each. In the case of long-serving Zionists, *watikim*,[27] and also *halutzim*, the organizers settled for lesser amounts, or even waived the dollar requirement altogether. The dollars could only be purchased in a neutral foreign country, of course, with the aid of relatives and friends; they had to be deposited with a bank in Zurich.

A substantial pool of staff was required to advise members of the public – who turned up each day in their hundreds at the Palestine Office – on all the various issues involved. I was one of these advisors. I was also on the commission that had to make the final decision on whether applications were to be approved. In our consultations we had to put straight many misguided and absurd notions, and destroy people's illusions. There

26 Plural of *halutz*; Hebrew for 'pioneer'. The term was used in Zionist discourse to refer to people who were or who trained to be agricultural labourers in settlements in Palestine.

27 Hebrew for 'veterans'; here Zionist veterans.

were also some amusing scenes. One day a little old woman of nearly 70 came and asked if we would take her with us to Apala, thinking this was some country overseas. Unfortunately, we had to tell her that at her age she was not up to coping with the exertions of such a journey, and could therefore not be taken with us.

Obviously it was not possible to accept more than a small proportion of the tens of thousands who had applied. We knew how difficult it was to organize such transports. In particular, we knew how difficult it was to get the ships. We did not have sufficient confidence in the Hapag Apala to believe that they could supply the ships. The only ships that could be considered – this was after the outbreak of war – were ships from neutral countries. But even in the neutral countries, shipping space was at a premium as a result of so many ships being sunk. Then there was the risk of sailing through war zones, and the threat of harsh penalties for the captain and crew for contravening the Palestinian immigration regulations.

Our surmise that Hapag would not be able to provide ships turned out to be right. So the Committees for Overseas Transports in Berlin and Vienna, supported by the Reich Association of Jews in Germany and the Joint [Distribution Committee], tried the same methods that had worked before to obtain ships for the earlier S.H. passages. This severely tested the patience of those who had been accepted for these later passages – including my wife and me. We were put off from week to week, and from month to month. One time we would be told that ships were there, Greek ships, but the Greek government had refused permission to sail; then we were told that the ships were permitted to sail, but no captain could be found. When a captain had been recruited, it then turned out that they couldn't get hold of a crew. When the crew had been hired, the Greek shipping company demanded an advance payment of 20,000 dollars; only after this had been paid would the ships be allowed to set sail from the port of Piraeus, bound for the mouth of the Danube on the Black Sea. But nobody was prepared to agree to that; one didn't trust the Greek crook. Then, when these difficulties had also been resolved, and the ships really had reached Tulcea at the mouth of the Danube, we were told that they had not yet been fitted out to accommodate a mass transport.

By now it was the summer of 1940. Italy had entered the war; the Mediterranean was now a war zone in its own right. France had been defeated. Hitler's invasion of England and his dictatorship over Europe looked likely to become a reality. And many feared that Mussolini would gain control of the entire Mediterranean, including Palestine. At any event, the situation was such that people had to give up hope of getting out of Germany now, or of getting to Palestine at all while the war was on. There was soon a rumour going around that all emigration would be blocked; then the word was that Jews up to the age of 45 would no longer be allowed to leave Germany. But the improbable became a reality, or as I said at the beginning: 'Lo Yanum velo Yishan …' Providence was vigilant, and smote the Nazi chiefs with blindness, so that they could not see how much they were damaging themselves by continuing to let Jews, especially young Jews, leave the country.

At the beginning of July 1940 the Gestapo ordered the Palestine Office to select 500 persons from the total number accepted for the S.H. passages; to submit the list of 500 names to it, the Gestapo, by nine o'clock the following morning; and to proceed with the dispatch of these 500 persons as quickly as possible. A commission (of which I was not a member) convened immediately, held an all-night session, and compiled the list of 500 names. This involved some very tough negotiations. The representative of each individual group fought hard to get as many from his own group as possible onto the list: representatives of the Halutzic youth movement, the Youth Aliyah, Bachad,[28] the Watikim, and other groups. There was already a sense that the impending Aliyah would be the last to get out of Nazi Germany, and that acceptance or rejection might well turn out to be a life or death decision.

My wife and I were among the 500. We had been included as members of the Watikim group. But belonging to the Watikim would not have been enough by itself. There were hundreds of Watikim apart from me. The deciding factor was that 200 dollars had been deposited in Zurich for us to pay for our passage. All those selected to travel were now required by the Palestine Office to sign a letter of indemnity. This letter pointed out the dangers and physical strains of the journey, excluded any liability for damages, and in particular emphasized that no liability could be assumed for arrival in Palestine. By signing the letter of indemnity, we were also confirming our full acceptance of the terms and conditions of carriage. On the basis of what had been learned from the earlier transports, these were aimed at maintaining the strictest discipline and unquestioning compliance with all instructions issued by those in charge of the transport.

Among those selected, there were a few who had anxieties or other reservations about undertaking the journey. Others were then selected to replace them, chosen from the large number who had protested about not being considered. On the final list approved by the Gestapo were 350 young persons and halutzim up to the age of 30, and 150 over the age of 30. The relatively large number of young persons and halutzim is explained by the fact that the S.H. transports were essentially organized for young people, who for obvious reasons are more valuable for the future development of the country than older people.

The 500 of us now prepared for our departure. The fact that a transport bound for Palestine was now about to set off in the middle of the war caused a real sensation among Berlin's Jews, and everyone was talking about it. Many were sceptical, and said the Gestapo would just deport us somewhere or other, while others said that even if the ships left port, we would never reach our destination; we would hit a mine, or be bombed from the air, or captured by the Italians and interned, or we would drift around for months on end at sea, unable to land anywhere – or else we would perish in some other way. I was expressly warned off by my friends, because I'd had several bouts of flu accompanied by a high fever, and had also had an accident in July that left me with a broken rib. But we refused to let all these sceptics and pessimists deter us. We were optimists, as befits Jews, and we had to be. And we had no other choice, now that the Gestapo had ordered the emigration of the 500.

First of all, we had to get our emigration papers in order. The Gestapo allowed us a few weeks for this. And there were numerous obstacles to be overcome. The tax offices checked very carefully to see that all our taxes, and in particular the Reich Flight Tax and the atonement fine, had been paid in full. The Jewish Community also had to certify that we had no tax arrears, and in particular that the Jewish emigration levy had been paid, which was intended to support Jews without means who were left behind in

28 Union of Religious Pioneers: Zionist youth movement combining adherence to orthodox religion and Zionist pioneering.

Germany.[29] I had another problem with the tax office that turned out to be difficult to resolve. The tax office had requested formal confirmation from the Reichsbank that it had no objections to the issue of a tax clearance certificate. I had duly notified the Reichsbank of claims for fees due to me by non-residents, and had registered the receipt of such claims. Some fees due were not recoverable, however. It took a lot of protracted negotiations with the Reichsbank to convince them that these fees really were irrecoverable. At first the Reichsbank suspected that I had deliberately not collected the amounts due because I wanted to keep the money abroad for its foreign exchange value.

Once all these obstacles had been successfully negotiated, and we had received our passports, we had to hand them in to the Palestine Office in order to obtain the necessary visa. We wanted to go to Palestine, so essentially what we needed was a visa from the British consulate. But for one thing, the British consulate was shut because of the war, and for another thing they would not have given us a visa because we didn't have certificates. But the Reich Association had made alternative provision. The consulate of *Paraguay* issued what we needed, for a hefty fee, which was paid by the Reich Association with the aid of the Joint [Distribution Committee]. The Joint [Distribution Committee] had also had to furnish guarantees that we would not, in actual fact, inflict ourselves on Paraguay.

Now there was only one thing missing: the exit visa issued by police headquarters, which was required by law for every border crossing.[30] It was issued without difficulty, as police headquarters already knew all about us and our plans. We could now have set sail at last, had it not been for a new difficulty that now presented itself. The Greek government suddenly refused to let us fly the Greek flag. Initially another flag could not be found – and we could not cross the open seas without a flag. So the Reich Association and the Palestine Office would not take responsibility for our departure. At this point the Gestapo intervened again, and on 3 August 1940 they ordered our departure in groups. They gave instructions that not one of the 500 was to be left in the Old Reich by 18 August. The first group was to leave the very next day.

Now things started to happen in earnest. The first group, a Halutzic group from the provinces, set off for Vienna as instructed. Other groups then followed. Before the departure of the Berlin group, the Reich Association and the Palestine Office arranged a farewell gathering, at which the composure and courage of the 500 were repeatedly acknowledged, as they faced an uncertain and hazardous future. One of the speakers at this farewell gathering was the head of the Reich Association, Dr Paul Eppstein, who was arrested by the Gestapo a few days later. They probably blamed him for having failed to accelerate the departure of the transport.[31]

My wife and I left with the last group on the evening of 17 August. In Vienna, where we had to stop over because the flag issue had not yet been resolved, all 500 were put up and fed in hotels, instead of in the expected mass accommodation. The costs were met by the Reich Association. Of course, nothing happened in Vienna either without the

29 On the emigration levy (*Auswandererabgabe*), see Doc. 45.

30 Under the terms of the Regulation on the Requirement for Passports and Visas and the Requirement for Identity Cards (10 Sept. 1939), the passports had to be stamped at the border crossing with a visa issued by an appropriate authority, usually the district police authority: *Reichsgesetzblatt*, I, 1939, pp. 1739–1740.

31 See Doc. 128.

knowledge and consent of the Gestapo. So our quartering in hotels also happened on orders from the Gestapo, not because they wanted to ease our departure from Hitler's Germany, but in order to fill the empty hotels of this former tourist city. For this reason, too, the Gestapo did not initially pressure us to move on. After a week or so of easy living, during which we were able to stroll about Vienna quite freely, although we were not permitted to frequent bars or restaurants, the picture changed. The hardships and discomforts of an S.H. now started. On orders from the Gestapo we had to vacate the hotels within a matter of hours, because visitors from out of town were arriving for the Vienna Fair, which was due to open on 1 September. We were now rehoused in accommodation belonging to the Jewish Community, which in the case of my wife and myself meant a school on Kasteletzgasse.[32] Here we all had to sleep on the floor of the classrooms, and put up with all the other discomforts and inconveniences of living in mass accommodation. Our freedom to come and go was also greatly curtailed – I'm not sure if this was on orders from the Gestapo, or because those in charge of our transport thought it best to avoid any trouble on the streets.

I have mentioned the people in charge before, and would like to say a little more about them. A young man of about 30 called *Erich Frank*, who had been a senior figure in the Hehalutz and had done most of the planning and preparations for the transport, was put in charge of our transport and had absolute authority over it.[33] Assisting him were two deputies, also young men from the Hehalutz. The participants were divided into groups. Each group was headed by a group leader, who was responsible for order and discipline within his group, and also looked after their well-being as far as that was possible, as well as ensuring that the instructions from the transport leadership were carried out. I was appointed to be one of these group leaders. One group was the Haganah,[34] consisting of 30 particularly fit young men, in effect a kind of police squad, whose job it was to maintain order and discipline – using brute force, if necessary.

This entire organization and its staffing were based on decisions taken by the large Palestine Office Commission, on which representatives of the Reich Association and the Jewish Community also had an important voice. By signing the letter of indemnity mentioned earlier, every participant had expressly accepted not only the terms and conditions of carriage, but also the leadership structure as described, and the leadership personnel appointed. A tight organization and discipline of this kind were absolutely essential for the highly unusual journey that we were about to undertake.

To go back to our stopover in Vienna: after what seemed like an endless period of waiting, which gave rise to wild rumours of every kind – there was even talk of our being repatriated to the Old Reich – the news eventually came through that the ships waiting

32 The correct spelling is 'Castellezgasse'. This school later served as an assembly point for Viennese Jews designated for deportation: see Doc. 144, fn. 5, and Doc. 151.

33 Dr Erich, also Ephraim, Frank (1909–1996), lawyer; deputy head of the Hehalutz in Berlin from 1935, and from Germany was actively involved in 1945 in the organization of illegal emigration to Palestine; he later lived in the Givat Chaim Ichud kibbutz, and established a legal department at its request, with the aim of representing kibbutz members who wished to pursue claims for compensation.

34 Hebrew for 'defence': Zionist paramilitary organization, founded in 1920 in the British Mandate for Palestine. It formed the core of the Israeli defence forces after the establishment of the state of Israel in 1948.

at the mouth of the Danube were now ready, and that the esteemed state of Panama had given consent for them to sail under its flag. Needless to say, all this had cost the Reich Association or the Joint [Distribution Committee] more money. Now we really thought that all our difficulties lay behind us. But then a new one arose, which we had not expected in the slightest. In order to travel on to Pressburg,[35] we needed Slovakian visas. This had never been a problem before, thanks to the efforts of a resourceful member of the Vienna Committee. But this time the authorities refused. The Vienna Gestapo now really did threaten to send us back to the Old Reich, if we had not moved on by 3 September. At the last minute we finally succeeded in obtaining the Slovakian visas, and on 3 September we travelled by special train from Vienna to Pressburg. At the border crossing station we were subjected to very thorough passport checks, customs checks, and foreign exchange controls. Selected men and women were body-searched. Cigarettes, food, medication, new cigarette lighters, books, and other items found in our luggage were confiscated.

In the late evening we set off again, and arrived at the port in Pressburg during the night. That same night we boarded a ship, which was to take us down the Danube as far as the Black Sea. It was a river cruise ship, the *Uranus*, belonging to the Danube Steamship Company. There were already 700 passengers on board – 'passengers' being a euphemism, of course. These were Jewish companions in misfortune, most of whom had been interned for the previous nine months in a camp near Pressburg, the so-called 'Patronka', a derelict cartridge factory. These people had been sent to Pressburg in December 1939 by the Vienna Committee, in the hope that they would be able to stay in Pressburg until arrangements could be made for their onward travel; but no sooner had they arrived than they were arrested by the Hlinka Guard and interned in the Patronka.[36] Among them were several hundred Poles, who had been in Sachsenhausen concentration camp. On the strength of formal undertakings from the Berlin Palestine Office that they would be put on the next S.H. transport, they had been released and taken to Vienna, so that they could join the transport to Pressburg and thus get out of Germany at least.

So it was these people from the Patronka that we met on board the *Uranus*, along with a number of native Viennese. The 700 also included 75 who had been sent straight to the ship from various jails by the Vienna Gestapo. We called the 700 Viennese the 'Vienna Transport', to distinguish them from us, the 500 who made up the 'Berlin Old Reich Transport'. So with 700 plus 500 we added up to 1,200 people altogether, on a ship that had been built to carry around 300 cruise passengers.

As well as all the people, their luggage also had to be stowed on the ship. The Viennese had a lot of luggage with them, while we Berliners had only been allowed to leave with what we could carry ourselves. Clearly, the space that was available to accommodate people and luggage was extremely limited. Every inch of floor space had to be used to provide spaces to sleep. Even the cabins designed for two people, where the older members of our party were accommodated, had six to eight occupants, which meant that the floor had to be used as well. The corridors were also used as places to sleep, and the deck too of course. Several hundred slept out on the deck, mainly the younger ones. This was only possible because we had the most *miraculous* summer weather for the whole of our

35 Bratislava.
36 Hlinka Guard: the armed wing of the antisemitic Slovak People's Party, founded before the First World War by the Catholic priest Andrej Hlinka (1864–1938).

voyage down the Danube. And when I say 'miraculous', I mean it literally; it was a miracle that we didn't have a *single* drop of rain. If it had rained at night, forcing the several hundred people sleeping on deck to come down below, the crowding below deck, where every inch of space was already occupied, would have become unbearable. And if it had rained constantly, it would have become impossible to continue the journey with 1,200 persons on board. Many of them would have had to leave the ship and go ashore. The countries along the Danube would not have permitted us to go ashore, however. We had no visas for these countries, and persons without visas are effectively non-persons. As Jewish emigrants, we were especially ostracized. Had it rained continually, an epidemic of colds and flu and other infectious illnesses would also have been inevitable; but as I say, we were blessed with a miraculously rain-free period. Such a thing, as the captain told us, was a rarity on the Danube. We were also largely spared other illnesses. Quite a few people suffered from bowel troubles, but nothing too serious. This was mainly due to the fact that the food on our Danube steamer was quite reasonable. The ship's Aryan catering manager bought fresh food supplies in various ports along the Danube – we were not allowed to enter the ports, so had to moor somewhere close by – and had them brought on board.

Leaving aside the many discomforts and disadvantages of having 1,200 people living together in a confined space – e.g. the sleeping arrangements, as already mentioned, having to fetch food, using the washrooms and toilets – life on our Danube steamer was pretty tolerable. There were even times when we felt like tourists on holiday – enjoying the architectural delights of Budapest, seeing Belgrade when it was all lit up for the king's birthday, and taking in the changing landscapes along the banks of the Danube. Of course, living together in such close proximity was bound to produce friction and arguments of all kinds. The Haganah had to intervene on many occasions, using force to deal with disorderly and ill-disciplined individuals. It started on the very first day. The Viennese, who were on the ship before us, had taken the cabins intended for us and commandeered other areas intended for our use. Some of the Viennese refused to leave; they claimed they had had a harder time of it than had we Berliners, after nine months in the Patronka and in the concentration camp before that. Their own leaders, in charge of the Vienna transport, didn't accept these arguments. As the interlopers still refused to move, they were forcibly ejected by the Haganah from the areas intended for the use of the Berliners.

In fact the Viennese and the Berliners had words with each other, and even came to blows, on an almost daily basis, and on one occasion it almost came to a stabbing. We group leaders often helped to settle disputes. My wife and I got on well with the Viennese. We were among the few older Berliners, only about 25 of us, who adhered to kosher principles. Among the Viennese there were 250. The shared interests that my wife and I had with such a large number of Viennese meant that we got along very peaceably together. There was, incidentally, no kosher kitchen on the ship, despite the large number of people – 350 – who wanted to eat kosher. Unlike all the others, who got a hot lunch every day, for the whole of our passage down the Danube we had to make do with hard-boiled eggs and tinned sardines – hardly a diet that nutritionists would recommend for one's calorie and vitamin intake.

On another occasion, when we were moored close to a port on the Danube, in this case the Bulgarian city of Rustchuk, we had an experience that filled our Jewish hearts with mortal fear and shredded our nerves. We saw the *Pencho*, moored about 200 metres from us. This was the ship I mentioned earlier, which had S.H. 5 on board. We had already heard that the *Pencho* was not seaworthy, and had broken down somewhere. We also knew that the ship had a number of Poles on board who had been released from a concentration camp on the strength of certificates issued by the Palestine Office in Berlin, and whose wives were travelling on our own ship. Based on the information they had, these women were extremely worried about the fate of their husbands. The people travelling on the *Pencho* recognized us as fellow sufferers, and tried to communicate with us by shouting across to us. On our ship everyone fell silent. We could make out that they were shouting: 'We are starving, send us bread and other food supplies.' We responded by shouting in unison: 'We'll send you something.' A collection was immediately held. Although we did not have an abundance of food ourselves, large quantities of bread, tinned sardines, chocolate, and cigarettes were collected. Everyone sensed that one of the greatest tragedies to afflict our people was being played out on that other ship. The women whose husbands were on the *Pencho* were particularly distressed. They wept, screamed, and pleaded with the leaders of our transport, as well as the ship's captain, to have their husbands transferred to our ship. But all their efforts were in vain. The captain explained that we could not have any contact with the other ship, as there were infectious diseases on board. It took a great deal of persuasion to get him to send across the food supplies we had collected – and then only after contacting the Bulgarian police.

The subsequent fate of the *Pencho* was also particularly sad. After it had been patched up some time later, and had reached the Aegean Sea, it was wrecked – smashed against the cliffs of an island. Some drowned, and the survivors were picked up by the Italians, taken to Rhodes, and interned there. A notice about these internees appeared last week in the *Hashavua*. Apparently these people, having suffered such a cruel fate, are to be transported back to Germany.[37]

I come now to our own voyage across the seas. By mid September our ship *Uranus* had reached Tulcea at the mouth of the Danube, the Romanian city that has lately been bombed frequently by Russian aircraft. In Tulcea we were transferred to one of the waiting Greek ships, the *Pacific*. The other two ships were the *Atlantic* and the *Milos*. The *Atlantic* was mainly carrying a contingent that had come from Danzig, while on board the *Milos* was a transport from Czechoslovakia. The passengers on board the *Atlantic* [were] the unfortunate wretches who were later transported to Mauritius. All three ships were now about to embark on the hazardous enterprise of getting to Eretz Israel.

The *Pacific* was a freighter of 700 tonnes, which was normally intended to carry about 50 people in addition to its cargo. When we boarded the ship, we were appalled to think that the 1,200 of us from the *Uranus* were supposed to find room on board. No words can adequately describe how everyone eventually managed to find a place to sleep in the tightest of spaces. The writer's line about being 'packed together in horrendous confinement' became a reality here.[38] Wherever a space could be found, wooden bunk

37 This could not be verified.

38 A reference to Friedrich Schiller's drama *Wallenstein* (1799), in which the Captain says: 'Neither forward nor back could they go, packed together in horrendous confinement' ('Nicht vorwärts konnten sie, auch nicht zurück, gekeilt in drangvoll fürchterliche Enge') (*Wallensteins Tod*, IV. x).

beds had been knocked up, two or three deep, with so little space between the beds that the occupants could only lie flat or kneel. The sexes were not segregated, and indeed could not be, for all kinds of different reasons. Some of the accommodation was really not fit for human beings. Two bunkers with no access to light or air, which were only designed for cargo, had to be put into service as dormitories. The decks were used as well. These had light and air in abundance, but at night they were very cold. Every inch of space on the floors of the narrow corridors was also used for sleeping. If you had to go to the toilet at night, you had to pick your way across the people sleeping on the floor.

Getting to the toilet and using it during the day was no joke either. There were generally so many people waiting to use it that you had to queue, and sometimes wait for up to an hour before it was your turn. Things got particularly bad for a while, when many people were suffering from diarrhoea accompanied by a fever. And again it was a miracle, given these toilet conditions, that there were no outbreaks of infectious diseases, and another miracle that we again had the most glorious summer weather for nearly the whole of our voyage on the *Pacific*. The Black Sea, which has the reputation of being stormy, was for days on end as calm and flat as the 'Neue See' lake in Berlin. The captain told us that he had only rarely seen it like this. We had just one stormy night. The storm was not even that bad, but the small and not altogether seaworthy ship was tossed and shaken so badly that we were close to sinking. The storm and a big wave even tore away a section of the ship's side. The water that came in was immediately bailed out by our fearless 'Haganah'. And we were shielded from further perils by a nearby Turkish bay, where we entered to await the end of the storm. So we suffered no loss of life. On the contrary, our human complement actually increased by one that fateful night: one of our travel companions gave birth to a child.

Our ship, I should add, was not at all properly equipped. The fact that we had to be grateful to have got out of Nazi Germany, and to have found a ship at all, had been callously exploited. The only compass on the ship didn't work. We had no sextant at all, nor the other standard nautical instruments or a radio set. As a result, the captain drifted off course on occasion; the stokers were not properly trained for the job either. We were often short of coal and machine oil. Consequently we sometimes crept along at the speed of an old Berlin cab horse pulling a 'second class taxi'. Despite all these handicaps, we got safely through the Bosporus, the Sea of Marmara, and the Dardanelles into the Aegean Sea.

A few more things about life on board the *Pacific*. It was a constant struggle to meet the most basic daily needs. We had to queue and wait for everything – washing, cleaning our teeth, shaving, fetching our meals three times a day, fetching drinking water, washing our clothes. Water for washing had to be hauled up from the sea for each individual, and drinking water was sometimes in such short supply that for days at a time none could be distributed; there was only enough for cooking. Some days there wasn't even any drinking water for cooking, and we had to use seawater instead, with its unpleasantly salty taste.

The business of fetching meals was particularly tiresome. Three times a day, hundreds of people shoved, or rather squeezed, past each other in the narrow corridors, where people spent much of their time on board anyway. Coming from one direction were those who had already collected their meal, and who were carrying hot tea or hot soup in their containers. And coming from the opposite direction were the others, who were on their way to collect their meals. It was another miracle that people were not scalded every day through bumping up against the hot containers of tea and soup. A few people did get scalded, but none of them seriously. Two more miracles: we didn't hit a mine, and we didn't meet any Italian ships. Strangely enough, we never saw another ship on all the seas that we sailed across. It felt as if we – and not Albion – 'ruled the waves'.

It was also a miracle that our ship survived when we held a 'neschef'[39] on deck in the Aegean Sea, with several hundred people in attendance. It was a reckless thing to do. The captain had always warned us against large gatherings on deck. The ship listed to the side where there were too many people standing, and then rolled back over towards the other side even more violently, so that pieces of luggage and anything else that wasn't tied down came crashing to the floor. We feared that if the ship rolled back over again, it would capsize. The captain shared our fear, but he was able, by skilfully moving people about to distribute the weight, to keep the ship on an even keel. If the ship had capsized, hardly anyone would have been rescued, as we were alone on the high seas, without radios, and with very few lifebelts on board.

A further dramatic incident also occurred without loss of life. As we were moored outside a harbour in order to take on food, water, and coal, five elderly men and women were standing at the railing looking across to the harbour town, leaning on a hatch that was used for loading and unloading cargo. Suddenly the hatch gave way, and the five plunged down into the sea. A dozen good swimmers immediately jumped in after them and rescued them.

By now we had entered the Mediterranean Sea. The tension was now rising, as we waited to find out whether we would reach our destination, whether we would finally see Eretz Israel, and whether we would see our children, our parents, and our friends again. We were constantly worried that our captain, who was still sailing without a compass, would take us to the coast of North Africa instead of to Eretz Israel. To make things worse, in the last few days of October we ran out of coal, and every scrap of wood that could be spared, including the improvised bunk beds, had to be used to fire the engines. This meant that nearly all the ship's passengers had to sleep on the floor now. Only the sick were allowed to keep their wooden beds. When the supply of wood was also about to run out, we faced the prospect, as from the next day, of being completely at the mercy of the weather and the wind and any new storms, without a compass, without a radio, and with no port in sight. Our nerves were stretched to breaking point.

And then the greatest of all miracles occurred, at first light on the morning of 1 November 1940. The captain said to those standing around him that the distinctive heights of Mount Carmel were now in sight in the far distance. Half a minute later, the entire ship knew. At first nobody could quite believe it, but a short time later we were able to make out Mount Carmel with the naked eye. Some were moved to tears, and others gave voice to their joy, but there was no loud cheering, and certainly no frenzy of celebration. We had a sense once again of having skirted the abyss many times over. There was an almost reverential silence as we lay at anchor some time later outside the port of Haifa.

I have come to the end of my tale. What happened next, our transfer to the *Patria*, the perils of the onward transport to Mauritius, the explosion on board the *Patria* and

39 Hebrew for 'celebration', 'party', 'ball'.

its consequences, our internment on the very day of the disaster, on 25 November 1940 – all this you already know. Exactly one hundred days after we embarked on our journey, we had reached our goal and set foot on the soil of Eretz Israel.[40]

DOC. 121
In his diary entries for September through to November 1940, Hans Baruch documents how he fled the Reich on a series of ships[1]

Handwritten diary of Hans Baruch,[2] entries for the period 2 September to 25 November 1940

Monday, 2 September 1940
23:00 – left for Prague
Masaryk Station
Customs control
Tuesday, 3 September 1940
10:00 – arrival in Vienna, Ostbahnhof
Onward to the Prater Quay. Here boarded the Danube steamer *Melk*[3]
Customs control before boarding the steamer
Wednesday, 4 September 1940
6:00 – departure of the *Melk*
9:00 – Heinburg
10:00 – docked in Bratislava
11:00 Budapest
Thursday, 5 September 1940
Hungary. Estergau
Ostřihom
Běhlehrad in the night (Belgrade)
Friday, 6 September 1940
Romania
Saturday, 7 September 1940
Afternoon, arrival in Ruse

40 On the explosion on board the *Patria*, and the internment of Jewish refugees in the then British Crown Colony of Mauritius, see Introduction, pp. 51–52, and Doc. 121, in particular fnn. 15, 16, and 18.

1 The original is privately owned; copy in IfZ-Archives, F 601. This document has been translated from German.

2 Hans, also Hanan Baruch (1920–2000); was born to parents in a so-called mixed marriage in Berlin; fled to Palestine on board the *Patria*, was initially placed in the refugee camp at Atlit, and volunteered to join the British army. When the war ended, he was stationed in Italy and travelled to Berlin to look for his parents, who had survived the war there; after the state of Israel was established, he worked until his retirement in the Israeli Ministry of Finance, where he rose to become a head of department.

3 A total of 1,880 Jews left Vienna on 3 Sept. 1940 on board the *Melk* and the *Uranus*; most of them were *halutzim* (Hebrew for 'pioneers') from Austria, the Protectorate of Bohemia and Moravia, and Danzig. The transports had been organized by Berthold Storfer and his Committee for Jewish Overseas Transports.

We saw the *Pentschau*[4]
Iron Gates above Ruse[5]
Monday, 9 September 1940
16:00 – departure from Ruse
Tuesday, 10 September 1940
Went ashore in Braila
Wednesday, 11 September 1940
Arrival of the *Melk* in Tulcea[6]
Saturday, 14 September 1940, 17:00/*Sunday*, 15 September 1940
Transferred to the freighter *Canisbay*.[7]
Left the ship in the night around 1:00. Around 17:00 some on board the transport taken to a camp
Monday, 23 September 1940
The *Canisbay* was renamed the *Milos*
Wednesday, 25 September 1940
Shortly before 10:00, all camp inmates suddenly ordered back to the ship. The last of them were transferred back shortly before 16:00. Two persons were arrested, but returned in the afternoon (Plaček, Berkovič)
Monday, 30 September 1940
In the morning the *Rozita* crew turned up;[8] straw mattresses and food supplies were brought on board over the following days
Saturday, 5 October 1940
The ship was readied for departure. The engines were inspected and repaired. Engines were made ready for operation, boilers fired
Monday, 7 October 1940
The rudder was checked. *Atlantic* (complement 1,500), the second transport ship, departed. An hour or so later, the *Pacific* (complement 1,000), the third ship.[9] 15:07 – the *Milos* (complement 700) left Tulcea. After an hour's sailing, we moored for the night downstream from Tulcea
Tuesday, 8 October 1940
Around 7:00 the *Atl.* was towed past. 10:57 – the *Milos* set sail downstream. 14:50 – the *Milos* reached the Black Sea at Sulina. Farewell, Europe! Sailed on after a short stop.
Wednesday, 9 October 1940
On the open sea. Many seasick

4 Correctly: *Pencho*. This refugee ship was detained temporarily at the Romanian–Bulgarian border: see also Doc. 120.

5 Iron Gates: gorge on the Danube, forming the border between Romania and Serbia.

6 Romanian port on the Danube.

7 Correctly: *Kenisbey*.

8 They had to wait for the *Rozita* to arrive, as this ship was bringing crews and equipment for the *Atlantic*, *Pacific*, and *Milos* refugee ships, which were waiting in the harbour to continue their journey. The original plan was for this ship to transport refugees on to Palestine as well.

9 The ships chartered by Berthold Storfer barely had room for 100 passengers each, the sanitary conditions were appalling, and the same was true of the food supply during the voyage. The *Milos* was the smallest of the three ships; of its 702 passengers, 652 came from the Protectorate of Bohemia and Moravia. On the voyage of the *Pacific*, see Doc. 120.

Thursday, 10 October 1940
Just before 8:50 entered the Bosporus. Istanbul denied entry to the harbour.[10] Sailed on through the very calm Sea of Marmara
Friday, 11 October 1940
Shortly before 5:30 passed through the Dardanelles. After a short stop sailed past Gallipoli. In the morning entered the Aegean Sea. Shortly before 17:30 we were off a Greek island near Sigri (Lesbos), awaiting a wire from Mytilene. Foreign currency was collected in order to buy food.
Saturday, 12 October 1940
Moored all day off the island. The captain conducted five weddings
Sunday, 13 October 1940
8:50 – we sailed on. After half an hour in stormy seas, turned back. Weddings conducted by a rabbi
Monday, 14 October 1940
7:30 – sailed on. Stormy seas. Towards 18:30 entered the Ionian Sea. The storm abated. 22:00 – people had to move elsewhere to bed down, as the upper deck was being sprayed with water by a strong side wind
Tuesday, 15 October 1940
We were cruising off Piraeus, but Piraeus refused us entry because of mines (!?).[11] We sailed on to Lavrion. 13:00 – arrived in Lavrion. We were given bread and water. The aid committee promised to help us[12]
Wednesday, 16 October 1940
Shortly before 10:00, we went alongside the jetty to take on fresh water.
Thursday, 17 October 1940
Spent the whole day taking on water and food.
Friday, 18 October 1940
In the afternoon we anchored in the middle of the harbour again.
Sunday, 20 October 1940
Telegram from the *Atl.*, saying she was lying off the coast of Crete with no coal, water, or food
Monday, 21 October 1940
6:20 – left Lavrion. 10:45 – entered harbour in Piraeus
Tuesday, 22 October 1940
Shortly before 22:00, left Piraeus and anchored in a more sheltered harbour (Salamis)
Wednesday, 23 October 1940
Towards evening, took on coal

10 The Turkish government cooperated with Britain in its efforts to stop illegal immigration into Palestine. Turkey was also keen not to let any Jewish refugees into the country unless arrangements for their onward travel were already in place. The Turkish parliament formalized this policy in a law, enacted on 12 Feb. 1941, which allowed Jewish refugees to pass through as long as they held a valid entry visa for their destination country.

11 As in the original.

12 The Jewish communities in the towns where the ships docked generally organized food and aid. The reference here may be to the Comité de Secours aux Réfugiés run by the Jews of Athens. The Greek secret police gave aid workers a free hand when it came to dealing with problems involving Jewish refugees on ships, and subsequently posed no significant obstacle to issuing visas.

Thursday, 24 October 1940
14:30 – departure. Heavy seas towards evening. Many seasick
Friday, 25 October 1940
Heavy seas towards evening. Some seasick.
Saturday, 26 October 1940
7:00 – we enter a harbour, Heraklion on Crete. Reunion with the *Atl.* I swam in the sea. *Pacific* also docked nearby. *Pentschau* stranded off Rhodes.
Sunday, 27 October 1940
17:00 – left port
Monday, 28 October 1940
Towards evening, our fellow passenger Nüssel was committed to the sea.
Tuesday, 29 October 1940
Calm sailing. From 16:00 could see Cyprus. We passed by Cyprus, but we turned around again in the night.
Wednesday, 30 October 1940
Shortly before 6:00, Cyprus in sight again. At 10:00 we entered harbour (Limassol). I went swimming.
Thursday, 31 October 1940
I went swimming. We took on bread. To buy coal we had to collect £150. We collected £100. Joined the Jewish army.[13]
Friday, 1 November 1940
Took on oranges, grapefruit, coal, bread, and pumpkins.
Saturday, 2 November 1940
Major delousing operation. Took on grapefruit, lemons, and coal. Due to leave. 14:10 – set sail. Choppy seas
Sunday, 3 November 1940
11:10 – stopped by coastguard boat; 14:00 – docked in Haifa.
Tuesday, 5 November 1940
Took on bread, meat, and fresh rolls. Air-raid alert in the afternoon
Wednesday, 6 November 1940
Some of those on the *Pacific* were transferred to the *Patria*. We expect to be transferred ourselves any day.[14] Bread, fresh rolls, coffee, jam, and honey taken on board.
Friday, 8 November 1940
Air-raid alert at lunchtime. *Pacific* fully disembarked.
Saturday, 9 November 1940
Shortly before 7:00, the first group of us transferred to the *Patria*.
Sunday, 10 November 1940
8:15 – I transferred to the *Patria*. Inspection, bath, registration of names
Monday, 11 November 1940
Nothing particular to report
Tuesday, 12 November 1940
Nothing particular to report. I moved into the catacombs (bunker)

13 Probably a reference to the recruitment of Jewish volunteers to separate Jewish units in the British army in the Middle East from July 1940.

14 The passengers on the *Milos*, the *Atlantic*, and the *Pacific* were all supposed to be transferred to the *Patria* passenger ship, which was moored in the harbour at Haifa.

Wednesday, 13 November 1940
Nothing particular to report.
Thursday, 14 November 1940
11:00 – air-raid alert
Friday, 15 November 1940
Nothing particular to report.
Saturday, 16 November 1940
Great events cast their shadow before them. Demonstrations against our deportation to an English colony.[15]
Sunday, 17 November 1940
Stayed in bed all day. Headache, diarrhoea, vomiting.
Monday, 18 November 1940
Felt better. Nothing particular to report.
Tuesday, 19 November 1940
Nothing particular to report.
Wednesday, 20 November 1940
Hunger strike from noon till midnight, in sympathy with a strike in Haifa to protest against our deportation.
Thursday, 21 November 1940
We received confirmation that we would not be remaining in Palestine. The plan is to send us to an English colony for the duration of the war. We don't know when or where.
Friday, 22 November 1940
In the evening a few brave souls (seven or eight?) attempted to escape, without success. As I have discovered, two halutzim managed to get ashore yesterday evening.[16]
Saturday, 23 November 1940
Some sort of commotion in the evening. Cause unknown. Again, a few tried to swim across.
Sunday, 24 November 1940
The ship is off limits for us, apart from the afterdeck. The doors have been nailed shut.
Monday, 25 November 1940
At 9:30 the *Patria* capsized.[17] Those who were rescued were put into a warehouse for the day, and later transferred to the Atlit camp.[18] Still no news about casualties, but some people I know are missing.[19]

15 The British Mandate administration sought to prevent all 3,552 passengers from entering the country, and planned to deport them instead to the island of Mauritius, a British colony in the Indian Ocean.

16 Many of the young pioneers tried to swim ashore after jumping overboard. They were picked up and interned.

17 The Yishuv leadership had hoped to prevent the disembarkation of the *Patria* by placing an explosive charge on board, but the explosion was too powerful and blew up the ship; see also Introduction, p. 51. (Yishuv was the term used for the organized Zionist Jewish community in the Land of Israel prior to the establishment of the State of Israel)

18 See Doc. 120, fn. 3.

19 Over 250 people died in the explosion. The survivors, together with the passengers from the *Atlantic* who had not yet been transferred to the *Patria*, were taken temporarily to the Atlit camp. The survivors from the *Patria* were eventually allowed to stay in the country, and the remaining Jews, some 1,500 in number, were shipped to Mauritius in Dec. 1940.

DOC. 122

On 2 December 1940 the mayor of Munich announces guidelines on public welfare for Jews who do not belong to the Reich Association of Jews in Germany[1]

Circular (for distribution to names on list I) issued by the mayor of Munich,[2] Department 6, signed City Councillor Ortner,[3] dated 2 December 1940[4]

Re: welfare for Jews.

The welfare department of the Israelite Religious Community of Munich has hitherto provided support not only for all Jews defined as such under § 5 of the First Regulation on the Reich Citizenship Law,[5] but also for Jews by faith of Aryan extraction. It has now been resolved that the welfare services provided by the Reich Association of Jews in Germany are to be restricted to those Jews who are members of the Reich Association of Jews by law under § 3 of the Tenth Regulation on the Reich Citizenship Law, or who have voluntarily chosen to join the Association. § 3 of the Tenth Regulation on the Reich Citizenship Law states the following:

(1) All Jews who are normally resident within the territory of the Reich, whether as subjects of the state or stateless persons, belong to the Reich Association.

(2) In the case of mixed marriages, the Jewish partner is a member only
   (a) if the husband is the Jewish partner and the marriage has produced no offspring, or
   (b) if the offspring of the marriage are classed as Jews.

(3) Jews of foreign nationality and Jews living in a mixed marriage who are not already members under (2) above are free to join the Reich Association.[6]

Accordingly, *public* welfare support is to be provided in case of need for:

(1) Jews who are living in mixed marriages with wives of Aryan extraction, where there are offspring of the marriage who are not classed as Jews (§ 5, sub-section II, of the First Regulation on the Reich Citizenship Law);

(2) Jewish women who are living in mixed marriages with Aryans, where the marriage has produced no offspring or only such offspring as are not classed as Jews;

(3) Jews of foreign nationality;

(4) Jews by faith of Aryan extraction.

1 StA Mü, Wohlfahrt 4599, fols. 1–3. This document has been translated from German.

2 Karl Fiehler (1895–1969) was mayor of Munich from 1933.

3 Karl Wilhelm Ortner (1901–1959), civil servant; employed in the welfare department of the Munich municipal administration from 1917 onwards; took part in the Beer Hall Putsch, 1923; joined the NSDAP and the SA in 1925; member of the SS, 1927–1929; headed the local Office for National Welfare in Munich, 1934–1940; was a councilman from 1935 onwards, and full-time city councillor, 1939–1945.

4 Receipt stamp of the welfare office, dated 10 Dec. 1940.

5 Section 5 of the First Regulation stipulated who was to be classed as a Jew under the terms of the Reich Citizenship Law: *Reichsgesetzblatt*, 1935, I, pp. 1333–1334; see also PMJ 1/210.

6 *Reichsgesetzblatt*, 1939, I, pp. 1097–1099, here p. 1097.

The above assumes that Jews listed under (1) to (3) are not voluntary members of the Reich Association of Jews in Germany, and that in the case of Jews listed under (1) and (2) the mixed marriage has not been dissolved as a result of the death of the Aryan party, divorce, or annulment.

Insofar as the welfare department of the Israelite Religious Community declines to continue providing support in the cases listed under (1) to (4), public welfare will have to step in again. Jews listed under (1) to (3), however, will have to produce written confirmation from the Reich Association of Jews in Germany (Munich branch) that they are not voluntary members of the Reich Association. Furthermore, these Jews are required to make the following signed declaration: 'I hereby declare that I

(1) am not a voluntary member of the Reich Association of Jews in Germany,
(2) will immediately inform the office if and when I do become a voluntary member of the Reich Association of Jews in Germany,
(3) will inform the office of any change in my family circumstances that requires me to become a member of the Reich Association of Jews in Germany in accordance with § 3, sub-sections I and II, of the Tenth Regulation on the Reich Citizenship Law.
(4) I understand that if I supply false information about my membership of the Reich Association of Jews in Germany, or about my family circumstances insofar as they affect membership, or about my wealth and earnings, I will be prosecuted to the fullest extent of the law.'

I will personally make the final decision on all applications for support from Jews and Jews by faith. The files are therefore to be forwarded to my office, after careful assessment of the applicant's need for assistance. The assessment of need must take special account of the applicant's fitness for work. Jews who are no more than 66⅔ per cent unfit for work are to be referred to the employment office.

I also call your attention to the Second Regulation on the Law on Changes to Forenames[7] issued by the Reich Ministry of the Interior on 17 August 1938, and to the announcement on the requirement to carry identity cards (departmental directive of 7 February 1929).[8]

Jews who fail to comply with this regulation are to be reported. It should be noted that Jews by faith of Aryan extraction are not affected by the regulations on the requirement to carry identity cards and on the adoption of a Jewish forename.

7 Correctly: Law on Changes to Surnames and Forenames; see PMJ 2/84.
8 The identity card was introduced in 1938 as a 'national identification document subject to police checks'. Following the Third Announcement on the Requirement to Carry Identity Cards (23 July 1938), Jews were required to carry this card on them at all times, with effect from 1 Oct. 1938: *Reichsgesetzblatt*, 1935, I, p. 922; see also PMJ 2/72.

DOC. 123

On 3 December 1940 the Head of the Reich Chancellery informs Gauleiter Baldur von Schirach that Adolf Hitler has approved the deportation of 60,000 Jews from Vienna[1]

Letter (marked 'secret!') from the Reich Minister and Head of the Reich Chancellery (Rk. 789 B g.), signed Dr Lammers, to the Reichsstatthalter in Vienna, Gauleiter von Schirach (received on 13 December 1940),[2] dated 3 December 1940 (copy)[3]

Dear Mr von Schirach,

As I am informed by Reichsleiter Bormann, the Führer has decided, on the strength of your report,[4] that the 60,000 Jews still living in the Vienna Reichsgau are to be deported to the General Government at the earliest opportunity – i.e. while the war is still ongoing – because of the current housing shortage in Vienna. I have communicated this decision of the Führer to the Governor General in Cracow and the Reichsführer SS, and kindly request you likewise to take note of it.

Heil Hitler!

Your very devoted

1 Copy in IfZ-Archives, PS-1950. Published in International Military Tribunal, *Der Prozess gegen die Hauptkriegsverbrecher vor dem Internationalen Militärgerichtshof, Nürnberg 14.11.1945–1.10.1946*, vol. 5 (Nuremberg: Sekretariat des Gerichtshofs, 1947), p. 343. This document has been translated from German.

2 Baldur von Schirach (1907–1974), writer and politician; joined the NSDAP in 1925; Reich youth leader of the NSDAP from 1931; member of the Reichstag in 1932; youth leader of the German Reich from 1933; state secretary in 1936; served in the war, 1939; Gauleiter and Reichsstatthalter in Vienna, and Reichsleiter for youth education from August 1940; responsible for the evacuation of German children from the cities to the countryside (*Kinderlandverschickung*) from Sept. 1940; sentenced to twenty years' imprisonment at the International Military Tribunal at Nuremberg in 1946, and released in 1966.

3 The document contains handwritten annotations and underlining.

4 On 2 Oct. 1940, during talks with Hitler on the General Government, Schirach had complained that there were still more than 50,000 Jews living in Vienna, and argued that they should become the responsibility of the Governor General, Hans Frank. The latter was opposed to this suggestion: Adler, *Der verwaltete Mensch*, p. 147.

DOC. 124
Kreiszeitung für die Ost-Prignitz, 4 December 1940: article on the genesis of the film *The Eternal Jew*[1]

How the film The Eternal Jew *came to be made. In the ghetto with the camera. The Jewish parasite people unmasked*
NSK[2] interview with Oberregierungsrat Dr Taubert

In the coming weeks the major documentary film about world Jewry, *The Eternal Jew*,[3] which was recently shown for the first time in Berlin, is set to expose all Volksgenossen to the truth about the Jew, his race, his nature, and his corrosive influence among the peoples. This occasion prompted an NSK editor to conduct an interview with Oberregierungsrat Dr Taubert – who conceived the idea for this film – about the making of this unique cinematic work.

How was it possible that at one time large sections of the German population were for so long blind or helpless in the face of the Jewish pestilence, which infected and permeated nearly every area of our national life with terrifying rapacity? That Jewish scum of the worst sort, freshly imported from Galicia, was able to take up residence in Germany with the impudence characteristic of their race, and that these crooks enjoyed here all the rights of long-established citizens as so-called 'German citizens of the Mosaic faith'? One of the main reasons for this disastrous phenomenon is to be found in the artful cunning with which Jews outwardly adapt to the customs and traditions of their host country, transforming themselves with astonishing speed from lice-infested Polish ghetto-dwellers to smooth salon Jews, and thus merging into the background and carrying on their business of exploitation behind a mask of respectability. Under the banner of another religion they sought to hide the otherness of their race, and to paper over the unbridgeable gulf that separates them from the Aryan host nation.

Worlds apart
If there are still any Volksgenossen left today whose anti-Jewish sentiments are based purely on the superficial view that the Jews had to be removed for economic reasons, because their influence here is pernicious, once they have seen the new documentary film on world Jewry, *The Eternal Jew*, they will fully grasp that the Jewish race is completely different, and gain the necessary clarity to see that our own race and the Jewish criminal rabble are literally worlds apart.

The main purpose and aim of this film is to show these polar opposites, the most extreme that one can possibly imagine. To rip the mask from the face of dissembling

1 'Wie der Film "Der ewige Jude" entstand', *Kreiszeitung für die Ost-Prignitz*, 4 Dec. 1940, p. 4. This document has been translated from German. The *Kreiszeitung für die Ost-Prignitz* was published from 1828 to 1943 in Wittstock/Dosse. In 1937 the paper had a circulation of 3,504 copies.

2 *Nationalsozialistische Parteikorrespondenz*: a news service set up in 1932, to which all German newspapers had to subscribe after 1933.

3 The propaganda film *Der Ewige Jude* was first screened in German cinemas in Sept. 1940. It was directed by Fritz Hippler, and the screenplay was written by Eberhard Taubert.

world Jewry, putting on its 'civilized' act, these wolves in sheep's clothing, and to show every last German Volksgenosse: *this is what they really look like*, these parasites on the human race! This is where they come from, out of the cesspool of stinking ghettos, those plague-boils of Europe!

The camera didn't bother them

Dr Taubert, who conceived the idea for this film, tells us about the preparatory work:

> We tried several years ago to film in the Polish ghettos. But the Polish government thwarted all our efforts, either because it was pressurized by the Jewish side, or because it thought it would be a poor advertisement for Poland, if the conditions there were put – literally – under the spotlight. So we were only able to start filming after the entry of German troops into the country. We begin the film with typical scenes of life in the Jewish quarters and in the filthy Jewish dwellings, and the thinking behind this is that once a person has seen one of these ghettos, he will never again want to go anywhere near a Jew, and he will be turned against the Jews for life.

It has to be said that this footage shot inside the ghetto captures the reality of life in the Jewish quarters of cities such as Cracow and Litzmannstadt;[4] the Jew rabble standing around in their hundreds in the filthy alleys, scheming and wheeling and dealing, did not feel in the least bothered by the cameraman. On the contrary, they probably felt honoured by this visit, and as we see in the film, their ugly Jewish mugs were grinning insolently into the camera lens. They regard the filthy conditions in which they live as something entirely natural, so that our disgusted reaction will always remain a mystery to them.

In the synagogue

In the film we also see for the first time some unique footage of a Jewish 'religious service' inside a synagogue. How did these scenes come to be filmed? Dr Taubert explains:

> The rabbi who led this 'religious service' was very happy to let the cameraman come into the synagogue, viewing the filming as a good way to promote the Jewish cause. What the German person, who has a rather different conception of a religious service, thinks of this and the fairground-like goings-on inside the synagogue, where people are still busy haggling and wheeling and dealing, is a question to which anyone viewing this film can provide the right answer. It was a similar case with the Jews who conduct their ritual prayers at home: it was not at all difficult to film them during this 'sacred rite'; for a few coins they were very happy to open their door to the cameraman. Examples such as these shed a revealing light in turn on Jewish character traits.

A very apt comparison

> Endowed with every physical and mental aptitude liable to make them enemies of humankind, they seek constantly to plague, afflict, and torment, and never cease to

4 The city of Łódź was renamed 'Litzmannstadt' in April 1940.

> inflict the most serious damage. As soon as they perceive that Man is helpless against them their audacity increases to a truly astonishing extent, and though it may almost drive us to distraction, it is tempting to laugh at their unbridled insolence.

A remarkably apt characterization of Jewry! And who wrote these lines? They are taken from *Brehms Tierleben*, and were in fact written about rats![5]

This example shows what astonishing parallels can be drawn between rats, as the parasites of the animal world, and the Jews, the bloodsuckers of humanity. The film *The Eternal Jew* shows us this similarity in their characteristics in an incredibly vivid manner. We see how the rat migrates throughout the entire world, the rat as the symbol of cunning, greed, and destruction, as the carrier of deadly diseases such as typhoid and the plague. And likewise we see how the Jews spread everywhere, living all over the world as parasites who do nothing but exploit and destroy, who are carriers of pestilences that sooner or later bring their host nations to their knees, both physically and morally.

There is no reaching an accommodation with the Jews

Dr Taubert finally points to the scenes of ritual slaughter, which were filmed shortly before the ban on ritual slaughter came into effect in the General Government. Understandably, these scenes have been cut from the short version of the film, on the grounds that they would be a severe test of the nerves for sensitive souls. Anyone who has ever seen such a Jewish ritual slaughter – which is, furthermore, carried out by rabbis as a 'sacred rite' – and been exposed to the sight of this monstrous bestiality and cruel animal torture, will forever feel a profound and amply justified inner loathing of these Jews, a physical revulsion, and will be sure to steer clear of him[6] in the future.

'There is no reaching an accommodation with the Jews; it is just a straightforward either/or.' This clear-sighted assessment, which the Führer wrote fifteen years ago in his book *Mein Kampf*,[7] has been taken to heart by the German people, and is starting to gain ground in most of the other nations of Europe as well. To ensure that every German Volksgenosse recognizes the clear and uncompromising stance that we must take against Jewry, and makes it his own, based on a thorough grasp of the Jewish question: such is the main purpose of the film *The Eternal Jew*.

H. Schwaibold[8]

5 Alfred Edmund Brehm, *Illustriertes Thierleben*, vol. 2 (Hildburghausen: Verlag des Bibliographischen Instituts, 1865, published in English as *Brehm's Life of Animals* (Chicago: A.N. Marquis & Company, 1896)), pp. 120 and 122. The quotation is inaccurate: in the first sentence cited here, instead of *Menschheit* (humankind) Brehm uses *Mensch* (man, human being), and the second sentence does not follow on directly from the first. Moreover, the author writes: 'if one were not almost driven to distraction by these wretched creatures' (*sich nicht halb zu Tode ärgern über die nichtswürdigen Tiere*), and 'audacity' (*Frechheit*) instead of 'insolence' (*Unverschämtheit*).

6 As in the original.

7 Adolf Hitler, *Mein Kampf*, trans. Ralph Manheim (London: Hutchinson, 1969 [German edn, 1925 1926]), p. 225.

8 Heinz Schwaibold (1913–2000), businessman and journalist; worked as a journalist in Britain, 1933–1935; joined the SS in 1934; honorary SS press officer, employed by the Eher publishing house in Berlin from 1936; joined the NSDAP in 1937; later became Reich main department head in the Reichsleitung of the NSDAP; served in the war, 1939–1940 and again from 1942; SS-Untersturmführer, 1941; worked as a sales director in Laupheim, in Biberach an der Riß, and elsewhere after 1945.

DOC. 125
On 4 December 1940 Adolf Eichmann regards the resettlement of nearly 6 million European Jews as the 'final solution to the Jewish question'[1]

Handwritten notes by Adolf Eichmann (initials), dated 4 December 1940[2]

The Jewish question[3]
I. Initial solution to the Jewish question through emigration (by transferring responsibility from the Jewish political organizations to the Security Police and SD).
(a) In the course of our efforts to promote emigration, the following number of people have emigrated to date:

From the Old Reich	since 1933	341,078 Jews
From the Ostmark	since 1938	135,547 Jews
From the Protectorate	since 1939	25,086 Jews
	In total	501,711 Jews

(b) To subsidise emigration, foreign exchange amounting to approximately *7,200,000 dollars* was raised, most of it in the form of donations from foreign Jewish organizations or from foreign relatives of the Jews, which was used to fund the emigration programme.
(c) Decline in the number of Jews as a result of natural attrition (since 1933 in the Old Reich, since 1938 in the Ostmark, since 1939 in the Protectorate):

Total mortality	70,792
Total births	13,756
Surplus of deaths over births	57,036

(d) The total number of Jews still living on the territory of the Reich (including the Protectorate), as defined under the Nuremberg Laws, is therefore *315,642 Jews*

II. *The final solution to the Jewish question*
Through resettlement of the Jews from the European economic area of the German people to a territory yet to be determined. Approximately *5.8 million Jews* fall within the scope of this project.

1 BArch, NS 19/3979, fols. 5–6. A facsimile is published in Susanne Heim and Götz Aly, *Bevölkerungsstruktur und Massenmord: Neue Dokumente zur deutschen Politik der Jahre 1938–1945* (Berlin: Rotbuch, 1991), pp. 26–27. This document has been translated from German.
2 The document was drafted in the offices of the Reich Commissioner for the Strengthening of Germandom. Himmler had commissioned it in preparation for his speech before the assembled Reichsleiter and Gauleiter on 10 Dec. 1940 (see Doc. 126).
3 Handwritten note: 'Immediate submission RFSS [Reichsführer SS]'.

DOC. 126

On 10 December 1940 Heinrich Himmler informs the Reichsleiter and Gauleiter of his settlement plans[1]

Handwritten notes by Heinrich Himmler

Presentation to the Reichsleiter and the Gauleiter in Berlin on 10 December 1940
A. Migration and settlement
Large-scale migration in the last eight years
Emigrants since 1933
I 873,483
Immigrants since 1933
II 530,713
Other
III 63,903
1,474,099[2]
Receiving provinces
1. Completed operation IV[3]
2. South Tyroleans – to be housed only temporarily[4]
3. Germans due to be resettled
Economic figures.
Assets 3,315 million
Payments from the DUT[5] 65 million V.
Tasks in the eastern provinces
1. *Size of farms*
Estates
Large farms
Farms
Smallholdings VI.
2. Overall area in the eastern provinces
3. *Area for woodland* 9,150 square km
Land 7 and 8 around 7,850 square km
Structuring of land[6]

1 BArch, NS 19/4007, fols. 175–184. This document has been translated from German.
2 Several handwritten corrections to the figure. Added together, the three figures come to a total of 1,468,099.
3 The meaning of the Roman numerals that appear at the end of the line from this point on is unclear.
4 For more on the resettlement of the German-speaking population from South Tyrol, see Introduction, p. 38.
5 Deutsche Umsiedlungs- und Treuhandgesellschaft mbH (DUT): German Resettlement Trust Company. The company was founded in Nov. 1939 to support so-called ethnic German settlers. It had the particular task of transferring confiscated goods and businesses in annexed west Poland. The DUT was part of Himmler's apparatus in his function as Reich Commissioner for the Strengthening of Germandom.
6 Points 2 and 3 were originally in reverse order.

4. *Area for ethnic Germans.*
at least ¼
5. *Area for Reich Germans*
No need to worry that too small, though not too large either
480,000 farming families VII
no *propaganda* Germanic immigrants
not army and individual military divisions
All villages mixed
Ethnic and Reich Germans
all ranks and divisions
no special conditions
New stock
Settlement of the
western provinces – Alsace-Lorraine by Baden and Palatinate.
B. Ethnic Germans
VIII
Romania 15.0 million inhabitants
1 million Jews
580,000 Germans
Transylvania, Banat, Romanian Old Kingdom
Ethnic group
People's League[7]
Departure of SS volunteers. Deployment in the West
Recovery of the lost Germans
Hungary 13 million inhabitants
1.5 million Jews
845,000 Germans
Hungarian uplands, Swabian Turkey,[8] western Hungary, Sathmar, Northern Transylvania, rump Bačka[9]
Ethnic group. Identification.
People's League
Yugoslavia 15.2 million inhabitants
170,000 Jews.
705,000 Germans.
Serbia, Bosnia, Croatia, Slovenia
Slovakia 3 million inhabitants
¼ million Jews.
160,000 Germans.
C. Overall task.
1. Germanizing the eastern provinces.
8 million Germans.

7 The People's League for Germandom Abroad (Volksbund für das Deutschtum im Ausland) represented the interests of the so-called ethnic German minorities.
8 A region in Hungary.
9 Main settlement areas of the German minority in Hungary.

8 million foreigners.
of whom 1 million can be Germanized
2. *German People's List*
Decree of 12 December 1940[10] IX
3. *Alongside agricultural settlement*
urban population and industry
Population density
4. *Cultivation of the East*
economic equality
labour service camps (female)
agricultural service of the Hitler Youth[11]
5. *Uncompromising implementation of German rule*
Use of labour resources
to consolidate German settlement – fight Polish intelligentsia
6. the General Government
pool of labour
for seasonal and occasional work.
7. *Jewish emigration*
and thus additional space for Poles
8. *Further immigration*
only fragments, which cannot realistically maintain themselves[12]
9. *Fortification of Germandom* in Europe
All are required to help.

10 The Decree of the Reichsführer SS and Reich Commissioner for the Strengthening of Germandom on the Examination and Selection of the Population in the Annexed Eastern Territories (12 Sept. 1940) mainly used 'racial' criteria to determine which population groups in the occupied areas were to be seen as 'German' or 'suitable for Germanization'. These groups could be included in different categories in the 'German People's List' (*Deutsche Volksliste*) and thereby acquire German nationality. In March 1941 a regulation was issued regarding the German People's List and German nationality in the annexed eastern territories: BArch, R 186/34, fol. 289–292, and *Reichsgesetzblatt*, 1941, I, pp. 118–120.

11 Agricultural Service (*Landdienst*), a division of the Hitler Youth, was intended to support the colonization of the occupied Eastern territories. It was founded in 1934 with the purpose of providing thousands of boys and girls aged between 14 and 18 with physical training through harvesting work, as well as political education. The aim was to create a 'pool' of people who could be used to form a new 'farming class'. In 1939–1940 around 26,000 young people were active in around 1,800 Agricultural Service groups.

12 This refers to those German-speaking minorities not living in enclosed settlement areas outside the areas then under German influence. The so-called fragmentary or scattered Germandom (*Splitter-* or *Streudeutschtum*) was to be resettled in the Old Reich or the annexed territories.

DOC. 127

On 12 December 1940 Reich Minister of the Interior Wilhelm Frick orders that Jewish psychiatric patients be transferred to the Jewish Psychiatric Hospital in Bendorf-Sayn[1]

Circular decree from Reich Minister of the Interior Frick,[2] Berlin, to the Reichsstatthalter in the Reich Gaue of the Ostmark, in the Sudetengau, in Danzig-West Prussia, and in the Warthegau, the state governments outside Prussia, the Reich commissioner for the Saar-Palatinate, the Oberpräsidenten and Regierungspräsidenten, the Chief of Police in Berlin, the mayor of the Reich capital Berlin, the police authorities, and the health authorities, dated 12 December 1940

Care of lunatics
Admittance of Jewish mentally ill patients to psychiatric hospitals.
Circular decree issued by the Reich Ministry of the Interior[3] dated 12 December 1940 (IV g 7123/40–5106)
(1) The arrangement up to now that Jews are accommodated together with Germans in psychiatric hospitals has led to complaints from the care staff and relatives of German-blooded patients, quite apart from the fact that it is intolerable for Germans to live side by side with Jews in this manner on a permanent basis.
(2) In order to rectify this deplorable state of affairs I hereby decree that, in the future, mentally ill Jews may only be admitted to the psychiatric hospital run by the Reich Association of Jews [in Germany] in *Bendorf-Sayn*, in the district of Koblenz.[4] I reserve the right to grant permission for the creation of further such fully Jewish and Jewish-run institutions, if necessary.
(3) If for reasons of public security it is necessary to admit a mentally ill Jew to a German psychiatric hospital, the patient should be transferred immediately to the Psychiatric Hospital in *Bendorf-Sayn*. The directors of the German psychiatric hospitals are obliged to ensure that this transfer takes place as soon as possible.
(4) This circular decree does not apply to mentally ill Jews who had already been admitted to German psychiatric hospitals before 1 October 1940 and who are still in the said homes at present. Specific instructions for the treatment of these patients will be issued.[5]

1 *Ministerialblatt des Reichs- und Preußischen Ministeriums des Innern*, vol. 51 (1940), pp. 2261–2262. This document has been translated from German.
2 Dr Wilhelm Frick (1877–1946), lawyer; in the Bavarian administration from 1903; headed the Political Police in Munich, 1919–1921, and the Criminal Police in Munich from 1923; detained for participation in the Beer Hall Putsch, 1923–1924; removed from office then reinstated, 1924; joined the NSDAP in 1925; Thuringian minister of the interior and of education, 1930–1931; Reich minister of the interior, 1933–1943; Reich Protector of Bohemia and Moravia from August 1943; sentenced to death at the International Military Tribunal at Nuremberg in 1946 and executed.
3 According to Henry Friedlander, the decree was written by Ministerialrat Dr Herbert Linden (1899–1945): Henry Friedlander, *The Origins of Nazi Genocide: From Euthanasia to the Final Solution* (Chapel Hill/London: University of North Carolina Press, 1995), p. 282.
4 The Jewish Psychiatric Hospital (Jüdische Heil- und Pflegeanstalt) in Bendorf-Sayn was founded in 1869 by the Jewish Jacoby family, who ran it until the Second World War.
5 Jewish psychiatric patients became victims of the so-called euthanasia programme in early 1940: see Doc. 85 and Glossary. The Jews grouped together in Bendorf-Sayn as a result of this decree were, however, initially kept alive. After the start of the systematic deportation of German Jews they were deported together with the Jews of Koblenz.

(5) All subordinate institutions or those subject to supervision are to be informed accordingly about the provisions of this circular decree.

Addendum for the State Ministry of the Interior in Munich: in response to the report dated 15 October 1940 – no. 5326 a 58,[6]

Addendum for the Oberpräsident (administration of the provincial association) in Hanover: in response to the report dated 29 October 1940 – 42a F 12a.[7]

DOC. 128
On 20 December 1940 Paul Eppstein records how his own detention was discussed when he was summoned to the Gestapo[1]

File note (Dr. E./My), signed Dr Eppstein, regarding his summons to the Gestapo Central Office, Berlin, Regierungsassessor Jagusch, on 20 December 1940 at 10 a.m.

2.[2] *Re*: protective custody Dr Paul Israel *Eppstein*
Regierungsassessor Jagusch stated that the grounds for protective custody were probably known to me. I replied that I was unaware of having failed to carry out an instruction from the Central Office,[3] and that perhaps there had been a misunderstanding regarding the design of the bulletin, about which a discussion had taken place with Hauptsturmführer *Dannecker.* I pointed out that, during the entire period in which I had to carry out the relevant tasks as commissioned by the Reich Association[4] and in accordance with the wishes of the authorities, there had never been any complaints in this matter, and that I would therefore appreciate being told the reason. Regierungsassessor Jagusch remarked that the handling of the bulletin matter had indeed given rise to complaints,[5] and that, moreover, the way orders were carried out or their delayed implementation had also given rise to complaints, as did appearing before the authorities without the knowledge of the department in charge, or in direct contravention of orders from this department. I pointed out that I was unaware of any of this, particularly regarding any appearances at the authorities, unless the complaints had been raised by staff, unbeknown to me, and I as the responsible head of department had to be held accountable for them. Regierungsassessor Jagusch thought that this may have been the case. In response to my question as to whether it might be possible to arrange a discussion with Sturmbannführer Eichmann on the matter, Regierungsassessor Jagusch replied, after making a telephone call, that such a discussion can take place in early January.

6 This report could not be found.
7 This report could not be found.

1 BArch, R 8150/45, fol. 101. This document has been translated from German.
2 The account begins here. The significance of the number is unclear.
3 Central Office for Jewish Emigration.
4 Reich Association of Jews in Germany.
5 Eppstein was accused of altering an article in the *Jüdisches Nachrichtenblatt*, after it had already been approved.

I remarked that, in contrast to the special circumstances surrounding the arrest of Dr Seligsohn, the general statement of reasons in the protective custody warrant did not contain any facts that would have explained the immediate need to make the arrest.[6] Regierungsassessor Jagusch noted that the grounds for my arrest were much more serious than in the case of Dr Seligsohn. I then remarked that this fact gives reason to hope that the internment of Dr Seligsohn will not last as long as mine. Regierungsassessor Jagusch noted in response that this question had to wait for the time being until the next discussion.

I requested the opportunity to meet with Sturmbannführer Eichmann on the grounds that, due to my protective custody, I felt hindered in continuing my work in any way and obliged to request release from my duties. Regierungsassessor Jagusch stated in response that this could not be considered and that he would instead reassign me to my work.[7]

DOC. 129
An emigrant describes the supply situation, the public mood, and conditions for the Jews in the Reich during the autumn and winter of 1940[1]

Account by an unknown author, dated 25 February 1941

The autumn and winter of 1940 in Germany

The following aims to give an account of the conditions that prevailed in the Third Reich during the autumn and winter of 1940. It is based for the most part on my own experiences, which have been supplemented by the observations and experiences of reliable sources. I should mention at the outset that I was born in southern Germany and resided in a larger city on the Rhine until the end of September [1940]. It was at this time that my wife and I set off for Berlin, in order to be able to make more concerted efforts to organize our departure. That was our stroke of luck. If we had returned to southern Germany, we would have been included in the evacuation of the Baden and Palatine Jews on 22 October and would now be in the Gurs camp.[2]

When we left Germany at the end of 1940, the war had already been going on for nearly one and a half years. This was evident by the fact that, particularly in Berlin, the military was the most conspicuous presence on the streets. One seldom saw a car driven

6 The protective custody warrant is not in the file. Eppstein was arrested on 15 August 1940 on the grounds that he had disobeyed orders from the Central Office for Jewish Emigration. This was probably related to the departure of an illegal transport to Palestine, which Eppstein did not want to authorize. However, the Gestapo ordered that the departure go ahead: see Doc. 120. Julius Seligsohn had been deported to Sachsenhausen concentration camp, as he was held responsible for a public protest by the Reich Association of Jews in Germany against the deportation of Jews from Baden and the Palatinate: see Doc 129, fn. 38.

7 Eppstein, who had been released from detention shortly before this summons, was consequently forbidden to handle any more emigration matters.

1 Wiener Library, Doc 1656/3/1/615, copy in YVA, O.2/421. On the accounts from the Wiener Library, see Doc. 88, fn. 1. This document has been translated from German.

2 On the deportations to southern France, see Docs. 111, 112, 113, and 115.

by a civilian. The passengers were mostly officers. Trains, elevated railways, and subways, as well as other transportation lines, were mainly used by soldiers. Military transports and trains carrying soldiers on leave tied up rail lines to such a large extent that the use of the railways for private purposes was heavily restricted. Large numbers of freight trucks hailing from all the occupied countries stood on the tracks. At one station I was able to make out French, Dutch, Belgian, Polish, and Czech trucks. The use of private cars was heavily restricted and complicated due to the shortage of petrol and oil. A great deal of effort, lots of documentation, visits to various authorities, and very good connections were required if one wanted to succeed in gaining permission to obtain fuel for one's car. When I needed a car to transport our luggage, I had to traipse around Berlin for over an hour before I found a taxi that would take me. The driver said that I had been lucky. He told me that due to the fuel shortage the taxi service was going to be suspended for a fortnight 'starting tomorrow'. I do not know whether it resumed after this period.

It was expected that directives calling on military bodies to limit fuel consumption as much as possible, both at home and behind the lines, would be issued as well.

The effects of the war, which included Germany being cut off from the main exporting countries, made themselves felt primarily in the supply of goods to meet the everyday needs of the population. Despite the extremely detailed collection of data on all food and daily goods, there was evidently a shortage in terms of the quantity and quality of the available goods. The figure announced by the government for the grain harvest of 1940 is considered by many to be inaccurate.[3] The rainy period that prevailed during the summer throughout most of Germany had a negative impact on the growth, flowering, and ripening of wheat and rye, so that – as I overheard an experienced farmer in the train saying to his travelling companion – one could expect only half the normal harvest. If the grain stockpiles actually do suffice until the next harvest, this will only be achieved by bringing the stocks found in France, Belgium, and Holland to Germany to feed its population. In addition to heavily milled grain flour, potato flour and other ingredients are used to bake bread, so that – as a baker told me – it takes a considerable amount of skill to bake bread that is in any way edible using the flour produced by the mills.

Potatoes seem to be the only thing that is not in short supply.

By contrast, vegetables are very scarce as a result of the poor summer. For this same reason there is hardly any fruit to be had. Apples and pears, the most important durable fruits, yielded a poor harvest, which was even more noticeable because no oranges were imported from Italy. In the Rhine valley, where fruit and vegetables are bountiful, there was still little sign of this in September. At that time there was still an abundance of stone fruit and berries. In Berlin, however, the shortage was keenly felt. Housewives experienced great difficulties, having to travel long distances and wait in long queues to

3 'Very good harvest. Despite the war and bad weather the expected yield is 24.6 million tones': *Völkischer Beobachter* (northern German edition), 11 Sept. 1940. On 3 August 1940 Goebbels noted in his diary that Herbert Backe from the Reich Ministry of Food and Agriculture had given him a report that assumed the grain harvest in 1940 would be mediocre, but that also pointed out that Germany still had large grain reserves at its disposal: *Die Tagebücher von Joseph Goebbels*, ed. Elke Fröhlich, part 1: *Aufzeichnungen 1923–1941*, vol. 8: *April–November 1940* (Munich: Saur, 1998), p. 250.

receive a bit of kale or cauliflower and a few apples or pears. Customer lists have been introduced in Berlin for vegetables. They are now expected to cover fruit, too.[4]

There was also a severe shortage of butter and all other fats. The amount available per capita (125 grams of butter per week) is far from sufficient. Oil, margarine, and other animal fats were rationed in very small quantities. Although the population was occasionally given special allowances of butter to raise its morale, and soldiers stationed in Holland, Denmark, and other countries had small quantities of fat and other food sent to their relatives – a practice that has probably stopped by now – this measure could only somewhat resolve the shortage for a brief period, but not for long. That there is a dire scarcity of fats cannot be denied. This is also the case with the meat supply. The 500 grams per capita weekly ration was in some cases handed out in the form of inferior quality sausage. The bones are included in the remaining amount, which means that each person barely receives more than 250 grams of meat a week. That which they do receive is of poor quality. The army administration takes the best of the animals for slaughter, so the civilian population receives only tough and dry meat from old cows and bulls. It is worth noting that as the meat shortage was particularly acute in the Sudetenland it also had to be supplied with meat, at least from southern Germany.

There is also a lack of milk. Whole milk was only given to children and expectant and nursing mothers. The rest of the population had to make do with skimmed milk, if such was available. Jews received none at all. Only in the rarest of cases could physicians obtain a milk allowance for the sick.

It was only possible to deliver the weekly egg allotted to each person at the appropriate time as long as the egg stocks in Holland and Denmark provided a sufficient supply. After these supplies were exhausted it was often another two weeks before eggs were distributed again.

Fresh and saltwater fish and fish products of all types were also scarce. It was not permitted to sell either these or game and poultry to Jews, but such provisions were also rare delicacies for 'Aryans', unless they were able to obtain them through secret connections at very high prices.[5]

The supply of preserved fruit and vegetables was frugal, too, and will increasingly disappear from the market as a consequence of the poor harvest. In June 1940 I enquired in at least ten shops and pharmacies about raspberry juice for someone who was seriously ill. I finally found some in a pharmacy whose former Jewish owner had sufficiently stocked up on it.

Sugar rations were also inadequate. Housewives were advised to make berry preserves and other types of jam without using sugar and to sweeten them just before consumption. Chocolate, chocolate confections, and other sweets were scarce and of very

4 Jews were allowed to purchase certain goods only upon presentation of a purchase permit or household identification card. They had to have these documents stamped by the retailer by a certain date. On the provisions in Berlin, see *Jüdisches Nachrichtenblatt* (Berlin edition), 25 Oct. 1940, p. 3. On similar provisions regarding customer lists in Vienna, see *Jüdisches Nachrichtenblatt* (Vienna edition), 14 June 1940, p. 4; on the customer lists, see also fn. 5.

5 According to the decree concerning the food supply of Jews, issued by the Reich Ministry of Food and Agriculture on 11 March 1940, Jews were not categorically excluded from purchasing skimmed milk, fish, poultry, and game, but they were to be excluded from buying these provisions if customer lists or other sale restrictions were introduced: IfZ-Archives, MA 1555–118, NID-14581.

poor quality. On the days when such products were distributed – they were not given to Jews[6] – customers would stand in long queues in front of the shops and wait until they opened. Cocoa, made from the shells of cocoa beans, was distributed in small quantities for children's food.

Rice, pearl barley, sago, pasta products, etc. were distributed in small quantities. The wine harvest was poor in both quantity and quality as a result of the poor summer. Since nearly all the available wine was confiscated by the army administration, only small quantities were offered for sale. A wine merchant told me that he would probably not be able to meet customer demand during the Christmas period. The small quantities of wine imported from Hungary, Italy, and Bulgaria were hardly sufficient to make up the shortage.

Cigars and smoking tobacco were also very scarce. Whether this was due to a lack of raw material or manpower, or both, is beyond my knowledge. This shortage was not felt so strongly in southern Germany, where the tobacco industry is based, although retailers there would not sell their customers more than five cigars at a time. In Berlin each customer received only two to three cigars per visit. In many of Berlin's cigar shops one could not buy any cigars at all on certain days of the week.

The lack of paper also had a particularly noticeable effect. Customers were advised to bring bags and other packing material with them when they went shopping. Grocers and butchers gladly accepted old newspapers from their patrons. Toilet paper was almost impossible to obtain. One shopkeeper told me, 'You'll just have to use the daily news!'

The same shortage existed for clothes as for food, drink, and tobacco. The so-called clothing ration card ensured, in theory, that everyone received the bare minimum of what they needed to protect their bodies against the elements. The quality of the textiles is so poor, because of the insufficient supply of wool and cotton, which makes it necessary to only use substitute fabrics, that the clothes people buy barely last only half as long as before. Prices, however, have remained at their previous level. In many cases they even went up for textiles and fabrics.

The most difficult thing was the supply of shoes. The biggest shortage was leather, which the army administration needed in vast quantities for every conceivable purpose. To purchase new shoes one had to obtain a special coupon,[7] and it was nigh on impossible to receive such a coupon without very good connections, unless one could prove that one was unable to report to work because of a complete lack of shoes. It therefore became fashionable in Germany for women to wear all sorts of wooden clogs, and in Berlin and other cities one could observe women from all walks of life wearing such clacking footwear. In addition, one would see men and women in worn-out shoes, which under normal circumstances would have been thrown out long ago. Having shoes repaired was also tricky. Shortly before we left Germany, everyone had to register as a customer with a shoemaker. Leather rations were so low that there were no more leather soles. Rubber soles (made of synthetic rubber), which are offered as a substitute, are of poor quality and only last for a short time.

6 On 11 March 1940 the Reich Ministry of Food and Agriculture had excluded Jews from receiving special food rations: see Doc. 36, fn. 7.

7 *Bedarfsschein*: special coupon for scarce goods.

Only on Sundays and holidays could a certain degree of elegance in attire be observed. The garments often date back to better times and painstaking attempts are made to preserve them, or they are newly purchased items, the splendour of which, one notices on closer inspection, will soon fade.

What also caught one's attention were the many fur coats, whose wearers looked utterly out of place in such attire. Since at that time fur coats could still be bought without special coupons and many women workers were unsure what to do with their income – they did not want to put their money in a savings bank – they invested it this way. Whether this form of capital accumulation is still possible today in the face of an ever-dwindling supply of raw furs is beyond my knowledge.

To prevent the actual situation from being all too conspicuous, shops are forced to decorate their display windows so that it looks as though everything is available in abundance. Thus, in many cases the display window is where most of a shop's wares can be found. Attached to the exhibited wares are often slips of paper saying 'sold'. If a customer wants to see an item in the display window, the shopkeeper or employee will tell him that none of the items in the window can be removed while they are on show.

In October 1940 a display window on Leipziger Straße in Berlin contained wonderful confectionary and chocolates that were labelled 'not for sale'. I could not tell whether the wares were real or just mock-ups. Through such means, for which the term 'Tarnung'[8] has recently been coined in the German language – to the best of my knowledge this term does not exist in other languages – those foreigners still sojourning in Berlin are to be misled into believing that everything is still available as before.

There is also a shortage of everything that tradesmen need to produce or repair all sorts of things. It is therefore a difficult and time-consuming endeavour to patch up damage to a water pipe, a machine, or a building. Replacement parts made from so-called raw materials are usually of such poor quality that they do not last long, and then the whole process starts over again. The army administration is said to have a sufficient supply of all durable goods. As to the quality of these goods, I am unable to judge. The army's needs are, however, so vast that an increasingly small proportion remains for the civilian economy. Allocations to this sector are getting smaller and smaller. A plumber and gas fitter told me as early as autumn 1939 that his guild barely receives 25 per cent of the goods they normally need.

Private sector construction has nearly ceased altogether. Necessary house repairs have to be put on hold. New public construction projects are way behind schedule. Only in the case of important buildings – those housing army supplies, for example – and accommodation for soldiers or workers in particularly vital enterprises are all necessary building materials delivered on time. But raw materials play a major role here as well.

The lack of materials is accompanied by a shortage of labour. Since millions of men are needed for military service and further millions must provide the vast amount of supplies required for the enormous war machine, the best employees are being taken out of the economy. The use of women, foreign workers, and prisoners of war cannot be regarded as a fully adequate replacement. Private industry is also suffering from an

8 German for 'camouflage'.

acute shortage of workers, and it is a moot point whether the upcoming harvest can be carried out in such a way as to provide sufficient food for the population for an entire year.

At the beginning of the war, laws aimed at preventing hoarding and illicit trading were enacted and subsequently tightened on several occasions. In some circumstances a person can even receive the death penalty for such crimes.[9] Nonetheless, a sizeable number of Volksschädlinge[10] break these laws every hour of every day. Illicit trading had already become incredibly widespread as early as autumn 1940, just as in 1914–1918. Every conceivable thing was sold on the black market. A particularly popular item was real bean coffee, which soldiers brought back with them or shipped from Holland. It found buyers at prices as high as RM 12 or even more for half a pound.

As was the case at the time of the First World War, farmers are gladly willing to exchange produce such as butter, eggs, and poultry for clothes and household goods on the sly, and shopkeepers in the city are more than happy to do such deals.

The restrictions that the population must endure with respect to food, clothing, and the comforts to which they are accustomed are not the only sacrifices that were demanded of them by the war. The RAF air raids are just as much of an ordeal and have caused great distress as far as the industrial cities along the Rhine, on the North Sea coast, and in Berlin. Along with the danger in which the cities attacked by enemy planes found themselves, the time spent in the air-raid shelters, often hours and sometimes nights on end, was extremely disruptive for people. The air raid wardens in Berlin had received orders to give suitable speeches to keep up the spirits of the people assembled in the cellars during the air raids.[11] One air raid warden took advantage of this opportunity to highlight Hitler's achievements. Among other statements, he enthusiastically exclaimed: 'Where would we be now if we didn't have Adolf Hitler?' A young girl replied: 'In bed.' Those present were paralysed with fear when they heard this audacious reply. The girl was handed over to the Gestapo the very next morning.

The worker who must often leave his apartment by five o'clock in the morning to arrive at work on time goes to work drowsy and ill-tempered after spending most of the night in the air-raid shelter – sometimes it was necessary to go to the shelter three or four times a night because the siren was sounded several times. Many working people have therefore stopped going to the air-raid shelters altogether.

The greengrocer is bad-tempered because after an air-raid night he must arrive at the market just as early as on other days. The only ones who derive an advantage from the air raids are the school children and teachers, since classes begin later depending on how long they are in the shelter.

The blackout rules are also bothersome and dangerous. From five o'clock in the afternoon a thick darkness reigned over the streets of Berlin, particularly during the short days of late autumn and winter. Those who had no urgent reason to go out chose to stay

9 In accordance with § 1 of the War Economy Regulation of 4 Sept. 1939, the retention of raw materials and food was deemed 'conduct detrimental to the war' and punishable with imprisonment or penal servitude; in particularly severe cases the death penalty could be imposed: *Reichsgesetzblatt*, 1939, I, pp. 1609–1613.

10 *Volksschädling*: 'vermin', people considered harmful to the German *Volk*.

11 These orders could not be verified.

at home. This state of affairs obviously makes any form of social life virtually impossible, including visits to concerts, the theatre, and the cinema.

It is difficult and almost impossible to give an account of the damage caused by the air raids, because the press is rarely allowed to report anything on this subject. Occasionally, official reports appear that play down the incidents and the number of victims whose lives were claimed. Government officials also immediately cordon off the bombed sites. It is certain that the RAF has caused a fair bit of damage. In Mannheim, for example, the bridge over the Rhine was closed because a bomb hit one side of it. Further bombs were dropped on and near the Lang machine factory, on the Lindenhof district, and on the various Baden Aniline and Soda Factory plants[12] situated on the west side of the Rhine. The top floor of a tenement building in Berlin between the Lehrter railway station and the Bellevue station on the elevated railway was completely destroyed. In October nearly all the glass panes of the lobby in the Lehrter station were destroyed. This damage was repaired as quickly as possible.

Around the same time a building on the old Kantstraße near the Charlottenburg railway station was severely damaged, which apparently resulted in the loss of many lives. Also noteworthy were the large number of notices put up in the stations of the elevated railway, stating that such and such a line was closed and giving information on the alternative route to be taken. It is not possible to report on the damage done in the area around Berlin and to the long-distance rail lines. There has been a lot of talk of destroyed factories and shut-down rail services. But these are unreliable reports that cannot be verified.

The treatment of Jews with respect to the air-raid shelters varied. In many buildings there were special air-raid shelters for non-Aryans, while in others they were allowed to use the same facilities as Aryans. Elsewhere, air raid wardens only made Jews go to the air-raid shelters out of fear that they might use their torches to send signals to the English pilots. In other buildings, Jews did not have to leave their apartments at all.[13] In one building a new tenant complained about the presence of Jews in the air-raid shelter, saying that it was unbearable for him. The Jews were subsequently expelled. The following night a bomb struck the shelter, killing and injuring a number of people. The Jewish residents who had to stay in their apartments remained unscathed.

How did the population respond to the conditions prevailing in Germany at that time? This question is not easy to answer because National Socialism had managed little by little to fully isolate the Jews in Germany and to put a stop to nearly all relations between the Aryan and non-Aryan population. That is the reason why the Jewish observer has few opportunities to establish the dominant sentiment among the population. One of the acts of Hitler and his accomplices was to rob the German people of their freedom. Those who did not willingly let themselves be silenced were deprived of their livelihood. The current mental state of German civil servants of all stripes is the best proof that this approach worked splendidly. I could observe this with remarkable clarity in the behaviour of my former acquaintances. Many of them, including some with whom I used to socialize and who had exchanged with me their most intimate confidences, gradually broke off contact with me. Others, as they passed me on the street, stopped at

12 This refers to the chemical concern BASF.

13 See also Doc. 109.

a shop window, looked at their watch or at something else, and acted as if they had not seen me. Only a few did not change how they acted and proved themselves, to the very end, to be upstanding, honourable men.

These are, however, only individual occurrences. The pervasive system of spying and informing created by National Socialism has brought about a situation where no one trusts anyone any more. Parents are afraid of being denounced by their children, and the presiding judge at the regional court, by his youngest clerk. Workers are careful to talk only about work-related matters with their colleagues. The system of informants is most established among women, who relay every small detail they observe at their neighbour's or friend's to the block warden, to the heads of the local Party branch, or to the Kreisleiter. This is how these offices receive more or less reliable information concerning the attitude of the population as a whole.

The behaviour of train passengers is interesting. Everyone either sits behind a newspaper or pretends to be asleep. Since no one trusts anyone, there is hardly ever any conversation. When two close acquaintances do carry on a conversation, the other passengers lie in wait behind their newspapers for them to say something incriminating. One rarely hears anyone joking around any more on Berlin's elevated trains. Everyone sits in silence and broods by himself.

To influence public opinion the National Socialist government, alongside the word-of-mouth propaganda circulated by the Party and its organizations, makes use of photographs, the radio, and the press. All three are firmly in the hands of the government and are closely monitored by it. The entire press has been forced into line. The largest newspapers in Berlin, as well as the *Frankfurter Zeitung*, do not really differ much from the smallest local papers, particularly because since the war began they have greatly reduced the number of pages as a result of the paper shortage.

On the whole, the population does not give too much credence to what the press reports. A soldier who returned home from the front in the winter of 1940 said that he only believed the date on the newspaper, and held everything else to be a sham. One could often hear people openly making similar remarks. Many had the same opinion of the wireless. Right at the start of the war the government made it illegal to listen to foreign broadcasters under penalty of severe punishment in the form of penal servitude.[14] Up until I left Germany, there had been announcements every week about sentences being issued to people who had listened to foreign broadcasters just the same and immediately spread the news. Many such listeners are now more careful and keep the foreign news to themselves. But in conversations with shopkeepers and other people one is often told things that could only have been learned from English or Swiss broadcasters.

It is understandable that many people, particularly those who have lived through different times, are extremely averse to this muzzling of free expression. In addition to this, many harbour bitter resentment against the government because of its hostile attitude towards positive Christianity.[15] I cannot comment on the extent of this disgruntlement, since it was not possible for me to pursue this matter in detail. It appears that a truce of sorts has been reached during the war. After its victorious conclusion, for which

14 See Doc. 2, fn. 10.

15 The author uses the Nazi propaganda term 'positive Christianity' here to refer to the majority of both Lutheran and Catholic Christians in Germany who were not opposed to the regime.

one hopes and in which the people are led to believe, the battle axe is likely to be dug up and wielded again.

In one area there is universal dissatisfaction among all sections of the population: the amount of taxes and levies. The remark 'I only work for the tax office' could already be heard before the start of the war from many businessmen. Now that the tax screw has been considerably tightened, dissatisfaction has grown even more.[16]

Also causing bitter resentment are the extensive powers that the National Socialist Party has gradually arrogated to itself. It, as well as the Secret State Police (Gestapo), which emerged from and is partly subordinate to the Party, has formed a parallel government that is more powerful than the actual government, whose organs, much to their considerable ire, frequently get the short end of the stick in cases of 'Party nepotism'. Since Party entities are authorized to summon non-Party members to appear before them, and issues relating to all aspects of public and economic life have to be relayed, these entities are generally feared and are regarded by most people as best avoided. A further disadvantage of the existence of this dual government is that one side passes the responsibility for newly issued decrees to the other. This manifests itself particularly in Jewish affairs. It was a common occurrence for the police authorities to declare, with respect to a new measure, that they knew nothing about the matter. They would go on to say that they had absolutely nothing to do with the measure and that it could only have come from the Party, while the Party would claim the police were responsible for it.

We know from the years 1914–1918 that a command economy and a comprehensive rationing scheme bring about universal disgruntlement. This feeling is now present again to at least the same degree. The housewife, especially in the cities, is ill-humoured when, in a state of exhaustion after hours of traipsing about and standing in queues to fetch what her coupons entitle her to buy, she anxiously realizes that the little she has obtained is not enough to put a hearty, wholesome meal on the table for her hard-working husband and growing children. Disillusionment has already set in among many who had previously worked zealously for the Women's League.[17]

Also out of sorts is the farmer's wife, whose husband is away doing military service and who must now manage the farm alone.

Drowsy, fatigued, and undernourished, the worker goes out to do strenuous labour, which normally demands ten hours, and frequently even more, of his time. In return he receives a meagre wage, from which one quarter to one third is deducted for taxes, insurance, contributions to the Party, etc. The extra food he receives for being a heavy labourer is insufficient to sustain the energy and strength that his work requires. He knows that in the Third Reich he has become a wage slave without rights, and regards the [German] Labour Front as a whip created by the government to keep him down. He is distrustful of the National Socialist slogans. I heard one worker telling another, in proper southern German dialect: 'Don't come to me with your Volksgemeinschaft, it's a massive swindle.' Another said: 'However it turns out, the workers will be the ones footing the bill.'

16 The War Economy Regulation (4 Sept. 1939) introduced a wartime surcharge on income tax as well as a war tax on beer, tobacco, spirits, and sparkling wine: *Reichsgesetzblatt*, 1939, I, pp. 1609–1613.

17 The National Socialist Women's League (Nationalsozialistische Frauenschaft) was the official women's organization of the NSDAP.

The farmer is dissatisfied because he is no longer allowed to freely dispose of what he has wrested out of the soil, and because he considers that he has to hand over too much. He regards the 'farmers' association' as an entity created for the purpose of causing him harm.[18] His biggest enemy is the local farmers' leader who has nothing but his own interest in mind.

The craftsman is dissatisfied because he is hampered in every possible way by the material shortage and because he lacks workers. The workers who have stayed with him are poorly skilled and do whatever they want. He speaks especially angrily of the guild master who, he feels, is lining his own pockets.

The shopkeeper is dissatisfied because he sees himself as being hindered by the new, often contradictory directives that are handed down daily and increasingly burden him with unproductive tasks. He is, as I heard with my own ears, no longer a retailer but a distributor who must be prepared for his shop to be closed down on account of some violation or other at any moment.

The industrialist is dissatisfied because he no longer has any say in his factory. Several of his employees are always busy studying and implementing the new directives issued by government agencies. (The pace at which the legislative machine works can be measured by comparing the length of the *Reichsgesetzblatt* and other bulletins published by government agencies over the past seven years with those from earlier years.) The Labour Front exercises constant control over his factory. Without its approval he is unable to hire or dismiss workers.

But there is also disgruntlement among intellectual workers, provided they are not employed by the state. For instance, a gentleman from a small town, who has occupied himself for quite some time with local history and genealogy, lamented to me about the poor quality of today's scholarly journals. I told him, 'But you all actually wanted it this way,' to which he replied, 'No, this isn't how we wanted it!'

As I already mentioned, it is not possible to report on the extent to which the handling of the church question increases dissatisfaction among all sections of the population.

The levity with which National Socialism deals with human life also arouses hatred and discontent in the broadest sections of the population. For a long time executions were a daily occurrence.

The killing in institutions of a large number of mentally ill people, idiots, epileptics, and others with mental deficiencies, whose lives were ended by [lethal] injections, caused particular agitation. Relatives were unceremoniously notified of the deaths. (This information is absolutely reliable.) The large number of sterilizations, performed on many people considered undesirable by the National Socialists, is also a subject about which one frequently hears disparaging comments.[19]

18 The Reich Food Estate (Reichsnährstand), the corporatist organization that operated under National Socialist agricultural policy, oversaw the production, distribution, and pricing of foodstuffs. It was divided into regional, district, and local farmers' associations.

19 On the so called euthanasia programme, see Introduction, pp. 32 f., and Glossary. The legal basis for forced sterilization was created as early as 14 July 1933 by the Law for the Prevention of Offspring with Hereditary Diseases. This law allowed sterilization to be performed on persons if it was considered highly probable that their offspring would suffer severe hereditary physical or mental defects: *Reichsgesetzblatt*, 1933, I, pp. 529–531. In total, approximately 400,000 people underwent forced sterilization.

I am unable to comment on public sentiment against the government because I had contact mostly with people who fiercely opposed it. The only ones who wholeheartedly supported the government were the beneficiaries of National Socialism, who grabbed good positions with its help, despite the fact that many of these people had previously led dubious lives. And now they do not want to lose their place on the gravy train. The system of 'fat cats' that the National Socialists wanted to stamp out when they seized power has run rampant since 1933. One businessman told me, 'The filth that has accumulated in the Third Reich has already eclipsed that which the November criminals[20] left behind.'

The population's behaviour before and during the war must be briefly touched upon. When the war broke out in September 1939, there was none of the enthusiasm we had experienced in the first days of August 1914. One listened to the radio reports with nervous suspense and desperately hoped that peace would be maintained. The vast majority of the population did not want war. Many had lived through the years 1914–1918 and still recalled the suffering caused during that period all too well. Even able-bodied young men were entirely lacking in enthusiasm. They bowed to the strong pressure. It was widely recognized among the population that Hitler had prepared the war long in advance and had frivolously entered into it at what was supposedly the most advantageous moment. The successes of the German forces in the summer of 1940 also produced little enthusiasm. People decorated their houses with flags because the Reich Minister of Propaganda had decreed this should be done, but there was no inner involvement. Everybody was thinking about their loved ones on the front, about the difficulties at home, and was anxious to see a quick end to this 'racket', regardless of who won. A triumphant optimism, which is particularly evident among public servants, appears to be the result of propaganda efforts by the Party aimed at keeping up public morale. The extent to which working people are confident of victory is demonstrated by the following isolated example:

A Jewish worker was discussing the political situation with his foreman and said: 'Now, hopefully, the war will soon be over.' – 'You're wrong about that,' the other said. 'The war is only just getting started. Just wait until spring when the English and American planes will be roaring above us, then we won't have anything to laugh about. Then we'll get what we deserve.'

In summary, it can be stated that there is a high level of dissatisfaction towards the government among broad sections of Germany's population. The straitjacket put around each and every person by the Party and the Gestapo, however, has made it impossible for this discontent to find distinct expression and for the masses to come together to put up a joint fight. Whether some sort of propaganda activity is being undertaken covertly to achieve this end is beyond my knowledge. The government is certainly not unaware of public sentiment. It is attempting to divert attention from the hostility of the masses through a historically unprecedented agitation against the Jews. By using the phrase 'There are no decent Jews', which the Party has brought to the remotest areas and issued as a slogan in all districts, the Jews were declared to be inferior. Public servants and their dependents were forbidden, under threat of disciplinary

20 *Novemberverbrecher*: a term used by far-right groups and parties to denounce the German politicians in the Weimar Republic who accepted the Treaty of Versailles.

action, to have contact with Jews and to make purchases in Jewish shops.[21] The Party made systematic efforts to force Jews out of all public offices and all branches of economic life, as well as the liberal professions. All the threats and use of force, however, did not suffice to prevent a large section of the non-Jewish population from continuing to have business and social contact with Jews, that is, until Reich Minister Funk forcibly excluded Jews from the economy in 1938 through legislative means.[22] One can only hint here at the appalling injustice inflicted upon Jews, with the help of German laws, through the so-called Aryanization of shops and the selling off of all property. This matter must be thoroughly addressed, but one must wait until a time when free access has been restored to court archives and other records. It is at that time that one must render an account of the incidents that befell Germany on 9 and 10 November 1938, purportedly brought about by the masses but in reality prepared well in advance and organized down to the last detail by National Socialism. Suffice to say that in those days tens of thousands of Jewish men were taken to the concentration camps in Dachau, Buchenwald, and other places, in many cases on the brink of death due to abuse suffered, while thousands perished from unspeakable torment; that a large number of Jews experienced the senseless destruction of the contents of their homes and shops; and that almost all Jewish places of worship went up in flames and with them things that are sacred to every Jew and whose value in many cases was irreplaceable from an artistic and historical perspective.[23]

With tears in my eyes I stood before the venerable synagogue in Worms, which in 1934 had celebrated its 900th year of existence. A feeling of deep melancholy swept over me every time I caught sight of the cracked, smoke-blackened walls of the magnificent temple on Berlin's Fasanenstraße, as I passed by on the elevated train.

The final link in the chain of the German Jews' suffering – there is only One who knows if this will be the very last link – is the transport of the Jews from Stettin to Lublin in spring 1940, which was followed on 22 October 1940 by the evacuation of Jews from Baden and the Palatinate to the Camp de Gurs in the French Pyrenees.[24]

When I left Germany in late 1940, there were still approximately 150,000 Jews living in the Old Reich, and more than half of those in Berlin, to where many had moved from all sections of Germany over the past few years. The overwhelming majority are people over the age of 50. Their situation was very sad in every respect. Only a small percentage still possessed sufficient assets to meet their basic needs. Most whittled away at their

21 Through a circular decree of 19 July 1937 (no. 52 124) the Baden Ministry of the Interior had already prohibited public servants from having contact with Jews: Joseph Walk (ed.), *Das Sonderrecht für die Juden im NS-Staat: Eine Sammlung der gesetzlichen Massnahmen und Richtlinien. Inhalt und Bedeutung*, 2nd edn (Heidelberg: C. F. Müller, 1996 [1981]), p. 196.

22 Particularly relevant here were the measures decreed by Göring as Plenipotentiary for the Four-Year Plan, such as the Regulation on the Registration of Jewish Assets, 26 April 1938 (*Reichsgesetzblatt*, 1938, I, p. 414: see also PMJ 2/29); the Regulation on the Reich Citizenship Law, 14 June 1938 (*Reichsgesetzblatt*, 1938, I, pp. 627–628: see also PMJ 2/42), which Funk also signed; and the Regulation on the Exclusion of Jews from German Economic Life, 12 Nov. 1938 (*Reichsgesetzblatt*, 1938, I, p. 1580: see also PMJ 2/143).

23 On the November pogroms, see PMJ 2, pp. 54–56, and particularly PMJ 2/123–126, 128–131, and 133–138.

24 On the deportations of Stettin's Jews, see Docs. 52 and 53; on the deportations to southern France, see Docs. 111, 112, 113, and 115, and PMJ 5/252.

assets and lived in constant worry that they would one day find themselves *vis à vis de rien*[25] or, if they did manage to emigrate, without any means. The wealthy few, whose numbers are constantly decreasing, are not able to support the have-nots, whose numbers are constantly increasing. Jews are barred from receiving public welfare.[26] Private charitable initiatives are hampered by the fact that the foreign exchange control offices of the tax offices have blocked pretty much all Jewish assets, and that people can only withdraw as much money from their bank as they are authorized to do so for their monthly living expenses. Employers are also required to pay their employees' salaries and wages into such blocked accounts.[27] People in need are looked after by the Reich Association of Jews in Germany, which has a limited jurisdiction to levy taxes for welfare and emigration purposes and to which emigrants, before leaving Germany, must pay an emigration tax based on the value of their assets. The Reich government recognizes the Reich Association as an organization to which the state authorities, particularly the Gestapo, issue directives concerning the Jews in Germany, and for the implementation of which it bears the responsibility. Many of its senior officials have already faced great difficulties because of their positions. Some were kept in custody for weeks for trivial reasons.[28]

Since there is a shortage of workers in every industry, a large number of Jews were integrated into the workforce in the summer of 1940. This was particularly the case in Berlin, where more than 20,000 Jewish men and women were put to work in factories and other enterprises. There was talk in October 1940 that this number should be substantially increased. Men up to the age of 60 and women up to the age of 50 were to be included. Understandably, many of these forced labourers really struggled to get to grips with the new situation, which was completely alien and unfamiliar to them. Many broke down after a short while and became ill. Others, however, once they had grown accustomed to the new way of life, felt fine and were glad not only to have something to occupy them but also to earn a bit of money. In many cases the wages were not at the same level as those of non-Jewish workers doing the same tasks.[29]

Few complaints were made about treatment by employers and other parties. Furthermore, relations with other fellow workers are reported to be favourable in every respect. Only a few physicians treating members of statutory health insurance schemes are said to have declared sick people to be in good health, even though their incapacity for work was conspicuously evident.

There were reports in Berlin of cases where non-Jewish labourers sent milk and other foods to their fellow workers who had not been granted a heavy labourer allowance.

As regards food supplies, the Jews, as already mentioned, are much worse off than the rest of the population. They are unable to obtain clothing coupons or special coupons for shoes.[30] Those who at the beginning paid a visit to the special coupon office for an

25 French in the original: 'left with nothing'.

26 The regulation issued by the Reich Ministry of the Interior on 19 Nov. 1938 excluded Jews from the public welfare system and directed them to seek aid from Jewish welfare organizations: *Reichsgesetzblatt*, 1938, I, p. 1649: see also PMJ 2/164 and Doc. 122.

27 On the use of so-called security orders (*Sicherungsanordnungen*) to block Jewish assets, see Doc. 17, fn. 5.

28 See Doc. 128.

29 See Docs. 108 and 114.

allocation of clothes or shoes were turned down with the comment: 'Go to Chamberlain, let him provide you with shoes and clothes.'[31] Larger Jewish communities set up clothing and shoe depots, where the better-off members, particularly the emigrants, donated what they could spare. These items were then handed out to those in need. Jews were also not given special allowances for food, such as real bean coffee, which was distributed for a short time from the supplies brought to Germany from Holland, etc.

In a number of cities Jews were only allowed to make purchases in certain shops, in others they were only allowed to shop at certain times, and in others both of these things were regulated. In Berlin the shopping time [for Jews] was 4–5 p.m.[32] There were no designated shops. The Jewish housewife must get done in an hour what her non-Jewish counterpart has the entire day to accomplish. There is no need to describe the haste with which Jewish women do their shopping and how tired and exhausted they are when they return home. The shopkeeper who sells goods to Jews outside the prescribed times or delivers goods to Jews must expect to be shut down.

It was particularly difficult for those in Berlin who had to visit the issuing office for food ration cards. My wife once found herself in this unpleasant situation. For Jews, the office in question was only open twice a week, and was located in a separate room. When my wife arrived there at around nine o'clock in the morning, two queues of at least 100 people had already formed in the courtyard. Those at the front of the queues were standing in the stairwell that led to the office. The rest had to wait for hours on end in the bitter cold as they inched forward. When my wife reached the top step and stood in front of the issuing office, the clock struck twelve and the office closed. She refrained from making a second attempt to visit the office.

Since the Jews are prohibited from entering restaurants, cinemas, theatres, and museums, and from using public libraries, there is a lack of intellectual stimulation and renewal. A social life is out of the question because of the air-raid regulations and because of the directive that forbids Jews from being on the streets after eight o'clock in the evening. Contacting one another by telephone is not possible. With only a few exceptions, all Jews' telephone lines were disconnected, starting on 1 October. Here it should also be noted that Jews were prohibited from using sleeping carriages and dining cars when travelling.[33]

In Berlin, there are Jewish cinemas as well as theatre performances and concerts organized by and for Jews, but these are not well attended.[34] It is understandable that exhausted and worn-out persons are not in the right frame of mind for such events, which are approved and monitored by the Gestapo.

The only Jewish newspaper still published, the *Jüdisches Nachrichtenblatt*, makes a pitiful impression. The unfortunate editor-in-chief is constantly under threat of imprisonment and can print only those stories that the Gestapo allows him or forces him

30 See Doc. 36, fn. 4.
31 Neville Chamberlain (1869–1949) was British prime minister from 1937 to 1940.
32 See Doc. 36, fn. 7.
33 On 28 Dec. 1938 Göring issued a directive that prohibited Jews from using sleeping carriages and dining cars: see PMJ 2/215. The ban entered into force through the Reich Minister of Transport's decree issued on 23 Feb. 1939. On the cancellation of telephone services for Jews, see Doc. 96.
34 On the events organized by the Jewish Culture League, see Docs. 14 and 105.

to.[35] For instance, when an English bomb fell on a Jewish old people's home in Berlin, the *Nachrichtenblatt* had to report in detail on how the German fire brigade diligently put out the fire at the Jewish old people's home caused by the English plane.[36]

Religious life is in an equally sorry state as the nurturing of cultural needs. In most towns where Jews still live, religious services cannot be held due to the shortage of places of worship and the lack of cantors and rabbis. Only in larger cities is it still possible to hold services. In Berlin some places of worship are still intact. Several of these, however, have been requisitioned in order to serve as clothing offices for the army administration, for example. The majority of Berlin's Jews are nonetheless still able to hold regular religious services. Concerns about the security and lives of Jews, however, prompted the Gestapo to issue a directive during the autumn holidays stipulating that the number of persons assembling in a synagogue at any one time could not exceed the capacity of its air-raid shelter. Even so, there continues to be a trace of religious life in Berlin and other cities where a large number of Jews are still present. Lamentable is the lot, on the other hand, of those scattered persons who still live in smaller towns where all forms of religious solace is lacking, where it is difficult to bury the dead, because no one wants to take the body to the cemetery and because many of the cemeteries, some of which are centuries old, have been desecrated and wrecked.

Many Jews also lack the necessary erudition and inner composure. Whereas their forefathers acquired fortitude by holding fast to tradition, which made outside pressure appear to be an ordeal imposed on them 'because of their sins', but one that they surmounted through sacrifice and proud defiance, a large number of today's traditionless generation are petty-minded and faint-hearted. They quarrel among themselves, and with the world and God. They consider their lineage to be a bothersome fetter and would willingly cast it off if that were somehow possible.

It is only when it comes to tax affairs that Jews are placed on a higher level than non-Jews. All Jews liable to income tax are assessed according to the higher tax band designated for unmarried men. The property tax is also calculated for Jews starting at a lower property value than is the case for other taxpayers. Recently, the income tax for Jews was increased by RM 15 per cent.[37] And this measure, as indicated in the statement accompanying this directive, aims to compensate for the 'social inferiority' of the Jews. The *New Yorker Staatszeitung und Herold* commented on the matter in a text box, writing that an alleged inferiority cannot be compensated for by money, and that the measure was nothing other than extortion.[38]

35 Leonhard (Leo) Kreindler (1886–1942), theatre critic and writer; from 1907 worked for the Jewish Community of Berlin; editor of the Berlin edition of the *Israelitisches Familienblatt*, 1925–1938; chairman of the Jewish Press Association, 1928–1931; director of the welfare department of the Reich Association of Jews in Germany and editor-in-chief of the *Jüdisches Nachrichtenblatt*; died of a heart attack in Nov. 1942 after his department was summoned to appear before the Gestapo.

36 This article could not be located.

37 As in the original; the correct meaning is 15 per cent. A regulation issued on 14 Dec. 1940 required Jews to pay a 15 per cent social compensation tax (*Sozialausgleichsabgabe*) on top of their regular income tax charges: *Reichsgesetzblatt*, 1940, I, p. 1666.

38 The German-language newspaper *New Yorker Staats-Zeitung und Herold* was published from 1934 to 1991. This article could not be located.

The present situation of Jews in Germany is worse than that of their forefathers in the Middle Ages. In those times they were given the opportunity at least to earn what was necessary for basic subsistence and their manifold taxes. In those times they enjoyed legal protection. Interference in their religious affairs was rare and it was possible for their home lives to be transfigured by a profound religious sublimity. By virtue of their misguided education, resulting from a mistaken world view, the present generation can still arrange their living quarters as the only place that affords them peace and tranquillity, but not as a site that allows for Jewish learning and the Jewish religion. The events of the last few years have made the German Jew a timid being who is 'put to flight by the sound of a windblown leaf',[39] as the Torah says. They are all afflicted by a psychotic anxiety which creates new rumours about imminent new measures every day, and these figments of the overwrought imagination are taken at face value and spread like wildfire, becoming more and more embellished in the process. In Berlin one calls such reports the 'Jewish word-of-mouth broadcast'.[40]

It is impossible to describe the distressing impact of the news about the evacuation of Jews from Baden and the Palatinate. A paralysing terror bore down on everyone. In Berlin the word-of-mouth broadcast spread the rumour that fellow Jews in Württemberg, Hesse, Frankfurt, and the Rhineland had suffered the same fate and that Jews everywhere should brace themselves to leave house and home. To be on the safe side, one gathered together and packed all the essential things one would need in the refugee camp.

After the misfortune that had befallen the Baden and Palatine Jews became known, the Reich Association of Jews in Germany called on the Jews in Berlin to observe a day of fasting, but was fined (RM 5,000 or 6,000) because this appeal had not been approved by the Gestapo.[41]

The psychotic anxiety reached its zenith in early November 1940. Rumours circulated that mass arrests would be carried out on 10 November and that the Gestapo was in the process of conducting raids aimed at seizing the food supplies and clothes of Jews. During this time, many Jewish men left Berlin to go into hiding with Aryan acquaintances. There they also hid money, food, and clothing. The 10th November came, and luckily nothing in particular happened.

The policies for Jews initiated and carried out by the masterminds behind National Socialism are by no means endorsed by the entire population. Although the clergy of all denominations, the university professors, the highest judges, and other prominent figures failed to muster the courage to speak out publicly against these monstrosities in the movement's early days, there are still broad circles of the population who regard these goings-on as repugnant and loathsome. This became particularly evident on 10 November 1938 as the SA and SS men, completely out of control, went on a rampage that filled

39 'As for those of you who are left, I will make their hearts so fearful in the lands of their enemies that the sound of a windblown leaf will put them to flight. They will run as of fleeing from the sword, and they will fall, even though no one is pursuing them' (Leviticus 26:36).

40 *Jüdischer Mundfunk*; *Mundfunk* is a play on the German word *Rundfunk*, meaning 'broadcasting service'.

41 The initiator and organizer of this protest was Julius Seligsohn, who was subsequently arrested and taken to Sachsenhausen concentration camp: see Doc. 128, fn. 6.

decent-minded people with outrage. Often one heard non-Jews say that their children would have to pay for what has happened to the Jews. One could cite touching examples of non-Jews' noble willingness to help Jewish friends and acquaintances. In many instances Aryans protected the lives and property of Jews, and supplied them with food and drink on those days on which provisions were impossible to come by. One rightfully said in Jewish circles that if the entire population were like its leaders, we would all have been killed long ago. Even today, there is hardly a Jew in Germany who doesn't have one or more Christian friends who help him as much as they possibly can. This is particularly the case in smaller places. Many non-Jews welcome the opportunity to thoroughly vent their discontent to Jews. They know they can do this without being betrayed.

It is also astonishing that most non-Jews are not even familiar with the measures that have been taken against the Jews. For instance, if one tells them that all Jews were required to hand in their silver, gold, and jewellery, they believe this to be a horror story. On the one hand, one regrets seeing emigrating Jews leave, particularly those who have been residents of a place for as long as one can remember. On the other hand, one envies them because they have the opportunity to escape this unbearable situation. The fact that *Der Stürmer* no longer plays the same role as it did in the early phase of the National Socialist regime is evidence that antisemitism is not as much of a draw as it was a few years ago. The paper's recurrent accounts of ritual murders and other horror stories no longer have the same impact as before. All government offices and enterprises still have to subscribe to it, but few read it any more.

Even among the wholly enslaved public service – particularly the older public servants who have known other times – there are still people for whom the treatment of the Jews is repugnant and who gladly help as much as they can within the limits of the fetters placed upon them. Others – this included public servants from the lower, middle, and upper classes – are also accommodating if one knows how to slip them, at the appropriate moment, a banknote commensurate with their rank and the service rendered. Those adept at bribery do as well in the Third Reich as anywhere else.

I myself was able to complete the formalities for my emigration without a hitch and encountered mostly goodwill at each government office. Only young public officials who obtained their posts through Party connections are rather unapproachable and seek to take their anger out on Jews. Such pathetic characters are not rare in Berlin. There are young officials there who are feared by the entire Jewish community.

With God's help, which clearly reigned over us, my wife and I were able to leave Europe and reach the land of freedom.

I take with me to the New World not only my memories of more than fifty happy years but also of the days of horror since 1933. They haunt me in my dreams. Filled with anguish, I think of those who must continue to live in Germany and who long for deliverance, but my thoughts are especially with my many friends and acquaintances languishing in the Camp de Gurs. My most fervent wish would be to be able to come quickly to their aid.

DOC. 130

Walter Mehring pays tribute to his dead friends in a New Year's poem, 1940/41[1]

Poem by Walter Mehring,[2] 31 December 1940

Part I: Odyssey out of Midnight X[3] – Marseilles, New Years 1940/41

On the door of my hut, the New Year pounds
A dozen times, and in hollowed tone
Of doom intones: 'These too are gone ...'
Hangs up a wreath and passes on his rounds.
The colors pale, plagued by the blight of lies.
Starved for the truth, the season token dies.
The richest fruitage in the season's yield
Was left to rot upon a German field.

Muehsam,[4] poet, firm promethean,
Was strangled, like a sick unwanted hound.
Ossietzky,[5] flung and flayed upon the ground,
Smiled and died, a proud unbeaten man.
He, having won the prize of Peace now gave
His gain to Death for peace within the grave.
The finest fruitage in the season's yield
Was left to rot upon a German field.

A letter flutters down; the script is blurred;
'Stupidities we once so roundly jeered
Fashion us history. And they are feared,
Applauded and bespeak the final word ...

1 Translation from German published in Walter Mehring, *No Road Back: Poems. English and German Text*, trans. S. A. De Witt, illus. George Grosz (New York: Samuel Curl, 1944), pp. 77–83. The poem is one of twelve 'Midnight Letters' (*Briefe aus der Mitternacht*).

2 Walter Mehring (1896–1981), writer, publicist, translator, and illustrator; co-founder of the political cabarets of Berlin, 1920; correspondent for *Die Weltbühne*, in Berlin and Paris, 1922–1928; journalist in Vienna, 1934–1938; fled to France after the Anschluss, and emigrated to the United States in 1941; returned to Europe in 1953, living first in Germany, then in Switzerland.

3 The 'Twelve Midnight Letters' are numbered.

4 Erich Mühsam (1878–1934), writer; worked at the weekly journal *Simplicissimus* from 1909; editor of the monthly journal *Kain: Zeitschrift für Menschlichkeit*, 1911–1914 and 1918–1919; played a leading role in the proclamation of the socialist Bavarian Council Republic in 1919, and thereafter was sentenced to 15 years' imprisonment; released in 1924; arrested by the SA in 1933, and murdered in Oranienburg concentration camp.

5 Carl von Ossietzky (1889–1938), publicist; from 1927 editor-in-chief of the weekly journal *Die Weltbühne*; imprisoned in Sonnenburg concentration camp in 1933; awarded the 1936 Nobel Peace Prize *in absentia*; died in a Berlin hospital as a result of mistreatment in the camp.

Forget … *Tucholsky*. …'[6] Then the Midnight Sun
Lit the fierce drink whereby he fell, self-done.
The richest fruitage of[7] the season's yield
Was left to rot upon a foreign field.

Then *Ernst Toller*,[8] companion since my youth,
Enriching everything he touched … the stage …
The gatherings of earnest folk … even the cage
That prisoned him … crusader for the truth …
Snuffed himself out under an alien sky
Far from the battle. We still wonder why …
The richest fruitage of the season's yield
Was left to rot upon a foreign field. …

In all this world there never was an inn
Quite like the one near Luxembourg, where we
Mixed Left and Right precept and policy,
While *Joseph Roth*[9] played master mind and Djinn.
A bearded prophet with a wine-drenched breath
Who very sagely drank himself to death.
The richest fruitage of the season's yield
Was left to rot upon a German field.

Just before our Paris fell, and I,
Released from jail discovered you again,
The exiled *Ernst Weiss*[10] tarried with us then,
Poet and surgeon, he knew how one should die.
He mixed himself a bane and quaffed it down
Before the croaking Huns flew into town. …
The richest fruitage in the season's yield
Was left to rot upon a foreign field.

The philosophic *Lessing*,[11] tried and slain,
And *Hasenclever*,[12] steeped in French esprit,
Dead in a French Dachau; grim comedy!

6 Kurt Tucholsky (1890–1935), journalist, writer, and literary critic; worked for the journal *Die Schaubühne* (later renamed *Die Weltbühne*), 1913–1933; Paris correspondent for the *Weltbühne* and the *Vossische Zeitung* from 1924; emigrated in 1930 to Sweden, where he committed suicide.

7 The inconsistent use of 'in' and 'of' in the refrain is present in the original text.

8 Ernst Toller (1893–1939), writer; played a leading role in the proclamation of the socialist Bavarian Council Republic in 1919, and thereafter was sentenced to five years' imprisonment; was stripped of German citizenship and emigrated to Switzerland, 1933; emigrated to Britain in 1934 and later to the United States, where he took his own life.

9 Joseph Roth (1894–1939), writer and journalist; from 1923 culture correspondent for the *Frankfurter Zeitung*, then its foreign correspondent in Paris, 1925–1929; emigrated to Paris in 1933.

10 Dr Ernst Weiss (1882–1940), writer, literary critic, and physician; worked for the *Berliner Börsen-Courier*; emigrated to Paris via Prague, 1933; committed suicide as German troops approached Paris.

Carl Einstein,[13] dreaming of a newborn Spain
Caught and hanged, a wild bird winged in flight. …
While *Olden*[14] drowned with Canada in sight. …
The richest fruitage of the season's yield
Was left to rot upon a foreign field.

Now *Horvarth*,[15] crushed beneath a stricken tree,
Cheated fate and exile: far too fine
A gem to lie before rapacious swine,
He died … a satyr-being, wildly free …
Twelve times the door is pounded; and it creaks.
Eleven are gone. And now the Reaper speaks:
The richest fruitage of the season's yield
Was left to rot upon a German field.

Within this hut, where days drag laggardly,
You in New York, and I in drab Marseilles,
Eking along on loans from day to day,
Munching on the sapless stuff of memory.
I bide the call to join the dead Eleven,
In some hard nether world, or gentler heaven.
The richest fruitage of the season's yield
Was left to rot upon a foreign field.

If one high boon were granted, I would dare
Command this New Year's Eve to carry here
Your living presence, firm, and sweet, and near;
That every nerve of mine twang quick and bare.
How I would breathe and sense you utterly,

11 Dr Theodor Lessing (1872–1933), philosopher and publicist; adjunct professor at the Hanover Institute of Technology; worked for the dailies *Prager Tagblatt* and *Dortmunder Generalanzeiger*; emigrated in 1933 to Mariánské Lázně (Marienbad) in Czechoslovakia, where he died after an assassination attempt by Sudeten German Nazis; author of works including *Der jüdische Selbsthass* (Jewish Self-Hatred) (1930).

12 Walter Hasenclever (1890–1940), writer; Paris correspondent for the *8-Uhr-Abendblatt*, 1924–1938; after 1933 lived in Yugoslavia, Britain, Italy, and the south of France; took his own life as German troops approached the Les Milles internment camp.

13 Carl Einstein (1885–1940), writer and art critic; emigrated to Paris in 1928; fought in the Spanish Civil War, 1936–1938; interned in France, 1940, and took his own life after his release, as German troops approached.

14 Rudolf Olden (1885–1940), journalist, lawyer, and historian; politics editor at the *Berliner Tageblatt*, 1924–1933; defence counsel at political trials in Berlin, including that of Carl von Ossietzky; emigrated to Czechoslovakia, 1933, and to Britain, 1934; died en route to the United States when his ship was torpedoed by a German submarine.

15 Ödön von Horváth (1901–1938), writer and playwright; worked for the satirical weekly *Simplicissimus*; emigrated to Austria in 1933, then to Switzerland in 1938; killed on the Champs-Elysées in Paris by a falling branch during a storm.

while love's deliriant potion heightened me.
But, ah, this wine I sip, tastes of the dead,
Pressed from a vintage, never harvested.

DOC. 131
On 3 January 1941 Kurt Rathenau from Berlin writes to his brother Fritz about what the censorship of letters means for him[1]

Handwritten letter from Dr Kurt Rathenau,[2] 115 Kurfürstenstraße, Berlin W. 62, to Fritz Rathenau,[3] dated 3 January 1941

Dear Fritz,

By now you will have received our joint New Year's wishes. The hour before the start of the New Year made us all think of those close to us but far away, and we all wished each other a Happy New Year for 1941!

I've read the lines you wrote on 18 December several times, and I thank you once again for taking all the time and trouble that you did. All of your news is of great interest to me, you can be sure of that. It's just that it's difficult, and not only for me, but for almost all of my acquaintances here – as you point out – to write long letters about ourselves, what we do and don't do, to write down our thoughts. The letters are only intended for the recipient, not for the censors, that's why. Not that I would have anything to fear or even hide, but one is utterly inhibited in revealing one's feelings to strangers, be they male or female. How easily can harmless sentences or words be misinterpreted by strangers who know neither the sender nor the recipient. Therefore, wherever possible, I avoid writing long epistles, as I cannot express myself either philosophically or historically. So it isn't secretiveness on my part, just a fear of censorship! – What would be the point of my wanting to tell you how annoying it is in everyday life that they cut off our telephone, after being used to having one with the same number at the same place for thirty years!

On 1 January, at about 8:30 in the morning, there was a quiet ringing and then it was all over![4]

Should I worry my head over why they are cutting off the telephones of non-Aryans instead of the many 'infrequent talkers' who maybe speak very rarely over the course of a month? – Why should I complain about how difficult it is for a housewife to buy the entire provisions needed for the household in just *one* hour! It has been decreed, and therefore we have to learn to live with it, like a lot of other things.[5] – Why get a heavy

1 Jüdisches Museum Berlin, 2001/106/054–982, Mappe 10. This document has been translated from German.

2 Dr Kurt Rathenau (b. 1880), businessman; lived in Berlin-Schöneberg; a partner in the firm Ernst Rosenberg und Co. GmbH, Berlin; deported to Minsk in June 1942 and later pronounced dead as of 31 Dec. 1944: see also PMJ 1/126.

3 Dr Fritz Rathenau (1875–1949), lawyer; member of the German People's Party (DVP); Regierungsrat in the patents office and in the Reich Statistical Office, 1909–1917; in the Prussian Ministry of the Interior, 1920–1933; Ministerialrat, 1927; transferred to the Prussian Directorate of Construction and Finance after 1933; dismissed in 1935; emigrated to the Netherlands in 1939; deported to Theresienstadt in 1943; lived in Bilthoven, near Utrecht, after 1945.

4 The reference is to the order issued on July 1940, cancelling Jews' telephone lines: see Doc. 96.

heart once again, adding further woes to one's nearest and dearest abroad when they have enough of their own?

Believe me, dear Fritz, it is so hard for everyone to come to terms with what is happening and what is allowed, that it takes strong nerves and a good dose of optimism to keep your chin up! Nobody can know how it feels for somebody else, not even those closest to them! Everyone has his deep sorrows of one sort or another. Nobody can gauge it, as no one knows how severe the pressure is on the other. – That's why I'm asking you not to take it the wrong way if my news seems a little sketchy. You cannot imagine how quickly we can rub people up the wrong way! You can find out what's really happening in the big wide world in the press, just like me!

Now for a few details: I have received no news of the marriage of Gilbert's sister; nor do I know Mrs Nelly; her interest in me just comes from the brief correspondence. I share your view that Papa G. must be generous-hearted given the differences between the present and future children-in-law, but the parents need not worry about Gilbert. That is a good sign for you too.

Yesterday I found out that your old great aunt, Mrs Lebmann, will turn 100 on 13 January!! Incredible; I'm sure you will write to her; I don't know her. Her son Georg Lebmann died eight days ago, at the age of 73! Moving on to talk about deaths: I don't know the date of José's death or who paid the costs for the funeral etc. He's buried in Stahnsdorf.

As regards Clara's will, I can't tell you anything today. I haven't been able to reach the lawyer Mr Bernd yet. I don't think he was allowed to continue working on Clara's affairs. Neither do I know whether he will give me information of any kind. Since the matter is not urgent, I would only write to Olga about how and where the execution of the will is taking place, whether she has considered all the points, and whether you should get involved. I would ask you to leave *me* completely out of it, if that is at all possible, please. Let it sink in slowly, after you have brought Olga's attention to things. The post from here and to here from the USA is very poor; sometimes it is completely disrupted. Therefore I would recommend that you write to Olga immediately, as no one knows how the USA will react during the course of world events. As far as I know, a mortgage was secured for the Gr. children. José's part will go to [...][6] Renée. – The reference number of Ludwig Clara's will is: Local Court Berlin-Mitte: 95 IV. 720.07.29.

The endowment dates from 10 November 1910, concluded by Judicial Counsellor Veit Simon.[7] – That's all on that for today. –

We were very happy to read Sophie's cheerful lines,[8] and Elsi[9] and I send our thanks. – A nice letter came from [...][10] also about you. –

Many warm wishes for today

Yours,

5 For restrictions on shopping hours, see Doc. 36, fn. 7.

6 One word is illegible.

7 Dr Heinrich Veit Simon (b. 1880), lawyer.

8 Sophie Rathenau, née Dannenbaum (1882–1973), emigrated to the Netherlands together with her husband Fritz Rathenau in 1939; was deported to Theresienstadt with him in 1943, lived in the Netherlands after 1945.

9 Else Rathenau, née von Peter (b. 1885), was deported to Minsk together with her husband Kurt Rathenau in June 1942 and later pronounced dead as of 31 Dec. 1944.

10 The name is illegible.

DOC. 132

On 6 January 1941 the South Westphalia Chamber of Industry and Commerce in Hagen requests permission from the Reich Minister of Economics to purchase land belonging to Dagobert Gottschalk, a Jew[1]

Letter from the South Westphalia Chamber of Industry and Commerce in Hagen, headquarters, signed President A. Hesterberg,[2] to the Reich Minister of Economics,[3] Berlin (received on 11 January 1941), dated 6 January 1941[4]

Re: *land purchase*

Together with the city of Hagen, we are the joint sponsors of the merchants' school, which consists of a vocational college, a commercial school, and a commercial college. The Chamber of Industry and Commerce owns the building. There is an opportunity to buy the adjacent plot of land. This is urgently needed, as it offers the only opportunity to extend the school. The plot belongs to the Jew Dagobert Gottschalk,[5] whose German nationality has in the meantime been declared void. During the course of the year 1939, with the cooperation of the Regierungspräsident,[6] we made an application to the Reich Ministry of Economics for this plot to be sold to us. The Reich Ministry of Economics granted this request, as shown in the copy of the attached letter from the Regierungspräsident of Arnsberg, dated 8 September 1939.[7] (The decree issued by the Reich Minister of Economics to the Regierungspräsident in Arnsberg is dated 1 August 1939 – III Jd. 3/16 449/39.[8]) Now that Gottschalk's complaint has been rejected and it has been established definitively that the senior public prosecutor in Hagen is conducting the sale of the land, we request:

(1) the issue of the permit pursuant to Article 7 § 1 of the implementing law to the BGB[9] for the purchase of the plot, entered in the Hagen land register, volume 97, page 2795, District Hagen, Cadastral District 43 no. 239/1, Hagen, Springmannstraße;

(2) the approval of an additional RM 30,000, entered in the supplement to the budget for the accounting year.[10]

1 BArch, R 3101/9556. This document has been translated from German.

2 Alex Hesterberg (1876–1956), factory owner; joined the NSDAP in 1931; co-owner, commercial manager, and senior partner of the company F. Hesterberg & Söhne, a drop-forging, screw, and nut manufacturer in Milspe; president of the South Westphalia Chamber of Industry and Commerce in Hagen, 1934–1943; honorary citizen of the town of Ennepetal.

3 Walther Funk.

4 The original contains handwritten annotations.

5 Dagobert Gottschalk (1879–1943), banker; partner of the Rossberg & Co. banking house in Hagen, imprisoned in Nov. 1936 for currency offences; fled to Amsterdam; convicted *in absentia* in 1937; arrested and brought to Germany in 1940; released due to unsuitability for prison; returned to the Netherlands; sent to Westerbork on 5 June 1943; from there deported on 20 July 1943 to Sobibor, where he was murdered.

6 The Regierungspräsident of Arnsberg from 1935 to Sept. 1941 was Dr Ludwig Runte (1896–1958).

7 In the letter Runte – with the agreement of the Reich Ministry of Economics – demanded that Gottschalk, who was living in Amsterdam, sell the land within four weeks to the Chamber of Industry and Commerce in Hagen: BArch, R 3101/9556.

8 This decree was not found.

9 *Bürgerliches Gesetzbuch*: German Civil Code.

10 Next to the last two points, the original contains a handwritten: 'Yes!' In a letter dated 22 Jan. 1941 the Reich Ministry of Economics approved the sale of the land: BArch, R 3101/9556.

DOC. 133

On 7 January 1941 the Steyrermühl paper factory and publishing company applies for compensation from the Reichsstatthalter of Upper Danube for losses resulting from Aryanization[1]

Letter from the Steyrermühl paper factory and publishing company (DirDa/MH),[2] signed, one signature illegible, Weber, to the Reichsstatthalter of Upper Danube, Department for De-Jewification, Linz an der Donau,[3] dated 7 January 1941[4]

De-Jewification of the Steyrermühl paper factory

We hereby submit the request for an investigation of the procedure, circumstances, and sale of our Vienna businesses, which were in our possession at the time of Austria's incorporation into the German Reich. We furthermore submit a claim to specify, on the basis of the investigation, the compensation for the losses we have incurred through the sale, and instruct the authorities in question to make arrangements for the compensation.

The claim concerns the following:

1. The sales of the newspaper publisher and the printing works at 5 Fleischmarkt, Vienna I, which continue to run today as a limited partnership known as the Ostmärkischer Zeitungsverlag, owned by the Herold publishing house in Berlin.

2. The Steyrermühl book and art printing press at 40–44 Gumpendorferstraße, Vienna, VI/6; buyer: M. Müller & Sohn, 39 Schelling-Straße, Munich 13.[5]

Our request is based on the following grounds:

At the time of the incorporation of Austria into the German Reich, the Steyrermühl paper factory and publishing company got a provisional director, Dr Leopold Winkler,[6]

1 YVA, O.30/96. This document has been translated from German.

2 Until 1938 Steyrermühl AG consisted of the Wiener Tagblatt group, to which a book publisher and eight newspapers (including the *Neues Wiener Tagblatt*) belonged, along with two printing presses and its own paper manufacturing facility. Originally, three pulp plants, a cellulose factory, several electricity plants, and a paper factory founded in Steyrermühl in around 1870 made up the public limited company, which had a staff of 1,500.

3 The sub-department IVc/W or Ib/J in the Reichsstatthalter's office, also called the 'Department for De-Jewification' (Entjudungsabteilung), was responsible for coordinating Aryanization in the Gau of Upper Danube. The head of the department from 1941 was Dr Ernst Lyro (1888–1954), lawyer; worked in the Reichsstatthalter's office as Oberregierungsrat from 1939; was also assigned to the Regierungspräsident in Aurich from July 1941 until Sept. 1942; after the war he worked in the finance department of the regional government of Upper Austria.

4 The original contains handwritten notes and a stamp of the Israelite Religious Community of Linz from the post-war period.

5 The Tagblatt group and the Steyrermühl book and art printing press were placed under the de facto control of the NSDAP's central publishing house Franz Eher Nachf., Munich. The Herold Verlags-GmbH functioned across the Reich as Eher's receiving company for the takeover of various newspaper publishers. The Munich book-trader M. Müller & Sohn printed publications for Eher, including the *Völkische Beobachter*.

6 Dr Leopold Winkler (1881–1949), lawyer; joined the NSDAP in 1933 and the SA in 1935; long-serving general secretary of the Steyrermühl publishing company and its head, 1938–1945; categorized as a 'lesser offender' in denazification proceedings after the war.

who worked back then as the chief cashier in the Vienna headquarters. Half of the members of the Steyrermühl supervisory board, which was consequently relieved of its responsibilities, were Jewish, although, according to the latest definition, one member who was apparently regarded as 100 per cent Jewish has turned out not to be. The sale of both businesses only went ahead after the failure of an appeal in the newspapers, signed by the acting manager, which sought to place a large number of shares into single ownership in order to form a majority shareholding. Furthermore, due to the regulations regarding the ownership of newspapers and publishing companies, a short-term deadline had been set, by which either Steyrermühl had to have been Aryanized or a sale had to have been carried out. Otherwise the publisher and the newspaper printing works would have to be closed down.[7] The present manager of the Ostmärkischer Zeitungsverlag, Dr Leopold Winkler, therefore conducted the sale of the publishing company as its acting director. The sale of the book and art printing works was subsequently initiated too, while the sale itself has already occurred during the tenure of Dr Winkler's successor, the new acting director.

During these processes the responsible authorities failed with regard to the following:

1. It was not investigated whether the possibility of sale was justified, considering the fact that at the time of the sale, on 2 August 1938, the registration of Jewish assets had already been undertaken and the Third Regulation to the Reich Citizenship Law of 14 June 1938[8] was also already in force. No investigation was conducted at this point as to whether the enterprise of the Steyrermühl paper factory and publishing company could be described as Jewish according to this regulation. However, an inspection of the registration of assets that took place in November 1938 showed that of a total of 105,000 shares, only 21,024 shares, less than a quarter of the total capital, were registered as Jewish shares. According to the terms in the regulation cited, clause 3b,[9] the business would have been regarded as non-Jewish due to the available declarations of assets. A recent investigation by the present company board in the spring of 1940 showed that of the shareholders, over 80 per cent[10] could be identified as Aryan shareholders, and it can be assumed that the majority of the rest of the unknown shareholders can also be regarded as Aryan.

2. As it was a non-Jewish company at the time of the sale in August 1938, the acting director was not authorized to activate the two legal transactions; nor was it necessary or obligatory to have the legal transactions approved by an authority deemed responsible due to the regulations valid at the time.

7 The directives issued by the Reich Press Chamber on 2 May 1938 aimed to assimilate the Austrian press with that of the Reich. On 2 August 1938 the Reich Press Chamber banned the publishing of newspapers by limited companies and decreed that each publisher could print only one newspaper. Furthermore, no newspapers were to be produced by printing companies 'whose owners or shareholders were not of German or related blood': *Zeitungs-Verlag*, no. 19, 7 May 1938, pp. 288–289.

8 The Third Regulation on the Reich Citizenship Law prescribed the criteria according to which a business was defined as Jewish: *Reichsgesetzblatt*, 1938, I, pp. 627–628.

9 According to Article I § 1(3b) of the Third Regulation, a business was deemed Jewish if more than a quarter of the capital belonged to Jews: *Reichsgesetzblatt*, 1938, I, pp. 627–628.

10 This figure is barely legible.

3. It has emerged from the audit conducted by the Danube Trust and Organization Company, Vienna I, that the purchase price for the publisher and the book and art printing press was in no way proportional to the actual value at the time. The two firms belonging to the company had been known to be developing healthily for decades with a net yield that allowed the paper and cellulose factory in Steyrermühl, Upper Danube, the means required for its expansion and refurbishment. It is common knowledge that after the dissolution of the economic area of the former Austro-Hungarian monarchy, the paper and cellulose factories fell upon hard times, as they were forced, at great cost, to sell off around half of their products abroad in order to be able to continue operating. The paper and cellulose factories were therefore running at a loss and in no position to be able to build up and renovate their factories in a short period of time. Steyrermühl is in the same position today and, due to the sale of the thriving parts of the business, has ended up in an even more difficult economic situation.

4. Regarding the sale itself, it is noted that the acting director brought two gentlemen from the former board of directors to the negotiations. However, due to the regulation regarding the appointment of the acting director, neither had these men co-decision rights nor were they in a position to draw up a valid board resolution. The position of the two gentlemen is characterized by the fact that, at the time, the acting director stated that either the publishing house should be sold in accordance with the conditions set by the buyer or the printing business would have to be closed down at the short notice given. The opinion of the acting director, which he expressed at the time and later also repeated, was that the damage to the company would be less if the publishing house were sold. Whether and to what extent this also applied to the book and art printing business cannot be established today.

Following a request by one of the shareholders at the annual general meeting in early 1940, the undersigned management board and the supervisory board of the company were assigned the task of arranging compensation for the damages incurred by the company and also by the shareholders of the business, using all means available. We also note here that, according to the information gathered in the spring of 1940, the number of Aryan shareholders was several hundred and the majority consisted of small savers and pensioners who for years had had to live off the income from their shares.

The supervisory board of the company decided to instruct the board to initiate the necessary procedure.

Finally, we refer to the statement of the Reichsstatthalter in Vienna, Settlement Agency of the Asset Transfer Office, dated 29 November 1940, which was sent from there to the NSDAP, Gau Economics Office, for the attention of the Gau economic advisor in Vienna regarding the same matter.[11]

On account of the available statements and the existing regulations regarding such sales and businesses from the period of upheaval,[12] we hereby apply for an investigation

11 This statement could not be located. From June 1939 the Vienna Asset Transfer Office (Vermögensverkehrsstelle), a state trust agency set up by Göring, was restructured and existed from Nov. 1939 as a 'settlement agency' (Abwicklungstelle), and later until 1945 as 'Section III De-Jewification' (Referat III Entjudung) in the Reichsgau of Vienna: see PMJ 2, p. 40, fn. 92.

12 The author is probably referring to the Anschluss of Austria to the Reich in March 1938 or the National Socialist assumption of power in Jan. 1933.

into and compensation for the damages incurred by our business. We request that this matter be given preferential, urgent treatment and are available should any further information or clarification be required.

Heil Hitler![13]

DOC. 134

Following his deportation from Stettin to Piaski, on 18 January 1941 Gerhard Michaelis asks the Reich Foreign Office to approve his family's emigration to Haiti[1]

Letter from Gerhard Israel Michaelis,[2] Piaski/Lublin, to the Reich Foreign Office, Berlin, dated 18 January 1941

Re: emigration of the following from the General Government to Haiti:
Gerhard Isr. Michaelis, born 20 July 1912 in Stettin, document no. 132/40 as substitute for identity card;
Paula Sara Michaelis,[3] née Perlinski, born 14 March 1877 in Berlin, identity card issued in Stettin, identity card no. A.00.992;
Else Sara Michaelis,[4] born 19 July 1899 in Lindow in der Mark, document no. 123/40 as substitute for identity card.

I request most cordially that the following appeal be processed and considered:

After many years of endeavouring to arrange emigration from Germany, on 12 January 1940 I finally succeeded in obtaining an entry permit to Haiti in Central America from the Haitian consulate general in Hamburg, as the attached photocopy shows.[5] I had completed all of the formalities in Stettin and was just about to commence my journey, which was due to take place at the end of February 1940, when we were resettled to the General Government on 12 February 1940. From our new home in Piaski near Lublin I immediately started preparing emigration for myself and my family, and I also managed to obtain an entry permit to Haiti for my sister and my mother.

The clearance certificates from the tax inspector of the Lublin region are already in our possession, and the foreign currency clearance certificates of the Foreign Exchange Office in Cracow are ready for us to pick up as well.

I would furthermore like to point out that my mother and my sister already had their boat tickets for Shanghai in August 1939 and only the outbreak of the war prevented them from travelling.

13 There is no reply in the file. The business was eventually merged with the Czech paper factory Pötschmühle, and the company headquarters were relocated from Vienna and Steyrermühl to Větřní (Wettern) near Český Krumlov (Krumau) on the Vltava river.

1 PA AA, R 99 368. This document has been translated from German.

2 Gerhard Michaelis (b. 1912), worked in the wine- and fruit-growing trade; deported from Stettin to Piaski on 12 Feb. 1940, and later pronounced dead.

3 Paula Michaelis, née Perlinsky (b. 1877), mother of Gerhard Michaelis; her husband, Dr Alfred Michaelis (1873–1940), physician, perished in Sachsenhausen concentration camp on 2 Feb. 1940; she was deported from Stettin to Piaski on 12 Feb. 1940 and later pronounced dead.

4 Else Michaelis (1899–1942), sister of Gerhard Michaelis; deported on 12 Feb. 1940 from Stettin to Piaski, where she perished on 2 March 1942.

5 PA AA, R 99 368.

Since the emigration of Jews from Germany is continuing as before, I would most courteously like to request that, as German subjects, we be permitted to emigrate from the General Government via Hamburg or Berlin. In the hope of receiving your confirmation very soon, I sign respectfully[6]

DOC. 135
On 20 January 1941 the SD's weekly situation report Meldungen aus dem Reich describes reactions to the film *The Eternal Jew*[1]

The Reichsführer SS and Chief of the German Police, the Chief of the Security Police and the SD, Office III:[2] Meldungen aus dem Reich, no. 155, dated 20 January 1941[3]

[...][4]
On reactions to The Eternal Jew, *a film for political enlightenment*

According to reports from all across the Reich, extensive coverage in the press and on the radio *led the public to eagerly await* the release of the documentary film *The Eternal Jew.*

According to numerous available reports, audiences repeatedly stressed that the pictorial evidence presented in the film along with its comprehensive overview of the Jews' life and activities fully met peoples' high expectations, and that it had a more enlightening, convincing, and memorable effect than much of the anti-Jewish literature. The *substantial extent to which the available pictorial material* has been *crafted to create a whole* has been widely acknowledged.

Reports from Munich, Koblenz, Schwerin, Danzig, Halle, Königsberg, Kiel, Neustadt/Weinstraße, Leipzig, Carlsbad, Potsdam, and Berlin indicated that the *cartographic and statistical presentation* of the proliferation of Jewry (the comparison with rats was picked out as being particularly impressive) and of the spread of their influence to all areas of life and all countries on earth was met with particular approval. The footage of the Jews in the USA drew particular attention. The audience was

6 On 1 March 1941 the Department for Internal Administration of the General Government's cabinet rejected the family's emigration 'as not desirable at present': ibid.

1 BArch, R 58/157, fols. 63–65. Published in Heinz Boberach (ed.), *Meldungen aus dem Reich 1938–1945: Die geheimen Lageberichte des Sicherheitsdienstes der SS*, vol. 6: *Meldungen aus dem Reich, Nr. 142 vom 18. Nov. 1940 – Nr. 179 vom 17. April 1941* (Herrsching: Pawlak, 1984), pp. 1917–1919. This document has been translated from German.

2 Office III (German Living Areas/SD Domestic) of the Reich Security Main Office (RSHA) was headed by Otto Ohlendorf (1907–1951).

3 The original is stamped 'Secret' and 'Personal – To be submitted immediately! This report is *personally* intended for the addressee and contains news material that is being sent *unverified* due to its topical nature.'

4 The first part of the report ('General') covers the wait-and-see attitude of the population towards the events of the war, as well as the allegedly imminent landing of German troops in Britain. The second part ('Cultural areas') reports on the effects of propaganda, press, and radio in Jan. 1941 as well as the coverage of the war in the German press.

surprised how openly the Jewish influence and Jewish dominance in the USA are shown (Schwerin, Carlsbad).

The scenes in which the Jew 'in his original form' and 'in his European version' was shown as a cosmopolitan (Leipzig) were particularly impressive, as were the extraordinarily effective *contrasts* (the Jewish ghetto – the march of the German youth at the Nuremberg rally). According to one report from Munich, there was unrestrained and enthusiastic applause during the film when the part of one of the *Führer*'s speeches was shown in which he predicted that a new war could only result in the end and the annihilation of Jewry.[5]

The *portrayal of the history of the Rothschild family*[6] had a particularly convincing effect everywhere, especially the evidence that individual family members have been naturalized in many different countries, allowing them to gain a foothold as recognized citizens in the most important countries. This portrayal and the contrasts of the different types of Jew throughout the world – as could be deduced from numerous conversations – have made it strikingly clear that the Jew, despite adapting externally to countries, languages, and living areas, nonetheless always remains a Jew.

Due to the particularly intense propaganda for the film and the impressive arrangement of the documentary visual evidence, the first showings attracted *extraordinary visitor numbers*. The population's interest often waned in certain regions, however, as the film was considered to have come out too soon after the major film *Jew Süss*.

As a large majority of the population had already seen the film *Jew Süss*, the various reports indicate that people frequently considered that the documentary film *The Eternal Jew* could not contribute anything particularly new. Accordingly, reports from Innsbruck, Dortmund, Aachen, Karlsruhe, Neustadt/Weinstraße, Bielefeld, Frankfurt am Main, and Munich stated that often only the more politically active part of the population went to see the documentary film, whereas typical filmgoers in some cases avoided it, and there was local word-of-mouth propaganda against the film and its highly realistic portrayal of Jewry.

In conversations, the revolting nature of what was shown, and in particular the scenes of ritual slaughter, were cited time and again as the chief reason not to go and see the film. The film was repeatedly described as 'an extreme strain on the nerves' (Neustadt/Weinstraße). Thus, audience figures chiefly in certain parts of the north-west, west, and south of Germany and the Ostmark fell very quickly. According to reports from western Germany and also from Breslau, individual audience members often left the cinemas disgusted in the middle of the screening, uttering phrases such as 'We've seen *Jew Süss* and have had enough of this Jewish filth!' There were isolated incidents of women and also some younger men fainting during the scenes of ritual slaughter.

The statement was often made that *Jew Süss* had already portrayed Jewry so convincingly that there really was no need for this new and even more glaring evidence in the documentary film shown immediately afterwards. On the other hand, a great number of statements have been heard, chiefly from politically active circles of the population,

5 Hitler's speech of 30 Jan. 1939 is documented in PMJ 2/248.

6 The Rothschild family was among the most important banking dynasties in nineteenth-century Europe. The company headquarters was M. A. Rothschild & Söhne in Frankfurt am Main.

describing the film as an extraordinarily impressive document that has been greeted most appreciatively.[7]

[...][8]

DOC. 136

On 20 January 1941 the Viennese cardinal Theodor Innitzer informs the Pope of his concern for the fate of 11,000 non-Aryan Christians[1]

Letter from Cardinal Innitzer,[2] Vienna, to Pope Pius XII,[3] dated 20 January 1941

Holy Father,

Grave pastoral concern induces me, Venerable Holiness, to put forward a request prompted by the shocking distress of many of my diocesans.

Approximately 11,000 non-Aryan Catholics are still living in Vienna today, a sizeable number of whom are worthy and devoted persons. Over the past few months the plight of these Catholics has become increasingly grave and pressing, whereas the prospect of receiving assistance has become dimmer and more hopeless.

What weighs heavily upon me is the fact that other communities, such as the Society of Friends,[4] the Swedish Mission,[5] and the Israelite Religious Community, are able to look after their non-Aryan charges much more effectively than we can because they have greater financial resources at their disposal.

The funds at our disposal have been depleted to such an extent by the utter failure from abroad that it is now barely possible to provide ample support.

As a consequence, in the past few weeks many of my non-Aryan diocesans have had to vacate their apartments and seek shelter in mass quarters. Moreover, our plans for

7 See also Doc. 124.

8 The third part ('Nationhood and public health') addresses the mood of the Czech population in the Sudetengau, as well as the new regulation on child benefit. The parts 'Administration and law' and 'Economy' follow.

1 Published in Pierre Blet et al. (eds.), *Actes et documents du Saint Siège relatifs à la Seconde Guerre mondiale: Le Saint Siège et les victimes de la guerre, janvier 1941 – décembre 1943*, vol. 8 (Vatican City: Vaticana, 1974), pp. 78–79. This document has been translated from German.

2 Theodor Innitzer (1875–1955), theologian; vice chancellor of the University of Vienna, 1928–1929; minister of social welfare, 1929–1930; archbishop of Vienna, 1932–1955; ordained cardinal, 1933; founded the Archiepiscopal Relief Agency for Non Aryan Catholics, 1940; from 1952 served as papal legate.

3 Dr Eugenio Pacelli (1876–1958), theologian and lawyer; entered the Papal Secretariat of State, 1901; professor at the Vatican's diplomatic academy, 1909–1914; ordained titular bishop and appointed apostolic nuncio to Bavaria, 1917; apostolic nuncio to the German Reich, 1920–1929; ordained cardinal, 1929; appointed cardinal secretary of state, 1930; elected pope in March 1939.

4 The Society of Friends was a Quaker organization based in London. It worked together with the Grüber Office, the St Raphael Society, and the Reich Association of Jews in Germany to assist non-Aryans and dissidents.

5 The Swedish Israel Mission was an initiative of the Swedish Evangelical Lutheran Church aimed at proselytizing Jews and supporting converted Jews. It had a presence in Vienna from 1920. From 1938 the Swedish Mission helped converts who were persecuted as Jews to secure safe passage out of Austria. In 1941 it was forced to close its Vienna offices on Seegasse.

providing passage out of the country have ended in failure or have not advanced beyond their humble beginnings, for example, the Brazil initiative.[6]

And now these sorely tried Catholics of my diocese are beset by an even greater danger. According to information that has come to me from a reliable source, all Jews living in Vienna – approximately 60,000 – are to be deported in the coming weeks.

Our most urgent task is, therefore, to wrest as many as possible from this terrible fate.

Encouraged by the most comforting Christmas message from Your Venerable Holiness,[7] I therefore do not hesitate to ask the Secretariat of State of the Venerable Holiness for help. I am thinking in particular of the procurement of foreign visas in order to enable at least some of the unfortunate to still depart at the last minute.

In the conviction that Your Holiness will take on my pressing worries as his own and provide assistance where possible, I implore the special blessing of the Venerable Holiness for my gravely afflicted diocesans.[8]

DOC. 137

On 21 January 1941 the Reichsstatthalter of Styria informs the Reich Minister of Food and Agriculture about the expropriation of Jewish agricultural landholdings[1]

Report from the Reichsstatthalter of Styria (Chief Land Settlement and Reallocation Authority), IVb-Gen. III, Bd. 1/98, signed p.p. Müller-Haccius,[2] Graz, to the Reich Minister of Food and Agriculture[3] (received on 28 January 1941), dated 21 January 1941[4]

Re: utilization of Jewish agricultural landholdings.
Case file: Decree of 28 Oct. 1940 – VIII B 2-14313/40.[5]
Enclosures: 1 list, 1 complete overview
Report prepared by: Regierungsrat *Leonhardt*[6]
I am sending you enclosed the overview of the Aryanized landholdings, current as of 1 January 1941. Of the total of the approximately 10,035 hectares of Jewish agricultural landholdings in the Reichsgau of Styria, about 7,802 hectares were de-Jewified up to

6 At the request of the St Raphael Society, Pope Pius XII had obtained from the Brazilian president 3,000 entry visas for Catholic-baptized non-Aryans. Brazil initially demanded a baptism certificate dating from before 1933, but it subsequently relaxed this rule. The rescue operation, however, began to falter when the first group of emigrants arrived in South America in May 1940 and it was discovered that most had only been baptized in 1939.

7 'Message de Noël du pape Pie XII', published in Pierre Blet et al. (eds.), *Actes et documents du Saints Siège relatifs à la Seconde Guerre mondiale: Le Saint Siège et la guerre en Europe, juin 1940 – juin 1941*, vol. 4 (Vatican City: Vaticana, 1967), pp. 307–313.

8 On 6 Feb. 1941 Innitzer received a reply from Cardinal Maglione, stating that since the introduction of the racist policies of National Socialism the Holy See had been seeking to alleviate the suffering of non-Aryan Catholics through, among other means, Catholic aid committees in Europe and America. He also stated that everything was being done to facilitate the emigration of 2,000 of the total of 3,000 non-Aryan Catholics who were to receive a Brazilian visa and to set aside a portion of the visas for non-Aryan Viennese Catholics: Blet et al., *Actes et documents*, vol. 8, pp. 92–94.

1 BArch, 3601/3267, fols. 286–287. This document has been translated from German.

1 January. The remaining 2,233 hectares are predominantly owned by Jews of foreign nationality.

Complete overview of the Aryanization of agricultural landholding pursuant to the regulation of 3 December 1938 (*Reichsgesetzblatt*, I, p. 206)[7]

District	Total area of agricultural landholdings (a) In Jewish ownership		(b) of which transferred to Aryan ownership		Percentage of Aryanized landholdings (col. 4) from the Jewish landholdings (col. 3)		Comments
	Total number	Area (ha)	Total number	Area (ha)	Total number	Area (ha)	
2	3		4		5		6
Bruck a/Mur	1	32	1	32	100	100	
Feldbach	2	21	1	7	50	33.3	
Fürstenfeld	5	729	2	472	40	65	
Graz-Land	9	209	4	195	44	94	
Wartberg	2	550	2	550	100	100	
Budenburg	4	5,086	3	4,038	75	80	
Leibnitz	5	153	2	10	40	0.6	
Leoben	1	18	1	18	100	100	
Wiezen	2	448	2	448	100	100	
Mürzzuschlag	9	1,541	5	1,120	55	73	
Oberwart	12	1,104	5	887	42	80	
Reiz	2	144	1	25	50	17	
Total amount in the district of the Chief Land Settlement Authority in the Reichsgau of Styria	54	approx. 10,035	29	approx. 7,802	approx. 54	approx. 78	

2 Dr Otto Müller-Haccius (1895–1988), lawyer, joined the NSDAP in 1933 and the SS in 1940; Regierungspräsident in Graz, 1939–1944; honorary professor in Graz, 1940; Oberpräsident in Silesia, 1944–1945; managing director of the Hanover Chamber of Industry and Commerce from 1949; CDU member of the Lower Saxony state parliament, 1963–1967 and 1970.

3 Richard Walther Darré.

4 The original contains handwritten notes; the first column of the table is illegible.

5 The Reich Ministry of Food and Agriculture (RMEuL) had instructed the Senior Settlement Authorities to prepare a detailed overview of the Aryanized landholdings as of 1 Jan. 1941 and then to submit additions and revisions every six months: decree issued by the RMEuL on 28 Oct. 1940, BArch, 3601/3267, fol. 3.

6 Dr Herbert Leonhardt (b. 1902), lawyer.

7 This is a reference to the Regulation on the Utilization of Jewish Assets, 3 Dec. 1938: *Reichsgesetzblatt*, 1938, I, pp. 1709–1712; see also PMJ 2/193. The regulation is published as no. 206, which explains the incorrect page reference in the original.

DOC. 138
On 21 January 1941 the SD's advisor on Jewish affairs in France notes that Reinhard Heydrich has developed, on Hitler's orders, a project for a 'definitive solution' to the Jewish question[1]

Memorandum by Theodor Dannecker, dated 21 January 1941 (copy)

'Central Office for Jewish Affairs' in Paris.

1. In accordance with the will of the Führer, the Jewish question within that part of *Europe* ruled over or controlled by Germany is to be brought to a definitive solution after the war.

The Chief of the Security Police and the SD[2] has already received from the Führer, via the Reichsführer SS or the Reich Marshal,[3] the assignment to submit a project for a final solution.[4] Owing to the extensive experience available at the offices of the *OdS*[5] and the SD and as a result of the preparatory work carried out over a considerable period, the essential elements of the project have already been defined. It has been submitted to the Führer and the Reich Marshal. The implementation will certainly be a mammoth task, the success of which can only be guaranteed through the most careful preparations. These must apply both to the work preceding the complete deportation of the Jews and to the meticulous planning of a settlement operation in the territory which is yet to be determined.

2. From the introductory description the enormous task imposed upon the office handling the Jews, initially in the occupied area of France but likewise in the other occupied parts of Europe, is self-evident: the visible identification of the Jews and their extraction from all spheres of life and all affairs of the state, followed by centrally controlled *administration of the Jews* and their property right up to deportation. Occupational restructing must be carried out in addition.

3. As many past examples have sufficiently shown, such a task can only be accomplished if there is a central leadership on hand to manage it.

In view of the conditions in France, which I assume to be well known, the task can only be accomplished if such central leadership takes up its goal-orientated work *as swiftly as possible*, consolidating all human resources in the process.

4. Before I explain the actual project of a 'Central Office for Jewish Affairs' in more detail, I would like to briefly elaborate on the present conditions. The Chief of the Military Administration in France[6] has, to a certain extent, laid the groundwork for the

1 CDJC, V-59; published as a facsimile in Serge Klarsfeld (ed.), *Recueil de documents des dossiers des autorités allemandes concernant la persécution de la population juive en France (1940–1944), de juin 1940 au 31 décembre 1941*, vol. 1 (Paris/New York: CDJC/Klarsfeld Foundation, 1979), unpaginated. This document has been translated from German.

2 Reinhard Heydrich.

3 Hermann Göring.

4 The text of the assignment has not survived.

5 Oberbefehlshaber der Sicherheitspolizei: Senior Commander of the Security Police.

6 General Alfred Streccius (1874–1944) had been appointed chief of the military administration in France in late June 1940, shortly after the armistice. On 25 Oct. 1940 General Otto von Stülpnagel (1878–1948) succeeded him as military commander in France.

launch of the anti-Jewish exclusion operation[7] by means of the directives against Jews which he has issued so far. It has become apparent, however, that the French authorities only adhere to the letter of the law – and, incidentally, even do that poorly! – and have no political understanding whatsoever of the necessity of a general cleansing. It is similar to the drama surrounding the implementation of the so-called Vichy Statute on Jews of 4 October 1940.[8]

No matter what sphere of life one observes, one always comes to the same conclusion, namely that one is dealing with decentralized, painstaking work. It should be evident that clearly targeted anti-Jewish propaganda is not possible under these circumstances.

It has therefore become an urgent necessity to establish the Central Office for Jewish Affairs, because otherwise a situation will occur where the day for actually carrying out the Jewish deportation will arrive and we will be faced with a nearly insurmountable task.

5. *Establishment and function of the Central Office for Jewish Affairs*

A previously untested combination of the various offices and components is necessary to address the problem. The following departments are planned:

(a) File registry, information provision, investigation (the special division for Jewish affairs at the Paris police headquarters, which has already started operations under our supervision, will be incorporated into this department!).

(b) Administration of all Jewish assets and handling of economic questions relating to Jews. (The 'Office du Controle des Administration provisoires', which also already exists, should be involved here.[9])

(c) 'Jewish Concentration Camp Affairs', on the basis of the law adopted by the French government on 4 October 1940, according to which Jews of foreign origin can initially be interned in special concentration camps.[10]

(d) Supervision of the work of the 'Compulsory Jewish Association', which has already essentially been established as an association that can be held accountable for all Jews,

7 Under the direction of Werner Best (1903–1989) in his function as chief of the civil administration under the military commander in France, in Sept./Oct. 1940, the military administration ordered, among other things, the registration of the Jewish population, the recording of their property, the labelling of all Jewish shops, and the registration of Jewish-owned businesses: Regulations on Measures against the Jews, 27 Sept. 1940 and 18 Oct. 1940, *Verordnungsblatt für die besetzten französischen Gebiete*, no. 9, 30 Sept. 1940, and no. 12, 20 Oct. 1940; see also the Introduction to PMJ 5.

8 The Statute on Jews (*Loi portant statut des juifs*), which was enacted by the Vichy government on 3 Oct. 1940 and based on the Nuremberg racial laws, defined who was deemed to be a Jew. The legislation also mandated the exclusion of Jews from public service, the armed forces, and numerous professions, as well as from radio, cinema, and journalism: 'Loi portant statut des juifs', 3 Oct. 1940, *Journal officiel*, 18 Oct. 1940, p. 5323.

9 This is a reference to the Service de Contrôle des Administrateurs Provisoires (SCAP), which was instituted in Dec. 1940. This office, which was initially attached to the Ministry of Industrial Production, had the role of overseeing the 'temporary administrators' who were tasked with the Aryanization of Jewish-owned businesses. Following the proposal by Dannecker, in June 1941 the SCAP was incorporated into the newly established Commissariat General for Jewish Affairs (Commissariat général aux questions juives). See fn. 14.

10 Pursuant to the law enacted by the Vichy government on 4 Oct. 1940, Jews of foreign nationality could be interned in concentration camps for no specific reason: 'Loi sur les ressortissants étrangers de race juive', *Journal officiel*, 18 Oct. 1940, p. 5324.

and which is also under our supervision.[11] (Also responsible for the redeployment operation!)
(e) Jews in the different spheres of life. In this respect the department will also be charged with *monitoring the implementation of the French Statute on Jews* of 4 October 1940.[12]
(f) Supervising the exclusively French Institute for the Study of Jewish Influence, which is also in the process of being established to serve as leverage against the French authorities and which is absolutely necessary in order to grasp the nature of the Jews and their influence.[13]
(g) Steering of anti-Jewish propaganda in line with the fundamental principles contained within the framework of the overall plan, which, in turn, ensue from the general activities of the 'Office for Jewish Affairs'. The office will be under French leadership.
This office must be in charge of administrative supervision,[14] in accordance with the tasks assigned to the Reichsführer SS/Chief of the Security Police and the SD[15] concerning the treatment of the Jews in Europe, and pursuant to the secret decree issued by the Wehrmacht High Command on 4 October 1940,[16] which, among other matters, transfers the responsibility of handling Jewish affairs to the representative of the Chief of the Security Police and the SD for Belgium and France.

11 The Union générale des Israélites de France (UGIF), which consolidated all Jewish organizations in France into a single administrative body, was established in its final form on 29 Nov. 1941.
12 Correctly: 3 Oct. 1940: see fn. 8.
13 At the behest of the Reich Minister of Public Enlightenment and Propaganda, the Institut d'étude des questions juives was founded on 11 May 1941 with the support of the German Propaganda Squad. The institute produced antisemitic brochures, organized conferences on the 'Jewish question', and published the newspaper *Le Cahier Jaune*.
14 In line with Dannecker's proposals, a Commissariat General for Jewish Affairs was established in March 1941. The commissariat was tasked with coordinating anti-Jewish measures in both occupied and non-occupied France. Xavier Vallat (1891–1972) was appointed its first director. A draft document on the establishment of a Central Office for Jewish Affairs is enclosed in the memorandum: CDJC, V-59.
15 As in the original. Himmler was the Reichsführer SS and Chief of the German Police and Heydrich was the Chief of the Security Police and the SD.
16 Decree of the Military Intelligence (Abwehr) of the Wehrmacht High Command, 4 Oct. 1940, concerning the deployment of the Security Police in the occupied territories: BArch, B 162/Vorl. AR-Z 18/61, Anl. 5, Handakten Bd. 10, fols. 26–27.

DOC. 139

On 23 January 1941 Max Schönenberg from Cologne writes to an acquaintance in the United States to ask for assistance in emigrating[1]

Letter from Dr Max Schönenberg, 23 Venloerstraße, Cologne, unsigned, to Mr Hirsch, dated 23 January 1941 (copy)[2]

Dear Mr Hirsch,

We hope that you and your family are well.

I do not know whether there is postal correspondence between you and Uncle Jacob and Aunt Evchen.[3] I am thus glad to avail myself of the opportunity to report on how they are faring.

Aunt is suffering more than ever. She has – day and night – a great deal of worry and work in caring for her husband. For Uncle Jacob has developed chronic intestinal trouble, which causes him – and her – many a fitful night due to colic attacks. After the attacks have subsided, Uncle is soon back in good form, while Aunt pays for the disturbances with physical and nervous ailments. Heddy[4] is employed in an office and cannot be there for them as much as before.

But this letter has, of course, another purpose.

Four years ago we asked you to take our son.[5] For understandable reasons you decided not to assume responsibility for a lad who had only recently grown out of childhood.

Since we already knew at that time that it would be impossible to subject a growing young man to the emotional strain caused by the local atmosphere here, we took him to Palestine, the only place at the time that was willing to accept him. As a result, the decision had been made for us too. Palestine would also have to be our future hope. In 1938, while we were preparing for the move, the doors there closed.[6] We had one less hope. Right around that time we discovered a distant – a very distant – relative in the United States. We contacted him and asked for assistance with our immigration. Back then, we could still have financed it with our own resources. The relative's sponsorship only needed to be a formal one. He went along with this. In the meantime, the situation, as you know, has changed fundamentally. Today, passage has to be paid in *foreign* currency, and on top of that, the American immigration authorities require one's means of subsistence to be fully guaranteed for several years. Our sponsor is evidently unable, or perhaps

1 NS-Dokumentationszentrum Köln, Briefe Max Schönenberg, record group 46. Excerpts printed in Rüther, *Köln im Zweiten Weltkrieg*, pp. 543–545. This document has been translated from German.

2 In the top-left margin is the handwritten note: 'From Dr Schönenberg, Cologne, to Dr Kaufmann, Shanghai.' Max Schönenberg sent this unsigned copy of the letter to his brother-in-law Julius in Shanghai.

3 Eva Leiser in Brussels.

4 Probably Hedwig Ehrlich, née Pels (1897–1942). Ehrlich was deported on 20 July 1942 to Minsk, where she was murdered.

5 Leopold Schönenberg (1920–2011), also known as Reuwen Schonenberg, emigrated in 1937 to Palestine, where he began an apprenticeship as a locksmith; later worked as a warehouse clerk for a construction company; lived in the suburb of Kiryat Haim in northern Haifa.

6 Jewish immigration into Palestine was in fact restricted by the British Mandate government in May of the following year: see Doc. 120, fn. 20.

unwilling, to do this. I cannot expect him to have familial feelings. His grandfather, who emigrated to America 105 years ago, was the brother of my mother-in-law's father. So it is not a very close connection there. We have, though, no familial connections whatsoever with you. And yet I intend – as you have realized by now – to appeal to you.

What gives me the courage to do this is our knowledge of your frequent acts of helpfulness and generosity. It gives us the hope that you will not heedlessly set aside our request. This hope is reinforced by the fact that we are at least not complete strangers. In her early years, your wife was connected by friendship to my wife[7] through Aunt Evchen. Your wife will verify that my mother-in-law and my wife are upright and worthy people. I believe I can say that I have held my own in life. And the friendship that Aunt Evchen and Uncle Jacob have always shown me does not, anyhow, speak against me. It takes courage to put to you a major request such as the one we have in mind. In normal times I would understand if you regarded this 'courage' as an 'impertinence' and left the request unheeded. But these are not normal times. The news of there no longer being any place for Jews in the German Reich must even have made its way across the ocean. The solution to the Jewish question in Germany is being, and will be, implemented uncompromisingly by the National Socialists with the same vigour and sense of purpose that is observable in everything they do. I do not need to prove this sentence to you.

[…][8]

It goes without saying that we would try to keep that sacrifice that we shall ask you to make as small as possible. We would exert all of our energy to find work and start earning a living in the United States as quickly as possible in order to draw as little as possible on the funds put at our disposal. We would strive to repay the expenses necessary for the crossing and the initial set-up. I can honestly promise only our good intentions. You can trust that we will uphold this promise as a debt of honour. My wife has already been learning dressmaking for a long time. Since I used to be a doctor, I can work as a nurse right away. I will also not shy away from taking on other work if it has prospects for success. I cannot initially allow myself to indulge in the dream of becoming a doctor again there, because this would require approximately two years of preparations, during which time I would not be able to earn my subsistence.

You will now want to know the extent of our wishes. The following figures are based on information from the local relief committee. According to this, we will need … US dollars for the crossing including the necessary baggage and … dollars[9] for ensuring the means of subsistence. The amount cited is greater than what is actually needed. But the American consulate requires a guarantee regarding these funds so that the immigrant does not become a burden on the American public in the event of unemployment.

It has not been easy for me, dear Mr Hirsch, to make this significant request of you. Up to now I have always been able to satisfy my pecuniary needs – and more – through my own efforts. But you understand that the tumultuous events of the last decade have created different conditions and different standards.

7 Erna Schönenberg.
8 A paragraph has been blacked out and is illegible.
9 The original contains blank spaces.

The fate of three people lies in your hands. We have confidence in you that you can and will assist us. Have confidence in us that your assistance will not be met with ingratitude.

My mother-in-law, my wife, and I send you and your wife best regards.

Yours,

DOC. 140

On 27 January 1941 the board of the Reich Association of Jews in Germany discusses assistance for non-Aryan Christians and the transfer of Jewish psychiatric patients to assembly centres[1]

Minutes of the board meeting of the Reich Association of Jews in Germany (I/Dr. Berl/Kl.), signed Dr Berliner,[2] 158 Kantstraße, Berlin-Charlottenburg, dated 27 January 1941[3]

1. Retired higher regional court judge Berthold Israel *Lehmann*,[4] who is already one of the assessors on the higher arbitration board, was appointed deputy chairman of the [same] arbitration board.
2. The community board ordered the head of the Hebrew school in Berlin, Mr *Baum*, to step down from his post, because his Aryan wife, who converted to Judaism at the time of their marriage, has now left the Jewish faith. A complaint from Baum addressed to the Reich Association concerning this matter was rejected.
3. Dr Eppstein is developing an education programme for extracurricular educational work with special emphasis on vocational training and occupational restructuring facilities, which is to be implemented on the basis of the guidelines adopted by the board. Under consideration of the outcome of the very extensive debate, Dr Eppstein was instructed to submit draft guidelines to the board.[5]
4. The Jewish Religious Association of *Hamburg*[6] was asked to remove the shipping containers in storage at the Hamburg Free Port from 700 persons who are still in Germany, and the approximately 5,000 packing cases from Jews who have already emigrated. It was decided to first contact the Reich Security Main Office in order to ensure that the Reich Association is informed of planned sales and is entitled to directly purchase

1 BArch, R 8150/2, fol. 67r–v. This document has been translated from German.
2 Dr Cora Berliner (1890–1942), economist; specialist for consumer protection in the Reich Ministry of Economics, 1919; Regierungsrat in the Reich Statistical Office, 1923; professor at Berlin's State Vocational Training Institute, 1930–1933; member of the board of the Reich Association of Jews in Germany, 1933–1942; deported to Minsk in June 1942, after which her whereabouts became unknown. It is unclear why Cora Berliner was listed as 'missing' on the list of inmates.
3 Present at the meeting were Dr Baeck (chairman), Dr Cohn, Dr Eppstein, Henschel, Dr Hirsch, Kozower, and Dr Lilienthal. Not in attendance were Dr Seligsohn, Dr Berliner, Brasch, Dr Fuchs, Fürst, Karminski, Löwenstein, Lyon, and Meyerheim
4 Berthold Lehmann (b. 1876), lawyer; higher regional court judge in Berlin; dismissed from his post in 1935; deported to Auschwitz in Jan. 1943; his further fate is unknown.
5 This document could not be located.
6 The Jewish Religious Association of Hamburg was established in 1937 from the merger of Ashkenazi communities; Dr Max Plaut was its director from 1938 to 1942. The organization was incorporated into the Reich Association of Jews in Germany at the end of 1942.

the textiles and leather goods in the packing cases, so as to stock up the Jewish clothing depots.[7]

5. The following decisions were made regarding assistance given to the Protestant members of the Reich Association by the Pastor *Grüber* Office:[8]

Emigration counselling will be provided forthwith by the Reich Association's Emigration Department, whereby the question of taking over the staff of the Pastor Grüber Office is still to be negotiated. Welfare assistance will be provided by the welfare offices of the Jewish religious congregations, but if necessary volunteer workers are to be recruited from this group of persons to carry out enquiries, pastoral care, and collection activities among the non-Aryan Christians.

6. A report was given on the transfer of mentally ill Jews to assembly centres and institutions of the General Government.[9] On the basis of the decree issued on 12 December 1940, the *Sayn*[10] Jewish psychiatric hospital has sole responsibility for mentally ill Jews who were admitted to psychiatric hospitals after 1 October 1940 or who are now newly admitted. An expansion of *Sayn* Jewish psychiatric hospital by setting up barracks is under consideration. Furthermore, invalids who were accommodated in psychiatric hospitals before 1 October are to be transferred, wherever possible, to the lunatic asylums, hospices, and old people's homes of the Reich Association.

DOC. 141
On 27 January 1941 Jan Springel is shot dead in Buchenwald[1]

Letter from the camp physician at Buchenwald concentration camp,[2] unsigned, to the commandant's office at Buchenwald concentration camp, dated 27 January 1941

Re: death of the prisoner (K.-Jud. 531.) Jan *Springel*[3]
born on 17 March 1915 in Zawiercie,
died on 27 January 1941, 10:30 a.m.

On 27 January 1941, at 10:30 a.m., the prisoner *Jan Springel* was shot dead after mounting violent resistance. The prisoner was hit by two pistol shots.

7 Some of the shipping containers at the Port of Hamburg were destroyed by air raids; others were confiscated by the Gestapo. The contents were auctioned.

8 The Grüber Office had been placed under Eichmann's supervision in 1939 and closed down in 1940. Between 1938 and 1940 it helped facilitate the emigration of more than 1,000 Jews who had converted to Christianity and their families: see also Doc. 47 and PMJ 2/267.

9 The alleged transfer of Jewish invalids to institutions of the General Government was only a cover-up; the invalids were murdered in the Reich. See Doc. 173 and Introduction, pp. 33–34.

10 Correctly: Bendorf-Sayn: see Doc. 127.

1 IPN, Sammlung KZ Buchenwald; copy in BwA, HKW 31, fol. 2, film 13 a. Reproduced as a facsimile in Stein, *Juden in Buchenwald*, p. 79. This document has been translated from German.

2 Dr Waldemar Hoven (1903–1948) and Dr Erich Wagner (1912–1959) were the camp physicians, 1939–1943 and 1939–1941, respectively. An assistant physician or a medical orderly probably drafted the letter.

3 Jan Springel (1915–1941), also known as Jona Szpringier, had been imprisoned in Buchenwald since 7 Nov. 1940.

1st entry wound: left side of the chest, 7 cm from the sternal line in the mammary gland region, 4 cm below the nipple. Exit wound: on the back near the scapular line, at the level of the costal margin of the eleventh rib.

2nd entry wound: left side of the chest, 1 cm to the left of the sternal line. Exit wound: 1 cm to the left of the scapular line, at the level of the first vertebra.

The cause of death was injury to the heart and lung inflicted by the first shot.

A traumatic force other than the aforementioned one can be ruled out definitively.

DOC. 142

On 30 January 1941 Hitler recalls his prophecy that in the event of a world war, European Jewry would be annihilated[1]

Excerpt from Adolf Hitler's speech at the Berlin Sportpalast on 30 January 1941 to mark the eighth anniversary of the National Socialists coming to power[2]

[…][3]

The year 1941 will be, I am convinced, the historic year of a great New Order in Europe! The aim can be no other than to make the world accessible to all, to break the privileges of the few, to break the tyranny of certain peoples, and, better still, their financial ruling powers. And this year will finally help us to truly secure the foundations for international understanding and a reconciliation of peoples at last!

I also do not wish to omit reference to the statement I have already made on one occasion, on 1 September 1939 in the German Reichstag, namely that if Jewry really thrusts the rest of the world into a general war, the role of Jewry in Europe will have been played out![4] They might still laugh at this today, just as they previously laughed at my domestic prophecies. The coming months and years will go to show that I was also right with this prophecy. But we can already see how our knowledge of race is capturing one nation after another, and I also hope that those peoples still standing against us as enemies today will one day recognize their bigger enemy within and form a large united front with us: the front of Aryan humankind against the international Jewish exploitation and the perversion of peoples!

This year, which came to an end on 30 January, was the year of the greatest successes, but also of many sacrifices. Even if the total number of dead and wounded is small compared to all previous wars, the sacrifice for every single family affected is nonetheless a heavy loss. We owe all of our devotion, our love, and our care to those who had to

1 DRA, 2 623 108. A heavily edited version was printed in the *Völkischer Beobachter* (northern German edition), 1 Feb. 1941, pp. 1–2, 4, and 7–8, here p. 8. This document has been translated from German.

2 The text is from the sound recording of the speech; total length of the speech: 95 minutes, 49 seconds.

3 In the first part of the speech Hitler talks about the origins of the National Socialist Movement, overcoming the Treaty of Versailles, and the causes of the Second World War. He furthermore warns the USA not to intervene in the war in Europe and stresses that the outcome of the war has already been decided in favour of the German Reich.

4 Hitler gave this speech on 30 Jan. 1939: see PMJ 2/248.

make these sacrifices. They have suffered that which generations before us also had to suffer. Yet every single German has also had to make sacrifices in other respects. The nation has toiled in every domain; in particular it is German women who have worked hard to substitute our menfolk.

Our people are filled with a wonderful sense of community! Our wish for today is that this spirit will stay with us in the coming year with all its strength. Let us vow to work for this community! We have faith and confidence that in serving this community we will achieve victory! And we pray that God will not forsake us in this struggle over the coming year! Deutschland Sieg Heil![5]

DOC. 143
In late January 1941 Elisabeth Butenberg from Rheydt is irritated by the conduct of Jews on the tram and submits suggestions for action to the head of the local NSDAP branch[1]

Letter from Mrs Butenberg[2] to Party Comrade Engels, head of the local NSDAP branch, Ludwig Knickmann local branch, Rheydt (received on 28 January 1941), dated January 1941 (copy)[3]

The Jewish question can only be solved if every German makes the task his *own*. In my opinion, what is required is that all activities in this regard should be absolute and radical. If, for example, it is still possible for a Jew to sit next to a German person on the *tram*, to rub up against him, or, as often happens to my daughter[4] and her friends who travel to the women's school in M[ünchen] Gladbach,[5] passengers are virtually undressed by the shamelessly lecherous looks of a Jewish layabout,[6] I regard all of this as an intolerable state of affairs for a racially aware German person. I therefore propose the following:

(1) separate 'compartments for Jews' are set up on the Reich Railways,
(2) Jews are to remain restricted to the front platform of the tram trailer,
(3) the use of trams without a trailer is hence forbidden to Jews.

I would be much obliged if you would put this proposal into practice at an opportune moment.[7]

Heil Hitler

5 Cries of 'Sieg Heil' follow, with a closing statement by Joseph Goebbels.

1 LAV NRW R, RW 58/14774. This document has been translated from German.
2 Probably Elisabeth Butenberg, née Gelling (1895–1944), housewife; married to procurator Franz Butenberg; moved to Dehrn, in the district of Limburg an der Lahn, in March 1942.
3 The original contains notes by the Düsseldorf Gestapo.
4 Ingeborg Butenberg (b. 1922).
5 Now Mönchengladbach in the German federal state of North Rhine-Westphalia.
6 Under this paragraph is a handwritten note: 'This concerns the Jew Jakob Schwalb, Rheydt, Hindenburgwall, born 20 Oct. 1880.' In Dec. 1941 Jakob Schwalb (1880–1942) was deported from Düsseldorf to Riga, where he perished.
7 Since Dec. 1938 Jews had been banned from using sleeping carriages and dining cars of the Reich Railways; there were no plans to introduce special compartments for Jews: see PMJ 2/215. For the discussion and implementation of a ban on Jews using public transport, see Docs. 158 and 222.

DOC. 144

On 2 February 1941 the Gestapo informs the head of the Israelite Religious Community of the impending deportation of Viennese Jews to the General Government[1]

File note, II-2.e, unsigned, regarding the visit by the head of the Israelite Religious Community of Vienna[2] to the Gestapo to see Regierungsrat Dr Ebner, with SS-Obersturmführer Brunner in attendance, on 1 February 1941, 12 noon, dated 2 February 1941

Regierungsrat *Dr Ebner* informed me of the following and issued me the instructions below:
(1) It is planned to resettle a portion of the Jews living in Vienna to the General Government. The Religious Community is to be kept out of this operation; its only task will be to carry out the instructions issued to it. Approximately 1,000 persons are to be sent away on each transport. The first transport will leave on 15 February, the second on 19 February 1941, and the subsequent ones on the Wednesday of every following week. The time has yet to be announced. The dispatch terminal will probably be Aspang Station.[3] The intention is to relocate 10,000 Jews to the General Government by May 1941. The Jews will be settled in small district towns in the Government. The names of these towns cannot be made known at this time.
(2) The registration of the Jews under consideration for assignment to the individual transports and the conduct of these transports are the responsibility of the Central Office for Jewish Emigration in accordance with the instructions issued to it by higher authority. Each emigrant can take along two suitcases or two bundles weighing no more than 50 kg. In particular, provisions must be made to ensure that each emigrant takes with him two good blankets and a second pair of shoes. On that score, the Religious Community should see to it that Jews who have more shoes will each make a pair available to the emigrants.
(3) The building at 35 Castellezgasse, II,[4] is designated as the assembly point for the emigrants. The Religious Community must vacate this building as soon as possible and remove all the furniture and fittings.[5] The abandoned telephone subscriber station in this building must be reported to the telephone exchange, with reference to the instructions from the Central Office for Jewish Emigration.
(4) The emigration of Jews to various countries overseas is continuing and must still be carried out by the Religious Community. Emigration to Yugoslavia is ruled out.

1 DÖW, 2562. Excerpts published in Adler, *Der verwaltete Mensch*, pp. 148–149. This document has been translated from German.
2 Josef Löwenherz.
3 Between Oct. 1939 and Oct. 1942, more than 50,000 Austrian Jews were deported from Vienna's Aspang Station to the ghettos and concentration camps in the eastern part of Europe.
4 Here and below, the writer is referring to Vienna's second municipal district, known as Leopoldstadt.
5 From 1923 the building at 35 Castellezgasse made its premises available to the Jewish Private Grammar School (*Gymnasium*), which from 1927 was known as the Chayes Grammar School. The primary school of the Jewish Religious Community was set up here for the 1935–1936 school year.

(5) The Central Office for Jewish Emigration in Vienna selects by family the persons who are to be designated for resettlement to the General Government. The persons designated for the transport concerned must lock their apartment, after which it will be sealed by the Gestapo. The apartment keys are to be handed in to the state bodies located in the building at 35 Castellezgasse, II. A cardboard tag must be attached to each apartment key. The apartment, the name of the apartment owner, and his date of birth must be clearly written on the tag. Each emigrant must take his food ration coupons to the building on Castellezgasse, II, and hand them in there. Cash may be taken along in unlimited amounts.[6] A Reichsbank official in the building at 35 Castellezgasse, II will exchange the Reichsmarks taken along by each person for zloty.
(6) Each Jew designated for emigration must compile and submit an accurate list of his assets, rights, and claims, and give the name and address of the current asset manager, so that the Gestapo can gift all these assets and settle up with the asset manager. The proceeds from the sale of these assets are intended to cover the costs of resettlement and emigration, as well as the definitive solution of the Jewish problem. It is not yet certain whether the assets will be gifted to one of the existing funds or one to be newly set up as a legal entity.
(7) The Religious Community must provide meals for those Jews who are designated for the transport and housed in the building at 35 Castellezgasse, II, until its departure. The expenses associated with these meals and with administration are to be managed separately. The Religious Community will receive separate contributions for this purpose from the Central Office for Jewish Emigration. The latter authority will also provide the ration coupons required for the meals, as well as the ration coupons for the food supplies to be taken on the journey, which must suffice for four days. Those Jews who are to be deported must be informed by the Religious Community that they should put their travel provisions away safely in a separate bag or in a small valise.

A practitioner for the sick[7] selected by the Central Office for Jewish Emigration will be assigned to each transport. This person may take along, in addition to the generally authorized luggage weighing 50 kg, the instruments and medications essential for the practice of his profession. Medical service in the building at 35 Castellezgasse, II, is to be provided by *Dr Biller*, the practitioner for the sick at the hospital of the Religious Community. If the Jews do not voluntarily comply with the summons of the Central Office for Jewish Emigration, orders will be given for them to be brought in by police authorities. In addition, these Jews must expect tougher measures.
(8) Three or four days before the departure of each transport the Religious Community will receive the lists of the Jews designated for this transport, so that they can be made aware of the orders issued. The orders issued to the Religious Community are to be combined in a pamphlet and handed out to the persons concerned.

From 1941 to 1945 the building served as an assembly camp for the Jews designated for deportation. From 1983 to 2008, it belonged to the Zwi Perez Chayes School, which reopened in 1980. Today it is a residential building.

6 The amount of money permitted was soon set at a maximum of 10 Reichsmarks.

7 *Krankenbehandler*: one of a small number of Jewish physicians who were allowed to treat Jewish patients after Jewish physicians lost their licence to practise medicine with effect from 30 September 1938.

(9) A prohibition is being issued to the Jews, forbidding them to leave Vienna without the express consent of the Central Office for Jewish Emigration. The Central Office for Jewish Emigration will issue additional certificates to Jews who are emigrating to other countries or travelling by order of the authorities.
(10) The Religious Community must compile a list of the Jews it is supporting and present it successively to the Central Office for Jewish Emigration. This list is to include Jews who receive free food supplies and, in addition, financial subsidies for rent, medical care, etc. The list must be drawn up by family, specifically in such a way that the family provider is named first and then the wife and children, with the exact address given.
(11) The younger persons designated for the transport should be instructed to help the elderly during the transport.
(12) The salaried employees of the Religious Community and their auxiliaries[8] whose services are required will be exempted from assignment to the transports.
(13) The occupational restructuring courses for adults and young people must be shut down at once. The teachers in the school at 35 Castellezgasse, II, who are no longer required, must be dismissed, as well as the retraining personnel.

DOC. 145

On 3 February 1941 Kurt Mezei notes in his diary that summonses for deportation have already been sent to Viennese Jews[1]

Handwritten diary of Kurt Mezei,[2] Vienna, entry for 3 February 1941

Monday, 3 February 1941
Events:
[I] have been lying in bed with a mild fever all day. The Polish operation has reached its climax. The first shipments have already been sent off![3]

Something dreadful has happened! The 'retraining' has – for what reason? – been shut down as of the 7th of this month.[4] What shall I do? It is terrible!

Thoughts:
What is happening with retraining is really awful! I heard hints as early as Sunday, but did not believe it. Now it has been officially confirmed today.

8 *Anstalter*: the term applied to the support staff of the salaried employees.

1 Jüdisches Museum Wien, Inv. No. 4465/3, Tagebuch von Kurt Mezei, Heft 1. This document has been translated from German.

2 Kurz Mezei (1924–1945), schoolboy; along with his twin sister, Ilse (1924–1945), attended the Chayes Grammar School (Gymnasium) in Vienna until it was closed down in Oct. 1938; took part in vocational retraining courses offered by the Israelite Religious Community (IKG); in 1940–1941 worked as an electrician and as an IKG messenger; transferred on 15 Oct. 1941 to 'Room 8', where he had to help with the administrative preparations for the deportations; shot by an SS unit on 12 April 1945. His sister had died previously in a bombing raid.

3 On the deportations of Viennese Jews to the General Government in the spring of 1941, see Docs. 144, 150, 151, and Introduction, pp. 39–40.

4 The retraining courses were discontinued in connection with the deportations: see Doc. 144.

DOC. 146

Völkischer Beobachter, 4 February 1941: article on the exclusion of Jews from the economy[1]

The de-Jewification of Europe

In the aftermath of the smoothly accomplished de-Jewification process in Germany, followed abroad with amazement and admiration, one European country after another addressed the Jewish question. The German model unleashed latent forces long at work in wide sections of Europe, particularly in its south-eastern part, and led to direct action on the part of the state leadership, or at least forced the government to concern itself in greater depth with the Jewish problem. However, comprehensive regulation has thus far not been introduced in any other country. It must not go unrecognized now that the elimination of Jewry is a *political measure* of the first order.

Certainly, Jewish influence was particularly obvious in the economy, but the dominant Jewish position in the press, the theatre and film industry, art and literature, as well as among lawyers, physicians, and pharmacists, was no less significant for völkisch life. The powerful position of Jewry was indeed based on the subtle, frequently disguised holding of decisive positions in business and industry, the cultural sphere, the legal system, and also the apparatus of the state – here the Jews mostly and preferably played the roles of *éminences grises*. Isolated measures in one area of völkisch life, therefore, can do just as little to solve the central problem as partial regulations in several or all areas. A complete purification and final völkisch liberation can be brought about only by the *elimination of all Jews*. The fact that the Jewish question can thereby be viewed and solved only in racial terms seems self-evident, on the basis of our experience. Unless all the signs are deceptive, the year 1941 will be characterized by the utter elimination of the Jews in the European economic area and will thus bring about the final breakthrough of all the völkisch forces.

There are three reasons motivating this opinion:

1. The economy of all European countries will increasingly be geared to the Axis powers. Germany is dominant by far in the foreign trade of all countries. The consequences of this situation for the development of the economic structure in other countries with regard to race are obvious. What German retailer and entrepreneur can still be expected to negotiate with Jews? It is therefore quite logical that the exclusion of Jews from the import and export business of the south-east European countries is the most advanced.

2. In addition, a revolutionary transition in economic thinking is taking place in all the countries of continental Europe, more in some places, less in others, here still tentative, there with vehement elemental force. And everywhere, though the adherents and beneficiaries of the fading Jewish liberal system are resisting with all their might, they are still unable to hold back the course of history any longer.

1 'Entjudung Europas', *Völkischer Beobachter* (northern German edition), 4 Feb. 1941, p. 2. This article has been translated from German.

Everywhere, German economic ideas are gaining ground. But they automatically lead to an elimination of Jewry. For National Socialist economic doctrine is not a theory of Mammonism, nor is it a catechism for earning money. Rather, it is the doctrine of the purposeful incorporation of the economy into the total organism of the nation state. It is no longer 'value neutral' in a liberalistic sense, but rather consciously and emphatically dedicated to a purpose. It unites those methods of the Jewish liberal and Jewish Marxist economic 'scientists' who broke up the life of the people and the nation into a mechanistic series of exchanges and economic price and value ratios. It knows no stabilized contrast between capital and labour, propertied and propertyless, state and economy. The essence of the German notion of economics lies, rather, in the 'realization of the natural economy based on labour, output, and property' (Prof. Hunke).[2] The primacy of policy, public interest before vested interest, the Führer principle[3] and the achievement principle, maintaining the peasantry in particular, liberation of work from its capitalist bondage, and emphasis on its moral value are, rather, the cornerstones of the new national economy. In contrast to the omnipotence of capital, 'stabilized' by Jews, we offer the particular value placed on labour.

3. The unavoidable consequence of such a revolutionary upheaval in intellectual thought must be a complete restructuring of the economic system. We already see the contours of a new economy beginning to take shape in every country. Some randomly selected examples of this are the reconfiguration of the Yugoslav national bank, the management of livestock production in Hungary, the restriction placed on the administrative councils in Romania, the punishment of economic saboteurs, the compulsory exploitation of unprofitable bauxite deposits, rebuilding of the foreign trade organization, and also the law for protection of the national economy in Turkey. Step by step the Jews are retreating, they are losing one bastion after another, one country after another is ridding itself of them, and many are astonished at the absence of economic convulsions and the continued functioning of the economic processes of production and distribution. It is quite the reverse. When the artificially woven Jewish veil of money and capital was rent, the parasitic nature of the Jews was revealed. Because they are incapable of truly independent creative achievements, the Jews generally held only managerial positions in commerce, finance, and banking, on the stock exchange, in the fields of insurance and transport, and the like. Capable Aryans did the work and provided the ideas. Such creative people were available in every business and so no 'gaps' arose after the exclusion of the Jews.

The distribution of the Jews

Below is an overview of the number of Jews, by continent and country:

2 Heinrich Hunke, *Grundzüge der deutschen Volks- und Wehrwirtschaft* (Berlin: Haude & Spenersche, 1938). The work was published in several editions in the period up to 1945. Heinrich Hunke (1902–2000) was considered one of the leading National Socialist economic ideologues.

3 An autocratic method of governmental organization whereby all power was concentrated in the hands of Hitler as Führer and extended downwards through each level of the hierarchy.

Number of Jews by continent

	In 1,000s	In %		
	1937	1937	1900	1880
Europe	10,270	60.4	82.1	88.4
America	5,110	30.0	11.0	3.3
Asia	939	5.5	3.9	4.5
Africa	666	3.9	2.8	3.6
Australia	30	0.2	0.2	0.2
total:	17,015	100.0	100.0	100.0

Around three fifths of all Jews are accounted for by Europe: the Ostjuden between the Baltic and the Black Sea alone total 8 million, and thus make up the densest Jewish population. The *massive emigration to America* that has been noticeable since the turn of the century is striking. The United States, with 4.5 million Jews, has more Jews than any other country, and New York, with 2.5 million Jews, more Jews than any other city in the world. The following table indicates the number of Jews in individual countries. The number of Jews in the Nordic states is small. The censuses in 1930 and 1931 revealed fewer than 15,000 Jews for Denmark, Norway, and Sweden together, representing around 1 per cent of the population.

Number of Jews in individual countries

	Date of last census or calculation or estimate	Number of Jews in 1,000s	Jews as % of the host people
Europe	1937	10,270	1.95
Belgium	1937	80	0.96
Britain	1937	340	0.72
Bulgaria	1934	48.8	0.80
France	1937	280	0.67
Greece	1937	90	1.06
Italy	1937	52	0.12
Yugoslavia	1937	75	0.49
Netherlands	1937	135	1.58
Poland	1937	2,300	9.64
Romania	1930	985	5.41
Soviet Russia (Europ. part)	1937	2,950	2.22
Turkey (Europ. part)	1937	60	4.76
Hungary	1930	444.6	5.01

In assessing the data, however, one must not lose sight of the fact that all the numbers given represent *minimum rates*, because the statistical surveys recorded *only the Jews by faith*. The actual number of Jews present in Europe might be several million higher. The orders of magnitude that we might be dealing with here are shown by the example of Romania: instead of the number of 985,000 Jews (before the cessions of territory), calculations made by various parties came up with almost 2 million Jews! The subjective nature of previous Romanian population censuses – there were many Jews among the census-takers – accommodated the well-known concealment efforts of the Jews, who frequently referred to themselves as Russians, Hungarians, or Romanians to make their population size and influence seem as insignificant as possible, with the result that more members of the Mosaic faith than Jews were counted. The share of the Jews by faith in the overall population was 4.2 per cent, but that of the 'Jews by race' who were counted was only 4 per cent! A truly grotesque result.

Dr A. Maelicke.[4]

DOC. 147

After receiving a message from the consulate dated 5 February 1941, Arthur and Johanna Cohen from Düsseldorf hope to be able to emigrate to the USA[1]

Letter from the US consulate in Stuttgart dated 5 February 1941, forwarded in a letter from Arthur and Johanna Cohen[2] from Düsseldorf to relatives, dated 8 February 1941

To the holder of registration number 19 478 AC[3]

You are hereby informed that the documents submitted by you for verification have been provisionally deemed sufficient, and that your case can be immediately considered, provided quota numbers are still available, as soon as proof is on hand that you would be able to travel to the United States if a visa were to be issued to you.[4]

The possibility to travel to the United States does not consist only in the fact that you are able to leave Germany. It also means that you have a way to obtain passage across the ocean and to reach the port of embarkation. In view of the currently very limited availability of tickets for ships, the deposit of a sufficient amount for your ocean crossing cannot be regarded as final proof of the possibility of travelling to the United States.

Once you have made firm preparations for the journey, you should present documentary evidence so that you can receive a summons to the consulate to submit the visa application.

The American Consul General

Valid only for Arthur and Johanna Cohen.

4 Dr Alfred Maelicke (b. 1911), economist and economic advisor; joined the NSDAP in 1937; Gau economic advisor in Berlin in 1938, involved in the Aryanization of Jewish businesses; manager and head of the Foreign Department of the Advertising Council for the German Economy, which was under the authority of the Reich Ministry of Public Enlightenment and Propaganda; Oberregierungsrat in 1944; author of a series of articles on Aryanization in the economic journal *Wirtschaftsblatt der Industrie- und Handelskammer zu Berlin.*

1 Mahn- und Gedenkstätte Düsseldorf, Briefe Familie Cohen. This letter has been translated from German.

2 Arthur Cohen (1888–1942), businessman; co-owner of J. & J. Cohen, a firm dealing in hides, the import of animal intestines, and butcher's equipment; imprisoned in Dachau concentration camp for six weeks following the November pogroms of 1938; married to Johanna (Aenne) Cohen, née Goldschmidt (1898–1942). Both husband and wife were deported to the Lodz ghetto on 27 Oct. 1941 and in Sept. 1942 to Chelmno, where they were murdered.

3 Because they were number 19,478 on the waiting list, Arthur and Johanna Cohen could not expect a visa and immigration to the USA until Oct. 1942.

4 The affidavit required for the Cohens to be allowed entry to the USA had been furnished by their cousin Ewald Kamp on 15 March 1940.

Düsseldorf, 8 February 1941.

My dears,[5]

Yesterday we received the letter above, dated 5 February, from the consulate in Stuttgart. You can imagine our joy, and we immediately contacted the Relief Association [of Jews in Germany] and, at its advice, immediately wrote to the American Express Company in Berlin to book places. In the next few days we will speak in person with the gentleman from the Relief Association and will cable you. Now, we hope, things will soon reach a point where we can travel, and we thank you so much, once again, for your great efforts. We will write to you again in the days ahead. Father's health continues to improve.

Warm regards, Yours, Arthur

My dears,

Indeed I need not describe to you how happy we were when we received the news. We have you to thank for everything, and you will surely be happy too when you hear the good news, and how happy Walter and Margot[6] will be when they get the good news. Once again, my most sincere thanks. Warmest regards to you all,

Yours, Aenne

DOC. 148
On 11 February 1941 Anna Samuel describes her growing distress to her friend Else Schubert[1]

Handwritten letter from Anna Samuel,[2] Berlin, to Else Schubert, dated 11 February 1941

My dear Else,

Doubtless, some lines are on the way from you to us again, you dear, faithful correspondent! Today we spent some quiet hours with the privy councillor's wife, whom you once visited in our company. She had, at last, news from Lisbon regarding her daughter in Palestine. She says that unfortunately no replies can be sent through *that* channel. Today I sorted out a bookcase, that is, I went through it to see what belongs to Hans.[3] I filled a cardboard box, and tomorrow it is the turn of the toy cupboard. That and

5 For practical reasons, the Cohens effectively wrote 'consolidated letters', which went to Leo Kamp (b. 1878) and were copied and forwarded by him to their children and to other relatives.

6 Arthur and Johanna Cohen had two children. Walter (b. 1924) was sent to boarding school in Britain in 1938. His sister Margot (b. 1926) came to Britain on a Kindertransport one year later.

1 Alte Synagoge Essen, AR.4733. Excerpts published in Genger, *Durch unsere Herzen*, pp. 132–133. This letter has been translated from German. Use of italics and abbreviated words as in the original: the meaning has been added in square brackets.

2 Anna Samuel, née Friedländer (1874–1942), head of the Jewish Women's Association in Essen until 1925; married to Dr Salomon Samuel, a rabbi in Essen. The couple moved to Berlin in 1932 and were deported to Theresienstadt in 1942.

3 Hans Samuel (b. 1902), the second-eldest son of the Samuels, had emigrated to Palestine.

everything that belongs to H., including the bench, goes, with your permission, to you. Possibly including the papers etc. that were left behind, in a crate, as freight, with Borchardt as the sender. Or do you have any other suggestions? You can look through the papers at your leisure whenever you have the time and the inclination, and throw away what you think is not worth keeping. There are, for example, photocopies of school certificates, including the music-teacher diploma etc. You never know when and where they will come in useful. Originals are probably in the crate (?),[4] which – we had confirmation – is stuck in Trieste – until the war ends! I know it will be in good hands with you. We will have to live somewhere so much smaller, whether any time soon is still uncertain.

After the *h*[uge] drain of money, called the 'social compensation tax', solely for *J*[ews], almost 100 [Reichsmarks] per month, we would like to live somewhere cheaper, but nothing has been found yet.[5] And perhaps – there are indications of it – we *must* get out quickly.

My husband would also like to send you some books, if you have no objection. In the home of the privy councillor's wife today, he read to us from an interesting book by Barth, a Swiss professor of theology.[6] His view of genuine faith.

Armgard's picture pleased us, she looks so delightfully happy. I wonder whether she, like Hede, will soon give you a son-in-law?[7] Warm congratulations to Hede and to you and your husband[8] on the fact that she found a job so quickly, so close to her sweetheart and her childhood home!

In vain my husband has requested more coal, first in writing and then verbally. This week we still have a supply. Leaving is *im*possible on account of the imminent *mandatory* moving-out date of 1 March. If we fail to find something suitable that quickly, we will put the things in storage. *One* room is going at present so we can take our time and keep looking, or travel. Everything is so uncertain! First I am immersing myself in putting things in order, which should not prevent me, however, from listening to music at Wachsmann's tomorrow afternoon. We are glad about the warmer weather, as then the gas stove will be enough to keep us from freezing to death.

It is really gratifying *that the Ogutsches* have had such an encouraging letter from *their* Edith.[9]

Yes, dear, a letter now would be as sweet as Turkish delight for us, we have been longing for one! Oh well! All this rummaging around makes one melancholy and is

4 As in the original.
5 See Doc. 129, fn. 37.
6 Karl Barth (1886–1968), Protestant theologian; critic of National Socialism, co-founder of the Confessing Church, and member of the National Committee for a Free Germany (NKFD); author of *Kirchliche Dogmatik* (from 1932).
7 Armgard and Hedwig, the daughters of Else Schubert.
8 Martin Schubert.
9 Wilhelm Ogutsch (1893–1944), rabbi; head cantor of the Jewish Community of Essen, and its rabbi from 1939; deported to Theresienstadt along with his wife Erna in 1942 and perished there in Feb. 1944. His wife survived and emigrated to the USA. Their ten-year-old daughter Edith had emigrated first to Britain and then to the USA.

difficult. Can I handle it, that is, am I doing it properly? *My's* things,[10] Ernst Samuel's things[11] – oh, I really am a bit at a loss. But it simply *must* be done! Every day I am glad to be free of worrying about lunch at least. – And it always does me good and calms me to have you as my friend! And four good children, thank God! But *so* far away![12] Yours,

DOC. 149
On 12 February 1941 Moritz Leitersdorf from Vienna receives a security order from the Reich Flight Tax Office[1]

Security order from the Inner City East Tax Office, Vienna, Reich Flight Tax Office, Vienna I, 2 Riemergasse, unsigned, to Mr Moritz Israel Leitersdorf and Mrs Bianka Sara Leitersdorf, 25 Türkenschanzstrasse, Vienna 18,[2] for the attention of Dr Rudolf Israel Braun, 4 Seilergasse, Vienna I,[3] dated 12 February 1941

Security Order[4]
A. Assessment of the security
My findings suggest that you will be leaving your residence – your permanent abode in the Austrian lands or elsewhere in the territory of the Reich. Pursuant to § 7 of the Reich Flight Tax Law I therefore request that you immediately furnish security *to the amount of 19,900 RM.*

This request is hereby issued also to your family members (wife, children), insofar as they have been jointly assessed with you or will be so assessed with respect to income tax or property tax. The security can, for example, be furnished by depositing money, by depositing or pledging securities or mortgages, or by means of surety (§§ 132 to 141 of the Reich Tax Code).

10 Dr Salomo Friedländer, pseudonym Mynona (1871–1946), philosopher, writer, and satirist; brother of Anna Samuel; contributor to publications including the expressionist journals *Der Sturm* and *Die Aktion*; emigrated with his family in 1933 to Paris, where he died in 1946 as a result of hunger and deprivation.
11 Anselm Ruest, born Ernst Samuel (1878–1943), writer and philosopher; youngest brother of Salomon Samuel; left Berlin in 1933 and emigrated to France; in various internment camps from 1940; released in 1943 and died from the consequences of his imprisonment.
12 All four of the Samuels' children were in Palestine: Ludwig (b. 1900) emigrated in 1933, Hans (b. 1902) in 1939, Eva (b. 1904) in 1932, and Edith (b. 1907) in 1939.

1 DÖW, 4671. This document has been translated from German.
2 Bianka (b. 1881) and Moritz Leitersdorf (b. 1873); lived in Vienna; deported from Vienna to Izbica on 9 April 1942; deported again, presumably to Belzec or Sobibor, where they were murdered.
3 Dr Rudolf Braun (1885–1963), lawyer; practised law in Vienna, 1917–1938; vice president of the Vienna Bar Association, chairman of the professional organization of lawyers, and board member of the Vienna Law Society after 1945.
4 The text states that this document replaces (a) the security order dated 2 October 1939 addressed to Moritz Israel and (b) the Reich Flight Tax notice dated 3 August 1939 addressed to Bianca Sara Leitersdorf. A security order (*Sicherheitsanordnung*) was used by the tax authorities to demand payment of the Reich Flight Tax, even before a claim to it had arisen, and the authorities demanded an up-front payment of the full amount, or other securities: Law on Changes to the Regulations on the Reich Flight Tax, 18 May 1934, Art. 1/4, *Reichsgesetzblatt*, 1934, I, p. 393.

This order is immediately enforceable.

The security has been calculated as follows:

Reich Flight Tax, which is due upon emigration: on the basis of my enquiries, the total assets belonging to you, your wife, and your children as of 1 January 1938 – including the added amounts under § 3(3) of the Reich Flight Tax Law and § 2(1) for (b) of the Regulation for Implementation of the Reich Flight Tax in Austria, dated 14 April 1938 – amounted to:

79,412 RM, of that one quarter	19,853 RM
Total:	19,853 RM
Rounded up:	19,900 RM

Further requirements:
I request that you and your wife report to this office within 5 days

B. Rights of appeal

You have the right to appeal against this security order to the regional tax director in Vienna, whose decision is final. The appeal can be submitted to me in writing or made verbally and placed on record. Appeals may only be made up to one month after service of the order, that is, after the day on which the order is posted. You must bear the costs of an unsuccessful appeal.

The validity of the security order will not be restricted by the filing of an appeal, and enforcement in particular will not be delayed.

§ 7 of the Reich Flight Tax Law

(*Reichssteuerblatt*, 1937, p. 1269; *Reichsgesetzblatt*, I, 1937, p. 1385; 1938, p. 389.)

(1) The tax office can require the furnishing of security if it deems this necessary to secure current or future claims purporting to the Reich Flight Tax, other taxes to be paid before emigration, and other payments related to tax laws. The following are considered to be future claims within the meaning of (1):

1. claims that have already arisen but are not yet due,
2. claims that have not yet arisen but are likely to result in the future.

(2) The security order, like a tax assessment notice, is enforceable (also provisionally enforceable). § 326([…][5]) of the Reich Tax Code does not apply.

(3) Appeals against this security order may be lodged with the regional tax director. His decision is final.

5 The number of the paragraph section is illegible.

UÖW 4671

Finanzamt Innere Stadt-Ost
Reichsfluchtsteuerstelle

Wien 1, 12. Februar 1941
Riemergasse 2
Fernsprecher: R-22-5-95, Hausanschluß

Rfl. Leitersdorf — Zimmer 512
Bitte, stets angeben!

Parteienverkehr nur Dienstag und Freitag von 9 bis 12 Uhr.

Sicherheiten nimmt die Vollstreckungsstelle entgegen, Einzahlungen nur im Wege der Postsparkasse auf Kontonummer A 43 167.

Nummer Ihres Kontos: 4380/H

An Herrn Moritz Israel Leitersdorf
und Frau Bianka Sara

Wien 18.,
Türkenschanzstraße 25

zu Händen von Herrn
Dr. Rudolf Israel Braun
Wien I.,
Seilergasse 4

Tritt an die Stelle
a) des Sicherheitsbescheids v.2.X.1939 an Moritz Israel und
b) des Reichsfluchtsteuerbesch.v.3.6.1939 an Bianca Sara Leitersdo

Sicherheitsbescheid

A. Festsetzung der Sicherheit

Meine Feststellungen lassen darauf schließen, daß Sie den Wohnsitz — gewöhnlichen Aufenthalt im Land Österreich oder im übrigen Reichsgebiet — aufgeben werden. Auf Grund des § 7 des Reichsfluchtsteuergesetzes*) ersuche ich Sie daher, sofort

in Höhe von 19.900.- RM

Sicherheit zu leisten. — Dieses Ersuchen ergeht hierdurch auch an Ihre Angehörigen (Ehefrau, Kinder), soweit sie mit Ihnen zur Einkommensteuer oder zur Vermögensteuer zusammen veranlagt worden sind oder zusammen zu veranlagen sind. — Die Sicherheit kann zum Beispiel durch Hinterlegung von Geld, durch Hinterlegung oder Verpfändung von Wertpapieren oder Hypotheken oder durch Bürgschaft geleistet werden (§§ 132 bis 141 der Reichsabgabenordnung).

Dieser Bescheid ist sofort vollstreckbar.

Die Sicherheit ist wie folgt errechnet worden:

Reichsfluchtsteuer, die mit der Auswanderung fällig wird: Nach meinen Ermittlungen betrug das Ihnen und Ihrer Ehefrau sowie Ihre Kinde gehörige Gesamtvermögen am 1. Januar 1938 — einschließlich der Hinzurechnungen gemäß § 3 Absatz 3 des Reichsfluchtsteuergesetzes und § 2 Absatz 1 zu b der Verordnung zur Durchführung der Reichsfluchtsteuer im Land Österreich vom 14. April 1938 —:

79.412.- RM, davon ein Viertel 19.853.- RM

Sonstige Ansprüche:
Ich ersuche um Ihr und Ihrer Ehefrau Vorsprache an Amtsstelle binnen 5 Tagen

RM

ergibt zusammen . 19.853.- RM

Aufgerundet . 19.900.-00 RM

B. Rechtsmittelbelehrung

Gegen diesen Sicherheitsbescheid steht Ihnen die Beschwerde an den Oberfinanzpräsidenten Wien zu, dessen Entscheidung endgültig ist. Die Beschwerde kann bei mir schriftlich eingereicht oder zu Protokoll erklärt werden. Dies kann nur bis zum Ablauf eines Monats nach der Zustellung des Bescheids, d. h. nach dem Tage, an dem der Bescheid zur Post gegeben ist, geschehen. Die Kosten einer erfolglosen Beschwerde haben Sie zu tragen.

Durch die Einlegung der Beschwerde wird die Wirksamkeit des Sicherheitsbescheids nicht gehemmt, insbesondere die Vollstreckung nicht aufgehalten.

*) Siehe Rückseite.

4671

Rfl. 7. (Reinschrift des Sicherheitsbescheids.) — 12. 39. — 3000. — Staatsdruckerei Wien. 12.466 39

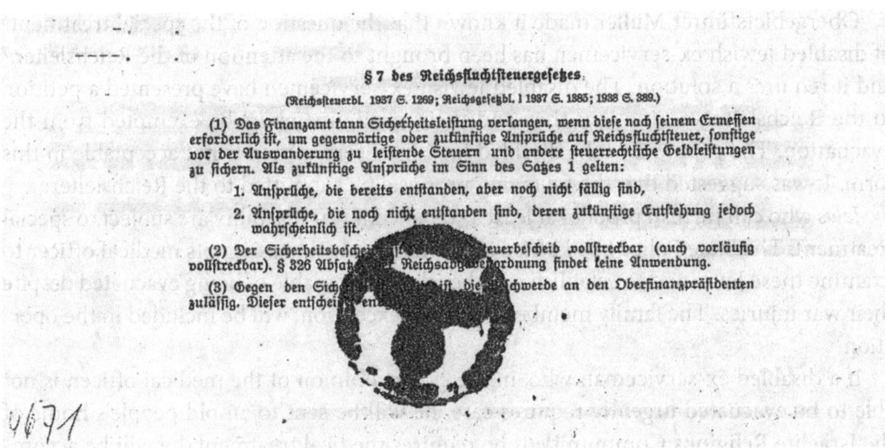
§ 7 des Reichsfluchtsteuergesetzes.

(Reichssteuerbl. 1937 S. 1269; Reichsgesetzbl. I 1937 S. 1385; 1938 S. 389.)

(1) Das Finanzamt kann Sicherheitsleistung verlangen, wenn diese nach seinem Ermessen erforderlich ist, um gegenwärtige oder zukünftige Ansprüche auf Reichsfluchtsteuer, sonstige vor der Auswanderung zu leistende Steuern und andere steuerrechtliche Geldleistungen zu sichern. Als zukünftige Ansprüche im Sinn des Satzes 1 gelten:

1. Ansprüche, die bereits entstanden, aber noch nicht fällig sind,
2. Ansprüche, die noch nicht entstanden sind, deren zukünftige Entstehung jedoch wahrscheinlich ist.

(2) Der Sicherheitsbesch[illegible] Steuerbescheid vollstreckbar (auch vorläufig vollstreckbar). § 326 Absa[illegible] Reichsabgabenordnung findet keine Anwendung.

(3) Gegen den Sich[illegible] ist die [illegible]schwerde an den Oberfinanzpräsidenten zulässig. Dieser entschei[illegible]en[illegible]

4671

DOC. 150

On 12 February 1941 a meeting is held at the office of the Obergebietsführer of the Hitler Youth in Vienna to discuss the deportation of the Viennese Jews[1]

Notes on the discussion in the office of Obergebietsführer Müller,[2] unsigned, Vienna, dated 12 February 1941

On 12 February 1941 a meeting took place in the office of Obergebietsführer Müller of the Hitler Youth at 2 Ballhausplatz, Vienna I. The discussion, which he chaired, dealt with the resolution of special questions that have arisen during the evacuation of the Jews from Vienna to the General Government. The participants in the discussion were:

Obergebietsführer Müller
Gaugeschäftsführer Laube[3]
Oberregierungsrat Dr David[4] and Party Comrade Augustin[5]
SS-Obersturmführer Brunner
Regierungsrat Dr Ebner.

1 DÖW, 1456. Published in Dokumentationsarchiv des österreichischen Widerstandes, *Widerstand und Verfolgung in Wien*, pp. 290–291. This document has been translated from German.

2 Herbert Müller (1910–1945); joined the NSDAP in 1931; head of the office of Reich Youth Leader Baldur von Schirach from 1934, and later head of the Central Office of the Reich Youth Leadership; Obergebietsführer of the Hitler Youth in Vienna from 1940; lost his life in a bombing raid on Vienna.

3 Heinrich Laube (b. 1894), cartographer; joined the NSDAP in 1931; member of the Fatherland Front, 1934–1938; Gaugeschäftsführer in Vienna; head of the Central Office of Housing and Settlement in the municipal administration of Vienna in 1942.

4 Dr Franz David (1881–1972), administrative official; worked for the municipal administration of the City of Vienna from 1906; joined the NSDAP in 1932; Oberregierungsrat; head of the Central Office for Housing and Settlement in the Vienna municipal administration in 1937, retired in 1943.

5 Theodor Augustin (b. 1906), waiter; joined the NSDAP in 1933; after 1938 worked for the Central Office for Housing and Settlement in the municipal administration of Vienna, where his tasks included allocating vacant housing and implementing the Law on Tenancy Agreements with Jews; sentenced to six months in prison for abuse of administrative authority in 1941.

Obergebietsführer Müller made it known that the question of the special treatment[6] of disabled Jewish ex-servicemen has been brought to the attention of the Reichsleiter,[7] and it requires a solution. The disabled Jewish ex-servicemen have presented a petition to the Reichsleiter, asking that they and their family members be exempted from the evacuation. The proposal of the disabled Jewish ex-servicemen is not acceptable in this form. It was suggested that the following proposal be submitted to the Reichsleiter:

Jews who can furnish proof of at least a 50 per cent war disability are subject to special treatment. The State Police head office in Vienna is asked to assign its medical officer to examine these Jews, and to establish whether they are capable of being evacuated despite their war injuries. The family members, without exception, will be included in the operation.

If a disabled ex-serviceman who, in the expert opinion of the medical officer, is not able to be evacuated urgently requires care, he will be sent to an old people's home of the Israelite Religious Community. If he requires medical treatment, he will be accommodated in the Rothschild Hospital.

Mixed marriages

(1) Husband a *Jew*, wife an Aryan – no children.
First, an attempt is made to make the wife aware of her racial obligations, and she is urged to seek a divorce. If the petition for divorce is filed, the Jew is included in the transport.
In this case, the wife is given special consideration with respect to matters of assets law. The Housing Office [however] does not take this case into account and performs resettlement within the municipal area.

(2) Husband an *Aryan*, wife a Jew – no children.
The household is regarded as Aryan. The Jewess is not included in the operation. The Housing Office does not carry out resettlement. If a petition for divorce is filed, the Jewess is included in the evacuation.

(3) No allowance is made for Jews who have adopted Aryan children.

Other special cases

(4) Stateless Jews, without exception, are included in the operation.

(5) Jews with foreign nationality are not included in the operation if they are able to furnish incontestable proof of their citizenship. (Valid passport or certificate of nationality.)

(6) Jews who are not capable of being evacuated because of serious illness or who are infirm and crippled are taken to either the Rothschild Hospital or a Jewish home for the elderly. The Jewish family members are evacuated.

(7) Former public servants who draw a pension are temporarily deferred [from evacuation] until the further payment of their pension is settled.

(8) Jews who are employed are evacuated irrespective of this circumstance.

(9) In each individual case, the Central Office closely examines whether there is an opportunity to emigrate in the near future. If there is such a possibility, the Jew is not included in the evacuation.

6 The German uses the term *Sonderbehandlung* here as a euphemism for deportation.
7 This refers here and in the following to Gauleiter and Reichsstatthalter Baldur von Schirach.

(10) Gaugeschäftsführer Laube asked to be informed in writing every time a Party Comrade approaches the State Police head office or the Central Office with written or oral requests, to exempt certain Jews from the evacuation.
(11) SS-Obersturmführer Brunner requested that resettlement of the Jews within the Gau territory be stopped, as the work of the Central Office is substantially hampered as a result.
(12) Jews who are nationals of this country and exempt from evacuation may possibly be relocated to a segregated area at a later time.
(13) Obergebietsführer Müller pointed out that the Reichsleiter alone reserves the right to issue orders for exemptions.

DOC. 151

On 15 February 1941 Paula Rosenberg writes about conditions in the assembly camp on Castellezgasse and her forced resettlement from Vienna to Opole Lubelskie[1]

Handwritten letters from Paula Rosenberg[2] to Oskar and Flora Stricker in Vienna[3] before and after her deportation from Vienna to Opole Lubelskie on 15 February 1941, undated

From the waiting camp in Vienna, Castellezgasse
Dear Oskar,

The conditions are worse than one can imagine. In each schoolroom there are as many as 75 people. Luckily I am in a small room with 14 people. The toilets barely flush, in the basement the washing facilities are under water, the drains are clogged, and all the corridors are full of people, even seriously ill people. Our mattresses were immediately taken away from us. I'm glad to be able to share two straw mattresses with four people. I don't know what could be done here to help. I'm not the kind of person who can't reconcile themselves to things, but these conditions are unimaginable. I have picked bugs off the wall myself, and they won't be the only ones.

I want to write down our information. Perhaps it will be of use somehow. *Heinrich Rosenberg born on 3 Oct. 1871 in Vienna. Paula Rosenberg, born on 29 May 1885 in Vienna, German Waiting List nos. 40 198 and 40 199, 9 August 1938. Affidavit provided by Dr Hans Rosenberg*, Silverstein and Furth.

1 YVA, O.75/187. This document has been translated from German.
2 Paula Rosenberg, née Gewitsch (b. 1885), housewife; married to Heinrich (Heinz) Salomon Rosenberg (b. 1871), businessman, Kommerzialrat ('commercial counsellor', honorary title bestowed on distinguished businessmen and philanthropists); owner of the 'Bernfeld & Rosenberg' company from 1900; briefly imprisoned in Buchenwald in 1938. The Rosenbergs' efforts to emigrate failed. They were deported to Opole Lubelskie in the General Government on 15 Feb. 1941 and from there presumably to either the Belzec or Sobibor extermination camp; declared dead after 1945.
3 Dr Oskar Stricker-Barolin (1886–1972), physician; served in the First World War from 1914; returned from captivity in 1920; barred from practising medicine in 1938; suicide attempt in the Gestapo building at Morzinplatz in Vienna; headed the Department of Urology at the Archduchess Sophie Hospital in Vienna from 1945.

If we all have to leave, I would be glad to go with Helene.[4] I still can't imagine her here with Eva and hope all the others will be spared this [and] we will keep our wits about us. I could certainly do with a rubber sock for soap. All our bags were immediately taken from us, so I could also do with needles and some thread, but just a bit. Supposedly one can deliver things at the gate or even ask for you to be fetched to talk. I would like some Kandiset[5] too.

I am in Room 6, Heinz is in Room 5.

Paula

We are thinking of you all and can only say that, thank God, we are in good health. It will be all right. I help here wherever I can. Notify Helene and Sosci too. It is indescribable, nowhere near enough of anything. So many of these poor people on their little bundles and this category, and this is what *we* have to be involved in.[6] If Helene is perhaps in need of a place to live at the moment, she should contact Mr Graber (Heinz's chess partner), 21 or 23 Seegasse, he might know of something.

Dearest Flora and dear Oskar,

We have just received both your cards and take great delight in them. We want to try to describe the conditions here to you. First, we were taken to Aspang Station[7] in Vienna at 3 a.m. in open lorries, and we did not leave there until 11:30 a.m. On top of that we were in railway carriages with no toilet and were not allowed to step outside. We were as resourceful as possible and used a glass during the 36-hour journey. In addition, we travelled the last 2 hours in open cattle trucks on a narrow-gauge railway. You are mistaken to think that provision had been made for anything. The village is like that bit when you go over the bridge into Gaaden.[8] incredible filth, low houses everywhere with shingle or thatched roofs. The population are Polish Jews who mainly speak Yiddish: Aryans had to leave their homes and live further away. We therefore have no idea whether there is any point learning Polish, because we have no opportunity at all to hear it. We spent the first two nights in a room in an indescribable inn with approximately thirty other persons, sitting on straw, and then, with the help of an acquaintance from Castellezgasse, a bed was found for us both in the home of very good people. However, it is a room that could only be compared to a cowshed back home (and I'm not exaggerating); at the same time we must be grateful to be here, because the people just let us live and eat with them, where we otherwise might completely starve to death. The free meals are meals in name only and consist of tea at around 10 a.m., if one is lucky enough to get it (we have tea from the evening in our thermos flask), a quarter of a loaf of bread per person, and at midday a ladle of some sort of watery soup, nothing else. In addition, we get various things from the people with whom we are staying. With money, everything can be got here, meat, poultry, eggs, as much as you want, sugar is very scarce and dear, as is fat, also white flour, very scarce and dear. The bread is black bread, but you get used to it.[9]

4 Probably: Helene Adelberg, née Gewitsch (1881–1942), deported on 14 June 1942 to Sobibor, where she was murdered.

5 An artificial sweetener.

6 Content as in the original.

7 See Doc. 144, fn. 3.

8 A district in Mödling, Austria.

The poor Jews have had their shops closed down, and they apparently live on illicit trade of some sort. It is thus completely inconceivable that we might earn anything. Last Friday when the second or third transport arrived (the second went to Kielce),[10] 300 places to sleep were set up in the temple, four bunks on top of one another, each for two persons, but 1,000 people arrived (around 10 p.m. as we did. This is probably so that no one sees these transports). Many wandered around all night, including numerous old people like Aunt Rosa. It is not known where they were all housed, and another 1,000 to 2,000 are already expected. The locals fear that a ghetto will be created here and the village sealed off, in which case no foodstuffs at all could come in. There are probably around 7,000 to 8,000 inhabitants. The village consists of a marketplace and a few wretched rows of houses. If we had money here we could, as I said, buy everything for ourselves. As regards the parcels, it is all fairly irrelevant, because we would just give it to our hostess. Naturally, tinned foods, for example, or cheese or fat would be quite good.[11] Some people have already received 3-kilo packages, whereas we have not received Uncle Josef's little parcel that he promised us. Things are probably different in each post office. As for clothes etc., we need nothing at the moment, unless it is to sell. Our shoes will probably do for this year, though not for next year. Long boots and short trousers would be best for here, and ideally the oldest things; one gets incredibly dirty. *As regards selling*, one allegedly gets 400–500 zloty for a suit, which is enough to live on for quite a while. One of our acquaintances here fortuitously found money in his coat, and so he is sorted here for quite some time. Helene need not send all the listed things to us at once, of course, because we'll mainly need them to sell – only if she has to leave suddenly. Thanks very much for the three letters from abroad. One was from Hans[12] (he thinks we're on our way to the USA); the Hungarian letter from a niece of Heinz's[13] (address Henrika Solgom, Budapest II, at *Olasfor*) gave us particular pleasure because a sweet letter from Madeleine was enclosed in it, but dated 23 September; and the third letter was from one of Hans's friends. We are very grateful to you for all your trouble. Oskar, did you pick up the letters yourself? Otherwise, shouldn't your address be on them?

Various people have already received cash remittances; how, I don't know, of course. In general, people have taken along far more luggage, even in large suitcases, and are now glad they did so. During the last night in Vienna, hope was still held out to us that

9 Added subsequently in the bottom margin: 'our colleague Dr Stettner has just told us that the bread is full of vitamins and very healthy'. Dr Siegfried Stettner (b. 1903), physician; was deported on 15 Feb. 1941 from Vienna to Opole Lubelskie, where he is presumed to have perished. According to a report for the Jewish Social Self-Help (JSS) dated 28 July 1941, he worked in the infirmary in Opole as a physician after his deportation: AŻIH, 211/762, fol. 15.

10 On 19 Feb. 1941 more than 1,000 Jews were deported from Vienna to Kielce in the Radom district.

11 Added later at the bottom of the page: 'it has just been announced that it is not permitted to send fat'.

12 Dr Hans August Rosenberg (1908–1982), physician; son of Paula and Heinrich Rosenberg; emigrated in 1938 with his wife Dr Ernestine Rosner Rosenberg (1912–1962) to Britain; from there they reached the USA in 1939. His sister Madeleine Anna Buchsbaum, née Rosenberg (b. 1911), emigrated to Britain in March 1939 and lived temporarily in the home of her brother in Manchester; she emigrated to the USA in 1947 and lived in New York.

13 Added later at the foot of the page: 'if a parcel arrives for her, it belongs to my sisters-in-law – Sosci knows them'.

we might be exempt from resettlement because of emigration, and those with a chance of emigrating were instructed to keep their luggage separate so that they could perhaps get away easily, and as a result these pieces of luggage, including ours, have not arrived to this day. They are allegedly on the current transport. As soon as we arrived, we had to pay 10 zloty as a head tax, so that one was left with only 30 zloty. Heinz wants to continue writing, one cannot possibly describe everything. If we stay here longer, we will surely all perish.

Why did you have to resettle Mother so quickly?

Much love, yours, Paula

International reply stamps are unfortunately not accepted. Please let everyone read the letter. Helene should also show it to our friends on Berggasse and Währingerstrasse.

I have to write something about the sanitary conditions too. There is *one* open latrine for ten persons in the village. Whenever too many people are queued up there, they simply squat somewhere on the road, in the evening, of course. Water is drawn from wells, without any pipes, from a depth of around 4–5 metres. The people carry home buckets, which they empty into a larger container in the straw room. Shoes are cleaned right there, and potatoes are washed in the same buckets. Dr Stettner thinks the local population must have incredibly strong immune systems if even one person is still alive here. Our hosts, husband, wife, and four children, had typhus last year, which they mention as if it was nothing out of the ordinary.[14]

The place where the free meals are distributed is around 10 minutes from where we live. For the time being, we do not want to inform the American consulate of our change of address, so that our case will not be dismissed as hopeless. The local population includes numerous Jewish tailors and cobblers, who would gladly do useful work. For example, the owner of the place where we live, working diligently, made a suit for a Christian Pole in the shortest time. If *you* don't mind, we would like to leave matters with the post as they have been so far. But if *you* want, we will have it sent on to us by the post office. We are very happy for you to have control over which letters for us are forwarded.

Dr Stettner has passed on regards from the family of grammar school teacher Dr Oppenheim. We were delighted by that and are very grateful to the Oppenheims and to Helene for instigating it. Dr Stettner, who has spoken very highly of you, said that fifteen Jewish patients were quartered in the local hospital. He said that the doctor in charge, an Aryan, told him that he could not allow this number to be exceeded. There had been plans to build a hospice with thirty beds, he said, but the Jewish Council had no funds, and it was evidently never built. Your suggestions have proved quite sensible. It has also been pointed out that in the event of an epidemic, isolation would be completely out of the question. The dangers (drinking water, typhus, etc.) were emphasized. If there was any intention to help the emigrants, then this help should be given, although the percentage of elderly and weak is very high. The general consensus is that the food is totally inadequate – unless one can buy additional rations for oneself. Relations between the members of the Jewish Council, the Ostjuden on the one hand and the Western Jews on the other hand, are also not as harmonious as they should be. By the same token, the Jewish Council's authority is diminished because those in its care have to watch it kow-

14 The next part is written in a different hand, evidently that of Heinrich Salomon Rosenberg.

tow to others.[15] When one sees the abject misery – also the primitive living conditions – of the local Jews, one is disinclined to reproach them, bearing in mind the words of Friedrich Hebbel in his famous poem:

What was to be read in your martyrs' bodies
When, torn to pieces, they were brought to light?
Only how hard the rack had been, of course;
One did not take their wounds for sins![16]

Warm regards to everyone,
Heinz and Paula

We would need a new *torch* (can't get batteries), *toilet paper, cologne or alcohol* for washing, and *Kandiset*. If my provisions are still available, the *rice, noodles, or anything else*. Letters are only sometimes opened by the Foreign Exchange Office to see whether there is money in them.

DOC. 152
A report for the American Jewish Joint Distribution Committee compiled in mid February 1941 describes Jewish forced labour in Berlin[1]

Report, marked 'strictly confidential, not to be published', compiled by an unknown author for the American Jewish Joint Distribution Committee, New York, Hotel Marcy, West End Avenue at 95th St (received on 14 May 1941), dated 6 May 1941, sent with compliments from Dr Alfred Wiener[2] on 13 May 1941[3]

Compulsory Labour Service for Jews in Berlin
Situation in mid February 1941
It is generally believed that the Jewish population of Berlin was saved from the transportation to Lublin (Poland) which was the fate of the Jews of Vienna,[4] by the fact that

15 In occupied Poland the Germans set up so-called Jewish Councils (*Judenräte*) or Councils of Elders (*Ältestenräte*) to carry out their orders and to organize Jewish life under German occupation. The first order for these councils to be set up was given by Heydrich in an express letter to the Einsatzgruppen leaders dated 21 Sept. 1939. In the General Government, Hans Frank, the governor general, issued a central directive to this effect for the General Government on 24 Nov. 1939: see the Introduction to PMJ 4.

16 'Der Jude an den Christen' (1857), in Friedrich Hebbel, *Sämtliche Werke*, vol. 2: *Gedichte und Prosa*, ed. Hansludwig Geiger (Berlin: Tempel, 1961), p. 350.

1 JDC 1933/44, 631, fols. 548–555. The original document is in English. Linguistic peculiarities have been retained.

2 Dr Alfred Wiener (1885–1964), publicist, association official, and politician; legal officer at the Central Association of German Citizens of the Jewish Faith (CV), 1919–1923; deputy director of the CV and deputy editor of the *C.V.-Zeitung*, 1923–1933; emigrated to the Netherlands in 1933; co-founder and director of the Jewish Central Office in Amsterdam, 1934–1939; director of the Wiener Library in London, 1939–1964.

3 Underlined by hand in the original.

4 On the deportation of Jews from Vienna, Moravská Ostrava, and Katowice in autumn 1939, see Doc. 16, fn. 9.

Berlin Jews are compelled to work in the Labour Service. In the beginning the labor service has been compulsory for women from about 20 to 45 years of age and for men from about 18 to 55 years of age. Some weeks ago this age limit had been raised by ten years, i.e. up to 55 years for women and up to 65 years for men.[5]

It is believed that out of these 70,000 to 80,000 Jews living to-day in Berlin more than one third, i.e. about 30,000, have to work in the labor service. Payment is made in accordance with the prescribed minimum tariffs and amounts to about 72 Pfennige an hour, while the non-Jewish workers as skilled craftsmen earn something between 90 Pfennige and 1 Reichsmark per hour.

On May 1, 1940 an order was published in the Berlin 'Juedisches Nachrichtenblatt' to the effect that all Jews of the above mentioned age, who had no occupation, should register as volunteers with the Jewish Community for assignment to the labor service.[6] The official name of the place of registration in the Oranienburger Street is: 'Use of labour (Arbeitseinsatz) of the Jewish Community, Berlin.' Those Jews who think that they are not physically fit for the prospective work, undergo recently a physical pre-examination by the Jewish Community. On the strength of the result of this examination the person is advised by the Community whether he should inform the Public Labor Distribution Office of his physical ailments. The extension of the Labor Office of the City of Berlin, which is competent for the Jews, is located at Fontane Street at Neukoelln.[7] Its director is Mr. Eschhaus, former chief of staff of a Jewish clothing firm in Berlin.[8]

The reporter has suffered from sciatica. At Fontane Street he was found to be fit for work and he was assigned to the rail road building firm Dudek at Spandau. The labor office generally puts together groups of 15 to 20 Jews and makes them work under a non-Jewish foreman. The firm Dudek employed about 10 groups, or about 100 to 150 Jews at various places in Berlin. The reporter who had never done physical work before, was assigned to the group 'Wedding', and had to stamp broken stones, to transport rails, to tighten screws, and so on. The working hours were from 9 a.m. to 5 p.m. with two interruptions of 15 minutes during which the laborers could eat their lunch which they had brought from home and could get drinks from the canteen. After a few days the reporter fell ill; he then did not attend the work principally on account of his shoes being completely broken. The firm applied to get work-shoes for him which he actually received. Thus he took up work again after about one week.

After four weeks during which the reporter had only worked ten days on account of his illness and lack of clothes – the work was done partly at Wedding and partly at

5 On the expansion of forced labour, see Introduction, pp. 42–43.

6 This order could not be found. There is no known issue of the *Jüdisches Nachrichtenblatt* (Berlin edition) dated 1 May 1940. Due to a bank holiday, the next issue did not appear until 4 May 1940 (nos. 35/36). On 21 May 1940 the *Jüdisches Nachrichtenblatt* (Berlin edition), p. 2, reported that those Jews between the ages of 18 to 55 (men) and between 18 and 50 (women) who had not signed up 'in the last few days of April 1940 and the first few days of May 1940' should do so immediately.

7 Correctly: Fontanepromenade in the Kreuzberg district of Berlin.

8 Alfred Eschhaus (1903–1945), clerk; first worked at the company Rothmann & Seligsohn; from 1933, salaried employee at the Berlin Employment Office; joined the SA in 1933 and the NSDAP in 1937; head of the Central Bureau for Jews at the Berlin Employment Office from 1939; sentenced to two years' imprisonment in 1942 on charges that included gross corruption; subsequently conscripted for military service; expelled from the NSDAP in 1943.

Hakenfelde, – he was assigned to the group 'Pape Street' where less heavy shovel work had to be done. His transfer was occasioned by the owner of the firm, who always was reasonable within the possible limits. The foreman, Mr. Piontek, however, was a sweater and an enraged antisemite. He often threatened the Jewish worker with his fist and tried to beat him. After this the Jewish worker stayed home and brought his complaint before the Labor Office and asked for transfer to another enterprise. He was informed that he could only be transferred to another place if his employer officially dismissed him. The worker then saw Mr. Dudek[9] and reluctantly he gave him notice, as he probably was afraid of getting into difficulties. In the worker's testimonial it was said, that he received notice because he was 'unfit for surface-building work.'[10]

Three days later the Jewish worker was assigned by the labor office to a country-rail firm at Falkensee together with ten other Jews. The work there was much lighter. Three men worked in the court (cleaning, arranging, etc.), three had to transfer the rails (those country rails are more easy to carry than ordinary rails) and three worked in the workshop at the screw-chase and boring-engines. He liked the work as he looked upon it as a preparations for his emigration and as a training. The foreman was especially kind. The reporter showed a photo on which the foreman was photographed together with the Jewish workers. He joined them when going to the canteen and when travelling home. The other workers too, [...][11] go to sports. They exchanged cigarettes, and beer was offered alternatively by Jews and non-Jews. The only antisemite was the senior chief, who always inveighed against the 'Jewish pack, who should have been drowned or hanged long ago.' The Jewish and non-Jewish workers acknowledged those outbursts with silence. When the foreman went on leave, he was replaced by the chief's son. He was an active member of the national socialist party and the Jews were very much afraid of him. But in opposition to his father, Mr. M. Grass, he was as kind as the foreman and he too went to the canteen together with the Jews, etc.

At the end of November, i.e. after about 5 months, the dismissal of the Jews employed with this firm took place. It was rumoured that these dismissals were carried through upon superior order, because Jews should only be employed in factories from now on.

Four days after his dismissal from the firm Grass, the Jewish worker was assigned to the 'Ready-to-drive group with the mayor of the Reichs Capital Berlin' (Gruppenfahrbereitschaft beim Oberbuergermeister der Reichshauptstadt Berlin). In view of the general shortage of cars and vehicles as well as of labor, it is the task of this institution to assign cars and labor to private firms or public institutions in cases of demand if the urgency of the matter is recognized.

Through this institution the reporter was assigned as a single person to a small coal-dealer at La[n]kwitz. There he worked together with non-jews only. They had to unload the coal from the train, to load it on the trucks and to deliver it to private houses. Also the son of the owner of the firm worked in the business; he had taken an active part in the campaign against Poland and was a member of the S.S. When he notice[d] that the Jewish worker was not strong enough for this hard work, he charged him with supervision of the other non-Jewish workers, i.e. he had to control the work, collect the money,

9 Probably Michael Dudek (b. 1884), building contractor; joined the NSDAP in 1932; lived in Berlin.
10 This refers to work on the trackbed and tracks in railway construction.
11 One word is illegible.

to write the receipts, to accept the tips – which were very abundant, as coal is a very much desired article, – and to distribute them equally in the evening. Here too, they had drinks in common at the pub and they had meals together.

The reporter had the impression that at many places workers welcomed Jewish laborers, because before them they had not to be cautious, but could have open discussions and express strong criticism. They preferred Jews to members of the party who spied and denounced them. The reporter has only found isolated cases of antisemitism. The air raid attacks made almost no impression. Hatred of England was more general than hatred of Jews.

Jewish workers can receive additional food-ration cards if their firm applies for them. Many firms are afraid of applying, but others do. Whether the application is approved depends entirely on the state of mind of the director of the respective office for ration-cards. Additional cards may be granted for especially hard work or for over-time work (i.e. workers who work more than 11 hours a day inclusive the time they need for the way to and from their working place).

Additional ration cards for

hard workers		*over time workers*	
500 gr. meat	weekly	100 gr. meat	weekly
1000 gr. bread	"	500 gr. bread	"
350 gr. fat	monthly	180 gr. fat	monthly

The use of tens of thousands of Jews in the Labor Service resulted in an acute shortage of efficient labour for the Jewish organisations. For, although the labor service is officially on a voluntary basis, there is practically a compulsion, and the authorities demand that every Jew submits to the service. Dispense is only given in extraordinary cases upon special application. The decrease in the efficiency of the Jewish Community organisations is chiefly to be explained by the fact that they are now compelled to employ even for important work unfit or extremely aged persons.

Some weeks ago a 'labor camp' has been established at Wuhlheide near Berlin, into which Jewish and non-Jewish 'unwilling workers and saboteurs' are put.[12] Particulars about conditions there are only known by the way to the reporter. Conditions are said to be not different from those prevailing in concentration camps.

12 The inmates at the 'work education camp' (*Arbeitserziehungslager*) for forced labourers in the northern section of Wuhlheide forest in Berlin had to work at the nearby plant of the firm AEG.

DOC. 153

On 19 February 1941 the Jewish Religious Community of Mainz provides information about the possibility of sending parcels to the Gurs camp in France[1]

Circular 3/41 from the Board of the Jewish Religious Congregation, Israelite Religious Community of Mainz, unsigned,[2] to the members of the Jewish Religious Community and of the Reich Association of Jews in Germany, Mainz, dated 19 February 1941

(1) *Sending parcels to the Camp de Gurs*[3]
The Darmstadt Foreign Exchange Office has given permission for the dispatch of parcels to the inmates of the Camp de Gurs, with the restriction that only the most necessary items, such as clothes etc., may be sent. All the items must have been worn. Rationed foodstuffs and dextrose are not permitted. The lists for shipment of items must be submitted in triplicate to the Foreign Exchange Office for approval. We recommend that this opportunity be taken advantage of only when parcels are being sent by relatives to relatives. *Maximum weight per parcel: 5 kg.*

(2) *Communication with the inmates of the Camp de Gurs*
The only permissible communication with persons in the Camp de Gurs, who are regarded by the postal service as non-internees, must go through the German Red Cross, Headquarters/Service Abroad, 2 Blücherplatz, Berlin SW 61. For such communication, special printed forms are mandatory, a limited number of which are available in our *administration building, Room 1.* Please pay special attention to the instruction sheet that is included with the forms.[4]

(3) *Changes of residence*
Changes of residence must be reported *immediately* after the move, in each case, to our *Department for Housing Maintenance.*

(4) *Religious services at 2 Horst Wessel Str.*
Starting on Friday, 21 February 1941, the evening religious service will start at 6 p.m. The Sabbath afternoon service will be held at 4 p.m. In consideration of the curfew, the service marking the end of the Sabbath will not take place until further notice.

(5) *Religious services on Purim at 2 Horst Wessel Str.*
On Wednesday, 12 March 1941 (Ta'anit Esther), the evening service begins at *6:30 p.m.*; on Thursday, 13 March, morning service (Purim) begins at 7:30 a.m.

1 CAHJP, D/Da1/5. This document has been translated from German.

2 The chairman of the board of the Jewish Community of Mainz was Fritz Löwensberg (1878–1944), businessman; owner of a hop wholesaling firm; was deported on 7 Feb. 1943 to Theresienstadt, where he perished.

3 On the deportations of more than 6,000 Jews from Baden, the Palatinate, and the Saarland to the internment camp in southern France, see Docs. 111, 112, and 113.

4 The instruction sheet is not in the file.

DOC. 154

On 20 February 1941 Martha Svoboda from Vienna describes her fears concerning the deportation of her parents to the General Government[1]

Handwritten diary of Martha Svoboda, Vienna, entry for 20 February 1941

My mood is always so bleak after visiting the grandparents. We know now that there is no age limit, everyone is being sent away, little children, the very old, even sick people are taken from the hospital and transported somewhere, into uncertainty, into misery.[2] The height of infamy: the religious community is required to provide food parcels, which are then handed out at the railway station by the National Socialist stewards; the whole thing is filmed and presented to foreign countries,[3] which are then also told how well the Jews are treated here and how content and happy they are to go to their new home. Poor, poor Mama![4] And I have to stand by and see how she becomes increasingly run-down, and cannot help her. Grete[5] in America, Paul[6] somewhere in Russia; I know how grievously she suffers from the thought that she may never see either of them again. I ask myself with dismay how the two old people will survive such a 'resettlement'. When will these terrible crimes be avenged at last! When will we be able to live again?

DOC. 155

On 20 February 1941 Malvine Fischer in Vienna asks her daughter in the USA to supply her with an affidavit as a matter of urgency[1]

Handwritten letter from Malvine Fischer,[2] Vienna, to Wilhelmine Weisz,[3] dated 20 February 1941

My dearest children,

Yesterday afternoon, to our great delight, we received the letter we had so yearned for, dated 13 January – which somewhat reassured us again. – We feel just the same as

1 The original is privately owned; copy in IfZ-Archives, F 601. This document has been translated from German.
2 On the deportations from Vienna, see Introduction, pp. 39–40, and Docs. 144 and 150.
3 This could not be verified.
4 Sara Müller (1867–1942); deported on 28 July 1942 to Theresienstadt, where she perished three months later.
5 Grete Wagschal, née Müller (1914–1998), sister of Martha Svoboda; emigrated to the USA; her final place of residence was in Denver, Colorado.
6 On the deportation of Paul Müller, the brother of Martha and Grete, see Doc. 27.

1 Leo Baeck Institute, AR 6651, Malvine Fischer Collection. Published in Edith Kurzweil, *Briefe aus Wien: Jüdisches Leben vor der Deportation* (Vienna: Turia + Kant, 1999), pp. 143–144. This document has been translated from German.
2 Malvine Fischer, née Schlesinger (b. 1878), housewife; originally from Rozsahegy in Hungary, and later lived in Vienna; deported on 3 Dec. 1941 from Vienna to Riga, where she is presumed to have perished.

you do, we worry when we get no post, although we are convinced that the delay is only down to the poor postal situation. – You will certainly not rejoice in my present letter, and please don't be angry with us if we upset you – when you are unfortunately so harassed yourselves, of course – but to whom can and should we turn in our great need – if not to our children? Mimerl – you have made so many impossible things possible, and we pray to God and hope that you will succeed again. You must supply us with an affidavit immediately – we hope that the relief committee there will provide it to you – because there is no more time to waste! I need not give you any detailed reasons – the consulate is now working at full steam, and we hope that your help will come in time. – We promise not to become a burden to you – we intend to work day and night to earn a living. – If you can't provide the affidavit for all four, then for the time being for us two. Ilka's[4] papers have still not arrived – I was with them both at the consulate today, to urge things along, because it will soon be a year since they submitted [the forms]. We beg you with all our might – not to delay – I know we can count on you, but every day is an eternity for us at this crucial time.

We have not seen Poldi since you left;[5] I went to see Lene, because I wanted to ask her some things, but she had already left to go to Hartl W. You can imagine my surprise. I will also telephone Anny and Poldi too. Today Matild[6] received news that Aunt Gisa in Paluaka[7] died on 11 February – she was a year younger than me – I would have been more easily spared – and I need peace and quiet, as my nerves are quite frayed. We are glad that you all have jobs again. – Work helps us get past all the bad things, I see this in my own case – if I didn't have my work at home, I would fall into despair. Matild is already working industriously on her departure – now it is just a matter of whether Fritz can send the boat ticket – I wish we were already at that point. Today Matild's neighbour Halpern was notified in a telegram from his children that they have made a down payment there for the boat ticket, and the departure is being worked on feverishly everywhere. Today I will keep this short – my mind is not really inclined to write. – Kiss the children for me, with hugs and kisses to you, Your parents.

I must add a few words and want to ask you to do whatever is possible.[8] I think I can manage to raise the travel expenses. I visited your parents[9] before they moved to Meidling, wanted to help them with the move, but I had so much legwork to do that I couldn't go back there. Both mums are very nervous, nonetheless one must not be

3 Wilhelmine (Mimi) Weisz, née Fischer (1900–2001), daughter of Malvine Fischer; housewife and seamstress; in 1921 married Ernst Weisz (1897–1992), retailer; the couple emigrated to the USA via Italy in 1940 and later lived in New York.

4 Ilka Donner, née Fischer (b. 1898), sister of Wilhelmine; was deported on 3 Dec. 1941 with her daughter Blanka Donner (b. 1922) to Riga; after 1945 declared dead by her brother Albin Fischer.

5 Poldi was a non-Jewish friend of Wilhelmine and Ernst Weisz.

6 Matilde Kort, née Fischer (b. 1886), sister-in-law of Malvine Fischer; deported on 11 Jan. 1942 from Vienna to Riga, where she is presumed to have perished.

7 Unclear; as in the original.

8 The last paragraph of the letter was written by Malvine Fischer's husband, Leopold Fischer (b. 1864), master carpenter; he was deported on 3 Dec. 1941 from Vienna to Riga, where he is presumed to have perished.

9 This is presumably a reference to the parents of his son-in-law Ernst Weisz.

despondent, one must take everything as it comes. I still hope that all will be well. We were happy to get Ditta's letter and learn that she is already helping with everything, and to read about Hansl, now called John.[10] Love and kisses, Your parents

DOC. 156

On 20 February 1941 Franz Heurich from Meiningen applies to the Foreign Exchange Office in Thuringia for a payment from Hermann Heimann's blocked account[1]

Letter from Franz Heurich,[2] 19 Fischergasse, Meiningen, to the Regional Tax Director for Thuringia,[3] Foreign Exchange Office,[4] Rudolstadt (received on 21 February 1941), dated 20 February 1941

Re: security order for Hermann Israel Heimann,[5] Meiningen, dated 12 September 1939, reference number: J.S. 143 Bo/Pa.[6]
Concerning the application of the aforementioned, dated 20 February 1941, for release under § 59 of the Foreign Exchange Law[7] of secured sums in the amount of RM 4,800.

On 31 January I paid a visit in person to the Foreign Exchange Office to ascertain whether the present application can be filed at all. I was told that the possibility of a permit exists, and it was left to my discretion to submit a corresponding application. I could not file the application until today, because I was not able to reach the applicant any sooner.

Regarding the application itself I would like to state the following:

From 1936 to 1939, I worked at the Jewish Firm Herbert Heinemann, Meiningen, as a bookkeeper. I had previously worked from 1926 to 1936 at *Gebr. Heinemann* (father of

10 Edith (Ditta) (1925–2016) and Hans (b. 1927), the children of Wilhelmine and Ernst Weisz, had gone to Belgium in Feb. 1939 on a Kindertransport and reached the USA in Sept. 1940 via France, Spain, and Portugal. Dr Edith Kurzweil, née Weisz, sociologist, later edited the *Partisan Review* and held a professorship at Adelphi University; her final place of residence was in New York. Hans Weisz, who Americanized his name to John Weiss in 1946, served in the US Army and then worked with his father in the marble trade; he resides in New Jersey and continues to oversee International Granite & Marble Corp. (IGM), the family marble business.

1 ThHStA, Der Oberfinanzpräsident Thüringen, Nr. 704, fol. 122r–v. This document has been translated from German.

2 Franz Heurich (1893–1952), chartered accountant; member of the German Democratic Party (DDP); worked as a bookkeeper at the Heinemann firm in Meiningen from 1926; faced legal proceedings in 1943 for subverting the war effort.

3 From 1936 the regional tax director was Dr Theodor Hillmer (1881–1961).

4 From 1937 the Foreign Exchange Office was headed by Dr Wilhelm Peine (b. 1901).

5 Hermann Heimann (b. 1876), retailer; emigrated to the USA in 1941 with his son Heinz Heimann (b. 1912).

6 On 12 Sept. 1939 Hermann Heimann received a security order from the Foreign Exchange Office under the regional tax director for Thuringia, instructing him to transfer his assets within five days into a 'secure account with limited availability' at a bank licenced to deal in foreign exchange. Beyond an allowance of 300 Reichsmarks per month, he could access his money only with the written permission of the Foreign Exchange Office: ThHStA, Nr. 704, fols. 96–97.

7 In accordance with § 59 of the Law on Foreign Exchange Control, the relevant foreign exchange office could dictate that the person concerned required permission to access his assets, if there were sufficient grounds to suspect that the assets would be removed from foreign-exchange control: *Reichsgesetzblatt*, 1938, I, p. 1742.

the aforementioned) as head bookkeeper. When this firm went bankrupt, I lost my job and was unable to find another position in Meiningen, as there is no demand here in this small place, which has no industry. Between 1936 and 1938 I was involved in handling the liquidation process for Gebr. Heinemann. This was not a full-time post and, as a sideline, I kept the books of the Herbert Heinemann Firm. Because this company, following the bankruptcy, had to pay in cash for all purchases of goods and was financially unsound, I abandoned my claim for salary in order to support the purchasing done by the firm, which could pay me only a low wage, and to make it possible to have goods in stock. Because I drew my salary from the liquidation, I was able to make this possible.

In November 1938 the action against the Jews took place, and on 31 December 1938 the Heinemann firm was closed. The Aryanization process yielded only enough to pay the suppliers, and I received not a penny in response to my claim, which had accumulated to RM 4,800. The owner of the Heinemann firm had thus become destitute and could not pay my claim.

This sum of RM 4,800 represents unpaid wages. It is thus something that I had to work hard for, very often in the evenings, and it is very hard for me to think that I worked for nothing. One may point out to me that I should have demanded my wages and had them paid, but on the other hand I could not foresee that, at the instance of the state, events would occur that would cheat me of my hard-earned money. The loss of the sum of RM 4,800 hits me very hard, particularly in today's world. I set myself up in business in 1939 by opening a stationery shop, because I could not undertake Aryanization as a result of insufficient funds, although I was the leading candidate for this for moral reasons alone, since I had worked for Heinemann for years, even before 1914. As a result of the war that has come about and the associated rationing, I receive virtually no paper supplies, with the result that my shop, which had shaped up quite well in 1939 and would have offered me a livelihood, now does not bring in enough for me to meet my obligations. This is due in part to the fact that my wife is seriously ill with diabetes and I have expenses of RM 150 per month for this illness.

Therefore, I could make good use of the sum of RM 4,800 now, to pay for [the costs associated with] my wife's illness. Several months ago I discussed this matter with Mr Hermann Israel Heimann, the applicant. I have known Mr Hermann Israel Heimann since 1909. As I have performed many services for him over the decades, he has offered to make good my loss of RM 4,800. He knows my situation and above all is aware of the illness of my wife and the substantial costs that inevitably arise from it. It is because of this that he has expressed his willingness to pay the RM 4,800 in question. Given the above, I most politely request – since the sum represents wages for work performed and I am in a particularly difficult position, in that I, in contrast to other Volksgenossen, have a considerable outlay for illness, which I cannot avoid – that you kindly approve the application for payment of the RM 4,800 from the restricted account of Hermann Israel Heimann.

I expressly attest herewith that my claim is genuine. The claim can also be substantiated by the balance sheet of the Heinemann firm, which is currently in the hands of the local tax office.

Heil Hitler![8]

8 On 4 March 1941 Franz Heurich's request was granted: ThHStA, Der Oberfinanzpräsident Thüringen, Nr. 704, fol. 125.

DOC. 157

On 25 February 1941 the Self-Help Organization of the Jewish Blind asks Josef Löwenherz for help in avoiding deportation to the General Government[1]

Letter from the Self-Help Organization of the Jewish Blind, signed Leo Damm, 35 Untere Augartenstraße, Vienna II, dated 25 February 1941

Esteemed Doctor,[2]

In our extreme distress we venture to submit to you the following request.

Based on the tender concern that you and your esteemed spouse[3] always displayed towards the blind, we hope that you will also understand the great difficulties in which we presently find ourselves and hold your protecting hand over us in this case also.

Our request has to do with the resettlement of the Jews. It is undeniable that the resettlement is difficult to bear for every one of our co-religionists. But it is equally undeniable that it hits the blind harder by far. A blind man who is taken out of his familiar environment and transplanted to one that is unknown to him is, in the truest sense of the word, a man who is lost. In the first transport, as many as three blind persons went astray. Currently there are two blind persons at Castellezgasse,[4] and it is to be feared that this unspeakably harsh lot will continue to befall the blind. To save the poorest of the poor, the blind, from the most terrible fate, we are turning to you, esteemed Doctor, with the respectful and most urgent plea: Help us!

All the blind of Vienna, who are united in our group and in whose name we address this plea to you, consider you as the only person who can bring salvation and help to them here and, because of your elevated status, as the person most ideally placed to do so.

We conclude our respectful request by expressing to you in advance our deeply felt gratitude for all that you do for us, and by voicing again the urgent plea: *Help us.*[5]

In respectful admiration

1 CAHJP, A/W 273, copy in Archiv der IKG Wien, MF A 3, frame 617. Excerpts published in Herbert Rosenkranz, *Verfolgung und Selbstbehauptung: Die Juden in Österreich 1938–1945* (Vienna/Munich: Herold, 1978), p. 260. This document has been translated from German.

2 This refers to Josef Löwenherz.

3 Sofie Löwenherz, née Schönfeld (1890–1981); from 1928, president of the Austrian branch of the Women's International Zionist Organization (WIZO) and headed the Jewish section of the National Women's Service (Nationaler Frauendienst), a relief organization founded in March 1934; emigrated to the USA with her husband in 1945.

4 This is the place where the Jews selected for deportation had to wait for their departure: see Docs. 144 and 151.

5 Josef Löwenherz was powerless to take action in this matter. The Israelite Religious Community of Vienna was required to submit each individual application for deferment from deportation, for example, in the case of essential employees, to the Central Office for Jewish Emigration for authorization.

DOC. 158
Travel restrictions for Jews are discussed in the Reich Ministry of Transport on 25 February 1941[1]

Transcript of the meeting on 25 February 1941 as an attachment to the letter (marked 'secret') from the Reich Minister of Transport (19 G/Vaap 11), p.p. signed Treibe,[2] to the Reich Minister of the Interior for the attention of Ministerialrat Dr Lösener, in triplicate; the Reich Minister of Labour for the attention of Regierungsrat Dr Graef; the Reich Minister of Justice for the attention of Ministerialrat Koffka; the Reich Marshal of the Greater German Reich, Plenipotentiary for the Four-Year Plan for the attention of Oberregierungsrat Dr Mann; the Deputy of the Führer, the liaison staff of the NSDAP, 64 Wilhelmstraße, Berlin W 8, for the attention of Landesgerichtsrat Dr Lampe; the Reich Minister of Aviation for the attention of Ministerialrat Dr Schleicher; the Reich Postmaster General for the attention of Ministerialrat Dr Schuster; the Reich Minister of Economics for the attention of Oberregierungsrat Dr Ottmann; dated 6 June 1941[3]

The question of restricting Jews from travelling on all means of transport was discussed in the Reich Ministry of Transport on 25 February 1941. In attendance were the departmental representatives whose names can be seen in the attachment.[4]

At the start of the meeting, the chair (Ministerialrat Dr *Friebe*)[5] explained the facts of the matter and made known the contents of the letters of the Reich Minister of the Interior dated 28 November 1940 and 11 January 1941.[6]

Ministerialrat Dr *Lösener* (Reich Ministry of the Interior)[7] and Oberregierungsrat Dr *Mann* (Office of the Plenipotentiary for the Four-Year Plan) confirmed that there had been no change in the meantime in the views represented in the letters mentioned. The secret decree issued by the Plenipotentiary for the Four-Year Plan[8] on 28 December 1938 was to remain in effect, i.e. no ban on Jews using railways, trams, suburban, city,

1 BArch, R 3001/20052, fols. 113–116. This document has been translated from German.
2 Paul Treibe (1876–1956), administrative official and lawyer; Regierungsrat in the Railway Directorate in Essen, 1918; headed the Fare and Traffic Department of the Main Administration of the Reich Railway (Reichsbahn), 1935; director of the Reich Railway, 1936; Ministerialdirigent in the Reich Transport Ministry (RVM), 1938; pensioned off in 1942.
3 The accompanying letter contains handwritten notes and instances of underlining.
4 Ministerialrat Dr Friebe, RVM, Dept. I (chair); Ministerialrat Reiser, RVM, Dept. I; Ministerialrat Büttner, RVM Dept. IV A; Ministerialrat Dr Genest, RVM Dept. V B; Ministerialrat Dr Lösener, Reich Ministry of the Interior Dept. I; Oberregierungsrat Dr Mann, Four-Year Plan; regional court judge Dr Lampe, Office of the Deputy of the Führer; Ministerialrat Koffka, Reich Ministry of Justice; Oberregierungsrat Dr Ottmann, Reich Ministry of Economics; Ministerialrat Dr Schleicher, Reich Aviation Ministry; Ministerialrat Dr Schuster, Reich Postal Ministry; Ministerialrat Dr Graef, Reich Labour Ministry.
5 Dr Kurt Friebe (b. 1896), lawyer; worked in the Reich Transport Ministry from 1933; deputy director of the Central Office for International Carriage by Rail in Berne, 1943.
6 These letters are not in the file. The Reich minister of the interior was Dr Wilhelm Frick.
7 Dr Bernhard Lösener (1890–1952), lawyer; worked first for the Customs and Tax Authorities; joined the NSDAP in 1930; in the Reich Ministry of the Interior from April 1933 to the end of 1942, specialist for 'Jewish affairs' there in Dept. I (constitution and legislation) from mid 1933; moved to the Reich Administrative Court in 1943; held in custody in connection with the attempt to assassinate Hitler on 20 July, 1944–1945; worked in the regional tax directorate in Cologne, 1949–1952.
8 Hermann Göring.

and underground lines, buses, and ferries for *short-distance travel* will be issued.[9] Ministerialrat Dr Lösener explained that the Jews, as a consequence of the special police restrictions imposed on their presence in public, are forced to use the railway and other means of transport over certain distances, particularly in order to meet their economic and cultural needs (such as using certain schools). This should not be prevented in the future either.

Ministerialrat Dr *Friebe*, with the assent of all present, took the view that one could not introduce the requirement for Jews to obtain police permission for travel over long distances solely for the railways. Rather, this measure should be extended to all means of transport, i.e. also to air and motor transport, as well as inland and maritime shipping.

Ministerialrat Dr *Schleicher* (Reich Ministry of Aviation)[10] made it known that there are at present no restrictions for Jews regarding the use of commercial aircraft, but that, in his opinion, such restrictions should also be introduced if the railways introduced them.

Ministerialrat Dr *Schuster* (Reich Postal Ministry)[11] stated that Reich Postal Service buses make local journeys only, and that they therefore must remain free of restrictions in accord with the principles of the Reich Minister of the Interior.

With regard to the legal implementation of the restriction for Jews concerning long-distance travel, Dr *Friebe* stated that this could not be achieved by revising the Rail Transport Regulations, because this would require a (police) regulation under public law, with provisions for severe penalties, up to imprisonment, in the event of non-compliance. By contrast, the *EVO*[12] is an implementing regulation on the Commercial Code under private law, and thus cannot introduce such provisions. As Jews are not to be prohibited from travelling altogether, but rather required to obtain a police permit, the best solution would be for the Reich Minister of the Interior, who is responsible for issuing police regulations, to issue such a police regulation for reasons of expediency. He stated that this solution was all the more necessary because Jews are to be required to obtain permits for *all* means of long-distance transport where the contract of carriage is often based exclusively on contracted law, as in the case of the bus service operated by the Reich Railways. It was the task of the Reich Railways and the other carriers to cooperate to the greatest possible extent in the implementation of this police regulation and to pass on reports of any violations, as well as to report any violations that they observe to the police authorities in charge of criminal prosecution.

Ministerialrat *Koffka* (Reich Ministry of Justice)[13] concurred fully with the statements made by Dr Friebe. In his opinion, too, the current issue is not to be resolved through transport law, but rather solely in the context of legislation pertaining to the

9 See PMJ 2/215.

10 Dr Rüdiger Schleicher (1895–1945), lawyer; Regierungsrat in the RVM, 1927; moved to the Reich Aviation Ministry, 1933; joined the NSDAP in 1933; Ministerialrat, 1934; headed the Institute for Aviation Law at the University of Berlin from 1939 as honorary professor, 1939; arrested and executed in connection with the attempt to assassinate Hitler on 20 July 1944.

11 Dr Fritz Schuster (b. 1897), lawyer; assistant judge at Königsberg local court from 1925; director of postal services in Leipzig, 1930; later Ministerialrat in the Reich Postal Ministry; joined the NSDAP in 1933; Ministerialdirigent, 1944; supervised the military mail service office; worked at the West German Postal Ministry from 1949.

12 *Eisenbahn-Verkehrsordnung*, Rail Transport Regulations: *Reichsgesetzblatt*, 1938, I, pp. 667–668.

Jews. The *EVO* is governed by the notion that carriers have a duty to convey passengers and goods. The exclusion from travel of passengers with diseases that constitute a risk to public health under § 9 of the *EVO* was issued exclusively to protect other passengers. However, the decisive factor in introducing the travel ban for Jews was not consideration for fellow passengers but rather other non-transport-related reasons, particularly the aspect of protection against sabotage and the question of the treatment of the Jews in public life in general.

Ministerialrat *Büttner* (RVM)[14] emphasized that, in his opinion, the implementation of the regulation by the transport offices will encounter great difficulties if no clear distinction is made between long-distance and short-distance travel. If no fixed kilometre limit was introduced, one could consider excluding Jews solely from using express trains and fast trains.

In the opinion of the chair (Dr Friebe) and the other participants at the meeting, limitation of the travel ban to the fast trains would be too narrow.

Ministerialrat Dr *Lösener* stated that he personally concurred with the view of the other participants at the meeting to the effect that the matter must be regulated not in the *EVO* but by a special police regulation for all means of transport in long-distance travel. He said that he was unable to make a binding statement as to whether his ministry is prepared to issue a corresponding police regulation as he is only in charge of the general political handling of the Jewish question, and the sole responsibility in this matter lies with the Security Police Department at the Office of the Chief of the German Police and Reichsführer SS, Department of Security Police (specifically, Regierungsassessor Jagusch). He said that he did not fail to recognize the difficulties involved in differentiating between long-distance travel and short-distance travel, and he was of the opinion that a flexible distinction must be drawn here, taking the individual case into account, which could be regulated in greater detail in an implementing provision for the planned police regulation. However, for practical reasons he was unwilling to endorse the proposal made by Ministerialrat *Reiser* (RVM) that identity cards for short-distance travel should be issued to Jews once and for all, because as a result of past experiences he does not wish to introduce any new sort of identity cards.

Ministerialrat Dr *Genest* (Reich Ministry of Transport)[15] stated that the question of the use of railway station dining facilities by Jews must be regulated along the same lines and in the same regulation as travel by Jews on long-distance transport in general, so that Jews, in the future, may only use station dining facilities and other subsidiary establishments of the Reich Railways (hairdressers' and barbers' shops) if in possession of a travel permit. He also regards such a regulation as necessary because conflicts with German Volksgenossen have arisen from the use of station dining facilities by Jews.

13 Johannes Koffka (b. 1882), lawyer; public prosecutor at Berlin Regional Court, 1911; higher regional court judge, 1922; division head in the Reich Ministry of Justice, 1924; Ministerialrat, 1929; member of the NSDAP.

14 Ernst Büttner (b. 1889), lawyer; first worked at Kiel Higher Regional Court; joined the NSDAP in 1939; from 1939 in the RVM; division head in the RVM's legal department; ministerial director in 1941.

15 Dr Genest, lawyer, Ministerialrat in the RVM from 1939; worked in Dept. IV B/88 (commercial law, advertising industry, taxes and levies).

There was general consensus that this proposal should also be taken into account in the regulation concerning the restriction of travel by Jews. This can come about most expediently by making the use of all means of transport in long-distance travel contingent on a police permit and by stipulating in the implementing regulation that 'use of the means of transport' also includes the use of their subsidiary establishments (station dining facilities, hairdressers' and barbers' shops, bookshops, newsagents, and other shops).

Regierungsrat Dr *Graef* (Reich Ministry of Labour)[16] stated that he agreed in principle with the envisaged regulation. Considering that increased use of transport by Jews is to be anticipated in the context of their labour deployment, he requested that the authority to issue travel permits in such cases be transferred from the police to the employment office, as outlined in the letter from the Reich Minister of the Interior dated 28 November 1940. All those present were in agreement with this.

Oberregierungsrat Dr *Ottmann* (Reich Ministry of Economics)[17] stated that, from the perspective of his ministry, he was wholly in agreement with the planned approach.

There was agreement that those Jews who live in privileged mixed marriages, as mentioned in the letter from the Reich Minister of the Interior dated 11 January 1941, are to be exempt from the travel bans. There was also unanimity as to how this concept should be defined.

Regional Court Judge Dr *Lampe* (Office of the Deputy of the Führer) was also of the view that the travel restriction for Jews on long-distance transport should be extended to all related means. He said that he had no objection to the planned regulation, but intends to forward the proposed regulation to a few Gauleiter to gauge their opinion, and wants to ask them about the experiences gained regarding the use of means of transport by Jews in short-distance travel. He will inform the Reich Minister of Transport and the Reich Minister of the Interior of the result of this survey, and asked for the final settlement of the matter to be deferred until then.[18]

16 Dr Walther Graef (b. 1895), lawyer; joined the SA in 1933; in judicial service at the local courts in Breslau and Namslau, 1934–1936; worked in the employment offices in Liegnitz, Brieg, Trebnitz, Beuthen, and Freiwaldau, 1936–1939; joined the NSDAP in 1937; worked at the Reich Ministry of Labour from 1940.

17 Dr Karl Ottmann (1892–1970), lawyer; with the Reich Railways from 1923; worked at the Reich Railways Directorate in Hanover, 1933–1939; joined the NSDAP in 1937; at the Reich Economics Ministry as liaison to the Reich Railways, 1940–1945; with the German Federal Railways (Deutsche Bundesbahn) from 1949; head of the central audit office for the German Federal Railways, 1952–1956.

18 On the restrictions concerning travel and means of transport that were ultimately introduced, see Doc. 222.

DOC. 159

On 1 March 1941 the head of the Political Department of the Reich Foreign Office comments on the extent to which action can be taken against foreign Jews[1]

Note by the head of the Political Department of the Reich Foreign Office (Pol. IX 585 to D III 1001), signed Woermann,[2] Berlin, dated 1 March 1941[3]

As far as I can remember, the Reich Foreign Office has always taken the view that, in view of German legislation, action against foreign Jews in Germany should only be taken in individual cases with the prior agreement of the Foreign Office.

In such cases, the position has always been adopted by Pol. IX[4] that such measures should not be taken against Jews who are subjects of the United States, mainly because the number of cases concerned is relatively small and the Americans should not be given the opportunity in this way to become spokesmen on the question of policy against foreign Jews in Germany. This should be the end of the matter.

The same would also apply by analogy to Americans in the occupied territories. This position was most recently expressed in the memo of Ministerial Director Wiehl[5] – head of Trade Policy [Department] 51, 1 March – with a note to the Reich Minister of Foreign Affairs[6] compiled following consultation with Envoy Luther. From this point of view, the policy against American Jews in France should be reviewed. For this purpose, the Germany Department has a copy of the letter written by the administrative staff of the military commander in France to the state secretary, dated 22 February of this year.[7]

Likewise, for non-American Jews a decision would have to be made on a case-by-case basis, though it can be stated from the outset that there are no political concerns regarding action against Hungarian Jews and Jews from the Balkan states.

Soviet Russians in Germany will be almost exclusively civil servants or staff from the trade mission etc., and for this reason action against them is out of the question. The same does not apply in the General Government, whereby it has to be ensured that no discrimination occurs.[8] With regard to the note submitted by the Swedish

1 PA AA, R 105 015. Published in *Akten zur Deutschen Auswärtigen Politik 1918–1945*, series D: *1937–1945*, vol. 12, no. 1 (Göttingen: Vandenhoeck & Ruprecht, 1969), pp. 169–170. This document has been translated from German.

2 Dr Ernst Woermann (1888–1979), lawyer; legation secretary in Paris, 1920, and in Vienna, 1925; consul in Liege, 1930; embassy counsellor in London, 1936; joined the NSDAP in 1937 and the SS in 1938, ministerial director and head of the Political Department in the Reich Foreign Office, 1938; SS-Oberführer, 1942; ambassador in China, 1943–1945; arrested at the end of the war, sentenced at the Nuremberg Military Tribunals to seven years' imprisonment in 1949, and released in 1950.

3 The original contains handwritten notes and underlining.

4 The 'America' desk at the Political Department of the Reich Foreign Office.

5 Emil Wiehl (1886–1960), lawyer; joined the Reich Foreign Office, 1920; legation secretary in London, 1921; legation counsellor, 1923; consul general in San Francisco, 1927, and in Pretoria (South Africa), 1933; joined the NSDAP, 1934; ministerial director and head of the Trade Policy Department at the Reich Foreign Office, 1937; retired from service, 1944.

6 See: *Akten zur Deutschen Auswärtigen Politik 1918–1945*, series D: *1937–1945*, pp. 167–168.

7 The file does not contain the copy of the letter.

8 In a letter dated 26 Feb. 1941, Woermann had noted that he had assured the first secretary of the Soviet embassy, Bogdanov, that Soviet Jews would be treated in exactly the same way as Jews from other third countries: PA AA, R 29 989, Nr. 321 638.

legation,[9] there are no grounds to grant Swedish Jews a special status. However, there should be no admission to them that they are being discriminated against in any way as compared with the Americans or any other countries. I would therefore consider it appropriate to leave the note unanswered, and to also act in a dilatory manner in the case of further reminders.

Hereby returned to the Germany Department[10] via Ambassador Dieckhoff.[11]

DOC. 160

On 5 March 1941 the Reich Security Main Office extends the opportunities for auctioning off the property of Jewish emigrants that has been confiscated prior to shipping[1]

Letter from the RSHA (IA II – Allgem. 1494/II), signed p.p. Dr Bilfinger, Berlin, to all Gestapo (head) offices with the exception of the Gestapo (head) offices in Graudenz, Bromberg, Posen, Hohensalza, Litzmannstadt, dated 5 March 1941[2]

Re: deprivation of German nationality in the case of Jewish emigrants; here, auction of household effects.

Reference: circular decrees dated 1 August 1940 (I A11 Allgem. 1450/40) and 24 September 1940 (I A 11 Allgem. 1433)[3]

I. Pursuant to the provisions in Point III of the circular decree dated 1 August 1940 (I A 11 Allgem. 1450/40), confiscated *household effects* belonging to emigrant Jews, against whom a denaturalization procedure has either been initiated or is being prepared, can

9 This note is not in the file.

10 Copy to: Acting Legation Counsellor Erich Albrecht (1890–1949), deputy head of the Legal Department at the Reich Foreign Office; head of the Trade Policy Department; Acting Legation Counsellor Reinold Freytag (1888–1962), section IX/America in the Reich Foreign Office; Envoy Curt Heinburg (1885–1964), head of section IVa/Balkans, Italy with Ethiopia; Envoy Dr Werner von Grundherr zu Altenhann und Weiherhaus (1888–1962), head of section for Scandinavia, Finland, and the Baltic in the Political Department of the Reich Foreign Office.

11 Dr Hans Heinrich Dieckhoff (1884–1952), diplomat; joined the Reich Foreign Office in 1912; legation counsellor in Constantinople, 1916–1918; ministerial director, 1930; headed the England-America Department from 1930 to 1936 and the Political Department at the Reich Foreign Office in 1936; ambassador in Washington, 1922–27 and again 1937–1938; joined the NSDAP in 1941; ambassador in Madrid, 1943–1944.

1 BArch, R 58/276, fol. 266r–v. This document has been translated from German.

2 Sent for information only to (a) the Inspector of the Security Police, (b) the Gestapo in Graudenz, Bromberg, Posen, Hohensalza, Litzmannstadt, (c) the Higher SS and Police Leaders (HSSPF), (d) the Senior Commander of the Security Police in Prague, (e) the SD (Main) Districts, (f) the Head of Group I A (a), (g) Section I B 1, (h) Section I F. At the top of the original there is the receipt stamp of the HSSPF West dated 11 March 1941, and at the bottom the official stamp of the Reichsführer SS and Chief of the German Police.

3 See Doc. 97, fn. 2. The decree 're: the deprivation of German nationality in the case of Jewish emigrants', dated 24 Sept. 1940, stipulated with reference to the directive of 1 August 1940 that financial assets above 5,000 Reichsmarks were to be seized by the State Police, in order to make them immediately unavailable to the Jewish emigrants: copy of the decree in LAB, A Rep 92 Nr. 336, fols. 1227–1228.

already be auctioned, providing that an imminent denaturalization is more or less certain.

I hereby agree that, in future, an auction of the confiscated *household effects* belonging to emigrant Jews can also occur in cases where the denaturalization process against Jewish emigrants has been started or is in preparation but cannot result in denaturalization according to the directives currently in force, and an auction seems necessary for economic reasons. Apart from that, the conditions in Point III, paragraphs 2 and 3, of the aforementioned circular decree dated 1 August 1940 shall apply *mutatis mutandis.*

II. Confiscations of household effects that take place in the course of a denaturalization process must be reported to me in all cases, with the proceeds of the auctioned items specified.

III. The decree is not intended for disclosure to district and local police authorities.

IV. All reports submitted to me concerning this issue have thus been addressed.

DOC. 161

Das Schwarze Korps, 6 March 1941: article on the continuing exclusion of Jews, initially in the Reich and then in Europe[1]

Slowly – but surely

We who are witnessing the epochal change in life and thought all too easily forget the individual milestones and markers along the path trodden. It is the sacred right of the revolutionary to eternally make demands. The thoughts of the German people are ahead of their time and are today concerned with what is still to come: with how we can go about peaceful construction, with housing and settlement matters, with questions concerning the cost of living and demand management, with how to shed the last liberal eggshells that still stick to our Volkskörper. There is enough to do, enough work, and enough requirements for many years and decades and as long as our contemporaries are alive. But it will always be advisable to gauge the laws of development from the path, lest we become ungrateful too easily and our concerned demands resemble the solely negative whining of those who are eternally dissatisfied.

A good example on both a large and small scale is provided by the Jewish question. In 1933 only a few with bold imaginations will have seriously believed that a country such as Germany could really be de-Jewified. Today we can already see the de-Jewification within the whole of Europe as a certainty. In 1933 there was still the occasional good German who would shake hands with a Jew without washing them in hot soapy water afterwards. Today, the separation has been performed so thoroughly that the mere thought of any kind of contact with Jews is completely unimaginable.

These are outward appearances, but how enormous must the spiritual development be that leads from simple antisemitism to complete eradication! And how difficult was

1 'Langsam – aber sicher', *Das Schwarze Korps: Zeitung der Schutzstaffeln der NSDAP. Organ der Reichsführung der SS*, issue 10, 6 March 1941, p. 7. This document has been translated from German. The weekly newspaper of the SS was published from March 1935 onwards and edited by Gunter d'Alquen. The initial circulation of 70,000 copies had increased to around 700,000 by 1939.

the struggle for each and every position, however small it may have been! This development was not opposed by those who were openly friendly towards the Jews – that would have resulted in an open fight and swift decision. It was the mental sluggishness of those who are unable to bring a thought process to an end if it is not spoon-fed to them.

Here is a smaller example within the larger one: even before the annual deadline the question as to whether a Jew could belong to a works community[2] was thrashed out in the courts. A completely absurd question, it should be said, for a works community is a part of the Volksgemeinschaft of the German national and racial family, so how would a Jew fit into that! Yet there was no procedure in place, no conditions or laws, and so time and time again, some labour courts conceded social rights for Jews, which National Socialism had won for its followers, not least against the Jewish demon.

Today, it is quite natural, indeed it is barely apparent and is hardly ever noticed, when the *labour court in Cologne* dismisses a case brought by a Jewish employee with the beautiful name *Hirsch Israel Hirsch* to claim holiday pay.[3] The Jew refers to a condition in the work regulations: '*The employee has the right to paid leave after belonging to a works community for an uninterrupted period of six months.*' In dismissing this case, the court reasons:

> *The claimant is a Jew. As such, he fundamentally has no part in the works community. If a Jew cannot belong to a works community, he has to be denied all rights directly derived from the works community, i.e. derived from the Germanic legal concept, according to which the employment relationship forms a community, a relationship between a leader and his followers imbued by the ideas of mutual loyalty, the employer's duty of care, and social honour.*

Is this self-evident? Is it self-evident that a Jew cannot be a member of this community, that he does not enjoy a right, which has always been fought and subverted by Jewry as a political factor? Yes, from today on this will be self-evident. Yesterday, it was not self-evident. Yesterday we were not as advanced in our thinking. And therefore the development can be traced back step by step. What is now self-evident was still a demand yesterday, and before that, it was a mere utopia.

Retrospectively, we recognize that the power of those who are half-hearted, inactive, and lacking in imagination was in each case much greater, how it increasingly dwindled in the course of developments and with each demand met, and how, following the breakthrough of the political revolution, the revolution in thinking is succeeding step by step in cleansing the space fought for and won.

Today, other European peoples are on the verge of radical transition. Those who believe this is happening too slowly may like to take note of the German example, whereby the inner transformation of people may progress slowly but is unswerving, as long as the pioneering flag-bearers do not lose heart.

2 *Betriebsgemeinschaft*: the workers and management as a collective.
3 This could not be verified.

DOC. 162

On 8 March 1941 Helene and Albin Fischer in Shanghai write to Mimi Weisz in the USA about their concerns regarding the prospect of taking in their parents from Vienna[1]

Letter from Helene and Albin Fischer,[2] Shanghai, to Mimi Weisz,[3] USA, dated 8 March 1941

Dearest Mimi,[4]

I received your letter just five minutes ago and am very happy that you are in the picture and have written to us. We only received the reports about your parents[5] five days ago and were quite devastated about it. Less because they want to leave Vienna (for living there is certainly no pleasure), but more because for three months we have been struggling with the insane local inflation and Albin being out of work for almost three months – or rather without earnings, as he did draw up quotes, but that was it – which has affected us very badly. Now, it is a tough prospect to think about two old people in need of rest coming here and having to count every slice of bread. I am also beside myself with worry about what is to happen with Blanka and Ilka.[6] I wrote to your parents straight away that, if it is an absolute *must*, they should by all means come here. If it is not a *must*, they should not come, as it would be right in the summer and that is almost a death sentence. Particularly for Mother, who could barely cope with the heat in Vienna. Now, as I am assuming that it really is a 'must', for how would she otherwise leave Ilka and Bl[anka], I have written that we will try to find her a place in a care home and pay extra so that it will be better for them. If they were to bring landing money,[7] however, they would not be accepted there, and we would take a small room. Mother should bring a paraffin stove, and it will just have to do. They would have to live in Hongkew, where everyone speaks German, it is cheaper and not as hot, and there are fewer mosquitoes. We cannot make any firm arrangements in advance and will just have to wait and see what circumstances they arrive in. There is no prospect of them continuing their journey any further to America, for who should pay for the journey? If they receive the affidavit in time, now would be a good time to go because they would receive money for the house on Schindlergasse, but that would be used up on the journey here and on the landing fee, and, for heaven's sake, they would have to leave some behind for Ilka and Bl[anka]. In US dollars, it is very cheap here, but unfortunately we earn Shanghai dollars, and that is really bad. Your parents could live modestly on 15–20 US dollars a month, which means they would need 300 Sh. dollars to live really modestly. If you could send *10 US* dollars a month, they could bring something, and we gave something, then it should be possible to keep them here. Unfortunately, the prospects here are very bad

1 Leo Baeck Institute, AR 6651, Malvine Fischer Collection. Published in Kurzweil, *Briefe aus Wien*, pp. 147–148. This document has been translated from German.

2 Albin Fischer (1894–1962), architect and engineer; married to Helene Fischer, née Billitzer (b. 1897). The couple emigrated to Shanghai at the end of 1938. Albin Fischer returned to Vienna after 1945.

3 Wilhelmine (Mimi) Weisz, sister of Albin Fischer.

4 The first letter is from Helene Fischer.

5 Malvine and Leopold Fischer.

6 Blanka and Ilka Donner.

7 For information on the landing fee and conditions for immigrants in Shanghai, see Doc. 100.

and if there should be a Japanese-American war, then we would probably lose touch completely.[8] Albin was a broken man: after all, he had to write and tell your parents the truth that I had been supporting the family almost single-handedly for months, and as you can imagine this hardly brings in a king's ransom, nor is it pleasant for him. In addition, it would be embarrassing for me if my parents[9] found out that we are not doing as well as they think. I receive very gloomy letters from my parents but they don't write anything specific. My mother doesn't want to burden me, but I am burdened anyway. Willi will be protecting Pauli from some of the aggravation; she writes that they lead the most secluded life in the world but they seem to have their peace and quiet.[10] He has advanced in his position, and is not serving in the war, so the worst has been avoided. By now, the war has advanced closer to Vienna,[11] and I am sure that Vienna will be bombed. The children, Albin, and I are well. The former are very well behaved and doing well at school.[12] Eva took part in a competition run by the Anti-Tuberculosis Society for secondary school pupils, and she won the second prize for her work here. She was very happy, particularly as she was in the newspaper and will receive some money for that. The difficult thing here is that we have to pay so much in school fees, when in America it is free of charge. There are no schools without fees here but schooling is not compulsory. If you so wish, you can happily grow up illiterate. I am working as usual, but unfortunately I am not getting any new work, which I so need. As I have already written, Albin is having a bad time, and if he has any dealings with clients, it is always with emigrants, and they are so vulgar that dealing with them is like doing penance. You write that we should look into the landing options for the parents and Ernst's family.[13] That is now impossible. Submitting a permit requires formalities, which take months. In view of the particular circumstances, there is the possibility of paying a certain sum to the Israelite Religious Community of Vienna (5,000–10,000 Reichsmarks per head), for which they will take care of travel, landing costs, etc. This can, of course, be overturned by the Japanese tomorrow, and nobody could do anything about it. You mustn't forget that we have just the same options with the Japanese authorities as we do with the Nazi authorities; we can't even get in. Since the travellers have to pass through Manchukuo, it is completely in the hands of the Japanese as to whether they arrive or not. Even a settlement permit won't help, if they are disinclined.[14] Nevertheless, it would be good to have one, but the waiting list already stretches into September. Without the data from Ernst's family and notification of their material circumstances, there is absolutely no point in

8 Following the Japanese occupation of Manchuria in 1931 and the invasion of China in 1937, relations between the USA and Japan had steadily deteriorated. The Japanese–American war began on 7 Dec. 1941 with the Japanese air strike on the US naval base in Pearl Harbor on Hawaii.

9 Probably: Sigmund (1855–1942) and Flora Billitzer (b. 1871); in July 1942 they were deported to Theresienstadt, where Sigmund Billitzer perished. In May 1944 Flora Billitzer was deported from there to Auschwitz, where she perished.

10 Helene's sister Pauli was married to an Aryan.

11 This is possibly a reference to the entry of German units into Bulgaria on 1 March 1941 to prepare for the invasion of Greece. On the same day, Bulgaria joined the Axis alliance. Tsar Boris III of Bulgaria signed the agreement in Vienna.

12 Eva and Miriam, the Fischers' two daughters.

13 This refers to the family of Ernst Weisz, the recipient's husband.

14 Manchuria was a formally independent empire in north-east China from 1932 to 1945, but controlled de facto by Japan.

making enquiries with the English police. What you write about Viki[15] is simply nonsense. Mimi, do you really believe that someone who was able to leave us all, and particularly his parents, to damn well die in Vienna, would suddenly help? What I am very happy about is that Ditta has the chance to continue learning. I am sending my love to both her and Hansl,[16] and am really sorry that our children have been torn away from all their relatives. So, goodbye, Mimi, we'll hear from each other again. Keep well. With much love, Helene

My dearest Mimi,[17]

To you, I would have written the truth earlier. I had a lot of work last year but never enough to take care of everything by myself. This year I took on my last job in January, which finished in February, and I took on a small job at the end of March,[18] which left me with earnings of $150. Rent (without heating) alone comes to $180. The renewed outbreak of war brought about a further deterioration.[19] Changing jobs is not possible: there are already more than enough salesmen, and I could not do any more to try and earn money. It would be impossible for Father to start working here, as he thinks he can, and Mother could not even pay for the bread as an outworker. Helene described everything correctly. The most dangerous thing is, and this we cannot write to the parents, the summer. Last year I was ready to drop and the death toll was considerable. But can one say something like that so bluntly? Of course there are all kinds of diseases, and the doctor, even if he charges very little, is too expensive. That is why I want to put the parents into a care home. It's just I have very little hope that this will be successful. We would have to help a lot because the food is poor and insufficient. But the other issue is the main problem. Ilka's and Blanka's future remains more of a puzzle. In a nutshell, Viki – = 0.00.[20] I will save my words. I would be the happiest person, if I could help. Your parents will have to take the same path as our folks.[21] Submitting papers takes more than just months; it's impossible to wait that long, but the process could be accelerated if $400 in gold could be put aside for each person here. None of us can do this. The most unfortunate thing that happened here is that all of Helene's jewellery (in other words, our reserves) was stolen. I ask you not to write home about this because it would upset mother-in-law terribly and change nothing. Please just give the children my love. I would really like to see what Hansl is like. If you have any news before we do (from our parents), please write. If you can, please also send some money, so that our parents can have something in reserve, because who knows what may change. With much love to you all, Albin

15 Viktor (Viki) Fischer (b. 1902), brother of Albin Fischer and Wilhelmine Weisz, emigrated to Brazil in 1936.
16 Edith Weisz, née Kurzweil, and Hans Weisz.
17 Albin Fischer added this handwritten note at the end of the page after his wife's letter.
18 As in the original. It is either a mistake or the undated handwritten letter was only added later.
19 He is possibly referring here to Italy entering the war in June 1940, as a result of which the sea route from Shanghai to Italy was cut off.
20 By this he probably means 'absolutely rubbish'.
21 This probably refers to the parents of his brother-in-law Ernst Weisz.

DOC. 163

On 12 March 1941 Martin Neugebauer is convicted by a court in Bielefeld for objecting to anti-Jewish comments[1]

Verdict of the Bielefeld Regional Court (5 K. Ms. /9/40), signed Meyer zu Schwabedissen,[2] Strümpler,[3] and Brandau,[4] dated 12 March 1941 (copy)[5]

In the name of the German people!
[Decision] in the criminal case against
unskilled worker Martin Neugebauer [living] in Gütersloh,[6] born on 1 November 1891 in Gütersloh,
charged with an offence against the Law on Treachery.

In the session on 12 March 1941 the Second Criminal Chamber of the Regional Court in Bielefeld, with the participation of Regional Court Director Meyer zu Schwabedissen as chairman, Regional Court Judge Strümpler, Regional Court Judge Brandau as associate judge, Public Prosecutor Dr Göke representing the prosecution, Judicial Secretary Köbbing as clerk of the registry,

passed the following judgement:

The accused is sentenced to a prison term of one year for an offence against § 2 of the Law on Treachery of 20 December 1934,[7] from which the remand period will be deducted. The defendant is to be placed in a psychiatric institution. The costs of the trial will be borne by the accused.

Grounds:

After leaving school, the accused temporarily attended the preparatory institute in Schildesche to prepare for a career in teaching. He then attended a commercial training course, went to the Bethel Institute to train as a missionary, and worked as a nurse. Following a stay at the Beuggen Institute of Pedagogy for teacher training, he was a student at the Academy of Music in Bielefeld. After that, until the outbreak of the World War, he worked in different commercial positions. He served in different units and pos-

1 BArch, R 3001/144089, fols. 10–12. This document has been translated from German.
2 Rudolf Meyer zu Schwabedissen (1889–1975), lawyer; regional court director at Bielefeld Regional Court; resident in Bielefeld from 1937; retired in 1957.
3 Paul Strümpler (b. 1901), lawyer; regional court judge in Bielefeld; resident of Bielefeld from 1934; joined the NSDAP in 1937; drafted into the navy, 1944; retired from Bielefeld Local Court as senior local judge, 1966.
4 Friedrich Brandau (b. 1901), lawyer; probationary judge, 1930; joined the SA in 1933; local and regional court judge from 1934; regional court judge in Bielefeld from 1936; joined the NSDAP in 1937; called up to the Wehrmacht, 1943; in 1959 declared dead as of 31 Dec. 1945.
5 The original contains handwritten underlining and an official stamp. The Senior Public Prosecutor Bielefeld forwarded a copy to the Reich Minister of Justice and chief public prosecutor in Hamm on 23 April 1941 with the information that the appeal submitted by the accused had been dismissed: BArch, R 3001/144089, fol. 9.
6 Martin Neugebauer (1891–1975), writer and journalist; joined the NSDAP in 1931; left it in 1933; sentenced on several occasions to terms of imprisonment for slander, sex crimes, and violations of the Law against Treacherous Attacks on State and Party and for the Protection of the Party Uniform, or *Heimtückegesetz* (20 Dec. 1934), 1936–1941; admitted to the local psychiatric hospital in Eickelborn, 1941, and released in 1945; freelance journalist for the *Gütersloher Zeitung*, 1952–1956.
7 See Doc. 10, fn. 5.

itions during the World War and upon his discharge held the rank of sergeant major second class. He initially showed enthusiasm for the revolution and exchanged letters with Rosa Luxemburg and [Karl] Liebknecht. He then participated in the fighting in the Baltic. After his return [to Germany], he served with the police for a while, which he gave up, allegedly due to moral conflicts. In the meantime, he had married in 1921. The marriage ended in divorce on the grounds of his wife committing adultery. After leaving the police force, he worked as a writer and as an agent for concerts for the blind and for magazines. He was in the Young German Order[8] and during that time filed a complaint against himself to clear himself of the allegation that he had participated in the betrayal of Schlageter.[9] In 1926 he was convicted of fraud and lewd misconduct. After serving his sentence, he spent several years travelling in the countries of the south-east and the Balkans. Following his return to Germany he again worked as a writer and newspaper agent. He joined the NSDAP in 1931, but left in January 1933 when he was due to be expelled for refusing to accept the concept of race and for other forms of dissent. He remarried at the beginning of January 1933. The marriage was an unhappy one. It was annulled in 1935, he being the guilty party as he was said to be a drinker and wanting to live off the income of his wife. In autumn 1934 he was sent to the Provincial Psychiatric Hospital in Gütersloh for observation, suffering from delusions that he was being persecuted. After that, he worked in factories and spent a fairly lengthy time abroad. In 1936 he was found guilty of bill-dodging and offensive behaviour towards women. After that, he had occasional work as a writer and started a job in Wiedenbrück. After attempting to commit a sex crime (§ 176, clause 3, *StGB*[10]) in 1937, he was sentenced to a year in prison. In spring 1939 he applied for work on the Siegfried Line.[11] In 1939 he was remanded in custody for making subversive comments and sentenced to five months in prison by the Cologne Special Court on 3 May 1940 on grounds of diminished responsibility for a violation of § 2 of the Law on Treachery of 30 December 1934.[12] This sentence was adjudged to have already been served while in remand custody. In April 1940 he started as a woodworker at the Henke carpentry firm in Gütersloh.

On the evening of 20 May 1940, he was in the Stieler Inn in Gütersloh. Various guests, including the witnesses Pieper, Schmidt, Hoffschild, and Grüschow,[13] were discussing the present war and started talking about who was to blame for it. Pieper was of the opinion that the Jews were to blame for the war. The accused then got involved in the

8 The Young German Order (Jungdeutscher Orden) was founded in 1920 as an association with a nationalist, anti-Bolshevik, and antisemitic thrust. Its political arm, the People's National Reich Association (Volksnationale Reichsvereinigung), merged with the German Democratic Party (DDP) to become the German State Party (Deutsche Staatspartei) in 1930. The order was dissolved in 1933.

9 This probably refers to the arrest of the Freikorps fighter Albert Leo Schlageter on 7 April 1923 in Essen. Schlageter was sentenced to death by a French military court for acts of sabotage against the occupying troops in the Ruhr region on 9 May 1923, and was executed the same month.

10 *Strafgesetzbuch*: the German Criminal Code.

11 Known as the 'Westwall' in German: a military defence system set up along the German–French border between 1938 and 1940.

12 Correctly: 20 December 1934. See fn. 14.

13 Ewald Pieper, engineer. Ernst Schmidt, employee of the National Socialist People's Welfare. Fritz Hoffschild, businessman in Gütersloh. Hugo Grüschow (b. 1900); joined the NSDAP in 1937; Kriminal-Oberassistent with the Gütersloh Criminal Police.

conversation and stated that the Jews bore absolutely none of the blame, and that the people were simply being told tales. Pieper stuck to his opinion that the Jews alone were to blame for all the recent wars and deserved to be beaten to death. The accused then leapt at him and yelled that he would defend every Jew who was attacked, even if it meant being shot to death. He continued to defend the Jews, but moderated his tone when he noticed the objections of those present and said he would defend anyone who was being unjustly attacked.

The accused admits making the aforementioned comments in the Stieler Inn. He was thereby defending Jews and did so intentionally. His statements are directed against the antisemitic position of the NSDAP and also against the laws and state directives based on the principle of race. Because if he wants to defend Jews who are being attacked, he is thus expressing his disapproval of the eradication of Jews from German national and business life and all measures made possible by that, and wants to try to obstruct them. Furthermore, by declaring that Jews have nothing to do with the outbreak of the current war, he is challenging the position of the state and the Party, according to which it is precisely Jewry that incited war and thereby brought it about. If he makes that out to be incorrect, he is fighting against the directives that were issued for the conduct of the war. His comments thus not only serve to subvert the closed front that is needed to defend against the dangers of the war and the unity of the people, but also to undermine the people's confidence in the political leadership. The accused wishes for his behaviour to be understood as loyalty to the state, and claims that through his attack on witness Pieper he only wanted to prevent steps being taken that could have had damaging consequences for the general public. His assertion that people were being told lies about the Jews being to blame for the war clearly demonstrates, however, that his intentions were of a different kind, namely to stir up hatred towards the leadership and to belittle it in a malicious fashion. He has also denounced the principle of race for a long time. This is what he wanted to reiterate in his comments in the Stieler Inn, as he did previously with his statements for which he was punished by the Cologne Special Court: a negative attitude towards the state.

The comments of the accused were made inside the Stieler Inn. It is unclear whether his comments might have been heard by any number of people, and thus whether they can be considered to have been made in public. Under the circumstances, they could at the very least have penetrated the public sphere. The accused should have taken this into account and assumed it to be the case.

The accused is accordingly found guilty of the offence against § 2(2) of the Law on Treachery of 20 December 1934. The Reich Minister of Justice has ordered prosecution under the decree of 28 August 1940 (III g – 424/40).[14]

At the time that the act was committed, the accused possessed only a diminished capacity to comprehend the illegal nature of the deed and to act accordingly (§ 51(2), *StGB*). According to the detailed and convincing report by the experts Dr Brunner[15]

14 Acts as defined by the Law on Treachery (*Heimtückegesetz*) were only prosecuted on the orders of the Reich Minister of Justice: see Doc. 10, fn. 5.

15 Probably: Dr Hans Joachim Brunner (b. 1900), physician; worked at the Provincial Psychiatric Hospital in Merxhausen, near Kassel, and in the Calmenhof/Idstein reform institution, 1928–1938; joined the NSDAP, 1933; junior doctor at the Bielefeld health authority from 1938; consultant psychiatrist from 1939.

and Dr Hartwich,[16] he is an unstable, devious, and unprincipled psychopath.[17] Both experts conclude this in agreement with Government Medical Officer Dr Kapp,[18] who gave a statement at the Cologne Special Court, on the basis of the erratic and volatile course of his life as described above, the discrepancy between his wishes and talents and his actual achievements and other conduct, and on his tendency towards an asocial lifestyle. In the view of the experts, the accused continues to be emotionally unstable and not in a position to control his emotions. This has shown itself not only in his sexual offences, but also in the offence in question here. He was under the influence of alcohol when he committed it, which caused him to become greatly agitated in the face of comments that he found inappropriate. He was unable to restrain himself and had to bring his objection to bear in a deranged manner. His tendency to showcase himself and his psychopathic reactions also played a part. His cognitive faculty was therefore in large part compromised and restricted when committing the offence.

This diminished capacity must be taken into account when determining the sentence. However, it must also be taken into account that the accused has allowed himself to make treacherous comments on several occasions and has been in trouble for this before. The current offence was committed only a short time after the verdict of the Cologne Special Court. The punishment did not therefore have a lasting impact on him. In addition, the accused has also committed criminal offences to an increasing degree in recent years. Under these circumstances, a prison sentence of one year seems a necessary but adequate atonement for his actions. The period spent on remand pending trial and his admission will be taken into account (§ 60, *StGB*).

The accused is a psychopath and suffers from an emotional disorder. The present offence is directly related to this. As the expert Hartwich correctly described, and as can be concluded from the course of his life up to now, the character and mental attitude of the accused cannot be reformed, by means of either punishment or medical treatment. It is therefore highly probable that he will break the law again in the future. In light of his moral transgressions, he has shown himself to have a weak moral core and thus even poses a risk to the public. Furthermore, a repetition of events such as those at issue here must be expected, bearing in mind his subversive tendencies. This danger must be prevented in the interest of public security. The accused must therefore be placed in a psychiatric hospital or institution, pursuant to § 42 of the *StGB*.[19]

The order for payment of costs results from § 465 of the *StPO*.[20]

16 Probably Dr Werner Hartwich (b. 1877), physician; worked at the Provincial Psychiatric Hospital in Gütersloh as a public health official from 1911, later as a chief physician there.

17 The expert opinions are not in the file.

18 Probably: Dr Franz Kapp (b. 1898), physician; from 1931, worked as a prison physician at Cologne-Klingelpütz prison; joined the NSDAP in 1933; senior public health official from 1939; consultant neurologist from 1939; posted to the Naugard juvenile detention centre, 1944.

19 § 42 of the Criminal Code set out measures for detaining and 'reforming offenders'.

20 *Strafprozessordnung*: Code of Criminal Procedure.

DOC. 164

On 17 March 1941 the emigration department of the Israelite Religious Community of Vienna points out the enormous significance of the retraining courses[1]

Letter from the emigration department of the Israelite Religious Community of Vienna, Advisory Centre for Vocational Training and Occupational Restructuring, signed Flesch,[2] 2/25 Seitenstettengasse, Vienna I, to office headquarters, for the attention of Dr Löwenherz, Vienna I, dated 17 March 1941

Honourable Office Director,

Should you, esteemed Office Director, deem the moment appropriate, it would be good to make an attempt to revive the retraining as quickly as possible, in the form outlined by me below.

The retraining courses run by the Israelite Religious Community have got Jewish people through the most difficult situations in the hardest times and, as a result of the many hours of work in the courses and the homework assignments, have left them little opportunity for brooding.

In particular young Jews (girls and boys) ought to be channelled into intense activity again as quickly as possible, to keep them from being unoccupied, left to their own devices, from idly wandering the streets, and thus running wild.

I venture to enclose a brief report which is intended to indicate how the retraining would be designed in the future.

Respectfully

Report
on the maintenance of skilled manual and industrial *work squads* by the Retraining Department.

The sudden shutdown of the retraining courses not only represented a very heavy blow for the course participants and instructors, but also had a most detrimental effect on the Jews collectively.[3]

At the time of its establishment, the sole purpose of the retraining programme was to create, for those willing to emigrate, the basis for them to establish a livelihood in the new country by virtue of learning manual occupations. Through retraining, many thousands who, unhappy and cast adrift, had lost all their vigour were given new heart and resilience. The huge mass of persons willing to be redeployed knew that manual labour would greatly add to their intellectual skills, and that the manual and industrial skills acquired in the courses would surely enable them to get ahead in their future destination country and avert the high risk of unemployment and destitution. The intensive

1 CAHJP, A/W 2509, copy in Archiv der IKG Wien, MF ZU 2, fols. 774–779. This document has been translated from German.

2 Hans Flesch (1895–1944?), engineer; head of the Advisory Centre for Vocational Training and Occupational Restructuring of the Israelite Religious Community of Vienna; deported on 1 Oct. 1942 to Theresienstadt and on 16 Sept. 1944 to Auschwitz, where he was murdered.

3 In the course of the deportations of the Viennese Jews to the General Government, the retraining courses had to be discontinued: see Docs. 144 and 145.

retraining programme provided capable unskilled labourers and often even qualified skilled workers. They all gladly took every available opportunity to leave the country, as they had no need to fear for their future. As a result of the occupations learned in the retraining courses, many thousands found incomes for themselves and their families and frequently were quickly enabled, on the basis of the income they attained, to have other family members join them in their new adopted homeland. All this is proof of the enormous significance of the retraining project for emigration during the initial period following its establishment.

In 1939, when the war began and emigration, until then a steady stream, began to slow down somewhat, it was once again the retraining programme that helped the Jewish community of the Ostmark to get through this difficult time. Those willing to be redeployed attended the courses in vast numbers and continued to take part in them until the point of emigration, but the majority remained until courses were officially suspended.[4] Apart from the fact that these participants, in 18 months of diligent work, admirably mastered their chosen trade, the course instructors adjusted themselves appropriately to the needs of the times and thoroughly adapted the syllabus of their courses to the wartime economy, as instructed by the administrators of the retraining programme.

Many materials are subject to wartime rationing and thus difficult to obtain. For the Jews, exclusionary laws were created, which would have had a catastrophic effect if it had not been for the retraining programme. After such a long period without earnings, the great majority of the Jews were unable to purchase any clothing, and in addition there was the clothing ration coupon and other ration coupons, which Jews were not permitted to receive.[5] In this way the retraining courses turned into training workshops, in which old garments that, in previous years, would have no longer been mended were patched together in an almost artful manner and made into wearable pieces of clothing again. The same is true with respect to millinery, linen, footwear, etc. etc.

In cooperation with the technical office, our retrained metalworkers, mechanics, carpenters, electrical engineering technicians, upholsterers and paperhangers, plumbers, and various other skilled craftsmen also maintained the facilities and buildings of the Israelite Religious Community and made the necessary repairs. Even the poorest could expect that any repairs they needed would be carried out as much as was possible in these course workshops, in connection with the welfare work of the Israelite Religious Community.

In the horticultural courses, three sites were used to conduct the allotment project of the retraining programme of the Israelite Religious Community, as a result of which the welfare institutions could additionally be provided with fresh vegetables. Even though the quantities yielded had little effect with relation to the amount consumed by the institutions, it was nonetheless important that around 150 adults and 200 adolescents were kept constantly busy and introduced to horticulture as an occupation.

4 From May 1938 to Feb. 1941, approximately 22,800 women and 22,500 men completed the occupational restructuring courses. An overview by occupation can be found in Rosenkranz, *Verfolgung*, p. 270.

5 On the ration coupons for clothing, see Doc. 36, fn. 4.

When barbers and hairdressers had to introduce a two-hour time slot for Jewish customers, and many shops of this kind even stopped serving Jews altogether,[6] it was once again the personnel of the retraining programme who lent a helping hand. From the standpoint of hygiene it was an absolute necessity to give the Jews who were looked after by the Israelite Religious Community an opportunity to maintain standards of personal hygiene and personal care free of charge in the workshops of the barbers and hairdressers, pedicurists, masseurs, etc.

As part of labour deployment – the retraining courses, these training workshops of the Israelite Religious Community – were then reshaped into work squads, which constituted the core for the workforce needed in the enterprises. The employment office (Jewish placement service) took men and women from our courses for all kinds of Aryan skilled craft and industrial businesses, and it turned out that they all, without exception, performed the tasks assigned to them most satisfactorily and repeatedly won commendation for their great knowledge. Numerous works managers approached the administrators of the retraining programme directly, asking them to send them workers, and every such wish could be quickly accommodated. Many of our retraining courses turned into home workshops for export firms, shoe factories, drapers, milliners, furriers, lingerie makers, weaving mills, mechanics, car mechanics, upholsterers and paperhangers, etc. etc.

The administrators of the retraining programme adapted the office to this activity and were constantly concerned with keeping these work squads at full strength at all times, finding a good replacement for everyone who left and thus continually maintaining a body of diligent workers. From individual businesses, even from the Institute for Natural Resources and Life Sciences, letters of commendation were sent to the administrators, proving that the path that had been taken was correct and that the reorientation of the retraining programme was important to the economy in general.

A further shutdown of the retraining programme would have a catastrophic effect on the entire Jewish community, but especially on the young people who have left school, who, without work and guidance, would lapse into idleness and thus also fall into bad ways. Hundreds of youngsters and thousands of older people too would be condemned to inactivity. Moreover, an organizational body would be lost, something that is of exceptional importance in these times, a body that seeks not only to help individual Jews but also to play a part in involving the Jews in the processes of labour and production at the right time and in the right place, and in this way to make suitable work squads available to the authorities in charge of this, as needed.

The costs of maintaining this retraining department would naturally be kept to a minimum. There are only a few Jews now who have not yet retrained. Discounts would have to be granted to these people for payment of the course fee, if they require them. All other course participants intended for the work squads would have to pay the full fee as long as they stay on the courses. In addition, the large number of courses previously available would be reduced. Instead, the administrators of the retraining programme

6 This could not be verified. Evidently the handling of these regulations varied from place to place. In Breslau, for example, from March 1940 Jews were allowed to go to a barber or hairdresser only at certain times: Moshe Ayalon, 'Jewish Life in Breslau, 1938–1941', *Leo Baeck Institute Yearbook*, vol. 41 (1996), pp. 323–345, here pp. 327–328.

would seek to retain, for each branch of trade, only the best course instructors with well-attended courses.

The formation of work squads, however, is also in the interest of the Israelite Religious Community because it is crucial, as it would definitely prevent our co-religionists from going downhill any further and becoming more impoverished.[7]

DOC. 165

On 18 March 1941 Luise Solmitz writes in her diary about a charge brought against her husband, who had failed to present his identity card unprompted[1]

Diary of Luise Solmitz,[2] Hamburg, entry for 18 March 1941

18 March 1941

New calamity? – Fr.[3] went to Police Constable Plischewski at Station 25 to add Aban {our dog}[4] to the register of dogs. I was supposed to go with him, {but} had things to do. If I had known what would happen, I would certainly have gone along. After all, the registration could also have been sent in by post. – Fr. was not yet back when Station 25 telephoned. – When I told Fr. about this later, he returned the call of his own accord, and I listened in. And what I heard was not pleasant. Was Fr. a non-Aryan? Well, then he had not shown his identity card as required, even though he was known to the authority concerned.[5] – He forgot to do so, he said. 'The law is the law. A charge is being brought against you.' – Silence on both sides. We are fortunately out of one difficulty, and now Fr. quite needlessly lets us in for a new, nasty one … I tried three times to speak with Mr {Police Inspector} Zille.[6] Finally I succeeded at Station 25. 'I am here on a very unpleasant matter …' He had already leapt to his feet, quite pale and agitated: 'At this moment I am reading the report that a charge has been brought against your husband – legal proceedings are under way.'

I was well aware of this. Nothing could retract it. That was not what I wanted either. Only to tell Mr Zille, who had always shown himself to be kind and friendly to us, that there was no malice on the part of Fr., who had indeed only wanted to hand something in, as one just puts something into the letter box, not to accomplish or obtain something surreptitiously. That the law is indeed the law. That there is, however, also an unwritten

7 The occupational restructuring courses were not resumed. Until July 1941 the Israelite Religious Community continued to offer language courses in preparation for emigration.

1 Staatsarchiv Hamburg, 622-1/140, 1, Bd. 32. This document has been translated from German.

2 Luise Solmitz, née Stephan (1889–1974), teacher in Hamburg; married to Friedrich Wilhelm Solmitz, who was considered a Jew under the Nuremberg Race Laws despite his conversion to Christianity.

3 Friedrich Wilhelm Solmitz (1877–1961), mechanical engineer and military officer; husband of Luise Solmitz; until 1920 in the army; subsequently senior engineer at a car factory in Berlin, then at the Deutsche Luftreederei airline, managed various metalworks in Berlin and Breslau from 1924.

4 The material in the curly brackets was added by Luise Solmitz after 1945, when she prepared a typewritten version of her originally handwritten diary: see also PMJ 2/5.

5 See Doc. 122, fn. 8.

6 Karl Zille (1884–1966), senior police constable in Hamburg; joined the NSDAP in 1937.

law, to which we all have been indebted at one time, which impels us to spare our fellow human beings unpleasantness, troubles, and hardship with a little wave of the hand. In this case, the question about the identity card and, as far as I'm concerned, a reprimand, a warning. I said there were mistakes that could not be made good: an engine driver who mistakes red for green and kills many people. I said that Fr., for almost six decades, was accustomed to going about without an identity card … Asked: 'Did it have to be a charge, straight away?' – Mr Zille was so touchingly kind and sympathetic … There is nothing, after all, better than a decent human being, even if he cannot help. One's spirits are lifted by the very fact of the good sentiments that are shown to one.

{What I could not write: Mr Zille – in charge of Station 25 – tiptoed to the door, peeked out into the corridor and let rip, although, with good reason, in hushed tones: 'You have no idea at all how dreadful it is to be spied on at every turn by subordinates.' He was their prisoner in his own police station, he said. I have never forgotten how he poured out his heart to me in complete confidence during those terribly dangerous times.}

We are saying nothing to Gisela[7] either about the {ill-fated} matter of the identity card or about the favourable matter of the statement of descent.

Gisela … in Blankenese, wanted to make a good job of it, set out early in the morning and spent 3½ hours in an ice-cold bunker … until the alarm sounded at 10:10 p.m. She quickly telephoned us here before she disappeared into the netherworld. For me, a terrible feeling to know that she was, of all things, near a railway station. All quiet until 15 minutes after midnight, then heavy anti-aircraft fire. Quiet again, all-clear signal at 10 minutes before 1:30 a.m. An anxious wait, with hot tea, for Gisela, who came home happily at 2 a.m.

DOC. 166

On 19 March 1941 State Secretary Wilhelm Stuckart records a discussion about the draft of the Eleventh Regulation on the Reich Citizenship Law[1]

Report (I c 5637 VII/40) from the Reich Minister of the Interior, p.p. signed Dr Stuckart,[2] dated 19 March 1941 (copy)

Re: draft of the Eleventh Regulation on the Reich Citizenship Law, with implementing regulation

In the discussion on 15 March 1941, it emerged that it was necessary to obtain a decision from the Führer for the time being regarding the envisaged measures against the Jews.[3] In preparation, the draft of an Eleventh Regulation on the Reich Citizenship Law and the draft of an implementing regulation are included, and a prompt response is requested.

The draft of the Eleventh Regulation on the Reich Citizenship Law consolidates the provisions with regard to the statelessness of Jews and the forfeiture of property. As

7 Gisela Solmitz (b. 1920), daughter of Luise and Friedrich Wilhelm Solmitz; later married a Belgian and settled in Brussels.

1 BArch, R 2/5980, fols. 53–58. This document has been translated from German.

forfeiture of property arises as a direct result of the loss of nationality, it seems reasonable to me to also base the forfeiture on the Reich Citizenship Law.

Only the fundamental provisions are incorporated in the draft, while the technical details, particularly the provisions concerning the onset and enforcement of the forfeiture of property, are dealt with in the implementing regulation.

Subject to the final opinion of the representative of the Reich Marshal,[4] agreement was reached in the discussion to the effect that the Jews living in privileged mixed marriages should also indeed lose their German nationality, but that the consequences associated with statelessness should eventuate in their case only if specifically so ordered. The question of whether additional groups of persons are to be exempted in general from the consequences of statelessness could not be addressed conclusively in the discussion. A prompt opinion on this is therefore requested.[5] The Reich Minister of Labour[6] is being asked here to consider in particular the question as to whether general exceptions for the areas covered by the Law on the Severely Disabled and the Reich Maintenance Law are deemed necessary.[7]

In the case of combat veterans of the World War, where an exception might come into consideration, it was pointed out during the discussion that no further exceptions for them have been envisaged in the legislation of recent years. In the enclosed draft, apart from privileged mixed marriages (§ 1 of the implementing regulation), no general exemptions are provided.[8]

The revocation of the Jews' nationality is intended to assign them to a lower status. If and when their situation ends up being improved in individual fields of law as a result of their statelessness, there was unanimous agreement that these legal consequences must be excluded. The Reich Minister of Justice[9] is already considering whether this viewpoint requires a special regulation for the Jews who become stateless, for example in the case of the sanctions for high treason, which are more severe for citizens than for stateless individuals.

2 Dr Wilhelm Stuckart (1902–1953), lawyer; joined the NSDAP in 1922; state secretary in the Prussian Ministry of Education from June 1933; state secretary in the Reich Ministry of the Interior (in charge of Department I, constitution and legislation) from 1935; joined the SS in 1936; participated in the Wannsee Conference, 1942; in US internment, 1945–1949; sentenced at the Nuremberg Military Tribunals to four years in prison (credited with time served while on remand), 1949.

3 See Doc. 184, fn. 7.

4 The Reich Marshal was Hermann Göring.

5 The opinion of Undersecretary Hering of the Reich Ministry of the Interior on a draft of the Eleventh Regulation on the Reich Citizenship Law was submitted on 7 July 1941. BArch, R 2/5980, fols. 62–66.

6 Franz Seldte (1882–1947).

7 The Law on the Employment of the Severely Disabled (6 April 1920) regulated various rights of the disabled, and the Law on the Maintenance of Military Personnel and Their Surviving Dependants in the Event of Injury while Serving, or Reich Maintenance Law (*Reichsversorgungsgesetz*) (12 May 1920), ensured the financial protection of the severely disabled: *Reichsgesetzblatt*, 1920, pp. 458–464 and pp. 989–1019.

8 In his written opinion, dated 30 April 1941, Göring requested a regulation for Jewish combat veterans 'that safeguards claims based on the laws pertaining to the severely disabled and on the Reich Maintenance Law etc., in exceptional cases and upon application': BArch, R 2/5980, fol. 126.

9 The acting Reich minister of justice from Jan. 1941 to August 1942 was Dr Franz Schlegelberger: see Doc. 240, fn. 5.

In the case of Jews living in this country, loss of nationality results in suspension of pension payments in accordance with § 120 of the German Civil Service Law. The extent to which use is to be made of the exemption provision envisaged in § 128 still requires clarification.[10] Please submit an opinion on this. It will be possible to make the provision through administrative channels.

Forfeiture of property affects Jews who lose German nationality if they have no habitual residence within the territory of the Reich or have subsequently given up their habitual residence within the territory of the Reich. Because the General Government is not part of the territory of the Reich, the Jews who are citizens and live there are subject to the provisions of property forfeiture.[11]

Forfeiture of property does not affect Jews who live in privileged mixed marriages, owing to their general exemption from the consequences of statelessness. Additional exceptions are not envisaged. At the wish of the representative of the Reich Minister of Finance,[12] in the determination of the debt liability of the Reich in § 3 of the implementing regulation, responsibility for claims for support under family law is explicitly excluded. § 7 of the implementing regulation affords an opportunity to resolve hardship cases.

In conclusion, I wish to point out that for the issuance of the regulation, practical considerations also are relevant, in addition to the general reasons that are intrinsic to the demographic development of the Greater German Reich and are stated in detail in my invitation letter of 13 March 1941 (I c 5637 VII/40 – 5016).[13] The withdrawal of the nationality of Jews living abroad means a significant easing of the burden on the diplomatic missions, which are relieved of the tasks associated with supporting this category of persons, such as the processing of applications for passport issue or extension and requests for readmission in the event of indigence. In addition, an urgently needed clarification of the situation for the Jews living in this country emerges as a result, in that they are now finally excluded from the people of the state. This thereby avoids a situation where the measures to be taken against the Jews, such as deportations etc., are to be carried out against state subjects, which would be awkward from a domestic policy perspective. In addition, the provisions regarding the forfeiture of the property of Jews living abroad signify an essential simplification of the process of liquidating this portion of the Jews' assets. Until now, action could only be taken here in connection with the deprivation of nationality under § 2 of the law of 14 July 1933 (*Reichsgesetzblatt*, I, p. 480), whereby, according to the wording of the law, in a given case it had to be ascertained that the Jew had acted subversively and harmed the interests of the Reich.[14] This time-consuming procedure, which unduly burdened the Reich departments concerned

10 German Civil Service Law, 26 Jan. 1937: *Reichsgesetzblatt*, 1937, I, pp. 39–70. According to § 128, payments ceased in the case of non-German nationals who were entitled to pensions or in cases where persons entitled to pensions had their residence outside the German Reich without this being approved by the highest administrative authority.

11 This refers to those Jews who were deported from the Reich to the General Government. This regulation applied also to the annexed territories.

12 Count Johann Ludwig Schwerin von Krosigk.

13 BArch, R 2/5980, fols. 46–48.

14 Under § 2 of the Law on the Revocation of Naturalization and the Deprivation of German Nationality (14 July 1933) subjects of the German Reich who were resident abroad could be deprived of their nationality if they engaged in political activity against the Reich.

(Reich Foreign Office, Reich Ministry of Finance, Reich Minister of the Interior,[15] Gestapo Central Office), would become obsolete as a result of the regulation and would be substantially simplified.

Because the Reich Foreign Office attaches great importance to having the regulation adopted in the same time frame as the implementation of the Aid to Britain Law by the USA, this must be done with the least possible delay.[16] I therefore request that statements be submitted to me by 26 March 1941.[17]

Copy

Implementing Regulation to the Eleventh Regulation on the Reich Citizenship Law of ...

On the basis of § 3 of the Eleventh Regulation on the Reich Citizenship Law of ... it is hereby decreed:

§ 1

(1) In the event of a mixed marriage, the consequences arising from loss of nationality under § 1 of the Eleventh Regulation on the Reich Citizenship Law do not apply

(a) to the Jewish spouse if the marriage produced offspring and these descendants are not deemed to be Jews, and also if the marriage no longer exists;

(b) to the Jewish wife, even if there are no offspring, for the duration of the marriage. This does not apply if both spouses and any issue of the mixed marriage have their habitual residence outside the territory of the Reich.

(2) The Reich Minister of the Interior can, in consultation with the Deputy of the Führer, order that the consequences arising from the loss of nationality nonetheless eventuate for the persons named in (1).

§ 2

(1) Forfeiture of property under § 2 of the regulation eventuates, in the case of Jews who do not have their habitual residence within the territory of the Reich when the regulation takes effect, at the moment the regulation comes into effect, and, in the case of Jews who later give up their habitual residence within the territory of the Reich, at the moment they give up their habitual residence.

(2) The assets of Jews who, on the basis of § 2 of the Law on the Revocation [of Naturalization] and the Deprivation of German Nationality of 14 July 1933 (*Reichsgesetzblatt*, I,

15 Dr Wilhelm Frick.

16 What the contemporary press called the 'Aid to Britain Law' (An Act to Promote the Defense of the United States) was passed by the US House of Representatives on 11 March 1941. Also in March 1941, US$7 billion was granted for assistance to allied countries: *Monatshefte für Auswärtige Politik*, vol. 8 (1941), pp. 237–242.

17 The report and the draft were sent to the Deputy of the Führer of the NSDAP for the attention of Oberregierungsrat Herbert Reischauer, the Reich Marshal of the Greater German Reich – Plenipotentiary for the Four-Year Plan – for the attention of Ministerialrat Dr Hans-Henning von Normann (b. 1903), the Reich Foreign Office for the attention of Legation Counsellor Franz Rademacher, the Reich Minister of Justice for the attention of Ministerialrat Dr Ruppert (presumably Dr Fritz Ruppert, b. 1887), the Reichsführer SS and Chief of the German Police in the Reich Ministry of the Interior, the Reich Security Main Office (RSHA) for the attention of Oberregierungsrat Rudolf Bilfinger, the Reich Ministry of Finance for the attention of Ministerialdirigent Trapp, and the Reich Ministry of Labour for the attention of Oberregierungsrat Hans Küppers (1907–1972). The Eleventh Regulation on the Reich Citizenship Law did not take effect until 25 Nov. 1941: *Reichsgesetzblatt*, 1941, I, pp. 722–724.

p. 480), have lost German nationality are forfeited to the Reich if they have not previously been declared to have been forfeited.

§ 3

(1) The Reich is liable for debts associated with the forfeited property only up to the amount of the marketable value of forfeited items that are under the control of the Reich. Liability for support claims under family law is excluded.
(2) Rights to items of the forfeited property are retained.
(3) In the event of insolvency, at the request of the regional tax director in Berlin or a creditor, bankruptcy proceedings with respect to the assets are instituted in accordance with the provisions of the Bankruptcy Code. The bankruptcy trustee is to be appointed in consultation with the lower administrative authority in charge of the property of the bankruptcy court, and is to be recalled at its demand.

§ 4

(1) All persons who have in their possession an item from the forfeited assets or who owe something to the legal estate must notify the regional tax director in Berlin of the possession of the item or the existence of the debt within one year of the property forfeiture having come into effect (§ 2(1)).
(2) Claims against the forfeited assets must be filed with the regional director in Berlin within one year of the property forfeiture having come into effect (§ 2(1)). Satisfaction of claims asserted after the deadline expires can be declined without the reasons being specified.

§ 5

(1) The Chief of the Security Police and the SD determines as to whether the prerequisites for forfeiture of property are met.
(2) The management and liquidation of the forfeited assets are the responsibility of the regional tax director in Berlin.

§ 6

(1) If the land registers are incorrect as a result of the property forfeiture, they are to be corrected at no charge at the request of the regional tax director in Berlin.
(2) The provisions of § 1(4, 5) of the Second Regulation on the Implementation and Amendment of the Law on the Granting of Compensation upon Confiscation or Transfer of Property of 18 March 1938 (*Reichsgesetzblatt*, I, p. 317) are to be applied accordingly.
(3) If a right affected by a correction in accordance with the aforementioned provisions does not appertain to confiscated property, the Reich must make good the loss hereby caused to the beneficiary. The extent to which lost profits are to be made good is decided by the judge, using reasonable discretion.

§ 7 To prevent hardship, the Reich Minister of Finance, in consultation with the Reich Minister of the Interior, can make a ruling to the contrary.

Berlin, dated …
The Reich Minister of the Interior
The Deputy of the Führer[18]
The Reich Minister of Finance

18 Rudolf Hess.

DOC. 167
At a meeting on 20 March 1941 in the Ministry of Propaganda, Adolf Eichmann mentions Hitler's instructions to Reinhard Heydrich to plan the 'definitive evacuation of the Jews'[1]

Reich Ministry of Propaganda memorandum (II G Bü/ Hu), initialled Bü,[2] Berlin, dated 21 March 1941

Re: evacuation of the Jews from Berlin.
On 20 March [1941] a discussion took place in the Ministry of Propaganda in the office of Party Comrade *Gutterer*,[3] in which representatives of the Reich Security Main Office and of Inspector General of Building *Speer* took part. Party Comrade Gutterer disclosed that Dr Goebbels, during a conversation at lunch with the Führer, was alerted to the 60,000–70,000 Jews still residing in Berlin. In this conversation it was stated that it is unacceptable that the capital of the National Socialist Reich continues even today to accommodate such a large number of Jews. A certain number of the Jews actively associate with and rent rooms to foreign students, journalists, and diplomats, and thus would have an opportunity to spread rumours detrimental to the state and to damage morale.[4]

Although the Führer did not himself conclude during this discussion that Berlin must be made free of Jews at once, Dr Goebbels is convinced that an appropriate evacuation proposal will surely meet with the Führer's approval.

Party Comrade *Eichmann* from the Reich Security Main Office said that Party Comrade *Heydrich* – who has been tasked by the Führer with the definitive evacuation of the Jews – presented to the Führer 8–10 weeks ago a proposal that has not yet been implemented, solely because the General Government cannot at present take in a Jew or a Pole from the Old Reich. However, there is on hand a written order of the Führer concerning the evacuation from *Vienna* of 60,000 Jews, whom the General Government must therefore still take in.[5] In Vienna, however, only 45,000 Jews are readily accessible at the moment, he said, and so it may be possible to remove the remaining 15,000 Jews from Berlin.

1 BArch, NS 18/1134, fols. 77–78. Published in Adler, *Der verwaltete Mensch*, pp. 152–153. This document has been translated from German.

2 Kurt Bühler (1910–1958), clerk; joined the NSDAP in 1930; worked in the Staff of the Deputy of the Führer (renamed the Party Chancellery in May 1941) from 1938; Reich main branch head responsible for propaganda, press, and lectures; detailed to Cracow to work in the NSDAP's General Government task force in July 1943.

3 Leopold Gutterer (1902–1996), Germanist and scholar of theatre studies; joined the NSDAP in 1925 and the SS in 1927; member of the SA, 1929–1933; Regierungsrat, 1933; ministerial director and head of Department II (propaganda) in the Reich Ministry of Public Enlightenment and Propaganda, 1938; SS-Brigadeführer, 1940; state secretary in the Reich Ministry of Public Enlightenment and Propaganda, 1941–1944; general manager of the Ufa film company, 1944; sentenced by a local tribunal to five years in a labour camp, 1948; granted early release; theatre director in Aachen, 1966.

4 Goebbels recorded this meeting in his diary: see Introduction, p. 55.

5 See Doc. 123.

Further, one must take into account the fact that every Jew who is fit for work is now needed for production, and that Jews suited for labour deployment, the number of whom is also not large, owing to the aging of the Jewish population, are hardly to be found at present. There is even a plan to transfer 42,000 male and 30,000 female Jewish workers from the Warthegau into the Reich on a temporary basis.[6]

He said that in Berlin the Jews have set up a gigantic apparatus for their cultural and economic self-administration, which employs 2,700 Jewish officials and salaried employees alone. The Jewish Reich Association has thus been ordered to dismiss 250 of its 1,000 employees, and the Jewish Community of Berlin to dismiss 700.

Of twenty-two Jewish homes for the elderly, the largest and most modern have been vacated, so that fifteen Jewish homes for the elderly remain at present.

The representative of Inspector General of Building Speer announced that 20,000 apartments are currently being used by Jews in Berlin. These apartments are needed by Speer as a reserve to be released in the event of possible major air-raid damage and later in order to enable the clearance of apartments that have to be demolished during the redevelopment of Berlin. Berlin currently has a shortage of 160,000–180,000 apartments. The outcome of the discussion was that Party Comrade Eichmann was requested to prepare a proposal for Gauleiter Dr Goebbels regarding the evacuation of the Jews from Berlin.[7]

During the discussion, someone also urged that a police regulation be issued forbidding Jews in Berlin to rent apartments to non-Jewish foreigners.[8]

As the Jews are evidently not adhering to the prescribed shopping hours in retail shops and are once again frequenting streets and establishments that are off limits to them, a crackdown is to be proposed, within the limits of the available police manpower.[9]

6 On 4 Feb. 1941 the Reichsstatthalter in Poznań, Arthur Greiser, had offered the Reich Minister of Labour 42,187 male and 30,936 female Jewish workers for the Reich. The Reich Minister of Labour revealed on 7 April 1941 that Hitler had personally prohibited the deployment of Jews from the General Government and the Warthegau in the Old Reich: BArch, R 3901/193, fols. 97–98.

7 See Doc. 203, fn. 3.

8 This could not be confirmed.

9 The Directive of the Berlin Chief of Police regarding Shopping Hours for Jews (4 July 1940) set these hours at 4–5 p.m.: see Doc. 36, fn. 7.

DOC. 168

On 20 March 1941 the Deputy Gauleiter of Vienna informs Police Chief Ernst Kaltenbrunner that every train going to the General Government should be used for deportation[1]

Letter from the Deputy Gauleiter of Vienna (Sch/G.), signed Scharizer,[2] to SS-Gruppenführer and Party Comrade Kaltenbrunner,[3] 8 Parkring, Vienna I, dated 20 March 1941[4]

Gruppenführer,

The Reichsleiter[5] telephoned me yesterday to say that he has spoken to the Reichsführer SS.[6] The Reichsführer has reached the following decisions:

(1) The expulsion of the Jews from Vienna is to be continued in this form: if at all possible, a railway truck carrying Jews is to be coupled to every train travelling into the General Government. Through Party Comrade Laube, I have already contacted President Töpfer[7] and the Emigration Office, Party Comrade Brunner, concerning this matter.

(2) The Jews who refused to clean the train coming from the General Government are to be sent to Mauthausen at once.[8]

(3) The Reichsführer has pledged to the Reichsleiter that in the future no more police forces will be withdrawn from Vienna. No agreement was reached with regard to police reinforcement.

Heil Hitler!

1 DÖW, 1456. Abridged version in Dokumentationsarchiv des österreichischen Widerstandes, *Widerstand und Verfolgung in Wien*, p. 294. This document has been translated from German.

2 Karl Scharizer (1901–1956), chemist; SA member, 1921–1926; joined the NSDAP in 1927; Gauleiter of Salzburg, 1932–1934; joined the SS in 1937; commissioner for settlement affairs in Austria, 1938; Reichstag delegate from 1938; deputy Gauleiter of Vienna from 1939; SS-Brigadeführer, 1941.

3 Dr Ernst Kaltenbrunner (1903–1946), lawyer; joined the NSDAP in 1930 and the SS in 1931; practised law in Linz from 1932; disbarred in 1936; member of the Reichstag from 1938; head of SS Main District Danube, 1938–1943; police chief in Vienna, 1940–1941; head of the Reich Security Main Office (RSHA) and Chief of the Security Police and the SD, 1943–1945; state secretary in the Reich Ministry of the Interior; SS-Obergruppenführer in the Waffen SS, 1944; sentenced to death at the International Military Tribunal at Nuremberg in 1946 and executed.

4 The original contains a receipt stamp with an illegible date, and the official stamp 'National Socialist German Workers' Party, Gauleiter of Vienna'.

5 Baldur von Schirach.

6 Heinrich Himmler.

7 Rudolf Töpfer (1882–1945), engineer; joined the NSDAP in 1938; president of the Reich Railways Directorate in Vienna from Oct. 1938.

8 This order was evidently not carried out.

DOC. 169

Letter, dated 26 March 1941, about the Reich Railways' attempts to purchase property in Frankfurt am Main that previously belonged to the Jewish Kaufmann brothers[1]

Letter (I 12 no. 185) from the Regierungspräsident,[2] property office of the General Tax Authorities, p.p. signed Prohasel,[3] Wiesbaden, to the Prussian Minister of Finance,[4] Berlin C2 (received on 30 March 1941), dated 26 March 1941[5]

Immediate!

Re: disposition of the premises at 8 Poststr. in Frankfurt am Main, confiscated by the Gestapo from Jewish possession (Salli and Leopold Kaufmann).[6]

Enclosures: 3 (land register record; calculation of value by the Prussian State Building Authority in Bad Homburg vor der Höhe, dated 18 January 1941; 1 site plan).[7]

Reporter: Regierungsrat Dr *Müller*.

No discount.[8]

The above property is situated opposite the main railway station in Frankfurt am Main and next door to an office building of the German Railways. The Railways Directorate in Frankfurt is interested in the purchase of this property inasmuch as it is compelled to expand its premises due to the need for increased space near the railway facilities.

For this reason, the Railways Directorate negotiated as early as 10 February 1939 with the tax office in Berlin Moabit,[9] which was dealing with the denaturalization case of Salli Kaufmann at that time. The Reich Railways Directorate was told that there was a prospect of the property being transferred.

As there was an unexpected delay to the confiscation proceedings, the trustee of the property, the lawyer Göllner in Frankfurt,[10] initially made vacant rooms on the first

1 GStAPK, I. HA Rep. 151 IA Nr. 8209, fol. 396r–v. This document has been translated from German.

2 Fritz von Pfeffer, born Friedrich Pfeffer von Salomon (1892–1968), Regierungspräsident of Wiesbaden from 1936 to 1943.

3 Gerhard Prohasel (1890–1976), lawyer; Regierungsdirektor under the Regierungspräsident in Oppeln; temporarily pensioned off and demoted for political reasons in 1933; worked for the Regierungspräsident in Wiesbaden from 1935; joined the NSDAP in 1937; exonerated by a denazification tribunal in 1949; later became a judge at Wiesbaden Administrative Court.

4 Dr Johannes Popitz (1884–1945), lawyer; at the Prussian Ministry of the Interior from 1914; at the Prussian Ministry of Finance, 1919–1929; head of the Department of Property and Transaction Tax, 1921–1925; state secretary, 1925–1929; Prussian minister of finance, 1933–1944; joined the NSDAP in 1937; tendered his resignation in 1938 because of the persecution of the Jews; convicted in 1944 as a conspirator in the attempt to assassinate Hitler on 20 July and executed.

5 The original contains handwritten notes and underlining, and official stamps.

6 Correctly: Sali Kaufmann (1873–1941), official broker at the stock exchange, imprisoned from April to June 1933, and Leopold Kaufmann (1878–1959), banker; they had already emigrated to the USA in 1937 and 1938, respectively.

7 The file does not contain these enclosures.

8 Handwritten addition.

9 The Berlin tax office in the Moabit-West district was in charge of confiscating the assets of Jewish emigrants throughout the Reich. In some cases the office, which had its own denaturalization department, proposed that certain Jews have their citizenship revoked on account of their economic situation.

floor of the property available to the Reich Railways on a rental basis. Over the course of time it also became necessary to repair the central heating system and make substantial repairs to the roof. This work was performed in view of the future purchase by the Reich Railways and at the expense of the Reich Railways. The Reich Railways has also borne the cost of heating the premises since 9 December 1939.

The assessed value of the property is RM 52,700. The value calculation prepared by the Prussian State Building Authority, dated 18 January 1941, along with the site plan, is enclosed. Accordingly, the value of the property is around RM 85,000. According to the enclosed land register record, the property is encumbered with a mortgage, converted into a land charge payable to the Frankfurter Sparkasse 1822 (the savings bank of the Polytechnic Society) totalling RM 84,000. The Reich Railways Directorate is prepared to purchase the property at the price of RM 84,000. It has incurred considerable expenses for the property thus far. Additional structural changes to the premises are still needed.

I therefore wish to endorse the conveyance of the property to the Reich Railways and ask that a decision be reached as quickly as possible, if necessary also with regard to whether the sales value is to be set at RM 85,000 in accordance with the valuation. The Reich Railways attaches great importance to gaining possession of the property as soon as possible.[11]

DOC. 170

Völkischer Beobachter, 27 March 1941: article on the opening of the Institute for the Study of the Jewish Question[1]

Independent research in the struggle against world Jewry
Alfred Rosenberg opened the Institute for the Study of the Jewish Question in Frankfurt/Main
Telegraphic report by our correspondent
R.J. Frankfurt/Main, 26 March
In the series of historic acts during this week,[2] there is an event of profound political and scholarly significance that cannot be overlooked: on Wednesday, Reichsleiter Alfred *Rosenberg*, the Führer's plenipotentiary for the supervision of the entire intellectual and ideological training and schooling of the NSDAP, opened the Institute for the Study of

10 Gerhard Göllner (1907–1980), lawyer; joined the NSDAP in 1933; practised law in Frankfurt from 1935; tasked by the Gestapo with the fiduciary management of the assets of Jews who had emigrated; worked as senior police administrator in Minsk and Riga, 1942–1944; classified as a 'follower' during denazification proceedings in 1948; defence counsel at the first Frankfurt Auschwitz trial, 1963–1965.

11 In a letter dated 12 April 1941 the Prussian Minister of Finance declared his assent to a sale of the property and issued the requisite authorization to the Regierungspräsident in Wiesbaden. The sale finally took place on 8 April 1942: GStAPK, I. HA Rep. 151 IA Nr. 8209, fols. 397r–v and 402r–v

1 'Freie Forschung im Kampf gegen das Weltjudentum', *Völkischer Beobachter* (northern German edition), 27 March 1941, p. 1. This document has been translated from German.

2 This probably refers to the heavy German bombing raids on Plymouth, Erwin Rommel's successful offensive in North Africa, and the accession of Yugoslavia to the Tripartite Pact.

the Jewish Question with an address on '*National Socialism and Scholarship*' and thereby inaugurated the first branch of the Advanced School, which is to be created after the war. The opening ceremony was attended by official delegations from nine European nations, in addition to high-ranking representatives of the Party, the state, the German academic world, and the Wehrmacht.

On Wednesday morning, in Frankfurt's magnificent Civic Hall, the Römer, the building in which numerous German emperors have been crowned, Gauleiter and Reichsstatthalter *Sprenger*[3] greeted the domestic and foreign guests of honour on behalf of the Party, following a solemn musical introduction. He firstly welcomed Reichsleiter Alfred *Rosenberg*. He then extended warm greetings to the representatives of the various governments and renewal movements: Slovak Minister of the Interior Alexander *Mach*; the representatives of Hungary, State Secretary *Kovacs* and Head of Department *Kultsar*; former Romanian minister Prof. *Cuza*; and the representatives of our allies Italy and Bulgaria. Sprenger then welcomed the head of the Nasjonal Samling,[4] Councillor of State Vidkun *Quisling*, and the head of the NSB in the Netherlands,[5] *Mussert*, as well as the delegations of the Danish National Socialist Workers' Party and the Flemish renewal movement.

Among the leading German guests of honour were Gauleiter *Florian* and Gauleiter *Eggeling* and Lieutenant General *Reinecke* as the representative of the Chief of the OKW,[6] Field Marshal *Keitel*. Officials from all Reich agencies and representatives of the organizations of the [National Socialist] Movement were in attendance alongside several vice chancellors of German universities and other prominent figures from German intellectual life. Among them, the Gauleiter singled out the venerable pioneer of racial thought Prof. Dr Hans F. K. *Günther* and Privy Councillor Eugen *Fischer* for a special welcome.

After tracing the great historical development of the old imperial city, Gauleiter *Sprenger* described the *systematic conquest of Frankfurt by the Jewish Gegenvolk*,[7] which, during the Systemzeit,[8] had celebrated genuine triumphs over Germany, suppressed by its enemies. The NSDAP in Frankfurt took up the fight against Jewish barbarism, mismanagement, and corruption by founding a local branch in the spring of 1924. The Gauleiter expressed his particular gratitude to Reichsleiter *Rosenberg* for the fact that now, through the opening of the new institute, the *city, liberated from the malign Jewish spirit*, has the first branch of the Advanced School within its walls.

On behalf of the city government, the mayor of Frankfurt, Staatsrat Dr *Krebs*, also cordially welcomed Reichsleiter *Rosenberg* and the guests. Frankfurt, the mayor continued, has the best prerequisites to offer for the creation of a broad-based centre for re-

3 Jakob Sprenger (1884–1945), postal official; joined the NSDAP in 1925; city councillor in Frankfurt, 1925–1933; member of the Reichstag from 1930; Gauleiter of Hesse-Nassau from 1932; Reichsstatthalter in Hesse from 1933; SA-Obergruppenführer, 1938; committed suicide in Tyrol while on the run.

4 Norwegian for 'National Union', the Norwegian fascist party founded in 1933.

5 Nationaal-Socialistische Beweging in Nederland, the Dutch National Socialist party which existed from 1931 to 1945.

6 Oberkommando der Wehrmacht: Wehrmacht High Command.

7 Literally 'anti-people'; derogatory term that distinguished between Jews and the German *Volk*.

8 German for 'system era': a term used by the National Socialists to refer disparagingly to the period of the Weimar Republic.

search into the Jewish question. He thanked Reichsleiter *Rosenberg* for the fact that the collections previously maintained here had been enriched by a unique specialized library on the Jewish question and by *immense holdings* that were confiscated from Jewish libraries and archives.

Reichsleiter Alfred Rosenberg was next to speak. (For the speech, see page 2.[9])

The Reichsleiter's address, which was accompanied and gratefully acknowledged by lively applause, was followed by a talk by Dr Wilhelm *Grau*,[10] the head of the institute, on 'Historical Attempts to Solve the Jewish Question'. Dr *Grau*, one of the leading experts on these problems, came to the conclusion *that Europe will find a solution to its Jewish question in this century.* (See also p. 2.)

Gauleiter and Reichsstatthalter *Sprenger* closed the opening ceremony by giving a salute to the *Führer*, which was met with enthusiastic applause. The event was accompanied by ceremonial music. Under the direction of the head conductor Dr *Konwitschny*,[11] the Municipal Opera and Museum Orchestra played the *Coriolan* Overture by Ludwig van Beethoven and the 'Solemn Prelude' by Alfred Jung. The guests of honour at the event assembled at lunchtime for a function hosted by Mayor Dr *Krebs*.

The representatives of the nine European nations who were present at the opening of the Frankfurt institute surely listened to the address of Reichsleiter Alfred Rosenberg with the feeling that they were witnessing a declaration of historic importance. In the life of the new Europe, scholarship and research are assigned their rightful rank, the rank of which they had been robbed by those very forces that were able to make out to the whole world that they were genuine representatives of scholarship.

From the first stirrings of antisemitism in Germany, but with greatly increased strength from the emergence of the National Socialist Movement in particular, the struggle against the intellectual renewal of the Reich was waged under the false colours of the defence of culture or the salvation of the German spirit from a cult of violence, and practically everyone who considered himself part of the 'scholarly community' joined in this refrain. Never has there been a cleaner sweep of these phoney ideologies, with their cunning spokesmen and their gullible supporters. The great lie has been revealed: the democratic apostles who spoke so highly of pure knowledge and independent research were neither inspired by the fanatical desire for truth nor free in their volition. Dependent on subversive, international forces that were well on the way towards subjugating the whole world, their quest was solely to aid and abet these elements and to forge poisoned weapons for them. Research in the sense of the Germanic drive for knowledge

9 The address is documented in excerpts. Rosenberg spoke about the plans for an Advanced School for doctrine and training in National Socialism and about the role the new institute was to play in those plans. He addressed the need to study the 'Jewish question' with regard to its historical development, as well as the influence of the Jews: *Völkischer Beobachter* (northern German edition), 27 March 1941, p. 2.

10 Dr Wilhelm Grau (1910–2000), historian; managing director of the Research Department for the Jewish Question at the Reich Institute for History of the New Germany, 1936–1938; joined the NSDAP in 1937; head of the Institute for the Study of the Jewish Question, 1941–1942; owner of a printing company in Alzey after 1945.

11 Dr Franz Konwitschny (1901–1962), musician and conductor; head conductor in Freiburg, 1933–1937; joined the NSDAP in 1937; chief musical director in Frankfurt, 1937–1945; chief musical director in Hanover, 1946–1949; headed the Gewandhaus Orchestra in Leipzig, 1949–1962, the State Orchestra in Dresden, 1953–1955, and the State Orchestra in Berlin, 1955–1962.

has not been fettered by National Socialism. Rather, it is only through National Socialism that it has been freed from the fetters in which it languished.

Jewry was only able to develop its power because it was able to deceive systematically as to its true nature with the aid of a corrupt or degenerate intellectual class. Now, however, it will be fought with the weapon of liberal scholarship. Decisive victories that have already been won in the political struggle will now receive their confirmation and profound, eternal justification through scholarship. But not in the sense that scholarship will be the handmaid of politics in the National Socialist state, subsequently delivering arguments for judgements already made. No, many a finding of future research may well diverge from what we believed in the political struggle, as Alfred Rosenberg states quite candidly. We need not fear such deviations. In the most fundamental and decisive respects, the inquisitive German mind will provide confirmation for what was anticipated by the active deed – after all, both arise from the same primal basis of German life.

But there are nations that are still grappling with the Jewish enemy of the world today or complying unwittingly with him, and to them, German scholarship will serve as a weapon and will strengthen them in the same way they have seen in our exemplary actions.

zZ.

DOC. 171

Weltkampf, 27 March 1941: Peter-Heinz Seraphim calculates the Jewish population of Europe and proposes its expulsion[1]

Demographic and economic policy challenges of an overall European solution to the Jewish question[2]

by *Peter-Heinz Seraphim*[3]

Consideration of the Jewish question in the context of demographic policy and economics extends geographically to all regions of the European continent as far as the eastern border of the Greater German sphere; it therefore concerns around 5.3 million people. In almost every country of Europe the Jewish question has played or plays a substantial role from an economic perspective, particularly with regard to industrial capital, banking capital, and commerce. But thus far there are no impeccable statistical surveys available that would permit an overall judgement as to what share the Jews have had, and still have today, in banking, in the ownership and turnover of industrial share capital, in the haulage industry and the like in Europe. In the absence of such findings, the attempt to make such estimates appears academically unsound. But this much may be said with some certainty: the small number of Jews in Scandinavia, for example, says little about

1 'Bevölkerungs- und wirtschaftspolitische Probleme einer europäischen Gesamtlösung der Judenfrage', *Weltkampf*, vol. 1 (1941), no. 1/2, pp. 43–51. This document has been translated from German.

2 Note in the original: 'Talk given on 27 March 1941 at the workshop of the Institute for the Study of the Jewish Question in Frankfurt am Main.'

3 Dr Peter-Heinz Seraphim (1902–1979), economist; editor of the *Königsberger Allgemeine Zeitung*, 1927–1930; worked at the Institute for East European Economics in Königsberg from 1930; joined the NSDAP and the SA in 1933; professor in Greifswald, 1940; editor of the journal *Weltkampf*, 1941–1943; director of studies at the Academy for Public Administration in Bochum after 1945; author of works including *Das Judentum im osteuropäischen Raum* (1938).

their actual influence on stock exchange transactions, and their shareholdings, their indirect political and intellectual influence. Let us take the example of the city of Frankfurt am Main until 1933. The share of Jews in the overall population, around 3–4 per cent, was of virtually no significance. In the commerce of this city, in market transactions, in stock trading, in the liberal professions, and at the university, however, the proportion of Jews involved was considerably larger. It can be said without exaggeration that a great part of these professions and these economic activities was under their control. The same is true for large parts of the European continent. In other words, the economic significance of the Jewish problem affects all the countries of Europe to varying degrees; it is a universal European problem. As a large-scale question of population policy, however, the Jewish problem is of genuine importance for only a portion of our continent. This is already evident from the fact that, of the aforementioned total number of 5.3 million Jews in Europe, excluding the USSR in its present borders, 3.3 million, or 62 per cent, are accounted for by the East European heartland of Jewry – the General Government, the reincorporated German eastern territories, Slovakia, Hungary, and Romania; 1.5 million Jews, or 29 per cent, by Germany's Old Reich, the Ostmark, the Sudetengau, and the Protectorate, as well as England, Holland, and France; and only 0.5 million Jews, or 9 per cent, by all the other countries of south-eastern, southern, western, and northern Europe.

We must bear in mind, however, that the Jewish problem in Europe is not the Jewish problem of the world at large. It is rather the case that Europe – excluding Russia – accounts for around ⅓ of the world's Jews; the USSR, another ⅓; the USA, ¼ of all the Jews in the world, while the tiny remainder is distributed throughout the other continents and countries.

Within Europe the Jewish problem is especially apparent in the *East*, not only on the basis of the absolute numbers concerned, but also in its relative significance as a large-scale problem. Here the share of Jews in the total population ranges between 6 and 12 per cent, averaging around 9 per cent, while in all other European countries the Jews make up only around 1 per cent of the total population. Therefore, only in the East is the Jewish problem a major issue for demographic policy!

But here, too, the Jews are unevenly concentrated. Even in the eastern and south-eastern areas of Europe, the Jews are an insignificant feature of the rural population. Around 81 per cent of all Jews live in the Jewish heartland of Eastern Europe, as outlined above. That is, 2.7 million Jews live in the towns but only 19 per cent, or 0.8 million Jews, in the countryside. Suffice to say that, with minor exceptions, these persons, statistically recorded as rural Jews, are not engaged in agriculture but pursue urban occupations, particularly trade. Given the predominantly agrarian structure of the eastern and south-eastern territories, this small number of Jews in the countryside is of major significance for demographic policy. In terms of population, Eastern Jewry too is only a significant factor in the towns. However, there Jewry is an important mass factor. Today, around 700,000 Jews are living in 14 larger cities in the General Government. In these cities, the Jews make up between 25 and 65 per cent of their overall population. Warsaw alone, a city of over 1 million inhabitants, is home to around 400,000 Jews, i.e. more than 30 per cent of its population are Jews. In the cities of the reincorporated German eastern territories too, especially if they had been part of the Russian state before the World War, the Jews represent a mass element.

Litzmannstadt, for example,[4] has 200,000 Jews, making up ⅓ of the total population. Bendzin, Sosnowitz, and Dambrowa together have 50,000 Jews, more than 40 per cent of the total population. In the cities south of the Carpathians as well – Pressburg[5] in Slovakia, Uzhorod, Munkacz in the Hungarian province of Subcarpathian Rus, in the northern Hungarian towns of Poprad, Bartha, Neutra,[6] Kaschau, and in the towns of Satmar, now incorporated into Hungary – we find Jewish ethnic groups that constitute 15, 20, 30 per cent and more of the total population of these cities. In Budapest the share of the Jews by race and Jewish Mischlinge is estimated at ⅓ of the total population of the Hungarian capital. A total of over 70,000 Jews live in the five Moldavian district cities of Dorohoi, Jassy, Roman, Vaslui, and Braila, i.e. more than 35 per cent of the overall population. According to the 1930 population census, in all the cities of the Moldavia region there were 140,000 Jews, or 24 per cent of the total population. In Bucharest there were at least 60,000 Jews. These examples should suffice to show that the Jewish question is one of mass dimensions for the urban parts of eastern Europe and some parts of south-eastern Europe.

This fact is of decisive importance for every practical solution to the Jewish question. In all the cities of central, southern, western, and northern Europe, an immediate exclusion – theoretically possible – or a deportation of the Jews would not create a void in terms of demographic policy. The outer appearance of the cities would not change at all. In essence, the property situation in the trade and industry sectors, in haulage and in shipping agencies, in banking and stock exchange transactions etc. would shift, and home ownership, cinema ownership, the notary profession, the medical profession, and more would be decisively affected. In the eastern part of Europe, the situation is different. Precisely because the Jewish question is a large-scale question there, a sudden solution to this question, possibly through expulsion, is proving to be especially difficult, and not only for technical reasons. Economically, too, it is difficult to implement, because one cannot imagine one third, indeed one half, of the cities' inhabitants to be simply gone from one day to the next, especially as this third or half previously accounted for 1/4, 4/5, or even 9/10 of urban, industrial, and commercial life. One must be aware that the Jew there is not only a capitalist, the owner of an anonymous parcel of shares. He is also to a large extent a consumer in the cities, he is involved in the production apparatus as a skilled craftsman to a not insignificant extent, and above all he has a decisive role in the distribution apparatus, namely through sub-distribution as a retailer, as a small shopkeeper, as well as for wholesale.

What emerges from this? By no means the conclusion that, because the Jewish problem in these regions is a large-scale question and therefore a phenomenon of especially great import, everything should stay as it was or be left to evolve for an unknown period of time. But one thing is clear: no country and no part of Europe can be responsible for a sustained threat to its economy – and indeed it is precisely in the cities where this threat comes to a head! Not in peacetime and even less so in wartime! This means that the removal of the Jewish element in the Jew-filled cities of the East can only be undertaken *as quickly as manpower replacements* for the Jews become available, once

4 From April 1940 the city of Łódź was renamed Litzmannstadt by the German occupiers.
5 Bratislava.
6 Poprad and Neutra belonged to Slovakia.

small traders and merchants are available to assume the economic functions previously held by Jews. This is undoubtedly possible, for within the peasant population of the Romanians, Magyars, Ukrainians, Slovaks, and Poles there is an 'excess pressure' in terms of population that is able to move indigenous elements into the place of the lower-middle-class Jewish elements. For years these second or third born peasants' sons of the native population have been prevented by the urban Jewish element from finding a way to get ahead in the cities. The cities were, so to speak, 'blocked' by the Jews. Now the moment seems to have come to break this monopoly! But it would be a misconstrual of reality if one were to conclude from this that first the removal of the Jews and then the entry of the members of the native peoples into the thus vacated jobs would be a smooth process. Not every farmer's son from Moldavia, Slovakia, or Galicia is a 'born retailer', and certainly no one who has not had thorough training is a 'born craftsman'! In practice, therefore, the method is this: *in Eastern Europe the Jew is to be replaced by non-Jews in the cities, through legal statutes and administrative measures, at the pace at which qualified non-Jews become available for this substitution.* In practical terms this means: training skilled craftsmen and commercial apprentices from the majority nation to serve as replacements for the Jews! The overarching principle remains: the Jew must give way if an equally qualified non-Jew is available! Vocational education, cooperative societies, and training of apprentices are the prerequisite, meaning rigorous, practical daily work. We have a number of examples precisely from Eastern Europe from the past decades, indicating that among young peasant peoples there are strong forces, which can effectively carry out such a replacement. To take just one example, let us consider the Ukrainian cooperative system in former eastern Galicia. Truly ingrained within the people, this system had managed for the most part to drive the Jew out of market towns and villages, and was poised to launch an economic offensive against the Jews in the cities through practical work. It would be pointless to delude oneself: as things stand today, the cooperative organizational apparatus and, more importantly, the völkisch, cooperative thinking of the native peoples of Eastern Europe have not yet developed to the point where a complete replacement for the Jewish merchant or tradesman is available. The creation of this replacement is the principal demand of every völkisch person who is serious about the practical implementation of his goals. But a further delusion must be cautioned against! One frequently tends to assume that solving the Jewish problem would likewise result in solving the problem of overpopulation in these regions. Filling the jobs of the Jews in urban areas, it is assumed, would provide the outlet that the native peoples require to release the population pressure in rural areas. And with the expulsion of the Jews, Eastern Europe would be restored to health with respect to its demographic policy problems. This is fundamentally wrong! *The population pressure of the peasantry of Eastern Europe is too great to be offset by the removal of the Jews from the cities.* Oberländer[7]

7 Dr Theodor Oberländer (1905–1998), economist and agronomist; joined the NSDAP in 1933; director of the Institute for East European Economics in Königsberg from 1934; professor in Greifswald, 1938; worked for the Abwehr (military intelligence service) headquarters for Military District VII in Breslau from 1939; professor in Prague, 1940–1945; stationed in Lwów, then in the Caucasus, 1941; co-founder of the League of Expellees and Dispossessed, 1950; West German minister for expellees, 1953–1960; resigned after accusations concerning his Nazi past; re-elected to the German Bundestag, 1963–1965.

and Franges[8] have furnished proof, for former Poland and for south-eastern Europe, of both the absolute and the relative population excess among the agricultural population. Their calculations indicate that there is an 'excess' of agricultural population amounting to 50–60 per cent of its current level! Above all, however, one must bear in mind that the majority of Jews in the Eastern European cities make their livelihoods in 'overcrowded' occupations, working as small-scale retailers or pedlars, as brokers and agents, in primitive crafts and in cottage industry. It would run completely counter to the interests of the economy of these countries to fill these jobs completely with non-Jews once the Jews are excluded. The objective, after all, is the organization of the industrial economy, the creation of a middle class that performs an economically useful function, that does not represent the 'misery of the urban proletariat', as we can observe it to a large extent among Jewry in these cities today.

The outcome of this reflection is:

1. Only in the cities of Eastern Europe is the Jewish problem a major question of relevance for demographic policy.
2. Because it is a major question there, one that calls into question the continued existence of the cities as municipalities and as economic hubs, caution is to be applied in the solution of the question.
3. However, even in these regions, the solution to the Jewish question must not be delayed or postponed.
4. Jews can be removed from these regions or cities to the extent that replacement workers from the native peoples are available to assume the economic functions previously performed by the Jews.
5. Replacement of the Jews is contingent on the schooling, education, and organization of the native peoples who succeed them.
6. Removing the Jews does not constitute a solution to the population problem of the native peoples.

What ways of solving the Jewish question as a large-scale demographic policy question are available, in practical terms? The answer is as follows:

1. Their *dissimilation*, without external and spatial separation from the host people.
2. Their *ghettoization*, whether in individual urban ghettos or in an area of Eastern Europe, to which first the Jews of Eastern Europe and later the Jews of all Europe would be transferred.
3. Their *removal from Europe* through the initiation of a systematic resettlement operation.

All three possibilities have their positive and negative aspects. The first, dissimilation without spatial segregation, is the simplest in practical and administrative terms. It has been employed up to now in the German Reich and, in a modified way, also in the General Government. It approaches the Jewish problem more from the political and economic aspect. *Its drawback is that Jewry survives as a foreign Volkskörper*, and among the native peoples at that. The Jew becomes a person with few rights, perhaps visibly marked, excluded from certain civil and political rights, placed in a special position

8 Otto Frangeš (1870–1945), Croatian agronomist; studied in Vienna and Leipzig; professor in Zagreb, 1921; Yugoslav minister of agriculture, 1929–1930; author of *Die Bevölkerungsdichte als Triebkraft der Wirtschaftspolitik der südosteuropäischen Bauernstaaten* (1939).

economically – but is not removed. The Jewish question remains a large-scale demographic question, with the sole difference that, owing to the restructuring within Jewry, the number of rich Jews decreases and the number of Jewish welfare recipients increases. The result can be the social impoverishment and restructuring of the Jews, but by no means the physical self-dissolution of Jewry, for the death of a people is never a quick death. Rather, it is a development that takes place over centuries, especially when it concerns 5.3 million people in Europe, not just an ethnic group of a few thousand or tens of thousands.

In addition, there is another point: as long as the Jews as a mass are found among the native people at the economic nerve centres, in the cities, it is exceedingly difficult to oversee the implementation of the laws that restrict or isolate them. It is, as everyone familiar with the Eastern European conditions in particular will confirm, virtually impossible to enforce such laws, first because the peoples living in these areas are by no means uniformly ready to disengage from the influence of the Jews, and second because the Jews are masters at interpreting, bending, and contravening such legal or administrative provisions. Disguise, bribery, the use of frontmen, and many other methods are, after all, familiar to the Jew through centuries of practice. In other words: a social, political, and economic exclusion of the Jews alone does not amount to a solution of the Jewish population problem, neither in the eastern part of our continent nor in the less 'Jew-saturated' regions to the west.

To what extent would such an isolation of the Jews, theoretically conceived for all of Europe, determine the *economic* position of the Jews and of their milieu? We know that the Jewish question, beyond the large-scale demographic policy problem, represents an economic problem of the first order. The breaking of Jewish influence has thus far been attempted in a purposeful manner only in the Greater German Reich. In a number of other countries, especially in south-eastern Europe, incipient efforts in the same direction can be discerned. Almost nowhere, however, has the problem been tackled uncompromisingly from the perspective of race. Usually there are external distinctions of a denominational sort, often notions of 'transitional provisions', assumptions of the protection of the 'acquired rights of persons of Jewish origin whose völkisch attitude is beyond question'. By no means should autonomous legislative actions of foreign states be measured strictly by German standards. But it must be stated quite objectively that the settlement of the Jewish question is only hampered by an attitude that, when looking at the problem, brings in some kind of economic competition with regard to the Jews. The stance on the Jewish question has, definitively, nothing to do with the economic competition between Jews and non-Jews. Its solution stands and falls with the recognition that Jewry is a *racial* alien body in a different, racially fully cohesive environment.

But what about the prerequisites for a potential solution to the European Jewish question from the economic perspective? Nowhere in Europe does the Jew have economic ties to the soil to any appreciable extent. Jewish farmers are rare, and we find Jewish tenant farmers only to a certain extent in north-eastern Hungary. The difficulties connected to finding a solution for masses of Jewish farmers will thus apply.

Is the Jew readily replaceable as a business manager, as an industrialist? Such difficulties can crop up in areas where most of the businesses in a certain sector, or perhaps an entire branch of industry, are in Jewish hands. These exist notably in parts of Eastern

Europe, where it is difficult to replace Jews because of the lack of suitable workers. However, aside from exceptions, these difficulties do not appear to be insurmountable, because almost every sector ought to have non-Jewish professionals available who can take the place of the Jew. For the skilled crafts replacements are only difficult to find in parts of Eastern Europe. In the other parts of our continent, the Jew does not play an appreciable role in these occupations. Far more complicated is the potential for replacing the Jews in the branch that is considered to be typically Jewish: trade. Here, indeed, replacing the Jew is in some cases not possible without friction and without economic losses. There is no reason to deny that such frictional losses have also undoubtedly occurred during the reorganization of the economy in the German Reich. But it can be stated that these difficulties have proved to be far fewer in practice than was to be anticipated in advance. Undoubtedly, the reorganization of the trade sector is made easier by the regulating influence of the state. Such an influence, through the state steering the operation, can prevent the private pursuit of gain from having an undesirable effect during the takeover of Jewish businesses. A rigorous survey, evaluating the assets and suitability – both objective and personal – of the individual who is taking over the business, appears to be necessary. The interposition of trustees is generally undesirable in general, as they are inclined to seek to take over only the assets of the business but to reject the liabilities, and they usually lack the desire to assume responsibility for profits. The situation is particularly difficult where Jews are over-represented in the trade occupation, with the result that previously there was practically a Jewish monopoly on the branch of trade concerned. Again, on the whole this should apply only to parts of Eastern Europe. There, transitional provisions are doubtlessly appropriate, even the very unsatisfactory solution of a non-Jewish trustee and a Jewish works manager, in order to prevent the branch of business from coming to a standstill. Naturally, the point of the operation is not to harm the economy through introducing immediate measures, but rather to avoid economic damage by replacing a Jew with a qualified non-Jew. In practice, this means that the Jew must *always* be replaced, but the *pace* of the process is determined by the existing opportunities for replacement. This should pose no difficulty for northern, southern, and western Europe, but for parts of Eastern Europe, difficulties must be anticipated.

For individual branches of the liberal professions (the Bar, the medical profession), difficulties are likewise to be expected. As a mass phenomenon they again affect only parts of Eastern Europe, while in other regions of our continent an exclusion of the Jews should endanger neither the functioning of the justice system nor healthcare in the state. Here, the problem lies more in the loss of individual Jews, not in the irreplaceability of the Jewish population element in these professional groups.

Let us turn to further possibilities of solving the Jewish question through population policy and economic measures. The second alternative goes one step further and is more consistent than mere dissimilation of the Jews: it involves their ghettoization. This is the process of physical isolation from the non-Jewish population. While the Jews survive as a mass within the non-Jewish settlement area, they are pushed together in Jewish enclaves and segregated through isolation from the non-Jewish population. It is customary to point out that this solution is the historically prevailing one, as the Jewish settlement area, the ghetto, was already in existence during the Middle Ages. This historical line of argument does not seem to apply. The ghetto of the Middle Ages was far more a *right* of the Jews than a compulsory measure. The Jews of the Middle Ages, to whom non-business dealings with goyim[9] were prohibited under religious law, were allowed to live in the Jewish residential community, which was simultaneously their day-to-day community and their religious community, their completely autonomous communal unit. The equivalent of the 'jus de non tolerando Judaeis'[10] was just as clearly the 'jus de non tolerando Christianis' in the Jewish residential district. The ghetto of the Middle Ages, in terms of its internal substance, was an essentially voluntary residential community, which, moreover, in no way ruled out commercial contact between Jews and non-Jews. Furthermore, one must recall that the medieval ghetto by no means completely fulfilled its alleged function of serving as a defensive wall against the Jews. Rather, from a very early stage we find complaints by non-Jewish citizens concerning the encroachment of Jews from the ghetto, constant proceedings between city councils and Jewish kahals[11] with the territorial sovereigns. We know that the Jews were able to overcome and practically to break down the ghetto walls through bribery, dishonest practices, and numerous subterfuges precisely where it was important to them from a business perspective. The present-day ghetto, should there be any point to it, would thus, in contrast to the medieval ghetto, be a compulsory ghetto, with no contact or possibility of contact with non-Jews. In practice, this means not only the erection of a ghetto wall but also the constant police surveillance of the entire ghetto boundary and a ban for non-Jews on entering or coming near the ghetto. In this case the ghetto would resemble a Jewish isolation zone, as exemplified by the distinctly transitional endeavour to create a ghetto for the Jews in Litzmannstadt.[12] If such a strictly closed ghetto is not created but only a ghetto wall is erected (as in Warsaw),[13] but at the same time a number of important authorities continue to have their offices in the part of town now declared a ghetto, and major arterial roads run through the ghetto, so that entering it cannot be prohibited, then the ghetto is largely ineffectual in practical terms. Full disassociation is achieved only to a very limited extent.

The creation of an urban ghetto in Europe, in practice, is uncommonly difficult. The cities are organic entities: transport lines, buses, and trams are designed to serve the entire urban area. Motorways cross or cut through the ghetto. Water, gas, and electricity are supplied through a common system. Readings must be taken to determine consumption. Repairs must be made. It is impossible to simply cut such a spatially significant part of a municipality (up to ⅓ of the living space) out of the municipal body. If it is done, the remaining part is also just a torso! The ghetto as a neighbourhood within an urban community, however, also implies a threat in many other respects. Disease can be spread despite there being a wall! Finally, the constant guarding of the ghetto by the police requires disproportionately large resources of manpower. Reducing the manpower needed, however, would mean allowing a reoccurrence of the threat of the ghetto boundary being violated in practice. A further objection to the closed urban ghetto

9 Plural of *goy*; Hebrew for 'non-Jew'.

10 Latin expression used in the Middle Ages and early modern times to refer to the ban on the settlement of Jews in certain cities and regions.

11 Plural of *kahal*; Hebrew for 'council'.

12 Friedrich Uebelhoer, the Regierungspräsident of Kalisch, who was in charge of Litzmannstadt, had expressly called the ghetto a 'transitional measure' when he ordered its creation at the end of 1939: see PMJ 4/54. However, it was in existence until August 1944.

13 The Litzmannstadt ghetto was more tightly closed off – especially in the initial phase – than the Warsaw ghetto, which was established in the summer of 1940. From 1940 the guards at Litzmannstadt had been ordered to fire at anyone trying to escape.

results from economic considerations: the urban ghetto cannot supply itself with industrial goods, or with raw materials and fuel, or with food.

Everything required would therefore have to be brought in. These imports might be small in per capita terms for the ghetto residents and might not exceed the subsistence level – but in their entirety they represent a perpetual, noticeable supply burden and, in practice, mean that the Jews are fed and maintained by the non-Jews. But providing food to the ghetto, of course, is inconceivable without the ghetto providing economic recompense. The only possible recompense would be the utilization of Jewish labour. To make use of this labour outside the ghetto contradicts the principle of the closed ghetto and the exclusion of the Jews. Their use in the ghetto, however, is possible only if the ghetto is supplied with machines and raw materials, a labour-service requirement is introduced, and its implementation is monitored, in short, if one adds to the external ghetto guard force an adequate internal guard and an organizational and supervisory staff consisting of a surely substantial number of non-Jewish supervisory personnel. It remains doubtful if this will yield any economic results as the workforce utilized is impelled solely by coercion from outside. The result of forced labour, however, always remains unsatisfactory in financial terms.

For most cities in the central, western, southern, and eastern parts of Europe, however, which have fewer Jews, a ghettoization of the Jews is out of the question, as the number of Jews is much too small to create such a Jewish collective. In practice, the potential alternative here would be – if one wants to go beyond the stage of political, social, and economic dissimilation – to remove the Jews from their previous residences and concentrate them at a number of points. In contrast to the approach in Eastern Europe, one would of course not choose existing cities but rather dwelling places created ad hoc. In principle, however, there would be little difference between such mandatory residences for Jews and the compulsory ghettos for the Ostjuden. A simple approach to counter the difficulties resulting from the creation of compulsory urban ghettos would be the proposal of demarcating a specific larger territory and concentrating the Jews of Europe there. The areas which one had in mind for this are those with a particularly high Jewish population and which can be reconfigured as closed Jewish settlements by moving in Jews and removing the non-Jewish population. These plans have a number of positive aspects, namely:

1. The population transfer operation can be spread out over time. Demographic and economic disturbances in the resettlement areas can be reduced or prevented.
2. As an end result, the Jews are radically removed from their previous areas of residence. This avoids the danger that even the closed urban ghetto poses. Difficulties of a local political nature, as instanced above, cease to apply.
3. The *resettlement* of the Jews into a larger territory affords the opportunity to alter their distribution by city and by country. The Jews do not need to be maintained by the non-Jews, as is the case in the urban ghetto. Instead, they have the opportunity to till the land themselves, to keep livestock, to grow food, and to feed themselves. It is well known that, in line with these plans, creation of such a 'Jewish reservation' in the eastern part of the present GG,[14] in the Lublin district, has frequently been contemplated, a reservation

14 General Government.

that could accommodate the Jews of the Greater German Reich and the remainder of the General Government, and possibly the Jews from the rest of Europe too at a later stage.[15] However attractive these plans may seem at first glance, the arguments against them are just as robust.

1. A concentration of the Jews in such a part of Europe (for example, in the present Lublin district) means a population transfer of around 5 million Jews who are to be resettled and 2.7 million non-Jews who are to be removed, including around 2¼ million Poles and 200,000 Ukrainians, in total a *population shift in Europe involving 7.7 million people*. The significance of this figure lies in the fact that the greatest population transfers in modern history (Greek–Turkish population exchange, forced expulsion of the Germans from Poland) affected 1 million people in each case, and that the German–Russian resettlements have thus far scarcely exceeded half a million people.

2. In addition, housing the resettled non-Jews in Europe is proving to be very difficult. In the overpopulated General Government, for example, this is impracticable, and migrant or seasonal labour is merely an interim solution. Resettlement to other parts of Europe is barely conceivable. The remaining option would be emigration. This would mean that non-Jews were forced to emigrate from Europe in order to settle Jews in Europe!

3. It must be investigated whether such a region would be adequate to accommodate all the Jews of Europe. Let us take the Lublin district as an example. It is 26,800 square km in area and has a population of around 2.7 million inhabitants, that is, an average density of 101 persons per square km. After deducting a clearly necessary protective strip approximately 10 km wide around the Jewish settlement district, there remains an area of around 25,000 square km which has approximately 2½ million inhabitants at present. If one theoretically assumes that all European Jews are concentrated in this area, the population would increase threefold in comparison with the present numbers, and the population density would reach a level of 320 inhabitants per square km. It would thus be far higher than that of the densely populated Old Reich, at 135 persons, and of England, at 271 persons per square km. And this in a region where not only all industry but also every sort of prerequisite for industry is lacking, and where agriculture, based on its current status, is already deemed to be 'overstaffed' by 40 per cent!

4. Like the urban ghettos, such a 'mass ghetto' is not able to sustain itself economically. It is dependent upon imports for its preservation. In short, the problems demonstrated there crop up again here, only to a greater extent.

5. There is no part of Europe that comes into question as a settlement area for the Jews. Particularly not in a distinctly peripheral region of Central Europe that borders on Euro-Asian megastate.

6. Guarding the external boundaries of such a gigantic ghetto would entail enormous staff costs, which, as fixed, non-productive costs, would place a burden on the country taking over the guard duty.

The last possible radical solution to the Jewish question through population policy measures is to initiate the *emigration of the Jews from Europe*.

15 There had temporarily been plans to create a 'Jewish reservation' in the eastern part of occupied Poland: see PMJ 4/65. In March 1940, however, Hitler rejected this idea: see the Introduction to PMJ 4. In connection with these considerations, around 5,000 Jews were deported to Nisko in the Lublin district in the autumn of 1939: see Doc. 16, fn. 9.

DOC. 172
On 27 March 1941 the SS leadership instructs the Minister of Science to have Martin Buber's doctorate revoked[1]

Letter from the Reichsführer SS and Chief of the German Police (A 15 b [new] – B. 555) in the Reich Ministry of the Interior, p.p. signed Engelmann,[2] to the Reich Minister of Science, Schooling, and Education[3] (received on 3 April 1941), dated 27 March 1941 (copy)

Re: revocation of the doctoral degree
Case file: none.
I have instituted proceedings against the Jew Martin Israel *Buber*,[4] born on 8 February 1878 in Vienna, last domestic residence: Heppenheim an der Bergstrasse, present abode: Palestine, for deprivation of his German nationality under § 2 of the law of 14 July 1933[5] (*Reichsgesetzblatt*, I, pp. 480 ff.).[6] *Buber* received his doctorate of philosophy from the University of Vienna in 1904.

I request that further arrangements be made with regard to revocation of his doctoral degree.[7]

1 DÖW, 8496. Published in Dokumentationsarchiv des österreichischen Widerstandes, *Widerstand und Verfolgung in Wien*, p. 261. This document has been translated from German.

2 Probably: Heinz-Günther Engelmann (1913–1999), lawyer; joined the NSDAP in 1937 and the SS in 1939; SS-Obersturmführer, 1941; detective chief superintendent; worked in Office V (Criminal Police) of the Reich Security Main Office.

3 Bernhard Rust (1883–1945), teacher; joined the NSDAP in 1925; member of the Reichstag, 1930–1945; Gauleiter of South Hanover-Braunschweig, 1932–1940; SA-Gruppenführer, 1933; Prussian state councillor, 1933; member of the Academy for German Law; Reich minister of education, 1934–1945; committed suicide.

4 Dr Martin Buber (1878–1965), philosopher of religion and writer; editor of various Jewish newspapers; professor of Jewish religious studies and ethics in Frankfurt, 1930–1933; head of the Liaison Office for Jewish Adult Education, 1933–1938; expelled from the Reich Chamber of Literature, 1935; emigrated to Palestine in 1938 and became a professor in Jerusalem.

5 Law on the Revocation of Naturalization and the Deprivation of German Nationality.

6 The original contains an insertion that is struck through: 'in connection with § 1 of the Law on the Deprivation of Nationality and the Revocation of Naturalization in the Ostmark, 11 July 1939 (*Reichsgesetzblatt*, I, page 1235)'.

7 Several such letters from the Reichsführer SS to the Minister of Science were the subject of a meeting at the University of Vienna on 8 May 1941, at which the doctoral degrees of eighteen Jews were revoked, including Martin Buber, whose citizenship was revoked on 26 May 1941: Michael Hepp (ed.), *Die Ausbürgerung deutscher Staatsangehöriger 1933–45 nach den im Reichsanzeiger veröffentlichten Listen* (Munich: De Gruyter, 1985), pp. 500–502.

DOC. 173

On 1 April 1941 Willy Cohn notes in his diary that he has heard of the murder of Jewish psychiatric patients in Chełm, near Lublin[1]

Handwritten diary of Willy Cohn, Breslau, entry for 1 April 1941

Breslau, Tuesday. Today was really a busy and exhausting day for me. Unfortunately, I haven't got much stamina! Waited a long time to fetch milk; bank; had the pleasure there of learning that 100 Reichsmarks from the school had been deposited. I am not greatly attached to money but, after all, one needs it to live. And in general, I have to be especially thankful that I am permitted to earn some. But at the bank something also made me feel very sad. I saw an elderly Jew paying an invoice from the mental asylum in Chelm near Lublin.[2] That is the institution where, it is said, all the Jewish mental patients are killed. Full of sympathy, I asked him whether he was paying for someone who, one hoped, was still alive. In reply he said that his wife, in any case, was no longer alive. I asked him where she had been previously: 'In Branißʼ,[3] and whether she had been completely insane, and he replied that she had been suffering from mania. It is horrible how the patients are dealt with. A former pupil of mine, Mamlok from Militsch, died there of circulation problems. Death announcements with such diagnoses are then simply sent by post. The news made me feel so low that I missed my tram stop later and rode too far.

Archive: continued sorting through the very interesting files from Sagan. If one only had time to look through them all. Susannchen[4] then turned up out of the blue, with Hanna Schmollny. They actually wanted to go to the Pottery Market and had got lost. At first I was somewhat startled, because I thought that Trudi[5] had a message for me, but then I was delighted. I could not work on my things today, which is no disaster anyway.

The pastor from Tarnowitz was here again. In the concentration camps, three persons die every night, it is said. Then, the next morning, the blankets of the deceased must be present at roll call. In Upper Silesia, the Poles have had their food rations cut by half. Noteworthy from the newspaper: the Italians admit to heavy losses in the naval battle in the Mediterranean. They have lost three cruisers, among other vessels.[6] In Yugoslavia a very intense anti-German movement has broken out! I think Italy will not take part much longer. But all the setbacks will affect us German Jews.

Went with the children to the Neumarkt. We thought that a pottery market was on, but that was not the case. Put both girls on the no. 18 tram. I myself took the no. 9 to the Community to fetch the food ration cards that Miss Silberstein obtained for us.

1 CAHJP, P88/102, fols. 119–123; abbreviated English translation published in Cohn, *No Justice in Germany*, pp. 347–348. This document has been newly translated from the original German.

2 The formerly Polish psychiatric institution in Chełm (Cholm), whose patients had already been murdered, was used as a cover address to conceal the murders of Jewish patients in the 'euthanasia' killing centres of the Reich. Family members were notified that the patient had died in the mental asylum in Chełm: see Introduction, p. 34, and Doc. 201.

3 The writer means the town of Branitz (Branice) in the district of Leobschütz (Głubczyce). In 1940, its psychiatric hospital had 1,600 patients.

4 Susanna Cohn.

5 Gertrud Cohn.

6 In the battle of Cape Matapan, the British Mediterranean Fleet sank three heavy cruisers and two destroyers of the Italian navy on 29 March 1941.

Talked to many people, and in the street I chanced to come across old Leß, whom I do not hold in very high esteem and who spoke with me about the comments in the news bulletin, then I talked for a long time with Dr Pex. He was very complimentary about Trudi's work in the course. I am certainly not very happy about it [the course], but at the same time I am glad that Trudi is finding recognition, which I certainly did not doubt would happen. Greeted Ella only in passing. Rode with Hannah Lemm, the rabbi's daughter, the pretty nurse, as far as Viktoriastraße. She seems to be a very reserved person. We chatted about her brother. They had three Red Cross letters recently from her brother in Jerusalem; he apparently attends school there. We are waiting so eagerly for news from the children![7]

DOC. 174

On 2 April 1941 Reinhard Heydrich announces that pensions are no longer to be paid to Jews abroad, owing to the anticipated 'solution to the general Jewish question'[1]

Letter from the Chief of the Security Police and the SD (IV A 3 c – No. 164/41 gen.), p.p. signed Jagusch, to the Reich Foreign Office, for the attention of the head of the Germany Department, SA-Standartenführer Envoy Luther, Berlin, dated 2 April 1941 (copy)[2]

Re: transfer of pension payments and procurement of documents for emigrants.
Reference: your letter dated 11 March 1941 – D III 1975 –.[3]
The solution to the general Jewish question, which is planned by the Reich government and is to be anticipated in the foreseeable future, and the revised nationality conditions for Jews, will also clarify the rights acquired by Jews from their previous employment status. In this regard, the payment of cash benefits from social insurance funds etc. to Jews under the present circumstances raises concerns for policing matters relating to security, especially as there is a justifiable suspicion that the eligible recipients are making these funds available to wholly or partially anti-German organizations or purposes. It would seem appropriate instead to have the respective pensions etc. that are due deposited into blocked accounts for exclusive use in this country.

Certificates and other identification documents that Jewish emigrants require for onward emigration are to be duly applied for directly from the offices within Germany that are responsible for issuing them.

I request that the German Red Cross headquarters in Berlin be informed accordingly.[4]

7 Wolfgang and Ernst Abraham Cohn.

1 PA AA, R 99 369, Nr. 5451, fol. 62r–v. This document has been translated from German.
2 The original contains handwritten notes, administrative stamps, and the official stamp of the Reichsführer SS and Chief of the German Police in the Reich Ministry of the Interior.
3 On 11 March 1941 the Reich Foreign Office had requested an opinion on the question of continued payment of pensions and related benefits to Jews interned in France: PA AA, R 99 369, Nr. 5451, fol. 59.
4 Many Jews interned in the Gurs camp approached the German Red Cross in the attempt to have official documents sent from the Reich for the purpose of emigration to the USA.

DOC. 175

Preußische Zeitung, 5 April 1941: article about the exhibition *The Eternal Jew* in Königsberg[1]

Jews unmasked ...
Exhibition 'The Eternal Jew' in Königsberg very well attended[2]

Wherever the Jew establishes himself, he constitutes a people within the people, a state within the state. The state's laws do not apply to him, for he must live according to his Jewish laws and act as the Jewish God demands of him. All his oaths before the courts are taken in pretence. To tell the truth is a mortal sin according to the Talmud, the Jewish code of law. He is a master of deceit, and so the peoples are simply unaware of the nature of the parasite feeding on their Volkskörper. If one does become aware of his corrosive influence, it is usually too late for resistance. The host people, of which he has made himself the ruler, is inevitably precipitated into ruin. Whatever the host people holds sacred, he drags into the dirt in the vilest way and ridicules.

The exhibition *The Eternal Jew*, which is on display *until 14 April* in Königsberg Town Hall and has attracted a large number of visitors, offers ample examples of the corrosive activity of the Jewish people. Whenever the Jew believes himself to be at the height of his power, he throws caution to the wind and reveals his true opinions and intentions with the cruellest brutality.

The caption for several pictures on one of the exhibition panels reads:

> Under Jewish leadership, the Marxist Popular Front government was established in France in 1936. Forty of its ninety members were Jews, and it unleashed a war of all against all. After it had come to power in the state, it destroyed the political might and economic strength of France and brought it to the point of complete collapse.[3]

The Jew abhors all military might, because this hinders him from achieving his goal of world dominance and also from unscrupulously plundering a nation. Around the turn of the century, France experienced the Dreyfus affair.[4] One of the exhibition panels gives also an account of this, titled 'The Dreyfus Affair – or Jewry vs. the French Army':

1 'Juden ohne Maske ...', *Preußische Zeitung*, 5 April 1941, p. 9. This document has been translated from German. The *Preußische Zeitung*, founded in 1931, was published in Königsberg as an official news bulletin of all Prussian state and municipal authorities. It ceased publication in 1945.

2 The travelling exhibition *The Eternal Jew* (*Der ewige Jude*) was opened on 8 Nov. 1937 by Joseph Goebbels in the German Museum in Munich and was shown in several cities. More than 300,000 people are said to have visited the exhibition by the end of Dec. 1937 alone.

3 The left-liberal Popular Front coalition, tolerated by the communists, formed the French government in 1936–1937 under Léon Blum (1872–1950).

4 The French officer Alfred Dreyfus (1859–1935), who was of Jewish descent, had been sentenced in 1894 to lifelong exile and imprisonment for treason for allegedly spying for the Germans. The 'Dreyfus affair' split French society for years into liberal supporters of Dreyfus and nationalist opponents. In 1906 the sentence was revoked.

> The French army was the last völkisch bastion standing in the way of Jewish dominance. This dominance had to be broken. The Jew Dreyfus, a captain on the general staff, is sentenced to deportation for life for his treason. Jewry perceived this sentence as a grave threat to its position of political power. By appealing the sentence and proving Dreyfus's supposed innocence, the army's influence was to be eliminated. World Jewry, bribery, corruption, and the removal of unwelcome governments and political figures are the weapons. In the fiercest struggle, the army was vanquished after twelve years. Dreyfuss was pardoned, and later the verdict against him was rescinded. His innocence could never be proved with certainty. But Jewry had won.

In the Jewish body of law, the Talmud, Pesachim 112, it says of the 'brave' Jewish soldiers: 'When you go to war, do not go first to the front, but rather, to the rear, so that you will be the first to return.'[5] Jewry has always adhered to this principle. Enough examples are still known to us from the [First] World War, relating how the Jew did indeed wear the uniform, kept himself in the rear, where he destroyed the resistance of the front by engaging in malicious rabble-rousing. The Jew Tucholsky expressed his notion of soldiership, one that all Semites fundamentally share with him, as follows:

> For three years I shirked my duty in the war as much as I could – and I regret not having had the courage shown by the great Karl Liebknecht to say no and refuse to serve in the military. Of this I am ashamed. So I did what most people did, I employed many strategies so as not to get shot and not to shoot.[6]

That is an authentically Jewish mindset. To take advantage of every right accorded him by his host people and even then to treat this with contempt, but to shirk the duties of a citizen. Woe to the people that fails to recognize the Jew hidden behind the mask of a man of integrity! The exhibition *The Eternal Jew* in Königsberg provides many convincing examples of Jewish hypocrisy and the appalling consequences for the peoples. Every German must be familiar with them in order to protect himself and his fatherland against them.

DOC. 176

On 21 April 1941 department head Walter Tießler informs the staff of the Deputy of the Führer about Goebbels's proposal for the visible identification of Jews[1]

Submission by Walter Tießler (initials, Ti/Wk),[2] Berlin, dated 21 April 1941

Submission

Because the evacuation of the Jews from Berlin unfortunately cannot proceed to the desired extent for the time being, Dr Goebbels has given instructions that proposals for

5 The quoted passage is in fact from Pesachim 113.

6 The statement by Kurt Tucholsky appeared in the weekly *Die Weltbühne*, 30 March 1926, in the article 'Wo waren Sie im Kriege, Herr –' (Where were you during the war, Mr – ?) under his pseudonym Ignaz Wrobel.

1 BArch, NS 18/1134, fol. 73. This document has been translated from German.

a badge for Jews be made to him. This badge should be worn either on the lapel and coat or in the form of an armband.[3]

Concerns that the foreign press might criticize us for this were dismissed by him for the very reason that the Polish women in Berlin also wear a P and the Jewish road workers wear yellow armbands.[4] Other than that, he views the measure as necessary because the Jews have become increasingly insolent over time. They do not observe the no-go area[5] at all, and in some cases they have even tried to encourage negative sentiments. For this reason they must be visibly marked and, if they fail to wear the badges, taken to a concentration camp.

DOC. 177

On 21 April 1941 the directors of Rosenthal Porcelain AG ask the Reich Ministry of Justice for permission to retain the name of the firm[1]

Letter from the board of Rosenthal Porcelain AG, signatures illegible,[2] Marktredwitz, to the Reich Ministry of Justice, for the attention of Landgerichtsrat Hefermehl,[3] dated 21 April 1941[4]

Dear Landgerichtsrat

Re: de-Jewification of company names

A regulation has been issued dated 27 March 1941,[5] stating that all company names derived from former leading Jewish figures of the enterprise in question must be changed within four months.

2 Walter Tießler (1903–1984), freight-forwarding manager; joined the SA in 1922 and the NSDAP in 1925; head of propaganda for the Gau of Halle-Merseburg, 1926–1930; worked with the Reichsleitung for propaganda in Munich, 1934; head of the propaganda department for the staff of the Deputy of the Führer, 1940; Party Chancellery liaison to Governor General Hans Frank, 1944; died in Munich.

3 As early as 1938 Goebbels had proposed making it compulsory for Jews to wear visible identification, but this had been rejected for foreign-policy reasons. The SD had also made corresponding proposals: see PMJ 2/149. The compulsory visible identification of the Jews was ultimately introduced on 1 Sept. 1941: see Doc. 212.

4 In accordance with a police regulation issued on 8 March 1940, Polish civilian workers deployed in the Reich were forced to wear a 'Polish badge' on their clothing: *Reichsgesetzblatt*, 1940, I, p. 555. The visible identification of Jewish road workers had not been made compulsory, but it was nonetheless practised in various firms and towns.

5 In Dec. 1938 the Berlin police chief had imposed a 'ban on Jews' (*Judenbann*) which applied to the city's government quarter, trade-fair grounds, public baths, and all sporting and cultural venues. Jews who lived in the vicinity of these places required a permit: *Jüdisches Nachrichtenblatt* (Berlin edition), 6 Dec. 1938, p. 2.

1 BArch, R 3001/20520, fols. 12–14. This document has been translated from German.

2 The directors of Rosenthal Porcelain AG were Paul Klaas and Otto Zöllner.

3 Dr Wolfgang Hefermehl (1906–2001), lawyer; joined the NSDAP and the SS in 1933; worked in the Reich Ministry of Justice, 1934–1945, lastly as Oberlandesgerichtsrat; SS-Hauptsturmführer, 1942; professor in Mannheim from 1956, in Münster from 1959, and in Heidelberg from 1961.

4 Parts of the original have been annotated and underlined by hand.

5 Regulation on Companies of De-Jewified Businesses (*Verordnung über Firmen von entjudeten Gewerbebetrieben*), 27 March 1941, *Reichsgesetzblatt*, 1941, I, p. 177.

Upon consulting you we learned that we would, in principle, come under this law if our company name represents nothing more than a purely personal connection to the name of the founder and former management board member Philipp Rosenthal.[6]

On the matter itself, we wish to point out from the outset that our company could never be regarded as non-Aryan, in that Privy Councillor Rosenthal and his family together did not own or control even 20 per cent of the company's capital. What is more, we take the view that the name 'Rosenthal Porcelain' has become a purely generic term in Germany and, above all, throughout the world, and that no connoisseur or purchaser would associate any thoughts of a personal nature with it. We gave clear evidence of our viewpoint on this as early as 1938 by changing the former company name – 'Porcelain Factory Philipp Rosenthal & Co. AG' – to 'Rosenthal Porcelain AG'.

For fifty years Rosenthal Porcelain has enjoyed a recognized international reputation and, particularly abroad, has come to epitomize porcelain of the highest quality. The name 'Rosenthal' in connection with porcelain has the same prestige in the world as the names of the internationally renowned factories of Sèvres, Royal Copenhagen, Wedgewood,[7] and Doulton.

The standing of the 'Rosenthal Porcelain' brand abroad is emphasized, in addition, by the fact that there are a number of company-owned branch offices and distributorships, for example, in America, Sweden, Norway, Italy, Romania, Hungary, and Switzerland.

Such a global brand can be readily destroyed by a stroke of the pen but it would take many years and enormous expenditure to rebuild. The harm done to the reputation of high-quality German products in the world by destroying the 'Rosenthal Porcelain' brand is, in any event, so substantial that applying to us a regulation that fundamentally is not geared to our company cannot be justified under any circumstances.

We therefore request that you concur with our opinion that the name 'Rosenthal Porcelain' is a generic term everywhere in the world, as in this case the regulation could not be applied to our organization or our company name.[8]

Heil Hitler!

6 Philipp Rosenthal (1855–1937) had founded the porcelain factory in 1879.
7 Correctly: Wedgwood.
8 After a lengthy exchange of letters, the Reich Ministry of Justice gave its consent on 25 August 1941: BArch, R 3001/20520, fol. 128.

DOC. 178

On 22 April 1941 the Reich Association of Jews in Germany and the Jewish Religious Communities of Vienna and Prague reach an agreement concerning the allocation of available places on ships bound for the USA[1]

Agreement between the Reich Association of Jews in Germany, Migration Dept./Relief Association, signed Victor Israel Löwenstein,[2] and the Israelite Religious Community of Vienna, p.p. signed Robert Israel Prochnik,[3] dated 22 April 1941

The Reich Association of Jews in Germany, Berlin
the Israelite Religious Community of Vienna
the Jewish Religious Community of Prague
agree:
(1) In continuation of the arrangement of 12 June 1940,[4] for the purpose of emigration to the USA the purchasing of space on ships by each of the organizations named will continue to be effected exclusively for joint distribution, in accordance with the proportions agreed upon.
(2) The assignment of the places on the ships will be based on the allocation formula:
Old Reich – 56⅔ per cent
Ostmark 33⅓ per cent
Protectorate – 10 per cent
Any places not needed by the Jewish Religious Community of Prague for emigrants from the Protectorate will go in equal parts to the Old Reich and the Ostmark.
(3) This agreement is valid for all newly arising passages, that is, both for ship spaces purchased by the JDC and for those made available by travel agencies, with the latter also including those spaces that individual emigrants obtain from travel agencies, if the amount contributed from the funds of one of the organizations to the costs of these passages exceeds $40 per person.

The ship spaces given on the enclosed list[5] are excluded, but the Reich Association of Jews in Germany will endeavour, to the best of its ability, to provide timely passage to emigrants from the Ostmark and the Protectorate whose visas are in danger of expiring in June.
(4) The validity of this agreement extends both to the ship routes currently at issue (for example, Lisbon) and also to any that may re-emerge in the future (for example, Japan),

1 YVA, O.7.Cz/128. This document has been translated from German.
2 Victor Löwenstein (1885–1943), procurator; head of the legal department of the Bayerische Hypotheken- und Wechselbank in Munich, 1922–1938; assigned to the board of the Relief Association of Jews in Germany in Berlin, 1938; worked for the emigration department of the Reich Association from 1939; lost his life in an air raid.
3 Robert Prochnik (1915–1977); was unable to complete his law degree after the Anschluss of Austria; employee of the Israelite Religious Community of Vienna from 1938; posted to Berlin in May, and returned to Vienna in 1941; deported to Theresienstadt in 1942; worked on the Council of Elders from 1943; employed by the American Jewish Joint Distribution Committee (JDC) in Munich and Paris after the war; later lived in London, where he was the manager of a steel plant.
4 In June 1940 the Jewish representatives had agreed to allocate tickets to Berlin, Vienna, and Prague for the passage by ship at a ratio of 5:1:1.
5 The list is in the file.

as well as to railway travel, if these means of transport can be used to reach the USA. A line of action regarding all the other immigration countries will be agreed upon in consensus.
(5) This agreement is effective as of today, but still requires the consent of the Jewish Religious Community of Prague, which has already declared its approval of the 10 per cent quota.
(6) This agreement can be terminated by any of the organizations involved, with a notice period of six weeks, after the expiry of a contract period of three months.

DOC. 179
On 3 May 1941 the VUGESTAP provides information in a leaflet about the arrangements for the public sale of Jewish property in Vienna[1]

VUGESTAP[2] instruction leaflet and authorization card, dated 3 May 1941

VUGESTAP
Vienna I, 24 Bauernmarkt

Instructions
The sale of personal and household effects of Jewish emigrants that have been confiscated by the Gestapo, State Police head office in Vienna, is being handled by the administrative centre established for this purpose, the 'Vugestap', 24 Bauernmarkt, Vienna I, in accordance with the following guidelines:
(1) Sales will be handled separately for furnishings (furniture, carpets, paintings) and everyday items (clothing, linen, tableware).
(2) Every Volksgenosse who wishes to purchase items must submit a corresponding application to the 'Vugestap'.
(3) The application forms (A for furniture, B for everyday items) will be given out to Volksgenossen by the local branches of the NSDAP*. Concurrently with the issue of the application form, the local branch will verify the reliability and worthiness of the applicant. After that, the applicant must submit the application to his works manager, who will corroborate the net monthly earnings stated in the application.
(4) The applications are to be filled out legibly, typed if possible, and then sent exclusively *by post* to the 'Vugestap', 24 Bauernmarkt, Vienna I. The forms cannot be submitted in person, and the 'Vugestap' is not open to the public.
(5) Despite the very extensive sales operation, it must be expected that the number of applicants will be so large that it will not be possible to allocate items to all bidders.

1 RGVA 1323k-2-445, copy ÖStA, record group: Historikerkommission. Published in Adler, *Der verwaltete Mensch*, p. 593. The two documents reproduced here (instruction leaflet and authorization card) have been translated from German.
2 Much of the property belonging to Jewish emigrants was stored with forwarding agents in Vienna, but with the outbreak of war it was not forwarded in most cases. The Vienna Gestapo established an organization to arrange the public auction of the property that was left behind. VUGESTA, also VUGESTAP, stood for 'Verkauf jüdischen Umzugsgutes Gestapo' (Gestapo Office for the Sale of the Personal and Household Effects of Jewish Emigrants). It commenced operation on 7 Sept. 1940.

The 'Vugestap', therefore, assumes no responsibility of any kind for guaranteeing that individual applications are taken into consideration.
(6) Each buyer is entitled to make purchases only for his own personal use and that of his family members. Any dealing in the goods acquired from the 'Vugestap' is strictly prohibited.
(7) The sale will take place on the grounds of the Vienna trade fair centre and specifically in livestock halls 1 and 2, Nordportalstrasse. Interested parties will receive a postcard informing them of the sale days. This card simultaneously serves as the buyer's authorization and must be handed in when he makes a purchase. *Sales prohibited without this authorization card.*
(8) The items will be offered for sale at prices determined by the estimated value and the selling fees, which have been kept extremely low. The prices written down must therefore be paid without additional surcharges; no auction will take place.
(9) The buyer will accept the purchased items in 'as is' condition and is obliged to have them removed within three days at his own expense and risk.
(10) The sale is carried out in exchange for cash payment. However, to enable less well-off Volksgenossen to purchase furnishings, a loan for the surplus amount can be granted if the purchase price is in excess of RM 300. This loan will total no more than twice the net monthly income and must be repaid in three to six instalments. The loan repayments are due in monthly instalments, calculated from the day of sale. No interest will be charged on the loan. An administrative fee of RM 1 per instalment will be charged, irrespective of the instalment amount. The items will remain the property of the 'Vugestap' until payment has been made in full.
(11) The sales operation will last for several months. Therefore, please refrain from making enquiries in the event that the authorization card has not arrived. The 'Vugestap' will endeavour throughout to issue only as many applications as there are items to be sold, in order to satisfy all applications, if possible. The applications will be processed in the order in which they are received by the 'Vugestap'.
* For members of the Wehrmacht, forms will be distributed by the superior military authorities.

Authorization no. ...*247*......
The addressee is entitled, on

4 May 1941, 9 a.m.—2 p.m.,

on the grounds of the trade fair centre, Südportalstraße, Hall 6 and South Hall,

to purchase used items during the sale of property by VUGESTA.

This authorization card is valid for no more than two accompanying persons and entitles the addressee only to purchase items for his personal use.

In addition, the items being offered for sale may be viewed on

3 May 1941, 3 p.m.—5 p.m.

— VUGESTA

VUGESTAP
Wien, I., Bauernmarkt 24.

Merkblatt!

Der Verkauf der von der Geheimen Staatspolizei, Staatspolizeileitstelle Wien beschlagnahmten Umzugsgüter jüdischer Emigranten erfolgt durch die hiefür organisierte Verwaltungsstelle „Vugestap" Wien, 1., Bauernmarkt 24, nach folgenden Richtlinien.

1.) Der Verkauf erfolgt getrennt nach Einrichtungsgegenständen (Möbel, Teppiche, Bilder) und Gebrauchsgegenstände (Kleider, Wäsche, Geschirr).

2.) Jeder Volksgenosse, der Gegenstände erwerben will, hat einen entsprechenden Antrag an die „Vugestap" zu stellen.

3.) Die Antragsformulare (A für Möbel, B für Gebrauchsgegenstände) werden durch die Ortsgruppen *) der NSDAP. an die Volksgenossen ausgegeben. Gleichzeitig mit der Ausgabe des Antragsformulares erfolgt die Bestätigung der Ortsgruppe über die Zuverlässigkeit und Würdigkeit des Antragstellers. Sodann hat derselbe den Antrag seinem Betriebsführer vorzulegen, der das Nettomonatseinkommen im Antrag bestätigt.

4.) Die Anträge sind gut leserlich, womöglich mit Schreibmaschine, auszufertigen, sodann ausnahmslos **per Post** an die „Vugestap" Wien, 1., Bauernmarkt 24, einzusenden. Persönliche Abgabe der Anträge oder Vorsprache bei der „Vugestap" ist ausgeschlossen.

5.) Trotz der äußerst umfangreichen Verkaufsaktion ist damit zu rechnen, daß die Zahl der Antragsteller derart groß sein wird, daß eine Zuteilung an alle Bewerber unmöglich ist. Die „Vugestap" übernimmt daher keinerlei Gewähr auf Berücksichtigung des einzelnen Antrages.

6.) Jeder Käufer ist nur berechtigt, zum persönlichen Gebrauch für sich und seine Angehörigen zu kaufen. Jeder Handel mit den von der „Vugestap" erworbenen Gütern ist strengstens verboten.

7.) Der Verkauf findet am Gelände der Wiener Messe und zwar in der Tierhalle 1 und 2, Nordportalstraße, statt. Die Interessenten werden von den Verkaufstagen mittels Karte verständigt, die gleichzeitig auch die Legitimationskarte des Käufers darstellt und beim Einkauf abgegeben werden muß. **Der Verkauf ohne Legitimationskarte ist ausgeschlossen.**

8.) Alle Gegenstände gelangen zu Preisen zum Verkauf, die aus dem Schätzwert und den äußerst niedrig gehaltenen Verkaufsspesen gebildet werden. Die angeschriebenen Preise sind daher ohne weitere Zuschläge zu bezahlen, eine Versteigerung findet nicht statt.

9.) Der Käufer übernimmt die erworbenen Gegenstände in ihrem tatsächlichen Zustand und ist verpflichtet, sie innerhalb von 3 Tagen auf seine Kosten und Gefahr abtransportieren zu lassen.

10.) Der Verkauf erfolgt gegen Barzahlung. Um jedoch minderbemittelten Volksgenossen die Erwerbung von Einrichtungsgegenständen zu ermöglichen, kann bei einem RM 300.— übersteigenden Kaufpreis für den Mehrbetrag ein Kaufkredit bewilligt werden. Dieser beträgt höchstens das zweifache Nettomonatseinkommen und ist in 3—6 Raten abzustatten. Die Kreditraten sind in Monatsraten vom Verkaufstag an gerechnet, fällig. Kreditzinsen werden nicht verlangt; für die Manipulation wird RM 1.— je Rate, ohne Rücksicht auf die Ratenhöhe, berechnet. Bis zur vollständigen Bezahlung bleiben die Gegenstände Eigentum der „Vugestap".

11.) Die Verkaufsaktion wird mehrere Monate dauern. Es sind daher Anfragen wegen nicht erhaltener Legitimationskarten zu unterlassen. Die „Vugestap" wird bemüht bleiben, im allgemeinen nur so viele Anträge auszugeben, als Gegenstände zum Verkauf kommen, um möglichst alle Anträge befriedigen zu können. Die Erledigung der Anträge erfolgt in der Reihenfolge ihres Einlaufes bei der „Vugestap".

*) Für Wehrmachtsangehörige erfolgt die Ausgabe durch die vorgesehenen militärischen Stellen.

Q 0485

86a

Legitimationskarte Nr. 247

Der Adressat ist berechtigt, am

4. Mai 1941, 9—14 Uhr,

im Messegelände Südportalstraße, Halle 6 und Südhalle,

gebrauchte Gegenstände anläßlich der Veräußerung durch die VUGESTA einzukaufen.

Diese Legitimation gilt für höchstens 2 Begleitpersonen und berechtigt nur zum Einkauf für den eigenen Gebrauch des Adressaten.

Außerdem ist die Besichtigung der zu kaufenden Gegenstände am

3. Mai 1941, 15—17 Uhr,

gestattet.

—VUGESTA

DOC. 180

On 6 May 1941 the management of Friedrich Krupp AG asks for permission to keep on two Jewish specialist workers[1]

Letter from Friedrich Krupp AG (H.V.Nr.-), signed Ihn,[2] to the German Labour Front, Social Responsibility Office, Chief Officer Schröder, dated 6 May 1941

Re: employment of Jews

Dear Mr Schröder,

In response to your kind letter of 25 April,[3] I would like to inform you that I have been working on the matter for quite some time now. As you will read below, it has not yet reached its conclusion. For the time being, I can say the following:

It is correct that two Jews are still employed at our cast steel foundry in Essen,[4] namely

1 Historisches Archiv Krupp, WA 41/8–88, fols. 14–16. This document has been translated from German.

2 Max Ihn (1890–1983); joined the Krupp concern as a trainee in 1919; assistant manager, 1933; head of personnel department, late 1934; deputy director, Oct. 1938, and then director, March 1941; arrested along with Alfried Krupp, 1945, and sentenced at the Nuremberg Military Tribunals to nine years' hard labour, 1947; released in 1951; later director general of the Gesamtmetall employers' association in Cologne.

3 In a letter dated 25 April 1941, the German Labour Front had asked Max Ihn to examine 'whether there is a possibility of removing the two Jews from Krupp': Historisches Archiv Krupp, WA 41/8–88, fol. 26.

4 The cast steel works founded by Friedrich Krupp in 1812 was the main production plant of the Krupp firm in Essen until 1945.

(1) the Jew Otto Israel *Wolf*,[5]
(2) the Jew Isaak *Kronenberg*.[6]

Wolf, born on 17 May 1877, has been employed in our cast steel works since 10 July 1906, that is, for approximately thirty-five years. From 11 September 1916 to 26 November 1918, Wolf was called up for military service. Wolf is employed as a precision steel press operator in the steel rim rolling mill, where around 300 employees work in two shifts.

Pressing the rolled steel rims to size is *specialized work*, which involves casting the red-hot rolled rims into their precise final dimensions. Knowledge of the shrinkage of the rolling material, proper assembly of the press, and knowledge of the pressing process itself are absolutely essential. Such specialized work requires a lengthy period of training and many years of experience. Wolf has performed this work conscientiously and impeccably for more than thirty years now. In his work, he does not come into direct contact with the other personnel. In addition, his conduct thus far has not given rise to any complaints whatsoever.

The management has made arrangements to train suitable junior personnel for these tasks, which require expertise akin to that of a skilled craftsman, but this training requires a minimum of one to two years. However, the training of new young workers is greatly hampered by the shortage of workers, absence due to illness, and conscription into the Wehrmacht, which has often made it necessary to redeploy the available manpower.

Kronenberg, born on 3 March 1878, has been employed in our cast steel works since 15 August 1905, that is, for more than thirty-five years. Kronenberg works in our crankshaft shop as a template fitter, repairing and producing templates and precision tools (objective gauges, pointer meters, and keying devices). The tasks involved are complex and require great precision, and a trained metalworker, after a three-month screening and qualifying period, needs at least a year of training in order to perform the task in a fully adequate manner. Only especially proficient metalworkers ever have the aptitude for these precision tasks.

Through many years of employment in the crankshaft workshop, Kronenberg has acquired considerable experience and he performs the tasks assigned to him to our complete satisfaction. In the specially equipped gauge room, which is the smallest department of the factory, work is done in rotating shifts. Generally, five workers are assigned to one shift and two to the other, so that Kronenberg does not come into contact with the rest of the firm's personnel. His conduct has thus far been faultless. His co-workers too, of whom the foreman above him and two template fitters are Party comrades, have thus far taken no exception to the employment of Kronenberg.

As a result of the short-term supply requirements of the Reich Ministry of Aviation, which have to be met by our crankshaft workshop, the firm cannot do without Kronenberg at the moment, as suitable replacement workers are not available.

In a letter dated 15 April of this year, the employment office in Essen, citing the stance taken by the local Kreisleiter, asked us to dismiss the aforementioned Jews and make

5 Otto Wolf (b. 1877), steel press worker; deported to Theresienstadt on 21 July 1942 and to Auschwitz on 28 Oct. 1944; survived.

6 Isaak, also Hermann, Kronenberg (1878–1942), metalworker; employed by Krupp, 1905–1926 and again from 1929 to 13 June 1942; deported on 15 June 1942 to Sobibor, where he was murdered.

them available to the employment office.[7] We then described the employment circumstances of the two Jews to the Kreisleiter in detail and, in this context, strongly emphasized that the extraordinary tasks assigned to us require us to retain every single worker, especially when, as in the present cases, these are specialized workers who cannot be replaced at this time. In view of the existing special circumstances, we asked the Kreisleiter to agree to the further employment of the Jews Wolf and Kronenberg, at least for the duration of the war. But the Kreisleiter does not have sole responsibility in this respect. It is the employment office that is in charge. We have therefore now submitted a request to the employment office in Essen, seeking permission to employ the men.

Of course we too fully accept the directives regarding the employment of Jews.[8] But specifically with respect to these two men, we are in such a difficult position that we have been forced in the first instance to submit a request for an exception.

I will write to update you once the matter has been concluded[9]

Heil Hitler!

DOC. 181

On 12 May 1941 the Jewish Religious Community of Cologne announces which buildings must be vacated[1]

Announcement by the Jewish Religious Association, Religious Community of Cologne, Housing Advisory Dept., signed Chairman Dr Albert Israel Kramer and Head of the Housing Advisory Dept. Siegfried Israel Bernhard,[2] to all Jews in Cologne, dated 12 May 1941

To all Jews in Cologne

In our circular of 3 May, it was already announced that, in addition to all Aryan buildings, a number of Jewish buildings must also be vacated. The directive of the authority has now been issued.[3]

All Jewish buildings on the right bank of the Rhine (Deutz, Kalk, and Mühlheim, etc.) and all Jewish buildings in the southern and western suburbs (Bayenthal, Marienburg, Zollstock, Klettenberg, Sülz, Lindenthal, Braunsfeld, and Müngersdorf) must be vacated,

7 The Kreisleiter was Peter Hütgens (1891–1945). The letter is in the file: Historisches Archiv Krupp, WA 41/8–88, fol. 30.

8 The employment office in Essen had previously referred to a decree of the Reich Ministry of Labour dated 20 Sept. 1939, which had supposedly not been published. According to the employment office, the decree stipulated 'that the Jews are to be deployed only in groups, separately from the rest of the personnel': ibid., fol. 34.

9 Both workers continued in their positions for a while (ibid., fols. 14–16), but were dismissed in June 1942: ibid., fol. 29.

1 NS-Dokumentationszentrum Köln, Rundschreiben an die jüdische Bevölkerung. Published in Zvi Asaria (ed.), *Die Juden in Köln von den ältesten Zeiten bis zur Gegenwart* (Cologne: Bachem, 1959), pp. 366–367. This document has been translated from German.

2 Probably: Siegfried Bernhard (b. 1896), head of the Housing Advisory Department of the Jewish Religious Community of Cologne; deported to Theresienstadt on 18 June 1942 and from there to Auschwitz on 28 Sept. 1944; declared dead.

3 The Gestapo directive is dated the same day: LAV NRW R, RW 18/5, fols. 48–49.

so that the housing of the Jews is limited to the Jewish buildings in the old town and the new town and the northern suburbs (Ehrenfeld, Nippes, etc.).

The authority further requires that both the Aryan and the aforementioned Jewish buildings must be vacated *by 1 June*, regardless of the existing notice periods and contracts.

We ask that you inform your landlord of this state of affairs at once, and that you communicate with us in the event of difficulties.

This directive requires an even more intense concentration of the Jews than was previously planned. It must now be assumed that, in principle, each family has the right to only one room, and that single persons must be accommodated together in larger numbers – depending in each case on the size of the room.

The result of this situation is as follows:

(1) All applications and the municipal transfer orders have become invalid, unless the relocation has already taken place.

(2) Within the next fortnight, everyone who is affected by the new regulation will receive a notification from us, stating what living quarters are assigned to him.

The owners of Jewish buildings or landlords of Jewish apartments will receive a copy of this transfer notification. It is pointed out in particular that no relocation may occur without our transfer notification. Contraventions must be reported.

(3) In view of the incredibly limited space available, no one – not even the owner of the building or the tenant remaining in his former apartment – may keep more furnishings than he can properly accommodate in the space assigned him in the future. (In the event of disagreements, the Housing Advisory Department must be informed immediately in writing.) *On the instructions of the authorities*, items of furniture that cannot be accommodated may not be sold. Instead, they must be stored under supervision, to avoid them being dumped.

The items are to be sold off gradually, for the benefit of the owner. Pricing is the responsibility of an officially appointed valuer.

(4) In preparation for the extensive rearrangement, the Housing Advisory Department will not offer consultation hours until further notice.

We are obliged to report to the State Police office all persons who fail to comply with the instructions to be issued by us – but we hope and expect that each individual will exhibit so great a sense of responsibility and discipline that there will be no cause for such reports.

DOC. 182

On 20 May 1941 the Reich Security Main Office issues guidelines concerning the emigration of Jews[1]

Letter from the RSHA (4b [Rz] [nec.] 2494/41 G (859)), p.p. signed Schellenberg,[2] Berlin, to all Gestapo (head) offices and for information to the SD (main) districts, dated 20 May 1941 (copy)[3]

Re: emigration of Jews from Belgium and from occupied and unoccupied France – emigration of Jews to unoccupied France from the territory of the Reich.
Reference: none.
Jews of German nationality who are currently in France and Belgium are requesting various authorities in the territory of the Reich to send documents to them, such as passports, police certificates, etc., for the purpose of emigration.

According to a notification from the Reich Marshal of the Greater German Reich,[4] the emigration of Jews from the territory of the Reich, including the Protectorate of Bohemia and Moravia, also during the war, is to be stepped up within the framework of existing opportunities, with due regard to the established guidelines for Jewish emigration.[5] As there are insufficient emigration opportunities for Jews from the territory of the Reich at present, primarily involving transit through Spain and Portugal, emigration of Jews from France and Belgium would entail a renewed curtailment of these opportunities. Considering these facts and in view of the undoubtedly imminent final solution to the Jewish question, emigration of Jews from France and Belgium is therefore to be prevented.[6] I request that the relevant domestic German authorities in your area of jurisdiction be informed that no documents are to be sent to Jews in France and Belgium for the purpose of emigration.

With regard to the emigration of Jews to unoccupied France from the territory of the Reich, including the Protectorate of Bohemia and Moravia, I inform you that as a general rule, in cases of a special nature, such as the relocation of Jews without means to relatives in unoccupied France, the emigration can be permitted once immigration authorization has been received from the French government, if there are no grounds to prevent the emigration in the interest of security. The decisive factor here is the judgement that authorization of the emigration of Jews to unoccupied France results in an advantage for the German Reich, even if only by virtue of the fact that a Jew leaves the territory of the Reich.

1 BArch, R 58/276, fols. 273–274. Excerpts published in Pätzold, *Verfolgung, Vertreibung, Vernichtung*, pp. 288–289. This document has been translated from German.
2 Walter Schellenberg (1910–1952), lawyer; joined the NSDAP and SS in 1933; worked in the SD from 1935; head of Division IV E (domestic counter-espionage), 1939–1941, and head of Office VI (foreign intelligence service) of the Reich Security Main Office (RSHA) and Oberregierungsrat from 1941; SS-Brigadeführer, 1944; police brigadier, 1944; sentenced at the Nuremberg Military Tribunals to six years in prison, 1949; released in 1950.
3 The copy was sent on 14 July 1941 by the Gestapo head office in Düsseldorf (B 4/71.02/1053/41 g), p.p. Dr Venter, to the field offices, the border police stations, the mayors of Krefeld, Neuß, and Viersen, the chiefs of police (with copies for the police offices), and the Landräte (with copies for the local police authorities).
4 Hermann Göring.
5 In its guidelines for accelerating Jewish emigration during the war, on 24 April 1940 the RSHA announced that Reich Marshal Göring explicitly supported such measures: see Doc. 71.
6 These instructions evidently refer to Jews of German nationality in France and Belgium.

If it becomes apparent in individual cases that immigration authorization was granted by the French government solely in view of certain advantages that would ensue for France as a result of the immigration of these Jews, permission for emigration is to be denied in these cases. In *each individual case*, however, the opinion of the Reich Security Main Office must be sought in advance.

An immigration of Jews from the other occupied countries in Europe to unoccupied France is not desirable, although it cannot always be prevented. An immigration of Jews into the territories occupied by us must be prevented, in view of the undoubtedly imminent final solution to the Jewish question.

DOC. 183

On 5 June 1941 a lawyer complains to the Regierungspräsident in Breslau about Jews being assigned to his client's building[1]

Letter from Dr Herbert Schmidt,[2] lawyer at the regional and local court in Breslau, notary, 13 Blücherplatz, Breslau 1, to the Regierungspräsident, for the attention of Inspector Hase, Breslau, dated 5 June 1941

My client, Mrs Berta *Olischewski*, here, *22 Freiburger Straße*, purchased the building at 22 Freiburger Straße in Breslau in October 1939 from the Jewish previous owner, the former solicitor Judicial Counsellor Siegfried Israel Friedländer,[3] and – as the result of a complaint lodged with the minister by the seller, Friedländer – did not enter into possession of the building until 1 July 1940, and pursuant to the decision of the Higher Regional Court *retrospectively* on 1 April 1940.[4] During the time between the conclusion of the purchase agreement and the conveyance, which firstly had to be forced by means of legal action, the seller, Friedländer, took additional Jews into the building as tenants without the knowledge and consent of the purchaser, Mrs Olischewski.

Before the conclusion of the purchase agreement, Mrs *Olischewski* had enquired of the government, and specifically of department head Mr *Hanifle*,[5] whether, if she bought the building, it would continue to be a Jewish one or not. The reply given to her was that the building, upon the transfer of the property into her hands, namely into Aryan hands, would be regarded as an Aryan building. Only upon receiving this information did Mrs Olischewski conclude the purchase agreement. Otherwise, she would have refrained from buying a Jewish building. After she had been recorded as the owner of the

1 Archiwum Państwowe we Wrocławiu, Rej. Wrocł., I/9976. This document has been translated from German.

2 Dr Herbert Schmidt (b. 1884), lawyer; joined the NSDAP in 1933; lawyer and notary in Breslau; member of the National Socialist Association of Legal Professionals.

3 Siegfried Friedländer (1868–1942), lawyer; lived in Breslau; deported on 12 June 1942 to Auschwitz, where he was murdered soon afterwards.

4 The files of the Breslau Higher Regional Court concerning the period in question have not survived.

5 Dr Rudolf Hanifle (b. 1893), lawyer and administrative official; Bezirkshauptmann in Zell am See from 1931; ousted from his post in 1938; worked for the Breslau government from 1939; worked in the office of the Reichsstatthalter in Salzburg from 1941; director of the regional office in Salzburg, 1951–1959.

building, she learned several months later that, contrary to the assurance given at the time, the building is regarded as a Jewish one, which now means that the Jewish Community plans to place additional Jews in the building as subtenants.

On behalf of Mrs Olischewski I ask that no more Jews be assigned to this building as tenants and subtenants.

The rooms in the building are currently leased to eight Aryan families and five Jewish families. As a result, there have already been detrimental consequences, inasmuch as the Jewish tenants are unruly, even threaten Mrs Olischewski's husband and brawl with each other, and subsequently the police have been repeatedly forced to intervene.

Naturally, the Aryan tenants suffer greatly in this situation, and these circumstances would escalate to an intolerable level if additional Jews were to be brought into the building. The Jews already living in the building now have around two or three subtenants, which naturally places an excessive strain on the rooms, particularly because the Jews do a brisk trade and business callers are constantly going in and out of their rooms. Both the Jewish tenants and their Jewish callers already feel that they are the absolute masters of the building. The Jewish Community has already stated that it can place anyone it wishes in the building and that the house owner herself has no say at all over this building.

At the time the building was purchased, a repair bill of RM 11,000 was imposed on the present owner, Mrs Olischewski, and specifically she had to pay RM 5,000 for prompt utilization and the remainder for carrying out the repairs within a period of five years. Because she did not have the RM 5,000 in ready cash, Mrs Olischewski was forced to take out a loan for this amount so that the repairs assigned to her could be carried out promptly. In this regard, she was expressly told that these repairs were required in order to get the building back into good condition for the prospective new Aryan tenants, for the intention was gradually to remove the Jewish tenants from the building. If, at the time, it had already been envisaged that the building would be treated as a Jewish one, this fee of RM 5,000 would not have been appropriate, for the Jewish tenants mean to harm the Aryan building owner wherever possible and to damage the building by defacing and putting things on the walls etc.; in particular they intend to let the apartments become as dilapidated as possible. Because all the apartments are let at a fixed rent, the building owner repeatedly has no other choice but to have all the repairs performed at her own expense. Taking on additional Jewish tenants would therefore cause the calamitous state of affairs described above to escalate beyond proportion and mean that the Aryan tenants, who are in the majority, would give up their apartments in this building as soon as possible. As a result, the building's owner would suffer severe losses.

Therefore, especially considering the assurance given by the government (Mr Hanifle) at the time that the building would be regarded as an Aryan one after purchase by Mrs Olischewski, I request that no more Jews be assigned to this building.[6]

Heil Hitler!

6 On 11 June 1941 the price control authority informed the Regierungspräsident on request that Mrs Olischewski had not been entered in the land registry as the owner until 10 August 1940 and that the building was accordingly to be regarded as Jewish. The apartments of the Jewish tenants, it was said, could 'not be vacated in the foreseeable future': Archiwum Państwowe we Wrocławiu, Rej. Wrocł., I/9976.

DOC. 184
On 7 June 1941 the Head of the Reich Chancellery informs Reichsleiter Martin Bormann that Hitler does not expect that Jews will still be living in Germany after the war[1]

Letter from Dr Hans Lammers (N.d.H. RMin.)[2] to the Head of the Party Chancellery, Reichsleiter Martin Bormann, currently at Obersalzberg, dated 7 June 1941 (copy)

Re: draft of an Eleventh Regulation on the Reich Citizenship Law concerning the statelessness of the Jews[3]

Esteemed Mr Bormann,

In a letter dated 8 April 1941, the Reich Minister of the Interior[4] sent me the draft of an Eleventh Regulation on the Reich Citizenship Law and an implementing regulation for it, and asked me to obtain a fundamental decision of the Führer regarding the measures against the Jews that are envisaged in the drafts.[5]

The Reich Minister of the Interior informs me that the office which you head played a decisive role in preparing the drafts.[6] I have presented both drafts to the Führer. I ask that you consult the enclosed copy of my letter to the Reich Minister of the Interior, which details the Führer's decision.[7]

For your information, I may add the following, in confidence: the Führer has not agreed to the issuance of the regulation proposed by the Reich Minister of the Interior primarily because he is of the opinion that there will be no more Jews in Germany after the war anyway, and that it is therefore not necessary to issue a regulation now that is hard to administer, takes up labour reserves, and yet fails to yield a fundamental solution.

Heil Hitler!

Your very devoted[8]

1 GStAPK, Rep. I-335-11-648, fols. 56–57. This document has been translated from German.
2 *Name des Herrn Reichsministers*: 'Name of the Reich Minister'.
3 See Doc. 166.
4 Dr Wilhelm Frick.
5 Nuremberg Document NG-299; IfZ-Archives, MA 1563/4. Published in abridged form in Adler, *Der verwaltete Mensch*, pp. 498–499.
6 The Party Chancellery was previously known as the Staff of the Deputy of the Führer. The office, which had been previously headed by Rudolf Hess, was under Hitler's direct authority from May 1941, with Martin Bormann as its head.
7 In a letter with the same date, Lammers informed the Reich Minister of the Interior that Hitler 'regarded as adequate a regulation that deprives those Jews of their German nationality who have their habitual abode abroad and declares their assets to have been forfeited to the Reich': GStAPK, Rep. I-335-11-648, fols. 54–56.
8 The Eleventh Regulation on the Reich Citizenship Law did not come into effect until 25 Nov. 1941: *Reichsgesetzblatt*, 1941, I, pp. 722–724.

DOC. 185

At a press conference on the evening of 22 June 1941, the Ministry of Propaganda issues guidelines for coverage of the war against the Soviet Union[1]

Notes taken at a press conference in the Reich Ministry of Propaganda, dated 22 June 1941[2]

[Point] 20. from the *press conference* on 22 June, evening:

1. Mr Suendermann,[3] Mr Fritzsche,[4] and Mr Bohrmann[5] from the Reich Foreign Office spoke about political commentary for the following days. Broadly speaking, the resulting guidance was as follows: one must not make the change of direction clear to the readers too abruptly. It must be done in stages.

First main question of the population: why a new campaign in the East now and not full effort towards the West? Answer emerges from the Fuehrer's proclamation.[6] Impossible to bring about a decision in the West as long as there is acute or overt danger from the East.

Second main question: why is the old anti-Comintern stance suddenly back again, after it had been abandoned.[7] On this, proceed in stages. At first, assessment of the political situation. Suited for this purpose is emphasis on the impact of the operation as an act of pan-European liberation. (With the restrictions in item 1 of the short version given earlier.) Place great emphasis on optimistic voices but do not support the expectation of a blitzkrieg. Solid conceptual basis required in the next phase. Do not repeat the old [anti-]Bolshevist arguments again, but make the problem adequately clear, in the same way in which the term plutocracy very quickly caught on

1 BArch, Zsg 102/32. This document has been translated from German.

2 The original contains handwritten underlining and is written entirely in lower case.

3 Helmut Sündermann (1911–1972), journalist; joined the NSDAP in 1930 and the SS in 1931; in the Reich Press Office of the NSDAP from 1931; head of the Press Political Office of the Reichsleitung of the NSDAP from 1934; member of the Reichstag and deputy press chief of the Reich government from 1942; in US internment, 1945–1948; owner of the Druffel publishing house from 1952 to 1972.

4 Hans Fritzsche (1900–1953), journalist; joined the NSDAP in 1933; at the Reich Ministry of Public Enlightenment and Propaganda from 1933; head of the German Press Department from 1939; ministerial director and head of the Radio Department from 1942; acquitted at the International Military Tribunal at Nuremberg, 1946; sentenced, as a 'major offender', to nine years in prison by a denazification tribunal, 1947; released in 1950; worked in the advertising industry from 1951.

5 Correctly: Dr Hans-Heinrich Bormann (1912–1994), lawyer in the Mecklenburg judicial service from 1934; joined the SA in 1933 and the NSDAP in 1937; in the Press Department of the Reich Foreign Office, Sept. 1939 to Sept. 1940 and from Oct. 1940; military service from Feb. to July 1942; worked as a lawyer and notary in Soltau from 1946; West German diplomatic service from 1957. consul in Bergen, 1964–1971, and embassy counsellor in Helsinki, 1973–1977.

6 Proclamation of the Führer to the German People on 22 June 1941, in Max Domarus, *Hitler: Reden und Proklamationen 1932–1945. Kommentiert von einem deutschen Zeitgenossen*, vol. 2 (Neustadt an der Aisch: Schmidt, 1963), pp. 1726–1732.

7 The Federation of German Anti-Communist Associations, or Anti-Comintern, had been founded in 1933 as a union of various anti-Communist leagues and was wholly financed by the Reich Ministry of Public Enlightenment and Propaganda. After the conclusion of the German-Soviet Non-Aggression Pact in August 1939, the Anti-Comintern was officially disbanded, and the publication of anti-Soviet works and films was prohibited. After the German invasion of the Soviet Union, the affiliate Nibelungen publishing house began publishing anti-Soviet works again.

in September 1939.[8] Finally, proceed with this, reiterating that the pact with Russia was never an ideological issue for us. We have never admired Soviet institutions, so no internal change of course either. National Socialism grew from the struggle against Bolshevism. Agitation was merely muted in a period of truce. Now there will be a return to the law under which it started. After all, absolute clarity regarding the nature of plutocracy and Bolshevism is required. Both have Jewish origins. The methods and aims are the same. One can have recourse to the old programme of the Comintern, to its role in Germany in 1918, memories from the Spanish Civil War, etc.

2. The population, spoiled by the previous successes, took a quick military victory for granted. These exaggerated expectations need to be countered skilfully.

3. The OKW issued guidelines for the wording of reports on military operations, which you will probably still receive orally through the state office. For the time being, the following from them:

The campaign is not being waged against the Russian people or the Russian army. Only Red Army and Red Navy, etc. In regional reporting speak of Lithuanians, Belorussians, Ukrainians, etc. Soviet Russians only in the region around Moscow, where it is justifiable.

Naturally, write about directions of operations and details only in accordance with the data from the Wehrmacht report. The disposition of the Red Army clearly reveals intentions to launch an offensive. In contrast to the Western campaign, do not conclude that the opponent has been defeated in the case of quick military successes. Possible attempt to withdraw to more favourable positions further to the rear. Continue to emphasize the fighting infantry units in the early stages, even once the armoured units and the Luftwaffe have started to play a major role again. Again, clearly signal the close relations among all parts of the Wehrmacht. Also, strongly emphasize navy operations in the Baltic.

Be certain to name General Antonescu[9] as commander-in-chief of the Romanian troops and Field Marshal Mannerheim[10] as commander-in-chief of the Finnish troops. Pay close attention to news about the war from the Allies.

If Hungary or Slovakia resists attack, skim over, [but if] reports come out do not hesitate to publish them.

Also during the Eastern Campaign, continue to pay particular attention to news about the progress of the battle for England. Announcements like the one yesterday about the Luftwaffe's great defensive success over the Channel must absolutely not be drowned out in future.

End

8 After the start of the war, Goebbels had introduced the term 'plutocracy' to denounce the Western democracies: see also *Tagebücher von Joseph Goebbels*, part 1, vol. 7, p. 241.

9 Ion Antonescu (1882–1946), Romanian military officer; appointed general, 1931; chief of the Romanian general staff from 1933; minister of war, 1937–1938; prime minister with absolute powers, 1940–1944; responsible for the deportation and murder of hundreds of thousands of Jews from the territories occupied by Romania; in Soviet internment, 1944; sentenced to death by the Romanian People's Court and executed, 1946.

10 Carl Gustav Emil Mannerheim (1867–1951), Finnish military officer; officer in the Russian army from 1889; commander-in-chief of the White Army in the Finnish Civil War, 1918; as regent he obtained recognition of Finland's sovereignty from the UK and the US, 1918–1919; field marshal, 1933; commander-in-chief of the Finnish army from 1939; president of Finland, 1944–1946.

DOC. 186

On 24 June 1941 Mr and Mrs Malsch inform their son of the closing of the US consulate in Stuttgart and the resulting hindrance to their emigration[1]

Handwritten letter from Mr and Mrs Malsch,[2] Düsseldorf, to their son, Wilhelm, and his wife, Trude,[3] dated 24 June 1941

My dear, dear children,

By now you will have probably received our letter of 19 June, in which we give you the address of the consulate in Stuttgart.[4] As of Thursday, 26 June, Stuttgart is closed. As we wrote to you, I had an appointment with the Relief Association here today. I went there anyway. There is a Mr Kluger[5] from Essen here now, for the local office. He had our files on hand. If nothing had come up, we would have cabled you. So, Mr Kluger looked through our files. He said, Mrs Malsch, you would have been dead certain to receive the visa, trust, bond, trip paid for, everything just as it should be. He said, I am taken aback myself, you were so close. The consul was just about to make another query with respect to Mr Marschütz. Everything in your case was fine. Now, unfortunately, nothing more can be done, we must wait and see what happens. Dear children, you simply cannot imagine how I felt. Are we then not to be reunited *at all*? It is just too awful, absolutely everything is going wrong for us. You got everything together with great effort and at great expense, and now that was all for nothing. It just doesn't bear thinking about. We have now been set back with everything, perhaps by years, and whether we will still be alive then, God only knows. Our heartfelt wish to see you again is what has kept us going, and who knows what will yet happen. I have never been so depressed in my life, everything has become so hopeless for us, for what else do we still have in the world besides you. Mr Marschütz wrote to us recently to say that he will now leave with us, he hopes. What is one to do, we must venture everything as it comes, but you can't know just how great a blow this is for us. I am terribly sorry for you. I think that if we had got there, I would have been unable to utter a syllable for the first few hours out of sheer joy. It was not meant to be. Please send a reply to us straight away. Your last letter was dated 21 May, since then we've heard nothing more from you. Every day we wait for post from you.

Dear little mouse. My warmest wishes on your 28th birthday, may the dear Lord continue to keep and protect you and bless you, and may you be granted health and happiness at the side of your dear Trudi. I cannot put in words all that I wish for you

1 USHMM, RG-10.086 /13 of 13. This document has been translated from German.

2 Amalie Malsch, née Samuel (1889–1942); married to the sales representative Paul Malsch (1885–1942). The couple lived in Düsseldorf and were deported to the Litzmannstadt (Lodz) ghetto on 27 Oct. 1941 in the first transport from Düsseldorf; they were murdered in Chelmno in May 1942.

3 Wilhelm Malsch, later William Ronald Malsh (1913–1994), only son of Amalie and Paul Malsch, emigrated at the end of 1935 or beginning of 1936 to Britain; from there he went to the USA in Jan. 1937 and married Trude in the summer of 1940.

4 This refers to the US consulate in Stuttgart, where the Malsches had applied for a visa.

5 Probably: Siegfried Kluger (b. 1899); lived in Essen and from 1941 headed the district office of the Reich Association of Jews in Germany; deported on 10 Nov. 1941 to Minsk, where he is presumed to have perished.

both as your mother. I am sending a big birthday kiss to you, dear Trudi, to pass on to Willy for me. Have a bit of a celebration. We certainly hoped to be able to join you this year, but it was not meant to be, fate willed it otherwise. Who knows when we will see each other again, let's continue to hope, it is the only thing we still have. Unfortunately, we're getting older and we're not getting any better-looking. Often I simply cannot believe that you are 28 years old now. We have not seen you two for 4½ years now, and who knows how much longer it will be. So, my dear children, keep having a good time, stay healthy and happy. We must wait and see what happens next and accept everything, however difficult it may be for us. It was not meant to be, the joy would have been too great for us. I send my love to all my loved ones, also my regards to Mrs Fraenkel.

Write back very soon. Hugs and kisses to you both from your loving and sorrowful mother.

My dear children. This is now the outcome of your effort, of our hopes and persistence. Unless a miracle happens, that the government there […][6] lets parents enter 'anyway', it can take a long time yet! Best, warmest wishes to you, dear Willy, on your birthday, stay healthy, stay at home during these times. Many hugs and kisses to you both, in abiding love, yours, Papa

DOC. 187

On 27 June 1941 the *Zeitschriften-Dienst* newsletter urges that links be drawn between the ideological conflict with the Soviet Union and the 'Jewish question'[1]

The ideological conflict with the Soviet Union

To create, in a way that is effective and convincing to readers, a link to the ideological struggle with the Soviet Union, a conflict which has been pushed into the background by the agreement of 1939,[2] it is first essential to lift the lid on the political and propagandistic machinations of the Soviets. The Red Book of the Anti-Comintern, *Why War with Moscow?*,[3] soon to be published by Nibelungen in Berlin, provides valuable material in this respect.

The best point of departure for the ideological discussion is the *treatment of the Jewish question*. After the conclusion of the Non-Aggression Pact of August 1939, the Ger-

6 A word is illegible.

1 'Die weltanschauliche Auseinandersetzung mit der Sowjet-Union', *Zeitschriften-Dienst: deutscher Wochendienst*, 27 June 1941, pp. 4–5. This document has been translated from German. Established in May 1939, the *Zeitschriften-Dienst* passed on the directives of the Reich Ministry of Public Enlightenment and Propaganda to magazine editors.

2 This refers to the German–Soviet Non-Aggression Pact signed by foreign ministers Ribbentrop and Molotov on 23 August 1939.

3 *Warum Krieg mit Moskau?*; correctly: *Warum Krieg mit Stalin? Das Rotbuch der Anti-Komintern* (Why a War with Stalin? The Red Book of the Anti-Comintern). The publisher Nibelungen brought out this book, although the Federation of German Anti-Communist Associations, or Anti-Comintern, founded in Oct. 1933, had already been dissolved in August 1939. See also Doc. 185, fn. 7.

man leadership had to expect that the influence of the Jewish elements in the political elite of the Soviet Union would gradually be curbed in order to make loyal, peaceful cooperation possible. It soon appeared, however, that the Soviets were by no means prepared to effect this transformation in the area of ideology and to break or at least restrict the absolute dominance of the Jews in the Soviet Union. The so-called fall of Finkelstein-Litvinov[4] was in reality only a change of function. Finkelstein reappeared in a key position, namely on the Central Committee of the CPSU, as head of its foreign policy division.[5] Admittedly, a few Jews vanished, but the most important ones remained and occupied new key posts. The Soviet Union, created by Jews, is still dominated by Jews even today.

The Red Book presents a wealth of authentic facts, unequivocally demonstrating the controlling influence of Jewry in the Party and state apparatus and in the cultural life of the Soviet Union. The real power in the Soviet Union rests exclusively in the hands of a tightly knit clique of power brokers, grouped around Stalin and organized by the Jew Kaganovich.[6]

The army of the Soviet Union, too, is completely under the influence of a Jewish ruling clique. The institution of the *political commissars* was created for the political 'education' and surveillance of the army. They were attached by the top army leadership to the troop commanders down to the smallest military unit level and were given very extensive powers.[7] These positions too were filled by Jews.[8] The Red Book mentions the most important names. The Jewification of the Soviet economic leadership, press, and cultural and academic life, the favouritism shown to the Jews in the annexed territories, and their decisive contribution to the work of subversion done by the Comintern everywhere in Europe provide a wealth of material.

In our cultural and scholarly journals, but especially in specialist journals, we no longer wish to deal with any special achievements of Soviet Russian science that may exist, nor, above all in economic and technical journals, do we wish to specify any production figures or to dispute in any detail any statistics of the Soviets from recent years.

4 Maksim M. Litvinov, born Meir (Max) Henoch Mojszewicz Wallach-Finkelstein (1876–1951), politician; Soviet foreign minister, 1930–1939; as such, responsible for a rapprochement with the Western powers; replaced by Molotov in May 1939. The National Socialist press usually referred to him as 'the Jew Finkelstein'.

5 Litvinov was a member of the Central Committee of the Communist Party of the Soviet Union (CPSU) until Feb. 1941, in Nov. 1941 he was named ambassador to the USA.

6 Lazar M. Kaganovich, born Kogan (1893–1991), politician; held top offices in the Central Committee of the CPSU, 1922–1925 and 1928–1930; first secretary of the Communist Party of the Ukrainian Socialist Soviet Republic, 1925–1928; head of the Moscow Party organization, 1930–1935; member of the Politburo of the CPSU, 1930–1957, and member of the State Defence Committee, 1942–1945; again first secretary of the Communist Party of the Ukrainian SSR, 1946–1947.

7 This refers to Red Army political officers, who were responsible for political education and orientation. The official position of political commissar had been abolished in July 1940 and was not reintroduced until July 1941. At lower levels, its equivalent was the *politruk* (Russian *politicheskii rukovoditel'*: 'political leader', the company-level political officer). The so-called Commissar Order (*Kommissarbefehl*) of the Wehrmacht, dated 6 June 1941, ordered that these personnel be shot upon capture: see the Introduction to PMJ 7 and Glossary.

8 In fact, only a fraction of the political commissars were of Jewish origin.

Instead, we wish to present in a convincing manner the disorganization induced by the Jews in the field of science and technology.

It is the task of the cultural, family-oriented, and entertainment magazines to demonstrate to their readers that, under the influence of the Jewish power-holders in the Soviet Union, there has been a failure to develop the frequently advertised '*proletarian culture*'. For literary journals, there is a good opportunity to prove that nihilism and anarchy, as manifested in political life and in pre-war literature, are the nucleus of Jewish Marxist subversion.

The same internal collapse of the Jewish Bolshevist ideology is proved in the military political sphere by the fact that there is now a frantic effort to mobilize, in the battle against the German Wehrmacht, the Soviet patriotism that has been cultivated for years. In dealing with the question of the Soviet army, the following must be taken into account: German propaganda has placed special emphasis on the strike capability of the Soviet army, particularly since 1935, when the build-up of a strong German Wehrmacht had to be accomplished. Let us not make the mistake of taking up reports from those days again. It is equally erroneous, of course, to minimize the significance of the world's largest army, measured by the number of soldiers.

DOC. 188
In the summer of 1941 an emigrant describes the situation of the Jews in Breslau in 1940–1941[1]

Account by an emigrant from Breslau, undated

Jewish life in the province of Silesia and in Breslau in 1940/41
Province
Small towns like Oels, Grottkau, Münsterberg, Cosel, and many others must be virtually free of Jews. In Liegnitz, too, there are only a few families. Eight, as I vaguely recall. Life there very unpleasant. In relative terms, best in the larger cities. Upper Silesia (Beuthen, Gleiwitz): no information, as for Breslau (am there approximately every three months), and limited freedom of movement. No significant migration to Breslau, I think. Earlier, at any event, the wealthy provincial Jews moved to Berlin, as long as migration was still possible – as the department head of the Community was content to inform me years ago. Without access to documents I cannot even give a rough estimate of how many provincial Jews recently immigrated to Breslau. A figure of between 200 and 500 is perhaps about right.
Current population in Breslau
Including the immigrants, around 6,000 to 7,000;[2] previously 18,000. Currently working there are

1 Wiener Library, Doc 1656/3/1/619, copy in YVA, 0.2/483: 'Jüdisches Leben in der Provinz Schlesien und in Breslau 1940/41'. This document has been translated from German. On the reports from the Wiener Library, see Doc. 88, fn. 1.

2 For the end of 1940 the statistical department of the Reich Association of Jews in Germany still reported 9,175 Jews for the Breslau district office.

(1) around 6 to 8 Jewish lawyers ('legal consultants')[3]
(2) around 40 to 50 Jewish doctors ('practitioners for the sick')[4] and around 15 dentists
(3) medical, legal, hospital, nursing, kitchen, administrative, domestic, etc. personnel
(4) all personnel of the Community administration in addition to the associated organizations and the Relief Association
(Regarding (3) and (4), now reduced by 40 per cent. Previously 1,400 as I vaguely recall (highly inexact)
(5) tailors, seamstresses, barbers, bathhouse staff, cobblers, hairdressers, and members of other occupations approved by the Regierungspräsident (in total, around 50 to 100).

Labour service

All males from 16 to 60 years of age and all females from 16 to 55 years of age are obliged to register, are examined by independent (Jewish) medical examiners, and have to work hard, and often long hours, sometimes doing the most menial tasks (sorting paper, rags, broken glass, etc. from the household waste collected by the Municipal Stables Administration, and shovelling snow). Mostly in suburbs or on the outskirts of the city. Wages RM 1, from which tram expenses, 30 pfennigs, are deducted. Daily wage. (Trip to and from work around 1 hour.) Others have to work in road construction and in other works and factories. I also know of a trained gardener, at the Linke-Hoffmann Works.[5]

The wages, including those of the gardener, are considerably below the pay for Aryan workers.

Almost across the board, the Jewish workers are treated impeccably by the business owners or other people in managerial positions, and by the supervisors, foremen, and other workmates. They all recognize the Jews' will to work and their achievements, and also take into consideration their lack of practical experience and the resulting lack of skills and physical abilities.

Quite a few illnesses as a result of overexertion. The Jewish hospitals have been merged and are over capacity (patients crammed together). Mischlinge and evacuees from Poland are also treated in the hospitals.

Most of the Jews are pale, gaunt, and shabbily dressed, including the formerly well-to-do ones, of course. In the street at least some of them are hard to identify and not immediately recognizable. This is less true of women. Of course, there are also so-called rich Jews, perhaps more than the individual intuitively assumes. At a real guess, I would say that today there are perhaps 150 to 200 with more than RM 100,000. Wealth only

3 Under the Fifth Regulation on the Reich Citizenship Law (27 Sept. 1938), Jews were barred from the legal profession. A very limited number were allowed to represent Jewish clients exclusively as so-called legal consultants (*Rechtskonsulenten*): *Reichsgesetzblatt*, 1938, I, pp. 1403–1406.

4 Under the Fourth Regulation on the Reich Citizenship Law (25 July 1938), the medical licences of Jewish physicians were revoked as of 30 Sept. 1938. Only a few Jewish doctors, as so-called practitioners for the sick (*Krankenbehandler*), were allowed to provide medical care to Jewish patients: *Reichsgesetzblatt*, 1938, I, pp. 969–970. See also PMJ 2/76.

5 Correctly: Linke-Hofmann Works AG, Breslau, rail vehicles manufacturer; founded in 1839 as a family owned enterprise, in 1871 converted into a joint stock company, and in 1897 into a public limited company; after 1945 the works were divided between the PAFAWAG train factory in Breslau and LOWA (the association of GDR-owned locomotive and train carriage enterprises) plants in Bautzen and Werdau. In 1958 they were re-established in the Federal Republic of Germany as Linke-Hofmann-Busch GmbH.

on paper. Blocked account, which is administered and overseen with unrelenting strictness by the extraordinarily malevolent officials in this department of the Foreign Exchange Office. The amount approved for release is very low.[6]

Trunks and other luggage belonging to the emigrants is confiscated and sold at public auction. Enquiries from the Gestapo. Especially aggressive in Frankfurt am Main. A very sympathetic freight-forwarding agent sent my luggage via Basel several weeks before my departure, so that when deregistering with the authorities on the day of my departure, I was able to notify the Gestapo that my luggage had been forwarded. The Gestapo was precisely informed with regard to the details of the forwarding agencies.

Increasingly large number of welfare recipients and constantly decreasing Jewish tax revenue.

Community no longer a public corporation but instead a private, incorporated association, under constant surveillance from the Gestapo. Community, institutions and foundations, and all other assets blended into the Reich Association, overseen by the Gestapo. The men in charge very parsimonious and not very pleasant. Payments often only made after threat of legal action. (My own experience as foundation head.) Justification: catastrophic situation of the Reich Association; perhaps the real reason: fear of the Gestapo.

Ghetto

Purely a ghetto in the mind, actual ghetto is feared. In Berlin, certain streets off-limits.[7] Not the slightest change on the electric tram in Breslau. Others in other cities, such as Dresden. In general, no hatred, but rather sympathy.

Official directives

Prohibited: access to most public parks and children's playgrounds, sitting on public benches (with the exception of seating in trams); barbers and hairdressers completely prohibited (resistance by individual barbers and hairdressers). Driving a car, very specific times and days for groceries and shops, precise stipulation of shopping hours and permitted purchases. Latest directive approximately three months ago: every Jew, when coming into contact with the authorities or with a private individual, while presenting his identity card, must state his full name, i.e. including his religious name, and add that he is a Jew.[8] (Matters of dispute: tram?) Apparently announced during the ideological training evenings. Pulses, fish, biscuits prohibited, no clothing ration cards. Sewing materials, up to 20 pfennigs.[9]

For emigrants

In Berlin I had to sign a declaration: no relative is permitted to accompany the emigrant to the train, and must therefore stay outside the railway premises. Curtains closed, no emigrant is permitted to stand by the window.

Appearance

A great many, mostly men, pale, gaunt, in shabby clothing, hard to recognize at first glance. Alleged statement by Hitler: in a few years there will be only Jewish cemeteries and scroungers in Germany. Leave with only a rucksack and 10 Reichsmarks.[10]

6 See Doc. 17, fn. 5.
7 See Doc. 176, fn. 5.
8 Most of the regulations mentioned varied by location. On the identity card requirement, see Doc. 122, fn. 8.
9 On such limitations, see Doc. 36, fn. 4.

Jewish life in Breslau

Board. (Führer principle.) Until a few months ago the chairman was City Councillor Less.[11] [He] emigrated somewhat surreptitiously, around May. (In common parlance: Germany without Hess. Breslau without Less.) Current board: (1) chairman: (retired) Regional Court Judge Dr Kohn,[12] genteel, knowledgeable, conscientious; (2) Community rabbi Dr Lewin:[13] keen intellect, extensive knowledge, brilliant orator, mastery of ideas and language, highly educated, also in the culture of the surrounding world, industrious, fast in his department, mostly welfare (thorough), but has been met with great hostility and is highly unpopular, has not a jot of emotion and lacks all connection with the individual; (3) the merchant Kaim,[14] very genteel, very calm, not overly humanitarian; (4) Orthodox Community rabbi Hamburger,[15] quiet, deeply religious, helpful, does good works (like his wife).

Relief Association

Separate from the Community, but internally connected, of course. After retirement of Regional Court Judge Dr Kohn, at present: (1) lawyer Dr Spitz;[16] (2) lawyer Dr Goldmann,[17] supposedly now released; (3) Pollak,[18] previously chairman of the Reich League of Jewish Combat Veterans in Breslau, now also liaison between Community and Relief Association on the one hand and Gestapo on the other hand. (Responsible, mostly unpleasant work.)

The personality, abilities, and actions of the gentlemen meet with extremely harsh criticism. In my assessment, somewhat unfairly. (Unfulfilled hopes owing to the unfavourable circumstances.) I have never had cause for complaint. On the contrary, however often I went there, despite the overburdening of the gentlemen, [I] always found a sympathetic ear and affability. I have heard some accounts of isolated substantiated complaints, but I am also suspicious of such portrayals. A boyhood friend told me that his journey to Shanghai fell through because *one* required visa had expired through the fault of the R[elief] A[ssociation], and his luggage was already in Shanghai. Another person, a doctor, complained that his emigration would have been unsuccessful if he

10 This could not be verified.

11 Georg Less (1871–1953), entrepreneur and municipal politician; chairman of the advisory board of the Chamber of Industry and Commerce and of the board of the Breslau City Bank; board member from 1932 and chairman, 1934–1941, of the Jewish religious community of Breslau; emigrated to Uruguay in 1941.

12 Dr Georg Kohn (1888–1944/1945?), regional court judge; last Community chairman in Breslau; deported to Theresienstadt on the last transport from Breslau on 16 June 1943; from there deported on 28 Oct. 1944 to Auschwitz, where he perished.

13 Dr Reinhold Lewin (1888–1943), rabbi; served as Reform rabbi in Leipzig, 1912, and in Königsberg, 1921–1938; editor of the *Königsberger Jüdisches Gemeindeblatt*, 1924–1938; rabbi in Breslau from 1938; deported in 1943 to Auschwitz, where he perished.

14 Emil Kaim (b. 1872), merchant in Breslau; deported to Theresienstadt in 1943; taken to Switzerland on a Red Cross transport in Feb. 1945.

15 Dr Bernhard Hamburger (b. 1875), rabbi; Orthodox rabbi at the Altglogauer Synagogue in Breslau until 1941; deported in 1942 to the Lublin district, where he is presumed to have perished.

16 Erich Spitz (b. 1882), lawyer, practised law in Breslau; worked at the advisory centre for emigrants; his subsequent fate is unknown.

17 Probably: Dr Max Goldmann (1887–1941), lawyer; deported on 25 Nov. 1941 to Kaunas, where he was murdered.

18 Probably: Max Pollack (1897–1941); deported on 25 Nov. 1941 to Kaunas, where he was murdered.

had not rectified, at the last moment, mistakes of the R[elief] A[ssociation] by taking action himself and through measures taken by the Hapag company. Here I heard that the ineptitude of the gentlemen, and particularly that of the first one, has put paid to the emigration of hundreds (?)[19] Perhaps the gentlemen (bureaucrats) are not sufficiently deft.

Working in the internal administration, the wife of a former lawyer, terrifically hard-working and overburdened, Mrs Mannsberg. Salaries cut to an almost unendurable extent for all workers at the Community and the associated organizations for the Relief Association. The clergy's salary completely withdrawn, incidentally, as reported, also that of clergymen of other religions. The aim is for them to be forced to take up some other occupation. (Russia.)

Jewish studies

The Fränckel Rabbinical Seminary[20] closed, also the library. All other libraries of the Community closed or dispersed, particularly as the building has been expropriated. So no Jewish studies at all. The new temple, built in 1863 and restored a few years ago, completely destroyed and razed to the ground on 10 November.[21] Now garages are to be built.

Latest directive from Goebbels: all pictures, collections, books that have antique value (thus also the old Talmud volumes) must be declared and apparently handed over. ([Further] details to be announced at a later stage.)[22]

Religious services

Services daily and on Sundays and holidays unless prohibited by the police, which reportedly has been the case only in 1939. In the old, dignified [White] Stork Synagogue, which reportedly has escaped destruction only thanks to the adjoining buildings. On the Day of Atonement, Reform service in the building of the former association of the 'Friends'. Apparently no harmony between the Orthodox Jews and the Reform Jews. (Conflict highly unnecessary at the present time.) Efforts to eliminate the Orthodox religious service. In winter, problems due to coal shortage.

Culture League

Efforts to arrange theatrical performances, concerts, and film screenings despite the greatest difficulties, stage in the 'Friends' House'. (See above.) Performances overcrowded, receive high praise. Only Jews admitted. Admission only on presentation of identity card.

19 Question mark in the original.

20 Jewish Theological Seminary of the Fraenckel Foundation, established in Breslau in 1854 as the first German rabbinical seminary. The seminary served as a model for setting up the Higher Institute for Jewish Studies in Berlin in 1870, as well as other rabbinical seminaries. It was closed in 1938 and the library's holdings were dispersed.

21 The New Synagogue was built between 1865 and 1872; after Berlin's main synagogue, it was the largest synagogue in Germany. On the night of 9 Nov. 1938, it was set ablaze and almost completely destroyed.

22 In accordance with § 2 of the Fifth Implementing Regulation to the Regulation on the Utilization of Jewish Assets (25 April 1941), the Reich Chamber of Fine Arts, as a purchasing body for cultural assets, decided whether Jewish-owned jewellery and art objects could be sold on the open market: *Reichsgesetzblatt*, 1941, I, p. 218.

DOC. 189
A lorry driver reports on the situation of the Jewish population in various German cities in mid 1941[1]

Anonymous report, undated

Jews in Germany in mid 1941
My own experiences and observations
The treatment of the Jews in Germany (Old Reich) varies greatly from place to place. What is permitted in one city is prohibited in another. In the handling of the different cases, things still depend on how well the official in question happened to sleep the night before. There are Gaue that are particularly notorious in the eyes of the world, but precisely in these places the treatment is actually not so bad. For example, in Leipzig, Jews are not allowed to go to public dining establishments (restaurants, cafés, etc.), while in Jena not a single venue of this type is off limits. In Berlin, signs are displayed at many restaurants: 'No entry for Jews' or at least 'Jews not welcome'. By contrast, all the hotels there are open to Jews. At least, no signs have been put up and in practice Jews have not been turned away. (The very few exceptions – Hotel Excelsior – confirm the rule.) On the other hand, I myself have had the experience in restaurants that co-religionists who were accompanying me were asked by the waiting staff: 'Are you a non-Aryan?' Upon receiving an affirmative answer, the waiter or waitress said, 'Then I have to ask the management whether I'm allowed to serve you.' (I assume, however, that the question was instigated by guests sitting nearby.)

Berlin, overall, is certainly the city in which the largest numbers of anti-Jewish signs are posted. At the directive of the Gauleitung, a big yellow sign is put up on every shop, not only grocery shops and the like: 'Merchandise on sale to Jews and for Jews only between 4 and 5 p.m.!'[2] It is hard to put into words what unpleasant consequences this shopping period of only one hour entails. For one thing, a housewife – as she is usually the one who must queue up – is far from able to do all her shopping in one hour. For another thing, and above all, most articles, groceries in particular, are already sold out by the afternoon. Another very typical sign, 'Goods in short supply and non-rationed items cannot be provided to Jews', is also found in quite a number of shops in the Reich capital. In this connection, I must add that the sale of fruit and milk [to Jews] has been prohibited for quite some time. (In other cities, the Jews at least get skimmed milk.) Absolutely all the chocolate shops, as well as the tobacconists, in Greater Berlin have signs stating 'No sales to Jews!' These signs and notices are all just a visible indication of the great shortage of commodities, and they all are posted only on instructions from higher up.

While I am on the subject of Berlin, I would like to report a few circumstances that I experienced there, in addition to other matters that are only implemented so severely

1 Wiener Library, Doc 1656/3/1/613; copy in YVA, O.2/419. This document has been translated from German. On the accounts from the Wiener Library, see Doc. 88, fn. 1.

2 In Berlin the shopping hours for Jews were set at 4–5 p.m.: see Doc. 36, fn. 7. Exceptions were regulated by the Police Supplementary Regulation to the Police Regulation on Shopping Hours for Jews (4 July 1940): *Amtsblatt für den Landespolizeibezirk Berlin nebst Öffentlichem Anzeiger*, 1940, no. 631, p. 230.

there. Berlin recently introduced a ban on Jews moving there. In Berlin, Jews' apartments must frequently be vacated for the SS. Often these apartments must be cleared out within 24 hours and, in addition, they must be renovated at the expense of the Jew who is moving out. Only one room is made available to Jews, for up to three persons.[3] In Berlin, all Jews, both men and women, between the ages of 16 and 65 are compulsorily conscripted for labour. The work is done in segregated squads. Standard wages are paid but the rates are very low, since these are mostly unskilled workers. Because of the high deductions – disability insurance, unemployment benefit, health insurance, taxes (always the highest [rate] for unmarried people), sometimes also military tax, and, for Jews and Poles, the special tax, the so-called social contribution amounting to 15 per cent of gross earnings – it is not unusual for a woman who does 48 hours of work to have take-home pay of RM 12 to 14 per week. If one now takes into account that transport costs also have to come out of this, one can imagine what is left.

The Jewish organizations, Reich Association [of Jews in Germany], religious community, etc. have been forced by the Gestapo to release a great part of their workers for the benefit of industry. Salaries in the Jewish offices have been forcibly cut to a minimum.[4]

The Jewish training workshops in Berlin were forced to close down in April 1941 in order to free up even the youngest people for the war industries. A young man of almost 18, a friend of mine, has been deployed in a lead works and has to work there all day with a sponge in his mouth; despite that, lead poisoning cannot be ruled out. There is only one means to prevent it: drinking large quantities of milk – that means also during working hours. The Aryan workers get milk supplied by the plant. For the Jews, milk provision has been forbidden.

A highly skilled mechanic, who had successfully trained in the largest optical works and had continued working there, had to be let go by his company in 1937. But to retain the good, well-trained technician, the company placed him in a smaller firm with which it was acquainted, in Berlin. Here, the specialist's qualities very soon become apparent, and he was put into the private lab of the firm's manager. (He worked alone there, separated from everyone else.) The man in question also invented several things here that produced good results for the firm, and for this reason he was of course also valued by his employer. He received a very decent monthly salary. Suddenly, in December 1940, the surprising order came via the German Labour Front: X must be dismissed immediately and must report to the employment office for placement elsewhere, as individual Jews are no longer to be employed. Soon afterwards, the man became the master craftsman in a Jewish department at Zeiss-Ikon,[5] and now he only takes home RM 30 a week – despite his responsible job. Several Aryan foremen and controllers work under him, but he is not allowed to tell them what to do, but he is held fully responsible for their work.

On 13 July 1941, coming back from Potsdam in the evening, I took the urban railway to Berlin. In the same railway carriage were two boys, who were behaving perfectly cor-

3 Content as in the original. The author presumably means that Jews had to live in one room, with up to three people sharing.

4 As of mid 1941, between 26,000 and 28,000 Jews had been deployed as forced labourers to more than 230 firms in Berlin. In August 1941 the Berlin Labour Administration recruited pensioners up to the age of 60 for forced labour: Wolf Gruner, *Judenverfolgung in Berlin 1933–1945* (Berlin: Stiftung Topographie des Terrors, 1996), p. 79.

5 Company manufacturing optical and photographic equipment, founded in 1926.

rectly and appropriately. Suddenly a man came up to them and asked: 'Are you Jews?' One child answered in the affirmative, and the reply was: 'And you're still sitting there? Get up quickly, or else something will happen.' Shocked, the children naturally stood up at once, and the man in question took a seat. A few fellow passengers were visibly indignant at the behaviour and tried to protest, but were silenced by a sharp remark from this great hero.

All transports of Jews who are emigrating leave from Berlin. (Even if a transport goes, for example, via Frankfurt, a Frankfurter must first travel to Berlin.) Three hours before the train departs, the participants in the transport must have assembled in the air-raid shelter, and they are not allowed to leave the shelter again before the departure time. Then the travellers, in a group, are led to the railway carriage. The curtains in the compartments must be kept closed. Relatives and friends are not allowed to come to the station to say goodbye.

Very harsh regulations apply to Jews elsewhere too, also in Leipzig, especially since the new mayor, Freyberg – formerly a Nazi minister in Braunschweig (but apparently sidelined there for being too capable) – has been in office. For example, in the trade fair city it had long been forbidden – before any other place even thought of it – to enter tobacconists' shops (once there was even a house search for cigars, cigarettes, etc. in Leipzig), to go to barbers and hair salons, to leave the city limits without explicit permission, to enter public parks. There was a ban on use of lodgings – with the exception of one specific small hotel – by Jews from out of town, and there were many other little forms of harassment. For the slightest causes, much harsher punishments were handed down than elsewhere. Two anti-Jewish authorities held sway there, and they tried to outdo one another wherever possible.[6]

Unexpectedly, a house search for money took place in Leipzig in February 1941. Anyone who had more than RM 500 at home was immediately taken away and later put in a concentration camp, without any hearing at all, of course.[7] I know of cases from other cities where thousands [of Reichsmarks] were found, and the people in question got off with two to four months in prison and were also released after serving their sentence. I should add here the fact that Jews who are sentenced to penal servitude are sent without further ado to a concentration camp after serving their sentences. In addition, in Leipzig there are especially tough restrictions on the luggage etc. that can be taken along by emigrants. There, for example, each person may take only one summer suit and one winter suit, two pairs of shoes and correspondingly little of everything else. In addition, everything has to be packed at the customs house. In other districts, by contrast, everything that had been recorded on the submitted list was allowed, except for the odd thing specified in a Reich order. The customs officials there also came to people's homes for the packing process.

6 An important role in the persecution of the Jews of Leipzig was played by the Central Agency for Jewish Affairs, which was connected to the city's Office for the Furtherance of Residential Construction and was soon known simply as the 'Jewish office' (*Judenstelle*). The second authority mentioned is possibly the Race Office of the NSDAP Kreisleitung.

7 After Felix Gebhardt (b. 1894) had become a case worker at the 'Jewish office' in Jan. 1941, he intensified the surveillance of the Leipzig Jews. Gebhardt constantly undertook inspections in the 'Jew houses'; if he found sizeable sums of cash or prohibited foodstuffs, he reported this to the Gestapo. In many instances the person concerned was sent to a concentration camp as a result.

In contrast to Berlin etc., I know of towns in the provinces where not a single anti-Jewish sign is posted. I remember one case, in April 1941, when a sign was put up on a Palm cigar shop in one of these towns: 'No sales to Jews'. After a few hours, however, it was gone again.

There were Gestapo main branches that deployed certain Jews in May 1939 as 'supervisors of the Jews' and furnished them with specific powers. Then, from this time on, most dealings with the Jews were handled only through the supervisors. The individual orders were delivered to the supervisor, and he had to pass them on. Indeed, he was made personally responsible for the implementation of each directive. (Incidentally, it was quite an unpleasant job, for the good people very often resisted the co-religionist in charge of them. They did not realize or perhaps were unwilling to accept how much more pleasant it was for them to deal with this man than with the Gestapo directly.)

All orders initially concerned all Jews by race, thus including those who were baptized or living in a mixed marriage. For the latter, there was a slight easing of a few restrictions later. In October 1939, radio sets were first confiscated across the board, without compensation, wherever there were Jewish members of the household. Later, upon application, mixed marriages in some cases were given permission again to buy a new radio (the first radio set continued to be impounded without any compensation), only there was a requirement that it must be possible for the Jewish household member to be excluded from listening to the broadcasts.[8]

In the summer of 1940 came the order that the additional given name (Israel, Sara) had to be included in the telephone directories. Shortly afterwards the telephones of the Jews were taken away altogether. The orders regarding air-raid shelters and limited times for going out are surely well known to you.[9]

In 1941 the Jewish partner in a mixed marriage also received the clothing ration card again. Likewise, his food ration cards, which he, like all Jews outside the big cities, had to collect at the food offices, were delivered again to him via the block administrators of the NSV. The Jewish partner was also exempted, for the time being, from the requirement that the letter 'J' must be printed on his food ration cards. In the provinces the food ration cards have a 'J' only in the centre – on the counterfoil – while in a number of large cities each individual small coupon has a 'J' printed on it. All other directives – apart from those listed above – continue to apply to all Jews by race.

Outside the big cities, Jews are required to buy in certain shops and at certain times. This applies to groceries in particular. The rule varies widely from place to place. In some cases, shopping is allowed for two hours in the afternoon, every day, while it is permitted elsewhere only twice a week in the early morning (this is definitely the best time, as the goods are always available in the morning). There are some towns where Jews receive the fish ration card. In other towns, they do not. In some cases, coupons

8 Decree of the Gestapo head office in Karlsruhe to the Landräte and chiefs of police in Baden, no. II B 4 – 22 032/39, dated 21 Sept. 1939, re confiscation of radio sets of Jews, published in Sauer, *Dokumente über die Verfolgung der jüdischen Bürger in Baden-Württemberg*, no. 400, pp. 179–180.

9 On the exclusion of Jews from the telephone service, see Doc. 96. In Sept. 1939 the Jewish communities were instructed to build their own air-raid shelters. In addition, Jews were forbidden to leave their homes after 8 p.m.: decree of the Gestapo head office in Karlsruhe to the Landräte and chiefs of police in Baden, no. II B 4 – 153 03/39, dated 10 Sept. 1939, re measures against the Jews, published ibid., no. 397, p. 176.

have been voided; that is, the articles available on this coupon are not to be given to Jews (chocolate, pulses, and other special allocations). Jewish veterans of the World War who can prove they were injured can obtain all the special allocations upon application, the approval of which, strangely enough, is in the hands of the Gestapo.

Men who are married to Jewish women have been discharged from military service. The same is true for Mischlinge of the first degree. Jews have had to withdraw from all insurance schemes and private health insurance plans.[10] Pensions – including state and municipal pensions – continue to be paid, in general. Here I can cite a case that is particularly interesting.

A Jew who had worked in an industrial plant for more than 30 years had to be dismissed several years ago at the age of 58. The firm, which had already been nationalized for some time, pays good pensions to its old employees. Right from when he was dismissed, our friend also received the statutory pension due to him. In February 1940 the man in question was sent to a concentration camp because of political statements he had made. His children, long since of legal age, nonetheless continued to receive the pension payments. Not only that: it turned out during an audit in early 1941 that the pension had been slightly miscalculated and was too low, and the back payments of the difference for the entire period of time were paid out to the daughter.

A full Jew is still working at the same plant today as a leading researcher. (To the best of my information, this man cannot be dismissed, on the basis of a Supreme Army Command order.)

However, with regard to another important plant, I know that the chief chemist, who was not to [be allowed to] emigrate because of his knowledge, was taken away to a concentration camp one day in November 1940. In the presence of his family members, it was explained to him that he would enjoy complete freedom in the camp and that he was to work in a chemical lab there. But a few weeks later, he 'suddenly' died.

A Jewish man who was employed in an Aryan business was collecting invoices for his firm one day. On this occasion, he allegedly said 'Heil Hitler!' at one point – though he vehemently denied this – and a young lady reported him to the Gestapo for this alleged salutation. She declared that she felt offended and insulted if a Jew merely uttered the name of our Führer. But the complaint was initially dropped by the Gestapo, with the explanation that it would be unworthy to punish a combat veteran who had been wounded multiple times and who had always displayed his nationalist convictions, even if, as in this case, he was a Jew. The 18-year-old girl, however, was not content with this and, through the Kreisleitung and even the Gauleitung, approached the superior authority of this Gestapo office. The result was that this Jew was, after all, picked up one day in the street and taken away there and then, without his wife and children being notified. He was sentenced to ten days in jail. When asked whether he was in agreement with the sentence – which was pronounced without any trial, of course – he told the Gestapo official, 'if you impose this, I surely have to be in agreement with it; only one question: which law am I being convicted under?' He received the prompt reply: 'You damned Jew-boy, you still dare to ask about laws, I ought to put you in Buchenwald now for keeps.' In contrast to other prisoners, he always had to report as Prisoner Jew X.

10 See Doc. 78, fn. 5.

In dealings with so-called official agencies – particularly with the tax offices – anyone who fails to use the additional given name Israel or Sara is sentenced to two weeks in prison, on average. Through relatives, I was told about a prisoner in the penitentiary in Untermaßfeld. This man – sentenced for race defilement – is addressed by the guards and fellow prisoners not by number or name, but as 'Jew'.

Upon request, Jews were also supplied with gas masks. Upon emigration, however, these items had to be returned.

In my last job I worked with French prisoners of war for almost a year. That went very well and without any friction. One day they were replaced with Serbian prisoners. When the Serbs learned one day that I was a Jew, one of them, who spoke German, declared that he wouldn't let Jews tell him what to do, and he made no end of trouble. For me and my operations manager, it was of course a very sticky situation. It was shortly before my emigration, and for this reason I left the job somewhat sooner than planned. Serious differences, which possibly could only have harmed me, were avoided as a result.

Incidentally, in this job, my last one, I worked as a lorry driver, and the district and regional farmers' associations wanted to enlist me. I emphasize this only to document the enormous shortage of workers. I was the only Jew in central Germany who had regained his driver's licence, after receiving express permission from the Ministry of the Interior – admittedly, only for the duration of the war.[11]

I must state that all the authorities behaved very correctly and politely when issuing certifications and other documents for emigration. Everything was taken care of as requested and also promptly and speedily, every time. The relevant foreign exchange office behaved most magnanimously when approving the luggage list.

Repeatedly, it has become apparent that the broad masses want nothing to do with rowdy and violent antisemitism and indeed are not even in agreement with it. But no one dares to say anything against it, let alone rebel. The fear is too great. The fear has become so great that many people try and avoid going to stand with a Jew in the street, while in the evening they are glad to visit him in his home.

11 The confidential letter from the Reich Ministry of Transport, dated 22 Feb. 1939, stated that driving licences and vehicle registrations issued to Jews were to be seized, except in the case of foreign Jews and in cases where seizure might be detrimental to the economy: Sauer, *Dokumente über die Verfolgung der jüdischen Bürger in Baden-Württemberg*, no. 324b, pp. 68–69.

DOC. 190
On 6 July 1941 Edith Hahn-Beer tells her boyfriend in Vienna about her labour deployment in Osterburg[1]

Handwritten letter from Edith Hahn-Beer[2] to Josef Rosenfeld,[3] dated 7 July 1941

My darling,

This is the first Sunday on which we are not cutting asparagus.[4] We didn't even know that until yesterday evening. Then he[5] finally called out: 'Sleep till noon tomorrow.' You can't imagine our joy. The way we feel is indescribable. My hands absolutely can't get used to the strain. They hurt so much that I can't close my hand and make a fist in the morning. I can't even feel my lower back any more. In the past few days we have worked very hard and very long hours. On Friday, people were already calling from the main road: 'It's time to go home!' However, our joy over the free Sunday is already muted, because four of us have to go and work for a few hours in the afternoon. Today hay is being transported, because the weather is good and so we are needed. The mowing is done with a machine, and then we have to gather the hay together with a wooden rake. I will certainly be one of the four, because I behaved very badly on Friday and now want to go in order to make up for that. On Friday afternoon he said that no one could go until everyone's work was done. I was through with my row at around quarter past seven. Then I helped Luci and was finished with the second row at quarter to eight. Then I couldn't bring myself to work any longer and went home. I knew that I should be working out of solidarity, but I was so worn out. Besides, I was very hungry, because I had brought nothing but a couple of crispbreads for my afternoon snack. So I went home. Four others had already gone home before me. He sent Frieda out of the field and ordered her to help his wife. The others kept on working. Frieda begged and cried, asking him to finally let us go. I begged him and then even his wife asked him. It was already 8:30. As he refused to relent, his wife went out to the field, took the hoe out of Lea's hands and did the work in her place. Then, at last, a few minutes later, he let us call it a day. The work was still not finished. It would have taken until 11 o'clock. I reproached myself for having gone home, but I was so terribly tired. The work was very hard. We had to cut the weeds out of the asparagus beds. Now the beds look quite different from the way they are in the photo. The spaces between the rows are all overgrown with weeds,

1 USHMM, RG-10.156, Acc. 1998.A.0079. Published in *'Ich will leben!' Briefe und Dokumente der Wiener Jüdin Edith Hahn-Beer*, ed. Angelika Schlüter (Münster: Ugarit, 1996), pp. 83–85. This document has been translated from German.

2 Edith Hahn-Beer (1914–2009), lawyer; studied in Vienna, forced labourer in Osterburg and Aschersleben, 1941–1942, then, under a false name, Red Cross helper in Brandenburg (Havel); judge and public prosecutor at the local court in Brandenburg after 1945; emigrated in 1948 to Britain, where she worked as housemaid, cook, and seamstress; emigrated to Israel in 1986; co-author (with Susan Dworkin) of *The Nazi Officer's Wife: How One Jewish Woman Survived the Holocaust* (New York: Harper Collins, 2012).

3 Dr Josef Rosenfeld (1913–1978), lawyer and Regierungsrat; was baptized in the Catholic Church and lived, without his Jewish origin becoming known, with his mother in Vienna; worked in the Vienna municipal administration after 1945.

4 From May 1941 Edith Hahn-Beer had to work as a farm hand in Osterburg (Altmark).

5 This refers to the overseer.

and on top of the mounded beds there is a whole meadow. And chopping all that out, including the roots, is not easy.

That's what it's like here now. We know we have to stay. We sent a telegram to the employment office in Vienna asking to be replaced, because we were promised, after all, that we could go home. This was the reply we got: 'No replacements will be sent. No promise was made.' That has completely knocked us for six. How are we supposed to endure it until the autumn? We really have nothing to eat except potatoes. Where are we supposed to find the strength? So I'm asking you, sweetheart, send me more pastries, because I don't eat them as treats but rather so that I can have enough to eat. Right now I have nothing at all to eat. Everything has already been devoured. Don't be angry with me, darling, for begging this way, but what am I to do. The first month you and Mama spoiled me, and now all that has gone. But my hunger has only increased, not decreased. Besides, I have already lost around 2 kg, and I would so much like to come home again. Sometimes, when I'm in the midst of the endless asparagus beds and doing some endless task, I have the feeling that I will never get away from here again. It seems like a fairy tale to me that I once sat in the library, studied, was a real person and had hopes. Now I am just a beast to be used and worn out. Can it ever be different? The hope that Uncle Roszi[6] will send the affidavit to me in time is another thing that I have given up on.

Will you be able to come here at some point? I've already written to you about it, but you didn't answer me.

Please, dear boy, send me another copy of every photo. Please!!! What do you think of Franz? In the picture with Franz is Mrs Teltscher. The girl by herself is Eva. The girl cutting asparagus is Luci. Please send me some film, too. Please.

I wanted to cut off a piece of bread for myself just now, but I can't manage it. My hands hurt too much. How will I be able to hold the rake again for four hours this afternoon?

I have not had a single line from Mama[7] all week long. Please go and see Mama and ask her why she doesn't write to me. Is she possibly angry because I tried to get parcels out of her too? Elsa[8] would surely part with bread coupons for my sake. It is very unpleasant for me to have to ask over and over again, but if I don't, I go hungry.

Lots and lots of kisses, your Bunny.

Would so love to see you. I just can't comprehend that I am not to see you all summer. I'm asking again for bread coupons.

No one has letter paper here, and therefore I can't write more to you.

6 Richard Hahn (b. 1881), Edith Hahn-Beer's uncle, and his wife, Roszi (combined into one person in the letter, perhaps in haste); lived in the USA and had already offered an affidavit to Edith Hahn-Beer previously. She had refused, however, as she wanted to stay in Vienna with Josef Rosenfeld.

7 Klothilde Hahn (1890–1942), seamstress; deported from Vienna to Minsk in June 1942 and murdered in Maly Trostenets.

8 Elsa Denner (b. 1924), artisan and restorer in Vienna. She was the sister of Edith Hahn-Beer's friend Christine (Christel) Beran, née Denner (1922–1992), a beautician; Christel Beran later gave her papers, which she had reported lost, to Edith Hahn-Beer, thus enabling her to live as a 'U-boat' (German for 'submarine'; term for someone living in Nazi Germany under a false, non-Jewish identity).

DOC. 191

On 12 July 1941 Felice Schragenheim asks the US consulate general in Berlin about opportunities for extending her visa[1]

Letter from Felice Schragenheim,[2] 102 Kurfürstendamm, Berlin-Halensee, unsigned, to the American consulate general, 21 Hermann-Göring-Straße, Berlin NW 7, dated 12 July 1941

Re: Quota Immigration Visa no. 23 989
I hereby inform you that my entry visa for the USA will expire on 18 July without my having been able to make use of it to date.

It was issued to me on the basis of a booking for the ship *Marques de Corillas*[3] that I had made through the American Express Company.[4] Because this ship did not sail on time, I changed the booking and since then have booked four other passages with the American Express Company that could not be put into effect, in some cases owing to the temporary Portugal suspension,[5] in other cases because the ship sailings were cancelled.

Most recently I had booked passage on the *Navemar*,[6] but its sailing was postponed as well and the departure date is still uncertain, so that I can no longer use the ticket.

I would be very grateful to you if you would tell me what the prospects are for a possible extension of the visa.

Respectfully[7]

1 Jüdisches Museum Berlin, Sammlung Wust-Schragenheim, Schenkung von Elisabeth Wust (2006/37/69). Published in facsimile in Erica Fischer, *Das kurze Leben der Jüdin Felice Schragenheim: 'Jaguar', Berlin 1922 – Bergen-Belsen 1945* (Munich: dtv, 2002), p. 89. This document has been translated from German.

2 Felice Schragenheim (1922–1945), had to leave school in Nov. 1938 before taking her school-leaving examination; afterwards made various efforts to emigrate; forced labourer for C. Sommerfeld & Co., a Berlin bottle-cap factory, Oct. 1941 to 1942; went into hiding in Berlin in Oct. 1942; arrested on 21 August 1944 and deported to Theresienstadt on 5 Sept. 1944 and from there to Auschwitz on 9 Oct. 1944; perished in Bergen-Belsen in March 1945. Her life was the subject of the film *Aimee & Jaguar* (1999), which is based on Erica Fischer's book of the same name.

3 Probably: *Marques de Comillas*; the ship sailed from Spanish ports to New York.

4 The freight-forwarding agency American Express Company, founded in the USA in 1850, had branches in Germany from 1907 and established itself as a transatlantic provider of financial and travel services.

5 On 24 April 1941 the Portuguese authorities had announced that no more transit visas would be issued.

6 The departure of SS *Navemar* from Cádiz (Spain) had been prohibited by the local authorities owing to faulty equipment. The ship did not put to sea until early August 1941, from Seville. Although the freighter offered accommodation for only 15 passengers, there were around 1,200 refugees on board. Several people died during the crossing.

7 In its reply, dated 15 July 1941, the embassy declined to extend the visa, pointing out that the processing of visa-related matters was discontinued until further notice: Jüdisches Museum Berlin, Sammlung Wust-Schragenheim, Schenkung von Elisabeth Wust, 2006/37/70.

DOC. 192

On 19 July 1941 Frida Neuber from Berlin writes to Bob Kunzig in Philadelphia to explain which forms he must fill out for her affidavit and how to do so[1]

Handwritten letter from Frida Neuber,[2] Berlin, to Bob Kunzig,[3] Philadelphia, dated 19 July 1941

My dear, kind Bob, now my suspense has been relieved at last: I received your lovely, most heartfelt letter of 27 June three days ago &[4] am extremely happy that nothing serious kept you from writing & you also are not angry with me for some reason. I had sent out another SOS call to you on 7 July, which you probably will have received in the meantime. Yes, things look quite different now & all my hopes appear to have burst like a soap bubble! From here, *nothing* can be done at the moment. I went to the Relief Association [of Jews in Germany] & to Hapag, and there I learned the following. Everything is being handled from Washington now & can be set in motion only by the persons providing the affidavits. You would have to write to the Visa Department of the State Department in W[ashington] and request that forms B & C be given to you from there. Form B must be filled out as follows:

Name: Friederike Johanna Neuber née Maison
Born on 6 November 1869 in Breslau
Religion: Protestant
Address: Berlin SO 16, at 66 II Engeldamm
Nationality: German state subject
Civil status: Widowed in 1912.
Family circumstances: Parents, 2 children and husband deceased, 3 surviving siblings living in Berlin, Clara Kramer née Maison,[5] widow, Berlin SO 16, 66 Engeldamm
Hermann Maison, widower,[6] Berlin SO 16, 66 Engeldamm
Robert Maison,[7] married, Berlin SO 16, 48 II Köpenickerstr.
Education: Until 1887 I attended the Viktoria School, a secondary school for girls
I have not had a job since 1930. I kept house for my brother.
Political connections: None
Punishments for political or other offences: *None*
Everything that refers to politics can be answered with *no.*
Previous stay in the States: I was in Philadelphia from December 1925 to July 1928 and lived in the home of Mrs Marie A. Lowe, 4622 Adams Ave.

1 Jüdisches Museum Berlin, Sammlung Frida Neuber, 2007/84/23. This document has been translated from German.
2 Friederike Johanna Neuber, née Maison (1869–1942); deported to Theresienstadt on 6 July 1942 and perished there on 20 Dec. 1942.
3 Robert Lowe Kunzig (1918–1982), lawyer; met Friederike Neuber during her three-year stay in Philadelphia. He supplied her with an affidavit and arranged her passage on a ship to the USA.
4 Use of ampersands as in the original.
5 Clara Kramer, née Maison (1867–1943), singing teacher; deported to Theresienstadt on 7 August 1942 and perished there on 7 April 1943.
6 Hermann Maison (1873–1942), manufacturer; deported to Theresienstadt along with his sister Friederike Neuber on 6 July 1942 and perished there on 25 August 1942.
7 Robert Maison (1874–1958), retailer; survived the war in Berlin.

Purpose of present entry: Permanent relocation to the USA.

All that & perhaps something more must be *entered by you* on Form *B*.

Form C requires the submission of affidavits by two sponsors, in the event that the immigrant must be supported, as is true in my case. I am writing all this down today, so that you have no need first to make further time-consuming enquiries. So, that is what I have learned from the Relief Association.

At Hapag I was told the following: At the moment one can immigrate to the USA only via Cuba, which naturally means a *substantial* increase in the travel costs & for this reason would probably be completely out of the question. You would have to get in contact *over there* with the *JDC* or *HIAS*,[8] both of which are Jewish institutions for emigrants, and they would possibly arrange whatever is necessary. The provisions regarding the route & immigration opportunities change quickly in times like these, of course. What I am describing for you is the way it is right now.

How can it be that Hapag informed me that you had paid in $420, when you actually paid $460? Did the $40 fall into the water when the payment was being transferred over here? Poor, dear boy, I hope you have not already had to forfeit this sum, but have instead recovered the entire 460.

So you are in Rangerhodge at the moment & are working there again. I know from Gr.'s descriptions that all of Maine is said to have marvellous scenery, with ocean & mountains combined to form the most spectacular views. I can easily believe that there in particular you will be reminded of our dear deceased especially often, but that is a good thing, it means you will always be in spiritual contact with her & she was reluctant to leave you as well. She wanted to follow your life, even without being visible to you, & to always stay by your side. That's what she told me on one occasion. On 12 July I was with you in spirit. Gr. has avoided much mental anguish. The difficult situation at present would have greatly depressed her again, you know. I am eager to hear where your parents & Mildred have gone & whether O. C. is [...].[9]

We live in real seclusion. Occasionally we go on little excursions to the nearby area, for example, to Treptow or Potsdam, places that you also know, but we face all kinds of obstacles & therefore I prefer to stay at home. Running the household is also difficult now, so I am tired after I have finished my day's work & like to have peace and quiet. I am now reading a German translation of A. T. Hobart's *Oil for the Lamps of China*, a book that interests me very much.[10] That is the finest thing for me, a good book & my peace and quiet!

I wonder whether this letter will still reach you. One does not know what the immediate future might bring, but I am not yet giving up the hope that everything will turn out well & I can be with you all soon. You will probably get this letter on 8 August. Yours took 19 days to reach me.

Goodbye, dear Bob, I thank you with all my heart for your kind words & ask that you get in touch briefly now and then, so that I know you are in good health and still

8 The Hebrew Immigrant Aid Society (HIAS) was founded in New York in 1898. In 1927 HICEM was founded to coordinate the work of the HIAS in New York, the Jewish Colonization Association (JCA) in Paris, and Emigdirect in Berlin, in order to make arrangements for Jewish emigration.

9 One word is illegible.

10 Alice Tisdale Hobart, *Oil for the Lamps of China* (Indianapolis: Bobbs-Merrill, 1933).

free. I worry a great deal about you when I don't hear anything. My regards, please, to *all* the family, your parents, Mildred, Aunt Else, Miss W., and last but not least Miss Schmidt, and for you a kiss along with the greetings

from your old aunt,[11] who loves you dearly

DOC. 193

Das Reich, 20 July 1941: inflammatory article by Joseph Goebbels, in which he warns the Jews that their judgement is nigh[1]

Mimicry

by Reich Minister Dr Goebbels

The Jews are known for having the knack of adapting themselves to their current surroundings or situation without losing their essential traits in the process. They engage in mimicry. They have a natural instinct for the dangers that threaten them, and their instinct for self-preservation also gives them, more often than not, the appropriate means and defence mechanisms with which to elude these dangers, if at all possible without any display of courage or risk to their life. It is very difficult to detect and expose their cunning, circuitous ways and secret paths. One must be a truly canny expert on the Jews if one wants to unmasl them. Their system, once one has seen through it, is extremely simple and primitive. It is characterized by a perfidious shamelessness, which is so successful because one does not usually consider it possible to be shameless to such a degree. Schopenhauer once said that the Jew is the master of the lie.[2] He has the repertoire of ways to twist the truth down to a fine art, and in the process he appears so confident that he has the audacity to tell even a harmless opponent the exact opposite of the facts, even when it is the most obvious thing in the world. He does this with such barefaced cheek that the listener suddenly begins to feel uncertain, and by then the Jew has usually already won.

In the language of the Jews, this is called chutzbah.[3] Chutzbah is a typically Jewish expression that cannot be translated into any other language, because what is meant by chutzbah is something that exist only among Jews. Other languages have not found it necessary to coin an equivalent expression, because other peoples are not familiar with what it signifies. It means, more or less, unlimited, impertinent, unbelievable insolence and shamelessness.

As long as we have the dubious pleasure of having to engage in polemics with the Jews, we will have an abundance of examples of the typically Jewish character trait that the Jews themselves call chutzbah. The coward becomes a hero and the honest, industrious, courageous man a despicable idiot or philistine. Gross, fat, sweaty stockbrokers play

11 Frida Neuber was not really Robert Kunzig's aunt. This was a ploy for immigration purposes.

1 'Mimikry', *Das Reich*, no. 29, 20 July 1941, pp. 1–2. Published in Joseph Goebbels, *Die Zeit ohne Beispiel: Reden und Aufsätze aus den Jahren 1939/40/41* (Munich: Zentralverlag der NSDAP/Franz Eher Nachf., 1941), pp. 526–528. This document has been translated from German.

2 Schopenhauer writes in a footnote: 'Jews [...] [are] great masters in lying': Arthur Schopenhauer, *Parerga und Paralipomena: Kleine philosophische Schriften*, vol. 2 (Berlin: A. W. Hayn, 1851), § 174.

3 Correctly: chutzpah, from *chuzpa*; Yiddish for 'audacity', 'impudence'.

the communist benefactors of mankind, and honourable soldiers are equated with wild beasts. Honest family life is ridiculed as a breeding institution, while companionate marriage is elevated to the highest ideal of human development. Revolting concoctions, representing all the filth that can spring from a human brain, are passed off as consummate art, while real works of art are derided as kitsch and satirized. Not the murderer, but rather his victim, is the guilty one now.

It is a system of public deception which, if applied long enough, superimposes a kind of intellectual and spiritual paralysis on an entire people and in the long run stifles all natural defence. Before National Socialism appeared, Germany was in the midst of this mortal danger. Had we not overcome it, had our people not come to its senses at the eleventh hour, our country would have been ripe for Bolshevism, the most diabolical infection that Jewry can bring upon a people.

Bolshevism too is an expression of Jewish chutzbah. Unruly Jewish party doctrinaires and wily Jewish capitalists came up with the most audacious coup imaginable. They took control of the so-called proletariat and, within its ranks, mobilized the class struggle by ruthlessly exaggerating real or purported social crises and evils. Then, with the help of the proletariat, they sought to achieve total Jewish dominance over a people. The crassest plutocracy makes use of socialism to establish the crassest dictatorship of money. With the help of the world revolution, this experiment, already a reality in the Soviet Union, was meant to be carried over to the other peoples, too. The result would then have been Jewish world domination.

The National Socialist revolution was a deathblow to this endeavour. Once the leading circles of international Jewry were made to realize that there could be no more talk of pursuing the Bolshevization of the individual European countries by agricultural means, they decided to wait for the great opportunity of an approaching war. Then, however, they wanted to choose their position so as to have the war last as long as possible. At its end, they would pounce on an exhausted, exsanguinated, and impotent Europe, and Bolshevize it through violence and terror. This is the goal which the tactics of Moscow's Bolshevists have been aiming for ever since the onset of this war. They intended to join in only once an easy and risk-free victory was ensured. Until then, however, they would tie down so many German forces that the Reich was incapable of striking a decisive blow in the West and ending the war quickly. One can imagine what a howl of rage was heard in the Kremlin when it was realized, one Sunday morning,[4] that the Führer had decided to rend this fine-spun web of lies and intrigues with one blow of the German sword.

Until then, the Jewish leaders of Bolshevism had cleverly been kept in the background, probably in the mistaken assumption that we could be fooled in that way. Litvinov and Kaganovich were scarcely seen in public any more. Behind the scenes, however, they were all the more active in their sinister work. There was an attempt to convey to us the impression that the Jewish Bolsheviks in Moscow and the Jewish plutocrats in London and Washington despised each other. In secret, however, they tightened all the more firmly the grasp with which they planned to crush us. That is proved by the very fact that, at the moment this infernal intrigue is unmasked, they are reconciled, in each

4 The day that the Wehrmacht invaded the Soviet Union, 22 June 1941, fell on a Sunday.

other's arms. The unwitting peoples on both sides, who surely are rubbing their eyes in disbelief at such an unaccustomed sight, are soothed by mutual tactful consideration.

In Moscow, for example, the Jews declare that the League of Atheists is a wrongful organization and disband it, even though honorary membership in it had been one of the first and noblest duties of all members of the Soviet elite only the previous day.[5] Religious freedom is supposedly to be ensured from now on in every part of the Soviet Union. Untruthful reports are sent out to the world's public, saying that there are prayers in the churches of Moscow again, along with other published deceptions. In London, by contrast, they cannot yet decide to play the Internationale on the radio every night, because, according to the subtle distinction drawn by Mr Eden,[6] the Bolsheviks are not allies but merely associates of England. The Internationale would have been a bit much even for the British people at this time. However, there is much eager praising of Stalin as the superior statesman and great social policy maker who can be compared only with Churchill. And in other ways one seeks ingenious connecting factors between the glorious styles of democracy practised in Moscow and London.

And at the same time – this is the remarkable thing – those blowing the trumpets on both sides are not so very wrong. They differ in the extreme only for someone who is unfamiliar with them. For the expert, however, they are as alike as two peas in a pod. Above all, it is the same Jews who set the tone and are the main speakers on both sides, whether openly or in secret. When they pray in Moscow and hasten to sing the Internationale in London, they are doing what they have always done. They are engaging in mimicry. They adjust to the current reality and situation, slowly, of course, and step by step, lest the peoples become suspicious and prick up their ears. And they are so angry with us primarily because we unmask them. They sense that we observe and recognize them. The Jew, you see, is secure only when no one sees through him. If he notices that someone has seen through his game, he loses his footing. The canny expert on Jews discerns that immediately from his railing and scolding and from his well-known Old Testament outbursts of hatred. We have endured such things so often by now that they have completely lost the appeal of originality for us. In our eyes, they are only of psychological interest now. We wait calmly and coolly for the moment when Jewish rage reaches its apex. Then Schmock[7] begins to flounder. He starts talking a lot of nonsense, and suddenly he betrays himself.

What is broadcast by Radio Moscow and Radio London today or is printed in the Bolshevist and plutocratic media simply beggars all belief. To maintain the proper tone and to adapt to the landscape, London always yields very tactfully to the Kremlin. The Moscow Jews *invent* the stories of lies and atrocities, and the London Jews *quote* and *circulate* them, quite innocently, of course, with a prim and proper demeanour, as if they

5 The League of Militant Atheists, closely associated with the Communist Party of the Soviet Union (CPSU), developed in 1929 from the Society of the Godless (Obshchestvo bezbozhnikov), founded in 1925. In early 1941 it had 3.5 million members from 100 countries. In the same year it ceased operations. It was officially abolished in 1947.

6 Anthony Eden, who had resigned his position as British foreign secretary in Feb. 1938 in protest at Britain's policy of appeasement towards Germany, returned to the British cabinet under Churchill in Sept. 1939, first as secretary of state for war and from Jan. 1940 as foreign secretary.

7 Schmock: pejorative term for a journalist or writer who is opportunistic and unprincipled, which gained currency through G. Freytag's comedy *Die Journalisten* (1854).

were merely satisfying a burdensome chronicler's duty. Clearly, the dreadful crimes in Lemberg that dismayed the whole world were not committed by the Bolsheviks, but rather were inventions of the Propaganda Ministry. It is quite irrelevant here that they are shown in living and moving images in German newsreels and thus made available to the entire world as pieces of evidence.[8] Needless to say, we suppress and terrorize the arts and sciences, while Bolshevism, by contrast, is a true stronghold of culture, civilization, and humanity. We personally take renewed delight in a characterization by Radio Moscow that is so vicious and base that it almost seems complimentary again. We assume that the Jewish spokesmen there still remember us from the good old days in Berlin. If their memory were not so short, they would also have to recall that all their insults are to no avail, and that, in the end, they will get a good thrashing, as the expression goes. They announce every evening that they want to beat the living daylights out of us, us and all the other Nazi swine. Yes, you want to, but can you, can you, Sir? There is something tragicomic about this matter. Wherever one lets the Jews have the floor, they give themselves airs and act as if they were on top of the world. But a short time later they fold up their tents again to take to their heels, fleeing the advancing German regiments. Qui mange du juif, en meurt![9]

One might almost say that the side on which they appear has already lost as a result. They are the best token of the coming defeat. They contain within themselves, inherently, the seed of ruin. In this war, they wanted to aim the last desperate blow at National Socialist Germany and at an awakening Europe. It will fall on the Jews themselves. Today we are already hearing, in spirit, the cry of the desperate and misguided peoples ring out all over the world: 'The Jews are to blame! It is the Jews' fault!'

The judgement that will descend upon them then will be formidable. We need contribute nothing to it. It will come about on its own, because it must come. Just as the fist of an awakening Germany once slammed down upon this racial filth, the fist of an awakening Europe will one day slam down on it as well. Then the Jews' mimicry will no longer be of avail to them either. Then they will have to face the consequences. The day when the peoples pass judgement on their subverters will have come.

The blow shall be struck then, inexorably and without mercy. The global enemy will fall, and Europe will have peace.

8 After the invasion of the Soviet Union the German media had received instructions to report extensively on massacres committed by the Soviet secret police (NKVD): see Doc. 185 and, on photographs from Lwów (Lemberg), Introduction, p. 60. On the pogroms in Lwów, see Doc. 195, fn. 21.

9 French in the original: 'whoever eats of the Jew will perish from it'.

DOC. 194

On 22 July 1941 Josef Löwenherz reports on the activities of the Israelite Religious Community of Vienna[1]

Report by the office director and head of the Israelite Religious Community of Vienna, signed Dr Josef Löwenherz, dated 22 July 1941

29th Weekly Report of the Israelite Religious Community of Vienna to date 22 July 1941.
(A) Activity report. Emigration.
In the period from 13 to 19 July 1941, 96 persons were processed by the Israelite Religious Community of Vienna. The countries of destination listed were:
1. *European countries*, 4: Sweden 3, Switzerland 1
2. *United States of North America*, 69
3. *Central and South American countries*, 23: Argentina 17, Cuba 6

In total, 56,986 persons have been processed to date with the help of the Israelite Religious Community of Vienna.

The following report relates to the activities of the individual offices.

I. Offices that are directly involved with emigration:

1. *Emigration advisory service.*
   Advice was provided to 440 persons, specifically to 415 regarding general emigration matters and to 25 persons regarding the shipment of goods.
2. *Correspondence department.*
   Three confirmations were relayed via the various HIAS[2] offices in the United States concerning affidavits that had been delivered directly to the American consulate general. In the case of other entry permits that have arrived for Central and South American countries, steps were initiated to obtain visas.
3. *Issuing of passport questionnaire forms.*
   In the past week, 19 questionnaire forms for submission of travel documents were handed out.
4. *Fee calculation office.*
   During this reporting period, fees were calculated in 53 cases, and the parties concerned were issued with a fee of RM 65,320.
5. *Document checking office.*
   There were 54 persons with 46 envelopes referred to the Central Office for Jewish Emigration. The number of daily referrals ranged between 5 and 20 persons, or 4 and 16 envelopes, respectively.
6. *Foreign exchange advisory office.*
   During the past week, 3 lists (584, 585, 586) with a total of 28 persons were submitted to the Central Office for Jewish Emigration or the Vienna Foreign Exchange Office, respectively, and allocation of $12,475.60 for ticket costs for journeys by sea was requested. An additional 29 requests for release of money from blocked accounts were submitted to the Vienna Foreign Exchange Office. In total, advice was provided to 235 persons.

1 CAHJP, A/W 114. This document has been translated from German.
2 Hebrew Immigrant Aid Society.

7. *Processing of emigrants.*
   With regard to the acquisition of American, Argentine, or Cuban entry permits, advice was provided to 971 persons. For emigrants to whose relatives overseas requests had been sent by telegraph, boat tickets and travel subsidies in the amount of $8,365 were received. The grand total of the travel subsidies and boat tickets received in this way amounts to $1,414,505.

II. Offices indirectly involved with emigration:

1. *Welfare department.*
   In the period from 13 to 19 July 1941, 2,296 persons received aid in the form of cash, and the amount of 19,783.37 Reichsmarks was paid out for this purpose, that is, 8.61 Reichsmarks per capita per month.
2. *Housing section.*
   In the period from 1 June to 15 July 1941, the Central Office for Jewish Emigration gave instructions for the vacating of 672 apartments containing 3,371 persons. By the deadline stated, 418 apartments could already be reported empty, while 254 apartments were being dealt with. A further number of apartments became available during the same time period owing to legal terminations [of the lease].

(B) Situation report.

In the course of the past week, it was possible to process a group of emigrants consisting of 113 persons, as part of the 20th transport along the Atlantic coast to Spain authorized by the Central Office for Jewish Emigration.

As previously reported, the financial requirements for these transports can be fulfilled primarily as a result of the cooperation of the American [Jewish] Joint Distribution Committee. Its European director, Mr *Troper*, left no stone unturned in Lisbon to enable the departure of the persons in question. As appeared from a telegram received on 17 July, in view of the closure of the American consulates in the Reich, the Jewish relief organizations are weighing the possibility of enabling the persons in question to obtain a visa for the USA in Marseilles, in accordance with the new rules.[3] With respect to children up to the age of 16, a way has apparently already been found to stave off the difficulties caused by the new rules. The Israelite Religious Community of Vienna is in constant contact with the American [Jewish] Joint Distribution Committee in New York and also with Mr *Troper* in Lisbon. Upon his request that he be made aware of the most significant problems for emigration from Vienna, the Israelite Religious Community of Vienna has requested by telegram that the negotiations include not only entry to the United States of America, but also the expansion of opportunities to emigrate to Central and South American countries, as well as the admission of larger groups to the settlements in San Domingo and Mindanao.

The Main Food Office in Vienna informed the Israelite Religious Community of Vienna on 10 July of this year that, in accordance with instructions that have been received, there is a plan to set up shops in the 1st, 2nd, 9th, and 20th districts, where foodstuffs are to be sold and issued exclusively to Jews. This introduction, it was said, would first be tested in the 1st and 9th districts by creating five sales outlets in each.

3 The US consulates in the Reich were closed in July 1941. At that time, there were still around 1,000–1,200 Jews in the Reich who were in possession of a US visa.

The Israelite Religious Community of Vienna was initially requested to assist as follows:

1. to name around one hundred persons to be employed in these businesses;
2. to assume collective liability in order to indemnify the sales outlet against all loss;
3. to assume full responsibility under commercial law, particularly with regard to the outgoing merchandise or food ration coupons.

As it was impossible for the Israelite Religious Community to accept material or even solely moral responsibility, the only task accomplished was the naming of persons who seemed suited, on the basis of their occupation at that time, to take over the running of such a sales outlet, and who were able to pay a certain sum as security. Further, the Israelite Religious Community of Vienna provided the names of more than one hundred persons to be employed in the individual sales outlets. On 20 July an official bulletin was sent by the Main Food Office in Vienna, Dept. B, to small distributors, announcing the following for the area of the Vienna Reichsgau:

'Beginning on 28 July 1941, a new arrangement for food supply in Jewish consumer groups in Vienna will take effect. Further details in this regard will be announced to small distributors through their district occupational group heads.'[4] According to what was previously reported, it is to be assumed that the new arrangement announced refers to the creation of special sales outlets for Jews.

In this connection, the Israelite Religious Community of Vienna ventures to point out that the previous method of supplying Jewish households, which was based on shopping hours, was maintained for almost more than two years[5] without any concerns arising as a result. Related to this observation is the request that, under the new arrangement now to be put into place, the Jewish consumers be allowed to receive the same food quantities due them as before, in accordance with the legal provisions.

The process of vacating apartments whose residents are to be resettled to parts of the 2nd, 9th, 20th, and 1st districts by order of the Central Office for Jewish Emigration has brought to light the following difficulties: only a very limited circle of persons has the opportunity to move into the apartments inhabited by Jews in the aforementioned districts. This is because allowances must repeatedly be made for disabled war veterans or for other persons where there are compelling reasons why a room must be retained for them. It must also be emphasized that, as a consequence of the age distribution of the Jewish share of the population, almost every apartment contains a bedridden invalid, including people with tuberculosis and infectious diseases. No less consideration must be given to married couples with small children, mixed marriages, and similar circumstances, to say nothing of the repeated refusals by building owners, managers, or caretakers of the buildings under consideration to accept new residents. In setting the deadlines for vacating the apartments, the difficulties associated with providing vehicles for resettlement purposes must also be taken into account.

It is therefore requested that additional parts of the 1st, 9th, and 2nd districts be made available for the purpose of settling new tenants there.

4 Haupternährungsamt Wien, Abt. B: 'Merkblatt an die jüdische Verbraucherschaft, einschließlich XXII. Bezirk, Mödling, Liesing, Atzgersdorf, Inzersdorf, Brunn am Gebirge, Mauer': CAHJP, A/W 2045.

5 As in the original.

DOC. 195

In late July 1941 Willy Cohn learns of mass murders of Jews in the occupied territories in the East[1]

Handwritten diary of Willy Cohn, Breslau, entries for 22 to 26 July 1941

22 July 1941

Breslau, Tuesday. Yesterday morning worked diligently in the cathedral library and gathered a good deal of material, especially for 'Dresden' and Saxony! In the afternoon slept very soundly and with [...].[2] Barber [...],[3] then to see Prof. Goerlitz,[4] who told me the following: he called on Chief Government Building Officer Stein[5] regarding my matter. As Stein was unavailable in the morning, he returned at lunchtime. Goerlitz told Stein more or less the following: he wanted me to be the last one affected by the measures concerning the vacation of apartments. Stein expressed agreement with this view. He then made a telephone call to an official whom he knew at the Pricing Office for Tenancy Agreements with Jews, who told him that they merely functioned as the agent for all these things, and that the decision was in the hands of the Pricing Office. Any Jew who now has a fairly unappealing apartment, he said, is in the best position, for if someone fancies an apartment, it is assigned to him! At any rate, Chief Government Building Officer Stein was unaware, as was the other office, that major eviction measures are now planned. That gave me some reassurance, and, in particular, it is also in the interest of all the Jews in Breslau. I was quite touched by the behaviour of Goerlitz and also of Chief Government Building Officer Stein, who has very rarely spoken to me and evidently has gained a favourable impression of me! Finally, and this is the greatest source of satisfaction for a scholar, objective research always finds a way and, even today, still finds recognition in 'Aryan' circles. Above all, I was delighted at people's willingness to help! Such things provide rays of hope in these times. Goerlitz also told me how decently the new mayor of Breslau, Dr Spielhagen,[6] behaved when he was to be put into a Jewish apartment. He had less gratifying things to tell me about the fate of the Romanian Jews. His

1 CAHJP, P 88/105, fols. 54–69; abridged English translation in Cohn, *No Justice in Germany*, pp. 362–364. This document has been newly translated from the original German.

2 Three words are illegible.

3 This name is illegible.

4 Dr Theodor Goerlitz (1885–1949), lawyer; city councillor and specialist for financial affairs in Thorn from 1916; minister in Oldenbourg, 1918–1921; its mayor, 1921–1932; head of the Institute for the Study of Magdeburg Municipal Law at the University of Breslau, 1941–1945; local court judge in Magdeburg, 1945–1947.

5 Dr Rudolf Stein (1899–1978), architect and curator of buildings and monuments; joined the NSDAP in 1932; municipal government building officer in Breslau.

6 Dr Wolfgang Spielhagen (1891–1945), lawyer; probationary judge, 1917; Regierungsrat in the Reich Ministry of Finance, 1922; Oberregierungsrat in the Office of the Reich Savings Commissioner, 1927; Ministerialrat at the Court of Auditors of the German Reich, 1936; joined the NSDAP in 1937; deputy mayor of Breslau from 1940; court-martialled and shot by order of Gauleiter Karl Hanke on 27 Jan. 1945.

nephew, a lieutenant in the air force, wrote that what was being done there was nothing less than butchery.[7] Spine-chilling!

Newspaper: increasing numbers of victories in the East, while in the West everything is apparently being destroyed. In Münster in Westphalia, allegedly only one church is still standing![8] In Schweidnitz, an Ursuline convent housing eighty nuns had to be vacated. In the evening, went to bed early, quite exhausted; had a very bad night.

23 July 1941
Breslau, Wednesday. Yesterday morning I went out with Trudi[9] at one point to get some fresh air. As long as it is still summer, one has to have a holiday feeling at least now and then. We walked along the railway embankment as far as the South Park and sat there for quite some time. There is a constant series of transport trains going along the bypass railway. Walked through the South Park, where we have not been for quite a long time. Many things have changed. For example, the lovely pavilion on the lake is no longer there! Down Kleinburgstr. and Wölflstr., where every spot is full of memories for me. On Kleinburgstr., Paschke's restaurant is gone, too. Dresdner Bank, then went to the school administration, too, regarding a teaching permit. Because the official servant concerned is on holiday, I can't go back there until next week! On the way home, I was accompanied by the physician Dr Juttmann, a man who has become somewhat strange. In the afternoon, worked industriously for the GJ.[10] After supper fetched the food ration cards from Miss Silberstein. I personally got none, because I have received parcels from abroad. In reality, I have recently received only 400 grams of cocoa on one occasion. At any rate, I have to go to the district office tomorrow and will lose valuable time as a result! They are trying to make our lives increasingly difficult! On the way home, got ice cream from […],[11] then sat on the balcony for a while!

24 July 1941
Breslau, Thursday. In the morning, worked quite hard on the GJ, then dictated letters to Trudi, went to the post office at midday, and in the afternoon was roused from my nap when Moritz Kalischer's mother brought a letter for me to translate from Spanish. As a result, lost the effect of a tablet and struggled a good deal in the afternoon. Worked diligently nonetheless. Post, also some [work] for the GJ and a bit on my memoirs, then went to visit the barber's. Miss Cohn brought the very sad news that the lawyer Polke[12]

7 On 22 June 1941 Romania, an ally of the German Reich, attacked the Soviet Union. Only a few days after the onset of war, Romanian and German units carried out numerous massacres of Jews. On 29 June 1941 around 13,000 Jews were murdered in the Romanian town of Iaşi (Jassy): see the Introduction to PMJ 7.

8 In July 1941 there were a number of major air raids on Münster.

9 Gertrud Cohn.

10 *Germania Judaica*. From 1939 Cohn was a contributor to the second volume of the *Germania Judaica*, which was, however, never published. He was supposed to write the sections on Silesia, Bohemia, Moravia, the Netherlands, and Brabant. Of his more than sixty contributions, only the article about Breslau has survived: Norbert Conrads, 'Die verlorene Germania Judaica: Ein Handbuch- und Autorenschicksal im Dritten Reich', *Berichte und Forschungen: Jahrbuch des Bundesinstituts für Kultur und Geschichte der Deutschen im östlichen Europa*, vol. 15 (2007), pp. 215–254, here pp. 215–229.

11 A word is illegible.

has been killed by an aerial bomb in Haifa. A terrible end! First fought for the German side in the World War, then carried off to Buchenwald by the Germans, and finally killed by a German aerial bomb in *Eretz Israel*. Bitter.[13]

Newspaper: description of the bombing raids on Moscow! Post: a very kind letter from Erna with good news about Wölfl. Erna has a plan to get him an affidavit for America. He is now doing some Latin and Greek again and is working in the office. Also from Steps (Stefan Brienitzer)[14] in Edinburgh, there was good news!

25 July 1941
Breslau, Friday. Yesterday was a very exhausting, albeit in some respects also very exhausting,[15] day for me. Early in the morning, first to the post office, then to the ration coupon distribution office to fetch my food ration cards. Nothing was subtracted from my coupons in exchange for the Chinese cocoa, but queuing up really exhausted me. I broke out in a sweat and was close to fainting. Unfortunately, my racial comrades displayed little discipline in their behaviour and, as a result, as I heard in the evening from Mr Foerder,[16] the Gestapo had to be called and a constable had to be sent for. Sad. When I left the ration coupon distribution office, I ran into Emil Kaim, who is a board member of the Synagogue Community. I told him it would be a good idea for the Community to send someone there, but he apparently did not heed my advice. Then, to the old Elisabeth Grammar School; spoke to the municipal architect Dubiel there about the Hebrew tombstone. He rang the photographer again, and he has agreed to get the picture ready now. Then I treated myself to some ice cream as refreshment and worked a bit longer in the official library. In the afternoon I was invited to have coffee with Professor Hermann Hoffmann.[17] Professor Hoffmann is a retired Catholic priest and lives in the convent of the Elisabethines on Antonienstraße. What calm and cleanliness there is in such a convent! I still recognize the atmosphere from my time in Trebnitz! It was a lovely afternoon. The main thing was not that there was real coffee with thickly buttered rolls and toasts,[18] but rather that there was such a fine intellectual atmosphere. We talked a great deal about scholarly works. We also exchanged books. I gave him a complete Mahzor,[19] which greatly delighted him. My gift from him was his great work on the history of the Jesuits

12 Max Moses Polke (1895–1941), lawyer and economist; practised law in Breslau from 1924; member of the Social Democratic Party of Germany (SPD); active in the Jewish Community of Breslau; imprisoned in a concentration camp after the November pogroms of 1938; in Dec. 1938 emigrated with his family to Palestine: see also PMJ 1/9 and PMJ 2/120.

13 The Luftwaffe launched bombing raids on the port at Haifa in June 1941.

14 Stefan (Steps) Brienitzer (b. 1928), son of the Breslau lawyer Günther Brienitzer; emigrated to Scotland in 1939.

15 The original repeats the word 'anstrengend' (exhausting) here. Presumably the author meant 'more exhilarating'.

16 David Foerder (1871–1943), retailer; treasurer of the Jewish House of Learning in Breslau; deported on 30 August 1942 to Theresienstadt, where he perished in March 1943.

17 Hermann Hoffmann (1878–1972), church historian and Catholic theologian; teacher of religion and schoolmaster in Breslau, 1907–1927; also taught at an adult education centre from 1919; co-founded the Catholic youth organization Quickborn-Arbeitskreis in 1917; worked as a pastor in Breslau until 1948; honorary doctorate from the University of Würzburg, 1958.

18 Zwieback: a kind of toasted crispbread made from sweetened twice-baked bread.

19 Prayer book for the Jewish holidays.

in Schweidnitz and many other things, including the doctoral thesis of Simonsohn! Professor Hoffmann wants to visit us too sometime. Now he is going to spend a fortnight relaxing at a castle near Troppau. In the evening I picked blackcurrants in order to do something completely different! […][20] rather dizzy. Unfortunately, everything is still an effort for me! Professor Hoffmann also told me the horrible news, barely comprehensible, that 12,000 Jews have been shot in Lemberg. The SS is said to have done it.[21]

26 July 1941

Breslau, Saturday. Yesterday morning worked with Miss Bohn, a bit of post, above all, dictated a large chunk of the memoirs. In the afternoon, did work for the GJ. Miss Witt was also here for some time regarding the Hebrew photocopies; however, she gleaned nothing from them. Trudi wrote diligently about the fleet of Charles I, barber Müller [about the] White Stork Synagogue; the mood there was rather gloomy; on Thursday, fifty-one Jews must be resettled in Thomasdorf near Rothenburg, not far from Görlitz;[22] notice has been given to vacate ten apartments; that is just the beginning of the operation, as the Community chairman, Dr Kohn, was told at the Gestapo office. It is evidently not this authority that wants this; it has come from elsewhere. The rationale is probably always the need for apartments. In his address that I did not hear, Rabb[i] Lewin[23] apparently has made the people quite upset again, so it would not surprise me if suicides were to occur tonight. I consider his behaviour to be very wrong! But I have no influence over him. Now we are only allowed to buy groceries between 11 and 1. Thus, every day brings new restrictions. The course of vengeance against the Jews!

On the [military] situation: the Russians seem to be selecting the southern part of Romania as the objective of their main offensive effort. They apparently intend to push forward to the Romanian oil centre. There is talk of one million losses on the German side!

20 Two words are illegible.

21 In the first few days after the occupation of Lwów on 30 June 1941, around 7,000 Jews were murdered in the city, most by SS-Einsatzgruppen, but others in the course of a pogrom in which local militias took part: see PMJ 7/16 and 18.

22 Correctly: Tormersdorf (Prędocice) on the Neiße river in Lusatia. A makeshift camp was erected here in 1941, which held as many as 700 Jews from Silesia.

23 Reinhold Lewin.

DOC. 196

On 31 July 1941 Göring authorizes Heydrich to prepare an 'overall solution to the Jewish question within the German sphere of influence in Europe'[1]

Letter from the Reich Marshal of the Greater German Reich, Plenipotentiary for the Four-Year Plan, Chairman of the Ministerial Council for the Defence of the Reich, signed Göring, Berlin, to Chief of the Security Police and the SD, SS-Gruppenführer Heydrich, Berlin, dated 31 July 1941[2]

In addition to the task already entrusted to you by the decree of 24 January 1939 – to bring the Jewish question, in the form of emigration or evacuation, to a solution that is as favourable as possible, in view of the prevailing circumstances[3] – I hereby instruct you to make all necessary preparations from an organizational, material, and financial perspective for an overall solution to the Jewish question within the German sphere of influence in Europe.

Insofar as this affects the powers and duties of other central authorities, these are to be involved.

I further instruct you to present to me, in the near future, an overall draft regarding the projected organizational, material, and financial measures required for the implementation of the intended final solution to the Jewish question.[4]

1 PA AA, R 100 857, fol. 189; also Latvijas Valsts Vēstures Arhīvs, Riga, P1026, opis 1, vol. 3, fol. 164. BArch, R 90/146, has a copy of the document, dated 8 July 1941. The version attached to Heydrich's letter of invitation to the Wannsee Conference has no date, but this is given in the accompanying letter, dated 29 Nov. 1941: PA AA, R100 857, fols. 187–188. In addition, Göring's desk calendar for 1941 contains the following entry for 31 July 1941: '6:15 p.m. Heydrich': IfZ-Archives, ED 180/5. Published in facsimile in sources including Jochen von Lang, *Das Eichmann-Protokoll: Tonbandaufzeichnungen der israelischen Verhöre* (Berlin: Severin und Siedler, 1982), and Gedenk- und Bildungsstätte Haus der Wannsee-Konferenz, *Die Wannsee-Konferenz*, p. 78. This document has been translated from German.

2 Eichmann stated after the war: 'the letter to Göring was undoubtedly drafted by me': Sassen-Interview, Transkript: BArch, ALLPROZ 6/103, Bd. 43, p. 393.

3 In his letter to the Reich Minister of the Interior dated 24 Jan. 1939, Göring wrote that the emigration of Jews from the Reich was to be facilitated using all possible means. Responsibility for preparations and coordination was assigned to the Reich Central Agency for Jewish Emigration under Heydrich's leadership: see PMJ 2/243.

4 A written version of this draft has thus far not been found. The only known related document is the protocol of the Wannsee Conference of 20 Jan. 1942, at which the questions referred to here were discussed: published in facsimile in Gedenk- und Bildungsstätte Haus der Wannsee-Konferenz, *Die Wannsee-Konferenz*, pp. 115–119.

DOC. 197

On 5 August 1941 Hermann Samter writes to Lisa Godehardt about roundups and arrests in Berlin[1]

Letter from Hermann Samter to Lisa Godehardt,[2] dated 5 August 1941

Dear Lisa,

Many thanks for the nice things! They tasted, and still taste, very good. – I have postponed my holiday by four weeks. Well, a lot can still happen before September. Last Thursday night between 9 and 11:30, more than 1,000 Jewish families in Berlin have had their house searched. The search was for money, gold, tomatoes, fruit, red wine, and anything else a Jew is not allowed to be in possession of nowadays. A note was made of anyone who was not at home. Anyone found in another apartment was immediately taken away, because a Jew has to be in his own apartment after 9 p.m. (But no one was told that in advance!) Also taken away on the spot were people who are fit for work but are not yet in labour deployment. There were a total of seventy arrests on this one evening. Now the speculation is beginning: is one allowed to go into the woods? etc. Incidentally, that's not such a ridiculous question, as has already become apparent. As you can see, one has major worries here. But perhaps the British air pirates will soon demonstrate that there are even worse things to worry about.

Kind regards,
also to your mother and Roswitha!

DOC. 198

On 5 August 1941 Paul Eppstein informs Josef Löwenherz in Vienna that Jewish males between the ages of 18 and 45 are no longer allowed to emigrate[1]

File note by the director of the Israelite Religious Community of Vienna, signed Dr Löwenherz, dated 5 August 1941, regarding a telephone conversation with Dr Eppstein, Reich Association, Berlin, on 5 August 1941 at 5:45 p.m.[2]

Dr *Eppstein* advises me of the following:

Today he was informed by the Central Office for Jewish Emigration in Berlin that males between the ages of 18 and 45 are not allowed to emigrate. This new directive is

1 Holocaust Memorial Center, Farmington Hills, MI; copy in YVA, o.2/30, fol. 6. Published in Samter, *Briefe*, p. 66. This document has been translated from German.

2 Lisa Godehardt, née Stadermann (1902–1980), daughter of the former housekeeper of Hermann Samter's parents, Karolina Stadermann (b. 1865); lived during the war in the Thuringian village of Breitenholz and supported Hermann Samter by sending him food parcels.

1 The original is privately owned; copy in DÖW, 8496. Published in Dokumentationsarchiv des österreichischen Widerstandes, *Widerstand und Verfolgung in Wien*, p. 276. This document has been translated from German.

2 The file note went to: 'Dr Murmelstein; foreign exchange advice; processing'.

already in effect for the 21st transport.[3] If males between 18 and 45 have been assigned to this transport, they are to be withdrawn from it. No exceptions are permitted.

This measure, which was previously administered in the Protectorate, is being extended to the entire Reich.

DOC. 199
On 11 August 1941 the emigrant Edgar Emanuel from Berlin writes to Ilse Schwalbe, describing the conditions in which Jews in Germany have to live[1]

Handwritten letter from Edgar Emanuel,[2] 1469 Lexington Ave. Apt. 51, New York City, to Ilse Schwalbe, 251 South 15th Street, San José/California, dated 11 August 1941

Dear Mrs Schwalbe, surely you will still remember us. We lived in the same building in Berlin, 10/II Sächsischestr. Before our departure, we had often talked with your mother,[3] who was also making preparations for emigration at that time. We left Berlin on 11 June and arrived in New York on 13 July after a lengthy odyssey. When we left, we promised your mother that we would get in contact with you. We would have done so sooner, but unfortunately my wife and I fell ill as a result of the previous agitation and possibly the unmanageable heat here in New York as well, and we were not able to undertake our assignments at once. As far as I know, your mother already had the affidavits, but needed to renew the paperwork. Now, however, as a result of the new provisions, much has probably changed.[4] Nevertheless, I would indeed advise everyone to keep working with undiminished vigour to get relatives out of the country. A life there is hardly possible any more. Every day, one must expect to have to vacate one's apartment within a few days. Shortly before we left, the owners of the apartment received the demand for their apartment to be vacated within a very short space of time. As for foodstuffs, Jews just got the stipulated rations. In every special distribution, for example, rice, coffee, tea, pulses, fruit, chocolate, tobacco products, poultry, milk etc., J[ews] were disregarded. They are not allowed to buy anything, nor may anything be sold to them. Shopping in general is permitted only between 4 and 5 in the afternoon. One can no longer go to a restaurant or café, can no longer sit down on a bench. An unwritten law says that one must be at home by 9 p.m.[5] Then the air-raid sirens, separate shelters for Jews. Often we sat together at night. Your mother was quite frantic because the papers requested had not arrived. She asked me to strongly urge you to do your utmost to get her out. We are remaining in New York for the time being, and if there is anything you want to know, please do not hesitate to write to me. What are the children up to?

3 The 21st emigration transport left Vienna on 7 August 1941 and went to North and South America via Spain and Portugal.

1 Jüdisches Museum Berlin, Sammlung Familie Korant Schwalbe Striem, 2006/57/479. This document has been translated from German.
2 Edgar Emanuel (1890–1967), retailer; emigrated to the USA in 1941.
3 Margarete Korant.
4 After July 1941 the USA admitted barely any Jewish refugees into the country.
5 See Doc. 4, fn. 9; Doc. 36, fn. 7; and Doc. 41, fn. 8.

For today, kind regards from my wife and daughter and me

NB Your mother has engaged an advisor for emigration matters over there, who relieves her of the most burdensome procedures. She has also learned tailoring, and she crafts animals out of oilcloth. Very nice. She's very hard-working.

DOC. 200

In a diary entry dated 12 August 1941 Friedrich Kellner criticizes legal arbitrariness with regard to Jews[1]

Handwritten diary of Friedrich Kellner, entry for 12 August 1941

12 Aug. 1941.

As we learned from a young lady living in Frankf[urt]-Rödelheim, the Rödelheim neighbourhood was subjected to quite a heavy attack on 6 or 7 August 1941. A large number of houses were destroyed. There were apparently few casualties. One must repeatedly note that it is scarcely possible to obtain reliable, objective reports. A great many of the inhabitants of a city that has been attacked are unwilling to survey the damage. They are sticking their heads in the sand. If I get leave, I will go in September to the areas that are being targeted by air strikes. Then I will know the score, at least to some extent, regarding 'minor damage to property'.

German judges appear to belong to a particular class of human being.

In a judgement issued by the Reich Fiscal Court on 23 July 1941 (VI a 34/41), it is ruled that *Jewish* hospitals are not exempt from land tax. The regional tax director stated that 'population' refers only to the *German* population. It is not a question of legal interpretation – the judgement states – but rather merely a matter of deciding *how the existing state of affairs is to be evaluated in accordance with the National Socialist world view.* (*Reichssteuerblatt*, 1941, p. 553)[2]

The 'independent' and 'regal' German judge has to concern himself not with the law, but rather solely with the *National Socialist world view.* And that world view truly has absolutely nothing to do with 'law'.

The law of present-day National Socialist Germany consists solely of *power* and *arbitrariness*!

1 The original is privately owned; copy in Archiv der Arbeitsstelle Holocaustliteratur an der Universität Gießen. Published in Kellner, *Tagebücher 1939–1945*, pp. 179–180. This document has been translated from German.

2 'RFH-Urteil vom 23. Juli 1941 VI a 34/41', *Reichssteuerblatt*, vol. 31, no. 62, 7 August 1941, no. 599, p. 553.

DOC. 201

On 13 August 1941 the Reich Association of Jews in Germany notifies its district offices that it must pay for the care and burial of the Jewish patients at the psychiatric hospital in Chełm[1]

Letter from Dr Conrad Israel Cohn, Reich Association of Jews in Germany, Welfare Department, Berlin-Charlottenburg, 158 Kantstraße, to the Jewish communities with more than 1,000 members and the district offices of the Reich Association of Jews in Germany, dated 13 August 1941

Re: invoices from the Cholm mental asylum[2]

It has been decided that we must pay the costs of the care and burial of mentally ill Jews who have been transferred to the Cholm mental asylum from the Old Reich, including the Sudetenland. The Cholm mental asylum will continue to send the bills as before to the religious congregations and district offices which were formerly responsible. Payment, however, will not be made by the individual religious congregations and district offices, but rather from here, in a separate procedure.

We ask the [Jewish] communities and district offices to forward to us, without delay, the invoices now in their possession from the Cholm mental asylum – including those they already submitted to us previously. An accompanying letter commenting on the individual cases must be enclosed with the invoices. In particular, precise information is required as to whether the mentally ill person concerned was a member of the Reich Association and whether the costs of care were previously borne in full or in part by the [Jewish] Community (district office). In cases where full or partial payment is to be made by individuals, the exact address of the person responsible for payment (family member, legal guardian, carer) must be provided. If applicable, reference must be made to existing pension entitlements.

If, in accordance with point 2 of our letter dated 12 June 1941,[3] legal guardians, caregivers or other persons have returned to the depositors any collected pension subsidies received for the period following evacuation, with the request that these sums and any future payments be transferred to the Cholm mental asylum, a specific note must be made of this. In addition, invoices from individuals paying in full are not to be returned to the Cholm mental asylum. Instead, they must be forwarded to us with precise information on the person responsible for payment. We will then have the sums from these payers refunded to us in a central special account. If invoices are received concerning non-members of the Reich Association (such as Mischlinge of the first degree who are not regarded as Jews etc.), these must also be forwarded to us with a note to this effect, so that we can then return them all to the (Cholm) mental asylum.

1 BArch, R 8150/7, fol. 222. This document has been translated from German.

2 The formerly Polish psychiatric hospital in Chełm (Cholm), where the patients had already been murdered, was used as a cover address to conceal the killings of Jewish patients in the 'euthanasia' killing centres in the Reich. Family members received notification that the patient had died in the Chełm psychiatric hospital. See Introduction, p. 34.

3 BArch, R 8150/7, fol. 223.

DOC. 202

Representatives of various ministries and the Security Police discuss 'tightening the definition of a Jew' at a meeting chaired by Adolf Eichmann in Berlin on 13 August 1941[1]

Memorandum, signed Dr Feldscher,[2] dated 13 August 1941 (copy)[3]

Re: Tightening[4] the definition of a Jew.

First note: In addition to the undersigned and several gentlemen from the [Reich] Security Main Office, Oberregierungsrat Reischauer,[5] representing the Party Chancellery, and Regional Court Judge Massfeller,[6] representing the Ministry of Justice, attended a meeting today at the Main Office of the Security Police, at 116 Kurfürstenstraße. The meeting, chaired by Sturmbannführer Eichmann, dealt with matters of European blood protection.

At the start, Sturmbannführer Eichmann read aloud the instructions given by the Reich Marshal[7] to SS-Gruppenführer Heydrich concerning preparations for the final solution to the European Jewish question.[8] Following this, he asked Oberregierungsrat Reischauer, as evidently arranged in advance, to outline the issue in brief, stating that Oberregierungsrat Reischauer had already acquired some experience through his dealings with other offices (?).[9]

Oberregierungsrat Reischauer said that, in the Reich, due to the uniform understanding of race and as a result of the educational work carried out in recent years, some things were achievable without the need for legislative measures that could not be implemented in other European countries without a clear legislative mandate. Therefore, he continued, it was necessary first and foremost to define in unambiguous terms the people of Jewish blood who are to be removed from the European peoples: the category of persons of Jewish blood. The most important question and the one to be discussed first, therefore, was that of *the definition of a Jew*. The opinion of the Party Chancellery

1 BArch, R 1501/3746a. This document has been translated from German.

2 Dr Werner Feldscher (1908–1979), lawyer; joined the NSDAP in 1931; district office manager for municipal policy; Oberregierungsrat in the Reich Ministry of the Interior; author of *Rassen- und Erbpflege im deutschen Recht* (1943); died in Dortmund.

3 The original contains handwritten annotations and underlining.

4 The German term here is *Verschärfung*, which implies that the definition is tightened but also given more effect.

5 Herbert Reischauer (b. 1909), lawyer; joined the NSDAP and the SS in 1932; section head on the staff of the Deputy of the Führer, 1936; Regierungsrat and head of training for the Reichsleitung of the NSDAP, 1938; SS-Obersturmbannführer, 1942; worked for the Reichsstatthalter of the Gau Wartheland from 1943, where he became senior Regierungsdirektor in 1944; missing as of Feb. 1945.

6 Franz Massfeller (1902–1966), lawyer; employed in the Prussian judicial service, 1929–1934, and in the Reich Ministry of Justice from 1934; Oberregierungsrat, 1942; categorized as 'exonerated' in denazification proceedings in 1949; Ministerialrat for family law in the Federal Ministry of Justice, 1951–1964; author of *Blutschutz- und Ehegesundheitsgesetz (Kommentar)* (Commentary on the Blood Protection and Marital Health Law) (1936).

7 Hermann Göring.

8 See Doc. 196.

9 Question mark in the original.

about the prevailing definition of a Jew in the Reich was well known, he said. The Chancellery considered the definition unsatisfactory. In particular, he said, the Chancellery was seeking to *relegate the Jewish Mischlinge of the first degree to the status of Jews*. Now the question must be posed as to whether one wished to recommend to the rest of Europe a definition of who is a Jew that differed from the one currently applicable in the Reich. In that case, if one were to retain the definition of a Jew currently in use in the Reich, the group of persons of Jewish blood who, in contrast to the rest of Europe, are not covered by this definition would be put on an equal footing with Jews by means of an administrative measure. This would mean that they can also be evacuated.[10]

In the course of the informal discussions that followed, the question was also posed as to whether it was in our interest to implement in every European country the tightened definition of a Jew that is sought, or whether it would be preferable to adapt the degree to which Jewish blood is excluded depending on the respective ethnopolitical circumstances.

Sturmbannführer Eichmann suggested setting up a task force to make preparations and examine these issues. In addition to the aforementioned participants, other departments should also be involved in this task force, depending on the issue to be discussed. There was all-round agreement with this proposal. This task force is to examine issues connected with blood protection in Europe and to draw up proposals which will form the basis for carrying out the task mentioned at the beginning. Apart from the Jewish question, protection against non-Jews of foreign blood will also be under discussion.[11]

The focus of the first meeting, scheduled for Tuesday, 19 August, at 4 p.m., is the question of defining the term Jew. (Retaining this definition in the Reich and applicability to the rest of Europe.)

10 The question is also addressed in the protocol of the Wannsee Conference held on 20 Jan. 1942: 'The figures listed for Jews in the different countries, however, pertain only to Jews by faith, as definitions of Jews along racial lines are still lacking to a certain extent.' Facsimile in Gedenk- und Bildungsstätte Haus der Wannsee-Konferenz, *Die Wannsee-Konferenz*, pp. 115–119, here p. 117.

11 The task force was established at the Reich Ministry for the Occupied Eastern Territories and was made up of representatives from the Reich Security Main Office, the Reich Ministry of Justice, the Reich Ministry of the Interior, the Office of the Four-Year Plan, and the Reich Foreign Office. There is evidence of meetings until Jan. 1942.

DOC. 203

New measures against the Jews in Berlin are discussed at a meeting at the Propaganda Ministry on 15 August 1941[1]

File note, dated 16 August 1941, regarding the meeting with State Secretary Gutterer, Berlin, on 15 August 1941[2]

State Secretary Gutterer expressed to representatives from all the ministries and other Party and state offices the need for new, more drastic measures against the Jews in Berlin. He began by pointing out that in recent weeks both officers and enlisted men had had the opportunity to speak with Dr Goebbels about their deployment in Russia, and they unanimously, as if by prior agreement, fail to understand why Berlin in particular still has such a large number of Jewish residents, who in many aspects are treated no differently than Aryan German Volksgenossen.

State Secretary Gutterer asked for suggestions for compulsory measures against the Berlin Jews,[3] which the Minister will have occasion to present to the Führer in the coming week.[4] Essentially, the debate revolved around the visible identification of the Jews in the territory of the Old Reich as well as, for example, in the General Government. Further, the discussion focused on placing restrictions on the Jews with regard to the distribution of foodstuffs. Those in attendance raised no objections to setting the daily rations for Jews at the level customary during the [First] World War. In addition, restrictions for the Jews are being considered with respect to the use of public transport (suburban train, underground, tram, etc.).[5]

It has repeatedly been observed – in this context, State Secretary Gutterer referred to his and Ministerial Director Hinkel's joint experience of attempting to find a building for the Reich Chamber of Culture – that the labour deployment of Jews has not yet yielded any satisfactory results at all. Of the total number of 70,000 Jews still living in Berlin, only 19,000 are working. The employment offices, in conjunction with the Chief of the Security Police,[6] are to go through these cases again thoroughly in an effort to direct an even greater percentage of the remaining 51,000 into more productive work so that other manpower can be freed up as a result.

State Secretary Gutterer will summon the invited representatives of the Party and the state again once the Minister returns from the Führer Headquarters.

1 BArch, R 56 I/132, fol. 4r–v. Excerpt in Pätzold, *Verfolgung, Vertreibung, Vernichtung*, p. 304. This document has been translated from German.
2 Parts of the original have been marked and annotated by hand.
3 In a note on the meeting, dated 18 August 1941, Lösener wrote: 'On the question of evacuating the Jews from the Old Reich, Sturmbannführer Eichmann additionally remarked that the Führer, in response to a proposal made by Obergruppenführer Heydrich, had rejected evacuations during the war. Consequently, he [Eichmann] was now having a proposal drafted that aimed at a partial evacuation of the larger cities.' Memorandum published in 'Dokumentation: Das Reichsministerium des Innern und die Judengesetzgebung', *Vierteljahreshefte für Zeitgeschichte*, vol. 9, no. 3 (1961), pp. 262–313, here p. 303.
4 Goebbels discussed these measures with Hitler on 18 August 1941. See Introduction, p. 64.
5 On these discussions, see Introduction, pp. 63 f.; on the implementation, see Docs. 213 and 222.
6 Reinhard Heydrich.

DOC. 204

On 17 August 1941 the Propaganda Ministry prepares a draft for Goebbels designed to obtain Hitler's assent to the compulsory visible identification of Jews in the Reich[1]

Draft by the Propaganda Ministry, Section Pro/2,[2] unsigned, Berlin, for the Reich Minister,[3] dated 17 August 1941[4]

To the Reich Minister
In the Eastern Campaign, the German soldier has experienced the Jews in all their baseness and vileness. His revulsion and resentment have increased substantially because Jews have maimed German soldiers and have shot them in ambushes.

When the soldier, with this experience fresh in his mind, comes home on leave, he is astounded and embittered by having to see the Jews – these true initiators of the war – walk freely in the streets. Further, he is forced to observe that they make purchases in the same shop as his wife; that his wife must share scarce commodities with the Jews; that the tradesmen, overburdened with work, perform work for Jews as well as Germans; that, despite the existing housing shortage, Jews still occupy apartments; that Jews take his seat on public transport and sit while he must stand; that they are still doing well financially and blatantly engage in stockpiling. For example, it has not escaped the attention of the Volksgenossen that the Jews, who are not entitled to fruit, have bought up a substantial portion of the Werder fruit crop. It becomes clear to the soldier that the Jew perceives the treatment accorded him as a rosy prospect and behaves with brazen confidence, and that, as an agent of incitement, he seeks to undermine the homeland's power of resistance.

It is clear that the soldier, when he comes back from the war, must no longer encounter any Jews. It is equally clear that stringent and prompt measures must be taken in the interim to avoid a poisoning of morale by such injustices. Efforts in this direction, however, fail on account of bureaucratic obstacles such as legalistic thinking, disputes over jurisdiction, and dawdling. The latter is still encouraged by the reasoning that the Jews will soon disappear anyway, and that it is therefore not worth making the regulatory apparatus run faster. Most regulations created before the war fail to deal adequately with the wartime situation and, in particular, the shortage of consumer goods. The people demand that quick, decisive steps be taken:

1) to subdue the Jew – only vigorous intimidation can bring the Jew to exhibit the requisite restraint;
2) to be able to keep tabs on the regulations issued, even with the few available surveillance personnel.

1 BArch, NS 18/1133, fol. 4. Excerpt published in Adler, *Der verwaltete Mensch*, pp. 50–51. This document has been translated from German.
2 Dr Eberhard Taubert was in charge of the section.
3 Joseph Goebbels.
4 The draft was sent to Goebbels via State Secretary Gutterer, with the wording: '*Re*: Jewish measures. I am sending enclosed the draft concerning Jews, intended for presentation by the Reich Minister to the Führer. Heil Hitler!' BArch, NS 18/1133., fol. 3. Goebbels met with Hitler the next day to discuss these issues. See Introduction, p. 64.

Requiring Jews to wear visible markers is, in the view of all the ministries and offices concerned, the central component of and precondition for every one of the urgently required measures against the Jews.

In the current political situation, consideration for foreign countries should no longer obstruct implementation. The introduction of visible identification is all the more justified, as the Poles are already required to wear identifying markers. With regard to foreign policy, this visible identification will have a beneficial effect, because it will be impossible to mistake foreigners for Jews. In addition, the south-east of Europe in particular will obtain a clear model for handling the Jewish question. Also, requiring the Jews to wear identifying markers will not give rise to disorderly conduct. Rather, it will put the Jew back in his place and thus eliminate any occasion for unrest.

On the question of visible identification of the Jews, a letter was sent today by Gruppenführer Heydrich to Reichsleiter Bormann, asking the latter to secure the assent of the Führer to the visible identification of the Jews. In this letter, it is stated that the Reich Marshal,[5] in response to a draft by SS-Gruppenführer Heydrich, has reached the decision that the matter must be presented to the Führer.[6]

In the enclosure, the most important immediate measures regarding the Jewish question are set forth in detail:

1) *Ban on Jews*
2) *Purchasing of goods by Jews*
3) *Skilled crafts services for Jews*
4) *Use of public transport*
5) *Surrender of everyday and luxury items*
6) *Compulsory [labour] service by Jews*
7) *Reduction of allowances for Jews*

The information presented demonstrates that these measures are possible only after the introduction of identifying markers for the Jews.

Heil Hitler!

1) *Ban on Jews*

In Berlin, a police regulation banned Jews from a number of prestigious residential streets and from visiting public baths, theatres, cinemas, restaurants, etc.[7] A special decree has rendered this regulation invalid.[8] With consideration for the German soldiers and the German Volksgenossen in general, the ban ought to be rigorously implemented from now on. In the process, it would also have to be prohibited for Jews to go beyond the municipal area or to go into the streets outside certain hours, unless they are working.

The visible identification of the Jews is a prerequisite for this measure.

5 Hermann Göring.
6 This letter could not be found.
7 See Doc. 176, fn. 5.
8 This could not be verified.

2) *Purchasing of goods by Jews*
At present the Jews shop in Aryan establishments. When so doing, they queue up together with German women. The Jews take advantage of the mood, already tense as a result of queuing in itself, and stir things up.

The German woman who works must do her shopping during the shopping hours for Jews, between 4 and 5 p.m.[9] She is forced to see that these Jews buy up the rest of the goods in stock that day, depriving her of them. The Jews avail themselves of the opportunity to shop in Aryan establishments so that they can gain possession of goods that are prohibited to them and can acquire scarce goods in unwarranted quantities.

In the shops in the Jewish areas, things have gone so far that the shopkeepers reserve goods for Jews that were once considered luxuries, but are now bought up by everybody to add some extra flavour to their mealtimes and are available only in small quantities for regular customers. The Jews, by offering higher prices, subvert the morality of the Aryan shopkeeper. In Berlin alone, in 12,000 instances, Jews and the corresponding shopkeepers have been punished for ordering and purchasing coffee and cocoa.

This sorry state of affairs can be rectified by allocating, city by city, all goods reserved for Jews to the Reich Association of Jews. Let the Reich Association work out how to distribute these goods to the consumer. This solution also eliminates the problem of Aryans coming into contact with Jews at a decisive point, in addition to allowing for more control over the consumption of non-rationed goods by Jews.

Apart from certain foodstuffs, the minimum subsistence level for Jews is adequately guaranteed by the supplies on hand in Jewish households. Thus, the question is why the Jew is allowed to buy goods at all, save pharmaceuticals, thereby depriving the German of them. Alcohol, tobacco products, photographic equipment, books, gramophone records, toys, perfumes, etc. are not essential items. Anything that must be conceded to the Jews can be supplied to them through the Reich Association. They must leave everything else to the Germans. We must therefore demand that German shops are made off limits to them. The consumer goods that are freed up in this way must be reserved to support the troops in the East.

Germans who then stoop to making purchases for Jews, and Jews who avail themselves of these helpers, must be made examples of and punished, and also named and shamed in the press.

The visible identification of the Jews is a prerequisite for this measure.

It must obviously be stipulated that Jews do not receive ration coupons for shoes and textile products.[10] But it is completely incomprehensible that even today they still continue to receive the same food rations as Germans, with the exception of the special allocations. Therefore, it has been urged that at least the meat rations, specifically for non-working Jews, be reduced to the level customary during the previous war (200 grams per week). The assertion that this would lead to the risk of epidemics can only be characterized as overly cautious, judging by the experiences of the previous war. At that time, the German drew half of the meat ration that is due today, and one

9 See Doc. 36, fn. 7.

10 As of the winter of 1939/1940, Jews were denied ration coupons for both clothing and shoes. See Doc. 36, fn. 4.

third of the fat ration. Bread was basically sawdust, and vegetables such as potatoes were replaced with turnips. Nonetheless, no epidemic occurred.

Besides the reduction of the meat ration, a decrease in the coal ration is advisable. The Jews, who bought up goods that were in short supply and thus deprived Germans of them during the *Systemzeit*,[11] are from now on to receive no more coal until the last German Volksgenosse has been supplied.

3) *Skilled crafts and trades service for Jews*

It is unacceptable that Germans must perform services for Jews. As long as the Americans had a sound sense of race, they refused to do the bidding of Negroes. For the German Volksgenosse as well, such an attitude towards Jews goes without saying.

In the course of adjusting Germany's economic life, Jews were forbidden to practise skilled crafts and trades. As a result, however, the German craftsman must serve the Jew as long as there are Jews in Germany. The German must wait for his shoes to be resoled because the Jew wants to have his shoes resoled. At the barber, the German must wait until the Jew has had his shave. Unrestricted visits to barber shops by Jews have an especially adverse effect in terms of propaganda, because experience has shown that such premises are centres of whispering campaigns.

The Reich Association of Jews must be tasked with ensuring that Jewish faces are shaved, Jewish shoes are resoled, etc.

The visible identification of the Jews is a prerequisite for this measure.

4) *Use of public transport*

Given the overburdening of public transport, it must be demanded that Jews only travel if they have police authorization. Such authorization should be granted only for travel to and from the workplace. On the trams, the front section of the platforms will be approved for Jews. On the urban railway, underground and Reich Railways, special compartments are to be set aside for Jews if and when regular travel to work in groups is concerned. Otherwise, Jews must stand. Taxis are to be prohibited for Jews.[12]

The visible identification of the Jews is a prerequisite for this measure.

5) *Surrender of everyday and luxury items*

The purchase and use of bicycles and tyres by Germans is restricted by regulations. Oddly enough, however, many Jews ride bicycles. If these are not being used for travel to work, they should be confiscated. Similarly, typewriters are to be taken away from the Jews, because they are urgently needed for German offices.

The visible identification of the Jews is a prerequisite for this measure.

Furthermore, the following items are to be confiscated from the Jews: cameras and photographic equipment, film projectors and films, books, gramophones and gramophone records, refrigerators, electric stoves, alcohol of every kind and tobacco products, handheld mirrors, playing cards and parlour games. The confiscated objects, after examination and inspection, should be used to support the troops in the East.

11 German for 'system era': a term used by the National Socialists to refer disparagingly to the period of the Weimar Republic.

12 The use of public transport by Jews was comprehensively regulated on 15 Sept. 1941. See Doc. 222.

With the instinct innate in them, the Jews have stockpiled provisions in good time and in large quantities. In the process of clearing out Jewish households, it should at the same time be ensured that stockpiled goods are confiscated for the benefit of wounded soldiers. Any unnecessary household effects should be sent to victims of bombing raids. The share of goods saved as a result of the purchase prohibition for Jews should be assigned to support the troops in the East.

6) *Compulsory [labour] service by Jews*

The outrageous state of affairs – Jews freeloading and lazing about while German women, even those with several children, work in munitions plants – has been remedied on paper. In practice, however, Jews are still hanging about, freeloading, in many cases on the strength of misleading medical certificates from Jewish doctors. A general muster of all Jews must be ordered to ascertain their fitness for work.[13] This thorough screening will simultaneously reveal which Jews are already to be considered ripe for deportation to the East and which Jews must, for now, remain included in the work process, which is so essential to the war effort. At the same time, it will reveal which Jews are not fully fit for work but can be used temporarily for light work or work as outworkers. Furthermore, it must be demanded that nationally standardized provisions regarding the compulsory service of Jews be issued at last.[14] It would have to be ensured that German employers do not make concessions to Jews out of misguided sympathy or in the erroneous belief that this will lead to increased efficiency. In particular, one must avoid enabling the Jews to obtain the social benefits that the German worker enjoys.

7) *Reduction of allowances for Jews*

The Jews demonstrate by their conduct that the monthly allowances they are permitted to draw from their sequestered assets and property, together with the remaining concealed funds, far exceed the appropriate minimum subsistence level. A rigorous curtailment must ensue, so that the Jew cannot buy over Germans who are weak in character. The Reich Security Main Office should be entrusted with calculating the rates.[15]

13 A general muster did not take place, but the labour deployment of the Jewish population had been repeatedly expanded prior to this. In July 1941, the Jewish Community in Berlin had to prepare a list of all Jewish women up to the age of 60 for the employment office, and shortly afterwards the labour administration enlisted in forced labour certain groups that had been spared thus far: all the pensioners in the Reich Association and the Community up to the age of 60 and women up to the age of 55.

14 The beginning of systematic deportation from the Reich obviated any further measures.

15 On these blocked accounts, from which Jews were permitted to withdraw only a fixed monthly sum, which could vary, see Doc. 17, fn. 5. The sum was not standardized nationwide before the deportations started, and thereafter the assets of deported Jews were seized by the Reich in any case.

DOC. 205

In mid August 1941 the Reich Security Main Office provides information on the treatment of Jews of foreign nationality[1]

Letter from the Reich Security Main Office (IVB 4 […][2] 76/41), p.p. signed Müller,[3] Berlin, to all Gestapo (head) offices, the Inspectors of the Security Police and the SD, the Senior Commander of the Security Police and the SD in Prague, and to the Higher SS and Police Leaders for their information, dated mid August 1941[4]

Re: treatment of Jews of foreign nationality
Ref: None
The question of how those Jews residing in Germany who hold *foreign nationality* are to be treated with respect to the provisions issued by the Security Police for German or stateless Jews has recently generated multiple queries. In the opinion of the Reich Foreign Office, there are no objections, from a foreign-policy perspective, to treating Jewish foreign nationals henceforth in the same manner as Jews of German nationality or stateless Jews. However, to avoid reprisals, the Reich Foreign Office requests that legal matters involving assets be excluded from this.

Regardless of this guideline, however, anti-Jewish measures of particular significance are to be made conditional upon my prior approval in every case. The corresponding reports that must be submitted to me are to be as detailed as possible.

In giving notice of this I would, however, like to point out, in order to allay any doubts, that this order is restricted *exclusively* to the implementation of police measures. If laws, regulations, and other provisions foresee a different treatment for Jews of foreign nationality, this must remain unchanged for the time being.

1 RGVA, 500k/1/329, copy in USHMM, RG-11.001M04, reel 72. This document has been translated from German.
2 Partially illegible.
3 Heinrich Müller.
4 Date partially illegible; sections of the original have been highlighted and annotated.

DOC. 206

On 19 August 1941 Goebbels notes that Hitler is seeing his prophecy of the annihilation of European Jewry come to fruition[1]

Diary of Joseph Goebbels, entry for 19 August 1941

19 August 1941 (Tuesday)
Yesterday:
[...][2]
With regard to the Jewish question, I am able to prevail upon the Führer completely. He agrees that we have to introduce a large, visible Jewish badge for all the Jews in the Reich, which the Jews must wear in public. This will then eliminate the danger that the Jews can engage in grumbling and defeatist talk without ever being recognized.[3] Also, if the Jews do not work, we will allocate smaller rations to them than to the German people in the future. That is only fair. Anyone who does not work should not eat. That's all we needed, that in Berlin, for example, only 26,000 of the 76,000 Jews are working, and the others live not only off the work, but also off the food rations of the Berlin population! In addition, the Führer approves my plan to deport the Berlin Jews from Berlin to the East as quickly as possible, as soon as the first opportunity for transport presents itself. There, they will be worked over in a harsher climate.[4]

Regarding the tobacco-related and confessional propaganda, the Führer completely shares my point of view. He has authorized me to issue a sharply worded circular to the Party, most strictly prohibiting the treatment of topics that are not directly essential to achieving victory.[5]

However, he intends to make an example of Bishop von Galen in Münster, if the excesses reported about his preaching are consistent with the facts. He instructed me to get this news into the English radio broadcasts, if possible. Next, in the press, we will pounce on it with indignation and declare that it could never happen and never did happen. Then, however, we want to have an investigation determine that Bishop Galen actually did say something of the sort, and the ensuing outburst of indignation from the entire nation will give us the welcome opportunity to proceed with the aforesaid bishop in accordance with the law. We will bring him before the People's Court and have him harshly sentenced.[6]

1 RGVA, Nachlass Goebbels, fond 1477, microfilm, 19 August 1941 (72 fols.). Published in *Die Tagebücher von Joseph Goebbels*, ed. Elke Fröhlich, part 2: *Diktate 1941–1945*, vol. 1: *Juli–September 1941* (Munich: Saur, 1996). pp. 255–272. This document has been translated from German.

2 In the preceding section, Goebbels writes about his assessment of the military situation and morale in the occupied territories of the Soviet Union. He describes his trip to the Führer Headquarters, where he met with Hitler, and talked with him about matters including the military and political situation of the Reich: RGVA, Nachlass Goebbels.

3 The requirement for German Jews to wear identifying markers was introduced on 1 Sept. 1941. See Doc. 212.

4 The systematic deportations to the East began across the Reich in Oct. 1941: see Doc. 223. The first Berlin transport arrived in the Litzmannstadt (Lodz) ghetto on 19 Oct. 1941.

5 Goebbels, in consultation with Bormann, sent such a circular to all NSDAP Reichsleiter and Gauleiter on 24 August 1941: BArch, NS 22/902.

6 The Bishop of Münster, Count Clemens August von Galen, had openly criticized the 'euthanasia' murders in a sermon on 3 August 1941. No charges were brought against him before the People's Court. See Introduction, p. 53.

But otherwise the Führer is determined to keep things quiet on the domestic front. I refer to the example of 1932, when we concentrated exclusively on gaining power and did not digress from this subject. So we must now concentrate exclusively on achieving victory. Problems of secondary significance should be filed away, for attention after the war.

The Führer is of the opinion that, in some circumstances, it is possible that peace will arrive quite suddenly. From our vantage point, we cannot accurately assess the situation in England at all. It is clear that things are at breaking point over there, wherever you look. When we achieved power, it was much the same. In our German thoroughness and objectivity, we have always overestimated the opponent, with the exception of the Bolshevists in this case. At that time too, in early January 1933, we believed ourselves to be further from power than ever. Four weeks later the Führer was Reich Chancellor. Perhaps it is similar here. Perhaps Churchill will one day experience his overthrow. Even today, he no longer really has any room for manoeuvre. His hands and feet are tied. When he tries now to wear down the German people with propaganda, this attempt is doomed to utter failure. England's situation is more than desperate. It just does not appear to us to be so, because Churchill boasts and swaggers so tremendously.

The USA is not ripe for war. Admittedly, Roosevelt has an interest in drawing out the war for as long as possible. But he lacks the desire and also the mandate to intervene in it. He is also likely to have difficulties in his alliance with Bolshevism. Big business and, above all, the Wall Street circles in the USA are opposed to it. One fears, probably not without good reason, a gradual infection of the American public as a result of it. Getting too cosy with Bolshevism is always to the disadvantage of the non-Bolshevists. The danger of Bolshevism can never be overestimated. If Bolshevism were then to become militant into the bargain, just as it confronts us today, then the danger would be a mortal one. We may not even realize yet how precarious our situation was in June of this year. Autumn would certainly have brought the explosion. Today the Führer is also convinced that Moscow and London have long since been in cahoots with each other. That does not mean that Stalin and Churchill are acting in concert. But they have assuredly had a common goal for a certain stretch of the way.[7] This goal is: the destruction of the Reich.

What it would have meant for us if the Bolshevist hordes had advanced into highly civilized Central and Western Europe is utterly indescribable. That actually ought to be a warning to our intellectuals, who, in many cases, are now floundering about with the objection that the Eastern Campaign was not necessary at all. They are unfamiliar with the danger of Bolshevism because they have never dealt with it. We are acquainted with it because we have already had Bolshevism at sword-point for years in our domestic political struggle. With the consent of the Führer, I will arrange for German intellectuals, economists, artists, and scientists to be brought in greater numbers to Bolshevist prison camps,[8] so that they can see there with their own eyes what a bad sort the Bolshevist is.

7 British–Soviet relations had been placed under great strain by the German–Soviet Non-Aggression Pact that was enacted in 1939. Since taking office in late 1940, the new British Foreign Secretary, Anthony Eden, had sought an improvement in relations, and from March 1941 both the British and the US governments had repeatedly warned the Soviet Union of a German invasion. On 12 July 1941, Britain and the Soviet Union concluded an agreement for joint action.

The anti-Bolshevist opinion is a fairly universal one in Europe. Admittedly, it is artificially concealed by English propaganda, but it is nonetheless clear and unambiguous. Above all, our Axis partners are extremely cooperative with us in this area. Spain, admittedly, has not yet brought itself to make a bold decision. Not much can be done with Franco. Where would we be now if we had taken Gibraltar with his approval last winter?[9] He is simply a reactionary general, not a revolutionary. Things are quite different with Italy. Mussolini is an anti-Bolshevist to the core, even if he cannot do very much with the Italian people.

Although the Führer is not optimistic about the internal situation in Italy, he is quite reassured. Mussolini will surely keep it in hand. Incidentally, the Duce will pay a visit to the Führer at the Headquarters in the next few days. A discussion of the overall situation has proved necessary again.[10] Pity that Mussolini's son was not killed in combat. Fascism could have really used that now.[11]

It is admirable how the German leaders are lending their support to the war today. For this reason, the Führer also emphasizes that, whenever sons of prominent National Socialists or military leaders are killed, this must also be made known to the German public. For example, the sons of Keitel and Dr Frick died heroic deaths in recent days.[12] The Führer is very glad that Harald also conducted himself and proved himself so splendidly in the battle of Crete.[13] Only in this way will it be possible to ask the people to make the gravest sacrifices over the long term. The people must know that its leaders are sharing these sacrifices.

I present to the Führer the case of the planned Italian film about Benghazi. The Italians intend to shoot a film about the conquest of Cyrenaica in which the military achievements of the German Wehrmacht only play a marginal role. They are even impertinent enough to request our cooperation on the project. I have already refused this on the quiet but will have it confirmed for me again by the Führer. Under no circumstances does he want such a film to reach the German public. However, he tells me to word the refusal diplomatically and to refer to the fact that, in this country, films that depict the interaction between various parts of the Wehrmacht are already leading to unpleasant statements and jealousies. That will be even more the case if the armed forces of two different nations feature in the film. Mussolini may need such a film for domestic Italian consumption. In Germany, it would be sure to have disastrous

8 This refers to camps for Soviet prisoners of war.

9 The Wehrmacht had planned the conquest of Gibraltar in August 1940, but Operation Felix could not be carried out as Spain remained neutral.

10 At the meeting between Hitler and Mussolini from 25 to 29 August 1941 at Hitler's 'Wolf's Lair' (*Wolfsschanze*) headquarters near Rastenburg, the topics under discussion included Britain's and the USA's contact with the Soviet Union.

11 Mussolini's son Bruno, a military pilot, was killed in a plane crash on 7 August 1941. The crash was caused by an equipment malfunction.

12 Lieutenant Hans-Georg Keitel (1919–1941), the youngest son of Chief of the Wehrmacht High Command Wilhelm Keitel, was killed in the Soviet Union in July 1941.

13 Harald Quandt (1921–1967), industrialist; stepson of Joseph Goebbels from the first marriage of his wife Magda, formerly Quandt, née Behrend; he took part in the invasion of Crete in 1941 as a paratrooper; in 1954 he took over the running of the Quandt corporation; Nicaraguan consul, 1957; died in a plane crash.

psychological consequences. Therefore, I will do my utmost to dissuade the Italians from this plan without alienating them.[14]

I brief the Führer on the food situation. It is not threatening at the moment, but it has some potential for crisis. Above all, the Wehrmacht in the occupied territories is receiving excessively high meat allowances, though at the expense of the hard-working civilian population. The Führer wants to tackle this problem after the Eastern Campaign; at the moment, the situation does not favour such action.

We talk about the Jewish problem. The Führer is convinced that his prediction in the Reichstag back then – that, should Jewry succeed once more in provoking a world war, it will end in the annihilation of the Jews[15] – is being confirmed. It is coming true during these weeks and months with an almost uncanny certainty. In the East, the Jews must pay for [their actions]. In Germany, they have, to some extent, already paid and will have to pay even more in the future. North America remains the last refuge. And there, sooner or later, they will also have to pay at some point.

Jewry is a foreign body among the civilized nations, and the Jews' activities during the past three decades have been so devastating that the reaction of the peoples is completely understandable, necessary. Indeed, one might almost say that it is by its very nature essential. At any rate, in a future world the Jews will not have much to laugh about. Even now, there is a pretty united front in Europe against the Jews. This is already becoming apparent throughout the European press, which indeed adheres to a thoroughly uniform opinion not only on this question, but also on many others.[16]

It is probably also due to the fact that we so readily succeeded in rather quickly disposing of the dangerous, explosive issues contained in the Eight-Point Declaration.[17] Now, we virtually control public opinion all over the continent. Churchill will not succeed in gaining any foothold here. And as to the Jewish question, one can state today, at any rate, that a man such as Antonescu, for example, is taking a far more radical tack in this matter than we have done thus far.[18] But I will not rest until we too have taken the last appropriate steps with regard to the Jews.

[…][19]

We sit together until 2 a.m., and I have the feeling that everything we had to discuss has been resolved or at least clarified. I then take my leave of the Führer. He is quite

14 Goebbels failed to put a stop to Augusto Genina's war propaganda film. *Bengasi* premiered in 1942 at the Venice Film Festival. A German-language version produced in 1943 was never released, as a result of the capitulation of the German and Italian troops in Northern Africa in May 1943.

15 See PMJ 2/248.

16 This refers to the European press in the German-occupied countries, as well as the states allied with Germany.

17 In the Atlantic Charter, which Roosevelt and Churchill had signed at a meeting on 14 August 1941, the two statesmen formulated an eight-point plan for future international relations policy, including the eschewal of territorial expansion. In addition, they emphasized the joint objective of putting an end to National Socialist rule.

18 On mass murders by Romanian units in the summer of 1941, see Doc. 195, fn. 7, and the Introduction to PMJ 7.

19 After this, Goebbels reports, among other things, on his talks with Hitler about further plans such as the reported leaflet drops on the Eastern Front. He writes that Hitler gave instructions to starve out a city that had burned its food supplies on Stalin's orders. He notes that, in general, Hitler favours a tougher policy in the occupied territories.

cordial and emotional. In my bunker there are still piles of work to which I must attend. But then I too will get some rest for a couple of hours.

The visit with the Führer was very productive. It will have an effect on the work of the next few days and weeks.

DOC. 207

Mr and Mrs Malsch write to their son and his wife in the USA on 20 August 1941, expressing their continued hopes of emigrating[1]

Handwritten letter from Mr and Mrs Malsch, Düsseldorf, 2 Karl-Antonstraße, to Mr and Mrs William R. Malsh, Los Angeles/California, 1129 (½) South Norton Ave., dated 20 August 1941

My dear children,[2]

On the 14th of this month we wrote to you + on the 16th your lovely letter, dated 31 July, arrived here, with the photo from the ranch.[3] It's a really nice picture. You two look great in it. The main thing is that you have recovered well, you are in good health and you are staying at home. We can't do anything at all from here because of the emigration [application]. As soon as an opportunity presents itself, we, like all the many other candidates, will be officially notified by the Relief Association [of Jews in Germany]. We'll just have to cross that bridge when we come to it. Autumn is slowly approaching now. In spring, when everything had turned green again, I hoped that I would not be seeing these same leaves fall. Now the leaves are falling, and my hope has proved false again. However, we are by no means discouraged. We take things as they are, as they come to us, with the stoicism that has become second nature to all of us here. One just puts up with everything, no longer gets upset about anything and says calmly: 'Oh, well!' Where are we to go? One day a way will surely be found for us to leave the country. We were glad to learn that Mr Maischutz arrived safely. It was no easy matter for an elderly gentleman. Give us the address of your sister Cilly sometime; we could write from here through the Red Cross. It also takes longer, of course. For more output, but especially for greater responsibility, everyone deserves more pay. Everything is getting more expensive over here too! Frida H's sister Betty and her husband are in Mexico. You should say nothing more about my operation; we have already half forgotten the matter. Everything is nicely healed and all right. We wrote to Uncle Ernst to wish him Happy New Year!![4] For today, love and lots of kisses from your Dad, who loves you very much.

It is too bad that we have not yet received a certificate of accreditation from the consulate.

My dear, beloved children. We were delighted to receive your lovely letter dated 30 July. The photo is beautiful, something different for once. We often did used to say 'Buffalo

1 USHMM, RG-10.086/13 of 13. This document has been translated from German.
2 The first letter is written by Paul Malsch.
3 In the original, there is a circled 'B' before the word.
4 In 1941, Rosh Hashanah (Jewish New Year), Yom Kippur (the Day of Atonement), and Sukkot (the Feast of Tabernacles) all fell in Sept./Oct.

Bill' to you, as we said so many things to you. We often talk about it. I am glad that you enjoyed the holidays so much. One must get out of the daily routine now and again, recharge one's batteries. Unfortunately, it is all over far, far too quickly. I am very, very distressed about our emigration, especially because we were once again so close to it. It is so sad that we can't be reunited, and my heart is so clinging to that. Will it ever be possible to see each other again and to get to know dear Trudi?

I must keep my mind off it, my dear boy, you know how I am. We certainly know that you are making every possible effort. We are unable *to do anything at all from here, unfortunately.* Again, one must just wait and see what happens. One is growing older, and one's nerves often get frayed, however much one fights against it. Our only remaining wish is to be with you soon. I envy all the people who are going to join their children. How lucky the Fenners[5] are, after all; the poor sick wife who can't even walk, but they are going to join their child. At any rate, keep us informed about everything. Everything that is to be done is arranged from there. My rheumatism is much better, thank God. It will be all right again. All in good time. If only we could just talk to each other, and if we could see you at some point. Now the holidays are approaching, and we are still so alone. How wonderful it used to be here with dear Gran, bless her soul. How happy she was, and what fun she had with you, especially when she went out with you on [...].[6] Everything, everything is over, all that remains is the memory. It was just so lovely when we were all still together. And back then in Meiningen, you had a really lovely childhood, dear boy, you had everything, and today I am glad it was like that. There is only one thing we still ask of the dear Lord. To see you again, then our greatest joy is complete. I pray for this every day. Did Uncle Karl give you the two pictures? Well, my dear children, stay healthy and happy. Write to us again very *soon*. For today, 10,000,000,000 hugs and kisses, your Mother who always loves you very much. Warm regards to Mrs Fraenkel and Brother Hans

DOC. 208

On 21 August 1941 the official in charge of Jewish affairs at the Reich Foreign Office learns that Hitler has agreed to the visible identification of the Jews[1]

Memorandum from the Reich Foreign Office, Section D III, signed by Rademacher, dated 21 August 1941, with a note by Undersecretary Luther, dated 22 August 1941[2]

Notes

SS-Sturmbannführer *Eichmann* from the Reich Security Main Office telephoned to inform me in confidence that SS-Gruppenführer *Heydrich* has received a telex from the Führer Headquarters, saying that the Führer has authorized the visible identification of the Jews in Germany.[3]

5 The married couple Josef (b. 1875) and Mary Fenner, née Katz (b. 1883), lived in Düsseldorf before emigrating to Buenos Aires in August 1941 to join their son Erwin (b. 1912).

6 One word is illegible.

1 PA AA, R 100 851, fol. 103r–v. This document has been translated from German.

2 The original contains handwritten annotations.

Eichmann asked for my opinion as to whether foreign Jews could be included. I told him that I think foreign Jews should absolutely be exempted. Otherwise it is to be feared that, in North America for example, there might be reprisals and German nationals would likewise be forced to wear an identifying marker.

I said that I would clarify the question of whether those Jews who are subjects of European nations could be included. Eichmann promised to furnish official information about their intentions as soon as he has the telex to hand.

I urge that a decision by the Reich Foreign Minister[4] be secured in this matter and that the following be proposed:

1) With regard to the occupied countries, to consent without further ado.

2) For the rest, however, to obtain the agreement of the European governments allied with Germany and the French government, and to advise them to implement a similar rule for their area of jurisdiction.[5]

3) Once the consent of these governments has been obtained, to instruct the Reich Security Main Office to formally extend the directive to all Jews, and to exempt Jews of non-European nationality only by means of an internal order to the relevant police authorities.

A protest by the Swiss or the Swedish governments is, in my view, no cause for alarm.

Herewith presented to Undersecretary Luther for his attention.

Original returned to
Party Comrade Rademacher, D III
In reply to my question, SS-Gruppenführer Heydrich told me today that Reich Minister Dr Goebbels presented the question of visibly identifying the Jews in Germany to the Führer several days ago, and in return received the Führer's decision that the Jews in Germany are to be required to wear an identifying marker.[6] This will take the form of a white/yellow armband. SS-Gruppenführer Heydrich simultaneously asked me to obtain a decision from the Reich Foreign Office with respect to foreign Jews living in Germany.

He would welcome the proposals set forth in your notes. Please prepare speaker notes for the Reich Foreign Minister.[7]

Berlin, 22 August 1941

3 This could not be found.

4 Joachim von Ribbentrop.

5 The Slovakian government introduced the requirement for Jews to wear identifying markers on 9 Sept. 1941; the Hungarian government resisted; in Bulgaria it was adopted in August 1942, but most Jews did not comply; Italy contemplated but did not implement the measure; the Vichy government under Pierre Laval rejected the measure in the spring of 1942, asserting that the existing anti-Jewish measures were adequate and that the French public would react with outrage.

6 See Doc. 206.

7 These speaker notes, dated 22 August 1941, are included in the file: PA AA, R 100 851, fols. 84–85.

DOC. 209
On 21 August 1941 the Israelite Religious Community of Nuremberg asks the Jewish population to donate money and goods[1]

Notifications issued by the Israelite Religious Community of Nuremberg, unsigned, 21 August 1941

Important notifications issued by the Israelite Religious Community of Nuremberg, 21 August 1941

1. To all: Read the notifications carefully and in full. This will save yourself and us a great deal of time and extra work. Make corresponding notes for yourself where necessary!

2. *Jewish Duty*: All members who have not yet discharged their 'Jewish Duty' should plan to pay their donation, specifying the particulars (from payroll tax, income tax, or wealth tax), either in cash at our administrative office, Room 2, or into the 'Jewish Duty' bank account, no. 49 067, at Commerzbank in Nuremberg. – The last house-to-house collection will take place on *Sunday, 14 September 1941*. Members who will not be at home should plan to leave the corresponding amount with their co-residents or authorize them to make payment. The 'Jewish Duty' will be completed by the end of September. To those who donated gladly, many thanks. We call upon the tardy to discharge their 'Jewish Duty' at once.[2]

3. *Religious services: Maintaining religious services* in their current form is in the interest of all members of our community. It is therefore urgently requested that you support us in the performance of this function by making further donations, in particular by making monthly contributions. The donations do not require a special permit from the foreign exchange office, nor are they set against the tax-free allowance. All that is required is a transfer to Dr Richard Israel Herz,[3] 'Religious' trust account, no. 49 065, at Commerzbank in Nuremberg. – May we hereby express our most cordial thanks to all donors for the sums provided thus far for this purpose.

4. *School bursaries and training workshop*: Owing to the closure of a number of Jewish schools in Bavaria, children are to be sent to school in other places. The Reich Association urges Community members to play an active role in helping to create vacancies and set up school bursaries. We ask that you open the door to the canvassers who will visit you soon and allow them to give you information. We expect that you will help secure a school education for our young people by making a donation.

5. *Change of address*: You are urgently reminded once again that every change of address must be immediately reported to the *tax office* and, if applicable, to the *foreign exchange office*. Failure to do so can result in prosecution. Likewise, it is absolutely essential to report this information to the administrative office of the Israelite Religious Community. Again, note the requirement to report the start of every new job and every change of workplace.

1 CAHJP, D/Nu2/1. This document has been translated from German.

2 The Jewish Duty (*Jüdische Pflicht*) was a donation drive. It was first carried out from June to Sept. 1941 as a counterpart to the Jewish Winter Relief. The Reich Association of Jews in Germany used the proceeds to support those in need.

3 Dr Richard Herz (1894–1943), lawyer; practised law in Nuremberg, 1921–1938; provided legal services to Jews in Fürth as a 'consultant' (*Konsulent*) after 1938; deported on 17 June 1943 to Auschwitz, where he perished.

6. *Labour deployment*: All persons who have started a new job since 28 May 1941 or who have changed their place of work, as well as all domestic workers, outworkers with an employment record book, and other employed persons for whom health insurance is compulsory, should, in their own interests, fill out the form below without delay and send it to the administrative office. (See form at the end of this notification!)
7. *Travel documents*: The documents officially required for a temporary stay outside one's permanent place of residence can be issued only if the corresponding travel tickets are presented. Issuance only between 9 a.m. and 12:30 p.m. The exchange of food ration cards *can take place only between 7 a.m. and 5 p.m.* at the food office in Luitpoldhaus, Room 9. For other matters as well, the food office is open to the public only during these hours.
8. *Textile supplies*: We repeat our request that, when households are dissolved, all articles destined for sale (clothing, linens, shoes, etc.) be offered first to our clothing store for purchase. In order to keep our clothing store running, which exclusively serves to supply the entire Jewish population, we are completely reliant – especially in view of the coming winter – on obtaining the goods in question from members, whether at no charge or in exchange for payment. Therefore, before you make any sales to other parties, please contact our clothing store regarding donation or sale in each individual case. For sales to the clothing store, the customary trade prices will be paid. Telephone: 63 027.
9. *Household items and tableware*: There is a constant need for kitchenware and home furnishings in order to set up our homes. Please think of our homes before disposing of these items elsewhere. To register for a collection of items: 6 Lindenaststraße, Room 1.
10. *Collection of scrap*: According to a notification from the Central Office, Jewish schools, by official directive,[4] must take part in the scrap collection drive. Collection will begin once the school holidays are over, that is, in early September. Community members are requested to prepare any scrap they have on hand (rags, paper, discarded metal, bones, etc.) for pick-up at the given time by the pupils of our primary school.
11. *Temporary stay in Berlin*: In a circular dated 12 August 1941, the Reich Association announced the following: 'Given the situation, it is pointed out that it is undesirable, as a matter of principle, for employees of the Reich Association or private individuals to accompany to Berlin any emigrants who are embarking on their journey from Berlin.'
12. Jewish assets: Sale of cultural assets in Jewish possession: according to a new regulation dated 25 April 1941,[5] the purchasing office for cultural assets is the Reich Chamber of Fine Arts, Berlin W. 35, at 6 Blumeshof. Only this office is authorized to determine whether jewellery and pieces of art owned by Jews can be sold. By official directive,[6] every community member who wishes to sell items of the sort described above must submit an application with precise details to the Gestapo office *via the administration of the Israelite Religious Community.*

4 The Reich Association conveyed this information in a circular to the heads of Jewish schools, religious communities, and the district offices of the Reich Association: undated draft, BArch, R 8150/6, fol. 179.
5 Fifth Implementing Regulation to the Law on the Utilization of Jewish Assets, 25 April 1941, *Reichsgesetzblatt*, 1941, 1, p. 218.
6 This directive could not be found.

13. *Reporting funds belonging to American citizens and persons who are residents of the USA*: Authorized representatives etc. are warned that all bank balances and claims must be reported *by 1 October 1941* on forms that will be handed out at the tax offices from early September.
14. *Tailor and dressmaker*: Mr Willi Israel *Ullmann*,[7] Fürth, 21 Hirschenstraße, is authorized to carry out repairs and alterations for Jews both inside the home and externally.
15. *Lessons*: Formerly private lessons are now being run by individual teachers under our supervision. As before, the classes take place in the school building, 25 Obere Kanalstraße:

English:
Intensive course: Miss Rothschild – Mr Weinheber,[8] 15 Hochstraße,
Beginners and elementary level: – Mr Weinheber, see above.
Intermediate: – Miss Plessner,[9] 27 Knauerstraße,
Advanced: – Mr Gosser,[10] 4 Kontumazgarten,
Modern Hebrew: Miss Rothschild, *Fürth*, 5 Marienstraße,
Spanish: Beginners: Mr Weinheber, see above.
Typing: Mr Weinheber, see above.

Timetables are available from the teachers upon request. We recommend active participation in the courses. In future, please send registration forms directly to the individual teachers.

Sewing course, Mrs Nachmann:[11] It is expected that Mrs Naumann will keep running this course, if there are sufficient numbers. Please send registration forms directly to Mrs Leontine Nachmann, 26 Lindenaststraße.

DOC. 210

In a letter to the Reich Foreign Office dated 28 August 1941, Adolf Eichmann mentions the 'approaching final solution, now in preparation'[1]

Letter from the Chief of the Security Police and the SD, p.p. signed Eichmann, Berlin, to the Reich Foreign Office, Department D V A,[2] Berlin, dated 28 August 1941[3]

Re: emigration of the Jew Werner Israel *Bauer*,[4] born in Mannheim on 9 December 1927, a resident of Frankfurt am Main, 87 Röderbergweg.
Ref: Your letter dated 14 August 1941[5]
Attachments: 2[6]
In response to your letter of 14 August 1941, I inform you that, from our standpoint, in view of the approaching final solution to the European Jewish question, now in prepar-

7 Willi Ullmann (b. 1902) was deported to Riga on 29 Nov. 1941.
8 Ludwig Weinheber (1904–1942), business graduate; deported on 24 March 1942 together with his wife Sophie Weinheber to Izbica, where he was murdered.
9 Hanna Plessner (b. 1904), nursery school teacher; deported on 29 Nov. 1941 to Riga, where she is presumed to have perished.
10 Siegmund Gosser (1884–1967), retailer; lived in a so-called mixed marriage and was not deported.
11 Leontine Nachmann, née Zinner (b. 1877); deported on 24 March 1942 to Izbica, where she is presumed to have perished.

1 PA AA, R 99 370, fol. 19. This document has been translated from German.

ation, both the emigration of Jews from France and the departure of Jews to France from the territory of the Reich, including the Protectorate of Bohemia and Moravia, must be prevented.[7]

For these reasons, I would ask you to reject the application of the Jewish Community in Frankfurt am Main for the issue of a transit visa.[8]

DOC. 211

On 31 August 1941 Arthur Cohen from Düsseldorf tells his cousin in New York about his unsuccessful efforts to emigrate[1]

Letter from Arthur Cohen, Düsseldorf, to Alfred and Christine Cohen,[2] dated 31 August 1941

My dears,

A few days ago Uncle Emil[3] sent us your letter, dear Alfred, dated 6 August, and added a few lines saying goodbye to us, as they intended to leave Berlin on 28 [August] and travel to Barcelona, where they would get a new American visa, he wrote. We're very glad that, after all the difficulties, the Koblenzers' efforts to emigrate have nonetheless been successful, not only for themselves, but also for you. When will we and the Krefelders also be at that point? If our emigration had gone as planned, we could have been ready to leave in a few weeks.

2 This probably refers to Dept. D V (Foreign Travel), which was headed from May 1940 by Dr Manfred Garben (1911–1984), economist; joined the NSDAP and the SA in 1931; in the German foreign service after 1934; section head in the Ribbentrop Bureau from 1937; legation counsellor, first class, 1942; military service, 1942–1943; rejoined the Reich Foreign Office as legation counsellor, 1943; worked as a farmer after 1945.

3 The original contains handwritten annotations and an official stamp.

4 Werner Bauer (b. 1927) emigrated to Belgium on 28 Feb. 1939; later returned to Mannheim. In 1941 he was placed in the children's home of the Jewish Community of Frankfurt am Main. His mother, Irma Bauer, while detained in Gurs internment camp, endeavoured to enable her son to leave the country and go to unoccupied France and from there to the USA. Werner Bauer was deported in 1942 and later declared dead.

5 Letter to the Chief of the Security Police and the SD, Dept. IV D 4, dated 14 August 1941, requesting a statement of opinion, in PA AA, R 99 370, fol. 22.

6 Letter from the Jewish Community of Frankfurt am Main, Dept. of Social Welfare, to the Wehrmacht High Command, Permit Office, Berlin, and telegram to the Relief Association in Frankfurt am Main regarding the departure of Werner Bauer for Marseilles, dates illegible, ibid., fols. 20–21.

7 See Doc. 182.

8 Werner Bauer's emigration application was definitively rejected by the Chief of the Security Police and the SD in a letter dated 18 Dec. 1941: PA AA, R 99 370, fol. 33.

1 Mahn- und Gedenkstätte Düsseldorf, Briefe Familie Cohen. This document has been translated from German.

2 Dr Alfred Cohen (1895–1974), lawyer; lived in New York. He paid a guarantee towards the emigration of his cousin Arthur Cohen and Arthur's wife, Aenne. The maiden name of Alfred's wife, Christine, was Monschan.

3 Emil Frank (1878–1954), retailer; lived in Wittlich, where he was a textiles retailer, and lastly in Koblenz; fled to Utica, New York, in Sept. 1941 via Spain and Cuba.

Unfortunately, dear Alfred, you appear to be right about the pointlessness of a temporary stay in Portugal, as our relatives in Oporto,[4] who wrote to the American [Jewish] Joint Distribution Committee in Lisbon, received the following information:

'With the closure of the American consulates in Germany, there is no possibility of emigration to the USA, at least at the present time. All visas must now be authorized in Washington. The consulate in Lisbon is unable to grant visas to people in Germany because they cannot obtain the requisite transit visa, which would enable them to come here first.'

From various quarters we heard that people with certificates of accreditation are given preference in the visa-granting process, but we have heard no positive news to that effect.[5] Uncle Leo[6] wrote to tell us that he would do everything possible to arrange a temporary stay for us in Cuba, but it is still doubtful whether the visa will still be issued by the Cuban legation in Berlin, as a result of the closure of the Cuban consulate. In the interim, we must console ourselves with the thought that there are so many others in the same situation, including the Krefelders, who wrote to us just recently and enclosed a letter from the dears in Worcester. We are happy that they are doing so well, and [I] hope you are in good health too, especially you, dear Alfred, as you have lost so much weight. In the course of the work I have been doing for a year now, I have certainly lost the same amount, but I feel well. It's a pity that I can't help you with your strenuous work, as I definitely have experience now in tackling such jobs. You can be glad about the success of your business. Eugen[7] really seems to have a top-notch position now, and the children will surely have a great deal of fun with their sweet Uncle Eugen. I hope you are well, enjoyed the holiday, and will meet up with Eugen and Lotte for the religious holidays, if at all possible.[8] This year too, unfortunately, we do not have the opportunity to wish them and Eugen's family well in person. But even so, they will know that we wish them all only the very best, as well as you, my dears. Father[9] is doing well. A few days ago, he was back in Cologne for the first time since his illness, and by himself at that. He has made another splendid recovery. On 9 September, Uncle and Aunt Lindheimer[10] in Krefeld have their golden wedding anniversary. Aunt was discharged from hospital a few weeks ago and can already get around quite well again. All good wishes, warm regards,

Your

4 This refers to a cousin of Aenne Cohen, née Goldschmidt.

5 The Cohens had received such a certificate on 5 Feb. 1941: see Doc. 147.

6 Leo Kamp (1878–1949), retailer; emigrated with his wife, Betty, née Pollag (1886–1980), and sons Ewald (1914–1986) and Rudolf Rudy (1910–2007) from Essen via Zurich to the USA.

7 Eugen Cohen, also Eugene Clifton (1895–1978), retailer; emigrated to Britain in 1939 with his wife, Lotte, née Rosenthal (b. 1909), and son Gerd, later Gerald Clifton (b. 1931).

8 In 1941 Rosh Hashanah (Jewish New Year), Yom Kippur (the Day of Atonement), and Sukkot (the Feast of Tabernacles) all fell in Sept./Oct.

9 Isaac Cohen (1859–1942), businessman, founder of J & J Cohen in Dusseldorf, a firm trading in hides, sausage casings, and butchery equipment; arrested on 11 Nov. 1938; deported to Theresienstadt on 21 July 1942 and perished there before the end of that month.

10 Pauline Lindheimer, née Reis(s) (1870–1942), lived in Krefeld with her husband, Josef Lindheimer (1859–1942), retailer; the couple owned a shop in Krefeld; on 25 July 1942 they were both deported via Düsseldorf to Theresienstadt, where they perished.

My dears, We hope you all are well, and we are in good health too, thank God. Naturally it pains us every time we realize that we had thought we could start our journey soon. But with God's help, the day will also come when we are reunited with our loved ones. I wish *all* of you only the best for the upcoming holidays. I hope the dear children will be together at Eugen's. Keep well and write again soon.

Most affectionately, Aenne

My dears,

I am fine again, praise God. On Wednesday I was in Cologne, after a long period in hospital,[11] [and] also spoke with Leopold.[12] Apart from […],[13] Siegmund[14] is doing fine so far, but he still thinks he can't get by on his money. I wish you well for the upcoming holidays. With warm regards, Isaac

DOC. 212

Police regulation, dated 1 September 1941, making it compulsory for Jews to wear an identifying badge[1]

Police Regulation on the Visible Identification of Jews
1 September 1941
Pursuant to the Regulation on the Police Regulations of the Reich Ministers, dated 14 November 1938 (*Reichsgesetzblatt*, I, p. 1582), and the Regulation on Legislative Authority in the Protectorate of Bohemia and Moravia, dated 7 June 1939 (*Reichsgesetzblatt*, I, p. 1039),[2] the following is decreed, in consultation with the Reich Protector of Bohemia and Moravia:

§ 1

(1) Jews (§ 5 of the First Regulation on the Reich Citizenship Law, 14 November 1935 – *Reichsgesetzblatt*, I, p. 1333)[3] aged six and above are forbidden to go out in public without wearing a Jewish badge.

(2) The Jewish badge consists of a palm-sized, six-pointed star made of yellow cloth and outlined in black, bearing the inscription 'Jew' in black. It must be worn visibly on the left side of the chest, and firmly sewn to the garment.

11 This refers to the Israelite Refuge and Hospital on Ottostrasse in Cologne.
12 Leopold Cohen (1862–1942), one of Isaac Cohen's four brothers, last lived in Cologne; deported on 27 July 1942 to Theresienstadt, where he perished soon afterwards.
13 The handwriting is illegible.
14 Siegmund Cohen (1856–1942), one of Isaac Cohen's four brothers, last lived in Cologne; deported to Theresienstadt on 27 July 1942 and perished there one month later; his wife, Henriette Cohen, had died in Cologne in 1941 at the age of 80.

1 'Polizeiverordnung über die Kennzeichnung der Juden', *Reichsgesetzblatt*, 1941, 1, p. 547. This document has been translated from German.
2 The two regulations mentioned here related to the jurisdiction of the Reich Minister of the Interior and the Reich Protector regarding police regulations issued in their respective spheres of control.
3 The term 'Jew' was defined in § 5 of the First Regulation on the Reich Citizenship Law (14 Nov. 1935): see PMJ 1/210.

§ 2
Jews are forbidden
(a) to leave the district in which they are resident without carrying on their persons a written permit from the local police authority;
(b) to wear medals, decorations, and other insignia.

§ 3
§§ 1 and 2 do not apply
(a) to Jewish spouses living in a mixed marriage, if the marriage has produced offspring and these offspring are not regarded as Jews, also in cases when the marriage ends or the only son was killed in the current war;
(b) to the Jewish wife in a childless mixed marriage, for the duration of the marriage.

§ 4
(1) Anyone who intentionally or negligently contravenes the prohibition stated in §§ 1 and 2 will be punished with a fine of up to 150 Reichsmarks or imprisonment for up to six weeks.
(2) Further police security measures, as well as penal provisions under which a greater penalty is issued, are unaffected.

§ 5
The police regulation also applies in the Protectorate of Bohemia and Moravia, with the stipulation that the Reich Protector of Bohemia and Moravia can adapt the provision under § 2(a) to the local circumstances in the Protectorate of Bohemia and Moravia.

§ 6
The police regulation will take effect two weeks after its promulgation.
Berlin, 1 September 1941.
The Reich Minister of the Interior
p.p.
Heydrich

DOC. 213

On 1 September 1941 the Gauleiter's Aryanization representative informs the Israelite Religious Community of Munich about the barracks camp in Milbertshofen[1]

Letter from the Gauleiter's Aryanization representative, signed by Hauptsturmführer Wegner,[2] Munich 22, to the Israelite Religious Community, Munich 15, dated 1 September 1941 (copy)

Re: accommodation for Jews
Parts of the barracks camp under construction in Milbertshofen[3] are already occupied. In the meantime, the prerequisites for further assignment to the camp have been met.

1 BArch, R 8150/114, fols. 110–111. This document has been translated from German.

Accordingly, barracks 5, 6, 7, 9, 11, and 16, with a total of approximately 300 beds, are available for occupancy.

Therefore, on the basis of my order dated 28 August 1941,[4] as many assignments as possible are to be made to the Milbertshofen Jewish settlement.

The following guidelines are to be followed for assignment to the camp:

1.) The collective lodging for Jews in Milbertshofen is called: *Jewish settlement in Milbertshofen.*

2.) The final number of occupants will be determined in due course.[5] The aforementioned barracks are now available for occupancy. The fee for using the Jewish settlement is *RM 3 per day* per person. This sum includes the costs of the fixtures that are made available, the costs of the extensive sanitary facilities, and the installation of the shared kitchen.

3.) As a rule, the people assigned to the settlement are to be evicted apartment occupants. They will be assigned in the sequence in which their notice of eviction is served. The sequence may only be changed on exceptional grounds and if authorized.

4.) To prevent future congestion, items of furniture and clothing brought into the settlement must be kept to an absolute minimum.

5.) Administrative payments will be settled on the basis of procedure at the Berg-am-Leim.[6] One of the inmates is to be put in charge of administrative work. All completed tasks must be presented for approval.

6.) *Mr Hugo Israel Railling*[7] is appointed as camp head of the Jewish settlement in Milbertshofen. Together with the leadership of the Israelite Religious Community, he is responsible for the proper management of the settlement.

7.) Internal regulation is subject to camp rules, which are yet to be compiled.[8]

2 Johann (Hans) Wegner (1905–1956), office worker; joined the NSDAP in 1929 and the SA in 1930; trustee for the government of Upper Bavaria and the Gauleiter's representative for Aryanization matters from 1939; drafted into the Wehrmacht in 1943; sentenced by a denazification tribunal to ten years in a labour camp in 1948; released in 1952.

3 From March 1941, Jewish forced labourers were made to build a camp in the Munich district of Milbertshofen. No one was allowed to leave the camp without permission. It later served as an assembly point for deportation to the East. The first transport, carrying around 1,000 Jews, departed for Kaunas on 20 Nov. 1941. The camp was dismantled in August 1942, after almost all the inmates had been deported.

4 This order could not be found.

5 Milbertshofen had been built for a maximum of around 1,000 Jews but was frequently over crowded.

6 Correctly: Berg am Laim. From Sept. 1941 to March 1943, the 'Jewish home' was located in the Convent of the Sisters of Mercy at 9 Clemens-August-Straße in Munich, where the last occupants of Milbertshofen were taken following the liquidation of the camp. As many as 300 persons lived there in extremely cramped conditions.

7 Correctly: Hugo Railing (b. 1886), businessman; co-owner, with his brother Siegfried, of the Hahn and Bach company in Munich from 1913 and, until its sale in 1936, also of the textiles company Münchner Textildruckerei GmbH in Großhadern; imprisoned in Dachau concentration camp after the November pogroms in 1938; deported to Piaski on 4 April 1942; subsequent fate unknown.

8 These camp rules could not be found.

DOC. 214

On 3 September 1941 Friedrich Mennecke writes to his wife about a trip to Dachau concentration camp, where he inspects prisoners and selects those to be murdered[1]

Letter from Friedrich Mennecke,[2] Hotel Bayrischer Hof, Munich, to his wife,[3] dated 3 September 1941, 8:30 p.m.

Dearest Mutti,[4]

At 8 p.m. I booked an urgent call to you, and until a short time ago I was waiting downstairs in the telephone room, but I am now ensconced in room 442, so that I can speak to you from here. Hopefully you'll be on the line soon! Are you already waiting for my call? And now right away the first question: 'Was there an air-raid warning last night? And you are all right?!' Soon I will hear it from you!

Hooray! 8:45 p.m.: I already got through to you! Oh, love, the aerial torpedo sounds so scary! Hopefully something like that won't happen again – or even something worse. Always go into the cellar right away so that you stay safe for me! I told you earlier all about things. The trip here was nice, but the train was packed after Frankfurt am Main, so I sat tight in my corner and just 'watched' the whole time. I met Dr Wischer[5] at the Schottenhamel Hotel, as well as Prof. Nitsche's[6] daughter, Mrs Wilhelm. Right away we were told that Steinmeyer[7] and I were staying at the 'Bayrischer Hof'. We went to the

1 HHStAW, Abt. 631A, Nr. 1652, fols. 129–132. Published in *Friedrich Mennecke, Innenansichten eines medizinischen Täters im Nationalsozialismus: Eine Edition seiner Briefe 1935–1947*, ed. Peter Chroust, vol. 1 (Hamburg: Hamburger Institut für Sozialforschung, 1987), pp. 198–200. This document has been translated from German.

2 Dr Friedrich (Fritz) Mennecke (1904–1947), psychiatrist; joined the NSDAP and the SS in 1932; junior physician at Bad Homburg von der Höhe, 1935; senior physician, 1938; chief physician and head of Eichberg regional psychiatric hospital, 1939; SS-Hauptsturmführer, 1940; from 1940 advisor to the 'euthanasia' programme; army doctor in the Wehrmacht, 1943; arrested and sentenced to death for murder by Frankfurt Regional Court in 1946; died in prison.

3 Eva Mennecke, née Wehlan (b. 1913), technical assistant; married Friedrich Mennecke in 1937; joined the NSDAP in 1940; arrested in 1945 for collaborating with her husband on the 'euthanasia' programme; released the same year.

4 German for 'mummy', colloquial term for 'wife'.

5 Dr Gerhard Wischer (1903–1950), psychiatrist; joined the SA in 1927; involved in screening 'people with hereditary diseases' in Arnsdorf psychiatric hospital from 1934; joined the NSDAP in 1937; medical officer and director of Waldheim psychiatric hospital, 1938; one of the doctors involved in selecting patients from this hospital to be murdered, 1941–1943; arrested in 1945; sentenced to death and executed in Waldheim in 1950.

6 Dr Paul Nitsche (1876–1948), psychiatrist; senior physician at the municipal psychiatric hospital in Dresden from 1908; director of Leipzig-Dösen psychiatric hospital, 1918–1928; professor, 1925; director of Pirna-Sonnenstein psychiatric hospital, 1928–1939; joined the NSDAP in 1933; director of Leipzig-Dösen psychiatric hospital, 1940; judge at the Higher Hereditary Health Court in Dresden; from 1940 advisor to the 'euthanasia' programme and its medical director from autumn 1941; sentenced to death by Dresden Regional Court in 1947 and executed in 1948.

7 Dr Theodor Steinmeyer (1897–1945), psychiatrist; joined the NSDAP in 1929; SA regimental physician; director of Ellen psychiatric hospital in Bremen from 1934; worked at Marsberg psychiatric hospital and the child and adolescent psychiatric hospital in Niedermarsberg from 1939; advisor to the 'euthanasia' programme from 1940; worked at its Berlin headquarters, 1941–1943; manager of Pfafferode psychiatric hospital in Thuringia from 1942, involved in the selection and murder of patients; committed suicide while in US captivity.

train station at 7 p.m. to pick up Prof. Nitsche (and Prof. Heyde),[8] as well as Mrs Nitsche. They didn't come, but right after we got back to Schottenhamel, Prof. Nitsche and his wife showed up with Bauer and 'hard-working Lieschen', who had come straight from Berlin. Dr Lonauer[9] had already arrived on Monday and is staying at the Hotel 'Rheinischer Hof'. Then I came straight here to move into my room, and it turns out that Steinmeyer and I are staying in Rooms 441–443 (two single rooms plus a bathroom). Then I went back to the train station and picked up St[einmeyer], who could barely speak because of a cold. Back here again and then back to Schottenhamel to the others. The Nitsche ladies had already retired, because they wanted to continue on to the Alps early today. We men stayed up chatting together until 11:30 p.m., including Director Dr Ratka[10] from the institution in Gnesen (Warthegau), the new one working with us. I slept very well and without interruption, but first I thought for a long time about my little Mutti. This morning at 7:45 a.m., Dr Lonauer picked us up in his Olympia. We drove straight out to Dachau in the two cars. But we didn't start work today, because the SS men first have to fill out the top sections of the forms. This began today, so that we can start with the inspections tomorrow. There are only 2,000 men and the job will be finished really quickly, as they are simply glanced at as they pass by, like on a conveyor belt. At 10 a.m. we drove back into Munich and at 11 we drove on to Starnberg, where we had lunch. Then we drove to Leoni along the eastern lakefront and first visited Berg Palace, where Ludwig II lived before he drowned himself. Then further by foot, to the place on the banks where he threw himself into the water, and further still to the Bismarck tower. There we had coffee and I wrote you today's card (Steinmeyer stayed by himself in Munich). At 6 p.m. we were back here, took a little tour of the city and then sat down at 7 p.m. for dinner in the local hotel restaurant. I had beefsteak for lunch (100 grams of meat), and this evening veal liver (50 grams of meat). From tomorrow we will have lunch and dinner in the camp. At 8 p.m. the others went out because some of them wanted to go to the cinema, and I booked the call and started to write. Steinmeyer left me a note to say where he would be until 8:30. Since that is already long past, now I just want to go to the Reß wine tavern, which is right next door. There I will write some more. Kisses – ahoy!!

9:50 p.m. 'Kunstgewerbehaus inn, Eberspacher wine tavern, leaseholder: Martin Modlmayer': this is the Reß wine tavern, very pleasant and well frequented. I just had the leaseholder sent over to me so that I could speak with him. This place is 100 m from my hotel, and they only do wine, but no Rheingau, only Niersteiner and Westhofner, so

8 Dr Werner Heyde (1902–1964), psychiatrist; joined the NSDAP in 1933; assistant in the Racial Policy Office of the NSDAP from 1934; joined the SS in 1936; from 1939 professor and director of Würzburg university clinic, medical director of the 'euthanasia' programme, 1939–1941; practised medicine in Flensburg after 1950 under the name Dr Fritz Sawade; chief expert at Schleswig Regional Social Court; arrested in 1959; committed suicide while awaiting trial.

9 Dr Rudolf Lonauer (1907–1945), psychiatrist; joined the NSDAP in 1933 and the SS in 1937; from 1938 manager of Niedernhart (Linz) psychiatric hospital; from 1940 head of Hartheim 'euthanasia' killing centre; advisor to the 'euthanasia' programme; SS-Hauptsturmführer, 1942; member of the Waffen SS from 1942; committed suicide with his wife.

10 Dr Viktor Ratka (1895–1966), psychiatrist; 'ethnic German'; senior physician at Lubliniec psychiatric hospital (in the Polish part of Upper Silesia), 1928; director of the Tiegenhof (Dziekanka) killing centre at Gnesen; joined the SA in 1940; SA staff surgeon; advisor to the 'euthanasia' programme from 1941; joined the NSDAP in 1943.

Rheinhessen, and a lot of Pfalz, Mosel, and red wine. Planes have been flying constantly over Munich for the past hour, but they are German training flights; the towers of the Mariahilf Church are beaming brightly. This wine tavern is a goldmine for sure. The Reß brothers will certainly bring in an overblown rent, because there is much more drinking done here than in Eberbach and Hattenheim put together. As I said to you on the phone earlier, I will get an earlier train on Sunday. I haven't made fixed plans yet. It will be the one that you mentioned. I'll call you from Wiesbaden or Eltville. Our provisions for the trip to Warsaw, liver sausage, butter, etc., can also be got together on Monday morning so that they are fresh to take with us. Some things can also be prepared beforehand for the sandwiches, which – please – you are to make.

I want to stop now, because Mr Steinmeyer just came over to keep me company. Please, my dear Mutti, stay healthy and safe for me!!! Always go swiftly into the cellar! My biggest, dearest kisses!

Your faithful Fritz-Pa.

DOC. 215

On 7 September 1941 Julius Jacoby reports to the Reich Association of Jews in Germany on the situation in the 'Jew houses' in Hanover[1]

Report by Julius Israel Jacoby,[2] Hanover, dated 7 September 1941 (copy)

Travel report
Re: resettlement campaign for the Jewish population in Hanover
On 6–7 September of this year, I travelled to Hanover at the behest of the Reich Association, and I have the following to report: the resettlement campaign has been completed. All of the Jews in Hanover (around 1,600) are now concentrated in fifteen houses.[3] Out of these fifteen accommodation sites, I visited six locations of different grades in order to gain an objective picture, along with Dr Schleisner[4] and in part with Community Secretary Herkovitz.[5]

1 BArch, R 8150/113, fols. 196–197. This document has been translated from German.
2 Julius Jacoby (1882–1943); Regierungsrat and building officer; employee of the welfare department of the Reich Association of Jews in Germany; deported on 17 March 1943 to Theresienstadt, where he perished.
3 At the beginning of September 1941, in the course of Operation Lauterbach, named after the Gauleiter of Southern Hanover-Braunschweig and Oberpräsident of Hanover, Hartmann Lauterbacher (1909–1988), more than 1,000 Jews had been forced to leave their homes within twenty-four to forty-eight hours and to move into six buildings (originally fifteen addresses were planned), the so-called Jew houses (*Judenhäuser*).
4 Dr Max Schleisner (1885–1943), lawyer; practised law in Hanover from 1912, board member of Hanover Jewish Community, and its first chairman from 1938 onwards; representative of the Reich Association of Jews in Hanover, 1939; emigration advisor for the Relief Association of Jews in Germany; deported on 17 March 1943 to Theresienstadt, where he perished four months later.
5 Correctly: Samuel Herskovits (1883–1944), community official; grew up in Transylvania; rabbinical training in Bratislava around 1903; emigrated to Hamburg around 1905; from 1909 worked in the office of the Jewish Community in Hanover; served as its secretary from 1924; deported on 30 June 1943 to Theresienstadt and on 27 July 1944 to Auschwitz, where he was murdered.

8 Bergstraße (previously offices of the Reich Association, the District Office of Hanover, a synagogue, and also a gymnasium).
Overcrowding. Bed next to bed, no space to pass between them. No segregation by sex; married and unmarried, old and young, children and infants are housed indiscriminately in the gymnasium and in narrow galleries. Emergency exits blocked. Tables and chairs are lacking due to a shortage of space. People mostly sit on the beds and also eat their meals there. Meals are prepared in a laundry room located 4 m below street level. Unhygienic storerooms. No air-raid shelter, because this space is being used for the kitchen and provisions. Four water taps and five toilets for all occupants, including employees of the Reich Association. Nowhere to do laundry. Of 134 people admitted, so far 90 have been housed, and with that it is already overcrowded.[6]
3 Lützowstr. (formerly a community centre and school).
Again, excessive occupancy, not even 3 m^2 of floor space per person. For example, in one room with 42 m^2 floor space there are five adults, a family of five, and a family of four, fourteen people altogether. People are also in the open attic, a major fire hazard. Multiple people are sharing one bed, tuberculosis patients. Adequate toilets, because there are six former school lavatories in the courtyard. Ninety-five people admitted, totalling 125 people with the previous inhabitants.[7]
12 Schelvinstr.[8] (older residential building, mixed with Aryan families)
Cooking is done in small kitchens, in which people actually have to live. Bedbugs, otherwise as it was before. Fifty-eight people admitted, totalling seventy-six people with those who already lived there.
61 Knochenhauserstr. (old half-timbered building, falling apart inside).
Bedbugs, rats, toilets are completely inadequate from a hygienic perspective. Four people and one child in a room of only 15 m^2. There is a severely crippled man among the occupants. Two Aryan families in the building. Twenty-nine people admitted, totalling thirty-five people with those who lived there previously.
24 Körnerstr.
In itself a good residential building in a good residential area, but the same overcrowding as mentioned above. Example: ten people and one child in a 30 m^2 room. One lavatory for thirty people. Windows partially blocked by furniture. Impeded ventilation. Aryan families in the same building. Ninety people admitted. With the previous 19 inhabitants, 109 people.[9]

6 Of the people who were crowded together at 8 Bergstraße, eighty-nine were deported to Riga on 15 Dec. 1941. Until 23 July 1942, approximately forty Jews still lived in the building, then sixteen of them were subsequently deported to Theresienstadt and the others had to move to other 'Jew houses'.

7 Teaching at the Jewish primary school was discontinued in Sept. 1941, when the building was repurposed as a 'Jew house'. Ninety-eight of the inhabitants were deported to Riga on 15 December 1941. Those who remained had to move to other 'Jew houses'.

8 Correctly: Scholvinstraße.

9 Non-Jewish tenants lived in the houses at 12 Scholvinstraße, 61 Knochenhauerstraße, and 24 Körnerstraße even after they were repurposed as 'Jew houses'. Most of the Jews quartered there had to leave Hanover in the first transport to Riga on 15 Dec. 1941. The rest had to move to other 'Jew houses'. Only 61 Knochenhauerstraße was vacated with the transport to Theresienstadt on 23 July 1942.

Israelite Hospital and Home for the Elderly, 14 Ellernstr.
Among the best accommodation on account of the sanitary facilities of the hospital being available. The patient ward has not been touched. The general attempt to carry out gender separation could not be entirely implemented. There are two married couples and individual people housed in each of three rooms. The hospital is already overcrowded as a result of necessary admissions.[10]
Summary:
With overcrowding and unhygienic conditions, there is a danger of epidemics. Prompt improvement appears necessary. This can only be achieved by approving more housing for the Jewish population. Dr Schleisner suggested houses at 5 Körnerstr. (a former home for the elderly), 11 and 12 Wisemannstr. (also property of the Reich Association, formerly the Simon Foundation). Furthermore, it would be useful if the accommodation of the Jewish population and the distribution of housing could be left to the Community, and longer deadlines afforded for redistribution.[11]

DOC. 216
In a letter dated 8 September 1941, Franz Bergmann from Neheim an der Ruhr criticizes the murder of psychiatric patients[1]

Letter, signed by Franz Bergmann, Neheim, to the Deputy General Command of the VI Army Corps,[2] Department of the Chief of Staff, Münster-Westphalia, dated 8 September 1941 (copy)[3]

Re: eradication of the mentally ill[4]
The murmurings about this grave and far-reaching problem are never-ending. They have now penetrated every home, ever since the Church, from a higher viewpoint, declared its religious and moral veto against it and described each such act as *vile murder.*[5]

The '*Hess affair*' did not depress and shock the people as a whole as much as this event has done.[6] Men who are gladly willing to make concessions in hopeless cases are quaking in the face of the horror that addresses them from this ice-cold, rationalistic,

10 Correctly: 16 Ellernstraße. The hospital remained in operation. The number of people accommodated here increased from around 90 to over 200. Of these, 52 were taken to Riga on 15 Dec. 1941, and the remaining 148 to Theresienstadt on 23 July 1942.
11 The deportation of the Jews of Hanover began in Nov. 1941. The number of 'Jew houses' was subsequently reduced, and the measures suggested in the report were never taken.

1 BArch, RH 14/46, fol. 47. Facsimile published in Bernward Dörner, *Die Deutschen und der Holocaust: Was niemand wissen wollte, aber jeder wissen konnte* (Berlin: Propyläen, 2007), p. 803. This document has been translated from German.
2 The chief of the general staff from Jan. 1941 to July 1942 was Hans Degen (1899–1971), a colonel on the general staff.
3 The original contains handwritten annotations and the stamp 'Secret!'
4 On the murder of institutionalized patients in the context of the 'euthanasia' programme, see Introduction, pp. 32 f.
5 This refers to the sermon delivered on 3 August 1941 by Count Clemens August von Galen, Bishop of Münster, who openly criticized the 'euthanasia' murders.
6 In May 1941, Rudolf Hess had flown to Scotland, allegedly to engineer peace negotiations with Britain. He remained in British captivity until the end of the war.

and uncompromising stance. There is also the feverish imagination that continues to spin the threads once they have been caught, already wreaking havoc in homes for cripples and the elderly, killing off people with tuberculosis and cancer, and not even stopping at the blessed head of the infirm mother. Indeed, this conduct has already been transferred from the imagination to our *field hospitals at the front*. In every conceivable variation, this rumour has pervaded German lands, weakening the people's morale most severely. Hope and faith in the benediction of the Party are melting away *like snow in the sun*. Germany cherished a sheer, unshakeable confidence, and it seems to want to carry this to the grave.

No one knows what induced our government to tread this path. Some say that the mental hospitals had to be cleared out because of the *many mentally-ill aviation officers*; others speak of *economic measures concerning our sustenance*. Yet all of this fails to have the desired effect. These objections are easily parried with reference to the *many millions of Jews* who are still in the country. Why is this scum of humanity still living while our patients are simply killed? Who here wants to advocate for the Jews?

Above all it is Party Comrade *Himmler* who the people are incriminating for this act. Whether rightly or wrongly, I cannot say of course. *They (the people) categorically reject this man, in whom they plainly see the incarnation of evil.* The extent to which the *international adversary* has contributed to this view is difficult to determine.

The *army and its leadership*, on the other hand, are highly regarded among the people. Here, a mighty tower of unconditional trust is being established. The army is, in a sense, the unmoveable rock in the drive of surging waves.

By contrast, people view the German *medical profession* with *unmistakable distrust*. People know very well that here there were always voices actively issuing propaganda for the eradication of the mentally ill. These voices maintained that the capital invested in the mentally ill should be freed up for other purposes, purposes that would bring doctors more active capital turnover. For the medical profession revealed its true face during the *Systemzeit*,[7] when the bank account was its all. This is of course an invalid generalization. Nevertheless, it seems that the morphine injection is set to become a horrifying symbol of the profession. People have recognized the devil's hoof and they are reacting accordingly.

Heil Hitler!

7 German for 'system era': a term used by the National Socialists to refer disparagingly to the period of the Weimar Republic.

DOC. 217

On 10 September 1941 Hermann Samter writes to Lisa Godehardt about the travel ban and the requirement for Jews to wear the yellow star[1]

Letter from Hermann Samter to Lisa Godehardt, dated 10 September 1941

Dear Lisa,

I just realized that I have not yet thanked you for the lovely sausage. It tasted excellent, as always, and made it much easier for me to manage with the ration book.

Is the *Koralle*[2] arriving regularly? Neither you nor your mother[3] wrote about it. –

Unfortunately, I postponed my holiday, and now it's over with travel: beginning on the 19th we are not allowed to leave our place of residence without written police authorization. So we can no longer even go to Potsdam or Bernau. Beginning on the same day, Jews have to wear a sewn-on, yellow Star of David the size of one's palm, with the inscription 'Jew'.[4]

Now I cannot buy a newspaper except between the hours of 4 and 5, or go for a meal at a restaurant, or visit Aryan acquaintances.

There are yet other unpleasant consequences that you can picture for yourself. But as far as I am concerned, people should have their fun.

Now we need to be home by 9 in the evening in any event, and by 8 from 1 October! –

I had a really nice letter from Sylvia and her Aunt Anke (do you know her?).

She also doesn't know why Lotte and Paul[5] are not in the USA yet. But both of them are said to be doing well.

Regards – also to your mother and Roswitha –

1 Holocaust Memorial Center, Farmington Hills, MI; copy in YVA, 0.2/30, fol. 7. Published in Samter, *Briefe*, p. 67. This document has been translated from German.

2 *Illustrierte Koralle: Bilderzeitung für Kultur und Sport, Natur und Reisen, Heimat und Ferne* (Magazine for Culture and Sport, Nature and Travel, Home and Abroad).

3 Karolina Stadermann.

4 See Docs. 212 and 222.

5 Charlotte and Paul Blumenfeld.

DOC. 218

The NSDAP's weekly slogan for 7 to 13 September 1941 evokes Hitler's prophecy that European Jewry would be annihilated in the event of a world war[1]

Weekly slogan of the NSDAP for 7 to 13 September 1941[2]

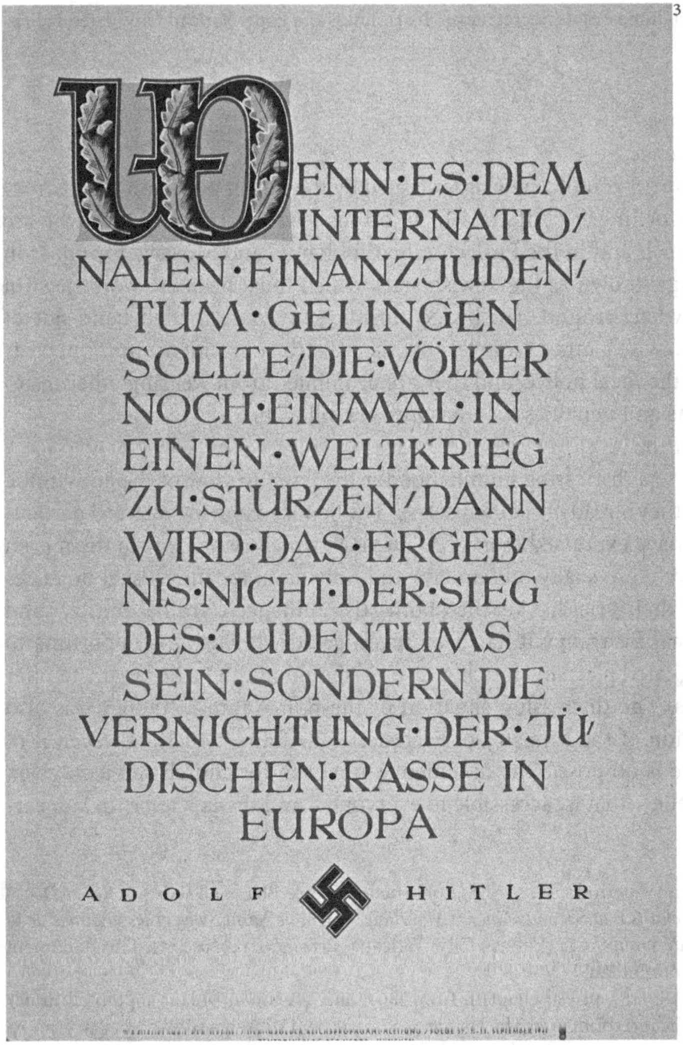

[3]

1 BArch, NSD 74/3. This document has been translated from German.
2 The weekly slogan of the NSDAP, which appeared between 1937 and 1944, always contained a quotation from Hitler or another leading Nazi, and these slogans were posted in public display cases. From 1939, there was a standardized weekly slogan across the Reich.
3 The text reads: 'If the international Jewish financiers should succeed in plunging the nations once more into a world war, then the outcome will not be the victory of Jewry but rather the annihilation of the Jewish race in Europe. Adolf Hitler.'

DOC. 219

On 13 September 1941 the apostolic nuncio tells Cardinal Luigi Maglione at the Vatican how humiliating it is for non-Aryan Christians in particular to be required to wear the yellow star[1]

Letter no. 1504 (42321) from Apostolic Nuncio Cesare Orsenigo,[2] Berlin, to His Most Reverend Eminence Cardinal Luigi Maglione,[3] State Secretary of His Holiness the Pope, Vatican City, dated 13 September 1941[4]

Re: new anti-Jewish laws

Most Reverend Eminence,

It is my duty to inform you of a new order issued by the Berlin police on the instructions of the Ministry for Internal Affairs, which forbids Jews aged six and over who are still resident in the Reich and in the Protectorate of Bohemia and Moravia to appear in public without a badge known as the 'Jewish star', which must bear the word 'Jew' in black against a yellow background. The badge must be sewn onto the left-hand side of the jacket. Jews are likewise banned from leaving their district of residence without written permission from the local police, and they are prohibited from wearing other insignia. A few exemptions and penalties for transgressors follow below.

I enclose a copy of the law.[5]

This law is of course a distressing humiliation for the Jews, in view of the antisemitic atmosphere in which they already find themselves. The baptised non-Aryans feel particularly bewildered and have expressed their great anguish, which remains with them even when they enter church, especially on Sundays and holy days, for their usual practices of devotion. News of their grief has reached both His Eminence Cardinal Innitzer and His Eminence Cardinal Bertram.[6] It has been investigated whether it is opportune to grant the Jews a designated place in church or even – should numbers be large – to offer them private services. The distressing situation of the non-Aryan Catholics was also brought to the attention of the Ministry of Ecclesiastical Affairs, which, however, is of the opinion that there is no possibility of leniency, not even for church services, given that these too are public – that is, accessible to everyone – and the law refers to 'appear-

1 ASV, A.E.S., Germania IV periodo, Bl. 50+RS. Published in Pierre Blet et al. (eds.), *Actes et Documents du Saint Siège relatifs à la Seconde Guerre Mondiale*, vol. 8: *Le Saint Siège et les victimes de la guerre, janvier 1941 – décembre 1942* (Vatican City: Vaticana, 1974), no. 149, p. 275 f. This document has been translated from Italian.

2 Cesare Orsenigo (1873–1946), priest; chaplain from 1897, later pastor in Milan; appointed titular bishop in 1922; apostolic internuncio in The Hague, 1922–1925, and subsequently in Hungary; apostolic nuncio in Berlin, 1930–1945.

3 Dr Luigi Maglione (1877–1944), Catholic theologian; acting papal representative at the League of Nations and envoy to Switzerland from 1918; appointed nuncio in 1920; from 1926 to 1935 nuncio in France; appointed cardinal, 1935; prefect of the Sacred Congregation of the Council, 1938; cardinal state secretary, 1939–1944.

4 The original contains handwritten annotations.

5 See Doc. 212.

6 Adolf Bertram (1859–1945), Catholic theologian; bishop of Hildesheim, 1906–1914; prince-bishop of Breslau from 1914; became cardinal in 1916, officially appointed in 1919; chairman of the Fulda Conference of Bishops, 1919–1945; archbishop of Breslau, 1930–1945.

ing in public'. His Eminence Signor Cardinal Bertram looked into the proposal of approaching the Minister for Internal Affairs with a petition, but fears that this is futile.

Kissing the Sacred Purple, I have the honour to remain Your Eminence's most humble and devoted servant[7]

DOC. 220
A poem, dated 14 September 1941, calls upon Jews to wear the yellow star with trust in God[1]

Mogen Dovid[2]

A newly shining star appears to light the sky
above this world of rage and hateful violence,
in which the air resounds with death's dejected cry,
in which your call, sweet peace, is hushed to silence,
in which the clarion sends a cruel and dreadful sound,
death floods the world as bloodily it rages.
And yet the star is old, though seemingly new-found:
the Maccabee[3] star, every Jew's star through the ages.

It's meant now as a penal load on each Jew's chest,
intended as a mark of malediction;
to rob us of life's joys we love the best;
reduce us to the sum of each affliction
that fills us with such worry, suffering and pain
far worse than in the days that were much older.
Yet we're devoted to that star, time and again.
We'll wear it ever firmly trusting God, and ever bolder.

It is the Mogen Dovid, bright and holy star,
to which we gaze aloft in supplication,
which roams forever in the heavens broad and far,
which stands as our millennia-old foundation.

7 The valediction is written by hand.

1 StA Mü, Familien 807. This document has been translated from German.
2 Ashkenazi pronunciation of Magen David, Hebrew for Shield of David. The poem was presumably written by Joseph Schachno, in whose literary estate it was found: Joseph Schachno (1876–1942), businessman; managed a womanswear business; moved from Nuremberg to Munich in 1935; deported on 22 July 1942 to Theresienstadt, where he perished.
3 Judas Maccabeus (died 160 BCE), Jewish freedom fighter in Judea, after whom the revolt of the Maccabees in the second century BCE is named; the rebellion was sparked by the religious edict of Antiochus IV, which required Jews to renounce their religion.

Not as a hurtful shame upon our chest it weighs.
Forever in God's nearness it's remaining.
We must be firmly mindful of this truth always:
The Mogen Dovid shines on high for us, unwaning.

But those who don't wear David's Star under duress –
the holy sign is not a duty for them –
they don't feel far from Judaism nonetheless,
Their Star of David's always in full sight, before them.
When in the coming days the shofar's[4] call sounds clear and bright,
we'll heed the message that the Mogen Dovid's giving:
The thing that now is meant to be our blight
shall be our star of hope as long as we are living.

Munich, 14 September 1941
Devoted and dedicated to Director Stahl[5]

DOC. 221
On 14 September 1941 Daniel Lotter from Fürth criticizes the introduction of the requirement for Jews to wear the yellow star[1]

Diary of Daniel Lotter,[2] Fürth, entry for 14 September 1941

Today Franz's[3] passing was commemorated in a very dignified and moving way in the service at St Michael's Church.

The losses in Russia are immense. Obituaries are piling up in the newspaper, and the mood in the country is becoming gloomy in view of the threat of a third winter of war. In conversation, one frequently hears that the war will not end well. The newspapers only report favourable things, of course, and the successes of our Wehrmacht in Russia

4 A shofar is a ram's horn that is blown on the Jewish High Holy Days of Rosh Hashanah (New Year) and at the end of Yom Kippur (the Day of Atonement). In 1941 both holidays fell in the second half of September.
5 Karl Stahl (1882–1944), qualified engineer and businessman; director of the winemaking company Vereinigte Keltereien AG from 1918; took over a wine wholesaler in 1937; his business was closed down after the November pogroms of 1938; co-founder and chairman of the Munich branch of the Reich League of Jewish Combat Veterans; on its board from March 1938; chairman of the Jewish Community of Munich, 1941; deported on 17 June 1942 to Theresienstadt, where he was a member of the Council of Elders; deported on 12 October 1944 to Auschwitz, where he was murdered.

1 Original privately owned; copy in IfZ-Archives, F 601; typewritten version in the Deutsches Tagebucharchiv in Emmendingen. This document has been translated from German.
2 Johann Daniel Lotter (1873–1953), lebkuchen baker; took over his parents' lebkuchen bakery in Fürth in 1897; joined the Masonic Lodge 'Truth and Friendship' in Fürth in 1901; on the supervisory board of a purchasing cooperative in Fürth; member of the church administration of the Evangelical-Lutheran parish of St Michael's from 1929.
3 Franz Segitz (1912–1941), Daniel Lotter's son-in-law; killed in action in the Soviet Union on 18 August 1941.

continue. St Petersburg is surrounded, and the toll of sunken English cargo ships remains very high. But bad news is also seeping through: England is trying to prise Italy away. The Duke of Aosta, a brother of the Italian king who was taken prisoner in Abyssinia, is said to have been sent to Italy on an aeroplane to take care of negotiations. Mussolini's four-day visit to the German headquarters is surely connected to these negotiations.[4]

Last Thursday, Roosevelt delivered a broadcast address. The wording has been withheld from the German public, as usual, but even according to German reports, its menacing and strident tone surpassed everything that the US president has said up to now.[5]

Japan – whose intervention in the war was to be reckoned with in the event of a US attack, according to the Tripartite Pact[6] – is conducting negotiations with America, initiated by Tenno's[7] special envoy to Roosevelt. A Japanese newspaper writes with utter composure: 'America's intervention in the European war is within the realm of possibility. First, however, America must sort out its relationship with Japan; the USA is not prepared for a two-front war.'[8] So the Japanese seem to consider it completely fine to bail out when favourable conditions are put in place for them.

Recently, the Volga Germans have been treated in the most inhumane manner, having already been reduced in number from 2½ million to 400,000 as a result of barbaric treatment by the Russians. They are set to be 'transplanted' to Siberia, which will surely mean the certain demise of these remaining brave German Volksgenossen.[9]

Of course nor do our rulers refrain from treating foreign races in an appalling manner. After taking from the German Jews their businesses, property, and most of their assets, and robbing them of every source of income, on 19 September a regulation is due to take effect that requires them to wear a yellow star with the inscription 'Jew', visible and tightly sewn on.[10] What they seek to achieve with such pointless and sadistic torments is a mystery to me. In order to have the regulation make a particularly malicious impact, they are implementing it on the so-called 'long day', the Day of Atonement and highest holy day of the Jews.[11]

4 Amedeo of Savoy, Duke of Aosta (1898–1942), viceroy of Italian-occupied Abyssinia from November 1937. In May 1941, he and his troops surrendered to the British army, and he was taken captive. On the meeting between Hitler and Mussolini in August 1941, see Doc. 206, fn. 10.

5 On 11 Sept. 1941 Roosevelt announced that he had granted the navy permission to attack German ships if they were approaching American waters or ships under the US flag: *New York Times*, 12 Sept. 1941, pp. 1 and 4. See also *Völkischer Beobachter* (northern German edition), 14 September 1941, p. 1, and *Frankfurter Zeitung*, 14 Sept. 1941, pp. 1–2.

6 On 27 Sept. 1940 the German Reich, Italy, and Japan concluded a pact in which they assured mutual recognition of the 'new order' that was to be created in Europe and East Asia.

7 Title of the Emperor of Japan; from 1926–1989 this was Hirohito (1901–1989).

8 The front page of the *Frankfurter Zeitung* on 14 Sept. 1941 reported on corresponding articles in the Japanese print media.

9 Between August and Oct. 1941, Stalin had the so-called Volga Germans deported from their home areas to Siberia and Central Asia. On 28 Oct. 1941, the Volga German Autonomous Soviet Socialist Republic (established in 1924) was dissolved.

10 See Doc. 212.

11 On 19 Sept. 1941, Rosh Hashanah (Jewish New Year) was imminent; Yom Kippur (the Day of Atonement) fell on 1 Oct.

DOC. 222

On 15 September 1941 the Reich Minister of the Interior restricts freedom of movement for Jews and sets out conditions applying to the use of transport[1]

Express letter (marked 'confidential! immediate! deadline! not suitable for publication!') from the Reich Ministry of the Interior (IV B 4 b Nr. 940/41–6), p.p. signed Heydrich, Berlin, to 1) all Gestapo (head) offices, 2) the Central Office for Jewish Emigration in Vienna, 3) the Central Office for Jewish Emigration in Prague, 4) the Reichsstatthalter and state governments, except for Prussia, 5) the Prussian Regierungspräsidenten (including Kattowitz and Zichenau, and the Chief of Police in Berlin), and 6) the Reich Commissioner for the Westmark, dated 15 September 1941

Re: Police Regulation on the Visible Identification of Jews, 1 September 1941 (*Reichsgesetzblatt*, I, p. 547)[2]
Enclosures: each – 2 – (models A, B).[3]
In order to implement the Police Regulation on the Visible Identification of Jews, issued on 1 September 1941 (*Reichsgesetzblatt*, I, p. 547), I hereby issue the following guidelines concerning the use of public transport, in consultation with the Reich Minister of Transport, the Reich Postmaster General, and the Reich Minister of Aviation:[4]

I. *Visible identification of Jews*
a) Instructions for wearing and distribution:
The badges are to be worn by Jews on the left-hand side of the chest, approximately at the level of the heart, tightly sewn on and visible at all times in public. The term 'public' includes private air-raid shelters, not only those that are accessible to everyone; this should be kept in mind as up to now a great many problems have arisen precisely in these shelters as a result of Jews not wearing the badges. Jews are to be instructed to always treat their badges with care, and to keep them clean. The Central Offices for Jewish Emigration in Berlin, Vienna, and Prague will be in charge of distributing the badges in cooperation with the Reich Association of Jews in Germany and the Jewish Communities of Vienna and Prague.
b) Violations:
Deliberate violations of the regulation or the corresponding implementing provisions, such as these, are to be punished categorically with protective custody. In the case of violations by Jews who cannot yet be held criminally responsible due to their young age, the Jewish guardian is liable to prosecution, according to the provisions of § 4 of the Supplementary Regulation to the Juvenile Criminal Law, dated 4 October 1940 (*Reichsgesetzblatt*, I, p. 1336).[5]

1 BArch, R 58/276, fn. 282–288. This document has been translated from German.
2 See Doc. 212.
3 BArch, R 58/276, fols. 289–290.
4 Julius Dorpmüller (1869–1945), Wilhelm Ohnesorge, and Hermann Göring.
5 According to § 4 of the Supplementary Regulation to the Juvenile Criminal Law, violation of the duty of supervision of persons under 18 years of age could be punished by six months' imprisonment or a fine, if the person to be supervised had committed a criminal offence that could have been prevented by supervision.

The offices of the state and civil administration must take all necessary steps to prevent unauthorized, unlawful excesses against the Jews who are now visibly marked with the badges. The Party Chancellery will ensure the same for the NSDAP. Strict measures will be taken against violations of this kind.

II. *Restriction on leaving the place of residence and use of transport (§ 2 of the regulation)*
Jurisdiction:
The Gestapo offices can allow Jews to leave their places of residence with a permit in order to attend to private affairs. This also includes granting permission to Jews who must leave their residential municipality on business as members of officially recognized Jewish organizations (for example, the Reich Association of Jews). Within the boundaries of the Reich Capital Berlin, the Chief of the Security Police and the SD (Central Office for Jewish Emigration in Berlin)[6] is responsible for authorizing business trips.

Under § 2 of the regulation, the Central Office for Jewish Emigration in Vienna will take over responsibility from the local police authorities for granting permission to leave the place of residence and for the use of public transport in the Vienna Reichsgau.

In all other cases, local responsibility for issuing written permission lies with the local police authority in the district where the applicant has his place of residence or, if he has no fixed abode, where he is currently staying. In municipalities under State Police administration, permission is granted by the State Police authorities.

a) *Prerequisites for granting permission to leave the residential municipality:*
Permits may only be issued to Jews who present one of the following identification documents: for German nationals, a passport, child identification card, identification card, or official photo identification card; for residents of the Białystok district, a passport or official photo identification card; for non-nationals of the Reich, a passport or a valid substitute, according to general German passport regulations.

Permits can only be granted upon proof of the irrefutable necessity of leaving the place of residence. Reasons may include: employment, attested by an official certificate from the employment office responsible; official summons or arrangements that make it necessary to leave the place of residence, which the Jew must likewise prove by submitting an official certificate to the issuing authority or office; essential business trips by members of officially recognized Jewish organizations; economic reasons, insofar as a certificate from the relevant Chamber of Industry and Commerce, Chamber of Skilled Crafts, or another official agency is presented; other personal or family reasons, such as serious illness or the serious illness or death of a close relative, whereupon in each individual case an official certificate (for example, from the medical officer) is to be produced.

b) *Prerequisites for granting permission for the use of means of transport outside the place of residence:*
In all cases, it is up to the issuing office to decide which means of transport the Jew is allowed to use, and this is to be noted in the permit. When taking this decision, the current transport situation is to be taken into consideration.

Accordingly, the use of taxis and hired cars (§ 39(1) to (4) of the Implementing Regulation to the Law on Passenger Transport by Land, dated 26 March 1935 – *Reichsgesetzblatt*, I,

6 The reference is to the Reich Central Agency for Jewish Emigration.

p. 473),[7] vehicles on inland roads and marine waterways, as well as aeroplanes, is not to be allowed as a general rule, i.e. only when there is an irrefutable necessity. Therefore, the use of taxis and hired cars (excluding hired omnibuses and hired lorries) is to be authorized regularly only for doctors; midwives; severely physically disabled people, particularly those with war disabilities (amputated legs, paralysed, etc.); people who are seriously ill and companions to people of German blood who are ill or physically disabled. The transportation of Jews by hired omnibuses or hired lorries can generally only be authorized in connection with the Jews' deployment in segregated work squads or similar circumstances, and the Jews' employer must submit a collective application for all individuals to the authority in charge. The use of vehicles on inland roads and marine waterways is likewise to be limited to what is absolutely essential. Air travel is, in principle, prohibited to Jews as well. Only in particularly urgent exceptional cases can an exception be made here. However, even in cases where the Jew has a police permit for air travel, it is still at Lufthansa's[8] discretion, as per the regulations previously in place, to exclude the Jew for reasons to do with the current transport situation. If Lufthansa is not to be granted this possibility of exclusion, it is to be informed of this in good time, in writing. Jews required to wear visible markers are completely excluded from transportation in excursion vehicles (§ 39(2) loc. cit.) and from the use of postal buses (§ 2(5) loc. cit.).[9]

If permission to use transport is necessary at all, Jews are therefore limited to the railway, tram (section II, number 1 of the Law on Passenger Transport by Land, dated 6 December 1937, *Reichsgesetzblatt*, I, p. 1319),[10] and transportation by land (section II, number 2, loc. cit.), as well as long-distance transport (§ 39(3) of the Implementing Regulation to the Law on Passenger Transport by Land, dated 26 March 1935, *Reichsgesetzblatt*, I, p. 473).[11] The licensing authority, the Reich Postal Service, and the Reich Railways can also limit this transportation of Jews to certain days, hours, and routes, or in other ways.[12]

Permits:

Permits are to be issued as per the attached sample A, free of charge. In the case of the collective transport of Jews, a collective permit is to be issued in the appropriate manner. Procurement is to be regulated locally, and it is to be left to the respective authorities whether the permits will be duplicated or printed.

Permission to leave the place of residence and to use transport is, as a rule, only to be granted in specific cases, with precise specifications of the length of time and the local area. In special cases, permission can be granted for a longer period, with a maximum validity of three months and within a specified transport network, as well as for repeated departure from the place of residence or repeated use of means of transport, if

7 The corresponding paragraph defines taxis, hired cars, and other vehicles: *Reichsgesetzblatt*, 1935, 1, pp. 473–479, here p. 478.

8 Under National Socialism Lufthansa was a state-owned airline.

9 Excursion vehicles are defined in the corresponding paragraph as 'omnibuses on public roads and squares that are kept ready for public transportation', while postal buses are defined as 'motor vehicles serving the routes of the Reich Postal Service'.

10 Section II of the law includes various special provisions regarding transportation conditions in trams and scheduled public transport services: *Reichsgesetzblatt*, 1937, 1, pp. 1319–1323.

11 Long-distance vehicles are defined in § 39(3) of the regulation: *Reichsgesetzblatt*, 1935, 1, pp. 473–479.

12 On travel restrictions for Jews, see Doc. 158.

the unavoidable necessity of this is proved. Permits cannot be extended; a new permit must be issued if required. The place and date, the official stamp, and the signature of the issuing official must all be included on the permit.

The Jew must return the permit to the issuing authority when it becomes invalid following the expiry of the prescribed period or after the completion of the Jew's travel outside the place of residence. Specific lists of the permits issued are to be kept by the issuing authority. Permits presented by the applicant as proof of the unavoidable necessity of leaving the place of residence etc. are to be added to the files, unless it is absolutely necessary to return them to the Jew in individual cases, whereupon a short note should be recorded in the file, along with transcripts of the presented permits, if possible.

Provision for the carriage of persons by means of transport and the use of transport facilities:

From the start of travel, or upon the purchase and inspection of tickets, Jews defined as such under the terms of the regulation are to show their police permit unprompted, along with official photo identification. If possible, the transport carrier or operator is to ensure that, upon the start of travel or upon the purchase of the ticket, utilization of the means of transport is indicated on the police permit by inscription or stamp, so that improper use is precluded. Jews are not allowed to use means of transport from which they are excluded by the transport carrier or operator; they must occupy specific seats in the means of transport if they are instructed to do so. Irrespective of further restrictions, Jews are allowed to use waiting rooms, restaurants, and other facilities within transport establishments only if they are allowed to make use of the means of transport itself.

c) *Local police permission for use of means of transport within the place of residence: General remarks*:

In substance the restrictions and guidelines regarding travel from the place of residence and use of transport outlined above must also be applied to the use of public transport by Jews within their places of residence, in order to prevent Jews from improperly and self-servingly using means of transport that must essentially be reserved for the German population. In all cases, local police authorities are responsible for granting this permission for the use of certain means of transport. Within the municipality of residence, Jews can only apply for police permission to use taxis and hired cars (including omnibuses and lorries for hire), as well as craft on inland waterways. These rules are to be strictly applied as a matter of course. Permits for the use of means of transport within the place of residence are to be issued as per the attached sample B, free of charge.

III. *Nationality*

Pending another provision, Jews of foreign nationality are not subject to the terms of the regulation, with the exception of Jews in the territories of Eupen-Malmedy and Moresnet who have Belgian nationality, and those who have Soviet-Russian nationality in the district of Bialystok, which has been incorporated into the province of East Prussia.[13]

13 On Eupen-Malmedy, see Doc. 83. The same conditions applied to Moresnet. After the invasion of the Soviet Union, on 1 August 1941 the district of Białystok was placed under the control of the Gauleiter of East Prussia, Erich Koch.

IV. *Subject to further provisions*
The right to issue additional ordinances is reserved. In respect thereof, measures that go further than those that have been established thus far should not be taken. Further provisions regarding the use of means of transport will be issued by the Reich Minister of Transport, the Reich Postmaster General, and the Reich Minister of Aviation. The Protectorate of Bohemia and Moravia is subject to a separate provision by the Reich Protector of Bohemia and Moravia.

Addendum:

a) To the Reichsstatthalter and state governments – with the exception of Prussia,
b) To the Prussian Regierungspräsidenten (including Kattowitz and Zichenau, and the Chief of Police in Berlin),
c) To the Reich Commissioner for the Westmark,
 – each individually –
 I request that subordinate authorities, particularly local police authorities, are immediately informed of these guidelines.
d) To the Reich Protector:
 I request that a corresponding order be issued in the Protectorate of Bohemia and Moravia. Copies of the local decrees in these territories are to be sent.
e) To the chiefs of the civil administration in Strasbourg, Metz, Luxembourg, Marburg, and Bled, *each individually*:
 With reference to my letter dated 1 September 1941 – Pol. S II A 2 Nr. 399/41 – 151,[14]
 I request that a corresponding order be issued. Copies thereof are to be submitted.
f) To the senior commanders of the Security Police and the SD in Strasbourg and Metz, the commanders of the Security Police and the SD in Marburg and Bled, as well as the Einsatzkommando in Luxembourg, *each individually*:
 This decree does not apply to those areas. As I already communicated, the Chief of the Civil Administration there is requested to issue a corresponding regulation on the visible identification of Jews.[15]

14 This letter is not in the file.

15 The letter was sent for information to the Plenipotentiary for the Four-Year Plan; Department I of the Reich Ministry of the Interior; the Reich Minister of Transport; the Reich Minister of Aviation; the Reich Foreign Office; the Reich Postmaster General; the Reich Minister of Economics; the Reich Minister of Labour; the Reich Minister of Public Enlightenment and Propaganda; the Party Chancellery; the Reich Protector of Bohemia and Moravia; the chief of the Order Police; the chiefs of the civil administration in Strasbourg, Metz, Luxembourg, Marburg, and Bled; the Bavarian State Ministry of the Interior; the Prussian Regierungspräsidenten; the chairman of the Reich Capital Berlin; the commissioners for defence of the Reich; the Higher SS and Police Leaders, except for Oslo, The Hague, and Cracow; department heads, group leaders, and specialists at the Reich Security Main Office, mailing list C; the Senior Commanders of the Security Police and the SD (BdS) in Prague, Strasbourg, and Metz; the inspectors of the Security Police and the SD; the border inspectors I to III; the Commanders of the Security Police and the SD (KdS) in Lower Styria, in Marburg, in South Carinthia and Carniola, and in Bled; the Einsatzkommando in Luxembourg; all SD (main) districts; and all Criminal Police (head) offices.

DOC. 223

On 18 September 1941 Heinrich Himmler informs Gauleiter Arthur Greiser of Hitler's wish to deport German Jews to the Litzmannstadt (Lodz) ghetto[1]

Letter from the Reichsführer SS (Tgb. Nr. /29/59/41), signed H. Himmler, to Gauleiter SS-Gruppenführer Greiser,[2] Posen, carbon copy with request for the attention of SS-Gruppenführer Heydrich, SS-Gruppenführer Koppe,[3] and SS-Gruppenführer Wolff,[4] dated 18 September 1941[5]

Dear Party Comrade *Greiser*,

It is the Führer's wish that the Old Reich and the Protectorate should as soon as possible be emptied and freed of Jews from west to east. To start, as a first step, I am therefore endeavouring to transport the Jews in the Old Reich and the Protectorate to the Eastern territories that recently became part of the Reich two years ago, if possible by the end of this year, and to deport them even further east next spring.

I intend to remove around 60,000 Jews for the winter from the Old Reich and the Protectorate to the Litzmannstadt ghetto, which, as I have heard, has room to take them in.[6] I ask you not only to understand this measure, which will doubtlessly entail difficulties and burdens for your Gau, but also to support it strongly in the interests of the Reich as a whole.[7]

SS-Gruppenführer Heydrich, who is to carry out this emigration of Jews, will contact you in due course either directly or through SS-Gruppenführer Koppe.

Heil Hitler!

Yours,

1 BArch, NS 19/2655. Published in Peter Longerich (ed.), with the assistance of Dieter Pohl, *Die Ermordung der europäischen Juden: Eine umfassende Dokumentation des Holocaust 1941–1945* (Munich: Piper, 1989), p. 157. This document has been translated from German.

2 Arthur Greiser (1897–1946), sales representative; joined the NSDAP and the SA in 1929, and the SS in 1931; deputy Gauleiter of Danzig, 1933–1939; president of the Danzig Senate, 1934–1939; Reichsstatthalter and Gauleiter of the Warthegau, 1939–1945; member of the Reichstag, 1940–1945; sentenced to death by a Polish court in 1946 and executed.

3 Wilhelm Koppe (1896–1975) was the leader of the SS Main District Warthe and Higher SS and Police Leader (HSSPF) in the Warthegau.

4 Karl Wolff (1900–1984) was Himmler's adjutant from Nov. 1935.

5 The original contains handwritten annotations and underlining.

6 From 16 Oct. to 3 Nov. 1941, close to 20,000 Jews from the Reich and the Protectorate of Bohemia and Moravia were deported to the Litzmannstadt ghetto. Most of them died in the ghetto or were deported to Chelmno in 1942 and 1944, as well as to Auschwitz-Birkenau in the summer of 1944, and murdered.

7 The choice of Lodz as a destination for deportation was probably made by Himmler after conversations with HSSPF Friedrich Wilhelm Krüger in the General Government on 2 Sept. 1941, and with HSSPF Koppe in the Warthegau two days later.

DOC. 224

In mid September 1941 an unknown Jewish author appeals to Bishop Galen of Münster to help the German Jews[1]

Anonymous letter from a Jew to Bishop Count Clemens August von Galen,[2] undated (prior to 19 September 1941)

Your Excellency,

It was with the greatest admiration for your heroic courage that I read the telegram[3] and the letter[4] you addressed to the minister with regard to the seizure of your monastery, and from my heart I wish your advocacy success!

Unfortunately, nowadays one is scarcely accustomed any more to people having the courage to stand up for justice! In your letter, you could at least speak of 'German people' who had been wronged. I have even had the right to be German taken from me!

The people looked on as the stealing – from the Jews – began in public. Now so many minds are confused; they no longer know what is allowed and what is not. Even the Catholics did not object to the inhumane treatment that has been meted out to us. People always talk of blood and soil.[5] Indeed, the soil *does* play a role in human development. I and many like me absorbed German culture from our fathers. I was consciously German with every breath; I volunteered for the war, and in 1933 it was my greatest sorrow that they wanted to take my fatherland from me, that I was not to be German any longer.

Since then, anguish upon anguish has piled up. We have learned to bear what we had thought to be unbearable. God has slowly accustomed us to the burden, the full force of which would initially have made us collapse. But that which is now to come once again appears unbearable! You will have heard that on 19 September a Jewish badge will be assigned to us, and no one will be allowed on the street without it.[6] We are at the mercy of the mob; anyone can spit on us, and we are not allowed to defend ourselves! And, oh how sadistic, they chose the beginning of our most sacred holidays for it! The dark ages are breaking into the full light of day! No one will come to our aid, and we will bear it, as indeed the poor people in the occupied territories have long had to bear it.

1 BAM, Generalvikariat Neues Archiv, Bischöfliches Sekretariat A 0–24. Published in *Bischof Clemens August Graf von Galen, Akten, Briefe und Predigten 1933–1946*, ed. Peter Löffler, vol. 2: *1939–1946* (Paderborn: Schöningh, 1996), no. 350, pp. 910–911. This document has been translated from German.

2 Count Clemens August von Galen (1878–1946), Catholic theologian; ordination to the priesthood in 1904; priest in Berlin until 1929, then in Münster; bishop of Münster, 1933–1946; openly criticized the 'euthanasia' murders in a sermon on 3 August 1941; appointed cardinal in 1946.

3 In a telegram to Lammers, head of the Reich Chancellery, dated 14 July 1941, von Galen had protested against the Gestapo's expropriation of Catholic church property in the diocese of Münster. See *Bischof Clemens August Graf von Galen*, no. 334, p. 852.

4 On 22 July 1941, von Galen thanked Lammers for his reply and again protested against the behaviour of the Gestapo. See *Bischof Clemens August Graf von Galen*, no. 337, pp. 864–866.

5 This is a reference to the National Socialists' ideological concept of *Blut und Boden*, according to which land, especially agricultural land, was inextricably linked to German blood.

6 See Doc. 212.

The German people, the German Wehrmacht stayed silent as the Gessler hat was raised.[7] You will know, Your Excellency, that in Poland, Lithuania, etc., it has already been this way for a long time: that every Jew wears an identifying badge, that he is not allowed on the pavement, and he has to greet every soldier, while the soldier is not allowed to return this greeting. That they are letting people in the ghettos slowly starve … Your Excellency, I would not say anything if they were to put us all against the wall and shoot us, but this slow torture, the degradation, that is inhuman! You will also know about the Jews currently being dragged away from Stettin, from Baden, from Breslau.[8]

The reason that I am speaking out is not because I consider all Jews to be angels. There are very bad and very good ones among them – just as there are among Germans. Forgive me for pointing out such obvious truths. I cannot formulate things in as polished a manner as you, Your Excellency, particularly as I am tormented and shaken to the core at the thought of the new misery that the 19th of September will bring for many thousands of people. Will someone come to relieve us?

I only want to hope one thing, namely that this letter does not cause you any difficulties. You do not know me, I do not know you. Only the absurd wish, the insane hope that somewhere a saviour will arise for us drives me to [write] this letter. God bless you!

DOC. 225

On 19 September 1941 Kurt Mezei notes in his diary that he wears the yellow star with pride[1]

Diary of Kurt Mezei, Vienna, entry for 19 September 1941

Friday, 19 September.
The grand premiere of the Jewish stars. At about 10 o'clock, I make my way to the *issuing office*,[2] where [I was] until 1 o'clock. I stand in front of the ration card office for almost the whole time, as I enjoy having people stare at me. I'm wearing my workman's overalls. Afterwards with Mimi, whom [I] meet in front of the issuing office, to the quay, from there go to the boarding house. From here to the hospital, and from there get the urban train home …

7 A term for a device whose purpose is to compel subservient behaviour. The name derives from the tale of Wilhelm Tell, in which Tell refuses to bow down to the cap of Hermann Gessler, the Austrian despot who governed Switzerland in the 1300s. Gessler then orders Tell to shoot an apple off the top of his son's head.

8 See Docs. 52, 112, and 113.

1 JMW, Inv. No. 4465/3, Tagebuch von Kurt Mezei, Heft 3. This document has been translated from German.

2 From Nov. 1940, food ration cards were issued to the Viennese Jews by this department of the Israelite Religious Community of Vienna (IKG). The entire Jewish population had to register here, as this was the only way for them to receive food ration cards.

At lunchtime Miry[3] pops in, in the *afternoon* write to Dad,[4] and do some darning. I'm in the *temple* at six o'clock (from today up to and including 10 October, the service starts at six o'clock) after first getting – and reading – a newspaper for Feldsberg, and at Mum's.[5] The service is without a choir today. I stand next to Murmelstein[6] – box.[7] At home in the evening with Ilse[8] & Edith. The latter has been wearing glasses since last week and is particularly grumpy today …

The Jewish star does not bother me at all, on the contrary: I wear it with pride![9]

DOC. 226

On 21 September 1941 Erwin Garvens from Hamburg writes in his diary about how appalled he is at the introduction of the yellow star[1]

Handwritten diary of Erwin Garvens,[2] Hamburg, entry for 21 September 1941

Sunday, 21 September (1941), the morning was just like the last few days […],[3] as a result of which we could not see much from the 'Alte Liebe'.[4] But it cleared up around midday, and after lunch we were able to go for a nice walk along the dyke with the Oldenburgs. We departed [by train] at 5:16. At first it was quite pleasant, but from Stade onwards it was unbelievably crowded with Sunday day trippers, so that we arrived in Hamburg

3 Probably: Marianne Neuwirth (1924–1942), deported on 14 Sept. 1942 to Maly Trostenets, where she was murdered.

4 Moritz, also Maurus, Mezei (1886–1944), journalist and writer; member of the Social Democratic Party of Germany (SPD) until the party was banned in 1934; fled to Hungary at the end of 1938 and to Italy in the summer of 1939; detained in the internment camp in Urbisaglia, 1940; detained in the Fossoli camp, Nov. 1943; deported to Auschwitz in April 1944 and murdered there that Sept.

5 Margarete Mezei (1899–1993), secretary; worked for the IKG, where one of her posts was as Benjamin Murmelstein's secretary; seriously injured in an air raid on 12 March 1945 but survived; worked for the IKG again after the war.

6 Dr Benjamin Murmelstein (1905–1989), rabbi; held leading posts in the IKG from 1938, including as head of the emigration department; deported in Jan. 1943 to Theresienstadt, where he was Jewish elder, 1944–1945; detained in custody in Czechoslovakia on suspicion of collaboration, 1945–1947; subsequently emigrated to Italy.

7 *Loge* in the original; possibly refers to an enclosed wooden seating area for the rabbi in a synagogue.

8 Ilse Mezei (1924–1945), twin sister of Kurt Mezei; attended a retraining course for musicians run by the IKG; worked on the IKG's switchboard, 1940–1941; died in an air raid on Vienna on 12 March 1945.

9 In the *Jüdische Rundschau* dated 4 April 1933 the writer and journalist Robert Weltsch (1891–1982) had called on German Jews to 'Wear the yellow patch with pride!' as a reaction to the boycott of 1 April 1933. See PMJ 1/25.

1 Staatsarchiv Hamburg, 622-1/124, 2 B 14. This document has been translated from German.

2 Dr Erwin Garvens (1883–1969), lawyer and writer; director of the audit office in Hamburg from 1926; Regierungsrat, 1930; sent into early retirement in 1933 with effect from 28 April 1934; joined the philanthropic Hamburg Patriotic Society in 1934, from which he was excluded in 1935, as his wife was classed as half-Jewish; worked as a notary's representative, 1942–1944; worked again briefly in the audit office, 1945–1946.

3 One word is illegible.

4 A jetty in Cuxhaven dating from 1732, which today serves as a viewing platform from which visitors can watch ships sailing along the River Elbe.

pretty exhausted at 9.29. Luckily we got a car fast – it was already dark – which drove us home quickly. In the evening, we noticed that we had each put on around three pounds in weight, and […][5] that this trip, our third in 1941, had satisfied and refreshed us the most, although the weather had not been particularly good.

It was just a pity that the really good autumn weather was only setting in now – once again to coincide with the start of the Jewish holiday. The Jews were given special attention from our glorious government this time: since 19 September all Jews, as long as they are not intermarried with Aryans, have to wear a large yellow star with the word 'Jew' written on it. Due to the aforementioned exception, relatively few of our acquaintances have been affected, which still does not prevent all decent-thinking people from being thoroughly ashamed of this barbaric measure. Personally, I view the stars as a hideous eyesore on the streets, especially as they are garish and ugly. Particularly now, during the holidays, you can see an especially large number of such stars in our district (Rotherbaum). One cannot help looking up at the people wearing them: without this label, one would never have realized that they are Jews; they have such 'neutral' expressions.

DOC. 227

On 21 September 1941 Alfred Rosenberg's adjutant notes that, for the present, Hitler has not planned any reprisals against German Jews as a reaction to the deportation of the Volga Germans[1]

Report (no. 34) by Dr Werner Koeppen,[2] SA-Standartenführer and personal aide, the Führer Headquarters, dated 21 September 1941

Lunch, 20 September
Guests: none
The Führer was extremely displeased with the Swedish government's attempt to buy part of the now-homeless Russian Baltic Sea fleet. He immediately gave the navy the order to prevent this under any circumstances.[3] The Führer sees new proof of hostility towards Germany in this bid by the Swedish government.[4] The Führer then made fun of English attempts to proclaim as lies the announcements in the German Wehrmacht report, dated 19 September, on the losses of its own troops in the campaign in the East. According to 'precise' English calculations, every German division would have suffered at least 100 losses every day, which would add up to 20,000 dead per day and a total of 18.2 million

5 Two words are illegible.

1 BArch, R 6/34a, fols. 20–22. Published in Martin Vogt (ed.), *Herbst 1941 im 'Führerhauptquartier': Berichte Werner Koeppens an seinen Minister Alfred Rosenberg* (Koblenz: Bundesarchiv, 2002), pp. 32–37.

2 Dr Werner Koeppen (1910–1994), teacher; joined the NSDAP and the SA in 1931; teacher at the SA Group School in Thurnau, 1935; adjutant to Alfred Rosenberg from 1937; liaison in the Reich Ministry for the Occupied Eastern Territories at the Führer Headquarters, 1941–1943; lived in Munich after 1945.

3 This could not be verified.

4 German–Swedish relations were tense because Sweden had refused to cooperate with the German navy and did not want to allow German troops to pass through Sweden to northern Finland.

dead since the beginning of the campaign in the East. The Führer instructed the Reich Press Chief to demonstrate to the entire world how ridiculous these stupid English calculations are.[5] – General Jodl[6] said that Afghanistan would certainly be the next country where the Russians and the English would celebrate their latest great victory! The English are trying to persuade Turkey that the Turks need fear neither the Russians nor the Germans in future, since both countries will end up killing each other. – The Americans are said to have built a new bomb. Apparently one large, thin-walled bomb contains a number of smaller bombs, which are strewn around upon the impact of the large bomb and then explode where they land.

In accordance with the telegram from Dr Leibbrandt,[7] which arrived early on 20 September,[8] I made my way that afternoon to Special Train Heinrich[9] to learn more details about the new border demarcation in the Grodno area.[10] Since Reich Minister Dr Lammers was already on his way to Berlin, I spoke to Reich Cabinet Advisor von Stutterheim.[11] I enclose a copy of the Führer's decree, signed on 18 September.[12] Since the original map with the borders is still with the Reich Marshal, it will be a few days until the Reich Chancellery can send the Führer's decree with the photocopy of the original map to the offices involved.[13]

On 21 September, I outlined the approximate border demarcation to Dr Leibbrandt by telephone, as far as this was possible with the available sketch. Only the southern part of the border is unclear, as north of Pruzany the border proposed by the Reich Marshal,[14] which runs north of the present valid border, runs through the town of Czeremcha and

5 This could not be verified.

6 Alfred Jodl (1890–1946), military officer; head of the Department for National Defence in the Reich Ministry of War, 1935; brigadier and head of the Military Operations Office in the Wehrmacht High Command, 1939; lieutenant general, 1940; colonel general, 1944; joined the NSDAP in 1944; in 1945 he signed the Wehrmacht's unconditional surrender in Reims as the representative of Karl Dönitz; sentenced to death at the International Military Tribunal at Nuremberg in 1946 and executed.

7 Dr Georg Leibbrandt (1899–1982), interpreter and diplomat; joined the NSDAP in 1933; head of the Eastern Department in the Foreign Policy Office of the NSDAP; head of Main Department I (Politics) in the Reich Ministry for the Occupied Eastern Territories, 1941–1943; ministerial director; attended the Wannsee Conference as the representative of the Reich Ministry for the Occupied Eastern Territories, 1942; imprisoned, 1945–1949.

8 This could not be found.

9 The Special Train Heinrich (*Sonderzug Heinrich*) was Heinrich Himmler's mobile field command train during the war. It was one of several special trains reserved for leading government and Wehrmacht officials while they were stationed on military fronts.

10 On 1 August 1941 the district of Białystok was set up, bordering on the Reich Commissariat Ostland. The territory around Grodno was allocated to the district of Białystok on 1 Nov. 1941.

11 Hermann von Stutterheim (1887–1959), lawyer and civil servant; Regierungsrat, 1919; legation counsellor and deputy Reichsrat representative in Berlin for Braunschweig and Anhalt, 1920–1934; personal advisor to the head of the Reich Chancellery, Hans Lammers, from 1934; joined the NSDAP in 1937; Reich Cabinet advisor from 1937.

12 In accordance with a decree issued on 18 Sept. 1941, Hitler assigned the district of Białystok to the Gauleiter of East Prussia, Erich Koch, without formally integrating the district into the Reich: Decree of the Führer on the Demarcation of the District of Białystok, BArch, R 43 II/604, fol. 186, and BArch, R 6/209, fol. 21.

13 This map can be found in BArch, R 6/209, fols. 22–23.

14 Hermann Göring.

reaches the Bug at Mielnik. Von Stutterheim also did not know whether the area between these two borders will now be returned to the Reich Commissariat Ostland by East Prussia, or whether Gauleiter Koch[15] prefers to stick with the old border, drawn by the Reich Ministry for the East, which runs through Pruzany and does not reach the Bug until just south of Mielnik. – As the implementing regulations in accordance with the Führer's decree are clearly in the hands of the Reich Minister for the Occupied Eastern Territories and those of the Reich Minister of the Interior, the parallel existence of two civil administrations in this area, as implied by Dr Leibbrandt, ought to be eliminated quickly.

Dinner, 20 September
Guests: none
One of the officers from the Führer Headquarters was in Nikolaev and inspected the newly built warships that have fallen into our hands there. The large 35,000-tonne battleship is completely undamaged. It was just about to be launched and could be completed with around two years of construction time. However, many drawings are missing. The ship's hull has been bolted almost to completion, the tank stations on the deck have already been fitted, and even the bases of the tank towers are already in existence. However, the submarines, destroyers, and 10,000-tonne cruise ships under construction are completely worthless and can only be scrapped, as the Soviets had burned the wooden parts of the slipways so that the heavy hulls have shifted and buckled. Luckily, however, a large number of individual parts and instruments were found in warehouses in Nikolaev.

So far, the Führer has not reached a decision as to whether reprisals should be taken against German Jews due to the treatment of the Volga Germans.[16] As Envoy von Steengracht[17] told me, the Führer is considering saving this measure for a possible American entry into the war.[18] The Reich Minister of Foreign Affairs is certainly also of the opinion that if something is to be done about the Volga Germans, it must occur within the next few days.

Reich Cabinet Advisor von Stutterheim informed me that the area between Dnjestr and Bug up to northern Mogilev-Podolsk has now finally been ceded to Romania.[19] The written statement on this matter has already been sent to the Reich Ministry for the East. He also deeply regrets the loss of Odessa and of the key railway link to Lemberg. At dinner I asked Envoy von Steengracht how this cession had come about, and he assured

15 Erich Koch (1896–1986), businessman and official at Reich Railways; joined the NSDAP in 1922; Gauleiter, 1928–1945, and Oberpräsident of East Prussia from 1933, member of the Reichstag, 1930–1945; SA-Obergruppenführer, 1938; chief of the civil administration in the district of Białystok, 1941–1944; Reich commissioner for Ukraine, 1942–1944; in 1949 extradited from a British prison to Poland, where he was sentenced to death in 1959. The sentence was later commuted to lifelong imprisonment; died in prison.

16 See Doc. 221, fn. 9.

17 Baron Dr Gustav Adolf Steengracht van Moyland (1902–1969), diplomat; joined the NSDAP in 1933; embassy attaché in London, 1936; consular secretary in the Reich Foreign Office, 1938; member of Ribbentrop's personal staff, 1940–1943; state secretary, 1943; sentenced at the Nuremberg Military Tribunals to seven years in prison, 1949; released in 1950.

18 Hitler had, however, already approved the deportation of the German Jews during the war. See Doc. 223 and Introduction, p. 39.

19 So-called Transnistria was under Romanian administration from August 1941.

me that it had occurred at the explicit wish of the Führer, contrary to the intention of the Reich Foreign Office (?).[20]

Military position, 21 September
There have been no major changes at the front. The Russians are retreating in the region around the Sea of Azov. We can count on capturing Melitopol soon. There is complete chaos in the pocket east of Kiev; we still have no clear picture of events. The 17th Army has advanced further towards Kharkov and has seized Krasnograd. Apart from disruptive artillery fire on both sides, all is quiet on the whole front of Army Group Centre front and on the Petersburg front, and both sides are engaged in redeployment. The Russian battleship *Marat* joined the fray unsuccessfully near Kronstadt. The conquest of Osel is progressing and should be completed in one or two days. There are no changes on the Finnish front. – In Africa there is heavy air activity by the English, with attacks on Bardia, Benghazi, and Tripoli: insufficient Italian convoy and ground defence. During the night of 20/21 September, 120 planes flew in on a wide front between the Baltic Sea and Heilbronn, without causing any great damage anywhere. Fifty planes targeted Berlin, but most were repelled by anti-aircraft guns.

DOC. 228

On 22 September 1941 the Reich Federation of German Newspaper Publishers proposes banning Jews from taking out newspaper subscriptions[1]

Letter from the Reich Federation of German Newspaper Publishers (Scht/Nt.)[2] to the Reich Postal Ministry,[3] dated 22 September 1941 (copy)[4]

Re: Jews as subscribers to German newspapers and magazines
For quite some time, German publishers have not been fulfilling direct orders by or for Jews. Jews wishing to purchase German newspapers and magazines have now found a way around this by ordering them by post.

The situation on the paper market is forcing publishing houses to make ever-increasing cuts. As a consequence of the cap on printing, it is no longer possible to supply enough newspapers to meet today's retail demand. Some news magazines have even been forced to refuse new subscriptions. Supplying print media to the troops is also starting to become very difficult.

20 Question mark as in the original.

1 BArch, R 55/1415, fols. 16–17. This document has been translated from German.
2 The Reich Federation of German Newspaper Publishers emerged in 1934 as the successor to the Association of German Newspaper Publishers. Its first chairman was Max Amann (1891–1957), also president of the Reich Press Chamber, into which the federation was incorporated.
3 Wilhelm Ohnesorge was the Reich postmaster general from 1937 to 1945.
4 On 15 Jan. 1942 the president of the Reich Press Chamber forwarded the copy together with other letters to the Reich Ministry of Public Enlightenment and Propaganda. The sender can only be seen in this letter: BArch, R 55/1415, fol. 14.

It is hard to see why Jews are still able to order any newspaper or magazine they like, while combat troops have to do without the information and the connections to back home that they can get from reading newspapers during their rest periods. We hereby wish to propose that a decree be issued ordering postal authorities to no longer accept subscriptions by or for Jews to daily or weekly newspapers and, as far as this is still possible, magazines, with immediate effect.

We are well aware of the considerable difficulties involved in implementing such an order in practice, as the Jew who, since the 19th of this month can be recognized by the yellow Star of David,[5] will often not appear at the counter in person. Nor will a name always reliably tell you whether someone is of non-Aryan origin, but it is out of the question to demand proof of Aryan heritage when a newspaper subscription is taken out. We can imagine, however, that the postmen, despite there being numerous temporary staff, are in the know regarding their own delivery districts. Therefore, if the radical exclusion of Jews as postal subscribers cannot be achieved immediately, a near complete rectification of the matter ought to be reached in this way in due course. However, an exception to the ban on accepting subscriptions must be made for the *Jüdisches Nachrichtenblatt*. This should be the only newspaper that Jews are allowed to purchase. It appears in a standardized edition over the entire territory of the Reich; a second edition exist for the territory of the Ostmark.[6] We would be most grateful if you would consider our request and inform us of your decision very soon.[7]

Heil Hitler!

5 See Doc. 212.

6 Along with the Berlin and Vienna editions, the *Jüdisches Nachrichtenblatt* also appeared in a Prague edition. See Doc. 273, fn. 1.

7 The president of the Reich Press Chamber referred to this letter in a circular (B II 4 8345/41 Dr. L/Wz, signed Anton Willi) and stressed that 'it [ought to] be clear to every single publisher, distribution company, and retailer that delivery to Jews is utterly out of the question as long as the needs of German customers cannot be met': BArch, R 55/1415, fol. 15. The Reich Ministry of Public Enlightenment and Propaganda referred to this on 16 Jan. 1942 and demanded that the Reich Press Chamber issue a prohibition accordingly: ibid., fol. 19. On 17 Feb. 1942 the Reich Security Main Office prohibited the purchase of newspapers by Jews: Walk, *Das Sonderrecht für die Juden im NS-Staat*, p. 364.

DOC. 229
In a letter to Shanghai, dated 24 September 1941, Max Schönenberg from Cologne describes the impact of the new anti-Jewish measures[1]

Letter from Dr Max Schönenberg, Cologne, to Julius Kaufmann, Shanghai, dated 24 September 1941[2]

My dears, dear Julius[3]

I'm sure you can't wait to hear from us right now. Firstly, it's our autumn holiday period,[4] which is bound to cause you concern after the experiences of recent years, and you'll also want to know how the new regulations are affecting us.[5] They have completely fulfilled our needs for New Year surprises this year; they cut very deeply into our life. There will be no more holidays or visits to relatives, as group travel permits can only be obtained on special occasions. This is particularly hard for Hedwig, who has often sought refuge with us in her loneliness. We won't be able to visit Regina and the Tützes so easily either.

The impact of being restricted to the city limits varies, depending on how big the town or city is. We can go on outings to the municipal woods and even to the edge of the Königsforst. I doubt whether all places offer such possibilities.

Wearing the yellow Star of David, or Jewish star, certainly has the desired effect of reinforcing the segregation. The first days went by well enough. The population of Cologne was tactful. A few silly schoolboys did not diminish this impression. The yellow Jewish symbol has not made people's blood boil. It is unlikely that events such as those of November 1938 will occur as spontaneous outbursts.[6]

Luckily, we Jews are showing a decent attitude and demeanour, almost without exception. I see men, women, and children walking the streets with their heads held high. We know that we do not need to feel ashamed of our Jewishness. We know that our tribe, our history, and our intellectual history do not compare unfavourably to others. We know that the stains on our image are no greater or darker than those on the image of others. We know that a large number of the faults we are accused of are the consequences of our political fate. And that is why I'm glad that our boy[7] in Palestine is among those helping to change the course of Jewish destiny. What I fought against as a student – building a Jewish national homeland – is what I long for today, and moreover, I have the audacious idea that within a consolidated Jewish state lies the opportunity for Jewry to liberate itself from the shackles that have paralysed it through its endless laws and bans.

It has been very interesting for me to observe different types. I have seen a striking number of people wearing the Star of David – both old and young – whom I would

1 NS-Dokumentationszentrum Köln, Briefe Max Schönenberg. Extracts published in Rüther, *Köln*, p. 552. This document has been translated from German.
2 In the original, '25.XI.' was written by hand.
3 'Dear Julius' was written by hand.
4 In 1941, Rosh Hashanah (Jewish New Year), Yom Kippur (the Day of Atonement), and Sukkot (the Feast of Tabernacles) all fell in Sept./Oct.
5 See Docs. 212 and 222.
6 See PMJ 2, pp. 53–59. PMJ 2 contains numerous documents about the November pogroms.
7 Leopold, also Reuwen, Schönenberg.

never have thought were Jews had it not been for this symbol. On the other hand, I have also seen a large number of people and been surprised because they were not wearing the yellow patch.[8]

DOC. 230

In a letter dated 24 September 1941 Margarete Korant from Berlin writes of her hopes of emigrating to Cuba and asks her daughter Ilse for help[1]

Handwritten letter from Margarete Korant, Berlin, to her daughter Ilse, dated 24 September 1941

My beloved child,

I have just come from the Relief Association, where I had to wait from eleven o'clock until half-past two despite having an appointment. After all that, the conversation then only lasted a couple of minutes. The gentleman in question was strongly in favour of cabling you again to say that you should speed up the Cuba matter and gave me, as you will have seen from the telegram, the same address of the New York lawyer that I gave you weeks ago. He confirmed to me that around $1,000 will be necessary, and that gives me a bit of hope again, since this is the kind of money we actually have. I told him straight away that this means you aren't in a position to pay for the passage as well, to which he replied that so far nobody had failed to emigrate simply because they couldn't afford the passage. So we can definitely count on the support of the Relief Association, perhaps with the help of the foundation. So do what you can *and as quickly as possible.* By the way, the Cuba advisor is a close acquaintance of Osw. Pick,[2] which is of course very welcome and probably also advantageous. It means that I don't always have to wait for hours and can leave things to him. I hope that he comes back in the next few days. My new tenants are not moving in until 10 October. Everything has been approved, also by the property manager. They are having the back room decorated, although the property manager advised against it, because you can't know how long they will live here. They seem very generous, however, which is of course very welcome. I have so much space now that I could have put up Aunt Hede[3] for a few days; what a pity! I haven't heard from O.[4] again, not even a few lines over the holidays.[5] By the way, on Tuesday I went round to Mrs R.'s[6] for coffee with two very nice ladies, whom I knew already of course, and in the evening I visited a friend of Adele's who lives nearby. But they are all just acquaintances, not friends. I hope to hear good news from you soon.

Lots of love and kisses, your Grandma-Mummy

8 The letter ends abruptly at this point, without a valediction.

1 Jüdisches Museum Berlin, Korant Schwalbe Striem Family Collection, 2006/57/299. This document has been translated from German.

2 Oswald Pick (b. 1880), businessman and lawyer; he was the Korant family's lawyer.

3 Hede Orgler, née Apt (1883–1944); Margarete Korant's sister, married to Alfred Orgler (1875–1944); lived in Oppeln, deported to Theresienstadt together with her husband on 21 April 1943; deported on 28 Oct. 1944 to Auschwitz, where she was murdered.

4 Oppeln.

5 This refers to Rosh Hashanah (Jewish New Year), which fell on 22 and 23 Sept. in 1941.

6 'Redlich' was added to the typed version.

DOC. 231

On 25 September 1941 the Reich Economics Minister informs the Reich Group for Industry of the regulations concerning the employment of *Mischlinge*[1]

Letter from the Reich Economics Minister (no. III WOS 1/18312/41), section head, Ministerialrat Dr Homann,[2] Regierungsrat Dr Mayer,[3] p.p. [initial h.], Berlin, to the Reich Group for Industry, 56/58 Tirpitz Ufer, Berlin West 35, dated 25 September 1941

Re: employment of Mischlinge in the administration of trade and industry organizations. On 9 July 1941 I received the following communication from the Economic Group for the Metal Industry:[4]

After checking with the Reich Group for Industry,[5] we recently employed a university graduate with a non-Aryan father and Aryan mother, as an assistant to our deputy managing director. The Labour Front, where we made enquiries, told us that the employment could go ahead, so long as the aforementioned gentleman had been accepted as a member of the German Labour Front. Since this was the case, and the member of staff simultaneously held Reich citizenship, we employed the gentleman, taking into consideration the condition of the Reich Group for Industry that we not use him in high-profile positions. However, the latter is unavoidable in the position that had to be filled. On the contrary, frequent participation in meetings and talks in many different areas of work is required. Moreover, the gentleman employed now demands that he be granted exactly the same status as the other members of the Economic Group, in particular as regards signature authorization etc.

The principle that Mischlinge who are not considered Jews according to the First Regulation on the Reich Citizenship Law[6] may work freely in trade and industry cannot simply be applied to employment in trade and industry associations, as they hold a special position within the private sector because of the special tasks assigned to them in connection with the war effort. In agreement with the Party Chancellery, I am therefore of the view that Mischlinge, at the very least, cannot be considered for posts in which they gain an insight into the management of the company, or which deal with tasks concerning the war economy. I therefore consider the employment of a Mischling as deputy to the managing director of an economic group to be problematic.

I ask that you inform the Economic Group for the Metal Industry of this and decide accordingly when confronted with similar cases.

1 BArch, R 3101/8936, fol. 508. This document has been translated from German.
2 Dr Fritz (Friedrich) Homann (1898–1981), lawyer; joined the NSDAP in 1933; Oberregierungsrat and section head in the Reich Ministry of Economics; Ministerialrat in 1940.
3 Probably Dr Friedrich (Fritz) Mayer (1901–1954), lawyer; worked for the auditing firm Bayerische Treuhandgesellschaft, 1932–1933; joined the NSDAP in 1933; section head in the Bavarian Regional Association of Agricultural Cooperatives (Raiffeisen), 1932–1937; lawyer for the Chamber of Industry and Commerce, Bayreuth, 1937–1939; department head in the Reich Ministry of Economics from 1939.
4 A subsidiary of the Reich Group for Industry.
5 From 1934, all trade and industry enterprises were placed in this Reich group. This brought an end to the self-administration of trade and industry.
6 First Regulation on the Reich Citizenship Law, 14 Nov. 1935, *Reichsgesetzblatt*, 1935, I, p. 1333, § 2(2). See also PMJ 1/210.

DOC. 232

Gauleiter Josef Grohé incites hatred against the Jews in a speech delivered in Cologne on 28 September 1941[1]

Speech by Gauleiter Josef Grohé[2] at a mass rally at Cologne trade fair centre on 28 September 1941

[…][3]

And while we are on this issue of aeroplanes, we have now begun turning the Jews out of the solidly built houses. [Applause.]

As you know, the Jew is the initiator of the war, the rabble-rouser in the whole world, and masses of them are still living here in Germany, spies in our own country. Wherever Germans have been living in enemy nations, they have long been arrested and imprisoned. We let our greatest enemy move about freely in our own country.

We could have put them behind bars! If we had lined them up against the wall, we would have been vindicated by history and by our own conscience. For the Jew was never a benefit to humankind, but only ever a source of harm.

The Jew is a born criminal and we know ourselves that among every people there are good and bad human beings, but that in all non-Jewish peoples the good element outweighs the bad, and that criminal natures are in the minority and are treated accordingly by the state. But the Jewish people is a people of criminals by birth; otherwise Christ wouldn't have called it the 'people of the devil'. He said, 'The devil is your father.'[4] And many, many centuries later, Luther said that there is no more wretched and dirty and bad and dangerous a people than these Jews.[5] And Schopenhauer called the Jews masters in the art of lying.[6]

One could cite evidence ad infinitum that the Jew has indeed been a criminal from the very beginning, as Christ called him. And there is a reason for this, of course: his ancestry. He is the scum of various primitive races; gathered inside him are all the bad features of those races which his primitive race mixed with. There are no good features left in him, and so he has only done bad things in the world.

1 NS-Dokumentationszentrum der Stadt Köln, Tk 134 and Tk 135, tape recording. This document has been translated from German.

2 Josef Grohé (1902–1987), sales employee; joined the NSDAP in 1925; publisher and editor-in-chief of the newspaper *Westdeutscher Beobachter* from 1926; Gauleiter of Cologne-Aachen and member of the Reichstag, 1931–1945; Reich commissioner in Belgium and northern France, 1944; went into hiding in 1945; held on remand, 1946–1950; sentenced by a denazification tribunal in Bielefeld to four and a half years' imprisonment in 1950, and released on account of time already served; afterwards worked as a sales representative.

3 The section of the speech published here begins at 35 minutes, 38 seconds. Beforehand, Grohé speaks about German–British relations. He claims that long before the outbreak of war, the British government had harboured a plan to remove the National Socialist government from power. Germany had been provoked by Britain's declaration of war. Grohé then tries to downplay the effects of the British air raids.

4 'You are of your father the devil' (John 8:44).

5 Martin Luther, *Von den Jüden und jren lügen* (On the Jews and their Lies) (Wittenberg, 1543). In the 1933 edition, published as a 'people's edition' by Hans Ludolf Parisius, the antisemitic treatise is divided into 394 articles. In articles 299–314, Luther calls for concrete action against the Jews.

6 See Doc. 193, fn. 2.

The eradication of this people could therefore be justified by anyone and at any time in history.

Adolf Hitler said in a speech before this war: 'If Jewry should succeed in plunging the nations once more into a war, the outcome of this war will be the complete expulsion of the Jews from Europe.'[7] [Applause.]

And in the meantime, they have succeeded in unleashing this new war. They may still be walking around freely, but that doesn't mean they have got away with it! The Jews … [Applause.]

Every single Jew will have to leave Europe. And since Mr Churchill does not want them, despite his many possessions around the world, nor is Mr Roosevelt opening his arms to welcome his friends, we ourselves will be forced to find a place somewhere in the world where the Jews will be concentrated.

In Cologne alone there are around 6,000 Jews that eat up our food; they largely do nothing but bother people. Now they have a Jewish star. You have seen the Jewish star, and many are now outraged and say, 'My God, I have never seen so many Jews in Cologne as now all of a sudden.'[8]

Well, there's a reason for that.

First of all, you don't always look the Jew in the face; after all, there's the saying that God already identified the Jews outwardly by their noses, which is the uniform God gave to the Jews. No, you don't always look them in the face, and there are also Jews with snub noses, you get that too. Among the eastern Galicians, the nose is usually different, and apart from that, one talks of the smell; well, when you're walking down the street, you aren't always walking against the wind. [Laughter.]

So the Jewish star was most expedient, and now we see how they are still walking around en masse. The reason why we are turning them out of the solidly built houses in Cologne is because for one thing we want to give solid apartments to our German Volksgenossen, whose apartments have been destroyed in air raids. [Applause.]

So the question here is: 'Who comes first?' Our German Volksgenosse, whose apartments the English have bombed to smithereens because of the war started by the Jews, or our enemy at home, the Jews? It's not really a question at all.

Nonetheless there are still people who say: 'Yes, but isn't that, isn't that against Christian charity?' Well, for one thing, the Jew has never known Christian charity, but rather said: 'An eye for an eye, a tooth for a tooth'! And second, that would mean that you couldn't punish a criminal, but we can do that, from a Christian point of view. Christ drove the Jews out of the temple with a whip. He didn't say: 'You are my brothers and you may commit crimes as you wish, and I will forgive you for that in the name of Christian charity.' He did something entirely different, because if that had been so, as some pastors would have us believe today, then the Jews wouldn't have nailed him to the cross. He must have been a very great enemy of the Jews, otherwise he wouldn't have been crucified and the crown of thorns would not have been placed on him.

We could simply turn the Jews out of the houses and leave them to their fate. We could say: 'Here, make sure that you get out of our way!' And think about what is hap-

7 In his speech in the Reichstag on 30 Jan. 1939, Hitler had prophesied not the expulsion but the annihilation of the European Jews: see Doc. 218 and PMJ 2/248.

8 At the end of 1941, 5,931 Jews were still living in Cologne.

pening: some of them are moving into one of Cologne's old forts, and barracks are being put up for the rest, brand new barracks like those that are being put up for our Wehrmacht, for our labour service, like the ones we need for our foreign labourers, like those we need for prisoner of war camps, and so on.[9] And so again we are treating the Jews so generously that you really have to be astounded at our own German good nature, which we confirm to ourselves through this. That's something that only the good-natured German can do.

For I don't need to tell you what the Jews did to ethnic Germans in the places where they lived. You know all about that from the reports, above all from Poland, and also from other regions, and now Russia, the Baltic countries. But we Germans are quite simply different and we are demonstrating that again here with regard to the Jews. At any rate, this way we can free up 1,000 solid apartments, and our housing crisis, the housing crisis of our Volksgenossen, is thereby alleviated to some extent. But it occurs to me: the Germans even go so far as – this is our own German authorities that are doing this – allowing a Jewish commission to come and see where their racial comrades from Cologne are going to be accommodated.[10] [Laughter.]

And the Jewish commission then submitted a report. And it states the following – this is very interesting, by the way – about the fort, about what they saw there. Until now, three Aryan families and twenty-five prisoners of war have been living in this fort – segregated, of course. The report notes that in the left wing of the fort, in four rooms, the plan is to install eight lavatories for women and another eight lavatories for men, along with urinals. The lavatories are separated from the corridor by a high wall. There are washing facilities for men and women, as well as several taps in the corridor. But what are missing, they want to point out, are baths and showers! [Laughter.]

Perhaps the Jews can be assimilated after all. We used to think that the Sarahs[11] would never in their lives wash their feet. [Laughter.]

And now all of a sudden they want to do so. And another thing: they say that the rooms all have to be given a fresh coat of paint, in a pale shade no less, and that the windows also need a fresh, light-coloured coat of paint. An insolent Jew dares to present this to us at a time when important work in Germany must be stopped because everyone has to work for the German war effort, when it has become practically impossible for a civilian to find a craftsman of any kind to do something that would be thoroughly desirable and justifiable, but which cannot be done because of the labour shortage. And the Jews want a bright coat of paint, to have the windows freshly painted in a light colour; they have the gall to demand that. They say the following about the barracks: 'In the barracks too, despite all the other useful fixtures, there are no facilities for bathing and showering. Moreover, every lavatory must have a door that can be closed from the inside;

9 Jews from Cologne who had been evicted from their apartments were forcibly rehoused to a barracks camp erected in an old fort in the district of Müngersdorf: see Introduction, p. 65.

10 Representatives of the Reich Association of Jews in Germany went to Cologne to inspect the camp, and on 9 Sept. 1941 submitted a report: BArch, R 8150/113, fols. 284–288. On the 'Jew houses' in Hanover, see also Doc. 215.

11 Presumably a reference to Jewish women. A decree issued in August 1938 obliged Jewish women with a first name of 'non-Jewish origin' to adopt the additional first name Sara.

the doors planned cannot be closed from the inside. Moreover, special rooms for children's day care and a special nursery [are required].' [Murmuring in the hall.]

So don't let anyone say again that we treat the Jews harshly! You have to ask yourself: How long will our patience last? [Applause.]

Finally, the report says that the path from the barracks to the latrines is too long and too arduous. We could well say, we could well say: fine, go ahead and do your mess beside your bed. But that isn't possible either. That isn't possible, because after all, they are coming here, to one of the most pleasant areas around Cologne, and because we have an interest in preventing a breeding ground for diseases from developing here, so the Jews have to keep to a certain standard of cleanliness; we will force them to do it. [Brief applause.]

And it is signed, among others, by a Dr Walter Israel Lustig,[12] [laughter] which is probably supposed to mean that the Jew is making fun of our German good nature. Oh, I think that the Jew has laughed long enough. His laughter will soon fade; we will not feel clean here until we are rid of him! When I talk about Jews, I have the feeling I need to wash my hands.

It really is the case that there is nothing more reprehensible and wretched in the world than the Jewish people, and there is nobody more good-natured than the German, who here again asks whether this can't be done a bit more gently. We don't treat pests like this, do we? And the Jew is nothing but a pest, a pest among the German people and a pest among other peoples.

But this war, which will bring victory for Germany, will bring the victory of the swastika over Europe, and with it the downfall of Jewry.

[…][13]

12 Lustig: German for 'funny'. The report was signed by Julius Jacoby and Walter Lustig (1891–1945). The latter was a physician who practised in Breslau, and from 1927 in Berlin; led the medical section of the police headquarters and was dismissed in Oct. 1933; worked for the Reich Association of Jews in Germany from July 1939, and was head of healthcare on its board, 1940–1941; led the investigation department for transport claims in the Jewish hospital from Dec. 1941; from 1943 led the 'Residue Reich Association' (the successor to the dissolved Reich Association of Jews in Germany); killed by the Soviet occupation regime under suspicion of being a collaborator.

13 The section of the speech published here ends at 47 minutes, 40 seconds. In the last part, Grohé talks about the inhumane conditions in the Soviet Union and the supposed social progressiveness and general superiority of the Germans, among other things. He concludes by appealing to the willingness of the German people to make sacrifices and for unconditional loyalty to Hitler.

DOC. 233

The Reich Association of Jews in Germany produces a summary of the emigration of Jews from the Old Reich between 1933 and 1941[1]

Statistics produced by the Reich Association of Jews in Germany

Emigration of Jews from the Old Reich
1933 to 1941
Scale
Since 1933, a total of 352,294 Jews have emigrated from the Old Reich. Emigration concerned the following main destination countries:

Africa	14,760
America	
North America	57,189
Central America	9,728
South America	53,472
Asia	16,374
Australia	4,015
Europe	143,326
Palestine	53,430
	352,294

Organization
The following organizations were active in supporting emigration from 1933: the Palestine Office of the Jewish Agency for Palestine, for emigration to Palestine; the Relief Association of Jews in Germany, for all other emigration; the Main Office for the Welfare of Jewish Migrants, for repatriation. The work of the three organizations was initially led by the Reich Representation of Jews in Germany; after the foundation of the Reich Association of Jews in Germany, it was merged with the latter's emigration department. Its main task consisted of identifying existing opportunities for emigration and creating new opportunities, as well as emigration counselling and the support of emigrants in need of assistance.

Funding
The financing of emigration in *Reichsmarks* was for the most part covered by the emigrants themselves. Insofar as they did not have the necessary means at their disposal, emigration was financed by the Reich Association.

The funds used by the Reich Representation or Reich Association to support those requiring financial assistance to emigrate (89,032) since 1933 amount to RM 20,494,864.67, with an annual total of:

1 BArch, R 8150/31, fols. 141–145. This document has been translated from German.

1933	RM	980,956.64
1934	RM	675,953.91
1935	RM	583,367.64
1936	RM	1,657,566.82
1937	RM	1,800,040.98
1938	RM	3,547,836.58
1939	RM	6,618,501.36
1940	RM	3,281,516.99
1 Jan. 1941 to 31 Oct. 1941	RM	1,347,123.75
	RM	*20,492,864.67*

Alongside the amounts in Reichsmarks, since the outbreak of war *foreign currency* has been required to provide evidence of funds and landing fees for passage by ship. These sums have mainly been provided by relatives or friends of the emigrants abroad via the Reich Association's emigration department. Where this was not possible, Jewish relief organizations abroad, in particular the American Joint Distribution Committee in New York, provided the required sums in foreign currency. Since 1 September 1939, the JDC has made a total of $2,193,810.28 available for the booking of passages.

The procurement of evidence of funds for emigration to *Palestine* took place largely by means of a *transfer* procedure, developed with the authorization of the Reich Economics Minister,[2] between the Palestine Trust Agency, Berlin, and Masvara Ltd., Tel Aviv, in collaboration with German and Palestinian banks, whereby German goods were exported to Palestine. Within the framework of the Palestine transfer, a total of RM 104,623,707.01 with a corresponding value of £5,440[3] (approximately) was transferred between 1933 and 1939.

In addition, procurement of evidence of funds and landing fees took place mainly via the *Altreu transfer* procedure, which has been carried out with the authorization of the Reich Economics Minister since 1937. Up to 1 September 1939, a total of 3,008 emigrants took part in this procedure and received a sum of foreign currency to the value of RM 5,131,000. This enabled the emigration of a further 2,845 persons without means within the framework of the *Altreu funding procedure.* Through overpayments in Reichsmarks based on a table staggered according to wealth classes and the number of persons emigrating together, the latter could be supplied with foreign currency to an exchange value of RM 1,234,000.

After this procedure was suspended (1 September 1939) the *Altreu passage* procedure was devised, under which foreign currencies from the Joint [JDC] were made available for the booking of passages in exchange for Reichsmarks, the sums calculated according to a table which was initially arranged in categories from RM 10 to 20, and later from RM 10 to 55, classified according to wealth and the number of persons emigrating together. From April 1940 until the end of October 1941, 987 persons took part in this procedure; their passage was procured for the equivalent sum of $154,233.29, for which a corresponding value of RM 3,698,569.43 was received by the Reich Association.

2 Walther Funk.
3 The reference is presumably to Palestinian pounds.

Implementation
The technical implementation of emigration can be broken down into the following phases:

From 1933 to the end of 1938:
Predominately emigration without financial support, primarily to Europe as a transit migration country; procurement of overseas passages in Reichsmarks; departure from German ports; return migration (repatriation) of Jews of foreign nationality; acquisition of labourer certificates for immigration into Palestine on the basis of professional training and occupational restructuring in agriculture, skilled crafts, and household management; from 1936, immigration ban in South Africa, previously the chartering of the Nord-Lloyd steamship *Stuttgart* carrying 540 emigrants to South Africa; from 1937, restrictions on immigration to South America, particularly to Brazil; in 1938, to Argentina and Colombia, and in contrast greater emigration to Bolivia and Chile; conference in Evian (July 1938);[4] settlements in the JCA[5] colonies in Argentina; group settlement projects for Brazil; further immigration restrictions.

From 1939 to 1 September 1939:
Setting up of the Central Office for Jewish Emigration in Berlin, standardization of emigration formalities (tax clearance certificates from the tax offices and municipal tax offices as a prerequisite for the issue of an emigrant passport, approval from the Foreign Exchange Office to take personal and household effects on the journey, closure of the employment records, introduction of the emigrant fee certificate), central monitoring, and guidance of emigration; regulation of the scale of emigration via instructions to the Central Office; increase in overseas emigration; restrictions on immigration to Palestine, special transports to Palestine;[6] increase in child emigration; setting up of the camp in Richborough for transit migrants;[7] from March 1939, average emigration of 9,000 persons per month; increase in emigration to the Far East (Shanghai), partly already on the condition of payment of passage in foreign currency; transit migration to European countries of persons awaiting visas for the USA; immigration ban in Cuba, previously departure of the Hapag steamer *St. Louis* carrying 900 passengers to Cuba who, because landing was not possible, were taken in by European countries.[8]

From September 1939 to April 1940:
Decline in emigration to European countries; passage bookings now only on foreign ships in foreign currency; departure predominantly from Italian ports; restrictions on

4 See Doc. 107, fn. 13.
5 Jewish Colonization Association.
6 See Doc. 120.
7 In 1938 a refugee camp (the 'Kitchener camp') was set up in Richborough outside Sandwich in Kent, Britain. It housed Jews and political refugees from the German Reich.
8 The cruise ship *St. Louis* had left Hamburg on 13 May 1939 bound for Cuba, carrying almost 1,000 Jewish passengers. The head of the Cuban immigration authorities had issued them entry permits without having been authorized to do so. The ship was then denied permission to dock in Havana at the end of May. The *St. Louis* headed back to Europe, with Belgium, France, the Netherlands, and Britain finally taking in 250 passengers each: see PMJ 2/290, 292, 297, and 316.

immigration to Bolivia and Chile; further emigration to the Far East; predominantly emigration to the USA.

From May 1940 to October 1940:
Decline in departures from Italian ports as a result of the ban on the issuing of Italian transit visas; use of overland routes to the Far East as well as departure to the USA from Japanese ports using the Trans-Siberian Railway; introduction of a transit depot for Manchukuo at the end of August; introduction of a Japanese transit depot in October 1940; attempts at departure from Petsamo by Finnish shipping lines; administrative restrictions on the issuing of American visas.

November 1940 to October 1941:
Creation of the possibility of departure from Portuguese and Spanish ports, particularly from Lisbon; attempts to reach Greece overland and from there via the Mediterranean to Lisbon, as well as overland through Switzerland, and from there by bus through France to Barcelona; setting up of emigrant mass transport, simultaneously for emigrants from the Ostmark and the Protectorate, through France to the ports of departure; booking of passages on American, Spanish, and Portuguese shipping lines; completion of 25 mass transports in special carriages for 5,945 emigrants, 4,808 of whom were from the Old Reich; predominance of emigration to the USA, since the issuing of visas was resumed in January 1941, until the issuing of visas was stopped (June 1941), and from then on greater emigration to Cuba and Ecuador; procurement of a relatively large number (around 800) of Cuban visa permits, of which the majority have yet to be used up.

Preparation for emigration
A total of 42 vocational or educational institutions for agriculture and forestry, 168 institutions for skilled crafts, 27 institutions for household management, and 12 institutions for the caring professions provided preparations for emigration. From 1933 to October 1941 a total of 66,546 persons were prepared for emigration in the course of vocational training and occupational restructuring; 33,751 received training in agriculture, 26,100 in skilled crafts professions, 4,350 in household management, and 2,337 in infant and child care.

Numbers remaining
Taking into account emigration and the tax surplus since 1933, as well as the resettlement transports in October 1941, there are currently around 151,000 Jews still present in the Old Reich, of whom 11 per cent are aged 18 years and under, 23.7 per cent are between 19 and 45 years old, 29.6 per cent are between 46 and 60 years old, and 35.7 per cent are over 60 years old.

DOC. 234

In autumn 1941 the émigré writer Stefan Zweig writes about an encounter with Sigmund Freud, during which the two talked about the persecution of the Jews[1]

Excerpt from Stefan Zweig's[2] memoirs written in exile, dated autumn 1941

During those hours I often spoke with Freud[3] about the horror of the Hitlerian world and the war. As a humane human being, he was deeply shocked, but as a thinker, he was in no way surprised at this terrible outburst of bestiality. He had always, he said, been berated for being a pessimist, because he had denied the power of culture over the drives. Now, his opinion that the elementary destructive drive in the human soul was ineradicable was being confirmed in the most appalling way – which of course he was not proud of. In the centuries to come, he said, perhaps a means would be found, at least in the communal life of nations, to supress these instincts. In daily life and in innermost nature, however, they existed as ineradicable forces that were perhaps necessary to maintain tension. What occupied him even more in his final days was the problem of the Jews and their current tragedy: here the scientist in him knew of no formula, and his lucid mind [had] no answer. A short while before he had published his study on Moses, in which he portrayed Moses as a non-Jew,[4] and with this attribution, which could barely be scientifically grounded, he had upset pious Jews just as much as the nationally minded. Now he was sorry to have published the book precisely in the midst of Jewry's most horrific hour: 'Now that everything is being taken from them, I also take from them their best man.' I had to agree that every Jew had now become seven times more sensitive, since even amidst this world tragedy they were the real victims, everywhere the victims, because they were distraught even before the blow, everywhere knowing that all bad things affect them first and seven times over, and that the most hate-maddened human being of all time wanted to humiliate them in particular and to drive them to the ends of the earth and under the earth. Week by week, month by month, more and more refugees arrived, and from week to week they were always even poorer and more distressed than those who came before them. The first, who had left Germany and Austria the fastest, had been able to salvage their clothes, their luggage, their effects and some of them even a bit of money. But the longer they had placed their trust in Germany, the more difficult it had been to tear themselves away from their beloved homeland, the harder they had been punished. First, the Jews had had their jobs taken away, had been banned from going to the theatre, to the cinema and museums, researchers from using

1 Stefan Zweig, *Die Welt von Gestern: Erinnerungen eines Europäers* (Stockholm: Bermann-Fischer Verlag AB, 1942), pp. 480–485. A published English translation exists as *The World of Yesterday: An Autobiography* (New York: Viking Press, 1945). This document has been newly translated from the original German.

2 Dr Stefan Zweig (1881–1942), author, dramatist, and translator; lived in Salzburg, 1919–1934; emigrated to Britain in 1934 and via the USA to Brazil in 1940; committed suicide together with his wife in 1942. His books were banned in Germany in 1936.

3 Dr Sigmund Freud (1856–1939), the founder of psychoanalysis; Zweig was in contact with Freud in exile.

4 The study *Der Mann Moses und die monotheistische Religion* was published in 1939, while Freud was in exile in London; it was his last work.

libraries: they had remained out of loyalty or apathy, out of cowardice or pride. They preferred to be humiliated at home than to humiliate themselves as beggars abroad. Then they had had their domestic servants taken away and the radios and telephones removed from their apartments, then their apartments themselves, then they had the Star of David compulsorily attached to their person; like lepers, everyone was to recognize them on the street, to avoid them and scorn them as outcasts, as pariahs. They were deprived of all rights, every kind of mental and physical violence was meted out to them with playful enjoyment, and for every Jew the old Russian folk saying had suddenly become a cruel truth: 'No one is safe from the beggar's bag and prison.' Whoever didn't go was thrown into a concentration camp, where German discipline broke down even the proudest, and then robbed him and shoved him out of the country with a single set of clothes and ten Reichsmarks in his bag, without asking where. And then they stood at the borders, then they begged at the consulates, and almost always in vain, because what country wanted the plundered, wanted these people who had been looted, these beggars? I will never forget the sight that presented itself to me when once I happened to be in a travel agency in London; it was stuffed full of refugees, practically all Jews, and every one of them wanted to go somewhere. It didn't matter to what country, to the ice of the North Pole or the burning sandpit of the Sahara, simply to get away, to move on, because the residence permit had expired, you had to move on, to move on with wife and child under foreign stars, to where the language was unfamiliar, among people whom you didn't know and who didn't want you. I met a man there from Vienna who was once a very rich industrialist, and also one of our most intelligent art collectors; I didn't recognize him at first, so grey, so old, so tired had he become. He feebly gripped the table with both hands. I asked him where he wanted to go. 'I don't know,' he said. 'Nowadays, who asks us what we want? You go where they still let you. Someone told me that you might be able to get a visa to Haiti or San Domingo.' My heart stopped; a tired old man with children and grandchildren, trembling in the hope of moving to a country that before then he had never seen properly on the map, just to be able to carry on begging his way and still to be foreign and useless! Next to him, a man asked with desperate eagerness how it was possible to get to Shanghai, he had heard that people were still being taken in by the Chinese. And so one pressed next to the other like this, former university professors, bank managers, retailers, proprietors, musicians, each willing to drag the pathetic ruins of his existence to anywhere over land and sea, to do whatever, to tolerate whatever, just away from Europe, just away, just away! It was a ghostly throng. But the most shocking thing for me was the thought that these fifty tortured human beings represented merely a scattered and very tiny vanguard of the huge army of five, eight, perhaps ten million Jews who behind them were getting ready to leave and pressing forwards; all those millions who had been robbed and then trampled by war, who were waiting for letters from the charitable organizations, for permits from the authorities and for travel money; a gigantic mass that, murderously startled and fleeing panic-stricken before Hitler's wildfire, was besieging the train stations and filling the prisons on all of Europe's borders; a people driven out entirely, banned from being a people, and yet still a people, which for two thousand years had yearned for nothing so much as to no longer have to roam, and to feel the earth, the quiet, peaceful earth, under its hurrying feet. But the most tragic thing in this Jewish tragedy of the twentieth century was that those who suffered it could no longer find meaning or blame in it. All the exiles of the Middle Ages, their fathers and ancestors, at least knew what they were suffering for: for their faith, for their law. They still possessed as the talisman of their soul what those today had long since lost, the unshakeable trust in their God. They lived and suffered under the proud illusion of being the chosen people of the creator of the world and humankind, and hence of being ordained for a special destiny and a special mission, and the promising word of the Bible was for them commandment and law. When they were thrown onto the pyre, they pressed their holy book to their breast, and because of this inner fire, did not feel the murderous flames so hotly. When they were driven across the lands, a last homeland remained to them: their homeland in God, from which no earthly power, no emperor, no king, no inquisition could expel them. As long as religion bound them together, they were still a community and therefore a force; when they were cast out and pursued, they were paying the penalty for having deliberately separated themselves from the other peoples of the earth by their religion, by their customs. But the Jews of the twentieth century had long since ceased to be a community. They had no common faith; they perceived their Jewishness more as burden than a source of pride and had no sense of mission. They lived removed from the commandments of their once-holy books, and they no longer wanted the old, common language. To settle down, to become members of peoples around them, to dissolve into the universal, this was their increasingly anxious effort, simply to have peace from all persecution, repose during the eternal flight. And so the one no longer understood the other, merged as they were into the other peoples, for a long time more French, German, English, Russian than Jewish. Only now, after they have all been thrown together and swept up like dirt on the streets, the bank managers from their Berlin palaces and the synagogue assistants from the Orthodox communities, the philosophy professors from Paris and the Romanian cabdrivers, the corpse washers and the Nobel laureates, the concert singers and the professional mourners, the writers and the schnapps distillers, the propertied and the propertyless, the big and the small, the pious and the enlightened, the profiteers and the sages, the Zionists and the assimilated, the Ashkenazi and the Sephardi, the just and the unjust, and behind them the distressed throng of those who thought they had long escaped the curse, the baptized and the mixed – only now, for the first time in centuries, have the Jews had a commonality forced upon them that they haven't felt for a long time: the commonality of exile that, since Egypt, has returned again and again. But why this fate, always for them and always only them? What was the reason, what was the meaning, what was the purpose of this senseless persecution? They were driven out of countries and given no country of their own. People said: Don't live with us. But one didn't say where they should live. People blamed them and refused them all means of atonement. And so during their flight they stared at one another with burning eyes – Why me? Why you? Why me with you, whom I do not know, whose language I do not understand, whose way of thinking I do not comprehend, with whom nothing connects me? Why all of us? And no one knew the answer. Even Freud, the most clear-sighted genius of our age, with whom I often spoke in those days, knew of no way, no meaning in this meaninglessness. But perhaps it is precisely Jewry's ultimate purpose, throughout its mysteriously enduring existence, to repeat over and over again Job's eternal question to God, so that it is not forgotten completely on Earth.

Part 2
Protectorate of Bohemia and Moravia

DOC. 235

On 15 March 1939 Camill Hoffmann describes the German invasion of Prague and reports on suicides among the Jewish population[1]

Handwritten diary of Camill Hoffmann,[2] entry for 15 March 1939

Overnight consultations with Hitler do not forestall the arrival of the German military; last night Mährisch Ostrau and Friedek (Witkowitz) occupied, as if it were necessary to pre-empt a Polish operation in this area; today the whole region of Bohemia and Moravia. The Czech state has ceased to exist. Hácha[3] has 'entrusted the destiny of the Czech people and country to the Führer of the German Reich', who will guarantee the Czechs 'the autonomy to develop a völkisch life befitting their particular characteristics'.[4] By morning the radio was reporting that the German military was invading from all directions; the first motorized units reached Invalidenplatz in Prague from Melnik between 10 and 11, and soon others followed: motor vehicles, tanks, artillery, field kitchens. The streets are full of people. It's a grey day, foggy, flurries of snow; the streets are icy. The invasion was undoubtedly a major operation. I took the bus into town; it got stuck at Graben. On the corner of Graben and Wenceslas Square a sea of people, barely held back by rows of policemen. Loud and sustained whistles from the crowd, then another *Kde domov můj,*[5] fists raised above [their] heads. If that happens again, I said to myself, there will be bloodshed. It's incredibly tense, the mood dark. Otherwise, the crowd is astonishingly disciplined. There has apparently been one death. A young man made a move to attack a German officer; according to another version, he spat at him; the officer immediately drew his revolver and shot him. Many suicides of Jews, many arrests. Even Hájek[6] was arrested by the Gestapo at 7 a.m. but released again after being interrogated.

1 Deutsches Literaturarchiv Marbach, HS.2002.0033.00047, copy in IfZ-Archives, F 147/1. Published in Camill Hoffmann, *Politisches Tagebuch 1932–1939*, ed. Dieter Sudhoff (Klagenfurt: Alekto Verlag, 1995), pp. 253–254. This document has been translated from German.

2 Camill Hoffmann (1878–1944), diplomat, journalist, cultural critic and poet; editor-in-chief of the *Dresdner Neueste Nachrichten*, 1912–1919; head of the press department of the Czechoslovak legation in Berlin, 1921–1938; department head at the Czech Ministry of Foreign Affairs, 1927; retired in 1939; deported in 1942 to Theresienstadt, where he worked in the 'press office' of the SS commandant's headquarters; his tasks included collecting newspaper clippings. Deported in 1944 to Auschwitz, where he was murdered.

3 Dr Emil Hácha (1872–1945), lawyer, journalist and translator; president of the Czecho-Slovak Republic, 1938–1939; president of the Protectorate of Bohemia and Moravia, 1939–1945; arrested on 13 May 1945, and died shortly afterwards in a prison hospital in Prague.

4 Hoffmann is citing Hácha's declaration, made at 3:55 a.m. on 15 March 1939, two hours before the Wehrmacht invaded. The declaration was drawn up by the German foreign minister, Joachim von Ribbentrop, on Hitler's orders. See Michael Freund, *Weltgeschichte der Gegenwart in Dokumenten: Geschichte des Zweiten Weltkrieges* (Freiburg: Herder 1954), p. 453, and Chad Bryant, *Prague in Black: Nazi Rule and Czech Nationalism* (Cambridge, MA: Harvard University Press, 2007), pp. 28–30.

5 'Where is my Home?', the Czech national anthem.

6 Jiří Hájek (1913–1993), politician and political scientist; member of the Youth Association of Czech Social Democrats; imprisoned from 1939 to 1945; from 1953, professor in Prague; ambassador to the United Kingdom, 1955–1958; representative of the Czechoslovak Socialist Republic (CSSR) at the UN, 1962–1965; Czechoslovak foreign minister, 1968; supported the Prague Spring; expelled from the Communist Party of Czechoslovakia (KSČ) in 1970.

Apparently they wanted to know about German secret informants. Traitors to the people. In the evening came the surprise announcement that Hitler had arrived at Prague Castle at 7.40 p.m. The Führer's standard on top of the Hradcany.[7] The rows of windows in the great halls lit up. He is receiving generals, officers, NS functionaries, ministers, probably just the Germans among themselves.

DOC. 236

Helga Weiss writes in her diary about the German invasion of Czecho-Slovakia on 15 March 1939[1]

Handwritten diary of Helga Weiss,[2] entry relating to 15 March 1939

[…]

It was 15 March 1939 when I was confronted with the reality of life for a second time. When I woke up in the morning, Mum[3] and Dad[4] were sitting by the radio with their heads bowed. At first I didn't know what had happened, but I soon worked it out as the newsreader's trembling voice could be heard from the radio, announcing: 'At 6:30 this morning, the German army crossed the Czechoslovak border.' I can still hear that voice clearly today. I didn't fully understand the meaning of those words, but I sensed that there was something terrible in them. The newsreader came back on the air several times. He urged residents to remain calm and collected. I stayed in bed for a bit longer. Dad came and sat next to me on the bed. He didn't say a word. I took his hand; I could feel it shaking. Dad was solemn, and you could tell that he was really upset. There was silence, broken only by the faint ticking of the clock. Something heavy hung in the air. No one wanted to break the awkward silence, so we stayed like that for several minutes. Then I got dressed and went to school. Mum took me that day. Along the way we encountered familiar and unfamiliar faces. You could read the same thing in everyone's eyes – fear, sadness and the question: 'What will happen next?'

7 The Prague Castle complex.

1 The original is held in a private collection; copy in Moreshet, D2, 215. This document has been translated from Czech. Helga Weiss began keeping a diary in Sept. 1938. She sometimes described events retrospectively, as with this entry. A slightly abridged translation of this diary entry is published in Helga Weiss, *Helga's Diary: A Young Girl's Account of Life in a Concentration Camp*, trans. Neil Bermel (London: Penguin, 2013), pp. 32–34.

2 Helga Weissová-Hošková, née Weiss (b. 1929), artist, illustrator, and teacher. She was deported with her parents to Theresienstadt on 7 Dec. 1941; she was then deported to Auschwitz in Oct. 1944, and from there via Freiberg, near Dresden to Mauthausen, where she was liberated by US troops in 1945. She returned to Prague in May 1945 and later studied art. She lives in Prague.

3 Irena Weiss, née Fuchs (1906–1990), dressmaker; she and her daughter were deported to Theresienstadt, Auschwitz, and Mauthausen, where they were later liberated. After 1945 she returned with her daughter to the apartment in Prague where she had lived before the war, and worked as a dressmaker in a state-owned enterprise.

4 Otto Weiss (1898–1944), salaried employee, originally from Pardubice; wounded in the First World War; after 1918 employed at the Länderbank in Prague; in Dec. 1941 deported to Theresienstadt and in Oct. 1944 to Auschwitz, where he was murdered.

Even at school it was sad that day. The usual cheerful chatter and carefree children's laughter had changed into frightened, anxious whispers. In the corridors and the classrooms you could see clusters of girls deep in conversation. When the bell rang, we went to our classrooms. Not much teaching went on that day. We were all distracted and breathed a sigh of relief when the bell rang again. We went home. Many of our parents were waiting for us. My mum also came to pick me up. On the way home, you could already see lots of German cars and tanks. The soldiers in them were poorly clad, and the cars themselves were made of thin metal. Even though they were poorly equipped, we were all terrified. The weather was awful that day. It rained, it snowed, the wind howled. It was as if nature was rebelling. So this is how we came under the 'protection' of the German Reich (without knowing how and from what). Slovakia succumbed to the temptation offered by the Germans and broke away from Bohemia, believing blindly that it would become an independent, free nation.[5] We also got a new name. Instead of Czechoslovakia, we were now called the Protectorate of Bohemia and Moravia.[6]

Since 15 March there hasn't been a single calm day.

DOC. 237
On 16 March 1939 Hermann Göring notifies the relevant authorities of his responsibility for all economic matters and prohibits 'unauthorized Aryanization measures'[1]

Express letter from Minister President Field Marshal Göring, signed by Göring, Plenipotentiary for the Four-Year Plan (St.M.Bev. Dev. 2560), to a) the Reich ministers, b) the Protector, c) the business groups of the Four-Year Plan, d) the general plenipotentiaries, e) Reich Commissioner Bürckel (for Moravia), and f) Reich Commissioner Henlein (for Bohemia),[2] dated 16 March 1939 (copy)

The specific issues that will arise with the incorporation of the Reich Protectorate of Bohemia and Moravia into the German economic area require, even more than was necessary with the incorporation of the Ostmark and the Sudetenland, a uniform direction. I therefore reserve the right to take decisions regarding all fundamental economic questions and ask that you inform me of your individual plans as soon as possible. In

5 The day after the 13 March 1939 meeting between Hitler and Jozef Tiso, who had been deposed as prime minister of Slovakia by the Czecho-Slovak government, the Slovak parliament voted unanimously for Slovakian independence.

6 Hitler issued a proclamation establishing the Protectorate of Bohemia and Moravia on 16 March 1939.

1 Copy in: NAP, sbírka filmů, film II 434 b/06075. Published in Miroslav Kárný and Jaroslava Milotová, *Anatomie okupační politiky hitlerovského Německa w 'Protektorátu Čechy a Morava': Dokumenty z období říšského protektora Konstantina von Neuratha* (Prague: Ústav československých a světových dějin ČSAV, 1987), doc. 52, pp. 129–131. This document has been translated from German.

2 Konrad Henlein (1898–1945), teacher; founded the Sudeten German Home Front in 1933; joined the SS in 1938; Reich commissioner for the Sudeten German territories, 1938–1939; Gauleiter from 1938; Reichsstatthalter of the Sudetenland from 1939; joined the NSDAP in 1939; head of the civil administration in Bohemia; Reich commissioner for defence in the Sudetenland, 1942–1945; SS-Obergruppenführer, 1943; committed suicide while in US internment.

particular, I ask that every plan related to the introduction of German economic and labour regulations be submitted in advance.

I would firstly like to draw your attention to the following points:

1) It is a well-known fact that Czechoslovakian industry is very export-oriented. The foreign exchange factors of which we are aware make it crucial to maintain this export trade. I request the Reich Minister of Economics[3] to take all measures that seem appropriate in order to achieve this aim. In particular, all existing contracts must firstly be completed on schedule by plants in Bohemia and Moravia, so that the foreign currency revenue is secured for the German economy as a whole.[4]

2) The buying-up of Bohemia and Moravia by German speculators from the Reich has, for the time being, been prevented by the executive authorities. In order to make proper use of the raw material reserves of Bohemia and Moravia, it is necessary, also with respect to the future, to take precautions in order to prevent such buying-up, which in practice can lead to the circumvention of German administrative procedures. Here I again request the Reich Economics Minister to devise appropriate measures.[5]

3) When it comes to major economic assets, in particular land, commercial enterprises, majority shareholdings, investments, etc., the change of ownership must be organized in a manner that corresponds to the interests of the German economy. For that reason, for the time being I reserve the right to approve any transactions of major assets (from half a million upwards). I request the Reich Economics Minister to ensure that the corresponding disclosure requirements and the conditions for approval are introduced, so as to allow ongoing supervision of the restructuring of ownership.[6]

4) Unauthorized Aryanization measures are to be prevented. I shall determine the timing, extent, and speed of any de-Jewification measures.[7]

5) Due to experiences in the Sudetenland, I urge all public sector consumers to maintain the utmost discipline where the services of residents of the country are required or wages are to be paid to them. Local wages and prices must be adopted as a general rule, and no comparisons are to be made with conditions in the German Reich. Excessive increases in this area could lead to severe setbacks.

6) In principle, efforts must be made to ensure that economic life continues without disruption. Trustees or commissioners are not to be deployed for individual businesses. If such a measure appears unavoidable in exceptional cases, the approval of the relevant minister must be obtained.

3 The Reich minister of economics was Walther Funk.

4 The industrial plants were of major significance to the German economy. According to estimates, between 9 and 12 per cent of German industrial production came from the Protectorate.

5 See Introduction, p. 24.

6 Göring subsequently arranged for Hans Kehrl to come to Prague for this purpose as representative of the Reich Ministry of Economics.

7 Göring feared that assets would be sold off at a loss, as had happened during the initial phase of the Anschluss of Austria. See PMJ 2, pp. 38–40.

DOC. 238

On 19 March 1939 the Oberlandrat in Mährisch-Budwitz orders the visible identification of Jewish shops[1]

Letter from the Oberlandrat of Mährisch-Budwitz, signed Dr Grazer,[2] to the Bezirkshauptmann[3] of Mährisch-Budwitz, Trebitsch, and Hrottowitz, dated 19 March 1939 (copy)

I intend to adopt a uniform approach to all matters related to the Jews in the districts under my authority – Mährisch-Budwitz, Trebitsch, and Hrottowitz. To this end, I decree the following:

Individuals are prohibited from taking action against Jews. Jewish shops in the aforementioned districts shall not be closed down by the authorities. It shall instead be left to the discretion of the public to avoid Jewish shops. Jewish retail premises are thus to be identified forthwith with signs measuring 20 cm x 50 cm. The signs shall read '*Jewish shop*' in both German and Czech.

I call upon the Bezirkshauptmänner to initiate the necessary steps in their districts without delay. I am to be notified of the implementation of this order by 23 March 1939.

DOC. 239

On 19 March 1939 Undersecretary Curt von Burgsdorff informs Gauleiter Josef Bürckel that synagogues in the Protectorate have been set on fire[1]

Report from Undersecretary von Burgsdorff,[2] Brünn, to Gauleiter Bürckel, Vienna, dated 19 March 1939[3]

1) Except for isolated attacks, there is complete calm in Moravia. The Oberlandräte have reported that they have been received courteously by the Czech authorities, and that they believe a good level of cooperation will develop.

1 NAP, ÚŘP, Armádní skupina 3, box 1; copy in USHMM, RG-48.005M, reel 2. This document has been translated from German.

2 Dr Oskar Grazer (1906–1991), lawyer; joined the NSDAP in 1932 and the SA in 1933; worked full-time for the SA, 1933–1936, and for the Bavarian Ministry of the Interior, 1937–1938; from Oct. 1938 to August 1939 acting Bezirkshauptmann, then Landrat in Znaim in Moravia, thereafter in Nikolsburg, and from March 1940 to 1942 in Tulln; transferred to the Party Chancellery, 1942; Gauhauptmann of Salzburg, 1944; founded the company Dr Grazer & Co. in Vienna in 1954.

3 Dr Viktor Souček (b. 1891), lawyer; Bezirkshauptmann of Mährisch-Budwitz from May 1938–1942; transferred to the regional office in Brünn in July 1942. Josef Navrátil served as the Bezirkshauptmann of Trebitsch from 1928 to 1942. Hrottowitz was only the seat of a judicial district and not an administrative unit.

1 NAP, ÚŘP, AMV 114-94-1, box 92. This document has been translated from German.

2 Dr Curt von Burgsdorff (1886–1962), administrative official; joined the NSDAP and was appointed SA-Gruppenführer, 1933; undersecretary and head of department in the Saxon Ministry of the Interior, 1933–1936; head of the office of the Reichsstatthalter in Vienna, 1938–1939; undersecretary in the office of the Reich Protector of Bohemia and Moravia, 1939–1942; governor of the Cracow district, 1943–1945; sentenced to three years' imprisonment in Poland in 1948; released in 1949.

3 The original contains handwritten notes, underlining, and corrections.

2) The main synagogues in Brünn, the synagogue in Olmütz, and the synagogue and the rabbi's house in Wsetin have been burned down. I have taken steps to prevent the second synagogue in Brünn from being set on fire. The Jews' shops have been marked with words such as 'Jew' and 'Jewish pig'. Even if it is quite correct to identify the Jewish shops, this has to be done properly and not by defacing them. I will therefore take up this matter with the local branch of the Party. The corresponding order was given to the acting police chief of Brünn, Party Comrade Dr Schwabe.[4] As Deputy Section Head Stahlecker has also confirmed to me, Reichsführer SS Himmler personally appointed Schwabe as acting police chief.

3) From time to time slight resistance makes itself felt, such as in Czech shops, where Czech customers are pointedly given better service than German ones. Even police officers on the streets occasionally do not respond to enquiries, giving no indication that they do not understand German. The swastika flags on both of the poles outside the Workers' Pension Institution[5] building in Brünn have been torn down. The German consulate has taken them in for safekeeping. The Gestapo is investigating the matter, particularly as the curtains on the ground floor of the building are not drawn back during the day despite it being working hours.

4) Unfortunately, unauthorized attempts at Aryanization are becoming noticeable. There are already signs on a large number of Jewish shops reading 'under temporary management'. On the basis of the Field Marshal's[6] decree, which has initially been communicated to me orally – according to which any type of intervention is prohibited, even in Jewish businesses – I intend to issue a corresponding regulation. In this regulation I shall prohibit the sale of Jewish businesses, because, after all, in 99 out of 100 cases such sales take place under pressure, and because I believe this will thereby significantly reduce the urge to take on the provisional management of Jewish businesses.[7]

5) As I have been informed, Landesstatthalter and Party Comrade Birthelmer[8] is seeking to merge the electricity industry in southern Moravia with that of the Lower Danube. Party Comrade Dadieu[9] appears to be making similar efforts with regard to the local mines.

4 Dr Karl Schwabe (1899–1946), lawyer; practised law in Brünn; sentenced to three years' imprisonment for espionage in 1922; joined the NSDAP in 1939; became police chief in Brünn on 14 March 1939; served in this capacity from 1939 to 1945; joined the SS in 1940; SS-Standartenführer, 1941; sentenced to death and executed by an Extraordinary People's Court in Czechoslovakia in 1946.

5 This is a reference to either the General Pensions Institution at 20 Kopalgasse or the Workers' Accident Insurance Institution for Moravia and Silesia at 51–55 Koliště.

6 Hermann Göring.

7 On 20 March 1939 the Chief of the Civil Administration in Brünn prohibited the sale of Jewish businesses in Moravia, and on 22 March 1939 the purchase, leasing, and giving away of Jewish real estate was also prohibited. There was no consistent policy on this issue in the Protectorate until the Regulation of the Reich Protector of Bohemia and Moravia on Jewish Assets was issued on 21 June 1939. See Doc. 247.

8 Heinz Adolf Birthelmer (1884–1940), engineer; joined the NSDAP in 1938; Landesstatthalter and Gau economic advisor for the Reichsgau of Lower Danube and chief executive of the electricity company Eisenstädter Elektrizitäts AG from 1938 to 1940.

9 Dr Armin Dadieu (1901–1978), chemist; appointed professor in 1932; joined the NSDAP in 1932 and the SS in 1936; deputy Landesstatthalter and Gauhauptmann of Styria, 1938; Göring's commis-

I intend to prevent these endeavours for the time being, because I have not been informed that these Party comrades have received corresponding instructions from you. If I am mistaken in this, please notify me at once. I would, however, consider it inexpedient if Party comrades outside the Chief of the Civil Administration's Economic Group received special assignments, because these could easily lead to their operating in parallel or against one another.

6) As Oberlandrat Reichelt in Ungarisch-Hradisch has informed me, there have been major demonstrations in Ungarisch-Hradisch (Uher. Hradiste), Göding (Hodonin), and Ungarisch-Brod (Uh. Brod, south-east of Ungarisch-Hradisch) as the result of rumours circulating among the populace that there are plans to cede the territory around Ungar. Hradisch, Ungar.-Brod, and Göding to Slovakia. According to the Oberlandrat, the news broadcast by the radio station in Pressburg[10] and the Slovakian news broadcasts by the Reich Broadcasting Station in Vienna have lent credence to the rumour.[11] I cannot rightly imagine the Reich Broadcasting Station doing that, but I would be grateful if you, as Gauleiter, would nonetheless issue an appropriate directive to the Reich Broadcasting Station in Vienna.

7) The news reports in the Czech press are not without interest. The *Venkov*, in particular, is running lead articles by the editor-in-chief, Halik,[12] who happens to be the press chief of the National Unity Party. The general thrust of the articles calls upon the Czechs to bring about the unconditional unity of the people and to combat any faint-heartedness and emotional turmoil. I believe I can read between the lines that, following the Führer's magnanimous proclamation, an attempt is being made to keep Czech nationhood as unified and as strong as possible.

8) In consultation with the Army Group, the Czech police are equipped with firearms to the extent required by their duties in the streets. This primarily means handguns, but also rifles in the case of the gendarmerie. Naturally, they remain without machine guns and other heavy weapons.

Heil Hitler!

sioner for mineral deposit research in Austria; SS-Oberführer, 1941; in 1948 fled via Italy to Argentina, where he worked as a government advisor on rocket development; from 1962 director of the Institute for Rocket Fuels in Stuttgart.

10 Bratislava.

11 In early March rumours had circulated in Göding that radical groups were preparing a coup in Slovakia and wanted to annexe Slovakia as well as Moravian Slovakia – which encompassed districts including Göding and Ungarisch-Hradisch – to Hungary. In response, the National Unity Party announced on 10 March 1939 that it would hold a major demonstration on 19 March in Brumow in support of a unified Moravia. However, the demonstration never took place.

12 Rudolf Halík (1881–1960), teacher, journalist, and politician; editor-in-chief of the Prague daily newspaper *Venkov*, 1938–1941; executive member of the Agrarian Party; found guilty of collaboration and sentenced to eighteen months and then ten years in prison in 1946 and 1948 respectively. Released in 1952.

DOC. 240

On 25 March 1939 a meeting is held at the Reich Ministry of the Interior to discuss the legal status of the Protectorate and guidelines for the treatment of the Jewish population[1]

Minutes (secret), unsigned, dated 25 March 1939[2]

Minutes of the state secretaries' meeting held at the Reich Ministry of the Interior on 25 March 1939.
Chair: State Secretary *Pfundtner*[3]
After the chair had opened the meeting, *State Secretary Dr Stuckart* began by pointing out that the purpose of the meeting was to inform the respective departments of the key principles governing the constitutional structure of the Protectorate. He then presented the attached draft, which addresses all the Führer's wishes in this respect, as well as the main constitutional issues that arise from them.

Following these remarks, *State Secretary Baron von Weizsäcker*[4] (Reich Foreign Office) noted that the Protectorate's envoy in Berlin would not be a member of the diplomatic corps and would not be accredited to the Führer and the Reich Chancellor.

With regard to handling border issues in the Protectorate, among the Berlin ministries, the Reich Foreign Office will be responsible where the borders with Slovakia and Poland are concerned. The Reich Ministry of the Interior will be in charge of border issues between the Protectorate and the Reich.

State Secretary Dr Schlegelberger[5] (Reich Ministry of Justice) was of the opinion that, in judicial terms, the agreements concluded between Czecho-Slovakia and the Reich may continue to apply as domestic law.

He stated that a swift clarification of the formalities of marriage in the Protectorate was needed.

With regard to the organization of German courts in the Protectorate, he considered it more expedient to establish a German senate at a Prague court rather than a higher regional court outside the Protectorate.

1 NAP, 109-1/88, fols. 1–8a. Published in Kárný and Milotová, *Anatomie*, docs. 1 and 2, pp. 1–17. This document has been translated from German.

2 The original contains handwritten underlining.

3 Johannes (Hans) Pfundtner (1881–1945), lawyer; after the First World War, initially worked in the Reich Ministry of Economics; lawyer and notary, 1925–1933; joined the NSDAP in 1932; state secretary in the Reich Ministry of the Interior, 1933–1943; retired in 1943; committed suicide in 1945. Editor of the academic journals *Das neue deutsche Reichsrecht* and *Die Verwaltungsakademie*.

4 Baron Ernst von Weizsäcker (1882–1951), diplomat; worked in the Reich Foreign Office from 1920; envoy to Oslo in 1931 and to Bern in 1933; undersecretary in the political department of the Reich Foreign Office, 1936; state secretary, 1938; joined the NSDAP in 1938; ambassador to the Vatican, 1943–1945; taken into custody in 1947 and sentenced to seven years' imprisonment at the Nuremberg Military Tribunals in 1949; released in 1950.

5 Dr Franz Schlegelberger (1876–1970), lawyer; worked in the Reich Ministry of Justice from 1918; Ministerialrat, 1921; honorary professor in Berlin, 1922; undersecretary, 1927; state secretary, 1931; joined the NSDAP in 1938; acting Reich minister of justice, Jan. 1941 – August 1942; sentenced to life imprisonment at the Nuremberg Military Tribunals in 1947; released in 1951.

It was furthermore noted that, in the Führer's view, German jurisdiction over German state subjects should extend not only to criminal law, but also to the domain of civil law, even where only *one* party (plaintiff or defendant) was a German national.[6]

State Secretary Colonel General Milch[7] (Reich Ministry of Aviation) reported that the Reich should assume responsibility for air traffic in the Protectorate, and that aviation law would need to be adapted accordingly.

State Secretary Kleinmann[8] (Reich Transport Ministry) emphasized that, in view of the Reich Railways' special responsibilities relating to the defence of the Reich, it was necessary to have directly appointed representatives of the Reich Railways present at the head offices of the Bohemian-Moravian Railways and to establish direct communication with these offices. State Secretary Dr Stuckart explained, that while one must distinguish between the special responsibilities of the Reich Railways and its general duties, it was, however, essential that the Reich Protector also be kept informed of affairs relating to the defence of the Reich, so business must, as a general rule, be conducted through him. Representatives of the Reich Railways and the other transportation agencies could be assigned to his office to deal with transport affairs.

State Secretary Zschintzsch[9] (Reich Ministry of Education) concurred with State Secretary Frank[10] from the Reich Protector's Office in declaring that the Protectorate's institutions of higher education must be included in the Reich budget as institutions of the Reich.

6 Regulation Concerning German Jurisdiction in the Protectorate of Bohemia and Moravia, 14 April 1939, *Reichsgesetzblatt*, 1939, 1, pp. 752–754; Regulation Concerning the Exercise of Criminal Jurisdiction in the Protectorate of Bohemia and Moravia, 14 April 1939, *Reichsgesetzblatt*, 1939, 1, pp. 754–758; Regulation Concerning the Exercise of Jurisdiction in Civil Proceedings in the Protectorate of Bohemia and Moravia, 14 April 1939, *Reichsgesetzblatt*, 1939, 1, pp. 759–760.

7 Erhard Milch (1892–1972), officer in the Luftwaffe; member of the board of directors of Deutsche Lufthansa AG, 1926; joined the NSDAP in 1933; state secretary of the Reich Ministry of Aviation in 1933; field marshal in the Luftwaffe, 1940; relieved of all duties after a conflict with Göring, 1945; sentenced to life imprisonment by a US military court in 1947; released in 1954; later worked as a consultant in the German aerospace industry.

8 Wilhelm Kleinmann (1876–1945), civil engineer; operations manager of the Katowice division of Prussian State Railways, 1920; joined the NSDAP in 1931; president of the Cologne division of the Prussian Reich Railways and deputy director general of the German Reich Railways, 1933, SA-Oberführer, 1934; state secretary in the Reich Transport Ministry, 1938–1942; chief executive of Mitropa, 1942.

9 Werner Zschintzsch (1888–1953), lawyer; member of the German National People's Party (DNVP), 1920–1922; section head at the Prussian Ministry of the Interior, 1924–1933; Ministerialrat from 1926; joined the NSDAP in 1933; Regierungspräsident of Wiesbaden, 1933–1936; joined the SS in 1936; state secretary in the Reich Ministry of Science, Schooling, and Education, 1936–1945; classified as a 'follower' in denazification proceedings, 1949.

10 Karl Hermann Frank (1898–1946); originally worked as a bookseller; deputy chairman of the Sudeten German Party (SdP), 1936–1938; joined the NSDAP and the SS in 1938; member of the Reichstag, 1938–1945; deputy Gauleiter of the Sudeten Gau, 1938–1939; state secretary of the Reich Protector of Bohemia and Moravia, 1939–1943; SS-Obergruppenführer 1943; Higher SS and Police Leader in Bohemia and Moravia, 1939–1944; German state minister for Bohemia and Moravia, 1943–1945; general in the Waffen-SS, 1944; executed by hanging in Prague in 1946.

State Secretary Syrup[11] (Reich Ministry of Labour) stressed that it was imperative for civil servants from the Reich working in the labour administration to be posted immediately to the Protectorate's agencies for the purpose of recruiting workers for Salzgitter[12] etc.

State Secretary Landfried[13] (Reich Ministry of Economics) reported that the plenipotentiaries of the Reich Ministry of Economics faced the same necessity.

It was determined that the civil servants from the Reich Ministry of Labour and the Reich Ministry of Economics posted to Prague may currently serve as representatives of the commander-in-chief of the army or of both army groups, and later as members of the Office of the Reich Protector. It was considered vital that these civil servants be placed under the authority of the Reich Protector and fully integrated into his office. Moreover, the greatest restraint was to be exercised in posting civil servants to Prague.

State Secretary Körner[14] and the representative of the Reich Forestry Office pointed out the necessity of standardizing hunting regulations and of adapting timber production in the Protectorate to the Reich's needs.

In response to a query from the representative of the Reich Ministry of Finance, it was stated that German state subjects in the Protectorate fell under the fiscal jurisdiction of the Protectorate authorities. It is still to be established which tax office Reich civil servants employed in the Protectorate have to pay their taxes to.

Following the announcement of a directive from the Führer on support for the ethnic Germans in the Protectorate, *State Secretary Pfundtner* closed the meeting by reiterating that the Reich Protector was the Führer's sole representative in the Protectorate, and that it was therefore *not* possible to post civil servants directly to the Protectorate's ministries. Representatives of the Reich departments would instead be incorporated into the Office of the Reich Protector. He further stated that their number should be kept as low as possible and that so long as the Commander-in-Chief of the Army[15] possessed executive power in the Protectorate, the departmental delegates in the Protectorate were to serve

11 Dr Friedrich Syrup (1881–1945), engineer, lawyer, and political scientist; worked in the Prussian civil service from 1905; president of the Reich Labour Administration, 1920–1927; president of the Reich Institute for Labour Placement and Unemployment Insurance, 1927–1932 and 1933–1938; Reich minister of labour, 1932–1933; joined the NSDAP in 1937; responsible for labour deployment under the Plenipotentiary for the Four-Year Plan, 1936–1942; state secretary in the Reich Ministry of Labour, 1939–1942; died in Soviet captivity.

12 This refers to the iron and steel complex at Salzgitter, operated by the Hermann Göring Works. It recruited forced labour from areas including the Protectorate. See Doc. 77, fn. 4.

13 Dr Friedrich Walter Landfried (1884–1952), lawyer; Regierungsrat in the Prussian civil service, 1920; Ministerialrat, 1925; undersecretary, 1932; state secretary in the Prussian Ministry of Finance, 1933–1943; state secretary in the Reich Ministry of Economics, 1939–1943; chairman of the supervisory board of numerous companies; acting president of the Prussian State Bank, 1945; interned in 1945.

14 Paul Körner (1893–1957), lawyer; joined the NSDAP in 1931 and the SS in 1932; member of the Reichstag, 1933 and 1936–1945; personal advisor to Göring, 1933; state secretary in the Prussian Ministry of State, 1933; deputy to Göring in his capacity as Plenipotentiary for the Four-Year Plan, 1936; SS-Obergruppenführer, 1942; sentenced to 15 years' imprisonment at the Nuremberg Military Tribunals in 1949; released in 1951.

15 Walter von Brauchitsch.

solely as representatives of the Commander-in-Chief of the Army or the Chief of the Civil Administration and were to be subject to their orders.

[...][16]

The consequences of an autonomous Protectorate are as follows:

1) Pursuant to Article 12, Czechoslovakian law hitherto in force shall remain in effect unless it contravenes the nature of the protection undertaken by the German Reich. A special statement clarifying that specific Czechoslovakian laws are still in effect is thus, in principle, unnecessary. Reich law does not automatically apply to the Protectorate. Future Reich legislation which is also to be enforced in the Protectorate must be explicitly applied to the Protectorate. Existing Reich law must be implemented in the Protectorate by decree if it is to apply there.

Czech laws which contravene the nature of the protection undertaken by the German Reich shall cease to have effect. The Reich Protector shall be the first to determine which laws shall cease to have effect.

2) The Protectorate shall have its own flag and its own official seal.

3) With the exception of ethnic Germans who, pursuant to Article 2, are German state subjects, the inhabitants of the Protectorate are subjects of the Protectorate. It is the will of the Führer that they shall not be treated as foreigners in relation to the Reich, whether at home or abroad. As subjects of the Protectorate, they instead count as German subjects with a special status. Therefore, the regulations concerning foreign passports, the police for foreigners, and residence and work permits do not apply to them. Nonetheless, a visa requirement shall be introduced for Protectorate subjects entering the Reich. There shall be no border controls on the border between the Protectorate and the Reich; the entry of Protectorate subjects without a visa shall instead be prevented through the imposition of severe penalties.

Czechoslovak subjects who hitherto had their legal residence abroad shall, in accordance with the will of the Führer, also become Protectorate subjects provided that they have a connection to the territory of the Protectorate – that is, possess rights of residence there. Marriages between Protectorate subjects and Reich subjects shall be subject to approval but will not be subject to the Law on Marriage with Foreigners. The Reich Minister of Justice[17] shall instead issue specific regulations for this matter.

The ethnic German inhabitants of the Protectorate are German state subjects and provisionally classed as Reich citizens in accordance with the Reich Citizenship Law.[18] In order that they may have access to all possible opportunities in the Protectorate, Reich citizens residing in the Protectorate will also need to retain or acquire the same rights as Protectorate subjects. It is still necessary to issue a specific regulation defining which persons are to be considered ethnic German inhabitants. The provisions of the Blood Protection Law, in particular the ban on marriage with Jews, shall also apply to ethnic German inhabitants. The prohibitions and penal provisions of the Blood Protection Law shall also apply to the Jews residing in the Protectorate, in the interests of German citizens of the Reich. The Marital Health Law and the Law for the Prevention of Offspring

16 The opening paragraphs of the appended draft dealt with the legal status of the Protectorate.

17 Dr Franz Gürtner (1881–1941) was Reich minister of justice from June 1932 to Jan. 1941.

18 Reich Citizenship Law, 15 Sept. 1935, *Reichsgesetzblatt*, 1935, 1, p. 1146. See also PMJ 1/198.

with Hereditary Diseases shall equally apply.[19] A clarifying regulation will be issued within the next few days.[20]

German state subjects residing in the Protectorate are subject to German jurisdiction. There are various ways to establish German jurisdiction in the Protectorate. One alternative would be to create consular courts. Due to the negative repercussions which doing so might have on the attitude of the Protectorate's government and population towards the Reich, this solution may be problematic. Instead, the Minister of Justice should examine the possibility of establishing German Reich courts for civil and criminal justice at the local level in those cities with a substantial number of German state subjects. These could then be grouped together under a Reich Regional Court in Prague, as well as a Higher Regional Court. The establishment of German tribunals and senates at Protectorate courts would probably not comply with the wording of the Führer's decree,[21] because this solution would merely establish a Protectorate jurisdiction implemented by Germans. Czech substantive law shall necessarily continue to apply to German state subjects in accordance with Article 12 of the decree, as otherwise there would be excessive interference in the economic structure of the Protectorate and it is not practicable to place the inhabitants of the Protectorate under different civil or criminal jurisdictions. However, Czech criminal law must be brought largely into line with German criminal law. The Minister of Justice and the Reich Protector are to examine how this alignment is to occur in practice, whether through the introduction of legislation or through relevant laws of the Protectorate. The law regulating political crime will have to be the German Reich criminal law and also applicable to subjects of the Protectorate. It shall be necessary to adjudicate such criminal offences before German courts. The relevant offices are asked to bear in mind the provisions concerning treason, high treason, and the like.

In connection with these questions concerning German subjects residing in the Protectorate, discussion is also required as to whether, as a rule, special arrangements should be introduced for the administration of the German-language enclaves. The larger language enclaves include: Brünn, with around 60,000 inhabitants; Iglau, with around 25,000 inhabitants; and Olmütz, with around 20,000 inhabitants. In addition, there are approximately 30,000 German subjects residing in the area around Mährisch-Ostrau.

In the first instance, it would be feasible to incorporate these areas into the Reich completely, with the exception of Iglau. It is still entirely unclear whether the Führer would agree to such a significant reduction in the Protectorate's size and such a weaken-

19 The Law for the Protection of German Blood and German Honour (15 Sept. 1935) prohibited marriages and extramarital sexual relations between Jews and non-Jews. See *Reichsgesetzblatt*, 1935, 1, pp. 1146–1147, and PMJ 1/199. The Law for the Protection of the Hereditary Health of the German People, or Marital Health Law (18 Oct. 1935) required persons intending to marry to submit a health certificate. See *Reichsgesetzblatt*, 1935, 1, p. 1246. The Law for the Prevention of Offspring with Hereditary Diseases (14 July 1933) permitted the sterilization of persons considered to be suffering from hereditary diseases, mental illness, or alcoholism. See *Reichsgesetzblatt*, 1933, 1, pp. 529–531.

20 This regulation could not be found.

21 Decree of the Führer and Reich Chancellor concerning the Protectorate of Bohemia and Moravia, 16 March 1939, *Reichsgesetzblatt*, 1939, 1, pp. 485–488.

ing of Germandom in Bohemia and Moravia. There are strong political considerations that speak in favour of incorporating the territory around Mährisch-Ostrau.[22]

It would also be possible to have the language enclaves remain associate parts of the Protectorate, while introducing German organizational law to these areas, in particular the constitutional law in the German Municipal Code. The cities of Brünn, Olmütz, and, if necessary, also Ostrau would then become municipal districts according to the German Municipal Code. The remaining German municipalities could potentially be consolidated into a German district under the leadership of a German Landrat. For reasons of expediency, the district would have to be organized according to the principles of our district law. Special arrangements would be required for the supervision of the municipal districts and the consolidated German district. This supervision could be entrusted to a German department in the Prague Ministry of the Interior, with the right of appeal to the Reich Protector. A feasible solution would be to create a separate German ministry within the Protectorate government, with responsibility for all German affairs. This would ensure, among other things, that a German has a seat in the Protectorate government. The extent to which the economic legislation of the German Municipal Code might be introduced into the numerous and varied financial relationships which would continue to exist between the Protectorate, the district, and the municipalities would require particular attention.

In addition to German organizational law, German school legislation must also be implemented for German state subjects, at least to some extent. German schools with German teachers and German curricula are the minimum requirements which must be fulfilled. The responsibility for school inspections would rest with the German ministry.

4) From the Reich's point of view, there is currently no particular interest in implementing racial legislation to protect the Czech people. Legislation to that effect is therefore not envisaged. In principle, it can be left to the Protectorate's government to decide whether and which measures should be taken against the Jews. The Jewish question in the Protectorate will likely develop of its own accord.

The Reich, however, does have an interest in preventing the Jews residing in the Protectorate from influencing the Protectorate's general relations with the Reich. The Führer has therefore decided that the Jews shall be eliminated from public life in the Protectorate. The responsibility for carrying out this task rests with the Protectorate government and is not the direct responsibility of the Reich. The Reich Protector will advise the government in Prague to take the necessary measures. These would include:

a) revocation of active and passive voting rights;
b) removal from public office;
c) removal from the press, radio and other activities which influence public opinion;
d) exclusion from specialist agencies to be set up for the maintenance of domestic security and order (Art. 7 of the Führer's decree);
e) prohibition of the possession of firearms and, in addition, a ban on the manufacture and trade of firearms.

22 Moravská Ostrava was not incorporated into the Reich but remained part of the Protectorate of Bohemia and Moravia.

With regard to the economy, no specific anti-Jewish measures will be issued by the Reich for the time being. Instead, it shall be up to the Protectorate government to take measures related to the exclusion of the Jews from the economy.

5) The civil servants of the Protectorate shall not be classed as Reich civil servants. Accordingly, the German Civil Service Law shall not be introduced in the Protectorate. The civil servants will also not take an oath of loyalty to the Führer. They should, however, submit a declaration of loyalty to the Reich, which the Reich Protector should prompt the Protectorate government to introduce. It is the will of the Führer that all public offices in the Reich stay barred to Protectorate subjects. Protectorate subjects can therefore become neither civil servants in the German Reich, nor officers in the German Wehrmacht, nor Party functionaries, nor holders of public office in trade and industry or in corporate and business organizations. Protectorate subjects are only eligible to hold office in those administrative branches which are administered autonomously by the Protectorate.

6) A separate Reich administration shall be set up in the Protectorate, but with a limited area of responsibility. It shall assume control over the armed forces and aviation, as well as customs administration, the security police, radio broadcasting, foreign exchange acquisition and – for the ethnic German inhabitants – judicial administration. All of the Reich's intermediary administrative branches shall fall under the remit of the Reich Protector. It is unlikely that a separate administration will be established for all the remaining administrative branches. This applies in particular to labour administration, the railways, the post office, and the entire transport system.

Article 8 of the Führer's decree, while granting the Reich direct supervision over transport, post, and telegraph systems, does not require these administrative branches to set up separate subordinate offices in the Protectorate. The concept of 'direct supervision', as it is generally understood, only entails briefing the administrative departments of the Protectorate on the guidelines of the corresponding Reich administrations and bringing them into line with the Reich's general and specialist institutions. To this end, these administrative departments can post individual inspectors and advisors to subordinate administrations in the Protectorate. These civil servants are responsible to the Reich Protector. A direct posting to the Prague ministries is, however, out of the question. Where possible, advisors will be assigned to the Reich Protector, who will also lead the supervision of the respective central Protectorate ministries. The Protectorate's railway, post, and telegraph systems must be coordinated in such a way that it is possible at any time, particularly in a crisis situation, for the Reich to integrate them into its own administration and management structure.

7) It cannot yet be ascertained whether the Oberlandräte who are currently in charge of general administration will remain in their posts. It is anticipated that their capacity to serve as citizenship authorities, as registration authorities, etc. will need to be maintained to some extent. As the executive authority, the Commander-in-Chief of the Army shall task the Oberlandräte with providing support to the Bezirkshauptmannschaften and lower-level specialized authorities. The Oberlandräte are responsible for several Bezirkshauptmannschaften. Should municipal authorities require support, special district commissioners can be appointed and supervised by the Oberlandräte. The Oberlandräte report to the Chief of the Civil Administration in the Army Group in which the entire civil administration will eventually be brought together, thereby avoiding any fragmen-

tation based on competences or other factors. District commissioners, Oberlandräte and the Chief of the Civil Administration are not to carry out administrative tasks themselves, but instead to supervise the administration of the Protectorate. The government of the Protectorate is to channel orders to subordinate authorities via the Oberlandräte. Oberlandräte may intervene in the administrative processes and transactions taking place between the Protectorate departments under their supervision and the government of the Protectorate. If the Oberlandräte object to the directives from the state government, they are also authorized to appeal to the Chief of the Civil Administration for a decision. The Oberlandräte have the power to revoke the directives of the Bezirkshauptmannschaften and, in urgent cases, to replace these with their own directives. The district commissioners occupy the same position between the Bezirkshauptmannschaften and the municipal authorities.

As already stated above, at present it is not possible to anticipate whether it will be necessary to maintain supervision of the Protectorate authorities on this scale.

8) It is the Führer's will that formally the Czechs are dealt with in a conciliatory manner, but in practical terms, they must be treated with the utmost severity and unrelenting rigour. It is not in the Czech character to understand conciliatory behaviour. The Czech tends to view any form of compliance as a sign of weakness. It goes without saying that their rigorous treatment should still be just. In all of their actions the government of the Protectorate as well as the subordinate offices must be conscious that supreme executive power rests with the Reich. On the other hand, however, this does not mean that there will be German intervention in each and every measure.

DOC. 241

Anonymous report on the situation of the Jewish population in the Protectorate up to the end of March 1939[1]

Report by an anonymous Dutchman, Prague, spring 1939

Report on the events in Prague on 15 March 1939

The Gestapo arrived in Prague at 9 a.m.; by 10 a.m. the arrests had already begun. Anyone holding any sort of leadership position was taken into custody. Only those in possession of the blue permit[2] were allowed to leave Czechoslovakia or cross back over the border.

The exit permit was, however, difficult to obtain. Whoever wishes to get one must queue up and wait at the Gestapo office, at 9 Perstyn. After one has waited for a long time, it can happen that the functionaries suddenly close the office on a whim. The hundreds

1 Wiener Library, Doc 1375/336–337. Published in Ben Barkow, Raphael Gross and Michael Lenarz (eds.), *Novemberpogrom 1938: Die Augenzeugenberichte der Wiener Library, London* (Frankfurt: Suhrkamp, 2008), pp. 881–890. This document has been translated from German.

2 The Gestapo was placed in charge of issuing the 'blue exit permits' (*Ausreisekarten*), which were introduced immediately after the establishment of the Protectorate. In the first few weeks, Jews could also still obtain such visas, but only if they had the requisite entry permit issued by another country.

of people waiting outside must then go home empty-handed. But most don't do that; instead, they stay where they are and keep waiting until the office reopens. Many queue overnight in snow, wind, and rain until the next morning and even longer, for hours and hours, until it is finally their turn. On 30 March, a sign went up announcing that Jews would no longer receive blue permits. A flourishing trade in these exit permits has since emerged. Cases are known in which thousands of korunas have changed hands. The original cost was around 2,000 korunas; by 31 March, as much as 50,000 korunas is said to have been paid.[3] The author of this report would like to point out in particular that the actual wording of the permit allows for a return to Czechoslovakia, but with Jews this section has often been crossed out, or else the permits still containing the return provision have been confiscated from Jews at the border, for example in Bentheim. This reporter received his permit through the intervention of the Dutch consulate in Prague.

The Gestapo distinguishes between 'genuine' and 'fake' foreigners. Genuine foreigners include, for example, Americans, Englishmen, Frenchmen, Dutchmen; fake foreigners are all Jews, Hungarians, Poles, and Yugoslavs. However, everyone needed this exit permit and, upon arrival, an entry permit from the German authorities. Even German state subjects must obtain an entry permit. In the case of business trips, they have to apply for the permit at the Reich Ministry of Economics and submit an endorsement from the Chamber of Commerce.

The Jews in Czechoslovakia have kept their passports for the time being. Incidentally, the 'J' has been added to these passports since January. Chvalkovsky[4] was summoned to Berlin back then, because Hitler's wishes concerning 'Aryanization' were not being implemented swiftly or precisely enough.[5] At that time, without any additional legislation, kosher butchering was suddenly prohibited – that is, it was simply made impossible by locking up the area set aside for this at the Prague slaughterhouse. The arrests were made by a Gestapo man and a Czech official, but these Czech officials were almost always Sudeten Germans. But all of them had a good command of Czech. Czech courses for military officers have apparently been running in Dresden for some time now.

On 14 March the atmosphere on the streets of Prague started to get noticeably tense. Bands of youths roamed the streets, clearly intent on inciting trouble. By the evening, it was no longer possible to speak Czech on the streets without being jostled. They mostly spat in the faces of people speaking Czech. It was said that the groups roving about were German students, but they were actually Henlein supporters[6] who had come specifically to Prague from the Sudetenland. Their ranks included not only youths, but also men between 40 and 45 years old. The author would like to describe how groups of twenty, thirty, or more people stirred up unrest in the most outrageously impudent manner.

3 According to the Regulation on the Rate of Exchange in the Protectorate of Bohemia and Moravia (21 March 1939), 1 koruna was equivalent to 10 Reichspfennigs. See *Reichsgesetzblatt*, 1939, 1, p. 555.

4 František Chvalkovský (1885–1945), lawyer; foreign minister of Czecho-Slovakia, 1938–1939; envoy of the Protectorate of Bohemia and Moravia in Berlin, 1939–1945; died in an air raid on Berlin.

5 Hitler and the Reich foreign minister, Joachim von Ribbentrop, received Foreign Minister Chvalkovský in Berlin on 21 Jan. 1939. During the talks, Hitler emphasized that Czecho-Slovakia could only exist in close dependence on the German Reich. Chvalkovský declared himself willing to make far-reaching concessions. Shortly thereafter, the Czecho-Slovakian government enacted tougher anti-Jewish legislation.

6 This is a reference to members and supporters of the Sudeten German Party (SdP), which was under the leadership of Konrad Henlein.

They crossed Wenceslas Square over and over again, harassing both Jews and Czechs. A terrible fight broke out in Heinrichsgasse, in which the Henlein people came off worse. On 14 March these people already knew exactly what was going on. Their greeting is said to have been 'Heil 15 March!' The demonstrations lasted well into the night. Several hundred police officers were stationed at Wenceslas Square and along Am Graben.

Late in the evening, the news arrived that German troops had occupied Ostrova (Mährisch-Ostrau) and were set to occupy Pilsen the following morning. They occupied Prague the next morning between 10 a.m. and noon. The first thing that happened was that the Gestapo drove up to the National Bank and seized the gold. Motorized troops made their way into Prague. The officers rode in open vehicles without side panels, such as are commonly used by the military. The population spat at them and shook their fists threateningly at the vehicles. The German military, however, was unruffled by this.

When the author of this report returned to his hotel, two Gestapo officers were there and demanded that the hotel provide them with twenty rooms: 'The rooms must be ready in two hours!' At 11 a.m. the hotel manager told him he had to vacate his room, because the entire floor was to be reserved for the Gestapo. At half past 11, another two Gestapo officers (in SS uniforms) came to demand that the entire hotel be vacated of guests and put at the Gestapo's disposal. After the hotel manager objected on the grounds that almost all the guests had gone out, he was given a deadline of 5 p.m. Other hotels (this was the Palace Hotel) were also seized. The Petschek building became the general staff's headquarters.[7]

Incidentally, the military behaved decently towards the public and did not bother anyone in particular. It was curious that all the books banned in Germany sold out soon after the German troops arrived. Books by Emil Ludwig,[8] for example, were snapped up immediately. The military officers apparently even bought Konrad Heiden's *Hitler*.[9] The Gestapo officers turned up with pre-prepared arrest lists in their briefcases, allowing them to begin making arrests shortly after their arrival. Henlein supporters who were in the know in Prague escorted the Gestapo automobiles on these round-ups. It is said that some 13,000 people were arrested in Czechoslovakia altogether. In the first two days, approximately 6,000 arrests were made in Prague. The first people to be arrested were the former mayor of Prague,[10] several department heads in the municipal administration, and various government officials. Jaksch[11] found refuge at the English Embassy.

7 The Wehrmacht commanders were housed in the former Petschek villa in the district of Bubeneč in Prague, which today serves as the seat of the US embassy in the Czech Republic. On the Petschek conglomerate, see Doc. 77 and Glossary.

8 Emil Ludwig, born Emil Cohn (1881–1948), writer, translator, lawyer, and editor; became well known for his biographies of Goethe (1920), Napoleon (1925), William II (1926), and Bismarck (1927). He emigrated to Switzerland in 1933, and to the United States in 1940.

9 Konrad Heiden, *Adolf Hitler: Eine Biographie*, 2 vols (Zurich: Europa Verlag, 1936–1937).

10 Petr Zenkl (1884–1975), politician; mayor of Prague, 1937–1939; arrested and deported to Buchenwald, 1939; mayor of Prague for a second time, 1945–1946; deputy prime minister of Czechoslovakia, 1946–1948; emigrated to the United States in 1948.

11 Wenzel Jaksch (1896–1966), mason and journalist; from 1924 executive member of the German Social Democratic Workers' Party (DSAP) and its chairman from 1938; in 1938 emigrated to Poland and later to Britain; unofficial representative of the Sudeten Germans in the Czechoslovak government in exile in London; director of the Office for Expellees, Refugees, and Evacuees in the State of Hesse, 1950–1953; president of the German League of Expellees, 1964–1966.

The *Prager Tagblatt* was occupied. Eight German regional court judges came to carry out enquiries. No instances of mistreatment are reported to have occurred during the arrests, but there were more than enough cases of rudeness and disrespect. Those arrested were initially sent to the prison in Pankrasz, and then to Sokol Stadium, where they were quartered in the cubicles installed for participants in sporting competitions. There is room there for 3,000 people. Many of those detained had to spend the night standing up because there was no room to lie down.

Life in Prague gradually began to 'normalize'. The shop signs were changed. The people took over Aryanization themselves. In the windows are signs reading 'pure Aryan shop' in Czech. Delivery vehicles were protected by simply painting over the company logo. On Wednesday, Hitler arrived in Prague. On Thursday, it was reported in every newspaper that the Chamber of Lawyers had instructed all Jewish lawyers to cease practising.[12] When one walked through the streets, all the shops, particularly the clothes shops, including the Christian ones, appeared to be closed. So much was being bought that shopkeepers began letting in just a few people at a time. They would then lock the doors and let the next people in after a while. Thus, people were stockpiling goods. People in Germany were buying their food here. Whole convoys of vehicles, loaded with food supplies, were departing for Germany.

On the third day following the occupation of Prague came terrible news about suicides among the Jewish population. Some thirty to forty suicides were occurring daily. So far, hospitals have admitted approximately 400 persons who attempted to commit suicide between 15 and 18 March. People were also arrested for completely non-political reasons. For example, the engineer Mr Freisinger,[13] who, with the permission of the Welfare Ministry in Prague, had organized and lawfully prepared the emigration of a group of 300 Jews to the Dominican Republic. The only difficulty was that there were people in the group who feared departing via Germany. Freisinger therefore negotiated with KLM in Holland[14] in order to secure air transport to Rotterdam. He was arrested for being the 'head of a group of emigrants'.

Mrs Schmolka[15] and Mrs Stein[16] were arrested as well.[17] All the money collected for the Sudeten German Jews was confiscated, which means that the Sudeten German Jewish refugees who have been living in Prague since last autumn will go hungry. In addition, all the wealthy people have been arrested. Even the lawyer Dr Stein, who had done a lot of work for Petschek, was arrested. Initially he managed to flee because he had been warned, but on the sixth day he handed himself in to the police.

12 On 15 March 1939, the newspaper *Pražský list* ran a front-page article titled 'No More Jewish Lawyers'. On 16 March 1939, the Reich Chamber of Lawyers barred Jewish lawyers in Prague from practising their profession. Shortly thereafter the ban was extended to Brno. All Jewish employees in the public administration were suspended from duty. See Franz Friedmann, 'Rechtsstellung der Juden im Protektorat Böhmen und Mähren, Stand: 31 Jul. 1942', in Helena Krejčová, Jana Svobodová and Anna Hyndráková (eds.), *Židé v Protektorátu: Hlášení Židovské nábotženské obce v roce 1942. Dokumenty* (Prague: Maxdorf, 1997), pp. 232–263.

13 Kurt Freisinger (1901–1942?), engineer; fled to Prague from the Sudeten territories in Oct. 1938. By order of the Germans, the Czech police detained Freisinger in Prague on 21 March 1939, but released him immediately afterwards. He was eventually deported to Theresienstadt on 24 April 1942 and from there on 28 April 1942 to Zamość, where he perished.

14 KLM: Koninklijke Luchtvaart Maatschappij, the Dutch national airline.

Many Jews have fled to Poland. However, Ostrova, the only escape route, was occupied by the Germans very early on, so the Jews found themselves trapped. It was under these circumstances that people smuggling began to take place in Ostrova, with Restaurant Grün and Café Union serving as the bases for the operation. For about ten days the process was as follows: those fleeing were smuggled into the coal mine tunnels and taken underground to Polish territory. The German authorities, however, discovered this passageway and blocked it. One now has to pay a large sum to be smuggled across the border. It reportedly costs 5,000 korunas to obtain safe passage to Poland. But the Sudeten German Jews no longer have so much money. They are borrowing 300 to 400 korunas from one another to flee.

Many Jews who were unable to cross the border have sought refuge in hospitals and sanatoria, where they believe they are safely out of the Gestapo's reach.

Several hundred of those who have escaped are in Częstochowa, while many have travelled on to Gdynia, from where they hope to reach England by ship. Many also fled to Yugoslavia, for which it was easy to obtain a visa.

Over the past few months, many Jews in Czechoslovakia have had themselves baptized just so that they can emigrate to South America. More still have baptism certificates that were procured through corrupt means. People have paid between 800 and 1,500 korunas for baptism certificates, depending on whether only the parents or also the grandparents are listed as Christians on the certificate.

Shortly after the start of the German occupation, regulations were issued concerning the Jews. All Jews residing in Bohemia and Moravia are required to register their assets by 15 April. Jews are not permitted to sell, transfer, or give away real estate. Shop owners may neither sell nor Aryanize their shops.[18] Jews are prohibited from entering cafés, cinemas, and theatres.[19]

The Czech view: once Hitler had arrived, Gajda[20] believed his time had come. On 15 March, he issued a proclamation urging the population to place themselves under his

15 Dr Marie Schmolka (Schmolková), née Eisner (1890–1940), association official; head of the refugee relief efforts of the Jewish Religious Community and the HICEM office in Prague; representative of Czechoslovakia's relief committee to the League of Nations; chairwoman of the Czechoslovak National Committee for Refugees from Germany, 1933–1938; imprisoned for two months in March 1939; emigrated after the outbreak of war to Britain, where she was involved in founding the National Council of Czechoslovak Jews.

16 Correctly: Hannah Steiner, née Dub (1894–1944), association official; president of the Czechoslovak branch of the Women's International Jewish Organization (WIZO); editor of the women's magazine *Blätter für die jüdische Frau*; co-founder of Jewish Refugee Relief in Prague; arrested in 1939; deported on 13 July 1943 to Theresienstadt, where she was active in the Women's Aid Service; on 16 Oct. 1944 deported to Auschwitz, where she was murdered.

17 After spurning offers of protection from various consulates, Marie Schmolka voluntarily handed herself in to the Gestapo in order to secure Hannah Steiner's release.

18 See Doc. 239, fn. 7.

19 The regional authorities in Prague did not issue a general ban on Jews attending cinema and theatre performances until 20 Feb. 1940. Jews in Prague had been prohibited from frequenting certain public establishments since 14 August 1939. See Friedmann, 'Rechtsstellung', pp. 245–246.

20 Radola Gajda, also known as Rudolf Geidl (1892–1948), professional soldier and politician; general of the Czechoslovak Legion in Russia; founded the National Fascist Community in 1925; leading figure in the Czechoslovak fascist movement; interned by the Soviets in 1945 and sentenced to two years' imprisonment in 1947.

leadership. There were originally plans to form a national guard, which Gajda was supposed to lead. These were thwarted by the Germans the very next day. Gajda has no say in matters, and Hácha has taken over the leadership. The population is learning from the fate of the Jews, but no conclusive judgement can be made regarding the mood of the Czech population. In any event, there is great disappointment and bitterness. It is reported that acts of sabotage have been carried out at the Skoda Works.

The author of this report adds the following personal experience:

After the Gestapo had already taken up quarters in the Palace Hotel, and he along with other guests had, with great difficulty, found private accommodation, the author felt compelled to return to the hotel to pick up his post. While the porter was picking out and handing over his letters, the SS men on duty in the lobby moved close to him and brusquely asked if he was Jewish, why he was in Prague, if he travelled often, etc. He was told to show his passport. Thereupon they said rudely, 'So you're Dutch! You think we can't get you, don't you?' They said that he should see to it that he returns to Holland, but that he must procure an exit permit just like everyone else. He responded in a calm but firm tone, whereupon the SS men backed down and even informed him in a relatively polite manner where he could obtain the 'blue permit'.

Addendum to the report from Prague

The following persons committed suicide between 15 and 18 March: Paul *Rittenberg* in Prague shot himself in the House of the Black Rose;[21] Dr *Beermann* and his wife from Carlsbad poisoned themselves.

DOC. 242

On 2 April 1939 Ilse Weber from Witkowitz writes to her friend Lilian about the daily discrimination against Jews and asks for her assistance[1]

Letter from Ilse Weber,[2] Witkowitz, to her friend Lilian,[3] dated 2 April 1939.

Dearest Lilian,

This is now no longer an *exchange* of letters, but rather more like keeping a diary which I send you to read. Well, you won't have time right now, but I do need to chat to you. The first and most important piece of news I have to tell you is that Elli[4] wrote to us this week with a positive suggestion. It concerns settlement in *Paraná*, Brazil, and by

21 Pavel Rittenberg (1912–1939), journalist; originally from Russia; journalist in Berlin, from where he fled to Prague in Sept. 1935 with his fiancée. The House of the Black Rose was the location of the travel agency for emigration.

1 The original is held in a private collection. Copy in IfZ-Archives, F 601. Published in Ilse Weber, *Wann wohl das Leid ein Ende hat: Briefe und Gedichte aus Theresienstadt* Ulrike Migdal ed., (Munich: Hanser Verlag, 2008), pp. 94–96. This document has been translated from German.

2 Ilse Weber, née Herlinger (b. 1903), children's author, radio playwright, translator. She was deported on 8 Feb. 1942 to the Theresienstadt ghetto and concentration camp, where she worked as a nurse in the children's hospital. While in the ghetto she wrote poems as well as songs that she sang to the children and other prisoners. She was deported from Theresienstadt to Auschwitz in autumn 1944; declared dead.

chance Elli got to speak to an influential person about us.[5] The airmail letter you had requested to send to her is thus no longer necessary, but if you've already written it, it's certainly not a tragedy. I would like to know more about Paraná; we were only able to find out what the encyclopaedia says about it, and that isn't much. I'd be very happy if we could leave here. Yet it's tough to go to a foreign country without any means, for one is not allowed to take anything.

It's difficult for you to picture our lives at present. Willi[6] is still going to the office and gradually liquidating the business. Hannerle[7] is going to school, but for how much longer is also uncertain, because there are plans to accommodate the German army in the schools. The children find the German soldiers very interesting. They can see them outside our window every morning performing their drills. The boys are already able to sing their songs. Tomorrow is Seder[8] evening, you know, that most festive evening of the year which commemorates the exodus of the Jews from Egypt. Der *Stürmer*, which is on display in all the bookstores, calls our Easter the 'Jewish celebration of murder'. One day I would like to have a word with the author of this and similar articles and ask why he writes them. For aren't we Jews unhappy enough as it is? And of all the malicious fabrications, the ritual [murder] myth is the basest and vilest. I can only believe that it must be awkward for the local Germans, who for decades have relished eating the matzos[9] given to them by their Jewish friends, to now read such things and act as if they believe them. We are invited to my mother-in-law's tomorrow evening. It was always wonderful at her place when all nine children and their wives, husbands, and children sat together around the long table. Last year Tommy,[10] being the youngest, asked the questions in Hebrew, and I was very proud of him. This year there will be several empty seats.

You've known me ever since my schooldays and have always been well informed about my friends, haven't you? These have included a great many German girls, and

3 Lilian von Löwenadler (b. 1903), daughter of a Swedish diplomat; Ilse Weber's penfriend. A longstanding friendship emerged from their correspondence. Lived first in Sweden before moving to Britain in 1940; died during the war from complications following surgery.

4 Elli Wendland, school friend of Ilse Weber; emigrated to Brazil.

5 In 1932, Oswald Nixdorf, a German tropical farming expert, and Hermann von Freeden purchased a plot of fertile rainforest in the Brazilian state of Paraná, where they founded the Roland (Rolândia) settlement for 400 German families. Many Jews also sought refuge there.

6 Willi Weber (1901–1974), gardener; Ilse Weber's husband; owned a debt collection agency; deported on 8 Feb. 1942 to Theresienstadt, where he worked as a gardener. He buried his wife's poems and songs before being deported to Auschwitz on 28 Sept. 1944 and retrieved them after the war. Returned in 1945 to Prague, where he worked for the Israeli embassy until 1967.

7 Hanuš Weber (b. 1931), journalist and interpreter; Ilse Weber's son, left Prague in 1939 on a Kindertransport; lived in Sweden with Lilian von Löwenadler's mother until 1945; returned to Prague in Nov. 1945 to live with his father; worked in radio broadcasting from 1955; later served as President Antonín Novotný's interpreter; emigrated in 1969 to Sweden, where he worked as a television journalist.

8 Hebrew: literally 'order', the term indicating the meal on the first evening of Pesach (Passover), which takes place according to a specific order indicated in the Mishna (the first part of the Talmud) and also involves reciting the Haggadah text.

9 Hebrew: unleavened flatbread that is integral to the Passover festival.

10 Tomáš Weber (b. 1934), youngest son of Ilse and Willi Weber; deported to Theresienstadt on 8 Feb. 1942 and from there to Auschwitz on 4 Oct. 1944; declared dead in 1947.

until recently we were still on good terms. But now when I bump into them, which can't be avoided in such a small town, they quickly look the other way. Only one of them has managed to smirk at me without saying hello, and *she*, interestingly enough, is the same person who years ago assured me, close to tears, that she would *never* forget it after I did a good turn for her. But there are also those people who instantly smile and say, 'Hello, Ilse', as well as *one* very special individual who makes a point of coming up to me and walking with me, although I find such heroism not in the least comforting. How does all of this make me feel? It hurts me wretchedly, Lilian, so wretchedly that I can't think of anything else the whole day, but at the same time I also wonder how *she* must feel when she doesn't greet me. I think every decent person would feel ashamed inside. Don't you think so too?

I still haven't received a reply from the Barbican Mission.[11] I even wrote in English. Perhaps that's why they didn't understand me? But if it hasn't reopened, I can't receive a reply. Lilian, wouldn't it be a good idea to write to the English consulate requesting that someone travelling to England take my Hanuš with them? But shouldn't *you* do that? I also wanted to ask you to let me know if he needs to bring anything in particular, perhaps bed sheets and pillowcases? Yesterday he received two nice outfits as gifts, so he is now well equipped for two years. And you shouldn't incur any unnecessary expenses because of him. I already owe you an enormous debt of gratitude. Even if it's somehow not possible for the child to come to you – you never know what may happen – I will always consider your offer to be genuine. We will never forget what you and Elli have done for us during these dark days. If it hadn't been for you two, we would have lost our faith in humanity. And I'm sending Hannerle to you with peace of mind and no concerns. I am firmly convinced that you will treat him with love and care, as if he were your own child. He should also go to school right away, shouldn't he? That's where he will best learn the language, as you will certainly speak German with him every now and then so that he doesn't feel too lonely. Even if we do emigrate, I would like him to remain with you at first. But these are questions which we can discuss once he is with you. He is looking forward to seeing you, even though he's afraid of being separated from us.

I haven't studied much in the past few weeks; to be frank, I have barely studied at all. But I haven't been able to concentrate.

One more thing: a friend of Lizzie's[12] arrived in London with her husband several days ago. He is a doctor, and she has two little girls, one of whom (a five-year-old) is being well looked after in a children's home. But she and her husband are living with the second child, who is still very young, in a wretched apartment. Apparently the little one is ill, and they are not doing well. Would you mind if I sent them your address? It just occurred to me that you know the husband. He is Dr Leo Hornung.[13] Perhaps you can help her out with some clothes from Gillian? They couldn't bring anything with

11 Founded in Britain in 1879, the Barbican Mission organized Kindertransport operations to Britain. The central aim of the organization was to give Jewish children a Christian upbringing.

12 Alice Gross, née Tobias (b. 1904); employed at the brewery in Moravská Ostrava; after 1939 worked for the Jewish Religious Community in Prague; deported with her son Daniel František (1937–1943) to Theresienstadt on 5 July 1943, and to Auschwitz on 15 Dec. 1943; perished at Stutthof concentration camp.

13 Dr Leo Hornung (b. 1902), doctor in Moravská Ostrava; emigrated to Britain shortly before the war.

them. And you might be invaded by Willi's relatives in the next few days. But don't be dismayed, my dear, and remember that they see a bit of me in you.

So now I've finished this letter, which has taken up my Sunday afternoon.

Give my regards to James. I'm sending my kisses to your daughter – How is she faring? And the warmest hugs and kisses to you from your Ilse.

Mama sends the warmest greetings.

I'm already looking forward to seeing you all! Hanuš[14]

DOC. 243

On 5 April 1939 Arnold Stein from Prague thanks Nicholas Winton for saving his daughter and asks for assistance with his own emigration from Prague[1]

Letter from Arnold Stein,[2] Prague II, Nekazanka 8/II, to Nicholas Winton,[3] dated 5 April 1939

Dear Mr Winton,

I would first and foremost like to express my most heartfelt gratitude to you for finding a place for my little Gerda.[4]

Gerda travelled with Mr Chadwick[5] to his mother's on the 14th and has already written us several enthusiastic letters. I consider the child to be very fortunate to have been taken in by these noble-minded, upstanding people.

There are now three of us: my wife,[6] my daughter from my first marriage,[7] and myself. It is certainly presumptuous to seek further assistance from you, and I should not like to abuse your goodwill. But perhaps you could provide us with some advice.

I have enclosed information about us so that, should it be needed, no delays will occur.[8] I would like to make it clear that should we be allowed to enter another country,

14 This last sentence was written by hand.

1 Copy in JMP, DP 43a/1. This document has been translated from German.

2 Arnold Stein (b. 1890), retailer; owned a shop in Carlsbad; fled to Prague in 1938; deported to Nisko by the Gestapo after a failed attempt to flee to Poland; probably fled to Lwów; subsequent fate unknown.

3 Sir Nicholas George Winton (1909–2015), stockbroker; together with the British Committee for Refugees from Czechoslovakia he organized the Czech Kindertransport, a rescue operation that brought 669 children, mostly Jewish, from the Protectorate to safety in Britain. Appointed Member of the Order of the British Empire (MBE) in 1983; knighted by Queen Elizabeth II in 2002.

4 Gerda Mayer, née Stein (b. 1927), writer and teacher; daughter of Arnold and Erna Stein; initially fled to Prague with her family in 1938; emigrated to Britain in 1939 with the help of Trevor Chadwick and lived with his family for several months; worked as an office employee and teacher; now lives in London.

5 Trevor Chadwick (1907–1979), teacher; involved in organizing the Czech Kindertransport in 1939; served in the Royal Navy; lived in Norway after 1945.

6 Erna Stein, née Eisenberger (1897–1943), fashion designer, second wife of Arnold Stein; owner of a knitwear factory in Carlsbad; deported to Theresienstadt in Oct. 1942, and then in Jan. 1943 to Auschwitz, where she perished.

7 Johanna (Hanna) Travnik, also Travnitschek (1920–2007), bank clerk; spent the war in Prague after being classed as a half-Jew; developed schizophrenia; hospitalized in a psychiatric clinic in Neuruppin after 1945.

8 The enclosure mentioned here is not in the file.

we would certainly be able to feed and fend for ourselves, because we do not shy away from *any kind* of work. If the knitting machines have arrived in England and we receive work permits (we've applied), we will be able to provide for ourselves right away. But even if permits are not issued for this purpose, we would surely be suitable to work as domestic servants (or in a similar capacity). Each of us will most gladly and willingly take on any kind of work. I've written down our skills on the enclosed sheet.[9]

Many thanks once again. I hope you will not consider me importunate, but in these grave times, one must pursue every opportunity so as not to reproach oneself at a later stage.

With my very best regards to you, also from my wife and daughter, and with my eternal gratitude and devotion

DOC. 244

On 26 and 27 April 1939 the diplomat George Kennan reports on conditions in Moravská Ostrava and on the situation of the Jews in particular[1]

Report (marked 'confidential, GFK/mhg') by George Kennan,[2] Moravská Ostrava, 26–27 April 1939 (carbon copy)

Report on conditions in the Moravská Ostrava district

Things seem to be very quiet just at present around Moravská Ostrava. Nearly all the German troops have left. They have apparently returned to Silesia. I suspect that the remaining garrison consists mostly of a Luftwaffe detachment which will doubtless be kept there indefinitely to operate the local airport. The commanding general of that district has been absent from his post most of the time during the last two weeks (apparently shooting in Silesia) and the parade in honour of Hitler's birthday was taken by a lieutenant of the air force, who seemed to be the ranking officer in town on that day.

The same quiet prevails on the Polish side. Only the normal garrisons are being maintained there. According to local inhabitants, no attempt has been made to fortify the Teschen district. It is my impression that the Poles do not intend to attempt any serious defense of this district in the event of war with Germany, but will probably fall back on the positions which they held and presumably fortified before Munich, when the Teschen district was still part of Czechoslovakia.[3]

Thus there were no signs on either side of any preparations for early hostilities.

9 The enclosure mentioned here is not in the file.

1 Princeton University Library, Public Policy Papers, Department of Rare Books and Special Collections, George Kennan Papers, Folder: From Prague After Munich: Diplomatic Papers, 1938–1940. Published in George F. Kennan, *From Prague After Munich: Diplomatic Papers, 1938–1940* (Princeton, NJ: Princeton University Press, 1968), pp. 131–134.

2 George F. Kennan (1904–2005), historian and diplomat; in the US diplomatic service from 1926, including postings in Tallinn, Riga, and Moscow; worked at the embassy in Prague, 1938–1939; then in Berlin from Sept. 1939; interned for five and a half months from Dec. 1941; subsequently worked at US embassies in Lisbon, London, and Moscow; briefly ambassador in Moscow, 1952, and in Belgrade, 1961–1963; taught at Princeton, Oxford, and Harvard.

As far as I could ascertain, there have been no frontier incidents in the usual sense along that border, since the German occupation of Moravská Ostrava. But one bit of shooting did – I am told – take place there and it is probably this which accounts for the wounded German soldiers whose presence in Olomouc and Prague hospitals was so often reported. It seems that the Germans asked for permission to move two trainloads of troops through Oderberg (Bohumin) across the Teschen district to Čadca, on the Polish-Slovak frontier, i.e., across the section of railway on Polish territory which the Germans themselves covet. The Poles granted permission after obtaining assurances from the Germans that the trains would not halt on the way and that there would be no debarkation of German troops on Polish territory. They placed no great confidence, however, in the sincerity of these assurances, and took measures of precaution to prevent these troops from establishing themselves along the route. When the movement took place, the Germans did attempt to unload their troops (this was probably right at the railway junction of Oderberg) and the Poles, who were ready for them, apparently opened fire and forced them to move on in a hurry.[4]

There can be no doubt, incidentally, of the German desire to get hold of this bit of railway. It is a section of the main connection between Berlin and Budapest, and the only section which is not really in German or Hungarian hands. It is the most convenient connection between Silesia and the German fortified zone in Slovakia. The railway station at Oderberg, only three or four miles from the German frontier, is one of the most important junctions in the vicinity, handling not only the Berlin–Budapest and Berlin–Istanbul trains but also trains between Warsaw, on the one hand, and Budapest, Prague, and Vienna, on the other. The Poles take the position that by building some twenty miles of new line in the Javorina Mountains, the Germans could easily provide a substitute route, but I am afraid that this suggestion is a little overoptimistic from both the technical and the political standpoint.

It is interesting to note that Moravská Ostrava, despite the relative scarcity of German troops, makes much more the impression of a Nazi city than do Prague and the other cities of the interior of Bohemia. The official German attitude toward the border towns with a sizeable percentage of Germans (in Moravská Ostrava it is scarcely more than twenty percent, but that seems to be enough) is apparently different from the attitude toward the purely Czech communities. In the latter there is no tendency at present to try to Germanize the Czechs. In the border communities, however, where nationality lines are vague and can be determined if at all only by language, the Germans seem to want to give the whole community a German National Socialist imprint. This was true of the communities in the Sudeten area. It is also true at present of Brno, Plzen, Olomouc, etc. Czechs in these communities, in contrast to the people in Prague, feel that if they are to please the authorities they must profess themselves to German culture and to the Nazi ideology.

3 A supplementary declaration to the Munich Agreement set the seal on the transfer of the Těšín (Teschen/Cieszyn) district to Poland. After an ultimatum was given to Czecho-Slovakia to cede the territory, it was occupied by Poland on 2 Oct. 1938. The formerly divided city of Těšín became the administrative seat of the newly established Polish district of Cieszyn.

4 This could not be verified.

The result is that in Moravská Ostrava the fascist greeting and the ubiquitous 'Heil Hitler' are used even by the Czech waiters in the hotels. Pictures of the Führer hang in the public places. Inhabitants are not encouraged to fly Czech flags. Whatever its racial composition may really be, the city is expected to behave like a German community.

This is particularly evident in the attitude toward the Jews. Expropriation of Jewish property has gone very far. The Gestapo is housed in the villa of the wealthiest Jewish merchants.[5] Jews are hounded out of all public places. One doctor, I am told, has attended thirty-three Jewish suicides since the occupation.

It should be added, however, that this complete Nazification of Moravská Ostrava is not solely the product of the recent occupation. There are many indications that the district was pretty well sold out to the Germans long before March 14. This is not surprising. It is an extremely drab industrial district with a dispirited and poverty-stricken proletariat, among whom the lines of nationality are unusually vague, even for Central Europe. There are many people who really cannot tell what their nationality is. Venality is almost universal, and there is little that cannot be obtained by a combination of bribery and intimidation. Many of the wealthier industrialists are Germans, and they were exerting pressure on their workmen in the direction of Germanization long before the occupation.

As a result of all this, a great deal of hedging in behalf of Germany took place during the months which followed Munich.[6] The local branch of the Czech secret police was actually subordinated to the Gestapo as early as January. Conversions to German nationality and to Nazi ideology were thick and fast. It became difficult to tell where Czech left off and German began. When the German troops finally entered the city (which was in the evening of March 14, before President Hacha had even arrived in Berlin), no one was much surprised. The real occupation had begun long before. The troops were just a finishing touch.

DOC. 245

On 2 May 1939 Undersecretary von Burgsdorff notes that Hitler has ordered that the Czechs should deal with the 'Jewish question' without German involvement[1]

Letter from the Reich Protector of Bohemia and Moravia,[2] signed Burgsdorff, Prague, dated 2 May 1939

Laws concerning Jews

The Reich Protector has spoken with the Führer about the introduction of the Nuremberg Laws.

5 The Gestapo had its headquarters in a building on ČSČK Street. The only Jewish-owned villa in Moravská Ostrava was on Sadova Street.

6 The author is referring to the Munich Agreement of 29 Sept. 1938, which enabled Hitler to incorporate the Sudetenland into the German Reich.

1 NAP, ÚŘP, I-3b-5801, box 388. Published in Kárný and Milotová, *Anatomie*, doc. 77, p. 203. This document has been translated from German.

The Führer has ordered that the Czechs should deal with the Jewish question themselves and that we should not interfere.

Moreover, the Reich Protector is of the opinion that the existing dynamic will cause the Jewish question to evolve in the way intended by the Nuremberg Laws.[3]

DOC. 246
On 11 May 1939 Prime Minister Alois Eliáš writes to the Reich Protector, Baron Konstantin von Neurath, with suggestions on how to approach the 'Jewish question'[1]

Letter from Alois Eliáš,[2] chairman of the government, Prague, to Baron Konstantin von Neurath, Reich Protector of Bohemia and Moravia, dated and received 11 May 1939[3]

Honourable Protector,

I hereby wish to inform you that the government is working intensively on the draft of a government regulation on the Jewish question. This is an extremely significant and urgent problem, which requires a rapid solution and a prompt announcement in the interest of an orderly development of the Protectorate, an opinion that you will certainly also share.

May I therefore suggest, honourable Protector, that the matter be prioritized and negotiated definitively in advance of the formal approval of the Ministerial Council, and that the positions of both parties are clarified by means of direct communication between the specialists authorized by you and my plenipotentiaries. I would be very grateful to you if such a negotiation could take place within the next few days, and if you could therefore be so kind as to inform me of your position with regard to my suggestion. With the highest esteem,[4]

2 Baron Konstantin Hermann Karl von Neurath (1873–1956), diplomat and politician; joined the NSDAP and the SS in 1937; ambassador to Rome, 1921–1930, and to London, 1930–1932; Reich foreign minister, 1932–1938; Reich Protector of Bohemia and Moravia, 1939 to 1943; sentenced to fifteen years' imprisonment at the International Military Tribunal at Nuremberg in 1946, released in 1954.

3 Handwritten note in the original: 'State Secretary Frank has been informed, so let things take their course for now.'

1 NAP, ÚŘP, I-3b-5801, box 388. Published in Kárný and Milotová, *Anatomie*, pp. 205–206. This document has been translated from German.

2 Alois Eliáš (1890–1942), professional soldier and politician; prime minister of the Protectorate of Bohemia and Moravia, 1939–1941; convicted of high treason in 1941 for having contact with the Czechoslovak government in exile, sentenced to death, and executed by firing squad.

3 There are handwritten notes in the original.

4 Enclosed with the letter was a 22-page draft: see Kárný and Milotová, *Anatomie*, pp. 205–206, and Introduction, p. 25. The government regulation was never approved. On 21 June 1939 the Reich Protector himself issued a corresponding regulation: see Doc. 247.

DOC. 247

In a regulation issued on 21 June 1939 the Reich Protector takes charge of measures to dispossess the Jewish population[1]

Regulation of the Reich Protector of Bohemia and Moravia on Jewish Assets, 21 June 1939[2]

The following orders are issued pursuant to Article 5 of the Decree of the Führer and Reich Chancellor concerning the Protectorate of Bohemia and Moravia, dated 16 March 1939:[3]

§ 1

(1) Jews, Jewish businesses, and Jewish associations require special written permission to exercise ownership over land, land rights, businesses, and investments in these, to exercise rights of ownership over securities of any kind, to lease land and businesses, and to transfer leasing rights of any kind. The same applies to obligations granting control over the aforementioned assets.

(2) If transactions resulting in obligation are authorized, this will also apply to the fulfilment of said obligations.

(3) Any legal acts that are in contravention to (1) or (2) or that are undertaken in order to circumvent these regulations will be considered void.

§ 2

(1) Permission as detailed in § 1 is to be authorized by the Reich Protector. He may confer this authority entirely or partially upon other agencies.

(2) If permission is to be granted by an authority other than the Reich Protector, then an appeal against the ruling may be addressed to the Reich Protector within a period of two weeks after the ruling has been issued. Appeals are to be lodged with the authority that issued the ruling. The Reich Protector can order that the right of appeal be waived under certain conditions.

§ 3 Jews, Jewish businesses, and Jewish associations must register with the Oberlandrat any agricultural land or forest that they own, co-own, or lease, by 31 July 1939.

§ 4

(1) Jews, Jewish businesses, and Jewish associations are prohibited from purchasing land and land rights, from holding stakes in businesses, and from purchasing securities, as well as from taking over and re-establishing businesses and from leasing land.

(2) The provision in § 1(3) shall apply accordingly.

§ 5

(1) Jews, Jewish businesses, and Jewish associations must register with the National Bank, or an authority nominated by it, any gold, platinum, or silver, as well as any precious stones and pearls that they own or co-own, by 31 July 1939.

(2) They are prohibited from purchasing, selling, and pawning the objects described in (1).

1 *Verordnungsblatt des Reichsprotektors*, 1939, no. 6, pp. 45–49. This document has been translated from German.

2 The regulation was published in German and Czech.

3 *Reichsgesetzblatt*, 1939, 1, p. 486. This article stipulated that the Reich Protector was to defend the interests of the Reich in the Protectorate and ensure compliance with Hitler's political instructions.

(3) The same applies to all other items of jewellery or pieces of art, insofar as the value of the individual objects or collections of objects exceeds the amount of 10,000 korunas.

§ 6 A Jew is classified as someone:

(a) who is descended from at least three grandparents who are full Jews according to race. A grandparent counts as fully Jewish if he or she belongs or has belonged to the Jewish religious community;

(b) also counting as Jewish is a Jewish Mischling who is descended from two fully Jewish grandparents,

1. who belonged to the Jewish religious community as of 15 September 1935 or joined it after this date;
2. who as of 15 September 1935 was married to a Jew or has married one since this date;
3. who is the offspring of a marriage concluded with a Jew [see (a)] after 15 September 1935;
4. who is the offspring of extramarital relations with a Jew [see (a)] and was born out of wedlock after 31 July 1936.

§ 7

(1) A business counts as Jewish if the owner is a Jew (§ 6).

(2) A general or limited partnership company counts as Jewish if one or more liable partners are Jews.

(3) A business operated by a legal person counts as Jewish:

(a) if one or more of the persons appointed as its legal representative, or one or more of the members of the management board or supervisory board, are Jews;

(b) if Jews hold a significant stake in terms of either capital or voting rights. A significant stake in terms of capital exists when over one quarter of the capital belongs to Jews; a significant stake in terms of voting rights exists if Jews hold half of the total number of votes.

(4) The provisions in (3) shall apply accordingly to companies regulated by mining law without legal capacity.

(5) If, in the case of a public limited company or a limited joint-stock partnership, there were no Jewish members on the board of directors, the management board, or the supervisory board as of 15 March 1939, then it is assumed that Jews do not hold a significant stake in terms of capital or voting rights (paragraph 3b). The opposite assumption applies if there were one or more Jewish members on the board of directors, the management board, or the supervisory board on the aforementioned date.

(6) A business also counts as Jewish if is effectively under the dominant influence of Jews.

(7) A subsidiary of a Jewish business counts as a Jewish business.

(8) A subsidiary of a non-Jewish business counts as a Jewish business if the manager or one of several managers of the subsidiary is a Jew.

§ 8 The provisions in § 7 shall apply accordingly to Jewish associations.

§ 9

(1) The Reich Protector may, where he considers it appropriate, appoint trustees, who shall carry out his instructions under his supervision. The Reich Protector may also recall intermediaries and receivers appointed on the basis of Protectorate regulations.

(2) Insofar as assets defined in § 1 of this regulation are concerned, the Reich Protector has the exclusive right to appoint trustees.
(3) The Reich Protector shall define the rights and duties of trustees.
(4) Insofar as the Reich Protector exercises his authority according to (1) and (3), the provisions in the Protectorate pertaining to intermediaries and receivers shall not apply.

§ 10

(1) Anyone acting in breach of this regulation or the provisions issued for its implementation shall be punished with imprisonment and/or a fine. Anyone contravening the provisions of this regulation or the provisions issued for its implementation shall also be punished.
(2) The attempt to do so is liable to punishment.
(3) Prosecution on the basis of other penal provisions is unaffected.
(4) Alongside the punishment, instructions may also be issued for assets to be confiscated, provided that they were the target of the criminal act. If no one individual can be prosecuted, then instructions to confiscate assets can also be issued independently.
(5) The general provisions of German Reich criminal law shall apply.
(6) The investigation and conviction of such criminal acts is incumbent upon the German courts, which are duly authorized under general Reich law.
(7) Furthermore, the provisions applicable to the German courts in the Protectorate shall apply, insofar as no alternative ruling is made.

§ 11

(1) The Reich Protector may issue provisions serving to implement or supplement this regulation.
(2) The regulations issued by the Chief of the Civil Administration in Brünn concerning the prohibition of unauthorized interventions in the economy of Moravia (20 March 1939) and the prohibition of the disposal of Jewish real assets in Moravia (22 March 1939), as well as the regulation issued by the Chief of the Civil Administration in Prague concerning decrees on Jewish assets of all kinds (29 March 1939) will be suspended with the entry into force of this regulation.

§ 12

(1) This regulation enters into force on 22 June 1939.
(2) The stipulations of §§ 1, 2, and 4 apply retroactively from 15 March 1939. Transactions requiring permission that have been concluded since that date will be considered null and void unless permission is granted retroactively.
(3) The exceptional permissions granted by the chiefs of the civil administration in Prague and Brünn in accordance with the regulations of 20, 22, and 29 March 1939 count as permissions as defined by this regulation. Persons already appointed by the Oberlandräte to act as trustees shall count retrospectively as trustees as defined in this regulation.

Prague, 21 June 1939.
The Reich Protector
of Bohemia and Moravia
signed Baron von Neurath

DOC. 248

Basler Nachrichten, 23 June 1939: article on the anti-Jewish regulation issued by the Reich Protector[1]

The progressive erosion of the autonomy of Bohemia-Moravia
Regulation on Jews issued without consulting the Czech government

Berlin, 23 June. (Private telegraphic dispatch.) There are only scattered reports in the Berlin press noting that the Reich Protector has placed the Aryanization of the Czech economy under his authority. A regulation that has just been issued and comes into force today, a measure *that immobilizes the Czech government*, is based *entirely* upon the stance[2] that informed the actions already taken in the Old Reich with regard to the Jewish question. Hence, the regulation revokes the Jews' right to participate in the economic life of Bohemia and Moravia and orders the appointment of trustees. Notably, it is explicitly emphasized that these trustees are '*solely subject to the Reich Protector's instructions and supervision*'.[3]

In addition, the aim of extending the Gleichschaltung of the Protectorate with the Reich is expressed in the fact that the German courts are given exclusive authority to impose the punishment imposed for any breaches of the regulation. This regulation on implementing Aryanization also enforces the general law of the German Reich. According to Reich law, the courts must hold proceedings and must also apply the provisions of German criminal law.

By statute, only the German proportion of the population in the Protectorate has hitherto been subject to the jurisdiction of German courts.[4] *Now, the first category of Czech citizens is included, which signifies a substantial change in the status of the Protectorate.*

Finally, the Czech Jews are required to register any gemstones and precious metals in their possession.

The regulation does not stipulate any requirement to surrender these items. This was also the case in the Old Reich when compulsory registration for Jews was first introduced.

1 *Basler Nachrichten*, no. 169, 23 June 1939, p. 2. The *Basler Nachrichten*, founded in 1844 as the successor to the *Avis-Blatt*, was published until 1977. The newspaper established itself as one of the leading dailies in German-speaking Switzerland. In 1977 it merged with the *National-Zeitung* to become the *Basler Zeitung*. This document has been translated from German.

2 Regulation of the Reich Protector of Bohemia and Moravia on Jewish Assets, 21 June 1939: see Doc. 247.

3 The German wording here differs slightly from that in the regulation.

4 Regulation on German Jurisdiction in the Protectorate of Bohemia and Moravia, 14 April 1939: *Reichsgesetzblatt*, 1939 I, pp. 752–754.

DOC. 249

Writing in the summer of 1939, Camill Hoffmann expresses the view that it is impossible to separate the Jews from the Czechs[1]

Report by Camill Hoffmann, undated [summer 1939][2]

The Jews among the Czechs

In the 'Protectorate' of Bohemia and Moravia, there is a rush to force the Jews out of public life, out of the economy, the academic professions, everywhere. What the Third Reich needed six years to accomplish, the Czechs are supposed to carry out in a few months, and without yet even having the equivalent racial laws. All under pressure from the Third Reich. The Jews have already disappeared from the state and municipal offices of the 'Protectorate', and the 'Aryanization' of banks, industrial companies, and businesses is also proceeding apace. The exodus of the Jews from the Protectorate – their number does not even amount to 1 per cent![3] – began immediately after the invasion by Hitler and is only suspended at present because the German Gestapo, which has established itself in the larger towns of the Protectorate, is not permitting the Jews to leave and is setting up controls that will be similar to the financial criteria for emigrants that were introduced in Germany. One knows that, in the Third Reich, all the antisemitic measures were and are the sole doing of the National Socialist Party, not of the population. One can say with utmost certainty that the Czechs, on the whole, are not antisemites. Nor has this changed, although the Czech press is obliged to adopt the anti-Jewish reports from the German press, and in public announcements it is said that the nation must be 'cleansed of foreign elements'. The development of the Czech nation in the nineteenth century and, above all, the tradition of humanism pursued by Masaryk[4] exclude any anti-Jewish sentiments. Insofar as antisemitic currents existed at all among the Czech nationalists, they resulted from the fact that the Jews in Prague and certain areas had – albeit *before* the Hitler regime in Germany – sympathized with Germandom and supported it. That factor is, of course, one to which the Nazis will never admit, let alone acknowledge publicly. But it is a fact that the German institutions in Prague, the German theatre, the German university, would have been unsustainable during the past decades, back in Austrian and then in Czechoslovak times, without the financial, political, and cultural assistance of the Jews. Today's Jews realize that the reproach of the Czech nationalists was justified, for Czech ground is now being attacked from some of the positions that were opened up to the Germans thanks to the support of the Jews. However, it was only a tiny, if wealthy, portion of the Jews that adopted this misplaced attitude in Bohemia and Moravia. A greater part took the view of Jewish nationalism (Zionism), and an even greater part professed allegiance to everything Czech. It is a bold

1 Deutsches Literaturarchiv Marbach, HS.2002.0033.00041. Published in Hoffmann, *Politisches Tagebuch*, pp. 274–277. This document has been translated from German.

2 Hoffmann sent his texts to his daughter Edith, who was living in Britain, in the hope of having them published there.

3 At the end of 1939, approximately 90,000 Jews were living in the Protectorate of Bohemia and Moravia, representing around 1 per cent of the total population.

4 Tomáš Garrigue Masaryk (1850–1937), first president of Czechoslovakia, 1918–1935.

undertaking to seek to implement a racist policy in the area of the former Austro-Hungarian monarchy. In no other region of Europe have the races been mixed to such a degree as here. In fact, at one time one could see it as the task of the Austro-Hungarian monarchy to avert the clash of the races and unite Germans, Slavs, and Italians under one roof. The late German minister in Czechoslovakia, Dr Spina,[5] spoke with good reason of the 'symbiosis' of peoples in the Lands of the Bohemian Crown. The population of Austria-Hungary was a mixed people, and in this respect, too, Czechoslovakia was the true heir of the monarchy. The extent to which Germans and Czechs have mixed for centuries is made clearest by the countless German surnames found among the Czechs and also by the countless Czech surnames that appear among the Sudeten Germans. In old Austria-Hungary, civil servants and military officers were so often transferred to regions other than those from which they came and so often married women of a different nationality that one cannot speak of a purity of ethnicity. It was not much different in Czechoslovakia. Anyone glancing through the Party membership list of the Sudeten German Nazis comes across so many Czech names that it seems simply grotesque when the Nazis add racial purity to their programme and even try to pass themselves off as Teutons. There was no defined ethnographic boundary in the lands of the present 'Protectorate' for a thousand years. It may be a strange phenomenon indeed that, on the one hand, the nationalism of the Czechs and the Germans assumed a distinct form and generated conflicts but, on the other hand, the symbiosis of the two peoples progressed. As a result, belonging to one nation or the other was not viewed as a mystery of blood, as the Nazis now want to view it, but rather as a decision based on free will and conscious affinity. In countries with such experiences, one understandably takes quite a sceptical view of racism. Were it not for German propaganda, the Sudeten Germans would have the same attitude towards racism as the Czechs. The Jews have now lived for more than a thousand years among this mixed population of Czechs and Germans. The famous synagogue in the Old Town of Prague, which has stood there for almost a thousand years, is a monument to the Jewish contribution to Bohemian culture. The Jews are closely bound up with the history of Bohemia. They were not only bankers, retailers, and scholars here; they were also farmers and skilled craftsmen. The many mixed marriages that were contracted in the nineteenth century in the territory of Czechoslovakia, and that have increased in number ever since, show how minimal antisemitism is among the Czech population. Implementing the Nuremberg Laws here would result in even more tragedies than in the Third Reich. But it is a mystery as to how the Czechs intend to go about 'cleansing foreign elements', for example, from their literature and art. The very attempt to resolve it implies self-abasement. The marvellous, noble equestrian monument to the country's patron saint and martyr, St Wenceslas, towers over Wenceslas Square in Prague. It is the work of the Czech sculptor Myslbek.[6] Myslbek was the son of a Czech father and a Jewish mother. Jaroslav Vrchlický is revered as one of the greatest

5 Dr Franz Spina (1868–1938), Slavist and politician; professor at the German University in Prague, 1921–1938; delegate in the Czechoslovak parliament, representing the League of Farmers, 1920; minister of public works, 1926–1929; minister of public health, 1929–1935; minister without portfolio, 1935–1938. As an opponent of Konrad Henlein's Sudeten German Party (SdP), he withdrew from the League of Farmers in 1938.

6 Josef Václav Myslbek (1848–1922), sculptor, founder of the modern school of Czech sculpture.

Czech poets.[7] He is not only the author of a significant lyrical and dramatic oeuvre and the translator of the most superb literature into Czech, but also an inspired linguistic innovator. One cannot imagine Czech intellectual life without his contribution to the modernization and enrichment of the Czech language. Vrchlický's real name was Emil Benda, and he was a Jewish-Czech Mischling. Another brilliant representative of Czech literature, the romantic poet Julius Zeyer, was a half-Jew.[8] The Czech Jew Rakous was a popular storyteller who drew on the life of the provincial Jews for his subject matter, which he enriched with a sage, charmingly rustic humour.[9] František Langer,[10] a Jew, who served in the Czechoslovak Legion and is a friend of the recently deceased Karel Čapek,[11] is one of the most successful modern Czech playwrights. *The Mounted Patrol*, his last drama, set in Siberia during the First World War, enthralled the Czech patriots – and has now vanished from the repertoire. Karel Poláček,[12] a Jew, is one of the wittiest Czech realist novelists, with a knack for depicting Jewish and Czech characters in an equally amusing fashion. Egon Hostovský,[13] whose nuanced social novels place him among the most gifted young writers in Czech-speaking Prague, is a Jew ... These are but a few names associated with successes that attest to their popularity. Until six months ago, it did not occur to any Czech to reject them as 'foreign elements'. On the contrary, they were welcomed as contributors to the national culture, who were owed grateful approbation for their every contribution. How are the Czechs to tear these pages from their body of literature today? It would be even more misguided than excluding Heinrich Heine, for example, from the canon of German literature, as the Nazis are now trying to do. But the example of the Jews' contribution to literature indicates how tightly interwoven the existence of the Czech Jews has been with the Czechs in Bohemia and Moravia until now, and how profound the involvement in the life of the Czech people is today, as the effort is made to remove the Jews from its midst.

7 Jaroslav Vrchlický, born Emil Bohuslav Frída (1853–1912), writer, poet, playwright, and translator.

8 Julius Zeyer (1841–1901), poet, writer, and playwright.

9 Vojtěch Rakous, born Adalbert Österreicher (1862–1935), writer and satirist; supported the cultural assimilation of the Jews living in Bohemia into Czech life.

10 František Langer (1888–1965), military physician, writer, and playwright; dramatist at the Vinohrady Theatre in Prague, 1935–1938; co-founder and intermittent chairman of the Czechoslovak PEN writers' association; emigrated to France in 1939 and later to Britain; returned to Czechoslovakia in 1945.

11 Dr Karel Čapek (1890–1938), writer, journalist, playwright, translator, and photographer.

12 Karel Poláček (1892–1945), writer and satirist; editor of the daily newspaper *Lidové noviny*, 1922–1933; worked for the Jewish Religious Community of Prague from 1939; deported to Theresienstadt on 5 July 1943 and to Auschwitz on 19 Oct. 1944.

13 Egon Hostovský (1908–1973), writer; civil servant in the Czechoslovak Foreign Office, 1937–1939; emigrated to France and Portugal in 1939; employee at the Czechoslovak Foreign Office, 1946–1948; emigrated to the USA in 1948; later worked as a journalist for Radio Free Europe.

DOC. 250
In early July 1939 the head of the Palestine Office in Prague reports on his two-month trip to Palestine[1]

Letter from the SD Headquarters in Prague (B1, Wo/Zb) to the head of the Reich Security Main Office, Special Office for Bohemia and Moravia,[2] Berlin, dated 7 July 1939

Re: report by the head of the Palestine Office in Prague, Edelstein,[3]
on his trip to Palestine.
Enclosure: 1.
Enclosed for your attention is a report compiled by the head of the Palestine Office in Prague, Jakob Edelstein, concerning a trip to Palestine in May–June 1939.[4]
Copy
Report on my trip to Palestine:
May–June 1939
My assignment:
As per the assignment given to me, it was my duty to establish contact with all the relevant authorities in Palestine in order to conduct extensive negotiations and thereby secure an appropriate share of the [immigration] certificates for the territory of the Protectorate. Furthermore, I was to make sure that the social and economic organizations in question take an interest in the emigrants from Protectorate territory, in order to facilitate their integration into Palestine.

Responsible authorities:
The following authorities are of crucial importance for the allocation of certificates:
1. Government of Palestine, Department for Migration;
2. Jewish Agency for Palestine;
3. Va'ad Haleumi, the central representative body of Palestinian Jewry;[5]
4. the economic and social authorities.

1 BArch, R 58/978, fols. 88–92. Published in Peter Heumos, *Die Emigration aus der Tschechoslowakei nach Westeuropa und dem Nahen Osten 1938–1945: Politisch-soziale Struktur, Organisation und Asylbedingungen der tschechischen, jüdischen, deutschen und slowakischen Flüchtlinge während des Nationalsozialismus. Darstellung und Dokumentation* (Munich: Oldenbourg Verlag, 1989), pp. 305–309. This document has been translated from German.

2 This office was headed by Gustav Jonak (1903–1985), lawyer; joined the Sudeten German Party (SdP) in 1936; lawyer in Moravská-Třebová, 1936–1938; SdP secretary general; joined the NSDAP in 1938; SS-Hauptsturmführer, 1939; Regierungsrat, 1939; sentenced to twelve years in prison by the Czechoslovak People's Court in 1947; released in 1955; later Ministerialrat in the Baden-Württemberg Ministry of the Interior.

3 Dr Jakob Edelstein (1903–1944), lawyer, association official, and Zionist; worked in the main office of Hehalutz from 1929, headed the Palestine Office in Prague from 1933, and was one of the main intermediaries between Czech Jews and the German administration; deported on 4 Dec. 1941 to Theresienstadt, where he was chairman of the Council of Elders, 1941–1943; deported in Dec. 1943 to Auschwitz, where he was shot dead on 20 June 1944, along with his wife and son.

4 The report is undated. Edelstein wrote it for the Gestapo in Prague and the emigration department of the Jewish Religious Community of Prague.

5 Va'ad Leumi (Hebrew: National Council) operated from 1920 until the founding of the State of Israel in 1948. It was the provisional government of the Jewish organized community in Palestine while Palestine was a British Mandate territory.

Government of Palestine: I was received by the heads of the Immigration Department of the government of Palestine. I have produced a detailed report on the work of the Palestine Office in the territory of the Protectorate. In particular, I pointed out that we have skilled human resources at our disposal. In so doing, I was able to refer to the fact that the persons who have thus far emigrated from the Protectorate territory have fully proved themselves in terms of both work and social interaction. The fact that the greatest percentage of our immigrants have withstood the process of occupational restructuring quite well, and that these people remain in the agricultural sector permanently, naturally made a strong impression on the government. The senior officials assured me that they want to help make sure that the Protectorate territory is given due consideration when it comes to conferring certificates.

Jewish Agency for Palestine: I had a series of talks with the board of the Jewish Agency for Palestine, during which I set out our requirements. In the process, I did not limit myself solely to asking for certificates from every category for Protectorate territory. Rather, I also requested that considerable attention be paid to the procurement of jobs in various European countries where our young people obtain temporary residence and, after an appropriate training period, are granted permission to enter Palestine. I provided the Jewish Agency for Palestine with detailed information about our work in the area of vocational counselling and occupational restructuring and about the registration of the Jewish children. I hope I was successful in gaining understanding and recognition of our concerns.

Va'ad Haleumi: the Jewish Community of Palestine has, as its supreme institution, the Va'ad Haleumi, which oversees all economic, social, and cultural affairs. I presented our wishes to the gentlemen in charge and asked that the immigrants from Protectorate territory be granted economic and social assistance. The cooperation of this body is of great importance, as a number of certificate categories can be applied only if the relatives in Palestine have found a permanent means of earning a living. This applies both to requests made for parents [to join children in Palestine] and to the accommodation of children.

Economic institutions: there are a number of institutions in Palestine that perform economic and social functions. Of significance here are, above all, the collectives in the countryside and the land-settlement societies. I paid visits to the administrators and also inspected several farming settlements. I studied the living conditions and the work ethic of the Jews who have settled there. I can state with satisfaction that the agricultural institutions have pledged their assistance to the integration of immigrants from the Protectorate territory. No less important are the enterprises, some of which were founded by citizens of the Protectorate. The entrepreneurs whom I visited gave me their word that they would give special consideration to emigrants from Protectorate territory when hiring new workers.

The most important figures I met during my aforementioned endeavours were: Sir Erwin Samuel,[6] Eliahu Dobkin,[7] Moshe Schapiro,[8] Dr Pinner,[9] Dr Georg Landauer,[10] Dr Förder,[11] Dr Wittkowski,[12] Moller,[13] Dr Werner Senator,[14] etc.

6 Correctly: Edwin Samuel, second Viscount Samuel (1898–1978), district officer in Palestine.

7 Eliahu Dobkin (1898–1976), association official; active member of Hehalutz in Russia, and from 1930 in Palestine; headed the immigration department of the Jewish Agency's Central Bureau for the Settlement of German Jews during the Second World War.

Certificate allocation and our share: the government of Palestine has issued a total of 10,350 certificates for the April–September 1939 schedule. Of that number, 5,000 are from the regular schedule and 5,350 from the refugee quota. Out of these certificates, the government has deducted 2,500 as payment on account for the April quota and so-called illegal immigration, so that only 7,850 certificates (persons) have become available for allocation.

The certificates are split into the following categories:

A/I 1,500, of which 320 are for tourists currently in Palestine (180 from Greater Germany and 140 from the rest of the world)
A/IV 70 (of which 23 have already been granted and 47 have yet to be allocated)
A/V 35
B/II 35
B/III 2,660, of these:
- 500 for children between the ages of 13 and 15;
- 900 for youngsters between the ages of 15 and 17,
- 500 for the university;
- 260 for technology;[15]
- 90 for Mikveh Israel;[16]
- 60 for Ben Shemen;[17]
- 150 for Wizo;[18]
- 40 for the Bezallel School;[19]
- 50 [for the] conservatoire;
- and the remainder for various institutions.

C 600
D 2,950 (this number also includes the persons in categories A/I, A/V and C.)

8 Correctly: Yeshayahu (Moshe) Schapira (1891–1945), manager of the Zerubavel Bank in Tel Aviv from 1933 to 1943.
9 Dr Ludwig Pinner (1890–1979), agronomist; from 1938 headed the Jewish Agency's department for the resettlement of small and medium-sized enterprises.
10 Dr Georg Landauer (1895–1954), lawyer and politician; general manager of the Zionist Federation for Germany and head of the Palestine Office in Berlin, 1929–1933; co-founder of the Reich Association of Jews in Germany, 1933; director of the Jewish Agency's Central Bureau for the Settlement of German Jews, 1934–1954; emigrated to the USA in 1953.
11 Dr Herbert Förder (1901–1970), banker; emigrated to Palestine in 1933; founder of the Rassco Rural and Suburban Settlement Company.
12 Dr Erwin Wittkowski (1904–1970), employee of the economic department of the Jewish Agency until 1942; later a bank manager.
13 Hans Moller (1896–1962), textile industrialist; from 1933 in Palestine; co-owner of the Ata Textile Company in Kefar Ata.
14 Dr Werner Senator (1896–1953), social worker and social policy-maker, initially in Berlin; secretary general of the European headquarters of the JDC in Paris, 1925–1930; board member of the Jewish Agency of Jerusalem, 1930–1935; from 1937 administrative official at the Hebrew University in Jerusalem and its executive vice-president from 1949 to 1953.
15 This refers to the Institute of Technology in Haifa, which was founded in 1912.
16 An agricultural school was established south-east of Tel Aviv in 1879.
17 The Ben Shemen youth village and agricultural school was founded in Palestine in 1927.
18 WIZO (Women's International Zionist Organization), established by Zionist women in London in 1920, advocated the training of Jewish women in Palestine.
19 Correctly: Bezalel School of Arts and Crafts, founded in Jerusalem in 1906. It was destroyed in the First World War and reopened in 1933.

The following certificates are allotted to the Protectorate:

Category:		Certificates:	Persons:
A/I		255	765
A/IV		5	10
A/V		15	45
B/II		7	14
B/III	children 13–15	70	70
	young persons aged 15–17	195	195
	students	164	164
C		81	220
D		110	110
		902	1,593

In addition, there is also the pledge with regard to indirect emigration to Palestine via vocational training in various countries, which concerns approximately 1,500 additional persons. As a result, our Palestine Office should be able to help more than 3,000 persons to emigrate from Protectorate territory by 30 September 1939. Of course, this work can succeed only if the corresponding technical prerequisites can be fulfilled within the Protectorate.

To estimate correctly the Protectorate territory's share in overall certificate allocation, it must be pointed out that we have had over 20% of the certificates designated for the entire world allotted to us.

Naturally, I dealt with all the schools cited in the report. Here I would particularly like to emphasize that the creation of a scholarship fund in Palestine was decided upon in order to enable poor students to continue their studies in the coming years.

Permanent representation in Palestine:
During my stay in Palestine, a Histradut Oley Bohemia and Moravia (Association of Emigrants from Protectorate Territory)[20] was created. This association cooperates closely with the Representation of Emigrants from the Old Reich and the Ostmark. Both bodies are recognized by the German consulate in Palestine.

My visit to the German consul:
The German consul in Haifa[21] was kind enough to receive me and accept a report that I produced on my activities in Palestine.

20 The association was the successor to Histadrut Oley Czechoslovakia, a Jewish trade union organization founded in 1921 by Czechoslovak immigrants.

21 The consul general of Palestine and the Transjordan from 1935 to 1939 was Walter Döhle (1884–1945).

DOC. 251

On 12 July 1939 the Wehrmacht Plenipotentiary contemplates the 'Czech problem' and advocates the expulsion of the Jews from the Protectorate[1]

Enclosure with the letter from the Plenipotentiary of the Wehrmacht to the Reich Protector of Bohemia and Moravia, no. 22/40 (W.B.6/39 top secret document, 12 July 1939), signed Friderici,[2] dated 12 July 1939 (copy 1 of 3 copies)[3]

Top-level issue.
Top secret. To be handled by officers only.
The Czech problem.
In the course of a thousand-year history, Germans and Czechs have lived in the Bohemian and Moravian regions. They have never loved each other. Mostly hated. It will be so for another thousand years, too, unless the problem is tackled in a completely new way. The previous methods have failed, regardless of whether they were employed by the old German emperors, the popes, the Habsburgs, or the Czechs themselves.

The cause of the mutual antipathy between the two peoples is rooted in issues of space and integral to the character of the peoples in question. It is pointless to quarrel over who was at fault. At any rate, the segment of the population in power at any one time utilized its strength to impose its national will on the segment of the population that was in an inferior position, to increase its own prosperity at the expense of the weaker segment and, in the process, to seek redress for wrongs previously suffered. That further stirred up the hatred of the weaker segment, which waited with cunning and impatience for the next opportunity to reverse the roles again. That was, and is, the interplay of forces in the territory of Bohemia and Moravia.

Today the German is the absolute master in Bohemian and Moravian territory, and he must decide how he should solve the problem for good. One thing is certain: he must assume decisive leadership. He must not leave things to chance. He must know what he wants, the final goal, and the method of achieving this goal. Given the existing thousand-year-old antagonisms, a policy of lenience and conciliation is just as wrong as a policy of petty political revenge and repression. Both have been tested over the course of history and have failed to achieve the goal.

The Czech views a policy of appeasement as a sign of weakness. It strengthens the militancy of national hatred. On the other hand, it is unlikely that one can suppress or even eradicate Czech nationalism, now a thousand years old, by brutal harshness, by a

1 NAP, MS, box 2076. Published in Kárný and Milotová, *Anatomie*, Doc. 13, pp. 49–56. This document has been translated from German.

2 Erich Friderici (1885–1964), military officer; military attaché to Hungary and Bulgaria, 1935–1937; Wehrmacht plenipotentiary to the Reich Protector of Bohemia and Moravia, 1939; infantry general, 1939–1941, commander of the Army Group South and of the security troops, 1941–1942; commander of Special Staff IV in the Army High Command (OKH), 1944; released from war captivity in 1947 and worked for an insurance firm.

3 The original contains handwritten underlining. The three copies were sent to the Wehrmacht High Command National Defence Branch, Army High Command Senior Quartermaster V, and General Staff Officer for Intelligence of the Chief of Army Armaments and Commander of the Reserve Army.

compulsory outward 'Germanization'. On the contrary, one will turn hatred of the Germans into the myth of the Czech soul. And the Czech-Slavic soul endures all repression and is still not destroyed as long as it lives in, and is led by, a large Czech community. There is only one solution: to eradicate this Czech community, both from the region and in intellectual terms, and, to this end, first to remove its highest tier from Bohemian/Moravian territory. The Czech intelligentsia is the implacable foe of Germany, less so the workers and farmers.

The radical method of physical eradication is not feasible under normal circumstances. It must be achieved in another way:

1) by emigration and dispersal;

2) by absorption into the Greater German sphere.

The preconditions for this, particularly at the present time, are not unfavourable.

On 1) the emigration problem:

a) The vast majority of the Czech people, workers and farmers, think less about Czech national goals than about the improvement of their social existence. If their wishes and demands in this matter are soon visibly and broadly enforced by Germany at the expense of their employers, the workers will speak up for Germany's leadership. The heavier burden that will ensue for the employer will make things difficult for him in economic terms. He will see his previous income dwindle and will then seek to emigrate. His place, and thus the leadership of the company, will be turned over to the German economic organism. Wages and profit margins will then be aligned with German conditions.

b) Extensive absorption of Czech seasonal workers into the German economy. In this way, the National Socialist and völkisch world view is brought into the lives of the Czech people. In the end, they will learn to feel and think as Germans do. This will annoy the current capitalist-minded businessman. He will no longer feel secure in his business and will leave. From an economic perspective, Bohemian-Moravian territory cannot in the long run be forcibly retained as an enclave under *special* wage and price conditions anyway. Rather, it will inevitably be absorbed into the German economic area. When this happens, the goal of eliminating the Czech economic leadership – this applies to both industry and agriculture – could thus easily be achieved. One only has to raise wages for a time and forcibly keep prices low. German firms could be assisted through subsidies. In agriculture, the influence of the Czech landowners must be broken by buying up or expropriating run-down estates.

c) The most vigorous implementation of the laws pertaining to Jews and measures to facilitate their emigration. In the long term, the harm done in political and völkisch terms by leaving the Jews in Protectorate territory and by their activities there would seem to be more serious than Jewish emigrants smuggling out a few millions. Antisemitic propaganda is completely geared towards the people in this respect.

d) Facilitation of any emigration of the Czech intelligentsia. The German missions abroad must simply be instructed to do everything possible, for example, to procure well-paid positions in distant parts of the world for Czech university professors, business leaders, political leaders, etc. naturally through intermediaries. All the relatives must follow. Example: as a result of the emigration of the *Petschek* family of industrial magnates in Prague, who owned eleven villas and other properties, quite a bit of space was created for Germandom to be established.[4]

A separate issue in this respect is the emigration of former Czech soldiers, which in my view must not be prohibited, but rather promoted by every possible means. Among the masses they will always be a source of anti-German propaganda unless they are placed under German influence through enlistment in the government forces. Nothing is more dangerous to German influence in the Protectorate than the uprooted retired former Czechoslovak officer, especially if he was or is a member of the Czechoslovak Legion. For he is the most active element. The risk of Czechoslovak legions being formed in hostile countries seems small by comparison.[5] By all accounts, things are not moving ahead. The legions will never be taken seriously as combat units. Such formations usually fall to pieces on their own. If the Czechs are denaturalized when they leave the Protectorate, we will be rid of them. And that is what counts. Similarly restless elements are the unemployed civil servants, particularly the teachers, who are mostly radically anti-German and are closely associated with the men of the Czechoslovak Legion.

As a result of the collapse of the Czechoslovak state, the elements from the Sudetenland and Slovakia, disappointed and embittered, have poured into the Protectorate and are presently – by all accounts – the nuclei of dissatisfaction and anti-German propaganda.

One must state from the outset that overall the absorption of Czech national elements into Germandom is not particularly desirable on the grounds of the race question itself. The misgivings that undoubtedly exist can, however, be dispelled for the following reasons:

a) Absorption concerns only a relatively small number in comparison with the 80 million inhabitants of Germany.
b) The population of Greater Germany is racially interspersed with the Slavic element in any case, without its Germandom being impaired.
c) Our Third Reich is internally so strong and unified that, especially with its present dynamic, it will simply sweep individual Czech elements along with it and swallow them up. Political harm cannot be inflicted to any appreciable extent if the Czech elements are dispersed and properly controlled.
d) The manpower, industriousness, and undemanding nature of the Czech element could be utilized to compensate for the shortage of skilled personnel in Germany and to set new challenges in this regard.

Considering the situation in the Protectorate, as described at the beginning, and in the interest of the greater goal of breaking up the Czech elite, the absorption of Czech elements into the Greater German sphere would have to be accepted as a necessary evil with regard to the following:

a) the appointment of Czech academics to positions at German universities;
b) the appointment of Czech economists to German firms;

4 On the Petschek family, see Doc. 77 and PMJ 2/91. The Prague branch of the family managed to anticipate the Aryanization process by selling to German consortia, thereby salvaging a great deal of their assets.

5 On 2 Oct. 1939 the Czech National Committee and the French prime minister Daladier signed an agreement on the formation of an independent Czechoslovak army in France. On 25 Oct. 1940 there followed an agreement between the Czechoslovak government in exile and Britain on incorporating the Czechoslovak air force into the Royal Air Force Volunteer Reserve.

c) the enlisting of technicians and skilled workers in Germany;
d) the exchange of doctors;
e) the establishment of Czech landowners as German farmers;
f) the admission of Czech students at German universities.
g) Also, in my view, specially selected former members of the Czechoslovak army can be safely employed in German private enterprises (excluding the arms industry).[6]

Should these elements fail to prove and adjust themselves, they can be sent back home without further ado. Given the adaptability of the Czechs, however, one must certainly expect that the majority will adjust after a period as *lone individuals* in the greater German territory, will be proud of their reputation and income, and, even in the next generation, will already feel themselves to be Greater Germans. German elements will be placed in the vacated positions in the Protectorate.

Concluding remarks

With a firm hand on the reins and without interference from secondary influences in the Protectorate, on the basis of the Führer's decree of 16 March 1939,[7] which is fully sufficient, but also on the basis of a simultaneously tenacious pursuit of the specified goals – the elimination of the Czech elite and the penetration of the German element – it will be possible in the foreseeable future to bring the Bohemian–Moravian territory *inwardly* into Greater Germany for all time, without major upheavals and without placing a strain on foreign policy. The healing of the thousand-year-old wound would thus not take place externally, through the formation of a thin skin of outward efforts at Germanization, whereby the pus in the wound can proliferate and burst out afresh, but rather through a proper healing from the inside, once the harmful bodies have been removed.

DOC. 252
On 15 July 1939 Reich Protector von Neurath sets up the Central Office for Jewish Emigration in Prague[1]

Letter from the Reich Protector of Bohemia and Moravia (no. 532/39), signed Baron von Neurath, Prague, to the Prime Minister in Prague,[2] dated 15 July 1939 (copy)[3]

Re: regulation of Jewish emigration from the Protectorate

Recently the need for the systematic management and implementation of Jewish emigration from the territory of the Protectorate of Bohemia and Moravia has become in-

6 Most plans for a solution to the 'Czech question' assumed that large numbers of Czechs could be Germanized by resettling them among the German population in the Reich. Such considerations subsequently played barely any role in practice. However, according to estimates, a total of 600,000 Czechs from the Protectorate and the Sudetengau were temporarily deployed as labourers in the Reich during the war.

7 Decree of the Führer and Reich Chancellor concerning the Protectorate of Bohemia and Moravia, *Reichsgesetzblatt*, 1939 1, pp. 485–488.

1 NAP, ÚŘP, I-3b 5811, box 389, fols. 8–10. This document has been translated from German.

2 Alois Eliáš.

creasingly apparent. In accordance with arrangements within the Reich, the centralized processing of all matters pertaining to Jewish emigration is thus also necessary in Protectorate territory. In order to encourage Jewish emigration and to speed up administration, a Central Office for Jewish Emigration must therefore be established in Prague.[4] It will have the following duties:

1) To create opportunities for emigration through negotiating entry permits with the relevant emigration organizations.
2) To procure the foreign exchange required for emigration.
3) To establish and supervise retraining sites.
4) To cooperate with travel agents and shipping companies to ensure that practical arrangements for departure are put in place.
5) To monitor Jewish political emigration organizations and other emigration organizations with regard to emigration.
6) To maintain constant contact with all German offices concerned with the emigration of Jews from the Protectorate, and with the offices of the Protectorate government.
7) To arrange standardized and accelerated procedure for the procurement of all documents and certifications necessary for emigration – while not encroaching upon the responsibilities of individual departments.

With regard to the emigration of the Jews from the territory of the Reich, it has only been necessary to guarantee cooperation between the individual agencies and the Jewish associations, but for emigration from the Protectorate, it is also essential to ensure close cooperation between the German offices and the respective departments of the Protectorate government. The Central Office thus has the task of ensuring a uniform and centralized approach to dealing with all questions, while nonetheless retaining the core responsibilities of individual heads of department, as mentioned above under point 7. As the Chief of the Security Police has been given central responsibility for Jewish emigration in the Reich, it is thus advisable to assign the responsibility for managing Jewish emigration in the territory of the Protectorate to the Commander of the Security Police under the Reich Protector of Bohemia and Moravia. I have accordingly put SS-Oberführer and Regierungsdirektor Dr Stahlecker in charge of the overall management of the Central Office for Jewish Emigration in Prague and granted him the necessary authority to perform his duties. In particular, he may require that civil servants needed by the individual offices are seconded to the Central Office for Jewish Emigration in Prague.

It is advisable to instruct all offices approached by Jews who are eager to emigrate that in the first instance they should forward all emigration requests immediately, without further independent disposition, to the Central Office for Jewish Emigration in Prague, and they must refer to this office all Jews who are eager to emigrate. In the future, Jews wishing to emigrate from the Protectorate must only approach the Central

3 The copy was sent to 'a) all subdivisions of the authority, b) the Commander of the Security Police, c) the Commander of the Order Police'.

4 The Central Office for Jewish Emigration in Prague (in 1942 renamed the Central Office for the Settlement of the Jewish Question in Bohemia and Moravia) was established on 26 July 1939, and was modelled on the Central Office for Jewish Emigration in Vienna. Hans Günther was appointed as its director. The Central Office was officially under the authority of the Commander of the Security Police and SD in Prague. In practice, responsibility lay with Adolf Eichmann, who was in charge of the 'Jewish affairs' section at the Reich Security Main Office.

Office for Jewish Emigration in Prague. This office will handle the subsequent process, procure in particular the documentation required from the relevant offices, and oversee the emigration once it is finalized.

This arrangement applies in the first instance to the city of Prague and the surrounding area. Arrangements for the remaining parts of Bohemia and Moravia will fall under the remit of the Central Office for Jewish Emigration in Prague.

With regard to the face-to-face meeting between SS-Oberführer Dr Stahlecker and the Prime Minister, I expect corresponding instructions to be issued to the offices of the Protectorate government, especially regarding the secondment of the civil servants required by the Protectorate government in order for individual departments to process Jewish emigration applications, and regarding the forwarding of all emigration applications to the Central Office for Jewish Emigration in Prague.

SS-Oberführer Dr Stahlecker is responsible for supervising the individual aspects of the procedure, in consultation with the Prime Minister's Office.

I am sending a copy of the decree for your attention and information.

Addendum for the Group for Cultural Policy Affairs: Please arrange for a suitable article to appear in the press.

DOC. 253
The Reich Protector receives an anonymous antisemitic letter on 25 July 1939[1]

Letter, unsigned and undated, to the Reich Protectorate, Prague (received on 25 July 1939)

With immediate effect, please prohibit Jews from entering Christian apartment buildings (even with tenants' rights!) and public parks. I refuse to let myself be provoked and further defiled at every turn by Jewish women and Jewish lawyers who, hand in glove with the judiciary and senior representatives, have destroyed me and my family! The Jews must not be allowed to leave the ghetto! Through procuring and defiling Christian women – before the very eyes of the women's fathers, husbands, and brothers, as it were – they 'buy' women for themselves, irrespective of whether these women are of presidents[2] or ordinary caretakers. And through the women they control the entire 'děvkocracy';[3] and because they are met with leniency they just become more and more brazen, because in Prague there are more and more rather than fewer of them, and the public parks (especially Letná[4]) are full of foreign Jews of all ages and all exoticitisms! Our young policemen are actively involved in procuring, and thus it is no wonder that so many women go 'missing'. Why aren't they sent to do harvest work, since they even own their own farms in the countryside? A corruption court has been established.[5] But the former powers that be have used the Restriction Law[6] to create positions for their

1 NAP, ÚŘP, I-3b-5801, box 388. This document has been translated from German.
2 As in the original: the meaning is presumably 'wives of presidents'.
3 *Děvka* is Czech for whore or prostitute; in the figurative sense someone who sells themselves.
4 A park in Prague on a hill of the same name.
5 Presumably this refers to the Commission to Combat Corruption, established in April 1939.
6 No details could be found.

nephews, brothers-in-law, and family friends, even walking all over the poor 'fools' and their families to do so, and this public procuring is not condemned – it is a family, and today it is not only the section heads who are 'on the take' – the honest ones were just restricted! There is also no criticism of the reorganization of the banks, the contributions of the villas, the stock-exchange robberies, the exemptions from military service, and all the corruption of the Jewified ochlocracy![7] We ask that you free us from Jewish Satanism, which is indeed becoming increasingly onerous – for reasons that are impossible to understand. One can barely move a muscle in one's own homeland and must even listen to threats of being expelled oneself!

DOC. 254
On 28 July 1939 the Oberlandrat in Tabor describes an attack upon Jews in Příbram[1]

Letter (no. Pol. 303, 1) from the Oberlandrat in Tabor for the district authorities in Tabor, Písek, Příbram, Benešov, Sedlčany, Milevsko, signed Dr Hertel,[2] to the Reich Protector of Bohemia and Moravia, Prague, dated 28 July 1939 (received on 29 July 1939)[3]

Re: excesses committed against the Jews in Příbram
The Bezirkshauptmann of Příbram reports to me that, on 22 July 1939, at around 8 p.m., two buses from Prague arrived in Příbram carrying approximately eighty men who were unknown in Příbram. The men proceeded to search various inns, looking for Jews. The Jews inside these pubs were chased out into the streets and beaten with rubber truncheons. Nine Jews were injured as a result. The perpetrators then proceeded to smash the display windows of Jewish shops. Eight windows of Jewish firms and one display window of an Aryan firm were demolished. Afterwards, the perpetrators reassembled and drove away in the direction of Prague.

The town's police and gendarmerie were unable to trace any of the troublemakers. The incident caused a sizeable commotion in the town. Driven by curiosity, many came to look at the scene of the damage. The Bezirkshauptmann reported that an on-duty German military patrol in Příbram, which was sighted after the incident, did not need to take any action. By around 10 p.m. the town was completely quiet.

According to the Bezirkshauptmann's report, the unknown perpetrators were members of the 'Vlajka' movement from Prague. The incident was linked solely to these unknown men. The population of Příbram was not involved. The Bezirkshauptmann expressly emphasizes that this applies to both the German and the Czech inhabitants. The

7 The term refers to mob rule.

1 ABS, 114-325-5, fol. 15r–v. This document has been translated from German.
2 Dr Gottfried Hertel (b. 1906), administrative official; joined the NSDAP in 1933; Regierungsrat in Pirmasens Regional Council, 1934–1938; joined the SA in 1938; seconded to the government of the Palatinate in Speyer, 1938; assigned to the Oberlandrat in Brünn in March/April 1939; acting Oberlandrat for the Brünn region in April/May 1939; initially acting Oberlandrat of Tábor from May 1939, then Oberlandrat; main department head in the regional authority for Bohemia in Prague from 1942.
3 The original contains handwritten corrections.

Bezirkshauptmann in Příbram has, of his own accord, informed the police headquarters in Prague. I have not taken any action thus far.

The reason for the incident, in my view, lies in the fact that a local Czech fascist leader of 'Vlajka' was allegedly brutally assaulted by two Jews at the beginning of July. In addition, the Příbram fascists are said to have been threatened with further violence by Jewish groups. This information was given to me by two Příbram fascists when they were submitting applications for firearms licences.

DOC. 255
On 28 July 1939 members of the Czech government report on their visit to Vienna's Central Office for Jewish Emigration[1]

Report, signed by Dr Baláž, department head in the Ministry of the Interior, and Karel Herr, senior official in the State Police Service,[2] dated 28 July 1939[3]

The Central Office for Jewish Emigration

On the orders of the Ministry of the Interior, the undersigned visited the 'Zentralstelle für jüdische Auswanderung'[4] at 32 Prinz-Eugen-Straße, Vienna, on 26 and 27 July 1939, and were informed about its role and facilities.

The Ministry of Social and Health Administration was represented during the visit by senior department heads *Dr Zavřel*[5] and *Dr Šlapák*,[6] who have both been assigned to the Institute for Refugee Support. The presentation was given by the senior commander of the Gestapo in Prague, Dr Stahlecker, and Gestapo commandants Dr Eichmann[7] and Günther. Commandant Günther[8] is head of the Zentralstelle in Vienna; Commandant Dr Eichmann, who organized the Zentralstelle in Vienna, is in charge of managing and organizing the Zentralstelle (Central Office) in the territory of the Protectorate of Bohemia and Moravia. The Central Office operates according to the following maxims: a) all matters pertaining to the emigration of Jews are concentrated in one location, thereby accelerating official procedures; b) the centralization of all of these departments will prevent important matters related to emigration from being overlooked or intentionally neglected; c) Jewish emigration is to be monitored.

However, the Central Office's failings are that: 1) the Central Office is intended solely for Jewish emigrants who voluntarily submit applications to emigrate; 2) the most im-

1 NAP, PP 42/Z-33/39, box 1575. This document has been translated from Czech.
2 Karel Herr (b. 1886), lawyer; chairman of the police department in Cheb, 1925, and later in Jablonec (Gablonz); police chief superintendent, 1931; chief of police in Užhorod (Ungwar), 1932; from 1937 chief of police in Carlsbad and Regierungsrat.
3 Parts of the original have been underlined by hand.
4 German: 'Central Office for Jewish Emigration'. In the original document, the author mainly uses the German term; in a few instances, the Czech designation ('Ústředna [pro židovské vystěhovalectví]') is used.
5 Probably Dr František Zavřel (1885–1947), lawyer and writer; worked for the Czechoslovak Ministry of Trade; department head, 1928; worked as a lawyer from 1931.
6 Dr Kamil Šlapák (b. 1897), lawyer and ministerial official.
7 Adolf Eichmann did not hold a doctorate.
8 Rolf Günther.

portant problem regarding Jewish emigration is unresolved, that being the question of which country will grant the emigrant an entry visa. The Zentralstelle itself does not arrange visas and leaves the procurement of a visa to the emigrant.

According to the statistical and schematic data, on 15 March 1938 there were 180,000 Jews in the Ostmark, 165,000 of whom were in Vienna and 15,000 in the provinces. As of 30 July 1939, the Zentralstelle statistics reported that 93,350 had emigrated from Vienna and 14,577 from the provinces. The number of those eligible for Jewish emigration should, however, be increased to include approximately 180,000 Jews of mixed blood; the Zentralstelle does not know whether any of those who fall into this category have already departed. However, the reported figures are clearly estimates; no information was given on the number of Jews who have emigrated via the Central Office, the number who have legally emigrated on their own, or how many have left the Ostmark illegally. The Central Office believes that only 3,784 Jews have emigrated to the Protectorate, but this figure suggests that the Central Office's statistics are sketchy, since according to rough calculations about 5,000–7,000 Jews emigrated from the Ostmark to Bohemia and Moravia in 1938.

According to the plans for the work of the Zentralstelle, the priority when it comes to Jewish emigration is cooperation between the Gestapo and Jewish organizations, namely with the Palestine Office, religious communities and the so-called Gildemes initiative[9] (which, according to the presentation, has emerged from a private, profit-oriented enterprise). These organizations also have their own staff on the Zentralstelle premises, with whom applicants must initially register and to whom they submit all of their application documents for checking. Jewish organizations procure entry visas independently of the Zentralstelle for the emigrants (or secure approval for such visas) and they organize group departures.

Anyone wishing to emigrate must obtain an application form from the Central Office, fill it out in duplicate, and add the required supporting documentation. They then report to the Jewish department (to the officials of the Jewish organizations). Once the application has been checked, the emigrant submits it to an official (Gestapo) at the Zentralstelle, who assigns it a number and inserts it in an official envelope bearing that number. Subsequently the emigrant applies to another official for the necessary character reference, and to a different official for a passport. The emigrant also applies for proof of residence (which is required to obtain a visa). The application and supporting documents are subsequently forwarded to the following departments: the criminal department (to which officials from police headquarters have been seconded), the Department of State Security, the Foreign Currency Police, the Economic Police, the criminal registry, the Department of Investigation, the Office of the Public Prosecutor, and the central authorities for combatting the trafficking of women and for recording the workshy and prostitutes.

The Economic Police include further subdivisions dealing with the postal service, social and public benefits, private debts, Aryanization, and the purchase of real estate.

9 Correctly: Gildemeester. The aid organization set up by the Dutchman Frank van Gheel Gildemeester had been commissioned by the Gestapo to accelerate the emigration of so-called non-Aryan Christians. The organization began its work in May 1938 and was dissolved at the end of 1939. See also PMJ 2/280.

The emigrant's application must be processed by all of the departments. If records are held at another department, the investigation department must track down the particular entry in the register using the fastest means possible. Each department marks on the official envelope whether it issues the required documents and whether investigations have indicated any objections [to the enquiry]. Subsequently, the departure tax [Fluchtsteuer] is calculated, and the passport and supporting documentation are issued so that the emigrant can obtain an entry visa (the emigrant only includes confirmation that an entry visa will be issued with the application) and travel ticket. Once the documents are issued, a deadline is set for the emigrant to depart, which must not exceed three months. The departure is monitored, and if the emigrant cannot adequately justify any delay to the departure, he or she is to be sent to a Jewish concentration camp. There, according to information provided by Dr Eichmann, he or she shall be required to take part in constant strenuous physical exercise.[10]

If the emigrant does not obey the order to leave even then, he or she shall be sent to a regular concentration camp.

The amount of the departure tax for Jews with assets over K 100,000 could not be ascertained even after specific enquiries. From one allusion, it could be inferred that Jews with assets of around K 100,000 (Mk 10,000) are left about K 50,000 (Mk 5,000) to found their departure. For Jews without assets, the departure tax totals Mk 5,010.[11] In addition to this tax, the emigrant must pay all the charges associated with issuing the passport and other official documentation. The period between the submission of the application and the issue of a passport ranges between ten and forty days. While the official process is under way, the emigrant is repeatedly summoned to the Zentralstelle to provide supplementary materials or to be questioned. The number of visitors per day (with the exception of Saturdays) is estimated at around 600 people. In order to ensure direct and prompt contact between the Zentralstelle and the applicant, the Zentralstelle instructs emigrants who live in the provinces to relocate to Vienna until the time of their departure. According to Dr Eichmann, a Central Office for Jewish Emigration is to be established in Prague for the region of Bohemia and in Brno for Moravia. To ensure direct contact, the Central Office also intends to have emigrants relocate to Prague or Brno. This measure can be based on regulation 16(1)(a) of government decree no. 14/1939 Slg. II, on the registration of assets and measures for restricting movement.[12]

10 'Jewish concentration camps' did not exist in Austria. The text probably refers to so-called re-education camps (*Umschulungslager*), which were controlled by the Central Office and increasingly developed into closely guarded labour camps.

11 This figure is difficult to make out, since it has been altered in the original: the first zero in '5,0010' has been either struck through or replaced with a dash. Thus, while it might have been altered to '5,010', the figure – in its amended form – could also feasibly be '5–10'.

12 Slg. is short for 'Sammlung' and refers to the compilation of laws and regulations of the Czech state. The reference is to § 14(1) (a) of the government regulation: 'Vládní nařízení ze dne 27. ledna 1939 o domovní evidenci obyvatelstva a některých opatřeních obmezujících jeho pohyb', cited in *Sbírka zákonů a nařízení republiky Česko-Slovenské*, no. 3, 4 Feb. 1939, pp. 13–16. According to this regulation, the regional, district, and state police were authorized to order people who had taken up residence in a municipality after 1 Jan. 1938 to relocate to a different locality specified by the police.

The Central Office's authority in issuing passports and character references and determining whether the emigrant is wanted for a crime or is subject to an arrest warrant falls under the remit of the relevant department of the Ministry of the Interior.

It is recommended that in issuing passports the Central Office provide each emigrant with a new passport and invalidate any passport issued previously. In order to determine whether the passport was issued by the Central Office for Jewish Emigration or by the former passport authorities for Aryan emigrants, it is proposed that passports issued by the Central Office are marked on the first page of the passport form with a letter 'V' in *red*, and passports issued by the passport offices for Aryan emigrants retain the *blue* letter 'V'. Passport applications are to be submitted in duplicate; one copy is to remain at the Central Office, and the second copy, with a record of the outcome, is to be stored at the police headquarters in Prague or Brno. The passport number (which corresponds to the number allocated upon submission to police headquarters) will be followed by a slash and the case number issued by the Central Office that handled the application. The same submission process and numbering method will be used for applications for character references. In order to determine whether an applicant has a criminal record, it is recommended that an enquiry be lodged with the prosecutor's office. The enquiry will not be sent to the public prosecutor's office or court, as is usually the case, but instead to the local gendarmerie or police department, as they will be able to make enquiries at the public prosecutor's office or court in the fastest way possible and report back promptly. Until now, enquiries sent to the public prosecutor's office or the courts have always required at least three weeks. Investigations in the areas covered by Prague and Brno will be assigned to the police departments associated with the Central Office.

Following a request made to the police headquarters in Prague by Dr Eichmann, the following police officials have been assigned to the Central Office in Prague: three trainee actuaries, one additional senior chancellery official, two[13] chancellery assistants, and eight investigators. As the police officers will be cooperating with the Gestapo authorities, it is also proposed that the Central Office be assigned one junior police officer and one motorcycle with a sidecar in order to expedite the processing of paperwork.

The Central Office for Jewish Emigration in Prague will commence operations on Monday, 31 July. It is located at 11 Dělostřelecká Street, Prague–Střešovice.[14]

Like the Vienna Central Office for Jewish Emigration, the Prague Central Office for Jewish Emigration also plans to force emigrants to leave by sending them to concentration camps. Where and how these camps will be set up has not become clear in the discussions held thus far. The matter will be a subject of discussion during the planned meeting at the Central Office in Prague, to take place at 10 a.m. on 31 July.[15]

Dr Stahlecker pointed out that the Central Office would not deal with Jews with foreign citizenship at all. He only stated that Jews holding Polish citizenship would be expelled and deported to Poland.

13 It is unclear from the original whether the figure is two or three here.

14 The headquarters of the Central Office were located on the premises of the former Dutch embassy in the Prague district of Střešovice.

15 The files contain no indication that this meeting took place on 31 July 1939. See Jaroslava Milotova, 'Die Zentralstelle für jüdische Auswanderung in Prag: Genesis und Tätigkeit bis zum Anfang des Jahres 1940', *Theresienstädter Studien und Dokumente*, vol. 4 (1997), pp. 7–30.

DOC. 256

On 3 August 1939 the Protectorate government's Ministry of the Interior orders the segregation of the Jewish population[1]

Letter from the headquarters of the Ministry of the Interior (no. 11. 206/39), unsigned, Prague, to the headquarters of the regional authorities in 1) Prague, and 2) Brünn, dated 3 August 1939 (copy)

Measures regarding contact between Jews and the rest of the population.
Circumstances have developed in such a manner that certain groups among the population are being incited to take unauthorized action against inhabitants of Jewish extraction. These incidents are often of a very serious nature (see for example the attempted bomb attacks which have been carried out in several locations) and can therefore jeopardize public safety in the entire surrounding area and cause a breach of the peace. In the interest of the safety of the entire population, such actions must not be tolerated, and as a preventative measure, it is necessary to ensure that anything which could cause such action is avoided. A number of authorities, which have apparently deemed it necessary to consider the views of certain circles, have introduced various police measures regarding the coexistence of the Jewish with the non-Jewish population, perhaps in order to nip a range of unauthorized actions in the bud. This type of solution to the aforementioned problem – one which is so inconsistent in its content, location, and timing – cannot be condoned, for on the one hand the manner in which the matter is being handled is not always in full accordance with existing legislation, and on the other hand it gives rise to the fear that certain authorities, driven by the wish to best fulfil the tasks arising from the matter at hand, may take their measures further than is actually necessary and in the public interest. This would lead to further irregularities in the whole affair, which is why it is necessary to bring about clarity and order in this matter and to indicate to the subordinate authorities the precise boundaries within which they are authorized to take measures of this kind.

In this regard, the subordinate authorities are to be instructed that they may issue regulations where it is absolutely necessary to uphold law and order, in the interest of public safety as well as law and order, pursuant to Article 3 of the Law on the Organization of Political Administration, 14 July 1927, Slg. no. 125,[2] whereby contact between the non-Jewish and the Jewish population in the public sphere can be provisionally regulated as follows:

1) The use of public facilities such as inns, restaurants, coffee shops, wine bars, public reading rooms, and suchlike is to be regulated – if need be in agreement with the relevant trade associations – so that visitors of non-Jewish extraction are not continually obliged to encounter visitors of Jewish origin for the duration of their visit or to spend time with

1 NAP, UŘP, ad I-3b 5800, box 392, fols. 828–831. This document has been translated from German.

2 Slg. stands for 'Sammlung', and refers to the compilation of laws and regulations of the Czechoslovak state. According to Articles 2 and 3 of the law referred to here, the Ministry for the Interior and the political authorities under its jurisdiction were able to take the steps necessary to secure public order and eliminate any disturbances of it, and to issue fines and prison sentences for any breach. See Law on the Organization of Political Administration, 14 July 1927, in *Sammlung der Gesetze und Verordnungen des Čecho-Slovakischen Staates*, vol. 2, no. 125 (1927), pp. 1599–1635.

them on the same premises. Depending on the location, the matter can be resolved by declaring certain public spaces inaccessible to visitors with Jewish origins, and where this is not viable, by reserving separate rooms for visitors of Jewish origin in these establishments. This regulation must be displayed in a clearly visible manner both in front of the establishments and on their premises.[3]
2) In public baths, visitors are to be allocated separate areas or time slots so that visitors of Jewish origin and of non-Jewish origin do not bathe together or use the shared facilities at the same time.
3) In publicly accessible bathing areas (swimming schools) special areas are to be allocated for visitors of Jewish origin and, where this is not possible, separate bathing areas are to be allocated.
4) Businesses and other commercial enterprises with owners or management of Jewish origin are to display a sign making it clearly visible to customers and the public that it is a 'Jewish shop' (Jewish business).
5) The day-to-day running of public institutions such as hospitals, infirmaries, poorhouses, and sanatoria, should be organized wherever possible so that the premises and facilities of these institutions are not used by Jews and non-Jews at the same time and so as to ensure that Jews and non-Jews are accommodated separately.

It should be emphasized that the prime objective of these measures is to guarantee the safety of persons of Jewish origin and their property, which is why these measures must go no further than the aforementioned purpose and public interest require. The measures must, however, be carried out in such a way as to genuinely guarantee complete security to persons of Jewish origin and their property.[4]

For the minister:

3 On 14 August 1939 the police headquarters in Prague issued a notice banning Jews from frequenting certain establishments in Prague. The owners were told to put up signs designating them as 'prohibited to Jews'. See Friedmann, 'Rechtsstellung', p. 246.

4 The Czech and German authorities still continued to issue unauthorized anti-Jewish regulations, which varied from region to region. See Doc. 258.

DOC. 257

On 10 August 1939 State Secretary Stuckart warns the Protectorate government not to take independent action to step up anti-Jewish policy[1]

Letter (secret) from the Reich Ministry of the Interior (I 1427 II/39 -g-/5012), p.p. signed Dr Stuckart, to the Reich Protector of Bohemia and Moravia, for the attention of Landrat Fuchs[2] – or his deputy in office – Prague, dated 10 August 1939[3]

Re: treatment of Jews in the Protectorate of Bohemia and Moravia

A large portion of the Czech population is seeking a solution to the Jewish question as quickly and as radically as possible along the lines of the measures being taken in the Old Reich. It will be necessary to align these endeavours with the interests of the entire Reich in this regard. To the extent that the Jewish question is a biological problem, I do not initially consider it is in the Reich's immediate interests to adopt special measures for the benefit of the Czech people. Until further notice, it will remain a matter for the Protectorate government to decide whether and which measures they wish to pursue in relation to blood protection. – As regards ethnic Germans, appropriate regulations are being prepared in accordance with Reich law. I refer to the draft regulation sent to you for the implementation of Article 2 of the Führer's decree of 16 March 1939.[4]

It is, however, very much in the interests of the Reich that Jews living in the Protectorate do not influence the general relationship of the Protectorate with the Reich or internal political developments within the Protectorate. I therefore deem it necessary to exclude Jews from public life in the Protectorate. The implementation of this task will be the duty of the Protectorate government. I propose that you recommend to the Protectorate government that it take the necessary measures. This would involve the following:

1) Withdrawal of active and passive suffrage.
2) Exclusion from public offices.
3) Elimination from the press, radio, and other institutions which may influence public opinion.
4) Elimination from Czech associations (Article 7 of the Führer's decree).[5]

1 NAP, ÚŘP, I-3b-5801, box 388, fols. 113 f, published in Kárný and Milotová, *Anatomie*, doc. 87, pp. 221–224. This document has been translated from German.

2 Dr Walther Kurt Fuchs (1891–1982), lawyer; senior civil servant in Ulm, 1923; senior civil servant in the Württemberg Ministry of the Interior, 1926; joined the NSDAP in 1933; head of the department for administration, justice, and teaching in Prague, 1939; ministerial director, 1940; put on leave in 1942, then chairman of the board of the Sarkese Bank in Prague. Appointed president of the administrative court in Stuttgart in 1956.

3 The original contains handwritten notes and underlining, as well as the official stamp of the Reich Ministry of the Interior.

4 Not in the file. Article 2 of the Führer's decree regulated the question of citizenship: 'ethnic German' residents of the Protectorate became citizens of the Reich, while others became 'subjects of the Protectorate'. See Decree of the Führer and Reich Chancellor concerning the Protectorate of Bohemia and Moravia, *Reichsgesetzblatt*, 1939, I, pp. 485–488, here p. 486.

5 Ibid., p. 487. Article 7 regulated the military status of the Protectorate and the establishment of its own associations.

5) As an extension of 4), prohibition of the ownership of weapons and the manufacture and trade of weapons.

The Reich has a further interest in not rushing the solution to the Jewish question in the Protectorate. The experience of the Old Reich clearly shows that the exclusion of the Jews, with their profound involvement in all areas of society, can only be without disadvantage for the general public if the process is suitably planned and not carried out too hastily. For this reason, I have strong misgivings regarding the draft of the government regulation on the legal status of the Jews, which you sent me a copy of in your letter dated 30 May 1939 – II B 10 469.[6] In my opinion, enacting this regulation would have an unfavourable effect on the general economic development of the Protectorate.

I consider that only a step-by-step approach is suited to the objective. The exclusion from public life detailed above would represent the first step. After implementing this measure, it would be necessary to decide which area can be tackled next. In particular, it will be necessary to examine whether it is possible to remove Jews from *leading positions in the economy.* This type of planned, step-by-step approach would correspond to the needs of the Czech population and is unlikely to trigger undesired repercussions affecting the overall development of the Protectorate and the progress towards the solution to the Jewish question in the Reich. The aim of Jewish policy is emigration. Overly hasty measures will only serve to hinder the achievement of this aim.

I request that you examine the above and communicate your views to me as soon as possible.[7]

Finally, I request that I am always involved in [decisions regarding] the regulations and measures concerning the Jewish question in the Protectorate. I attach great importance to ensuring that Jewish policy, for which I am responsible, is also consistent in the Protectorate.

DOC. 258

On 12 August the Chief of Police in Brünn announces anti-Jewish measures[1]

Announcement by the Chief of Police in Brünn (no. 2111 39 Präs[2]), signed Dr Schwabe, dated 12 August 1939[3]

Official announcement

Pursuant to the stipulations of the decree issued by the headquarters of the Ministry of the Interior on 3 August 1939 no. 11 206,[4] and the decree no. 30 732 Präs issued by the

6 Draft of the government regulation of 4 July 1939 on the legal status of the Jews: NAP, ÚŘP, I-3b-5801, box 388, fol. 150–157, published in Kárný and Milotová, *Anatomie*, doc. 87, pp. 221–224.

7 After lengthy discussions, the regulation was finally issued on 24 April 1940. See Government Regulation on the Legal Status of Jews in Public Life, 4 July 1939, in *Sammlung der Gesetze und Verordnungen des Protektorates Böhmen und Mähren vom 24 April 1940*, no. 136 (1940), pp. 395–403.

1 MZAB, B 251/522/4080, box 45. The announcement was published in the *Volksdeutsche Zeitung Brunn*, 17 August 1939. This document has been translated from German.

2 Präsidium; German for 'headquarters'.

3 The announcement appeared in German and in Czech.

4 See Doc. 256.

headquarters of the regional authorities in Brünn on 5 August 1939,[5] in accordance with Article 5 of the law no. 123 S.d.G.u.V.,[6] issued on 14 July 1927, with a view to maintaining public order, peace, and public safety, as well as in the interests of personal and material safety with regard to contact between Aryans and non-Aryans in the areas covered by the police headquarters in Brünn, I hereby order the following:

I. Jews are not permitted to enter inns or coffee houses which have put up notices to this effect. Such establishments are to draw attention to this accordingly. Inns which do not display such information should make provision to ensure either that Jewish visitors have a dedicated room at their disposal or, if the inn only consists of one room, that a specific section of this room is reserved for them. This section is to be marked accordingly. The same applies to dance halls, unless special rules are listed in this announcement, and to public reading rooms.

II. Jews are only allowed to attend theatre productions, concerts, film screenings, and other performances and events if this is expressly announced at the venue itself and, if necessary, also through other channels.

III. In public institutions such as hospitals, maternity hospitals, sanatoria, infirmaries, poorhouses, and suchlike, Jews and Aryans are to be kept strictly separate and accommodated in such a way that encounters between Jews and Aryans are avoided wherever possible, also on the way to and from their rooms or beds. Jews are completely prohibited from entering private establishments of this kind if the establishment concerned specifies this. Should this not be the case, the same arrangements should apply as to public establishments of this kind.

IV. Jews are banned from entering all parks. One exception to this is the park at Winterhollerplatz, the Glacis, but only in the section between Pressburgerstrasse and Karpfengasse.

V. Jews are forbidden to frequent or use all public baths and outdoor swimming pools. Exceptions to this are the Charlottenbad in Pressburgerstrasse, in Brünn, and the 'Riviera' in the Schreibwalde neighbourhood, on Mondays from morning to evening.

VI. Jews may not decorate their houses, apartments, shops, business premises, enterprises, vehicles, etc. with any flag other than the Jewish flag (blue and white with the Star of David), nor may they wear any personal emblems intended to identify them as members of any other group but the Jewish nation.

VII. Jewish shops, businesses, and enterprises of every kind, including those not governed by trade regulations, in particular lawyers' offices, doctors' practices etc., must be clearly marked as such. The identification must feature the wording: 'Jewish shop – židovský obchod' or 'Jewish business – židovský závod', or 'Jewish enterprise – židovský podnik' and be displayed as follows:

5 According to a decree dated 5 August 1939, the district and police authorities were to issue regulations governing contact between Jews and non-Jews 'in the interests of public safety and law and order'. See MZAB, B 251/522/4080, box 45.

6 Slg. stands for 'Sammlung' and refers to the Compilation of Laws and Regulations of the Czechoslovak State. According to Article 5 of the Law on the Organization of Public Administration, 14 July 1927, political authorities could also issue regulations within their jurisdiction in areas which by law were assigned to the local police if said regulations affected several municipalities, or if the municipality in question did not implement the necessary order in time. See Law on the Organization of Political Administration, 14 July 1927, in *Sammlung der Gesetze und Verordnungen des Čecho-Slovakischen Staates*, vol. 2, no. 125 (1927), pp. 1599–1635.

1) on business premises, in such a way that the wording is posted, in black letters, 12 cm high, on a yellow background (vertical poster):
   a) 25 cm above the door handle of every entrance door giving access to the business, and
   b) in the geometric centre of every display window;
2) on business stationery, in letters at least as large as those used in the letterhead, in a different colour to the standard print;
3) with businesses under provisional management, I shall take a decision on a case-by-case basis.

For the purpose of judging whether a person is to be classed as a Jew or whether a shop, business, or enterprise is to be labelled as Jewish, the clauses in §§ 6–8 of the Regulation of the Reich Protector of Bohemia and Moravia on Jewish Assets, dated 21 June 1939, shall apply.[7]

The above orders are to be implemented with immediate effect.

The responsibility for ensuring that these measures are implemented lies solely with police headquarters.

Failure to comply with these regulations will lead to prosecution under Article 3 of the law no. 125 S.d.G.u.V. issued on 14 July 1927, and result in fines of K 10 to K 5,000 or imprisonment of between twelve hours and two weeks.[8]

Brünn, 12 August 1939
The Chief of Police
Dr Schwabe, m.p.[9]

DOC. 259

In its weekly report, dated 19 August 1939, the Jewish Religious Community of Prague outlines its endeavours to arrange emigration from the Protectorate[1]

Weekly report (no. 4) from the executive secretary of the Jewish Religious Community of Prague, for the period 13–19 August 1939, signed Franz Weidmann, dated 19 August 1939

1) Emigration

1,508 portfolios (forms to accompany emigration documents) have been sold. 489 persons have been referred to the Central Office for Jewish Emigration in Prague.

2) Offices indirectly involved in the emigration process

a) Welfare

3,305 persons have received aid from the Social Institute of the Jewish Religious Community of Greater Prague.[2] 5,178 midday meals have been distributed.

7 See Doc. 247.
8 Law on the Organization of Political Administration, 14 July 1927.
9 *Manu propria* (Latin): '(signed) with one's own hand'.

1 YVA, 0.7/53. This document has been translated from German.
2 The Jewish Religious Community of Prague set up the Social Institute in 1935 in order to centralize its welfare activities. The institute supported impoverished Jews in the Prague area by providing them with financial assistance, food, and clothing.

b) Situation report

With the consent of the Gestapo, the heads of the provincial communities were summoned to Prague on Sunday 13 August 1939 and told to inform members of their communities that they have to transfer their residence to Prague on the instruction of the Central Office for Jewish Emigration in Prague.[3] Furthermore, they were instructed to send statistics on membership levels, the existing Jewish organizations, and the retraining courses offered by their communities to the Jewish Religious Community as soon as possible. Once this material has been processed accordingly, it will be sent to the Central Office for Jewish Emigration in Prague.

The decree issued by the Chief of Police in Prague on 14 August 1939 regarding the presence of Jews in public,[4] as well as the identical decrees issued in the provinces, has made it plain to Jews living in the Protectorate just how serious the situation is. This week we noted an even higher number of requests for information on emigration opportunities.

This week also saw the start of the relocation of Jews from the provinces to Prague, and thus the housing department began its work on 17 August this year. The plan to establish the emigration department of the Jewish Religious Community of Prague has already been completed, and the individual sections will begin their work as required. In agreement with the Central Office for Jewish Emigration in Prague, the chairman of the community, Dr Kafka, and Mrs Schmolka, who has been appointed chief emigration advisor, travelled to Paris and London on 19 August this year to conduct negotiations regarding the creation of emigration opportunities and to discuss the question of the funding of the Prague Religious Community. In many cases, we have noted that people who already have an opportunity to emigrate cannot make use of this opportunity, as they are unable to receive their emigration documents in time, and, in many cases, the consulates refuse to extend the deadline for entry. From next week, we will be in a position to communicate exact statistical data in the weekly reports.[5]

3 See also Doc. 252, fn. 4.

4 Announcement by the police headquarters in Prague, dated 14 August 1939, concerning the ban on Jews entering public establishments in Prague, as well as the regulations on the use of public baths and other public institutions such as hospitals, infirmaries, poorhouses, and sanatoria. See Friedmann, 'Rechtsstellung', p. 246.

5 In the subsequent weekly reports, the Jewish Religious Community of Prague reported on how many applications had been processed by their emigration department and how many had been assigned to the Central Office for Jewish Emigration. See YVA, O.7/53.

DOC. 260
On 21 August 1939 the Jewish Religious Community of Prague reports on the catastrophic situation of the Jews and on Eichmann's rule in the Protectorate[1]

Report by the Jewish Religious Community of Prague, unsigned, dated 21 August 1939[2]

The Jewish question
I. Jews in the Czechoslovak Republic
Up until the events in Munich,[3] there was no Jewish problem to speak of in the Czechoslovak Republic. In the peace treaties [of 1919], the country had already pledged that it would not differentiate between its citizens on the basis of race, religion, or nationality, and it enshrined this principle in its basic law, the Constitutional Charter. This principle and this pledge were indeed fully recognized and respected. It should be emphasized that this was not merely forced compliance with a legal and contractual obligation. Rather it corresponded to the character of the Czech nation and all of its administrative and political officials, who never distinguished between people on the basis of their origin or religion, but only according to their abilities. One can thus say that there was a truly ideal coexistence between Jews and non-Jews in the Czechoslovak context. Even the events in the neighbouring German Reich, which affected German Jewish citizens so profoundly, had no noticeable impact on how the Czech nation viewed the Jewish question. This was also reflected in the fact that a large number of the Jewish people fleeing Germany and especially Austria found at least temporary shelter in Czechoslovakia.

Masaryk's conduct in the Polná affair brought about an ideological and practical resolution of the Jewish question within the Czech national context.[4] His uncompromising stance against antisemitism even convinced the last few people who up to that point had apparently not understood that antisemitism is just a cover for other aims.

The 1921 census made it possible to determine the number of Jews, i.e. people identifying with the religion. Moreover, legal regulations made it possible for Jews who viewed their Judaism not only as a religion, but also as a nationality (Zionists), to register as Czechoslovak citizens of Jewish nationality.

1 VHU Prag, 140/19; copy in USHMM, RG-48.004M, reel 3. This document has been translated from the original Czech. The version of this document in the German edition of this series is based on the contemporary translation into German found in the USHMM copy; there are some content discrepancies between the original Czech and the translation into German.

2 According to Stanislav Kokoška, the report was compiled by the Jewish Religious Community of Prague for the Czechoslovak government in exile. See 'Zwei unbekannte Berichte aus dem besetzten Prag über die Lage der jüdischen Bevölkerung im Protektorat', in *Theresienstädter Studien und Dokumente*, vol. 4 (1997), pp. 31–49.

3 This is a reference to the Munich Agreement of 29 Sept. 1938, which enabled Nazi Germany to annexe portions of Czechoslovakia.

4 In 1899, following the murder of a Catholic girl in Polná, a small town in the Bohemian-Moravian Highlands, the Jewish shoemaker Leopold Hilsner was charged with ritual murder. Tomáš Garrigue Masaryk, later the first president of the Czechoslovak Republic, publicly defended him. Hilsner was sentenced to death; his sentence was later commuted to life in prison. See Introduction, p. 16.

Region	Number of Jews	% of total population	% of Jewish population living in
Bohemia	79,777	1.19	22.51
Moravia	37,989	1.43	10.72
Silesia	7,317	1.09	2.07
Slovakia	135,918	4.55	38.36
Subcarpathian Rus	93,341	15.39	26.34
Total	354,342	2.6	100.00

Most Jews were concentrated in Prague, home to 31,863 Jews; in Brno, 10,904 Jews; Moravská Ostrava, 7,584 Jews; followed by Pilsen and České Budějovice.

The national distribution of Czechoslovakian citizens of Jewish faith in 1921 was as follows:

Country	Czechoslovak	Ruthenian	German	Hungarian	Jewish	Other
Bohemia	37,234	36	26,058	424	10,983	304
Moravia-Silesia	6,116	9	13,671	190	18,630	423
Slovakia	29,136	171	8,738	21,584	71,018	188
Subcarpathian Rus	717	3,528	262	6,863	79,560	713

The number of Jews in the western parts of the Czechoslovak Republic fell rapidly, a sociological phenomenon that can be seen generally around the world. The causes are to be found in the relatively low Jewish birth rate; in the fact that Jews are abandoning the Jewish religion, which is perhaps the only distinguishing statistical marker; and in their entry into matrimony with non-Jewish persons, which corresponds to the natural coexistence among people whose central issue is human qualities, not religion or race.

In the 1930 census, the number of Jews had thus already fallen: Bohemia, 76,301; Moravia-Silesia, 41,250; Slovakia, 136,737; Subcarpathian Rus, 102,542.

II. From the Munich Agreement to the establishment of the Protectorate.

Based on statistical findings on the number of Jews in Bohemia and Moravia from around 1930, one can observe a steady decline in the number of Jews, with an average annual fall of 6.15 per cent. Based on this finding, one can estimate that, as of 1 July 1938, there were about 71,000 Jews in Bohemia and 38,000 Jews in Moravia. Of this number, about 25,000 lived in the territory ceded to Germany in the Munich Agreement.

Since it is impossible to obtain exact statistical data for the subsequent period, one has to rely on estimates. After the surrender of territory to Germany, about 90 per cent of the Jews living in the ceded territory moved to the remaining territories of Czechoslovakia, i.e. about 20,000 people. In addition, according to rough estimates, the number of Jews rose as a result of about 6,000 people moving to Bohemia and Moravia from Austria and the German old Reich.

At the same time, of course, emigration was already well under way, which resulted in a further decline in the number of Jews. In terms of religion, the number of Jews declined considerably in this period, because a significant number, fearing future developments in a Central Europe surrendered to the interests of Germany, abandoned the Jewish religion and were baptized. However, this issue is of no significance to further contemplation of the Jewish problem, as racial indicators must now be used to determine the number of Jews.

During the Second Republic, as the period between Munich and the establishment of the Protectorate is called, circumstances changed somewhat. It became ever clearer that there was increasing interference into the affairs of what was still an independent country by neighbouring Germany, which sought a solution to the Jewish question according to Nazi principles here as well. Under the influence of these principles, some elements among the Czech people viewed antisemitism as a means of personal enrichment. This was especially the case among attorneys and physicians, who wanted to get rid of their Jewish colleagues in the first months of 1939. But then, as now, government circles and broad sectors of society were not willing to change anything in the principles of the Constitutional Charter, which did not distinguish between citizens on the grounds of race or religion.

Following the decision regarding autonomy of Slovakia and Subcarpathian Rus, the number of Jews in Bohemia and Moravia increase, because of the significant number who fled there. Their numbers cannot be estimated even roughly.[5]

III. The Protectorate of Bohemia and Moravia.
After Bohemia and Moravia were incorporated into the German Reich, Reich officials announced that the Jewish question was among the questions which would be left to the autonomous Czech government to resolve, as the German government was not interested in interfering in this issue.

Nonetheless, direct and indirect political pressure was exerted on Czech political circles to reach a solution to the Jewish question that corresponded to the principles of the Third Reich. Národní souručenství[6] therefore set up a commission for the solution to the Jewish problem, and the government also addressed the question in a special ministerial committee.[7] The general thrust of these discussions was that Jews who had lived in the territory of the Protectorate for generations and who claimed Czech nationality would be granted almost complete civil equality. As reported in the press, after lengthy negotiations, the government presented its proposals to solving the Jewish question to Reich Protector Neurath for approval in early May 1939. Instead of approving the proposals, however, the Office of the Reich Protector, based on the special powers it had been granted by the Reich Government, or more specifically by Adolf Hitler, issued its own set of Jewish laws in a regulation dated 21 June 1939, which came into effect on the same day.[8] The new laws were published in the newspaper *Der Neue Tag*, formerly *Prager Tagblatt*.[9] This was the first

5 In July 1939, a total of 22,033 Jewish refugees were living in the Protectorate, of whom 18,673 came from the areas annexed by the German Reich, 428 from Poland, 164 from Hungary, 142 from Slovakia, and 2,626 from other territories: Jaroslav Šíma, *Českoslovenští přestěhovalci v letech 1938–1945* (Prague: Societas, 1945), doc. 4.

6 National Solidarity: the only political party permitted by the Germans in the Protectorate of Bohemia and Moravia.

7 See Introduction, p. 24, and Doc. 246.

8 See Doc. 247.

9 *Der Neue Tag* was founded in 1939 as the successor to the daily newspaper *Prager Tagblatt*. It functioned as a publication organ of the Reich Protector of Bohemia and Moravia as well as other German agencies.

official infringement of the rights of the autonomous Czech government to address issues relating to citizens of the Protectorate independently.

The above regulation, issued on 21 June 1939, primarily governed the question of who is considered a Jew under the law. A Jew is anyone who, according to racial principles, is descended from at least three Jewish grandparents, and further those of mixed race who are descended from two Jewish grandparents and were members of the Jewish religious community as of 15 September 1939, or were married to a Jew, or were the product of a marriage with a Jew or an extramarital affair with a Jew. At the same time, it was stipulated that a company could be classed as Jewish if it had at least one Jew on the management or supervisory boards, or if at least one Jew was authorized to legally represent the company.

Through this regulation, Jews were banned from acquiring titles to real estate, businesses, company shares, securities, and leaseholds. At the same time, they were ordered to report to the appropriate Oberlandrat (that is, the administrative authorities of the German Protectorate) by 21 July 1939 to register the agricultural and forestry land they owned, co-owned, or held leases on. It was further ordered that Jews are obliged to register with the National Bank of the Protectorate of Bohemia and Moravia all objects in their ownership or co-ownership made of gold, platinum, or silver, as well as precious stones and pearls, regardless of value, as well as jewellery and pieces of art, if the price of the single object or collection of such objects exceeds 10,000 korunas. At the same time, Jews were prohibited from acquiring such objects.

Finally, it should be noted that any transgressions and all acts in breach of this regulation are punishable under German law and dealt with by the German courts. Non-Aryan lawyers have been prohibited from practising law, and commissioners have been appointed to run Jewish companies.

In around mid July 1939, the German authorities, or rather the German secret police (henceforth the Gestapo), which are in charge of this agenda, refused to permit Jews to travel abroad. In the month of June, Obersturmführer Eichmann took charge of the Gestapo, the department for the Jewish question. Up until then, he had been the decision-making official in charge of the Jewish question in Vienna and in the Ostmark. This Eichmann is furnished with exceptional authority and allegedly reports directly to Himmler.[10] He came to Prague for the purpose of ridding the Protectorate of Jews. Eichmann set about this task with great zeal. Since, as he says, he cannot negotiate with each Jew separately, he recognizes a total of four people as spokesmen for Jewry in the Protectorate, or rather people to whom he gives orders and will grant an audience. They are the chairman of the Jewish Religious Community of Prague, Dr Emil Kafka; the secretary of this same Community, Dr František Weidmann; and two representatives of the Palestinian Office, Dr Kahn[11] and Secretary Edelstein.[12] First of all he sent Dr Weid-

10 Eichmann set up the Central Office in Prague and was its de facto head until the end of 1939, when Heydrich placed Section IV D 4 in the Reich Security Main Office under his control and Eichmann was transferred to Berlin. His immediate superior in this function was again Heydrich, who was in turn accountable to Himmler.

11 Franz Kahn (1895–1944), lawyer and association official; secretary general of the Zionist Organizations of Czechoslovakia, 1921–1938; opened the 18th World Zionist Congress in Prague in 1933; on 28 Jan. 1943 deported to Theresienstadt and on 4 Oct. 1944 to Auschwitz, where he was murdered.

12 Jakob Edelstein.

mann to Vienna for twenty-four hours so that he could view the facilities there for Jewish emigration. Upon his return, he issued an order to immediately set up an emigration department at the Jewish Religious Community of Prague. About eighteen different questionnaires were issued, which each Jew who wants to emigrate – the official term is: der auswanderungslustige Jude[13] – must complete. Questionnaires must be filled out using a typewriter and only in German. The Jewish Religious Community of Prague is obliged to make sure that the questionnaires are filled out completely and accurately, and is obliged to calculate a levy on Jewish assets amounting to between 1/2 of the total assets and 20 per cent of the assets, which encompasses everything the émigré owns, i.e. including clothing and even the clothes on their back. The purchase price has to be listed for items purchased after 1 September 1938; the estimated price must be given for other items. When the émigré has everything prepared, they will receive a pass from the Religious Community allowing them to report to the Zentralstelle für jüdische Auswanderung,[14] the office run by the Gestapo, or rather Eichmann and his colleagues Günther,[15] Bartl, Nowak, and Fuchs, at the time and date designated by the Community. This is also where officials from individual Czech authorities have their offices, i.e. the police, the tax offices, etc., as Eichmann has ordered that henceforth no office may issue any official confirmation of the payment of taxes, certificate of good conduct, passport, etc. to Jews. Jews receive all of these certificates only through the Zentralstelle, and only if they want to emigrate. This ban in itself has caused numerous difficulties, as in many cases Jews need tax and police documents for purposes other than emigration and have practically no chance of obtaining them.

The Zentralstelle has exclusive authority, which means that it is the only body that can give permission to emigrate. Branch offices are not and will not be established. For this reason, every Jew has to move to Prague before emigrating, because at the same time it was decreed that the Zentralstelle may grant permission to emigrate only to Jews who are registered with the police as residents of Prague. This order, however, is bound up with another question – the order that all Jews in the Protectorate be concentrated in Prague, which we will discuss below.

In addition to the 1/2–20 per cent levy on assets, Jews departing for another country must pay another tax on the items they are taking abroad. This tax amounts to 26 per cent of the value of these items. This is calculated on the basis of the estimated price for items purchased before 1 September 1938 and the purchase price for items bought later. Generally, the principle applies that the only items that may be taken abroad are items purchased before 1 September 1938.[16] The only exceptions are objects purchased as a replacement for worn clothing and undergarments, as well as objects purchased by the emigrant for emigration (furniture, equipment, etc.). Objects made of gold, silver, or platinum, precious stones, and pearls may be exported only according to the following specifications: one's own wedding ring and the wedding ring of a deceased spouse, a silver wristwatch or pocket watch, used silverware – two four-piece sets com-

13 German in the original: 'the Jew with an inclination to emigrate'.
14 German in the original: 'Central Office for Jewish Emigration'.
15 Hans Günther.
16 This appears to be the correct meaning, although the original Czech states that it is not possible to take these items.

prising a knife, fork, tablespoon, and teaspoon per person – and silver objects weighing up to 40 grams per item, up to a total weight of 200 grams per person. Valuables purchased before 1 September 1938, such as optical equipment, radios, refrigerators, typewriters, musical instruments, etc., may also be taken abroad. So much for the formalities.

However, the Jewish Religious Community of Prague bears yet another responsibility. It has guaranteed that 250 Jews willing to emigrate will report to the Zentralstelle every day to apply for an emigration permit; this number is later to be increased to 300 people a day. With considerable effort, the emigration department can currently prepare about 220 people for emigration per day. That this is possible at all is due to the fact that many people had obtained visas earlier and then could not emigrate, since they were refused permission by the Gestapo. But it is certain that this number of people will soon be exhausted. As it is currently next to impossible to obtain emigration opportunities, the Jews are facing a genuine catastrophe, since Eichmann is certain that every Jew will use any opportunity to emigrate once they have been arrested two or three times. Eichmann intends to create a mood among Jews here such that they would be happy if he just allowed them to emigrate at all, even with little more than the shirt on their back. This is why people and 'travel agencies' that focus on exporting Jews en masse are supported. Eichmann has allowed various dubious people who organize very expensive transports abroad to relocate their offices to Prague. These are the infamous illegal transports to Palestine, South America, etc. The international press has run detailed reports on the suffering of Jewish people on board the *St. Louis* heading to Cuba[17] or the expedition that criss-crossed the Mediterranean for three months without being allowed to anchor.[18] Letters from those on board refer to endless misery. Entirely typical reports say they suffered from a lack of water to drink or wash with and a lack of food throughout the voyage, with the result that they lost up to 16 kilos over the course of three months. On the ship there were two cabins for eight people, and about 800 people were transported altogether. Today this expedition, organized by a travel agency at the House of the Black Rose in Prague, is quarantined in Beirut and its fate is uncertain. Another such voyage is now being planned by Mr Handler,[19] a special favourite of Eichmann's, on Lützovova Street.[20] He has about 800 people ready, and if anyone wants to abandon their intention to depart with this expedition, they face arrest by the Gestapo.

17 On the voyage of the *St. Louis*, see Doc. 233, fn. 8.

18 The refugee ship *Frossoula* set sail from Sulina for Palestine at the end of May 1939 carrying around 650 Jewish refugees, all of them from the Protectorate. After a long odyssey at sea and the outbreak of an epidemic on board, the ship was quarantined in Beirut in July 1939. At the end of Aug. 1939, the *Tiger Hill* took over the refugees, but it ran aground on 1 Sept. 1939 off Tel Aviv. In the process of breaking the British naval blockade, two passengers were killed. Upon arrival, most of the refugees were briefly interned.

19 Probably: Arieh Händler (1915–2011), official in the Orthodox Bachad (Union of Religious Pioneers) youth movement; worked in the main office of Bachad in Berlin; on multiple occasions he was given special permission by the Gestapo to leave the country in order to explore possibilities for setting up Hachsharah centres abroad and thus emigration; arrived in Palestine in 1938, and later went to London for Bachad.

20 Now Opletalova Street.

Jewish physicians under the age of 45 are not permitted to emigrate.

With regard to the Jewish emigration tax, it should be added that this is formally levied for the benefit of Jews without means, in order to provide them with the funds to finance their emigration, but in actual fact this tax is collected by the Gestapo and it is uncertain what it is used for.

In addition to organizing emigration, Eichmann is truly doing everything necessary to rid the Protectorate of Jews. He is creating the necessary mood among Jews to make them truly 'auswanderungslustig'.

First and foremost he has ordered that all Jews must move to Prague, which means that all Jews from the entire Protectorate, wherever they live and whatever their occupation, are to be concentrated in Prague. If we estimate the approximate number of Jews at 120,000 people, we must consider that two thirds of them live outside Prague. This means that about 80,000 Jews are to move to Prague, or probably more, because this number rises significantly if one uses race as a measure and includes mixed marriages. This means that the livelihoods of these people will be destroyed. Eichmann works on the basis that it is not up to him to take care of what these people will do for a living or where they will live; if ten to fifteen Jews are living in a single room in Prague, they will try to emigrate more quickly. This de-Jewification of the rural areas is set to begin immediately, with at least 200 people moving to Prague daily. There is no need to state what a tragedy this is on a human level.

Eichmann is applying here in the Protectorate the same procedure he used in the Ostmark: of the 15,000 Jews scattered throughout the countryside, 500 remain, as far as we know; the others are either in Vienna, in jail, abroad, or dead. For him the difference in numbers is immaterial.

All interventions, all appeals are in vain: the law is as Eichmann orders it. And implementation has started. Individual German authorities in the countryside summon rabbis and Jewish community officials and give them tight deadlines for Jews to liquidate their assets and immediately move to Prague.[21] There are known cases in which Jews had to move out of their own homes within twenty-four hours and were not even allowed to take all their belongings with them. Their assets, savings, etc. were confiscated. In the city of České Budějovice in particular, the authorities have been very rigorous so far in this respect.

Slowly, Jews in the Protectorate are coming to realize that they may have fewer problems once they no longer have any possessions; then it will not be possible to take anything away from them. This view has probably given rise to a new saying in Prague's German Jewish community. 'Dalles in Prague is worth millions' (Dalles is the Jewish expression for destitution). It is bitter irony.

IV. Czechs and antisemitism.

In spite of all of this official pressure, the broadest levels of Czech society remain unaffected by antisemitism. On the contrary, it can be said that today they understand more than ever that operations against the Jews are a front to pursue personal goals great and small. For this reason, they have taken a stance against antisemitism and are fighting,

21 It turned out that the relocation of all Jews to Prague was not feasible, and so the measures were not implemented.

in the true sense of the word, against those Czech individuals who have put themselves in the service of the Germans for personal gain and seek to foster an aggressive antisemitism. Only those elements who did not hesitate at the decisive historical moment to leave Národní souručenství and serve foreign interests have descended to this level. Based on numbers, these are two small groups of fascists, the Vlajka group and men from the Aryan Cultural Union.[22] These are numerically unimportant groups propped up by support from German finance and the German press who want to stir up unrest, come to power with help from the Germans, and then rule over their people according to German orders and the principles of Hitler's National Socialism.

They are the ones who initiate operations against the Jews in cafés by sending their supporters there to attend anti-Jewish demonstrations for 30 to 100 korunas per evening; they are the ones who initiate demonstrations at outdoor swimming polls; they are the ones who give the German authorities the opportunity to demand that autonomous Protectorate offices prohibit Jews from entering public baths, parks, public spaces, etc.[23]

And yet these people completely disregard the damage they are doing to their own nation.

V. Economic and national consequences of German antisemitism in the Protectorate.
The purpose of all of these German operations is to transfer Jewish property into German hands. This is already evidenced by the fact that Jews are not allowed to sell their possessions without permission from the German authorities. This permission is not granted unless the buyer is a German Aryan. Therefore, the rapid and forcible removal of the Jews in the rural areas and in the Protectorate as a whole is just a means to get Jewish assets into German hands and for Germans to replace the Jews, even in areas that are otherwise entirely Czech. The process is already well under way. It is most clearly evident with regard to agricultural property. The former national land registry office, its district offices, and its allocation commissioners are now truly under German control, i.e. run by the Aryanization institute which appoints German trustees for Jewish property and transfers this property into German hands, usually free of charge.[24]

The same procedure is undertaken for designated industrial businesses. The district authorities register Jewish property and businesses and issue announcements with the names and addresses of these companies, inviting Aryans to apply to take them over.[25]

22 The National Aryan Cultural Union in Prague was established in June 1939 under the chairmanship of Dr Stanislav Babický with the aim of influencing cultural conditions in the Protectorate according to an Aryan perspective. The Union was active until 1942, though it was not officially dissolved until 25 July 1945.

23 See Doc. 258.

24 The Land Office was initially a department of the Czechoslovak Ministry of Agriculture, but it was controlled by the Chief of the Security Police and was instructed to ensure that all the land in the Protectorate was transferred into German hands. 'Aryanization institute' probably refers to Section VII a ('De-Jewification') in the Office of the Reich Protector. Aryanization was used in the Protectorate of Bohemia and Moravia as a means of Germanization, and so it was overwhelmingly Germans who profited from it: see Introduction, p. 25.

25 Such changes in ownership were regularly announced in the daily press: see, for example, Doc. 294.

The announcements literally state that interested parties should negotiate directly with the Jewish owners concerned, but if these make trouble, the interested party should contact the authorities, who will make arrangements to remedy the situation.

VI. Conclusion

The Jews in the Protectorate find themselves in a catastrophic situation, through no fault of their own and without the Czech nation bearing any guilt or being party to their suffering in any way. On the contrary, the Czech people, true to their humane and ethical traditions, and themselves severely impacted, are helping their Jewish compatriots endure this difficult time.

In spite of this, however, the Jews are now forced to request foreign assistance as a matter of particular urgency, since their position is deteriorating from day to day and from hour to hour: they are becoming impoverished and devastated, having no refuge, no place to take shelter. Whereas Jews from Austria and Germany could still flee to Czechoslovakia, Jews in the Protectorate have no place to run; they are caught in a trap, a giant concentration camp from which there is no escape without outside help.

Most of all, Jews in the Protectorate need to be given the opportunity to emigrate, they need a place where they can at least preserve their mere lives. More than ever before, the Jewish question is becoming a Central European question of ethics and humanity. By sacrificing Czechoslovakia, the last area of Central Europe where a Jew was treated as a person has vanished. Now Jews call out for help to simply save their lives. They believe that in the future the sacrifices will not be forgotten that both they and the Czech people made – the people with whom they shared sorrow and joy.

And together with and as a part of the Czech nation, they retain hope for the future.

DOC. 261
On 15 September 1939 State Secretary Karl Hermann Frank attempts to quash anti-Jewish violence carried out by ethnic Germans[1]

Letter from the Reich Protector of Bohemia and Moravia 'marked confidential', No. I 1a-7520, p.p. signed State Secretary K. H. Frank, Prague, to: a) the Gauleitung of Lower Danube, for the attention of Gauleiter Dr Jury[2] or his official representative, Vienna; b) the Gauleitung of Upper Danube, for the attention of Gauleiter Eigruber[3] or his official representative, Linz; c) the Gauleitung of Bavarian Ostmark, for the attention of Gauleiter Wächtler[4] or his official representative, Bayreuth; d) the Gauleitung of the Sudetenland for the attention of Gauleiter Henlein or his official representative, Reichenberg: dated 15 September 1939[5]

In the territory of the Protectorate there have been excesses against Jews, not just in recent months, but also in particular since 1 September 1939, which certainly not only involved Czech elements, but also primarily ethnic Germans as well. In some cases, the ethnic Germans even appeared wearing the uniform of the Party divisions and not only were responsible for injuring persons and causing material damage by smashing windows, but also attacked the police units of the administrative authority of the Protectorate, forcibly preventing them from intervening.

This behaviour on the part of the German population in the Protectorate must be described as undignified and, moreover, it has had the disastrous after-effect of providing new and significant sustenance to French and English radio propaganda since the war began. It is a well-known fact that, as soon as the war broke out, English and French radio stations passionately dedicated themselves to prophesying to the Protectorate's Czech population in no uncertain terms that their day of 'liberation from the German yoke' was nigh, and to inciting them against the German Reich and its authorities. Particularly on 8 and 9 September 1939 this propaganda pounced on the violent excesses of ethnic Germans.[6] I therefore repeat my request, in the most urgent tone, to communicate to the ethnic German population through the channels of the Party offices and

1 MZAB, B 251/522/4080, box 45. This document has been translated from German.
2 Dr Hugo Jury (1887–1945); physician in Frankenfels, 1913–1919; joined the NSDAP in 1931; deputy regional head of the illegal NSDAP in Austria, 1936–1938; arrested several times; joined the SS in 1938; member of the Reichstag and Gauleiter from 1938, from 1940 also Reichsstatthalter of Lower Danube; committed suicide shortly before the Allied occupation of Austria after the war.
3 August Eigruber (1907–1947), mechanic and labourer; joined the NSDAP in 1928; Gauleiter of Upper Austria, 1936–1938; arrested several times; joined the SA and the SS in 1938; member of the Reichstag and Gauleiter from 1938, from 1940 also Reichsstatthalter of Upper Danube; arrested in 1945, charged in the Mauthausen trial in 1946, and sentenced to death; executed in 1947.
4 Fritz Wächtler (1891–1945); worked as a primary school teacher; joined the NSDAP and the SA in 1926; deputy Gauleiter of Thuringia, 1932–1935; Thuringian state minister of the interior and deputy minister president, 1933–1936; from 1933 member of the Reichstag; Gauleiter of the Bavarian Ostmark Gau from 1935; on Bormann's orders, shot dead by an SS commando before the end of the war for abandoning his duties.
5 The original contains an official stamp: The Reich Protector of Bohemia and Moravia.
6 This could not be verified.

their divisions just how disastrous participation in these kinds of brutal attacks is. This information must be absorbed in such a way as to prevent the occurrence of similar attacks in future.[7]

DOC. 262

On 27 September 1939 the Regional Psychiatric Hospital in Jihlava provides notification of its measures against Jewish patients[1]

Letter from the Regional Psychiatric Hospital, Jihlava (no. 282), signed Krátký, to the Regional Office, Dept. IV/9, Brno (received on 28 September 1939), dated 27 September 1939[2]

Re: segregation of patients – Jews from Aryans
Re: number 33 192/IV/9, dated 14 September 1939[3]
Attachments: 2[4]
In reference to the letter m ref. no. 33 192/IV/9 dated 14 September 1939, the undersigned directorate hereby states that it has successfully separated non-Aryan patients here at the hospital.

This concerned ten men and nine women. Two isolation rooms in infirmary ward II were adapted for the men and two isolation rooms in infirmary ward V were adapted for the women. They are strictly divided from the other patients. They use separate sinks located directly in the rooms. Dishes (plates, bowls, and cups) are set apart from the others and washed separately.

The non-Aryan patients also use separate lavatories. Strict separation, with separate staff in a separate ward, was not feasible, both because the institute is over capacity and due to the insignificant number of non-Aryan patients. In principle, there would be no objections to the Brno directorate's proposal for Jewish patients to be concentrated at the provincial hospital in Kroměříž, but [the undersigned] would like to note that the question of potentially evacuating the Jihlava hospital remains current, and it would therefore be practical to reserve a facility to isolate the Jews in Kroměříž for any patients evacuated from the Jihlava hospital.[5]

7 Frank sent copies to the Oberlandräte, the Moravia group in Brünn, and to the Senior Commander of the Security Police in the Office of the Reich Protector, 'requesting acknowledgement'. He added that Reich police may only intervene 'if the property or lives of Reich Germans are in danger or there is a threat to businesses which are necessary for the war effort and for everyday life, and must be allowed to operate without interruption'.

1 MZAB, ZÚ Brno, B 40 III, box 6972. This document has been translated from Czech.
2 The original contains handwritten notes, an official stamp, and the following handwritten addition: 'The transfer of non-Aryan patients to the hospital in Kroměříž is, as he originally thought, not possible yet, since the Kroměříž hospital has to set aside 460 beds for military use.'
3 This is not in the file.
4 These attachments are not in the file.
5 Handwritten addition in the original: 'Deadline: 10 Jan. 1940.' Handwritten addition underneath: 'The deadline has been cancelled because the entire Jihlava hospital has been allocated. Record for the permanent file. 17 Jan. 1940.'

DOC. 263
A Jewish woman who has emigrated to the Netherlands describes the situation in the Protectorate at the beginning of October 1939[1]

Report by an unknown author, dated 6 December 1939 (copy)[2]

The situation in the Protectorate of Bohemia and Moravia in early October 1939.
I. Economy
1. Food. When I got to Holland, everyone asked me, quite astonished: But you look quite well?[3] People imagine that there is a real famine. But one must consider what an unbelievably bountiful country the former Czechoslovak Republic was, and then one will understand that it is indeed an achievement of the first order to bring it within the space of six months to the point where it lacks almost all foodstuffs and everything is rationed. The food situation in the Protectorate is still much better than in the Old Reich and the Sudetenland, and incomparably better than in the former Austria. The first things to be in short supply were sugar and butter. Coffee and tea followed soon thereafter, and now there is already a shortage of everything. According to the ration cards, one gets, for example, 10 grams of butter per day per person. For young children somewhat more, 300 grams of meat per week, and in addition 200 g of smoked meat or ham, etc. Anyone who knew Prague before will barely be able to imagine that there are empty smoked-foods shops there and that, long before rationing, there was often not a scrap of ham left by 6 p.m. Just before rationing began, people of course stockpiled a great deal. The first rationing measure was the introduction of ration cards, which restricted each shopper to a specific shop. This was intended to make it impossible to go from one shop to the next, buying items to squirrel away. In addition, every shop was then supposed to be allocated precisely the quantity of goods needed for the number of customers.[4] The rules are circumvented wherever possible; the shop assistants show preference to Czechs and Jews and sell larger rations to them than to the Germans, who are told that there is simply nothing left. In the countryside the bulk of the butter and eggs, even on the small farms that are not geared towards sales, is requisitioned. Bringing food from the countryside into town is prohibited.[5] Whipping cream is no longer allowed. During the first week of the war, there was a sudden shortage of cigarettes. A great many tobacconists were sold out all day long, and the others doled out only two or three cigarettes per person. The supplies were evidently requisitioned for the army. A few days later the situation improved, but one gets no more than ten cigarettes, and sales to women and children are officially prohibited.
2. Textile industry. The textile shops are allowed to sell, per month, only 60 per cent of the volume of sales from the same month in 1937 (a miserable year). In practice, this

1 NAP, Fond Hubert Ripka 50–44, fols. 122–129. This document has been translated from German.
2 The original contains handwritten notes and the following text in Czech: 'Copy of a letter sent by a female emigrant from Prague, who fled from the Protectorate to Holland in mid October.' The account was partially incorporated into the report on Germany by the Social Democratic Party in exile (Sopade), dated 7 April 1940. See Doc. 64, fn. 15.
3 Syntax as in the original.
4 This could not be verified.
5 This directive was issued at the local level in each case. On the differences in the food supply between urban and rural areas, see also Doc. 288.

means that by nine in the morning all the shops display the following signs: Today's quota sold out. At the same time, they were not allowed to let any employees go, the shops cannot be locked up, the lights must be on; in short, the same set-up, but without any sales. People who cannot go shopping before 9 a.m. have no opportunity at all to buy a pair of stockings. The manufacture of fabrics for women and of fine table and bed linens has been officially discontinued altogether, and other branches of industry are likely to follow in the very near future.
3. Arms industry. All arms factories and associated branches of industry operate under German management under great pressure. The Škoda Works are under the supervision of Göring's brother.[6] The SS stands guard day and night in front of Českomoravská Kolben-Daněk.[7] Of all the major companies, only Baťa[8] has preserved an element of independence. But the Textiles Law applies in large part to Baťa, and the company is suffering terribly as a result of the shortage of raw materials.
4. Banks. The three big German banks – Union Bank, Böhmische Escomptebank and Kreditanstalt, and Länderbank – were incorporated into Dresdner Bank.[9] The Länderbank, for example, dismissed all Jews on 1 September, and all Czechs on 1 October. A money transfer from one part of the Greater German Reich to another is completely impossible. People who left their assets in the Sudetenland in September of last year and moved to Prague have no way of getting hold of any of their property. However, if they want to emigrate, they have to hand over this property or pay high taxes on it.

During the first week of the war, the price of cigarettes and beer rose by 20 per cent, and signs were put up everywhere, saying that the price difference would be used to benefit the German Reich. Beer consumption dropped rapidly.

II. Politics.
The only Czech party allowed, Národní souručenství, has completely changed in character. Quite apart from the policy decisions that the leaders of this movement make or have to make, the members (and this means practically all Aryans, as the pressure is so strong that simply everyone must join) wear emblems primarily as a demonstration against the German emblems. One cannot wear any other emblem, only the old Czech flag, and you see a lot of them, and this is a way of demonstrating that Prague is a Czech city and will remain so. The Gajda[10] group and Vlajka, bankrolled by the Germans, direct the antisemitic propaganda. At intervals a new newspaper appears, because every paper closes down after a very short time. Some people will continue to buy anything

6 Albert Günther Göring (1895–1966), engineer; brother of Hermann Göring; head of exports for the Škoda Works in Pilsen; worked in Munich as a writer and translator after 1945.

7 This Czech–German industrial syndicate, founded in 1926, was one of the leading Czech heavy engineering companies. It produced turbines, locomotives, and motor vehicles. It was nationalized after 1945.

8 The shoe firm established by Tomáš Baťa in Zlín in 1894 moved its headquarters to Canada in 1939, and the section of the company that remained in Czechoslovakia was nationalized after 1945.

9 The Bohemian Union Bank and the Böhmische Escomptebank had already been acquired by Deutsche Bank and Dresdner Bank, respectively, in 1938, after running into economic difficulties as a result of losing their branches in the Sudetenland to Deutsche Bank. The Escomptebank was reorganized by Dresdner Bank. The Länderbank was acquired by the Escomptebank in July 1939 and merged with it in Dec. 1939.

10 See doc. 241, fn. 20.

that is new. After two or three issues, nobody reads it any more. Because they are paid by the Germans, these two groups are so despised that the desired outcome, namely the exertion of influence upon the Czech population, has completely failed to materialize. Today, after six months of the Protectorate's existence, the Germans must see that they have made no progress at all in their attempt to win over the Czechs. On the contrary, the part of the Czech population that may, before March, have viewed an understanding with the Germans as feasible in principle has quickly become convinced of the contrary after experiencing the Germans' methods at first hand. Yet the Germans, with an uncanny accuracy, undertake everything that is bound to make the worst possible psychological impact on the Czechs. This includes, for example, the introduction of German language signs on all public buildings and the announcement of tram stops in German. In opposition to this compulsory Germanization and rising prices and many other things, a passenger strike for the tram was announced for a specific day, passed on by word of mouth. The notification was so complete that even days before the event there was no one left to inform, simply because everyone already knew about it. It also went perfectly at the time when people were going to work; the workers walked long distances, and the trams were empty. Then there was a German radio broadcast at 8 a.m.: the Czechs are going on strike today to demonstrate that they are unwilling to travel on the trams with Jews. That confused things, of course; one no longer knew whether the strike should be cancelled or not, and from then on it was only very sporadically successful.[11] The spreading of information works wonderfully well. Despite the threat of penal servitude for listening to foreign radio broadcasts and even the death penalty for the dissemination of foreign news,[12] people listen avidly wherever there is, or still is, a radio (radios belonging to Jews have been confiscated).[13] Usually Paris and London, above all the Czech reports and the speeches of Beneš,[14] Jan Masaryk,[15] etc. It is thus all the more important that the reports in the foreign broadcasts are both serious and reliable. For example, the information about the great riots in the Protectorate, which did not correspond to the facts, did a great deal of harm, because such reports are likely to shake people's trust in foreign reporting in general.[16] Sabotage and passive resistance are the order of the day. Around one week before the war started, large red placards appeared on every street corner, warning that acts of sabotage would be severely punished. In the suburbs, these warnings were repeatedly torn down, until ultimately, in some cases,

11 The strike organized by the resistance groups Political Centre (Politické ústředí) and Petition Committee 'We Will Remain Faithful' (Petiční výbor 'Věrni zůstaneme') took place in Prague on 30 Sept. 1939, the anniversary of the Munich Agreement.

12 This could not be verified. It is certainly true that the anti-Czech policy of the German government in the Protectorate became markedly more stringent after the war began, and Czechs too were shot dead for taking a stand and resisting.

13 On 22 Sept. 1939 the Jews in Prague were ordered to hand in their radio sets. Around 12,000 radios were handed in within two days.

14 Edvard Beneš (1884–1948), politician; foreign minister, 1918–1935; president of Czechoslovakia, 1935–1938; fled to London, 1938; after the war served as president again until his death.

15 Jan Masaryk (1886–1948), son of Czechoslovak president Tomáš Garrigue Masaryk; Czechoslovak ambassador to Britain, 1925–1938; resigned in protest against the Munich Agreement, 1938; remained in London during the Second World War as a member of the government in exile. After 1945, foreign minister of Czechoslovakia; died in 1948 after an unexplained fall from a window at the Ministry of Foreign Affairs.

16 See fn. 4.

guards were posted day and night in front of them. On 1 September many hundreds of people were arrested.[17] They were members of the previous governments; Beneš supporters; groups of Legion members; figures from the press, radio, and all the associations of the former republic; almost the entire editorial staff of *České slovo* [and] the former Czechoslovak press agency, the head of which was meanwhile shot for sabotage.[18] All those who had already been arrested in March were arrested again, as were many more. Of the many taken into custody, only very few were released again immediately. There continue to be sporadic releases, but the majority, as the relatives have been told in no uncertain terms, will remain in protective custody for [the] duration of the war. The more prominent figures were mostly taken to the concentration camp in Buchenwald. These included, for example, the former mayor of Prague, Dr Zenkl; Hájek, a head of department at the Ministry of Foreign Affairs (whose whereabouts are unknown, however);[19] Plamínková (Pankrác), a senator;[20] Kurt Sitte;[21] Dr Matoušek;[22] Přikryl;[23] and many others. The Gleichschaltung of the Czech press, of course, took place straight away in March. At first, seeking to deflect the attention of the censors once and for all, the Czech press even vied with the German press. Since then things have changed considerably. The Czech press can indeed print nothing other than what it gets from the press agency, but it strictly limits itself to the official announcements and refrains from any commentary and from all strong language of the sort to be found in the German newspapers. Of all the press, *Lidové noviny* has known best how to maintain a certain standard even in this situation.[24] The news from the press agency has to be translated verbatim. In the process, the most hilarious situations arise whenever things are translated that are simply ridiculous in Czech usage. Whether it is done by Germans who do not know enough Czech, or whether the Czechs do it intentionally to make a mockery of the press, I do not know. For example, one newspaper printed this sentence: 'Moje jméno je zajíc

17 At the start of the war, the Gestapo arrested somewhere between 2,000 and 3,000 members of the Czechoslovak ruling classes in Operation Albrecht I.

18 This could not be verified. The daily newspaper *České slovo* began publication in 1908. The editors-in-chief were Dr Václav Crha (Prague) and Karel Režny (Moravská Ostrava). The Czechoslovak press agency ČTK continued to operate in the Protectorate under German management. Many of the former employees were active in the Czech underground movement.

19 Jan Hájek (1883–1969), journalist and politician; member of the Czechoslovak delegation to the Paris peace negotiations, 1919; head of the press and information department at the Ministry of Foreign Affairs from 1919; arrested in March 1939 and interned in various concentration camps until the end of the war; placed in custody in 1956 for alleged coup attempts; amnestied in 1960.

20 Františka Plamínková (1875–1942), author and campaigner for women's rights; co-founder of the Czech Committee for Women's Suffrage, 1905; senator in the Czechoslovak National Assembly from 1925; arrested during Operation Albrecht I and released after a few weeks; rearrested in 1942 and murdered on 30 June in the notorious Pankrác prison in Prague.

21 Dr Kurt Sitte (1910–1961), physicist; lecturer at the Medical School of the German University in Prague, 1935; emigrated to the USA in 1939, and thereafter to Israel.

22 Dr Josef Matoušek (1906–1939), historian, archivist, and journalist; executed for his alleged co-instigation of the Prague student protests in the autumn of 1939.

23 This may refer to the engineer Bohumil Přikryl, chairman of the Czechoslovak League of Human Rights.

24 The oldest daily newspaper still existing in the Czech Republic was founded in Brno in 1893. In the 1920s and 1930s it was the liberal-democratic mouthpiece of President Masaryk's supporters. The newspaper ceased publication in 1952. It was reactivated as an underground newspaper in 1988. In 1990 it was relaunched as a daily.

a já o ničem nevím', a literal translation of 'My name is Hare, I know nothing'.[25] An article in *České slovo* about England discusses the rise in grocery prices in England, and the writer reports on the resulting public dissatisfaction. The final sentence is: 'A lze očekávat, že stížnosti ze strany obecenstva přinesou nějaké ovoce' ('And it is to be expected that the complaints of the public will be fruitful', but literally translated, 'will carry fruit'). On the eve of 28 September, St Wenceslas Day, there was a strong police presence throughout the city centre; by the evening the St Wenceslas monument was already piled high with flowers and heavily guarded. In the morning, a huge crowd of people thronged around the monument but were allowed to approach it only in turns. It was now difficult to put even a little flower anywhere on the monument. Towards midday there were clashes with police, with the result that access to the monument was completely blocked in the afternoon. The next morning all the flowers had been cleared away, except for four flowerpots.

That same day, when it was declared in England and France that Czechs are not enemy aliens, the Protectorate government issued a regulation to the effect that Czech passports and Protectorate passports are no longer valid for travel abroad; anyone who wants to travel must apply for a Reich German passport. Incidentally, that also brings in 180 k. per passport.[26]

III. Jews[27]

Neither the Nuremberg Laws nor any other Reich law pertaining to Jews have been officially introduced thus far in the Protectorate.[28] In practice, however, the same things are imposed, only with far less success, as there is a complete lack of public engagement. One of the principles is that Jews should emigrate. The fact that it was utterly impossible to obtain an exit permit for such a long time was due to the need to first work out a regulation to establish the ways in which one could 'legally' get the most money from the emigrants. Now a procedure had been established. The process begins at the Religious Community, which was designated as the general Jewish legislative authority.[29] One receives a portfolio containing approximately thirty different forms, which one must fill out with the utmost care. No sheet may be creased, no word written by hand (as the portfolio is a lovely brown colour, it is frequently also called 'Mein Kampf'). Then the various forms go to the various offices, tax offices etc. At the Ministry of Finance, one must pay for every item that one wants to take with them, and after as many offices as possible have demanded sums as large as possible, one is summoned a second time to the emigration office to fetch the documents and the exit permit. If one has tax arrears,

25 The German idiom 'Mein Name ist Hase, ich weiss von nichts' is used to express feigned ignorance about a subject.

26 On 19 Jan. 1940 the *Jüdisches Nachrichtenblatt* (Prague edition) ran a front-page article reporting that these newly requested Reich German passports had to include the addendum 'Protectorate of Bohemia and Moravia'.

27 The following section was included in the Sopade reports on Germany in 1940. See *Deutschland-berichte der sozialdemokratischen Partei Deutschlands*, pp. A48–A50.

28 The regulation of the Reich Protector issued on 21 June 1939 introduced into the Protectorate the definition of a Jew according to the Nuremberg Laws. See Doc. 247.

29 The Central Office for Jewish Emigration assigned the Jewish Religious Community of Prague numerous tasks associated with the supervision of the Jews in the Protectorate. See Introduction, p. 26, and Docs. 259 and 260.

one does not get out at all. In many cases, it is especially difficult to get the economic clearance certificate. Doctors, chemists, nurses, etc. are not allowed to leave at all. There is a Reichswehr uniform that has an insignia with the words: Jewish doctor. At the last minute, the Gestapo office often levies a fee, which is usually very high and is in no way determined by calculating assets, but rather set arbitrarily. This is the substitute for the Reich Flight Tax, which has not yet become law.[30]

No regulation for the Jews is officially announced or published in the press. Everything is done through the Religious Community, which must simply be regarded as an official authority; and yet, the Religious Community is not permitted to say where the directives come from, nor to make them known by telephone or post. Instead, the information must be passed round from one person to the next. However, no one knows whether that will change now, after the unsuccessful wooing of America. On the Day of Atonement, the most solemn Jewish holy day, a registry of all the Jews had to be compiled within twenty-four hours, with detailed information on assets, age, etc., and all radios belonging to Jews had to be handed in.[31] That meant that not only the whole Religious Community, but also all Jewish organizations, orphanages, etc., and a great many Jewish individuals had to run from house to house on this holiday, from early morning until night, to carry out this directive. One did not even get confirmation that the radios had been handed in. One day a curfew was issued for all Jews, which forbade them to be out after 8 p.m.[32] But it was not observed, and even the Jewish coffee houses do not close at 8 p.m. In Prague, there is no known instance of anyone being stopped or punished for breaking the curfew. Outside the capital, however, things are said to be much worse, and various incidents have occurred (in Pilsen, for example). The ban on non-segregated restaurants and coffee houses and [on Jews entering] all public establishments was introduced in mid August.[33] With regard to the coffee houses, at first most of the big coffee houses on St Wenceslas Square declared themselves to be Jewish businesses, and in the first few days the German Aryans were actually unable to go to any coffee houses at all. The Czechs boycotted the Aryan businesses and openly went to the Jewish ones. Then this was officially changed, but now most of the coffee houses have Jewish sections, and new ones are opening daily because it is a particularly good business. Thus far there have been no raids on Jewish coffee houses in Prague. Cinema visits are completely prohibited to Jews. Jews are only allowed to go to public baths and libraries on certain days and at certain times.[34] One fears that, in the near future, food supplies, clothing, typewriters, etc. will be confiscated to benefit the Winter Relief drive,[35] but thus far the rumours are unconfirmed. If a German likes an apartment,

30 On 23 Nov. 1939 the government issued the regulation on the emigration tax. The tax amounted to 25 per cent of assets for emigrants whose assets exceeded 200,000 korunas or who had a taxable income of 140,000 korunas in the tax year 1938. See Friedmann, 'Rechtsstellung', p. 235.

31 In 1939 Yom Kippur fell on 23 Sept.

32 The Gestapo imposed the curfew in Sept. 1939. See Friedmann, 'Rechtsstellung', p. 262.

33 See Doc. 259, fn. 4.

34 Implementation of these measures varied from region to region and they were introduced at the Protectorate level by the decree issued by the Czech Ministry of the Interior on 3 August 1939. See Doc. 256.

35 The Winter Relief Agency started as a joint initiative of private welfare organizations. It came under the control of the National Socialist People's Welfare in 1933. It turned away all Jews.

the Jewish tenants are given notice within the hour. Jewish shops must be labelled as such, but the public purposely buy from Jewish shops. However, the Jewish grocery shops get far smaller allocations of foodstuffs than the Aryan ones, and gradually, of course, this is the case for all goods that are becoming scarce. The intention is that this will force the Jewish business people to declare bankruptcy. But plans are no different for Czech business people either; hence, for example, the Textile Law. In short, in every respect a boycott of Jews from above, without the slightest cooperation from the Czech public, who have learned to see the Jewish population as fellow sufferers.

IV. Czechs

The optimism of the Czech population is indomitable. It goes way beyond the bounds of what seems objectively possible. From time to time, one comes up with a date on which 'everything will be all right again', and when the date is past, one simply dreams up another one. One such date was 28 October.[36] But even the objective response to the general situation is calm and measured. Generally speaking, one cannot completely close one's mind to the notion that a war in the previous year could have meant a fate for Prague like the one Warsaw has suffered. To some extent, this reconciles one with the sad thought of having to be in enemy territory today. And one trusts that it will not remain like this for long. But one has not forgotten the events of the previous year. There was not a great deal of sympathy for Poland; the memory of its attitude during last year's conflict is still too clear.[37] The Russians have lost absolutely none of their popularity – on the contrary. One senses and knows that the Germans will be the ones deceived in the end. Beneš is and will remain the president of our republic, and his speeches on the radio and Masaryk's speeches are heard by thousands and regarded as authoritative political information. Sabotage and passive resistance are the essential weapons. But one part of sabotage is also ridiculing all regulations etc., which finds expression in cast-iron humour. The practice of calling out the tram stops in German has provided endless scope for this. Some examples: someone simply does their own translation of the various street names, and these are then called out by the passengers on the tram – for example, nám. Petra Osvoboditele [Peter the Liberator Square] is called Platz Peters des Gefreiten [Lance Corporal Peter Square]; Hitlerplatz: Hlídej Prázdné Náměstí is called Hüt-Leer-Platz [Empty Hats Square]; Myslíková is called Spekuliergasse [Speculation Alley]; Střešovice is called Dachau (*střecha* = *Dach* [roof], and also that is where the emigration office of the Gestapo is located); Na Zbořenci is called Siegfriedlinie [Siegfried Line];[38] and there are many more. Or a conductor calls out: 'Lange Gasse, Dlouhá třída, lange Gasse aby měli radost!'[39] At one stop where a great many people try to board a carriage that is already

36 On 28 Oct. 1939, Czechoslovak Independence Day, Czechs wearing small ribbons in the national colours held a demonstration in Prague city centre. Karl Hermann Frank accused the Protectorate police of failing to take action, ordered the German SS and police to intervene, and even himself took part in violence against passers-by.

37 Immediately after the conclusion of the Munich Agreement, Poland delivered an ultimatum to Czechoslovakia on 30 Sept. 1938 and occupied the Těšín (Teschen, Cieszyn) region shortly afterwards. See Doc. 244, fn. 3.

38 The Siegfried Line was a 400 mile stretch of fortifications forming Nazi Germany's western line of defence during the Second World War.

39 *Lange Gasse* (German); *dlouhá třída* (Czech): 'long street'; *aby měli radost!* (Czech): 'so that they can be happy!'

full, the conductor calls out: 'Pánové, nenastupujte, vždyť vidíte, že tu nemáme žádný životní prostor.' (Now gentlemen, don't pile in; you can certainly see there's no Lebensraum here.) Or the passengers say: 'eine Fahrkarte, jízdenku prosím',[40] etc., etc. All the conductor has to do is to call out 'waiterr' instead of 'dále' to the driver and the entire tram is in fits of laughter.[41] A wonderful example of sabotage was provided by the Czech police themselves. One day it was ordered that all citizens must carry with them proof of citizenship (to facilitate identification upon arrest, one assumes).[42] Few people have such documents; huge crowds of people went to the police authorities; many new documents had to be printed. When the first lot of people went to pick up the completed documents, they were told to come back at a later date, because all the documents that had already been prepared had to be destroyed; they had been printed only in Czech instead of in German and Czech. And that at a time when all public buildings already had to have signs giving the German names first! Anyone could have worked out for themselves that the identification papers should also be in two languages, but because that had not been made explicit to the police, they preferred to do twice the work and thereby inflict quite a loss on the state. A German in the street asked the way to the castle; the Czech replied: 'You don't know that? And yet you've been living here for 1,000 years?' For months on end there was not a single bookshop in Prague that did not display a book titled *History of the Maffia*[43] in a clearly visible spot in its window.

Long ago, the Czechs came up with a jokey way of referring to dubious news: JPP, meaning 'jedna paní povídala' ('a woman told me'). But now they say DPP: 'druhá paní povídala, protože ta jedna už sedí' ('the other woman told me, because the first one is already locked up'). In a Czech middle school, a teacher asked on the first day whether any non-Aryan pupils were present. Two boys got to their feet. Then the teacher explained that, for the Czechs, there can and will be no difference in the treatment of Aryans and non-Aryans and he asked the pupils to treat the two boys just the same, as would have been the case before. Then he asked the children to say nothing about what he had said, not even to their parents, because it could have negative consequences for him in the present circumstances. An enormous display of courage in front of 14-year-old children. The automotive section of *Národní politika* ran a report on a test drive of the new Tatra[44] to Italy, followed by the Italians' views on the new oscillating axle of the motor vehicle. It continued: 'The Italians, who until now were genuine advocates of the fixed axle, nonetheless recently became convinced that an oscillating axle, which can be turned in any direction, is preferable after all.'[45] This item did not escape the eyes of the censors, and the newspaper was suspended for two days.[46] The new Protectorate stamps are another story. Beyond doubt, the image on the stamp is quite clearly in the shape of

40 *Eine Fahrkarte*: German for 'a ticket'; *jízdenku prosím*: Czech for 'a ticket, please'.

41 'Waiterr' (German: correctly *weiter*); *dále*; (Czech): 'keep going'.

42 On 19 July 1940 the front page of the *Jüdisches Nachrichtenblatt* (Prague edition) reminded readers that every Jew must carry 'proof of citizenship'.

43 Maffia: a secret organization that came into being during the First World War under the leadership of Edvard Beneš; its aim was to create a sovereign Czech state.

44 Tatra: a Czech car manufacturer.

45 The original German is a play on words: *Achse* means both axle (of a vehicle) and axis (as in the Axis powers).

46 This could not be verified.

the former region of Bohemia, and the cloud in the top right-hand corner is in the shape of the former republic (the 50-haléř stamp),[47] but the various heads of Masaryk, Beneš, and other leaders of the Czech people are more imagined than actually there. On the whole, the resilience of the Czechs remains unbroken, and resistance to the Nazis grows stronger by the day, despite all the propaganda and being cut off from foreign countries.

V. Nazis.
During the first days of the war, no enthusiasm could be detected among the Germans. The younger cohorts in the military left Prague. Older reservists came, people who had taken part in the last war and knew what awaited them. Among the SA and the SS and the various formations, one can clearly detect their fear of being sent to the front; in short, the mood was sombre, and the faces were long and gloomy. After the victory in Poland (the capture of Warsaw was reported as fact every day for more than a week), the atmosphere improved somewhat. With regard to the alliance with Russia, people are very perplexed; after all, it is not so easy to suddenly present this turnaround to a people who have been schooled for years in opposition to Bolshevism. Only in a state like Germany, where simply everything is based on blind trust in the leadership, where the Führer saves every supporter the trouble of thinking, is it possible that something of this sort does not immediately lead to open revolt. It festers within, however, and will one day have dire consequences. The opposition between the Party and the Reichswehr can hardly be concealed anymore. The Reichswehr has got its way, for example, by ensuring that the clause in the Military Law which stipulates that even Jews can be called up for active service in the event of a war, is enforced to the extent that all Reich German, Austrian, and Sudeten German Jews have already been entered in the muster rolls.[48] On this occasion, the Jews were addressed as 'comrade'; no distinction was made between Jews and Aryans. When one Jew, asked his name, answered: 'Karl Israel X' (all Jewish men must have the name Israel added to their passport; all Jewish women, the name Sara), the official replied: 'Your name is Karl X, you are not at the Gestapo here.' All the medical examinations of Jews for military service are performed against the will of the Gestapo. Obviously to keep sentiment against the SS etc. from growing too strong, all the SS have worn the uniform of the SS Dispositional Troops[49] since the outbreak of the war; apart from the epaulettes, it is indistinguishable from the Reichswehr uniform. One cannot find out very much about treatment in the German prisons, when asked, the people who come out reply only: 'Once was enough; I'm not going to talk about it.' Nonetheless, one then learns from a few that they were beaten. All of them, Aryans as well as Jews, come out pale and full of hatred. If the prisoners are guarded by the Czech police, they do well. The wardens and the prisoners are fellow sufferers, after all, and stand against a common enemy. Apart from psychological blunders and petty annoyances, in general one has the feeling that the Nazis want to keep the Protectorate in a good mood as much as possible. When the news of the alleged uprisings was broadcast on the radio, the Protectorate government, as is already known, invited a group of foreign journalists to travel to the Protectorate. This trip was a comedy of the first order.

47 Haléř = cent; 1 Czech koruna = 100 haléř.
48 Muster roll: a list of all the inhabitants of a locality eligible for military service.
49 SS-Verfügungstruppe, armed SS regiments that were the precursor to the Waffen-SS.

Up until then, dancing had been prohibited everywhere in the Greater German Reich. On that day, Gestapo officials hastened from one venue to the next to announce that dancing was allowed today. Upon leaving the hotel, the journalists were greeted in the street by music playing in the square. In this way, one 'entertained' the members of the foreign press and proved to them how calm and content the Protectorate is.[50]

All of these facts are correct primarily for Prague, as I was in another part of the Protectorate and heard only occasional authentic reports. The fact is that everything is far worse and more blatant outside the capital; for example, for a time there was a plan to move all the Jews out of the provinces and into Prague and Brünn, and to make them 'emigration-ready' here. The forced resettlements had in fact already begun, but were halted quite abruptly one day, probably when the plan for forced resettlement into Poland emerged. At the time when this began, I was no longer in the Protectorate.[51] In economic terms, there are probably no major differences between Prague and the rest of the Protectorate.

Addendum to 1)
Since the war broke out, there have, of course, been ration coupons for petrol. Several weeks ago, however, all motor car owners had to apply for permission to keep driving, and only in a few cases (doctors, vehicles for businesses essential to the war effort) was this granted. The other motor cars had to be garaged, only the vehicles of the Reichswehr and the Gestapo can be used without restrictions. Taxis can run only every other day, so the number of taxis is thus in practice reduced to 50 per cent, and the bus service is extremely limited. Companies with more than one taxi are only allowed to have one in use at a time. Cross-country journeys by taxi are completely prohibited.[52]

DOC. 264

On 9 October 1939 employees of the Reich Security Main Office meet in Mährisch-Ostrau to discuss the deportation of its Jewish population[1]

Memorandum (Dan/Pr.), Dannecker, Mährisch-Ostrau, dated 11 October 1939[2]

Re: work in M. Ostrau
1. Notes:
On 9 October 1939, a meeting took place at the office of the head of the State Police Field Office in M. Ostrau, Detective Superintendent Wagner.[3] In addition to Wagner,

50 To discount reports in the British media about demonstrations and street brawls, twenty-seven members of the press from neutral countries were invited to the Protectorate in Sept. 1939.
51 On the deportations to Nisko in the Lublin district, see Doc. 16, fn. 9.
52 This could not be verified.

1 NAP, 101-653 1a. This document has been translated from German.
2 The original contains handwritten corrections and additions.
3 Gerhard Wagner (b. 1906); joined the NSDAP and the SA in 1931 and the SS in 1935; detective superintendent from 1936 and head of the State Police Field Office in Moravská Ostrava from 1939; sentenced to three years in a penal institution in 1941 for covertly reselling Jewish-owned motor vehicles.

SS-Hauptsturmführer Eichmann, SS-Hauptsturmführer Günther, SS-Oberscharführer Dannecker, and Party Comrade Brunner were present.

During the meeting, SS-Hauptsturmführer Eichmann clarified the significance and purpose of the task as well as possible solutions:

In accordance with an order by SS-Oberführer Müller from the Gestapo Central Office in Berlin, one transport of Jews from M. Ostrau and one from Kattowitz are to be organized as soon as possible and in such a way that these transports can be deployed as a sort of preliminary detachment to the area designated to receive the first transports, i.e. the Rozwadow–Annopol–Krasinik area, south-west of Lublin.[4] This advance detachment of Jews has the task of constructing a village made up of barracks, which is envisaged as a transit camp for all subsequent transports. The precise location of the camp will be chosen at that end, but it will probably be situated in the vicinity of the Rozwadow railway junction.[5]

In contrast to the subsequent transports to be carried out, in which the age and gender of the Jews being resettled will not be taken into account, the Jews in the advance detachment will consist exclusively of male Jews with restricted means who are fully fit for work. In addition, it is important to include in the transport Jewish engineers, builders, craftsmen of all sorts, and at least ten Jewish doctors who are fully equipped to provide medical care. During the meeting on 9 October 1939 Detective Superintendent Wagner stated that it was definitely possible to procure a large part of the materials needed for building the barracks etc. through the Witkowitz Ironworks or through his local contact there.

Advance measures: (a) already completed:

The State Police Field Office in M. Ostrau has in its possession the declarations of assets submitted by all the Jews living in the region. The Jews have been deprived of general discretionary power over their assets. They can now [only] withdraw RM 150 from their accounts each week without special permission.

Following a local directive, the Jewish Religious Community of M. Ostrau submitted a list of male Jews between the ages of 17 and 55. It only includes so-called impoverished Jews who are completely fit for work and lists the first and last names, dates of birth, citizenship, and whether they are single or married. Among the 1,030 Jews listed are only 19 of Slovak nationality, 7 of Hungarian nationality, and 1 of Russian nationality. The Jewish Religious Community is at present reportedly producing a breakdown of this list by occupation.

In addition, the Jewish Religious Community of M. Ostrau, following an order issued locally, submitted construction plans along with a list of materials for building the barracks. It is noted that these proposals are very extensive. However, since the intention here is to always house the Jews on two levels in the barracks, 50 per cent of the Jewish proposals can be discounted from the outset.

In accordance with a prior instruction issued to the Jewish Religious Community by Party Comrade Brunner, the Jews in M. Ostrau have already donated to the Jewish Reli-

4 On Müller's directive, see Introduction, p. 39.

5 The camp was built in Zarzecze near Nisko on the San River. On the deportations, see Doc. 16, fn. 9, and Introduction, p. 39.

gious Community in M. Ostrau the sum of RM 300,000 from the blocked accounts; this money is intended to go towards the construction of retraining camps to facilitate emigration.

In addition, there are lists on hand of the materials stored with the ten Jewish builders located here, which can also be used as building materials and tools for constructing the barracks.

In accordance with local instructions, the Jewish Religious Community has, with immediate effect, set up an on-call service that can be contacted round the clock. A complete census of all Jews over the age of 14, using the questionnaires of the Central Office for Jewish Emigration in Prague, is under way and will be completed by 14 October 1939. The Jews must each submit two photos and must voluntarily declare that they are registering for retraining of their own accord, for the purpose of their emigration.

With regard to the technical implementation of the transport, it was stipulated that the Jewish Religious Community of M. Ostrau must immediately assign a Jewish transport manager, who will in turn appoint a Jewish steward for each railway carriage. The Jews must be allocated to the railway cars in such a way that the individual groups of skilled craftsmen and the unskilled labourers, respectively, will travel in separate groups from the outset, wherever possible. As a result, once at the destination one can smoothly and immediately deploy the manpower needed for unloading while the other Jews can be ordered to begin construction at once.

Before the transports depart, a two-metre-long wooden plank must be put up in front of each railway carriage. Small labels showing the numbers of Jews being transported are to be affixed to these planks with drawing pins, numbered consecutively from the locomotive to the end of the train. The Jews designated for a particular railway carriage must line up in three rows behind the plank to which the corresponding number of labels are affixed. Each steward will have a list (one original, three carbon copies) in a binder, giving the names of the Jews in his railway carriage. The transport manager must carry a complete list, in addition to lists (also prepared in quadruplicate) indicating the contents of the individual railway carriages that are transporting materials.

The local contact of the field office in M. Ostrau, engineer Mach, was consulted with regard to planning the barracks and procuring the building materials and other materials. Mach drew up plans for the barracks and the blockhouse for the guards, respectively. Together with his brother, he will also arrange the procurement of the other items needed, such as tools, stoves, cooking pots, etc. With regard to the procurement of wood, the engineer Mach has established contact with two firms located in Slovakia.

The transport issues have also been resolved. The provision of the necessary locomotives was promised as early as 9 October 1939 by the transport commandant's office in Oppeln, Transport Officer Captain Wiehle. In addition, a telephone conversation with the representative of Captain Wiehle on 10 October 1939 revealed that the Kracow–Tarnowitz–Mielec–Rozwanow railway lines are open to traffic.

According to a telephone message from SS-Oberführer Dr Stahlecker on 10 October 1939, the Reich Protector has also given his approval again for the resettlement of the Jews from the Protectorate. He has merely made it a condition that receiving and distributing the Jews in Poland must be organized without a hitch.

With regard to the provision of the guard squads, SS-Untersturmführer Tröstel[6] was instructed to assemble, without delay, a guard squad with a manpower ratio of 1:10 at the Central Offices for Jewish Emigration in Prague and Vienna. He was further instructed to prepare a list of all the materials and foodstuffs to be procured. SS-Untersturmführer Grävenig has already tasked Vienna with the procurement of these items. In addition, there is a possibility of also obtaining a guard squad with a manpower ratio of 1:10 from the Border Police station in M. Ostrau. The equipment for these guards would mostly be procured in M. Ostrau.

(b) Not yet completed:

To ensure the timely completion of this initial 'model transport', a relatively large number of freight trucks must be moved immediately onto a works siding at the Witkowitz Ironworks. This will avoid the doubling of work that would occur through initially storing the […][7] material in sheds or the like, which would mean that loading could only take place during a second cycle of work.

It is also important to step up efforts to procure wood from Slovakia. The difficulties arising with regard to foreign exchange legislation can doubtless be dealt with by Detective Superintendent Wagner. However, an option in this case is to procure freight trucks which could be attached to the transport train, so that reloading would be necessary.

A further problem is the procurement of the requisite heating materials, both for the guard barracks and for the Jews themselves.

A decision from the senior commander must still be obtained as to whether the sixty Jews of Polish nationality who are imprisoned here will be included in the first transports. We must bear in mind that these Jews will have been weakened by their imprisonment and that it would be advisable for them to be put on one of the subsequent transports. A large part of the materials and foodstuffs needed for the guard squads will be procured in M. Ostrau itself, considering that conditions are more favourable here. SS-Sturmbannführer Post will lend support in this respect.

The RM 300 per head that the Jews are permitted to take with them must be exchanged, without fail, no later than 14 October 1939 at the Reichsbank in Kattowitz, where sufficient quantities of zloty are available.

At the same time, the Jews must be given an exact plan for their transport to the site where they will board the train (divided into time periods) and for the boarding process itself. This plan will serve to make transport to the site as inconspicuous as possible, and should firstly make the Jews themselves principally responsible for its orderly implementation. This is necessary in the interest of retaining a certain 'voluntary nature' and also in order to make the departure of the transport as inconspicuous as possible. The Jews are to be instructed to arrive to board the train without any accompanying relatives.

The Jewish Religious Community must pay 50 k. for every Jew included in the transport. How it goes about collecting the money is its own affair.

6 Presumably: Wilhelm Tröstl (1906–1972), carpenter; served in the Austrian armed forces, 1925–1931; joined the NSDAP and the SA in 1932 and the SS in 1933; SS-Untersturmführer, 1938; employed by the Asset Transfer Office in Vienna; later joined the Wehrmacht; Oberleutnant, 1944; sentenced by a Czechoslovak People's Court to two and a half years in prison and forfeiture of assets in 1948.

7 One word is illegible.

DOC. 265
RČS, 23 October 1939: article on the disguised deportation of the Jews from Moravská Ostrava[1]

German methods
On 11 October this year, the Jewish Religious Community of Moravská Ostrava published a summons in *České slovo* and *Mähr[ische] Landeszeitung*[2] for all male Jews between the ages of 14 and 70 to report to the Religious Community. There they received emigration questionnaires which they were to complete and submit the next day. Upon submitting the questionnaires, they had to sign a statement requesting permission to undergo voluntary vocational retraining in a camp. At the same time, all Jewish physicians and Jewish business owners were told to submit immediately an itemized inventory list on 11 October of this year. Physicians then had to surrender all their medical inventory in excess of the most essential needs. In this regard, an ordinance was issued that all males were to report to the riding school on Tuesday, 18 October 1939, and bring with them the items on a list that was published at the same time.[3] The ordinance dispensed with any age limits. It was merely stipulated that anyone aged 17 to 70 should report to the riding school, and anyone under 17 and over 70 directly to the Religious Community. In addition to this information, the ordinance contained a number of instructions on how the Jews should behave upon entering the designated sites.

At the same time as this ordinance was issued, all the stock at Jewish grocery stores and also at a number of other shops was confiscated on the grounds that it was no longer required in view of the departure of the Jews.

The Jews thus affected were permitted to retain, in addition to the movable assets mentioned on the list, as stipulated by the Gestapo, RM 300 or 3,000 korunas; the remainder of their assets were confiscated. This campaign was later expanded to Frýdek-Místek, where the Religious Community received orders at 12 noon on Monday, 16 October 1939, that all males aged 14 and above should report to the riding school in Moravská Ostrava at 8 a.m. on Tuesday, 17 October, to be placed in a retraining camp.

On the surface, this entire operation is carried out in a way that gives one the impression that it has been organized by the Religious Community itself, and the Gestapo is merely giving its kind permission. In fact, however, the campaigns are carried out by the Gestapo itself, and the religious communities are mere executive bodies working under the looming threat that if they don't comply with the orders, these issues will be resolved by the Gestapo itself, and the functionaries themselves will be arrested and executed.

All of these acts directed against the Jews pursue just one aim: to take possession of their assets, if they have any left, and to settle Germans from the Reich in place of the

1 'Německé metody', *RČS*, 23 Oct. 1939; BArch, R 55/20966, fols. 48–50. This document has been translated from Czech. *RČS* was one of many Czechoslovak underground newspapers. There were forty-seven such publications in Prague alone.

2 The *Mährisch-Schlesische Landeszeitung* was founded in 1939 and appeared as the successor to two daily newspapers, the *Ostrauer Zeitung* and the *Morgenzeitung*. The editor-in-chief was Robert Keßler. In 1944, it had a circulation of around 23,000.

3 *Mährisch-Schlesische Landeszeitung*, 16 Oct. 1939, p. 4; *České slovo* (Ostrava edition), 16 Oct. 1939, p. 1.

forcibly expelled Jews. In this way, the German element is to penetrate purely Czech territories. The Jews are at the mercy of the German authorities, since their officials have received strict orders that they must not appeal to the Czech authorities or to any other authorities except the Zentralstelle für die jüdische Auswanderung.[4] According to information obtained from well-placed sources within the Prague Gestapo, the above operation will gradually be extended to the entire Protectorate and implemented with the greatest possible speed.

DOC. 266

In October 1939 the émigré Heimann Stapler reports on how the situation of the Jews in the Protectorate has worsened since the outbreak of the war[1]

Report by Heimann Stappler,[2] dated October 1939[3]

Situation report from Prague.
It should first be noted that precisely at the time of our departure, that is, 13–15 October 1939, the situation of the Jews in the Protectorate worsened considerably, and the already difficult situation is threatening to escalate into a veritable catastrophe. Those in positions of authority were surely informed by our representatives at the Congress[4] of the conditions prior to the outbreak of war, and therefore only the measures taken after 1 September will be discussed.

The wartime events that have occurred have had a disastrous effect on the Jews in the Protectorate, and there is a danger that this clearly valuable section of Jewry will be completely destroyed[5] and enslaved. Of concern are the approximately 82,000 persons there who were listed as full Jews during the registration of non-Aryans. Of that number, approximately 16,000 are between 6 and 24 years of age. In addition, there are 15,000 to 20,000 non-Aryans according to the Nuremberg Laws, who were also placed under the supervision of the Religious Community.

Characteristic of the restrictions imposed on the Jews is that these were not introduced by regulations from either the Germans or the Czech authorities, but rather through an oral order issued by the Gestapo to the Religious Community in Prague, which in turn had to instruct all the other religious communities to implement the restrictions.

4 German in the original: Central Office for Jewish Emigration.

1 YVA, O.7.Cz/367. This document has been translated from German.

2 Correctly: Heimann Stapler (1880–1956), engineer; after graduating worked for the state railway of the Austro-Hungarian monarchy as a building commissioner and from 1918 for the administration of the Czechoslovak State Railway as a technical director; representative of Czechoslovakia at the Zionist World Congress in Vienna, 1925; emigrated to Palestine aboard the *Galil* with his wife and two children in March 1939; worked there as a bookkeeper.

3 The original contains handwritten corrections.

4 This refers to the World Jewish Congress.

5 The German source uses the word 'Vernichtung', which commonly refers to the physical annihilation of the Jews, but here to their dispossession and economic ruin.

On 1 September 1939 the religious communities were directed to implement the following measures:

1) Registration of all Polish or Poland-born Jews within twenty-four hours.[6]

2) Curfew for Jews after 8 p.m. Ordered to be implemented within four hours.[7]

3) Handing in of radio sets, ordered on 22 September, that is, on Erev Yom Kippur,[8] at 4 p.m., with instructions to transfer the radios to the religious communities on Yom Kippur itself. Exceptions allowing the radios to be handed in by 10 a.m. on the day after Yom Kippur were granted only under certain specified circumstances. In Prague, where around 7,000 radios were handed in, the handover process at the religious communities lasted from 8 a.m. on Yom Kippur until 10 a.m. the next day, without interruption. All night long, hundreds of people queued in front of the premises of the Religious Community with their radios. Owners were not permitted to be issued receipts for the radios they had surrendered. Instead, the radios were numbered upon receipt, registered, and then taken in furniture vans for storage in warehouses designated by the Gestapo.[9] In quite a number of towns Jews were also required to hand in their typewriters at the same time.

4) During the same period, orders were given for the registration of the assets of all those who were classed as Jews and non-Aryans under the Nuremberg Laws.[10] The relevant forms issued by the Religious Community of Prague had to be distributed to all Jews on Yom Kippur and collected again the next day. For the religious communities outside the capital, the deadline was set in such a way that the completed forms had to be sent to Prague by messenger, where the overall registration had to be undertaken within a maximum of two days. For this, the deadline that had been set was midnight on 25 September, that is, two days after Yom Kippur.

For the implementation of all of these restrictions, verbally mandated by the Gestapo, a staff of around 1,000 persons had to be made available in Prague each time, as the most severe reprisals against the Jews and mass arrests were threatened if implementation failed to occur on time. The Chief Rabbinate, therefore, in consideration of these circumstances, permitted the violation of the sacrality of Yom Kippur.

On the first day of Rosh Hashanah[11] the police appeared in front of the synagogues and arrested all those who could not prove they were not nationals of Poland. All those whose place of origin was Poland are still in custody today. Particularly tragic was the fate of the Jews in towns with a large number of German inhabitants, such as Mährisch-Ostrau, Brünn, Olmütz, Iglau, Pilsen. Apart from the fact that all the synagogues in these towns had been burned to the ground, there were mass arrests of Jews there. The majority were released after some time, of course, but were arrested again after the war started and sent to the Dachau and Buchenwald concentration camps. Among them were quite a number of people to whom [immigration] certificates had been issued, as well as two

6 In mid Sept. 1939 the employees of the Jewish Religious Community of Prague had to visit every house and apartment in order to register Jews with Polish citizenship: 'Jüdische Kultusgemeinde Prag, Sonderaktionen', in Krejčová et al., *Židé v Protektorátu*, pp. 226–229, here p. 226.

7 See Doc. 263, fn. 31.

8 The day preceding Yom Kippur.

9 See Doc. 263, fn. 12.

10 See Doc. 247.

11 Rosh Hashanah (Jewish New Year) fell on 14 Sept. in 1939.

children who were destined for the Youth Aliyah. In a number of large towns, such as Mährisch-Ostrau and Friedek, the Gestapo seized the Jews' cash, and in many cases simply took it without issuing a receipt, and the same was true for their jewellery. In Friedek all the Jews were summoned to appear at the Gestapo office, where they had to hand over their cash and jewellery without any acknowledgement of receipt. They also had to sign a declaration stating that they were placing their houses under the trusteeship of an Aryan. Simultaneously, they were ordered to relocate to Prague. The heaviest blow, however, came at the time of our departure. Namely, the Gestapo announced that the Jews from the *Protectorate* were to be resettled in Poland, where reservations were to be set up. This measure has already been carried out in Mährisch-Ostrau, a town that had to make available 1,000 men between the ages of 17 and 55, who were sent away as early as 18 October.[12] To implement the complete plan for resettling the Jews, Edelstein[13] was reassigned to M. Ostrau by the Gestapo and was ordered to take along enough clothing for three or four weeks. At the same time, Friedmann[14] was also sent with him from Vienna to Ostrau, and it was hinted to him that additional representatives of the Palestine Office might be transferred to Ostrava. The Jews who were deported to Poland will be used to construct barracks, and once these are completed, the deportation of the family members is scheduled to begin.

Gestapo Central Office for Jewish Emigration

The Central Office was created at the end of July, with the aim of facilitating the procedure required for emigration.[15] In reality, this office has become a veritable hell for those who are forced to appear there in person with their so-called portfolios. These portfolios contain seventeen questionnaires with around 600 questions that must be answered. This emigration office has branches in the Palestine Office for emigration to Eretz and the Religious Community of Prague for emigration to the rest of the world. All persons who are in line for emigration must relocate to Prague before submitting the portfolios.[16] The aforementioned branch offices for emigration are now the most important instruments of the entire organization, and they employ a whole team of people, some of whom are assigned to provide information about filling in the questionnaires, while others are given the task of copying the questionnaires themselves, as they must be typed in duplicate and may be neither folded nor crumpled in any way, lest the person presenting them get a slap in the face at the Central Office. But these technical difficulties are trivial in comparison with the objective difficulties that arise in answering the questions contained in the questionnaires.

These questionnaires are primarily intended to record all the assets of the emigrant, using the tax declarations of the past three years as a basis. Total assets are defined as

12 In Oct. 1939 approximately 1,300 Jews from Moravská Ostrava were deported to Nisko in the Lublin district. Approximately 190 survived the war. On the deportations of Jews from Vienna, Moravská Ostrava, and Katowice, see Doc. 16, fn. 9; on the plans for a 'Jewish reservation', see Doc. 39 and Introduction, pp. 39–41.

13 This refers to the head of the Palestine Office in Prague, Jakob Edelstein.

14 Richard Friedmann (1906–1944), association official; worked at the Israelite Religious Community of Vienna from 1929; transferred to the Jewish Religious Community in Prague in 1939; deported in 1943 to Theresienstadt and in 1944 to Auschwitz-Birkenau, where he was shot dead.

15 See Doc. 252.

16 This provision was rescinded soon thereafter because it was impossible to implement in practice.

including not only real taxable assets but also life insurance policies, household effects that emigrants are leaving behind or taking with them, jewellery, assets abroad, even if there is proof that these are unrecoverable, above all also property holdings in present-day German territory regarding which the emigrant no longer has the right of disposal, because they are under trusteeship anyway. All these assets, including notional ones, are regarded as wealth and are included in the calculation of the levy. Anyone who owns real estate, business ventures, or a shop cannot be permitted by the branch offices, that is the Palestine Office and the Religious Community, to complete the portfolios, even if he has been guaranteed a certificate, until he liquidates his company or places it under trusteeship. From that alone one can gather what exceptionally great sacrifices are demanded of people wishing to emigrate, who, given the current difficulties of obtaining a visa for Palestine,[17] are by no means convinced that they will actually be able to leave the country. It must also be mentioned, however, that those who have handed in the portfolio and receive the so-called exit permit must emigrate while it remains valid. Otherwise, they are at risk of being deported to a concentration camp. But that is not the only difficulty. In addition, there is the financial risk (which often concerns the very last reserves of those who are to emigrate), which is considerable, because those petitioning for certificates must pay all the levies before receiving the exit permit. If they fail to obtain the visa, 100 per cent of the money is lost. For assets which, as mentioned above, include everything – even the handkerchief an emigrant takes with him and the shoes on his feet – these levies are:

up to K	10,000	½%	Jew tax
	50,000	2%	
	200,000	4%	
	500,000	5%	
	1,000,000	10%	and over
	1,000,000	20%	

This Jew tax is prescribed by the Jewish Religious Community of Prague and is collected by the Gestapo upon issuance of the exit permit and the passport (the emigrants now receive German passports, as the old Czech passports have been declared invalid). Besides this tax, the Czech Ministry of Finance collects a levy for the removals office, specifically 20 per cent for items that were acquired before 1 September 1938 and 100 per cent for all items acquired after 1 September 1938, based on the purchase price. This includes all items that have been acquired for emigration itself, such as tools, suitcases, crates, etc., for which 100 per cent of the purchase price is collected. The same rate also applies for paintings, carpets, furs, and silver which, however, emigrants are only permitted to take with them to a limited extent (two silverware settings and 200 grams of other silver objects per person, gold wedding rings, and a silver watch). All other jewellery as well as stocks and bonds in bank safes or security deposit accounts must be surrendered, and prior to the presentation of the portfolios at that. At the same time, the would-be emigrants are forced to pay the fees for both the deposit account and the safe for two years in advance.

17 In May 1939 the British Mandate government had issued strict immigration quotas for Palestine.

Particularly great difficulties arise for the refugees who come from the Sudetenland, where they have left behind substantial assets. Even if they have the requisite means to obtain an A/I certificate[18] in Prague, they cannot emigrate because of the high levies on the assets remaining in the Sudetenland. These levies often exceed their assets in Prague, which are the only ones permitted to be used for payment of the levies. Then no funds remain for the transfer. A considerable number of persons are ruled out as a result, persons to whom certificates had already been promised, but who can no longer make aliyah on account of the aforementioned circumstances. One is thus forced to draw on other seekers of A/I certificates who had been considered for a later stage, with preference being given to people who have already liquidated [their assets] and thus are 'ready' for their portfolios to be submitted. In evaluating applications for the purpose of allocation, it is not only a person's Zionist past that is taken into account. The capacity of the persons concerned to integrate is also taken into consideration. While all other criteria are equal, people who are potential recruits for specialized industries or for settlement in the countryside are favoured as a result of the contracts signed with Yakhin or RASSCO,[19] all other things being equal.

Now, a bit more about the way the portfolios are submitted. The Pal[estine] Office and the Jewish Religious Community are forced to 'deliver' a certain number of emigrants to the Central Office every day. At first it was 200, then 100, then 80, and now 40 every day. If these goals were not met, there was hell to pay for Edelstein and the representative of the Religious Community. The shortfall with respect to the number of would-be emigrants delivered had to be 'made up for' the next day. Otherwise the Gestapo threatened to close the Central Office for [Jewish] Emigration and to take reprisals against those in charge. Incidentally, just at the time of our departure Edelstein was informed by the Gestapo that the latest instruction received by the Gestapo from the authority to which it is accountable was that the emigration of the Jews must not be interfered with, but must not be promoted either. What that will mean in practice is impossible to say today.

On the question of aliyah from the last schedule.[20]

From the most recent schedule, around 1,200 persons here are making aliyah, of whom 212 have already emigrated, so that there are still around 1,000 emigrants to be processed. The Pal[estine] Office is in possession of all the A/I certificates, with the exception of the five certificates that are to be directly allocated by the sokhnut.[21] Of the B/III certificates, 50 and 18 are missing; the latter are blocked at the English consulate in Berlin. In addition, 60 D certificates and 20 student certificates are missing.[22]

18 Capital of at least £1,000 sterling was the prerequisite for such a certificate. A/I certificates were also known as capitalist certificates.

19 The Yakhin settlement company bought up agricultural acreage and distributed it to settlers. The RASSCO (Rural and Suburban Settlement Company) construction firm, founded in 1934, mainly built houses for German immigrants in Palestine and later operated in the general construction industry.

20 List of certificates issued for emigration to Palestine.

21 *Ha-sokhnut ha-yehudit*; Hebrew for 'Jewish Agency'. This refers to the Jewish Agency for Palestine, which represented the Jewish population in dealings with the British Mandate government in Palestine.

In order to accomplish the aliyah that rapidly, it is essential the difficulties in issuing Palestinian visas in Trieste be eliminated as quickly as possible, so that the emigrants are not in danger of failing to be confirmed by the English consul in Trieste. That was the case this time for one A/I certificate and three D certificates, which were rejected because their Palestinian visa had already expired. One should investigate the possibility of sending an official from the shipping company in Prague with the passports to Trieste, to present them there in person for attestation, and to bring them back to Prague again, or the possibility of obtaining group visas, with the exception of visas for A/I certificate holders. In addition, the Pal[estine] Office in Trieste ought to be instructed to arrange a more precise fixing of the dates for ship sailings, so that the emigrants who are destined for departure can arrive on time, without having to take precautionary measures.[23]

DOC. 267

On 26 January 1940 the managing director of Villeroy & Boch expresses his interest in two Jewish malthouses in Olmütz[1]

Letter from Boch-Galhau,[2] managing director of the company Villeroy & Boch (B/R 1/152), 6 Leipziger Straße, Dresden N 6, to the Oberlandrat in Olmütz,[3] Protectorate of Bohemia and Moravia (received on 28 January 1940), dated 26 January 1940[4]

Re: Aryanization of malthouses

Now back in Dresden, I would like to express my sincere thanks for giving me and Mr Roscher[5] the opportunity for such detailed discussions.

22 B/III certificates were awarded to secondary school students whose means of subsistence were assured until they took up an occupation. As a rule, D certificates were given to wives, parents, or children who had been 'requested' by a relative living in Palestine, who then also had to guarantee their means of subsistence. A student certificate was awarded to those who could prove that admission to an institution of higher education recognized by the government in Palestine (such as the University of Jerusalem) was guaranteed, as well as living expenses and educational expenses for at least two years.

23 The following addendum appears at the end: 'For immediate intervention with the Machleketh [Hebrew: 'department'] for Aliyah in Jerusalem. The D-certificate holders Pohl/2 persons, Löwit/1 person have visas which expired on 16 September 1939!'

1 NAP, NSMPO, box 286. This document has been translated from German.

2 Dr Luitwin von Boch-Galhau (1906–1988), engineer; general manager and senior partner of the firm Villeroy & Boch from 1932; honorary citizen of Mettlach on the Saar river.

3 Marius Molsen (1899–1971), lawyer; junior lawyer in the government of Schleswig from 1923; member of the Wetzlar regional council from 1926; joined the NSDAP in 1933; Regierungsrat at the police headquarters in Stettin from 1933; mayor of Stettin, 1933–1935; Oberlandrat in Olmütz from 1939; Ministerialrat at the Reich Ministry of the Interior, 1943; lived in Flensburg after 1945.

4 The original contains handwritten annotations.

5 Michael Roscher (dates of birth and death unknown); chief executive of Villeroy & Boch AG in Dresden in 1932; director of the head office in Mettlach following the dissolution of the limited company in Dresden in 1935; retired in 1954. The head office was moved back to Dresden in 1939 and relocated to Mettlach in July 1940.

I hereby also declare in writing that, as the sole individually liable partner in the family-owned company Villeroy & Boch,[6] I am interested in purchasing the Hermann Brach Malthouse in Olmütz and the Ed. Hamburger & Son Malthouse in Olmütz, which are currently in the process of Aryanization.[7]

As the accounting reports for the two firms are not yet available, we suggested waiting for the rendering of these accounting reports, and then conveying them to the persons seriously interested in acquiring these two plants and asking these persons to submit a bid. I am sincerely grateful to you for having accepted this suggestion, because we hereby have the opportunity to look into every last detail of the issues, some of which are incredibly complex, associated with the purchase of such significant companies under the current circumstances. I look forward to examining the accounting reports once they are available to you.

As I have already explained in person, I am primarily interested in the *Hermann Brach Malthouse*. Admittedly, the buildings at this plant are not particularly good, and the arrangement of the buildings also leaves something to be desired, because it is obvious that they were put up in stages as the operation was expanded. As a result, it was impossible to stick to a clearly defined purpose, as one would envisage when building a new plant. The Brach plant, however, has modern processing machinery and good materials-handling equipment in the form of bucket conveyors, elevators, and screw conveyors, and so, in my opinion, more efficient operations will be possible there.

My impression is that the structural condition of the buildings at the *Hamburger & Son Malthouse* is better, and the basic aspects of the facilities are better maintained, yet on the other hand, the machinery is less modern and efficient and the materials-handling equipment is far inferior to that at the Brach plant.

I have described to you in detail the reasons explaining my firm's interest in acquiring a malthouse, though this interest must certainly seem strange at first glance. In addition, a partner in our firm (a family member), Baron Georg von Zedlitz und Leipe[8] in Prinsnig Post, Groß Tinz near Liegnitz, has substantial brewery interests and possesses both the appropriate education and the corresponding skills in the brewing and malt trade; and as Baron Zedlitz would be put in charge of any Olmütz malt plant acquired by us, the prerequisites for ensuring that the plant is run correctly as a business and that the technical aspects run smoothly would thereby be fulfilled.

In our acquisition plan, we are pursuing a long-term investment, not merely a temporary capital investment, and by no means a speculation. Sufficient capital is available

6 The company was founded by François Boch as a porcelain factory in Lorraine in 1748 and merged with the Nicolas Villeroy company in 1836 to create the Villeroy & Boch Ceramic Works. The production centres in Breslau, Dresden, and Torgau were expropriated after 1945, and the firm acquired several enterprises in West Germany, Canada, Argentina, France, Portugal, Italy, and Switzerland. It was converted into a joint-stock company in 1987.

7 The Hermann Brach Malthouse in Olmütz was founded in 1872 and the company Eduard Hamburger & Sohn in 1884. The latter belonged to Otto Erich Heynau, who fled to Belgium. Hans Swrschek managed the assets of the company. In addition to Villeroy & Boch, two malthouses – one in Langensalza and the other, Wolff Sons, in Erfurt – expressed an interest in acquiring Eduard Hamburger & Son.

8 Baron Georg von Zedlitz und Leipe (1891–1966), estate owner in Silesia; lived in Wiesbaden after the war.

both for the acquisition of such a plant and also for any investments that may become necessary, as well as for financing barley purchases, malt storage, and the sales transaction. We regard it as a self-evident national duty that a plant in the Protectorate should be managed by our firm according to both the national and the ethnopolitical perspectives of the Reich.

I look forward to receiving further news.[9]

Heil Hitler!

DOC. 268

On 1 February 1940 the Oberlandrat in Iglau provides information on the lack of progress concerning Aryanization[1]

Report by the Oberlandrat in Iglau[2] (secret, file Z.: R V 41/40 g.), unsigned, to the Reich Protector of Bohemia and Moravia in Prague, via the Office for Moravia in Brünn, dated 1 February 1940 (excerpt)[3]

Re: administrative report for January 1940
Enclosures: 3 copies
[…][4]
c) Aryanization
Aryanization has come to an almost complete standstill. This situation can, however, no longer be attributed solely to the lack of potential buyers, but rather to an unmistakable reticence on the part of Jewish owners. A great many Jewish business owners are under the delusion that the tide might turn again. Therefore, they are trying to keep hold of their property wherever possible.

Despite this reticence by the Jews, I do not consider it advisable to introduce compulsory Aryanization with a fixed deadline across the board. Given the ongoing difficulty of finding suitable potential buyers, the economy would suffer extremely adverse effects if universal compulsory Aryanization were introduced.

The appointment of trustees *across the board* has failed due to a lack of suitable personnel. From an economic standpoint, such appointments can only be justified if diligent, autonomous trustees are available for each individual business.

9 In early April 1940 the official in charge, Dr Diehler, informed the head office of Villeroy & Boch that there were no objections to the start of sales negotiations, but that the price offered was far below its estimated market value. After Villeroy & Boch withdrew its offer, the entrepreneurs Göhler and Weiß had their bid for Ed. Hamburger & Son accepted. The Brach firm was sold to the Hamburg shipping company Horn & Stinnes. See NAP, NSMPO, box 286.

1 NAP, ÚŘP, I-1a 1803, box 280, fols. 11–12. This document has been translated from German.
2 Eugen Fiechtner (1908–1988), lawyer; joined the NSDAP in 1930; articled clerk at Waiblingen local court in 1932; employed by the Württemberg interior administration from 1937; appointed Oberlandrat in Iglau from 1939; transferred in 1942 for abuse of office; deployed at the front in 1944; returned to Stuttgart from Soviet captivity, 1946.
3 The original contains the handwritten addition: 'Tgb. – B 152/40 g'.
4 The first part of the report deals with the general political situation in the Iglau district in Jan. 1940.

On the other hand, it should certainly be possible to appoint trustees who have authorization to sell as the opportunity arises to businesses that are ripe for Aryanization. By 'ripe' for Aryanization I mean, in this context, businesses for which a suitable candidate has already been found. With these businesses, there is a guarantee that Aryanization can be carried out step by step, taking economic requirements into account, without harming the overall economy. At present, the businesses in a district that have not yet been Aryanized and are not managed by trustees are overseen by representatives, who are generally employees of these firms. The Jew can scarcely continue to have a harmful influence here.

The categorical ban on the assignment of trustees for the purpose of selling, however, completely closes off what seems to me to be the only suitable way of accelerating the continued implementation of the Aryanization process at present. Today, at any rate, I cannot expect significant progress to be made in the foreseeable future with regard to transferring Jewish business assets into Aryan hands. Even the Reich Economic Aid Programme[5] will not reach its potential unless one has the chance to carry out compulsory Aryanization in a given case at a given time. In addition, two of the most significant Jewish textile factories in my district, Münch & Son in Triesch[6] and Gabriel Kärger in Iglau,[7] have been appropriated by the State Police, so that Aryanization negotiations basically cannot be conducted at all for these firms. For the Kärger firm, however, a definitive confiscation has not yet been declared.

Aryanizations of agricultural land and property have not been carried out, as a matter of principle. The compulsory administrations were, wherever possible, extended also to smaller businesses (butchers, innkeepers, mills, and the like).

[…][8]

5 The Reich Economic Aid Programme (Reichswirtschaftshilfe) issued financial guarantees as a means of providing assistance to German enterprises seeking loans to enable them to take over businesses in the occupied territories.

6 Adolf Münch (1805–1877) founded a textile factory in Hodice near Třešť (Triesch) in 1860. Rudolf Münch (1884–1939) took over the running of the firm in 1909 and moved the production of suit fabrics and Persian carpets to Třešť in 1926. Shortly after the German invasion, he was arrested and killed by the Gestapo. The authorities confiscated the business and appointed Alois Felker from Jihlava as trustee.

7 Gabriel Kärger founded a knitwear manufacturing firm in Jihlava in 1901. On 1 Feb. 1939 Kärger emigrated to Britain with his family. The firm's assets were seized, and Paul Witter of Düsseldorf took over the management of the firm.

8 Section 'd) Price control' follows.

DOC. 269

On 9 February 1940 the Reich Protector outlines further procedures for expropriating Jewish businessmen[1]

Express letter (marked 'strictly confidential') from the Reich Protector of Bohemia and Moravia (II/1/Jd 3452/40), p.p. signed Dr Bertsch,[2] Prague, to a) the Oberlandräte and b) the Moravia Group,[3] dated 9 February 1940[4]

Guidelines concerning the Regulation of the Reich Protector of Bohemia and Moravia on the Exclusion of Jews from the Economy of the Protectorate, issued on 26 January 1940.[5]
I. General
The regulation has decisive significance for the progress of de-Jewification in the Protectorate. It allows for the de-Jewification of the Protectorate economy and the transfer of previously Jewish businesses into non-Jewish hands by means of legal compulsion. The rudiments of this process were already present in § 9 of the Regulation on Jewish Assets, dated 21 June 1939, as § 15 of the Second Implementing Decree expressly provided that trustees could also be appointed for the sale or liquidation of the business.[6] Thus far, little use has been made of this option, which was intended to be used only in exceptional cases. This new regulation too is to be applied only when the transfer of a Jewish enterprise to a non-Jew is necessary for general economic reasons and cannot be achieved either through a contract or in the desired form, and there are special reasons to justify the accelerated transfer of the business to a non-Jewish owner.

The new regulation makes it possible:

1) to prohibit Jews from running commercial operations. The prohibition applies

a) to economic sectors in general, as has been brought into force by the First Implementing Decree,[7] which was announced at the same time as the regulation, and which concerns the textile, footwear, and leather goods trade, and peddling and all itinerant trade with effect from 30 April 1940,

1 NAP, ÚŘP II.-l-ref4, box 578/1, fols. 608–609; copy in USHMM, RG-48.008M, reel 43. This document has been translated from Czech.

2 Dr Walter Bertsch (1900–1952), administrative official and lawyer; joined the NSDAP in 1933 and the SS in 1938; head of Dept. II (Economics and Finance) in the Office of the Reich Protector, 1940; minister of economics and labour in the Protectorate, 1942–1945; SS-Brigadeführer, 1944; incarcerated in 1945 and sentenced to life imprisonment in 1948 by the Czechoslovak National Court; died in prison in Brno.

3 The 'Moravia Group' developed from the Office of the Head of the Civil Administration. As an administrative unit, it stood between the Office of the Reich Protector and the Oberlandräte and mediated between them.

4 The original contains official stamps of the Reich Protector of Bohemia and Moravia.

5 *Verordnungsblatt des Reichsprotektors*, 1940, no. 7, pp. 41–43.

6 Under § 9 of the Regulation of the Reich Protector of Bohemia and Moravia on Jewish Assets (21 June 1939) the Reich Protector was authorized to appoint trustees for Jewish enterprises: see Doc. 247, and the Second Implementing Regulation of the Reich Protector in Bohemia and Moravia concerning the Regulation on Jewish Assets, Art. VII (Legal Status of Trustees), § 15 (Purport and Exercise of Rights), *Verordnungsblatt des Reichsprotektors*, 1939, no. 39, pp. 318–323.

7 First Implementing Decree to the Regulation of the Reich Protector in Bohemia and Moravia on the Exclusion of Jews from the Economy of the Protectorate, 26 Jan. 1940, *Verordnungsblatt des Reichsprotektors*, 1940, no. 7, p. 43.

b) to individual businesses as per a special prohibition order, which I reserve the right to issue.

2) To forcibly transfer Jewish businesses to non-Jewish ownership.

The registration of assets for Jewish businesses and the registration of Jewish shareholdings, as mandated in the Fourth Implementing Decree to the Regulation on Jewish Assets issued on 21 June 1939, are important instruments for procuring the requisite documentation.[8]

The powers granted by the new regulation are exhaustive. Individual cases aside, the extent and pace at which they are to be applied will be determined by directives I will issue in future.

II. Procedure

1)

a) Whether a business is to be liquidated or transferred to non-Jewish ownership is determined by whether there is a need for the business to continue to exist. Ethnopolitical considerations can play a decisive role here. To transfer a business into German hands can be an important factor in favour of the German ethnic population in German spheres of interest, despite the existence of overcrowding in the economic sector concerned. However, ethnopolitical considerations might make it necessary to close down a thriving business in the interest of other German-owned businesses.

b) The businesses affected by this compulsory de-Jewification must be notified as to whether they are to be liquidated or sold. The notifications are to be served to all owners of Jewish commercial operations. In the case of public limited companies, the notifications are to be sent to the members of the management board; in the case of private limited companies, they must be sent to the management. If these persons are absent, notification is to be served by means of publication in the newspapers 'Der Neue Tag' and 'Národní Politika'.[9]

c) If the business is to be liquidated, the owner must be told to begin the liquidation process on the day of the prohibition. He is to be informed that in accordance with §§ 1 and 5 of my Regulation on Jewish Assets of 21 June all disposal is still subject to approval. You are to monitor the progress of the liquidation process. Beginning on the day the prohibition takes effect, goods may no longer be sold. They must be disposed of in accordance with § 6(1) of the regulation. There must be no sell-off prior to this date. I will give details of the office responsible at a later date.

d) If the business is to be transferred into non-Jewish hands, the owner must be assigned a deadline by which the business must be sold. In the process, conditions can be imposed with regard to who the desired buyer should be. He must be informed that the sale nonetheless requires approval in accordance with §§ 1 or 5 of my Regulation on Jewish Assets of 21 June 1939.

e) Sale trustees and liquidation trustees must be appointed if reasonable doubts exist concerning the proper implementation of the prescribed measures by the Jewish

8 Fourth Implementing Decree to the Regulation of the Reich Protector in Bohemia and Moravia on Jewish Assets, 7 Feb. 1940, *Verordnungsblatt des Reichsprotektors*, 1940, no. 7, pp. 45–47.

9 The conservative *Národní politika* was published from 1883 to 1945 and was one of the leading Czech-language dailies. The editor-in-chief was Dr Jan Scheinost.

owner. It must be ensured that the guidelines for the trustees as well as any supplements are known to the appointed and yet to be appointed trustees at all times. The trustees in charge of the liquidation and sale are to be provided with the special guidelines intended for them *in addition* to the general guidelines.

As a matter of principle, care must be taken to ensure that the trustee is not the buyer. The same principle applies in cases where the trustee is an employee of the buyer.

f) Also affected by the regulation are Jewish businesses that are engaged in bankruptcy proceedings. In these cases, the notifications and conditions are to be addressed to the official receiver. He must be told that my Regulation on the Exclusion of Jews from the Economy of the Protectorate must be taken into account in the bankruptcy proceedings. If the sale of the business is envisaged, a trustee for the sale must be appointed.

g) In every case, I reserve the right to de-Jewify and to appoint trustees of all kinds for businesses owned by foreign nationals.

2) With regard to the approval of sales applications, I refer to my guidelines concerning the Regulation on Jewish Assets.

It must be ensured that any sum accruing to the Jew is paid into a blocked account. I must stress here that approvals can always be made subject to conditions. Such conditions could be a lower purchase price or a compensatory levy paid to a designated office yet to be determined. Contributions of all kinds to other offices are prohibited, without exception. If approval is withheld or if it is granted under a condition, the notification must contain the legal information on the right of appeal.

As a rule, it is the Jewish proprietor who must liquidate the business, and therefore the sum paid to him must, as a rule, not exceed the liquidation value. If a trustee was assigned to the business, the liquidation value at the time of the trustee's appointment will be used, if the liquidation value at the time of sale is lower. Withdrawals by the owner in the interim, if they exceed the usual rate of interest, are to be deducted.

In most cases, paying merely the liquidation value would mean an enrichment of the buyer. In such cases a compensatory levy should always be collected from the buyer, which should generally amount to 70 per cent of the difference between the liquidation value and the fair market value on the day of sale. Special circumstances justify deviations upwards and downwards. Goodwill is usually excluded from the calculation when determining the fair market value.[10]

An appraiser must always be called upon to determine the values. The fee will be paid by the sellers and buyers proportionately.

3) In cases where sale trustees are assigned or where the Jewish owner has asked for a prospective buyer to be procured, it must be ensured that only *one* prospective buyer applies. If there are several potential buyers, the most suitable one must be selected and granted permission to negotiate with the sale trustee. The permission must generally be limited to a period of four weeks. The trustee is only allowed to negotiate with persons who are in possession of such a permit. A permit can only be granted to a new applicant if negotiations with the previous applicant have failed. The old permit must then be withdrawn.

10 Goodwill refers to the intangible assets of a company, such as the projected earnings, customer potential, quality of management, significance within the industry, etc.

DOC. 270

Washington Post, 11 February 1940: article on the increasingly stringent anti-Jewish policies in the Protectorate[1]

Nazis Extend Drive to Oust Moravia Jews. 'Aryanizing' of Shops By April Decreed; Migration Advised.

Prague, Feb. 10. – Jews in the protectorate of Bohemia and Moravia, who hitherto have escaped the full scope of Germany's anti-Jewish laws, were informed today of measures that will reduce them to the state of impoverished helplessness suffered by their brothers in Germany.

(There were 126,310 Jews in Czecho-Slovakia before the Nazi invasion.[2])

By April 1, they were told, all Jews' shops must be 'Aryanized' or be closed by the government and goods confiscated while all other Jews' businesses, unless urgent reason for their continued existence can be satisfactorily proved, will be terminated.[3]

Jewels Must Be Sold

Jews will be forbidden to earn their living by peddling goods from house to house. Their jewellery, gold, silver, plating and other articles of value must be sold to a state-appointed firm while they must emigrate as soon as possible to escape arrest.

These decrees were issued today by the protector, Baron von Neurath, who in his decrees of last June indicated that in the protectorate Jews would meet the same fate as those in Germany. German authorities said the Jews had failed to take the hint to pack up their goods and leave.

'Too many of them are still here so other methods of forcing emigration must be brought to bear,' it was said.

The decree for closing Jews' shops includes all textile, clothing, shoe and leather goods stores. Confiscated goods, it is understood, will go to the Hageda[4] firm which has been appointed the 'Aryyanization'[5] concern. It also will buy Jews' jewelry. Pressure to induce emigration is also being brought by other means, notably by one well known in the Reich – personal interviews with Gestapo authorities. In recent weeks numerous individuals were called to Gestapo headquarters and questioned as to why they still were in [the] protectorate. All the interviews terminated in the admonition to get out. If necessary by illegal means.

1 *Washington Post*, 11 Feb. 1940, p. 11.

2 Around 118,000 people classed as Jews according to the Nuremberg Laws came under German rule following the Wehrmacht invasion.

3 See Doc. 269.

4 Correctly: Hadega. Hadega was founded as a subsidiary of the Kredit- und Wirtschaftsgemeinschaft Wige GmbH as a trading company for raw materials and colonial goods. From 1940 to 1945 the company was responsible for buying up precious metals, gemstones, and coins owned by Jews. The capital came from the funds of the Kreditanstalt der Deutschen (the largest German banking institution in Czechoslovakia), into which the profits were also paid.

5 Spelling as in the original.

DOC. 271

In the spring of 1940 the Jewish Agency in Jerusalem learns of the despair of the Jews in Mährisch-Ostrau and of their relatives in the Zarzecze camp[1]

Report, unsigned, no date[2]

1. The Situation of the Jews in Mährisch-Ostrau

At the beginning of 1939, Mährisch-Ostrau had around 8,000 Jewish inhabitants. Today the number is only approximately 2,200. Only around 400 of them are males. A majority of the Jewish population is disproportionately old; the others are women and children whose heads of household were deported in the autumn of the previous year. The Jewish Community of Mährisch-Ostrau has suffered unlike any other community in the Protectorate or in the Greater German Reich. The Jews in Mährisch-Ostrau have lost their assets by having had their jewellery, cash, bank books, typewriters, cameras, radios, cars, etc. taken from them. They are not in possession of their immovable assets either, as these are under compulsory administration. The shops are almost all Aryanized or run by acting managers.

The Jews of Mährisch-Ostrau are no longer in gainful employment; of the 2,200 persons mentioned, 1,500 live on welfare benefits provided by the [Jewish] Religious Community of Mährisch-Ostrau. Under the most difficult conditions, this Religious Community has created institutions and facilities that have become a model for other communities in the Protectorate: two soup kitchens, two homes for the elderly, one outpatient facility, retraining courses, social and youth welfare programmes, including youth welfare. Currently a Jewish hospital is also being set up, which one cannot manage without.

But the Jewish Religious Community of Mährisch-Ostrau, from its own resources, has also provided all the Poland transports with medical supplies and building materials, with foodstuffs and equipment, although only around 1,400 of the approximately 20,000 persons deported from Vienna, Teschen, etc. were from Mährisch-Ostrau itself, excluding Witkowitz and the surrounding areas.[3] As a result, the financial situation of the Jewish Religious Community of Mährisch-Ostrau is catastrophic and largely dependent on Prague.

The despair of the women and the demoralization of the children grow from day to day, as the heads of the households are absent, and there is still no news at all from some of them. The number of those who are reliant on the support of the Religious Community increases daily.

2. The Poland transports.

Last autumn, three transports went 'voluntarily' from and through Mährisch-Ostrau to the retraining camp in Poland.

1 CZA, S 26/1546, fols. 231–232. The holdings include the reports and correspondence of the Jewish Agency. This document has been translated from German.
2 The report must have been written prior to the closure of the camp in Zarzecze in April 1940.
3 The number given is too high. In the autumn of 1939, more than 5,000 Jews were deported from Vienna, Moravská Ostrava (Mährisch-Ostrau), and Katowice to the vicinity of Nisko on the San river in the Lublin district. See Introduction, p. 39, and Doc. 16, fn. 9.

They included around 1,400 Jewish men from Mährisch-Ostrau.

In the camp at Zarzecze near Nisko on the San river, the untrained and unprepared pioneers from Ostrau created from nothing, under the most difficult conditions – when they arrived, there was only an open meadow, with no shelter of any kind – a camp that can be held up as a kind of model establishment.

In the meantime, a majority have left the camp, some voluntarily, some involuntarily, and many hundreds are now in what is today Russia, with no contact with their relatives and no hope. Around 310 Ostrava Jews, along with men from Vienna and Teschen, etc., still remain in the camp itself and in the surrounding area. All of these people will have to leave the camp sooner or later, as was also the case in Sosnowitz.

3. The solution to Ostrau's Nisko problem

The men are forbidden from returning to the Protectorate, even if they want to emigrate with their families. The Protectorate authorities regard the deported Jews as having emigrated, and all the Jewish offices in Prague have been forbidden from doing anything for Nisko. For this reason it is difficult, if not impossible, for the Protectorate Jews to broach this problem abroad or to provide help or appeal for help.

In fact, the problem of the Ostrau camp inmates in Nisko and the surrounding area is the most urgent one of all at the moment. This is acknowledged by all the agencies in the know, even by the representatives of the Polish Jewish community, which is also suffering gravely, of course.

The Slovak Republic is willing to admit the 310 Ostrau camp inmates from Nisko and the surrounding area to Slovakia if, among other things, their living expenses are guaranteed from *abroad* for three months in advance and if it is guaranteed that they will continue their journey within that time. As both questions are mainly financial ones, this matter has not yet been settled.[4]

The construction of the camp in Nisko has shown that the men would be able to engage in agricultural work in San Domingo.[5] The family members, women, and children in the Protectorate would likewise be willing to do such work. Only a small fraction have genuine opportunities to emigrate.[6]

4 In the original, the following was crossed out by hand: 'The Religious Community of Mährisch-Ostrau is trying to transfer ½ million korunas to Slovakia. Whether this transfer will take place is doubtful, firstly in terms of making the funds available, secondly on account of the clearing system for the Protectorate and Slovakia, and thirdly on account of the ban on doing anything for Nisko.'

5 In the spring of 1940, the American Jewish Joint Distribution Committee began to build a settlement in the Dominican Republic for refugees from Europe.

6 When the camp in Zarzecze was closed down, the surviving Jews from Vienna and Mährisch-Ostrau were able to return to their places of origin.

DOC. 272

On 5 March 1940 the Senior Commander of the Security Police objects to the introduction of identifying badges for Jews in the Protectorate[1]

Letter, dated 5 March 1940, from the Reich Protector of Bohemia and Moravia, Senior Commander of the Security Police (no. II-635/40- BdS), p.p. signed Suhr,[2] Prague, to Group I/3[3] in the Office of the Reich Protector in Bohemia and Moravia, Prague[4]

No. II – 635/40 – BdS
Re: introduction of a special badge for Jews
Case file: letter dated 21 February 1940 – *I 3 b 1376/40- 3040*[5]
In my view, the introduction of a special badge that must be visibly worn by the Jews in public is completely undesirable. A regulation of this kind has thus far been avoided in the rest of the territory of the Greater German Reich, in line with explicit instructions from senior authorities. Only in the General Government has such a measure been necessary, owing to the special circumstances. However, conditions in the Protectorate of Bohemia and Moravia are by no means the same as in the General Government. Therefore, until a general regulation for the entire territory of the Reich is adopted, I consider the introduction of a Jewish badge in the Protectorate to be inappropriate.[6]

1 NAP, ÚŘP, I-3b 5851, fol. 579. This document has been translated from German.
2 Friedrich Suhr (1907–1946), lawyer; joined the NSDAP and SS in 1933; headed Section II A 3 (Legal Affairs) at the Reich Security Main Office from 1940; worked in the 'Jewish affairs' section of the Reich Security Main Office, 1941–1942; leader of Sonderkommando 4b and Einsatzkommando 6 (both part of Einsatzgruppe C), 1942–1943; senior commander of the Security Police and the SD in Toulouse, and later senior commander of the Security Police and the SD in France from 1943; Oberregierungsrat, 1944; committed suicide in prison.
3 Group I/3's tasks included citizenship issues as well as race and so-called blood-protection matters.
4 The original contains handwritten annotations, underlining, and official stamps.
5 On 21 Feb. 1940 a memorandum from the Reich Protectorate had been sent to the Senior Commander of the Security Police in the Office of the Reich Protector, with a request for his opinion regarding the fact that Jews in the territory of the Reich were not required to wear identifying badges and that such a requirement was also not regarded as useful. See NAP, URP, I-3b 5851, fol. 579.
6 See also Docs. 316 and 315. The compulsory visible identification of Jews in the Protectorate was not introduced until a corresponding regulation was adopted for the entire Reich in Sept. 1941. See Doc. 212.

DOC. 273

Jüdisches Nachrichtenblatt, 8 March 1940: interview with Franz Weidmann on the tasks of the Jewish Religious Community of Prague[1]

Increased activity of the Jewish Religious Community of Prague. Facing new tasks. Conversation with the executive secretary, Dr F. Weidmann

The Jewish Relief Organization and its accomplishments. – Solution to the emigration question. – Concern for children and the elderly. – Closest cooperation with the Zionist Central Association.[2]
– Enormous financial challenges.
Prague, 5 March 1940.

The cataclysmic events of recent times have brought the wide-ranging work of the Jewish Religious Community of Prague to the forefront of public attention. The interest shown in the range of activities of this body is definitely welcome, for, like every effort dedicated to the common good, the work of the Religious Community also requires the active participation of as many sections of the Jewish population as possible. In these times, the officials bear a special responsibility. Their task is neither easy nor rewarding either. But because it is a matter not only of acquitting oneself of the tasks, but also of the way in which this is done, we have asked the executive secretary, Dr F. *Weidmann*, to answer a few questions for our freelance reporter. In the following we convey the information he provided.

How is the Religious Community structured today?

> The entire organization of the Religious Community is based on the principle of personal responsibility. Each section head is fully responsible to the central administration for the accomplishments and activities of his department; the Community works in close cooperation with the Zionist Central Association's Palestine Office. Deliberations take place on a daily basis, in the course of which the current issues of the day are discussed in detail and all the important guidelines are provided.

How do you envisage the solution to the Jewish emigration question in the Protectorate?

> The emigration of the Jews from the Protectorate already began under the Second Republic. It increased considerably after the events of March 1939,[3] particularly after the creation of the 'Central Office for Jewish Emigration, Prague.' From March to December 1939,[4] over 19,000 Jews emigrated from the Protectorate. The outbreak of

1 *Jüdisches Nachrichtenblatt* (Prague edition), no. 10, 8 March 1940, pp. 1–2. This document has been translated from German. The Prague edition of the *Jüdisches Nachrichtenblatt* was published from 1939 to 1945 as the official organ of the Jewish Religious Community of Prague, under German censorship. The newspaper was published in German and in Czech, and the final issue appeared on 26 Jan. 1945.

2 In 1939 the various individual Zionist organizations and institutions were merged to form the Zionist Central Association, which arranged for the emigration of Jews from the Protectorate. It was dissolved on 10 May 1941.

war did not bring the vast wave of emigration to a halt. Emigration was, of course, greatly obstructed by the loss of opportunities to emigrate to England and the English dominions, so that we were forced to turn our attention to all overseas countries. We were successful in this for the most part, so that the majority of transports to overseas destinations were considerable. The implementation itself was possible only with the aid of the Jewish committees in neutral countries and support from the JDC.[5] It was and is the JDC in particular that makes the necessary grants available. In January 1940 around 1,000 persons emigrated, so that in just under seven months, 25 per cent of the Jews had already left the Protectorate.[6]

We have major problems to solve in this regard. In particular, we have to house elderly people whose children have already emigrated and, in addition, we take charge of the children whose parents have already left the Protectorate or must emigrate without their children. The children themselves stay in children's homes until the parents can submit an application from their new home for their children to join them. Therefore, both children's homes and homes for the elderly have been opened as a solution to this important matter. In the period from 10 to 16 February alone, no fewer than 3,471 persons received information about emigration opportunities from the 'promotion of emigration' department.

What experience have you gained through setting up the 'Central Office for Jewish Emigration, Prague'?

The creation of this office greatly simplified all the emigration options. It means that it is now possible to secure all the necessary documents. The emigrant does not need to run from one office to the next; instead, all the documents he requires for emigration are provided and dealt with here. It now takes no more than two weeks from the day the portfolio is submitted until the day the exit permit is issued.[7] The Jewish Religious Community and the Palestine Office are involved in the organization of the 'Central Office'. They arrange all emigration matters and, because of the creation of the 'Central Office', they also have a way of recording all the emigrants. The expanded decree of the Reich Protector, stating that the 'Central Office for Jewish Emigration, Prague' is now responsible for the entire territory of the Protectorate,[8] was welcomed by the Religious Community, as it made it possible to introduce a uniform procedure for recording all Jewish emigrants and facilitated the straightforward processing of all cases.

How did you manage to set up the entire Jewish relief organization in such a short time?

Before 15 March 1939, the Jewish relief organization was in the hands of the Jewish Institute of Social Affairs. Enormous sums had to be raised in recent months. The

3 On 15 March 1939, the Wehrmacht occupied Czecho-Slovakia. The Czech part was declared a Protectorate by Hitler and the Slovak part became independent.

4 See Docs. 252 and 255.

5 American Jewish Joint Distribution Committee (JDC).

6 In 1940 around 6,000 Jews emigrated from the Protectorate. Overall, 26,093 Jews managed to leave the Protectorate by 15 July 1943; 19,016 emigrated in 1939 alone.

7 On the portfolios containing the official forms for submission of the documents required for emigration, as well as the exit permits (*Durchlaßscheine*), see Docs. 263 and 266.

8 Regulation of the Reich Protector of Bohemia and Moravia on the Supervision of the Jews and Jewish Organizations, 5 March 1940, in *Verordnungsblatt des Reichsprotektors*, 1940, no. 11, p. 77.

Jewish Religious Community of Prague now spends more on social welfare *in one week* than all seven Prague religious communities together used to spend in *one year*. That represents a fifty-fold increase in ongoing expenditure. Now the entire relief organization is being centralized in stages at the Institute of Social Affairs. Trained officials work in accordance with precise guidelines, which are designed so that one no longer feels that he is accepting charity any more. The principles differ from the previous ones: today, productive assistance no longer means getting someone into the economic system. Instead, it must involve procuring an opportunity to emigrate. For this reason, the Jewish Institute of Social Affairs helps all poor co-religionists to emigrate. The relief effort itself takes on greater dimensions daily. Thus far, support has been granted to 10,000 individuals in need. But other urgent problems have been solved as well. A large public soup kitchen has been set up, which feeds 2,000 people a day. The Religious Community has taken direct control of all social institutions and welfare organizations. Around 1,000 persons are housed in homes for the elderly, children's homes, and apprentices' hostels. The outpatient facility is used by more than 1,000 persons each week. A hospital has been established, and the creation of a second one is under way. A tuberculosis sanatorium will be built in the near future. Finally, an outpatient service for bedridden patients has been organized.[9]

How is it possible to raise all the necessary funds today?

It is incredibly difficult to raise the funds. The funds are primarily obtained from the religious tax and collections, and through financial aid from the JDC, which is extremely difficult to secure. But all the expenses of the Religious Community are covered in full. There is thus no need to touch the reserves.

Do you have new plans with regard to the increased range of activities of the Religious Community?

Once the winter is over, the emigration department will probably begin organizing the worker transports to overseas destinations, so far as this is possible. And the associated work will be undertaken at an accelerated pace. The retraining courses will be expanded with the addition of special agricultural courses intended to prepare emigrants for their work in their new homeland.

What are the next tasks of the Jewish Religious Community of Prague?

At present, we are dealing with the reorganization of all the provincial communities, especially with regard to financial and social management. Simultaneously work is being done to centralize emigration from the entire Protectorate by including all the provincial communities.

9 The outpatient clinic was initially located in Karlsgasse and was moved to Kelleygasse on 15 Sept. 1940 due to the increasing numbers of patients. The outpatient clinic for tuberculosis patients remained in Karlsgasse and was the only site in the Protectorate that provided care to Jews suffering from tuberculosis. The Jewish Religious Community of Prague ran a Jewish hospital with thirty-seven beds in Katharinengasse. It opened on 1 Dec. 1939. In June 1940 a second hospital with fifty beds was set up in the former orphanage in Laibachgasse.

Has cooperation with the Palestine Office yielded any specific results?

Cooperation with the Zionist Central Association has contributed a great deal to the success of the work. We work together in a brotherly way, and the warm relationship will also develop further in the future. We talk through current issues together and all decisions are made jointly.

What guidelines are used to select personnel for the Religious Community?

Experience has shown that major problems have to be solved almost exclusively by career officials, not by volunteers. The work must be attended to day and night. For this reason, it was necessary to adopt an extremely rigorous approach to the selection of the official staff we employ. Based on the principle of personal responsibility, strict guidelines for recruitment are applied, not only concerning the most important positions but also for the most minor officials. Professional qualities, energy, and circumspection are crucial, but a close connection to the Jewish problem is also an important consideration. Despite a relatively small administrative staff, tremendous things have thus been achieved. If the field of activity of the Religious Community has increased by a factor of around twenty to twenty-five, the increase in the number of officials, by contrast, is only twelve-fold.

DOC. 274
On 17 March 1940 Robert Weinberger writes to Richard Schindler, asking him to speed up his aliyah[1]

Handwritten letter from Dr Robert Weinberger,[2] Přerov, to Richard Schindler,[3] dated 17 March 1940

Dear Richard,

First, my warmest regards! Above all, I have to comment on the question of my aliyah, and it is difficult for me to write about it.[4] Do I really need to start by saying that I would very gladly make aliyah as soon as possible and together with most of the plugah?[5] I hardly think so. And I am also convinced that, under different circumstances, my aliyah would be a matter of course.

1 JMP, DP 35. This document has been translated from German.

2 Dr Robert Weinberger (1913–1977), lawyer; practised law in Brno; deported on 4 Dec. 1941 to Theresienstadt, where he worked in the labour office from 1944 to 1945 and was a member of the Council of Elders; took part in the 'Documentation Campaign' initiated by the Czech branch of Hehalutz to secure documents from Theresienstadt that had been collected in the ghetto; emigrated in 1949 to Israel, where he worked as a bookkeeper and financial manager.

3 Richard Schindler (1916–2008), lawyer; member of the Jewish pioneer group Maccabi Hatzair; deported to Theresienstadt on 13 July 1943 and to Auschwitz on 1 Oct. 1944; liberated from the Buchenwald satellite camp in Meuselwitz. After 1945 worked in the glass industry in Czechoslovakia; later emigrated to Israel and was a colonel in the Israeli army.

4 In a letter dated 14 March 1940, Richard Schindler had asked Robert Weinberger to postpone his aliyah in view of his responsibility for the group: JMP, DP 35.

5 Hebrew for 'company'; the different Zionist youth movements used various terms for groups of the same age. The term plugah was used by Maccabi Hatzair, the group to which Weinberger belonged.

The continuity of the group must be maintained. Of course. But can I be the right man for it, having been a member of MH[6] for less than a year and having worked for the group for only just over two months now? Imagine my situation: I come to Brünn in November for aliyah hofesh,[7] the promised aliyah does not come about, and while other haverim[8] do retraining courses, I make myself available to work for the group. I conduct a kvutzah,[9] I am involved in publishing cultural materials, I have been madrich[10] of a class at the YouAl school[11] for several days now.

I admit that I'm not bad at this work. But I only see this as a provisional arrangement, and I never abandon the thought of my aliyah as the next goal.

As I said, I have been working for the group for two months, and now I'm supposed to be indispensable? I can't believe that.

Perhaps I need not tell you in greater detail how much it would matter to me not to make aliyah together with the haverim of Baderech,[12] with whom I was in the Hachsharah programme. Georg Lustig[13] has also written to tell you that the plugah is not indifferent to the matter either, and I must also point out that Gert has said that the Bund[14] will release me to make aliyah, taking into account the interest of the plugah.

I don't want to make a final decision here. For the time being, I'm just asking you to reflect upon things with the haverim again, and I hope to discuss the matter thoroughly in Verměřovice with Gert, who is due to come for the opening of the camp.

As to the camp,[15] I want to tell you that I spoke with Fricek in Kojetín yesterday. He went to Verměřovice today to make arrangements for everything.

I have one request for you. there will be eleven haverot in the camp (in addition to the ten listed in the register, Lilly Hirsch[16] from Brünn). I would consider it quite important to have a madrichah[17] in the camp. A haverah who has already been in a Hachsharah programme could perform a very important function there, and I thought of Máňa Steinová, who would surely be well-suited to this position. I think that financial difficulties cannot be insurmountable, especially as, in my opinion, it is *absolutely neces-*

6 Abbreviation for Maccabi Hatzair; Hebrew for 'Young Maccabi'. The youth movement of the Zionist World Sports Organization Maccabi, established in 1929; it focused on Zionist ideals and sports, promoting aliyah and pioneering in Palestine.

7 Hebrew: here 'freedom'; the author is probably referring to his release from commitments to the movement in anticipation of making aliyah in the near future.

8 Plural of *haver*, Hebrew for 'friend'; in modern Hebrew also 'member', 'comrade'.

9 Hebrew for 'group', in the sense of Zionist movements being organized as a kind of socialist commune; here: group of Zionist pioneers who are preparing for aliyah.

10 Hebrew for 'instructor' or 'guide', here head of a Zionist youth group.

11 Youth Aliyah school.

12 Hebrew for 'on the way'; here the name of a group.

13 Possibly Jiří Lustig (1912–1944), student; worked as a farm hand, 1940; deported on 8 April 1942 to Theresienstadt and from there on 28 Sept. 1944 to Auschwitz, where he perished.

14 The General Jewish Bund was founded in Vilna (Vilnius) in 1897. The Bund was a secular socialist party that campaigned for equal rights for Jews and the recognition of Jewish nationality in the diaspora, and was opposed to Zionism.

15 This refers to a Hachsharah camp.

16 Lilly Hirschová (1921–1942); employed as a household help and on a Hachsharah programme in Myslibořice, 1940; deported on 5 Dec. 1941 from Brno to Theresienstadt and from there on 15 Jan. 1942 to Riga, where she perished.

17 Hebrew term for a female guide or peer group leader, here head of a Zionist youth group.

sary to have a haver who has Hachsharah experience and Zionist and Bund training in the camp. So you should definitely send Máňa or another suitable haverah out to me!

I hope everything else in the camp will run smoothly.

Warmest regards and greetings from

DOC. 275
In a letter dated 7 April 1940, Ilse Weber tells Gertrude von Löwenadler about the restrictions on her everyday life in Prague[1]

Letter from Ilse Weber, Prague, to Gertrude von Löwenadler,[2] dated 7 April 1940

Dear Aunt Gertrude,

Thank you *very much* for your kind letter of 28 March, which I received today. I think I will create all kinds of work for you once Lilian has left, but I am convinced that you will be happy to do it, because your boys were also in a foreign country and you were glad to hear about them. And *to me*, 'post from Sweden' means everything: joy, diversion, consolation; these letters must even replace the cinema, radio, and theatre for me. Maybe you still remember how fond I am of music. Music is just as essential in my life as food and drink. (By the way, do you still have your mandolin?) And now I can't go to a single concert, can't listen to the radio; my guitar is my only friend, and since I'm not often in the mood to sing, the guitar is not the right thing either. After 8 p.m. I am not allowed to go out in the street any more, and that is tough now that summer is here.[3] Willi[4] is at work all day, of course; a short walk after supper used to give us our only chance to chat with one another undisturbed. Now that chance is gone. We are left with little in which we can still take pleasure. Had I not left my old home, I would surely have died of despair, humiliation, and hopelessness. *Here*, however, things are still better. The city is incredibly beautiful, especially the neighbourhood where we live, known as the 'Vineyards'. Narrow lanes and alleys, with lovely villas and splendid gardens, which are terraced, as all the streets go uphill and downhill. Everything is quiet and peaceful – and all so curiously familiar, even if one is seeing it for the first time! *Home*. I sense again and again how deeply rooted I am here, contrary to all the assertions that we do not belong here. Mama[5] even yearns for the 'ancestral home',[6] although she experienced such incredibly tough and difficult times there. Just now she was weeping because she felt homesick.

1 The original is privately owned; copy in IfZ-Archives, F 601. Published in Weber, *Leid*, pp. 113–115. This document has been translated from German.

2 Gertrude von Löwenadler, mother of Ilse Weber's friend Lilian. After Lilian von Löwenadler's death, Gertrude took Ilse Weber's son Hanuš into her home in Sweden.

3 See Doc. 241, fn. 19, and Doc. 263, fn. 31.

4 Willi Weber.

5 Ilse Weber's mother Therese Herlinger, also Herlingerová, née Bellak (1866–1942), singer; married the widower Moritz Herlinger, 1895; worked in her husband's hotel; deported on 12 May 1942 to Theresienstadt and on 19 Oct. 1942 to Treblinka, where she was murdered.

6 Ilse Weber's grandfather called the Herlingers' house the 'ancestral home' (German: *Erbrichterei*, 'hereditary judge's estate') after it had come into the family's possession.

Yesterday, Sunday, I was at our cemetery to visit the grave of my mother-in-law,[7] who died here in January. I was very fond of her; she was a wonderful woman. She could only write and read Yiddish and had no formal education at all, but on the other hand, in terms of nobleness of heart, she was better than a queen. She had nine children, and five of them are fleeing; she could not survive the separation from them. Now she has it quite nice at the Olšan cemetery. And I adore cemeteries above everything. I walk past the graves of strangers and dream about the fates of those who lie in them. On top of one weather-beaten gravestone yesterday, a blackbird was singing so prettily; I had never heard the like. I went up close to the bird, but it paid no attention and kept on singing. The man lying in the grave had already been dead for thirty-five years and had a ludicrously Jewish name. It was so comforting that the blackbird nonetheless sang its song on top of his grave. It was only bad in the new section, where two, three, and often even *four* names with the same date of death appear on freshly dug mounds. There one needs no powers of imagination to guess the grievous fate.

Is Carl-Axel's wife nice? She is Hungarian, isn't she, and *they* suffer particularly from homesickness, of course. It will be hard for her when Acki is away from her for so long. But her boy looks as if he would not leave her much time for herself. He is quite handsome! Does he look like Acki or his wife? And how are Ocki's children? These questions seem so strange even to me, because I last saw the 'boys' when they were 9 and 13, respectively, and I still picture them in the same way.[8]

What is Acki's job? Is he doing well? You must be very happy and grateful for your children; just imagine how atrocious it is for Jewish mothers who have a husband and children so far away, usually without the slightest hope of seeing them again. Take my mum, for example: Ernst[9] is somewhere in Russian captivity, Oscar[10] is in Palestine, and *we* are supposed to go to San Domingo. And Mutzi,[11] who for the time being is still running the old people's home in Ostrau, has an affidavit for America. And what is to become of Mum is still a mystery. Yet her fate is the standard fate of Jewish mothers.

You write that you have copied that one particular set of baby's clothes so many times. What a pity that all the cute things I sent to Sweden when Alistair was born have been returned. They were quite adorable things, which my sister-in-law knitted. Now they are lying in my cupboard, and Alistair is outgrowing them.

Hanuš wrote to me on Saturday. I am – despite all my longing for him – so happy that he has had this marvellous year in Sweden, which was so extremely beneficial for his health and maybe also his character. He loves his 'brothers and sisters' very much,

7 Jetty Weber (1870–1940).

8 Carl-Axel and Oscar von Löwenadler, Gertrude von Löwenadler's sons.

9 Ilse Weber's brother Ernst Herlinger (1900–1995), distiller; worked in Berlin, 1921–1933; returned to Moravská Ostrava, 1933; briefly detained, 1939; fled to Poland; fought for the Czechoslovak army in exile, the French Foreign Legion, and the British armed forces; returned to Czechoslovakia after the war; emigrated to Britain in 1948.

10 Ilse Weber's brother Oscar Mareni, born Herlinger (1907–2011), bookkeeper; studied in Vienna; emigrated to Palestine in 1935; served in the Africa Corps of the Royal Air Force; worked in the office of the mayor of Jerusalem.

11 Ilse Weber's half-sister Bettina (Mutzi) Herlinger (b. 1892) was deported on 30 Sept. 1942 from Ostrava to Theresienstadt and on 26 Oct. 1942 to Auschwitz, where she is presumed to have perished.

but especially the little boy. You must tell me a great deal more about him, dear Aunt Gertrude, when you see him again upon departure. The only thing that distresses me is that Lilian, who is already short of money anyway, has more expenses because of him. I have no idea how we can ever repay her for this.

My little rascal[12] is just coming home for lunch. Since he is not allowed to attend kindergarten because he lacks an Aryan certificate and I have little time for him, he seeks his amusement outdoors. Luckily we live in a good area, and he only plays with nice children. He is naturally quite independent and grown-up of course, quite unlike 'Hannerle'. He is quite different in general. But humorous.

I've had a lovely hour chatting to you, and I want to post the letter by airmail this afternoon. You'll write to me soon to say how long it took to reach you, won't you? My warmest regards to you and also to your boys!

Yours,

DOC. 276

On 31 May 1940 the Brünn Gestapo informs the Reich Protector about the Jews in the internment camp in Eibenschitz[1]

Letter from the Gestapo, State Police head office in Brünn (B. No. II B 2–7465/40), p.p. signature illegible,[2] Mozartgasse 3, Brünn, to the Reich Protector in Bohemia and Moravia – Office for Moravia, dated 31 May 1940

Re: Jewish camp in Eibenschitz.[3]
Case file: letter dated 24 May 1940 – file ref. II – 4082.[4]
The Jewish camp in Eibenschitz located in a former Jewish leather factory, the Sinaiberger[5] firm, was placed under State Police surveillance during the occupation of Bohemia and Moravia. It is a camp for Jews, in which predominantly impoverished and ill Jews of both sexes are quartered, persons who would become a burden on the public. According to the ruling by the Central Office for Jewish Emigration in Prague, the Jewish camp in Eibenschitz, among others, is set to become a so-called infirmary camp.

Closure of the Jewish camp in Eibenschitz is not to be anticipated in the near future. The camp is under constant supervision by the State Police. No complaints have been made thus far.–

12 Ilse Weber's younger son, Tommy Weber.

1 MZAB, B 251/523/4082, box 46. This document has been translated from German.
2 From July 1939 to April 1941 the head of the Gestapo head office in Brünn was Günther Herrmann (1908–2004).
3 The refugee camp in Eibenschitz was set up in Oct. 1938. After the occupation of Czechoslovakia, it was converted into an internment camp for Jews. In March 1942 the Jews were deported from Eibenschitz to the assembly camp in Brünn.
4 The letter requests that the Gestapo head office in Brünn consider closing the camp: MZAB, B 251/523/4082, box 46.
5 The firm Max Sinaiberger und Söhne had ceased operations in 1930 on account of financial difficulties.

DOC. 277
On 4 June 1940 Alice Henzler asks to be recognized as a *Mischling*[1]

Transcript (II-3-2079/40), v. g. u.[2] Alice Henzler,[3] Prague, dated 4 June 1940

As summoned,[4] the divorcée Alice *Henzler*, née Eichner, resident at 7 In der Grube, Prague II, appears and states upon questioning:

I was born in Lazy on 22 September 1907, the daughter of Leo Eichner and his wife Erna, née Wechsberg. Although both of my parents were of the Jewish faith and I too was recorded in the Jewish civil registry, my upbringing was a purely German one. I was sent by my parents to a German school, and I attended the German Catholic convent school in Orlau and the German high school for girls, the German Association's Progressive Grammar School for Girls in Mährisch-Ostrau. As a result of this education, I have always considered my mindset to be completely German and have acted as such. Among other things, I was a member of the German Cultural Association[5] and the German Beskids Club.[6] During my marriage I was baptized in accordance with the Protestant rite on 30 May 1935. As a child, I had absolutely no idea that Jewish blood flowed through my veins, and I never had the slightest connection to the Jewish faith. As a result of my convent education, I became deeply religious in the Christian sense, so that the later receipt of baptism was merely an expression of my inner convictions. It was only a short time ago that I learned that my attachment to the German people and the Christian world view runs much deeper than a purely emotional feeling. When my mother noticed how deeply affected and unhappy I was to be now considered a Jew, she revealed to me that I am, in fact, the illegitimate daughter of the Aryan Dr Franz *Pokorny*. She had had an affair with him, she said. But in the civil registry I am recorded as the legitimate daughter of Leo Eichner. My mother made a binding statement on 13 February of this year in Prague, attested by the notary Dr Alois Frenzl, saying that I am the child of Dr Pokorny.

In reality, therefore, I am not a full Jew, but rather a Mischling of the first degree. I am no longer to be regarded as a member of the Jewish race within the meaning of the Regulations of 21 June 1939.[7] My wish and my every desire is to be allowed to feel once again that I am a German and to avow myself as such.

In May 1936 I married the ethnic German Ferdinand Henzler[8] in Mährisch-Ostrau, and before my marriage I left the Jewish religious community. My husband always worked prominently for the advancement of völkisch causes. Given his völkisch activ-

1 NAP, 101-653-6. This document has been translated from German.
2 German: 'read aloud, approved, signed'.
3 Alice Henzlerová, née Eichner (1907–1942), was deported in Sept. 1942 to Theresienstadt and one month later to Treblinka, where she was murdered.
4 On 12 May 1940 the Moravská Ostrava office of the Brünn Gestapo had asked the Prague Gestapo to investigate this case: NAP, 101-653-6.
5 The organization, established in 1919 as an association of Germans in Bohemia and Moravia, had aimed to strengthen Germandom in the Bohemian and Moravian areas of settlement.
6 The club, the name of which refers to the Beskid Mountains, was founded in 1893 and based in Moravská Ostrava. The club was German in character. It had around 3,500 members in 1926.
7 See Doc. 247.

ities and his position as the only German senior official at the mine in Mährisch-Ostrau, it became necessary to annul the marriage. The decision was decreed final by the German district court in Mährisch-Ostrau on 14 December 1939.[9]

In October 1939 I petitioned the Reich Chancellery to request that I be acknowledged as a Mischling of the first degree. I was thereby informed that, as a citizen of the Protectorate, I should approach the Reich Protector in Prague. I immediately sent a corresponding petition to the Reich Protector in Prague, and shortly thereafter I received three questionnaires from the Oberlandrat in Mährisch-Ostrau. I answered the questions and returned the forms on 23 April. To date I have received no further information from the Oberlandrat in Mährisch-Ostrau.[10]

DOC. 278

On 10 June 1940 the Oberlandrat in Jitschin sets out measures to evict Jews from their apartments and to concentrate them in separate residential areas[1]

Letter (Gesch. No. 5-8-0) from the Oberlandrat in Jitschin,[2] unsigned, to the Bezirkshauptmänner in the Oberlandratsbezirk Jitschin,[3] dated 10 June 1940 (copy)

Re: vacating Jew apartments

When inspecting Jewish businesses and Jewish apartments, I have established that the Jews, particularly in the towns in the district, usually have the largest and best apartments. By contrast, the non-Jewish population, including the German population in

8 Ferdinand Henzler (b. 1892), engineer; member of the Sudeten German Party (SdP) and the NSDAP; moved to Poland, where he worked in Katowice as the manager of the Satura firm, 1940; expelled from the Party by the NSDAP district court in Český Těšín in June 1943 on account of his marriage to a Jewish woman.

9 The decision is not included in the file.

10 At the foot of the petition is the following comment: 'The alleged progenitor of the Henzler woman, Dr Franz Pokorny, born 20 Nov. 1870 in Srch. near Pardubitz, formerly residing in Lazy, died in 1932 in a sanatorium in Prague. Hüssel, detective sergeant.' The petition was rejected on the grounds that there were fundamental suspicions concerning the information supplied: NAP, 101-653-6.

1 NAP, ÚŘP, AMV 114-184-5, box 182. This document has been translated from German.

2 Adolf Möller (b. 1901), administrative official; in the Prussian administrative service from 1925; joined the NSDAP and the SS in 1933; acting mayor of Beuel on the Rhine in 1933; political department head in the Cologne government, 1933–1935; Regierungsrat in 1935; in the Merseburg government, 1935–1937; in the Arnsberg government, 1937/38; head of the department for economics in the Carlsbad government from Oct. 1938 to March 1939; Oberlandrat of Jičín from March 1939.

3 Copies of the letter were sent for the information and attention of the Gestapo in Mladá Boleslav and Jičín, to the NSDAP Kreisleitungen in Prague and Hradec Králové, and to the heads of the local NSDAP branch in the Oberlandratsbezirk Jitschin. The officials were informed that: 'In the utilization of the living space being vacated, consideration is to be given primarily to people recognized as ethnic Germans. Oversized Jewish apartments can, if necessary, be made available to several ethnic German families or also, in exchange for smaller apartments, to German housing interests. If ethnic Germans do not or no longer come into consideration, I request that contact be made with the local Reich German offices for the purpose of housing their employees.'

particular, in many cases live in apartments that are far too small for their family circumstances, and are often in a disgraceful condition.

Considering this unfair distribution of living space, it is justified and necessary to merge the apartments of the Jews in order to free up living space for the non-Jewish population. Similarly, uncompromising measures must be taken to rid the Jews of any second apartments. This must be brought about by housing several Jewish families that previously had apartments of their own in a single apartment. In the process, vacant and otherwise unusable buildings – such as factory or agricultural premises, storage space, and the like – can also be used in place of apartments, in many cases. The legal basis for these measures is the National Defence Law.[4]

When Jewish families' apartments are merged, care must be taken, whenever possible, to ensure that Jewish families are housed in specific streets or buildings. This is intended to prevent the Jew apartments from being scattered around the entire urban area.

In terms of procedure, these measures are to be taken in such a way that the Bezirkshauptleute first contact the heads of the local Jewish religious communities and initially leave it to these heads to submit proposals of their own accord. If these proposals do not meet the requirements, additional conditions are to be imposed on the heads of the Jewish religious communities. It is self-evident that above all the best and finest apartments must be vacated. In addition, the heads of the Jewish religious communities are to be involved as appropriate, under official supervision, in the process of merging apartments.

Apartments that become free in this way are destined primarily for Germans in the area who have inadequate or poor-quality apartments. To this end, the Bezirkshauptleute must communicate with the relevant heads of the local NSDAP branches and with the German district or municipal representatives, so that the names of those interested in apartments can be indicated to them from the German side. Utilization of the vacated apartments may take place only with the written consent of the head of the relevant local NSDAP branch. Any living space that is not required by Germans is to be made available to the Czech population.

The measures set forth above are intended primarily for the towns in the district. However, an influx of Jews from these towns into the rural communities in connection with these measures must be avoided at all costs. Accordingly, if need be, the same measures must also be carried out in those rural communities in which apartments are inhabited by Jews, even if no Germans live in the place in question.

You are to report to me on the result of your actions by 30 June and, at the same time, to indicate how many formerly Jewish apartments it has been possible to vacate and to whom these apartments were assigned. I expect you to avoid being influenced by false sentimentality with regard to the measures I have ordered. Instead, keep in view the objective necessity of putting an end to the generally desperate housing situation.

4 The Czech National Defence Law, issued in May 1936, originally served to protect the country against the threat presented by National Socialist Germany. The category of 'nationally unreliable person' (*staatlich unzuverlässige Person*), which was introduced in this law, was often used against Sudeten Germans: *Sammlung der Gesetze und Verordnungen des Čecho-Slovakischen Staates*, 1936, no. 131/1936 Sb.

Addendum for Bezirkshauptmänner in Jungbunzlau and Jitschin:
Before carrying out the measures ordered, you are also to communicate with the Gestapo.[5]

DOC. 279

On 12 June 1940 the Jewish Religious Community of Německý Brod asks its members to donate textiles to the Jewish Hospital in Prague and announces bans on the use of certain facilities[1]

Circular (5/40) from the Jewish Religious Community of Německý Brod[2] (ref. no. 356/40), signed Willy Mahler,[3] dated 12 June 1940

We hereby inform you of the following:

Use of train station restaurants.
By order of the Reich Protector, Jews may use train station restaurants only if they are railway passengers.

Please note that checks will be carried out to make sure the train station restaurants are in fact frequented only by passengers.[4]

Charity campaign for the hospital under construction
Our Prague central office has called on us to collect various textiles to supply the Jewish hospital in Prague.

We are to provide pillows, pillowcases, sheets, towels, blankets, mattresses, etc. Notify us of the items you can spare and donate to this cause, and we will have them collected and provide you with written confirmation of collection.

We expect that this voluntary collection of textiles for our hospital and hospice will meet with your full understanding.

5 On 29 June 1940 the Reich Protector told the Oberlandrat in Jičín that he must first communicate with the Central Office for Jewish Emigration in Prague and should not take any similar action for the time being. On 4 July 1940, Möller informed the Senior Commander of the Security Police and the SD in Prague about the measures carried out thus far: NAP, ÚŘP, AMV 114-184-5, box 182.

1 JMP, DP 78 Pokorna. This document has been translated from Czech.
2 In 1945 Německý Brod was renamed Havlíčkův Brod after Karel Havlíček Borovský, one of the leading figures in the Czech nationalist movement in the nineteenth century.
3 Willy Otto Mahler (1909–1945), trader; worked in his parents' flour-trading business in Německý Brod; authorized representative of the Jewish Religious Community of Německý Brod; deported on 13 June 1942 to Theresienstadt, where he worked in the postal and financial administration; deported to Auschwitz in Sept. 1944; perished at Dachau concentration camp.
4 On 30 April 1940, the Czechoslovak Ministry of Transport announced that only Jews and non-Jews who were actually travelling were permitted to use train station restaurants: NAP, PMR 1590, box 588.

Use of the swimming pool in Německý Brod prohibited
The Německý Brod Municipal Office has informed us that, with immediate effect, Jews are prohibited from using the swimming pool in Německý Brod.

Please take heed of our communication.

On behalf of the
Jewish Religious Community of Něm[ecký] Brod
Willy Mahler
Current authorized representative.

DOC. 280

On 13 June 1940 the Oberlandrat in Olmütz asks the Reich Protector for a decision regarding anti-Jewish initiatives on the part of the Kreisleitung[1]

Letter (Gesch.-Z. Pol. IV/5) from the Oberlandrat in Olmütz, signed Molsen, to the Reich Protector of Bohemia and Moravia, Prague (received on 17 June 1940), via the Office for Moravia in Brünn (received on 15 June 1940), dated 13 June 1940[2]

Re: Jewish question
The Kreisleitung in Olmütz has presented me with the following proposals for further measures against the Jews:

(1) fixed shopping hours,
(2) the identification of Jews with armbands,
(3) the establishment of a ghetto.

I have informed the Kreisleiter that I cannot designate fixed shopping hours because it is impossible to monitor compliance with such measures owing to the limited capacity of the Gestapo and the police forces. The other measures suggested are beyond my jurisdiction. I therefore present them with the request that a decision be taken.[3]

1 NAP, ÚŘP, I-3b-5851, fol. 580. This document has been translated from German.
2 The original contains handwritten annotations.
3 On the basis of a decree issued by the regional authorities in Prague on 23 July 1940, the district authorities were responsible for regulating shopping hours. The proposed hours were from 10.30 a.m. to 1 p.m. and from 3 p.m. to 5 p.m. See NAP, ÚŘP, AMV 114-184-5. Jews in the Protectorate were not required to wear visible identification until this was made compulsory throughout the Reich in Sept. 1941: see Doc. 212. Theresienstadt, the first ghetto in the Protectorate, also serving as a concentration camp, was established in Nov. 1941.

DOC. 281

Die Judenfrage, 1 July 1940: article on the exclusion of the Jews in the Protectorate from society and economic life[1]

The Jewish question in the Protectorate of Bohemia and Moravia
The Jews in former Czechoslovakia
Before 1933 the number of Jews in what was then Czechoslovakia totalled around 200,000. Since that time their number has grown by around one third, owing to the massive influx of Jews from the Reich. Population shifts have occurred as a result of moving, relocation, and the emigration that followed the break-up of the Czechoslovakian entity. As a result, we can only estimate the number of Jews living in each territory of the former Czech lands, especially seeing as a considerable portion of the Jews by race displayed the well-known propensity for concealing their völkish attributes or their confession. Czech sources maintain that in the period from October 1938 to March 1939, 21,000 Jews emigrated from Czechoslovakia, which had been reduced in size following the Munich decrees.[2] There may still be over 150,000 Jews living within the borders of the present-day Protectorate of Bohemia and Moravia.[3]

The Jewish question in the Czech-dominated multi-ethnic state was a problem not so much of numbers as of *political, cultural, and economic magnitude*. Regardless of whether some of the Jews behaved like Zionists and others like assimilationists, they all enjoyed the goodwill of the Masaryk and Beneš regimes, which were infested with Freemasons. As late as 1938, there was hardly a Czech daily that was not under Jewish influence, at least indirectly. The situation was not much different in *book publishing* or the *film industry*. The failure of Czech foreign policy, which had been oriented towards the Western powers; the dissolution of the old non-state; and the establishment of the Protectorate of Bohemia and Moravia as part of the Greater German Reich brought about an entirely new state of affairs for the Czech people, also with regard to the Jewish question. The elimination of Jewry from the Reich inevitably disrupted the Jews' status in the reorganized Czechoslovak territory. But the insight of the Czechs themselves, following all the experiences and disappointments of the recent past, also led them to *abandon their previous forbearance towards the Jewish population*, which, as everywhere else, had never been particularly widespread among the masses of the Czech people, anyway.

1 *Die Judenfrage*, nos. 15/16, 1 July 1940, pp. 76–78. The journal, first published in 1937 by the Antisemitische Aktion (formerly the Institute for the Study of the Jewish Question), was originally called *Mitteilungen über die Judenfrage* (Announcements on the Jewish Question). From 1940 it was known as *Die Judenfrage* and from 1941 it was published, usually every two weeks, as *Die Judenfrage in Politik – Recht – Kultur und Wirtschaft* (The Jewish Question in Politics – Law – Culture and the Economy). Publication was abruptly discontinued in 1943. This document has been translated from German.

2 This refers to the Munich Agreement of 29 Sept. 1938: see Glossary.

3 According to a survey conducted by the Jewish Religious Community of Prague, in June 1942 there were 91,995 Jews still living in the Protectorate of Bohemia and Moravia on 30 June 1940. See Krejčová et al., *Židé v Protektorátu*, pp. 51–66, here p. 51.

Jewish attempts at camouflage in the Protectorate
The attitude of the Jews after the establishment of the Protectorate on 15 March 1939 was profoundly characteristic. At first, panic broke out among them. But when they noticed that there was no risk to life and limb, their insolence returned and they did all that they could to slip through the cracks, which were still quite large at first. The Aryanization measures, above all in commercial life, that were introduced by the authorities in response to the *antisemitic mood of the population*, which was growing daily, were not consistent or drastic enough. This meant that the Jews promptly adopted their usual *camouflage strategies*. Many a shop belonging to a Jew in possession of a baptismal certificate was declared to be Aryan. In other cases, the frontman ploy was adopted, leading a Czech newspaper (*Praszky list*, late March 1939) to write: 'The difference is, at most, that a paid Aryan helper stands behind the counter, that old Sarah at the till has vanished, and the Jewish boss does not enter the shop to collect the money until after closing time.'[4] At first, the old Jewish custom of marrying an Aryan woman and having the business transferred into her name was of course practised here as well.

In the Czech political offices and organizations, opinions about the measures to be employed against the Jews, and specifically about the *boundaries of the term 'Jew'*, were *by no means uniform*. Initially, in many cases, there was a tendency to view the problem too one-sidedly, namely, as an economic and denominational one, and to a lesser extent as a racial one.

The Reich Protector brings clarity
After the Czech debates went on for months without producing a clear result, the *Regulation of the Reich Protector of Bohemia and Moravia on Jewish Assets*, dated 21 June 1939,[5] brought about a gratifying clarity. Although the regulation primarily concerns economic questions, at the same time it states clearly for the first time who is to be considered a Jew in the Protectorate. The definition conforms to the *Nuremberg Laws* and forms the unalterable basis for all the directives and measures that will concern the Jewish population of the Czech ethnic area in the years to come. The regulation created a solid legal basis concerning the assets in Jewish hands: *Jewish-owned property* may only be transferred with special permission from the Reich Protector. Furthermore, Jews, Jewish businesses, and Jewish associations are prohibited from *purchasing plots of land, acquiring and creating business establishments*, and from being *involved in such created businesses. Precious metals* and *gemstones* in the possession of Jews must be registered with the National Bank. The provisions of the regulation are retroactive to 17 March 1939. *Transactions requiring approval* that were concluded in the meantime became inoperative unless subsequent approval had been granted. The publication of the regulation was met with a *lively response in the Czech press*: 'The law is thorough and clear and signifies the long-awaited economic resolution of the Jewish question in the Protectorate. The regulation has been met with a favourable response from the Czech public. Both in economic circles and in broad segments of the Czech population, the change in a state of affairs that has long been criticized by the people was perceived as a relief' (*Expres*, 22 June 1939).[6]

4 'Bráníme se potupě být spoluvinníky židovských rejdů' *Pražský list*, 30 March 1939, p. 1. The newspaper article, however, refers to an 'old Jewess' rather than 'old Sarah'.
5 See Doc. 247.

'Time really was high for the regulation on the cleansing of Jewish elements from economic life' (*Pražský list* from the same date).[7] The significance of the new arrangement is also underlined by the fact that, according to conservative estimates, the value of Jewish assets in the Protectorate amounted to 17 million korunas in 1939. In the meantime, several *implementing decrees* to this regulation have been issued in addition, notable elements of which include the requirement to deposit *securities* and – with a few specific exceptions – objects made of *precious metals* and *gemstones* in a personal security deposit account at a bank licensed to deal in foreign exchange;[8] and also the requirement for the official registration of *Jewish landed property*, rights to ownership over plots of land, *stocks*, *shares*, and *investments* of every sort. Finally, Jewish enterprises, including craftsmen's establishments, must register all the *domestic and foreign assets* in their possession as of 31 December 1939.[9]

Elimination from economic life
While all of these provisions, in connection with strict sanctions, primarily enable the control and oversight of the actual remaining material capacity of the Jews in the Protectorate, the goal of *excluding them from the economy* is being rigorously pursued through the *Regulation of the Reich Protector of 26 January* of this year and the corresponding supplementary decrees.[10] These make it possible to forbid Jewish enterprises *to conduct commercial operations* of any kind. In such cases, they are to be shut down and liquidated. As of 30 April 1940, Jews are completely excluded from the *textiles, footwear, and leather goods trades.* As of the same date they have also been forbidden to engage in *peddling* and all *itinerant trade.* The *film industry* has also been made free of Jews – a development of immense cultural significance. The implementing decree of 19 March of this year states succinctly that 'Jewish companies in the film industry are forbidden to engage in commercial activity of any kind … as of 15 April 1940'.[11] *Film production* and *film distribution* had already been almost completely Aryanized during the previous year. That also applied to the 92 per cent (!)[12] share of Jewish salaried employees in these film-industry sectors, which thereafter had openings for unemployed Czech officials. The heavily overstaffed film-distribution sector in the Protectorate (there were fifty-seven establishments in Prague – more than in the Old Reich – and eighteen of them were Jewish) was thus now greatly simplified and tightly consolidated.

6 'Protižidovská nařízení v našem hospodářství', *Expres*, 22 June 1939, p. 1.
7 'Židi nebudou vyhazovat naše lidi na dlažbu', *Pražský list*, 22 June 1939, p. 1.
8 According to the Fifth Implementing Decree to the Regulation of the Reich Protector of Bohemia and Moravia on Jewish Assets (2 March 1940), within two weeks the Jews had to put their shares and securities into a deposit account in their name at a bank licensed to deal in foreign exchange. See *Verordnungsblatt des Reichsprotektors*, 1940, no. 12, p. 81.
9 Fourth Implementing Decree to the Regulation of the Reich Protector of Bohemia and Moravia on Jewish Assets (7 Feb. 1940), ibid., no. 7, p. 45.
10 Third Implementing Decree to the Regulation of the Reich Protector of Bohemia and Moravia on Jewish Assets (26 Jan. 1940), ibid., no. 7, p. 44.
11 Second Implementing Decree to the Regulation of the Reich Protector of Bohemia and Moravia on the Exclusion of the Jews from the Economy of the Protectorate (19 March 1940), ibid., no. 14, p. 89.
12 Exclamation mark in the original.

Segregation in public life
The segregation of the Jews from the rest of the population in the public life of the Protectorate had already progressed quite far by the middle of last summer. The local administrative authorities adopted uncompromising measures along these lines. The *Prague* regulation was officially announced on 14 August.[13] The announcement made by the police chief of the Protectorate capital served as a model for the other local authorities in the country. The *Brünn* directives,[14] made public at the same time, to some extent went even further than the Prague directives, which specified that Jews are prohibited from going to a range of specified *public houses or inns*. These establishments are required to display a sign reading 'No admittance to Jews'. The same rule applies to other public houses under Aryan ownership, unless it is possible to restrict Jewish patrons to designated areas and to segregate them in a conspicuous and unmistakable manner. Jewish public houses must be marked with a conspicuously placed sign reading '*Jewish business*'. The arrangements for *public baths* are regulated in the same way. In the *healthcare system* and *in care for the poor* and *the elderly*, too, opportunities for contact between Aryans and Jews are to be prevented by means of suitable precautionary measures. Finally, Jewish shop owners in general were instructed to display signs reading 'Jewish shop'.

There was a report from Prague on *25 April* on the publication of an *additional government regulation* that further governs the legal status of Jews.[15] On the basis of this regulation, they are to be excluded from *public service*, *the liberal professions*, and *political life*. Dismissal from public service must take place within three months. Jews working in the liberal professions must be struck from the occupational registers. Two per cent of the Jewish *lawyers* and *doctors* who are currently licensed to practise can keep their licences should there be a need thereof.

DOC. 282

On 12 July 1940 Josef Lichtenstern informs Hehalutz in Geneva about how Jews in the Protectorate are being prepared for emigration[1]

Letter from Josef Lichtenstern,[2] c/o Hehalutz, Dlouhá 41/I, Prague I, to the Hehalutz Geneva Office, Geneva, 125 rue de Lausanne, dated 12 July 1940

Dear Haverim,[3]

I confirm receipt of your letter of 2 July[4] and hasten to reply. Please attribute the absence of our letters to the fact that we did not know for certain whether you would stay there in future or not.

Naturally, the present standstill in emigration creates major new problems for us. We have a well-led movement here that is strong in terms of organization. It is especially

13 See Doc. 259, fn. 4.
14 See Doc. 258.
15 The Government Regulation on the Legal Status of Jews in Public Life was issued on 4 July 1939 and came into force on 24 April 1940. See Doc. 257, fn. 7.

1 Lavon Institute, Labour Archives, III-37 A-l-36, fol. 112. This document has been translated from German.

interesting that the members of Hehalutz account for around 28 per cent of the overall membership of the Zionist Central Association. Nonetheless, at present our movement still lacks internal cohesion and the desired level of culture. Our occupational restructuring work is organized as follows. We have placed groups of ten to twenty-five persons with individual farmers who have fairly large acreage. Apart from considering membership in the various movements, great attention has been paid to the composition of the groups. Nonetheless, even now there are frequent social conflicts within the groups, so that we are often forced to change the arrangements. In this way, we have placed around 720 persons in 56 groups. Over the course of the next week, we will take over a so-called training farm. This is a large, extremely well-managed estate on which all the previously employed workers will continue to have work. We will integrate an additional 100 workers, who will live in barracks and must also work in the fields. These 100 persons can be replaced by a new group after three months. The German authorities have made this estate available to us for retraining purposes. We hope that this new endeavour will succeed and offer us some certainty regarding our retraining work for the winter. We expect that around 1,200 persons will be assigned to the training farm during harvest time.

For our intensive cultural training activities, however, we lack suitably trained staff and also, particularly, the active contact with the local population. Unfortunately, nothing can be changed in this regard at the moment.

I look forward to receiving your news again and extend my warm regards

P.S. The applicant for student emigration, Jakob Wurzel,[5] is not from the Shomer youth movement, but rather from the Blue-White youth movement.[6] I think that this information is important for you, so that you know how the allocation of possible certificates should be made.

2 Josef (Sepl) Lichtenstern (1915–1945), civil servant; member of the German-speaking Zionist movement Tchelet Lavan; after its merger with the Czech El Al in Feb. 1939, worked in the joint leadership; sought to emigrate that May; deported to Theresienstadt on 13 July 1943 and to Auschwitz on 18 Dec. 1943, involved in setting up the so-called children's barracks in Birkenau; deported to Schwarzheide/Brandenburg on 1 July 1944; perished during a death march.

3 Plural of *haver*, Hebrew for 'friend'; in modern Hebrew also 'member' or 'comrade'.

4 M. Orenstein, Hehalutz, Geneva Office, to the Department for Vocational Training and Preparation for Emigration to Palestine in Prague, 2 July 1941; Lavon Institute, Labour Archives, III-37 A-l-36, fol. 110.

5 Jakob (Jacques) Wurzel (1919–1945), state employee and electrical engineer; active member of the Zionist movement; member of Tchelet Lavan; attempted to emigrate in 1939; worked as a teacher from 1940, firstly in Prague, then in Moravská Ostrava; deported to Theresienstadt on 29 March 1942, where he organized Hebrew courses; deported to Auschwitz on 28 Sept. 1944; liberated in Augsburg in 1945; married in Prague in Sept. 1945, and died shortly afterwards of tuberculosis.

6 Shomer: abbreviation of Hashomer Hatzair. The Blue-White movement was the largest Zionist youth movement in the Weimar Republic and the precursor to El Al.

DOC. 283
Jüdisches Nachrichtenblatt, 26 July 1940: Oskar Singer writes about the significance of the Central Office for Jewish Emigration in Prague[1]

A year of reorganization and emigration
July 1939 – July 1940
O. S.[2] Only in retrospect do we have the opportunity for an objective and fair appraisal of events. At the moment they occur we may certainly adopt a certain stance, but such reactions are always governed by emotion, and an assessment at that stage has all the disadvantages of haste. Only gradually, once emotion gives way to reason, does logic come into its own. It is from this perspective that we must now examine, now that a year has passed, an event of profound significance for the Jews in Bohemia and Moravia, namely the creation of the 'Central Office for Jewish Emigration in Prague'.[3]

We wish to record only plain facts, for it is only in this way that we can obtain a clear picture. To obtain an accurate impression of the tasks of the Central Office for Jewish Emigration, we must look back at the status of the Jews before the creation of the Central Office.

In psychological terms, the Jews in Bohemia and Moravia were completely unprepared for what happened on 15 March 1939.[4] When it came to misjudging the political situation, the Jews were certainly in the same boat as many others, but before the Protectorate was established the *majority* of the Jews did not consider the ensuing ramifications. The desire to emigrate, the awareness of fighting a losing battle, was not yet widespread within Jewry. Even so, a great many Jews sought to leave the country, and today one can say that the Czech authorities placed in charge of overseeing Jewish emigration tried very hard to cope with the unprecedented task. Even at this stage of historical development, some of the Jews in Bohemia and Moravia were able to draw conclusions from the altered situation and leave the country.

However, the date 15 March signifies a turning point not only for world politics but also for the Jews. It was on this day that they first came face to face with intransigency with respect to Jewish questions. Until then, the Jew in Bohemia and Moravia was acquainted with these questions only as more or less emotionally engaged observers of a gripping drama. When the German troops invaded, the fiction abruptly became reality. A fully fledged shock was inevitable. The Jews were not sufficiently prepared to calmly take in this turn of events.

1 *Jüdisches Nachrichtenblatt* (Prague edition), 26 July 1940, p. 3. This document has been translated from German.

2 Dr Oskar Singer (1893–1944), lawyer, journalist, and writer; lawyer in Neu-Oderberg and co-owner of a forwarding company; moved to Prague in 1933; wrote for the Jewish journal *Selbstwehr*; editor-in-chief of the *Jüdisches Nachrichtenblatt* in Prague, 1939–1941; deported to the Lodz ghetto on 26 Oct. 1941, where he worked in the archives of the Jewish Elder and co-authored the ghetto chronicle; deported to Dachau via Auschwitz and Sachsenhausen in August 1944; perished at the Dachau satellite camp in Kaufering.

3 See Doc. 252.

4 This was the day that the Wehrmacht invaded Prague; the Protectorate of Bohemia and Moravia was proclaimed the following day. See also Docs. 235 and 236.

Jewish life in this area had always been structured quite loosely. There were religious communities all over the country, which had a sort of confederation in the form of the 'Supreme Council', but nonetheless were essentially autonomous. There was the Zionist Organization, which was certainly more tightly organized, but encompassed only a fraction of the Jews. And there were a great many large and small Jewish associations – all of this without any uniform leadership. The religious communities confined themselves to the fostering of religious life and, within their modest scope, dealt with local welfare duties. In terms of politics and world view, fragmentation and indifference prevailed among the Jews.

The Prague Community immediately recognized the danger of the situation. First, it attempted to combine forces in order to cope with the problems of social welfare and emigration, which had now become pressing for the community at large. The utter lack of authority, however, came home to roost. The inevitable consequences in the context of the authoritarian state require no further explanation. The available institutions proved to be too weak. They were only able, at a pinch, to provide the outline of a new structure. Added to that was the fact that the fledgling Jewish leadership suddenly saw itself almost completely cut off from relief organizations in foreign countries. With the heightened tension in world politics, there was an increasing danger that Jewish self-help would fail. There was still peace, but the Jews had to worry about what was to come.

Under these circumstances, the question of whether to emigrate still seemed to be marginal to discussion. A private matter, a matter of opinion, so to speak. Vague notions prevailed with regard to the attitude of the German authorities towards the heightened Jewish problem in this territory, and one nurtured vague, false hopes for a regional solution. The lack of targeted press coverage made the situation all the more complicated. During this stage, at the end of July, the 'Central Office for Jewish Emigration in Prague' was created. At a single stroke, the overall situation became clear. The question of the emigration of all Jews immediately moved to the forefront, now no longer as a matter for debate but rather as a categorical imperative. A categoric solution was formulated and elevated to the status of the only applicable maxim. Soon afterwards a newspaper was launched, tasked with effectively conveying to the Jewish masses the idea of obligatory emigration and of explaining all the individual problems associated with it. The general emigration requirement became common knowledge all the more rapidly once the Jewish regulations that then ensued provided the corresponding impetus. With the exclusion of Jews from economic life, the social welfare tasks of the community soared to unanticipated levels.

The Central Office alone was authorized and able to create the preconditions for dealing with these tasks. A decisive step, therefore, was the centralization of operations and the authoritative restructuring of the Jewish Religious Community of Prague. This community was reorganized in line with its area of responsibility, which was expanding daily. It became a model for all the other communities and soon functioned as an advisory body. Now, with the support and under the supervision of the Central Office, the crucial assistance of the Jewish relief organizations in neutral foreign countries could be operationalized. The provision of cash, foreign currency, tickets (boat tickets for departures overseas), employment contracts; the establishment of contact with overseas relatives of the emigrant; the regulation of communication by telegram – methods were now established to deal with these and many other matters. Overcoming the enormous problem of social relief work was the next aspect of this huge complex of emigration issues. Things started to develop rapidly. The assignment of additional tasks and thus even greater responsibility to the Religious Community of Prague was merely a logical progression of events. This came about through extending the powers of the 'Central Office for Jewish Emigration'.

The significance of the Regulation of the Reich Protector of 5 March 1940 on the Supervision of the Jews and Jewish Organizations culminated in the Central Office *acquiring the right to supervise all Jews in Bohemia and Moravia* and in the Religious Community of Prague being assigned the right to issue directives. Since this regulation, therefore, the Central Office has been the *sole* competent authority for all Jewish affairs.[5] To a certain extent, this legal position has resulted in new organizational measures for all the communities; in other cases, measures that already existed in practice have been legalized.

The Jewish Religious Community of Prague has thus obtained, by decree, an administration to which all the communities in the countryside are also subordinated, on the basis of this authority to issue directives. The authority exerted by the Religious Community of Prague derives from the power of the Central Office. The existence of this authority is something new in the history of diaspora Jewry. It is the profound wish and firm hope of the administration that it shall operate only for the good of the Community.

DOC. 284

On 8 August 1940 the SD Main District Prague reports on the banning of National Solidarity activities and on the friendliness towards Jews in Pilsen[1]

Daily report from the Security Service (SD) of the Reichsführer SS, SD Main District Prague, no. 182/40, p.p. signed Wolf,[2] Prague, dated 8 August 1940

Daily report
(Strictly confidential, for official use by the individual recipient only)
I. General situation and mood.
The vast majority of the Czech population reacted somewhat indifferently to the banning of the activities of the Greater Prague District of *National Solidarity*.[3] It only caused

5 Under § 2 of the Regulation of the Reich Protector of Bohemia and Moravia on the Supervision of the Jews and Jewish Organizations (5 March 1940), all Jewish organizations, foundations, and funds – with the exception of the legal entities specified in § 7 of the Regulation of the Reich Protector of Bohemia and Moravia on Jewish Assets (21 June 1939) – were overseen by the Central Office for Jewish Emigration in Prague. See *Verordnungsblatt des Reichsprotektors*, no. 11, 1940, pp. 77–79.

1 NAP, ÚŘP, AMV 114-312/1–3. This document has been translated from German.
2 Martin Wolf (b. 1908); trained as a teacher; joined the NSDAP and the SS in 1933; head of Dept. II 121 (far left-wing movement) at the SD Main Office; SS-Sturmbannführer in the SD Main District Prague from 1939; pronounced dead by Rendsburg Local Court in 1952.
3 Národní souručenství (National Solidarity Party). On 7 August 1940 a notice was published in several Prague newspapers ordering the closure of the Prague district branch of Národní souručenství because of anti-German activities and the arrest of Kreisleiter Dr Josef Nestával (1900–1976).

a major stir among the intelligentsia and the NS [National Solidarity] officials themselves. In these circles, the ban was portrayed as the latest evidence of German arbitrariness and as the start of the complete dissolution of NS. In some instances, intellectuals commented that if NS were to cease to exist, they would simply join Vlajka to demonstrate Czech 'indomitability' to the Germans.

Naturally, Vlajka and other right-wing opposition groups welcomed the news of this measure. To some extent, one sees a great opportunity as having now arrived. Rys[4] is now glad to have already broken off the negotiations with NS some time ago. As a direct consequence of the Gestapo measure, a decline in the wearing of NS badges could be observed throughout Prague.

But also outside these right-leaning opposition groups, the announcement of the banning of the activities of the Greater Prague NS gave rise to heightened criticism of National Solidarity more generally. It is consistently reported from Prague and Budweis that the action taken against NS has been met with satisfaction by Czech workers, due to their dissatisfaction with NS, which has allegedly accomplished nothing in terms of social policy. In addition, it is frequently pointed out that the NS administrative offices have generated almost no activity whatsoever for quite some time now, and the influence of NS on the Czech public has invariably declined. When the banning of National Solidarity activities was announced, the editorial staff of several large Prague dailies (*Večer*, *Národní práce*, *Venkov*, *A Zet*, and the smallholders' newspaper *Lidový deník*) immediately filed an application for permission to omit the phrase 'Newspaper of National Solidarity' from their mastheads and replace it with a different one.[5] In addition, a similar decision was made by the administrative board of *Národní politika*.[6] On the part of the government, efforts are being made to slow these developments. Governor Eliáš told two editors, who had claimed that NS would never bring about a real Czech Volksgemeinschaft and gain the Germans' trust, that they were mistaken. With regard to dropping the subtitle 'Newspaper of NS', Eliáš maintained that the banning of the activities of the NS district of Greater Prague was only a minor episode, and that he even trusted that the activity ban for the NS district of Olmütz would be rescinded in the near future. It is noteworthy that the editor-in-chief of the *A-Zet*[7] justifies his application for the removal of the subtitle 'Newspaper of NS' in the following terms: 'The newspaper represents the position adopted by the state president and therefore cannot serve an institution that has flouted this.'

4 Jan (also Josef) Rys-Rozsévač (1901–1946), journalist and politician; joined the fascist group Vlajka in 1936. Under his leadership, Vlajka merged with numerous affiliated groups in the Protectorate on 11 Oct. 1939 to form the Czech National Socialist Camp – Vlajka. After Vlajka was disbanded in 1942, he was deported to Dachau as an 'honour prisoner' (*Ehrenhaftling*). In 1945 he was extradited to Prague, where he was hanged the following year.

5 From 8 August 1940 most Czech newspapers were published without the subtitle, which had been introduced on 31 March 1939 on the orders of Národní souručenství.

6 Conservative Czech daily newspaper published from 1883 to 1945.

7 This presumably refers to Dr Jaroslav Křemen. The newspaper *A-Zet*, which appeared twice daily, was first published in 1928. It had a circulation of approximately 100,000 in 1944.

II. Individual events

For the month of September, the NS association 'Joy of Life'[8] in *Pilsen* is arranging a festival featuring traditional dress. Participants will include performers in traditional costume from the Chod region,[9] Hanna,[10] the Ostrau region, and the Strakonitz region.

The *Pilsen* municipal authority has appointed Dr Pilz,[11] who was arrested on 1 September 1939 and was recently released from a concentration camp, as chairman of the municipal welfare office. Pilz was widely known as a member of the Czechoslovak Legion, a Social Democratic official, and a dangerous Marxist.

A Czech landlord (a former member of the Czechoslovak Legion) in *Pilsen* recently gave notice to three Czech families, alleging that they had had frequent disputes. The real reason, however, was obviously the pro-German stance of these three families.

From Pilsen comes a report that, among the Czech population, not only is there no discernible opposition to the Jews, but there is a constantly growing pro-Jewish sentiment. For example, the park[12] designated for the Jews is now frequented by a great number of Czechs, in contrast to previous times. These Czechs frequently converse with the Jews in a lively and genial manner.

The *Moldautein* garrison of government troops deployed seventy-three men to assist with the harvest in the districts of Moldautein and Pisek.

On 7 August *Olmütz* city council received an anonymous malicious postcard from Prague, which showered abuse on Germandom because of the heightened measures against the Jews.

The Chodové pilgrimage scheduled for 11 August in *Taus* (Oberlandratsbezirk Klattau) was not authorized by the Oberlandrat.

In *Pschestitz* (Oberlandratsbezirk Klattau), when new street signs were put up, the old street signs were taken away by a vintage steamroller decorated with flowers. Apparently the Czech population greeted the old signs with shouts of 'Zdar' in many cases.[13]

In *Bresnitz* (Oberlandratsbezirk Klattau), Czech workers from the Old Reich who were on holiday spoke very favourably about the labour conditions in the Old Reich and said that they were not thinking of taking up jobs in their homeland again. In Bresnitz workers now greet people solely with the Hitler salute.

8 The association Radost ze života, which was affiliated with Národní souručenství, published the magazine *Pestrý týden* and had taken up the cause of social equality.

9 The region around the city of Domažlice in south-western Bohemia, the inhabitants of which were known as the Chodové.

10 Hanakia; region in Moravia, situated between the cities of Olomouc, Kroměříž, Prostějov, and Vyškov.

11 Dr Josef Pilz (1897–1970/1971), lawyer and Social Democratic politician; member of the Czechoslovak Legion in Russia, 1917–1920; member of parliament and senator in Czechoslovakia; from 1938 worked for Pilsen municipal authority; director of the Western Bohemian Museum in Pilsen after 1945.

12 According to an announcement made by the police headquarters in Pilsen on 30 April 1941, the only park Jews were permitted to frequent was Obcizna (now Štruncovy sady). See Ivan Martinovský et al., *Dějiny Plzně v datech od prvních stop osídlení až po současnost* (Prague: Lidové noviny, 2004), p. 334.

13 Czech for 'success', 'hail'.

In *Wsetin* and *Wal. Meseritsch* (Oberlandratsbezirk Mährisch-Ostrau), there has been a significant shortage of meat, potatoes, and milk for several days now. In Pardubitz too, potatoes have not been available since early this week, which a whispering campaign mistakenly blames on attempts by the German Wehrmacht to buy up the supplies.

DOC. 285

On 17 August 1940 Norbert Meissner from Triesch writes to his son Franz to describe how the family is pulling together[1]

Handwritten letter from Norbert Meissner,[2] Triesch, to Franz Meissner,[3] Denmark, dated 17 August 1940

81st letter
My dearest child! There is no need to further describe how pleasant it is to receive two letters from you this week, namely, those dated 2 and 8 August. However, we find your reproach unjust because, as you can see from the numbering, two more letters dated 5 and 8 August are on their way. Surely you will have received one of them in the meantime. After what you told us, we have certainly not been writing with the same frequency, as we always had to presume that our notes would no longer get to you, given that it takes 8–12 days for a letter to arrive. But you can see that we have even taken this risk to keep you from worrying. Besides, you know how one now waits for news in particular, whether from you, Ossi, or Otto,[4] or from whomever, in order to hear something definitive. For example, Ossi wrote to us on the 4th to say that the first group, which you are also in, will depart in four days' time, even giving the location of the final destination. After that, news arrived from you about the delays concerning the Swedish visa and 100 per cent certainty and again today a further postponement of three weeks owing to Turkish reluctance. According to other accounts, the departure has been postponed indefinitely. That strengthens our firm resolve to write diligently once again, to keep you informed. Above all, I want to tell you that our dear Leo[5] arrived unexpectedly yesterday

1 USHMM, Acc. 2 004 692.1, Frank Meissner papers, letter no. 81. This document has been translated from German.
2 Norbert Meissner (1884–1944), factory owner; lived in Vienna until 1903; owned engineering works in Třešť (Triesch); head of the Jewish Religious Community in Třešť, 1925–1930; employed from 1939 by the Jewish Religious Community in Jihlava, where he was in charge of Třešť; deported on 18 May 1942 from Třebíč to Theresienstadt and in Oct. 1944 to Auschwitz, where he was murdered.
3 Dr Franz, also Frank, Meissner (1923–1990), agricultural economist; active in the Zionist youth movement from 1937; emigrated to Denmark in Oct. 1939; fled from the Gestapo to Sweden in late 1943; reached Britain in Sept. 1944; returned briefly to Jihlava in 1946; emigrated to the USA in 1949; held various posts (including a lectureship) at San José State University and at the UN in Argentina.
4 Presumably the twins Otto and Julius Grünberger, cousins of Franz Meissner. Otto Grünberger (1900–1945), pharmacist; deported to Theresienstadt in 1943; perished in Dachau on 9 May 1945. Julius Grünberger (1900–1944), engineer; deported on 24 Nov. 1941 from Prague to Theresienstadt, where he was a member of the Council of Elders; subsequently deported to Auschwitz.
5 Leo Meissner (1920–1944), mechanical engineer; son of Norbert and Charlotte Meissner; deported to Theresienstadt on 18 May 1942 and in Oct. 1944 to Auschwitz, where he was murdered.

for a few days, as he, Sonja,[6] Erne[7] and Gustl Drechsler,[8] and the two Brünners[9] were put on leave by the landowner. The corn, barley, and wheat have been reaped, and threshed, and some has even been sold. On the other hand, the oats are still stacked in piles outside, and are even still standing in some fields, and cannot be brought in on account of the daily rainfall. There is not enough for thirteen people to do on the farm, which is why the leave came about. If good weather comes soon, they will be summoned by telegram. Of further interest to you are the arrangements made to house Uncle Hilbert's[10] family here in the front apartment, because he also expects to have to give up his apartment on account of the ongoing sales negotiations for the factory. It is still quite uncertain when exactly the relocation is to take place, but the apartment has to be brought into good condition while the weather is still halfway summery. The rear apartment is left for us as a furniture warehouse, so to speak, as we are moving everything from the front to the back, with the exception of a three-piece suite. Yesterday we had the dining room and kitchen painted, and today we are doing a thorough house clean so that we can set up the furniture tomorrow afternoon. You can imagine what a mess we are living in. And as a result, we have moved Grandfather to the Grünbergers and Leo to Höditz. As soon as we have moved, Uncle will begin the building alterations. The hall will be made into a kitchen with a stove for cooking and heating. As the sketch shows, the built-in hall cupboard will be partly dismantled – thick lines mean it stays, crossed out means it will be removed. *Sketch crossed out*,[11] it's better if the part near the window stays, also the complete upper parts with the drawers, and the stove is installed in the middle, and the plain part by the entrance. The large room will be used as a living room, combined with the study, and the little room will be made into the bedroom. All the other furniture will be stored. I hope that being together will be good for us. From the next issue of the *Jüdische Nachrichten* you will learn that Peter can no longer go to school.[12] Yesterday I was with Dr Singer[13] in Telč to discuss arrangements with the gentlemen there, so that together we can secure one or two teachers for our youngsters; naturally we must wait for directives and guidelines from Prague. At any rate, this is another major concern for us and especially for parents with school-age children. Since I've mentioned the newspaper, are you receiving it weekly? Please write about this and

6 Sofie (Sonja) Meissner, née Pick (1922–1944), housekeeper and midwife; deported together with her husband, Leo Meissner, on 18 May 1942 to Theresienstadt and on 16 Oct. 1944 to Auschwitz, where she was murdered.

7 Fritz, also Bedřich, Drechsler (b. 1915); studied medicine; after 1939 his family moved from Jihlava to Prague; deported to the Lodz ghetto on 16 Oct. 1941, where he worked as an auxiliary physician; liberated from Dachau.

8 Gustav Drechsler (1918–1944), brother of Fritz Drechsler; after 1939 he moved with the family from Jihlava to Prague; deported from there on 16 Oct. 1941 to the Lodz ghetto, where he perished.

9 Moses Brünner (b. 1869); lived with his brother Gustav in Jihlava and later moved to Vienna; subsequent fate unknown. Gustav Brünner (1866–1942); owner of a business in Jihlava; forced to move to Třešť in early 1941 and then to Třebič, from where he was deported to Theresienstadt on 18 May 1942; he perished there shortly afterwards.

10 Hilbert Grünberger (1896–1945), factory owner; held shares in his brother-in-law Norbert Meissner's business and was employed there as a labourer following the German invasion in March 1939; deported to Theresienstadt on 18 May 1942 and to Auschwitz on 1 Oct. 1944; murdered in Dachau on 6 Feb. 1945.

11 Abrupt start to sentence as in the original. The sketch drawn in this section was crossed out.

also tell me whether Mrs Nielsen received the cushion. Your letter of 8 August gave us great pleasure because of the excursion you described to us so beautifully, with everything associated with it, and we hope to hear further good news.

Regards to the Nielsen family.

Love and kisses, your father, Norbert.

Mum is very busy helping and apologizes for not writing herself.[14] Grandfather and Leo are not here.

DOC. 286

On 17 August 1940 State Secretary Karl Hermann Frank rejects the proposal from several Oberlandräte to ghettoize Jews in the Protectorate and to require them to wear visible identification[1]

Letter from the Reich Protector of Bohemia and Moravia (BdS. II – 1305-6/40), p.p. signed Frank, Prague, to all Oberlandräte, for the information of a) Departments I (Group 3) and II, b) the Office for Moravia (received on 19 August 1940), c) the Party liaison office, d) the Gestapo head offices in Prague and Brünn, and e) the Central Office for Jewish Emigration, dated 17 August 1940[2]

Recently, in a number of districts, various local authorities have issued directives that partly worked towards restricting the Jews' freedom of movement, and partly pursued housing policy objectives relating to the Jewish problem.[3] Because such directives often take only local interests into account and are not geared towards the concerns of the rest of the territory of the Reich, it is not only the coherence of such measures that suffers. It is instead often the case that they involve increased expenditure to look after the Jews concerned and thus place a heavy burden on the resources of the emigration fund.

I again urge that anti-Jewish measures of fundamental significance be taken only after prior consultation with the Senior Commander of the Security Police (Central Office for Jewish Emigration). Centralized handling of all Jewish questions is also necessary in order to monitor the directives issued. As the German police in the Protectorate lack sufficient personnel under the given conditions, the monitoring of such Jewish measures must be left to the Protectorate police. This fact also speaks in favour of the centralized regulation of such directives.

12 On 7 August 1940 the Protectorate government ordered that Jewish children be excluded from state schools from the beginning of the next school year. See Friedmann, 'Rechtsstellung', pp. 261–262.

13 Presumably Dr Alfred Singer (1897–1944), physician; Red Cross chairman in Třešť; barred from his profession in 1939; forced to move to Prague with his family in 1942; deported on 22 Dec. 1942 to Theresienstadt, where he worked in the Jewish self-administration; deported on 23 Oct. 1944 to Auschwitz, where he perished.

14 Charlotte, also Karolina, Meissner, née Grünberger (1894–1944), local government employee and accountant; married Norbert Meissner in 1918; deported to Theresienstadt on 18 May 1942 and on 16 Oct. 1944 to Auschwitz, where she was murdered.

1 MZAB, B 251/523/4082, box 46. This document has been translated from German.

2 The original contains handwritten underlining and official stamps.

3 See Docs. 258 and 278.

For guidance, I hereby inform you that, at my suggestion, the following measures to restrict the Jews' freedom of movement have been mandated by the Protectorate government or are in the process of being mandated:

(1) a ban on visiting various public parks,[4]

(2) a ban on attending sporting events,[5]

(3) a ban on the use of dining cars and sleeping carriages,[6]

(4) a regulation on the carriage of Jews in trams,[7]

(5) a regulation on shopping hours,[8]

(6) the closure of non-segregated inns (separate dining sections for Jews).[9]

I will make known, in each case, the contents of the directives issued by the Protectorate government. Absolutely no exceptions are to be issued that exempt individuals from compliance with such directives.

Neither the visible identification of Jews with armbands or badges, a topic that was raised for discussion by individual Oberlandräte, nor the establishment of ghettos or the grouping together [of Jews] in specific apartments or residential neighbourhoods can be considered at present.

DOC. 287

On 30 August 1940 Holleschau town council orders the introduction of compulsory labour and other anti-Jewish measures[1]

Letter from the Oberlandrat (No. Pol-), signed Bayerl,[2] Zlin, to the Reich Protector of Bohemia and Moravia, Prague (received on 3 September 1940), via the Office for Moravia, Brünn (received on 31 August 1940), dated 30 August 1940[3]

Re: anti-Jewish measures in Holleschau.
Reference: Decree of 10 July 1940, no. 3 b – 5498.[4]
Holleschau town council has resolved:

1) To ask the Jewish Religious Community to remove the fence around the synagogue for use as scrap iron.

4 A decree was issued on 17 May 1940 prohibiting Jews from entering all public parks. See Friedmann, 'Rechtsstellung', p. 246.

5 The exclusion of Jews from Aryan associations and the ban on attendance at sporting events had been announced as early as 1939: ibid.

6 On 7 August 1940 the Central Office for Jewish Emigration issued an order prohibiting Jews from using sleeping carriages and dining cars on the Reich and Protectorate Railways: ibid., p. 247.

7 On 12 Sept. 1940 the police headquarters in Prague issued a directive stating that Jews could only travel in the rear carriage of trams. If the tram had no rear carriage, Jews were not allowed to travel: ibid.

8 In a circular decree issued on 23 July 1940, the regional authority in Prague designated the following fixed shopping hours for Jews: 10:30 a.m.–1 p.m. and 3 p.m.–5 p.m. See NAP, 114-184-5, fol. 36r–v.

9 See also Doc. 258.

1 NAP, ÚŘP, I-3b 5850, copy in USHMM, RG-48.005M, reel 4. This document has been translated from German.

2) To provide the municipal swimming pool with a sign reading 'Jews prohibited'.

The instructions were also enforced at the same time. With regard to compulsory labour for the Jews in Holleschau, the town council has decided to ask the district authority for permission to introduce compulsory labour for Jews and to prohibit Jews from keeping Aryan maids. However, because this concerns normative regulations regarding the Jews' circumstances, the district authority in Holleschau is to refer the matter to the regional authority in Brünn for assessment.

For the time being, I have refrained from taking action against the town of Holleschau, which is attempting on its own initiative to resolve fundamental questions regarding the Jewry in public life. In the interest of a uniform resolution of such questions throughout the Protectorate, I would ask that instructions be issued stating that local authorities in the Protectorate are not authorized to deal with such matters.[5]

DOC. 288
On 4 October 1940 Alžběta Salačová in Prague receives an anonymous antisemitic letter[1]

Anonymous letter sent by women from Mšeno to Alžběta Salačová,[2] Prague, dated 4 October 1940[3]

You stinking Jewesses!

You come here to steal our meat, eggs, fruit, and poultry. We won't put up with that!![4]

You stay in a hotel that is no place for Jews. If you turn up here again, we'll call the Gestapo, who'll chuck you out of the Aryan hotel and then we'll get the Gestapo in Prague to come and search your homes.

This is your last warning!!

From the poor women of Mšeno[5] who you're robbing.

2 Dr Josef Bayerl (b. 1894), administrative official; worked in the Bavarian administration from 1922; Regierungsrat, 1923; employed at the Bavarian State Ministry of the Interior, 1925; district official in Hammelburg, 1926–1933; worked for the district office in Freising, 1933–1938; joined the NSDAP in 1937; Landrat in Parsberg, 1938; Kreishauptmann in Brünn from April to Nov. 1939; Oberlandrat in Prostějov from Nov. 1939, later in Zlín, and from 1942 in Brünn.

3 The original contains handwritten marks and annotations.

4 In the letter dated 10 July 1940, the Reich Protector had asked the Oberlandrat in Zlín for a detailed report on the measures taken against the Jews in Holleschau: NAP, ÚŘP, I-3b 5850, copy in USHMM, RG 48.005M, reel 4.

5 Such instructions had already been issued. See, for example, Doc. 286.

1 Copy in JMP, DP 45d. This document has been translated from Czech.

2 Alžběta Salačová (1909–1973); married the Aryan lawyer Vladimír Salač in 1936 in Prague. They officially separated in 1939 in order to avoid the problems associated with being in a mixed marriage. Following the birth of their son Ivan Martin in July 1942, Salač had the divorce annulled. On 25 Jan. 1943, Alžběta Salačová and her son were deported to Theresienstadt. Until their liberation in May 1945, they were supplied with clothing, food, and cigarettes by Salač, who had moved to a nearby area.

3 The Czech original contains numerous spelling mistakes.

4 The urban population attempted to obtain foodstuffs in the countryside: see Doc. 263.

5 Mšeno is near Mělník in Central Bohemia.

DOC. 289
Writing in his diary on 6 October 1940, the teenager Jiří Münzer describes how he came to embrace Zionism[1]

Handwritten diary of Jiří Münzer,[2] entry for 6 October 1940

Sunday, 6 October 1940
After a long time, I've again decided to note a few things down in my diary. I say 'note', for if I were to write down everything that has happened recently, both to me personally and in general, I'd have to write a whole set of books. However, as I don't have the talent of a writer, I don't know how that would turn out. First, then, my inner transformation.

I have turned from an apathetic individual into a Jew, and this awareness gives and will give direction to my entire life. My Zionism is genuine and I will always be true to it, of that I am absolutely certain. I've come to know a proud, confident Judaism and I now devote all of my time to it, and will live and work for it. I believe that I will look through this diary some day in my homeland, in Palestine.

Until February of last year I actually didn't have a clue about Zionism. I was completely indifferent towards my Judaism, and I was not at all aware of national Judaism. My mother was in the WIZO and my uncle Milan Kollman, who is now with Žanka and Jona in Kfar Ata[3] in Eretz, has always been a Zionist, but it had no effect on me. Not until this year, when I basically lost my footing, did I come to know my people.

One Sunday at the end of February I stayed in Hradec Králové, and Jirka Fränkl[4] and Míla Frischmannová[5] told Dad[6] they would be going to a meeting that afternoon and asked if I wanted to come and have a look. I knew that El Al was in Hradec, and I had also been invited to the Wednesday meetings before, but it never interested me in the slightest. But I didn't have anything to do that Sunday, and as Mum had already tried more than once to get me to go along, I went. I made my way to the synagogue

1 JMP, DP 79. Published *Dospívání nad propastí: Deník Jiřího Münzera 1936–1942* (Prague: Radioservis, 2002), pp. 44–49. This document has been translated from Czech.

2 Jiří Münzer (1923–1943), lived in Hohenbruck; member of the Zionist organization El Al in Hradec Králové; worked in a factory; deported from Hradec Králové to Theresienstadt on 21 Dec. 1942; volunteered for the transport to Auschwitz on 6 Sept. 1943 in order to accompany his girlfriend Ilsa Polláková; murdered in Auschwitz.

3 Milan Kollmann (1897–1975), physician; worked as a paediatrician in Hradec Králové; emigrated to Palestine in 1939 with his wife Žanka (also known as Jeanne) Kollmann, née Klepetarova (d. 1985), who worked as a gym teacher at a school in Hradec Králové, and his son Jona (b. 1929), a graphic designer; worked as a paediatrician in Kfar Ata (now Kiryat Ata).

4 Jiří (Jirka) Fränkl (1921–1994), teacher and writer; deported from Hradec Králové to Theresienstadt on 21 Dec. 1942 and on 18 Dec. 1943 to Auschwitz, where he worked in the children's block; transported to Schwarzheide on 1 July 1944 for forced labour; liberated by the Red Army during the death march to Lübeck; worked as a teacher after 1945; emigrated with his family to Britain in 1968; wrote works including a memoir on Jiří Münzer and his girlfriend Ilsa Polláková.

5 Kamila (Míla) Frischmannová (b. 1925); teacher; active in the Zionist movement; deported to Theresienstadt on 21 Dec. 1942 and to Auschwitz on 15 Dec. 1943; liberated from Bergen-Belsen; studied languages and worked as a teacher.

6 Dr Leo Münzer (1885–1943), lawyer; worked for the Czechoslovak state railways; deported with his wife Ida Münzerová on 21 Dec. 1942 to Theresienstadt, then on 6 Sept. 1943 to Auschwitz, where he was murdered.

and once there into the secretariat, where I met Ilsa Polláková[7] and Bibi Peters. After a while, the others came. They were celebrating the end of a week of organization – šavua irgun[8] – and everyone was wearing white hultsot.[9] Jirka F. led the sichos[10] in Netsah,[11] which I understandably couldn't follow at all. The following people were in El Al at that time: Jirka Fränkl, Ilsa Polláková as the Rosh Gdud[12] and Madricha,[13] Bibi Peters, Míla Fuchsová, Rutka Fürtková,[14] Jirka Brod[15] as more or less active haverim.[16] Herbert Pechts and later Hela Kantůrková came for a while as guests. Then Karel Rosenbach[17] and me.

Not all of them were there for the closing of the week of organization. Though I liked the sichos, especially the singing, it didn't make a particularly strong impression on me. It was none other than Jirka himself who persuaded me to sign up for the Youth Aliyah a few days later. So, I first had decided to leave for Palestine, and only later did the real awareness come, and a spiritual transformation occurred in me such as I had never experienced before. Through this I became fully human.

Since then I have regularly gone to sichos and have become an increasingly active participant in all our projects. Sichos was usually [delivered] by Ilsa, and several times by Mr Nohel or Mr Lüftschitz[18] as guests. Jirka was already preparing for his school leaving exam, so he didn't have much time for the activities of the organization.

On 24 March, I went to Stéblová for my first pegisha,[19] which made a deep impression on me; Ota Klien from Prague made an especially strong impression. Beda Kraus[20] from Náchod and Viki Feder and Jenda Parkus[21] from Kolín were also at the pegisha. We spent the night in Stéblová and, as I already said, this pegisha really made a strong

7 Ilsa Polláková, née Töpfer (b. 1917), student; active member of the Zionist movement; deported on 21 Dec. 1942 from Hradec Králové to Theresienstadt, then, along with her mother, on 6 Sept. 1943 to Auschwitz, where she was murdered; pronounced dead after the war.

8 Czech transcription of 'shvua ha'irgun', the week of organization.

9 Plural of *hultzo*, Hebrew for 'shirt'.

10 Ashkenazi pronounciation of the Hebrew 'sihot', plural of 'siha'; 'talks, discussions'.

11 Hebrew for 'eternity'. It is unclear what the organization meant by this; it was perhaps the term for a room.

12 Hebrew for 'head of the group'.

13 Hebrew for 'peer group leader' (female).

14 Ruth, also Rutka, Fürthová, also Fuerthová (1921–1943); lived in Stěžery; active member of the Zionist movement; deported to Theresienstadt on 21 Dec. 1942, then on 20 Jan. 1943 to Auschwitz, where she was murdered.

15 Jiří (Jirka) Brod (1922–1943); lived in Kratonohy; active in the Zionist movement; initially deported to Theresienstadt, then on 29 Jan. 1943 to Auschwitz, where he was murdered.

16 Plural of *haver*; Hebrew for 'friend'; in modern Hebrew also 'member', 'comrade'.

17 Karel Rosenbach (b. 1923); lived in Libníkovice; active in the Zionist movement; initially deported to Theresienstadt, then to Raasiku on 1 Sept. 1942; subsequently perished.

18 Probably: Edvard Lüftschitz (1884–1944), engineer; employed by the Czech railways; moved from Hradec Králové to Prague with his wife and daughter in 1921; initially deported to Theresienstadt, then on 28 Oct. 1944 to Auschwitz, where he was murdered.

19 Hebrew for 'assembly'; plural: *pegishot*.

20 Bedřich (Beda) Kraus (1920–1943); lived in Náchod; active in the Zionist movement; worked on various farms after the start of the war; deported to Theresienstadt on 17 Dec. 1942, then on 6 Sept. 1943 to Auschwitz, where he was murdered.

21 Jan (Jenda) Parkus (1921–1942); lived in Kolín; active in the Zionist movement; deported to Theresienstadt on 13 June 1942 and from there to Auschwitz, where he perished.

impression on me. We later had several more pegishot in Stéblová, of which the last one on 24 June was especially good. On Saturday (the 23rd) we had supper together at our place (our parents were in the Bohemian-Moravian Highlands).[22] Avi Fischer from Prague was also there.

On 14 July, we held Bechinat habagrut[23] at our place again, and that day I basically took over the role of Rosh Gdud from Jirka. Three days later a ve'ida[24] took place in the Makabi gym in Prague. The German police showed up, took everyone's identity cards away, and prohibited our activities. Since then only Hebrew lessons have been allowed. Our work is thus very much restricted and more difficult, but we're persevering nonetheless.

I won't write any more about my Zionism, which has become the purpose of my life, and I'll switch to everyday things that have changed so much since I last wrote. Almost all the changes have something to do with the current political situation.

Last time I got as far as the establishment of the Protectorate. At the end of August 1939, Germany entered into a non-aggression pact with Russia, and on 1 September 1939 war broke out, with Germany on one side and Poland, France, and England on the other. Poland soon fell and Germany and Russia divided it up. Then there was relative calm for a long time and the war was limited to sinking ships and local fighting on the western border and the Maginot Line. This spring Germany occupied Denmark and Norway, where there was fighting for a longer period. Then Belgium, Holland, and Luxemburg were conquered, after which the German military entered France and soon occupied Paris. The Maginot Line was broken in many places and France surrendered.

Prior to this, Italy entered the war alongside Germany. Following the French capitulation, there has been no front in Europe; only in Africa is there fighting along the borders with Egypt and Ethiopia. Italy recently conquered British Somalia. The battle in the air is raging in Europe, and London is bombarded on a daily basis. Many attacks are concentrated on Gibraltar as well.[25] Paradoxical events have resulted, for instance the French are bombing Gibraltar. Haifa is also sometimes targeted by Italian air strikes. In the winter, Russia fought in Finland and occupied part of the country. Lithuania, Latvia, and Estonia have also fallen to the USSR. Romania was carved up a month ago. The USSR had occupied Bessarabia previously; now Hungary got Transylvania and Bulgaria [got] southern Dobruja. In Romania itself the Iron Guard has come to power and Carol, the former king, has fled to Switzerland.[26] So those are pretty much the political developments in Europe.

Developments inside the Protectorate are governed by the overall situation. All memorials to the World War and the republic have disappeared; everything is in two lan-

22 Stretch of land in eastern Bohemia.

23 Hebrew for 'school leaving examination'; can also refer to an initiation ceremony.

24 Annual assembly of the Federation of Zionist Youth, a union of the groups Maccabi Hatzair, Hashomer Hatzair, Bnei Akiva, Tchelet Lavan, and El Al.

25 This probably took place against the backdrop of the German Reich's plans beginning in Aug. 1940 to conquer the outpost of Gibraltar. See Doc. 206, fn. 9.

26 On 6 Sept. 1940 King Carol II of Romania was forced to abdicate and go into exile. Prime Minister Antonescu established the authoritarian National Legionary State in partnership with the fascist Iron Guard party, which he brought into the government.

guages. The main changes, of course, concern the Jews. Apart from that, goods are in very short supply, and everything is rationed and can only be obtained using ration coupons.

The restrictions imposed on Jews are constantly increasing. Dad of course has long since retired. We aren't allowed to enter any pubs, cafés, hotels, cinemas, theatres, parks, snack bars, swimming pools, outdoor pools, playgrounds, etc.; in some places it's also prohibited to go into the forest (here, one can still do so for the time being); our designated shopping hours are from ten thirty till one and from three till five; we aren't allowed to be outdoors after eight o'clock or take taxis; in Prague one may only ride in the rear carriage of the tram. We aren't allowed to get out more than 1,500 korunas per week (so far, I've had my weekly wage of 36.45 korunas paid into my bank account, since it is not permitted to give Jews cash), we did not get any coupons for clothing, and last year on Yom Kippur we had to hand in our radio. In some cities Jews have had to move out of their apartments and we, too, live in constant uncertainty as to how long we will be able to live here and how long we will receive money. We had to surrender our jewellery to the bank and there are many, many more restrictions of all sorts, and every week new ordinances are posted. All Jewish businesses are either Aryanized or under temporary management; physicians either have to stop practising medicine or may only treat Jews. Our position is deteriorating more and more as time goes on. Jewish children may not be admitted to any schools, even primary schools.[27] (Recently a seminar for teachers at Jewish schools was held in Prague; from here, Ilsa and Jirka F. took part.)

Now for something about employment. When I last wrote, I was still in the fifth year of grammar school. Then I was on holiday for a month and on 31 July 1939 I started my apprenticeship at the Kanders' in Třebechovice as a decorator. I enjoy the work and I'm not bad at it. I worked[28] with a team at a table; the group leader was Mr Hampl, then there was the seamstress Mrs Konečná and the machine lubricator Ema Charvátová. Next to me is group leader Hajn, with Cás and Barvíř on the other side. I attended the first year of a continuing education school in Třebechovice; now I'm not allowed into the second year, though, but I don't mind because school is on Saturday afternoon. This spring a commissioner came to the factory, barred the Kanders from entering, and fired foreman Diamant and his assistants – both Jews. Mr Hampl became the foreman and we now have Pultr as group leader. This week a new commissioner came. I now consider this work a sideline because in Palestine I will work in the fields, although it's still good even for a halutz[29] to know a trade.

I'm learning Hebrew from Emil Müller. I had four hours on my own, and now I will have Hebrew together with Míla, Zuza, and Mr Werner.[30] I'm also learning English with Mr Munk, and now at my advanced age I've started to learn piano, in exchange for which I give Mum Hebrew lessons. In addition, I have learned how to type a bit on the typewriter

27 See, for instance, Docs. 247; 259, fn. 4; 263; and 286, fnn. 4, 7, and 8.

28 Change of tense as in the original.

29 Hebrew for 'pioneer'. The term was used in Zionist discourse to refer to people who were or who trained to be agricultural labourers in settlements in Palestine.

30 Probably: Rudolf Werner (1897–1944), trader; lived in Hradec Králové, where he owned a business; was initially deported to Theresienstadt, then on 29 Sept. 1944, to Auschwitz where he was murdered.

I bought last August. I read a lot now, mostly Zionist and Jewish things. Not many magazines, though I am the director of the Jewish reading group in Třebechovice and distribute magazines in the local yeshiva every week.

I don't go on trips very often now, because there's no food and there's barely anywhere I'm allowed to stay. The last time we went on a big trip was with Mum when we went to Paris in 1937; I've got notes about it somewhere else. In the summer of 1938 I spent a fortnight in Liberec learning German at the Königsteins'. This past winter I went skiing several times (always on Sundays) at Tábor [Hill] near Lomnice, usually with Zbyněk Petřík (who now regularly comes to my place on Saturday evenings) and Jirka Vosmek.

At the start of this year's holidays, Bibi and I went on a nice cycling trip (five days); first to Seč and then to Svratky in the Bohemian-Moravian Highlands. We enjoyed it tremendously, and then I spent four days at the Peters' in Prague.

I'm finishing for today; I hope to continue again soon.

DOC. 290

On 27 October 1940 the writer Jiři Orten lists the restrictions to which Jews are subjected[1]

Text by Jiři Orten,[2] 27 October 1940

Bans

Last night it took me a long time to get to sleep, and I lay awake thinking about and going over in my head all of the bans that somehow affect me, even in minor ways. And because it's Sunday morning, it's been snowing for the second day in a row, and I'm not due to travel to Košíře[3] for a few hours, I'm going to write down all the bans that I can recall, and when I write them down I'm going to leave a really large space underneath for the ones that will be added after today. Unfortunately, I don't have any sources to hand that I could use as a guide and so the way they are put together and the sequence are more or less random. So, these are the bans:

I am not allowed to leave the house after eight o'clock in the evening.[4]

I am not allowed to rent an apartment of my own.[5]

1 Literární archiv Památníku národního písemnictví, record group Jiří Orten, př. č. 30/79, inv. č. 1, Žíhaná kniha,13.12.1939–9.12.1940. Published in *Deníky Jiřího Ortena: Poesie – myšlenky – zápisky*, ed. Jan Grossman (Prague: Československý spisovatel, 1958). This document has been translated from Czech.

2 Jiří Orten, also Ohrenstein (1919–1941), writer and literary critic; leading representative of the so-called war generation of Czech writers; studied acting at the state conservatoire, 1937–1940; expelled in 1940 because of his Jewish background; died as a result of a road accident.

3 A suburb of Prague.

4 See Doc. 263, fn. 35.

5 *Jüdisches Nachrichtenblatt* (Prague edition), 13 Sept. 1940, p. 1.

I am not allowed to move anywhere except to Prague I or Prague V – and even then only as a subtenant.[6]

I am not allowed to go to wine bars, cafés, pubs, cinemas, or theatres or to attend concerts, apart from those designated for me.[7]

I am not allowed to go to parks or gardens.[8]

I am not allowed to go to municipal forests.[9]

I am not allowed to go beyond the district of Prague.

So I am not allowed to go home, to Kutná Hora, or anywhere else unless I get special permission from the Gestapo.[10]

I am not allowed to travel in motorized trams – only in the rear carriage, and if it has doors in the centre, only in the rear half.[11]

I am not allowed to go shopping anywhere apart from between 11 a.m. and 1 p.m. and between 3 p.m. and 5 p.m.[12]

I am not allowed to perform in the theatre or be otherwise publicly active.[13]

I am not allowed to be a member of any associations.[14]

I am not allowed to attend any school.[15]

I am not allowed to associate with members of Národní souručenství[16] and they are not allowed to associate with me; they are not allowed to greet me or to stop to speak with me about anything except when necessary (while shopping, etc.).[17]

6 On 25 Oct. 1940 the Prague police headquarters prohibited the Jewish residents of Greater Prague from moving within or away from the district. Only the Central Office for Jewish Emigration could issue a certificate of exemption via the Jewish Religious Community. See announcement by the police headquarters in Prague, cited in Helena Petrův, *Právní postavení židů v Protektorátu Čechy a Morava (1939–1941)* (Prague: Sefer, 2000), p. 109.

7 See Doc. 241, fn. 19.

8 See Doc. 286, fn. 4.

9 *Jüdisches Nachrichtenblatt* (Prague edition), 6 Sept. 1940, p. 3.

10 See fn. 6.

11 The ban was issued on 12 Sept. 1940. See Friedmann, 'Rechtsstellung', p. 247.

12 See ibid., fn. 8.

13 This ban was possibly communicated orally. Shortly thereafter, on 7 Dec. 1940, the Czech Ministry of the Interior issued a regulation instructing the regional offices in Prague and Brno to make arrangements to exclude Jews from cultural life. Thus, licences were only granted to those theatres that did not appoint Jews as directors, actors, etc. See NAP, PMR 1590, box 588.

14 See Doc. 286, fn. 5.

15 A decree issued by the Ministry of Education and Culture on 12 July 1939 prohibited Jews from attending German primary and secondary schools, while a ministerial decree of 7 August 1940 prohibited them from attending schools where Czech was the language of instruction. Jewish schools were closed down in July 1942. See Friedmann, 'Rechtsstellung', p. 232–363.

16 National Solidarity: the only political party permitted by the Germans in the Protectorate of Bohemia and Moravia.

17 See Doc. 256.

DOC. 291

On 25 November 1940 the SD Main District Prague warns State Secretary Karl Hermann Frank that German influence in Triesch is at risk from the influx of Jews[1]

Letter from the SD Main District Prague, B SA 63, signed Böhme,[2] Prague-Bubeneč, to the State Secretary in the Office of the Reich Protector of Bohemia and Moravia, SS-Gruppenführer Frank, Prague, dated 25 November 1940 (copy of a copy)

Re: situation in Triesch with regard to ethnic policy
Case file: None.
Triesch, a town of more than 6,000 inhabitants situated on the southern edge of the Iglau ethnic enclave, developed with increasing vigour during the years of the Czechoslovak state as a result of Jewry, which always had a strong presence. In the mid seventeenth century, Triesch, even according to Czech sources, was still half German. It is common knowledge that the south church in Triesch used to be called 'the German church'. Until the end of the World War, there was still a German-Jewish primary school in Triesch. Back then, Triesch was an insignificant little rural town, which only acquired a certain prominence just before the World War, when it was declared a judicial district town (the northern part of the present judicial district of Triesch was previously under the authority of the district of Iglau, the southern part under the authority of the district of Teltsch).

After the reorganization of the Oberlandratsbezirk Iglau, the judicial district of Trietsch was now separated from the political district of Iglau and assigned to the political district of Teltsch. After the foundation of Czecho-Slovakia, the population grew significantly; the town became a centre of Communism, which evidently was heavily promoted by the resident Jewry. The continued strength of Communism in Triesch today is proved by the arrests made by the State Police in the course of penetrating the illegal KSČ in recent weeks. The present tendency to make Triesch the gathering point for all the Jews who are still resident and unwelcome in the Iglau region appears all the more dangerous. The Germans in Triesch have recently complained strongly that they continually notice new Jewish faces, people who obviously feel quite at ease in Triesch and are establishing an active existence. These Jews attend the Triesch Synagogue in large numbers and have also established separate Jewish schooling for their children, supervised by the Triesch rabbi Strauss, who is latterly said to even have assistance from a Jewish teacher. The classes are held in the apartment of the Jew Norbert Meissner in Triesch.[3]

1 ABS, 114-187-6, fols. 126–127. This document has been translated from German.
2 Horst Böhme (1909–1945?), businessman; joined the NSDAP and the SS in 1930; senior commander of the Security Police and the SD in Prague, 1939–1942; responsible for the Lidice massacre, 1942; police attaché in Bucharest, 1942; head of Einsatzgruppe B in Belarus, 1943; SS-Oberführer, 1944; lost without trace in Königsberg, April 1945.
3 Usually four children attended the classes, which were probably conducted by Dr Anna Spitzerová (1909–1942) or Dr Evžen Ornstein (1897–1942?).

The clustering of the Jews in Triesch is also encouraged by the German authorities, as is proved, for example, by the instruction issued by the office of the Oberlandrat to the sole licensed Jewish physician in the Iglau region, Dr Kürschner in Iglau,[4] requiring him to move his practice to Triesch. The influx of Jews into Triesch is also furthered by the fact that many have their legal residence there. Despite leaving Triesch many years ago, they are now going back there because they have the right of domicile. This development seems inadvisable on ethnopolitical grounds as it would result in the creation of a Jewish centre on the edge of the Iglau ethnic enclave, in a town that is, moreover, a well-known communist stronghold. A highly passive attitude towards German directives is already apparent among the Czech population, for example concerning the dual-language labelling of shops, which predominantly display only the proprietor's name, but no indication of the type of shop.

Starting points for active efforts to promote Germandom in Triesch, which is situated on the Iglau–Triesch–Teltsch–Datschitz–Zlabings (Lower Danube) road, are the large estate of Baron Wenzel Sternbach;[5] Norbert Meissner's Jewish business (enamel works),[6] now in the hands of a German trustee, which is to be bought by the Alexander Works in Remscheid; and several smaller businesses. Today there are just over fifty persons of German ethnic origin in Triesch, including a relatively large number of mixed marriages. It is the location of an NSDAP block. The German children attend the German school in Iglau; some of them live in Iglau, and some of them travel there and back every day by train. Most of the younger children speak German poorly, if at all. A kindergarten privately established by Baroness Sternbach is now defunct. The overall social situation of the Germans in Triesch is poor, as they belong, by and large, to lower occupational categories. Housing conditions, too, are in line with that. The few Germans are often simultaneously members of the Party, the BDO, the DAF etc.[7] The formations are poorly represented in Triesch. The Germans lack the suitable premises they need for a positive community life; in addition, there is the strong boycott by the Czechs, which continues to largely prevent a more self-confident bearing on the part of the Germans. This also explains why the Germans usually use the Czech language in Czech administrative offices. In the event of an expansion of German influence along the Bohemian-Moravian Highlands to the Gau of Lower Danube, Triesch, as one of the major centres in this region, would have to be given priority.

4 Dr Milan Kürschner (b. 1899), physician; licensed as a Jewish physician for Jihlava (Iglau), Třešť (Triesch), and Telč (Teltsch); deported from Prague to Theresienstadt on 31 Jan. 1945 for forced labour in a segregated unit; returned to Jihlava after 1945 and resumed work as a physician.

5 Here and below, this should be: Sternberg. The family of the counts of Sternberg had had extensive landholdings in Bohemia and Moravia since the Middle Ages and was one of the leading aristocratic families in Bohemia. The town of Třešť had been in the family's possession since 1831. Following the Second World War, the property was nationalized after the family fled to Austria.

6 See Doc. 297.

7 BDO: Bund Deutscher Osten (League of the German East). This organization, founded in 1933, was among the pillars of National Socialist ethnopolitical activity. DAF: Deutsche Arbeitsfront (German Labour Front).

DOC. 292

On 12 December 1940 Undersecretary von Burgsdorff calls for the Jews to be removed definitively from the wholesale and retail trade by 31 March 1941[1]

Express letter (marked 'secret') from the Reich Protector of Bohemia and Moravia (II/1 Jd – 107/40g), p.p. signed Dr von Burgsdorff, to a) the Oberlandräte and b) the administrative office for Moravia, dated 12 December 1940

Re: progress on de-Jewification

The removal of Jews from the wholesale and retail trade is particularly urgent because the value of a firm is decisively influenced by the personal skill and productivity of the proprietor. When management under a trustee goes on too long, there is naturally a danger that the assets of the company will be exhausted, in particular because of the difficulty of acquiring new inventory, and that customers will be lost and the business becomes worthless. Thus the firm no longer offers any incentive to a bidder. Additionally, it has been shown that violations of pricing and management regulations occur particularly frequently in businesses managed by a trustee. These dangers can only be avoided by finding suitable bidders for commercial operations as quickly as possible, and transferring the businesses over to them. Where this does not appear possible, above all because of the war, for the reasons cited above it is usually not in the interests of the later bidder to keep operations running for him. Instead, as a rule it seems more appropriate to cease operations, and to ensure that the expired business licence can be restored immediately to a suitable purchaser at a later stage. In this way, ethnopolitical concerns are fully taken into account.

The de-Jewification of the wholesale and retail trade must therefore be completed by 31 March 1941. A third implementing decree to the Regulation of the Reich Protector on the Exclusion of Jews from the Economy of the Protectorate of 26 January 1940[2] will be enacted in which, with effect from 31 March 1941, Jews and Jewish companies will be forbidden from managing economic concerns of the following kinds:[3]

a) wholesale and retail on behalf of one's self or a third party,
b) public houses or accommodation businesses,
c) insurance companies,
d) shipping,
e) haulage and storage,
f) travel operators and agencies,
g) tour-guiding businesses,
h) transport and haulage companies of any kind, including the rental of vehicles and carts,
i) banks and currency exchange,
j) pawnbroking,
k) credit bureau and debt collection agencies,

1 JMP, DP 22/7. This document has been translated from German.

2 *Verordnungsblatt des Reichsprotektors*, 1940, no. 7, p. 41.

3 The third implementing decree was enacted on 10 Jan. 1941: *Verordnungsblatt des Reichsprotektors*, 1941, no. 2, pp. 13–14.

l) surveillance,
m) vending machine installation,
n) advertisement agency,
o) housing, property, mortgage brokering,
p) marriage bureaus.

The de-Jewification procedure is to be based on experiences with Jewish textile and leather retail businesses (I.D.E.).[4] To guarantee a smooth implementation, by *15 January 1941* at the latest trustees are to be appointed for those operations in which there is a danger of goods being displaced. In particular, the trustee has the task of supervising operations to prevent the dispatch of goods or other discrepancies. Because of the low number of suitable trustees, I agree that one trustee can be appointed for several businesses at the same time. Immediately upon appointment, the trustee must produce an inventory of the warehouse. The business is to be kept closed until the completion of this inventory. Under no circumstances may the business be used for more than a few days. After that, operations should be resumed under the trustee's supervision up until 31 March 1941. The entire wholesale and retail trade is affected by the de-Jewification process. Commercial sales from such businesses are not permitted after 31 March 1941. To the extent that the portion of the business allocated to trade is predominant (for example in tailoring enterprises), the entire business is to be closed down.

A certificate of exemption in accordance with § 5(2) of the Regulation of the Reich Protector on the Exclusion of Jews from the Economy of the Protectorate is to be granted only in the following cases:

1) if a suitable bidder is available on 31 March 1941, and the transfer of the company to this prospective buyer is to be expected shortly;
2) if no suitable bidder is available yet, but it is absolutely necessary for the business to continue operating in order to supply the population, and there is a firm guarantee that a trustee will continue to run the business in accordance with regulations.

In the above cases it should be ensured that the expiring business licence for liquidated companies cannot be reissued, so that there is no ethnopolitical damage. The district authorities that grant business licences are to take the appropriate precautions in this respect. The same holds true for the relocation of another company to the businesses premises of a company that has closed down (see the announcements by the Ministry of Industry, Trade, and Commerce, 30 October 1940, no. 757 on limiting the establishment and expansion of wholesale companies, no. 768 on limiting the establishment and expansion of retail companies, official gazette no. 255, 31 October 1940). If suitable bidders come forward during the subsequent period, especially those who have been discharged from military service, it is to be ensured that the expired business licences can be immediately granted to them.

By way of exception, I agree that trustees can also be allowed to bid for wholesale and retail companies. This is, however, not to be made known to the trustees before the inventory has been drawn up. In cases where a trustee is authorized to purchase the company he is managing, examination of the sale contract by an auditor is essential.

4 The meaning of this abbreviation could not be ascertained.

For all remaining companies, the de-Jewification is to be implemented as rapidly as possible. Here as well, the aim must be to complete the de-Jewification by 31 March 1941. Regarding the treatment of Jews of foreign nationality, I refer to the decree of 31 October 1940 (II/1 Jd 37 432/40).[5] My prior approval is thus still required only for Jews of Italian, Russian, and American (USA) nationality.

My prior approval is not required for the compulsory de-Jewification that is to be undertaken on the basis of this decree.

By 30 April 1941, I request a report on how many Jewish companies:

1) have been closed on the basis of this decree, and
 a) are already liquidated
 b) are undergoing liquidation
2) have been transferred to non-Jewish ownership
3) are being operated by a trustee and
 a) there is a prospective buyer
 b) there is no prospective buyer.

This decree also applies to food and agricultural companies, as well as the forestry and timber trade.

DOC. 293
In 1940 Bedřich Kolín writes an ironic poem about the 'advantages' of being a Jew in the Protectorate[1]

Poem by Bedřich Kolín, Prague, 1940

1940 F.R.[2]

Blessed, o blessed the life of a Jew.

Once, as an official, the Jew had tough work,
'Good morning!' he'd say to his boss, a big jerk.
But now, without worries, he carelessly capers,
untroubled by balance sheets, numbers and papers,
not peeved that vacations come always too late,
o blessed, o blessed, today a Jew's fate.

A Jew who's an entrepreneur – likewise he's
now living more comfortably, much more at ease.
No more of the threats and the risk his work brings,
because the commissioner handles those things.
He isn't involved any more, not a jot.
O blessed, o blessed, is now a Jew's lot. •

5 This could not be found.

1 JMP, DP 79, Bedřich Kolín. This document has been translated from German.
2 Handwritten note.

Once, buying goods, a Jew always debated
to make sure the prices were not overstated.
Now neither tailor nor cobbler can con him,
junk shoes from merchants have no effect on him.
He has no 'body';[3] can't trick him, nohow,
blessed, o blessed, a Jew's life is now.

Once, sitting through films – was a Jew even able?
He was so sick and tired of dull old Clark Gable,
and always that Garbo – they weren't worth two damns,
he wished he did not have to watch all those hams.
A small note now spares him the ticket desk queue.[4]
Blessed, o blessed, to be now a Jew.

Once the Jew asked: Shall we spend Christmas in
Karlovy Vary or Špindlerův Mlýn?
Now he sits tight at his home with his spouse,
or might go to Střešovice,[5] near their house.
Isn't that splendid, isn't that great?
Blessed, o blessed, today a Jew's fate.

To make his name known in the arts, once a Jew
needed to labour all day and night through.
To earn a name these days, it taxes him not.
His name's Israel, doesn't that hit the spot?
O blessed, o blessed, today a Jew's lot.

The Jew spent last New Year's in typical vein:
first movie, then Šroubek, then out for champagne.
He's blithe as a kid now, his time's better spent,
those spots 'not accessible' where he once went.
Invited to friends' homes, it's tickety-boo!
Blessed, o blessed, the life of a Jew.

Once, if a Jew came home late in the night,
he'd clash with his wife, she would scold him all right.
Now he's no need for excuses to say,
for oh, how the hours at night slip away.
Now, what a joy, he's reliable from eight.
O blessed, o blessed, today a Jew's fate.

3 Czech: 'points'. The German equivalent ('Punkte') was added by hand. The term may refer to rations.

4 Handwritten addition: 'No access for Jews'.

5 A district of Prague.

Getting up early was really not pretty
when there was shopping to do in the city.
Now there's a chance to have long dreamy snores
without wasting hours for visiting stores.
If there are simply no goods to be had,
all that saved money can make you so glad.
Life was so hard with expenses to pay,
blessed, o blessed, a Jew's life today.

It's nicer to ride the last car of the tram
than up in the front one, where other folks cram.
That Jewish salon's not the worst of all places,
you've never before met so many new faces,
Mr Kohn, Mrs Pick, Mr Schwarzkopf, Mrs Stein,
o blessed, o blessed, Jews' life is so fine.

Why does a Jew need to go to the park,
and what's at the sports field that's worth a remark?
To take a nice dip that's refreshing and cool,
is it vital to mix with the folks at the pool?
That saying of old is now proven anew,
the coffeehouse is the sole place for a Jew.
So let us all sing it and cheer it and yell,
blessed, o blessed, a Jew lives so well.

DOC. 294

Der Neue Tag, 4 January 1941: announcement of the Aryanization of Salomon Trau's company in Proßnitz[1]

Announcement by the Reich Protector in Bohemia and Moravia, p.p. signed Pritzel, dated 27 December 1940, published on 4 January 1941

The Reich Protector of Bohemia and Moravia
Public notification
No. II/1 Jd. 44 509/40.
Pursuant to § 3 (2) of the Regulation of the Reich Protector on the Exclusion of Jews from the Economy of the Protectorate, dated 26 January 1940 (BBl. RProt. p. 41), I grant authorization for the company

1 *Der Neue Tag*, 4 Jan. 1941, p. 12. The daily newspaper *Der Neue Tag* appeared from 1939 to 1945 as an official publication of the German administration of the Protectorate of Bohemia and Moravia in Prague. This document has been translated from German.

Salomon Trau,[2]
factory for women's and girls' coats, Proßnitz,
to be transferred to non-Jewish ownership. I therefore order the proprietor, Salomon *Trau*, whereabouts unknown, to sell the company by 15 January 1941.

Upon the expiration of this deadline without effect, a trustee will be appointed for the sale in order to protect the interests of the proprietor of the firm.

Prague, 27 September 1940.
Reich Protector
of Bohemia and Moravia
p.p. signed: Pritzel

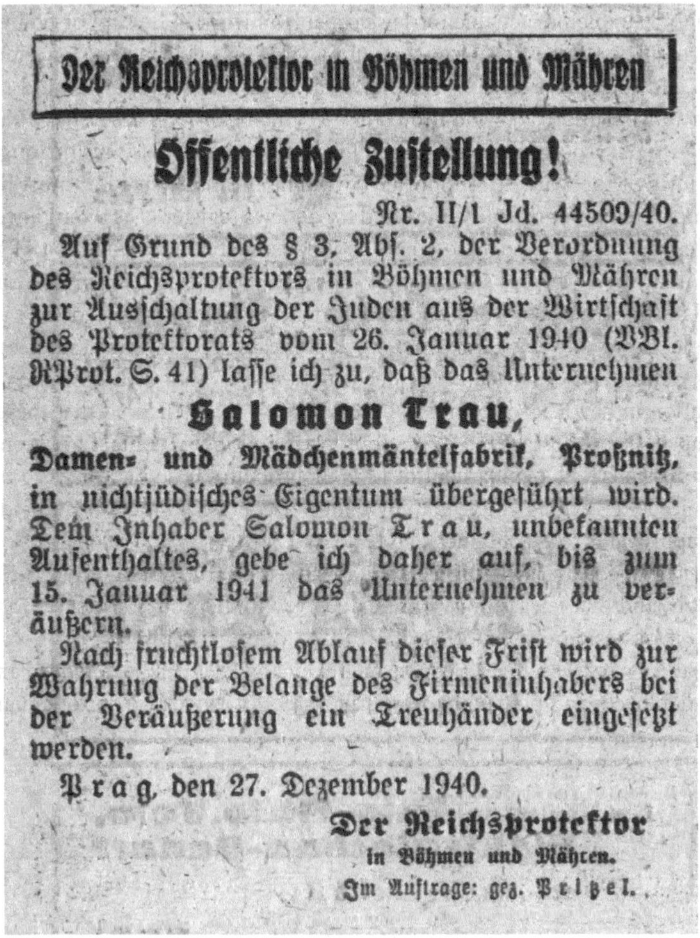

Der Reichsprotektor in Böhmen und Mähren

Öffentliche Zustellung!

Nr. II/1 Jd. 44509/40.

Auf Grund des § 3, Abs. 2, der Verordnung des Reichsprotektors in Böhmen und Mähren zur Ausschaltung der Juden aus der Wirtschaft des Protektorats vom 26. Januar 1940 (VBl. RProt. S. 41) lasse ich zu, daß das Unternehmen

Salomon Trau,

Damen- und Mädchenmäntelfabrik, Proßnitz,

in nichtjüdisches Eigentum übergeführt wird. Dem Inhaber Salomon Trau, unbekannten Aufenthaltes, gebe ich daher auf, bis zum 15. Januar 1941 das Unternehmen zu veräußern.

Nach fruchtlosem Ablauf dieser Frist wird zur Wahrung der Belange des Firmeninhabers bei der Veräußerung ein Treuhänder eingesetzt werden.

Prag, den 27. Dezember 1940.

Der Reichsprotektor
in Böhmen und Mähren.
Im Auftrage: gez. Pritzel.

2 Salomon Trau (b. 1879), businessman; Polish citizen; until 1918 partner in the garment manufacturing company Süsskind and Trau in Prostějov, and from 1918 proprietor of a women's and girls' coat factory that employed up to 273 workers from 1918; escaped to Poland in April 1939. The firm was managed in trust from Nov. 1939 and ultimately purchased by Robert Hanisch in 1941.

DOC. 295

On 13 January 1941 the Oberlandrat calls on the head of the employment office in Pardubitz to assign Jews to forced labour[1]

Letter from the Oberlandrat for the political districts of Pardubitz, Chrudim, Hohenmauth, Leitomischl and Politschka, Chotieborsch,[2] Department of Labour and Social Affairs (Tgb. no. 0550 Ha/W), p.p. signed, signature illegible, Pardubitz, to the head of the employment office in Pardubitz (received 13 January 1941), dated 13 January 1941

Subject: placement of Jews.
Reference:
It is neither desirable nor tenable for Jews capable of work to be supported by receiving unemployment assistance, for it is to be assumed that they will become long-term benefit recipients and thus place a heavy strain on unemployment assistance funds. The need for labour in various areas of the Protectorate, which cannot be met, has already made it necessary to put emergency recruitment measures in place. It is thus no longer acceptable that Jews fit for work are supported by public means. Instead, it must be ensured that an employment opportunity is created for all Jews registered as unemployed as soon as possible. For this purpose, road construction, excavation, development of green spaces, or similar are to be considered first, because members of all professions can be employed for these types of work, and manual labour for Jews is indeed to be welcomed. In principle, however, they should not work alongside Aryans, but rather be grouped into work details and deployed at the construction sites separately from Aryans. If accommodation in barracks or camps is necessary, it is to be ensured that these barracks are built apart from those of the Aryans, and that no kind of contact between Jews and Aryans is possible. The deployment of Jews in agricultural operations is to be avoided for the time being. Should their employment be seen as desirable in individual cases, my prior approval is to be obtained.

I request that construction projects suitable for the deployment of Jews be identified immediately, and that Jews fit for work be deployed to these sites. Strict standards are to be applied in assessing fitness for work.

By 27 January 1941, I request a report on how many Jews can be deployed and/or how many are deployed, and how many were still in receipt of welfare on 10 January 1941.[3]

1 JMP, DP 49/4. This document has been translated from German.

2 Dr Rudolf Schultz von Dratzig (b. 1897); Oberlandrat in Pardubitz, 1940–1943.

3 The following has been added in Czech at the end of the document: 'copy of this letter given to all branch offices and agencies to report according to the last paragraph. 20 Jan. 1941.' On 27 Jan. 1941 the Pardubitz employment office reported to the Oberlandrat that eleven Jews had thus far been placed in excavation and construction sites in its district: JMP, DP 49/4.

DOC. 296
On 14 January 1941 Undersecretary von Burgsdorff rejects the Protectorate government's request to exempt forty-one designated persons from anti-Jewish provisions[1]

Letter from the Reich Protector of Bohemia and Moravia (no. 13 B – 10 711), pp. signed Dr von Burgsdorff, Prague IV, to the Prime Minister,[2] Prague (received 16 January 1941), dated 14 January 1941[3]

Re: application for exemption from the legal effects of the Government Regulation on the Legal Status of Jews in Public Life, pursuant to § 3 of the Government Regulation, SdGuv. no. 136/40.[4] In response to the letter dated 21 December 1940, Zl. 3978/1590/7/40 S. M. R.[5] Your explanations could not convince me that it would be in the general interest to exempt the specified persons[6] from the legal effects of the Regulation on the Legal Status of Jews in Public Life. Before I address your suggestions more closely, I request that in the individual cases you inform me of the particular facts that indicate that a certificate of exemption should be considered in the cases you name. In particular, I request that you state the areas of life in which the persons named seek continued activity, and from which Jews are eliminated on the basis of the aforementioned Government Regulation, § 4 subsections 1 and 3.[7] Here I would ask you to bear in mind that, from the point of view of the general public, only particularly compelling reasons can justify any deviation from the ruling set out in the Government Regulation. General considerations as such – for example that there were or are no objections to the persons who work in business being involved in associations and organizations of social, cultural, and economic life, especially as they are integrated with the rest of the population as a result of their family connections – I perceive as just as irrelevant as the single fact that children from a racially mixed marriage exist, justifying an exemption for the wife from [the prohibition against] participating in organizations of social, cultural, and economic life (§ 4 (3), loc. cit.).[8]

1 NAP, PMR-S, 1590/7, box 589. This document has been translated from German.
2 Alois Eliáš.
3 The original contains various official stamps.
4 The government regulation included measures to remove Jews from public life, for example bans on employment. According to § 3, Jews could be exempted by the president if an application was submitted by the Protectorate government and approved by the Reich Protector: Government Regulation on the Legal Status of Jews in Public Life, 4 July 1939, in *Sammlung der Gesetze und Verordnungen des Protektorats Böhmen und Mähren*, 24 April 1940, no. 136, 1940, pp. 395–403.
5 On 21 Dec. 1940, in response to a negative reply, the Czech government had requested that exemptions not be rejected on principle but rather individual cases examined: NAP, PMR-S, 1590/7, box 589.
6 By mid Oct. 1940, around 1,000 applications for exemption had been received. The government had selected forty-one petitions and forwarded these to the Reich Protector: ibid.
7 According to § 4 (1) of the government regulation, Jews were to be excluded from the judiciary and public administration, and according to (3), from participation in political life as well as from all associations and other organizations: *Sammlung der Gesetze und Verordnungen des Protektorats Böhmen und Mähren*, pp. 395–403.
8 As in the original. In a number of follow-up letters, the Office of the Reich Protector rejected exemptions for individual professional groups. On 4 Oct. 1941 it finally announced that no one on the list could be granted exemption from the provisions of the Government Regulation on the Legal Status of Jews in Public Life, 4 July 1939: Miroslav Kárný, 'Die Ausschaltung der Juden aus dem öffentlichen Leben des Protektorats und die Geschichte des "Ehrenariertums"', in *Theresienstädter Studien und Dokumente*, 1998, pp. 4–40, here pp. 27 ff.

DOC. 297

On 1 February 1941 Charlotte and Norbert Meissner from Triesch inform their son Franz about the Aryanization of the family business[1]

Letters from Charlotte and Norbert Meissner, Triesch, to Franz Meissner, St Taaroje, Pr. Fakse, Gribsbjerg, Denmark, dated 1 February 1941

121st letter

My dearest Franzi,

Your letter of 20 January arrived the day before yesterday, and today a really old letter arrived, dated 3 [January] and addressed to dear Leo.[2] We immediately forwarded the latter to Höditz, because as of today, Saturday 1st, dear Leo is no longer employed by Dr Singer and will not be coming to Triesch. Thank goodness you are doing well and everything is carrying on as normal for you. We are also in good health, and over the last few days the gentlemen from Remscheid have taken over the factory, and so my days left there are numbered.[3] I will probably be given notice on 15 February, with the six weeks required by law, and will leave the post on 1 April. Well, I have been expecting this, and so I was not surprised. Dear Uncle[4] will stay on up there as an advisor for a while; it is just he has to vacate the apartment on 15 February for the engineer who will run the factory. Now we have made some progress again. If only the weather for the relocation were better. Since yesterday we have had the most dreadful weather, as tends to be the case here. There is a terrible storm, and the streets are all blocked with snow. The trains are also really delayed, and I fear that the winter will be harsher again where you are as well. Well, let us hope nonetheless that it will not stay like that much longer, as the toughest of all the months is already behind us, after all. Hopefully we will already find out tomorrow in Höditz whether the books have already been sent off to you from Prague, so that they can bring you joy again. Today, in the letter to Leo, you also wrote that reading gives you such pleasure, and it is so commendable that you spend all of your free time doing this. Your cousin Peter is such a bookworm too and always prefers to stay at home alone with a book.[5] Whenever your aunt rushes home to him, as she usually does, she finds him with a book, and he has absolutely no desire to see her. He only wants to read; not even studying and completing assignments give him such pleasure. Well, am I wrong to say that he is just like Franzi? He is a very clever boy, and you might really enjoy it if you could chat with him one day. I look forward to having him here with us; it's just that he is sometimes so boisterous that it's impossible to calm him

1 USHMM, Acc. 2 004 692.1, Frank Meissner papers, letter no. 121. This document has been translated from German.

2 Leo Meissner.

3 This refers to the family business owned by Norbert Meissner. The engineering works was founded in 1923 and had seventy-nine employees in 1939. On the Aryanization of the company, see also Doc. 291.

4 Hilbert Grünberger.

5 Peter, also Petr, Grünberger (1932–1944); deported to Theresienstadt on 18 May 1942, along with his parents, Hilbert and Eleonora (Elly) Grünberger, and from there on 1 Oct. 1944 to Auschwitz, where he was murdered. The Grünberger family had moved into the Meissners' home. See Doc. 285.

down. Oh, you were like that in your day; now that's all in the past. You have since become extremely serious, and indeed you have already been through enough grave things in your young life. May you always just be healthy and not lose heart.

Today I still have to go to the funeral of Mr Leirich,[6] the father of my office colleague. You will surely remember him; as a child you were quite often at their home with Anna. Keep well, lots of love and kisses,

Mum.

Lots of love and kisses from your dear Grandfather. And kind regards to the Nielsen family.

My dear child,

In your letter of 20 January you again expressed several wishes, which we will gladly fulfil, provided no obstacles present themselves. Naturally we will make inquiries first, so as to be on the safe side. The knife and wallet are feasible, but we can't fulfil the third request because, as you may know, we no longer have such objects in our possession. If you lack the item and have savings, then buy it for yourself there; if not, we will endeavour to replace it with an inferior version. As Mum has already told you, your book order was already forwarded last week, and we are curious to find out whether it has been dispatched. If so, you will soon receive the shipment. Today's letter is the third one we have written to you this week, and so it is no wonder that there is little to write about. I don't really understand why your departure has been delayed by the refusal of the visa when, after all, the first transport took the same route.[7] The circumstances are such that each day brings new regulations. One must exercise patience and sit tight. Just don't become impatient. In the last letter I also suggested that you number your letters, and as you see from the confirmation of the one received today, the letter dated 3 January has arrived today, after the one dated 20 January. I want to tell you before you leave that you can send short letters of twenty-five words through the German Red Cross, even from Palestine. Make inquiries in good time at the League in Copenhagen.[8]

Tomorrow, as usual, we will be in Höditz, where time always passes so quickly for us because it is so pleasant to chat.

Keep well, love and kisses,

Your devoted Father

6 František Leirich (1864–1941), factory worker at the Meissner firm.

7 Franz Meissner was waiting to emigrate to Palestine.

8 The Danish division of the Women's International League for Peace and Freedom had supported the Youth Aliyah group in Denmark.

DOC. 298

On 4 February 1941 Gert Körbel from Prague informs Nathan Schwalb in Geneva about the preparatory courses for emigration from the Protectorate[1]

Letter from Gert Körbel,[2] Na Zderaze 14, Prague II, to Nathan Schwalb,[3] Boulevard des Philosophes 12, Geneva, dated 4 February 1941

Dear Nathan,

I hereby confirm receipt of your letters dated 6 and 20 January.[4] Many thanks for them. So, I returned from my trip a few days ago and have now gained quite a good overview. The few retraining groups are developing well, despite the rather harsh winter conditions. I have also regained optimism with regard to the older group. It is very, very difficult of course, but we will nonetheless succeed in really acquiring a core group of such people. I spent a somewhat longer time with what is unfortunately at present the only group of younger people. They have only been together in this configuration for a short time, and therefore it is difficult to make a judgement. At any rate, however, the group is quite good in terms of its attitude to work and its cultural work (Hebrew, in particular). Naturally, the human interaction between them is not yet as close and warm as it should be. But because everyone is making a genuine effort, we will certainly make some progress here too.

Other than that, we are now already beginning to prepare to set up the retraining site in the spring. In doing so, our chief principle will be shared responsibility, [and] decentralization. We want to apply this principle in every way possible, right from when the groups are being put together. We will try hard to locate the groups belonging to a particular social set as close together as possible. At present, developments point to the emergence of two centres for new settlements. The younger group is already very active: they are discussing the retraining plans, making plans for the future, and studying. In general, a number of friendships have emerged between the people of our retraining programme. Even now, when so many are not in the process of retraining, they have maintained contact with each other, sometimes through letters, sometimes in person. – We are also in relatively close contact with all the people, which is very important with regard to setting up the next retraining site. Above all, we encourage them to diligently learn Hebrew, to read good books, and the like. We already have a very good overview of our people's proficiency in Hebrew, and next time I will be able to tell you even more

1 Lavon Institute, Labour Archives, III-37A-1-138B, fol. 133r–v. This document has been translated from German.

2 Jiří, also Gert, Körbel (b. 1919), student; moved from Brno to Prague in 1939; began attempts to emigrate to Peru at the end of that year; deported on 10 August 1942 to Theresienstadt, where he worked as an educator and was a member of Hehalutz; deported to Auschwitz on 19 Oct. 1944; probably perished in the labour camp in Litoměřice.

3 Nathan Schwalb (1908–2004), trade unionist; studied law in Lwów; emigrated to Palestine in 1929; employee of Hehalutz in Prague and Vienna, 1938–1939; helped establish the World Centre of the Hehalutz movement in Geneva; together with the American Jewish Joint Distribution Committee, World Jewish Congress, and the Swiss Red Cross, helped organize relief operations for the Jews in the German sphere of influence; returned to Palestine in 1945; from 1946, worked for the Union of Hebrew Labourers in Eretz Israel (Histradut), a Jewish trade union organization.

4 The letter dated 20 Jan. 1941 is included in the file: Lavon Institute, Labour Archives, fol. 131.

about this. In any event, one can already say that the general level has improved quite a lot, and that there are already a substantial number who are fairly advanced here (over fifty by now), and that there is good reason to hope that the upturn will continue. Everyone in the retraining programme will now do a month of Hebrew. An intensive course will be held here in Prague, there will be exams, etc.

The girls in the retraining programme posed a certain problem, even during the previous year. We are now looking after them more, and above all we have also seen to it that most of them learn how to cook and to run a household properly.

Today I also want to tell you something about the young generation, about the younger ones. The retraining courses offered by Youth Aid[5] are quite successful. In Prague and Ostrau, they really are going just as we wish; all the instructors there are young. In Brünn and Olmütz, some are young, some are professors. In Brünn, where courses have been offered for two years now, we have become fairly well established. In Olmütz, where the courses began just recently, we have only had partial success thus far. During my stay there, I had a chance to take part in a teachers' meeting, and on that occasion I made several suggestions for reorganization according to our principles. Elsewhere too we are seeing to it that the youngsters are being prepared for their future – that, above all, they learn Hebrew and choose productive occupations.

To finish, something about emigration. Erich[6] has already written to tell you how things stand with the youngsters. My own case has still not been decided. But it is clear that we are doing everything possible so that we don't lose out on certificates.

I think this letter will give you an idea of how things stand, and I hope you will write again soon.

By the way, it may interest you to know that I also received news from Willi Smulovits not long ago.

With warm regards,

Your

5 Jewish Youth Aid, a division of the Central Zionist Association, took in young people between the ages of 12 and 17, prepared them for emigration in Prague and Brno, and, along with the Jewish Religious Community, set up Youth Aliyah schools in Prague and Brno.

6 Presumably: Dr Erich Oesterreicher (1910–1944), lawyer; practised law in Olomouc; one of the Hehalutz leaders; deported in Dec. 1941 to Theresienstadt, where he was head of the central labour office; deported in Oct. 1944 to Auschwitz, where he was murdered.

DOC. 299

On 12 February 1941 Olga Keller writes to Walter Jacob about her emigration and her new life in Bolivia[1]

Letter dated 12 February 1941, from Olga Keller,[2] Casilla de Correo 334, La Paz, Bolivia, to Walter Jacob,[3] until 14 February in General Roca 1654, Florida (FCCA), from 15 February in Buenos Aires, Montevideo 1306, dep. 22, Argentina.

Dear Mr Walter Jacob,

Your letter gave me such great pleasure. I have known for quite a long time, of course, that you are the director of the German theatre – I follow your work in the *Argentinisches Tageblatt* – and I also read in that paper that you have married Lotte Reger.[4] (Please give her my warm regards – I can still recall every one of her roles from my time in Teplitz.) But in the general pessimism that overwhelms everyone at times, I have done nothing to resume contact with you. Hence my great delight that there still exists such a thing as human interest. Incidentally, I experienced the same thing once before, not all that long ago. Do you still remember Arne Laurin,[5] the editor-in-chief of the *Prager Presse*? One fine day I got a letter from him; he is now working at the Czechoslovak consulate general in New York. It had been sent via post restante and came into my hands by chance. Someone or other had told this friend that I was in Bolivia, and he tried to find me, without having an address. Since then we have been corresponding regularly, and the letters are at times really very interesting.

I assume you don't know how our circle, or the remnants of it, came to disband. It was like this: on the evening of 14 September 1938 we were sitting together, as usual, in Dr Neubauer's[6] home, Hurrle,[7] Dr Knöpfmacher[8] – his wife had already fled with the little boy to Prague when previous disturbances occurred – and also a married couple, who were otherwise not part of our circle. There was the usual commotion in

1 Archiv der Berendsohn Forschungsstelle für deutsche Exilliteratur, PWK Korr. 1941, folders I, J, K. Published in Paul Walter Jacob and Frithjof Trapp (eds.), *Reunion der Überlebenden: P. Walter Jacobs Korrespondenz mit Freunden und Kollegen 1939–1949* (Hamburg: Walter-A.-Berendsohn-Forschungsstelle für deutsche Exilliteratur, 2005), pp. 74–79. This document has been translated from German.

2 Olga Keller, actress; fled from Teplitz-Schönau to Prague in Sept. 1938; emigrated to Bolivia via Italy in 1939, and later lived in Oruro.

3 Paul Walter Jacob, pseudonym Paul Walter (1905–1977), actor, dramaturge, and writer; worked at theatres in Koblenz, Lübeck, Cologne, and Essen, 1929–1933; dismissed in 1933; emigrated to Paris in 1933 and to Prague in 1936; worked at theatres in Teplice-Šanov and Prague, 1936–1938; emigrated to Argentina in 1939; co-founder and director of the Free German Theatre in Buenos Aires from 1939; returned to Germany in 1950; director of the Municipal Theatres of Dortmund until 1962.

4 Liselott (Lotte) Reger (1899–1972), actress; worked at the municipal theatre in Teplice-Šanov, 1928–1938; emigrated in 1939 to Argentina, where she married Paul Walter Jacob, who became her second husband, the same year; co-founder of the Free German Theatre in Buenos Aires; actress in the Federal Republic of Germany after 1949.

5 Arne Laurin, born Arnošt Lustig (1889–1945), journalist and politician; editor-in-chief of the *Prager Presse*; founder and head of a press archive on the German question, 1921–1938; emigrated to the USA in 1938; worked at the Czechoslovak consulate general in New York; editor of the press service of the Czechoslovak National Assembly in Paris.

the streets: there had been shouting and 'rallies' for days.[9] One evening Dr Riethof[10] was driving us home in his car when the vehicle was surrounded by a crowd in front of the theatre – we could not move an inch forward or backward. The people shook their fists menacingly and shouted, 'Off to Palestine with you; you deserve to die a miserable death.' I have been good at hating ever since, but that evening all I could do was stare, completely devoid of hatred, at the twisted faces. They were just kids, all barely 17 years old. On the evening at the Neubauers', we kept going out onto the balcony to discuss how we might get home. Perhaps you will ask why we did not just stay at home in the first place on such evenings, but in those days, more than ever, one felt the need to be together. Incidentally, we were pretty much the only Jewish families to have stayed; our men thought it cowardly to flee – until that evening. Let me describe our mood. The radio was almost the only voice in the room. Suddenly the telephone rang, and Hurrle was summoned [to answer it]. I don't know what it was he found out; at any rate, he came back into the room, deathly pale, and said: 'You have to go to Prague this instant. I will drive the Neubauers, the rest of you need to find some way to get a car.' We couldn't get anything else out of him, and as his barely concealed anxiety indicated to us that there was a real danger, we all hastened to pack up our things. It was 11 p.m. Do I need to tell you how we packed a bag at home with the help of the maid, roused from her sleep, just some undergarments and a couple of dresses? We let the child sleep until Dr Knöpfmacher came with a car to fetch us. It was 1 a.m. by then. Suitcase, child, and dog under my arm, we left the apartment as it was – do you still remember? – and went downstairs. Two Czech policemen stood at the front door with guns at the ready: 'Where do you want to go in the middle of the night?' 'To Prague, we are Jews.' 'Just go to bed; nothing will happen, we'll protect you,' these good men said and, deeply moved, we shook their hands. By the way, they had also taken their wives and children to Prague – just to be on the safe side! This drive through the night – it was foggy, no one said a word; here and there the shadow of a tank emerged – it was eerie. But, dear Jacob, not one of us had a sense of irrevocability at the time. Then there was a grotesque little scene. In Prague there was not a room to be had, literally, and the middle classes from the towns of the Sudetenland, if they were Jewish, spent that night sitting on the steps in front of the railway station, because every place was closed at that hour.

As an aside, my husband drove back that night, because he considered it beneath him to leave his post because it had become perilous. Curious male notions of honour! Besides, Dr Knöpfmacher drove back too, and then his 17-year-old son was in the camp

6 Dr Bernard Neubauer (b. 1889), surgeon.

7 Curth Hurrle (1907–1974), dramaturge and director; joined the NSDAP in 1933; worked for the Munich Kammerspiele and in radio broadcasting in Stuttgart; director of the municipal theatres in Teplice-Šanov and Most, where he employed many emigrants; artistic director in Neiße in 1940 and later in Gliwice; artistic director of the Bavarian State Operetta in Munich after 1945.

8 Presumably: Dr Friedrich (Fritz) Knöpfmacher (1886–1957), lawyer.

9 Spurred on by the Sudeten German Party (SdP) under Konrad Henlein, in Sept. 1938 demonstrators became increasingly vocal in their calls for the incorporation of the Sudeten German territories into the German Reich. In the process, there were growing numbers of antisemitic attacks. Thousands of Jews fled from the Czech peripheral regions to the Bohemian heartland.

10 Presumably Dr Georg Riethof, factory owner.

in Oranienburg for several months, without his parents being able to receive any word from him.

Director Hurrle continued to act in a most friendly manner. He brought carpets and other valuables to the Neubauers from their apartment by car, and each time these trips could have cost him more than just his job. May then he also be forgiven for having 'betrayed' his Lili now and then. I have a delightful anecdote about that, which I will gladly tell you some day, if you like – discretion becomes an absurdity when one person is in Palestine and the other is a theatre director in Teplitz.

And the story is so amusing that it extends beyond the individuals themselves. I don't know what has become of the other acquaintances.

We have ended up here. We did not manage to get our furniture to Prague, and I have no idea what has become of it. Our child[11] went to England on a Kindertransport. Then the war broke out and every opportunity to communicate or to see each other again was taken away. It's easy to write such a sentence, but try to read between the lines. Then the visa for Bolivia. Then an interesting interlude with the German authorities – I will gladly tell you about that too, some day – and then all of our luggage was confiscated at the railway station because 'insufficient taxes had been paid on it'. It contained everything we had acquired for emigration with the money we had left; from Teplitz we only had the few things from the night we had fled. We travelled without any luggage, just two pairs of pyjamas in a small suitcase, one change of clothes, a dress for me and another suit for my husband, besides the one he was wearing – just what we had taken along as hand luggage for three days in Genoa before being able to unpack the big suitcases on the ship. And that is also the sum of our possessions to this very day! Our suitcases were released later, after our relatives had made great sacrifices to pay a large sum for this purpose, only to have them loaded onto the *Orazio*[12] and, uninsured, sink along with it. (Insurance had to be paid in dollars, and that was impossible for our folk to do.) Dear Mr Jacob, please believe me when I say that when I heard this news, I had a good laugh for the first time since my emigration. I had already reconciled myself to being a poor wretch, and the adverse fate of our last remaining possessions was not without a truly comical side.

We have also been lucky in another respect. Our child came here aboard the last Italian ship – the girl had travelled alone through half of Europe and across two seas, and I was overjoyed to greet her in Arica.

Here – I would have to write many pages to tell you about this place; it is a very interesting country. A country of contrasts with respect to society, landscape, and culture. Indians in ancient traditional attire, and streamlined motor cars, tropics and glaciers. It may interest you that I am writing a book about Bolivia for a North American publishing house. What else are we doing? We have not yet succeeded in earning a living. All day long, in grimy overalls, we stir soft soap and washing soda, and we live in a room that I would like to tell you about one day as well. The only thing that has not suffered is my sense of humour – at least I have two pairs of stockings that are still intact, and when I put on my travel suit I still look like an elegant woman. What one misses most

11 Sonja Keller.

12 The Italian liner *Orazio*, used on the Genoa–Valparaíso (Chile) route, sank in Jan. 1940 with more than 100 passengers on board, including a great many Jewish refugees.

of all here – apart from money, of course – is people with whom one could converse. The greatest riffraff have emigrated to this place, petty bourgeois and small-town individuals in the way they live and in their souls. And pedlars – just between us, we are indeed a wretched little community! That is why it did me so much good to hear from you. Incidentally, I am in touch with many friends of old, for example, Dr Keller[13] from the *Prager Tagblatt*, who has been through a real odyssey. With one shirt in his briefcase, he fled across the Polish border, and is in England at the moment; he has a number of university job offers in the bag, and has not been granted entry to any country. I am looking around for your leading man. It would be a joy for me to give someone the chance to work in his profession again, and to live in a cultured city. I have already tracked one down. He lives in Santa Cruz and works as a teacher, and he was in the ensemble that performed the *Mousetrap* in Berlin.[14] You will hear about him. Perhaps I will even place an advert in the newspaper.

With regard to the newspaper: Dr Schück is utterly charming towards me; he really helps me in a kind way with my journalistic work. He is also helping me to write for America, and you can imagine what a few dollars mean here, where one of these things is worth 60 bolivianos and one person can live for a whole month on 10 dollars. Please put in a good word for me there, if you have not already done so. I don't know Dr Schück personally, and he treats me like a friend.

Now don't go off somewhere in the world again and lose touch, but instead let me know how you and Mrs Reger are in terms of life and work, what it is like to be in Buenos [Aires], and what plans you have concerning work. You unfortunately forgot to enclose the list of premieres in your letter, but I know all of them from the *Argentinisches Tageblatt*. You won't believe how the likes of us follow such things.

I am using a new typewriter for the first time to write to you today. An acquaintance lent it to me. My own, as you know, is at the bottom of the ocean. So forgive me for the typing errors. I would be most grateful if you could suggest a way for me to earn money with the typewriter. It seems to be the only work of which I am really capable.

Warmest regards to you both from my husband and me, and get in touch again soon!
Yours,

Wurmser[15] is in Cochabamba and has a lending library there.

13 Dr Rudolf Keller (1875–1964), journalist and biochemist; editor of the newspapers *Prager Tagblatt* and *Aussiger Tagblatt*; head of a scientific laboratory in Prague, 1925–1938; honorary doctorate from the University of Basel; emigrated to the USA via Britain in 1939 and worked at the Madison Foundation.

14 In 1931–1932 the Theatre Troupe 1931 had performed the play *The Mousetrap* ('Die Mäusefalle') by Gustav von Wangenheim (1895–1975) in the Berlin artists' colony.

15 Ernst Wurmser (1882–1950), actor and director; acting engagements in Prague, Berlin, Vienna, Breslau, Opava, and Brno, and collaborated on approximately thirty silent and ninety sound films from 1917 to 1933; director and actor in Teplice-Šanov, 1937–1938; emigrated to Bolivia in 1939; acting engagements at the Free German Theatre in Buenos Aires from 1941.

DOC. 300

On 13 February 1941 Wilhelm Wrbka reaffirms his wish to buy the Rix fashion house in Mährisch-Ostrau[1]

Letter from Wilhelm Wrbka,[2] Mährisch-Ostrau, to the Reich Protector of Bohemia and Moravia, Prague, dated 13 February 1941 (copy)

Re: de-Jewification of the Rix fashion house in Mährisch-Ostrau.[3]
File reference no. II/1 Jd. 40 204/40.
The NSDAP Kreisleitung in Mährisch-Ostrau has instructed me to submit a proposal to the Office of the Reich Protector that will make it possible for local applicants to acquire the Rix fashion house.

As you are aware, I am myself applying to purchase the Rix fashion house, but I received notice on 16 November 1940, file reference no. II/1 Jd. 40 204, that the only authorized candidate for the purchase is Mr Alfred Wieland, Halle/Saale.[4] The official responsible orally stated the following reasons for deferring my interest in the purchase:

(1) Mr Alfred Wieland declared his interest in the acquisition earlier than I did.

(2) My plan does not guarantee financing in the event of an Aryanization.

With regard to 1), I wish to point out that I have been attempting to purchase the Rix fashion house since May 1939, and with the express endorsement of the relevant departments, namely the office of the Oberlandrat and the NSDAP Kreisleitung. The fact that the Bohemian Union Bank[5] wrote to your office on my behalf on 11 October 1940 concerning my interest in the purchase does not mean that my interest only arose at that time. Rather, the letter from the Bohemian Union Bank, as its contents indicate, had the specific purpose of making it known to you that, considering the position of the Jew Rix,[6] a sale on a commercial basis is not possible. Instead, Aryanization can only be carried out by appointing a trustee for the sale. An inquiry to the NSDAP Kreisleitung and the office of the Oberlandrat will suffice to confirm the validity of my claims that I presented my acquisition plan to the authorities in Mährisch-Ostrau as early as May 1939 without objections being raised there.

With regard to 2), when it comes to the impression that arose there, to the effect that financing is not guaranteed in the event of my acquiring the firm, I venture to point out that my application was declined even before I was asked to supply proof of funds. Allow me to point out that I myself am able to mobilize 1 million korunas from my own re-

1 NAP, ÚŘP-ST, 109-6-62, box 113, fols. 21–22. This document has been translated from German.
2 Wilhelm Wrbka (1896–1945), retailer and department store owner; joined the NSDAP in 1939; trustee of the Rix company.
3 The fashion house was sold by the company's founder, Julius Rix, to Adolf Lüftschitz in 1906. The firm was one of the largest and most prestigious fashion houses in Czechoslovakia and had several branches. In the 1930s the firm had approximately 250 employees.
4 This notification is not included in the file.
5 The Bohemian Union Bank played a leading role in the Aryanization of numerous firms in the Protectorate. See also Doc. 263, fn. 9.
6 This refers to Adolf Lüftschitz (1874–1943), who changed his name to Rix for business reasons after he had purchased the fashion house. He was deported from Moravská Ostrava to Theresienstadt on 26 Sept. 1942 and then to Auschwitz on 18 Dec. 1943.

sources. In addition, the factory owner Emmerich Machold[7] in Freudenthal has made a binding commitment to place a sum of 5 million korunas at my disposal for the Aryanization of the Rix fashion house. I enclose a copy of the agreement I concluded to this effect with Mr Emmerich Machold.[8] As a result, the sum of 6 million korunas, which is sufficient to ensure the financing, is immediately available. I would also be able to procure an additional sum, should this be required, through an intra-family loan from my uncle, Baron Karl von Baillou.[9] Under these circumstances and considering that I have worked for the firm for twenty years, I ask that my request be granted and that I be approved as an applicant to purchase the Rix fashion house.

Heil Hitler![10]

DOC. 301

On 26 February 1941 the Jewish Religious Community of Prague has to issue a summons requiring Jews to clear snow[1]

Summons from the Jewish Religious Community of Prague, dated 26 February 1941[2]

This summons must be brought with you.

P.T.

With reference to the Government Regulation, dated 23 January 1941,[3] and the Regulation of the Reich Protector, dated 5 March 1940,[4] you are summoned by order of the Central Office for Jewish Emigration in Prague (Office of the Senior Commander of the Security Police at the Office of the Reich Protector of Bohemia and Moravia) to appear on Friday, 28 February 1941, *punctually* at 8:05 a.m. in front of the military guardroom at the entrance to the Prague-Ruzin military airfield. You will be engaged in clearing snow at the Ruzin airfield for *eight* hours on this day. Prepare yourself accordingly (dress warmly, take food with you).

We explicitly bring to your attention the fact that every recipient of *this letter must fully comply with the summons*, or else expect serious legal consequences. The day and time are to be strictly observed.

7 Emmerich Machold (b. 1894), business manager; joined the NSDAP in 1938; owner of a textile factory and an agricultural estate in Bruntál (Freudenthal) in Moravian Silesia. During the war the factory initially employed 200 and later 300 Jewish women from the Auschwitz concentration camp.

8 This is not included in the file.

9 Correctly: Baron Carl von Baillou (1882–1953), landowner and owner of a private library in Hustopeče and Kolešovice. Wilhelm Wrbka was married to the baron's niece, Baroness Irene Sophie Antonine von Baillou (b. 1902).

10 Wrbka's efforts were unsuccessful. As the Reich Protector of Bohemia and Moravia had stated in an express letter dated 9 Feb. 1940, trustees were not permitted to apply. See Doc. 269.

1 JMP, DP 78 Jachnin, folder 4. This document has been translated from German.

2 The summons was written in German and in Czech.

3 Government Regulation on Measures to Control the Workforce, 23 Jan. 1941, *Sammlung der Gesetze und Verordnungen des Protektorates Böhmen und Mähren vom 3.2.1941*, no. 46 (1941), pp. 111–123.

4 Regulation of the Reich Protector of Bohemia and Moravia on the Supervision of the Jews and Jewish Organizations, *Verordnungsblatt des Reichsprotektors*, 1940, no. 11, pp. 77–79.

You reach the airfield on the number 11 tram, last stop Wokowitz, and from there you go by foot. The travel time from the city centre to Wokowitz is approximately 45 minutes, and the walk from Wokowitz to Ruzin takes 30–40 minutes. Special attention is also drawn to the fact that you are to refrain from using the bus both on the way there and on the way back.

DOC. 302

In February 1941 Rudolf Stier and Helmut Schmidt emphasize that Jews are no longer permitted to play a role in the economy of the Protectorate of Bohemia and Moravia[1]

Foreword to the book *Die Ausschaltung der Juden aus der Wirtschaft des Protektorats Böhmen und Mähren* (The Exclusion of the Jews from the Economy of the Protectorate of Bohemia and Moravia) by Rudolf Stier[2] and Helmut Schmidt[3]

The vital force of a people, as a living organism, and thus a people's justification for existence, is most clearly demonstrated in its recognition of all influences that are harmful to it and the application of its will to eliminate this harm. The German people has had the good fortune, in its times of direst need, to have had a man who has recognized the symptoms of disease in the German people with great clarity and who has successfully communicated this insight to the entire German people and called on its power of resistance to eliminate this harm. It was with this recognition that the recovery process of the German people in all areas began and in doing so preserved the people from downfall. In 1933 the ideological principles of National Socialism became the principles of the German people. Eight years of National Socialist rule have proved the validity of the National Socialist principles and with this demonstrated the vital force of the German people on an unimagined scale. All along, National Socialism has regarded the influence of the Jews on the German people as a source of major harm and, as a result, soon after the taking of power made its aim the complete elimination of Jewish influence on the German people. Once the Jews had been removed from the political and cultural life of the German people, their exclusion from economic life followed.

By enacting the Nuremberg Laws,[4] the National Socialist state clearly expressed its attitude towards Jewry. German economic life, then completely dominated by Jewish influence, could eliminate this influence only by excluding the Jews. As the Jews were unwilling to withdraw voluntarily from the economy, their exclusion had to be accomplished through official measures.

1 Rudolf Stier and Helmut Schmidt, *Die Ausschaltung der Juden aus der Wirtschaft des Protektorats Böhmen und Mähren: Kommentar zu den Verordnungen des Reichsprotektors über das jüdische Vermögen und zur Ausschaltung der Juden aus der Wirtschaft des Protektorats: Zusammenstellung der übrigen ergangenen Verordnungen nach dem Stande vom 15. März 1941* (Prague: Böhmisch-Mährische Verlags- und Druckerei, 1941). This document has been translated from German.

2 Dr Rudolf Stier (b. 1907); joined the NSDAP in 1931; SA-Obersturmführer; Regierungsrat in the Reich Ministry of Economics; from autumn 1939, head of Section VII a ('De-Jewification') in the Office of the Reich Protector.

3 Helmut Schmidt was a probationary civil servant in the Office of the Reich Protector.

4 See PMJ 1/198, 199, 201, 212, and 223.

In the territory of the Old Reich, in the Ostmark, and in the Sudetenland, the de-Jewification of the economy can be regarded as complete.

When, after the disintegration of the Czechoslovak Republic, the current president, Hácha, placed the Bohemian and Moravian lands under the protection of the German Reich,[5] it became apparent that these regions were afflicted by Jewish influence to an even greater degree than in the Old Reich. All intellectual and economic life was completely in thrall to the Jews. How strong the influence was in the economy in particular is indicated by the fact that the value of Jewish assets in the Bohemian and Moravian lands alone almost equalled the value of formerly Jewish assets in the Old Reich. The Greater German Reich, at the moment it began to share responsibility for the lands of Bohemia and Moravia, therefore extended to these lands as well its intention of eliminating the harmful influence of Jewry on the people. The de-Jewification of trade and industry thus begins at the moment of the incorporation of Bohemia and Moravia into the Greater German Reich.

In numerous provisions which have been harmonized with the laws and decrees of the Reich, the Reich Protector has laid the foundations for the exclusion of the Jews from the economy.[6] It is the purpose of the present commentary to explain them. At the time of publication of the present work, a potential buyer has been found for almost all Jewish enterprises. However, the acquisition of Jewish commercial enterprises raises a host of problems for the purchaser. Our views on these issues are stated in the commentary, whereby substantial importance is placed on providing explanation and not encumbering the commentary with legal considerations. It is intended rather as a practical guide for every purchaser. This is all the more necessary because the acquisition of commercial enterprises is taking place at a time when the Greater German Reich, in a war that was forced upon it, must fight for its existence, and when many regulations regarding the wartime economy and control of raw materials exert a decisive influence upon the acquisition of a commercial enterprise and, in particular, on its value.

Further, the explanatory comments on the regulations and decrees of the Reich Protector go into great detail on the de-Jewification of real estate and the exclusion of Jews from the occupation of sales representative.

Finally, the rights and duties of the trustees of Jewish enterprises are explained in detail.

May this work contribute to the complete and rapid liberation of the lands of Bohemia and Moravia from Jewish influence and thus enable them to integrate fully into the German Reich and its economy.

5 See Introduction, p. 14.

6 The Regulation of the Reich Protector of Bohemia and Moravia on Jewish Assets (21 June 1939) prohibited Jews from acquiring plots of land as well as commercial enterprises and securities, and decreed that trustees should be appointed to administer Jewish assets: see Doc. 247. The regulation was followed by nine implementing decrees and additional regulations: see Doc. 269.

DOC. 303
On 10 April 1941 the Aryan Society in Bohemia and Moravia submits proposals to Prime Minister Eliáš on how to deal with the Jewish population[1]

Letter (registered post) from the Aryan Society in Bohemia and Moravia,[2] Czech Institute for the Study of Jewry in Bohemia and Moravia, signed Koči-Rmen,[3] Prague II, 525, to the Government of the Protectorate of Bohemia and Moravia, Prime Minister's Office, for the attention of the Head of Government Mr Eliáš,[4] Prague, dated 10 April 1941[5]

Re: official registration of Jews in the Protectorate, Jewish identity cards, keeping statistics, visible identification of Jews

Since time immemorial, the Czech nation in all the Bohemian lands has been strongly anti-Jewish. Its clear position against Jews was not, however, based on any theories, but was the only possible consequence of the destructive and subversive actions of this degenerate race. Every uncorrupted historian can provide proof of this, from the measures to defend our nation taken by the princes and later kings of the Přemyslid[6] dynasty up to the time of the Habsburg monarchy. The Jewish race is also the only race in the whole world that at all times, in the documented history of mankind, encompassing about five millennia, *has always sparked blind hatred among all individuals.* This hatred stems from the eternal *destructiveness* of this race, always practically and scientifically verified over and over again, in the fields of culture, society, politics, and economic life, something which is anchored in its invariable hereditary racial characteristics – its criminal nature; the malevolence of its firmly upheld petrified religion; its social and racial peculiarity; its low-grade fertility; its lack of creative ability and its adaptive parasitism, physical degeneration, monstrous sexuality, and pathological morbidity; its insane mysticism; its cowardice with regard to combat; laziness etc., etc.

Jewry will never blend in with its environment; nowhere does it become the fellow worker of its host people or even a loyal servant of its conqueror. Even in Biblical times it was the case that the rulers of Egypt and Babylon let them [the Jews] go, or rather expelled them from captivity, since in the long term they are of no permanent use, even as slaves, due to their racial incompatibility with every other race then and now. Since those times, the history of their wanderings is a constant alternation between planting the diabolical seed of Judaism among the peoples and remaining subject to the curse meted out to them on account of their anti-human characteristics. All other races have come a long way and have undergone their own creative and remarkable development regarding freedom of conscience and the development of moral codes, only Judaism never did. For over ten years, I have studied Judaism. In this time I have lifted the secrets

1 Copy in JMP, DP 59. This document has been translated from Czech.

2 The Aryan Society in Bohemia and Moravia, which sought to prevent all Jewish influence on life in Bohemia and Moravia, repeatedly approached both the Czech interior ministry and the Reich Protector's Office for permission to set up an official association, but never received it.

3 B. Koči-Rmen, journalist and writer.

4 Mr Eliáš is referred to in the original with the title 'Ing.', denoting a graduate in engineering.

5 The letterhead is written in Czech and German.

6 A Bohemian royal dynasty that ruled over the duchy and later kingdom of Bohemia from the ninth to the early fourteenth century.

which both presidents of the former republic[7] kept hidden, as it was not the Czech people, but international and domestic Jewry that ruled in the former Czechoslovakia. In the process, I became convinced that, like a number of known living or recently extinct relicts in the animal kingdom, Judaism is also a *fossilized race* with living conditions entirely different from the environment in which it lives and which operates not for the benefit but to the detriment of the environment: not having the ability to adapt to the environment, it attempts to *forcibly change the conditions of the environment to its own needs.* Meanwhile, influenced by their religion, the Jews are endowed with a pathological megalomania that hardens their utopian vision that, despite all their negative characteristics and typical Jewish laziness, 45 million Jews will take control over 2,500 million other men!

However, this utopia was able to become reality not because the Jews are, as the 'chosen people', endowed with the protection from divine providence, or due to their superhuman characteristics (which, on the contrary, are below the human average), but because for centuries and in all countries they have been allowed to work towards the goal that has been defined by their religion, through the inattention of humanity, warned by their best leaders to no avail. The independent nations posed the greatest barrier to them. Therefore, everywhere they severed the roots of tradition, art, [and] national consciousness, [and] replaced them with a grey, uniform internationalism in all sectors and expressions of national existence, all the way through to the sciences. They themselves fostered their national distinctiveness so energetically and exclusively that even today we do not know much about them, and they have endured as a closed racial tribe despite the diversity of the environment of Europe, Asia, America, of West and East. They have weakened and led the arts, politics, sociology, economy, etc., etc. astray by having the fallacies they have instilled into mankind apply to everyone else except themselves. As one example representing thousands of others: a number of Judaized Euro-American biologists, blinded by Jewish gold and career ambitions, still today assert that racial science 'is baseless' – despite the proof Judaism itself poses for the validity of racial science, despite Mendel's discoveries,[8] despite the validity of heredity in the animal and plant kingdoms that is proved each and every day, despite the proven connection between animals and man, despite the fact that one can verify the laws of heredity in the descendants of a regular pedigree bull.

But despite these scholarly good-for-nothings (scholarly, because university professors, after all, can't be called feeble-minded, and good-for-nothings, because instead of lighting the way of their nation, they are leading it down into the Jewish mire in exchange for personal gain), the development of true science will advance just like the German military, regardless of the Jewish 'army' in Palestine.

Thanks to the genius of Adolf Hitler, the Jewish danger that would have threatened European man in one or two generations has been definitively averted. The fossilized race will die out, that is clear. The problem we Czechs have in the Protectorate is how to separate our own Czech nation from the Jews without incurring damages in the

7 The author means the Czechoslovak presidents Tomáš Garrigue Masaryk (1850–1937) and Edvard Beneš (1884–1948).

8 The author means the principles of inherited genetic characteristics, named after the monk and scientist Gregor Mendel (1822–1884), who first described some of the laws of heredity.

process and despite the continued contact [with the Jews], *which the current measures, which only exist on paper and which are thus far incomplete, have not managed to prevent.* After the war there will certainly be a pan-European solution to Jewish emigration. But we also need immediate measures *right now,* and it is the right and the obligation of the Czech Protectorate government.

Reserving the right, as in all previous submissions to the authorities, for additional proposals, we demand the following:

I. *The complete registration of Jews on the entire territory of the Protectorate of Bohemia and Moravia is to be immediately ordered and implemented in the shortest possible period of time.* Aryan persons living with a Jew or Jewess in matrimony or in the same household are also to be considered Jews. Jews are not to be allowed to have Aryan servants or foster children etc. at all.

II. *Apart from the central registration sites to be designated by the Ministry of the Interior, partial lists of registered Jews, arranged both alphabetically and according to their place of residence, are to be made freely available to Aryans for perusal upon presentation of identification in designated separate rooms at the political office of the first instance.* These lists are to correspond to the administrative districts. The office will initiate an expedited procedure to investigate remarks by Aryans made in writing and submitted unstamped regarding information they discovered on the lists or clear suspicions as to whether additional persons should also be on the list. Concealing a person's Jewishness is to be punished, and all newly identified Jews are to be recorded in the main registry.

III. *All Jewish persons and their spouses, as well as persons living in the same household, regardless of their race, are to be issued a 'Jewish card' with a photo for a set fee, which they must show whenever required to present personal identification, including on non-official business.*

IV. *Jewish identity cards are to be numbered in a sequence, so the last card issued will be marked with the total number of cards issued to date. The central registration office is to implement this. Every Jew and person considered a Jew must state the number in all official communications with the public authorities.*

V. *So that the rest of the Aryan population, for now at least in written communications, are aware they are dealing with a Jew, Jews must put a capital – Ž.*[9] *– with a full stop and underlined, before their actual name in all written materials, as well as on the nameplate on the door of their residence. The doors of rooms where, for example, a single Jew resides must be marked either in the above fashion or with a Star of David.*

VI. *Changes to the Jewish names of Jews are to be prohibited by the relevant authorities with immediate effect. Jews who have previously received permission to change Jewish or Jewish-sounding names shall be required by law to use both names (to prevent misunderstanding among Aryans) and add the above-mentioned Ž. After full registration has been completed, Aryans who present full Aryan documentation and confirmation from the main registration office that they are not on the list of Jews, or have no more than one sixteenth Jewish blood, will be permitted to change their Jewish names to Aryan ones.*

VII. *Changes within the Jewish population which are important for the state and the broader public are to be kept on file and systematically monitored by the State Statistical*

9 For *Žid*, the Czech word for 'Jew'.

Office. This especially concerns the exact determination of the number of Jews in the various professions in the [former] Republic and, in relation to the present time, emigration, sickness levels, and all other fields important for the economy, politics, sociology, racial biology, etc. Instead of earlier imprecise reports made by Jews themselves, all measures must be based on figures from the relevant offices and central registers. The data is to be made available to all interested parties.

VIII. *The inconsistency arising from Jews being baptized is to be resolved by prohibiting the conversion of Jews to Aryan denominations.* Jews are only to be allowed to be members of the Jewish faith or to belong to no religion. Jewish conversion to Aryan religious denominations contravenes the public interest and the prohibition of Aryans mixing with Jews, and contradicts the scientific finding that, upon converting, the Jew does not surrender his faith, for which he continues to work by breaking down the environment which he has entered as an equal through conversion.

IX. *By law, Jews are to be excluded from all places where their presence, though temporary, causes revulsion among or danger for Aryans – primarily in spa resorts, hairdressers, and consulting Aryan physicians – by a direct ban.*[10] So far nothing has been done with regard to this important point. Given that there are a sufficient number of authorized Jewish physicians, it is absurd for Jews to be permitted to consult an Aryan physician, whatever the nationality. Other bans are also fully justified, given the marked proliferation of venereal and other diseases among Jews.

As orders and bans issued against Jews are mere words without the appropriate sanctions, *we demand that punishments be set for violations of all the above points, in the form of both fines and imprisonment, whereby the principles of probation are to be generally disregarded, given the evil that Judaism represents. All the costs necessary for the implementation [of the bans] are to be borne by the Jews.*

We ask that the relevant authorities issue an order to prepare to clear out the centres of Prague and other large cities and to resettle the Jews into designated districts, the costs of which the Jewish community is to bear. A number of the above proposals have already been implemented in many European countries.[11]

With Czech greetings

I am sending the original carbon copy to the Reichsprotektoramt,[12] Abt. f. d. Politik, und jüdische,[13] for inspection.

10 From 26 June 1941, Jews were only allowed to go to the hairdresser between 8 a.m. and 10 a.m., in accordance with a regulation issued by the police headquarters in Prague. On 13 June 1942, the Ministry of Economics and Employment issued a decree prohibiting Jews with health insurance, as well as their relatives, from consulting Aryan doctors: Friedmann, *Rechtsstellung*, pp. 249 and 256.

11 The first ghetto in occupied Poland was established in Oct. 1939 in Piotrków Trybunalski. The Lodz ghetto was sealed off on 30 April 1940 and the Warsaw ghetto was surrounded with a fence in Nov. 1940: see the Introduction to PMJ 4, as well as, for example, PMJ 4/54, 180, 183, and 193.

12 German in the original: 'Office of the Reich Protector'.

13 Name of department in German and incomplete in the original: 'Department of Politics, and Jewish'.

DOC. 304

On 16 April 1941 State Secretary Karl Hermann Frank clarifies the conditions under which the property belonging to Jews is to be sold in order to finance their emigration[1]

Letter (marked 'confidential') from the Reich Protector of Bohemia and Moravia (Tgb. No. B.d.S. I 189/41), p.p. signed Frank, to (a) Departments I and II; (b) Groups I/1, I/2, I/3, II/1 D; (c) the Office for Moravia; (d) all Oberlandräte; and (e) the Central Office for Jewish Emigration in Prague, dated 16 April 1941[2]

Re: Securing of financial means for Jewish emigration; property acquisition by the Emigration Fund for Bohemia and Moravia.[3]
Reference: Decree dated 20 June 1940 – Tgb. B.d.S. I 1282/40.[4]
There appears to be no clear idea among individual Oberlandräte of the purpose and aim of the property acquisition effected by the Emigration Fund for Bohemia and Moravia in the implementation of my aforementioned circular decree, and the concern was raised that a delay in fulfilling the ethnopolitical tasks of the Oberlandräte could result if the Emigration Fund is involved in the transfer of Jewish-owned buildings and land into Aryan hands. To ensure the complete consistency of the tasks on both sides, the following is resolved:

The basic principle behind my Regulation on the Supervision of the Jews and Jewish Organizations, issued on 5 March 1940, is to promote Jewish emigration and secure the financial means required for this purpose. The funds that accrue to the Central Office on the basis of this regulation, however, constitute only part of the funds required for organizing and enabling the emigration of Jews without assets. Substantial means have been sent from abroad to the Central Office for Jewish Emigration. However, these sources have completely dried up since the beginning of the war. In order to now be able to continue the work on the previous scale also in wartime and, even more importantly, to create even now the capital base for a process of increased emigration once the war is over, the Senior Commander of the Security Police, as head of the Central Office for Jewish Emigration, *also had to ensure that new sources of money were found in time, as significant Reich funds would otherwise have had to be utilized.*

The course of action that suggested itself was to make the Jews themselves raise the money, i.e. to take it from their assets. That led to the idea of not only putting the assets of the religious communities and other Jewish organizations, foundations, and funds to use for the purpose, but also of using Jewish-owned houses and land for these purposes.

1 NAP, ÚŘP, I-3b-5810. This document has been translated from German.
2 The original contains handwritten notes and stamps of the Reich Protector.
3 The Emigration Fund for Bohemia and Moravia was founded by the Reich Protector by means of the Regulation on the Supervision of the Jews and Jewish Organizations (5 March 1940). The fund was supervised by the senior commander of the Security Police and the SD, Walter Stahlecker. The fund's financial resources (with an initial capital of more than 11 million korunas) were held in the account of the Central Office for Jewish Emigration at the Bohemian Union Bank in Prague: *Verordnungsblatt des Reichsprotektors*, 1940, no. 11, pp. 77–79.
4 This could not be found. It may refer to the Decree on the Securing of Financial Means for Jewish Emigration (14 June 1940).

But there was also another occurrence that urgently called for a fundamental solution to the question of transferring Jewish properties into Aryan hands. The benefits of the sale, usually at a low price, of Jewish-owned houses and land – owing to imminent emigration or the elimination of regular income through work, the Jewish owner is often under pressure and sells his property even below its actual real value – did not accrue to the general public, but instead to individuals, and not even always the most deserving ones at that. Frequently, Czechs were also the beneficiaries of this plight of the Jews.

The creation of a kind of receiving company for Jewish property was therefore urgently necessary for ethnopolitical reasons as well, especially as, owing to the state of war, neither German capital nor appropriately qualified German buyers can currently be found in sufficient numbers. In the meantime, the centralized acquisition of Jewish-owned properties by the Emigration Fund has not only eliminated all speculative buying and selling, *but has also made possible a future form of divestiture that can be adapted to the prevailing public and ethnopolitical concerns while eliminating agents' profits etc.*

With appropriately coordinated cooperation between the Oberlandräte and the Central Office for Jewish Emigration, it is entirely possible to take local circumstances and ethnic policy requirements into account in this process. The Emigration Fund is instructed to proceed with a sale in cases involving properties for which a German applicant who is economically qualified and unobjectionable in ethnopolitical terms is already available. At the same time, he must abide by the mandatory guidelines for resale. These guidelines are, in the main:

(1) The sale of formerly Jewish properties is not to be accelerated for the time being, as the price trend after the war is not yet clear. In addition, subsequent competition by applicants currently in military service must be taken into consideration.

(2) Sales are to be undertaken now if there is:

(a) a public interest,

(b) an ethnopolitical interest in the acquisition of the property on the part of a specific applicant.

(3) The assessment of the purchaser will be made by the relevant Oberlandrat. The assessment must take into account the following considerations:

(a) The buyer must be an Aryan, a resident, and, as a rule, a subject of the Reich.

(b) The buyer must pay a price commensurate with the real value of the property.

(c) To prevent the properties from being used for undesirable (speculative) purposes, the reason for purchase and the capacity for efficient management must be examined.

(d) The German buyer, with his family and his business, should make his home in the Protectorate, if possible. The situation must be avoided whereby the purchase serves merely as a capital investment and the management remains in Czech hands.

These guidelines allow the justified wishes of German Volksgenossen to be taken into consideration without compromising the public interest, which must also be fully protected here.

This decree must be regarded as confidential and is not intended for circulation.

DOC. 305

On 17 April 1941 the Reich Protector explains the procedure for the labour deployment of Jews to the Ministry of Social Welfare and Health Administration[1]

Letter from the Reich Protector of Bohemia and Moravia (no. II 4a – 5431/41), p.p. signed Dr Bertsch,[2] Prague, to the Ministry of Social Welfare and Health Administration, Prague, dated 17 April 1941 (copy)[3]

Re: labour deployment of Jews; here: procedure
Case file: your letter of 13 February 1941 – E 4120-13/2[4]
I have instructed the Jewish Religious Community, in preparation for labour deployment, to have all Jews examined in order to determine their fitness for work. These examinations will presumably be completed by 25 April 1941, so that a comprehensive overview of the Jews available for deployment is then on hand.[5] Until then, no placement of Jews is to occur, unless this concerns Jews who worked for businessmen the previous year and are to be rehired by them.

To keep the scheduled labour deployment of Jews from being disrupted by special measures, I ask that the employment offices be instructed to proceed along the following lines:

(1) The selection of workplaces suitable for Jews is made only by the employment offices. The Jewish Religious Community and the Jewish employment offices are not permitted to have contact with employers directly. All vacant positions for Jews must be reported to you and may not be filled with Jews without your approval.

(2) All male Jews may be deployed only in groups, which are to be housed separately from Aryan workers. During their employment Jews are not permitted to work with Aryans. The employers are to be held responsible for ensuring compliance with these provisions. In the event of violations, the employer is to be denied permission to employ Jews. The employment offices must continuously monitor compliance with these provisions.

(3) Male Jews, provided the conditions of (2) are met, may be employed in agricultural concerns if domestic workers cannot be procured. Jews may not be deployed individually in agricultural concerns; a group must include at least ten Jews.

(4) Jewish girls, if at all possible, should be deployed in Jewish households as domestic servants or in agriculture as farmhands – in the latter case, however, only in groups in

1 NAP, ÚŘP, I-3b-5813. This document has been translated from German.
2 Dr Walter Bertsch (1900–1952), lawyer; joined the NSDAP in 1933; minister of labour and economics in the Protectorate of Bohemia and Moravia from 1942; SS-Brigadeführer, 1944; sentenced to life imprisonment in Czechoslovakia in 1948; died in prison.
3 The copy was sent 'for careful attention' to the Oberlandräte in Bohemia and Moravia (via the Group for Moravia in Brünn) and to Group I 3 B (including race and blood protection, civil status). The original contains handwritten annotations.
4 This is not included in the file.
5 The examination revealed that 4,173 Jews could be conscripted for heavy labour, 3,960 Jews for moderately heavy labour, and 3,398 Jews for light work. The Religious Community classified 1,087 Jews as unfit for work: Letter from Group Leader II/4 (Employment and Social Affairs) to Group I 1 a (ethnopolitical matters), 31 July 1941, in NAP, ÚŘP, I-3b-5813.

accordance with the provisions under (2). Work as a domestic servant or household help and gardening work on farms is prohibited. My consent must be obtained prior to the deployment of Jewish girls for work in business or industry.
(5) The placement of Jews is exclusively the task of the relevant employment offices. The Jewish employment office will inform you of the number of Jews available for labour deployment and will support you in assigning Jews to individual projects. For specific projects, you may order the Jewish employment office to name a certain number of Jews who are fit for work, who are thereafter to be placed by the local employment office concerned. Jews are not to be placed without your prior consent.
(6) The Jewish work details will be led by Jewish work detail leaders, who are selected by the Jewish Religious Community. The activities of the individual work details will also be overseen by persons specifically designated by the Jewish Religious Community.

I request a report by 30 June 1941 on the number of Jews deployed in the individual employment office districts.[6]

DOC. 306
On 7 May 1941 Charlotte and Norbert Meissner write to their son Franz about the imminent deployment of the Jews in Triesch as labour[1]

Letter from Charlotte and Norbert Meissner, Triesch, to Franz Meissner, c/o Reinhold Nielsen, St Taaroje, Pr. Fakse, Gribsbjerg, Denmark, dated 7 May 1941

139th letter
Dearest Franz. We are not so much concerned, rather longing for a letter from you so much, because we are terribly curious to learn how your emigration is coming along.[2] Now of all times, as we are waiting for news from you, the post has to be so slow. But we have resigned ourselves in the certain hope that all is well with you which, thank God, is also true for us. I wrote you a postcard two days ago so that you will not be completely without news from us, as we have also been late in writing because we have not had any post from you. Hopefully it won't take too long now.

Leo[3] is working this week as a clerk for Dr Böhm.[4] It's because medical examinations for labour service are taking place for all men between the ages of 18 and 50 (you must have read about it in the news). Most people are classed as Group I and are to be used for building roads and railways in the Protectorate.[5] Our children received definite notification yesterday to go to the Obora estate near Pilsen, and they are due to be called up

6 This is not included in the file.

1 USHMM, Acc. 2 004 692.1, Frank Meissner papers. This document has been translated from German.
2 Franz Meissner wanted to relocate to Palestine.
3 Leo Meissner.
4 Dr Ernst, also Arnolt, Böhm (1903–1944), physician in Telč (Teltsch); deported from Třebíč (Trietsch) to Theresienstadt on 22 May 1942, and from there on 23 Oct. 1944 to Auschwitz, where he was murdered.
5 Those who were examined were divided into four groups in accordance with their physical fitness. See Doc. 305.

in a week or two.[6] There will be seven boys and three girls in this group. The same man has two more farms, which are only an hour away from each other, and schoolmates will be deployed on all three farms. We are naturally very happy about this solution, as the children will be with some of their good old friends again and will have Berta Steiner[7] along this time as a good cook. But we will be really anxious, of course, because we have already become so accustomed to the children and will be by ourselves again now. Luckily, the resettlement from Höditz will not take much longer, as Pospicha's[8] handing over of the lower rooms is definite at last, and his relocation is dependent only on the repair work for Pokorny. This is apparently due to be completed before the end of the week. Then we will first have to undertake all the work in our home, because, despite the thorough overhaul at that time, there is still a great deal to be done, such as the electric rewiring, installing the stove, etc. Should the weather become warmer and more favourable by then, everything ought to be finished quickly. We had to stop working in the garden, as the weather is rainy and cold, and with the early frosts every day, it would have made no sense to do any planting. We just have to wait until the Three Ice Saints have gone.[9] Luckily, I have some supplies of wood, so I am busy chopping wood for several hours every day.

As always, stay healthy, love and kisses, your devoted Father.

My dear child. We always longingly await the postman, but on Saturday it will already be two weeks since your last letter arrived. I hope everything is fine with you and only the post is to blame for our having to wait so long. We would so dearly like to know whether the League[10] has granted permission for your relocation. I thought about you a lot on 1 May, and wondered whether you have already left the Nielsens' home. I don't want to worry unnecessarily, because it does not make much sense; at such a distance one achieves nothing by worrying. Now I will continue to be patient and am convinced that, once again, at least two letters will arrive at the same time.

I have already grown used to not going to the office and have nicely filled up the whole day with work. Unfortunately, it has become so cold again that we had to stop working in the garden at Hauser's, and I am afraid the plants will freeze, as the temperatures are below freezing every night. In the fields, too, the planting is proceeding very slowly, because it often rains and the soil is still really wet. I hope that things are better now for all you there and I'm sure that you are further along with the work than the farmers here. Gustl Stransky,[11] who works for Foitl, is teaching us how to work the fields.

6 This could not be verified.

7 Berta Steiner (1920–1942), cook; applied for emigration to the USA on 1 April 1939. In the summer of 1941 her family was forcibly resettled in Moravské Budějovice; deported from Třebíč to Theresienstadt on 22 May 1942 and three days later to Lublin, where she perished.

8 An employee at the Meissner firm.

9 Meissner uses the term 'drei Eismänner' (three ice men), but he presumably means the 'drei Eisheiligen' (three ice saints), St Pancras, St Servatius, and St Mamertus. In countries including Germany and Austria the traditional belief is that their days (11, 12, and 13 May) bring a cold snap and the last frost of the year.

10 See Doc. 297, fn. 8.

11 Gustav (Gustl) Stránský (1899–1942) worked in Mr Foitl's pub in Třešť during the war, and was then forced to move in with the Meissner family; deported from Třebíč to Theresienstadt on 18 May 1942 and one week later to Lublin, where he perished.

Now the dear children, too, will soon start their summer work, and we hope things will go well for them and that they will once again learn more about agriculture.

Today we received a letter from Uncle Friedl and Ernst again and are happy that they are both doing really well, and that Ernst also has had good news from his parents and siblings. Have you written to your uncle again recently? If not, then do so, so that you stay in contact with him. A postcard from Mella Eckstein,[12] Fritz Eckstein's mother,[13] also came today. We correspond with her really often now, as we sent parcels to her brother in the [General] Government in Poland, where he is now with his wife. In addition, we received letters from Vienna yesterday and today, from Aunt Rose and Uncle Emil.[14] Unfortunately, dear Uncle is not in good shape at all; his heart is causing him great problems, and Aunt is very worried about him. He can't work at all; even the few things that he helped Aunt with in the household are too difficult for him. It is the greatest pity when one is not healthy. For Easter we sent him a young goat, and he can't thank us enough for it; the poor man is still so tense that he can only eat certain things. It is not easy for Aunt to get hold of something for him these days. He now goes to the hospital twice a week and gets injections. Hopefully his condition will improve as a result.

Dear Sonja has just arrived, so I want to finish for today. We are, thank God, in good health and hope to have news from you very soon now, and will then answer your letter right away. I think that your chances of leaving the country are very slim, as things currently stand. But one must not lose heart; it may just be for the best. Stay healthy, lots of love and kisses from your devoted Mum.

DOC. 307

On 31 May 1941 the district authority in Ungarisch-Brod issues instructions to segregate Jews and identify their homes with signs[1]

Announcement (no. 458/2-präs.) issued by the district authority of Ungarisch-Brod, dated 31 May 1941

Official announcement

Pursuant to Articles 2 and 3 of the Law on the Organization of the Political Administration, 14 July 1927, no. 127 S.d.G.u.V.,[2] the following instructions are hereby issued for the town of Ungarisch-Brod:

12 Amálie Ecksteinová, née Schwarz (1874–1942), milliner; before 1920 owned a corsetry shop in Mariánské Lázně, then lived in Prague; deported from Prague to Theresienstadt on 7 May 1942 and on 9 May 1942 to Sobibor or Ossowa, where she perished.

13 Fritz, also Bedřich, Eckstein (1917–1942), civil servant; married in Nov. 1941; deported on 10 Dec. 1941 from Prague to Theresienstadt; on 9 May 1942 deported from there to Sobibor or Ossowa, where he perished.

14 Emil Meissner (1881–1944), brother of Norbert Meissner; in Russian captivity after the First World War; returned home in 1920; later lived in Vienna; deported to Theresienstadt on 24 Sept. 1942 and on 12 Oct. 1944 to Auschwitz, where he was murdered.

1 MZAB, B 251/522/4080, box 45. This document has been translated from German.

2 *Sammlung der Gesetze und Verordnungen des Čecho-Slovakischen Staates* (Compilation of Laws and Regulations of the Czecho-Slovak State).

1) All Jewish houses must be identified with a sign stating 'Jew house' in clearly legible letters. All Jewish apartments must be identified with a notice stating 'Jew apartment' in clearly legible letters. This sign must be affixed to the outside door and to the other doors giving access to the Jewish apartment. The signs must measure 30 x 20 cm. The letters must be 3 cm high. The sign must be written in black letters on white paper.
2) The Jews may leave their homes only when absolutely necessary, and must carry personal identification documents with them at all times. Jews must always be able to substantiate the reason for leaving their home.
3) The Jews are required to wear the light yellow armband, measuring 10 cm across, on their left arm at all times.
4) Jewish homes may only be entered by persons who can prove that they are there on official business, or that they are carrying out some other important work for building purposes or for the Public Hygiene Police, the Fire Police, or the Security Police. Visiting Jews for any other purpose is strictly forbidden.
5) The Jews are required to ensure that their houses and apartments are kept scrupulously clean and tidy. All Jewish homes must be thoroughly cleaned from top to bottom by the deadline of 15 June 1941.
6) Because Jewish homes will be inspected for cleanliness, Jews are ordered to grant access to housing inspectors whenever required.
7) The Jews are required to maintain stringent standards of personal hygiene. The men must always have shaved heads and be clean-shaven. Women must also have their heads shaved if an infectious disease or lack of hygiene is detected.
8) Because it is in the public interest that Aryans do not carry out any domestic work in Jewish households, it is hereby decreed that Jews are not permitted to employ any Aryan person as of 1 July 1941. Aryans employed up to now in Jewish households must report to the employment office in Ungarisch-Brod.
9) The Jews can send and receive all mail only via the Jewish Religious Community in Ungarisch-Brod. The Jewish Religious Community is to guarantee that there is no inappropriate content.
10) All these provisions shall also apply to the Jewish wives of Aryan persons.
Non-compliance with these provisions will be punishable under Article 3 of the aforementioned law, with a fine of K 10–5,000 or with imprisonment of between twelve hours and fourteen weeks. The entire Jewish community will act as a guarantor for the payment of such fines. The provisions come into force on the day of their publication.

DOC. 308

In her diary entry for 22 June 1941, Eva Roubíčková expresses the hope that the German forces will be defeated following their invasion of the Soviet Union[1]

Diary of Eva Roubíčková,[2] entry for 22 June 1941

Sunday, 22 June 1941
Russia at war with Germany! Since four o'clock this morning. Hitler gave the order to his soldiers and they are marching into Russia. It came as a complete surprise; we had no idea. Only the day before yesterday, all the papers were reporting on the great friendship. Went rowing with Eva,[3] Vera, and Peter. We are in high spirits; this is a blow for the Germans. Now they are ranting against both the Bolsheviks *and* the Jews. Communism must be eradicated. Went to see Peter this afternoon; he showed us his range of cosmetic products and perfumes, most interesting. I promised Mum I would call in later. Everyone is full of hope.

DOC. 309

On 5 July 1941 the provisions of the Blood Protection Law come into force in the Protectorate with retroactive effect[1]

Third Implementing Regulation to the Law for the Protection of German Blood and German Honour.
5 July 1941
Pursuant to § 6 of the Law for the Protection of German Blood and German Honour of 15 September 1935 (Reichsgesetzbl. I, p. 1146)[2] and Article 13 of the Decree of the Führer and Reich Chancellor concerning the Protectorate of Bohemia and Moravia, dated 16 March 1939 (Reichsgesetzbl. I, p. 485),[3] the following orders are hereby issued in agreement with the Reich Protector of Bohemia and Moravia:

1 Eva Mändl Roubíčková, *'Langsam gewöhnen wir uns an das Ghettoleben': Ein Tagebuch aus Theresienstadt*, ed. Veronika Springmann, in collaboration with Wolfgang Schellenbacher (Hamburg: Konkret Literatur, 2007), pp. 37–38. This document has been translated from German.
2 Eva Mändl Roubíčková (b. 1921–2013), secretary and translator; fled with her family from her home town of Žatec to Prague in Sept. 1938; deported to Theresienstadt on 17 Dec. 1941. After the war she was reunited with her fiancé in Prague; they married and had two children. She worked as a secretary and translator from 1957 to 1973, and did various other jobs thereafter.
3 Eva Glauber (1922–1944), from Dresden; friend of Eva Roubíčková; deported from Prague to Theresienstadt on 30 July 1942 and in Dec. 1943 to Auschwitz, where she was murdered.

1 *Reichsgesetzblatt*, 1941, I, pp. 384 f. This document has been translated from German.
2 On the basis of Section 6 of the law, the Reich Ministry of the Interior, in consultation with the staff of the Führer and the Reich Ministry of Justice, issued the necessary legal and administrative regulations for the implementation and amendment of the law. See PMJ 1/199.
3 On the basis of Article 13 of the decree, the Reich Ministry of the Interior, in consultation with the other Reich ministries involved, gave instructions for the appropriate legal and administrative regulations to be implemented in the Protectorate of Bohemia and Moravia. See *Reichsgesetzblatt*, 1939 I, p. 488.

§ 1 The provisions of the Law for the Protection of German Blood and German Honour of 15 September 1935 (Reichsgesetzbl. I, p. 1146), and of the First Implementing Regulation to this law of 14 November 1935 (Reichsgesetzbl. I, p. 1334),[4] shall also apply to the Protectorate of Bohemia and Moravia with effect from the entry into force of the Decree of the Führer and Reich Chancellor concerning the Protectorate of Bohemia and Moravia, dated 16 March 1939 (Reichsgesetzbl. I, p. 485). The Amending Regulation to the First Implementing Regulation to the Blood Protection Law of 16 February 1940 (Reichsgesetzbl. I, p. 394) shall also apply.[5]

§ 2

(1) In the Protectorate of Bohemia and Moravia, as in the Reich, the definition of who is a Jew and who is a Jewish Mischling shall be made in accordance with § 2, subsection 2, and § 5 of the First Regulation on the Reich Citizenship Law of 14 November 1935 (Reichsgesetzbl. I, p. 1333).[6]

(2) From the entry into force of this regulation, a Jewish Mischling with two full-Jewish grandparents, who is a subject of the Protectorate, is classed as a Jew, subject to the conditions set forth in § 5, subsection 2, of the First Regulation on the Reich Citizenship Law.

§ 3 In the case of marriages between German state subjects and Protectorate subjects, Protectorate subjects shall be treated like German state subjects for the purpose of applying the regulations on the prohibition of marriages because of Jewish blood (§ 1 of the Law for the Protection of German Blood and German Honour; §§ 2 to 4 and § 6 of the First Implementing Regulation to this law)

§ 4 Those provisions which, under the terms of § 15 of the First Implementing Regulation to the Law for the Protection of German Blood and German Honour, are applicable to stateless persons shall also apply to those stateless persons who have their domicile or usual residence abroad, if they were previously Protectorate subjects.

§ 5 Subjects of the Protectorate are not foreign nationals within the meaning of the provisions set forth in Section 1 above.

Berlin, 5 July 1941

The Reich Minister of the Interior[7]
p.p. Dr Stuckart
The Head of the Party Chancellery
M. Bormann
The Reich Minister of Justice
Tasked with the management of affairs
Dr Schlegelberger

4 The First Implementing Regulation to the Law for the Protection of German Blood and German Honour (14 Nov. 1935) supplemented the provisions of the Blood Protection Law of 15 Sept. 1935, including those relating to marriages between Jewish *Mischlinge* and Aryans. It also defined the circumstances under which a household was to be classified as Jewish within the meaning of the law. See *Reichsgesetzblatt*, 1935, I, pp. 1334–1336.

5 The Regulation of 16 Feb. 1940 amended section 11 of the First Regulation of 14 Nov. 1935 by the addition of subsection 2, according to which only the male spouse would be prosecuted for so-called race defilement. See *Reichsgesetzblatt*, 1940, I, p. 394.

6 See PMJ 1/210.

7 Dr Wilhelm Frick.

DOC. 310

Večerní České slovo, 5 July 1941: article calling for more restrictions on Jews[1]

Complaints regarding Jewish impudence. Jews secretly in managerial positions in Aryan businesses. Jews who have taken up cycling upset the sense of public decency.

Jews have been put in their rightful place in economic and social life through corresponding regulations. They initially crawled away, but now, once again, complaints are mounting about how many Jews are ignoring and circumventing the regulations, finding help from a number of Aryans. *Árijský boj*[2] has reported on a number of such cases. In Prague–Letná there is a logistics company where the Jew Popovský, a former dancer, continues to have the final say, despite the company being Aryan.[3] The Jew Popovský negotiates with business associates, advises on the payment of staff wages, signs business correspondence, and is paid his wages cash in hand, even though the law states that his account should be blocked.[4] A number of Jews occupy managerial positions in the coal industry; many Jews continue to run their businesses over the phone and with the assistance of Aryans, who offer their services. Complaints are coming in from the countryside regarding the provocative and morally offensive behaviour of Jews – and especially Jewesses – who have recently taken up cycling, and about how Jews enjoy watching young people, of course mostly girls, play games and sports, etc. Some Jews and Jewesses go shopping at prohibited times, visit parks, open-air swimming pools, etc., relying on the fact that they won't be recognized because Jews are not required to wear identifying badges. Decisive action is required to stamp out Jewish impudence.

1 'Stížnosti na troufalost Židů', *Večerní České slovo*, 5 July 1941, p. 3. This document has been translated from Czech. The newspaper *Večerní České slovo* appeared from 1919 to 1945 in Prague and had a circulation of 400,000. The editors-in-chief were Emanuel Vajtauer, V. Brejnik, and, from 1944, K. Werner.

2 *Árijský boj* ('Aryan Battle'), the main newspaper of the Anti-Jewish League, was the successor to the periodical *Štít národa* ('Shield of the Nation'). Rudolf Novák was its editor-in-chief from 1940 to 1945.

3 Probably Bedřich Popovský (1908–1942), dancer and dance teacher; one of the most successful pre-war dancers in Czechoslovakia; won the World Amateur Ballroom Dance Championship with his partner, Božena Vandasová, in Prague in 1934; deported to Theresienstadt on 28 April 1942, then on 9 May 1942 to Sobibor, where he was murdered.

4 See Doc. 269.

DOC. 311

On 28 July 1941 the Oberlandrat in Tabor complains about the local Jewish population and calls for drastic measures[1]

Letter (marked 'confidential!') from the Reich Protector of Bohemia and Moravia, I 1 a,[2] p.p. signed Dr Strobl,[3] to Group I 3[4] at the same address, Prague, dated 28 July 1941[5]

Re: administrative reports from the Oberlandräte for July 1941
Please find attached the relevant section of the administrative report of 21 July 1941 from the Oberlandrat in Tabor, no. I/218,[6] for your attention and further action.

Sign-ups for Germandom have declined by 50 per cent during the month under review. It is too early to tell whether this is a temporary phenomenon or a permanent one.

Recently there have been particular complaints about Jewish behaviour. We are hearing reports from all sides claiming that they are constantly flouting the curfew, while the Czech authorities dare not intervene. Although the Gestapo have already arrested a number of Jews, they cannot be everywhere at once. The Jews have become extremely insolent again, and they are stirring up trouble, as usual. I believe that drastic measures are urgently needed. In particular, Jews living out in the country should be made to leave the villages and small towns. It is well known that the rural population is particularly susceptible to Jewish influence, as the farmers are generally financially dependent on the Jews in one way or another. Despite all the problems of housing them, we need to keep reminding ourselves that this is the only way to make a real start on instituting a political settlement. By contrast, any leniency is seen by both Jews and Czechs as a sign of weakness. The measures undertaken by the employment offices to get male Jews into work cannot completely resolve the problem. They are very welcome nonetheless.

1 NAP, ÚŘP, I-3b 5850, fols. 521–523. This document has been translated from German.
2 Group I/1's remit included general political affairs and ethnopolitical matters.
3 Dr Guido Strobl (b. 1910), lawyer; practised law in Jihlava (Iglau) in 1936; joined the Sudeten German Party (SdP) and then the NSDAP in 1938; worked in the Price Setting Office for the Sudeten German territories from Nov. 1938 to March 1939; employed at the Office of the Reich Protector from March 1939; appointed Bezirkshauptmann for Budweis in 1942; acting head of the Wittingau district authority from Nov. 1942; worked in the Office of the State Minister for Bohemia and Moravia in 1944; joined the Waffen SS in Nov. 1944.
4 Group I/3's remit included matters relating to citizenship, race, and so-called blood protection.
5 The original contains handwritten annotations.
6 The file contains only this excerpt.

DOC. 312

On 29 July 1941 the Oberlandrat in Brünn proposes that Jews be forbidden to ride bicycles[1]

Letter from the Oberlandrat in Brünn, for the districts of Brünn and the suburbs (incl. Seelowitz), Boskowitz, Tischnowitz, Wischau,[2] p.p. signed [signature illegible], to the Reich Protector of Bohemia and Moravia, Prague, sent via the Office for the Region of Moravia, Brünn (received on 31 July 1941), dated 29 July 1941

Re: use of bicycles by Jews

The NSDAP Kreisleitung for Brünn has repeatedly approached me to suggest that Jews should be forbidden to use bicycles. This was prompted by various reports indicating that the Jewish population has for some time been using bicycles a great deal. It has been widely observed that Jews are learning to ride bicycles and practising their riding skills.

Among those sections of the population that used to ride bicycles for financial or work-related reasons, but now have to do without them because of the shortage of tyres, there is indignation at the fact that idle Jews have the use of bicycles for sport and possibly also for foraging trips.

I therefore ask you to consider whether it might be possible to prohibit Jews from using bicycles at all.[3]

1 MZAB, B 251/522/4080, box 45. This document has been translated from German.
2 Dr Oskar Hofmann (b. 1900), administrative officer; active in the NSDAP from 1921; joined the SA in 1933; employed at the Bavarian Ministry of the Interior from 1934; rejoined the NSDAP in 1937; appointed Oberregierungsrat in the Office of the Reich Protector in 1939; in charge of the conduct of official business for the Oberlandrat in Brünn from June 1940; appointed to the regional authority in Brünn in 1942; president of the Board of Youth Education in Bohemia and Moravia from 1943.
3 See Doc. 316.

DOC. 313

On 31 July 1941 Undersecretary Kurt von Burgsdorff issues instructions prohibiting local agencies from taking individual action against Jews in the Protectorate[1]

Letter from the Reich Protector of Bohemia and Moravia (B. No. BdS – I – 2256/41), p.p. signed Dr von Burgsdorff, Prague, to all Oberlandräte, dated 31 July 1941[2]

Re: anti-Jewish measures
Ref: Decree of 17 August 1940 – B.d.S. – II – 1305-6/40[3]
Although we have been explicitly informed and instructed, both in general terms through the above decree and in specific terms through numerous individual orders, that local measures against the Jews are not permitted, nor are they effective, and that any anti-Jewish measures may only be carried out with the prior consent of the Senior Commander of the Security Police, anti-Jewish measures relating to assets or persons have recently been undertaken again by individual Oberlandräte or, with their approval, by German government commissioners, Party agencies, and even by Czech district authorities. Hence, for example, instructions have been issued for the confiscation of typewriters, bicycles, and items of furniture, and Jews have been forbidden to leave their homes for any reason, or to open their windows, or to air their bedding at open windows, or to do all kinds of other everyday things – even though compliance with such prohibitions cannot be adequately policed, and indeed is not always practicable anyway.[4]

The point that is completely overlooked here is that, in the main, only the executive authority in the Protectorate is available to monitor compliance, and we cannot count on support from the local population, given the pro-Jewish sympathies of a substantial number of Czechs. Not only are such prohibitions ineffective, but they also often verge on the ridiculous. I refer you, for example, to an announcement in *Der Neue Tag* on 31 July 1941 regarding anti-Jewish measures in Klattau, which even discusses the correct storage of shaving brushes.[5]

Furthermore, the effect of ill-judged articles in the daily press has repeatedly been to mobilize certain elements that, under the guise of cracking down on the Jews, are in fact pursuing their own, sometimes criminal, interests (looting, destruction of Jewish property). Although the growing resentment against all things Jewish is undoubtedly understandable, particularly in the light of events in the Eastern theatre of the war, we

1 MZAB, B 251/522/4080, box 45. Published in Jaroslava Milotová and Miroslav Kárný, 'Od Neuratha k Heydrichovi: Na rozhrání okupační politiky hitlerovského Německa v "Protektorátu Čechy a Morava"', *Sborník archivních prací*, vol. 39, no. 2 (1989), pp. 281–394, doc. 20, pp. 322–324. This document has been translated from German.

2 The letter was circulated for information purposes to Departments I, II, and IV of the Moravia Office, Groups I/1 and I/3, the Party Liaison Office, the Gestapo Headquarters in Prague, the Gestapo Headquarters in Brünn, and the Central Office for Jewish Emigration in Prague. The original contains handwritten annotations and underlining.

3 See Doc. 286.

4 See also Doc. 307.

5 *Der Neue Tag*, 31 July 1941, p. 3. Under the terms of an order issued by the district authority in Klatovy, one of the many restrictions imposed on the Jews was the requirement for barbers to keep the shaving kit for Jews separate from the shaving kit used for Aryans; contravention of this and other restrictions was punishable by a fine or imprisonment.

have to prevent individuals from seeking a solution to the Jewish problem through more or less drastic local initiatives.

In line with the policy towards the Jews pursued in the rest of the Reich, the Senior Commander of the Security Police[6] has either ordered a whole series of restrictive measures against the Jews himself, or arranged for such measures to be imposed by the government of the Protectorate. The strict policing of these measures would undoubtedly guarantee the effective suppression of the Jewish element. But as long as the Jews are not identified with visible markings, all prohibitions will suffer from the shortcomings already described. The Jewish problem is constantly under the closest scrutiny of both the Commander of the Security Police and other agencies of mine that address issues concerning Jews, and we continue to consult with the central agencies in the Reich, so that the groundwork has already been done for the major decisions on these matters that will need to be taken once the Eastern campaign is concluded. Until such time, however, the general political interests of the Reich must be respected. I must insist on absolute discipline in this regard.

I therefore draw this matter urgently to your attention once again, and am holding the Oberlandräte personally responsible for ensuring that my instructions are adhered to. In particular:
1) all pecuniary measures (securing and confiscation of Jewish assets) are to be left to the offices of the Gestapo or the Commander of the Security Police, on the basis of existing legal and administrative instructions,[7]
2) the full wording of all other anti-Jewish restrictions must be submitted to the Senior Commander of the Security Police for decision prior to their entry into force or promulgation.

Addendum for the Party Liaison Department:[8]
Please see to it that the leaders of the various Party organizations are briefed accordingly, as individual operations conducted by the SA at the end of June, particularly in Moravia, and in some cases even in conjunction with Czechs, also resulted in instances of looting and theft.[9]

6 Horst Böhme.
7 This refers principally to the Regulation of the Reich Protector of Bohemia and Moravia on Jewish Assets, issued on 21 June 1939; the Regulation of the Reich Protector of Bohemia and Moravia on the Exclusion of the Jews from the Economic Life of the Protectorate, issued on 26 Jan. 1940; and their respective implementing regulations. See Docs. 247 and 269.
8 The NSDAP did not establish a separate Gauleitung in the Protectorate, but assigned its various regions to the Party organizations in the neighbouring Gaue of Sudetenland, Bavarian Ostmark, Upper Danube, and Lower Danube, thus giving their respective Gauleiter a say in the affairs of the Protectorate. In order to coordinate the measures issued by the four Gaue, a Party Liaison Department was established in the Office of the Reich Protector on 30 Jan. 1940.
9 No further details available.

DOC. 314

On 14 August 1941 the Reich Minister of the Interior informs the Head of the Reich Chancellery that there are no further objections to the visible identification of Jews in the Protectorate[1]

Letter from the Reich Minister of the Interior[2] (Ie 163 I-III/41/5012), Berlin, to the Reich Minister and Head of the Reich Chancellery,[3] Berlin, dated 14 August 1941 (copy)[4]

Re: visible identification in the Protectorate
Response to the letter of 18 July 1941 – Rk. 10 588 B –[5]
With regard to introducing identifying markers for Jews, the Reich Marshal announced at a meeting of Gauleiter on 6 December 1938 that the Führer had decided against it, and he explained the reasons for this decision.[6] Following last year's review of the matter, I refer you to my letter of 24 July 1940 – I 1401 VII/VIII/40g – 5012.[7] The Führer's decision related to the territory of the Reich as it was then constituted.

In the meantime, the political situation has completely changed. Now that the foreign policy situation is clear, it seems to me – subject to the position taken on this by the Foreign Office, which you have no doubt asked them to clarify – that we no longer need to consider the repercussions for our foreign policy. More to the point, conditions in the Protectorate of Bohemia and Moravia are completely different from those in the Old Reich. I also think it not without significance that in the General Government, as well as in small areas of the annexed Eastern territories, Jews have been required to wear identifying markers since the conclusion of the Polish campaign.[8]

I therefore have no objections to the visible identification of Jews in the Protectorate of Bohemia and Moravia, but I think we need to find out first whether this is likely to result in an increased drain of Jewish manpower from enterprises in the Protectorate which cannot be compensated for by other workers in view of the acute labour shortage.[9]

1 NAP, ÚŘP, I-3b 5851, box 389, fols. 596 f. Published in Milotová and Kárný, *Od Neuratha k Heydrichovi*, doc. 31, pp. 346 f. This document has been translated from German.

2 Dr Wilhelm Frick.

3 Dr Hans Lammers.

4 Forwarded to the Reich Protector of Bohemia and Moravia (received 24 August 1941). At the end of the document: 'For your information I attach a copy to the telex L.S.D. L.A. Prague no. 1375, dated 16 July 1941, addressed to Reich Minister Dr Lammers. Signed on behalf of Dr Stuckart. Witnessed: [signature illegible] Ministerial Registry.' The original contains handwritten annotations. The telex mentioned here from Karl Hermann Frank to Lammers, dated 16 July 1941, is published in Pätzold, *Verfolgung, Vertreibung, Vernichtung*, p. 294.

5 This letter is not in the file.

6 On 6 Dec. 1938 Göring explained that Hitler had objections to the visible identification. He was said to reject the idea partly because he did not want to jeopardize foreign relations. See Götz Aly and Susanne Heim, 'Staatliche Ordnung und organische Lösung: Die Rede Hermann Görings "über die Judenfrage" vom 6. Dezember 1938', *Jahrbuch für Antisemitismusforschung*, vol. 2 (1993), pp. 378–404.

7 This letter is not in the file. Regarding the discussions on the visible identification of Jews in the Reich, see Introduction, pp. 63–64.

8 Regulation on the Visible Identification of Jews and Jewesses in the General Government, 23 Nov. 1939, *Verordnungsblatt Generalgouvernement*, 1939, no. 8, 30 Nov. 1939, p. 61: see also PMJ 4/49.

9 The ruling applicable to the entire German Reich, including the Protectorate, pre-empted any separate ruling for the Protectorate. See Doc. 212.

DOC. 315

On 20 August 1941 State Secretary Frank asks Reich Protector von Neurath to confirm by telephone that he approves the introduction of identifying armbands for the Jewish population[1]

Telex no. 952/41 (marked 'secret'), signed Frank, to Reich Protector Baron von Neurath, Leinfelden, via SD Main District Stuttgart, dated 20 August 1941 (copy)[2]

Your Excellency. I request your approval to have Jews in the Protectorate to be visibly identified with armbands. The Jews are becoming more brazen by the day. Constant violations of our regulations pertaining to Jews are a daily occurrence. We are getting reports from every quarter on the anti-Reich activities of the Jews, which are getting worse by the hour. They are forming little cliques in public bars, restaurants, and cafés, despite a ban on entry; they are discussing enemy radio news bulletins with Czech groups; and they are inciting the local population against us. Jewish black marketeers and racketeers are plying their trade openly in the streets. Oberlandräte, other Reich offices, Party agencies, and other organizations, including Czech groups, are calling for the visible identification of Jews to be introduced as a matter of urgency. Luxembourg has just introduced visible identification for Jews.[3] A meeting with the undersecretaries and departmental heads concluded in unanimous approval. We expect the measure to have a positive impact. Please telephone to confirm your approval.[4]

Heil Hitler!

DOC. 316

On 14 September 1941 Jiří Münzer writes about the impending introduction of the yellow star for Jews and the ban on them leaving their places of residence[1]

Handwritten diary of Jiří Münzer, entry for 14 September 1941

This was one of the saddest weeks I've ever lived through. It was announced that we'll have to wear stars and we won't be allowed to leave our place of residence.[2] I'd welcome the badges – why shouldn't I show everyone that I'm a Jew and proud of it – if we could

1 YVA, 0.7.Cz/4. Published in Milotová and Kárný, *Od Neuratha k Heydrichovi*, doc. 34, p. 350. This document has been translated from German.
2 The original contains handwritten comments and annotations.
3 The Regulation concerning the rules for Jewish Life in Luxembourg, dated 29 July 1941, introduced the requirement for Jews to wear a yellow armband before similar legislation was implemented in the Old Reich.
4 Neurath telephoned the same day to approve Frank's proposal: Milotová and Kárný, *Od Neuratha k Heydrichovi*, pp. 350–351. The requirement for Jews to wear visible identification was introduced in the Protectorate at the same time as legislation making this mandatory throughout the Reich. See Doc. 212.

1 JMP, DP 79. Published in Münzer, *Dospívání nad propastí*, pp. 87 f. This document has been translated from Czech.
2 The compulsory visible identification of Jews was also introduced in the Protectorate with a regulation issued on 1 Sept. 1941: see Doc. 212. On 15 Sept. 1941, the Reich Ministry of the Interior supplemented the regulation with an express letter forbidding Jews from leaving their places of residence: see Doc. 222.

only stay in Hradec. However, this means that I'm not allowed to leave Třebechovice, and no one can come to Třebechovice from there, so we're completely cut off. I keep thinking about it all the time. This is the first ban that has really got to me; it's really struck at my heart, right at my innermost being.

Now I see how little material things matter to me if I can simply be with the people I love. I feel a sense of helpless anger that I can't change anything and there is no end to any of this.

I'm not a jealous person, but on this occasion I am: though I'm truly delighted that the Mahlers[3] have found an apartment, I'm awfully jealous of them. They are going to live with Dr Neu[4] about a hundred steps from the house where Ilsa[5] lives, while I'm thirteen kilometres from Hradec and am not allowed to go there.

That was already [bad] enough, and once I had more or less come to terms with it and told myself that the week always flew by and I'd be in Hradec on Saturday and Sunday, then this came along.

Grandma is still unwell, and she's not getting any help at all.

During the week I was at home every day, and I was at Ilsa's on four of the evenings. Yesterday we had sichos[6] at the Frischmanns' – Jirka[7] spoke about the period before Christ. I am also sad not to be able to go to sichos any more, but I won't stop working.

We didn't have our Hebrew lesson today because the teacher has already moved – I went to the hospital to see Grandma this morning. Uncle Otta[8] came too; he and I went to meet Granddad.

In the afternoon I popped in to see the Müllers and Bertík, and then I was at Ilsa's till evening. We weren't in a particularly jolly mood.

This week Jews were also ordered to hand in their bicycles and typewriters – I gave notification of my typewriter and bicycle.[9] Nothing new in the war.

3 Probably: Maximilian Mahler (1886–1944), engineer; deported from Hradec Králové to Theresienstadt on 21 Dec. 1942. Otylie Mahlerová, née Nohel (1889–1944), housewife; deported from Hradec Králové to Theresienstadt on 21 Dec. 1942, then on 16 Oct. 1944 to Auschwitz, where she was murdered.

4 Probably: Dr Julius Neu (1887–1943), lawyer; deported on 21 Dec. 1942 from Hradec Králové to Theresienstadt, where he perished two and a half months later.

5 Ilsa Polláková.

6 Hebrew for 'talks'.

7 Probably Jiří (Jirka) Fränkl or Jiří (Jirka) Brod.

8 Ota Klepetář (b. 1900), dentist; deported on 9 Dec. 1942 from Pardubice to Theresienstadt and from there on 23 Jan. 1943 to Auschwitz, where he perished.

9 Towards the end of 1941, Jews in the Protectorate were required to hand in their bicycles and typewriters to the Jewish Community: H. G. Adler, *Theresienstadt, 1941–1945: The Face of a Coerced Community*, trans. Belinda Cooper (Cambridge: Cambridge University Press, 2017 [German edn, 1955]), p. 11.

DOC. 317

On 18 September 1941 State Secretary Hubert Ripka of the Czechoslovak government in exile in London sides with the Jews in the Protectorate[1]

B.B.C. – Czechoslovaks News Talk
Thursday 18th September, 1941 9:45 p.m. By Dr. Hubert Ripka,[2] Under secretary for Foreign Affairs.

So Hitler has forced the Jews in our country, too, always to appear in public with a special distinguish[ing] mark by which they should be easily distinguished from the others. Thus it is to be made easier for the Nazi mob and the rabble of the Vlajka[3] and of Tuka and Mach[4] to hurl themselves on the wretched defenceless Jews whenever they wish. It was not sufficient for these barbarians to rob and plunder the Jews, cruelly to persecute them and sadistically to torture them; no, over and above this they now expose them by publicly distinguishing them from the others to daily insults and brutal caprice.

It will remain the terrible shame of the German nation that it has allowed itself to be misled by the monstrous racial doctrine and that such a vast party has fallen victim to bestial anti-Semitism. In this, of course, there also lies the most visible expression of their feeling of inferiority; for only he who is not sure of himself, has not sufficient self-confidence in himself, needs to raise himself in his own eyes and those of others above everyone else. German anti-Semitism, which Hitler has exploited to whip up the basest and often diseased and perverted instincts, is an expression of the typical disintegration and endeavours to overcome these not only [by] boastfulness, but also by brute force against others. Incidentally, what is a disgusting shame for the Germans in all this, a shame for which they will bitterly atone, is an honour for the persecuted Jews: for why should the Nazis torture, exile, rob and kill the Jews if they were not afraid of their intelligence, cleverness and talent?

If the Jewish distinguishing mark is now also being introduced into our lands[5] we wish to tell you, Czech and Slovak friends, that we believe you will do nothing for which you have to be ashamed one day. We are convinced that you do not forget your honourable privilege in belonging to the nation of Masaryk, who educated all of us to be revolted by debasing anti-Semitism and who also in this way contributed to making our nation a spiritually advanced and self-confident nation, whose members of [the] Jewish race

1 CZA, C2/96 – 15.9.1941. The document is a transcript of a radio broadcast. The original document is in English.

2 Dr Hubert Ripka (1895–1958), journalist and politician; editor of the Czechoslovak Legion newspaper *Národní osvobození*, 1925–1930; editor of the newspaper *Lidové noviny*, 1930–1938; emigrated to Britain in 1940; state secretary for foreign affairs in the Czechoslovak government in exile in London, 1940–1945; returned to Prague in 1945; minister for foreign trade until 1948, then emigrated to Britain again.

3 See Docs. 254 and 284.

4 Vojtěch Tuka (1880–1946); prime minister of the Slovak Republic, 1939–1944, and its foreign minister from 1940; sentenced to death and executed in Czechoslovakia in 1946. Aleksander (Šaňo) Mach (1902–1980), interior minister and deputy prime minister of the Slovak Republic, 1940–1945.

5 A decree issued on 1 Sept. 1941 had made it mandatory for Jews in the Reich and the Protectorate to wear visible identification in the form of a yellow star. See Doc. 212.

are able or unable to be excellent patriots and decent people, just as its members of different racial origin are also able or unable to be so.

We here abroad are well informed about everything that is happening at home. Therefore, we also know well how everyone has behaved and is behaving towards the Jews. It fills us with justified pride when we can announce to the civilised world that our people behaves towards the persecuted Jews with Christian sympathy and profoundly human understanding for their cruel hardships. And we are happy that the German anti-Semites are joined only by a handful of rascals, who speak Czech and Slovak but have sold their souls to their slave-drivers.

Czechoslovak Jews, we think of you with sincere sympathy in these days. We know of your sufferings, and we carefully assemble all the data about the way in which you are persecuted and the people who persecute you. We know that they are driving you out of the towns, that they are restoring the ghetto, that they imprison you in concentration camps and torture you there to death; we know what happens in the so-called labour camps at Nemecky Brod, Terezin near Chocen,[6] and elsewhere where even the older and invalid Jews are driven and where they must work eleven hours a day under the most shameful food and lodging conditions; we know what fell work is being wrought by the criminal Mach, how he is driving Jews from Pressburg and the other towns, even the small ones, how he steals their property and drives them like beasts into huts where they will suffer from cold, filth and hunger.[7] We know everything, even the details. We cannot help you for the present. But we tell the world about your sufferings, and we assure you that they will not be forgotten.

To-day they wish to designate you publicly by a mark of shame. But the yellow star of David is a sign of honour which all decent people will respect. I recall the words of the profoundly faithful Catholic of Jewish origin, the writer Alfred Fuchs,[8] whom the Nazis tortured to death. For his Catholic zeal he received a Papal distinction. He then said: If the Germans introduce a Jewish badge in our country, I shall wear it with demonstrative pride beside my Papal distinction.[9] Jewish friends, strengthen your minds in faith in the victory of justice. To-day it is already certain, and it is no longer in the invisible future. You will live to see the day of liberation and just retribution.

6 The mention of Německý Brod is probably a reference to the retraining centre in nearby Linden. The Jewish community was required to send a certain number of men there. The reference to Theresienstadt (Terezin) is evidently a mistake, since at the time in question there was no camp or ghetto. There were, however, rumours that a ghetto might be built.

7 From 1940, numerous anti-Jewish laws were enacted in Slovakia under Vojtěch Tuka and Šaňo Mach. The culmination of these policies was the 'Jew Code', enacted on 9 Sept. 1941, which was closely modelled on the Nuremberg Laws.

8 Dr Alfred Fuchs (1892–1941), poet, journalist, translator and literary critic; editor of the *Prager Abendblatt*; senior director of the press department at the headquarters of the Czech government's ministerial council; wrote on religious matters, in particular Judaism and Catholicism; was murdered in Dachau concentration camp.

9 This could not be verified.

DOC. 318

In her diary entry for 19 September 1941, Eva Roubíčková records the reactions to her wearing the yellow star[1]

Diary of Eva Roubíčková, entry for 19 September 1941

Friday, 19 September 1941
Went to work at half-past seven wearing the star.[2]
People either ignored it or smiled, but in any event they behaved better than I would have expected.

In the workshop they were all surprised that I am a Jew, and they were very decent about it. After work I went to see Mama;[3] Lotte[4] was there too. Then met up with Benny[5] and went with him to Eva's.[6]

Ernst and Danny[7] were there as well.

Everyone is talking about how decently people have behaved.

Word has come from England that the Czechs should be especially nice to their Jewish compatriots, and that they should do whatever they can to make this humiliation easier to bear.[8] Many people greet Jews in the street, speak to them, and make the conscious decision to walk side by side with them for a while, which is, of course, an act of provocation against the Germans.

1 Published in Roubíčková, *Langsam*, p. 47. This document has been translated from German.
2 A regulation of 1 Sept. 1941 made it compulsory for Jews in the Protectorate to wear visible identification in the form of a yellow star. See Doc. 212.
3 The writer is referring to the mother of her then fiancé, Richard Roubíček, namely Marie Roubíčková, née Gibian (1889–1943), housewife; married to a lawyer; deported from Prague to Theresienstadt in Sept. 1942 and then to Auschwitz in Dec. 1943.
4 Lotte, also known as Lota Singerová, née Roubíčková (1913–1943), student and housewife; sister of Richard Roubíček; lived in Vizovice, near Zlin; was married to a businessman and factory owner, and had two children. She was deported from Prague to Theresienstadt on 8 Sept. 1942 and on 15 Dec. 1943 to Auschwitz, where she perished.
5 Benny Grünberger (1922–1942); on 22 Oct. 1942 deported from Theresienstadt to Treblinka, where he was murdered.
6 Eva Glauber.
7 Benny Grünberger's brother Danny was caught by the Gestapo while attempting to flee to Hungary in 1943 and subsequently executed along with his parents. See Roubíčková, *Langsam*, pp. 139–142, entry for 22 July 1943.
8 See Doc. 317.

DOC. 319

On 21 September 1941 Jiří Münzer describes Czech reaction to the Jews wearing the yellow star[1]

Handwritten diary of Jiří Münzer, entry for 21 September 1941

So, it's the last Sunday in our apartment – and then that'll be it. I've now somewhat come to terms with it all.

This week I was at home every day and at Ilsa's every evening.[2]

Yesterday we had sichos[3] at the Pollaks' – we just read and talked.

This morning I was at Grandma's – she's feeling a bit better – and then at Ilsa's. I also spent the afternoon with Ilsa and we went to the temple – it was Erev Rosh Hashanah.[4]

Since Friday we've been wearing the stars,[5] and the Czechs' reaction to them has been better than expected. We are constantly watching to see how people behave, and it must be said that despite the constant provocations in the newspapers and the inflammatory articles, the Czech citizens have acted impeccably so far. Of course, everyone is looking us up and down and we're attracting attention at the moment, but I haven't heard any derogatory remarks over the past three days, quite the opposite – people are showing their sympathy and strangers now greet us. It was only today that some boys from the Hitlerjugend[6] shouted out something to Ilsa and me as we left the temple. The ban on leaving one's place of residence hasn't come in yet; it's only in Pardubice that they've already got it [in writing].[7]

Each of us received just one star, a nice orange-coloured one with the word *Jude*[8] printed in black. It has to be worn stitched to the left-breast side of the jacket. Workers got two, so I've got two. Jews married to Aryans do not have to wear it, so Otta[9] hasn't got a star.

We're moving on Wednesday, but I won't go to the factory[10] then; I'll go back in on Thursday.

In Russia the Germans have occupied Kiev and Poltava.

1 JMP, DP 79. Published in Münzer, *Dospívaní nad propastí*, pp. 88–89. This document has been translated from Czech.
2 Ilsa Polláková.
3 Ashkenazi pronunciation of the Hebrew 'sihot', plural of 'siha'; 'talks, discussions'.
4 Hebrew for 'evening before New Year'. In the original, Erev is written in Hebrew and Rosh Hashanah in Czech.
5 See Doc. 318, fn. 2.
6 German in the original: 'Hitler Youth'.
7 On 15 Sept. 1941 the Reich Ministry of the Interior issued a general ban on Jews leaving their places of residence. See Doc. 222.
8 German in the original: 'Jew'.
9 Ota Klepetář.
10 Münzer worked in Stanislav Kauder's factory.

DOC. 320

On 28 September 1941 Eva Roubíčková records Reinhard Heydrich's arrival in the Protectorate[1]

Handwritten diary of Eva Roubíčková, entry for 28 September 1941

Sunday, 28 September 1941
Met up with Käthe[2] in town; all of a sudden, they announced a state of emergency in all the larger towns in the Protectorate.

Nobody knows the reason; things must be happening that they are not telling us about. Sabotage.

A new Reich Protector, Heydrich, has arrived – Himmler's deputy.[3] He will clamp down much harder. This means that things are not going as well as the Germans claim. Was at the cemetery in the Old Town, and the Jewish Museum, then Käthe came back to ours, then was at Peter's with Eva and Benny.[4]

Had a great time.

1 Published in Roubíčková, *Langsam*, p. 49. This document has been translated from German.
2 Probably: Käthe Fuchs, née Neumann (b. 1921), state employee; an acquaintance of Eva Roubíčková's from Vienna, who had emigrated to Prague; married with two children; survived the war and later returned to Prague.
3 Konstantin von Neurath was suspended from office in Sept. 1941, accused of being too lenient. He did not submit his formal resignation until August 1943. His successor, as acting Reich Protector, was Reinhard Heydrich.
4 Eva Glauber and Benny Grünberger.

Glossary

Affidavit (of support)
: Legal document showing proof of financial support by a US citizen or permanent resident that was required to obtain a visa to the United States. The affidavit was difficult to acquire and presented a major bureaucratic obstacle to emigration.

Aliyah (Hebrew for 'ascent')
: Jewish emigration to Palestine with the Zionist aim of establishing a Jewish homeland. Aliyah Aleph referred to legal emigration and Aliyah Beth to illegal emigration organized from the mid 1930s, in defiance of the restrictions placed by the British government on Jewish immigration into Palestine.

Altreu (Allgemeine Treuhandstelle für die jüdische Auswanderung GmbH; General Trust Agency for Jewish Emigration)
: Agency established in May 1937 to support emigration to countries other than Palestine (in addition to the Paltreu-Haavara, which had been responsible for Palestine since 1933). Emigrants could transfer a fixed amount of Reichsmarks into an Altreu account, in return for which they received foreign currency at a markdown of 50 per cent.

American Jewish Joint Distribution Committee (JDC, Joint)
: Committee founded in the United States in 1914 to coordinate the relief efforts of American Jewish aid organizations. It provided funding and aid to Jews and Jewish organizations, especially in Eastern Europe. Following the outbreak of the Second World War, its efforts extended to Nazi-occupied and Nazi-controlled territories, including the ghettos, where it supported schools, orphanages, cultural institutions, and other important areas of Jewish life.

Anschluss
: Annexation of Austria by Nazi Germany in March 1938.

Anti-Comintern Pact
: Agreement concluded between Germany and Japan (25 November 1936), and then between Italy, Germany, and Japan (6 November 1937), directed against the Communist International (Comintern) and specifically against the Soviet Union. The signatories pledged to safeguard each other's interests in the event of an attack by the Soviet Union and to refrain from entering into political treaties with the Soviet Union.

Aryan (*Arier*)
: Term used to describe the peoples supposedly descended from the Indo-Europeans. It was used in Nazi Germany to support the thesis of the inequality of human races and the superiority of those with 'German and related blood' over 'non Aryan races', above all Jews.

Aryanization (*Arisierung*)
: The process of expropriating Jews and excluding them from a 'racially purified' economy. It involved the confiscation or liquidation of Jewish property, assets and businesses and the forced transfer of these to Aryans or to the Reich.

Asset Transfer Office (Vermögensverkehrsstelle, VVSt)
Office founded in May 1938, headed by Walter Rafelsberger, which oversaw the Aryanization and liquidation of Jewish businesses in Austria. By mid August 1939 there were no more Jewish-owned businesses in Vienna.

Beer Hall Putsch
The failed attempt by Adolf Hitler and other right-wing opponents of the Weimar Republic to seize power in Germany on 8–9 November 1923 in Munich.

Bezirkshauptmann
Highest administrative rank within a district administration (*Bezirkshauptmannschaft*) in the Protectorate of Bohemia and Moravia.

Blocked account (*Sperrkonto*)
Special account holding the liquid assets of Jews who had emigrated. The accounts were set up because German financial policy prohibited Reichsmarks from being removed from Germany without heavy penalties. Due to the depreciation of the Reichsmark, the contents of these accounts had little value outside Germany.

British Mandate for Palestine
League of Nations mandate granted to Britain in 1922. The Mandate ended on 15 May 1948, one day before the proclamation of the State of Israel.

Central Office for Jewish Emigration (Zentralstelle für jüdische Auswanderung)
Institution established first in Vienna in August 1938 by the Security Police and SS Security Service to facilitate and expedite the emigration of Jews from Nazi-controlled territories. There were four such offices, set up in Vienna (1938), Prague (1939), Berlin (1939), and Amsterdam (1941). Adolf Eichmann headed the offices in Vienna and Prague.

Commander of the Security Police and SD (Kommandeur der Sicherheitspolizei und des SD, KdS)
Commander of the combined Gestapo, Criminal Police, and SD operating on the regional level in the occupied territories and, during the final phase of the war, also inside the Reich; subordinate to the Senior Commander of the Security Police (BdS).

Commissar Order (*Kommissarbefehl*), also known as Guidelines for the Treatment of Political Commissars (*Richtlinien für die Behandlung politischer Kommissare*)
Order issued by the Wehrmacht High Command on 6 June 1941, in contravention of international law, instructing the Wehrmacht that Red Army political commissars should be summarily executed rather than taken as prisoners of war. The order was suspended in May 1942.

Criminal Police (Kriminalpolizei, Kripo)
Criminal investigation force that, together with the Gestapo, constituted the Security Police (Sipo). The Kripo mainly dealt with non-political crimes including offences against the war economy (black market activity, slaughtering animals without permit, contravention of the rationing regulations), rape, murder, and arson. It was also heavily involved in the persecution of marginalized groups such as Sinti and Roma and homosexuals.

Czechoslovak Legion
Voluntary military force composed of ethnic Czechs and Slovaks. It was formed in Russia in 1914 to fight on the side of the Entente powers in the First World War, with the aim of winning their support for the independence of Bohemia and Moravia

and the Slovak territories from the Austro-Hungarian Empire. The Legion played a key role in the foundation of the Czechoslovak Republic and its members made up a significant part of the new Czechoslovak army.

Denazification (*Entnazifizierung*)

Allied efforts to remove Nazis and Nazi ideology from public life and to re-educate Germans and Austrians after 1945. In 1946 the Western Allies transferred the responsibility for denazification to the local administration in their zones of occupation. The newly-established West German state concluded the process in the early 1950s. In the Soviet zone, denazification efforts ended in March 1948.

Einsatzgruppen

Units of the Security Police (and SD), first deployed during the occupation of Austria and the Sudetenland in 1938. They were instructed to monitor political activity and to identify and arrest political enemies. Following the invasion of Poland (1939) and the Soviet Union (1941), they were tasked with eliminating racial and political enemies, and operated as mobile killing units as the German armed forces advanced into Eastern Europe. Einsatzgruppen were formed and deployed as the Germans occupied more countries.

Einsatzkommando

Subunits of the Einsatzgruppen, created in 1938. In the occupied Soviet Union they were assigned to one of the three Rear Area Army Groups.

Eretz Israel (Hebrew for the 'Land of Israel' or the 'Holy Land')

Biblical term used in Jewish writings to refer to Palestine. The Zionist movement sought to establish a state in Eretz Israel within the British Mandate for Palestine in order to revive the Jewish people as a modern nation and provide a refuge for diaspora Jews. Zionists in the diaspora often used the shortened version, 'Eretz'.

Ethnic Germans (*Volksdeutsche*)

People of German descent with a shared language and culture living beyond German borders. Under National Socialism, the term distinguished ethnic Germans from Reich Germans (*Reichsdeutsche*), who were German citizens.

'Euthanasia' programme

National Socialist programme to murder patients with psychiatric illnesses or mental or physical disabilities, led by the head of the Chancellery of the Führer, Philipp Bouhler, and Hitler's personal physician, Karl Brandt. The murders were initiated by Hitler's 'mercy killing decree' of autumn 1939, which authorized doctors to terminate the lives of people deemed 'unworthy of life'. Between January 1940 and August 1941, over 70,000 patients were murdered in six purpose-built killing centres in Germany and Austria. Hitler stopped the programme in August 1941 as a result of widespread protests, especially from the churches. However, the 'euthanasia' killings continued until the end of the war, both in the German Reich and in German-occupied territories. Between 1939 and 1945 some 200,000 people were murdered in Germany and Austria, and around 100,000 others were killed elsewhere in occupied Europe.

Four-Year Plan

A series of economic measures initiated by Hitler in 1936 and managed by the Office of the Four-Year Plan under the leadership of plenipotentiary Hermann Göring. The plan aimed to prepare Germany for war within four years. It focused on the rearmament of Germany and the mobilization of the economy, and aimed to make the country more self-sufficient in terms of raw materials.

Gau (NSDAP term for 'region')

The largest NSDAP administrative category below Reich level. After the National Socialists assumed power in 1933, the Gaue increasingly replaced the individual states (Länder) as the effective regional subdivision of the Third Reich. As the regional units of the NSDAP, the Gaue were divided into Kreise (districts), consisting of 'local branches' (Ortsgruppen, covering several villages or towns), 'cells' (Zellen), and 'blocks' (Blöcke, neighbourhoods within the cells). The number of Gaue varied over time, with new ones created following territorial annexations.

Gaugeschäftsführer

Senior regional official, subordinate to a Gauleiter.

Gauhauptmann

Reichsgau official and representative of the Gauleiter and the Reichsstatthalter, responsible for the administration of a Gau.

Gauleiter ('Gau leader')

Head of an NSDAP Gau.

General Government

Area of central Poland that became one of the three territorial units created following the German invasion of Poland in 1939. It was divided into four districts – Cracow, Warsaw, Lublin, and Radom – to which Galicia was added in August 1941. The General Government was a central site of the mass extermination of European Jews.

General Plan East (*Generalplan Ost*)

A plan commissioned by the Reich Security Main Office in 1941 that envisaged a racial reordering of Eastern Europe through the deportation of 30–50 million Slavs from Poland, the Baltics, and the Soviet Union, and the repopulation of these lands with approximately 10 million ethnic Germans over a period of 30 years.

German Labour Front (Deutsche Arbeitsfront, DAF)

Compulsory National Socialist organization of workers and employers, set up to replace trade unions following their dissolution in 1933. It had approximately 22 million members.

German Reich (Deutsches Reich; German Empire)

From 1871 to 1945 official term for Germany, comprising Imperial Germany (Kaiserreich, 1871–1918), the Weimar Republic (1918–1933), and the Third Reich (1933–1945).

German–Soviet Non-Aggression Pact (also known as the Molotov–Ribbentrop Pact or Hitler–Stalin Pact)

Treaty between Nazi Germany and the Soviet Union, signed in Moscow on 23 August 1939 by foreign ministers Joachim von Ribbentrop and Vyacheslav Molotov, stipulating that neither signatory would attack the other. It also contained a secret protocol that provided for the division of Poland and parts of East Central Europe into Soviet and German spheres of interest.

Gestapo (abbreviation for Geheime Staatspolizei; Secret State Police)

Secret State Police in Nazi Germany and German-occupied Europe, established by Hermann Göring in 1933 with the aim of combating internal 'enemies of the state'. From 1934 it was led by Heinrich Himmler and in 1936 it became part of Reinhard Heydrich's Security Police. In 1939 the Security Police merged with the SD to form the Reich Security Main Office (RSHA). Thereafter it became known as RSHA Amt IV and was headed by Heinrich Müller. It was divided into five departments: (a) Political Opponents, (b) Sects and Churches, (c) Administration and Party Affairs, (d) Occupied Territories, (e) Security and Counter-intelligence. By the end of 1944 the Gestapo had a staff of 32,000.

Gleichschaltung ('synchronization' or 'enforced coordination')
Synchronization of all areas of life (political parties, professional associations, cultural organizations, etc.) and their subordination to National Socialist ideology.

Greater German Reich (Großdeutsches Reich)
Unofficial designation for Nazi Germany after the Anschluss of Austria in 1938 and including all annexed territories.

Grüber Office
Aid agency set up by the Provisional Church Government of the Berlin Confessing Church in September 1938 and run by Pastor Heinrich Grüber. It assisted Protestant Christians persecuted on grounds of race to emigrate from Germany. It was shut down by the Gestapo in December 1940, and Grüber and his staff were arrested and sent to concentration camps. After 1945 Grüber reopened his office to help Holocaust survivors and deportees returning home.

Haavara Agreement (Hebrew for 'transfer' agreement)
In effect between 1933 and 1939, an agreement between the Jewish Agency for Palestine and Nazi Germany that enabled Jewish emigrants to receive German goods in Palestine in exchange for money they deposited in Germany and was also intended to promote German exports. The arrangement made it possible for emigrants to indirectly transfer a part of their assets without the National Socialist state incurring foreign exchange costs. The Berlin-based Paltreu was responsible for overseeing the financial transactions. Nearly 140 million Reichsmarks were transferred to Palestine while the agreement was in force.

Hachsharah (also hakhsharah; Hebrew for 'preparation')
Occupational and agricultural training of young Jews on Zionist collective farms in preparation for emigration to Palestine.

Haganah (Hebrew for 'defence')
Zionist paramilitary organization, founded in 1920 in the British Mandate for Palestine. It formed the core of the Israel Defense Forces following the establishment of the State of Israel in 1948.

Hehalutz (Hebrew for 'the pioneer')
Organization founded in the United States in 1905 to prepare *halutzim* (pioneers) for life in Palestine. A German branch was established in 1922.

Hermann Göring Reich Works (Reichswerke Hermann Göring)
Industrial conglomerate set up in July 1937 to exploit Germany's low-grade domestic iron ores. It grew rapidly beyond its initial purpose as Göring used it as a vehicle for taking over other industrial assets which the state needed for war preparations and for setting up new state-owned businesses.

Higher SS and Police Leaders (Höhere SS- und Polizeiführer, HSSPF)
Representatives of Himmler, appointed by him from 1937, responsible for ensuring police control and coordinating the activities of the Security Police, the SD, the

Order Police, the Waffen SS, and local auxiliary police units in all occupied territories and, to a limited extent, in the Reich.

Hofrat ('court councillor')

Professional title for senior civil servants in Austria, roughly equivalent to the rank of Ministerialrat in Germany. It was also an honorary title bestowed on deserving individuals by the Austrian state.

Israelite Religious Community of Vienna (Israelitische Kultusgemeinde, IKG)

Jewish umbrella organization authorized by the Austrian government in 1852 to manage the religious, educational, and philanthropic affairs of the Jewish population in Vienna and the Jewish community of Austria, including the establishment and upkeep of synagogues, the supervision of religious rituals and traditions, the care of the elderly, and the maintenance of Jewish charities and cemeteries. It also served as the official registrar of Jewish births, deaths, marriages, and conversions in Vienna from 1794 to 1938. In 1938 it came under the control of the Central Office for Jewish Emigration in Vienna and the Gestapo, and was forced to organize the emigration and deportation of Austria's Jews. The IKG exists to this day.

Jew houses (*Judenhäuser*)

Buildings to which Jews in the German Reich were forced to move following eviction or as a result of financial hardship. Conditions were often squalid and overcrowded.

Jewish Agency for Palestine ('Jewish Agency')

Agency founded in 1929 to represent Jewish interests in the British Mandate for Palestine. It cooperated with the British Mandate government and advised it on socio-economic issues. The Jewish Agency served as the political leadership of the Jewish community in Palestine until the establishment of the State of Israel in 1948. It also worked to help Jews emigrate to Palestine under the Haavara Agreement.

Jewish Council (*Judenrat*)

A Jewish council established on German orders in Jewish communities in Nazi-occupied Europe. The councils were set up under a decree issued after the invasion of Poland in September 1939. Their main aim was to ensure the implementation of Nazi orders and regulations, and they were in charge of transferring Jews from their homes to ghettos and providing services to maintain everyday life in the ghettos (housing, medical supplies, food distribution). From 1940 they were ordered to provide workers for forced labour camps and were later also required to prepare lists with names of Jews to be deported to extermination camps.

Jewish Culture League (Jüdischer Kulturbund)

Organization founded in 1933, and known until 1935 as the Culture League of German Jews (Kulturbund deutscher Juden), which supported and promoted Jewish music, art, theatre, and publishing for Jewish-only audiences after the Nazis had excluded Jews from German cultural life. By 1935 the league had thirty-six branches and over 70,000 members.

Jüdisches Nachrichtenblatt

News bulletin established by order of the Reich Ministry of Propaganda and Public Enlightenment following the pogroms of November 1938. It replaced all Jewish newspapers in circulation up to that point. The bulletin informed the Jewish population of new antisemitic laws and regulations as they were issued.

Kindertransport ('children's transport')
Rescue operation that helped approximately 10,000 children, most of them Jewish, to flee the German Reich and the Protectorate of Bohemia and Moravia for Britain between 1938 and 1940. Transports were organized and carried out by the Refugee Children's Movement and the Central British Fund for German Jewry (now World Jewish Relief), with the support of Dutch aid organizations. Several thousand more children found refuge in the Netherlands, Belgium, France, Switzerland, and Sweden. After the invasion of Czechoslovakia, the programme also included children from this country; as many as 669 children from Czechoslovakia were rescued in an operation organized by the British stockbroker Nicholas Winton on the eve of the Second World War.

Kreisleiter ('district leader')
Head of an NSDAP Kreis.

Kreisleitung ('district leadership')
Leadership of an NSDAP Kreis.

Landeshauptmann
Austrian rank equivalent to the minister president of a German state.

Landgerichtsrat
Professional title for a judge at a Landgericht, a mid-level district court in Germany. More than a mere job title, it also denoted the bearer's rank within the German judiciary.

Landrat
Civil service official in charge of a rural district.

Minister president (Ministerpräsident)
Head of a German state within the Reich.

Ministerial director (Ministerialdirektor)
Head of a department within a ministry or other high-level governmental agency.

Ministerialdirigent
Civil service rank subordinate to ministerial director.

Ministerialrat
Civil service rank subordinate to Ministerialdirigent.

Mischling ('half-caste' or person of 'mixed blood')
Classification under Nazi racial law to describe an individual of combined Aryan and non-Aryan, particularly Jewish, descent. The Nuremberg Laws of 1935 categorized *Mischlinge* according to the number of Jewish grandparents: *Mischlinge* of the first degree ('half Jewish' – one Jewish parent or two Jewish grandparents) and *Mischlinge* of the second degree ('quarter Jewish' – one Jewish grandparent). In order to prevent the birth of children of 'mixed blood', marriage was effectively prohibited between Aryans and '*Mischlinge* of the first degree' (those with two Jewish grandparents).

Mixed marriage (*Mischehe*)
Marriages between Jews and non-Jews, prohibited by the Nuremberg legislation of 1935 in order to preserve the 'racial purity' of the *Volksgemeinschaft*. In 1938 mixed marriages were subdivided into 'privileged' (Jewish wife married to a non-Jewish husband, or if there were children who were raised as Christians and under the age of eighteen) and 'non-privileged' (when the children were considered Jews, the

couple was childless, or a Jewish husband was married to a non-Jewish wife). Jews in both types of mixed marriages suffered under most of the anti-Jewish measures that applied to 'full Jews', although they were not deported from Germany systematically.

Munich Agreement

Agreement ratified on 29 September 1938 by Germany, Italy, Britain, and France at a conference in Munich, held without Czech representation. It permitted German annexation of the Sudetenland, a territory with a majority ethnic German population that was included as part of newly created Czechoslovakia after the First World War. The agreement was a gesture of appeasement towards Hitler.

Národní souručenství (National Solidarity)

Political party founded in March 1939 by Emil Hácha following the establishment of the Protectorate of Bohemia and Moravia in the Czech lands. It was the only political party authorized by the Germans in the Protectorate. All adult male residents of the Protectorate had to join; Jews and women were excluded.

National Socialist People's Welfare Organization (Nationalsozialistische Volkswohlfahrt, NSV)

A social welfare organization founded in Berlin in 1933. Its welfare work was restricted to 'valuable' members of the *Volksgemeinschaft* and included annual charity drives for the poor, funding holiday homes for mothers, food distribution to large families, the evacuation of children from urban areas, and assistance to bombing victims during the war.

November pogrom(s) (also known as Kristallnacht or the 'Night of Broken Glass')

Series of state-orchestrated anti-Jewish pogroms across the entire German Reich on the night of 9–10 November 1938 and in the days that followed, during which hundreds of synagogues and thousands of Jewish businesses were looted and demolished. At least 91 people were killed and hundreds committed suicide. Approximately 25,000 Jewish men were arrested and sent to concentration camps, where hundreds of them died.

NSDAP (Nationalsozialistische Deutsche Arbeiterpartei; National Socialist German Workers' Party or Nazi Party)

Anti-Marxist, antisemitic, and racist political party founded in Munich in 1919 as the Deutsche Arbeiterpartei (German Workers' Party) and renamed in 1920. Adolf Hitler became its leader in July 1921. In July 1933 the NSDAP became the only legal political party in the German Reich. In 1945 there were between 8 and 8.5 million NSDAP members.

Nuremberg Laws

Laws proclaimed at the annual Nazi Party rally in Nuremberg in September 1935. They comprised two pieces of legislation: the Reich Citizenship Law and the Law for the Protection of German Blood and German Honour. These excluded German Jews from Reich citizenship and prohibited them from marrying or having sexual relations with persons of 'German or related blood'. Further ancillary ordinances concerning these laws led to the disenfranchisement of Jews and deprived them of most political rights.

Obergebietsführer ('senior area leader')

High-ranking official in the Hitler Youth.

Oberlandesgerichtsrat
Professional title for a judge at an Oberlandesgericht (Higher Court); *see* Landgerichtsrat

Oberlandrat
Post established within the German occupation administration in the Protectorate of Bohemia and Moravia, directly responsible to the Reich Protector. The Oberlandrat's office was in charge of administering the local German population and also served as the supervisory authority for the Czech district administrations (Bezirkshauptmannschaften).

Oberlandratsbezirk
A regional administrative district of the Protectorate under the authority of one or more Oberlandräte. Each Oberlandratsbezirk covered several Czech district administrations (Bezirkshauptmannschaften).

Oberpräsident
Official in charge of a Prussian province, in the Third Reich usually also a Gauleiter.

Oberregierungsrat
Senior civil service rank in a ministry or other government agency. More senior than Regierungsrat, often the head of a department.

Occupational restructuring *(Berufsumschichtung)*
Movement that emerged in the second half of the nineteenth century within liberal Jewish discourse in Germany and aimed to improve Jews' employment opportunities and emigration chances by training them for work in agriculture and skilled crafts. Its proponents sought to counter the high proportion of Jews in certain professions (i.e. academia and trade) and direct them into fields in which they were permitted to work.

Old Reich (Altreich)
Germany within its 1937 borders, prior to the annexation of Austria in March 1938 and of the Sudetenland in October of the same year.

Order Police (Ordnungspolizei, Orpo)
German uniformed police between 1936 and 1945 composed of the urban police (Schutzpolizei), municipal police (Gemeindepolizei), and the rural police (Gendarmerie). The Order Police was initially administered by the Interior Ministry; it was merged with the SS in 1936. During the war, it was in charge of policing the civilian population in the occupied territories and was also directly involved in killing operations as part of the 'final solution'.

Ostjuden ('Eastern Jews')
Yiddish-speaking, mainly non-assimilated Jews who had migrated from Eastern Europe, particularly Poland, to Western Europe, North and South America, and Palestine from the nineteenth century onwards. The term initially emerged as a result of the division between these Jews and the emancipated Jews in the countries to which they migrated. *Ostjuden* were early targets of the Nazi regime and the negative stereotype associated with them played a central role in Nazi propaganda.

Ostmark
Name for Austria following its annexation to the German Reich in March 1938 until 1942, when the designation was changed to 'Alpen- und Donau Reichsgaue' (Reichsgaue of the Alps and Danube).

Palestine Office (Palästina-Amt)
Branch of the Jewish Agency for Palestine (in Germany and other countries) that helped Jews prepare for and organize their emigration to Palestine. The Palestine Office distributed the immigration certificates required by the British Mandate for Palestine.

Petschek group
Coal-mining, manufacturing, and trade conglomerate with companies in Germany, Czechoslovakia, and Austria. The majority shareholder was the Jewish Petschek family. The group resisted Aryanization until December 1938, when the firm's holdings were put into Aryan trusteeship and placed under the control of the Hermann Göring Works.

Political commissar
A Soviet military officer responsible for the morale and the ideological education of the troops from the regimental level upwards. Political commissars were considered the ideological backbone of the Soviet Army, and antisemites held the majority of them to be Jewish. The position was temporarily suspended from mid 1940 to mid 1941.

Political Police
Common term for the Secret Police of the German states in the nineteenth and twentieth centuries. The Prussian Secret Police was renamed the Gestapo in 1933.

Protective custody (*Schutzhaft*)
Arrest and detention of persons suspected of acting against the state's interests, carried out without warrant or judicial review. The Gestapo in particular used protective custody as an instrument to crush dissent and to enforce Nazi racial and social policy. Those arrested were either imprisoned or sent to concentration camps.

Regierungsassessor
Junior civil service rank attained after passing the qualifying examinations for the civil service.

Regierungsbezirk
Administrative subdivision in larger German states, especially in Prussia and Bavaria, the level above Kreis (district).

Regierungspräsident
Civil service official in charge of a Regierungsbezirk.

Regierungsrat
Senior civil service rank in a ministry or other government agency, subordinate to Oberregierungsrat.

Reich Central Agency for Jewish Emigration (Reichszentrale für jüdische Auswanderung)
Agency set up in January 1939 in Berlin on the instructions of Hermann Göring to centralize and accelerate all work connected with Jewish emigration from Germany. It was officially headed by Reinhard Heydrich.

Reich Citizenship Law (*Reichsbürgergesetz*)
One of the Nuremberg Laws proclaimed in September 1935. The Reich Citizenship Law did not strip Jews of their German citizenship but introduced a new distinction between 'subject of the state' (*Staatsangehörige*) and 'Reich citizen' (*Reichsbürger*); only those with 'German or related blood' could be the latter.

Reich Commissioner for the Strengthening of Germandom (Reichskommissar für die Festigung deutschen Volkstums, RKF, RKFDV)

Office held by Heinrich Himmler from 7 October 1939 with the task of resettling ethnic Germans resident abroad in the newly annexed territories and eradicating the 'harmful influence' of non-German groups on the Reich. The RKFDV played an important role in the ethnographic restructuring of German-dominated Europe, which included deportation and mass murder.

Reich Flight Tax (*Reichsfluchtsteuer*)

Emigration tax, introduced during the Weimar Republic to prevent capital flight during the Great Depression, which increasingly targeted Jews forced to flee Nazi Germany. At first the tax only applied to emigrants with assets worth over 200,000 Reichsmarks, but from 1934 it was extended to those with assets of 50,000 Reichsmarks or more. Initially levied at a rate of 25 per cent, in 1938 the rate increased to 90 per cent.

Reich Germans (*Reichsdeutsche*)

Designation commonly used during the National Socialist period to distinguish Reich citizens who were residents of the German Reich from Reich citizens who were resident abroad (*Auslandsdeutsche*) and from foreign citizens with German ethnicity (*Volksdeutsche*, ethnic Germans). After the annexation of Austria in March 1938, Austrian citizens also acquired the status of *Reichsdeutsche*.

Reich Protector of Bohemia and Moravia

Head of the Protectorate of Bohemia and Moravia. The Reich Protector enjoyed the protection and the rights of the head of state, and acted as Hitler's representative.

Reich Security Main Office (Reichssicherheitshauptamt, RSHA)

Office created by Heinrich Himmler on 27 September 1939 by merging the SD and the Security Police, and headed by Reinhard Heydrich. The RSHA played an important role in the regime's policies of persecution and extermination. It was responsible for intelligence gathering and criminal investigation. Through the work of Section IV D 4 (later IV B 4), run by Adolf Eichmann, it was instrumental in the implementation of the 'final solution'.

Reichsgau

Administrative subdivision in some of the territories annexed to the German Reich between 1938 and 1945, including Austria and western and northern Poland.

Reichsgesetzblatt (*Reich Law Gazette*, RGBl)

Official gazette in the German Reich that published laws and regulations.

Reichsleiter ('Reich leader')

The most senior political rank in the NSDAP, second only to the Führer. Hitler appointed Reichsleiter to oversee a range of portfolios (propaganda, law, finance, foreign policy). They were collectively designated as the Reich leadership (Reichsleitung).

Reichsstatthalter ('Reich governor')

Political officials appointed to head the Länder (German states) and implement political orders from Hitler after 1933. The Gauleiter frequently also served as Reichsstatthalter.

SD (abbreviation for Sicherheitsdienst; SS Security Service)
Intelligence service of the SS and NSDAP, founded in 1931 by Heinrich Himmler and headed by Reinhard Heydrich. Its tasks included the detection and surveillance of those classed as political and ideological enemies, especially Jews, communists, Social Democrats, and Freemasons. In 1939 it was incorporated into the Reich Security Main Office (RSHA) along with the Security Police (Gestapo and Criminal Police). It played an instrumental role in the planning and implementation of the 'final solution'.

Security Order (*Sicherheitsanordnung*)
Legal instrument introduced in 1936 to access Jewish emigrants' capital and could be issued as soon as it was suspected that someone was going to emigrate. The regulations were tightened with the Law on Foreign Exchange Control of 12 December 1938. Jewish taxpayers subsequently had to transfer their capital to security accounts at a bank licensed to deal in foreign exchange and required authorization to access it.

Security Police (Sicherheitspolizei, Sipo)
One of the two police branches after Himmler's reorganization of the entire police apparatus in 1936 (the other being the Order Police). The Security Police was headed by Reinhard Heydrich between 1936 and 1942 and consisted of the Gestapo and the Criminal Police. It was incorporated into the Reich Security Main Office in 1939.

Senior Commander of the Security Police (*Befehlshaber der Sicherheitspolizei*, BdS)
Head of the Reich Security Main Office field office in an occupied territory during the war; also subordinate to the Higher SS and Police Leaders.

Sonderkommando
Subunit of the Einsatzgruppen operating in the rear of the German armies.

Sopade
The exiled executive of the Social Democratic Party of Germany (SPD) that operated in Prague (1933–1938), Paris (1938–1940), and London (until 1945). It collected and analysed reports and newspaper articles about the political, cultural, economic, and social situation in Germany, which it published on a monthly basis from May 1934. The Sopade reports are among the most valuable historical sources about public opinion in Nazi Germany.

SS (abbreviation for Schutzstaffel; 'protection squadron')
Paramilitary force established in 1925, under the leadership of Heinrich Himmler from 1929. From 1934 it was responsible for running the concentration camps and from 1941 for the extermination camps.

SS-Verfügungstruppe (SS Dispositional Troops)
Combat units of the SS formed in 1934 and trained along the same lines as the Wehrmacht; precursor to the Waffen SS.

Staatsrat ('state councillor')
Member of the Prussian State Council.

State minister (*Staatsminister*)
Head of a ministry in a state government.

State secretary (*Staatssekretär*)
The most senior rank of permanent civil service official in a ministry. There were sometimes several state secretaries in one ministry.

Sudeten German Party (Sudetendeutsche Partei, SdP)
Party founded by Konrad Henlein in October 1933. After the parliamentary elections in May 1935, the SdP became the strongest party in Czechoslovakia. It became increasingly Nazified from 1937 and worked with Nazi leaders on integrating German-speaking parts of Bohemia and Moravia into the Third Reich.

Undersecretary (*Unterstaatssekretär*)
Civil service official within a ministry; rank below state secretary.

Vlajka (Czech for 'Flag')
A Czech fascist and nationalist movement founded by the philosophy professor František Mareš in the late 1920s. Vlajka became politically active in the 1930s and called for the complete Nazification of Bohemia and Moravia after 1938. Its members carried out assaults on Jews, and organized protests against the Czech presidents Tomáš Masaryk and Edvard Beneš. The movement had approximately 13,000 members in 1939. It was disbanded in 1942 and its leaders were imprisoned in Dachau concentration camp as 'privileged prisoners'.

Volga Germans
Ethnic Germans invited by Catherine the Great in 1762/1763 to colonize underdeveloped land on the banks of the Volga river and to introduce more advanced agriculture methods to rural Russia. They were given the freedom to practise their religion and to retain their culture and language, and were immune from conscription. In 1941 they were considered potential collaborators and a large number of them were sent to Central Asia, Siberia, and Kazakhstan. Many moved to Germany in the 1980s and 1990s.

völkisch (literally 'folkish'; roughly meaning 'ethno-nationalist')
Term dating back to the nineteenth century and denoting the organic unity of people bound by blood, soil, history, and culture. In the second half of the nineteenth century the central tenet of *völkisch* thinking was a racial ideology that later became a key element of National Socialism.

Völkischer Beobachter
Official newspaper of the NSDAP from December 1920 to 30 April 1945. It initially appeared as a national edition published in Munich; a Berlin edition and a northern German edition were added in 1933, followed by a Viennese edition in 1938. By 1944 it had a circulation of 1.5 million copies.

Volksgemeinschaft (usually translated as 'people's community' or 'national community')
Under National Socialism, the notion of a racially homogeneous, 'Aryan' national community, restricted to those of 'German blood'. The concept evoked a utopian order that promised material well-being and self-fulfilment, and provided Nazi functionaries with a framework for social engineering.

Volksgenosse/-in ('ethnic comrade')
Member of the German *Volksgemeinschaft*.

Volkskörper ('people's body' or 'body politic')
Under National Socialism, the notion of a biologically defined collective body of the German people. The concept distinguished between individual bodies deemed to be of (hereditary) 'value' or 'non-value', and provided Nazi functionaries with a framework for determining policies to cultivate certain elements within society and to eradicate others.

Wehrmacht

Collective term for the German armed forces – army, air force (Luftwaffe), and navy – from 1935 to 1945. The Wehrmacht was the successor to the Reichswehr (1919–1935). The Armed Forces High Command (Oberkommando der Wehrmacht, OKW) under Wilhelm Keitel coordinated military activities, although each of the three military branches had their respective high command: OKH (army), OKM (navy), and OKL (air force).

Westmark

Gau created in December 1940 from the Bavarian Rhine Palatinate, the Saarland, and parts of Lorraine.

World Jewish Congress (WJC)

International organization founded in Geneva in August 1936 with the backing of the American Jewish Congress (AJC). It was set up with the aim of promoting Jewish unity, supporting the establishment of a Jewish national home in Palestine, campaigning for political and economic equality for Jews across Europe, and combatting Nazism and antisemitism. The organization is still in operation today.

Yom Kippur (Hebrew for 'Day of Atonement')

The most sacred holiday in the Jewish calendar, celebrated in autumn on the tenth day of the Hebrew month Tishri. It is a day of penance, fasting, and synagogue services.

Youth Aliyah

A department of the Jewish Agency for Palestine formed in 1932 with the aim of helping Jewish children and young people in Europe to emigrate to Palestine.

Zionism

Movement that originated in Central and Eastern Europe in the late nineteenth century and advocated the re-establishment of a Jewish nation in what is now Israel.

Approximate Rank and Hierarchy Equivalents

NSDAP and Civil Service

NSDAP	Civil Service
Reichsleiter	Staatssekretär
–	Oberpräsident (only in Prussia)
Gauleiter	Unterstaatssekretär
Hauptbefehlsleiter	Ministerialdirektor
Oberbefehlsleiter	Regierungspräsident
Befehlsleiter	–
Hauptdienstleiter	Ministerialdirigent
Oberdienstleiter	–
Hauptbereichsleiter	Ministerialrat
Kreisleiter	
Oberbereichsleiter	Regierungsdirektor
Bereichsleiter	–
Hauptgemeinschaftsleiter	Amtsrat
Ortsgruppenleiter	
Obergemeinschaftsleiter	Oberinspektor
Gemeinschaftsleiter	Inspektor
Haupteinsatzleiter	–
Einsatzleiter	–
Hauptbereitschaftsleiter	Obersekretär
Oberbereitschaftsleiter	Sekretär
–	Verwaltungsassistent
Bereitschaftsleiter	–
–	Assistent
Hauptarbeitsleiter	Assistent
Oberarbeitsleiter	Amtsgehilfe
Arbeitsleiter	–
Oberhelfer	–
Helfer	–
Polit. Leiter-Anwärter	–

Source: Michael Buddrus, *Totale Erziehung für den totalen Krieg: Hitlerjugend und nationalsozialistische Jugendpolitik* (Munich: De Gruyter, 2003).

SS, Wehrmacht, British Army, US Army

SS	Wehrmacht	British Army	US Army
–	Reichsmarschall	–	–
Reichsführer-SS	Generalfeldmarschall	Field Marshal	General of the Army
SS-Oberstgruppenführer	Generaloberst	–	General
SS-Obergruppenführer	General der Waffengattung (Infanterie, Artillerie, etc.)	General	Lieutenant General
SS-Gruppenführer	Generalleutnant	Lieutenant General	Major General
SS-Brigadeführer	Generalmajor	Major General	Brigadier General
SS-Oberführer	–	Brigadier	–
SS-Standartenführer	Oberst	Colonel	Colonel
SS-Obersturmbannführer	Oberstleutnant	Lieutenant Colonel	Lieutenant Colonel
SS-Sturmbannführer	Major	Major	Major
SS-Hauptsturmführer	Hauptmann	Captain	Captain
SS-Obersturmführer	Oberleutnant	First Lieutenant	First Lieutenant
SS-Untersturmführer	Leutnant	Second Lieutenant	Second Lieutenant
SS-Sturmscharführer	Stabsoberfeldwebel	Regimental Sergeant Major (Warrant Officer Class 1)	Sergeant Major
–	Oberfähnrich	–	Senior Officer Candidate
SS-Hauptscharführer	Oberfeldwebel	Staff Sergeant Major (Warrant Officer Class 1)	Master Sergeant
SS-Oberscharführer	Feldwebel	Warrant Officer Class 2	Technical Sergeant
–	Fähnrich	Ensign	Officer Candidate
SS-Scharführer	Unterfeldwebel	Staff Sergeant	Staff Sergeant
SS-Unterscharführer	Unteroffizier	Sergeant	Sergeant
–	Stabsgefreiter	Corporal (senior)	–
–	Obergefreiter	Corporal	Corporal

SS-Rottenführer	Gefreiter	Lance Corporal	Acting Corporal
SS-Sturmmann	Obersoldat	Private (senior)	Private First Class
SS-Mann	Soldat	Private	Private
SS-Anwärter	–	–	–

Sources:
SS/Wehrmacht ranks Heinz Antzt, *Mörder in Uniform: Organisationen, die zu Vollstreckern nationalsozialistischer Verbrechen wurden* (Munich: Kindler, 1979).
Wehrmacht/US army ranks: Tim Ripley, *The German Army in World War II, 1939–1945* (Hoboken: Taylor and Francis, 2014).
Wehrmacht/British army ranks: Ben H. Shepherd, *Hitler's Soldiers: The German Army in the Third Reich* (New Haven: Yale University Press, 2017).

Security Police (SIPO)
Sicherheitspolizei (SIPO)
Reichsführer SS und Chef der deutschen Polizei / Reichsführer SS and Chief of the German Police
Chef der SIPO / Chief of the SIPO
Kriminaldirigent / SIPO commissioner
Reichskriminaldirektor / SIPO Reich assistant commissioner
Regierungs- und Kriminaldirektor / SIPO commander
Kriminalrat / detective chief superintendent
Kriminalkommissar / detective superintendent
Kriminalinspektor / detective inspector
Kriminalobersekretär / detective chief sergeant
Kriminalsekretär / detective sergeant
Kriminaloberassistent / detective chief constable
Kriminalassistent / detective constable
Kriminalassistentenanwärter / detective constable candidate

Source: Hans-Christian Harten, *Die weltanschauliche Schulung der Polizei im Nationalsozialismus* (Paderborn: Ferdinand Schöningh, 2018).

List of Abbreviations

§	section (of a German law, code, or regulation)
§§	sections (of a German law, code, or regulation)
ABS	Archiv bezpečnostních složek (Archive of the Czech Security Forces)
AdK	Akademie der Künste (Academy of Arts)
AdR	Archiv der Republik (Archive of the Austrian Republic)
AEG	Allgemeine Elektrizitäts-Gesellschaft (General Electric Company)
AG	Aktiengesellschaft (public limited company)
AP	Associated Press
Art.	article (of a German law, code, or regulation)
ASV	Archivio Segreto Vaticano (Vatican Secret Archives)
AVG	Allgemeines Verwaltungsverfahrensgesetz (General Administrative Procedure Law)
AŻIH	Archiwum Żydowski Instytut Historyczny (Archives of the Jewish Historical Institute), Warsaw
b.	born
BADV	Bundesamt fur zentrale Dienste und offene Vermögensfragen (Federal Office for Central Services and Unresolved Property Issues)
BAM	Bistumsarchiv Münster (Archives of the Diocese of Münster)
BArch	Bundesarchiv (German Federal Archives)
Bd.	Band (volume)
BdS	Befehlshaber der Sicherheitspolizei (Senior Commander of the Security Police)
BGB	Bürgerliches Gesetzbuch (German Civil Code)
BLHA	Brandenburgisches Landeshauptarchiv (Brandenburg Main State Archives)
BwA	Archiv der Gedenkstätte Buchenwald (Archive of the Buchenwald Memorial)
CA	California
CAEJR	Committee for the Assistance of European Jewish Refugees, Shanghai
CAHJP	Central Archives for the History of the Jewish People, Hebrew University of Jerusalem, Israel
CDJC	Centre de Documentation Juive Contemporaine (Contemporary Jewish Documentation Center), Paris
CDU	Christlich Demokratische Union Deutschlands (Christian Democratic Union of Germany)
CPSU	Communist Party of the Soviet Union
ČSAV	Československá akademie věd (Czechoslovak Academy of Sciences)
CSSR	Czechoslovak Socialist Republic
CV	Centralverein deutscher Staatsbürger jüdischen Glaubens (Central Association of German Citizens of the Jewish Faith)
CZA	Central Zionist Archives
d.	died
DAF	Deutsche Arbeitsfront (German Labour Front)
DAP	Deutsche Arbeiterpartei (German Workers' Party)
DBG	Deutsches Beamtengesetz (German Civil Service Law)
DDP	Deutsche Demokratische Partei (German Democratic Party)
DFG	Deutsche Forschungsgemeinschaft (German Research Foundation)

DGT	Deutscher Gemeindetag (German Council of Municipalities)
DIAG	Deutsche Industrie AG (German Industry AG)
DNVP	Deutschnationale Volkspartei (German National People's Party)
DÖW	Dokumentationsarchiv des Österreichischen Widerstandes (Documentation Centre of Austrian Resistance), Vienna
DP	Deutsche Partei (German Party)
DRA	Deutsches Rundfunkarchiv (German Broadcasting Archives)
DSAP	Deutsche Sozialdemokratische Arbeiterpartei (German Social Democratic Workers' Party)
DSP	Deutschsoziale Partei (German Social Party)
DVP	Deutsche Volkspartei (German People's Party)
e.V.	eingetragener Verein (registered charitable / non-profit society)
EZA	Evangelisches Zentralarchiv (Evangelical Central Archives)
fol.	folio (of an archival source)
fr.	frame
geh.	geheim (secret)
Gestapa	Geheimes Staatspolizeiamt (Secret State Police Central Office)
Gestapo	Geheime Staatspolizei (Secret State Police)
Gen. Gov.	General Government
GmbH	Gesellschaft mit beschränkter Haftung (private limited company)
GStAPK	Geheimes Staatsarchiv Preußischer Kulturbesitz (Secret State Archives Prussian Cultural Heritage Foundation)
HHStAW	Hessisches Hauptstaatarchiv (Hessian Main State Archives)
HIAS	Hebrew Immigrant Aid Society
HICEM	amalgamation of *H*IAS, *I*CA, and *Em*igdirect
HSSPF	Höhere(r) SS- und Polizeiführer (Higher SS and Police Leader(s))
IfZ-Archives	Archiv des Leibniz Instituts für Zeitgeschichte München – Berlin (Archives of the Leibniz Institute for Contemporary History)
IGCR	Intergovernmental Committee on Refugees
IKG	Israelitische Kultusgemeinde (Israelite Religious Community of Vienna)
Inv. No. / Inv.	inventory number(s)
IOBB	Independent Order of B'nai B'rith
IPN	Instytut Pamięci Narodowej (Institute of National Remembrance, Warsaw)
ISG	Institut für Stadtgeschichte Frankfurt am Main (Institute for the History of Frankfurt)
JCA (also ICA)	Jewish Colonization Association
JDC	American Jewish Joint Distribution Committee
JMB	Jüdisches Museum Berlin (Jewish Museum Berlin)
JMP	Jewish Museum Prague
JMW	Jüdisches Museum Wien (Jewish Museum Vienna)
JSS	Jewish Social Self-Help (Jüdische Soziale Selbsthilfe)
k.	Koruna ('crowns', Czechoslovak currency)
KdS	Kommandeur der Sicherheitspolizei (Commander of the Security Police)
KPÖ	Kommunistische Partei Österreichs (Communist Party of Austria)
KSČ	Communist Party of Czechoslovakia
KZ	Konzentrationslager (concentration camp)
LAB	Landesarchiv Berlin (Berlin State Archive)
LA Graz	Landesarchiv Graz (Graz City Archives)

LAV NRW R	Landesarchiv Nordrhein-Westfalen, Abt. Rheinland (North Rhine-Westphalia State Archives, Rhineland Department)
lic.	licentiate degree
lic. habil.	licentiate degree with qualification to enter German academia
mbH	mit beschränkter Haftung (limited liability company)
MdI	Ministerium des Innern (Ministry of the Interior)
Mk.	(Reichs)mark
MZAB	Moravský zemský archiv Brno (Brno Moravian Land Archives)
NAP	Národní archiv (National Archives of the Czech Republic, Prague)
NACP	National Archives at College Park, Maryland
NDR	Norddeutscher Rundfunk (Northern German Broadcasting)
NS	National Socialist
NSDAP / N.S.D.A.P.	Nationalsozialistische Deutsche Arbeiterpartei (National Socialist German Workers' Party)
NSK	Nationalsozialistische Partei-Korrespondenz (National Socialist Party Correspondence)
NSV	Nationalsozialistische Volkswohlfahrt (National Socialist People's Welfare Organization)
OKH	Oberkommando des Heeres (Army High Command)
OKW	Oberkommando der Wehrmacht (Wehrmacht High Command)
OSE	Œuvre de Secours (Children's Aid Society)
ÖStA	Österreichisches Staatsarchiv (Austrian State Archives)
ÖStA/AdR	Österreichisches Staatsarchiv / Archiv der Republik (Austrian State Archives / Archive of the Austrian Republic)
PA AA	Politisches Archiv des Auswärtigen Amts (Political Archives of the Federal Foreign Office)
PMJ	*The Persecution and Murder of the European Jews by Nazi Germany, 1933–1945*
p.p.	*per procurationem* (by proxy)
r–v	recto and verso (of an archival source)
RAF	Royal Air Force
RFSS	Reichsführer-SS
RG	record group
RGASPI	Rossiiskii gosudarstvennyi arkhiv sotsial'no-politicheskoji istorii (Russian State Archive of Socio-Political History)
RGBl.	*Reichsgesetzblatt* (Reich Law Gazette)
RGVA	Rossiiskii gosudarstvennyi voennyi arkhiv (Russian State Military Archives)
RM	Reichsmark(s)
RMdI	Reichsministerium des Innern (Reich Ministry of the Interior)
RMEuL	Reichsministerium für Ernährung und Landwirtschaft (Reich Ministry of Food and Agriculture)
RPM	Reichspostminister/-ium (Reich Postal Ministry/Minister)
RSHA	Reichssicherheitshauptamt (Reich Security Main Office)
RuSHA	Rasse- und Siedlungshauptamt (Race and Settlement Main Office)
RVM	Reichsverkehrsminister/-ium (Reich Transport Ministry/Minister)
RWM	Reichswirtschaftsministerium (Reich Ministry of Economics)
SA	Sturmabteilung (Storm Troopers)
SD / S.D.	Sicherheitsdienst (SS Security Service)
S.d.G.u.V.	*Sammlung der Gesetze und Verordnungen* (Compilation of Laws and Regulations)

SdP	Sudetendeutsche Partei (Sudeten German Party)
S.H.	Sonder-Hachsharah (Special Hachsharah)
SIG	Schweizerischer Israelischer Gemeindebund (Swiss Federation of Jewish Communities)
SOAL	Státni oblastni archiv Litoměřice, pobočka Most (State District Archives, Most)
Sopade	Sozialdemokratische Partei Deutschlands im Exil (Social Democratic Party of Germany in Exile)
SPD	Sozialdemokratische Partei Deutschlands (Social Democratic Party of Germany)
SS	Schutzstaffel ('Protection Squadron')
StA	Stadtarchiv (City Archives)
StA Ma	Stadtarchiv Mannheim (Mannheim City Archives)
StA Mü	Stadtarchiv München (Munich City Archives)
StA Wü	Stadtarchiv Würzburg (Würzburg City Archives)
StGB	Strafgesetzbuch (German Criminal Code)
StPo	Strafprozessordnung (Code of Criminal Procedure)
Str.	Straße (street/road)
Tgb.	Tagebuch (diary/journal)
ThHStA	Landesarchiv Thüringen (Thuringia State Archives)
trans.	translated by
USHMM	United States Holocaust Memorial Museum
USSR	Union of Soviet Socialist Republics
v.	verso (of an archival source)
VHÚ Praha	Vojenský historecký ústav (Military History Institute) Praha, Prague
Viag / VIAG	Vereinigte Industrieunternehmungen AG (United Industrial Enterprises)
VKP	All-Union Communist Party
WIZO	Women's International Zionist Organization
YVA	Yad Vashem Archives
Zl	Złoty (Polish currency)

List of Archives, Sources, and Literature Cited

Primary Sources

Archives

Alte Synagoge Essen, Old Synagogue Essen
American Joint Distribution Committee Archives (JDC), New York
Archiv bezpečnostních složek (ABS, Archive of the Security Forces), Prague
Archiv der Akademie der Künste (AdK, Academy of Arts), Berlin
Archiv der Arbeitsstelle Holocaustliteratur an der Justus-Liebig-Universität Gießen (Archives of the Working Group on Holocaust Literature at the Justus-Liebig-Universität Gießen), Gießen
Archiv der Gedenkstätte Buchenwald (BwA, Archive of the Buchenwald Memorial)
Archiv der Israelitischen Kultusgemeinde Wien (IKG, Archives of the Israelite Religious Community of Vienna), Vienna
Archiv der Walter A. Berendsohn Forschungsstelle für deutsche Exilliteratur (P. Walter Jacob Archive at the Archives of the Walter A. Berendsohn Research Centre for German Exile Literature), Hamburg
Archiv des Leibniz Instituts für Zeitgeschichte München – Berlin (Archives of the Leibniz Institute for Contemporary History), Munich
Archives d'Etat de Genève (State Archives of Geneva), Geneva
Archives of the Leo Baeck Institute, New York (LBI), at the Jüdisches Museum Berlin
Archivio Segreto Vaticano (ASV, Vatican Secret Archives), Vatican City
Archiwum Państwowe w Gdańsku (State Archives in Gdańsk)
Archiwum Państwowe we Wrocławiu (State Archives in Wrocław)
Archiwum Żydowski Instytut Historyczny (AŻIH, Archives of the Jewish Historical Institute), Warsaw
Bistumsarchiv Münster (BAM, Central Archives of the Diocese of Münster)
Brandenburgisches Landeshauptarchiv (BLHA, Brandenburg Main State Archives), Potsdam
Bundesamt für zentrale Dienste und offene Vermögensfragen (BADV, Federal Office for Central Services and Unresolved Property Issues), Berlin
Bundesarchiv (BArch, German Federal Archives), Berlin
Central Archives for the History of the Jewish People (CAHJP), Jerusalem
Central Zionist Archives (CZA), Jerusalem
Centre de Documentation Juive Contemporaine (CDJC, Contemporary Jewish Documentation Center), Paris
Deutsches Literaturarchiv (German Literature Archive), Marbach
Deutsches Rundfunkarchiv (DRA, German Broadcasting Archives), Frankfurt
Dokumentationsarchiv des Österreichischen Widerstandes (DÖW, Documentation Centre of the Austrian Resistance), Vienna
Evangelisches Zentralarchiv in Berlin (EZA, Evangelical Central Archives)
Geheimes Staatsarchiv Preußischer Kulturbesitz (GStAPK, Secret State Archives Prussian Cultural Heritage Foundation), Berlin
Hessisches Hauptstaatsarchiv (HHStAW, Hessian Main State Archives), Wiesbaden
Historisches Archiv Krupp (Krupp Historical Archive), Essen
Holocaust Memorial Center, Farmington Hills, Michigan
Institut für Stadtgeschichte Frankfurt am Main (ISG Frankfurt, Institute for the History of Frankfurt)
Instytut Pamięci Narodowej (IPN, Institute of National Remembrance), Warsaw
Jewish Museum in Prague (JMP)

Jüdisches Museum Berlin (JMB, Jewish Museum Berlin)
Jüdisches Museum Wien (JMW, Jewish Museum Vienna)
Landesarchiv Berlin (LAB, Berlin State Archives)
Landesarchiv Graz (LA Graz, Graz City Archives)
Landesarchiv Nordrhein-Westfalen, Abt. Rheinland (LAV NRW R, North Rhine-Westphalia State Archives, Rhineland Department), Düsseldorf
Landesarchiv Thüringen (ThHStA, Thuringia State Archives)
Latvijas Valsts Vēstures Arhīvs (Latvian State Historical Archives), Riga
Lavon Institute, Labour Archives, Tel Aviv
Literární archiv Památníku národního písemnictví (Archive of the Museum of Czech Literature), Prague
Mahn- und Gedenkstätte Düsseldorf (Düsseldorf Site of Remembrance and Commemoration)
Moravský zemský archiv v Brně (MZAB, Brno Moravian Land Archives)
Moreshet Holocaust and Research Center, Givat Haviva
Národní archiv (NAP, National Archives of the Czech Republic in Prague)
National Archives at College Park (NACP), Maryland
NS-Dokumentationszentrum der Stadt Köln (NS Documentation Center of the City of Cologne)
Österreichisches Staatsarchiv, Archiv der Republik (ÖStA/AdR, Austrian State Archives, Archives of the Republic), Vienna
Österreichisches Staatsarchiv (ÖStA Austrian State Archives), Vienna
Politisches Archiv des Auswärtigen Amts (PA AA, Political Archives of the Federal Foreign Office), Berlin
Princeton University Library
Rossiiskii gosudarstvennyj arkhiv sotsial'no-politicheskoi istorii (RGASPI – Russian State Archive of Socio-Political History), Moscow
Rossiiskii gosudarstvennyi voennyi arkhiv (RGVA, Russian State Military Archives), Moscow
Staatsarchiv Hamburg (State Archives of the Free and Hanseatic City of Hamburg)
Stadtarchiv Bonn (Bonn City Archives)
Stadtarchiv Leipzig (StA Leipzig, Leipzig City Archives)
Stadtarchiv Mannheim (StA Ma, Mannheim City Archives)
Stadtarchiv München (StA Mü, Munich City Archives)
Stadtarchiv Würzburg (StA Wü, Würzburg City Archives)
Státní oblastní archiv Litoměřice, pobočka Most (SOAL pobočka Most, State Regional Archives Litomerice, Most district)
Steiermärkisches Landesarchiv (Styrian Provincial Archives), Graz
United States Holocaust Memorial Museum (USHMM), Washington, DC
Vojenský historicý ústav Praha (VHU, Military History Institute, Prague)
Wiener Library, London
Yad Vashem Archive (YVA), Jerusalem

Newspapers and Magazines

Allgemeine Heeresmitteilungen
Amtliche Mitteilungen der Reichsmusikkammer
Amtsblatt für den Landespolizeibezirk Berlin
Aufbau
Basler Nachrichten
Bundesgesetzblatt für die Republik Österreich
České slovo
Das Reich
Das Schwarze Korps: Zeitung der Schutzstaffeln der NSDAP. Organ der Reichsführung der SS
Der Neue Tag
Der Stürmer
Deutscher Reichsanzeiger und Preußischer Staatsanzeiger
Die Judenfrage
Expres
Frankfurter Zeitung
Journal officiel
Jüdisches Nachrichtenblatt
Kreiszeitung für die Ost-Prignitz

Leipziger Neueste Nachrichten
Leitmeritzer Tagblatt
Mährisch-Schlesische Landeszeitung
Mansfelder Zeitung
Ministerialblatt des Reichs- und Preußischen Ministeriums des Innern
Mitteilungsblatt der Stadt Warschau
Monatshefte für Auswärtige Politik
Nachrichtendienst des Deutschen Gemeindetags
Neue Zürcher Zeitung
New York Times
Pražský list
Preußische Zeitung
RČS
Reichsgesetzblatt
Reichssteuerblatt
Sbírka zákonů a nařízení republiky Česko-Slovenské
Schawe Zion
The Times
Večerní České slovo
Verordnungsblatt des Reichsprotektors in Böhmen und Mähren (VBl. RProt.)
Verordnungsblatt für die besetzten französischen Gebiete
Verordnungsblatt Generalgouvernement (GG)
Völkischer Beobachter
Washington Post
Weltkampf
Zeitschriften-Dienst: deutscher Wochendienst

Diaries and Memoirs

Behrend-Rosenfeld, Else R., *Ich stand nicht allein: Erlebnisse einer Jüdin in Deutschland 1933–1944*, 3rd edn (Cologne: Europäische Verlagsanstalt, 1979).

Braach, Emilie, *Wenn meine Briefe Dich erreichen könnten: Aufzeichnungen aus den Jahren 1939–1945*, ed. Bergit Forchhammer (Frankfurt am Main: Fischer, 1987).

Brod, Max, *Streitbares Leben 1884–1968* (Munich: F.A. Herbig, 1969).

Cohn, Esther, and Martin Ruch, *'Inzwischen sind wir nun besternt worden': Das Tagebuch der Esther Cohn (1926–1944) und die Kinder vom Münchener Antonienheim* (Norderstedt: Books on Demand, 2006).

Cohn, Willy, *No Justice in Germany: The Breslau Diaries, 1933–1941*, trans. Kenneth Kronenberg (Stanford, CA: Stanford University Press, 2012 [German edn, 2006]).

Freund, Elisabeth, *Als Zwangsarbeiterin in Berlin: Die Aufzeichnungen der Volkswirtin Elisabeth Freund*, ed. Carola Sachse (Berlin: Akademie, 1996).

Goebbels, Joseph, *Die Tagebücher von Joseph Goebbels*, part 1: *Aufzeichnungen 1923–1941*, vol. 7: *Juli 1939–März 1940*, ed. Elke Fröhlich (Munich: Saur, 1998).

Goebbels, Joseph, *Die Tagebücher von Joseph Goebbels*, part 1: *Aufzeichnungen 1923–1941*, vol. 8: *April–November 1940*, ed. Elke Fröhlich (Munich: Saur, 1998).

Goebbels, Joseph, *Die Tagebücher von Joseph Goebbels*, part 1: *Aufzeichnungen 1923–1941*, vol. 9: *Dezember 1940–Juli 1941*, ed. Elke Fröhlich (Munich: Saur, 1998).

Goebbels, Joseph, *Die Tagebücher von Joseph Goebbels*, part 2: *Diktate 1941–1945*, vol. 1: *Juli–September 1941*, ed. Elke Fröhlich (Munich: Saur, 1996).

Hahn-Beer, Edith (with Susan Dworkin), *The Nazi Officer's Wife: How one Woman Survived the Holocaust* (New York: Harper Collins, 2012)

Hoffmann, Camill, *Politisches Tagebuch 1932–1939*, ed. Dieter Sudhoff (Klagenfurt: Alekto, 1995).

Kellner, Friedrich, *My Opposition: The Diary of Friedrich Kellner, a German against the Third Reich*, ed. Robert Scott Kellner (Cambridge: Cambridge University Press, 2018).

Klemperer, Victor, *I Shall Bear Witness: The Diaries of Victor Klemperer, 1933–1941*, trans. Martin Chalmers (London: Weidenfeld & Nicolson, 1998 [German edn, 1995]).

Klepper, Jochen, *Unter dem Schatten deiner Flügel: Aus den Tagebüchern der Jahre 1932–1942* (Giessen: Brunnen, 1997).

Klüger, Ruth, *Landscapes of Memory: A Holocaust Girlhood Remembered* (London: Bloomsbury, 2004 [German edn, 1994])

Mändl Roubíčková, Eva, *'Langsam gewöhnen wir uns an das Ghettoleben': Ein Tagebuch aus Theresienstadt*, ed. Veronika Springmann in collaboration with Wolfgang Schellenbacher (Hamburg: Konkret Literatur, 2007).

Mannheimer, Max, *Spätes Tagebuch: Theresienstadt – Auschwitz. Warschau – Dachau* (Munich: Pendo, 2009).

Meyring, Else, 'Deportation aus Stettin', in Andreas Lixl-Purcell (ed.), *Erinnerungen deutsch-jüdischer Frauen 1900–1990* (Leipzig: Reclam, 1992), pp. 307–332.

Münzer, Jiří, *Dospívání nad propastí: Deník Jiřího Münzera 1936–1942* (Prague: Radioservis, 2002)

Rosenberg, Alfred, *The Political Diary of Alfred Rosenberg and the Onset of the Holocaust*, ed. Jürgen Matthäus and Frank Bajohr (Lanham, MA: Rowman & Littlefield, 2015).

Schramm, Percy E. (ed.), *Kriegstagebuch des Oberkommandos der Wehrmacht (Wehrmachtführungsstab)*, vol. 1: *1. August 1940–31. Dezember 1941*, compiled and annotated by Hans-Adolf Jacobsen (Frankfurt am Main: Bernhard & Graefe, 1965).

Tausk, Walter, *Breslauer Tagebuch 1933–1940*, ed. Ryszard Kincel ([East] Berlin: Rütten & Loening, 1975).

Weiss, Helga, *Helga's Diary. A Young Girl's Account of Life in a Concentration Camp* (London: Penguin, 2013).

Works Published before 1945

Brehm, Alfred Edmund, *Illustriertes Thierleben*, vol. 2 (Hildburghausen: Verlag des Bibliographischen Instituts, 1865).

Fürstenthal, Ernst, *Abraham* (Berlin: Jüdische Buch-Vereinigung, 1936).

Goebbels, Joseph, *Die Zeit ohne Beispiel: Reden und Aufsätze aus den Jahren 1939/40/41* (Munich: Zentralverlag der NSDAP/Franz Eher Nachf., 1941).

Goetsch, Paul, *Das Reichsgesetz über das Auswanderungswesen vom 9. Juni 1897* (Hamburg: Lütcke/Wulff, 1898)

Heiden, Konrad, *Adolf Hitler: Eine Biographie*, 2 vols (Zurich: Europa Verlag, 1936/1937)

Herzl, Theodor, *The Prague Jews between Two Nations* (1897), cited in Wilma Iggers (ed.), *The Jews of Bohemia and Moravia: A Historical Reader*, trans. Wilma Iggers, Káča Poláčková-Henley, and Kathrine Talbot (Detroit: Wayne State University Press, 1992 [German edn, 1986]).

Hitler, Adolf, *Mein Kampf*, trans. Ralph Manheim (London: Hutchinson, 1969 [German edn, 1925–1926]).

Hunke, Heinrich, *Grundzüge der deutschen Volks- und Wehrwirtschaft* (Berlin: Haude & Spenersche, 1938).

Lexikon der Juden in der Musik: Mit einem Titelverzeichnis jüdischer Werke, Veröffentlichungen des Instituts zur Erforschung der Judenfrage Frankfurt a. M., vol. 2 (Berlin: Hahnefeld, 1940).

Lösener, Bernhard, and Friedrich A. Knost (eds.), *Die Nürnberger Gesetze mit den Durchführungsverordnungen und den sonstigen einschlägigen Vorschriften* (Berlin: Decker, 1942).

Mehring, Walter, *No Road Back: Poems. English and German Text*, trans. Samuel Aaron De Witt, illus. by George Grosz (New York: Samuel Curl, 1944).

Reichsbund jüdischer Frontsoldaten, *Die jüdischen Gefallenen des deutschen Heeres, der deutschen Marine und der deutschen Schutztruppen 1914–1918: Ein Gedenkbuch* (Berlin: Der Schild, 1932).

Sammlung der Gesetze und Verordnungen des Čecho-Slovakischen Staates 1927, vol. 2, no. 125/1927.

Sammlung der Gesetze und Verordnungen des Čecho-Slovakischen Staates 1936, no. 131/1936.

Sammlung der Gesetze und Verordnungen des Protektorates Böhmen und Mähren vom 24. April 1940, no. 136, 1940.

Sammlung der Gesetze und Verordnungen des Protektorates Böhmen und Mähren vom 3. 2. 1941, no. 46, 1941.

Schopenhauer, Arthur, *Parerga und Paralipomena: Kleine philosophische Schriften*, vol. 2 (Berlin: A. W. Hayn, 1851).

Seligsohn, Julius Ludwig Israel, *Die Einwanderung nach U.S.A.* (Berlin: Jüdischer Kulturbund in Deutschland, 1940).

Stier, Rudolf, and Helmut Schmidt, *Die Ausschaltung der Juden aus der Wirtschaft des Protektorats Böhmen und Mähren: Kommentar zu den Verordnungen des Reichsprotektors über das jüdische Vermögen und zur Ausschaltung der Juden aus der Wirtschaft des Protektorats: Zusammenstellung der übrigen ergangenen Verordnungen nach dem Stande vom 15. März 1941* (Prague: Böhmisch-Mährische Verlags- und Druckerei, 1941).

Tisdale Hobart, Alice, *Oil for the Lamps of China* (Indianapolis: Bobbs-Merrill, 1933).

Wertheimer, Martha, *Dienst auf den Höhen* (Berlin: Jüdische Buch-Vereinigung, 1937).

Zweig, Stefan, *Die Welt von Gestern: Erinnerungen eines Europäers* (Stockholm: Bermann-Fischer Verlag AB, 1942).

Primary Source Collections

Akten zur Deutschen Auswärtigen Politik 1918–1945, series D: *1937–1945*, vol. 4 (Baden-Baden: Imprimerie Nationale, 1951).

Akten zur Deutschen Auswärtigen Politik 1918–1945, series D: *1937–1945*, vol. 10 (Göttingen: Vandenhoeck & Ruprecht, 1963)

Akten zur Deutschen Auswärtigen Politik 1918–1945, series D: *1937–1945*, vol. 12, no. 1 (Göttingen: Vandenhoeck & Ruprecht, 1969)

Barkow, Ben, Raphael Gross, and Michael Lenarz (eds.), *Novemberpogrom 1938: Die Augenzeugenberichte der Wiener Library, London* (Frankfurt: Suhrkamp, 2008).

Behnken, Klaus (ed.), *Deutschlandberichte der Sozialdemokratischen Partei Deutschlands (Sopade) 1934–1940*, vol. 7 (Frankfurt am Main: Zweitausendeins, 1980)

Berenstein, Tatiana, and Adam Rutkowski, 'Dokument o konferencji w Urzędzie Policji Bezpieczeństwa z 21 IX 1939 r.', *Biuletyn Żydowskiego Instytutu Historycznego*, vol. 49, no. 1 (1964).

Blet, Pierre, et al. (eds.), *Actes et documents du Saint Siège relatifs à la Seconde Guerre mondiale*, vol. 4: *Le Saint Siège et la guerre en Europe, juin 1940 – juin 1941* (Vatican City: Vaticana, 1967).

Blet, Pierre, et al. (eds.), *Actes et documents du Saint Siège relatifs à la Seconde Guerre mondiale*, vol. 8: *Le Saint Siège et les victimes de la guerre, janvier 1941 – décembre 1943* (Vatican City: Vaticana, 1974).

Boberach, Heinz (ed.), *Meldungen aus dem Reich 1938–1945: Die geheimen Lageberichte des Sicherheitsdienstes der SS*, vol. 6: *Meldungen aus dem Reich, Nr. 142 vom 18. Nov. 1940 – Nr. 179 vom 17. April 1941* (Herrsching: Pawlak, 1984).

Broszat, Martin (ed.), *Bayern in der NS-Zeit*, vol. 1: *Soziale Lage und politisches Verhalten der Bevölkerung im Spiegel vertraulicher Berichte* (Munich: Oldenbourg, 1977).

Die Namensliste der 1940 aus dem Regierungsbezirk Stettin deportierten Juden (Rostock: Geschichtswerkstatt Rostock, 2009).

'Dokumentation: Das Reichsministerium des Innern und die Judengesetzgebung', *Vierteljahrshefte für Zeitgeschichte*, vol. 9, no. 3 (1961), pp. 262–313.

Dokumentationsarchiv des österreichischen Widerstands, *Widerstand und Verfolgung in Tirol 1934–1945: Eine Dokumentation*, vol. 1 (Vienna/Munich: Österreichischer Bundesverlag/Jugend und Volk, 1984).

Dokumentationsarchiv des österreichischen Widerstands, *Widerstand und Verfolgung in Wien 1934–1945: Eine Dokumentation*, vol. 3: 1938–1945 (Vienna: Österreichischer Bundesverlag, 1984)

Domarus, Max, *Hitler: Reden und Proklamationen 1932–1945. Kommentiert von einem deutschen Zeitgenossen*, vol. 2 (Neustadt an der Aisch: Schmidt, 1963).

Domarus, Max, and Patrick Romane (eds.), *The Essential Hitler: Speeches and Commentary* (Wauconda, IL: Bolchazy-Carducci, 2007).

Freund, Michael, *Weltgeschichte der Gegenwart in Dokumenten: Geschichte des Zweiten Weltkrieges* (Freiburg: Herder, 1954).

Genger, Angela (ed.), *Durch unsere Herzen ziehen die Jahrtausende: Briefe von Anna und Salomon Samuel 1933–1942* (Düsseldorf: Patmos, 1988).

Hahn-Beer, Edith, *'Ich will leben!' Briefe und Dokumente der Wiener Jüdin Edith Hahn-Beer*, ed. Angelika Schlüter (Münster: Ugarit, 1996).

Heim, Susanne, and Götz Aly, *Bevölkerungsstruktur und Massenmord. Neue Dokumente zur deutschen Politik der Jahre 1938–1945* (Berlin: Rotbuch, 1991).

International Military Tribunal, *Der Prozess gegen die Hauptkriegsverbrecher vor dem Internationalen Militärgerichtshof, Nürnberg 14.11.1945–1.10.1946*, vol. 5 (Nuremberg: Sekretariat des Gerichtshofs, 1947).

Jacob, Paul Walter and Frithjof Trapp (eds.), *Reunion der Überlebenden: P. Walter Jacobs Korrespondenz mit Freunden und Kollegen 1939–1949* (Hamburg: Walter A. Berendsohn-Forschungsstelle für deutsche Exilliteratur, 2005).

Kaden, Helma (ed.), *Europa unterm Hakenkreuz: Die faschistische Okkupationspolitik in Österreich und der Tschechoslowakei (1938–1945)* (Berlin: Deutscher Verlag der Wissenschaften, 1988).

Kafka, Franz, *Briefe 1902–1924* (Frankfurt am Main: Fischer, 1958).

Kafka, Franz, *Letters to Friends, Family and Editors*, trans. Richard Winston and Clara Winston (New York: Schocken, 1977 [German edn, 1958]).

Kárný, Miroslav and Jaroslava Milotová (eds.), *Anatomie okupační politiky hitlerovského Německa v 'Protektorátu Čechy a Morava': Dokumenty z období říšského protektora Konstantina von Neuratha* (Prague: Ústav Českosloven. a Světových Dějin ČSAV, 1987).

Kennan, George F., *From Prague after Munich: Diplomatic Papers, 1938–1940* (Princeton, NJ: Princeton University Press, 1968), pp. 131–134.

Klarsfeld, Serge (ed.), *Recueil de documents des dossiers des autorités allemandes concernant la persécution de la population juive en France (1940–1944), de juin 1940 au 31 décembre 1941*, vol. 1 (Paris/New York: CDJC/Klarsfeld Foundation, 1979).

Koehl, Robert Lewis, *RKFDV: German Resettlement and Population Policy, 1935–1945: A History of the Reich Commission for the Strengthening of Germandom* (Cambridge: Harvard University Press, 1957).

Kommission zur Erforschung der Geschichte der Frankfurter Juden, *Dokumente zur Geschichte der Frankfurter Juden 1933–1945* (Frankfurt am Main: Kramer, 1963).

Krausnick, Helmut (ed.), 'Denkschrift Himmlers über die Behandlung der Fremdvölkischen im Osten (Mai 1940)', *Vierteljahrshefte für Zeitgeschichte*, vol. 5 (1957), pp. 194–198.

Krejčová, Helena, Jana Svobodová, and Anna Hyndráková (eds.), *Židé v Protektorátu: Hlášení Židovské náboženské obce v roce 1942. Dokumenty* (Prague: Maxdorf, 1997).

Kreutzer, Michael, *'Die Gespräche drehten sich auch vielfach um die Reise, die wir alle antreten müssen.' Leben und Verfolgtsein der Juden in Berlin-Tempelhof. Biographien, Dokumentation* (Berlin: Evangelischer Kirchenkreis Tempelhof, 1988).

Kulka, Otto Dov and Eberhard Jäckel (eds.), *The Jews in the Secret Nazi Reports on Popular Opinion in Germany, 1933–1945*, trans. William Templer (New Haven, CT/London: Yale University Press, 2010 [German edn, 2004]).

Kurzweil, Edith, *Briefe aus Wien: Jüdisches Leben vor der Deportation* (Vienna: Turia + Kant, 1999).

Lang, Jochen von, *Das Eichmann-Protokoll: Tonbandaufzeichnungen der israelischen Verhöre* (Berlin: Severin und Siedler, 1982).

Löffler, Peter (ed.), *Bischof Clemens August Graf von Galen: Akten, Briefe und Predigten 1933–1946*, vol. 2: *1939–1946* (Mainz: Matthias-Grünewald, 1988).

Longerich, Peter (ed.), *Die Ermordung der europäischen Juden: Eine umfassende Dokumentation des Holocaust 1941–1945* (Munich/Zurich: Piper, 1989).

Lotz, Wolfgang (ed.), *Die Deutsche Reichspost 1933–1945: Eine politische Verwaltungsgeschichte. Ausgewählte Dokumente* (Koblenz: Bundesarchiv, 2002).

Löwenherz, Josef Israel, *Vollständiger Bericht von Dr. Löwenherz über die Tätigkeit Eichmanns und Brunners in Wien–Prag–*

Berlin, 1938–1945, compiled by Tuviah Friedman (Haifa: Institute of Documentation in Israel, 1995).

Maršálek, Hans, *Die Geschichte des Konzentrationslagers Mauthausen: Eine Dokumentation* (Vienna: Österreichische Lagergemeinschaft Mauthausen, 1980).

Mennecke, Friedrich, Innenansichten eines medizinischen Täters im Nationalsozialismus: Eine Edition seiner Briefe 1935–1947, ed. Peter Chroust, vol. 1 (Hamburg: Hamburger Institut für Sozialforschung, 1987).

Nationale Kommission für die Veröffentlichung diplomatischer Dokumente der Schweiz, *Diplomatische Dokumente der Schweiz 1848–1945*, vol. 13: *1939–1940* (Bern: Benteli, 1991).

Orten, Jiří, *Deníky Jiřího Ortena. Poesie – Myšlenky – Zápisky*, ed. Jan Grossman (Prague: Československý spisovatel, 1958).

Pätzold, Kurt (ed.), *Verfolgung, Vertreibung, Vernichtung. Dokumente des faschistischen Antisemitismus 1933 bis 1942* (Leipzig: Reclam, 1991).

Präg, Werner, and Wolfgang Jacobmeyer (ed.), *Das Diensttagebuch des deutschen Generalgouverneurs in Polen, 1939–1945* (Stuttgart: Deutsche Verlags-Anstalt, 1975).

Rürup, Reinhard (ed.), *Der Krieg gegen die Sowjetunion 1941-1945: Eine Dokumentation* (Berlin: Argon, 1991).

Samter, Hermann, *'Worte können das ja kaum verständlich machen': Briefe 1939–1943*, ed. Daniel Fraenkel, commissioned by Yad Vashem, trans. Tamar Avraham (Göttingen: Wallstein, 2009). English language edition: *To Be a Jew in Berlin: The Letters of Hermann Samter, 1939–1943* (Jerusalem: Yad Vashem, 2012).

Sauer, Paul (ed.), *Dokumente über die Verfolgung der jüdischen Bürger in Baden-Württemberg durch das nationalsozialistische Regime 1933–1945*, vol. 2 (Stuttgart: W. Kohlhammer, 1966).

Schrader, Ulrike (ed.), *'...so froh, dass Ihr draußen seid': Die Briefe der Familie Inow, Wuppertal* (Wuppertal: privately published, 2005).

Šíma, Jaroslav, *Českoslovenští přestěhovalci v letech 1938–1945* (Prague: Societas, 1945).

Stadtarchiv Mannheim, *Die Judenverfolgung in Mannheim 1933–1945*, compiled by Hans-Joachim Fliedner, vol. 2: *Dokumente* (Stuttgart: W. Kohlhammer, 1971).

Trial of the Major War Criminals before the International Military Tribunal Nuremberg 14.11.1945–1.10.1946, vol. 31 (Nuremberg: Internationaler Militärgerichtshof, 1948).

Vogt, Martin (ed.), *Herbst 1941 im 'Führerhauptquartier': Berichte Werner Koeppens an seinen Minister Alfred Rosenberg* (Koblenz: Bundesarchiv, 2002).

Walk, Joseph (ed.), *Das Sonderrecht für die Juden im NS-Staat: Eine Sammlung der gesetzlichen Massnahmen und Richtlinien. Inhalt und Bedeutung*, 2nd edn (Heidelberg: C. F. Müller, 1996 [1981]).

Weber, Ilse, *Wann wohl das Leid ein Ende hat: Briefe und Gedichte aus Theresienstadt* ed. Ulrike Migdal (Munich: Hanser Verlag, 2008).

Secondary Literature

Absolon, Rudolf, *Die Wehrmacht im Dritten Reich*, vol. 5: *1. September 1939 bis 18. Dezember 1941* (Boppard am Rhein: Boldt, 1988).

Adam, Uwe Dietrich, *Judenpolitik im Dritten Reich* (Düsseldorf: Droste, 1972).

Adler, H. G., *Der verwaltete Mensch: Studien zur Deportation der Juden aus Deutschland* (Tübingen: Mohr, 1974).

Adler, H. G., *Theresienstadt 1941–1945: The Face of a Coerced Community*, trans. Belinda Cooper (Cambridge: Cambridge University Press, 2017 [German edn, 1955]).

Aly, Götz, *Die Belasteten: 'Euthanasie' 1939–1945. Eine Gesellschaftsgeschichte* (Frankfurt am Main: Fischer, 2013).

Aly, Götz, *'Final Solution': Nazi Population Policy and the Murder of the European Jews*, trans. Belinda Cooper and Allison Brown (London: Arnold, 1999 [German edn, 1995]).

Aly, Götz, and Peter Chroust, *Cleansing the Fatherland: Nazi Medicine and Racial Hygiene*

(Baltimore, MD: Johns Hopkins University Press, 1994).

Aly, Götz, and Susanne Heim, *Architects of Annihilation: Auschwitz and the Logic of Destruction*, trans. A. G. Blunden (London: Weidenfeld & Nicolson, 2002 [German edn, 1991]).

Aly, Götz, and Susanne Heim, 'Staatliche Ordnung und organische Lösung: Die Rede Hermann Görings "über die Judenfrage" vom 6. Dezember 1938', *Jahrbuch für Antisemitismusforschung*, vol. 2 (1993), pp. 378–404.

Anderl, Gabriele, *9096 Leben: Der unbekannte Judenretter Berthold Storfer* (Berlin: Rotbuch, 2012).

Anderl, Gabriele, 'Die "Zentralstellen für jüdische Auswanderung" in Wien, Berlin und Prag – ein Vergleich', *Tel Aviver Jahrbuch für deutsche Geschichte*, vol. 23 (1994), pp. 275–299.

Anderl, Gabriele, and Walter Manoschek, *Gescheiterte Flucht: Der jüdische 'Kladovo-Transport' auf dem Weg nach Palästina 1939–1942* (Vienna: Verlag für Gesellschaftskritik, 1993).

Anderl, Gabriele, and Walter Manoschek, 'Die Geschichte des Kladovo-Transports 1939 bis 1942', in Alisa Douer, *Kladovo: Eine Flucht nach Palästina* (Vienna: Mandelbaum, 2001), pp. 10–16.

Anderl, Gabriele, Dirk Rupnow, and Alexandra-Eileen Wenck, *Die Zentralstelle für jüdische Auswanderung als Beraubungsinstitution* (Vienna: Oldenbourg, 2004).

Asaria, Ziv (ed.), *Die Juden in Köln von den ältesten Zeiten bis zur Gegenwart* (Cologne: Bachem, 1959).

Ascher, Abraham, *A Community under Siege: The Jews of Breslau under Nazism* (Stanford, CA: Stanford University Press, 2007).

Ayalon, Moshe, 'Jewish Life in Breslau, 1938–1941', *Leo Baeck Institute Yearbook*, vol. 41 (1996), pp. 323–345.

Baader, Gerhard, 'Auf dem Weg zum Menschenversuch im Nationalsozialismus', in Carola Sachse (ed.), *Die Verbindung nach Auschwitz: Biowissenschaften und Menschenversuche an Kaiser-Wilhelm-Instituten* (Göttingen: Wallstein, 2003), pp. 105–157.

Bachrach, Susan and Dieter Kuntz (eds.), *Deadly Medicine: Creating the Master Race* (Washington, DC: United States Holocaust Memorial Museum, 2004).

Bajohr, Frank, 'Hamburgs "Führer": Zur Person und Tätigkeit des Hamburger NSDAP-Gauleiters Karl Kaufmann (1900–1969)', in Frank Bajohr and Joachim Szodrzynski (eds.), *Hamburg in der NS-Zeit: Ergebnisse neuerer Forschungen* (Hamburg: Ergebnisse, 1995), pp. 59–91.

Bajohr, Frank, 'Vom antijüdischen Konsens zum schlechten Gewissen: Die deutsche Gesellschaft und die Judenverfolgung 1933–1945', in Frank Bajohr and Dieter Pohl, *Der Holocaust als offenes Geheimnis: Die Deutschen, die NS-Führung und die Alliierten* (Munich: C.H.Beck, 2006), pp. 15–79.

Bajohr, Frank, 'Die wirtschaftliche Existenzvernichtung und Enteignung der Juden: Forschungsbilanz und offene Fragen', *Theresienstädter Studien und Dokumente*, vol. 13 (2006), pp. 348–365.

Bankier, David, *Die öffentliche Meinung im Hitler-Staat. Die 'Endlösung' und die Deutschen: Eine Berichtigung* (Berlin: Berlin Verlag Spitz, 1995).

Bankier, David, *The Germans and the Final Solution: Public Opinion under Nazism* (Oxford: Blackwell, 1992).

Barkai, Avraham, *From Boycott to Annihilation: The Economic Struggle of German Jews, 1933–1943*, trans. William Templer (Hanover, NH: University Press of New England, 1989 [German edn, 1988]).

Barkai, Avraham, Paul Mendes-Flohr, and Steven M. Lowenstein, *Deutsch-jüdische Geschichte in der Neuzeit*, vol. 4: *Aufbruch und Zerstörung 1918–1945* (Munich: C.H.Beck, 1997).

Beker, Avi (ed.), *The Plunder of Jewish Property during the Holocaust* (Basingstoke: Palgrave, 2001).

Benz, Wolfgang, 'Typologie der Herrschaftsformen in den Gebieten unter deutschem Einfluß', in Wolfgang Benz, Johannes Houwink ten Cate, and Gerhard Otto (eds.), *Die Bürokratie der Okkupation: Strukturen der Herrschaft und Verwaltung im besetzten Europa* (Berlin: Metropol, 1998), pp. 11–25.

Bergen, Doris L., *The Holocaust: A New History* (Stroud: History, 2016).

Berger, Natalia (ed.), *Where Cultures Meet: The Story of the Jews of Czechoslovakia* (Tel Aviv: Beth Hatefutsoth, 1990).

Berner, Margit, '"Judentypologisierungen" in der Anthropologie am Beispiel der Bestände des Naturhistorischen Museums, Wien', *Zeitgeschichte*, vol. 32, no. 2 (2005), pp. 111–116.

Bodensieck, Heinrich, 'Das Dritte Reich und die Lage der Juden in der Tschecho-Slowakei nach München', *Vierteljahrshefte für Zeitgeschichte*, vol. 9 (1961), pp. 249–261.

Boelcke, Willi A., *Kriegspropaganda 1939–1941: Geheime Ministerkonferenzen im Reichspropagandaministerium* (Stuttgart: Deutsche Verlags-Anstalt, 1996).

Böhler, Jochen, *Auftakt zum Vernichtungskrieg: Die Wehrmacht in Polen 1939* (Frankfurt am Main: Fischer Taschenbuch, 2006).

Bondy, Ruth, 'Chronik der sich schließenden Tore: *Jüdisches Nachrichtenblatt – Židovské listy* (1939–1945)', *Theresienstädter Studien und Dokumente*, vol. 7 (2000), pp. 86–106.

Bondy, Ruth, *'Elder of the Jews': Jakob Edelstein of Theresienstadt* (New York: Grove Press, 1989).

Botz, Gerhard, *Wohnungspolitik und Judendeportation in Wien 1938 bis 1945: Zur Funktion des Antisemitismus als Ersatz nationalsozialistischer Sozialpolitik* (Vienna/Salzburg: Geyer, 1975).

Brandes, Detlef, 'Deutsche Propaganda und Stimmung der tschechischen Bevölkerung im Protektorat Böhmen und Mähren 1939–1945', in Michal Anděl et al. (eds.), *Propaganda, (Selbst-)Zensur, Sensation: Grenzen von Presse- und Wissenschaftsfreiheit in Deutschland und Tschechien seit 1871* (Essen: Klartext, 2005), pp. 149–178.

Brandes, Detlef, 'Nationalsozialistische Tschechenpolitik im Protektorat Böhmen und Mähren', in Detlef Brandes and Václav Kural (eds.), *Der Weg in die Katastrophe: Deutsch-tschechisch-slowakische Beziehungen 1938–1947* (Essen: Klartext, 1994), pp. 39–56.

Brandes, Detlef, 'Politische Kollaboration im "Protektorat Böhmen und Mähren"', in Joachim Tauber (ed.), *'Kollaboration' in Nordosteuropa: Erscheinungsformen und Deutungen im 20. Jahrhundert* (Wiesbaden: Harrassowitz, 2006), pp. 453–462.

Brandes, Detlef, *Die Tschechen unter deutschem Protektorat*, vol. 1: *Besatzungspolitik, Kollaboration und Widerstand im Protektorat Böhmen und Mähren bis Heydrichs Tod, 1939–1942* (Munich/Vienna: Oldenbourg, 1969).

Brechtken, Magnus, *'Madagaskar für die Juden': Antisemitische Idee und politische Praxis 1885–1945* (Munich: Oldenbourg, 1997).

Breitman, Richard, and Alan M. Kraut, *American Refugee Policy and European Jewry, 1933–1945* (Bloomington, IN: Indiana University Press, 1987).

Brenner, Michael, 'Jewish Culture in a Modern Ghetto: Theater and Scholarship among the Jews of Nazi Germany', in Francis R. Nicosia and David Scrase (eds.), *Jewish Life in Nazi Germany: Dilemmas and Responses* (New York: Berghahn, 2012), pp. 170–184.

Browning, Christopher R., *The Final Solution and the German Foreign Office: A Study of Referat D III of Abteilung Deutschland, 1940–1943* (New York: Holmes & Meier, 1978).

Browning, Christopher R., with contributions by Jürgen Matthäus, *The Origins of the Final Solution: The Evolution of Nazi Jewish Policy, September 1939 – March 1942* (Lincoln, NE: University of Nebraska Press, 2004).

Bryant, Chad, *Prague in Black: Nazi Rule and Czech Nationalism* (Cambridge, MA: Harvard University Press, 2007).

Buchholz, Marlis, *Die hannoverschen Judenhäuser: Zur Situation der Juden in der Zeit der Ghettoisierung und Verfolgung, 1941 bis 1945* (Hildesheim: August Lax, 1987).

Burleigh, Michael, *Death and Deliverance: 'Euthanasia' in Germany, 1900 to 1945* (London: Pan, 2002).

Čapková, Kateřina, *Czechs, Germans, Jews? National Identity and the Jews of Bohemia*, trans. Derek and Marzia Paton (New York: Berghahn Books, 2012 [Czech edn, 2005]).

Černý, Václav, *Kultur im Widerstand: Prag 1938–1945*, vol. 1: *1938–1942* (Bremen: Kafka-Presse, 1979).

Cesarani, David, *Eichmann: His Life and Crimes* (London: William Heinemann, 2004).

Conrads, Norbert, 'Die verlorene Germania Judaica: Ein Handbuch- und Autorenschicksal im Dritten Reich', *Berichte und Forschungen: Jahrbuch des Bundesinstituts für Kultur und Geschichte der Deutschen im östlichen Europa*, vol. 15 (2007), pp. 215–254.

Dagan, Avigdor, 'The Czechoslovak Government-in-Exile and the Jews', in Avigdor Dagan, Gertrude Hirschler, Lewis Weiner et al. (eds.), *The Jews of Czechoslovakia: Historical Studies and Surveys*, vol. 3 (Philadelphia: Jewish Publication Society of America, 1984), pp. 449–495.

Dagan, Avigdor, Gertrude Hirschler, Lewis Weiner et al. (eds.), *The Jews of Czechoslovakia: Historical Studies and Survey*, 3 vols. (Philadelphia: Jewish Publication Society of America, 1968–1984).

Dahm, Volker, 'Kulturelles und geistiges Leben', in Wolfgang Benz (ed.), *Die Juden in Deutschland 1933–1945: Leben unter nationalsozialistischer Herrschaft* (Munich: C.H.Beck, 1988), pp. 75–267.

Demetz, Peter, *Prague in Danger: The Years of German Occupation, 1939–1945: Memories and History, Terror and Resistance, Theater and Jazz, Film and Poetry, Politics and War* (New York: Farrar, Straus and Giroux, 2008).

Dillmann, Hans-Ulrich, and Susanne Heim, *Fluchtpunkt Karibik: Jüdische Emigranten in der Dominikanischen Republik* (Berlin: Ch. Links, 2009).

Dörner, Bernward, *Die Deutschen und der Holocaust: Was niemand wissen wollte, aber jeder wissen konnte* (Berlin: Propyläen, 2007).

Dreyfus, Jean-Marc, 'Alsace Lorraine', in Wolf Gruner and Jörg Osterloh (eds.), *The Greater German Reich and the Jews: Nazi Persecution Policies in the Annexed Territories, 1935–1945*, trans. Bernard Heise (New York/Oxford: Berghahn, 2015 [German edn, 2010]), pp. 316–339.

Dublon-Knebel, Irith, 'Der Bericht der Marianne Wachstein', in *Schnittpunkt des Holocaust: Jüdische Frauen und Kinder im Konzentrationslager Ravensbrück: Wissenschaftlicher Begleitband zur Ausstellung* (Berlin: Metropol, 2009).

Dunkhase, Jan Eike, *Werner Conze: Ein deutscher Historiker im 20. Jahrhundert* (Göttingen: Vandenhoeck & Ruprecht, 2010).

Eckart, Wolfgang, *Man, Medicine and the State: The Human Body as an Object of Government Sponsored Medical Research in the 20th Century* (Stuttgart: Steiner, 2006).

Evans, Richard J., *The Third Reich at War, 1939–1945* (London: Allen Lane, 2008).

Fedorovič, Tomáš, 'Jüdische geisteskranke Patienten aus dem Protektorat Böhmen und Mähren zwischen nationalsozialistischer "Euthanasie" und Holocaust (1939–1945)', in Michal Šimůnek and Dietmar Schulze (eds.), *Die nationalsozialistische 'Euthanasie' im Reichsgau Sudetenland und Protektorat Böhmen und Mähren 1939–1945* (Prague: Mervart, 2008), pp. 199–236.

Fischer, Erica, *Das kurze Leben der Jüdin Felice Schragenheim: 'Jaguar', Berlin 1922 – Bergen-Belsen 1945* (Munich: dtv, 2002).

Förster, Jürgen, 'Ideological Warfare in Germany, 1919 to 1945', in Militärgeschichtliches Forschungsamt, *Germany and the Second World War*, vol. 9/1: *German Wartime Society, 1939–1945: Politicization, Disintegration, and the Struggle for Survival*, trans. Derry Cook-Radmore, Ewald Osers, Barry Smerin, and Barbara Wilson (Oxford: Oxford University Press, 2008 [German edn, 2004]), pp. 485–670.

Förster, Jürgen, 'Operation Barbarossa as a War of Conquest and Annihilation', in Militärgeschichtliches Forschungsamt, *Germany and the Second World War*, vol. 4:

The Attack on the Soviet Union, trans. Dean S. McMurry, Ewald Osers, and Louise Willmot (Oxford: Oxford University Press, 1996 [German edn, 1983]).

Frankl, Michal, 'The Background of the Hilsner Case: Political Antisemitism and Allegations of Ritual Murder, 1896–1900', *Judaica Bohemiae*, vol. 36 (2000), pp. 34–118.

Frankl, Michal, 'Tschechien', in Wolfgang Benz (ed.), *Handbuch des Antisemitismus: Judenfeindschaft in Geschichte und Gegenwart*, vol. 1: *Länder und Regionen* (Munich: Saur, 2008), pp. 364–370.

Freeden, Herbert, *Jüdisches Theater in Nazideutschland* (Tübingen: Mohr, 1964).

Friedlander, Henry, *The Origins of Nazi Genocide: From Euthanasia to the Final Solution* (Chapel Hill, NC/London: University of North Carolina Press, 1995).

Friedländer, Saul, *Nazi Germany and the Jews*, vol. 2: *The Years of Extermination, 1939–1945* (New York: HarperCollins, 2007).

Friedländer, Saul, *Prelude to Downfall: Hitler and the United States, 1939–1941*, trans. Aline B. Werth and Alexander Werth (New York: Knopf, 1967 [French edn, 1966]).

Friedländer, Saul, *When Memory Comes* (New York: Farrar, Straus and Giroux, 1979).

Friedman, Saul, *No Haven for the Oppressed: United States Policy Toward Jewish Refugees, 1938–1945* (Detroit, MI: Wayne State University Press, 2017).

Friedmann, Franz, 'Rechtsstellung der Juden im Protektorat Böhmen und Mähren, Stand: 31 Jul. 1942', in Helena Krejčová, Jana Svobodová and Anna Hyndráková (eds.), *Židé v Protektorátu: Hlášení Židovské náboženské obce v roce 1942. Dokumenty* (Prague: Maxdorf, 1997), pp. 232–263.

Gallagher, Hugh Gregory, *By Trust Betrayed: Patients, Physicians, and the License to Kill in the Third Reich* (Arlington, VA: Vandamere, 1995).

Gebhart, Jan and Jan Kuklík, *Velké dějiny zemí Koruny české*, vol. 15a: *1938–1945* (Prague: Paseka, 2006).

Gedenk- und Bildungsstätte Haus der Wannsee-Konferenz, *Die Wannsee-Konferenz und der Völkermord an den europäischen Juden: Katalog der ständigen Ausstellung* (Berlin: Gedenk- und Bildungsstätte Haus der Wannsee-Konferenz, 2006).

Gerlach, Christian, 'The Wannsee Conference, the Fate of German Jews, and Hitler's Decision in Principle to Exterminate All European Jews', trans. Stephen Duffy, *Journal of Modern History*, vol. 70, no. 4 (December 1998 [German edn, 1997]), pp. 759–812.

Goeschel, Christian, *Suicide in Nazi Germany* (Oxford/New York: Oxford University Press, 2009).

Goshen, Seev, 'Eichmann und die Nisko-Aktion im Oktober 1939', *Vierteljahrshefte für Zeitgeschichte*, 29 (1981), pp. 74–96.

Gottwaldt, Alfred, and Diana Schulle, *Die 'Judendeportationen' aus dem Deutschen Reich 1941–1945* (Wiesbaden: Marixverlag, 2005).

Grode, Walter, *Die 'Sonderbehandlung 14f13' in den Konzentrationslagern des Dritten Reiches: Ein Beitrag zur Dynamik faschistischer Vernichtungspolitik* (Frankfurt am Main/New York: Peter Lang, 1987).

Gruner, Wolf, 'Das Protektorat Böhmen und Mähren und die antijüdische Politik 1939-1941: Lokale Initiativen, regionale Maßnahmen, zentrale Entscheidungen im "Großdeutschen Reich"', *Theresienstädter Studien und Dokumente*, vol. 12 (2005), pp. 27–62.

Gruner, Wolf, *The Holocaust in Bohemia and Moravia: Czech Initiatives, German Policies, Jewish Responses* (New York/Oxford: Berghahn, 2019).

Gruner, Wolf, *Jewish Forced Labor under the Nazis: Economic Needs and Racial Aims, 1938-1944*, trans. Kathleen M. Dell'Orto (New York: Cambridge University, 2006 [German edn, 1997]).

Gruner, Wolf, *Judenverfolgung in Berlin 1933–1945* (Berlin: Stiftung Topographie des Terrors, 1996)

Gruner, Wolf, *Öffentliche Wohlfahrt und Judenverfolgung: Wechselwirkung lokaler und zentraler Politik im NS-Staat 1933 bis 1942* (Munich: Oldenbourg, 2002).

Gruner, Wolf, 'Von der Kollektivausweisung zur Deportation der Juden aus Deutschland: Neue Perspektiven und Dokumente', in Birthe Kundrus and Beate Meyer (eds.), *Die Deportation der Juden aus Deutschland: Pläne – Praxis – Reaktionen 1938–1945* (Göttingen: Wallstein, 2004), pp. 21–62.

Gruner, Wolf, *Zwangsarbeit und Verfolgung: Österreichische Juden im NS-Staat 1938–45* (Innsbruck: Studien Verlag, 2000).

Grynberg, Anne, *Les camps de la honte: Les internés juifs des camps français 1939–1944* (Paris: La Découverte, 1991).

Hampel, Jens, 'Das Schicksal der jüdischen Bevölkerung der Stadt Iglau 1938–1942', *Theresienstädter Studien und Dokumente*, vol. 5 (1998), pp. 70–99.

Hanke, Peter, *Zur Geschichte der Juden in München zwischen 1933 und 1945* (Munich: Stadtarchiv, 1967).

Haumann, Heiko, *A History of East European Jews*, trans. James Patterson (New York: Central European University Press, 2002 [German edn, 1998]).

Hebbel, Friedrich, *Sämtliche Werke*, vol. 2: *Gedichte und Prosa*, ed. Hansludwig Geiger (Berlin: Tempel, 1961).

Heiber, Helmut, 'Der Generalplan Ost', *Vierteljahrshefte für Zeitgeschichte*, vol. 6 (1958), pp. 281–325.

Heiber, Helmut, 'Zur Justiz im Dritten Reich: Der Fall Eliáš', *Vierteljahrshefte für Zeitgeschichte*, vol. 3 (1955), pp. 275–296.

Heim, Susanne (ed.), *Plant Breeding and Agrarian Research in Kaiser-Wilhelm-Institutes 1933–1943: Calories, Caoutchouc, Careers* (Dordrecht: Springer, 2008).

Heim, Susanne, 'Vertreibung, Raub und Umverteilung. Die jüdischen Flüchtlinge aus Deutschland und die Vermehrung des "Volksvermögens"', *Beiträge zur nationalsozialistischen Gesundheits- und Sozialpolitik*, vol. 15: *Flüchtlingspolitik und Fluchthilfe* (Berlin: Schwarze Risse; Göttingen: Rote Strasse, 1999), pp. 107–138.

Heinemann, Isabel, *'Rasse, Siedlung, deutsches Blut': Das Rasse- und Siedlungshauptamt der SS und die rassenpolitische Neuordnung Europas* (Göttingen: Wallstein, 2003).

Heinemann, Isabel, 'Wissenschaft und Homogenisierungsplanungen für Osteuropa: Konrad Meyer, der "Generalplan Ost" und die Deutsche Forschungsgemeinschaft', in Isabel Heinemann and Patrick Wagner (eds.), *Wissenschaft – Planung – Vertreibung: Neuordnungskonzepte und Umsiedlungspolitik im 20. Jahrhundert* (Stuttgart: Franz Steiner Verlag, 2006), pp. 45–72.

Hepp, Michael (ed.), *Die Ausbürgerung deutscher Staatsangehöriger 1933–45 nach den im Reichsanzeiger veröffentlichten Listen* (Munich: De Gruyter, 1985).

Herbert, Ulrich, *Best: Biographische Studien über Radikalismus, Weltanschauung und Vernunft 1903–1989* (Bonn: J.H.W. Dietz, 1996).

Herbert, Ulrich, 'Der deutsche Professor im Dritten Reich: Vier biografische Skizzen', in Karin Orth and Willi Oberkrome (eds.), *Die Deutsche Forschungsgemeinschaft 1920–1970: Forschungsförderung im Spannungsfeld von Wissenschaft und Politik* (Stuttgart: Franz Steiner Verlag, 2010), pp. 483–502.

Herbert, Ulrich, *Hitler's Foreign Workers: Enforced Foreign Labor in Germany under the Third Reich*, trans. William Templer (Cambridge: Cambridge University Press, 2006 [German edn, 1999]).

Herbert, Ulrich, Karin Orth, and Christoph Dieckmann (eds.), *Die nationalsozialistischen Konzentrationslager: Entwicklung und Struktur*, 2 vols. (Göttingen: Wallstein, 1998).

Herbst, Ludolf, *Das nationalsozialistische Deutschland 1933–1945: Die Entfesselung der Gewalt. Rassismus und Krieg* (Frankfurt am Main: Suhrkamp, 1996).

Herf, Jeffrey, *The Jewish Enemy: Nazi Propaganda during World War II and the Holocaust* (Cambridge, MA: Harvard University Press, 2006).

Heumos, Peter, *Die Emigration aus der Tschechoslowakei nach Westeuropa und dem Nahen Osten 1938–1945: Politisch-soziale Struktur, Organisation und Asylbedingungen der tschechischen, jüdischen, deutschen und slowakischen Flüchtlinge während des Nationalsozialismus. Darstellung und Dokumentation* (Munich: Oldenbourg, 1989).

Hilberg, Raul, *The Destruction of the European Jews*, 3rd edn, vol. 1 (New Haven, CT/ London: Yale University Press, 2003 [1961]).

Hildesheimer, Esriel, *Jüdische Selbstverwaltung unter dem NS-Regime* (Tübingen: Mohr, 1994).

Hillgruber, Andreas, *Die gescheiterte Großmacht: Eine Skizze des Deutschen Reiches 1871–1945* (Düsseldorf: Droste, 1980).

Hillgruber, Andreas, *Hitlers Strategie: Politik und Kriegsführung 1940–1941* (Frankfurt am Main: Bernard & Graefe, 1965).

Hinz-Wessels, Annette, 'Jüdische Opfer der "Aktion T4" im Spiegel der überlieferten "Euthanasie"-Krankenakten im Bundesarchiv', in Maike Rotzoll et al. (eds.), *Die nationalsozialistische 'Euthanasie'-Aktion 'T4' und ihre Opfer: Geschichte und ethische Konsequenzen für die Gegenwart* (Paderborn: Schöningh, 2010), pp. 143–146.

Hocheneder, Franz, *H.G. Adler (1910–1988): Privatgelehrter und freier Schriftsteller* (Vienna: Böhlau, 2009).

House of the Wannsee Conference, *The Wannsee Conference and the Genocide of European Jews: Catalogue of the Permanent Exhibition*, trans. Caroline Pearce (Berlin: House of the Wannsee Conference, 2009)

Hürter, Johannes, *Hitlers Heerführer. Die deutschen Oberbefehlshaber im Krieg gegen die Sowjetunion 1941/42* (Munich: Oldenbourg, 2006).

Iggers, Wilma (ed.), *The Jews of Bohemia and Moravia: A Historical Reader*, trans. Wilma Iggers, Káča Poláčková-Henley, and Kathrine Talbot (Detroit: Wayne State University Press, 1992 [German edn, 1986]).

Jäckel, Eberhard, *Hitler's World View: A Blueprint for Power*, trans. Herbert Arnold (Cambridge, MA: Harvard University Press, 1981 [German edn, 1969]).

Jäckel, Eberhard, 'Der Mord an den Juden als historisches Problem', in Eberhard Jäckel and Jürgen Rohwer (eds.), *Der Mord an den Juden im Zweiten Weltkrieg* (Frankfurt am Main: Fischer, 1987), pp. 15–16.

Jacobsen, Hans-Adolf, 'Kommissarbefehl und Massenexekutionen sowjetischer Kriegsgefangener', in Martin Broszat, Hans-Adolf Jacobsen, and Helmut Krausnick, *Anatomie des SS-Staates*, vol. 2 (Olten/ Freiburg im Breisgau: Walter-Verlag, 1965), pp. 161–279.

Jansen, Hans, *Der Madagaskar-Plan: Die beabsichtigte Deportation der europäischen Juden nach Madagaskar* (Munich: Herbig, 1997).

Jersak, Tobias, 'Die Interaktion von Kriegsverlauf und Judenvernichtung: Ein Blick auf Hitlers Strategie im Spätsommer 1941', *Historische Zeitschrift*, vol. 268, no. 2 (1999), pp. 311–374.

Johnson, Eric Arthur and Karl-Heinz Reuband, *What We Knew: Terror, Mass Murder, and Everyday Life in Nazi Germany; an Oral History* (Cambridge, MA: Basic Books, 2005).

Kaplan, Marion A., *Between Dignity and Despair: Jewish Life in Nazi Germany* (New York/Oxford: Oxford University Press, 1998).

Kárný, Miroslav, 'Die Ausschaltung der Juden aus dem öffentlichen Leben des Protektorats und die Geschichte des "Ehrenariertums"', *Theresienstädter Studien und Dokumente* (1998), pp. 7–40.

Kárný, Miroslav, 'Die "Judenfrage" in der nazistischen Okkupationspolitik', *Historica*, vol. 21 (1982), pp. 137–192.

Kárný, Miroslav, *'Konečné řešení': Genocida českých židů v německé protektorátní politice* (Prague: Academia, 1991).

Kárný, Miroslav, 'Zur Statistik der jüdischen Bevölkerung im sogenannten Protektorat', *Judaica Bohemiae*, vol. 22, no. 1 (1986), pp. 9–19.

Kašák, Karel, *'Češi v koncentračním táboře Dachau', in Almanach Dachau: Kytice událostí a vzpomínek* (Prague: Calve, 1946), pp. 14–22.

Kaufmann, Doris (ed.), *Geschichte der Kaiser-Wilhelm-Gesellschaft im Nationalsozialismus: Bestandsaufnahmen und Perspektiven der Forschung* (Göttingen: Wallstein, 2000).

Kepplinger, Brigitte, Gerhart Marckhgott, and Hartmut Reese (eds.), *Tötungsanstalt Hartheim* (Linz: Oöla, 2008).

Kershaw, Ian, *Fateful Choices: Ten Decisions that Changed the World, 1940–1941* (London: Penguin, 2007).

Kershaw, Ian, *Hitler, 1936–1945: Nemesis* (London: Penguin, 2009).

Kershaw, Ian, *Hitler, the Germans, and the Final Solution* (New Haven, CT: Yale University Press, 2008).

Kestenberg-Gladstein, Ruth, *Neuere Geschichte der Juden in den böhmischen Ländern* (Tübingen: Mohr, 1969).

Kieval, Hillel J., 'Bohemia and Moravia', in Gershon David Hundert (ed.), *The YIVO Encyclopedia of Jews in Eastern Europe*, vol. 1 (New Haven, CT: Yale University Press, 2008), pp. 202–211.

Kieval, Hillel J., 'Death and the Nation: Ritual Murder as Political Discourse in the Czech Lands', in Maurice Godé, Jacques Le Rider, and Françoise Mayer (eds.), *Allemands, Juifs et Tchèques à Prague de 1890 à 1924: Actes du colloque de Montpellier, décembre 1994* (Montpellier: Université Paul-Valery, 1996), pp. 83–99.

Kieval, Hillel J., 'The Lands Between: The Jews of Bohemia, Moravia, and Slovakia to 1918', in Natalia Berger (ed.), *Where Cultures Meet: The Story of the Jews of Czechoslovakia* (Tel Aviv: Beth Hatefutsoth, 1990), pp. 23–51.

Kieval, Hillel J., *Languages of Community: The Jewish Experience in the Czech Lands* (Berkeley: University of California Press, 2000).

Kieval, Hillel J., *The Making of Czech Jewry: National Conflict and Jewish Society in Bohemia, 1870–1918*, (New York/Oxford: Oxford University Press, 1988).

Klee, Ernst, *'Euthanasie' im Dritten Reich: Die 'Vernichtung lebensunwerten Lebens'*, 2nd edn (Frankfurt am Main: Fischer, 2010 [1983]).

Kovtun, Jiří, *Tajuplná vražda: Případ Leopolda Hilsnera* (Prague: Sefer, 1994).

Korb, Alexander, *Intertwined Genocides: Mass Violence in Western Yugoslavia during the Second World War* (Oxford: Oxford University Press, 2019).

Král, Václav, *Otázky hospodářského a sociálního vývoje v českých zemích v letech 1938–1945*, 3 vols. (Prague: Nakladatelství Československé akademie věd, 1957–1959).

Krausnick, Helmut, Martin Broszat, and Hans-Adolf Jacobsen, *Anatomy of the SS-State*, trans. Richard Barry, Marion Jackson, Dorothy Long et al. (London: Collins, 1968 [German edn, 1965])

Krejčová, Helena, 'Juden in den 30er Jahren des 20. Jahrhunderts', in Marek Nekula and Walter Koschmal (eds.), *Juden zwischen Deutschen und Tschechen: Sprachliche und kulturelle Identitäten in Böhmen 1800–1945* (Munich: Oldenbourg, 2006), pp. 85–102.

Krejčová, Helena, 'Spezifische Voraussetzungen des Antisemitismus und antijüdische Aktivitäten im Protektorat Böhmen und Mähren', in Jörg K. Hoensch, Stanislav Biman, and L'ubomir Liptak (eds.), *Judenemanzipation – Antisemitismus – Verfolgung in Deutschland, Österreich-Ungarn, den Böhmischen Ländern und in der Slowakei* (Essen: Klartext, 1999), pp. 175–194.

Kreutzmüller, Christoph, Ingo Loose, and Benno Nietzel, 'Nazi Persecution and Strategies for Survival: Jewish Businesses in Berlin, Frankfurt am Main, and Breslau, 1933–1942', *Yad Vashem Studies*, vol. 39, no. 1 (2011), pp. 31–70.

Kulka, Otto Dov, '"Public Opinion" in Nazi Germany and the "Jewish Question"', *Jerusalem Quarterly*, vol. 25 (1982), pp. 121–144.

Kulka, Otto Dov, 'The Reichsvereinigung and the Fate of the German Jews, 1938/1939–1942', in Arnold Paucker, *Die Juden im nationalsozialistischen Deutschland, 1933–1943: The Jews in Nazi Germany, 1933–1943* (Tübingen: J. C. B. Mohr, 1986), pp. 353–363.

Küpper, René, *Karl Hermann Frank (1898–1946): Politische Biographie eines sudetendeutschen Nationalsozialisten* (Munich: Oldenbourg, 2010).

Kwiet, Konrad, 'Nach dem Pogrom: Stufen der Ausgrenzung', in Wolfgang Benz (ed.), *Die*

Juden in Deutschland 1933–1945: Leben unter nationalsozialistischer Herrschaft (Munich: C.H.Beck, 1988), pp. 545–659.

Kwiet, Konrad, 'The Ultimate Refuge: Suicide in the Jewish Community under the Nazis', *Leo Baeck Institute Yearbook*, vol. 29 (1984), pp. 135–167.

Laharie, Claude, *Le camp de Gurs 1939–1945: Un aspect méconnu de l'histoire du Bearn* (Pau: Infocompo, 1985).

Leichsenring, Jana, *Die Katholische Kirche und 'ihre Juden': Das 'Hilfswerk beim Bischöflichen Ordinariat Berlin', 1938–1945* (Berlin: Metropol, 2007).

Lichtenstein, Erwin, *Die Juden der Freien Stadt Danzig unter der Herrschaft des Nationalsozialismus* (Tübingen: Mohr Siebeck, 1973).

Lifton, Robert, *The Nazi Doctors: Medical Killing and the Psychology of Genocide* (New York: Basic, 1988).

Lipstadt, Deborah E., *Beyond Belief: The American Press and the Coming of the Holocaust, 1933–1945* (New York: Free Press, 1986).

Longerich, Peter, *'Davon haben wir nichts gewusst!': Die Deutschen und die Judenverfolgung 1933–1945* (Munich: Siedler, 2006).

Longerich, Peter, *Holocaust: The Nazi Persecution and Murder of the Jews*, new edn, trans. Shaun Whiteside (Oxford: Oxford University Press, 2010 [German edn, 1998]).

Longerich, Peter, *The Unwritten Order: Hitler's Role in the Final Solution* (Stroud: Tempus, 2001).

Löw, Andrea, 'Die frühen Deportationen aus dem Reichsgebiet von Herbst 1939 bis Frühjahr 1941', in Susanne Heim, Beate Meyer, and Francis R. Nicosia (eds.), *'Wer bleibt, opfert seine Jahre, vielleicht sein Leben': Deutsche Juden 1938–1941* (Göttingen: Wallstein, 2010), pp. 59–76.

Ludwig, Hartmut, *An der Seite der Entrechteten und Schwachen: Zur Geschichte des 'Büro Pfarrer Grüber' (1938 bis 1940) und der Ev. Hilfsstelle für ehemals Rasseverfolgte nach 1945* (Berlin: Logos, 2009).

Madajczyk, Czesław (ed.), *Vom Generalplan Ost zum Generalsiedlungsplan* (Munich/New Providence/London/Paris: Saur, 1994).

Maier, Clemens, '*Das Jüdische Nachrichtenblatt 1938–1943*: Instrument der Verfolgung und Mittel der Selbstbehauptung', in Eleonore Lappin and Michael Nagel (eds.), *Deutsch-jüdische Presse und jüdische Geschichte: Dokumente, Darstellungen, Wechselbeziehungen*, vol. 2 (Bremen: Edition Lumière, 2008), pp. 163–179.

Maierhof, Gudrun, *Selbstbehauptung im Chaos: Frauen in der jüdischen Selbsthilfe 1933–1943* (Frankfurt am Main/New York: Campus, 2002).

Mallmann, Klaus-Michael, 'Der qualitative Sprung im Vernichtungsprozeß: Das Massaker von Kamenez-Podolsk Ende August 1941', *Jahrbuch für Antisemitismusforschung*, vol. 10 (2001), pp. 239–264.

Mallmann, Klaus-Michael, and Bogdan Musial (eds.), *Genesis des Genozids: Polen 1939–1941* (Darmstadt: Wissenschaftliche Buchgesellschaft, 2004).

Manoschek, Walter, *'Serbien ist judenfrei!': Militärische Besatzungspolitik und Judenvernichtung in Serbien 1941/42* (Munich: Oldenbourg, 1993).

Marrus, Robert, and Robert O. Paxton, *Vichy France and the Jews* (New York: Basic Books, 1981).

Maršálek, Pavel, *Protektorát Čechy a Morava: Státoprávní a politické aspekty nacistického okupačního režimu v českých zemích 1939–1945* (Prague: Karolinum, 2002).

Martinovský, Ivan, et al., *Dějiny Plzně v datech od prvních stop osídlení až po současnost* (Prague: Lidové Noviny, 2004).

Mastný, Vojtěch, *The Czechs under Nazi Rule: The Failure of National Resistance, 1939–1942* (New York: Columbia University Press, 1971).

Matthäus, Jürgen, 'Operation Barbarossa and the Onset of the Holocaust, June–December 1941', in Christopher R. Browning, with contributions by Jürgen Matthäus, *The Origins of the Final Solution: The Evolution of Nazi Jewish Policy, September 1939 – March*

1942 (Lincoln, NE: University of Nebraska Press, 2004), pp. 244–308.

Matthäus, Jürgen, 'Verfolgung, Ausbeutung, Vernichtung: Jüdische Häftlinge im System der Konzentrationslager', in Günter Morsch and Susanne zur Nieden (eds.), *Jüdische Häftlinge im Konzentrationslager Sachsenhausen, 1936 bis 1945* (Berlin: Edition Hentrich, 2004), pp. 64–90.

Maurer, Trude, 'Vom Alltag zum Ausnahmezustand: Juden in der Weimarer Republik und im Nationalsozialismus', in Marion Kaplan (ed.), *Geschichte des jüdischen Alltags in Deutschland: Vom 17. Jahrhundert bis 1945* (Munich: C.H.Beck, 2003), pp. 347–470.

Mayer, Michael, *Staaten als Täter: Ministerialbürokratie und 'Judenpolitik' in NS-Deutschland und Vichy-Frankreich. Ein Vergleich* (Munich: Oldenbourg, 2010).

Meyer, Beate, *A Fatal Balancing Act: The Dilemma of the Reich Association of Jews in Germany, 1939–1945*, trans. William Templer (Oxford: Berghahn, 2013 [German edn, 2011]).

Meyer, Beate, 'The Fine Line between Responsible Action and Collaboration: The Reichsvereinigung der Juden in Deutschland and the Jewish Community in Berlin, 1938--1945', in Beate Meyer, Hermann Simon and Chana Schütz (eds.), *Jews in Nazi Berlin: From Kristallnacht to Liberation*, trans. Caroline Gay and Miranda Robbins (Chicago: University of Chicago Press, 2009 [German edn, 2000]), pp. 310–363.

Meyer, Beate, *'Jüdische Mischlinge': Rassenpolitik und Verfolgungserfahrung 1933–1945* (Hamburg: Dölling und Galitz, 1999).

Meyer, Beate, 'Der Traum von einer autonomen jüdischen Verwaltung: Die Reichsvereinigung der Juden in Deutschland. Auswanderer und Zurückbleibende in den Jahren 1938/39–1941', in Susanne Heim, Beate Meyer, and Francis R. Nicosia (eds.), *'Wer bleibt, opfert seine Jahre, vielleicht sein Leben': Deutsche Juden 1938–1941* (Göttingen: Wallstein, 2010), pp. 21–38.

Meyer, Beate, Hermann Simon and Chana Schütz (eds.), *Jews in Nazi Berlin: From Kristallnacht to Liberation*, trans. Caroline Gay and Miranda Robbins (Chicago: University of Chicago Press, 2009 [German edn, 2000]).

Michaelis, Herbert, and Ernst Schraepler (eds.), *Ursachen und Folgen: Vom deutschen Zusammenbruch 1918 und 1945 bis zur staatlichen Neuordnung Deutschlands in der Gegenwart*, vol. 14: *Das Dritte Reich: Der Angriff auf Polen. Die Ereignisse im Winter 1939–1940* (Berlin: Wendler, 1969).

Milotová, Jaroslava, 'Die Zentralstelle für jüdische Auswanderung in Prag: Genesis und Tätigkeit bis zum Anfang des Jahres 1940', *Theresienstädter Studien und Dokumente, vol. 4 (1997), pp. 7–30.*

Milotová, Jaroslava, 'Zur Geschichte der Verordnung Konstantin von Neuraths über das jüdische Vermögen', *Theresienstädter Studien und Dokumente*, vol. 9 (2002), pp. 75–115.

Milotová, Jaroslava, and Miroslav Kárný, 'Od Neuratha k Heydrichovi: Na rozhrání okupační politiky hitlerovského Německa v "Protektorátu Čechy a Morava"', *Sborník archivních prací*, 39 (1989), vol. 2, pp. 281–394.

Mommsen, Hans, and Susanne Willems (eds.), *Herrschaftsalltag im Dritten Reich: Studien und Texte* (Düsseldorf: Schwann, 1988).

Moser, Jonny, '"Nisko": The First Experiment in Deportation', *The Simon Wiesenthal Center Annual*, 2 (1985), pp. 1–30.

Moser, Jonny, *Nisko: Die ersten Judendeportationen* (Vienna: Steinbauer, 2012).

Müller, Rolf-Dieter, *Hitlers Ostkrieg und die deutsche Siedlungspolitik: Die Zusammenarbeit von Wehrmacht, Wirtschaft und SS* (Frankfurt Main: Fischer, 1991).

Němec, Peter, 'Das tschechische Volk und die nationalsozialistische Germanisierung des Raumes', *Bohemia*, vol. 32 (1991), pp. 424–455.

Němeček, Jan, 'Das tschechoslowakische politische Exil in London und die "jüdische

Frage"', *Theresienstädter Studien und Dokumente*, vol. 9 (2002), pp. 347–366.

Nicosia, Francis R., and Jonathan Huener (eds.), *Medicine and Medical Ethics in Nazi Germany: Origins, Practices, Legacies* (New York/Oxford: Berghahn, 2004).

Nietzel, Benno, 'Die Vernichtung der wirtschaftlichen Existenz der deutschen Juden 1933–1945: Ein Literatur- und Forschungsbericht', *Archiv für Sozialgeschichte*, vol. 49 (2009), pp. 561–613.

Niven, Bill, *Hitler and Film: The Führer's Hidden Passion* (New Haven/London: Yale University Press, 2018), pp. 163–184.

Nowak, Kurt, 'Widerstand, Zustimmung, Hinnahme: Das Verhalten der Bevölkerung zur "Euthanasie"', in Norbert Frei (ed.), *Medizin und Gesundheitspolitik in der NS-Zeit* (Munich: Oldenbourg, 1991), pp. 235–249.

Oexler, Otto Gerhard, and Winfried Schulze (eds.), *Deutsche Historiker im Nationalsozialismus* (Frankfurt am Main: Fischer, 1999).

Ofer, Dalia, *Escaping the Holocaust: Illegal Immigration to the Land of Israel, 1939–1944* (New York/Oxford: Oxford University Press, 1990).

Ofer, Dalia, 'Die illegale Einwanderung nach Palästina: Politische, nationale und persönliche Aspekte (1939–1941)', *Beiträge zur nationalsozialistischen Gesundheits- und Sozialpolitik*, vol. 15 (1999): *Flüchtlingspolitik und Fluchthilfe*, special issue, pp. 9–38.

Ofer, Dalia and Hannah Weiner, *Dead-End Journey: The Tragic Story of the Kladovo-Šabac Group* (Lanham, MD: University Press of America, 1996).

Oprach, Marc, *Nationalsozialistische Judenpolitik im Protektorat Böhmen und Mähren: Entscheidungsabläufe und Radikalisierung* (Hamburg: Kovač, 2006).

Orth, Karin, *Das System der nationalsozialistischen Konzentrationslager: Eine politische Organisationsgeschichte* (Hamburg: Hamburger Edition, 1999).

Osterloh, Jörg, 'Sudetenland', in Wolf Gruner and Jörg Osterloh (eds.), *The Greater German Reich and the Jews: Nazi Persecution Policies in the Annexed Territories, 1935–1945*, trans. Bernard Heise (New York/Oxford: Berghahn, 2015 [German edn, 2010]), pp. 68–98.

Osterloh, Jörg, and Harald Wixforth, 'Die "Arisierung" im Protektorat Böhmen und Mähren', in Harald Wixforth, *Die Expansion der Dresdner Bank in Europa* (Munich: Oldenbourg, 2006), pp. 306–350.

Overy, Richard, *1939: Countdown to War* (London: Allen Lane, 2009).

Pěkný, Tomáš, *Historie Židů v Čechách a na Moravě*, 2nd edn (Prague: Sefer, 2002).

Peschanski, Denis, *La France des camps: L'internement, 1938–1946* (Paris: Gallimard, 2002).

Petersen, Hans-Christian, *Bevölkerungsökonomie – Ostforschung – Politik: Eine biographische Studie zu Peter-Heinz Seraphim (1902–1979)* (Osnabrück: Fibre, 2007).

Petrův, Helena, *Právní postavení židů v Protektorátu Čechy a Morava (1939–1941)* (Prague: Institut Terezínské iniciativy, 2000).

Pickhan, Gertrud, '"Niemandsland": Die Briefe der Greta Schiffmann und das Schicksal einer jüdischen Familie, ausgewiesen aus Dortmund im Oktober 1938', *Beiträge zur Geschichte der Stadt Dortmund und der Grafschaft Mark*, vol. 91 (2001), pp. 170–201.

Pingel, Falk, *Häftlinge unter SS-Herrschaft: Widerstand, Selbstbehauptung und Vernichtung im Konzentrationslager* (Hamburg: Hoffmann und Campe, 1978).

Pohl, Dieter, 'The Holocaust and the Concentration Camps', in Jane Caplan and Nikolaus Wachsmann (eds.), *Concentration Camps in Nazi Germany: The New Histories* (London/New York: Routledge, 2010), pp. 149–166.

Pohl, Dieter, 'The Murder of Ukraine's Jews under German Military Administration and in the Reich Commissariat Ukraine', in Ray Brandon and Wendy Lower (eds.), *The Shoah in Ukraine: History, Testimony, Memorialization* (Bloomington: Indiana University Press, 2008), pp. 23–76.

Pohl, Dieter, 'Schauplatz Ukraine: Der Massenmord an den Juden im

Militärverwaltungsgebiet und im Reichskommissariat 1941–1943', in Norbert Frei, Sybille Steinbacher, and Bernd C. Wagner (eds.), *Ausbeutung, Vernichtung, Öffentlichkeit: Neue Studien zur nationalsozialistischen Lagerpolitik* (Munich: Saur, 2000), pp. 135–173.

Polian, Pavel, 'Hätte der Holocaust beinahe nicht stattgefunden? Überlegungen zu einem Schriftwechsel im Wert von zwei Millionen Menschenleben', in Johannes Hürter and Jürgen Zarusky (eds.), *Besatzung, Kollaboration, Holocaust: Neue Studien zur Verfolgung und Ermordung der europäischen Juden* (Munich: Oldenbourg, 2008), pp. 1–19.

Priemel, Kim Christian, *Flick: Eine Konzerngeschichte vom Kaiserreich bis zur Bundesrepublik* (Göttingen: Wallstein, 2007).

Proctor, Robert, *Racial Hygiene: Medicine under the Nazis* (Cambridge, MA: Harvard University Press, 1989).

Pross, Christian, and Götz Aly, *Der Wert des Menschen: Medizin in Deutschland 1918–1945* (Berlin: Edition Hentrich, 1989).

Rabinovici, Doron, *Eichmann's Jews: The Jewish Administration of Holocaust Vienna, 1938–1945*, trans. Nick Somers (New York: John Wiley, 2014 [German edn., 2000]).

Reuband, Karl-Heinz, '"Jud Süß" und "Der ewige Jude" als Prototypen antisemitischer Filmpropaganda im Dritten Reich: Entstehungsbedingungen, Zuschauerstrukturen und Wirkungspotential', in Michal Anděl et al. (eds.), *Propaganda, (Selbst-)Zensur, Sensation: Grenzen von Presse- und Wissenschaftsfreiheit in Deutschland und Tschechien seit 1871* (Essen: Klartext, 2005), pp. 89–148.

Rickman, Gregg J., *Conquest and Redemption: A History of Jewish Assets from the Holocaust* (Piscataway, NJ: Transaction, 2014).

Rieß, Volker, *Die Anfänge der Vernichtung 'lebensunwerten Lebens' in den Reichsgauen Danzig-Westpreußen und Wartheland 1939/40* (Frankfurt am Main/New York: Peter Lang, 1995).

Rigg, Bryan Mark, *Hitler's Jewish Soldiers: The Untold Story of Nazi Racial Laws and Men of Jewish Descent in the German Military* (Lawrence, KS: University Press of Kansas, 2002).

Röder, Werner and Sybille Claus (eds.), *Biographisches Handbuch der deutschsprachigen Emigration nach 1933* (München: Saur, 1980–1983).

Rogge-Gau, Sylvia, *Die doppelte Wurzel des Daseins: Julius Bab und der Jüdische Kulturbund Berlin* (Berlin: Metropol, 1999).

Röhm, Eberhard, and Jörg Thierfelder, *Juden – Christen – Deutsche*, vol. 3: *1938–1941* (Stuttgart: Calwer, 1995).

Rohwer, Jürgen, 'Jüdische Flüchtlingsschiffe im Schwarzen Meer – 1934 bis 1944', in Ursula Büttner (ed.), *Das Unrechtsregime: Internationale Forschung über den Nationalsozialismus*, vol. 2: *Verfolgung, Exil, belasteter Neubeginn* (Hamburg: Christians, 1986), pp. 197–248.

Rosenkranz, Herbert, *Verfolgung und Selbstbehauptung: Die Juden in Österreich 1938–1945* (Vienna/Munich: Herold, 1978).

Rössler, Mechthild, and Sabine Schleiermacher (eds.), *Der 'Generalplan Ost': Hauptlinien der nationalsozialistischen Planungs- und Vernichtungspolitik* (Berlin: Akademie Verlag, 1993).

Rothkirchen, Livia, 'Czechoslovak Jewry: Growth and Decline. Part I: 1918–1939', in Natalia Berger (ed.), *Where Cultures Meet: The Story of the Jews of Czechoslovakia* (Tel Aviv: Beth Hatefutsoth, 1990), pp. 107–115.

Rothkirchen, Livia, *The Jews of Bohemia and Moravia: Facing the Holocaust* (Lincoln, NE: University of Nebraska Press, 2005).

Rothkirchen, Livia, 'Zur ersten authentischen Nachricht über den Beginn der Vernichtung der europäischen Juden', *Theresienstädter Studien und Dokumente*, vol. 9 (2002), pp. 338–340.

Rovit, Rebecca, *The Jewish Kulturbund Theatre Company in Nazi Berlin* (Iowa City: University of Iowa Press, 2012).

Rupnow, Dirk, *Judenforschung im Dritten Reich: Wissenschaft zwischen Politik, Propaganda und Ideologie* (Baden-Baden: Nomos, 2011).

Rüther, Martin, *Köln im Zweiten Weltkrieg: Alltag und Erfahrungen zwischen 1939 und 1945* (Cologne: Emons, 2005).

Safrian, Hans, *Eichmann's Men*, trans. Ute Stargardt (New York/Cambridge: Cambridge University Press, 2010).

Schine, Robert S., *Jewish Thought Adrift: Max Wiener (1881–1950)* (Atlanta: Scholars, 1992).

Schmidlin, Antonia, *Eine andere Schweiz: Helferinnen, Kriegskinder und humanitäre Politik 1933–1942* (Zurich: Chronos, 1999).

Schmidt-Hartmann, Eva, 'Übersicht über die nationalsozialistische "Endlösung der jüdischen Frage" in den böhmischen Ländern', in Ferdinand Seibt (ed.), *Die Juden in den böhmischen Ländern* (Munich: Oldenbourg, 2002), pp. 321–322.

Schmuhl, Hans-Walter, *Rassenhygiene, Nationalsozialismus, Euthanasie: Von der Verhütung zur Vernichtung 'lebensunwerten Lebens' 1890–1945* (Göttingen: Vandenhoeck & Ruprecht, 1987).

Schneider, Hubert, *Die 'Entjudung' des Wohnraums: 'Judenhäuser' in Bochum, die Geschichte der Gebäude und ihrer Bewohner* (Berlin/Münster: Lit, 2010).

Schulze Wessel, Martin, 'Entwürfe und Wirklichkeiten: Die Politik gegenüber den Juden in der Ersten Tschechoslowakischen Republik 1918 bis 1938', in Dittmar Dahlmann and Anke Hilbrenner (eds.), *Zwischen großen Erwartungen und bösem Erwachen: Juden, Politik und Antisemitismus in Ost- und Südosteuropa 1918–1945* (Paderborn: Schöningh, 2007), pp. 120–135.

Seibt, Ferdinand, 'Tausend Jahre jüdische Geschichte in Böhmen und Mähren', in Ferdinand Seibt, *Deutsche, Tschechen, Sudetendeutsche: Analysen und Stellungnahmen zu Geschichte und Gegenwart aus fünf Jahrzehnten* (Munich: Oldenbourg, 2002), pp. 49–62.

Shlain, Margalit, 'Jakob Edelsteins Bemühungen um die Rettung der Juden aus dem Protektorat Böhmen und Mähren vom Mai 1939 bis Dezember 1939', *Theresienstädter Studien und Dokumente*, vol. 10 (2003), pp. 71–94.

Simonsohn, Berthold, 'Sein Andenken wird weiterleben', *Jüdische Sozialarbeit*, vol. 4, no. 3/4, (18 Sept. 1959), pp. 23–26.

Šisler, Stanislav, 'Příspěvek k vývoji a organizaci okupační správy v českých zemích v letech 1939–1945', *Sborník archivních prací*, vol. 2 (1963), pp. 46–95.

Sládek, Oldřich, 'Standrecht und Standgericht: Die Gestapo in Böhmen und Mähren', in Gerhard Paul and Klaus-Michael Mallmann (eds.), *Die Gestapo im Zweiten Weltkrieg: "Heimatfront" und besetztes Europa* (Darmstadt: Primus, 2000), pp. 317–339.

Sládek, Oldřich, *Zločinná role gestapa: nacistická bezpečnostní policie v českých zemích 1938–1945* (Prague: Naše Vojsko, 1986).

Sofsky, Wolfgang, *The Order of Terror: The Concentration Camp*, trans. William Templer (Princeton: Princeton University Press, 1999 [German edn 1993]).

Spoerer, Mark, *Zwangsarbeit unter dem Hakenkreuz: Ausländische Zivilarbeiter, Kriegsgefangene und Häftlinge im Deutschen Reich und im besetzten Europa 1939–1945* (Stuttgart: Deutsche Verlags-Anstalt, 2001).

Spring, Claudia, 'Vermessen, deklassiert und deportiert: Dokumentation zur anthropologischen Untersuchung an 440 Juden im Wiener Stadion im September 1939 unter der Leitung von Josef Wastl vom Naturhistorischen Museums Wien', *Zeitgeschichte*, vol. 32, no. 2 (2005), pp. 91–110.

Stein, Harry, *Juden in Buchenwald 1937–1942* (Weimar: Gedenkstätte Buchenwald, 1992).

Steinweis, Alan, *Studying the Jew: Scholarly Antisemitism in Nazi Germany* (Cambridge, MA: Harvard University Press, 2006).

Stoltzfus, Nathan, *Hitler's Compromises: Coercion and Consensus in Nazi Germany* (New Haven, CT/London: Yale University Press, 2016).

Stompor, Stephan, *Jüdisches Musik- und Theaterleben unter dem NS-Staat* (Hanover: Europäisches Zentrum für Jüdische Musik, 2001).

Strauss, Herbert, 'Jewish Autonomy within the Limits of National Socialist Policy: The

Communities and the Reichsvertretung', in Arnold Paucker, *Die Juden im nationalsozialistischen Deutschland, 1933–1943 / The Jews in Nazi Germany, 1933–1943* (Tübingen: J. C. B. Mohr, 1986), pp. 125–152.

Strauss, Herbert A., 'Jewish Emigration from Germany: Nazi Politics and Jewish Responses, Part I', *Leo Baeck Institute Yearbook*, vol. 25 (1980), pp. 313–361.

Strauss, Herbert A., 'Jewish Emigration from Germany: Nazi Politics and Jewish Responses, Part II', *Leo Baeck Institute Yearbook*, vol. 26 (1981), pp. 343–409.

Streit, Christian, *Keine Kameraden: Die Wehrmacht und die sowjetischen Kriegsgefangenen 1941–1945*, 4th edn (Bonn: Dietz, 1997).

Süß, Winfried, *Der 'Volkskörper' im Krieg: Gesundheitspolitik, Gesundheitsverhältnisse und Krankenmord im nationalsozialistischen Deutschland 1939–1945* (Munich: Oldenbourg, 2003).

Šustek, Vojtěch, 'Die nationalsozialistische Karriere eines sudetendeutschen Historikers', in Alena Míšková, Josef Pfitzner, and Vojtěch Šustek (eds.), *Josef Pfitzner a protektorátní Praha v letech 1939-45*, vol. 1 (Prague: Scriptorium, 2000), pp. 71–109.

Sywottek, Jutta, *Mobilmachung für den totalen Krieg: Die propagandistische Vorbereitung der deutschen Bevölkerung auf den Zweiten Weltkrieg* (Opladen: Westdeutscher Verlag, 1976).

Szalet, Leon, and Winfried Meyer, *Baracke 38: 237 Tage in den 'Judenblocks' des KZ Sachsenhausen* (Berlin: Metropol, 2006).

Teschner, Gerhard J., *Die Deportation der badischen und saarpfälzischen Juden am 22. Oktober 1940: Vorgeschichte und Durchführung der Deportation und das weitere Schicksal der Deportierten bis zum Kriegsende im Kontext der deutschen und französischen Judenpolitik* (Frankfurt am Main/New York: Peter Lang, 2002).

Tomaszewski, Jerzy, *Auftakt zur Vernichtung: Die Vertreibung polnischer Juden aus Deutschland im Jahre 1938* (Osnabrück: Fibre, 2002).

Tooze, Adam, *The Wages of Destruction: The Making and Breaking of the Nazi Economy* (London: Allen Lane, 2006).

Toury, Jacob, 'Die Entstehungsgeschichte des Austreibungsbefehls gegen die Juden der Saarpfalz und Badens (22./23. Oktober 1940, Camp de Gurs)', *Jahrbuch des Instituts für deutsche Geschichte Tel Aviv*, vol. 15 (1986), pp. 431–464.

Trevor-Roper, H.R. (ed.), *Hitler's War Directives 1939–1945* (London: Pan Books Ltd, 1966).

Vogel, Detlef, 'German Intervention in the Balkans', in Militärgeschichtliches Forschungsamt, *Germany and the Second World War*, vol. 3: *The Mediterranean, South-East Europe, and North Africa 1939–1941*, trans. Dean S. McMurry, Ewald Osers, and Louise Willmot (Oxford: Oxford University Press, 1995 [German edn, 1984]), pp. 417–511.

Wachsmann, Nikolaus, *KL: A History of the Nazi Concentration Camps* (London: Little, Brown, 2015).

Walker, Mark, Karin Orth, Ulrich Herbert, and Rüdiger vom Bruch (eds.), *The German Research Foundation, 1920–1970: Funding Poised between Science and Politics* (Stuttgart: Steiner, 2013).

Weil, Jiří, 'Klagegesang für 77 297 Opfer', in Jiří Weil, *Leben mit dem Stern*, trans. Bettina Kaibach (New York: Farrar, Straus and Giroux, 1989 [Czech edn, 1949]), pp. 337–386.

Weinberg, Gerhard L., *A World at Arms: A Global History of World War II*, 2nd edn (Cambridge: Cambridge University Press, 2005).

Weindling, Paul, *Victims and Survivors of Nazi Human Experiments: Science and Suffering in the Holocaust* (London: Bloomsbury, 2015).

Weinreich, Max, *Hitler's Professors: The Part of Scholarship in Germany's Crimes against the Jewish People* (New York: Yiddish Scientific Institute, 1946).

Weiss, Yfaat, *Deutsche und polnische Juden vor dem Holocaust: Jüdische Identität zwischen Staatsbürgerschaft und Ethnizität 1933–1940* (Munich: Oldenbourg, 2000).

Weissweiler, Eva, *Ausgemerzt! Das Lexikon der Juden in der Musik und seine mörderischen Folgen* (Cologne: Dittrich, 1999).

Weitkamp, Sebastian, *Braune Diplomaten: Horst Wagner und Eberhard von Thadden als Funktionäre der 'Endlösung'* (Bonn: Dietz, 2008).

Werle, Gerhard, *Justiz-Strafrecht und polizeiliche Verbrechensbekämpfung im Dritten Reich* (Berlin/New York: Walter de Gruyter, 1989).

Wetzel, Juliane, 'Auswanderung aus Deutschland', in Wolfgang Benz (ed.), *Die Juden in Deutschland 1933–1945: Leben unter nationalsozialistischer Herrschaft* (Munich: C.H.Beck, 1988), pp. 413–498.

Wiehn, Erhard R. (ed.), *Oktoberdeportation 1940: Die sogenannte 'Abschiebung' der badischen und saarpfälzischen Juden in das französische Internierungslager Gurs und andere Vorstationen von Auschwitz* (Konstanz: Hartung-Gore, 1990).

Wildman, Sarah, *Paper Love: Searching for the Girl My Grandfather Left Behind* (New York: Penguin, 2014).

Wildt, Michael, *An Uncompromising Generation: The Nazi Leadership of the Reich Security Main Office*, trans. Tom Lampert (Madison, WI: University of Wisconsin Press, 2010 [German edn, 2002]).

Wlaschek, Rudolf W., *Juden in Böhmen: Beiträge zur Geschichte des europäischen Judentums im 19. und 20. Jahrhundert* (Munich: Oldenbourg, 1997).

Wyman, David S., *Paper Walls: America and the Refugee Crisis, 1938–1941* (Amherst: University of Massachusetts Press, 1968).

Yahil, Leni, *The Holocaust: The Fate of European Jewry, 1932–1945*, trans. Ina Friedman and Haya Galai (New York: Oxford University Press, 1990 [Hebrew edn, 1987]).

Yahil, Leni, 'Madagascar – Phantom of a Solution for the Jewish Question', in George Mosse and Bela Vago (eds.), *Jews and Non-Jews in Eastern Europe* (New York: Wiley, 1974), pp. 315–334.

Zimmermann, Moshe, *Deutsche gegen Deutsche: Das Schicksal der Juden 1938–1945* (Berlin: Aufbau, 2008).

Zuccotti, Susan, *The Holocaust, the French, and the Jews* (Lincoln, NE: University of Nebraska Press, 1999).

Index

Newspapers and periodicals are included in the index only if the text contains information about them (e.g. publication period, editors), and not if they are merely mentioned or cited as a source.

Protectorate of Bohemia and Moravia
Sudetenland
Borders in 1937
Borders of the Oberlandratsbezirke after the territorial reform of 1940 (in the Protectorate of Bohemia and Moravia)
District borders after the territorial reform of 1940
Reichenberg
Aussig
(Ústí nad Labem)
Turnau
Münchengrätz
Raudnitz
Melnik
Jungbunzlau
Laun
Kralup
Neuenburg
Karlsbad
Schlan
Brandeis
Sudetenland
Annexed by the German Reich, Oct. 1938
Kladno
Prague
Böhmisch Brod
Rakonitz
Ritschan
Kolin
Prag-Land
PRAGUE
Kralowitz
Beraun
Eule
Kuttenberg
Horschowitz
Beneschau
Rokitzan
Pibrans
Pilsen (Plzeň)
Wlaschim
Pibrans
(Příbram)
Seltschan
Ledetsch
Pilsen
Tabor
Pilgrams
Pschestitz
PILSEN
Blatna
Protectorate of B
Annexed by the German Reich, Ma
Taus
Mühlhausen
Klattau
Pisek
BUDWEIS
Kamnitz
GERMAN
REICH
Schüttenhofen
Strakonitz
Moldautein
Wittingau
Wodnian
Regensburg
Budweis
Böhmisch Budweis
(České Budějovice)
Passau
AUSTRIA
Annexed by the German Reich, M
Linz
0
20
40
60
80
100 km